CASES AND MATERIALS

CONTRACTS

SEVENTH EDITION

by

E. ALLAN FARNSWORTH
Late Alfred McCormack Professor of Law
Columbia University

WILLIAM F. YOUNG
James L. Dohr Professor of Law Emeritus
Columbia University

CAROL SANGER
Barbara Aronstein Black Professor of Law
Columbia University

NEIL B. COHEN
Jeffrey D. Forchelli Professor of Law
Brooklyn Law School

RICHARD R.W. BROOKS
Professor of Law
Yale Law School

FOUNDATION PRESS

© 1965, 1972, 1980, 1988, 1995, 2001 FOUNDATION PRESS
© 2008 By THOMSON REUTERS/FOUNDATION PRESS

395 Hudson Street
New York, NY 10014
Phone Toll Free 1–877–888–1330
Fax (212) 367–6799
foundation–press.com

Printed in the United States of America

ISBN 978–1–59941–030–2

TEXT IS PRINTED ON 10% POST CONSUMER RECYCLED PAPER

WFY: *To Phyllis and AN3E*

CS: *To Anna and Michael*

NBC: *To Amy, Emily, Liz and Claudia*

RRWB: *To Heidi, Travers, Tilly, and, of course,*
Trudy and James

*

PREFACE

The course in Contracts serves at least two purposes. It is a law school's first course in commercial law, and so provides the foundation for advanced offerings in the area, and ultimately for professional practice. It has also a more ambitious function, for teachers have long believed—rightly, we think —that contract law is exceptionally well suited to the development of a "legal mind": respect for sources, skepticism of loose generalizations, and disciplined creativity in the use of legal materials.

Judicial opinions are the major component of this casebook and are intended as the primary vehicle for instruction. But they are not the only vehicle. The book also features relevant statutes (notably parts of the Uniform Commercial Code), and formulations of the common law expressed in the Restatement of Contracts.

To facilitate understanding, we have provided commentaries at various points, especially at the outset of a chapter or section. A number of principal cases are preceded by "Introductions" that provide settings for the cases in history, in law, in commerce, and the like. At appropriate points the book includes perspectives on some major categories of transactions, such as family agreements, real-estate transactions, and sales of goods. Some topics are presented largely in text, especially those dominated by legislation or by commercial practice.

Through notes and problems, students are provided with tests of their understanding, opportunities for reflection, connections among principles and cases, and sometimes simply with sidelights. Students are asked repeatedly how litigation might have been prevented by skillful counseling or drafting.

The book contains an array of questions about competing policies, and of opinions about them. These, we believe, are essential to an understanding of the law of contracts, as of other bodies of law. We have sought to avoid pressing on readers our individual conceptions of broad social policy.

CAROL SANGER
W. F. YOUNG
NEIL B. COHEN
RICHARD R. W. BROOKS

New York
July, 2008

*

ACKNOWLEDGMENTS

The previous edition of this casebook included the following statement:

> Our indebtedness to scores of distinguished scholars in Contracts (including especially E.W. Patterson, a progenitor of this book) will be evident. We have profited immeasurably over the years, from the responses of generous colleagues and a host of imaginative and energetic students."

This edition extends our indebtedness. We acknowledge, most particularly, the enormous contributions of E. Allan Farnsworth, whose influence remains powerful not only in this casebook but in the larger world of contracts scholarship and practice. We have added a biographical note for Allan, in the tradition of this book, that attempts to capture the breadth of his work and his stature in the field.

We thank the following colleagues for their comments on this and earlier editions: Barbara Black, Scott Burnham, Marvin Chirelstein, Larry Garvin, Tom Joo, Gerald T. McLaughlin, and Kerry MacIntosh.

We also express deep gratitude to the following research and editorial assistants: Maureen Siedor, Lynn Beller, Sarah Bishop, Aliza Hochman, Caroline Lukaszewski, Gerald Moody, John Nann, Mary Pyrdum, Cina Santos, Justin Schwab, Paul Simon, and Karthik Srinivasan.

*

SUMMARY OF CONTENTS

*

TABLE OF CONTENTS

xiii

CHAPTER 9   Basic Assumptions: Mistake, Impracticability and Frustration --- 807

*

TABLE OF CASES

Principal and digested cases are in bold type. Non-principal cases are in roman type. References are to Pages.

CONTRACTS

NOTE ON EDITING

In presenting the materials in this book the editors have used the following conventions.

Cases. Descriptions and restatements of the facts of a case, and any insertion within an opinion, if prepared by the editors, are enclosed in brackets. Some opinions are presented with minor adjustments in format and style. A statutory reference in an opinion is as given by the court, except as otherwise noted.

Citations. The Restatement, Second, of Contracts (1980) is referred to simply as "Restatement," except when it is compared with the initial Restatement of Contracts (1932). References to the initial Restatement carry a designation such as "original" or "first." The Uniform Commercial Code is cited, often, as "UCC," or "the Code." All references to Article 1 of the UCC are to the 2001 Revised Text. (That version and its predecessor, as well as Article 2 of the UCC and the proposed amendments to it, and the Restatement and other useful sources, are found in the paperback *Selections for Contracts* (*Selections*) that accompanies this text.) The United Nations Convention on Contracts for the International Sale of Goods, sometimes referred to as the Vienna Convention, is cited as "CISG."

In general, parallel citations to cases in materials reproduced, including opinions, have been deleted unless they carry information (*e.g.*, a page reference). A citation to a decision does not include, normally, an indication of subsequent case history having no effect on the merit or authority of the decision cited, or of an opinion associated with it (*e.g.*, "certiorari denied").

Notes and Problems. When a question or problem is accompanied by a reference to a case, the reference is intended only to support a line of thought, or an analogy, and not to supply "the answer."

Footnotes. The lettering of a footnote reference within an opinion or other quoted text indicates that the note was inserted by the editors; numbering indicates a quoted footnote. When a footnote in an opinion or other reproduced text has been omitted, the footnotes retained have been renumbered in sequence.

Pronouns and Gender. To avoid occasional awkwardness or confusion in distinguishing one party from another, we have, when useful, characterized promisors as women and promisees as men.

CHAPTER 1

BASES FOR ENFORCING PROMISES

SECTION 1. ENFORCEABLE PROMISES: AN INTRODUCTION

Most people have an informal sense of contracts. Almost everyone of consenting age has entered into a contract, often with little hesitation or ceremony. Consider, for example, the arrangement you have with your cell phone company or the agreement established when you accepted the offer of admission from your law school. Yet while there may be a common sense notion of contracts and of contracting, this book provides more formal content to that general understanding. We are interested in what "contract" means as a matter of law.

The Restatement of Contracts, Second, defines contract as "a promise or set of promises for the breach of which the law gives a remedy, or the performance of which the law in some way recognizes as a duty." Restatement § 1. Not all promises are legally binding; the law does not provide a remedy for every broken promise. There may, of course, be moral or social sanctions for breaking a promise, but our primary inquiry here concerns the distinctive contributions of *law*. And how does the law determine which promises to enforce?

We take up that question with two cases that focus on the promise itself. The first considers whether a binding (or enforceable) promise was created by a doctor's assertion that he would make an injured hand "one hundred percent perfect." The second case queries whether an enforceable promise should be found in the printed materials of a boat manufacturer, stating that its boats could attain a "maximum speed of 30 miles per hour." These cases begin our exploration of why some promises are found to be enforceable and others not. We then turn to the issue of how law enforces promises, taking an initial look at remedies for breach.

Beyond the "why" and "how" of promissory enforcement, these opening materials also serve as an introduction to the question of "where" the law of promissory obligation is to be found: the basic sources and authorities that govern most contract cases. We have already mentioned the influential Restatement of Contracts, a comprehensive statement of general common law contract principles first promulgated by the American Law Institute (ALI) in 1932. The Restatement, Second, appeared in 1980. In this book, unless otherwise indicated, a reference to the "Restatement" refers to the Restatement, Second. While not enacted law itself, the Restatement has been aptly described by a former ALI director as "common law 'persuasive authority' with a high degree of persuasion." Herbert Goodrich, 241, 244–45 *Field Centenary Essays* (1949). For more on the history of the Restatements, see the Selections for Contracts.

1

In addition to the Restatement, statutes are a second important source of authority, particularly Article 2 of the Uniform Commercial Code, which, as we shall see in the next case, governs all cases involving the sale of goods. We highlight various sources of law as we encounter them below.

Of course, the primary sources relied on in this casebook are judicial opinions, or the common law, and we begin our investigation of promises with a well-known case, Hawkins v. McGee.

Hawkins v. McGee

New Hampshire Supreme Court, 1929.
84 N.H. 114, 146 A. 641.

■ BRANCH, J. The operation in question consisted in the removal of a considerable quantity of scar tissue from the palm of the plaintiff's right hand and the grafting of skin taken from the plaintiff's chest in place thereof. The scar tissue was the result of a severe burn caused by contact with an electric wire, which the plaintiff received about nine years before the time of the transactions here involved. There was evidence to the effect that before the operation was performed the plaintiff and his father went to the defendant's office, and that the defendant, in answer to the question, "How long will the boy be in the hospital?" replied, "Three or four days, not over four; then the boy can go home and it will be just a few days when he will go back to work with a good hand." Clearly this and other testimony to the same effect would not justify a finding that the doctor contracted to complete the hospital treatment in three or four days or that the plaintiff would be able to go back to work within a few days thereafter. The above statements could only be construed as expressions of opinion or predictions as to the probable duration of the treatment and plaintiff's resulting disability, and the fact that these estimates were exceeded would impose no contractual liability upon the defendant. The only substantial basis for the plaintiff's claim is the testimony that the defendant also said before the operation was decided upon, "I will guarantee to make the hand a hundred per cent perfect hand or a hundred per cent good hand." The plaintiff was present when these words were alleged to have been spoken, and, if they are to be taken at their face value, it seems obvious that proof of their utterance would establish the giving of a warranty in accordance with his contention.

The defendant argues, however, that, even if these words were uttered by him, no reasonable man would understand that they were used with the intention of entering "into any contractual relation whatever," and that they could reasonably be understood only "as his expression in strong language that he believed and expected that as a result of the operation he would give the plaintiff a very good hand." It may be conceded, as the defendant contends, that, before the question of the making of a contract should be submitted to a jury, there is a preliminary question of law for the trial court to pass upon, i.e. "whether the words could possibly have the meaning imputed to them by the party who founds his case upon a certain interpretation," but it cannot be held that the trial court decided this question erroneously in the present case. It is unnecessary to determine at this time whether the argument of the defendant, based upon "common knowledge of the uncertainty which attends all surgical operations," and the improbability that a surgeon would ever contract to make a damaged part of the human body "one hundred per cent perfect," would, in the absence of countervailing considerations, be regarded as conclusive, for there were other factors in the present case which tended to support the contention of the plaintiff. There was evidence that the defendant repeatedly solicited from the plaintiff's father the opportunity to perform this operation, and the theory was advanced by plaintiff's counsel in cross-examination of defendant that he sought an opportunity to "experiment on skin grafting," in which he had had little previous experience. If the jury accepted this part of plaintiff's contention, there would be a reasonable basis for the further conclusion that, if defendant spoke the words attributed to him, he did so with the intention that they should be accepted at their face value, as an inducement for the granting of consent to the operation by the plaintiff and his father, and there was ample evidence that they were so accepted by them. The question of the making of the alleged contract was properly submitted to the jury.

[The Court then discussed the proper measure of damages and, finding that the trial court's instructions regarding damages to the jury were erroneous, ordered a new trial. We take up the question of damages in Section 2.]

NOTES

(1) *One Hundred Percent.* Dr. McGee made a number of statements to the boy's father regarding the outcome of treatment, but it does not appear that Dr. McGee actually used the word "promise." What makes a statement a promise? Consider the role of language, its context, and the nature of the transaction. See Restatement §§ 2 and 4. What result if a surgeon, before performing reconstructive knee surgery, tells the patient that "the operation could give you a knee that was stronger than before" and that the patient would, "if committed, play basketball again"? See Anglin v. Kleeman, 665 A.2d 747 (N.H.1995).

(2) *Policy Considerations.* In a well-known case involving plastic surgery gone wrong, the court observed that "[i]t is not hard to see why the courts should be unenthusiastic or skeptical about contract theory [in such a case]." Sullivan v. O'Connor, 296 N.E.2d 183 (Mass.1973). Is judicial skepticism about recovery in contract warranted? Why? What other theories of recovery might an aggrieved plaintiff try? What factors might contribute to a decision to bring one sort of claim rather than another? The *Sullivan* case is presented on p. 14 below.

(3) *Statutory Override.* Common-law rulings by judges sometimes give way to opposing judgments by legislatures. In this regard, consider the following. In 1971, the Michigan Supreme Court affirmed a judgment for damages for breach of contract against a surgeon who, according to his patient's testimony, had said before a stomach operation, "After this operation, you can throw your pillbox away" and "Once you have an operation it takes care of all your troubles." Guilmet v. Campbell, 188 N.W.2d 601 (Mich.1971). Three years later, the Michigan legislature enacted a statute providing that an "agreement promise, contract, or warranty of cure relating to medical care or treatment" is void unless evidenced by a signed

writing. 31 Mich.Comp.L.Ann. 566132(g). We note the interplay between courts and legislatures at various points throughout this book.

Bayliner Marine Corp. v. Crow

Supreme Court of Virginia, 1999.
257 Va. 121, 509 S.E.2d 499.

■ KEENAN, JUSTICE. In this appeal, the dispositive issue is whether there was sufficient evidence to support the trial court's ruling that the manufacturer of a sport fishing boat breached an express warranty and implied warranties of merchantability and fitness for a particular purpose.

In the summer of 1989, John R. Crow was invited by John Atherton, then a sales representative for Tidewater Yacht Agency, Inc. (Tidewater), to ride on a new model sport fishing boat known as a 3486 Trophy Convertible, manufactured by Bayliner Marine Corporation (Bayliner). During an excursion lasting about 20 minutes, Crow piloted the boat for a short period of time but was not able to determine its speed because there was no equipment on board for such testing.

When Crow asked Atherton about the maximum speed of the boat, Atherton explained that he had no personal experience with the boat or information from other customers concerning the boat's performance. Therefore, Atherton consulted two documents described as "prop matrixes," which were included by Bayliner in its dealer's manual.

Atherton gave Crow copies of the "prop matrixes," which listed the boat models offered by Bayliner and stated the recommended propeller sizes, gear ratios, and engine sizes for each model. The "prop matrixes" also listed the maximum speed for each model. The 3486 Trophy Convertible was listed as having a maximum speed of 30 miles per hour when equipped with a size "20x20" or "20x19" propeller. The boat Crow purchased did not have either size propeller but, instead, had a size "20x17" propeller.

At the bottom of one of the "prop matrixes" was the following disclaimer: "This data is intended for comparative purposes only, and is available without reference to weather conditions or other variables. All testing was done at or near sea level, with full fuel and water tanks, and approximately 600 lb. passenger and gear weight."

Atherton also showed Crow a Bayliner brochure describing the 1989 boat models, including the 3486 Trophy Convertible. The brochure included a picture of that model fully rigged for offshore fishing accompanied by the statement that this model "delivers the kind of performance you need to get to the prime offshore fishing grounds."

In August 1989, Crow entered into a written contract for the purchase of the 3486 Trophy Convertible in which he had ridden. The purchase price was $120,000, exclusive of taxes. The purchase price included various equipment to be installed by Tidewater including a generator, a cockpit cover, a "Bimini top," a winch, a spotlight, radar, a navigation system, an icemaker, fishing outriggers, an automatic pilot system, extra fuel gauges, a second radio, and air conditioning and heating units. The total weight of the added equipment was about 2,000 pounds. Crow did not test drive the boat after the additional equipment was installed or at any other time prior to taking delivery.

When Crow took delivery of the boat in September 1989, he piloted it onto the Elizabeth River. He noticed that the boat's speed measuring equipment, which was installed in accordance with the contract terms, indicated that the boat's maximum speed was 13 miles per hour. Crow immediately returned to Tidewater and reported the problem.

During the next 12 to 14 months, while Crow retained ownership and possession of the boat, Tidewater made numerous repairs and adjustments to the boat in an attempt to increase its speed capability. Despite these efforts, the boat consistently achieved a maximum speed of only 17 miles per hour, except for one period following an engine modification when it temporarily reached a speed of about 24 miles per hour. In July 1990, a representative from Bayliner wrote Crow a letter stating that the perform-ance representations made at the time of purchase were incorrect, and that 23 to 25 miles per hour was the maximum speed the boat could achieve.

In 1992, Crow filed a motion for judgment against Tidewater, Bayliner, and Brunswick Corporation, the manufacturer of the boat's diesel engines. Crow alleged, among other things, that Bayliner breached express warran-ties, and implied warranties of merchantability and fitness for a particular purpose.

At a bench trial in 1994, Crow, Atherton, and Gordon W. Shelton, III, Tidewater's owner, testified that speed is a critical quality in boats used for offshore sport fishing in the Tidewater area of Virginia because of the distance between the coast and the offshore fishing grounds. According to these witnesses, a typical offshore fishing site in that area is 90 miles from the coast. Therefore, the speed at which the boat can travel to and from fishing sites has a major impact on the amount of time left in a day for fishing.

Crow testified that because of the boat's slow speed, he could not use the boat for offshore fishing, that he had no other use for it, and that he would not have purchased the boat if he had known that its maximum speed was 23 to 25 miles per hour. . . .

The trial court entered judgment in favor of Crow against Bayliner on the counts of breach of express warranty and breach of implied warranties of merchantability and fitness for a particular purpose. . . . On appeal, we review the evidence in the light most favorable to Crow, the prevailing party at trial.

Crow argues that the "prop matrixes" he received created an express warranty by Bayliner that the boat he purchased was capable of a maxi-mum speed of 30 miles per hour. We disagree.

Code § 8.2–313 provides, in relevant part:

Express warranties by the seller are created as follows:

(a) Any affirmation of fact or promise made by the seller to the buyer which relates to the goods and becomes part of the basis of the bargain creates an express warranty that the goods shall conform to the affirmation or promise.

(b) Any description of the goods which is made a part of the basis of the bargain creates an express warranty that the goods shall conform to the description.

The issue whether a particular affirmation of fact made by the seller constitutes an express warranty is generally a question of fact. See id., Official Comment 3; Daughtrey v. Ashe, 243 Va. 73, 78, 413 S.E.2d 336, 339 (1992). In Daughtrey, we examined whether a jeweler's statement on an appraisal form constituted an express warranty. We held that the jeweler's description of the particular diamonds being purchased as "v.v.s. quality" constituted an express warranty that the diamonds were, in fact, of that grade. Id. at 77, 413 S.E.2d at 338.

Unlike the representation in Daughtrey, however, the statements in the "prop matrixes" provided by Bayliner did not relate to the particular boat purchased by Crow, or to one having substantially similar characteristics. By their plain terms, the figures stated in the "prop matrixes" referred to a boat with different sized propellers that carried equipment weighing substantially less than the equipment on Crow's boat. Therefore, we conclude that the statements contained in the "prop matrixes" did not constitute an express warranty by Bayliner about the performance capabilities of the particular boat purchased by Crow.

Crow also contends that Bayliner made an express warranty regarding the boat's maximum speed in the statement in Bayliner's sales brochure that this model boat "delivers the kind of performance you need to get to the prime offshore fishing grounds." While the general rule is that a description of the goods that forms a basis of the bargain constitutes an express warranty, Code § 8.2–313(2) directs that "a statement purporting to be merely the seller's opinion or commendation of the goods does not create a warranty."

The statement made by Bayliner in its sales brochure is merely a commendation of the boat's performance and does not describe a specific characteristic or feature of the boat. The statement simply expressed the manufacturer's opinion concerning the quality of the boat's performance and did not create an express warranty that the boat was capable of attaining a speed of 30 miles per hour. Therefore, we conclude that the evidence does not support the trial court's finding that Bayliner breached an express warranty made to Crow.

[The Court also found that Bayliner had not violated the "implied warranty of merchantability" provided in UCC § 2–314. Discussion of implied warranties is left to Chapter 5.]

Reversed and final judgment.

NOTES

(1) *Express Warranties.* According to Crow, what promise had Atherton broken? By what means had the supposed promise been made? What if Atherton had

told Crow during their negotiations that "in my opinion this boat will go 30 miles per hour no trouble"? See UCC § 2–313(2). Why should an express warranty result if the seller did not intend to make one?

(2) *UCC Primer.* Article 2 of the Uniform Commercial Code (UCC or "the Code") is the primary source of law for transactions involving the sale of goods. The Code itself is the product of the American Law Institute and the National Conference of Commissioners on Uniform State Laws (NCCUSL). Versions of the Code have been enacted across the country by state legislatures, and by Congress for the District of Columbia. Transactions covered by Article 2 include not only sales between merchants but also those between merchants and consumers, as in *Bayliner.* As we shall see, in a number of areas the Code provides special rules for merchants, who are assumed to be more sophisticated and more familiar with commercial practices than are consumers. Determining whether a party is a merchant is therefore an important preliminary question. Article 2 defines merchant to include not only "a person who deals in goods of the kind" but also one who "by his occupation holds himself out as having knowledge or skill peculiar to the goods involved in the transaction." UCC § 2–104(1). We return to the significance of a party's status as a merchant throughout the book.

What are "goods" under Article 2? The starting point is UCC § 2–105(1). What are "things ... which are movable"? Is land "goods"? Is a 10–ton printing press "goods"? What if in the case above, Crow had custom-ordered his boat so that at the time of the contract the boat had not been built? See UCC § 2–105(2). The application of Article 2 is often called into question in contracts that involve both goods and services. Article 2 does not apply, for example, to a contract to paint the exterior of a house, even though a small amount of paint (goods) will be transferred, because the goods component of the contract is incidental. Should Article 2 apply to a "hybrid contract"—that is, a contract involving both the sale of goods and the provision of services, or a contract involving both the sale of goods and the sale of property other than goods, such as real estate? What about a contract that includes both the sale and installation of an appliance such as a washing machine? What about a catering contract, in which the customer is both buying the food and paying for wait staff? We look more closely at the problem of hybrid contracts in Chapter 8.

Finally, it is important to keep in mind that the Code does not wholly supplant the common law. UCC § 1–103(b) states that "Unless displaced by the particular provisions of [the Code], the principles of law and equity ... supplement its provisions." UCC § 1–103(b) provides a lengthy list of principles of law and equity that may supplement the Code, including such principles as capacity to contract, duress, and mistake. For an interesting discussion of the concept of supplementation, see Comment 2 to UCC § 1–103.

(3) *Implied Warranties.* Suppose that another purchaser contracted with Bayliner for the sale of a speed boat and that, as in the principal case, the contract was silent with regard to the boat's speed. Assuming that there had been no brochure or other printed materials or any discussion of speed between the parties prior to the sale, would any promise have been broken if when the purchaser revved the engine of his new boat, it was able to achieve a maximum speed of only two miles per hour? See UCC § 2–314 (2). Which of the provisions of that subsection might apply? The matter of a seller disclaiming warranties is addressed in Chapter 6.

PROBLEM

Canine Conundrum. Melissa bought a puppy from Peter, a rancher whose dog had just had a litter, for $300. The next day Melissa took the puppy to a veterinarian for a check up. The vet diagnosed a minor urinary infection and prescribed a week-long course of antibiotics. Melissa has brought a claim against Peter in small claims court for breach of warranty. Is she likely to succeed? See *Nuijens v. Novy*, 543 N.Y.S.2d 887 (N.Y.Just.Ct., 1989). What if Melissa had bought the puppy from a kennel intending to breed it, and a week later her veterinarian accurately informed her, upon examining the puppy, that it was incapable of reproduction? *Dempsey v. Rosenthal*, 468 N.Y.S.2d 441 (N.Y. 1983). What additional facts might you want to know in determining whether or not a warranty had been breached?

SECTION 2.   REMEDYING BREACH

We all know what it means to keep a promise. Simply put, it means doing what was promised. But what does it mean to *enforce* a promise? Restatement § 1 defines a contract in terms of both a legal duty to perform a promise and the provision of remedy if performance does not occur. How does the law determine the appropriate remedy? Although the answer is taken up in detail in Chapter 7, some consideration of remedies is useful at the outset to get a sense of what is at stake for the parties when a promise is broken.

The cases that follow introduce two fundamental assumptions made by courts in providing remedies. The first is that the law is primarily concerned with *relief* of aggrieved promisees and not with *punishment* of promisors. The second assumption is that the primary purpose of the remedy is to put the promisee in the position it would have been in had the promise been performed. The promisee is often said to receive "the benefit of the bargain" and the interest that is protected in this way is called the *expectation interest*. The complexities of figuring out just how to measure that interest are tested in *Naval Institute*, our next case.

NOTE

Theories of Enforcing Promises. Although the primary focus of this casebook is contract doctrine—that is, the basic rules and practices that comprise contract law—contract *theory* is not entirely unrelated to our endeavor and we will from time to time refer to it in order to illuminate aspects of contract law. A central concern of contract theory is the question of why law *should* enforce certain promises.

A number of theoretical justifications have been proposed to answer this question and each directs us to a set of underlying values served by contract doctrine. Some theories turn principally on protecting the promisee's reliance on the promise or on respecting the promisor's autonomy or will to make binding promises. Other theoretical justifications look to economic efficiency, predictability, fairness, social justice and morality. All of these concerns resonate in contract law although to some extent they take us out of the realm of positive contract law, or more commonly, doctrine. This has been a matter of concern for some, including Oliver Wendell Holmes[a] who unhappily noted that "[n]owhere is the confusion

---

a. Oliver Wendell Holmes, Jr. (1841–1935) practiced law in Boston, served briefly as professor of law at Harvard, and then for twenty years as justice and later chief justice between legal and moral ideas more manifest than in the law of contract." Oliver Wendell Holmes, The Path of the Law, 10 Harv. L. Rev. 457 (1897). Still, as you read the cases going forward, it is worth bearing in mind the competing normative values that justify the legal enforcement of promises.

United States Naval Institute v. Charter Communications, Inc.

United States Court of Appeals, Second Circuit, 1991.
936 F.2d 692.

■ KEARSE, CIRCUIT JUDGE: This case returns to us following our remand in United States Naval Institute v. Charter Communications, Inc., 875 F.2d 1044 (2d Cir.1989) ("Naval I"), ... for the fashioning of relief in favor of plaintiff United States Naval Institute ("Naval") against defendant Charter Communications, Inc., and Berkley Publishing Group (collectively "Berkley"), for breach of an agreement with respect to the publication of the paperback edition of The Hunt For Red October ("Red October" or the "Book"). On remand, the district court awarded Naval $35,380.50 in damages [and] $7,760.12 as profits wrongfully received by Berkley.... Naval appeals from so much of the judgment as failed to award a greater amount as profits.... Berkley cross-appeals from the judgment as a whole and from such parts of it as awarded moneys to Naval. For the reasons below, we reverse the award of profits; we affirm the award of damages....

I. Background

... Naval, as the assignee of the author's copyright in Red October, entered into a licensing agreement with Berkley in September 1984 (the "Agreement"), granting Berkley the exclusive license to publish a paperback edition of the Book "not sooner than October 1985." Berkley shipped its paperback edition to retail outlets early, placing those outlets in position to sell the paperback prior to October 1985. As a result, retail sales of the paperback began on September 15, 1985, and early sales were sufficiently substantial that the Book was near the top of paperback bestseller lists before the end of September 1985.

Naval commenced the present action when it learned of Berkley's plans for early shipment, and it unsuccessfully sought a preliminary injunction. After trial, the district judge dismissed the complaint. He ruled that Berkley had not breached the Agreement because it was entitled, in accordance with industry custom, to ship prior to the agreed publication date. On appeal, we reversed. Though we upheld the district court's finding that the Agreement did not prohibit the early shipments themselves, we concluded that if the "not sooner than October 1985" term of the Agreement had any meaning whatever, it meant at least that Berkley was not

of the Supreme Judicial Court of Massachusetts. In 1902 President Theodore Roosevelt appointed him to the Supreme Court of the United States, where the quality of his dissenting opinions won him the title of the "Great Dissenter." He resigned because of his great age in 1932. His most famous work is *The Common Law* (1881), based on a series of lectures.

allowed to cause such voluminous paperback retail sales prior to that date, and that Berkley had therefore breached the Agreement. Naval I, 875 F.2d at 1049–51. Accordingly, we remanded for entry of a judgment awarding Naval appropriate relief.

On the remand, Naval asserted that it was entitled to recovery for copyright infringement, and it sought judgment awarding it all of Berkley's profits from pre-October 1985 sales of the Book; it estimated those profits at $724,300. . . . Berkley, on the other hand, [contended] that Berkley could not be held liable for copyright infringement . . .; it argued that Naval therefore had at most a claim for breach-of-contract [and] argued that the profits attributed to it by Naval were inflated. . . . [On remand, the district judge] concluded that Naval was entitled to recover damages for copyright infringement, comprising actual damages suffered by Naval plus Berkley's profits "attributable to the infringement," 17 U.S.C. § 504(b).

The court calculated Naval's "actual damages from Berkley's wrongful pre-October 'publication' " as the profits Naval would have earned from hardcover sales in September 1985 if the competing paperback edition had not then been offered for sale. July 17 Order at 8. Noting the downward trend of hardcover sales of the Book from March through August 1985, the court found that there was no reason to infer that Naval's September 1985 sales would have exceeded its August 1985 sales. The court calculated Naval's lost sales as the difference between the actual hardcover sales for those two months, and awarded Naval $35,380.50 as actual damages.

The district judge held that Berkley's profits "attributable to the infringement" were only those profits that resulted from "sales to customers who would not have bought the paperback but for the fact it became available in September." July 17 Order at 10. He found that most of the September paperback sales were made to buyers who would not have bought a hardcover edition in September, and therefore only those September sales that displaced hardcover sales were attributable to the infringement. Berkley's profit on the displacing copies totaled $7,760.12, and the court awarded that amount to Naval. . . .

II.   Discussion

A.   Naval's Claim of Copyright Infringement

[The court rejected this claim because an exclusive licensee cannot be liable for infringing the copyright conveyed to it, even though it is liable for breach of contract.]

B.   Contract Damages . . .

Since the purpose of damages for breach of contract is to compensate the injured party for the loss caused by the breach, 5 Corbin On Contracts § 1002, at 31 (1964), those damages are generally measured by the plaintiff's actual loss, see, e.g., Restatement (Second) of Contracts § 347 (1981). While on occasion the defendant's profits are used as the measure of damages, see, e.g., Cincinnati Siemens–Lungren Gas Illuminating Co. v. Western Siemens–Lungren Co., 152 U.S. 200, 204–07 (1894), . . . this generally occurs when those profits tend to define the plaintiff's loss, for an award of the defendant's profits where they greatly exceed the plaintiff's loss and there has been no tortious conduct on the part of the defendant would tend to be punitive, and punitive awards are not part of the law of contract damages. See generally Restatement (Second) of Contracts § 356 comment *a* ("The central objective behind the system of contract remedies is compensatory, not punitive."); *id.* comment *b* (agreement attempting to fix damages in amount vastly greater than what approximates actual loss would be unenforceable as imposing a penalty); *id.* § 355 (punitive damages not recoverable for breach of contract unless conduct constituting the breach is also a tort for which such damages are recoverable).

Here, the district court found that Berkley's alleged $724,300 profits did not define Naval's loss because many persons who bought the paperback in September 1985 would not have bought the book in hardcover but would merely have waited until the paperback edition became available. This finding is not clearly erroneous, and we turn to the question of whether the district court's finding that Naval suffered $35,380.50 in actual damages was proper.

In reaching the $35,380.50 figure, the court operated on the premise that, but for the breach by Berkley, Naval would have sold in September the same number of hardcover copies it sold in August. Berkley challenges that premise as speculative and argues that since Naval presented no evidence as to what its September 1985 sales would have been, Naval is entitled to recover no damages. It argues alternatively that the court should have computed damages on the premise that sales in the second half of September, in the absence of Berkley's premature release of the paperback edition, would have been made at the same rate as in the first half of September. Evaluating the district court's calculation of damages under the clearly erroneous standard of review, . . . we reject Berkley's contentions.

The record showed that, though there was a declining trend of hardcover sales of the Book from March through August 1985, Naval continued to sell its hardcover copies through the end of 1985, averaging some 3,000 copies a month in the latter period.[a] It plainly was not error for the district court to find that the preponderance of the evidence indicated that Berkley's early shipment of 1,400,000 copies of its paperback edition, some 40% of which went to retail outlets and led to the Book's rising close to the top of the paperback bestseller lists before the end of September 1985, caused Naval the loss of some hardcover sales prior to October 1985.

As to the quantification of that loss, we think it was within the prerogative of the court as finder of fact to look to Naval's August 1985 sales. Though there was no proof as to precisely what the unimpeded volume of hardcover sales would have been for the entire month of September, any such evidence would necessarily have been hypothetical. But it is not error to lay the normal uncertainty in such hypotheses at the door of the wrongdoer who altered the proper course of events, instead of at the door of the injured party. See, e.g., Lamborn v. Dittmer, 873 F.2d 522,

---

a. It is unclear where Judge Kearse got the figure of only "some 3,000 copies a month" used in the paragraph after the next, but it might be a misprint for 30,000, an approximation of the August figure.

532–33 (2d Cir.1989); Lee v. Joseph E. Seagram & Sons, Inc., 552 F.2d 447, 455–56 (2d Cir.1977).... See generally ... Restatement (Second) of Contracts § 352 comment *a* ("Doubts are generally resolved against the party in breach."). The court was not required to use as the starting point for its calculations Naval's actual sales in the first half of September, *i.e.*, those made prior to the first retail sale of the paperback edition. Berkley has not called to our attention any evidence in the record to indicate that the sales in a given month are normally spread evenly through that month. Indeed, it concedes that "[t]o a large degree, book sales depend on public whim and are notoriously unpredictable...." (Berkley brief on appeal at 31 n. 15.) Thus, nothing in the record foreclosed the possibility that, absent Berkley's breach, sales of hardcover copies in the latter part of September would have outpaced sales of those copies in the early part of the month. Though the court accurately described its selection of August 1985 sales as its benchmark as "generous[ ]," it was not improper, given the inherent uncertainty, to exercise generosity in favor of the injured party rather than in favor of the breaching party.

In all the circumstances, we cannot say that the district court's calculation of Naval's damages was clearly erroneous. ...

Conclusion

... For the foregoing reasons, we reverse so much of the judgment as granted Naval $7,760.12 as an award of Berkley's profits. In all other respects, the judgment is affirmed.

NOTES

(1) *Measuring Promisee's Loss.* How did the district court go wrong in awarding Berkley's profits on pre-October paperback sales to Naval Institute? How does that award square with protecting Naval's expectation interest? How does it square with assumption that the law's concern is with relief of promisees and not punishment of promisors?

(2) *Conceptualizing Disgorgement.* Are there any cases where "the defendant's profits ... tend to define the plaintiff's loss," as Judge Kearse put it? Professor E. Allan Farnsworth[a] described cases like *Cincinnati Siemens–Lungren,* cited as an example, in the following way:

"Suppose that a seller of a business makes a valid contract not to compete with the buyer and then breaks the covenant by operating a competing business. If the buyer claims damages ..., the court will often receive evidence of the profits that the seller made from the competing business as evidence of the profit that the buyer lost as a result of the breach. But a court will not assume that the buyer could have made the same sales that the seller did...." Your Loss or My Gain? The Dilemma

a. E. Allan Farnsworth (1928–2005) was an eminent contract law scholar. He taught for fifty years at the Columbia Law School, from which he graduated in 1952. He represented the United States in matters of international trade law at the United Nations and at UNIDROIT. In 1971, following Professor Robert Braucher, Farnsworth became the Reporter for the Restatement, Second, of Contracts. Now in its third edition, his treatise *Farnsworth on Contracts* is a standard text. Farnsworth was an editor on three editions of this casebook. In 2004, he published *Alleviating Mistakes: Reversal and Forgiveness for Flawed Perceptions*.

of the Disgorgement Principle in Breach of Contract Cases, 94 Yale L.J. 1339, 1366 (1985).

In other words, where the breaching promisor's profits match the amount the promisee would have gained had the promise been performed, disgorgement may be ordered. In such a case disgorgement and expectation produce the same figure. Nonetheless, the purposes of the two measures of recovery are distinct. Protecting the promisee's expectation interest "undoes" the breach with regard to the promise; the effect of disgorgement is to "undo" the breach with regard to the promisor, who must forego the gains of the breach.

(3) *Disgorgement in Non–Contract Cases.* Disgorgement of profits is not uncommon in non-contract cases. Note that the district judge "concluded that Naval was entitled to recover damages for copyright infringement, comprising actual damages suffered by Naval *plus Berkley's profits* 'attributable to the infringement.' 17 U.S.C. § 504(b)." This provision of the Copyright Act requires the infringer to disgorge profits to prevent the infringer from unfairly benefiting from a wrongful act.

(4) *Puzzler.* Why was the transaction in *Naval Institute* not governed by Article 2 of the Code?

————

THE PURPOSE OF REMEDIES: THREE PROTECTED INTERESTS

The court in *Naval Institute* sought to compensate Naval by calculating the extent of profits it lost on account of Berkley's breach of promise. This amount, and no more, constituted Naval's expectation interest. As expressed in Restatement § 344(a), the goal or purpose of protecting a promisee's expectation interest is to put the promisee "in as good a position as he would have been in had the contract been performed."

One way to accomplish this is for courts to compel performance of what was promised, using the remedy known as specific performance. However, specific performance is often unavailable (promised goods may be no longer available) or undesired (would young Charlie Hawkins have wanted Dr. McGee to give it another try?). In addition, ordering a party to do what was promised might require continuing judicial supervision, a task courts are reluctant, and perhaps ill-equipped, to take on, especially when the performance involves a service or a performance that extends over time. These considerations lead to another assumption animating contract remedies in the United States: the appropriate form of relief is compensation for the breach, rather than requiring the promisor to perform. Courts order specific performance only sparingly, and in cases where compensation is "inadequate." See Restatement § 359. The classic case for specific enforcement concerns the sale of land, since courts have traditionally regarded each tract of land as unique and therefore not susceptible to substitution.

If the law is to remedy breach by compensating the promisee, what amount of money should the promisor pay? We have already encountered one answer: whatever it takes to protect the promisee's expectation interest, or, as expressed in Restatement § 344(a), the amount necessary to put the promisee "in as good a position as he would have been in had the contract been performed." On this account, the promisee's injury consists in being worse off than if the promise had been performed, and expectation damages "undo" the effect of breach on the promisee.

There are two other interests that damages may protect: reliance and restitution. A promisee has a reliance interest if it has changed its position to its detriment in reliance on the promise. The promisee may, for example, have incurred expenses in preparing to perform. The promisee's injury consists of being worse off than if the promise had not been made. Reliance damages protect the promisee's interest in "being reimbursed for loss caused by reliance." Restatement § 344(b). As that section explains, reliance damages put the promisee "in as good a position as he would have been in had the contract not been made."

The promisee has a restitution interest to the extent that the promise conferred a benefit on the promisee. The promisee may, for example, have given the promisor a down payment or performed some work. Restatement § 344(c) describes the restitution interest as the promisee's "interest in having restored to him any benefit that he has conferred on the other party." Judicial remedies that protect this interest have the effect of "undoing" the promise by putting the *promisor* in the position in which it would have been had the promise not been made. For more on the three interests, see the pioneering article cited by the court in the following case, Lon Fuller & William Perdue, Jr., The Reliance Interest in Contract Damages, 46 Yale L.J. 52, 53–57 (1936). For criticism, see Richard Craswell, Against Fuller and Perdue, 67 U.Chi.L.Rev. 99 (2000).

In the following case, the Supreme Judicial Court of Massachusetts considered how these three interests—expectation, reliance, and restitution—play out in the context of an action brought against a cosmetic surgeon for his failure to improve the claimant's appearance as he had promised to do. Our focus in *Sullivan* is not on the promise, as it was in *Hawkins*, but on the nature of the remedy.

Sullivan v. O'Connor

Supreme Judicial Court of Massachusetts, 1973.
363 Mass. 579, 296 N.E.2d 183.

[Alice Sullivan alleged she had entered into a contract with Dr. James O'Connor for plastic surgery "to enhance her beauty and improve her nose," but that her appearance had been worsened by surgery on her nose performed by Dr. James O'Connor. She charged him with negligence and with breach of contract. A jury awarded her $13,500 on the latter count, rejecting her charge of negligence. The evidence provided support for findings as follow. O'Connor had promised Sullivan that, in two operations, he would make her nose shorter and more pleasing in relation to her other features. Having failed in that, he performed a third operation. Sullivan remained disfigured; and her appearance could not be improved by further surgery. Sullivan had paid a fee to O'Connor, and hospital expenses, amounting to $622.65. She was a professional entertainer, as O'Connor had known. She failed to demonstrate, however, that she had lost employment by reason of her change of appearance.

O'Connor appealed, contending that the trial judge had erred in instructing the jury about the issue of damages. Sullivan had also objected to those instructions, on the ground that the judge had not instructed the jury that she was entitled to the difference between the value of her nose as promised and the diminished value of her nose after the operations. However, Sullivan indicated on appeal that she was willing to waive that objection if the appellate court denied O'Connor's appeal.

The opinion describes the instructions about damages given to the jury, and O'Connor's objections to them.]

■ KAPLAN, JUSTICE. . . . The judge instructed the jury, first, that the plaintiff was entitled to recover her out-of-pocket expenses incident to the operations. Second, she could recover the damages flowing directly, naturally, proximately, and foreseeably from the defendant's breach of promise. These would comprehend damages for any disfigurement of the plaintiff's nose— that is, any change of appearance for the worse—including the effects of the consciousness of such disfigurement on the plaintiff's mind, and in this connection the jury should consider the nature of the plaintiff's profession. Also consequent upon the defendant's breach, and compensable, were the pain and suffering involved in the third operation, but not in the first two. As there was no proof that any loss of earnings by the plaintiff resulted from the breach, that element should not enter into the calculation of damages.

By his exceptions the defendant contends that the judge erred in allowing the jury to take into account anything but the plaintiff's out-of-pocket expenses (presumably at the stipulated amount). The defendant excepted to the judge's refusal of his request for a general charge to that effect, and, more specifically, to the judge's refusal of a charge that the plaintiff could not recover for pain and suffering connected with the third operation or for impairment of the plaintiff's appearance and associated mental distress.

The plaintiff on her part excepted to the judge's refusal of a request to charge that the plaintiff could recover the difference in value between the nose as promised and the nose as it appeared after the operations. However, the plaintiff in her brief expressly waives this exception and others made by her in case this court overrules the defendant's exceptions; thus she would be content to hold the jury's verdict in her favor.

We conclude that the defendant's exceptions should be overruled . . .

[In an omitted part of the decision, the Court discussed whether a doctor's promise should be unenforceable on policy grounds, concluding that the law allows "actions based on alleged contract, but insist[s] on clear proof . . . that a given result was promised." The Court then turned to the question of damages.]

If an action on the basis of contract is allowed, we have next the question of the measure of damages to be applied where liability is found. Some cases have taken the simple view that the promise by the physician is to be treated like an ordinary commercial promise, and accordingly that the successful plaintiff is entitled to a standard measure of recovery for breach of contract—"compensatory" ("expectancy") damages, an amount intended to put the plaintiff in the position he would be in if the contract had been performed, or, presumably, at the plaintiff's election, "restitution" damages, an amount corresponding to any benefit conferred by the plaintiff upon the defendant in the performance of the contract disrupted by the defendant's breach. See Restatement: Contracts § 329 and comment *a*, §§ 347, 384(1). Thus in Hawkins v. McGee, 84 N.H. 114, 146 A. 641, the defendant doctor was taken to have promised the plaintiff to convert his damaged hand by means of an operation into a good or perfect hand, but the doctor so operated as to damage the hand still further. The court, following the usual expectancy formula, would have asked the jury to estimate and award to the plaintiff the difference between the value of a good or perfect hand, as promised, and the value of the hand after the operation. (The same formula would apply, although the dollar result would be less, if the operation had neither worsened nor improved the condition of the hand.) If the plaintiff had not yet paid the doctor his fee, that amount would be deducted from the recovery. There could be no recovery for the pain and suffering of the operation, since that detriment would have been incurred even if the operation had been successful; one can say that this detriment was not "caused" by the breach. But where the plaintiff by reason of the operation was put to more pain than he would have had to endure, had the doctor performed as promised, he should be compensated for that difference as a proper part of his expectancy recovery. It may be noted that on an alternative count for malpractice the plaintiff in the *Hawkins* case had been nonsuited; but on ordinary principles this could not affect the contract claim, for it is hardly a defense to a breach of contract that the promisor acted innocently and without negligence. The New Hampshire court further refined the *Hawkins* analysis in McQuaid v. Michou, 85 N.H. 299, 157 A. 881, all in the direction of treating the patient-physician cases on the ordinary footing of expectancy. . . .

Other cases, including a number in New York, without distinctly repudiating the *Hawkins* type of analysis, have indicated that a different and generally more lenient measure of damages is to be applied in patient-physician actions based on breach of alleged special agreements to effect a cure, attain a stated result, or employ a given medical method. This measure is expressed in somewhat variant ways, but the substance is that the plaintiff is to recover any expenditures made by him and for other detriment (usually not specifically described in the opinions) following proximately and foreseeably upon the defendant's failure to carry out his promise. Robins v. Finestone, 308 N.Y. 543, 546, 127 N.E.2d 330. . . . This, be it noted, is not a "restitution" measure, for it is not limited to restoration of the benefit conferred on the defendant (the fee paid) but includes other expenditures, for example, amounts paid for medicine and nurses; so also it would seem according to its logic to take in damages for any worsening of the plaintiff's condition due to the breach. Nor is it an "expectancy" measure, for it does not appear to contemplate recovery of the whole difference in value between the condition as promised and the condition actually resulting from the treatment. Rather the tendency of the formulation is to put the plaintiff back in the position he occupied just before the parties entered upon the agreement, to compensate him for the detriments he suffered in reliance upon the agreement. This kind of intermediate pattern of recovery for breach of contract is discussed in the suggestive article by Fuller and Perdue, The Reliance Interest in Contract Damages, 46 Yale L.J. 52, 373, where the authors show that, although not attaining the currency of the standard measures, a "reliance" measure has for special reasons been applied by the courts in a variety of settings, including noncommercial settings. See 46 Yale L.J. at 396–401.[1]

For breach of the patient-physician agreements under consideration, a recovery limited to restitution seems plainly too meager, if the agreements are to be enforced at all. On the other hand, an expectancy recovery may well be excessive. The factors, already mentioned, which have made the cause of action somewhat suspect, also suggest moderation as to the breadth of the recovery that should be permitted. Where, as in the case at bar and in a number of the reported cases, the doctor has been absolved of negligence by the trier, an expectancy measure may be thought harsh. We should recall here that the fee paid by the patient to the doctor for the alleged promise would usually be quite disproportionate to the putative expectancy recovery. To attempt, moreover, to put a value on the condition that would or might have resulted, had the treatment succeeded as promised, may sometimes put an exceptional strain on the imagination of the fact finder. As a general consideration, Fuller and Perdue argue that the reasons for granting damages for broken promises to the extent of the expectancy are at their strongest when the promises are made in a business context, when they have to do with the production or distribution of goods or the allocation of functions in the market place; they become weaker as the context shifts from a commercial to a noncommercial field. 46 Yale L.J. at 60–63.

There is much to be said, then, for applying a reliance measure to the present facts, and we have only to add that our cases are not unreceptive to the use of that formula in special situations. We have, however, had no previous occasion to apply it to patient-physician cases.[2]

1. Some of the exceptional situations mentioned where reliance may be preferred to expectancy are those in which the latter measure would be hard to apply or would impose too great a burden; performance was interfered with by external circumstances; the contract was indefinite. See 46 Yale L.J. at 373–386; 394–396.

2. In Mt. Pleasant Stable Co. v. Steinberg, 238 Mass. 567, 131 N.E. 295, the plaintiff company agreed to supply teams of horses at agreed rates as required from day to day by the defendant for his business. To prepare itself to fulfill the contract and in reliance on it, the plaintiff bought two "Cliest" horses at a certain price. When the defendant repudiated the contract, the plaintiff sold the horses at a loss and in its action for breach claimed the loss as an element of damages. The court properly held that the plaintiff was not entitled to this item as it was also claiming (and recovering) its lost profits (expectancy) on the contract as a whole. Cf. Noble v. Ames Mfg. Co., 112 Mass. 492. (The loss on sale of the horses is analogous to the pain and suffering for which the patient would be disallowed a recovery in Hawkins v. McGee, 84 N.H. 114, 146 A. 641, because he was claiming and recovering expectancy damages.) The court in the *Mt. Pleasant* case referred, however, to Pond v. Harris, 113 Mass. 114, as a contrasting situation where the expectancy could not be fairly determined. There the defendant had wrongfully revoked an agreement to arbitrate a

The question of recovery on a reliance basis for pain and suffering or mental distress requires further attention. We find expressions in the decisions that pain and suffering (or the like) are simply not compensable in actions for breach of contract. The defendant seemingly espouses this proposition in the present case. True, if the buyer under a contract for the purchase of a lot of merchandise, in suing for the seller's breach, should claim damages for mental anguish caused by his disappointment in the transaction, he would not succeed; he would be told, perhaps, that the asserted psychological injury was not fairly foreseeable by the defendant as a probable consequence of the breach of such a business contract. See Restatement of Contracts, § 341, and comment *a*. But there is no general rule barring such items of damage in actions for breach of contract. It is all a question of the subject matter and background of the contract, and when the contract calls for an operation on the person of the plaintiff, psychological as well as physical injury may be expected to figure somewhere in the recovery, depending on the particular circumstances. The point is explained in Stewart v. Rudner, 349 Mich. 459, 469, 84 N.W.2d 816. Cf. Frewen v. Page, 238 Mass. 499, 131 N.E. 475; McClean v. University Club, 327 Mass. 68, 97 N.E.2d 174. Again, it is said in a few of the New York cases, concerned with the classification of actions for statute of limitations purposes, that the absence of allegations demanding recovery for pain and suffering is characteristic of a contract claim by a patient against a physician, that such allegations rather belong in a claim for malpractice. See Robins v. Finestone, 308 N.Y. 543, 547, 127 N.E.2d 330; Budoff v. Kessler, 2 A.D.2d 760, 153 N.Y.S.2d 654. These remarks seem unduly sweeping. Suffering or distress resulting from the breach going beyond that which was envisaged by the treatment as agreed, should be compensable on the same ground as the worsening of the patient's condition because of the breach. Indeed it can be argued that the very suffering or distress "contracted for"—that which would have been incurred if the treatment achieved the promised result—should also be compensable on the theory underlying the New York cases. For that suffering is "wasted" if the treatment fails. Otherwise stated, compensation for this waste is arguably required in order to complete the restoration of the status quo ante.[3]

dispute with the plaintiff (this was before such agreements were made specifically enforceable). In an action for the breach, the plaintiff was held entitled to recover for his preparations for the arbitration which had been rendered useless and a waste, including the plaintiff's time and trouble and his expenditures for counsel and witnesses. The context apparently was commercial but reliance elements were held compensable when there was no fair way of estimating an expectancy. See, generally, annotation, 17 A.L.R.2d 1300. A noncommercial example is Smith v. Sherman, 4 Cush. 408, 413–414, suggesting that a conventional recovery for breach of promise of marriage included a recompense for various efforts and expenditures by the plaintiff preparatory to the promised wedding. . . .

3. Recovery on a reliance basis for breach of the physician's promise tends to equate with the usual recovery for malpractice, since the latter also looks in general to restoration of the condition before the injury. But this is not paradoxical, especially when it is noted that the origins of contract lie in tort. See Farnsworth, The Past of Promise: An Historical Introduction to Contract, 69 Col.L.Rev. 576, 594–596; Breitel, J. in Stella Flour & Feed Corp. v. National City Bank, 285 App.Div. 182, 189, 136 N.Y.S.2d 139 (dissenting opinion). A few cases have considered possible recovery for breach by a physician of a promise to sterilize a patient, resulting in birth of a child to the patient and spouse. If such an action is held maintainable, the reliance and expectancy measures would, we think, tend to equate, because the promised

In the light of the foregoing discussion, all the defendant's exceptions fail: the plaintiff was not confined to the recovery of her out-of-pocket expenditures; she was entitled to recover also for the worsening of her condition,[4] and for the pain and suffering and mental distress involved in the third operation. These items were compensable on either an expectancy or a reliance view. We might have been required to elect between the two views if the pain and suffering connected with the first two operations contemplated by the agreement, or the whole difference in value between the present and the promised conditions, were being claimed as elements of damage. But the plaintiff waives her possible claim to the former element, and to so much of the latter as represents the difference in value between the promised condition and the condition before the operations.

Plaintiff's exceptions waived. Defendant's exceptions overruled.

NOTES

(1) *Applying the Interests.* Assign the following round numbers to Sullivan's claim: doctor's fee $300; hospital fee per operation $100; pain and suffering per operation $3,000; increase in value of appearance if enhanced as promised $20,000; loss in value of appearance due to disfigurement $10,000. What would be the amount of Sullivan's claim if based on her restitution interest? On her reliance interest? On her expectation interest? How did the trial court calculate her damages?

(2) *Lost Opportunities as Reliance.* It can be argued that by relying on O'Connor, Sullivan lost the opportunity to deal with another doctor, who would presumably have done a competent job so that she would have been in the same position as if O'Connor had performed as promised. What if Sullivan could prove she had lost professional engagements as a result of surgeries? Why not take such a loss into account in calculating Sullivan's reliance interest? Because it would deprive the court of a middle ground to avoid an "excessive" and "harsh" recovery? Because lost opportunities are too speculative? Keep your eyes open for the relatively rare instances where courts take account of lost opportunities.

(3) *The Case of the Request for Restitution.* Not all plaintiffs have shared the view of the court in *Sullivan* that "a recovery limited to restitution seems plainly too meager." When two oil companies sued the United States for its breach of lease contracts giving them rights to explore for and develop oil off the North Carolina coast, what they sought was restitution of $156 million that they had paid in return for the contracts. Their award of summary judgment was reversed by the Court of Appeals. The Supreme Court reversed and remanded.

The Court observed that when the United States makes contracts, its rights and duties are governed generally by the law applicable to contracts between private individuals, as reflected in the Restatement. "We agree that the Government broke its promise ... and it must give the companies their money back.... And it must do so whether the contracts would, or would not, ultimately have

---

condition was preservation of the family status quo....

It would, however, be a mistake to think in terms of strict "formulas." For example, a jurisdiction which would apply a reliance measure to the present facts might impose a more severe damage sanction for the wilful use by the physician of a method of operation that he undertook not to employ.

4. That condition involves a mental element and appraisal of it properly called for consideration of the fact that the plaintiff was an entertainer. Cf. McQuaid v. Michou, 85 N.H. 299, 303–304, 157 A. 881 (discussion of continuing condition resulting from physician's breach).

proved financially beneficial to the companies. The Restatement illustrates this point as follows:

> A contracts to sell a tract of land to B for $100,000. After B has made a part payment of $20,000, A wrongfully refuses to transfer title. B can recover the $20,000 in restitution. The result is the same even if the market price of the land is only $70,000, so that performance would have been disadvantageous to B. . . .

If a lottery operator fails to deliver a purchased ticket, the purchaser can get his money back—whether or not he eventually would have won the lottery. And if one party to a contract . . . advances the other party money, principles of restitution normally require the latter, upon repudiation, to refund that money." Mobil Oil Exploration & Producing Southeast v. United States, 530 U.S. 604, 624 (2000) (Breyer, J.).

THE ECONOMICS OF REMEDIES: AN INTRODUCTORY NOTE

As noted on pp. 8–9, Oliver Wendell Holmes, Jr. expressed his concern about the confusion of law and morality in no uncertain terms. Holmes advocated an approach to contracts informed more by external legal sanctions than by moral intuitions: "The duty to keep a contract at common law means a prediction that you must pay damages if you do not keep it, and nothing else." *The Path of the Law* at 458. The promisor's obligation under this approach was reduced to a choice between performing a specified act and paying for its non-performance.

Though often characterized as immoral, Holmes's "perform-or-pay" approach might be better understood as an *amoral* system, where "[p]rices do the work of morals" in guiding behavior.[a] Holmes joins a long line of political theorists—including Hobbes, Bentham and Adam Smith—all of whom understood sanctions as useful means of enlisting self-interested individual behavior to promote social welfare. Consider in this regard this excerpt from Adam Smith in *The Wealth of Nations*:

> [M]an has almost constant occasion for the help of his brethren, and it is vain for him to expect it from their benevolence only. He will be more likely to prevail if he can interest their self love in his favour, and shew them that it is for their own advantage to do for him what he requires of them. Whoever offers to another a bargain of any kind, proposes to do this: Give me that which I want, and you shall have this which you want, is the meaning of every such offer; and it is in this manner that we obtain from one another the far greater part of those good offices which we stand in need of. . . . We address ourselves, not to their humanity but to their self love, and never talk to them of our own necessities but of their advantages. Nobody but a beggar chooses to depend chiefly upon the benevolence of his fellow citizens.

An Inquiry into the Nature and Causes of the Wealth of Nations 11 (1811 ed., bk. 1, ch. II).

Building on Smith's claim to mutual gain through self-interested motivations and Holmes's perform-or-pay vision of contracts, scholars from

---

a. Samuel Bowles, Policies Designed for Self-interested Citizens May Undermine "The Moral Sentiments": Evidence from Economic Experiments, 320 Science 1605 (2008).

a school of thought known as law and economics have developed a distinctive approach to contract remedies. This school of thought has achieved substantial influence in the last forty years, and has enabled scholars and jurists to examine the economic effects of legal remedies. Most notably, they have observed that a promisor will exercise an "option" to breach and pay expectation damages instead of performing when it is in her economic interest to do so. That is, she will breach when her gain from breaching exceeds the amount of damages she will have to pay to leave the promisee just as well off as he would have been had the promisor performed. In principle, then, breaches of this sort make promisors better off without making promisees worse off.

This observation, known as the "efficient breach hypothesis," may be illustrated with a simple example. Say a promisor has promised to sell a piece of machinery to a promisee. The machinery will cost the promisor $300 to produce and is worth $1,000 to the promisee (the maximum amount the promisee is willing to pay for it). Exchange will produce $700 of surplus since the promisee's value of the machinery ($1,000) is greater than the promisor's costs to produce it ($300). Say they agreed on a price of $600. This means the promisor gets $300 of the surplus (the $600 price minus her costs of $300) and the promisee gets $400 (the $1000 value to him of the machinery minus the $600 price). At the time they enter into the contract, the performance is mutually advantageous.

Now the twist. Assume that at some date before performance a second buyer approaches the promisor and offers $1200 for the machinery. The promisor has only one unit and cannot procure another. Suppose further that the promisee and the second buyer are unable to transact with each other, perhaps because neither knows of the other's existence and it would be too costly for them to identify each other. The question then becomes, should the promisor sell the machinery to the first buyer (the promisee) as agreed or should he sell the machinery to the second buyer at the higher price? The efficient breach hypothesis says the latter course is the better economic option for all parties involved. Why? The promisee will be fully compensated for his expectation by the payment of $400 in damages (since that is the amount that the promisee would have gained from the promisor's full performance). The second buyer gets the machinery that she values at least as much as $1200. Finally, if the promisor had performed the original contract she would have gained $300 ($600 sale price minus $300 cost to produce), but by breaching the contract and selling to the second buyer the promisor is left with a gain of $500, even after paying expectation damages to the promisee ($1200 sale price minus $300 cost to produce minus $400 damages paid to the promisee). This suggests that, under the assumptions of this example, the promisor can break her promise and enjoy a gain, without leaving the promisee any worse off.

Transactions that make no one worse off, while making someone else better off, are called Pareto-improving, so named after the 19th century Italian economist Vilfredo Pareto. Pareto-improvement is an important measure of what economists identify as efficiency, but it is not the only one. Suppose that, in the example above, the promisor breaks her promise to the promisee and sells the machinery for $1200. As we noticed, the machinery then ends up in the hands of the second buyer, who values it more than the promisee. At this point, even *without* compensating the promisee, the result satisfies another conception of efficiency known as Kaldor–Hicks efficiency.

Note, however, that unless the promisee receives at least his expectation damages, this outcome would not be Pareto-improving. Without this compensation, the promisee is worse off on account of the breach. Compensating the promisee for the breach is irrelevant under the Kaldor–Hicks approach, so long as the promisor's gains from the breach exceed the promisee's loss. Yet we should not lose sight of distinctions between economic theories and rules of law. The irrelevance of compensating the promisee may be a plausible feature of economic efficiency—it is certainly not irrelevant to law.

Our discussion of efficiency thus far has focused only on the moment when a party decides whether to breach. Economics, however, is the study of incentives broadly conceived and the question of whether parties have incentive to act efficiently will arise at every point where contracting parties make choices. These include searching for contractual partners, entering into a contract, relying on a contract, and so forth. Economic analysis cannot identify a single remedy, whether money damages or specific performance, that satisfies the demands of efficiency at all points concerning the transaction. This does not deprive economic analysis of value, however; it merely highlights the inevitable trade-offs that occur even within the singular perspective of efficiency.

The economics of remedies is essential to the study of contracts. Contract remedies provide incentives that guide behavior. At the same time, of course, other principles, such as morality and fairness, also guide contractual behavior. For example, the promisor who has been offered $1200 by the second buyer might decide that the harm to her reputation and self-esteem of breaking her promise to sell the machinery to the promisee is worth more to her than the $200 gain. On some accounts, this may be factored into her economic calculation of the cost to her of the breach. On other accounts, her decision is guided by independent moral considerations not reducible to an economic calculus. Happily, we need not choose one approach over the other; behavior is guided by many considerations. Whether economic efficiency is compatible with other normative objectives, like fairness, is a topic of debate. See Richard R.W. Brooks, The Efficient Performance Hypothesis, 116 Yale L.J. 568 (2006).

NOTES

(1) *Efficient Breach and the Bench.* How has the concept of efficient breach been received in practice by judges? Since the early 1980s, there have been a hundred or so cases that expressly employ the term. For example, Judge Richard Posner,[a] discussing efficient breach in relation to an award of punitive damages, observed that "if the promisor has discovered that his performance is worth more to someone else," then "efficiency is promoted by allowing him to break his promise, provided he makes good on the promisee's actual losses. If he is forced to pay more than that, an efficient breach may be deterred, and the law doesn't want to bring about that result." Patton v. Mid–Continent Systems, Inc., 841 F.2d 742, 750 (7th Cir.1988).

a. Richard Allen Posner (1939–), after clerking for Justice William Brennan and occupying several legal positions in the federal government, taught briefly at Stanford University Law School and then for more than a decade at the University of Chicago Law School. In 1981 he was appointed to the United States Court of Appeals for the Seventh Circuit, where from 1993 to 2000 he served as Chief Judge. His many books include the influential Economic Analysis of Law. Judge Posner maintains a personal website, http://home.uchicago.edu/?rposner/.

Other courts have also taken account of the concept. In refusing to enforce a contract upon a finding that one company had struck too struck too hard a bargain with another, a California court stated: "Hard bargaining, 'efficient' breaches and reasonable settlements of good faith disputes are all acceptable, even desirable, in our economic system. That system can be viewed as a game in which everybody wins, to one degree or another, so long as everyone plays by the common rules. Those rules are not limited to precepts of rationality and self-interest. They include equitable notions of fairness and propriety which preclude the wrongful exploitation of business exigencies to obtain disproportionate exchanges of values. Such exchanges make a mockery of freedom of contract and undermine the proper functioning of our economic system." Rich and Whillock, Inc. v. Ashton Development, Inc., 157 Cal.App.3d 1154, 1159 (Ct.App.1984).

How should "notions of fairness and propriety" guide the law of remedies? Have you seen any examples of this in the cases so far?

(2) *The Economics of Naval Institute.* Suppose that in August Berkley, noting the downward trend in Naval's hardcover sales, had estimated that by jumping the gun and shipping its paperback edition early as it did, it would gain at least $100,000 from pre-October sales while the loss to Naval would be no more than $40,000. Assuming that its estimates were accurate, and that Naval receives an award for its expectation damages, what is the gain to Berkley by breaching its contract with Naval? What factors, financial and other, might affect Berkley's decision about whether or not to ship the paperbacks early and breach the contract?

PUNITIVE DAMAGES

White v. Benkowski

Supreme Court of Wisconsin, 1967.
37 Wis.2d 285, 155 N.W.2d 74.

[In 1962, Virgil and Gwynneth White bought a house that lacked its own water supply but was connected by pipes to a well on the adjacent property of Paul and Ruth Benkowski. The Whites entered into a written contract with the Benkowskis under which the Benkowskis promised to supply water to the Whites' home for ten years unless the municipality supplied it, the well became inadequate, or the Whites drilled their own well. In exchange, the Whites agreed to pay the Benkowskis $3 a month and half the cost of any future repairs or maintenance. Although the relationship between the neighbors began as a friendly one, by 1964 it had deteriorated and become hostile. During March and June, the Benkowskis shut off the water supply on nine occasions for periods in the late afternoon and early evening that were, according to Mrs. White's records, well under an hour. Mr. Benkowski claimed this was done either to allow accumulated sand in the pipes to settle or to remind the Whites that their water use was excessive. The Whites sued the Benkowskis for breach of contract, seeking compensatory and punitive damages. The jury found the Benkowskis has shut off the water maliciously in order to harass the Whites. It awarded the Whites compensatory damages of $10 and punitive damages of $2000. On motions after the verdict, the award was reduced to $1 in compensatory damages and no punitive damages. The Whites appealed.]

■ Wilkie, Justice. Two issues are raised on this appeal.

1. Was the trial court correct in reducing the award of compensatory damages from $10 to $1?

2. Are punitive damages available in actions for breach of contract?

Reduction of Jury Award

The evidence of damage adduced during the trial here was that the water supply had been shut off during several short periods. Three incidents of inconvenience resulting from these shut-offs were detailed by the plaintiffs. Mrs. White testified that the lack of water in the bathroom on one occasion caused an odor and that on two other occasions she was forced to take her children to a neighbor's home to bathe them. Based on this evidence, the court instructed the jury that:

"... in an action for a breach of contract the plaintiff is entitled to such damages as shall have been sustained by him which resulted naturally and directly from the breach if you find that the defendants did in fact breach the contract. Such damages include pecuniary loss and inconvenience suffered as a natural result of the breach and are called compensatory damages. In this case the plaintiffs have proved no pecuniary damages which you or the Court could compute. In a situation where there has been a breach of contract which you find to have damaged the plaintiff but for which the plaintiffs have proven no actual damages, the plaintiffs may recover nominal damages.

"By nominal damages is meant trivial-a trivial sum of money."

Plaintiffs did not object to this instruction. In the trial court's decision on motions after verdict it states that the court so instructed the jury because, based on the fact that the plaintiffs paid for services they did not receive, their loss in proportion to the contract rate was approximately 25 cents. This rationale indicates that the court disregarded or overlooked Mrs. White's testimony of inconvenience. In viewing the evidence most favorable to the plaintiffs, there was some injury. The plaintiffs are not required to ascertain their damages with mathematical precision, but rather the trier of fact must set damages at a reasonable amount. Notwithstanding this instruction, the jury set the plaintiffs' damages at $10. The court was in error in reducing that amount to $1.

The jury finding of $10 in actual damages, though small, takes it out of the mere nominal status. The award is predicated on an actual injury. This was not the situation present in Sunderman v. Warnken.[1] Here there was credible evidence which showed inconvenience and thus actual injury, and the jury's finding as to compensatory damages should be reinstated.

Punitive Damages

"If a man shall steal an ox, or a sheep, and kill it, or sell it; he shall restore five oxen for an ox, and four sheep for a sheep."[2]

Over one hundred years ago this court held that, under proper circumstances, a plaintiff was entitled to recover exemplary or punitive damages.[3]

---

1. (1947), 251 Wis. 471, 29 N.W.2d 496.
2. Exodus 22:1.
3. McWilliams v. Bragg (1854), 3 Wis. 377 (*424).

In Wisconsin compensatory damages are given to make whole the damage or injury suffered by the injured party. On the other hand, punitive damages are given "... on the basis of punishment to the injured party not because he has been injured, which injury has been compensated with compensatory damages, but to punish the wrongdoer for his malice and to deter others from like conduct."[4]

Thus we reach the question of whether the plaintiffs are entitled to punitive damages for a breach of the water agreement.

The overwhelming weight of authority supports the proposition that punitive damages are not recoverable in actions for breach of contract. In Chitty on Contracts, the author states that the right to receive punitive damages for breach of contract is now confined to the single case of damages for breach of a promise to marry.[5]

Simpson states:

"Although damages in excess of compensation for loss are in some instances permitted in tort actions by way of punishment ... in contract actions the damages recoverable are limited to compensation for pecuniary loss sustained by the breach."[6]

Corbin states that as a general rule punitive damages are not recoverable for breach of contract.[7]

In Wisconsin, the early case of Gordon v. Brewster[8] involved the breach of an employment contract. The trial court instructed the jury that if the nonperformance of the contract was attributable to the defendant's wrongful act of discharging the plaintiff, then that would go to increase the damages sustained. On appeal, this court said that the instruction was unfortunate and might have led the jurors to suppose that they could give something more than actual compensation in a breach of contract case. We find no Wisconsin case in which breach of contract (other than breach of promise to marry) has led to the award of punitive damages.

Persuasive authority from other jurisdictions supports the proposition (without exception) that punitive damages are not available in breach of contract actions. This is true even if the breach, as in the instant case, is willful.

Although it is well recognized that breach of a contractual duty may be a tort, in such situations the contract creates the relation out of which grows the duty to use care in the performance of a responsibility prescribed by the contract. Not so here. No tort was pleaded or proved.

Reversed in part by reinstating the jury verdict relating to compensatory damages and otherwise affirmed. Costs to appellant.

NOTES

(1) *Questions.* Why was only $10 awarded to the Whites as compensatory damages? What did that amount represent? How was it calculated? How did the jury come up with the $2000 punitive damage award?

4. Malco, Inc. v. Midwest Aluminum Sales (1961), 14 Wis.2d 57, 66, 109 N.W.2d 516, 521.

5. 1 Chitty, Contracts, (22d ed. 1961), p. 1339.

6. Simpson, Contracts, (2d ed. hornbook series), p. 394, sec. 195.

7. 5 Corbin, Contracts, p. 438, sec. 1077.

8. (1858), 7 Wis. 309 (*355).

Why shouldn't punitive damages be awarded in such a case? What effect would the availability of punitive damages have on parties tempted to breach their contracts? Would it make sense to award punitive damages in cases where the breach was malicious, as in *White*, or should the law be indifferent as to why a party fails to perform? How might the possibility of a punitive damage award affect a party's decision to *enter* into contract?

(2) *Nominal Damages.* A plaintiff who proves a breach of contract but fails to prove damages is traditionally awarded nominal damages (six cents or one dollar); as Judge Posner has observed, "for reasons we do not understand every victim of a breach of contract, unlike a tort victim, is [so] entitled." Chronister Oil Co. v. Unocal Ref. & Mktg., 34 F.3d 462, 466 (7th Cir.1994). Such an award may serve as a declaration of the plaintiff's rights and may also carry with it an award of court costs.

(3) *Flirting with Punitive Damages.* Although not traditionally granted for breach of contract, punitive or exemplary damages may be granted for tortious conduct that is sufficiently "outrageous." See Restatement, Second, of Torts § 908 (1979). Some courts have departed from the strict rule that denies punitive damages for breach of contract when the breach is accompanied by "fraudulent" conduct or by an "independent" tort sufficiently outrageous to justify such damages. See generally Restatement § 355; 3 *Farnsworth on Contracts* § 12.8 (2d ed.1998).

The trend in judicial decisions toward greater use of punitive damages has been most noticeable in connection with claims against insurers for vexatious refusal to settle insurance claims. See Comunale v. Traders & Gen. Ins. Co., 328 P.2d 198 (Cal.1958); Vernon Fire & Cas. Ins. Co. v. Sharp, 349 N.E.2d 173 (Ind.1976). In 1984, the Supreme Court of California suggested that the new tort of "bad faith breach" might extend beyond insurance cases. In Seaman's Direct Buying Service v. Standard Oil Company of California, 686 P.2d 1158 (Cal.1984), a would-be oil dealer claimed punitive damages from an oil company that had refused to honor its contract. In remanding the case for erroneous jury instructions, the court in dictum defined a new tort where a party to a contract "in addition to breaching the contract ... seeks to shield itself from liability by denying, in bad faith and without probable cause, that the contract exists." But a tort action would be available for breach of contract, the court said, only where there was a "special relationship" similar to that between insurer and insured.

The suggestion that the tort of "bad faith breach" could occur outside the insurance field triggered much academic discussion and much litigation in California courts. In 1988, a differently composed Supreme Court of California dealt a severe blow to the new tort by denouncing the "uncritical acceptance" by some California courts "of the insurance model into the employment context, without careful consideration of the fundamental policies underlying the development of tort and contract law in general or of significant differences between the insurer/insured and employer/employee relationships." In Foley v. Interactive Data Corp., 765 P.2d 373 (Cal.1988), the court refused to apply *Seaman's* to an employer's discharge of an employee holding his job at the pleasure of his employer. In 1989, a Ninth Circuit opinion explained that *Foley* "solidly reaffirms the notion that the bad faith denial of the existence of contract is a cause of action wholly distinct from the breach of the covenant of good faith and fair dealing." Air–Sea Forwarders, Inc. v. Air Asia Co., 880 F.2d 176, 187 (9th Cir.1989). *Seaman's* has had little impact in other states.

———

REMEDIES IN PRACTICE

In providing promisees relief through money damages, the law by and large ignores the costs of obtaining that relief. To be sure, the successful claimant may ordinarily recover its court costs, but these are typically quite modest. But in contrast to the situation in many countries, the successful claimant in the United States is usually not allowed to recover its attorney's fees from the losing party. Thus even winning parties are left to pay their own, often substantial, lawyers' fees, as well as the many other costs of litigation. These may include the cost of enforcing a judgment. This helps to explain why many disputes are settled out of court or not initiated in the first place.

Where the transaction is a substantial one between business people, the cost of litigation may not seem overwhelming in relation to the amount in dispute or in relation to the precedential value of a judicial decision. But what of the typical consumer transaction in which the stakes are often smaller, whether the aggrieved party is the merchant (often trying to collect) or the consumer (perhaps refusing to pay)?

Of the two, the merchant is in the better position. The merchant is likely to have enough disputes to have them handled in bulk by specialists in collection. The merchant engages professionals such as lawyers or trade associations to write the contract, which may provide for liquidated damages and for attorney's fees; such provisions are likely to be sustained so long as the fees are reasonable. The merchant may also be able to provide for security, as by taking a deposit where goods have not been delivered or by preserving the right to repossess goods that have been delivered. Indeed, the law's concern has been not that the merchant can do too little but too much in disputes with consumers.

In contrast, the consumer is unlikely to know or be able to afford a lawyer. The consumer could not have changed the contract's terms or even known what changes were desirable. Depending on how trusting the merchant has been, the consumer may be able to stop payment on a check or to refuse to pay for goods delivered on credit, but even here the consumer risks action by the merchant's specialists in collection. It is not that "the customer is always right." Customers may be wrong. The problem is that the consumer and the merchant stand on an unequal footing in attempting to show who is right.

A variety of solutions, many procedural in nature, have attempted to even out disparities in a consumer's ability to bring or to defend claims. One solution is to "sweeten the pot" by increasing the successful consumer's recovery through statutes that allow civil penalties, multiple (*e.g.*, treble) damages, or attorney's fees. Another solution is to facilitate the representation of consumers by providing free or inexpensive legal services, by allowing them to join with claimants in class actions, or by having a public agency handle the claim and distribute any recovery to the aggrieved consumers.

Still other mechanisms for reducing the costs and complexities of litigation for consumers focus on the forum. For example, small claims courts and non-judicial forms of dispute resolution such as arbitration are generally cheaper and offer more flexible and informal procedures than those applied in standard litigation. Whether arbitration *always* favors "the little guy" is a question we take up in Chapter 6, Limits on the Bargain.

NOTES

(1) *Efficient Breach and the Costs of Enforcements.* The efficient breach hypothesis ignores the cost to the parties of enforcing rights. How might taking those costs into account change the analysis? For example, what if it is very costly for the promisee to pay for an attorney, to prove the performance was defective, or to prove the amount of its damages?

(2) *Arbitration Primer.* An arbitration tribunal is typically constituted for a single dispute, and is discharged upon making an award. Commonly the tribunal has either one or three members. Many institutions, notably trade associations and chambers of commerce, engage in the administration of arbitrations, including promulgation of procedural rules and the appointment of arbitrators. Two of the most important of these are the International Chamber of Commerce in Paris and the American Arbitration Association (AAA) in New York.

The AAA recommends the following arbitration clause for insertion in all commercial contracts: "Any controversy or claim arising out of or relating to this contract, or the breach thereof, shall be settled by arbitration administered by the American Arbitration Association under its Commercial Arbitration Rules, and judgment on the award rendered by the arbitrator(s) may be entered in any court having jurisdiction thereof."

As mandated by the Federal Arbitration Act and widespread state statutes, courts commonly grant specific performance to provisions like this, dismissing claims within the description, and enforcing, within wide limits, arbitration awards.

(3) *The Costs of Justice.* In one respect, the cost of obtaining relief in court is subsidized by the availability of the public machinery of justice. Litigants are not charged, except as tax payers, for the services of judges or juries in resolving their disputes. In contrast, arbitration is paid for by the parties themselves. A number of states have also authorized the practice of "private judging," in which the parties agree to choose and pay for a private adjudicator, typically a retired judge, to hear the case. See Cal.Civ.Proc. Code §§ 638–645.2. Sometimes referred to as "rent-a-judge," private judging combines aspects of arbitration with the judicial authority of the courts. While alternative adjudicatory fora are mainly a subject for procedure courses, we consider the costs of justice in Chapter 6 in connection with mandatory arbitration clauses and class actions.

(4) *The "Work of the Law Machine at the Margin."* Professor Karl Llewellyn[a] concluded "that the real major effect of law will be found not so much in the cases in which law officials actually intervene, nor yet in those in which such intervention is consciously contemplated as a possibility, but rather in contributing to, strengthening, stiffening attitudes toward performance as what is to be expected and what 'is done'.... This work of the law machine at the margin, in helping keep the level of social practice and expectation up to where it is, as against slow canker, is

a. Karl Nickerson Llewellyn (1893–1962) practiced law in New York for two years, and taught law at Yale, Columbia, and Chicago law schools. He was well-known for his contributions to the field of jurisprudence, as one of the school of "legal realists," and also to the fields of commercial law and contracts. He was Chief Reporter of the Uniform Commercial Code, and the author of many books, including The Bramble Bush: On Our Law and Its Study, which was written especially for first-year law students.

probably the most vital single aspect of contract law. For in this aspect each hospital case is a case with significance for the hundreds of thousands of normal cases." Llewellyn, What Price Contract?—An Essay in Perspective, 40 Yale L.J. 704, 725 n. 47 (1931). For a discussion of the nonlegal sanctions that may encourage promisors to keep their promises, see David Charny, Nonlegal Sanctions in Commercial Relationships, 104 Harv.L.Rev. 373 (1990).

SECTION 3. CONSIDERATION AS A BASIS FOR ENFORCEMENT

(A) FUNDAMENTALS OF CONSIDERATION

What promises should the law enforce? In a well known article, legal philosopher Morris Cohen suggested that

> [t]he simplest answer is that of the intuitionists, namely, that promises are sacred per se, that there is something inherently despicable about not keeping a promise, and that a properly organized society should not tolerate this.... There can be no doubt that from an empirical or historical point of view, the ability to rely on the promises of others adds to the confidence necessary to social intercourse and enterprise.

At the same time, Cohen thought it very doubtful that "many of us would want to live in an entirely rigid world in which one would be obliged to keep all one's promises instead of the present more viable system, in which a vaguely fair proportion is sufficient. Many of us indeed would shudder at the idea of being bound by every promise, no matter how foolish, without any chance of letting increased wisdom undo past foolishness. Certainly, some freedom to change one's mind is necessary for free intercourse between those who lack omniscience." Morris Cohen, The Basis of Contract, 46 Harv.L.Rev 553, 571–74, 580–583 (1932). Courts have agreed. As noted in Mills v. Wyman, p. 50 below, "[g]eneral rules of law established for the protection and security of honest and fair-minded men, who may inconsiderately make promises without any equivalent, will sometimes screen men of a different character from engagements which they are bound in *foro conscientiae* to perform."

If we accept the argument that not all promises should be legally enforceable, we are left with the question of which ones are. We begin here with an historical perspective, for the question of enforceability under early English law was closely tied to the common law actions of covenant, debt, and assumpsit, and even today no adequate answer can ignore this aspect of legal history.

The first of these actions, *covenant*, was used to enforce contracts made under seal. Once a written promise was sealed and delivered, the action of covenant was available to enforce it, and it made no difference whether the promisor had bargained for or received anything in exchange for the promise, or whether the promisee had in any way changed position in reliance on it. In medieval England, the seal was a piece of wax affixed to the document and bearing an impression identifying the person who had executed it. At first its use was confined to the nobility, but later it spread to commoners. With the growth of literacy and the use of the personal signature as a means of authentication, the requirement of formality was so eroded that a seal could consist of any written or printed symbol intended to serve as a seal. The word "Seal" and the letters "L.S." (*locus sigilli*) were commonly used for this purpose.

Two functions performed by such legal formalities as the seal have been described by Professor Lon Fuller[a] as "evidentiary," that is, providing trustworthy evidence of the existence and terms of the contract in the event of controversy, and "cautionary," that is, bringing home to the parties the significance of their acts—inducing "the circumspective frame of mind appropriate in one pledging his future." Fuller, Anatomy of the Law 36–37 (1968); Fuller, Consideration and Form, 41 Colum.L.Rev. 799, 800 (1941). With the erosion of the solemnity of the seal, it became doubtful that it performed either of these functions well. Consequently, the distinctive effect of the seal on the enforceability of promises has been abolished in roughly half of the states of the United States and has been seriously curtailed in the rest. The most recent of these assaults on the seal came with the enactment of the Uniform Commercial Code, which "makes it clear that every effect of the seal which relates to 'sealed instruments' as such is wiped out insofar as contracts for sale are concerned." Comment 1 to UCC § 2–203. Where the seal still retains some effect, it is often limited to raising a rebuttable presumption of consideration or making applicable a longer period of limitations. What supplanted the seal as the primary criterion of the enforceability of a promise was the circumstance that the promise was, or was not, given in exchange for something, or consideration. The contours of the criterion are featured below. At this point it is enough to say that an uncle's promise to his nephew to pay the nephew's way through law school is not one supported by consideration; not, that is, if the only reward for the uncle's promise is a warm glow of satisfaction.

The criterion of consideration has been partially supplanted, in its turn, by other criteria of enforceability, such as reliance. These too are developed in the following sections.

The second of the three common law actions—debt—was used to enforce some types of unsealed promises to pay a definite sum of money. These included a promise to repay money that had been loaned and a promise to pay for goods that had been delivered or for work that had been done. Since these were situations in which the contemplated exchange was completed on one side, they appealed to the primitive notion that the promisor (or debtor) had something belonging to the promisee (or creditor) that the former ought to surrender. The proprietary element present in

---

a.   Lon L. Fuller (1902–1978) had a long teaching career at Oregon, Illinois, Duke, Columbia, and, for the last three decades of his life, at Harvard, where he taught contracts and jurisprudence. In philosophical works he presented alternatives to positivist attitudes toward law, sometimes using partly-fanciful cases in imaginary and contrasting opinions. See, e.g., Fuller, The Case of the Speluncean Explorers, 62 Harv.L.Rev. 616 (1949). His article, with one of his students, William Purdue, on the reliance interest in contracts prompted an extensive reexamination of the subject. It is cited on p. 14 below.

this notion is reflected in the popular expression that a depositor who is owed money by a bank "*has* money in the bank." What the promisee had given the promisor was sometimes called the "*quid pro quo*" and, as the underlying principles of contract law developed, the promisor's obligation in debt was considered to rest upon receipt of a *benefit* from the promisee.

The third and ultimately the most important common law action, *assumpsit*, grew out of cases in which the promisee sought to recover damages for physical injury to person or property on the basis of a consensual undertaking. In one such case a ferryman who undertook to carry the plaintiff's horse across a river was held liable when he overloaded the boat and the horse drowned. In another a carpenter who undertook to build a house for the plaintiff was held liable when he did so unskillfully. The underlying theme of these decisions was that of misfeasance—the promisor, having undertaken (*assumpsit*) to do something, had done it in a manner inconsistent with that undertaking to the detriment of the promisee. The decisions did not go so far as to impose liability for nonfeasance—where the promisor had done *nothing* in pursuance of the undertaking—for example, where the carpenter in the case just put had failed to build the house at all. It was not until the latter half of the fifteenth century that the common-law courts began to make this extension. When they did, they imposed a requirement, analogous to that in the misfeasance cases, that the promisee must have incurred a *detriment* in reliance on the promise—as where the owner had changed position by selling an old house in reliance on the carpenter's promise to build a new one.

Finally, by the end of the sixteenth century, the courts made a second major extension of the action of assumpsit and held that a party that had given only a promise in exchange for the other's promise had incurred a detriment by having its freedom of action fettered, since it was bound in turn by its own promise. By this circular argument, the common law courts began to enforce exchanges of promises. Here is the opinion in what is said to be the earliest case recognizing that a promise, not even partly performed, could be consideration for a return promise:

> Note, that a promise against a promise will maintain an action upon the case, as in consideration that you do give me £10 on such a day, I promise to give you £10 such a day after.

Strangborough v. Warner, 4 Leo. 3 (Queen's Bench 1588). See Holdsworth, Debt, Assumpsit and Consideration, 11 Mich.L.Rev. 347, 351 (1913).

Eventually, the action of assumpsit was allowed to supplant that of debt for the enforcement of promises that would previously have been enforced only in the latter action. By the beginning of the seventeenth century, the common law courts had succeeded in developing the action of assumpsit as a general basis for the enforcement of promises. By that time, the term "consideration" had come to be used as a word of art to express the sum of the conditions necessary for such an action to lie. It was therefore a tautology that a promise, if not under seal, was enforceable only where there was "consideration," for this was to say no more than that it was enforceable only where the action of assumpsit would lie. Bound up in the concept of consideration were several elements. Most important, from the *quid pro quo* of debt came the idea that there must have been an exchange arrived at by way of bargain. To the extent that debt inspired the concept of consideration, there was the notion that there must be a *benefit* to the promisor. To the extent that assumpsit inspired it, there was the notion that there must be a *detriment* to the promisee.

The cases that follow refine our understanding of the doctrine of consideration and of its development into this century. The concept of benefit and detriment have receded but the centrality of a bargained-for exchange between the parties remains, lending at least some support to the claim of the English legal historian, F.W. Maitland, that "The forms of action we have buried, but they still rule us from their graves." Frederic W. Maitland, *The Forms of Action at Common Law 2* (1936 ed.). For a thorough treatment of this historical background, see A.W. Brian Simpson, *A History of the Common Law of Contract* (1975). See also Patrick S. Atiyah, *The Rise and Fall of Freedom of Contract* (1979); Farnsworth, The Past of Promise: An Historical Introduction to Contract, 69 Colum.L.Rev. 576 (1969). In any event, consideration has long been a fundamental feature of a contractual relationship; decades ago it was called "the glue that binds the parties to a contract together." In re Owen, 303 S.E.2d 351 (N.C.App.1983).

TYPICAL CATEGORIES OF AGREEMENTS

Throughout the nineteenth century, text writers on contract law devoted considerable attention to specific types of agreements, such as contracts with common carriers, innkeepers, and for pawns and pledges, that were on the periphery of general contract law. When, in 1920, Samuel Williston[a] launched the first edition of his magisterial contracts treatise, he announced that he sought to "treat the subject of contracts as a whole, and to show the wide range of application of its principles." Not surprisingly, this conception of a body of contract law generally applicable to agreements of all sorts was confirmed in 1932, when the ALI promulgated its original Restatement of Contracts, for which Williston served as Reporter. A federal court of appeal has most recently affirmed this view. In response to a party's plea to limit an earlier holding to cases involving software, the judge responded, "Where's the sense in that? ProCD is about the law of contracts, not the law of software." Hill v. Gateway, 105 F.3d 1147 (7th Cir.1997). (The case appears at p. 215 below.) Consistent with this concep-

a. Samuel Williston (1861–1963) joined the faculty of the Harvard Law School in 1890, after practicing law for a short period in Boston, and taught there until his retirement in 1938. His principal fields were contracts and sales. His multi-volume work, A Treatise on the Law of Contracts, was first published in 1920 and became one of the most widely used legal treatises in the United States. He was the Reporter for the Restatement of Contracts and the draftsman of several uniform laws, including the Uniform Sales Act.

tion, this book seeks to show how such principles apply to a wide variety of transactions.

At the same time, many transactions fall into recognizable categories, in which lawyers sometimes specialize and which sometimes develop distinctive rules and practices. We note five such categories here: contracts for sales of goods, real estate transactions, construction contracts, employment agreements, and family contracts. In this book, when a case involving one of these five categories appears, it is preceded by a description of some of the features that characterize such agreements and some of the common questions that they raise. To be sure, other types of agreements appear throughout the book; these include franchise and distributorship contracts, publishing contracts, government contracts, and consumer contracts. You may want to observe and organize distinctive features of these categories as well.

But now to the first of our five typical categories: Family Contracts.

———

FAMILY CONTRACTS

The agreement in the following venerable case—an uncle's promise to a nephew made during a family celebration—is typical of agreements between relatives and others in close personal relationships. Unlike most commercial agreements, family agreements are frequently oral, may not be preceded by significant bargaining, and are often informal and lacking in detail. They may not be of great economic moment except, of course, to the parties themselves. Family agreements often involve matters and relationships long understood to be outside the proper scope of judicial intervention. An initial question is therefore whether a promise made between family members is enforceable at all, a question that explains the presence of a number of such cases in this chapter.

The traditional answer has been No. Goods or services provided from one family member to another were assumed to be gifts motivated by altruism, not bargains motivated by gain. Furthermore, as an English court explained in denying a wife recovery on her husband's promise of a stated monthly allowance, "[I]t would be the worst possible example to hold that agreements such as this resulted in legal obligations which could be enforced in the Courts," for "each house is a domain into which the King's writ does not run and to which his officers do not seek to be admitted." Balfour v. Balfour, [1919] 2 K.B. 571, 579 (Court of Appeal 1919). An American court justified a similar decision by declaring that to enforce such a promise would "open an endless field for controversy and bickering." Graham v. Graham, 33 F.Supp. 936 (E.D.Mich.1940).

In recent years, the differences between family agreements and commercial ones have narrowed as contractual relationships among intimates have found increasing legal acceptance. Sophisticated contracts, now often drafted by lawyers, are used to order matters once considered wholly unsuited for private agreement or public enforcement. Thus parties, married and unmarried, now arrange aspects of their relationships from start to finish through pre-nuptial agreements, cohabitation contracts, and divorce and property settlements. People also contract with one another to create families through surrogacy contracts, open adoption agreements, and the sale of genetic material. We explore several such agreements in later chapters, but begin here with a relatively straightforward promise from uncle to nephew.

Hamer v. Sidway

Court of Appeals of New York, 1891.
124 N.Y. 538, 27 N.E. 256.

Appeal from an order of the general term of the supreme court in the fourth judicial department, reversing a judgment entered on the decision of the court at special term. The plaintiff presented a claim to the executor of William E. Story, Sr., for $5,000 and interest from the 6th day of February, 1875. She acquired it through several mesne assignments from William E. Story, 2d. The claim being rejected by the executor, this action was brought.

It appears that William E. Story, Sr., was the uncle of William E. Story, 2d; that at the celebration of the golden wedding of Samuel Story and wife, father and mother of William E. Story, Sr., on the 20th day of March, 1869, in the presence of the family and invited guests, he promised his nephew that if he would refrain from drinking, using tobacco, swearing, and playing cards or billiards for money until he became 21 years of age, he would pay him the sum of $5,000. The nephew assented thereto, and fully performed the conditions inducing the promise. When the nephew arrived at the age of 21 years, and on the 31st day of January, 1875, he wrote to his uncle, informing him that he had performed his part of the agreement, and had thereby become entitled to the sum of $5,000. The uncle received the letter, and a few days later, and on the 6th day of February, he wrote and mailed to his nephew the following letter:

Buffalo, Feb. 6, 1875.

"W.E. STORY, JR.:

"DEAR NEPHEW—Your letter of the 31st ult. came to hand all right, saying that you had lived up to the promise made to me several years ago. I have no doubt but you have, for which you shall have five thousand dollars as I promised you. I had the money in the bank the day you was 21 years old that I intend for you, and you shall have the money certain. Now, Willie, I do not intend to interfere with this money in any way till I think you are capable of taking care of it and the sooner that time comes the better it will please me. I would hate very much to have you start out in some adventure that you thought all right and lose this money in one year. The first five thousand dollars that I got together cost me a heap of hard work.... It did not come to me in any mysterious way, and the reason I speak of this is that money got in this way stops longer with a fellow that gets it with hard knocks than it does when he finds it. Willie, you are 21 and you have many a thing to learn yet. This money you have earned much easier than I did besides acquiring good habits at the same time and you are quite welcome to the money; hope you will make good use of it. I was ten long years getting this together after I was your age. Now, hoping this will be satisfactory, I stop. . . .

Truly Yours,
"W.E. STORY.

"P.S.—You can consider this money on interest."

The nephew received the letter and thereafter consented that the money should remain with his uncle in accordance with the terms and conditions of the letters. The uncle died on the 29th day of January, 1887, without having paid over to his nephew any portion of the said $5,000 and interest.

■ PARKER, J. The question which provoked the most discussion by counsel on this appeal, and which lies at the foundation of plaintiff's asserted right of recovery, is whether by virtue of a contract defendant's testator William S. Story became indebted to his nephew William E. Story, 2d, on his twenty-first birthday in the sum of five thousand dollars. The trial court found as a fact that "on the 20th day of March, 1869, . . . William E. Story agreed to and with William E. Story, 2d, that if he would refrain from drinking liquor, using tobacco, swearing, and playing cards or billiards for money until he should become 21 years of age, then he, the said William E. Story, would at that time pay him, the said William E. Story, 2d, the sum of $5000 for such refraining, to which the said William E. Story, 2d, agreed," and that he "in all things fully performed his part of said agreement."

The defendant contends that the contract was without consideration to support it, and, therefore, invalid. He asserts that the promisee by refraining from the use of liquor and tobacco was not harmed but benefited; that that which he did was best for him to do independently of his uncle's promise, and insists that it follows that unless the promisor was benefited, the contract was without consideration, a contention which, if well founded, would seem to leave open for controversy in many cases whether that which the promisee did or omitted to do was, in fact, of such benefit to him as to leave no consideration to support the enforcement of the promisor's agreement. Such a rule could not be tolerated, and is without foundation in the law. The Exchequer Chamber, in 1875, defined consideration as follows: "A valuable consideration in the sense of the law may consist either in some right, interest, profit, or benefit accruing to the one party, or some forbearance, detriment, loss, or responsibility given, suffered, or undertaken by the other." Courts "will not ask whether the thing which forms the consideration does in fact benefit the promisee or a third party, or is of any substantial value to any one. It is enough that something is promised, done, forborne, or suffered by the party to whom the promise is made as consideration for the promise made to him." Anson's Prin. of Con. 63.

"In general, a waiver of any legal right at the request of another party is a sufficient consideration for a promise." Parsons on Contracts, 444.

"Any damage, or suspension or forbearance of a right, will be sufficient to sustain a promise." Kent, Vol. 2, 465, 12th Ed.[a]

Pollock, in his work on contracts, page 166, after citing the definition given by the Exchequer Chamber already quoted, says: "The second branch of this judicial description is really the most important one. Consideration means not so much that one party is profiting as that the other abandons some legal right in the present or limits his legal freedom of action in the future as an inducement for the promise of the first."

Now, applying this rule to the facts before us, the promisee used tobacco, occasionally drank liquor, and he had a legal right to do so. That right he abandoned for a period of years upon the strength of the promise of the testator that for such forbearance he would give him $5000. We need not speculate on the effort which may have been required to give up the use of those stimulants. It is sufficient that he restricted his lawful freedom of action within certain prescribed limits upon the faith of his uncle's agreement, and now having fully performed the conditions imposed, it is of no moment whether such performance actually proved a benefit to the promisor, and the court will not inquire into it, but were it a proper subject of inquiry, we see nothing in this record that would permit a determination that the uncle was not benefited in a legal sense. Few cases have been found which may be said to be precisely in point, but such as have been support the position we have taken.

In Shadwell v. Shadwell, 9 C.B.N.S. 159, an uncle wrote to his nephew as follows:

"MY DEAR LANCEY—I am so glad to hear of your intended marriage with Ellen Nicholl, and as I promised to assist you at starting, I am happy to tell you that I will pay you 150 pounds yearly during my life and until your annual income derived from your profession of a chancery barrister shall amount to 600 guineas, of which your own admission will be the only evidence that I shall require.

> "Your affectionate uncle,
> "CHARLES SHADWELL."

It was held that the promise was binding and made upon good consideration.

a. James Kent (1763–1847) began practice after three years as an apprentice and was active in Federalist politics. Hamilton introduced him to the writings of European authors on the civil law, which were to influence his later work. In 1793, largely through his Federalist connections, he was made Professor of Law in Columbia College. He attracted few students, and soon resigned to become a judge on the New York Supreme Court, then the highest court in the state. In 1814 he became Chancellor. Upon his retirement in 1823, he lectured again at Columbia for three years. Out of these lectures grew the "Commentaries on American Law," in four volumes, which became one of the most important American law books of the century. (It is the source of the quotation above.) Kent lived to prepare six editions; subsequent ones were revised by others. For his work on the Court of Chancery, he has been called the creator of equity in the United States.

In Lakota v. Newton, an unreported case in the Superior Court of Worcester, Mass., the complaint averred defendant's promise that "if you (meaning plaintiff) will leave off drinking for a year I will give you $100," plaintiff's assent thereto, performance of the condition by him, and demanded judgment therefor. Defendant demurred on the ground, among others, that the plaintiff's declaration did not allege a valid and sufficient consideration for the agreement of the defendant. The demurrer was overruled.

In Talbott v. Stemmons, 89 Ky. 222, the step-grandmother of the plaintiff made with him the following agreement: "I do promise and bind myself to give my grandson, Albert R. Talbott, $500 at my death, if he will never take another chew of tobacco or smoke another cigar during my life from this date up to my death, and if he breaks this pledge he is to refund double the amount to his mother." The executor of Mrs. Stemmons demurred to the complaint on the ground that the agreement was not based on a sufficient consideration. The demurrer was sustained and an appeal taken therefrom to the Court of Appeals, where the decision of the court below was reversed. In the opinion of the court it is said that "the right to use and enjoy the use of tobacco was a right that belonged to the plaintiff and not forbidden by law. The abandonment of its use may have saved him money or contributed to his health; nevertheless, the surrender of that right caused the promise, and having the right to contract with reference to the subject-matter, the abandonment of the use was a sufficient consideration to uphold the promise." Abstinence from the use of intoxicating liquors was held to furnish a good consideration for a promissory note in Lindell v. Rokes, 60 Mo. 249. The cases cited by the defendant on this question are not in point. . . .

[In an omitted part of the opinion the court held that the action was not barred by the statute of limitations because under the uncle's letter he held the money in trust and not merely as a debtor.] Order reversed and judgment of special term affirmed.

NOTES

(1) *Benefit, Detriment, and Bargain.* What was the consideration for the uncle's promise to pay $5,000? How did the court's definition of detriment differ from that urged by the defendant? What role do benefit and detriment play under Restatement §§ 71 and 79? Was there consideration for the uncle's promise under those sections? How clear is it that there was consideration for promise of the affectionate uncle in Shadwell v. Shadwell ("My dear Lancey . . .")?

(2) *Holmes and the "Bargain Theory" of Consideration.* Oliver Wendell Holmes, Jr., an early advocate of the "bargain theory" of consideration later espoused in the Restatement, spoke of "reciprocal conventional inducement": "It is said that consideration must not be confounded with motive. It is true that it must not be confounded with what may be the prevailing or chief motive in actual fact. A man may promise to paint a picture for five hundred dollars, while his chief motive may be a desire for fame. A consideration may be given and accepted, in fact, solely for the purpose of making a promise binding. But, nevertheless, it is the essence of a consideration, that, by the terms of the agreement, it is given and accepted as the motive or inducement of the promise. Conversely, the promise must be made and

accepted as the conventional motive or inducement for furnishing the consideration. The root of the whole matter is the relation of reciprocal conventional inducement, each for the other, between consideration and promise." Holmes, *The Common Law* 293–94 (1881).

Holmes reaffirmed this when he went on the bench: "[T]he promise and the consideration must purport to be the motive each for the other, in whole or at least in part. It is not enough that the promise induces the detriment or that the detriment induces the promise if the other half is wanting." Holmes, J., in Wisconsin & Michigan Railway Co. v. Powers, 191 U.S. 379 (1903). Compare Restatement § 71(2) with § 81(1).

(3) *"Sufficiency" of Consideration.* The term "sufficient consideration" appears at several points in Hamer v. Sidway. The Restatement, First, embodied a concept of the "sufficiency" of consideration. Although consideration did not have to be "adequate," it had to be "sufficient." See the Restatement, First, §§ 76–81. The Restatement, Second, abandoned this concept. Under its terminology the question is simply whether there is "consideration," with no qualifying adjective. See Restatement § 79. In declining to assess whether a particular lease provision was inadequate, one court relied on the "time-honored principle" that an informed decision by a party "that what it is receiving is worth what it is giving may not later be second-guessed by that party, nor may the party ask a court to engage in such post-hoc revisionism." GLS Development v. Wal–Mart Stores, 944 F.Supp. 1384 (N.D.Ill. 1996). Whether or not consideration can ever be so paltry as to suggest impermissible overreaching by one of the parties is taken up in Chapter 4.

(4) *Peppercorn.* Under the bargain theory of consideration, can a gratuitous promise be made enforceable by a mere token payment, arranged by the parties for the sole purpose of satisfying the requirement of consideration? Holmes concluded that since courts would not in general "inquire into the amount of such consideration . . . , consideration is as much a form as a seal." Krell v. Codman, 28 N.E. 578 (Mass.1891). The term "peppercorn" is often used to deride consideration that is of trifling value.

Will such a device be given effect? There is some authority, most of it old, that it will be. *E.g.*, Thomas v. Thomas, 2 Q.B. 851, 114 Eng.Rep. 330 (1842). Illustration 1 to the Restatement, First, § 84 reads:

> A wishes to make a binding promise to his son B to convey to B Blackacre, which is worth $5,000. Being advised that a gratuitous promise is not binding, A writes to B an offer to sell Blackacre for $1. B accepts. B's promise to pay $1 is sufficient consideration.

The Restatement, Second, takes the opposite view. Illustration 5 to § 71 reads:

> A desires to make a binding promise to give $1,000 to his son B. Being advised that a gratuitous promise is not binding, A offers to buy from B for $1,000 a book worth less than $1. B accepts the offer knowing that the purchase of the book is a mere pretense. There is no consideration for A's promise to pay $1,000.

For a case in support of this illustration, see Fischer v. Union Trust Co., 101 N.W. 852 (Mich.1904).

(5) *Promise for Performance or Promise for Promise?* In the principal case, the uncle promised to pay his nephew in exchange for his nephew's *refraining* from various vices, and not for his nephew's *promise* to refrain. See Restatement § 71(1). Why might the uncle have sought actual performance rather than his nephew's promise? Distinctions between contracts in which the promise is exchanged for

performance and those in which two promises are exchanged are discussed at p. 67 below and again in Chapter 2 in connection with contract formation. Agreements in which only one party makes a promise are often called *unilateral* contracts; agreements in which each party makes a promise to the other are often called *bilateral*. Bilateral contracts are much more common and economically significant than unilateral contracts. Why might this be?

(6) *Hamer Lives.* In Dahl v. HEM Pharmaceuticals, 7 F.3d 1399, 1404 (9th Cir.1993), a drug company promised a year's free supply of an experimental drug to subjects who participated in a one-year clinical trial to test the drug's efficacy. Dahl participated for the full year, at which time HEM refused to supply the drug any further, claiming its promise to do so was unsupported by consideration. On appeal, the court said: "Somehow the category of unilateral contracts appears to have escaped HEM's notice. The deal was, 'if you submit to our experiment, we will give you a year's supply of Ampligen at no charge.' This form of agreement resembles that in the case taught in the first year of law school, Hamer v. Sidway ..."

PROBLEM

Discounting Retirement. Thomas Hurley has worked as general superintendent for Marine Contractors for eight years, during which time Marine has made annual payments into an Employee Retirement Plan and Trust Fund, a legally separate entity whose sole trustee is also the president of Marine. Hurley now plans to leave Marine, and is entitled under the terms of the trust to payment of his vested share after a five year waiting period. Marine wants Hurley to make a binding promise to Marine not to compete with it after he leaves its employ. In return, Marine's president, as trustee, is willing to have the trust pay Hurley his vested share immediately. Will payment by the trust to Hurley be consideration for Hurley's promise to Marine? Does the answer depend on whether you are looking for a benefit, a detriment, or a bargain? See Marine Contractors Co., Inc. v. Hurley, 310 N.E.2d 915 (Mass.1974).

————

GRATUITOUS PROMISES

Suppose that the uncle in *Hamer* had given his nephew $5,000 in cash at the golden wedding anniversary and had told him that it was a gift that he could keep on condition that he refrain from drinking, smoking, swearing, and gambling until he was twenty-one. Surely the nephew, having met the condition, could have kept the money if the uncle's executor had attempted to get it back. Why, if the law recognizes gratuitous *transfers*, with or without strings attached, should it not recognize gratuitous *promises*? Why did the court have to find that there was consideration? What explains the reluctance to create a regime of enforceable gift promises? We have already seen the suggestion that social cooperation might best be achieved by a system of "free enterprise." Is it the fact that gratuitous promises serve no useful economic function? Do gift promises raise dangers as to proof?

What sorts of rules would you suggest if it were thought desirable to enable promisors to make enforceable gratuitous promises? To what extent should those rules take account of such factors as the promisor's motives, the social utility of the promise, the formality with which it was made and the availability of alternate means of making gifts?

NOTES

(1) *Sweetheart Stadium?* A group of taxpayers in Washington State sought to enjoin a bond ordinance enacted to raise money for a new stadium for the Seattle Mariners, a baseball team. They argued that the consideration received by the city under the terms of the stadium lease between the city and the team was so "grossly inadequate" as to make the lease a gift, one prohibited under the state constitution, which forbids gifts of public monies to private organizations. The taxpayers pointed to such provisions as profit-sharing (with little expectation of profit), nominal rent, and easy-out terms for the team.

Noting that "courts do not inquire into the adequacy of consideration," the Washington Supreme Court found consideration in the Mariners' obligations to play home games, maintain the stadium, and share profits. It affirmed the trial court's declaratory order validating the bonds. King County v. Taxpayers of King County, 949 P.2d 1260 (Wash.1997).

Is the traditional contract standard for consideration appropriate in the context of a constitutional challenge? A dissent in the stadium case argued that the traditional standard failed to accomplish the objective of the constitutional prohibition: "If a public official may transfer $100 of the taxpayer property for a $5 return to the taxpayer, they are $95 poorer. The return is inadequate regardless of the legal sufficiency of the consideration. The purpose of the [constitutional] provision is to avoid transactions which plunder the public purse to the benefit of private corporate wealth." *Id.* at 1278. Dissenting justices would have required a trial on the question of the adequacy of the return.

(2) *Changing One's Mind.* One argument against enforcing gratuitous promises is that enforcement leaves no room for a promisor's regret or for changed circumstances. But might not some reasons for changing one's mind be anticipated and accommodated? French and German laws, for example, permit the revocation of *gifts* by means of implied conditions in cases where the donor is subsequently impoverished (German law), or cases of "donee ingratitude" (French law). See John P. Dawson, *Gifts and Promises* (1980) at 53, 140–141. Consider also an Israeli rule that permits revocation of a gift *promise*, even after reliance by the promisee, "if the retraction is warranted by disgraceful conduct towards the [promisor or the promisor's family]," 22 Laws of State of Israel 113. Is it significant in these latter cases that the promisee appears to have had some responsibility for the promisor's regret? For a thorough investigation of the subject, see Farnsworth, *Changing One's Mind: The Law of Regretted Decisions* (2000).

Fiege v. Boehm

Court of Appeals of Maryland, 1956.
210 Md. 352, 123 A.2d 316.

■ DELAPLAINE, JUDGE. This suit was brought in the Superior Court of Baltimore City by Hilda Louise Boehm against Louis Gail Fiege to recover for breach of a contract to pay the expenses incident to the birth of his bastard child and to provide for its support upon condition that she would refrain from prosecuting him for bastardy.

Plaintiff alleged in her declaration substantially as follows: (1) that early in 1951 defendant had sexual intercourse with her although she was unmarried, and as a result thereof she became pregnant, and defendant acknowledged that he was responsible for her pregnancy; (2) that on September 29, 1951, she gave birth to a female child; that defendant is the father of the child; and that he acknowledged on many occasions that he is its father; (3) that before the child was born, defendant agreed to pay all her medical and miscellaneous expenses and to compensate her for the loss of her salary caused by the child's birth, and also to pay her ten dollars per week for its support until it reached the age of 21, upon condition that she would not institute bastardy proceedings against him as long as he made the payments in accordance with the agreement; (4) that she placed the child for adoption on July 13, 1954, and she claimed the following sums: Union Memorial Hospital, $110; Florence Crittenton Home, $100; Dr. George Merrill, her physician, $50; medicines $70.35; miscellaneous expenses, $20.45; loss of earnings for 26 weeks, $1,105; support of the child, $1,440; total, $2,895.80; and (5) that defendant paid her only $480, and she demanded that he pay her the further sum of $2,415.80, the balance due under the agreement, but he failed and refused to pay the same.

Defendant demurred to the declaration on the ground that it failed to allege that in September, 1953, plaintiff instituted bastardy proceedings against him in the Criminal Court of Baltimore, but since it had been found from blood tests that he could not have been the father of the child, he was acquitted of bastardy. The Court sustained the demurrer with leave to amend.

Plaintiff then filed an amended declaration, which contained the additional allegation that, after the breach of the agreement by defendant, she filed a charge with the State's Attorney that defendant was the father of her bastard child; and that on October 8, 1953, the Criminal Court found defendant not guilty solely on a physician's testimony that "on the basis of certain blood tests made, the defendant can be excluded as the father of the said child, which testimony is not conclusive upon a jury in a trial court." Defendant also demurred to the amended declaration, but the Court overruled that demurrer.

Plaintiff, a typist, now over 35 years old, who has been employed by the Government in Washington and Baltimore for over thirteen years, testified in the Court below that she had never been married, but that at about midnight on January 21, 1951, defendant, after taking her to a moving picture theater on York Road and then to a restaurant, had sexual intercourse with her in his automobile. She further testified that he agreed to pay all her medical and hospital expenses, to compensate her for loss of salary caused by the pregnancy and birth, and to pay her ten dollars per week for the support of the child upon condition that she would refrain from instituting bastardy proceedings against him. She further testified that between September 17, 1951, and May, 1953, defendant paid her a total of $480.

Defendant admitted that he had taken plaintiff to restaurants, had danced with her several times, had taken her to Washington, and had brought her home in the country; but he asserted that he had never had sexual intercourse with her. He also claimed that he did not enter into any agreement with her. He admitted, however, that he had paid her a total of $480. His father also testified that he stated "that he did not want his mother to know, and if it were just kept quiet, kept principally away from his mother and the public and the courts, that he would take care of it."

Defendant further testified that in May 1953, he went to see plaintiff's physician to make inquiry about blood tests to show the paternity of the child; and that those tests were made and they indicated that it was not possible that he could have been the child's father. He then stopped making payments. Plaintiff thereupon filed a charge of bastardy with the State's Attorney.

The testimony which was given in the Criminal Court by Dr. Milton Sachs, hematologist at the University Hospital, was read to the jury in the Superior Court. In recent years the blood-grouping test has been employed in criminology, in the selection of donors for blood transfusions, and as evidence in paternity cases. The Landsteiner blood-grouping test is based on the medical theory that the red corpuscles in human blood contain two affirmative agglutinating substances, and that every individual's blood falls into one of the four classes and remains the same throughout life. According to Mendel's law of inheritance, this blood individuality is an hereditary characteristic which passes from parent to child, and no agglutinating substance can appear in the blood of a child which is not present in the blood of one of its parents. The four Landsteiner blood groups, designated as AB, A, B, and O, into which human blood is divided on the basis of the compatibility of the corpuscles and serum with the corpuscles and serum of other persons, are characterized by different combinations of two agglutinogens in the red blood cells and two agglutinins in the serum. Dr. Sachs reported that Fiege's blood group was Type O, Miss Boehm's was Type B, and the infant's was Type A. He further testified that on the basis of these tests, Fiege could not have been the father of the child, as it is impossible for a mating of Type O and Type B to result in a child of Type A.

Although defendant was acquitted by the Criminal Court, the Superior Court overruled his motion for a directed verdict. In the charge to the jury the Court instructed them that defendant's acquittal in the Criminal Court was not binding upon them. The jury found a verdict in favor of plaintiff for $2,415.80, the full amount of her claim.

Defendant filed a motion for judgment n.o.v. or a new trial. The Court overruled that motion also, and entered judgment on the verdict of the jury. Defendant appealed from that judgment.

Defendant contends that, even if he entered into the contract as alleged, it was not enforceable, because plaintiff's forbearance to prosecute was not based on a valid claim, and hence the contract was without consideration. . . .

It was originally held at common law that a child born out of wedlock is *filius nullius,* and a putative father is not under any legal liability to contribute to the support of his illegitimate child, and his promise to do so is unenforceable because it is based on purely a moral obligation. . . .

However, where statutes are in force to compel the father of a bastard to contribute to its support, the courts have invariably held that a contract by the putative father with the mother of his bastard child to provide for the support of the child upon the agreement of the mother to refrain from invoking the bastardy statute against the father, or to abandon proceedings already commenced, is supported by sufficient consideration. Jangraw v. Perkins, 77 Vt. 375, 60 A. 385; Beach v. Voegtlen, 68 N.J.L. 472, 53 A. 695; Thayer v. Thayer, 189 N.C. 502, 127 S.E. 553, 39 A.L.R. 428.

In Maryland it is now provided by statute that whenever a person is found guilty of bastardy, the court shall issue an order directing such person (1) to pay for the maintenance and support of the child until it reaches the age of eighteen years, such sum as may be agreed upon, if consent proceedings be had, or in the absence of agreement, such sum as the court may fix, with due regard to the circumstances of the accused person; and (2) to give bond to the State of Maryland in such penalty as the court may fix, with good and sufficient securities, conditioned on making the payments required by the court's order, or any amendments thereof. Failure to give such bond shall be punished by commitment in the jail or the House of Correction until bond is given but not exceeding two years. Code Supp.1955, art. 12, § 8.

Prosecutions for bastardy are treated in Maryland as criminal proceedings, but they are actually civil in purpose. . . . Accordingly a contract by the putative father of an illegitimate child to provide for its support upon condition that bastardy proceedings will not be instituted is a compromise of civil injuries resulting from a criminal act, and not a contract to compound a criminal prosecution, and if it is fair and reasonable, it is in accord with the Bastardy Act and the public policy of the State.

Of course, a contract of a putative father to provide for the support of his illegitimate child must be based, like any other contract, upon sufficient consideration. . . .

In 1867 the Maryland Court of Appeals, in the opinion delivered by Judge Bartol in Hartle v. Stahl, 27 Md. 157, 172, held: (1) that forbearance to assert a claim before institution of suit, if not in fact a legal claim, is not of itself sufficient consideration to support a promise; but (2) that a compromise of a doubtful claim or a relinquishment of a pending suit is good consideration for a promise; and (3) that in order to support a compromise, it is sufficient that the parties entering into it thought at the time that there was a *bona fide* question between them, although it may eventually be found that there was in fact no such question.

We have thus adopted the rule that the surrender of, or forbearance to assert an invalid claim by one who has not an honest and reasonable belief in its possible validity is not sufficient consideration for a contract. 1 Restatement, Contracts, sec. 76(b). We combine the subjective requisite that the claim be *bona fide* with the objective requisite that it must have a reasonable basis of support. Accordingly a promise not to prosecute a claim which is not founded in good faith does not of itself give a right of action on an agreement to pay for refraining from so acting, because a release from mere annoyance and unfounded litigation does not furnish valuable consideration.

Professor Williston was not entirely certain whether the test of reasonableness is based upon the intelligence of the claimant himself, who may be an ignorant person with no knowledge of law and little sense as to facts; but he seemed inclined to favor the view that "the claim forborne must be neither absurd in fact from the standpoint of a reasonable man in the position of the claimant, nor, obviously unfounded in law to one who has an elementary knowledge of legal principles." 1 Williston on Contracts, Rev. Ed., sec. 135. We agree that while stress is placed upon the honesty and good faith of the claimant, forbearance to prosecute a claim is insufficient consideration if the claim forborne is so lacking in foundation as to make its assertion incompatible with honesty and a reasonable degree of intelligence. Thus, if the mother of a bastard knows that there is no foundation, either in law or fact, for a charge against a certain man that he is the father of the child, but that man promises to pay her in order to prevent bastardy proceedings against him, the forbearance to institute proceedings is not sufficient consideration.

On the other hand, forbearance to sue for a lawful claim or demand is sufficient consideration for a promise to pay for the forbearance if the party forbearing had an honest intention to prosecute litigation which is not frivolous, vexatious, or unlawful, and which he believed to be well founded. Snyder v. Cearfoss, 187 Md. 635, 643, 51 A.2d 264; Pullman Co. v. Ray, 201 Md. 268, 94 A.2d 266. Thus the promise of a woman who is expecting an illegitimate child that she will not institute bastardy proceedings against a certain man is sufficient consideration for his promise to pay for the child's support, even though it may not be certain whether the man is the father or whether the prosecution would be successful, if she makes the charge in good faith . . . .

Another analogous case is Thompson v. Nelson, 28 Ind. 431. There the plaintiff sought to recover back money which he had paid to compromise a prosecution for bastardy. He claimed that the prosecuting witness was not pregnant and therefore the prosecution was fraudulent. It was held by the Supreme Court of Indiana, however, that the settlement of the prosecution was a good consideration for the payment of the money and it could not be recovered back, inasmuch as it appeared from the evidence that the prosecution was instituted in good faith, and at that time there was reason to believe that the prosecuting witness was pregnant, although it was found out afterwards that she was not pregnant. [The court's summary of a similar decision on similar facts in Illinois is here omitted. Heaps v. Dunham, 95 Ill. 583, 590.]

In the case at bar there was no proof of fraud or unfairness. Assuming that the hematologists were accurate in their laboratory tests and findings, nevertheless plaintiff gave testimony which indicated that she made the charge of bastardy against defendant in good faith. For these reasons the

Court acted properly in overruling the demurrer to the amended declaration and the motion for a directed verdict.

As we have found no reversible error in the rulings and instructions of the trial court, we will affirm the judgment entered on the verdict of the jury.

Judgment affirmed, with costs.

NOTES

(1) *The Objective Requisite.* What was the consideration for Fiege's promise? Boehm's forbearance to press a claim that later turned out to be invalid? According to the Restatement, First, § 76, "forbearance to assert an invalid claim ... by one who has not an honest and reasonable belief in its possible validity" is not consideration. Examine Restatement § 74(1). What has happened to the requirement of the Restatement, First, that the forbearing party have a reasonable belief in its position? On a close reading of *Fiege*, does it appear that the Restatement, Second, rule is substantially identical to the rule of the case?

(2) *Nondisclosure.* What important information did Boehm fail to disclose to Fiege when he made his promise? Is it arguable that her failure amounted to a misrepresentation? Misrepresentation by non-disclosure is dealt with at p. 352 below. Could Boehm have enforced promises for child support against two promisors? What facts might warrant her belief in the "possible validity" of claims against both?

(3) *Legal Claims and Legal Ethics. Fiege* concerned the issue of forbearance on a claim in a personal context. The settlement of doubtful claims is of significant economic importance in connection with nuisance litigation or "strike suits." These are defined as lawsuits with a sufficiently low chance of prevailing at trial that they would not have been brought but for the prospect of settlement. Why are frivolous suits not always met with blanket refusals to negotiate? A legal economist has observed that "since refusing to take a valid claim seriously can be quite costly, a frivolous plaintiff may be able to take advantage of the defendant's uncertainty regarding the claim's validity to extract a substantial settlement." Avery Katz, The Effect of Frivolous Lawsuits on the Settlement of Claims, 10 Intl.Rev.L. & Econ.3,4 (1990).

What is a lawyer's responsibility with regard to filing dubious pleadings? Rule 11(b) of the Federal Rules of Civil Procedure provides that by presenting a pleading to a court, an attorney certifies that to the best of his or her knowledge, after a reasonable inquiry, the pleading "is not being presented for any improper purpose, such as to harass or to cause unnecessary delay or needless increase in the cost of litigation." An attorney further certifies, by virtue of a pleading, that there is evidentiary support for any fact it asserts. Courts may order sanctions against attorneys who violate Rule 11(b). Comparable rules about state court pleadings are prevalent.

PROBLEM

Stairway to Heaven. Ralston was injured when she fell on a negligently maintained church stairway. An adjuster for the church's insurance company called on her and promised that it would pay all her expenses if she would refrain from suing the church or the insurer. When the insurer failed to pay, she sued the company on its promise. The insurer argued that because under existing law churches and charitable organizations are immune from liability for their torts,

Ralston could not have won a judgment against the church. The trial court agreed and sustained the insurer's demurrer to the Ralston's complaint. What result on Ralston's appeal? How does the insurer's argument resemble that of Fiege in the main case? How does it differ? Should this distinction matter? See Ralston v. Mathew, 250 P.2d 841 (Kan.1952).

———

(B) THE REQUIREMENT OF EXCHANGE: ACTION IN THE PAST

Feinberg v. Pfeiffer Co.

Saint Louis Court of Appeals, Missouri, 1959.
322 S.W.2d 163.

Action on alleged contract by defendant to pay plaintiff a specified monthly amount upon her retirement from defendant's employ. The Circuit Court, City of St. Louis, rendered judgment for plaintiff, and defendant appealed.

■ DOERNER, COMMISSIONER. This is a suit brought in the Circuit Court of the City of St. Louis by plaintiff, a former employee of the defendant corporation, on an alleged contract whereby defendant agreed to pay plaintiff the sum of $200 per month for life upon her retirement. A jury being waived, the case was tried by the court alone. Judgment below was for plaintiff for $5,100, the amount of the pension claimed to be due as of the date of the trial together with interest thereon, and defendant duly appealed.

The parties are in substantial agreement on the essential facts. Plaintiff began working for the defendant, a manufacturer of pharmaceuticals, in 1910, when she was but 17 years of age. By 1947 she had attained the position of bookkeeper, office manager, and assistant treasurer of the defendant, and owned 70 shares of its stock out of a total of 6,503 shares issued and outstanding. Twenty shares had been given to her by the defendant or its then president, she had purchased 20, and the remaining 30 she had acquired by a stock split or stock dividend. Over the years she received substantial dividends on the stock she owned, as did all of the other stockholders. Also, in addition to her salary, plaintiff from 1937 to 1949, inclusive, received each year a bonus varying in amount from $300 in the beginning to $2,000 in the later years.

On December 27, 1947, the annual meeting of the defendant's Board of Directors was held at the Company's offices in St. Louis, presided over by Max Lippman, its then president and largest individual stockholder. The other directors present were George L. Marcus, Sidney Harris, Sol Flammer, and Walter Weinstock, who, with Max Lippman, owned 5,007 of the 6,503 shares then issued and outstanding. At that meeting the Board of Directors adopted the following resolution, which, because it is the crux of the case, we quote in full:

"The Chairman thereupon pointed out that the Assistant Treasurer, Mrs. Anna Sacks Feinberg, has given the corporation many years of long and faithful service. Not only has she served the corporation devotedly, but with exceptional ability and skill. The President pointed out that although all of the officers and directors sincerely hoped and desired that Mrs. Feinberg would continue in her present position for as long as she felt able, nevertheless, in view of the length of service which she has contributed provision should be made to afford her retirement privileges and benefits which should become a firm obligation of the corporation to be available to her whenever she should see fit to retire from active duty, however many years in the future such retirement may become effective. It was, accordingly, proposed that Mrs. Feinberg's salary which is presently $350.00 per month, be increased to $400.00 per month, and that Mrs. Feinberg would be given the privilege of retiring from active duty at any time she may elect to see fit so to do upon a retirement pay of $200.00 per month for life, with the distinct understanding that the retirement plan is merely being adopted at the present time in order to afford Mrs. Feinberg security for the future and in the hope that her active services will continue with the corporation for many years to come. After due discussion and consideration, and upon motion duly made and seconded, it was—

"Resolved, that the salary of Anna Sacks Feinberg be increased from $350.00 to $400.00 per month and that she be afforded the privilege of retiring from active duty in the corporation at any time she may elect to see fit so to do upon retirement pay of $200.00 per month, for the remainder of her life."

At the request of Mr. Lippman his sons-in-law, Messrs. Harris and Flammer, called upon the plaintiff at her apartment on the same day to advise her of the passage of the resolution. Plaintiff testified on cross-examination that she had no prior information that such a pension plan was contemplated, that it came as a surprise to her, and that she would have continued in her employment whether or not such a resolution had been adopted. It is clear from the evidence that there was no contract, oral or written, as to plaintiff's length of employment, and that she was free to quit, and the defendant to discharge her, at any time.

Plaintiff did continue to work for the defendant through June 30, 1949, on which date she retired. In accordance with the foregoing resolution, the defendant began paying her the sum of $200 on the first of each month. Mr. Lippman died on November 18, 1949, and was succeeded as president of the company by his widow. Because of an illness, she retired from that office and was succeeded in October, 1953, by her son-in-law, Sidney M. Harris. Mr. Harris testified that while Mrs. Lippman had been president she signed the monthly pension check paid plaintiff, but fussed about doing so, and considered the payments as gifts. After his election, he stated, a new accounting firm employed by the defendant questioned the validity of the payments to plaintiff on several occasions, and in the Spring of 1956, upon its recommendation, he consulted the Company's then attorney, Mr. Ralph Kalish. Harris testified that both Ernst and Ernst, the accounting firm, and Kalish told him there was no need of giving plaintiff the money. He also stated that he had concurred in the view that the payments to plaintiff were mere gratuities rather than amounts due under a contractual obligation, and that following his discussion with the Company's attorney plaintiff was sent a check for $100 on April 1, 1956. Plaintiff declined to accept the reduced amount, and this action followed. Additional facts will be referred to later in this opinion. . . .

Appellant's next complaint is that there was insufficient evidence to support the court's findings that plaintiff would not have quit defendant's employ had she not known and relied upon the promise of defendant to pay her $200 a month for life, and the finding that, from her voluntary retirement until April 1, 1956, plaintiff relied upon the continued receipt of the pension installments. The trial court so found, and, in our opinion, justifiably so. Plaintiff testified, and was corroborated by Harris, defendant's witness, that knowledge of the passage of the resolution was communicated to her on December 27, 1947, the very day it was adopted. She was told at that time by Harris and Flammer, she stated, that she could take the pension as of that day, if she wished. She testified further that she continued to work for another year and a half, through June 30, 1949; that at that time her health was good and she could have continued to work, but that after working for almost forty years she thought she would take a rest. Her testimony continued:

"Q. Now, what was the reason—I'm sorry. Did you then quit the employment of the company after you—after this year and a half? A. Yes.

"Q. What was the reason that you left? A. Well, I thought almost forty years, it was a long time and I thought I would take a little rest.

"Q. Yes. A. And with the pension and what earnings my husband had, we figured we could get along.

"Q. Did you rely upon this pension? A. We certainly did.

"Q. Being paid? A. Very much so. We relied upon it because I was positive that I was going to get it as long as I lived.

"Q. Would you have left the employment of the company at that time had it not been for this pension? A. No.

"Mr. Allen: Just a minute, I object to that as calling for a conclusion and conjecture on the part of this witness.

"The Court: It will be overruled.

"Q. (Mr. Agatstein continuing): Go ahead, now. The question is whether you would have quit the employment of the company at that time had you not relied upon this pension plan? A. No, I wouldn't.

"Q. You would not have. Did you ever seek employment while this pension was being paid to you—A. (interrupting): No.

"Q. Wait a minute, at any time prior—at any other place? A. No, sir.

"Q. Were you able to hold any other employment during that time? A. Yes, I think so.

"Q. Was your health good? A. My health was good."

It is obvious from the foregoing that there was ample evidence to support the findings of fact made by the court below.

We come, then, to the basic issue in the case. While otherwise defined in defendant's third and fourth assignments of error, it is thus succinctly stated in the argument in its brief: "... whether plaintiff has proved that she has a right to recover from defendant based upon a legally binding contractual obligation to pay her $200 per month for life."

It is defendant's contention, in essence, that the resolution adopted by its Board of Directors was a mere promise to make a gift, and that no contract resulted either thereby, or when plaintiff retired, because there was no consideration given or paid by the plaintiff. It urges that a promise to make a gift is not binding unless supported by a legal consideration; that the only apparent consideration for the adoption of the foregoing resolution was the "many years of long and faithful service" expressed therein; and that past services are not a valid consideration for a promise. Defendant argues further that there is nothing in the resolution which made its effectiveness conditional upon plaintiff's continued employment, that she was not under contract to work for any length of time but was free to quit whenever she wished, and that she had no contractual right to her position and could have been discharged at any time.

Plaintiff concedes that a promise based upon past services would be without consideration, but contends that there were two other elements which supplied the required element: First, the continuation by plaintiff in the employ of the defendant for the period from December 27, 1947, the date when the resolution was adopted, until the date of her retirement on June 30, 1949. And, second, her change of position, i.e., her retirement, and the abandonment by her of her opportunity to continue in gainful employment, made in reliance on defendant's promise to pay her $200 per month for life.

We must agree with the defendant that the evidence does not support the first of these contentions. There is no language in the resolution predicating plaintiff's right to a pension upon her continued employment. She was not required to work for the defendant for any period of time as a condition to gaining such retirement benefits. She was told that she could quit the day upon which the resolution was adopted, as she herself testified, and it is clear from her own testimony that she made no promise or agreement to continue in the employ of the defendant in return for its promise to pay her a pension. Hence there was lacking that mutuality of obligation which is essential to the validity of a contract. . . .

Consideration for a promise has been defined in the Restatement of the Law of Contracts, Section 75, as:

"(1) Consideration for a promise is

    (a) an act other than a promise, or

    (b) a forbearance, or

    (c) the creation, modification or destruction of a legal relation, or

    (d) a return promise,

bargained for and given in exchange for the promise."

As the parties agree, the consideration sufficient to support a contract may be either a benefit to the promisor or a loss or detriment to the promisee. . . .

[The rest of the opinion is set out at p. 94, below. There Feinberg prevails on her contention that the defendant's promise resulted in a "change of position" on her part.]

NOTES

(1) *The Missing Ingredient.* Feinberg conceded "that a promise based on past services would be without consideration." Why was it so clear to everyone that her 37 years of service, prior to the resolution of December 27, 1947, could not be consideration for Pfeiffer's promise?

(2) *Drafting.* Suppose that Max Lippman had called in his lawyer in December, 1947, and said, "I want you to draw up a resolution that will make sure that Mrs. Feinberg will get a pension of $200 a month as long as she lives." How might the lawyer have drafted such a document? Would it have helped to include the words, "*in consideration of* her many years of long and faithful service"?

MORAL OBLIGATION

Mills v. Wyman

Supreme Judicial Court of Massachusetts, 1825.
3 Pick. 207, 20 Mass. 207.

[Levi Wyman, age 25, fell ill on his return from a sea voyage and, being poor and in distress, was cared for by Daniel Mills for about two weeks. A few days later, after all Mills's expenses had been incurred, Seth Wyman, Levi's father, wrote Mills promising to pay those expenses. When Seth Wyman decided not to pay, Mills sued him. From a direction of nonsuit, Mills appealed.]

■ PARKER, C.J. General rules of law established for the protection and security of honest and fair-minded men, who may inconsiderately make promises without any equivalent, will sometimes screen men of a different character from engagements which they are bound in *foro conscientiae* to perform. This is a defect inherent in all human systems of legislation. The rule that a mere verbal promise, without any consideration, cannot be enforced by action, is universal in its application, and cannot be departed from to suit particular cases in which a refusal to perform such a promise may be disgraceful.

> The promise declared on in this case appears to have been made without any legal consideration. The kindness and services towards the sick son of the defendant were not bestowed at his request. The son was in no respect under the care of the defendant. He was twenty-five years old, and had long left his father's family. On his return from a foreign country, he fell sick among strangers, and the plaintiff acted the part of the good Samaritan, giving him shelter and comfort until he died. The defendant, his father, on being informed of this event,

influenced by a transient feeling of gratitude, promises in writing to pay the plaintiff for the expenses he had incurred. But he has determined to break this promise, and is willing to have his case appear on record as a strong example of particular injustice sometimes necessarily resulting from the operation of general rules.

It is said a moral obligation is a sufficient consideration to support an express promise; and some authorities lay down the rule thus broadly; but upon examination of the cases we are satisfied that the universality of the rule cannot be supported . . .

A deliberate promise, in writing, made freely and without any mistake, one which may lead the party to whom it is made into contracts and expenses, cannot be broken without a violation of moral duty. But if there was nothing paid or promised for it, the law, perhaps wisely, leaves the execution of it to the conscience of him who makes it. It is only when the party making the promise gains something, or he to whom it is made loses something, that the law gives the promise validity . . .

[T]here seems to be no case in which it was nakedly decided, that a promise to pay the debt of a son of full age, not living with his father, though the debt were incurred by sickness which ended in the death of the son, without a previous request by the father proved or presumed, could be enforced by action.

For the foregoing reasons we are all of opinion that the nonsuit directed by the Court of Common Pleas was right, and that judgment be entered thereon for costs for the defendant.

NOTES

(1) *The Case Against "Moral Obligation."* Mills v. Wyman accurately reflects the traditional common law view that a promise made in recognition of a "moral obligation" arising out of a benefit previously received is not enforceable. A benefit conferred before a promise is made can hardly be said to have been given in "exchange" for the promise. Williston noted further that "it is essential that the classes of promises which are [enforceable by law] shall be clearly defined. The test of moral consideration must vary with the opinion of every individual. Indeed, as has been said, since there is a moral obligation to perform every promise, it would seem that if morality was to be the guide, every promise would be enforced and if the existence of a past moral obligation is to be the test, every promise which repeats or restates a prior gratuitous promise would be binding." 1 Williston, *Treatise on the Law of Contracts* § 148 (1st ed. 1920).

(2) *Recognized Exceptions.* As the court acknowledged in *Mills*, in certain exceptional situations the common law does enforce certain promises made in recognition of what could be viewed as a "moral obligation." These include a promise to pay a debt no longer legally enforceable because the statutory period of limitations has run, and a promise by an adult reaffirming a promise made when the promisor was a minor and that could have avoided on that ground. A promise to pay a debt that has been discharged in bankruptcy constitutes a third exception. See Restatement §§ 82 and 83. What appears to explain these exceptions? (The enforceability of a promise to pay a debt unenforceable because of the promisor's discharge

in bankruptcy is now subject to additional requirements under the Bankruptcy Code. 11 U.S.C. § 524(c), (d).) On reaffirmation by minors, see Note 2, p. 314 below.

Webb v. McGowin

Court of Appeals of Alabama, 1935.
27 Ala.App. 82, 168 So. 196.

Action by Joe Webb against N. Floyd McGowin and Joseph F. McGowin, as executors of the estate of J. Greeley McGowin, deceased. From a judgment of nonsuit, plaintiff appeals.

■ BRICKEN, PRESIDING JUDGE. This action is in assumpsit. The complaint as originally filed was amended. The demurrers to the complaint as amended were sustained, and because of this adverse ruling by the court the plaintiff took a nonsuit, and the assignment of errors on this appeal are predicated upon said action or ruling of the court.

A fair statement of the case presenting the questions for decision is set out in appellant's brief, which we adopt.

"On the 3d day of August, 1925, appellant while in the employ of the W.T. Smith Lumber Company, a corporation, and acting within the scope of his employment, was engaged in clearing the upper floor of Mill No. 2 of the company. While so engaged he was in the act of dropping a pine block from the upper floor of the mill to the ground below; this being the usual and ordinary way of clearing the floor, and it being the duty of the plaintiff in the course of his employment to so drop it. The block weighed about 75 pounds.

"As appellant was in the act of dropping the block to the ground below, he was on the edge of the upper floor of the mill. As he started to turn the block loose so that it would drop to the ground, he saw J. Greeley McGowin, testator of the defendants, on the ground below and directly under where the block would have fallen had appellant turned it loose. Had he turned it loose it would have struck McGowin with such force as to have caused him serious bodily harm or death. Appellant could have remained safely on the upper floor of the mill by turning the block loose and allowing it to drop, but had he done this the block would have fallen on McGowin and caused him serious injuries or death. The only safe and reasonable way to prevent this was for appellant to hold to the block and divert its direction in falling from the place where McGowin was standing and the only safe way to divert it so as to prevent its coming into contact with McGowin was for appellant to fall with it to the ground below. Appellant did this, and by holding to the block and falling with it to the ground below, he diverted the course of its fall in such way that McGowin was not injured. In thus preventing the injuries to McGowin appellant himself received serious bodily injuries, resulting in his right leg being broken, the heel of his right foot torn off and his right arm broken. He was badly crippled for life and rendered unable to do physical or mental labor.

"On September 1, 1925, in consideration of appellant having prevented him from sustaining death or serious bodily harm and in consideration of the injuries appellant had received, McGowin agreed with him to care for and maintain him for the remainder of appellant's life at the rate of $15 every two weeks from the time he sustained his injuries to and during the remainder of appellant's life; it being agreed that McGowin would pay this sum to appellant for his maintenance. Under the agreement McGowin paid or caused to be paid to appellant the sum so agreed on up until McGowin's death on January 1, 1934. After his death the payments were continued to and including January 27, 1934, at which time they were discontinued. Thereupon plaintiff brought suit to recover the unpaid installments accruing up to the time of the bringing of the suit.

"The material averments of the different counts of the original complaint and the amended complaint are predicated upon the foregoing statement of facts." . . .

The action was for the unpaid installments accruing after January 27, 1934, to the time of the suit. . . .

1. The averments of the complaint show that appellant saved McGowin from death or grievous bodily harm. This was a material benefit to him of infinitely more value than any financial aid he could have received. Receiving this benefit, McGowin became morally bound to compensate appellant for the services rendered. Recognizing his moral obligation, he expressly agreed to pay appellant as alleged in the complaint and complied with this agreement up to the time of his death; a period of more than 8 years.

Had McGowin been accidentally poisoned and a physician, without his knowledge or request, had administered an antidote, thus saving his life, a subsequent promise by McGowin to pay the physician would have been valid. Likewise, McGowin's agreement as disclosed by the complaint to compensate appellant for saving him from death or grievous bodily injury is valid and enforceable.

Where the promisee cares for, improves, and preserves the property of the promisor, though done without his request, it is sufficient consideration for the promisor's subsequent agreement to pay for the service, because of the material benefit received. . . .

In Boothe v. Fitzpatrick, 36 Vt. 681, the court held that a promise by defendant to pay for the past keeping of a bull which had escaped from defendant's premises and been cared for by plaintiff was valid, although there was no previous request, because the subsequent promise obviated that objection; it being equivalent to a previous request. On the same principle, had the promisee saved the promisor's life or his body from grievous harm, his subsequent promise to pay for the services rendered would have been valid. Such service would have been far more material than caring for his bull. Any holding that saving a man from death or grievous bodily harm is not a material benefit sufficient to uphold a subsequent promise to pay for the service, necessarily rests on the assumption that saving life and preservation of the body from harm have only a sentimental value. The converse of this is true. Life and preservation of the body have material, pecuniary values, measurable in dollars and cents.

Because of this, physicians practice their profession charging for services rendered in saving life and curing the body of its ills, and surgeons perform operations. The same is true as to the law of negligence, authorizing the assessment of damages in personal injury cases based upon the extent of the injuries, earnings, and life expectancies of those injured.

In the business of life insurance, the value of a man's life is measured in dollars and cents according to his expectancy, the soundness of his body, and his ability to pay premiums. The same is true as to health and accident insurance.

It follows that if, as alleged in the complaint, appellant saved J. Greeley McGowin from death or grievous bodily harm, and McGowin subsequently agreed to pay him for the service rendered, it became a valid and enforceable contract.

2. It is well settled that a moral obligation is a sufficient consideration to support a subsequent promise to pay where the promisor has received a material benefit, although there was no original duty or liability resting on the promisor. [Cases cited.]

The case at bar is clearly distinguishable from that class of cases where the consideration is a mere moral obligation or conscientious duty unconnected with receipt by promisor of benefits of a material or pecuniary nature.... Here the promisor received a material benefit constituting a valid consideration for his promise.

3. Some authorities hold that, for a moral obligation to support a subsequent promise to pay, there must have existed a prior legal or equitable obligation, which for some reason had become unenforceable, but for which the promisor was still morally bound. This rule, however, is subject to qualification in those cases where the promisor having received a material benefit from the promisee, is morally bound to compensate him for the services rendered and in consideration of this obligation promises to pay. In such cases the subsequent promise to pay is an affirmance or ratification of the services rendered carrying with it the presumption that a previous request for the service was made....

4. The averments of the complaint show that in saving McGowin from death or grievous bodily harm, appellant was crippled for life. This was part of the consideration of the contract declared on. McGowin was benefited. Appellant was injured. Benefit to the promisor or injury to the promisee is a sufficient legal consideration for the promissor's agreement to pay....

5. Under the averments of the complaint the services rendered by appellant were not gratuitous. The agreement of McGowin to pay and the acceptance of payment by appellant conclusively shows the contrary....

From what has been said, we are of the opinion that the court below erred in the ruling complained of; that is to say in sustaining the demurrer, and for this error the case is reversed and remanded.

Reversed and remanded.

■ SAMFORD, JUDGE (CONCURRING). The questions involved in this case are not free from doubt, and perhaps the strict letter of the rule, as stated by judges, though not always in accord, would bar a recovery by plaintiff, but following the principle announced by Chief Justice Marshall in Hoffman v. Porter, Fed.Cas. No. 6,577, 2 Brock. 156, 159, where he says, "I do not think that law ought to be separated from justice, where it is at most doubtful," I concur in the conclusions reached by the court.

[Part of the short opinion of the Supreme Court of Alabama, denying certiorari, is set out next.]

■ FOSTER, JUSTICE.... The opinion of the Court of Appeals here under consideration recognizes and applies the distinction between a supposed moral obligation of the promisor, based upon some refined sense of ethical duty, without material benefit to him, and one in which such a benefit did in fact occur. We agree with that court that if the benefit be material and substantial, and was to the person of the promisor rather than to his estate, it is within the class of material benefits which he has the privilege of recognizing and compensating either by an executed payment or an executory promise to pay. The cases are cited in that opinion. The reason is emphasized when the compensation is not only for the benefits which the promisor received, but also for the injuries either to the property or person of the promisee by reason of the service rendered.

Writ denied.

NOTES

(1) *The Case for "Moral Obligation."* "Courts have frequently enforced promises on the simple ground that the promisor was only promising to do what he ought to have done anyway. These cases have either been condemned as wanton departures from legal principle, or reluctantly accepted as involving the kind of compromise logic must inevitably make at times with sentiment. I believe that these decisions are capable of rational defense. When we say the defendant was morally obligated to do the thing he promised, we in effect assert the existence of a substantive ground for enforcing the promise.... The court's conviction that the promisor ought to do the thing, plus the promisor's own admission of his obligation, may tilt the scales in favor of enforcement where neither standing alone would be sufficient. If it be argued that moral consideration threatens certainty, the solution would seem to lie, not in rejecting the doctrine, but in taming it by continuing the process of judicial exclusion and inclusion already begun in the cases involving infants' contracts, barred debts, and discharged bankrupts." Fuller, Consideration and Form, 41 Colum.L.Rev. 799, 821–822 (1941).

(2) *Reform by Statute.* New York law does not recognize "moral obligation" as an equivalent of consideration, but a New York statute enacted in 1941 and now found in General Obligations Law § 5–1105 provides: "A promise in writing and signed by the promisor or by his agent shall not be denied effect as a valid contractual obligation on the ground that consideration for the promise is past or executed, if the consideration is expressed in the writing and is proved to have been given or performed and would be a valid consideration but for the time when it was given or performed."

How would the New York statute have affected the preceding cases? Would the common recital "for value received" satisfy the New York statute? Would you favor the adoption of that statute by other states? What about the adoption of a statute enacting Restatement § 86?

————

(C) THE REQUIREMENT OF BARGAIN

Kirksey v. Kirksey

Supreme Court of Alabama, 1845.
8 Ala. 131.

The plaintiff was the wife of defendant's brother, but had for some time been a widow, and had several children. In 1840, the plaintiff resided on public land, under a contract of lease, she had held over, and was comfortably settled, and would have attempted to secure the land she lived on. The defendant resided in Talladega County, some sixty or seventy miles off. On the 10th October, 1840, he wrote to her the following letter:

"Dear Sister Antillico,—Much to my mortification, I heard that brother Henry was dead, and one of his children. I know that your situation is one of grief and difficulty. You had a bad chance before, but a great deal worse now. I should like to come and see you, but cannot with convenience at present.... I do not know whether you have a preference on the place you live on or not. If you had, I would advise you to obtain your preference, and sell the land and quit the country, as I understand it is very unhealthy, and I know society is very bad. If you will come down and see me, I will let you have a place to raise your family, and I have more open land than I can tend; and on account of your situation, and that of your family, I feel like I want you and the children to do well."

Within a month or two after the receipt of this letter, the plaintiff abandoned her possession, without disposing of it, and removed with her family, to the residence of the defendant, who put her in comfortable houses, and gave her land to cultivate for two years, at the end of which time he notified her to remove, and put her in a house, not comfortable, in the woods, which he afterwards required her to leave.

A verdict being found for the plaintiff, for $200, the above facts were agreed, and if they will sustain the action, the judgment is to be affirmed, otherwise it is to be reversed.

■ ORMOND, J. The inclination of my mind is that the loss and inconvenience which the plaintiff sustained in breaking up and moving to the defendant's, a distance of sixty miles, is a sufficient consideration to support the promise to furnish her with a house, and land to cultivate, until she could raise her family. My brothers, however, think that the promise on the part of the defendant was a mere gratuity, and that an action will not lie for its breach. The judgment of the court below must therefore be reversed, pursuant to the agreement of the parties.

NOTES

(1) *Conditional Gift or Bargained–For Exchange?* How did the court read the words, "If you will come down and see me, I will let you have a place to raise your family"? As words of bargain for an exchange or as a condition to a gratuitous promise? What factors (language, circumstances, indications of intent) make the sentence appear more like the promise of a gift? More like a proposal of a bargain?

(2) *Lunchtime at Tiffany's.* A father and his daughter became estranged after her mother divorced the father, and the daughter refused to see her father. The father then wrote to his daughter: "If you will meet me at Tiffany's next Monday at noon, I will buy you the emerald ring advertised in this week's *New Yorker*." The daughter met her father at Tiffany's, but he did not buy her the promised ring. Bargained-for exchange or conditional gratuitous promise?

Williston put this case: "If a benevolent man says to a tramp, 'If you go around the corner to the clothing shop there, you may purchase an overcoat on my credit,' no reasonable person would understand that the short walk was requested as the consideration for the promise; rather, the understanding would be that in the event of the tramp going to the shop the promisor would make him a gift." This first appeared in 1 Williston, *A Treatise on the Law of Contracts* § 112 (1st ed.1920). Is the situation of the daughter distinguishable from that of the tramp?

(3) *The Million Dollar Swipe.* While vacationing at Atlantic City, New Jersey, Rena Gottlieb went to a promotional booth at the Tropicana Casino and joined the Tropicana's Diamond Club by filling out a simple application. She received a card that club members swipe before playing any machine. The swipe provides information about members' gambling habits, which is then used by the casino's marketing department to tailor its promotions. Diamond Club members are entitled to one free spin daily of the Fun House Million Dollar Wheel. After swiping in, Gottlieb spun the wheel, which landed on the million dollar mark. Tropicana refused to pay on the ground that there was no consideration for her participation in the Diamond Club promotion. She sued the Tropicana Casino and Resort for $1,000,000. *Held*: For plaintiff. Gottlieb v. Tropicana Hotel and Casino, 109 F.Supp.2d 324 (E.D.Pa.2000):

"Ms. Gottlieb had to go to the casino to participate in the promotion. She had to wait in line to spin the wheel. By . . . allowing her [Diamond Club card] to be swiped into the casino's machine, she was permitting the casino to gather information about her gambling habits. Additionally, by participating in the game, she was a part of the entertainment that casinos, by their very nature, are designed to offer to all of those present. All of these detriments . . . were 'the requested detriment[s] to the promisee induced by the promise' of Tropicana to offer her a chance to win $1 million. Tropicana's motives in offering the promotion were 'in nowise altruistic.' Tropicana offered the promotion in order to generate patronage of and excitement within the casino. In short, Ms. Gottlieb provided adequate consideration to form a contract with Tropicana." The case was remanded to determine the factual question of whether the marker firmly landed on the million-dollar mark, or immediately fell off, as the Casino claimed.

PROBLEM

Jailhouse Rock. Steve Jennings, a prisoner in Texas, was a faithful listener to radio station KSCS, which regularly broadcast that it played "at least three-in-a-row, or we pay you $25,000. No bull, more music on KSCS." Jennings sued KSCS, alleging that each time it played "five-in-a-row" it played only three songs, followed by a brief commercial, and then only *two* songs, but that when he notified KSCS on specific occasions of this they refused to pay him $25,000. He also alleged that he then stopped listening to KSCS. KSCS has moved to dismiss on the ground that there was no consideration for its promise. What decision? See Jennings v. Radio Station KSCS, 96.3 FM, Inc., 708 S.W.2d 60 (Tex.App.1986).

EMPLOYMENT AGREEMENTS

The next case introduces the category of personal service or employment agreements. For more than six centuries, important aspects of the employment relationship, such as the period of service, were governed by statute. For example, the Statute of Laborers, 23 Edw.III (1349), imposed a duty to work on most able-bodied adults, and later Elizabethan enactments established a minimum one-year duration for all employment contracts. Agreements between master and servant, as the parties were then called, shifted to a contractual model as industrialization and the philosophy of *laissez faire* took hold. A detailed account of the rise of bargaining, including collective bargaining, and of current statutory regimes such as minimum-wage, safety, or anti-discrimination law, is left to courses on labor and employment law.

Our concern here is how basic contract principles play out in the circumstances of employment, including decisions about hiring and firing. We focus particularly on "at-will" employees, those whose employment agreements are terminable by either party at any time and for any reason, or no reason at all. As you read the employment cases that follow, consider how background policies regarding the right to work or the prevention of idleness have influenced the development of common law contract doctrine.

We begin with the problem of bargained-for exchange between employers and employees when, as is often the case, the terms of the agreement are not entirely settled at a single moment. Determining these terms is crucial to deciding whether an employee has been wrongfully fired. In our first case, however, the shoe is on the other foot, and it is the employer who seeks to enforce the promise of an at-will employee. The term at issue concerns post-employment conduct, specifically the employee's broken promise not to compete with his former employer.

Lake Land Employment Group of Akron, LLC v. Columber

Supreme Court of Ohio, 2004.
101 Ohio St.3d 242, 804 N.E.2d 27.

■ MOYER, C.J. Lake Land Employment Group of Akron, LLC ("Lake Land"), appellant, initiated this action by filing a complaint asserting that its ex-employee, appellee Lee Columber, had breached a noncompetition agreement the parties had executed. The agreement provided that for a period of three years after his termination of employment Columber would not engage in any business within a 50–mile radius of Akron, Ohio, that competed with the business of Lake Land. Lake Land further claimed that Columber's employment with Lake Land terminated in 2001 and that he thereafter violated the terms of the noncompetition agreement. Lake Land sought money damages and an order prohibiting Columber from engaging in any activities that violated the noncompetition agreement.

Columber answered and admitted that he had been employed by Lake Land from 1988 until 2001. He further admitted that he had signed the noncompetition agreement and that following his discharge from Lake Land he had formed a corporation that is engaged in a business similar to that of Lake Land. Columber pled lack of consideration in his answer. Columber moved for summary judgment, claiming that the noncompetition agreement was unenforceable ... and that the restrictions in the agreement were overly restrictive and imposed an undue hardship on him.

Columber could remember very little about the presentation or execution of the noncompetition agreement. He could not remember whether he had been told that his continued employment was dependent upon execution of the agreement or whether he had posed questions about the restrictions it contained. He testified that he vaguely remembered signing the agreement after his employer presented it to him and told him to read and sign it. He acknowledged that he had read the agreement, but had not talked to an attorney or anybody else about it. The at-will relationship of the parties continued for ten years thereafter.

The trial court granted summary judgment in Columber's favor. It found no dispute that Columber had been employed by Lake Land beginning in 1988 and that Columber signed the agreement in September 1991. It further found no dispute that there "was no increase of salary, benefits, or other remunerations given as consideration for Columber signing the non-competition agreement" and "no change in his employment status in connection with the signing of the noncompetition agreement." The trial court concluded that the noncompetition agreement lacked consideration, and was unenforceable. The trial court therefore found it unnecessary to determine the reasonableness of the temporal and geographical restrictions in the noncompetition agreement.

The court of appeals affirmed. It certified a conflict, however, between its decision and [those of other Ohio districts courts]. The certified issue is "Is subsequent employment alone sufficient consideration to support a covenant-not-to-compete agreement with an at-will employee entered into after employment has already begun?"

I   Legal Background

Generally, courts look upon noncompetition agreements with some skepticism and have cautiously considered and carefully scrutinized them. Ingram, Covenants Not to Compete (2002), 36 Akron L.Rev. 49, 50. Under English common law, agreements in restraint of trade, including noncompetition agreements, were disfavored as being against public policy, although partial restraints supported by fair consideration were upheld ... In a society in which working men entered skilled trades only by serving apprenticeships, and mobility was minimal, restrictive covenants precluding an ex-employee from competing with his ex-employer "either destroyed a man's means of livelihood, or bound him to his master for life." *Raimonde v. Van Vlerah* (1975), 325 N.E.2d 544.

Modern economic realities, however, do not justify a strict prohibition of noncompetition agreements between employer and employee in an at-will relationship. "The law upholds these agreements because they allow the parties to work together to expand output and competition. If one party can trust the other with confidential information and secrets, then both parties are better positioned to compete with the rest of the world. . . . By protecting ancillary covenants not to compete, even after an employee has launched his own firm, the law 'makes it easier for people to cooperate productively in the first place.' " KW Plastics v. United States Can Co. (Feb. 2, 2001), M.D. Ala. Nos. Civ. A. 99–D–286–N and 99–D–878–N, 2001 WL 135722, quoting Polk Bros., Inc. v. Forest City Ent., Inc. (C.A.7, 1985), 776 F.2d 185, 189. . . .

Jurisdictions throughout the country are split on the issue presented by the certified question. See, generally, Annotation, Sufficiency of Consideration for Employee's Covenant Not to Compete, Entered into after Inception of Employment (1973), 51 A.L.R.3d 825. As summarized by the Supreme Court of Minnesota, "cases which have held that continued employment is not a sufficient consideration stress the fact that an employee frequently has no bargaining power once he is employed and can easily be coerced. By signing a noncompetition agreement, the employee gets no more from his employer than he already has,[1] and in such cases there is a danger that an employer does not need protection for his investment in the employee but instead seeks to impose barriers to prevent an employee from securing a better job elsewhere. Decisions in which continued employment has been deemed a sufficient consideration for a noncompetition agreement have focused on a variety of factors, including the possibility that the employee would otherwise have been discharged, the employee was actually employed for a substantial time after executing the contract, or the employee received additional compensation or training or was given confidential information after he signed the agreement." (Citations omitted.) *Davies & Davies Agency, Inc. v. Davies* (Minn. 1980) 298 N.W.2d 127, 130.

More recently, some courts have found sufficient consideration in an at-will employment situation where a *substantial* period of employment ensues after a noncompetition covenant is executed, especially when the continued employment is accompanied by raises, promotion, or similar tangible benefits. 6 Lord, Williston on Contracts (4th Ed.1995), Section 13:13. These courts thereby implicitly find that the execution of a noncompetition agreement changes the prior employment relationship from one purely at will. Id. at 577–584. In effect, these courts infer a promise on the part of the employer to continue the employment of his previously at-will employee for an indefinite yet substantial term. Under this approach,

---

1. Note, however, that an at-will employee does not already have a right to come to work in the future at all, let alone under past terms of employment. Although both parties may very well contemplate continuation of the relationship, either may terminate it at any time.

however, neither party knows whether the agreement is enforceable until events occur after its execution.

This diversity of approach to the issue is reflected in opinions of the courts of appeals of this state. . . .

II   Formation of Binding Contract

[In a passage omitted here the court reviewed some elementary characteristics of contract law, and of at-will employment agreements.]

. . . [E]ither an employer or an employee in a pure at-will employment relationship may legally terminate the employment relationship at any time and for any reason. *Mers v. Dispatch Printing Co.* (1985), 19 Ohio St.3d 100, 103, 19 OBR 261, 483 N.E.2d 150. In the event that an at-will employee quits or is fired, he or she provides no further services for the employer and is generally entitled only to wages and benefits already earned.

It follows that either an employer or an employee in an at-will relationship may propose to change the terms of their employment relationship at any time. If, for instance, an employer notifies an employee that the employee's compensation will be reduced, the employee's remedy, if dissatisfied, is to quit. Similarly, if the employee proposes to the employer that he deserves a raise and will no longer work at his current rate, the employer may either negotiate an increase or accept the loss of his employee. In either event the employee is entitled to be paid only for services already rendered pursuant to terms to which they both have agreed. Thus, mutual promises to employ and to be employed on an ongoing at-will basis, according to agreed terms, are supported by consideration: the promise of one serves as consideration for the promise of the other.

The presentation of a noncompetition agreement by an employer to an at-will employee is, in effect, a proposal to renegotiate the terms of the parties' at-will employment. Where an employer makes such a proposal by presenting his employee with a noncompetition agreement and the employee assents to it, thereby accepting continued employment on new terms, consideration supporting the noncompetition agreement exists. The employee's assent to the agreement is given in exchange for forbearance on the part of the employer from terminating the employee.

We therefore hold that consideration exists to support a noncompetition agreement when, in exchange for the assent of an at-will employee to a proffered noncompetition agreement, the employer continues an at-will employment relationship that could legally be terminated without cause.

III   Caveat

We concur in the view that in cases involving noncompetition agreements, "as in other cases, it is still believed to be good policy to let people make their own bargains and their own valuations." 15 Corbin on Contracts (Interim Ed.2002) 96–97, Section 1395. Professor Corbin suggests that courts should inquire into the sufficiency of consideration in cases involving noncompetition agreements by examining the extent and character of the consideration received by the promisor-employee, "even though we do not do so in ordinary contract cases." Id. at 94–95.

Our decision today does no more than recognize that consideration exists where an at-will employer and an at-will employee continue their employment relationship, rather than terminate it, after the employer imposes a new requirement for employment, i.e., execution of a noncompetition agreement by the employee. While we are not prepared to abandon our long-established precedent that courts may not inquire into the adequacy of consideration, we do not disagree with Corbin's conclusion that the validity of a restraining contract such as a noncompetition agreement should be "determined by weighing as best we can the sum-total of all factors standing together." Id. at 97. We simply recognize that weighing of these factors should not be performed in the context of an inquiry concerning the sufficiency of consideration. That balancing instead should occur in the context of our established precedent recognizing that only reasonable noncompetition agreements are enforceable....

Our refusal to sanction judicial inquiry into the adequacy of consideration in cases similar to the one at bar does not exclude consideration of other requisites of a contract. It remains the law that noncompetition agreements, like other purported contractual arrangements, may be voidable or unenforceable for reasons other than lack of consideration....

IV   Disposition

Both Columber and his employer had a legal right to terminate their at-will employment relationship when Columber was presented with the noncompetition agreement in 1991. Neither party exercised that legal right to terminate the employment relationship, and, in fact, Columber continued working for the appellant for an additional ten years. Accordingly, the noncompetition agreement is not void for lack of consideration, and summary judgment in Columber's favor should not have been entered on that basis.

Although the trial court erred in entering summary judgment based on its determination that the noncompetition agreement lacked consideration, it must yet determine whether the noncompetition agreement is reasonable pursuant to controlling precedent. We therefore reverse the judgment of the court of appeals and remand the cause for further proceedings.

Judgment reversed and cause remanded.

■ RESNICK, J., DISSENTING. Courts everywhere are sharply divided on the present certified issue. However, I adhere to the principle that continued employment in an at-will situation does not by itself constitute consideration. I respectfully dissent.

As the majority confirms, "a contract is not binding unless supported by consideration," which is generally defined as "a detriment to the promisee or a benefit to the promisor." Thus, in order for the September 1991 noncompetition agreement executed between appellant, Lake Land Employment Group of Akron, LLC, and appellee, Lee Columber, to be binding, either Lake Land must have given something for it or Columber must have received something in return. Yet, when all is said and done, the only difference in the parties' employment relationship before and after September 1991 is the noncompetition agreement.

The majority's holding that "[c]onsideration exists to support a non-competition agreement when . . . the employer continues an at-will employment relationship . . ." belies itself. If the same at-will employment relationship continues, where is the consideration? The employer has relinquished nothing, since it retains exactly the same preexisting right it always had to discharge the employee at any time, for any reason, for no reason, with or without cause. The employee has gained nothing, for he has not been given or promised anything other than that which he already had, which is "employment which need not last longer than the ink is dry upon [his] signature." *Kadis v. Britt* (1944), 224 N.C. 154, 163, 29 S.E.2d 543. It is precisely because the same at-will employment relationship continues that there is no consideration.

In fact, the majority endeavors to transform this mutual exchange of nothing into consideration by formulating such artful euphemisms as "forbearance on the part of an at-will employer from discharging an at-will employee," "mutual promises to employ and to be employed on an ongoing at-will basis," and "a proposal to renegotiate the terms of the parties' at-will employment." But in the end, the employer simply winds up with both the noncompetition agreement and the continued right to discharge the employee at will, while the employee is left with the same preexisting "nonright" to be employed for so long as the employer decides not to fire him. The only actual "forbearance," "proposal," or "promise" made by the employer in this situation is declining to fire the employee until he executes the noncompetition agreement.

Moreover, the majority's holding and supporting rationale would allow the enforcement of a noncompetition agreement that was exacted from an employee who, at the time of execution, had already acquired all the knowledge his or her position affords and who was fired the day after affixing his or her signature to the document. In cryptic fashion, the majority is essentially holding that a restrictive covenant may henceforth be exacted from an at-will employee without any supporting consideration . . .

Since the noncompetition agreement in this case lacked consideration and therefore was unenforceable, I would affirm the judgment of the court of appeals.

■ PFEIFER, J., DISSENTING. I concur with Justice Resnick's dissent—an employer's agreement not to terminate an employee if the employee signs a noncompetition agreement does not constitute consideration. It constitutes coercion.

But the majority has found otherwise. In doing so, the majority must acknowledge that the execution of a noncompetition agreement for which forbearance from discharge is the consideration alters the at-will nature of the employment relationship. Any promise of continued employment removes the employment from the realm of an at-will relationship. For some undefined time, the employer must continue to employ the signer of the agreement. How long a period is enough? The absence of a specified term for the forbearance from discharge will leave courts to determine what period is reasonable.

NOTES

(1) *Questions.* What is the significance of Columber's status as an at-will employee in the court's determination that his promise not to compete was supported by consideration? Do you agree with Judge Moyer or Justice Resnick (a "mutual exchange of nothing")? Does the majority opinion rest on policy considerations, the straightforward application of doctrine, or both? What policy considerations weigh in favor of Columber? In favor of Lake Land Employment?

(2) *Dueling Dissents.* Although Justice Pfeifer professed to agree with Justice Resnick, the two dissents appear to disagree with regard to the effect of the court's ruling. Justice Resnick concludes that "in the end, the employer simply winds up with both the noncompetition agreement and the continued right to discharge the employee at will." Contrast Justice Pfeifer's understanding that "the execution of the noncompetition agreement . . . alters the at-will nature of the employment relationship." How does it do so? If Judge Pfeifer is right, how would a court go about deciding what period of time is reasonable? If these are opposing views, which is the more favorable to employees?

(3) *Opposing Decisions.* The Supreme Court of Minnesota has held that "where no raises or promotions resulted, where other employees with similar access were not asked to sign, the mere continuation of employment . . . is not enough." Jostens, Inc. v. National Computer Systems, Inc., 318 N.W.2d 691, 703–04 (Minn. 1982). The decision, and others, reflect judicial hostility to promises not to compete. Only a few months after *Jostens*, the same court said: "We look upon restrictive covenants with disfavor, carefully scrutinizing them because they are agreements in partial restraint of trade." National Recruiters, Inc. v. Cashman, 323 N.W.2d 736, 740 (Minn.1982). Judicially imposed constraints on such agreements are discussed further in the materials on public policy in Chapter 4.

EMPLOYEE HANDBOOKS

In *Lake Land Employment*, the question was whether or not the *employee's* promise not to compete was supported by consideration. Questions about the term of employment also arise with regard to the enforceability of *employers'* promises, often in the context of employee handbooks. Typically, and often some time after they have been hired, employees receive handbooks setting out company policies on matters ranging from vacation schedules to job security. Is the employer bound by these policies? Most employees do not bargain for the policies, and many may not have read or in some cases even received a handbook. The following case is illustrative.

Mettille, a loan officer and at-will employee at the Pine River State Bank, was fired by the bank president, Griffith, for serious deficiencies in processing over $600,000 worth of loans. Griffith had earlier prepared and distributed a printed Employee Handbook with information on various bank policies including "job security" and "disciplinary policy." In firing Mettille, Griffith failed to follow Handbook rules relating to "disciplinary policy." Mettille argued that Griffith was bound by those policies. Griffith countered that the handbook was intended only as a source of information for employees on bank procedures and that, in any case, it could not be part of an employee's employment contract because it was unsupported by consideration. In an action by Mettille against the bank, he won a money judgment.

The Supreme Court of Minnesota affirmed the judgment, stating: "An employer's offer of a unilateral contract may very well appear in a personnel handbook as the employer's response to the practical problem of transactional costs. Given these costs, an employer, such as the bank here, may prefer not to write a separate contract with each individual employee. . . . Mettille's continued performance of his duties despite his freedom to quit constitutes an acceptance of the bank's offer and affords the necessary consideration for that offer, with the bank gaining the advantages of a more stable and, presumably, more productive work force." Pine River State Bank v. Mettille, 333 N.W.2d 622, 627–30 (Minn.1983).

The Court compared this approach with its cases holding that employee noncompete covenants signed after the initial employment contract "are not enforceable absent a showing of independent consideration involving something more than just continued services." The Court noted that, with regard to the covenants not to compete, "a different public policy is at play, namely, the law's disfavor with restraints on trade, so that noncompete covenants are treated as a special circumstance and, therefore, these cases are not decided strictly according to the principles of contract formation."

NOTES

(1) *Promise or Policy?* Not all representations in a handbook become terms of an at-will employee's contract. The court found that Pine River State Bank's statements about job security, as distinguished from its disciplinary policy, were "no more than a general statement of policy" in contrast to the "definite language" used to set out the disciplinary policy.

(2) *Modifications of Employee Handbooks.* To the extent that the terms of an employee handbook become part of an employment contract, can an employer unilaterally change or modify its terms so as to reduce the employee's rights? Several courts have answered No. "If the disclaimer modifies an existing employment contract requiring termination for cause, the employer must provide consideration to make the disclaimer effective." Worley v. Wyoming Bottling Company, Inc., 1 P.3d 615, 621 (Wyo.2000); see also Doyle v. Holy Cross Hospital, 708 N.E.2d 1140 (Ill.1999). The modification of contract terms is examined more generally in Chapter 4.

(3) *An Administrative Law Model?* In re Certified Question (Bankey v. Storer Broadcasting), 443 N.W.2d 112 (Mich.1989), the court held that an employer *may* alter the terms of employment for existing employees by unilaterally changing its written policy statements even without prior notification to the employees that it has reserved the right to do so. In that case the employer had replaced an existing "discharge for cause" provision with a term providing for employment "at the will of the company." The court held that as long as the new policy was applied

consistently, the employees were bound. Explaining that the purpose of the change was "to promote an environment conducive to collective productivity," the court stated that it is "[t]he benefit to the employer of promoting such an environment, rather than the traditional contract-forming mechanisms of mutual assent or individual detrimental reliance, [that] gives rise to a situation 'instinct with obligation.' "

In answer to a similar certified question from the Ninth Circuit, the Arizona Supreme Court held that an employer *cannot* unilaterally change a handbook provision. The Arizona court rejected *Bankey* as using an "administrative law model." The court stated: "We do not agree that a party to a contract containing a term that proves to be inconvenient, uneconomic, or unpleasant should have the right, like an administrative agency, 'to change the rules prospectively through proper procedures.' " Demasse v. ITT Corp., 984 P.2d 1138, 1149 (Ariz.1999).

REWARDS

The sheriff of Dallas County, A.H. Ledbetter, offered a reward of $500 for the capture and return of an escaped convict, one Vann. After capturing Vann and bringing him in, S.H. Broadax sued for the reward. The trial court dismissed the petition, believing that it omitted a fact essential to the claim. On appeal, this question was certified to the Texas Supreme Court: "Was notice or knowledge to plaintiff of existence of the reward when the recapture was made essential to his right to recover?" The answer given was Yes: A reward offer "may be accepted by anyone who performs the service called for when the acceptor knows that it has been made and acts in performance of it, but not otherwise." Broadnax v. Ledbetter, 99 S.W. 1111 (Tex.1907). Put in terms of Restatement § 71(2), the service that Broadnax rendered was not given by him in exchange for Ledbetter's promise. Although the details of offer and acceptance are not taken up until the next chapter, it may help to know now that it is often possible to express the same principle either in terms of "consideration" or of "offer and acceptance." Offer and acceptance can be understood as the mechanism by which consideration is exchanged.

Could Broadnax have recovered if he had captured Vann while ignorant of the reward but had learned of it before returning him to jail? Is his solution to release Vann and recapture him? See Restatement § 51. Could Broadnax have recovered if he had known of the reward but had captured Vann and turned him in because he was a close friend and wished to save him from mob violence? See Restatement § 81(2). For a case where three sets of claimants—including the attorney with whom the outlaw had conferred—sought unsuccessfully to recover the same reward, see Taft v. Hyatt, 180 P. 213 (Kan.1919).

NOTES

(1) *Comparative Perspective.* Under the law of some countries, such as Germany, a promise of reward is treated "not as an offer which would require acceptance in order to ripen into a contract, but as a unilateral jural act which as such is effective and binding without acceptance." 1 Rudolf B. Schlesinger (ed.), *Formation*

of Contracts: A Study of the Common Core of Legal Systems 101–02 (1968). Would such a concept be a desirable one in our law? See Choice v. City of Dallas, 210 S.W. 753 (Tex.Civ.App.1919).

(2) *Employment Cases As Analogous?* As pointed out earlier, an employee may not have read, or even received, the employer's handbook. Is that fatal to a claim by the employee based on a provision in the handbook? Reviewing the general requirement of reward cases that the promise must induce the performance, the Supreme Court of Iowa declined to follow it in a case in which the employee had received but not read the handbook provisions in question: "Although this holding is a departure from the traditional 'bargain-theory' contract analysis, we think it produces 'the salutary result that all employees, those who read the handbook and those who didn't, are treated alike.' Farnsworth, Developments in Contract Law During the 1980's: The Top Ten, 41 Case W.Res.L.Rev. 203, 209 (1990)." Anderson v. Douglas and Lomason Co., 540 N.W.2d 277, 285 (Iowa 1995). What if the employee had not received the handbook?

PROBLEM

The One that Didn't Get Away. Diamond Jim III, a rockfish, was tagged and placed in the Chesapeake Bay in June by the American Brewery in connection with its Third Annual American Beer Fishing Derby. Under the Derby's well-publicized rules, the person who caught Diamond Jim III would receive a cash prize of $25,000. In August, William Simmons went fishing in the Bay. He had heard of the contest, but did not have it in mind on that day. He caught Diamond Jim III and, although at first Simmons took little notice of the tag, he realized upon reexamining it a half hour later that he had caught the prize fish. Is Simmons entitled to the prize? See Simmons v. United States, 308 F.2d 160 (4th Cir.1962). Note that Simmons, not the brewery, contended that the prize was a gift. Does the identity name of the other party suggest a reason for that?

———————

(D) PROMISES AS CONSIDERATION

The cases presented so far have focused on contracts in which the promisor has sought performance in exchange for a promise. As mentioned in Note 5, pp. 38–39 above, these are called unilateral contracts. Yet we have already seen courts come to recognize that the consideration for a promise could be found in a return promise, even in one not even partly performed. Contracts where both parties make promises are called bilateral contracts. See Restatement § 71. Indeed, Comment *a* to Restatement § 75 informs us that "the promise is enforced by virtue of the fact of the bargain, without more."

This raises an underlying question regarding enforceability. What rationale lies behind the enforcement of a promise when it has not been shown that the promisee has conferred a benefit upon the promisor or done anything in reliance on the promise? If one of the parties to an exchange of promises has second thoughts about the transaction the instant after the exchange has occurred, why should that party not be allowed to retract its promise? Consider again the various theories of enforcement described above at p. 8.

We now look more closely at the question of what constitutes a promise, pausing for a moment to introduce some contract terminology.

NOTES

(1) *Conditional Promises.* A promisor who seeks a *promise* in return is not, to be sure, unconcerned with the *performance* of the return promise. Suppose for example, that a buyer promises to pay $100,000 in exchange for a seller's promise to convey a tract of land. The difference between this buyer's situation and that of a promisor such as Sheriff Ledbetter in Broadnax v. Ledbetter, p. 66 above, is that this promisor wants a return promise in *addition* to the transfer of land. Ledbetter's assurance that he would not have to pay the reward unless Vann is returned to captivity follows from the doctrine of consideration itself. His promise to pay the reward was not enforceable unless Vann was captured and returned: that is what he bargained for. How can one who bargains for a return promise, as the buyer above has done, be assured that its performance (paying the money in this instance) will not be due until the other party has performed (executing a deed in this instance)? The solution to this problem is considered in detail in Chapter 8, but a brief explanation may be helpful now.

The solution involves the concept of a *condition*. A promise is conditional if its performance will become due only if a particular event, known as a "condition," occurs. This does not mean that the promise is not binding until the event occurs, but only that the event must occur before the promisor must perform. Insurance contracts provide good examples of *express* conditions. If a home owner pays $1,000 to an insurance company in exchange for the company's promise to pay the owner $100,000 if the owner's house suffers serious fire damage, the company has made an enforceable promise. But the company will owe nothing unless the house suffers serious fire loss within the year. Fire damage to the house is a condition of the company's promise to pay.

When a party makes a promise in exchange for a return promise, it can be protected by making its promise conditional on performance by the other party. Even if the contract does not so provide, the court may impose a condition by implication. Under such a "constructive condition of exchange," one party's duty to perform is not triggered until the other party has performed. For example, where promises are not typically performed at the same time, as in personal service contracts, the usual rule is that the work is made a condition of payment.

(2) *Rights and Duties.* The relationships between the parties in unilateral and bilateral contracts can be analyzed in terms of *right* and *duty*. A is said to have a *right* that B shall do an act when, if B does not do the act, A can initiate legal proceedings against B, and B in such a situation is said to have a *duty* to do the act. *Right* and *duty* are correlatives. In this strict sense there can never be a *right* without a *duty,* nor a *duty* without a *right.* The *right-duty* relationship is one between two parties. The *right* describes the relationship from one end and the *duty* from the other. Since, in a "unilateral" contract, there is a promise on one side only, there is a *duty* on one side only, and a *right* on the other side; and since in a "bilateral" contract there is a promise on each side, there is a *right* and a *duty* on each side.

For the precise use of terms such as *right* and *duty* the legal profession is indebted to the work of Professor Wesley Newcomb Hohfeld,[a] whose system of

a. Wesley Newcomb Hohfeld (1879– 1918) practiced law briefly in San Francisco   before joining the Stanford law faculty in 1905. In 1914 he left Stanford to teach at

"Hohfeldian terminology" is set forth in *Fundamental Legal Conceptions* (1923). Review the language of Restatement § 1. How does it incorporate the language of right and duty?

————

WHAT CONSTITUTES A PROMISE?

It has long been clear that the consideration for a promise can be found in a return promise. The Restatement informs us that, with some exceptions, "a promise that is bargained for is consideration if the promised performance would be consideration." Restatement § 75. But what exactly counts as a promise? The following cases explore how courts determine from language and context whether a performance has in fact been promised or whether only the *illusion* of performance has been held out.

Strong v. Sheffield

Court of Appeals of New York, 1895.
144 N.Y. 392, 39 N.E. 330.

[Action on a promissory note. A judgment for plaintiff, Benjamin B. Strong, against defendant, Louisa A. Sheffield, was reversed by the General Term of the Supreme Court.

Benjamin Strong brought this action against Louisa Sheffield, his niece. Strong had sold a business to her husband, Gerardus ("Rard"), on credit. Later, the buyer's debt was embodied in a promissory note, payable on demand. Mrs. Sheffield endorsed the note, an act which the law treats as a promise to pay if her husband, the "maker" of the note, did not. What, if anything, she got in exchange for that was a matter in issue.

The trial court gave judgment for Strong. That was reversed on a first appeal. Then Strong appealed.]

■ ANDREWS, C.J. The contract between a maker or endorser of a promissory note and the payee forms no exception to the general rule that a promise, not supported by a consideration, is nudum pactum. The law governing commercial paper which precludes an inquiry into the consideration as against bona fide holders for value before maturity, has no application where the suit is between the original parties to the instrument. It is undisputed that the demand note upon which the action was brought was made by the husband of the defendant and endorsed by her at his request and delivered to the plaintiff, the payee, as security for an antecedent debt owing by the husband to the plaintiff. The debt of the husband was past

Yale until his death at the age of thirty-nine. He made a lasting contribution to legal literature through his development of the eight terms of "Hohfeldian terminology" in his book Fundamental Legal Conceptions. Corbin wrote, "He was a severe taskmaster, requiring his students to master his classification of 'fundamental conceptions' and to use accurately the set of terms by which they were expressed. They found this, in the light of the usage of the other professors [at Yale], almost impossible." Their resistance resulted in a petition to the President of Yale that Hohfeld's appointment not be extended. The petition was ignored and generations of law students have continued to master Hohfeld's terms.

due at the time, and the only consideration for the wife's endorsement, which is or can be claimed, is that as part of the transaction there was an agreement by the plaintiff when the note was given to forbear the collection of the debt, or a request for forbearance, which was followed by forbearance for a period of about two years subsequent to the giving of the note.

[According to the record in the case, Mrs. Sheffield was reluctant to endorse the note.[a] Strong testified that he had said: "Rard, I will give you my word as a man ... that if you will give me a note, with your wife's endorsement ... I will not pay that note away; I will not put it in any bank for collection, but I will hold it until such time as I want my money...." Strong testified also that Gerardus had said, on delivering the note, "You won't pay this note away?", and that Strong answered, "No, I will keep it until such time as I want it." An example of "paying the note away" would have been for Strong to sell the note, giving the buyer the right to collect it on demand.]

There is no doubt that an agreement by the creditor to forbear the collection of a debt presently due is a good consideration for an absolute or conditional promise of a third person to pay the debt or for any obligation he may assume in respect thereto. Nor is it essential that the creditor should bind himself at the time to forbear collection or to give time. If he is requested by his debtor to extend the time, and a third person undertakes in consideration of forbearance being given to become liable as surety or otherwise, and the creditor does in fact forbear in reliance upon the undertaking, although he enters into no enforceable agreement to do so, his acquiescence in the request, and an actual forbearance in consequence thereof for a reasonable time, furnishes a good consideration for the collateral undertaking. In other words, a request followed by performance is sufficient, and mutual promises at the time are not essential unless it was the understanding that the promisor was not to be bound, except on condition that the other party entered into an immediate and reciprocal obligation to do the thing requested.... The note in question did not in law extend the payment of the debt. It was payable on demand, and although being payable with interest it was in form consistent with an intention that payment should not be immediately demanded, yet there was nothing on its face to prevent an immediate suit on the note against the maker or to recover the original debt....

In the present case the agreement made is not left to inference, nor was it a case of request to forbear, followed by forbearance, in pursuance of the request, without any promise on the part of the creditor at the time. The plaintiff testified that there was an express agreement on his part to the effect that he would not pay the note away, nor put it in any bank for collection ... [The court then quoted Strong's testimony as recited above.] Upon this alleged agreement the defendant endorsed the note. It would have been no violation of the plaintiff's promise if, immediately on receiving the note, he had commenced suit upon it. Such a suit would have been an assertion that he wanted the money and would have fulfilled the condition of forbearance. The debtor and the defendant, when they became

a. The record on appeal indicates that Benjamin Strong was Louisa Sheffield's uncle. He had sold his business on credit to Louisa's husband, Gerardus, and then sought Gerardus' note with Louisa's endorsement as security for the debt. Louisa was reluctant to endorse her husband's note because she had her own successful business and did not want to hurt her credit by having it known that she had undertaken a debt of her husband.

parties to the note, may have had the hope or expectation that forbearance would follow, and there was forbearance in fact. But there was no agreement to forbear for a fixed time or for a reasonable time, but an agreement to forbear for such time as the plaintiff should elect. The consideration is to be tested by the agreement, and not by what was done under it. It was a case of mutual promises, and so intended. We think the evidence failed to disclose any consideration for the defendant's endorsement, and that the trial court erred in refusing so to rule.

The order of the General Term reversing the judgment should be affirmed, and judgment absolute directed for the defendant on the stipulation with costs in all courts.

Ordered accordingly.

NOTES

(1) *Questions.* Restatement § 77 mentions the "illusory" or "apparent" promise as a type that is not consideration. Did Strong make any promise of substance? Could he have been held liable for breach of contract in any circumstances?

(2) *Drafting.* Suppose that Louisa Sheffield had written to Strong: "I will be responsible for my husband's debt if you will not bother him about it for two years." Would she have been liable to Strong if he had done nothing about the note for that period? What difference is there between this situation and the case as it stands? The precise rule of this case is reversed by UCC § 3–303(b).

(3) *Sexually Transmitted Debt.* Why might Louisa have agreed to endorse Gerardus' note in the first place? Empirical studies suggest that spouses, and perhaps particularly wives, commonly co-sign or otherwise act as sureties for the debts of the other spouse, and many of them may be less experienced in financial matters than Louisa Sheffield was. For a study of surety spouses in England, see Belinda Fehlberg, *Sexually Transmitted Debt* (1997), suggesting that spousal promises to act as sureties should be subject to special scrutiny. Do you agree? See also Barclay's Bank v. O'Brien, 4 All E.R. 417 (House of Lords, 1993). We return to the question of pressuring in bargaining in Chapter 4.

PROBLEM

The Case of the Unexpected Heir. Under the terms of their divorce settlement agreement, Gerald kept the family farm and Nancy took mortgages on the farm to secure periodic payments that Gerald was to make to her. Gerald later had financial difficulties and sought to refinance previous bank loans, but he found that he could not do so because of Nancy's mortgages. Nancy agreed to give up her right to any additional payments and to satisfy the mortgages in return for Gerald's promise to make a will leaving the farm to their son Ronn, reserving the right to sell a portion of the land in order to continue farming if "future economic exigencies require." Although Gerald made a will and obtained refinancing as promised, Nancy began foreclosure proceedings. She argued that Gerald's promise was illusory because he had reserved a right to convey the farm. Should Nancy prevail? See Harrington v. Harrington, 365 N.W.2d 552 (N.D.1985).

CONTRACTS FOR THE SALE OF REAL ESTATE

Sales of land and other real estate transactions, including leases, are often of considerable complexity. The following case, in which a developer sought to buy land in order to construct a shopping center, is an example. A commercial transaction of this kind typically involves not only the buyer (often called "purchaser") and at least one seller (often called "vendor") and their agents, but also third parties such as lenders, title companies, and potential lessees of the completed development. Each contributes to the intricacy of the transaction.

Real estate transactions are of great moment not only to the economy but also to the individual parties, such as homeowner and prospective homeowner. For many, the most financially significant transaction of a lifetime is the purchase or sale of a home. Certainly as an historical matter, land has been regarded as a uniquely valuable form of wealth. For these reasons, contracts for the sale of real estate are characterized by more formality than, say, contracts for the sale of goods. Even in residential sales, the parties are frequently represented by lawyers and the required documents are lengthy and detailed.

After an initial agreement of sale, a number of other events commonly take place before the formal "closing," at which a deed is exchanged for the payment of the price. The intervening activities involve the development of information, including a check of the seller's title to the property, the buyer's obtaining financing, and—as in the case that follows—lining up enough satisfactory tenants to make the prospective shopping center viable. It is not uncommon for a deal to fall apart during the period (formally called the executory interval) between the contract signing and the closing.

Mattei v. Hopper

Supreme Court of California, 1958.
51 Cal.2d 119, 330 P.2d 625.

■ Spence, Justice. Plaintiff [Mattei] brought this action for damages after defendant [Hopper] allegedly breached a contract by failing to convey her real property in accordance with the terms of a deposit receipt which the parties had executed. After a trial without a jury, the court concluded that the agreement was "illusory" and lacking in "mutuality." From the judgment accordingly entered in favor of defendant, plaintiff appeals.

Plaintiff was a real estate developer. He was planning to construct a shopping center on a tract adjacent to defendant's land. For several months, a real estate agent attempted to negotiate a sale of defendant's property under terms agreeable to both parties. After several of plaintiff's proposals had been rejected by defendant because of the inadequacy of the price offered, defendant submitted an offer. Plaintiff accepted on the same day.

The parties' written agreement was evidenced on a form supplied by the real estate agent, commonly known as a deposit receipt. Under its terms, plaintiff was required to deposit $1,000 of the total purchase price of

$57,500 with the real estate agent, and was given 120 days to "examine the title and consummate the purchase." At the expiration of that period, the balance of the price was "due and payable upon tender of a good and sufficient deed of the property sold." The concluding paragraph of the deposit receipt provided: "Subject to Coldwell Banker & Company obtaining leases satisfactory to the purchaser." This clause and the 120–day period were desired by plaintiff as a means for arranging satisfactory leases of the shopping center buildings prior to the time he was finally committed to pay the balance of the purchase price and to take title to defendant's property.

Plaintiff took the first step in complying with the agreement by turning over the $1,000 deposit to the real estate agent. While he was in the process of securing the leases and before the 120 days had elapsed, defendant's attorney notified plaintiff that defendant would not sell her land under the terms contained in the deposit receipt. Thereafter, defendant was informed that satisfactory leases had been obtained and that plaintiff had offered to pay the balance of the purchase price. Defendant failed to tender the deed as provided in the deposit receipt.

Initially, defendant's thesis that the deposit receipt constituted no more than an offer by her, which could only be accepted by plaintiff notifying her that all of the desired leases had been obtained and were satisfactory to him, must be rejected. Nowhere does the agreement mention the necessity of any such notice. Nor does the provision making the agreement "subject to" plaintiff's securing "satisfactory" leases necessarily constitute a condition to the existence of a contract. Rather, the whole purchase receipt and this particular clause must be read as merely making plaintiff's performance dependent on the obtaining of "satisfactory" leases. Thus a contract arose, and plaintiff was given the power and privilege to terminate it in the event he did not obtain such leases. (See 3 Corbin, Contracts (1951), § 647, pp. 581–585.) This accords with the general view that deposit receipts are binding and enforceable contracts. (Cal.Practice Hand Book, Legal Aspects of Real Estate Transactions (1956), p. 63.)

However, the inclusion of this clause, specifying that leases "satisfactory" to plaintiff must be secured before he would be bound to perform, raises the basic question whether the consideration supporting the contract was thereby vitiated. When the parties attempt, as here, to make a contract where promises are exchanged as the consideration, the promises must be mutual in obligation. In other words, for the contract to bind either party, both must have assumed some legal obligations. Without this mutuality of obligation, the agreement lacks consideration and no enforceable contract has been created.... Or, if one of the promises leaves a party free to perform or to withdraw from the agreement at his own unrestricted pleasure, the promise is deemed illusory and it provides no consideration.... Whether these problems are couched in terms of mutuality of obligation or the illusory nature of a promise, the underlying issue is the same—consideration....

While contracts making the duty of performance of one of the parties conditional upon his satisfaction would seem to give him wide latitude in avoiding any obligation and thus present serious consideration problems, such "satisfaction" clauses have been given effect. They have been divided into two primary categories and have been accorded different treatment on that basis. First, in those contracts where the condition calls for satisfaction as to commercial value or quality, operative fitness, or mechanical utility, dissatisfaction cannot be claimed arbitrarily, unreasonably, or capriciously . . . , and the standard of a reasonable person is used in determining whether satisfaction has been received. . . . However, it would seem that the factors involved in determining whether a lease is satisfactory to the lessor are too numerous and varied to permit the application of a reasonable man standard as envisioned by this line of cases. Illustrative of some of the factors which would have to be considered in this case are the duration of the leases, their provisions for renewal options, if any, their covenants and restrictions, the amounts of the rentals, the financial responsibility of the lessees, and the character of the lessees' businesses.

This multiplicity of factors which must be considered in evaluating a lease shows that this case more appropriately falls within the second line of authorities dealing with "satisfaction" clauses, being those involving fancy, taste, or judgment. Where the question is one of judgment, the promisor's determination that he is not satisfied, when made in good faith, has been held to be a defense to an action on the contract. . . . Although these decisions do not expressly discuss the issues of mutuality of obligation or illusory promises, they necessarily imply that the promisor's duty to exercise his judgment in good faith is an adequate consideration to support the contract. None of these cases voided the contracts on the ground that they were illusory or lacking in mutuality of obligation. Defendant's attempts to distinguish these cases are unavailing, since they are predicated upon the assumption that the deposit receipt was not a contract making plaintiff's performance conditional on his satisfaction. As seen above, this was the precise nature of the agreement. Even though the "satisfaction" clauses discussed in the above-cited cases dealt with performances to be received as parts of the agreed exchanges, the fact that the leases here which determined plaintiff's satisfaction were not part of the performance to be rendered is not material. The standard of evaluating plaintiff's satisfaction—good faith—applies with equal vigor to this type of condition and prevents it from nullifying the consideration otherwise present in the promises exchanged.

Moreover, the secondary authorities are in accord with the California cases on the general principles governing "satisfaction" contracts. . . . "A promise conditional upon the promisor's satisfaction is not illusory since it means more than that validity of the performance is to depend on the arbitrary choice of the promisor. His expression of dissatisfaction is not conclusive. That may show only that he has become dissatisfied with the contract; he must be dissatisfied with the performance, as a performance of the contract, and his dissatisfaction must be genuine." (Restatement, Contracts (1932), § 265, comment *a*.)

If the foregoing cases and other authorities were the only ones relevant, there would be little doubt that the deposit receipt here should not be deemed illusory or lacking in mutuality of obligation because it contained the "satisfaction" clause. However, language in two recent cases led the trial court to the contrary conclusion. The first case, Lawrence Block Co. v. Palston, 123 Cal.App.2d 300, 266 P.2d 856, 858, stated that the following two conditions placed in an offer to buy an apartment building would have made the resulting contract illusory: "O.P.A. Rent statements to be approved by Buyer" and "Subject to buyer's inspection and approval of all apartments." These provisions were said to give the purchaser "unrestricted discretion" in deciding whether he would be bound to the contract and to provide no "standard" which could be used in compelling him to perform. 123 Cal.App.2d at pages 308–309, 266 P.2d at pages 861–862. However, this language was not necessary to the decision. . . .

The other case, Pruitt v. Fontana, 143 Cal.App.2d 675, 300 P.2d 371, 377, presented a similar situation. The court concluded that the written instrument with a provision making the sale of land subject to the covenants and easements being "approved by the buyers" was illusory. It employed both the reasoning and language of *Lawrence Block Co.* in deciding that this clause provided no "objective criterion" preventing the buyers from exercising an "unrestricted subjective discretion" in deciding whether they would be bound. 143 Cal.App.2d at pages 684–685, 300 P.2d at page 377. But again, this language was not necessary to the result reached. The buyers in *Pruitt* refused to approve all of the easements of record, and the parties entered into a new and different oral agreement. The defendant seller was held to be estopped to assert the statute of frauds against this subsequent contract, and the judgment of dismissal entered after the sustaining of demurrers was reversed.

While the language in these two cases might be dismissed as mere dicta, the fact that the trial court relied thereon requires us to examine the reasoning employed. Both courts were concerned with finding an objective standard by which they could compel performance. This view apparently stems from the statement in *Lawrence Block Co.* that "The standard 'as to the satisfaction of a reasonable person' does not apply where the performance involves a matter dependent on judgment." 123 Cal.App.2d at page 309, 266 P.2d at page 862. By making this assertion without any qualification, the court necessarily implied that there is no other standard available. Of course, this entirely disregards those cases which have upheld "satisfaction" clauses dependent on the exercise of judgment. In such cases, the criterion becomes one of good faith. Insofar as the language in *Lawrence Block Co.* and *Pruitt* represented a departure from the established rules governing "satisfaction" clauses, they are hereby disapproved.

We conclude that the contract here was neither illusory nor lacking in mutuality of obligation because the parties inserted a provision in their contract making plaintiff's performance dependent on his satisfaction with the leases to be obtained by him.

The judgment is reversed.

NOTE

Satisfied? If, after signing the deposit receipt, Mattei had changed his mind about the purchase, could he have avoided liability simply by saying that he was "dissatisfied" with the deal? Would Hopper have been bound if Mattei had inserted a clause permitting him to do this? The meaning of "good faith" is explored further in later chapters.

After negotiations, parties often leave some matters for their lawyers. Do you see a difference in legal effect between a provision that says "subject to my lawyer's approval of our agreement" and one that says "subject to my lawyer's approval of documents tendered when the deal is closed"?

CONTRACTS FOR THE SALE OF GOODS

You have already been introduced, preliminarily, to this category of Contracts in the *Bayliner* case on p. 4 above. The next case involves a contract for the sale of a different sort of goods—jet fuel. Such contracts have long been regarded as distinctive, as evidenced by the reduction of the common law of sales to statutory form in England in 1893 by the Sale of Goods Act and in the United States in 1906 by the Uniform Sales Act, later replaced by the UCC. The law of international sales has now also been codified in the United Nations [Vienna] Convention on the International Sale of Goods (CISG). (The Convention is also found in Selections for Contracts.)

Article 2 of the Code, the statutory authority for all domestic sale of goods cases, reflects the characteristics of commercial sales transactions in a number of ways. In contrast to contracts for the sale of real estate, agreements to buy and sell goods are often made quickly and informally, increasingly electronically or by telephone, so that the requirements for contract formation tend to be less demanding. The parties are often "repeat players" who have dealt with similar goods and often with each other over time, so that their particular understandings as well as customs and practices within the trade may give added content to their agreements. Terms and entire forms are standardized. The nature of goods themselves is significant. In contrast to real property, goods are considered fungible, one item of a particular sort understood to be as good as any other. There is a general assumption that goods of all sorts are available on the market. Market price therefore plays an important role in the calculation of damages in Article 2. In reading the following case, consider which of the characteristics just described plays a role in the decision.

Eastern Air Lines, Inc. v. Gulf Oil Corporation

United States District Court, Southern District of Florida, 1975.
415 F.Supp. 429.

■ JAMES LAWRENCE KING, DISTRICT JUDGE. Eastern Air Lines, Inc., hereafter Eastern, and Gulf Oil Corporation, hereafter Gulf, have enjoyed a mutually advantageous business relationship involving the sale and purchase of aviation fuel for several decades.

This controversy involves the threatened disruption of that historic relationship and the attempt, by Eastern, to enforce the most recent contract between the parties. On March 8, 1974 the correspondence and telex communications between the corporate entities culminated in a demand by Gulf that Eastern must meet its demand for a price increase or Gulf would shut off Eastern's supply of jet fuel within fifteen days.

Eastern responded by filing its complaint with this court, alleging that Gulf had breached its contract and requesting preliminary and permanent mandatory injunctions requiring Gulf to perform the contract in accordance with its terms. By agreement of the parties, a preliminary injunction preserving the status quo was entered on March 20, 1974, requiring Gulf to perform its contract and directing Eastern to pay in accordance with the contract terms, pending final disposition of the case.

Gulf answered Eastern's complaint, alleging that the contract was not a binding requirements contract, was void for want of mutuality, and, furthermore, was "commercially impracticable" within the meaning of Uniform Commercial Code § 2–615; Fla.Stat. §§ 672.614 and 672.615.

The extraordinarily able advocacy by the experienced lawyers for both parties produced testimony at the trial from internationally respected experts who described in depth economic events that have, in recent months, profoundly affected the lives of every American.

The Contract

On June 27, 1972, an agreement was signed by the parties which, as amended, was to provide the basis upon which Gulf was to furnish jet fuel to Eastern at certain specific cities in the Eastern system. Said agreement supplemented an existing contract between Gulf and Eastern which, on June 27, 1972, had approximately one year remaining prior to its expiration.

The contract is Gulf's standard form aviation fuel contract and is identical in all material particulars with the first contract for jet fuel, dated 1959, between Eastern and Gulf and, indeed, with aviation fuel contracts antedating the jet age. It is similar to contracts in general use in the aviation fuel trade. The contract was drafted by Gulf after substantial arm's length negotiation between the parties. Gulf approached Eastern more than a year before the expiration of the then-existing contracts between Gulf and Eastern, seeking to preserve its historic relationship with Eastern. Following several months of negotiation, the contract, consolidating and extending the terms of several existing contracts, was executed by the parties in June, 1972, to expire January 31, 1977.

The parties agreed that this contract, as its predecessor, should provide a reference to reflect changes in the price of the raw material from which jet fuel is processed, i.e., crude oil, in direct proportion to the cost per gallon of jet fuel.

Both parties regarded the instant agreement as favorable, Eastern, in part, because it offered immediate savings in projected escalations under the existing agreement through reduced base prices at the contract cities; while Gulf found a long term outlet for a capacity of jet fuel coming on stream from a newly completed refinery, as well as a means to relate anticipated increased cost of raw material (crude oil) directly to the price of the refined product sold. The previous Eastern/Gulf contracts contained a price index clause which operated to pass on to Eastern only one-half of any increase in the price of crude oil. Both parties knew at the time of contract negotiations that increases in crude oil prices would be expected, were "a way of life", and intended that those increases be borne by Eastern in a direct proportional relationship of crude oil cost per barrel to jet fuel cost per gallon.

Accordingly, the parties selected an indicator (West Texas Sour); a crude which is bought and sold in large volume and was thus a reliable indicator of the market value of crude oil. From June 27, 1972 to the fall of 1973, there were in effect various forms of U.S. government imposed price controls which at once controlled the price of crude oil generally, West Texas Sour specifically, and hence the price of jet fuel. As the government authorized increased prices of crude those increases were in turn reflected in the cost of jet fuel. Eastern has paid a per gallon increase under the contract from 11 cents to 15 cents (or some 40%).

The indicator selected by the parties was "the average of the posted prices for West Texas sour crude, 30.0–30.9 gravity of Gulf Oil Corporation, Shell Oil Company, and Pan American Petroleum Corporation". The posting of crude prices under the contract "shall be as listed for these companies in Platts Oilgram Service—Crude Oil Supplement . . ."

"Posting" has long been a practice in the oil industry. It involves the physical placement at a public location of a price bulletin reflecting the current price at which an oil company will pay for a given barrel of a specific type of crude oil. Those posted price bulletins historically have, in addition to being displayed publicly, been mailed to those persons evincing interest therein, including sellers of crude oil, customers whose price of product may be based thereon, and, among others, Platts Oilgram, publishers of a periodical of interest to those related to the oil industry.

In recent years, the United States has become increasingly dependent upon foreign crude oil, particularly from the "OPEC" nations most of which are in the Middle East. OPEC was formed in 1970 for the avowed purpose of raising oil prices, and has become an increasingly cohesive and potent organization as its member nations have steadily enhanced their equity positions and their control over their oil production facilities. Nationalization of crude oil resources and shutdowns of production and distribution have become a way of life for oil companies operating in OPEC nations, particularly in the volatile Middle East. The closing of the Suez Canal and the concomitant interruption of the flow of Mid–East oil during the 1967 "Six–Day War", and Libya's nationalization of its oil industry during the same period, are only some of the more dramatic examples of a trend that began years ago. By 1969 "the handwriting was on the wall" in the words of Gulf's foreign oil expert witness, Mr. Blackledge.

During 1970 domestic United States oil production "peaked"; since then it has declined while the percentage of imported crude oil has been steadily increasing. Unlike domestic crude oil, which has been subject to price control since August 15, 1971, foreign crude oil has never been subject to price control by the United States Government. Foreign crude oil prices, uncontrolled by the Federal Government, were generally lower than domestic crude oil prices in 1971 and 1972; during 1973 foreign prices "crossed" domestic prices; by late 1973 foreign prices were generally several dollars per barrel higher than controlled domestic prices. It was during late 1973 that the Mid–East exploded in another war, accompanied by an embargo (at least officially) by the Arab oil-producing nations against the United States and certain of its allies. World prices for oil and oil products increased.

Mindful of that situation and for various other reasons concerning the nation's economy, the United States government began a series of controls affecting the oil industry culminating, in the fall of 1973, with the implementation of price controls known as "two-tier." In practice "two-tier" can be described as follows: taking as the bench mark the number of barrels produced from a given well in May of 1972, that number of barrels is deemed "old" oil. The price of "old" oil then is frozen by the government at a fixed level. To the extent that the productivity of a given well can be increased over the May, 1972, production, that increased production is deemed "new" oil. For each barrel of "new" oil produced, the government authorized the release from price controls of an equivalent number of barrels from those theretofore designated "old" oil. For example, from a well which in May of 1972, produced 100 barrels of oil; all of the production of that well would, since the imposition of "two-tier" in August of 1973, be "old" oil. Increased productivity to 150 barrels would result in 50 barrels of "new" oil and 50 barrels of "released" oil; with the result that 100 barrels of the 150 barrels produced from the well would be uncontrolled by the "two-tier" pricing system, while the 50 remaining barrels of "old" would remain government price controlled.

The implementation of "two-tier" was completely without precedent in the history of government price control action. Its impact, however, was nominal, until the imposition of an embargo upon the exportation of crude oil by certain Arab countries in October, 1973. Those countries deemed sympathetic to Israel were embargoed from receiving oil from the Arab oil producing countries. The United States was among the principal countries affected by that embargo, with the result that it experienced an immediate "energy crises".

Following closely after the embargo, OPEC (Oil Producing Export Countries) unilaterally increased the price of their crude to the world market some 400% between September, 1973, and January 15, 1974. Since the United States domestic production was at capacity, it was dependent upon foreign crude to meet its requirements. New and released oil (uncontrolled) soon reached parity with the price of foreign crude, moving from approximately $5 to $11 a barrel from September, 1974 to January 15, 1974.

Since imposition of "two-tier", the price of "old oil" has remained fixed by government action, with the oil companies resorting to postings reflecting prices they will pay for the new and released oil, not subject to government controls. Those prices, known as "premiums", are the subject of supplemental bulletins which are likewise posted by the oil companies and furnished to interested parties, including Platts Oilgram.

Platts, since the institution of "two-tier" has not published the posted prices of any of the premiums offered by the oil companies in the United States, including those of Gulf Oil Corporation, Shell Oil Company and Pan American Petroleum, the companies designated in the agreement. The information which has appeared in Platts since the implementation of "two-tier" with respect to the price of West Texas Sour crude oil has been the price of "old" oil subject to government control.

Under the court's restraining order, entered in this cause by agreement of the parties, Eastern has been paying for jet fuel from Gulf on the basis of the price of "old" West Texas Sour crude oil as fixed by government price control action, i.e., $5 a barrel. Approximately 40 gallons of finished jet fuel product can be refined from a barrel of crude.

Against this factual background we turn to a consideration of the legal issues.

I

The "Requirements" Contract

Gulf has taken the position in this case that the contract between it and Eastern is not a valid document in that it lacks mutuality of obligation; it is vague and indefinite; and that it renders Gulf subject to Eastern's whims respecting the volume of jet fuel Gulf would be required to deliver to the purchaser Eastern.

The contract talks in terms of fuel "requirements".[1] The parties have interpreted this provision to mean that any aviation fuel purchased by Eastern at one of the cities covered by the contract, must be bought from Gulf. Conversely, Gulf must make the necessary arrangements to supply Eastern's reasonable good faith demands at those same locations. This is the construction the parties themselves have placed on the contract and it has governed their conduct over many years and several contracts.

In early cases, requirements contracts were found invalid for want of the requisite definiteness, or on the grounds of lack of mutuality. Many such cases are collected and annotated at 14 A.L.R. 1300.

As reflected in the foregoing annotation, there developed rather quickly in the law the view that a requirements contract could be binding where the purchaser had an operating business. The "lack of mutuality" and "indefiniteness" were resolved since the court could determine the volume of goods provided for under the contract by reference to objective evidence of the volume of goods required to operate the specified business. Therefore, well prior to the adoption of the Uniform Commercial Code, case law generally held requirements contracts binding. See 26 A.L.R.2d 1099, 1139.

---

1. "Gulf agrees to sell and deliver to Eastern, and Eastern agrees to purchase, receive and pay for their requirements of Gulf Jet A and Gulf Jet A–1 at the locations listed...."

The Uniform Commercial Code, adopted in Florida in 1965, specifically approves requirements contracts in F.S. 672.306 (U.C.C. § 2–306(1)).

"(1) A term which measures the quantity by the output of the seller or the requirements of the buyer means such actual output or requirements as may occur in good faith, except that no quantity unreasonably disproportionate to any stated estimate or in the absence of a stated estimate to any normal or otherwise comparable prior output or requirements may be tendered or demanded."

The Uniform Commercial Code Official Comment interprets § 2–306(1) as follows:

"2. Under this Article, a contract for output or requirements is not too indefinite since it is held to mean the actual good faith output or requirements of the particular party. Nor does such a contract lack mutuality of obligation since, under this section, the party who will determine quantity is required to operate his plant or conduct his business in good faith and according to commercial standards of fair dealing in the trade so that his output or requirements will approximate a reasonably foreseeable figure. Reasonable elasticity in the requirements is expressly envisaged by this section and good faith variations from prior requirements are permitted even when the variation may be such as to result in discontinuance. A shut-down by a requirements buyer for lack of orders might be permissible when a shut-down merely to curtail losses would not. The essential test is whether the party is acting in good faith. Similarly, a sudden expansion of the plant by which requirements are to be measured would not be included within the scope of the contract as made but normal expansion undertaken in good faith would be within the scope of this section. One of the factors in an expansion situation would be whether the market price has risen greatly in a case in which the requirements contract contained a fixed price. Reasonable variation of an extreme sort is exemplified in Southwest Natural Gas Co. v. Oklahoma Portland Cement Co., 102 F.2d 630 (C.C.A.10, 1939)."

Some of the prior Gulf–Eastern contracts have included the estimated fuel requirements for some cities covered by the contract while others have none. The particular contract contains an estimate for Gainesville, Florida requirement.

The parties have consistently over the years relied upon each other to act in good faith in the purchase and sale of the required quantities of aviation fuel specified in the contract. During the course of the contract, various estimates have been exchanged from time to time, and, since the advent of the petroleum allocations programs, discussions of estimated requirements have been on a monthly (or more frequent) basis.[2]

---

2. A requirements contract under the U.C.C. may speak of "requirements" alone, or it may include estimates, or it may contain maximums and minimums. In any case, the consequences are the same, as Official Comments 2 and 3 indicate. Comment 2 is set out in the text above. Comment 3 provides:

"If an estimate of output or requirements is included in the agreement, no quantity unreasonably disproportionate

The court concludes that the document is a binding and enforceable requirements contract.

II
Breach of Contract

[The court determined that Eastern's performance under the contract "did not constitute a breach of its agreement with Gulf" and was "consistent with good faith and commercial practices as required by U.C.C. § 2–306."

III
Commercial Impracticability

[The court concluded that Gulf was not excused on the ground of commercial impracticability. See p. 848 below.]

IV
Remedy

Having found and concluded that the contract is a valid one, should be enforced, and that no defenses have been established against it, there remains for consideration the proper remedy.

The Uniform Commercial Code provides that in an appropriate case specific performance may be decreed. This case is a particularly appropriate one for specific performance. The parties have been operating for more than a year pursuant to a preliminary injunction requiring specific performance of the contract and Gulf has stipulated that it is able to perform. Gulf presently supplies Eastern with 100,000,000 gallons of fuel annually or 10 percent of Eastern's total requirements. If Gulf ceases to supply this fuel, the result will be chaos and irreparable damage.

Under the U.C.C. a more liberal test in determining entitlement to specific performance has been established than the test one must meet for classic equitable relief. U.C.C. § 2–716(1). . . .

It has previously been found and concluded that Eastern is entitled to Gulf's fuel at the prices agreed upon in the contract. In the circumstances, a decree of specific performance becomes the ordinary and natural relief rather than the extraordinary one. The parties are before the court, the issues are squarely framed, they have been clearly resolved in Eastern's favor, and it would be a vain, useless and potentially harmful exercise to declare that Eastern has a valid contract, but leave the parties to their own devices. Accordingly, the preliminary injunction heretofore entered is made a permanent injunction and the order of this court herein.

NOTES

(1) *Drafting and Price Fluctuations.* Under a fixed-price requirements contract, the seller runs a risk that if the market price rises, the buyer's requirements will

to it may be tendered or demanded. Any minimum or maximum set by the agreement shows a clear limit on the intended elasticity. In similar fashion, the agreed estimate is to be regarded as a center around which the parties intend the variation to occur."

escalate. (Part II of the court's opinion discusses the limited protection that the concept of good faith affords against this risk.) Does the Code suggest any drafting techniques that a seller might use to reduce this risk? Did Gulf succeed in avoiding this risk by making a flexible-price requirements contract?

(2) *Output Contracts.* In contrast to a "requirements" contract, an "output" contract is one that calls on the seller to deliver and the buyer to take all of the goods, or all of a certain sort, that may be produced by the seller. Output contracts are often bracketed with requirements contracts in discussion as presenting problems common to arrangements in which exclusivity is part of the bargain.

INTRODUCTION TO *WOOD v. LUCY*

The cases so far have focused on statements that at least one of the parties regarded as an express promise. The following case concerns a promise that the court agrees was not "expressed in so many words" but instead, was "fairly to be implied." What was it implied from? In the discussion of Hawkins v. McGee in Note 1, p. 3 above, you were asked to consider the language, context, and nature of the transaction in determining whether Dr. Hawkins's statement was a promise. As you read Judge Cardozo's famous opinion below, consider again how those factors contribute to the court's decision that despite the absence of an explicit statement or promise, the writing is nonetheless "instinct with obligation"?

Wood v. Lucy, Lady Duff–Gordon
Court of Appeals of New York, 1917.
222 N.Y. 88, 118 N.E. 214.

Appeal from Supreme Court, Appellate Division, First Department.

Action by Otis F. Wood against Lucy, Lady Duff–Gordon. From a judgment of the Appellate Division (177 App.Div. 624, 164 N.Y.Supp. 576), which reversed an order denying defendant's motion for judgment on the pleading, and which dismissed the complaint, plaintiff appeals. Reversed.

■ CARDOZO, J.[a] The defendant styles herself "a creator of fashions." Her favor helps a sale. Manufacturers of dresses, millinery, and like articles are glad to pay for a certificate of her approval. The things which she designs, fabrics, parasols, and what not, have a new value in the public mind when issued in her name. She employed the plaintiff to help her to turn this vogue into money. He was to have the exclusive right, subject always to her approval, to place her indorsements on the designs of others. He was also to have the exclusive right to place her own designs on sale, or to license others to market them. In return she was to have one-half of "all profits and revenues" derived from any contracts he might make. The exclusive right was to last at least one year from April 1, 1915, and thereafter from year to year unless terminated by notice of 90 days. The plaintiff says that he kept the contract on his part, and that the defendant broke it. She

---

a. Benjamin Nathan Cardozo (1870–1938) practiced in New York City after law school. He served as judge and later chief judge of the New York Court of Appeals, for which most of his significant opinions were written. President Hoover appointed him to Supreme Court of the United States in 1932, upon Holmes's retirement. Cardozo's best known jurisprudential work is a series of lectures entitled *The Nature of the Judicial Process* (1921).

placed her indorsement on fabrics, dresses, and millinery without his knowledge, and withheld the profits. He sues her for the damages, and the case comes here on demurrer.[b]

The agreement of employment is signed by both parties. It has a wealth of recitals. The defendant insists, however, that it lacks the elements of a contract. She says that the plaintiff does not bind himself to anything. It is true that he does not promise in so many words that he will use reasonable efforts to place the defendant's indorsements and market her designs. We think, however, that such a promise is fairly to be implied. The law has outgrown its primitive stage of formalism when the precise word was the sovereign talisman, and every slip was fatal. It takes a broader view today. A promise may be lacking, and yet the whole writing may be "instinct with an obligation," imperfectly expressed (Scott, J., in McCall Co. v. Wright, 133 App.Div. 62, 117 N.Y.S. 775; Moran v. Standard Oil Co., 211 N.Y. 187, 198, 105 N.E. 217). If that is so, there is a contract.

The implication of a promise here finds support in many circumstances. The defendant gave an exclusive privilege. She was to have no right for at least a year to place her own indorsements or market her own designs except through the agency of the plaintiff. The acceptance of the exclusive agency was an assumption of its duties. Phoenix Hermetic Co. v. Filtrine Mfg. Co., 164 App.Div. 424, 150 N.Y.S. 193; W.G. Taylor Co. v. Bannerman, 120 Wis. 189, 97 N.W. 918; Mueller v. Mineral Spring Co., 88 Mich. 390, 50 N.W. 319. We are not to suppose that one party was to be placed at the mercy of the other. Hearn v. Stevens & Bro., 111 App.Div. 101, 106, 97 N.Y.S. 566; Russell v. Allerton, 108 N.Y. 288, 15 N.E. 391. Many other terms of the agreement point the same way. We are told at the outset by way of recital that:

"The said Otis F. Wood possesses a business organization adapted to the placing of such indorsements as the said Lucy, Lady Duff–Gordon, has approved."

The implication is that the plaintiff's business organization will be used for the purpose for which it is adapted. But the terms of the defendant's compensation are even more significant. Her sole compensation for the grant of an exclusive agency is to be one-half of all the profits resulting from the plaintiff's efforts. Unless he gave his efforts, she could never get anything. Without an implied promise, the transaction cannot have such business "efficacy, as both parties must have intended that at all events it should have." Bowen, L.J., in The Moorcock, 14 P.D. 64, 68. But

b. In dismissing the complaint, the Appellate Division explained that "the plaintiff by this contract promises to collect the revenues derived from the indorsements, sales and licenses and to pay the cost of collecting them out of his half thereof, and to account to the defendant each month. But this promise on his part is not binding on him unless he places indorsements, makes sales or grants licenses, and nowhere in the contract has he bound himself to get these indorsements, or make the sales or grant the licens- es.... It is quite apparent that in this respect the defendant gives everything and the plaintiff nothing and there is a lack of mutuality in the contract.... In fact the plaintiff in the nature of the case could not perform any of his various dependent agreements unless he placed indorsements, made sales or granted licenses to manufacture. And as the contract did not bind him to do any of these things, there is no provision of the contract which the defendant could enforce against him." 164 N.Y.S. at 577.

the contract does not stop there. The plaintiff goes on to promise that he will account monthly for all moneys received by him, and that he will take out all such patents and copyrights and trademarks as may in his judgment be necessary to protect the rights and articles affected by the agreement. It is true, of course, as the Appellate Division has said, that if he was under no duty to try to market designs or to place certificates of indorsement, his promise to account for profits or take out copyrights would be valueless. But in determining the intention of the parties the promise has a value. It helps to enforce the conclusion that the plaintiff had some duties. His promise to pay the defendant one-half of the profits and revenues resulting from the exclusive agency and to render accounts monthly was a promise to use reasonable efforts to bring profits and revenues into existence. For this conclusion the authorities are ample. . . .

The judgment of the Appellate Division should be reversed, and the order of the Special Term affirmed, with costs in the Appellate Division and in this court.

[Three judges dissented.]

NOTES

(1) *Questions.* What is the rationale for the implication of a promise? To what extent does it turn on the fact that Lady Duff–Gordon gave Wood "an exclusive privilege"? On other of the "many circumstances" referred to by Cardozo? How does the statement of the rule in UCC § 2–306(2) guide your analysis? (Would the UCC, if enacted at the time, have applied to the case?)

(2) *Corbin and Llewellyn on Cardozo.* Professor Arthur Linton Corbin[a] wrote this of Cardozo: "It cannot be said that he made any extensive changes in the existing law of contract. To state the facts of the cases, the decision, and the reasoning of the opinion will not show the overthrow of old doctrine or the establishment of new. Instead, it will show the application of existing doctrines with wisdom and discretion; an application that does not leave those doctrines wholly unaffected, but one that carries on their evolution as is reasonably required by the new facts before the court. When Cardozo is through, the law is not exactly as it was before, but there has been no sudden shift or revolutionary change." Mr. Justice Cardozo and the Law of Contracts, 39 Colum.L.Rev. 56, 56–57, 52 Harv. L.Rev. 408, 408–09, 48 Yale L.J. 426, 426–27 (1939).

Professor Karl Llewellyn used Wood v. Lucy to illustrate Cardozo's mastery in presenting the facts of a case. "You must remember that Cardozo was a truly great advocate, and the fact that he became a great judge didn't at all change the fact that he was a great advocate. And if you will watch, in the very process of your listening to the facts, you will find two things happening. The one is that . . . you arrive at the conclusion that the case has to come out one way. And the other is, that it fits into a legal frame that says, 'How comfortable it will be, to bring it out that way. No trouble at all. No trouble at all.' " Llewellyn quoted the first five sentences of the opinion, noting how the defendant "is subtly made into a nasty person," and then

a. Arthur Linton Corbin (1874–1967) practiced law in Colorado for four years after his graduation from law school in 1899. He taught at the Yale Law School from 1903 until his retirement in 1943, and became a leading authority on the law of contracts. His eight-volume treatise, *Corbin on Contracts*, which began to appear in 1950, ranks as one of the great legal treatises. He also served as Special Advisor, and as Reporter for the Chapter on Remedies, for the First Restatement of Contracts.

continued: "Does this sound ... like a business deal? Does a business deal sound like a legally enforceable view? Nothing is being said about that. But watch it grow on you. And if I hadn't stopped to tell you about it, it would have grown until you just took it, without a word." Llewellyn, A Lecture on Appellate Advocacy, 29 U.Chi.L.Rev. 627, 637–38 (1962). Can you give a similar reading to other parts of the opinion?

A copy of the contract in Wood v. Lucy is found in *Selections*. Might Cardozo have drawn his characterization of the defendant from the contract drafted by Lady Duff–Gordon's lawyer?

(3) *Termination Clauses.* Parties often use termination clauses to reduce the risks that they assume by contracting. The contract in Wood v. Lucy was, for example, terminable by either party without liability after one year. (As Judge Richard Posner has noted, "a year can be a long time in the fashion business." Posner, *Cardozo: A Study in Reputation* 96 (1990).)

If a termination clause is read as giving a party the power to terminate at any time at will, without more, that party's promise will be held to be illusory. For example, a license agreement for the manufacture of Orange Crush gave the licensee the exclusive right and the duty to manufacture the soft drink in a specified territory, but provided that the licensee could terminate the contract at any time. In a suit by the licensee against the licensor, the court held that the licensee's promise was not consideration for the licensor's because the licensee "did not promise to do anything and could at any time cancel the contract." Miami Coca–Cola Bottling Co. v. Orange Crush Co., 296 F. 693 (5th Cir.1924).

If, however, a termination clause is read as requiring that notice be given some period of time before the termination becomes effective, or be given in writing, or in some other way restricts the right of termination, the promise will not be held to be illusory.

(4) *Termination Under the Code.* UCC § 2–309(3) requires "reasonable notification" for termination, except on the happening of an agreed event. What if a termination clause explicitly negates any duty of notification? As to this, Comment 8 to the section says: "An agreement dispensing with notification or limiting the time for the seeking of a substitute arrangement is, of course, valid under this subsection unless the results of putting it into operation would be the creation of an unconscionable state of affairs." Termination clauses are considered again in later chapters.

———

SUBSTITUTES FOR CONSIDERATION

The doctrine of consideration has been subjected to attacks for more than two centuries. Why, critics ask, should a promisor not be able to make a binding promise without receiving something in return from, and without reliance by, the promisee? Attempts at reform have focused on this problem, particularly with regard to gratuitous promises, and various substitutes have been suggested.

As long ago as 1765, in a case involving past consideration, Lord Mansfield[a] declared that a writing might substitute for consideration: "The

a. William Murray, first Earl of Mansfield (1705–1793), was a rival of William Pitt the Elder in school, in Parliament and in politics. He favored strict measures with the ancient notion about the want of consideration was for the sake of evidence only: for when it is reduced into writing ... there was no objection to the want of consideration.... In commercial cases amongst merchants, the want of consideration is not an objection." Pillans and Rose v. Van Mierop and Hopkins, 97 Eng.Rep. 1035 (Kings Bench 1765). His rule was short lived, for thirteen years later it was rejected by the House of Lords, which concluded that, "All contracts are, by the laws of England, distinguished into agreements by specialty [*i.e.*, agreements under seal], and agreements by parol; nor is there any such third class as some of the counsel have endeavored to maintain, as contracts in writing. If they be merely written and not specialties, they are parol, and a consideration must be proved." Rann v. Hughes, 101 Eng.Rep. 1014 (House of Lords 1778). Nonetheless, the view that the formality of putting a promise in writing should operate as an alternative to consideration continued to have appeal, and gained new vitality—particularly in connection with gratuitous promises—when the abolition of the seal raised the doctrine of consideration to even greater prominence.

A few states have general statutes that facilitate the making of binding gratuitous promises by recognizing some form of writing as a substitute for consideration. (Hark back to the seal on pp. 29–30.) One such statute, the Model Written Obligations Act, proposed by the National Conference of Commissioners on Uniform State Laws, provides:

> A written release or promise hereafter made and signed by the person releasing or promising shall not be invalid or unenforceable for lack of consideration, if the writing also contains an additional express statement, in any form of language, that the signer intends to be legally bound.

Only Pennsylvania and Utah adopted this act, and Utah later repealed it. According to one of Utah's code commissioners, there was "no more vicious statute in the written laws of any civilized nation" since it would "enable confidence men and swindlers to enforce written promises ... which they may obtain from the unwary." See Report to the Governor (1933), quoted in Note, 3 Utah L.Rev. 73, 95 n.166 (1952). A 1937 recommendation of the English Law Revision Commission that a similar statute be adopted was also rejected. What explains legislative reluctance to recognize written gratuitous promises as binding?

A more common variety of general legislation is typified by a California statute that makes a writing presumptive evidence of consideration. Cal. Civ.Code § 1614 (West 2001). In addition, Article 2 of the Uniform Commercial Code dispenses with the requirement of consideration in certain

---

American rebels. His friend Alexander Pope helped him practice advocacy and later praised his eloquence in verse. Dr. Johnson said of him, "much can be made of a Scot if caught young." Mansfield achieved greatness as a judge, being Lord Chief Justice from 1756 to 1788. One of his chief services was in rationalizing mercantile law. In commercial cases he made effective use of special "juries" of merchants, whose advice about their practices was sometimes instrumental in transforming custom into law.

limited circumstances, as indicated on p. 176 and Note 2, pp. 327–328 below.

Civil law countries commonly have procedures by which a promisor may appear before a notary, a lawyer who holds an appointment from the state and who has no counterpart in common law countries, and make an irrevocable gratuitous promise. See Arthur T. von Mehren, Civil Law Analogues to Consideration: An Exercise in Comparative Analysis, 72 Harv.L.Rev. 1009, 1057–62 (1959). One explanation offered for the refusal by the American legal system to provide a similar mechanism is paternalism, the view that a promisor's preferences regarding the enforceability of the promise should be disregarded for the promisor's own good. See Farnsworth, Promises and Paternalism, 41 Wm. & Mary L.Rev.385 (2000). We consider the general question of whether legal constraints on a party's ability to contract are better understood as paternalism or protection in Chapters 4 and 6.

NOTE

"Furthering Economic Activity." In a provocative article, Professors Daniel Farber and John Matheson proposed a rule that would enforce any promise "made in furtherance of an economic activity;" See Beyond Promissory Estoppel: Contract Law and the Invisible Handshake, 52 Chi.L.Rev. 903, 929 (1985); see also Edward Yorio and Steve Thel, The Promissory Basis of Section 90, 101 Yale L.Rev. 111 (1991). Farber and Matheson argued that because firms commonly make promises for which they expect economic benefits—the promise to keep a plant open, for example—without receiving any specific bargained-for exchange but with the expectation of eventual economic benefit, such promises should be enforced. They concluded that a "rule that enforces promises designed 'to induce the creation of economic activity' simply 'reinforces the traditional free-will basis of promissory liability, albeit in an expanded context of relational and institutional interdependence.'" Farber and Matheson suggest that courts are already implementing the proposed rule using reliance to enforce commercial promises in cases where the plaintiff has shown little or no reliance at all; see Vastoler v. American Can Co., cited in Note 3, p. 96 below. For criticism of the empirical basis of their argument, see Robert Hillman, Questioning the New Consensus on Promissory Estoppel: An Empirical and Theoretical Study, 98 Colum.L.Rev. 580 (1998).

In their proposal Farber and Matheson drew a clear line between gratuitous promises that further economic activity and those that don't. "Unlike promises made in an economic setting, [non-commercial gratuitous promises] are not generally made to coordinate activities or generate reliance beneficial to the promisor. The presumption of utility that underlies our proposed enforcement of promises in furtherance of economic activity thus does not apply ..." Why is it that non-commercial gift promises find no haven, even among proposals that would abandon consideration in commercial dealings?

PROBLEM

Reviewing the Situation. Grateful for various forms of personal assistance (driving, shopping, and so on) received from a close friend over the years, Jack Tallas, a retired businessman, wrote out a memorandum stating his intention to change his will to make the friend "an heir for the sum of $50,000." Tallas had the memorandum notarized and gave a notarized copy of the memo to his friend to keep. When Tallas died never having changed his will, the friend sued his estate for $50,000. Assuming, as the court did, that there was no fraud, duress, or misrepresentation, is there any legal basis to support the friend's claim? Consideration?

Moral obligation? The writing? The notarization? If your answer is "None of the above," why should the promise not be enforced? Is the concern that the cautionary or evidentiary functions performed by consideration, p. 30 above, have not been met? What more could Tallas have done? See DeMentas v. Tallas, 764 P.2d 628 (Utah 1988).

SECTION 4.   RELIANCE AS A BASIS OF ENFORCEMENT

This section examines the role of reliance on a promise as a basis for the enforcement of the promise separate and distinct from consideration. We have already considered reliance as one interest a court might protect when providing a remedy to an aggrieved promisee. The focus here, however, is not on reliance as a form of relief, but rather as a theory for enforcing promises in the first place. As we shall see, to recognize this function of reliance may ameliorate injustices that would otherwise result from a want of consideration. At the same time, recognizing reliance also risks unfair or unsatisfactory outcomes. In reading the following cases, compare the advantages and limitations offered by reliance as a ground for enforcing promises with those offered by consideration.

Ricketts v. Scothorn
Supreme Court of Nebraska, 1898.
57 Neb. 51, 77 N.W. 365.

■ SULLIVAN, J. In the District Court of Lancaster county, the plaintiff, Katie Scothorn, recovered judgment against the defendant, Andrew D. Ricketts, as executor, of the last will and testament of John C. Ricketts, deceased. The action was based upon a promissory note, of which the following is a copy: "May the first, 1891. I promise to pay to Katie Scothorn on demand, $2,000 to be at 6 per cent. per annum. J.C. Ricketts." In the petition the plaintiff alleges that the consideration for the execution of the note was that she should surrender her employment as bookkeeper for Mayer Bros., and cease to work for a living. She also alleges that the note was given to induce her to abandon her occupation, and that, relying on it, and on the annual interest, as a means of support, she gave up the employment in which she was then engaged. These allegations of the petition are denied by the administrator.

The material facts are undisputed. They are as follows: John C. Ricketts, the maker of the note, was the grandfather of the plaintiff. Early in May—presumably on the day the note bears date—he called on her at the store where she was working. What transpired between them is thus described by Mr. Flodene, one of the plaintiff's witnesses: "A. Well, the old gentleman came in there one morning about nine o'clock, probably a little before or a little after, but early in the morning, and he unbuttoned his vest, and took out a piece of paper in the shape of a note; that is the way it looked to me; and he says to Miss Scothorn, 'I have fixed out something that you have not got to work any more.' He says, 'none of my grandchildren work, and you don't have to.' Q. Where was she? A. She took the piece of paper and kissed him, and kissed the old gentleman, and commenced to cry.'' It seems Miss Scothorn immediately notified her employer of her intention to quit work, and that she did soon after abandon her occupation. The mother of the plaintiff was a witness, and testified that she had a conversation with her father, Mr. Ricketts, shortly after the note was executed, in which he informed her that he had given the note to the plaintiff to enable her to quit work; that none of his grandchildren worked, and he did not think she ought to. For something more than a year the plaintiff was without an occupation, but in September, 1892, with the consent of her grandfather, and by his assistance, she secured a position as bookkeeper with Messrs. Funke & Ogden. On June 8, 1894, Mr. Ricketts died. He had paid one year's interest on the note, and a short time before his death expressed regret that he had not been able to pay the balance. In the summer or fall of 1892 he stated to his daughter, Mrs. Scothorn, that if he could sell his farm in Ohio he would pay the note out of the proceeds. He at no time repudiated the obligation.

We quite agree with counsel for the defendant that upon this evidence there was nothing to submit to the jury, and that a verdict should have been directed peremptorily for one of the parties. The testimony of Flodene and Mrs. Scothorn, taken together, conclusively establishes the fact that the note was not given in consideration of the plaintiff pursuing, or agreeing to pursue, any particular line of conduct. There was no promise on the part of the plaintiff to do, or refrain from doing, anything. Her right to the money promised in the note was not made to depend upon an abandonment of her employment with Mayer Bros., and future abstention from like service. Mr. Ricketts made no condition, requirement, or request. He exacted no quid pro quo. He gave the note as a gratuity, and looked for nothing in return. So far as the evidence discloses, it was his purpose to place the plaintiff in a position of independence, where she could work or remain idle, as she might choose. The abandonment by Miss Scothorn of her position as bookkeeper was altogether voluntary. It was not an act done in fulfillment of any contract obligation assumed when she accepted the note.

The instrument in suit, being given without any valuable consideration, was nothing more than a promise to make a gift in the future of the sum of money therein named. Ordinarily, such promises are not enforceable, even when put in the form of a promissory note.... But it has often been held that an action on a note given to a church, college, or other like institution, upon the faith of which money has been expended or obligations incurred, could not be successfully defended on the ground of a want of consideration.... In this class of cases the note in suit is nearly always spoken of as a gift or donation, but the decision is generally put on the ground that the expenditure of money or assumption of liability by the donee on the faith of the promise constitutes a valuable and sufficient consideration. It seems to us that the true reason is the preclusion of the defendant, under the doctrine of estoppel, to deny the consideration....

Under the circumstances of this case, is there an equitable estoppel which ought to preclude the defendant from alleging that the note in controversy is lacking in one of the essential elements of a valid contract? We think there is. An estoppel in pais is defined to be "a right arising from acts, admissions, or conduct which have induced a change of position in accordance with the real or apparent intention of the party against whom they are alleged." ... According to the undisputed proof, as shown by the record before us, the plaintiff was a working girl, holding a position in which she earned a salary of $10 per week. Her grandfather, desiring to put her in a position of independence, gave her the note, accompanying it with the remark that his other grandchildren did not work, and that she would not be obliged to work any longer. In effect, he suggested that she might abandon her employment, and rely in the future upon the bounty which he promised. He doubtless desired that she should give up her occupation, but, whether he did or not, it is entirely certain that he contemplated such action on her part as a reasonable and probable consequence of his gift. Having intentionally influenced the plaintiff to alter her position for the worse on the faith of the note being paid when due, it would be grossly inequitable to permit the maker, or his executor, to resist payment on the ground that the promise was given without consideration. The petition charges the elements of an equitable estoppel, and the evidence conclusively establishes them. If errors intervened at the trial, they could not have been prejudicial. A verdict for the defendant would be unwarranted. The judgment is right, and is

Affirmed.

NOTES

(1) *Questions.* What if, during the brief exchange between Ricketts and Scothorn, Ricketts had not mentioned work at all, but had simply handed his granddaughter the promissory note? (Note that Ricketts's promise to Scothorn is found in the promissory note, not in the conversation between them.) What result if the conversation took place as it did, and Scothorn decided to keep on working but relied on the promise by buying a horse so that she could get to work more conveniently? Might another court have found a bargained-for exchange and so have enforced Ricketts's note as a promise supported by consideration? Compare, particularly, Hamer v. Sidway, p. 34 above. How might Ricketts have structured his promise so as to ensure its enforcement?

(2) *Kirksey Revisited.* Would the reasoning of the court in *Ricketts* support a recovery by the sister-in-law, the promisee, in *Kirksey,* above?

––––––––

THE DEVELOPMENT OF PROMISSORY ESTOPPEL

Holmes said, "It would cut up the doctrine of consideration by the roots, if a promisee could make a gratuitous promise binding by subsequently acting in reliance on it." Commonwealth v. Scituate Savings Bank, 137 Mass. 301, 302 (1884). Nevertheless, a number of 19th and early 20th century cases, including *Ricketts,* recognized reliance as a basis for the enforcing of promises. For the most part, these cases fall into the following four categories.

Family Promises. As in *Ricketts*, a promise is made by one family member to another, on which the other relies. Many such cases have involved a promise to leave the family farm to the son who stays and works the property, or to the daughter who doesn't marry but cares for her aging parents instead. For a catalogue of reasons why such promises traditionally failed as enforceable contracts, see Hendrik Hartog, Someday This Will All Be Yours: Inheritance, Adoption, and Obligation in Capitalist America, 79 Ind.L.J. 345 (2004).

Promises to Convey Land. The recipient of a promise to convey land relied on it by moving onto the land and making improvements. An early example is Freeman v. Freeman, 43 N.Y. 34 (1870). Would the facts in *Kirksey*, above, have brought that case within this category?

Promises Coupled with Gratuitous Bailments. A person to whom the owner of something entrusts its possessions makes a promise to the owner respecting the property, on which the owner relies. The leading case is Siegel v. Spear & Co., 138 N.E. 414 (N.Y.1923). Siegel bought furniture on credit from Spear, giving Spear a mortgage on it and agreeing not to remove it from his apartment without Spear's consent until it was paid for. When he decided to leave the city for the summer, Siegel saw Spear's credit man, McGrath, who agreed to store the furniture free of charge. When Siegel stated that he would first have to get some property insurance, McGrath responded that it wouldn't be necessary: "I will do it for you; it will be a good deal cheaper; . . . when you get the next bill—you can send a check for that with the next installment." Siegel then sent the furniture to Spear's storehouse, where, a month later it was destroyed by fire. It had not been insured. Siegel sued Spear, won, and Spear appealed. The Court of Appeals affirmed. Although the gratuitous bailment itself imposed no duty on Spear to insure the furniture, such a duty arose from McGrath's promise followed by the delivery of the furniture by Siegel.

Charitable Subscriptions. A person promises to contribute to a not-for-profit organization. In that case enforcement may be regarded as particularly desirable as a means of allowing decisions about the distribution of wealth to be made at an individual level. As one court put it, "This promise was made to a charitable corporation, and for that reason we are not confined to the same orthodox concepts which once were applicable to every situation arising within a common law jurisdiction. There can be no denying that the strong desire on the part of the American courts to favor charitable institutions has established a doctrine which once would have been looked upon as legal heresy." Danby v. Osteopathic Hosp. Ass'n of Delaware, 104 A.2d 903, 904 (Del.Ch.1954). It is sometimes possible to enforce a promise of charitable contribution by finding an exchange among subscribers of promises for the benefit of (and enforceable by) the charitable organization, especially when one subscriber appears as the "bellwether" of the flock and has promised a large sum on condition that other subscribers raise a specified amount. See Congregation B'Nai Sholom v. Martin, 173 N.W.2d 504 (Mich.1969). (How could you draft a pledge form to help your favorite charity take advantage of this possibility?) Courts have also enforced such a promise by finding that the charity has done or has promised to do something in exchange for the subscriber's promise.

The most widely known and influential decision on charitable subscriptions rests on this last ground and contains only dictum concerning the effect of reliance. The case is Allegheny College v. National Chautauqua County Bank of Jamestown, 159 N.E. 173 (N.Y.1927). Mary Yates Johnston promised to pay $5,000 to Allegheny College by a writing denoted an "Estate Pledge" that stipulated that "this gift shall be known as the Mary Yates Johnston memorial fund, the proceeds from which shall be used to educate students preparing for the ministry." The sum was not payable until 30 days after her death, but $1,000 was paid while she was alive and set aside by the college for the specified purpose. She later repudiated her promise, and after her death, the college brought an action against her executor for the unpaid balance. Writing for the New York Court of Appeals, Cardozo found consideration for her promise in the return promise of the college to set up the memorial fund which arose "by implication" from its acceptance of the $1,000. "The college could not accept the money and hold itself free thereafter from personal responsibility to give effect to the condition." In the course of his opinion, Cardozo went out of his way to speak to the effect of reliance. "[T]here has grown up of recent days a doctrine that a substitute for consideration or an exception to its ordinary requirements can be found in what is styled 'a promissory estoppel'.... Whether the exception has made its way in this state to such an extent as to permit us to say that the general law of consideration has been modified accordingly, we do not now attempt to say. Cases such as Siegel v. Spear & Co.... may be signposts on the road. Certain, at least, it is that we have adopted the doctrine of promissory estoppel as the equivalent of consideration in connection with our law of charitable subscriptions." For a detailed account of the case, see Alfred S. Konefsky, How to Read, or at Least Not Misread, Cardozo in the *Allegheny College* Case, 36 Buffalo L.Rev. 645 (1987).

RESTATEMENT, FIRST, § 90

Cardozo's dictum in *Allegheny College* was surely influenced by what was to become Restatement, First, § 90, the text of which had been considered at the annual meeting of the American Law Institute in 1926. It reads:

§ 90.   Promise Reasonably Inducing Definite and Substantial Action

A promise which the promisor should reasonably expect to induce action or forbearance of a definite and substantial character on the part of the promisee and which does induce such action or forbearance is binding if injustice can be avoided only by enforcement of the promise.

Although the section avoids the use of the term "promissory estoppel," it states in general terms the principle that had been applied in the four categories of cases just described. Its remarkable impact is suggested by its role in the following cases.

During the discussion of Restatement, First, § 90 on the floor of the American Law Institute, Samuel Williston, as Reporter, stated: "Either the promise is binding or it is not. If the promise is binding it has to be enforced as it is made. As I said to Mr. Coudert, I could leave this whole thing to the subject of quasi contracts so that the promisee under those circumstances shall never recover on the promise but he shall recover such an amount as will fairly compensate him for any injury incurred; but it seems to me you have to take one leg or the other. You have either to say the promise is binding or you have to go on the theory of restoring the status quo." 4 American Law Institute Proceedings, Appendix, 103–04 (1926).

Do you agree with Williston?

Feinberg v. Pfeiffer Co.

Saint Louis Court of Appeals, Missouri, 1959.
322 S.W.2d 163.

[The facts and the first part of the opinion in this case are at p. 46 above. The court there rejected Mrs. Feinberg's contention that her continuation in the employ of Pfeiffer Co. from December 27, 1947, the date of the resolution, until the date of her retirement, June 30, 1949, was consideration for Pfeiffer's promise to pay her $200 per month for life upon her retirement. In this portion of the opinion, the court considered Mrs. Feinberg's second contention, that the promise was enforceable because of her reliance on it, "*i.e.,* her retirement, and the abandonment by her of her opportunity to continue in gainful employment."]

■ DOERNER, COMMISSIONER. . . . But as to the second of these contentions we must agree with plaintiff. By the terms of the resolution defendant promised to pay plaintiff the sum of $200 a month upon her retirement.

[The court quoted Restatement, First, § 90.] Was there such an act on the part of plaintiff, in reliance upon the promise contained in the resolution, as will estop the defendant, and therefore create an enforceable contract under the doctrine of promissory estoppel? We think there was. One of the illustrations cited under Section 90 of the Restatement is: "2. A promises B to pay him an annuity during B's life. B thereupon resigns a profitable employment, as A expected that he might. B receives the annuity for some years, in the meantime becoming disqualified from again obtaining good employment. A's promise is binding." This illustration is objected to by defendant as not being applicable to the case at hand. The reason advanced by it is that in the illustration B became "disqualified" from obtaining other employment *before* A discontinued the payments, whereas in this case the plaintiff did not discover that she had cancer and thereby became unemployable until *after* the defendant had discontinued the payments of $200 per month. We think the distinction is immaterial. The only reason for the reference in the illustration to the disqualification of A is in connection with that part of Section 90 regarding the prevention of injustice. The injustice would occur regardless of when the disability occurred. Would defendant contend that the contract would be enforceable if the plaintiff's illness had been discovered on March 31, 1956, the day before it discontinued the payment of the $200 a month, but not if it occurred on April 2nd, the day after? Furthermore, there are more ways to become disqualified for work, or unemployable, than as the result of illness. At the time she retired plaintiff was 57 years of age. At the time the payments were discontinued she was over 63 years of age. It is a matter of common knowledge that it is virtually impossible for a woman of that age to find satisfactory employment, much less a position comparable to that which plaintiff enjoyed at the time of her retirement.

The fact of the matter is that plaintiff's subsequent illness was not the "action or forbearance" which was induced by the promise contained in the resolution. As the trial court correctly decided, such action on plaintiff's part was her retirement from a lucrative position in reliance upon defendant's promise to pay her an annuity or pension. [The court quoted from *Ricketts v. Scothorn*, p. 89 above.]

The Commissioner therefore recommends, for the reasons stated, that the judgment be affirmed.

■ Per Curiam. The foregoing opinion is adopted as the opinion of the court. The judgment is, accordingly, affirmed.

PROBLEM

Parallel Pension Promise? In January, 1972, Edward J. Hayes announced his intention to retire from Plantations Steel the following July after 25 years of continuous service. About a week before his retirement, he had a conversation with a Plantations Steel officer who said that, though Hayes was not eligible for a pension, the company "would take care" of him. Hayes retired and sought no other employment, and the company paid him $5,000 a year through 1976. When payments were discontinued on the ground that the promise was unsupported by consideration, Hayes sued, relying on *Feinberg*. What result? Do the facts in Hayes's case differ significantly from those in Feinberg's? Hayes v. Plantations Steel Co., 438 A.2d 1091 (R.I.1982).

––––––––

RESTATEMENT, SECOND, § 90

In view of the great influence that § 90 of the Restatement, First, has had, § 90 of the Restatement, Second, set out below, merits a particularly careful reading. Note the addition of the second sentence of Subsection (1) and the deletion in the first sentence of the requirement that the reliance be of "a definite and substantial character." How might these two changes be related? Note also the liberalization in Subsection (2) of the rule as to charitable subscriptions.

§ 90.   Promise Reasonably Inducing Action or Forbearance

(1) A promise which the promisor should reasonably expect to induce action or forbearance on the part of the promisee or a third

person and which does induce such action or forbearance is binding if injustice can be avoided only by enforcement of the promise. The remedy granted for breach may be limited as justice requires.

(2) A charitable subscription or a marriage settlement is binding under Subsection (1) without proof that the promise induced action or forbearance.

NOTES

(1) *Measure of Recovery.* Fuller and Perdue posed the following hypothesis:

An uncle promises his nephew $1,000 as a gift. The nephew decides to go into business, and, reserving the promised sum for use in paying his rent, spends a large sum of money laying in a stock of goods. The uncle declines to perform his promise; the nephew is forced to abandon his plans, and sells his stock of goods at a sacrifice of $2,000.

See Lon L. Fuller & William R. Perdue, Jr., The Reliance Interest in Contract Damages, 46 Yale L.J. 52, 80 (1936).

How much should the nephew recover in the preceding hypothetical case?

(2) *Charitable Subscriptions Revisited.* How does the rule of Restatement, Second, § 90(2) differ from Cardozo's dictum in *Allegheny College*, at p. 93 above? Several courts have refused to apply § 90(2) and continue to require a showing of reliance. One such case involved the ownership of the papers of Dr. Martin Luther King Jr. In a 1964 letter, Dr. King named the Boston University Library as the repository of his papers, and authorized their removal to Boston University on a yearly basis. His letter stated further that "In the event of my death, all such materials deposited with the University shall become from that date the absolute property of Boston University." Coretta Scott King, Dr. King's widow, later sought to recover his papers on the ground that his statement was at best a gratuitous promise. A Massachusetts jury found for the University and King appealed. *Held*: Affirmed.

The court held that either consideration or reliance was required and that the jury could have concluded that the University's efforts in caring for the papers constituted reliance on Dr. King's promise to transfer ownership of the papers at the time of his death. King v. Trustees of Boston University, 647 N.E.2d 1196 (Mass.1995). What other forms of reliance might the University have shown? Advertising itself to scholars as the repository of the King papers? For a case in which the same court found no injustice in declining to enforce an oral promise to give $25,000 to a synagogue, see Congregation Kadimah Toras–Moshe v. DeLeo, 540 N.E.2d 691 (Mass.1989)

(3) *Detriment.* In discussing Section 90, courts often speak of detriment, as if reliance were not sufficient. Does Section 90 mention "detriment"?

In Vastoler v. American Can Co., 700 F.2d 916 (3d Cir.1983), Vastoler sued his employer for breach of a promise of greater pension benefits, on which he claimed he had relied in taking a promotion from an hourly lithographer to a salaried supervisor. The trial court granted summary judgment for the employer on the ground that, because the promotion had been to Vastoler's financial advantage, there was a "complete absence of any detriment, let alone a substantial one." The Court of Appeals reversed, concluding that there was "a genuine issue of material fact . . . concerning Vastoler's detrimental reliance upon the Company's promise." The court noted that Vastoler "asserted that he remained with [the] Company because of his pension benefits." It also found "that the trial judge erred in failing to recognize that absorption of the stress and anxiety inherent in supervisory positions could be one of the factors that constitutes detrimental reliance." This explains, the court said, "why some qualified people do not want to be President of Fortune 500 corporations, nominee for the Presidency of the United States, or foreman of their plants."

Was the court, in effect, applying a rule similar to that of Restatement, Second, § 90(2)? The court in *Vastoler* used reliance to enforce a promise where the plaintiff seemed to show little or no reliance. Does the case suggest that courts may in fact be implementing the Farber and Matheson proposal discussed in the Note at p. 88?

(4) *Decline and Fall.* In the provocatively titled *The Death of Contract*, Professor Grant Gilmore[a] described the "decline and fall" of "the general theory of contract," as espoused by Langdell, Holmes, and Williston. He referred to "the Restatement's schizophrenia" and quoted from the Restatement, First, § 75 (found in Feinberg v. Pfeiffer Co. at p. 49 above), and Restatement, First, § 90 (p. 93 above).

"Perhaps what we have here is Restatement and anti-Restatement or Contract and anti-Contract.... The one thing that is clear is that these two contradictory propositions cannot live comfortably together: in the end one must swallow the other up.... Clearly enough the unresolved ambiguity in the relationship between [the two sections] has now been resolved in favor of the promissory estoppel principle of § 90 which has, in effect, swallowed up the bargain principle of § 75. The wholly executory exchange where neither party has yet taken any action would seem to be the only situation in which it would be necessary to look to § 75—and even there, as the Comment somewhat mysteriously suggests, the 'probability of reliance' may be a sufficient reason for enforcement without inquiring into whether or not there was any 'consideration.' ... Speaking descriptively, we might say that what is happening is that 'contract' is being reabsorbed into the mainstream of 'tort.' " Gilmore, *The Death of Contract* 61–65, 72, 87 (1974).

Gilmore's remark about the "wholly executory exchange where neither party has yet taken any action" has not gone unnoticed. An English contracts scholar, Professor Patrick Atiyah, has argued that the case for enforcing such exchanges is not compelling and that "there are signs of an increasing reluctance to impose liability in wholly executory contracts, that is, on promises which have neither been paid for, nor relied upon." Patrick S. Atiyah, *Promises, Morals and Law* 5–6 (1981). Can you find any of those signs? See Melvin Eisenberg, The Bargain Principle and Its Limits, 95 Harv.L.Rev. 741 (1982).

PROBLEM

Applied Measures of Recovery. Assuming that each of the following plaintiffs were allowed to recover under the rule stated in Restatement § 90, which of them might appropriately be limited to recovery based on the reliance interest? Katie Scothorn? Anna Feinberg? Antillico Kirksey?

———

a. Grant Gilmore (1910–1982), once a teacher of French, practiced law in New York for two years before teaching law at Yale and for some years at Chicago. He was a principal architect of Article 9 of the Uniform Commercial Code, which deals with secured transactions, and wrote a two-volume work on that subject as well as shorter works on admiralty, contracts, and legal history.

COHEN v. COWLES MEDIA COMPANY, 479 N.W.2d 387 (Minn.1992) (en banc). [Dan Cohen, an associate of a gubernatorial candidate, informed reporters for the Minneapolis Star and the Pioneer Press Dispatch of the arrest for unlawful assembly and the conviction for shoplifting of the opposing candidate for lieutenant governor. Although the reporters promised to keep Cohen's identity confidential, the newspapers' editors overruled those promises. When the stories were published, Cohen was fired by his advertising firm, and he sued the publishers of the papers for breach of contract.

The jury awarded Cohen $200,000 in compensatory damages, but the Minnesota Supreme Court held that, though the papers may have had a moral and ethical commitment to keep their source anonymous, the parties were not thinking in terms of a legally binding contract. It also held that to allow Cohen to recover under the doctrine of promissory estoppel would violate the papers' First Amendment rights. The Supreme Court of the United States granted certiorari and held that the First Amendment was not offended by use of the doctrine to enforce confidentiality agreements because it had only "incidental effects" on news gathering and reporting. It remanded the case to the Supreme Court of Minnesota.

Citing Restatement § 90(1), that court affirmed the jury's $200,000 verdict on the grounds of promissory estoppel, concluding that the promise must "be enforced to prevent an injustice."]

■ SIMONETT, JUSTICE.... It is perhaps worth noting that the test is not whether the promise should be enforced to do justice, but whether enforcement is required to prevent an injustice. As has been observed elsewhere, it is easier to recognize an unjust result than a just one, particularly in a morally ambiguous situation. Cf. Edmond Cahn, The Sense of Injustice (1964). The newspapers argue it is unjust to be penalized for publishing the whole truth, but it is not clear this would result in an injustice in this case. For example, it would seem veiling Cohen's identity by publishing the source as someone close to the opposing gubernatorial ticket would have sufficed as a sufficient reporting of the "whole truth."

Cohen, on the other hand, argues that it would be unjust for the law to countenance, at least in this instance, the breaking of a promise. We agree that denying Cohen any recourse would be unjust. What is significant in this case is that the record shows the defendant newspapers themselves believed that they generally must keep promises of confidentiality given a news source. The reporters who actually gave the promises adamantly testified that their promises should have been honored. The editors who countermanded the promises conceded that never before or since have they reneged on a promise of confidentiality. A former Minneapolis Star managing editor testified that the newspapers had "hung Mr. Cohen out to dry because they didn't regard him very highly as a source." The Pioneer Press Dispatch editor stated nothing like this had happened in her 27 years in journalism. The Star Tribune's editor testified that protection of sources was "extremely important." Other experts, too, stressed the ethical importance, except on rare occasions, of keeping promises of confidentiality. It was this long-standing journalistic tradition that Cohen, who has worked in journalism, relied upon in asking for and receiving a promise of anonymity.

Neither side in this case clearly holds the higher moral ground, but in view of the defendants' concurrence in the importance of honoring promises of confidentiality, and absent the showing of any compelling need in this case to break that promise, we conclude that the resultant harm to Cohen requires a remedy here to avoid an injustice. In short, defendants are liable in damages to plaintiff for their broken promise. . . .

NOTE

Questions. The case above was the second time the Supreme Court decided the matter. In its initial decision (*Cohen I*), the Court concluded that although "the newspapers may have had a moral and ethical commitment to keep their sources anonymous, . . . this was not a situation where the parties were thinking in terms of a legally binding commitment." Do you agree? A dissenting judge in *Cohen I* argued that "the news media should be compelled to keep their promises like anyone else" and should therefore be liable "on either a contract or promissory estoppel theory." If, as the majority suggested in *Cohen I,* the newspapers's commitment was only "moral and ethical," was Cohen justified in relying on it?

A context of bargaining for many problems gives some assurance that the promisors made them with serious intent. Reliance on a promise may well give some assurance that the recipient took it seriously, but does not demonstrate that the promisor *meant* it so. Is there anything in Section 90 that warrants a court taking account of the degree of circumspections that accompanied the making of a promise? As to the reporters concerned in Cohen's case, can it be doubted that both he and they took seriously their promise of confidentiality? With only a little strain, one might suppose that they struck a bargain about the matter.

PROBLEM

The Ear of the Beholder. In 1977, the Township of Ypsilanti, Michigan, created an industrial development district for General Motors' Willow Run plant and subsequently gave it a series of property tax abatements. Prior to the 1988 abatements, Harvey Williams, the plant manager, made the following statement as part of General Motors' presentation.

> Good evening, my name is Harvey Williams and I am the plant manager of the Buick Oldsmobile Cadillac group's Willow Run plant. We are pleased to have this opportunity to appear before the Ypsilanti Township Board of Trustees. This application for an industrial facilities exemption certificate is for an investment totalling $75,000,000.00 for machinery and equipment. This will enable our plant to assemble a new full size car in the 1991 model year. This new rear wheel drive car is substantially larger than our current model. And specifically it will generate major booth, oven and conveyor changes in the paint shop and assembly line process, changes in the body, trim and chassis department. This change will also provide additional flexibility at our assembly plant. Essentially we would now have the capability to produce either front or rear wheel drive cars with minimum modifications to our facility. Upon completion of this project and favorable market demand, it will allow Willow Run to continue production and maintain continuous employment for our employees. I would like to introduce Russell Hughes, our controller, who will review pertinent charts pertaining to our request.

In 1991, General Motors announced that, because of record losses, it had decided to consolidate the work done at Willow Run with that done at Arlington, Texas, and to close the Willow Run plant. The Township sought and obtained an injunction barring General Motors from transferring production from the Willow Run plant, and General Motors appealed.

How would you argue the case for the Township? For General Motors? Where in Williams's speech do you find a promise? See Charter Township of Ypsilanti v. General Motors Corp., 506 N.W.2d 556 (Mich.App.1993). See also Local 1330, United Steel Workers v. United States Steel Corp., 631 F.2d 1264 (6th Cir.1980).

D & G Stout, Inc. v. Bacardi Imports, Inc.
United States Court of Appeals, Seventh Circuit, 1991.
923 F.2d 566.

■ CUDAHY, CIRCUIT JUDGE. D & G Stout, Inc., operating at all relevant times under the name General Liquors, Inc. (General), was distributing liquor in the turbulent Indiana liquor market in 1987. When two of its major suppliers jumped ship in early 1987, General faced a critical dilemma: sell out at the best possible price or continue operating on a smaller scale. It began negotiating with another Indiana distributor on the terms of a possible sale. Bacardi Imports, Inc. (Bacardi), was still one of General's remaining major suppliers. Knowing that negotiations were ongoing for General's sale, Bacardi promised that General would continue to act as Bacardi's distributor for Northern Indiana. Based on this representation, General turned down the negotiated selling price it was offered. One week later, Bacardi withdrew its account. Realizing it could no longer continue to operate, General went back to the negotiating table, this time settling for an amount $550,000 below the first offer. The question is whether General can recover the price differential from Bacardi on a theory of promissory estoppel. The district court believed that as a matter of law it could not, and entered summary judgment for defendant Bacardi. We disagree, and so we remand for trial.

I.

General was (and D & G Stout, Inc., is) an Indiana corporation with its main place of business in South Bend. Bacardi is a corporation organized in New York and doing business primarily in Miami, Florida. General served at Bacardi's will as its wholesale distributor in Northern Indiana for over 35 years. During the 1980s, liquor suppliers in Indiana undertook an extensive effort to consolidate their distribution, the effect of which was to reduce the number of distributors in the state from approximately twenty in 1980 to only two in 1990.

General weathered the storm until April 1987, when two of its major suppliers withdrew their lines, taking with them the basis of more than fifty percent of General's gross sales. By June, General recognized that it must choose between selling out and scaling back operations in order to stay in business. Despite the recent setbacks, General calculated that remaining operational was possible as long as it held on to its continuing two major suppliers, Bacardi and Hiram Walker.

About this time (and probably in connection with the same forces concentrating distribution) Bacardi lost its distributor in Indianapolis and southern Indiana. Bacardi decided to convene a meeting on July 9, 1987, of applicants for the open distributorship. General's president, David Stout, attended the meetings as an observer, with no designs on the new opening. Stout did intend to seek assurances from Bacardi about its commitment to General in Northern Indiana. While in Indianapolis, Stout was approached by National Wine & Spirits Company (National), which expressed an interest in buying General. Stout agreed to begin negotiations the following weekend. Stout also received the assurances from Bacardi he sought: after listening to Stout's concerns and hearing about his contemplated sale of General, Bacardi emphatically avowed that it had no intention of taking its line to another distributor in Northern Indiana. This promise was open-ended—no one discussed how long the continuing relationship might last.

During the ensuing two weeks, General carried on negotiations with National to reach a price for the purchase of General's assets. Bacardi kept in close contact with General to find out whether it would indeed sell. The negotiations yielded a final figure for Stout to consider. On July 22 and again on July 23—with negotiations concluded and only the final decision remaining—Stout again sought assurances from Bacardi. The supplier unequivocally reconfirmed its commitment to stay with General, and Stout replied that, as a result, he was going to turn down National's offer and would continue operating. Later on the 23rd, Stout rejected National's offer. That same afternoon, Bacardi decided to withdraw its line from General.

General learned of Bacardi's decision on July 30. The news spread quickly through the industry, and by August 3, Hiram Walker had also pulled its line, expressing a belief that General could not continue without Bacardi on board. By this time, sales personnel were abandoning General for jobs with the two surviving distributors in Indiana (one of which was National). General quickly sought out National to sell its assets, but National's offer was now substantially reduced. The ensuing agreement, executed on August 14 and closed on August 28, included a purchase price $550,000 lower than the one National offered in mid-July. Stout's successor company brought suit under the diversity jurisdiction against Bacardi, claiming that the supplier was liable by reason of promissory estoppel for this decline in the purchase price. Judge Miller entered summary judgment for Bacardi, holding that the promises plaintiff alleged were not the type upon which one may rely under Indiana law. Plaintiff appeals.

II.

We have generally stated General's version of the facts, many of which are undisputed. On appeal, Bacardi does not argue the facts and is apparently willing to rest on Judge Miller's legal analysis. Both parties also agree with Judge Miller that Indiana law governs this case and we do not question this conclusion. Before us then is the legal question whether the plaintiff has alleged any injury which Indiana's law of promissory estoppel redresses.

Indiana has adopted the Restatement's theory of promissory estoppel:

A promise which the promisor should reasonably expect to induce action or forbearance on the part of the promisee and a third person and which does induce such action or forbearance is binding if injustice can be avoided only by the enforcement of the promise. The remedy for breach may be limited as justice requires.

Restatement (Second) of Contracts § 90(1) (1981); Eby v. York–Division, Borg–Warner, 455 N.E.2d 623, 627 (Ind.App.1983); Pepsi–Cola General Bottlers, Inc. v. Woods, 440 N.E.2d 696, 698 (Ind.App.1982). The district judge dismissed the complaint on the ground that Bacardi's alleged promise was not one on which it should reasonably have expected General to rely.

The district court first noted that the relationship between General and Bacardi had always been terminable at will. Because Bacardi's promises that it would continue to use General as its distributor contained no language indicating that they would be good for any specific period,[1] the court reasoned that the relationship remained terminable at will. It then concluded that the promise was not legally enforceable, and thus was not one on which General reasonably might rely. We agree with each of these conclusions but the last. Notwithstanding the continuation of an at-will relationship between Bacardi and General, the promises given between July 9 and July 23 were not without legal effect.

In Indiana, as in many states, an aspiring employee cannot sue for lost wages on an unfulfilled promise of at-will employment. Pepsi–Cola, 440 N.E.2d 696; accord Ewing v. Board of Trustees of Pulaski Memorial Hosp., 486 N.E.2d 1094, 1098 (Ind.App.1985) (employment contract for indefinite tenure is unenforceable for future employment). Because the employer could have terminated the employee without cause at any time after the employment began, the promise of a job brings no expectation of any determinable period of employment or corresponding amount of wages. The promise is therefore unenforceable under either a contract or a promissory estoppel theory in an action for lost wages. Nevertheless, lost wages are not the only source of damages flowing from a broken promise of employment, enforceable or not. Indiana courts acknowledge certain damages as recoverable when the employer breaks a promise of employment, even if the employment is to be terminable at will. For example, in Eby v. York–Division, Borg–Warner, 455 N.E.2d at 627, a plaintiff who gave up a job and moved from Indiana to Florida on a promise of employment sued for recovery of preparation and moving expenses incurred on the basis of the promise. The Indiana appellate court reversed the lower court's summary judgment for the defendant employer, holding that the plaintiff employee had stated a cause of action for promissory estoppel. The court found that the defendant could have expected the plaintiff and his wife to move in reliance on the promise of employment and therefore might be liable for

---

1. Given the context of the promise, we see a plausible argument that the promise was one for a term, namely that Bacardi would stay on at least until the rush toward consolidation passed. But the district judge found differently, and we need not question his factual conclusion in light of our legal analysis.

reneging. See also Pepsi–Cola, 440 N.E.2d 696; accord Lorson v. Falcon Coach, 214 Kan. 670, 522 P.2d 449 (1974).

Our review of Indiana law thus leaves us a simple if somewhat crude question: are the damages plaintiff seeks here more like lost future wages or like moving expenses? We can better answer the question if we determine why Indiana draws this distinction. Unlike lost wages, moving expenses represent out-of-pocket losses; they involve a loss of something already possessed. It would be plausible, although not very sophisticated, to distinguish between the loss of something yet to be received and the loss of something already in hand. But this is not precisely where Indiana draws the distinction, nor where we would draw it if it were our choice to make. *Eby* itself involved not only moving expenses, but wages lost at plaintiff's old job during the few days plaintiff was preparing to move. 455 N.E.2d at 625. Those wages were not out-of-pocket losses: plaintiff had no more received those wages than he had received wages from his promised employment.

In fact, the line Indiana draws is between expectation damages and reliance damages. In future wages, the employee has only an expectation of income, the recovery of which promissory estoppel will not support in an at-will employment setting. In wages forgone in order to prepare to move, as in moving expenses themselves, the employee gave up a presently determinate sum for the purpose of relocating. Both moving expenses and forgone wages were the hopeful employee's costs of positioning himself for his new job; moving expenses happen to be out-of-pocket losses, while forgone wages are opportunity costs. Both are reliance costs, not expectancy damages.

Thus, the question has become whether the loss incurred from the price drop was attributable to lost expectations of future profit or resulted from an opportunity forgone in reliance on the promise. At first blush, the injury might seem more like the loss of future wages. Bacardi was a major supplier whose business was extremely valuable to General. While the loss of this "asset" might cause a decline in General's market value as measured by the loss of future income from the sale of Bacardi's products, this loss is not actionable on a promissory estoppel theory. Those damages would presumably be measured by the present value of General's anticipated profit from the sale of Bacardi's products, and Indiana will not grant relief based on promissory estoppel to compensate an aggrieved party for such expectancy damages. Lost future income expected from an at-will relationship, whether from wages or from profits, is not recoverable on a theory of promissory estoppel, and neither is the present value of such losses.

But the fact is that recovery of lost profits is not a question before us. Bacardi's account was never an "asset" that National could acquire by purchasing General. As counsel for the defendant candidly but carefully explained, National never assumed that it would retain the Bacardi account by buying General; in fact, National assumed the opposite. Bacardi's major competitor in the rum distilling business distributed through National, and the two top distillers in a given category of liquor would not choose the same distributor. Both before and after Bacardi decided to withdraw its products, all National wanted from General were its assets other than the Bacardi account. But Bacardi's repudiation of its promise ostensibly affected the price of General's business so drastically because, as everyone in the industry understood, General's option to stay in business independently was destroyed by Bacardi's withdrawal of its account. Thus, through its repudiation, Bacardi destroyed General's negotiating leverage since General no longer had the alternative of continuing as an independent concern. Presumably, after Bacardi's withdrawal General's only alternative to selling to National was to liquidate. Thus, Bacardi's repudiation turned General's discussions with National from negotiations to buy a going concern into a liquidation sale. Instead of bargaining from strength, knowing it could reject a junk-value offer and carry on its business, General was left with one choice: sell at any price.

Under these facts, General had a reliance interest in Bacardi's promise. General was in lively negotiations with National and it repeatedly informed Bacardi of this fact. A price was agreed upon, and based on that figure, Stout had to decide whether to close his doors or continue operating. General had a business opportunity that all parties knew would be devalued once Bacardi announced its intention to go elsewhere. The extent of that devaluation represents a reliance injury, rather than an injury to General's expectation of future profit. The injury is analogous to the cost of moving expenses incurred as a result of promised employment in *Eby* and *Pepsi–Cola.*

Nor were these promises merely meaningless restatements of an understood at-will relationship. With its current business opportunity, General stood at a crossroads. Circumstances foreshadowed a costly demise for the company, but it was able to negotiate an alternative. Far from confirming the obvious, Bacardi wrote its assurances on a clean slate with full knowledge that General was just as likely to reject the offered relationship as embrace it. That this was the situation is indicated most clearly by Bacardi's repeated calls to check on Stout's impending decision. Bacardi reassured Stout of its commitment in full knowledge that he planned to reject National's offer and with the reasonable expectation that an immediate pull out would severely undermine General's asking price. Like the plaintiffs in *Eby* who moved based on the promise of a job, General incurred a cost in rejecting the deal that was non-recoverable once Bacardi's later decision became known.

There may always exist the potential for a quandary in a promissory estoppel action based on a promise of at-will employment. When could Bacardi terminate the relationship with General without fear of liability for reliance costs, once it made the assurances in question? Obviously we do not hold that General and Bacardi had formed a new, permanent employment relationship. How long an employee can rely on the employer's promise is not a matter we can decide here. The issue is one of reasonable reliance, and to the extent that there might be questions, they should be for trial.

III.

We have, of course, reviewed this case in the posture of summary judgment. General's allegations still must be proven at trial. However, under Indiana law, we think that Bacardi's promise was of a sort on which General might rely, with the possibility of damages for breach. For that reason the judgment of the district court is

Reversed and remanded.

NOTES

(1) *Questions.* What exactly was the promise on which General relied? What was the nature of General's reliance? Was Bacardi's statement that "it had no intention of taking its line to another distributor" a promise? Why did the at-will doctrine not make any reliance by General unreasonable from the start?

(2) *Outcome on Remand.* Judge Cudahy recited General's claim that "Bacardi emphatically avowed that it had no intention of taking its line to another distributor in Northern Indiana." On remand, however, the district court found as a fact that Bacardi's promise had been "contingent on future events" since it was "subject to the conditions that General would continue to meet Bacardi's expectation in sales and no market changes would occur." Nevertheless, the district court held that "the conditional nature of Bacardi's commitment does not make General's reliance unreasonable." The court awarded General "damages incurred in reliance on Bacardi's promise" equal to "the difference between National's initial offer and the final sale price"—a total of $394,050. The damages awarded look suspiciously like the "lost opportunities" denied to the plaintiff in Sullivan v. O'Connor; see Note 2, p. 19 above. Can you distinguish the two cases with regard to the availability of lost opportunities in one, but not the other?

SECTION 5.   RESTITUTION AS AN ALTERNATIVE BASIS FOR RECOVERY

To this point, we have been concerned with recovery based on the enforcement of promises. We turn now to an entirely different basis of recovery—the prevention of unjust enrichment even when there has been no promise. This area of law is called restitution, and the subject of restitution is vast. Indeed restitution has its own Restatement and is often taught as a separate course. Yet because restitution problems are often inseparable from contract problems, a few basics are indispensable.

The underlying premise is this: "gains produced through another's loss are unjust and should be restored." John P. Dawson, The Self–Serving Intermeddler, 87 Harv.L.Rev. 1409 (1974). For example, if a person over-pays a bill by mistake, the recipient owes restitution in the amount of the excess payment. Liabilities like that are often predicated on "contracts implied in law." A limiting principle, however, is that one who acts officiously in conferring a benefit cannot get restitution from the recipient. One so acting is often called a *volunteer*, or *intermeddler*.

An illustration to the Restatement of Restitution § 112 gives this rather obvious example:

> During A's absence and in the belief that A will be willing to pay for the work, B improves A's land, which is worth and is offered for sale at $5000, to such an extent that upon A's return he sells the land for $8000. B is not entitled to restitution from A.

No one, that is, "should be required to pay for benefits that were 'forced' upon him." Dawson, as quoted above.

According to Professor Dawson, that precept "is often stated with more than the needed vigor, perhaps in an effort to neutralize the beguiling effect of the unjust enrichment principle, which postulates that gains produced through another's loss are unjust and should be restored." The following cases pose difficult problems in drawing the line between deserving claimants on one hand, and the intermeddlers on the other.

Further attention must be paid to vocabulary. Sometimes, as in the opinion that follows, the term "quasi contract" is used to describe a ground for recovering money in an action at common law, when the claim is not based on a true contract but instead seeks redress for unjust enrichment. "Quantum meruit" (as much as he deserved) describes a type of action used for centuries in enforcing duties of payment for services. A related action for the worth of goods was "quantum valebant" (as much as they were worth). The term "quantum meruit" is often used interchangeably (if inexactly) with "quasi-contract." "Restitution" is a broader term used to embrace all of the grounds for recovery based on unjust enrichment. Recall that "restitution" is also used in contract cases to describe one measure of damages. See discussion at p. 14 above.

Cotnam v. Wisdom

Supreme Court of Arkansas, 1907.
83 Ark. 601, 104 S.W. 164.

Action by F.L. Wisdom and another against T.T. Cotnam, administrator of A.M. Harrison, deceased, for services rendered by plaintiffs as surgeons to defendant's intestate. Judgment for plaintiffs. Defendant appeals. Reversed and remanded.

Instructions 1 and 2, given at the instance of plaintiffs, are as follows: "(1) If you find from the evidence that plaintiffs rendered professional services as physicians and surgeons to the deceased, A.M. Harrison, in a sudden emergency following the deceased's injury in a street car wreck, in an endeavor to save his life, then you are instructed that plaintiffs are entitled to recover from the estate of the said A.M. Harrison such sum as you may find from the evidence is a reasonable compensation for the services rendered. (2) The character and importance of the operation, the responsibility resting upon the surgeon performing the operation, his experience and professional training, and the ability to pay of the person operated upon, are elements to be considered by you in determining what is a reasonable charge for the services performed by plaintiffs in the particular case."

■ HILL, C.J. ... The first question is as to the correctness of [the first] instruction.... [T]he facts are that Mr. Harrison ... was thrown from a street car, receiving serious injuries which rendered him unconscious, and while in that condition the appellees were notified of the accident and summoned to his assistance by some spectator, and performed a difficult operation in an effort to save his life, but they were unsuccessful, and he died without regaining consciousness. The appellant says: "Harrison was never conscious after his head struck the pavement. He did not and could not, expressly or impliedly, assent to the action of the appellees. He was without knowledge or will power. However merciful or benevolent may have been the intention of the appellees, a new rule of law, of contract by implication of law, will have to be established by this court in order to sustain the recovery." Appellant is right in saying that the recovery must be sustained by a contract by implication of law, but is not right in saying that it is a new rule of law, for such contracts are almost as old as the English system of jurisprudence. They are usually called "implied contracts." More properly they should be called "quasi contracts" or "constructive contracts." See 1 Page on Contracts, sec. 14; also 2 Page on Contracts, sec. 771.

The following excerpts from Sceva v. True, 53 N.H. 627, are peculiarly applicable here: "We regard it as well settled by the cases referred to in the briefs of counsel, many of which have been commented on at length by Mr. Shirley for the defendant, that an insane person, an idiot, or a person utterly bereft of all sense and reason by the sudden stroke of an accident or disease may be held liable, in assumpsit, for necessaries furnished to him in good faith while in that unfortunate and helpless condition. And the reasons upon which this rests are too broad, as well as too sensible and humane, to be overborne by any deductions which a refined logic may make from the circumstances that in such cases there can be no contract or promise, in fact, no meeting of the minds of the parties. The cases put it on the ground of an implied contract; and by this is not meant, as the defendant's counsel seems to suppose, an actual contract—that is, an actual meeting of the minds of the parties, an actual, mutual understanding, to be inferred from language, acts, and circumstances by the jury—but a contract and promise, said to be implied by the law, where, in point of fact, there was no contract, no mutual understanding, and so no promise. The defendant's counsel says it is usurpation for the court to hold, as a matter of law, that there is a contract and a promise, when all the evidence in the case shows that there was not a contract, nor the semblance of one. It is doubtless a legal fiction, invented and used for the sake of the remedy. If it was originally usurpation, certainly it has now become very inveterate, and firmly fixed in the body of the law. Illustrations might be multiplied, but enough has been said to show that when a contract or promise implied by law is spoken of, a very different thing is meant from a contract in fact, whether express or tacit. The evidence of an actual contract is generally to be found either in some writing made by the parties, or in verbal communications which passed between them, or in their acts and conduct considered in the light of the circumstances of each particular case. A contract implied by law, on the contrary, rests upon no evidence. It has no actual existence. It is simply a mythical creation of the law. The law says it shall be taken that there was a promise, when in point of fact, there was none. Of course this is not good logic, for the obvious and sufficient reason that it is not true. It is a legal fiction, resting wholly for its support on a plain legal obligation, and a plain legal right. If it were true, it would not be a fiction. There is a class of legal rights, with their correlative legal duties, analogous to the obligations quasi ex contractu of the civil law which seem to lie in the region between contracts on the one hand, and torts on the other, and to call for the application of a remedy not strictly furnished either by actions ex contractu or actions ex delicto. . . ."

In its practical application it sustains recovery for physicians and nurses who render services for infants, insane persons, and drunkards. . . . And services rendered by physicians to persons unconscious or helpless by reason of injury or sickness are in the same situation as those rendered to persons incapable of contracting, such as the classes above described. . . . The court was therefore right in giving the instruction in question. . . .

There was evidence in this case proving that it was customary for physicians to graduate their charges by the ability of the patient to pay, and hence, in regard to that element, this case differs from the Alabama case [Morrisette v. Wood, 123 Ala. 384, 26 So. 307]. . . . This could not apply to a physician called in an emergency by some bystander to attend a stricken man whom he never saw or heard of before; and certainly the unconscious patient could not, in fact or in law, be held to have contemplated what charges the physician might properly bring against him. In order to admit such testimony, it must be assumed that the surgeon and patient each had in contemplation that the means of the patient would be one factor in determining the amount of the charge for the services rendered. While the law may admit such evidence as throwing light upon the contract and indicating what was really in contemplation when it was made, yet a different question is presented when there is no contract to be ascertained or construed, but a mere fiction of law creating a contract where none existed in order that there might be a remedy for a right. This fiction merely requires a reasonable compensation for the services rendered. The services are the same be the patient prince or pauper, and for them the surgeon is entitled to fair compensation for his time, service, and skill. It was therefore error to admit this evidence, and to instruct the jury in the second instruction that in determining what was a reasonable charge they could consider the "ability to pay of the person operated upon."

It was improper to let it go to the jury that Mr. Harrison was a bachelor and that his estate was left to nieces and nephews. This was relevant to no issue in the case, and its effect might well have been prejudicial. While this verdict is no higher than some of the evidence would justify, yet it is much higher than some of the other evidence would justify, and hence it is impossible to say that this was a harmless error.

Judgment is reversed, and cause remanded.

■ BATTLE and WOOD, JJ., concur in sustaining the recovery, and in holding that it was error to permit the jury to consider the fact that his estate would go to collateral heirs; but they do not concur in holding that it was error to admit evidence of the value of the estate, and instructing that it might be considered in fixing the charge.

NOTES

(1) *Questions.* Would the result have been different if Dr. Wisdom had treated Harrison in response to a call from Harrison's daughter, who had said, "Give him the best care you can and I will pay you for it"? What fee would Dr. Wisdom have been entitled to from the daughter under those circumstances? For a case rejecting Cotnam v. Wisdom on the issue of the admissibility of the patient's ability to pay, see In re Agnew's Estate, 231 N.Y.S. 4 (Surrogate's Ct.1928). Are there grounds, policy or otherwise, for admitting such evidence?

(2) *Gratuitousness.* Ordinarily, when a bystander renders first aid, or another service, to an accident victim, or when someone acts to protect another's property from loss by fire or other casualty, courts assume that the services were intended to be gratuitous. Thus if a passing motorist finds an injured pedestrian on the highway, administers first aid and takes the injured person to a hospital, there is a presumption of gratuity which will ordinarily bar recovery. However, the presumption may be rebutted if the services are excessively expensive or burdensome to the person rendering them, as when one goes out of one's way a hundred miles to take an injured person to a hospital. The presumption may also be overturned if the person rendering them does so in a business or professional capacity, as in *Cotnam*, when a passing physician treats an injured person.

(3) *Webb v. McGowin Revisited.* Recall the court's argument in *Webb* that saving life has "material, pecuniary" value, supported by the fact that "physicians practice their profession charging for services rendered in saving life." Would Webb have had a claim against McGowin on the authority of *Cotnam* and other like cases?

Recall, too, the Alabama court's reliance on Boothe v. Fitzpatrick, the case of the promise "to pay for the past keeping of a bull which had escaped . . . and been cared for." Aside from the promise by the owner of the bull, would the keeper of the bull have had a claim against its owner? Might the keeper's *belief* in such a claim have helped to justify enforcement of the owner's promise to pay a reasonable amount? Might Webb's *belief* in a claim against McGowin (even if he had no such claim) help to justify enforcement of McGowin's promise to pay $15 every two weeks? See Fiege v. Boehm, p. 40 above.

(4) *Comparative Recompense.* Consider the doctrine known to civil law systems (those derived from Roman law) as *negotiorum gestio* ("management of the affairs [of another]"). It provides that a person who, without invitation but in compelling circumstances, takes charge of the affairs of another, is entitled to compensation for services rendered in the other's interest. How does this doctrine differ from that in Cotnam v. Wisdom? What problems do you see in the application of such a doctrine? See Samuel J. Stoljar, Negotiorum Gestio § 251 (1984), in 10 International Encyclopedia of Comparative Law.

PROBLEM

The Suggestion Box. Schott, an employee of Westinghouse, twice submitted an idea concerning the construction of circuit breaker panels pursuant to a Westinghouse program inviting its employees to submit suggestions for cash awards. On the suggestion form, above the line for the employee's signature, appeared the stipulation, "I agree that the decision of the local Suggestion Committee on all matters pertaining to this suggestion ... will be final." The Committee twice rejected Schott's suggestion, stating that it would require heavy preliminary expenditures but would be reconsidered if circuit breaker redesign was undertaken for other reasons. Within a year, however, Westinghouse had made the suggested change but refused to pay Schott, explaining that it had been made as "the result of independent action taken without knowledge of your suggestion." What factors weigh in Schott's favor in an action against Westinghouse for unjust enrichment? What facts favor Westinghouse? Might Schott have a claim for breach of contract? In Schott v. Westinghouse Electric Corp., 259 A.2d 443 (Pa.1969), two judges answered the last question with a "Yes."

Callano v. Oakwood Park Homes Corp.

Superior Court of New Jersey, 1966.
91 N.J.Super. 105, 219 A.2d 332.

■ COLLESTER, J.A.D. Defendant Oakwood Park Homes Corp., (Oakwood) appeals from a judgment of $475 entered in favor of plaintiffs Julia Callano and Frank Callano in the Monmouth County District Court.

The case was tried below on an agreed stipulation of facts. Oakwood, engaged in the construction of a housing development, in December 1961 contracted to sell a lot with a house to be erected thereon to Bruce Pendergast, who resided in Waltham, Massachusetts. In May 1962, prior to completion of the house, the Callanos, who operated a plant nursery, delivered and planted shrubbery pursuant to a contract with Pendergast. A representative of Oakwood had knowledge of the planting.

Pendergast never paid the Callanos the invoice price of $497.95. A short time after the shrubbery was planted Pendergast died. Thereafter, on July 10, 1962 Oakwood and Pendergast's estate cancelled the contract of sale. Oakwood had no knowledge of Pendergast's failure to pay the Callanos. On July 16, 1962 Oakwood sold the Pendergast property, including the shrubbery located thereon, to Richard and Joan Grantges for an undisclosed amount.

The single issue is whether Oakwood is obligated to pay plaintiffs for the reasonable value of the shrubbery on the theory of *quasi*-contractual liability. Plaintiffs contend that defendant was unjustly enriched when the Pendergast contract to purchase the property was cancelled and that an agreement to pay for the shrubbery is implied in law. Defendant argues that the facts of the case do not support a recovery by plaintiffs on the theory of *quasi*-contract.

Contracts implied by law, more properly described as *quasi* or constructive contracts, are a class of obligations which are imposed or created by law without regard to the assent of the party bound, on the ground that they are dictated by reason and justice. They rest solely on a legal fiction and are not contract obligations at all in the true sense, for there is no agreement; but they are clothed with the semblance of contract for the purpose of the remedy, and the obligation arises not from consent, as in the case of true contracts, but from the law or natural equity. Courts employ the fiction of *quasi* or constructive contract with caution. 17 C.J.S. Contracts § 6, pp. 566–570 (1963).

In cases based on *quasi*-contract liability, the intention of the parties is entirely disregarded, while in cases of express contracts and contracts implied in fact the intention is of the essence of the transaction. In the case of actual contracts the agreement defines the duty, while in the case of *quasi*-contracts the duty defines the contract. Where a case shows that it is the duty of the defendant to pay, the law imparts to him a promise to fulfill that obligation. The duty which thus forms the foundation of a *quasi*-contractual obligation is frequently based on the doctrine of unjust enrichment. It rests on the equitable principle that a person shall not be allowed to enrich himself unjustly at the expense of another, and on the principle of whatsoever it is certain a man ought to do, that the law supposes him to have promised to do. St. Paul Fire, etc., Co. v. Indemnity Ins. Co. of No. America, 32 N.J. 17, 22, 158 A.2d 825 (1960).

The key words are *enrich* and *unjustly*. To recover on the theory of *quasi*-contract the plaintiffs must prove that defendant was enriched, *viz.,* received a benefit, and that retention of the benefit without payment therefor would be unjust.

It is conceded by the parties that the value of the property, following the termination of the Pendergast contract, was enhanced by the reasonable value of the shrubbery at the stipulated sum of $475. However, we are not persuaded that the retention of such benefit by defendant before it sold the property to the Grantges was inequitable or unjust.

Quasi-contractual liability has found application in a myriad of situations. See Woodruff, Cases on Quasi–Contracts (3d ed. 1933). However, a common thread runs throughout its application where liability has been successfully asserted, namely, that the plaintiff expected remuneration from the defendant, or if the true facts were known to plaintiff, he would have expected remuneration from defendant, at the time the benefit was conferred. See Rabinowitz v. Mass. Bonding & Insurance Co., 119 N.J.L. 552, 197 A. 44 (E. & A. 1937); Power–Matics, Inc. v. Ligotti, 79 N.J.Super. 294, 191 A.2d 483 (App.Div.1963); Shapiro v. Solomon, 42 N.J.Super. 377, 126 A.2d 654 (App.Div.1956). It is further noted that *quasi*-contract cases involve either some direct relationship between the parties or a mistake on the part of the person conferring the benefit.

In the instant case the plaintiffs entered into an express contract with Pendergast and looked to him for payment. They had no dealings with defendant, and did not expect remuneration from it when they provided the shrubbery. No issue of mistake on the part of plaintiffs is involved. Under the existing circumstances we believe it would be inequitable to hold defendant liable. Plaintiffs' remedy is against Pendergast's estate, since they contracted with and expected payment to be made by Pendergast when the benefit was conferred.... A plaintiff is not entitled to employ the legal fiction of *quasi*-contract to "substitute one promisor or debtor for another." Cascaden v. Magryta, 247 Mich. 267, 225 N.W. 511, 512 (Sup.Ct. 1929).

Plaintiffs place reliance on De Gasperi v. Valicenti, 198 Pa.Super. 455, 181 A.2d 862 (Super.Ct.1962), where recovery was allowed on the theory of unjust enrichment. We find the case inapposite. It is clear that recovery on *quasi*-contract was permitted there because of a fraud perpetrated by defendants. There is no contention of fraud on the part of Oakwood in the instant case.

Recovery on the theory of *quasi*-contract was developed under the law to provide a remedy where none existed. Here, a remedy exists. Plaintiffs may bring their action against Pendergast's estate. We hold that under the facts of this case defendant was not unjustly enriched and is not liable for the value of the shrubbery.

Reversed.

NOTES

(1) *Questions.* Which, if any, of the players in the case was enriched by the transaction? Did the Callanos suffer a loss? Why did the Callanos not sue Pendergast's estate? Why not the Grantges? What other things might the Callanos have done differently?

(2) *The Case of the Contractor's Claim.* Paschall's built a bathroom onto the Doziers' house at the request and on the credit of their daughter, Mrs. Best, who lived with them, and with the knowledge and consent of the Doziers. Paschall's was unsuccessful in collecting from Mrs. Best, who was subsequently adjudicated a bankrupt, and sued the Doziers on a theory of restitution. The trial court sustained the Doziers' demurrer and dismissed the complaint, and Paschall's appealed. *Held:* Reversed and remanded "to the trier of facts to determine whether or not the defendant has been so unjustly enriched at the detriment of the complainant so as to require him to make compensation therefore."

The court granted that it may be "the general rule" that "an implied undertaking cannot arise against one benefitted by the work performed, where the work is done under a special contract with another. . . . However, the situation is dissimilar where a person furnishes materials and labor under a contract for the benefit of a third party, and that contract becomes unenforceable or invalid. . . . [W]e think that before recovery can be had against the landowner on an unjust enrichment theory, the furnisher of the materials and labor must have exhausted his remedies against the person with whom he had contracted, and still has not received the reasonable value of his services." Paschall's, Inc. v. Dozier, 407 S.W.2d 150 (Tenn.1966). See also Idaho Lumber, Inc. v. Buck, 710 P.2d 647 (Idaho App.1985).

Can this case be distinguished from *Callano*? One writer suggests: "Where benefit is conferred on a stranger through performance of one's own contract various intermediate solutions could be thought of. The most plausible would be to permit restitution of the benefit to the stranger when the remedy of the gain-producer against his own obligor had failed or was certain to fail. Restitution would then serve as a surrogate, being held in reserve to insure the gain-producer against deficits in the return promised him." John P. Dawson, The Self–Serving Intermeddler, 87 Harv.L.Rev. 1409, 1457–58 (1974). To what extent are *Callano* and *Paschall's* consistent with this suggestion? For an analysis in economic terms, see Anthony Kronman and Richard Posner, *The Economics of Contract Law* 59–64 (1979).

(3) *Measure of Recovery.* If recovery is allowed in cases like *Callano* and *Paschall's*, how should it be measured? The Restatement offers two alternatives:

"the reasonable value to the [defendant] of what he received in terms of what it would have cost him to obtain it from a person in the claimant's position" and "the extent to which the [defendant's] property has increased in value or his other interests advanced." See Restatement § 371. Which measure would be more generous? Do we know that on selling the lot to the Grantges, Oakwood got a price enhanced by the value of the shrubbery? Should it matter?

(4) *Mechanics' Liens. Callano* introduces a problem of great practical importance: the rights of subcontractors on construction jobs. Commonly in such cases, two contracts are involved, one between an owner and a general contractor, and another between the general contractor and a subcontractor. It is clear that if, after the subcontractor has performed, it is not paid by the general contractor, it has no contractual right to payment from the owner. It is also clear, under reasoning like that of *Callano*, that it has no right to restitution from the owner, even though its work has conferred a benefit on the owner.

Every state legislature has addressed the situation in statutes commonly called "mechanics' lien" laws. They protect laborers, materialmen, contractors and others who make improvements on real property, by giving them a lien on that property to secure payment for those improvements.

Why did the Callanos and Paschall's not have mechanics' liens on the properties concerned? Although a New Jersey statute provides for a lien on property for improvements, including "planting thereon any shrubs," it applies only to "debts contracted by the owner." N.J. Stat.Ann. § 2A:44–66(g). Oakwood, not Pendergast, was the "owner" of the property. Similarly, a Tennessee statute provides for a lien where improvements have been made on a house, but only by "contract with the owner or his agent." Tenn.Code Ann. § 66–11–102(a).

(5) *Wrestling With Unjust Enrichment.* The court in *Callano* observed that Oakwood might have been accountable if it had perpetrated a fraud. Compare Ventura v. Titan Sports, Inc., 65 F.3d 725 (8th Cir.1995). Jesse Ventura, in 1987 a wrestler and "heel commentator," hired Barry Bloom to negotiate his contract with Titan Sports, owners of The World Wrestling Federation. (According to the court, "[a] heel commentator is a color commentator who plays the role of 'the bad guy.' ") Bloom asked for royalties for any videotape sales in which Ventura appeared but was told that only "feature" performers got royalties. Wanting to secure the job with Titan, Ventura agreed to waive any claim to royalties. When Ventura found out that other non-feature performers were getting royalties, he brought an action for fraud, misappropriation of publicity rights, and unjust enrichment. The jury awarded Ventura $800,000 on the latter claim. On appeal, Titan argued that the express contractual provision waiving royalties barred Ventura's claim for unjust enrichment. *Held*: Affirmed. The court said: "Had Ventura known that Titan did not abide by its stated policy, he would not have accepted a deal which did not compensate him for [the sale of his likeness].... The fraud rescinded or set aside the contract, opening the door to his quantum meruit claim."

————

PYEATTE v. PYEATTE, 661 P.2d 196 (Ariz.App.1982) [Charles Pyeatte and Margrethe Pyeatte were married in 1974. The couple agreed that Margrethe would "put Charles through law school without his having to work" and that when he had graduated, he would put her through graduate school on the same terms. Thus Charles attended law school and Margrethe worked to pay the bills. (Sometime during Charles's third year,

Margrethe lost her job and the couple lived on their savings for that period.) Charles was graduated in 1977, passed the bar, and became an associate at a law firm. In April, 1978, Charles informed Margrethe that he wanted a divorce. She had not yet started graduate school. She sued for breach of their agreement to put one another through school.

The trial court found that the couple's agreement was a valid contract and awarded Margrethe $23,000. On appeal, Charles argued that the agreement was too indefinite to be enforceable. Margrethe countered that she was entitled to recover in restitution. The Arizona Court of Appeals granted her claim for restitution and Charles appealed.]

■ CORCORAN, JUDGE: ... Although we found that the spousal agreement failed to meet the requirements [of definiteness] of an enforceable contract, the agreement still has importance in considering appellee's claim for unjust enrichment because it both evidences appellee's expectation of compensation and the circumstances which make it unjust to allow appellant to retain the benefits of her extraordinary efforts.

[The court then addressed the question "whether restitution on the basis of unjust enrichment is appropriate in the context of the marital relationship."] No authority is cited to the court in support of the proposition that restitution as a matter of law is inappropriate in a dissolution proceeding. In Wisner [v. Wisner, 631 P.2d 115, 123 (Ariz.App.1981)], we observed that "[i]n our opinion, unjust enrichment, as a legal concept, is not properly applied in the setting of a marital relationship." ... Our observation was directed to the wife's claim in that case for restitution for the value of her homemaking services during the couple's 15–year marriage and for the couple's reduced income during the husband's lengthy training period. Where both spouses perform the usual and incidental activities of the marital relationship, upon dissolution there can be no restitution for performance of these activities. Ibid. Where, however, the facts demonstrate an agreement between the spouses and an extraordinary or unilateral effort by one spouse which inures solely to the benefit of the other by the time of dissolution, the remedy of restitution is appropriate....

The portion of the judgment in the amount of $23,000 is reversed and remanded for proceedings in accordance with this opinion.

NOTES

(1) *Questions.* What did the lower court's award of $23,000 represent? How should the lower court calculate Margrethe's recovery for unjust enrichment? Suppose that the Pyeattes had not divorced until ten years after Charles' graduation from law school, during which time Margrethe had lived as the wife of a successful law firm partner. Would such facts affect her restitutionary claim? How?

(2) *Restitution Between Spouses.* Restitutionary claims between spouses have traditionally failed because the services of each are presumed to be gratuitous. As the Supreme Court of North Carolina explained, the rule denying restitution "is particularly applicable where a husband makes improvements to his wife's land because of the presumption that the improvements constitute a gift." Wright v. Wright, 289 S.E.2d 347 (N.C.1982). The assumption of a gift extends to other family relationships as well. The Pennsylvania Supreme Court refused to grant restitution

to an adult son despite evidence of his father's promise to pay for the son's labor, observing that "we do not infer a contract of hiring, because the principle of family affection is sufficient to account for the family association. . . ." Hertzog v. Hertzog, 29 Pa. 465, 468 (Pa.1857).

(3) *Restitution Without Benefit of Clergy.* When a sexual relationship between unmarried cohabitants is included among the benefits bestowed, courts have generally refused to grant restitution on public policy grounds. See Hewitt v. Hewitt, 394 N.E.2d 1204 (Ill.1979). Restitution has been permitted when sexual services were found to be severable from other forms of enrichment, such as improvements to property. In Watts v. Watts, 405 N.W.2d 303 (Wis.1987), the Supreme Court of Wisconsin held that "unmarried cohabitants may raise claims based upon unjust enrichment following the termination of their relationship where one of the parties attempts to retain an unreasonable amount of the property acquired through the efforts of both." It has been suggested that unmarried cohabitants may have greater success than married ones in recovering in restitution because the background assumption of marital gratuitousness is absent.

CHAPTER 2

CREATING CONTRACTUAL OBLIGATIONS

SECTION 1. THE NATURE OF ASSENT

What kind of assent to a bargain is necessary to bind a party? Different answers are given by two contrasting theories of contract, commonly described as "objective" and "subjective." They are illustrated by the following excerpts, the first from Judge Learned Hand[a] and the second from his colleague Judge Jerome Frank,[b] concurring in a case in which Hand wrote the opinion of the court.

According to Hand: "A contract has, strictly speaking, nothing to do with the personal, or individual, intent of the parties. A contract is an obligation attached by the mere force of law to certain acts of the parties, usually words, which ordinarily accompany and represent a known intent. If, however, it were proved by twenty bishops that either party when he used the words intended something else than the usual meaning which the law imposes upon them, he would still be held, unless there were some mutual mistake or something else of the sort." Hotchkiss v. National City Bank of New York, 200 F. 287, 293 (S.D.N.Y.1911).

According to Frank: "In the early days of this century a struggle went on between the respective proponents of two theories of contracts, (a) the 'actual intent' theory—or 'meeting of the minds' or 'will' theory—and (b) the so-called 'objective' theory.[1] Without doubt, the first theory had been

a. Learned Hand (1872–1961) was admitted to the practice of law in New York in 1897, appointed to the United States District Court for the Southern District of New York in 1909 and to the United States Court of Appeals for the Second Circuit in 1924. He retired in 1951, after having sat on the bench longer than any other federal judge. Justice Cardozo called him "the greatest living American jurist," and he was so regarded by many of his contemporaries. His extrajudicial utterances may be sampled in The Spirit of Liberty (1952) and The Bill of Rights (1958).

b. Jerome New Frank (1889–1957) practiced in Chicago and New York for more than twenty years before going to Washington in 1933, where he served first as a government lawyer and then as a member and later chairman of the Securities and Exchange Commission. In 1941 he was appointed to the United States Court of Appeals for

the Second Circuit. He also lectured at the Yale Law School and was associated with the philosophy of law known as "legal realism." One of his best known books is Law and the Modern Mind (1930).

1. "The 'actual intent' theory, said the objectivists, being 'subjective' and putting too much stress on unique individual motivations, would destroy that legal certainty and stability which a modern commercial society demands. They depicted the 'objective' standard as a necessary adjunct of a 'free enterprise' economic system. In passing, it should be noted that they arrived at a sort of paradox. For a 'free enterprise' system is, theoretically, founded on 'individualism'; but, in the name of economic individualism, the objectivists refused to consider those reactions of actual specific individuals which sponsors of the 'meeting-of-the-minds' test purported to

carried too far: Once a contract has been validly made, the courts attach legal consequences to the relation created by the contract, consequences of which the parties usually never dreamed—as, for instance, where situations arise which the parties had not contemplated. As to such matters, the 'actual intent' theory induced much fictional discourse which imputed to the parties intentions they plainly did not have.

"But the objectivists also went too far. They tried (1) to treat virtually all the varieties of contractual arrangements in the same way, and (2), as to all contracts in all their phases, to exclude, as legally irrelevant, consideration of the actual intention of the parties or either of them, as distinguished from the outward manifestation of that intention. The objectivists transferred from the field of torts that stubborn anti-subjectivist, the 'reasonable man'; so that, in part at least, advocacy of the 'objective' standard in contracts appears to have represented a desire for legal symmetry, legal uniformity, a desire seemingly prompted by aesthetic impulses. Whether (thanks to the 'subjectivity' of the jurymen's reactions and other factors) the objectivists' formula, in its practical workings, could yield much actual objectivity, certainty, and uniformity may well be doubted. At any rate, the sponsors of complete 'objectivity' in contracts largely won out in the wider generalizations of the Restatement of Contracts and in some judicial pronouncements." Ricketts v. Pennsylvania R. Co., 153 F.2d 757, 761 (2d Cir.1946). See also Lawrence Solan, Contract as Agreement, 83 Notre Dame L. Rev. 353 (2007).

Does either theory alone adequately explain the decision in the following principal case?

Lucy v. Zehmer

Supreme Court of Appeals of Virginia, 1954.
196 Va. 493, 84 S.E.2d 516.

■ BUCHANAN, JUSTICE. This suit was instituted by W.O. Lucy and J.C. Lucy, complainants, against A.H. Zehmer and Ida S. Zehmer, his wife, defendants, to have specific performance of a contract by which it was alleged the Zehmers had sold to W.O. Lucy a tract of land owned by A.H. Zehmer in Dinwiddie county containing 471.6 acres, more or less, known as the Ferguson farm, for $50,000. J.C. Lucy, the other complainant, is a brother of W.O. Lucy, to whom W.O. Lucy transferred a half interest in his alleged purchase.

The instrument sought to be enforced was written by A.H. Zehmer on [Saturday,] December 20, 1952, in these words: "We hereby agree to sell to

cherish. 'Economic individualism' thus shows up as hostile to real individualism. This is nothing new: The 'economic man' is of course an abstraction, a 'fiction.' "

W.O. Lucy the Ferguson Farm complete for $50,000.00, title satisfactory to buyer," and signed by the defendants, A.H. Zehmer and Ida S. Zehmer.[a]

The answer of A.H. Zehmer admitted that at the time mentioned W.O. Lucy offered him $50,000 cash for the farm, but that he, Zehmer, considered that the offer was made in jest; that so thinking, and both he and Lucy having had several drinks, he wrote out "the memorandum" quoted above and induced his wife to sign it; that he did not deliver the memorandum to Lucy, but that Lucy picked it up, read it, put it in his pocket, attempted to offer Zehmer $5 to bind the bargain, which Zehmer refused to accept, and realizing for the first time that Lucy was serious, Zehmer assured him that he had no intention of selling the farm and that the whole matter was a joke. Lucy left the premises insisting that he had purchased the farm.

Depositions were taken and the decree appealed from was entered holding that the complainants had failed to establish their right to specific performance, and dismissing their bill. The assignment of error is to this action of the court....

The defendants insist that the evidence was ample to support their contention that the writing sought to be enforced was prepared as a bluff or dare to force Lucy to admit that he did not have $50,000; that the whole matter was a joke; that the writing was not delivered to Lucy and no binding contract was ever made between the parties.

It is an unusual, if not bizarre, defense. When made to the writing admittedly prepared by one of the defendants and signed by both, clear evidence is required to sustain it.

In his testimony Zehmer claimed that he "was high as a Georgia pine," and that the transaction "was just a bunch of two doggoned drunks

a. Here is a photocopy from the record:

[Front]

[Back]

bluffing to see who could talk the biggest and say the most." That claim is inconsistent with his attempt to testify in great detail as to what was said and what was done. It is contradicted by other evidence as to the condition of both parties, and rendered of no weight by the testimony of his wife that when Lucy left the restaurant she suggested that Zehmer drive him home. The record is convincing that Zehmer was not intoxicated to the extent of being unable to comprehend the nature and consequences of the instrument he executed, and hence that instrument is not to be invalidated on that ground. C.J.S. Contracts, § 133, b., p. 483; Taliaferro v. Emery, 124 Va. 674, 98 S.E. 627. It was in fact conceded by defendants' counsel in oral argument that under the evidence Zehmer was not too drunk to make a valid contract.

The evidence is convincing also that Zehmer wrote two agreements, the first one beginning "I hereby agree to sell." Zehmer first said he could not remember about that, then that "I don't think I wrote but one out." Mrs. Zehmer said that what he wrote was "I hereby agree," but that the "I" was changed to "We" after that night. The agreement that was written and signed is in the record and indicates no such change. Neither are the mistakes in spelling that Zehmer sought to point out readily apparent.

The appearance of the contract, the fact that it was under discussion for forty minutes or more before it was signed; Lucy's objection to the first draft because it was written in the singular, and he wanted Mrs. Zehmer to sign it also; the rewriting to meet that objection and the signing by Mrs. Zehmer; the discussion of what was to be included in the sale, the provision for the examination of the title, the completeness of the instrument that was executed, the taking possession of it by Lucy with no request or suggestion by either of the defendants that he give it back, are facts which furnish persuasive evidence that the execution of the contract was a serious business transaction rather than a casual, jesting matter as defendants now contend. . . .

If it be assumed, contrary to what we think the evidence shows, that Zehmer was jesting about selling his farm to Lucy and that the transaction was intended by him to be a joke, nevertheless the evidence shows that Lucy did not so understand it but considered it to be a serious business transaction and the contract to be binding on the Zehmers as well as on himself. The very next day he arranged with his brother to put up half the money and take a half interest in the land. The day after that he employed an attorney to examine the title. The next night, Tuesday, he was back at Zehmer's place and there Zehmer told him for the first time, Lucy said, that he wasn't going to sell and he told Zehmer, "You know you sold that place fair and square." After receiving the report from his attorney that the title was good he wrote to Zehmer that he was ready to close the deal.

Not only did Lucy actually believe, but the evidence shows he was warranted in believing, that the contract represented a serious business transaction and a good faith sale and purchase of the farm.

In the field of contracts, as generally elsewhere, "We must look to the outward expression of a person as manifesting his intention rather than to his secret and unexpressed intention. 'The law imputes to a person an intention corresponding to the reasonable meaning of his words and acts.' " First Nat. Exchange Bank of Roanoke v. Roanoke Oil Co., 169 Va. 99, 114, 192 S.E. 764, 770.

At no time prior to the execution of the contract had Zehmer indicated to Lucy by word or act that he was not in earnest about selling the farm. They had argued about it and discussed its terms, as Zehmer admitted, for a long time. Lucy testified that if there was any jesting it was about paying $50,000 that night. The contract and the evidence show that he was not expected to pay the money that night. Zehmer said that after the writing was signed he laid it down on the counter in front of Lucy. Lucy said Zehmer handed it to him. In any event there had been what appeared to be a good faith offer and a good faith acceptance, followed by the execution and apparent delivery of a written contract. Both said that Lucy put the writing in his pocket and then offered Zehmer $5 to seal the bargain. Not until then, even under the defendants' evidence, was anything said or done to indicate that the matter was a joke. Both of the Zehmers testified that when Zehmer asked his wife to sign he whispered that it was a joke so Lucy wouldn't hear and that it was not intended that he should hear.

The mental assent of the parties is not requisite for the formation of a contract. If the words or other acts of one of the parties have but one reasonable meaning, his undisclosed intention is immaterial except when an unreasonable meaning which he attaches to his manifestations is known to the other party. Restatement of the Law of Contracts, Vol. I, § 71, p. 74. . . .

An agreement or mutual assent is of course essential to a valid contract but the law imputes to a person an intention corresponding to the reasonable meaning of his words and acts. If his words and acts, judged by a reasonable standard, manifest an intention to agree, it is immaterial what may be the real but unexpressed state of his mind. C.J.S. Contracts, § 32, p. 361; 12 Am.Jur., Contracts, § 19, p. 515.

So a person cannot set up that he was merely jesting when his conduct and words would warrant a reasonable person in believing that he intended a real agreement. . . .

Whether the writing signed by the defendants and now sought to be enforced by the complainants was the result of a serious offer by Lucy and a serious acceptance by the defendants, or was a serious offer by Lucy and an acceptance in secret jest by the defendants, in either event it constituted a binding contract of sale between the parties. . . .

The complainants are entitled to have specific performance of the contract sued on. The decree appealed from is therefore reversed and the cause is remanded for the entry of a proper decree requiring the defendants to perform the contract in accordance with the prayer of the bill.

Reversed and remanded.

NOTES

(1) *Jesting and Bluffing.* What result if the price for the farm had been $50 rather than $50,000? In Keller v. Holderman, 11 Mich. 248 (1863), Holderman, as a

"frolic and banter," gave Keller a $300 check for a watch worth about $15. Holderman had no money in the bank and intended to insert a condition in the check rendering him not liable. This he neglected to do. Keller sued Holderman on the check and had judgment. Holderman appealed. *Held:* Reversed.

"When the Court below found as a fact that 'the whole transaction between the parties was a frolic and a banter, the plaintiff not expecting to sell, nor the defendant intending to buy the watch at the sum for which the check was drawn,' the conclusion should have been that no contract was ever made by the parties. . . ." How does this use of the price differ from that of a peppercorn discussed above at Note 4, p. 38?

Note that the Zehmers, in addition to contending that "the whole matter was a joke," contended that the writing "was prepared as a bluff or dare to force Lucy to admit that he did not have $50,000." What result if Lucy, knowing this, had "called their bluff" by raising the money from his brother? Should a distinction be made between jesting on the one hand, and bluffing or daring on the other?

(2) *The Right Stuff.* John Leonard watched a television commercial touting a range of items ("Pepsi Stuff") that consumers could acquire by redeeming "Pepsi Points" from specially marked packages of the soft-drink. The commercial showed a suburban high school student getting ready for school while using various items from the Pepsi collection, as the required number of Pepsi Points appeared in subtitles ("SHADES 175 PEPSI POINTS"; "LEATHER JACKET 1450 PEPSI POINTS"). The scene then switched to the student's school, as a Harrier jet came into view and landed next to a bike rack. The cockpit opened and the student stepped out, holding a Pepsi as the words "HARRIER JET 7,000,000 PEPSI POINTS" appeared on the screen. Leonard obtained an official order form from the Pepsi Stuff catalogue, which did not list the Harrier, and sent away for one Harrier Jet. He enclosed 15 Pepsi Points and a check for $700,000. (Pepsi permitted consumers to buy additional points for 10 cents a point.) Pepsi returned Leonard's check explaining that the "Harrier jet in the Pepsi commercial is fanciful and simply intended to create a humorous and entertaining ad." *Held*: For Pepsico.

Noting "the obvious absurdity of the commercial," the court held that "no objective person could reasonably have concluded that the commercial actually offered consumers a Harrier jet. . . . The commercial is the embodiment of what defendant [Pepsi] appropriately characterizes as 'zany humor.' " "In light of the Harrier Jet's well documented function in attacking and destroying surface and air targets, . . . depiction of such a jet as a way to get to school in the morning is clearly not serious. . . ." Leonard v. Pepsico, 88 F.Supp.2d 116, 129 (S.D.N.Y.1999) (Kimba Wood, J.).

Price also played a role in the decision. "The cost of a Harrier jet is roughly 23 million dollars, a fact of which plaintiff was aware. . . . Even if an objective, reasonable person were not aware of this fact, he would conclude that purchasing a fighter plane for $700,000 is a deal too good to be true." *Id.*

Do you agree? What result under the holding in *Lucy*? The case is discussed further at Note 2, p. 135 below, in connection with offers.

(3) *Proving Subjective Intent.* If a party's subjective intent is to play any role in contract law, how is that intent to be proved?

One way is to exalt the objective over the subjective. As Grant Gilmore explained, "If . . . the actual state of the parties' minds is relevant, then each litigated case must become an extended factual inquiry into what was 'intended,' 'meant,' 'believed,' and so on. If, however, we can restrict ourselves to the 'externals' (what the parties 'said' or 'did'), then the factual inquiry will be much simplified." Gilmore, *The Death of Contract* 42 (1974).

Contract law's preference for the objective has not, however, completely solved the problem of proof. Suppose, for example, that Lucy had actually known that the Zehmers were joking even though this was not objectively apparent. Does this mean that a witness's testimony as to intent simply goes unchallenged? A number of safeguards suggest that the answer is No. These include: the availability of pretrial discovery to reveal prior inconsistent statements or other such evidence; confidence in a jury's ability to discern when a witness is untruthful; and the fact that the person whose intent is at issue may well be a corporation or other organization leading to the possibility of conflicting sources of information regarding intent, such as testimony from disaffected former employees or email trails.

INTENT TO BE BOUND

The preceding materials suggest that a promisor may not be bound if the promise, whether from its content or the circumstances of its making, is insufficiently serious to indicate the promisor's intent to be bound. What other factors have made courts and, on occasion, legislatures reluctant to enforce a statement on the ground that no binding promise was intended? One area, touched upon in Chapter 1, concerns optimistic statements made by doctors to patients. See Notes, p. 3 above. In an omitted passage from Sullivan v. O'Connor, the court expressed concern that "patients may transform such statements into firm promises in their own minds...." Statements made for social purposes or among family members provide a second category in which the promisor may not have intended to make a legally enforceable promise.

In thinking further about the nature or quality of assent necessary to make a promise binding, consider Professor Edwin Patterson's suggestion that "A good legal rule as to the enforceability of promises should make contracting available to non-lawyers who will take the pains to clarify their ideas as to what they want to contract about; yet it should not make contracting so easy that it hooks the unwary signer or the casual promisor. The first may be called freedom *to* contract, the second, freedom *from* contract. These are, of course, counsels of perfection." Patterson, An Apology for Consideration, 58 Colum.L.Rev. 929, 958 (1959).[a] In proceeding through this book, look for instances in which courts have suppressed one of these freedoms. What instances have you encountered so far?

NOTES

(1) *Dining Together.* Should a court enforce a promise made for a social purpose, such as a promise to be a guest at a dinner party? Would it make a difference if the host had gone to considerable expense to make elaborate preparations in honor of the guest?

a. Edwin W. Patterson (1889–1965) practiced for fours years in Kansas City and then taught at Texas, Colorado, Iowa and Columbia. He was one of the Advisers for the Restatement of Restitution. Among his writings are books on contracts, insurance and jurisprudence, including four editions of the predecessor of this casebook.

What if the broken promise was one to marry and the plaintiff's expenses had included a wedding dress and the rental of a hall for the reception? See Ferraro v. Singh, 495 A.2d 946 (Pa.Super.1985). What result if the wedding expenditures were not allocated by tradition (bride pays), but by an express agreement? See DeFina v. Scott, 755 N.Y.S.2d 587 (Sup.Ct. N.Y.C. 2003).

(2) *Hunting Together.* Two friends, Mitzel and Hauck, went duck hunting in a car driven by Hauck. While taking a curve on a country road at 74 miles per hour, Hauck lost control and crashed the car, injuring Mitzel, who then sued Hauck. South Dakota law provides that "no person transported . . . as a guest" has a cause of action against the driver for negligence. Mitzel testified that he was not a guest: "I told him I would accompany him on this trip to look for ducks. I would take my time and go along on this trip and look for ducks on the agreement he would take the car." From a judgment for Hauck, plaintiff appealed. *Held*: For Hauck.

"It is not every agreement that results in a binding, legally enforceable contract. Neither party may intend the writing to be a contract; it must contemplate the assumption of legal rights and duties. . . . This is not to say . . . that contracts may not be implied in fact or in law . . . [Yet to] spell out a contract from this hunting trip of these young men . . . would 'transcend reality,' and transform this sport and similar social affairs to a new legal field. . . . It was not a commercial arrangement or one that removed [plaintiff] from his status as a guest." Mitzel v. Hauck, 105 N.W.2d 378, 380 (S.D.1960).

(3) *Living Together.* What effect should be given promises made between spouses or cohabitants? In Balfour v. Balfour, p. 33 above, the court denied the wife recovery on her husband's promise to pay her an allowance on the ground that such promises "are not contracts because the parties did not intend that they should be attended by legal consequences." This strict traditional view persists in a reluctance to enforce agreements between husband and wife, although it has been relaxed considerably.

As for unmarried couples, one court has said that "[o]rdinary contract principles are not suspended . . . for unmarried persons living together, whether or not they engage in sexual activity." Boland v. Catalano, 521 A.2d 142 (Conn.1987).

———

"GENTLEMEN'S AGREEMENTS"

Can the parties who have exchanged promises prevent courts from enforcing their agreements? Consider this question in connection with two significant situations where such "gentlemen's agreements" have been used.

One arises in "firm-commitment underwriting" of corporate stock, a transaction in which the corporate issuer sells an entire issue of stock outright to a group of underwriters, who in turn sell to a larger group of dealers, who then sell to the public. Under the Securities Act of 1933, a registration statement containing specified information about the stock, the issuer and the underwriters must be filed with the Securities and Exchange Commission before the stock is offered to either the dealers or the public. Before going to the substantial trouble and expense of preparing and printing a registration statement, the issuer wants some assurance of the availability of the underwriters. The underwriters, however, are not willing to make an enforceable promise to purchase the stock, since that would subject them to the risk of an adverse change in the market during the time before the registration statement takes effect. The solution has been found in having the underwriters write to the issuer a "letter of intent," which is then signed by the issuer, and which sets out, often in considerable detail, the terms of the proposed underwriting, but states that "no liability or obligation of any nature whatsoever is intended to be created as between any of the parties hereto." Such a clause was given effect in Dunhill Securities Corp. v. Microthermal Applications, Inc., 308 F.Supp. 195 (S.D.N.Y.1969).

Bonus and death benefit plans afford a second situation in which "gentlemen's agreements" are used. The employer may want to disclose the plan in order to take advantage of the resulting incentive, but may want to keep its administration within its uncontrolled discretion. In Mabley & Carew Co. v. Borden, 195 N.E. 697 (Ohio 1935), an employer gave an employee a certificate promising that a specified death benefit would be paid to her designated beneficiary if she was still employed at the time of her death, but stating that "it carries no legal obligation whatsoever or assurance or promise of future employment, and may be withdrawn or discontinued at any time by this Company." The court held that, in spite of this language, the employer was liable to the beneficiary. Why should this language be treated differently from that of the "letter of intent"? Cf. Spooner v. Reserve Life Ins. Co., 287 P.2d 735 (Wash.1955), distinguishing bonus plans from death benefit plans. See generally Wendell Holmes, The Freedom Not to Contract, 60 Tul.L.Rev. 751 (1986).

"FORMAL CONTRACT CONTEMPLATED"

Not infrequently, particularly following complex negotiations, parties agree on what they consider to be the essential terms of a contract and leave details to be worked out, often by their lawyers, in connection with the preparation of a final, formal document that they expect to sign. If one of the parties then refuses to sign the formal document, can the other enforce their agreement?

The answer may depend on whether the parties intended to conclude their agreement earlier. As to that, and how to determine their intent, see Consarc Corp. v. Marine Midland Bank, N.A., 996 F.2d 568, 570 (2d Cir.1993). "The tension between the concepts—contract arises upon meeting of the minds, no binding contract absent a writing—has resulted in courts struggling to resolve these inherently conflicting notions. From this judicial effort have evolved two widely-accepted common law principles: (a) that absent an expressed intent that no contract shall exist, mutual assent between the parties, even though oral or informal, to exchange acts or promises is sufficient to create a binding contract; and (b) that to avoid the obligation of a binding contract, at least one of the parties must express an intention not to be bound until a writing is executed."

In Winston v. Mediafare Entertainment Corp., 777 F.2d 78 (2d Cir. 1985), the court listed "several factors that help determine whether the parties intended to be bound in the absence of a document executed by both sides." These factors are: "(1) whether there has been an express reservation of the right not to be bound in the absence of a writing; (2) whether there has been partial performance of the contract; (3) whether all of the terms of the alleged contract have been agreed upon; and (4) whether the agreement at issue is the type of contract that is usually committed to writing." Despite such guidance, cases involving this question are frequently before the courts.

NOTES

(1) *Open Terms.* For a further treatment of the factors in *Winston,* see Teachers Ins. & Annuity Ass'n v. Tribune Co., discussed on p. 239 below. The court distinguished two types of binding agreements yet to be memorialized. In one, there are both agreed and open terms and the parties are bound to "negotiate the open terms in good faith toward a final contract incorporating the agreed terms." How does this distinction affect the third factor listed in *Winston?* Some courts have sought to distinguish between open terms that are "deal breakers" and those that are not. See A/S Apothekernes Laboratorium v. I.M.C. Chemical, 873 F.2d 155 (7th Cir.1989). How might a party make certain, throughout negotiations, that every open term is a deal breaker? See Budget Marketing, Inc. v. Centronics Corp., 927 F.2d 421 (8th Cir.1991).

(2) *Of Oil and Honor.* The most celebrated of the cases about "formal contract contemplated" concerned a so-called "handshake deal" between the Pennzoil Company and the Getty Oil Company. Getty, having negotiated a sale of stock to Pennzoil, refused to perform and sold the stock to Texaco, Inc. Pennzoil's first legal sally was an attempt to charge Getty with breach of contract in Delaware. When that failed, Pennzoil shifted its ground to Texas and sued Texaco there for interfering with the alleged Getty contract. This action produced a verdict against Texaco for $10.53 billion and (after much maneuvering, including a reduction of $2 billion in the jury's punitive-damage award and a visit to the Supreme Court of the United States) led to Texaco's bankruptcy. Its bankruptcy petition was designed to effectuate a $3 billion settlement agreement between the parties. For a description of the Pennzoil–Getty dealings see Texaco, Inc. v. Pennzoil Co., 729 S.W.2d 768 (Tex.App.1987). See also T. Petzinger, Oil and Honor: The Texaco–Pennzoil Wars (1987).

(3) *Ethics in Educating a Client.* When a party's intent is key to a determination regarding formation, how is a lawyer to ascertain a client's state of mind at the earlier time? It is popular wisdom that a client's report regarding intent may be influenced by what the client knows of the law. Hence there are situations in which it is at least questionable for a lawyer to give legal advice "to assist his client in developing evidence relevant to the [client's] state of mind." See Code of Professional Responsibility (Ethical Consideration 7–6). Precepts issued by the American Bar Association emphasize, however, that a lawyer *may* properly assist a client in that way, and "may discuss the legal consequences of any proposed course of conduct with a client." Rule 1.2(d) of the Model Rules of Professional Conduct.

For a colloquy on the question "whether it is proper to give your client legal advice when you have reason to believe that the knowledge you give him will tempt him to commit perjury," see Monroe Freedman, Professional Responsibility of the Criminal Defense Lawyer: The Three Hardest Questions, 64 Mich.L.Rev. 1469, 1478–82 (1966), and John Noonan, The Purposes of Advocacy and the Limits of Confidentiality, 64 Mich.L.Rev. 1485, 1488 (1966). In a later book, Prof. Freedman conceded that there comes a point where "nothing less than 'brute rationalization' can purport to justify a conclusion that the lawyer is seeking in good faith to elicit truth rather than actively participating in the creation of perjury." Freedman, *Lawyers' Ethics in an Adversary System* 73, 75 (1975).

Although the problem has drawn attention chiefly in connection with defense preparations in criminal matters, in which intent is often a critical fact, counsel's explanation of the law might also bear on a client's recollection regarding contract formation. Recall Mitzel, Note 2, p. 123 above, who testified that he went duck hunting "on the agreement" that his friend would drive.

Whether or not a contract has been formed often depends on choosing between conflicting accounts of a conversation. Recall the conflicting testimony in Lucy v. Zehmer. Does the decision in that case ease or intensify qualms that lawyers may have about educating their clients about contract law?

SECTION 2. THE OFFER

The process by which the parties arrive at a bargain varies widely according to the circumstances. It is common to assume that it involves two distinct steps: first, an offer by one party and, second, an acceptance by the other. In practice, the process of contract formation is often more complicated and muddled. "[H]owever suited [the rules of offer and acceptance] may have been to the measured cadence of contracting in the nineteenth century, they have little to say about the complex processes that lead to major deals today.... During the negotiation of such deals there is often no offer or counter-offer for either party to accept, but rather a gradual process in which agreements are reached piecemeal in several 'rounds' with a succession of drafts.... When the ultimate agreement is reached, it is often expected that it will be embodied in a document or documents that will be exchanged by the parties at a closing...." Farnsworth, Precontractual Liability and Preliminary Agreements: Fair Dealing and Failed Negotiations, 87 Colum.L.Rev. 217, 219 (1987). The UCC addresses the issue explicitly in section 2–204: "An agreement sufficient to make a contract for sale may be found even though the moment of its making is undetermined."

Nonetheless, it is useful at least to begin with the assumption of a clear offer followed by a clear acceptance.

What then is an offer? Corbin gave this answer: "An offer is ... an act whereby one person confers upon another the power to create contractual relations between them.... It must be an act that leads the offeree reasonably to believe that a power to create a contract is conferred upon him.... It is on this ground that we must exclude invitations to deal or acts of mere preliminary negotiation, and acts *evidently* done in jest or without intent to create legal relations. All these are acts that do not lead others reasonably to believe that they are empowered 'to close the contract.'" Corbin, Offer and Acceptance, and Some of The Resulting Legal Relations, 26 Yale L.J. 169, 181–82 (1917). See also Restatement § 24. It may be helpful to keep Corbin's view in mind as you read the next three cases.

Owen v. Tunison

Supreme Judicial Court of Maine, 1932.
131 Me. 42, 158 A. 926.

Action by W.H. Owen against R.G. Tunison for breach of contract.

■ BARNES, J. This case is reported to the law court, and such judgment is to be rendered as the law and the admissible evidence require.

Plaintiff charges that defendant agreed in writing to sell him the Bradley block and lot, situated in Bucksport, for a stated price in cash, that he later refused to perfect the sale, and that plaintiff, always willing and ready to pay the price, has suffered loss on account of defendant's unjust refusal to sell, and claims damages.

From the record it appears that defendant, a resident of Newark N.J., was, in the fall of 1929, the owner of the Bradley block and lot.

With the purpose of purchasing, on October 23, 1929, plaintiff wrote the following letter:

"Dear Mr. Tunison:

"Will you sell me your store property which is located on Main St. in Bucksport, Me. running from Montgomery's Drug Store on one corner to a Grocery Store on the other, for the sum of $6,000.00?"

Nothing more of this letter need be quoted.

On December 5, following, plaintiff received defendant's reply apparently written in Cannes, France, on November 12, and it reads:

"In reply to your letter of Oct. 23rd which has been forwarded to me in which you inquire about the Bradley Block, Bucksport, Me.

"Because of improvements which have been added and an expenditure of several thousand dollars it would not be possible for me to sell it unless I was to receive $16,000.00 cash.

"The upper floors have been converted into apartments with baths and the b'l'dg put into first class condition.

"Very truly yours,
"[Signed] R.G. Tunison."

Whereupon, and at once, plaintiff sent to defendant, and the latter received, in France, the following message:

"Accept your offer for Bradley block Bucksport Terms sixteen thousand cash send deed to Eastern Trust and Banking Co Bangor Maine Please acknowledge."

Four days later he was notified that defendant did not wish to sell the property, and on the 14th day of January following brought suit for his damages.

Granted that damages may be due a willing buyer if the owner refuses to tender a deed of real estate, after the latter has made an offer in writing to sell to the former, and such offer has been so accepted, it remains for us to point out that defendant here is not shown to have written to plaintiff an offer to sell.

There can have been no contract for the sale of the property desired, no meeting of the minds of the owner and prospective purchaser, unless there was an offer or proposal of sale. It cannot be successfully argued that defendant made any offer or proposal of sale.

In a recent case the words, "Would not consider less than half" is held "not to be taken as an outright offer to sell for one-half." Sellers v. Warren, 116 Me. 350, 102 A. 40, 41.

Where an owner of millet seed wrote, "I want $2.25 per cwt. for this seed f.o.b. Lowell," in an action for damages for alleged breach of contract to sell at the figure quoted above, the court held: "He [defendant] does not say, 'I offer to sell to you.' The language used is general, and such as may be used in an advertisement, or circular addressed generally to those engaged in the seed business, and is not an offer by which he may be bound, if accepted, by any or all of the persons addressed." Nebraska Seed Co. v. Harsh, 98 Neb. 89, 152 N.W. 310, 311, and cases cited in note L.R.A. 1915F, 824.

Defendant's letter of December 5 in response to an offer of $6,000 for his property may have been written with the intent to open negotiations that might lead to a sale. It was not a proposal to sell.

Judgment for defendant.

NOTE

Offer v. Non-offer. In his letter of November 12, did Tunison indicate an intention to empower Owen "to close the contract"? Consider the language "it would not be possible for me to sell it unless I were to receive $16,000 cash." Was the problem in the statement a matter of the price or of Tunison's intent to sell or both? What result if Tunison had said, "I will sell for $16,000"? What if he had said, "I will not entertain an offer for less than $16,000"? Could Tunison have expected Owen to respond with an offer of more than $16,000? If your answer is No, was it not reasonable for Owen to infer that he could close the deal by acceding to that price?

PROBLEM

Neighborly Buy-out. In May, Joseph Oliver spoke individually to several neighbors about his plans to dispose of his ranch. On June 13, one of them, J.W. Southworth who Oliver knew had long wanted to buy the property, asked Oliver if his plans for selling "continued to be in force." Oliver responded that he expected soon to be able to put a price on the property. Southworth then said that he had the money available, that Oliver "didn't have to worry," and that "everything was ready to go." Four days later, Oliver sent a letter to four neighbors, including Southworth, enclosing "the information that I had discussed with you," as follows:

> Selling [ranch as described] at the assessed market value of . . . $324,419.
> Terms available—29% down—balance over 5 years at 8% interest. Negotiate sale date for December 1, 1976 or January 1, 1977. . . .

Has Oliver made an offer to sell his ranch? See Southworth v. Oliver, 587 P.2d 994 (Or.1978). Assume that his letter began: "I am sending this letter to you and three other neighbors." Develop reasoning that is based on that sentence and that leads to this conclusion: None of the recipients could have understood, reasonably, that the letter was an offer. See Southworth v. Oliver, 587 P.2d 994 (Or.1978).

———

HARVEY v. FACEY, [1893] A.C. 552 (Privy Council) (Jamaica). [Harvey and another, solicitors in Kingston, were interested in a piece of property known as Bumper Hall Pen. Facey, the owner, had been engaged in negotiations for its sale to the town of Kingston for £ 900. Harvey telegraphed Facey, who was on a journey, "Will you sell us Bumper Hall Pen? Telegraph lowest cash price—answer paid." Facey replied by telegram, "Lowest price for Bumper Hall Pen £ 900." Harvey answered, "We agree to buy Bumper Hall Pen for the sum of nine hundred pounds asked by you." Harvey sued for specific performance of this agreement and for an injunction to restrain the town of Kingston from taking a conveyance of the property. The trial court dismissed the action on the ground that the agreement did not disclose a concluded contract; the Supreme Court of Jamaica reversed; the defendants appealed to the Judicial Committee of the Privy Council.]

■ LORD MORRIS. . . . [T]heir Lordships concur in the judgment of Mr. Justice Curran that there was no concluded contract between the appellants and L.M. Facey to be collected from the aforesaid telegrams. The first telegram asks two questions. The first question is as to the willingness of L.M. Facey to sell to the appellants [i.e. Harvey]; the second question asks the lowest price, and the word "telegraph" is in its collocation addressed to that second question only. L.M. Facey replied to the second question only, and gives his lowest price. The third telegram from the appellants treats the answer of L.M. Facey stating his lowest price as an unconditional offer to sell to them at the price named. Their Lordships cannot treat the telegram from L.M. Facey as binding him in any respect, except to the extent it does by its term, viz., the lowest price. Everything else is left open, and the reply telegram from the appellants cannot be treated as an acceptance of an offer to sell to them; it is an offer that required to be accepted by L.M. Facey. The contract could only be completed if L.M. Facey had accepted the appellants' last telegram. It has been contended for the appellants that L.M. Facey's telegram should be read as saying "yes" to the first question put in the appellants' telegram, but there is nothing to support that contention. L.M. Facey's telegram gives a precise answer to a precise question, viz., the price. The contract must appear by the telegrams, whereas the appellants are obliged to contend that an acceptance of the first question is to be implied. Their Lordships are of opinion that the mere statement of the lowest price at which the vendor would sell contains no implied contract to sell at that price to the persons making the inquiry. . . . [Reversed and the judgment of the trial court restored.]

NOTES

(1) *More Analysis of Communications.* Is it significant that Harvey presumably knew that he was not the only potential buyer for Bumper Hall Pen? What result if

Harvey's first telegram had read, "What is the lowest price at which you will sell me Bumper Hall Pen?" Redraft Facey's telegram so that it clearly would have been an offer.

(2) *Addressee of Offer.* Generally, an offer can be accepted only by the person the offeror has invited to furnish the consideration. Although one might expect this principle to have frequent application, as when an offer is addressed to an enterprise that may have changed its corporate identity, in fact, there are few cases exemplifying the principle. Why might that be so?

In a 19th–century case, Boulton, the manager of a leather "pipe hose" business, bought out the owner, Brocklehurst. Later on the same day a regular customer named Jones, who had a running account with Brocklehurst, sent him an order for merchandise. Boulton received the order and supplied the goods without notifying Jones of the change of ownership. When Jones refused to pay, Boulton sued for the price. *Held:* for Jones. "When a contract is made, in which the personality of the contracting party is or may be of importance, as a contract with a man to write a book, or the like, or where there might be a setoff, no other person can interpose and adopt the contract." Boulton v. Jones, 157 Eng.Rep. 232 (1857) (Exchequer Chamber) (Bramwell, B.).

Was the personality of Brocklehurst likely to be of importance in this transaction? In sales transactions generally?

PROBLEM

Cats and Dogs. Dr. Johnson, president of the All Pet Animal Clinic, wrote the following letter to Dr. Hopper, an employee:

> I have learned that you are considering leaving us to take over the small animal part of Dr. Meeboer's practice in Laramie.

> When we negotiated the terms of your employment, we agreed that you could leave upon 30 days' notice, but that you would not practice small animal medicine within five miles of Laramie for a three-year period.

> I am willing to release you from the non-competition agreement in return for a cash buy-out. I have worked back from the proportion of the income of All–Pet which you contribute and have decided that a reasonable figure would be $40,000, to compensate the practice for the loss of business which will happen if you practice small-animal medicine elsewhere in Laramie.

> If you are willing to approach the problem in the way I suggest, please let me know and I will have the appropriate paperwork taken care of.

Is this letter an offer? See Hopper v. All Pet Animal Clinic, 861 P.2d 531, p. 557 below.

Fairmount Glass Works v. Crunden–Martin Woodenware Co.

Court of Appeals of Kentucky, 1899.
106 Ky. 659, 51 S.W. 196.

Action by the Crunden–Martin Woodenware Company against the Fairmount Glass Works to recover damages for breach of contract. Judgment for plaintiff, and defendant appeals. Affirmed.

■ HOBSON, J. On April 20, 1895, appellee wrote appellant the following letter:

"St. Louis, Mo., April 20, 1895. Gentlemen: Please advise us the lowest price you can make us on our order for ten car loads of Mason green jars, complete, with caps, packed one dozen in a case, either delivered here, or f.o.b. cars your place, as you prefer. State terms and cash discount. Very truly, Crunden–Martin W.W. Co."

To this letter appellant answered as follows:

"Fairmount, Ind. April 23, 1895. Crunden–Martin Wooden Ware Co., St. Louis, Mo.—Gentlemen: Replying to your favor of April 20, we quote you Mason fruit jars, complete, in one-dozen boxes, delivered in East St. Louis, Ill.: Pints, $4.50, quarts, $5.00, half gallons, $6.50 per gross, for immediate acceptance, and shipment not later than May 15, 1895; sixty days' acceptance,[a] or 2 off, cash in ten days. Yours truly, Fairmount Glass Works.

"Please note that we make all quotations and contracts subject to the contingencies of agencies or transportation delays or accidents beyond our control."

For reply thereto, appellee sent the following telegram on April 24, 1895:

"Fairmount Glass Works, Fairmount, Ind.: Your letter twenty-third received. Enter order ten car loads as per your quotation. Specifications mailed. Crunden–Martin W.W. Co."

In response to this telegram, appellant sent the following:

"Fairmount, Ind., April 24, 1895. Crunden–Martin W.W. Co., St. Louis, Mo.: Impossible to book your order. Output all sold. See letter. Fairmount Glass Works."

Appellee insists that, by its telegram sent in answer to the letter of April 23d, the contract was closed for the purchase of 10 car loads of Mason fruit jars. Appellant insists that the contract was not closed by this telegram, and that it had the right to decline to fill the order at the time it sent its telegram of April 24. This is the chief question in the case. The court below gave judgment in favor of appellee, and appellant has appealed, earnestly insisting that the judgment is erroneous.

We are referred to a number of authorities holding that a quotation of prices is not an offer to sell, in the sense that a completed contract will arise out of the giving of an order for merchandise in accordance with the proposed terms. There are a number of cases holding that the transaction is not completed until the order so made is accepted. 7 Am. & Eng.Enc.Law (2d Ed.) p. 138; Smith v. Gowdy, 8 Allen, Mass., 566; Beaupre v. Telegraph Co., 21 Minn. 155. But each case must turn largely upon the language there used. In this case we think there was more than a quotation of prices, although appellant's letter uses the word "quote" in stating the prices

a. In this context the word "acceptance" is not used to denote a response to an offer. Rather, here it refers to a form of commitment used to assure payment in sixty days.

given. The true meaning of the correspondence must be determined by reading it as a whole. Appellee's letter of April 20th, which began the transaction, did not ask for a quotation of prices. It reads: "Please advise us the lowest price you can make us on our order for ten carloads of Mason green jars.... State terms and cash discount." From this appellant could not fail to understand that appellee wanted to know at what price it would sell ten car loads of these jars; so when, in answer, it wrote: "We quote you Mason fruit jars ... pints $4.50, quarts $5.00, half gallons $6.50, per gross, for immediate acceptance; ... 2 off, cash in ten days,"—it must be deemed as intending to give appellee the information it asked for. We can hardly understand what is meant by the words "for immediate acceptance," unless the latter was intended as a proposition to sell at these prices if accepted immediately. In construing every contract, the aim of the court is to arrive at the intention of the parties. In none of the cases to which we have been referred on behalf of appellant was there on the face of the correspondence any such expression of intention to make an offer to sell on the terms indicated.... The expression in appellant's letter, "for immediate acceptance," taken in connection with appellee's letter, in effect, at what price it would sell it the goods, is, it seems to us, much stronger evidence of a present offer, which, when accepted immediately, closed the contract. Appellee's letter was plainly an inquiry for the price and terms on which appellant would sell it the goods, and appellant's answer to it was not a quotation of prices, but a definite offer to sell on the terms indicated, and could not be withdrawn after the terms had been accepted.

[The court quoted further from Crunden–Martin's telegram of April 24 and a letter in which it gave "specifications": shipment not later than May 15; first carload to contain 55 gross quart jars and other specified quantities of pint and half-gallon jars; and "The jars and caps to be strictly first-quality goods." Referring to the latter expression, Fairmount observed that it was not in its offer of April 23, and contended that, because the offer had not been "accepted as made", Fairmount was not bound. The court observed that this objection came late in the day. The court further stated: "Crunden–Martin offers proof tending to show that these words, in the trade in which parties were engaged, conveyed the same meaning as the words used in Fairmount's letter and were only a different form of expressing the same idea. Fairmount's conduct would seem to confirm this evidence." (In this quotation the parties' names have been substituted for "appellant" and "appellee.")]

Appellant also insists that the contract was indefinite, because the quantity of each size of the jars was not fixed, that ten car loads is too indefinite a specification of the quantity sold, and that appellee had no right to accept the goods to be delivered on different days. The proof shows that "ten car loads" is an expression used in the trade as equivalent to 1,000 gross, 100 gross being regarded as a car load. The offer to sell the different sizes at different prices gave the purchaser the right to name the quantity of each size, and, the offer being to ship not later than May 15th, the buyer had the right to fix the time of delivery at any time before that.... The petition, if defective, was cured by the judgment, which is fully sustained by the evidence.

Judgment affirmed.

NOTES

(1) *The Fairmount Letter.* Suppose that Fairmount's letter of April 23 had not been in response to a preliminary letter from Crunden–Martin. Would the result have been the same? What significance should be attached to the use of the expression "we quote you" in the Fairmount letter? What facts make "quote" mean "offer"?

(2) *The Salt–Trade Case.* Consider the foregoing questions in relation to the decision in Moulton v. Kershaw, 18 N.W. 172 (Wis.1884). Kershaw wrote to Moulton:

> In consequence of a rupture in the salt trade we are authorized to offer Michigan fine salt in full car load lots of 80 to 95 barrels, delivered at your city at 85 cents per barrel to be shipped per C. & N.W.R.R. Co. only. At this price it is a bargain as the price in general remains unchanged. Shall be pleased to receive your order.

Moulton immediately wired Kershaw, "Your letter of yesterday received and noted. You may ship me two thousand barrels Michigan fine salt as offered in your letter." Kershaw failed to ship the salt, and Moulton sued for breach of contract. The trial court overruled Kershaw's demurrer and Kershaw appealed. *Held:* Reversed. "The language is not such as a business man would use in making an offer to sell ... a definite amount of property." Moulton v. Kershaw, 18 N.W. 172 (Wis.1884).

Suppose Kershaw's communication to Moulton had read, "we are authorized to offer one to twenty-five carloads Michigan fine salt," etc. Would the result have been different? What would be the objection to construing Kershaw's communication as an offer to sell any reasonable quantity of salt—say one to twenty-five car load lots—leaving it to the offeree to name the precise quantity? Has not Kershaw committed himself in advance to supply any reasonable quantity? What result if Kershaw's communication had read, "we are authorized to offer you all the Michigan fine salt you will order," etc.?

ADVERTISEMENTS AS OFFERS

Proposals are sometimes addressed to a very wide audience. Advertisements by sellers to the general public provide a familiar example. Are such proposals offers? The general rule is that an advertisement is not an offer, but rather an invitation by the seller to the buyer to make an offer to purchase.

What about reward notices, which are also typically made to a general audience? Do they empower the offeree to "close the contract," in Corbin's phrase? What does Broadnax v. Ledbetter, discussed on p. 66 above, suggest?

If advertisements were held to be offers, what would be a store's position if the demand for its advertised wares exceeded its supply? Might the problem of unexpected demand be solved if sellers were required to have on hand a reasonable supply of advertised merchandise? Another solution might require "first come, first served" to be read into every advertisement. This appears to be the approach of French law, under which "the great majority of authorities consider such a proposal to be an offer, even if it can be accepted only by one of those to whom it is addressed. But such an offer is subject to the condition, as to each offeree, that it has not already been accepted by a quicker-acting offeree." 1 Rudolf B. Schlesinger (ed.), *Formation of Contracts: A Study of the Common Core of Legal Systems* 359 (1968). Which approach do you prefer? Which better protects the parties' expectations?

Whether an advertisement can *ever* be an offer is considered in the next case.

———

LEFKOWITZ v. GREAT MINNEAPOLIS SURPLUS STORE, 86 N.W.2d 689 (Minn.1957). [The Great Minneapolis Surplus Store published the following advertisement in a Minneapolis newspaper:

> Saturday 9 a.m.
> 2 Brand New Pastel
> Mink 3–Skin Scarfs
> Selling for $89.50
> Out they go
> Saturday, Each $1.00
>
> 1 Black Lapin Stole ...
> Beautiful,
> worth $139.50 ...... $1.00
> First Come
> First Served [a]

Lefkowitz was the first to present himself on Saturday and demanded the Lapin stole for one dollar. The store refused to sell to him because of a "house rule" that the offer was intended for women only. Lefkowitz sued the store and was awarded $138.50 as damages. The store appealed.]

■ Murphy, Justice.... On the facts before us we are concerned with whether the advertisement constituted an offer, and, if so, whether the plaintiff's conduct constituted an acceptance. There are numerous authori-

a. The text of the ad appeared as one of scores of boxed items in a full-page ad featuring widely varying type sizes. A snippet from the page, somewhat reduced in size, is reproduced here:

ties which hold that a particular advertisement in a newspaper or circular letter relating to a sale of articles may be construed by the court as constituting an offer, acceptance of which would complete a contract.... The test of whether a binding obligation may originate in advertisements addressed to the general public is "whether the facts show that some performance was promised in positive terms in return for something requested." 1 Williston, Contracts (rev. ed.) § 27. The authorities above cited emphasize that, where the offer is clear, definite and explicit, and leaves nothing open for negotiation, it constitutes an offer, acceptance of which will complete the contract.... Whether in any individual instance a newspaper advertisement is an offer rather than an invitation to make an offer depends on the legal intention of the parties and the surrounding circumstances.... We are of the view on the facts before us that the offer by the defendant of the sale of the Lapin fur was clear, definite, and explicit, and left nothing open for negotiation.... The defendant contends that the offer was modified by a "house rule" to the effect that only women were qualified to receive the bargains advertised. The advertisement contained no such restriction. This objection may be disposed of briefly by stating that, while an advertiser has the right at any time before acceptance to modify his offer, he does not have the right, after acceptance, to impose new or arbitrary conditions not contained in the published offer....

Affirmed.

NOTES

(1) *More Facts.* The store's advertisement was actually the second one by the store to which Lefkowitz had responded. The first, published a week earlier, was: "3 Brand New Fur Coats Worth to $100.00/First Come First Served/$1 Each." To Lefkowitz's claim based on that ad the court answered that the ad was not an offer because the word "to" made the value of the coats "speculative and uncertain." This ruling is criticized in Ian Ayres and Robert Gertner, Filling Gaps in Incomplete Contracts: An Economic Theory of Default Rules, 99 Yale L.J. 87, 105–106 (1989).

On the first occasion the Store had also refused to sell to Lefkowitz, saying that by a "house rule" the offer was intended for women only; sales would not be made to men. Considering this additional fact (and putting aside questions of discrimination), do you agree with the court's decision that he could recover under the second advertisement?

(2) *Case Comparison.* In Leonard v. Pepsico, described at Note 2, p. 121, the would-be purchaser of the Harrier jet, relying on *Lefkowitz*, argued that the Pepsi Stuff television commercial was an offer. The court held it was not: "First, the commercial cannot be regarded in itself as sufficiently definite, because it specifically reserved the details of the offer to a separate writing, the Catalog.[1] The commercial itself made no mention of the steps a potential offeree would be required to take to accept the alleged offer of a Harrier Jet. The advertisement in *Lefkowitz*, in contrast, 'identified the person who could accept.' Second, even if the Catalog had included a Harrier Jet among the items that could be obtained by redemption of Pepsi Points, the absence of any words of limitation such as 'first

---

1. It also communicated additional words of reservation: "Offer not available in all areas. See details on specially marked packages."

come, first served,' renders the alleged offer sufficiently indefinite that no contract could be formed." 88 F.Supp.2d at 124.

(3) *Consumer Protection.* In Geismar v. Abraham & Strauss, 439 N.Y.S.2d 1005 (Dist.Ct.1981), a disappointed shopper sued a department store that had advertised a set of china dishes regularly priced at $280 for only $39.95, but had refused to sell them at that price. The court held that since the advertisement was not an offer, there was no breach of contract. But it went on to hold that she could recover $50 under a New York statute providing that any person "injured" by advertising "which is misleading in a material respect" is entitled to recover actual damages or $50, whichever is greater. Many other states have enacted laws dealing with false advertising, such as the Uniform Deceptive Trade Practices Act. In addition, Section 5 of the Federal Trade Commission Act (15 U.S.C. § 45) declares "unfair or deceptive acts or practices" to be unlawful as a matter of federal law.

Consumers may also be protected by bait-and-switch legislation that makes unlawful "the disparagement by acts or words of the advertised product" and "the failure to have available ... a sufficient quantity of the advertised product to meet reasonably anticipated demands, unless the advertisement clearly and adequately discloses that supply is limited...." 16 C.F.R. 238.3.

(4) *Competitive Bidding.* A contracting party may fix the contract price, leave it to negotiation, or determine it by competitive bidding. A party who chooses to determine it by competitive bidding may invite open bids at an auction, as is often done in the sale of goods or land, or may invite sealed bids, as is common in the letting of building contracts.

If a party invites competitive bids, is this an offer to be accepted by the highest bidder when the bid is made? Or is it merely an invitation for offers by bids that can then be accepted or rejected by the one who has invited them? The law has taken the latter view, that it is the bidder who makes the offer. Can you see why? This is the general rule stated in UCC § 2–328 with respect to the sale of goods by auction. Under that section the auctioneer may, however, make an offer by advertising the sale to be "without reserve." Note that if the sale is "without reserve," the auctioneer is bound not to withdraw after a bid is made, but the bidder is not similarly bound. Local statutes may also govern auction sales.

The rather elaborate provisions of UCC § 2–328 are, of course, expressly applicable only to the sale of goods. UCC § 2–102. Might they be extended by analogy to the sale of land? Comment 1 to UCC § 1–103 considers that possibility: "The courts have often recognized that the policies embodied in an act are applicable in reason to subject-matter that was not expressly included in the language of the act ... and did the same where reason and policy so required, even where the subject-matter had been intentionally excluded from the act in general.... Nothing in the Uniform Commercial Code stands in the way of the continuance of such action by the courts." See Chevalier v. Town of Sanford, 475 A.2d 1148 (Me.1984), a land auction case in which the court reasoned by analogy to UCC § 2–328.

Although UCC § 2–328 describes a sale by auction as "complete when the auctioneer so announces by the fall of the hammer or in other customary manner," thousands of auctions daily are now concluded with a click rather than a hammer, as buyers bid on on-line auction websites such as e-Bay. Millions of auctions can be found at any time on that and other sites, governed by a set of rules that bidders and sellers agree to as a condition of using the site.

PROBLEM

The Midas Touch. In 1985, as part of the Liberty–Ellis Island Commemorative Coin Act, the United States Mint produced a limited run of 500,000 gold five dollar coins. Announcements were sent to lists of coin collectors, who were informed that "[i]f the Mint receives your reservation by December 31, 1985, you will enjoy a favorable Pre–Issue Discount saving you up to 16% on your coins." The Mint received over 756,000 orders, and a number of buyers were sorely disappointed when their order forms were returned. (The court noted that many buyers "developed a more serious case of disappointment when it became apparent that the gold coins had increased in value by approximately 200% with the first months of 1986.") Two such buyers, Mary and Anthony Mesaros, sued for breach of contract, arguing that their order forms ("YES, please accept my order for the U.S. Liberty Coins I have indicated. I understand that all sales are final. Verification of my order will be made by the Department of Treasury, US Mint . . .") were acceptances of the Mint's advertised offer. Did the Mesaros have a contract with the United States? See Mesaros v. United States, 845 F.2d 1576, 1578 (Fed.Cir.1988).

CONSTRUCTION CONTRACTS

Construction contracts are the last of the "typical categories" of cases highlighted here. Given the construction industry's significant role in the economy, such agreements are of great importance. In consequence, disputes arising from construction contracts often result in litigation. The resulting opinions, including that in the next case, are an important source of the common law of contracts. The complexity of the typical transaction, with a general contractor perched between an owner and a subcontractor, invites sophisticated analysis that is often useful by analogy in other transactions involving intermediaries, such as brokers or middlemen. See Note 2, p. 463.

Some of the most intractable disputes in construction contracts involve claims of improper performance. This is not surprising given the length of time required to build a particular project and the difficulty of complying with the details of plans and specifications; such claims are dealt with in later chapters. We begin with offer and acceptance, which, for major construction projects, typically involve a bidding process in which general contractors compete with each other by submitting bids that are in turn based on bids received from subcontractors, who also compete with each other. Bidding is particularly common, as in the following case between a contractor and a school district, when the construction is for a branch of government rather than a private landowner. Government construction contracts are often subject to additional statutory requirements concerned with such policy issues as fiscal responsibility to taxpayers; see discussion on p. 463.

MISTAKEN BIDS

The next case involves the not uncommon situation of a contractor who has made an error in a bid submitted on a project. It is not hard to understand why mistakes occur with some regularity in construction bids. Not only must the contractor solicit, select, and coordinate bids from multiple subcontractors across the building trades in exact compliance with the owner's specifications, but, as the following excerpt explains, the entire process occurs within a short and frequently pressured time frame:

"Subcontractor and supplier bidders may fear that their bids will be undercut by their competition, so they often wait to submit their bids until the last hour or two before the general contractor's bid is due. Frequently, a subcontractor or materialman will discover after submitting his bid that he has made a mistake, perhaps because one of the general contractors informs him that he is either substantially higher or substantially lower than other bidders. He must then frantically review the plans (if he still has access to them), correct his mistake, and telephone his corrected price to all concerned.

"While this last-minute subcontractor bidding is being received, the general contractor is collating and comparing the prices and the qualifying restrictions that he has received, adding in factors for his own workforce and supervision, and adjusting the total as later prices are received by phone. His final bid will probably be typed on the bid form while he stands impatiently over the typewriter with car keys in hand, hoping that traffic will not delay him on his way to the bid opening. When he arrives at the appointed place with his sealed bid envelope, he may make a quick call to his office to learn whether any substantial price cuts were received after he left. If any were, he will have to decide quickly whether he can risk using the lower price (Is it a mistake? Does he believe the subcontractor can perform?), or whether he can still be competitive if he decides not to use the lower price. If he decides to use it, he may write on the outside of his bid envelope 'Deduct X dollars' and he will be bound by that writing as a reduction of the enclosed bid." Comment, The Subcontractor's Bid: An Option Contract Arising Through Promissory Estoppel, 34 Emory L.J. 421, 425–28 (1985).

Contractors sometimes shop around among the subcontractors to secure a lower price. The construction industry regards such "bid shopping" with opprobrium, whether it occurs before or after the award. Subcontractors regard it with particular distaste when it occurs after the successful general contractor's bargaining position has been strengthened by the award.

One objection to bid shopping is that it results in an undesirable decrease in competition, because subcontractors will pad their bids so that they can lower them later when bid shopping occurs, inflating the general contractor's bid to the ultimate disadvantage of the owner. Is this objection convincing if, as the excerpt suggests, there is a countervailing tendency among general contractors to discount their estimates on subcontractor's bids in anticipation of bid shopping?

An opposing objection is that bid shopping results in an undesirable *increase* in competition—that subcontractors will be driven to bid so low (bid-chopping) that they will be operating at a loss and tempted to use substandard work and materials, again to the ultimate disadvantage of the owner. Is this risk greater in the construction industry than in other areas of the economy?

An owner may combat post-award bid shopping by requiring that general contractors list their prospective subcontractors in their bids. This requirement has been more common, however, in government than in private contracts. Why do not more private owners require listing if bid shopping is to their ultimate disadvantage? Subcontractors, whose self-interest is clearer, have attempted to combat bid shopping by organizing themselves into "bid depositories," although such concerted efforts raise problems under the antitrust laws. They have also tried to combat pre-award bid shopping by waiting until the last possible moment to submit their bids. The resulting haste with which the general contractor must then prepare its own bid may, of course, cause the general contractor to make the kinds of errors that gave rise to the next case. For more background, see Franklin M. Schultz, The Firm Offer Puzzle: A Study of Business Practice in the Construction Industry, 19 U.Chi.L.Rev. 237 (1952), an illuminating empirical study of bidding practices in the construction industry in Indiana.

Elsinore Union Elementary School District v. Kastorff

Supreme Court of California, 1960.
54 Cal.2d 380, 6 Cal.Rptr. 1, 353 P.2d 713.

■ SCHAUER, JUSTICE. Defendants, who are a building contractor and his surety,[a] appeal from an adverse judgment in this action by plaintiff school district to recover damages allegedly resulting when defendant Kastorff, the contractor, refused to execute a building contract pursuant to his previously submitted bid to make certain additions to plaintiff's school buildings. We have concluded that because of an honest clerical error in the bid and defendant's subsequent prompt rescission he was not obliged to execute the contract, and that the judgment should therefore be reversed.

Pursuant to plaintiff's call for bids, defendant Kastorff secured a copy of the plans and specifications of the proposed additions to plaintiff's school buildings and proceeded to prepare a bid to be submitted by the deadline hour of 8 p.m., August 12, 1952, at Elsinore, California. Kastorff testified that in preparing his bid he employed work sheets upon which he entered bids of various subcontractors for such portions of the work as they were to do, and that to reach the final total of his own bid for the work he carried into the right-hand column of the work sheets the amounts of the respective sub bids which he intended to accept and then added those amounts to the cost of the work which he would do himself rather than through a subcontractor; that there is "a custom among subcontractors, in bidding on jobs such as this, to delay giving . . . their bids until the very last moment";

---

a. The surety in this case issued a "bid bond." A standard form of bid bond as promulgated by the American Institute of Architects, obligates the surety to pay "the difference not to exceed the penalty hereof [*i.e.*, the amount of the bond] between the amount specified in said bid and such larger amount for which the Obligee may in good faith contract with another party to perform the Work covered by said bid."

that the first sub bid for plumbing was in the amount of $9,285 and he had received it "the afternoon of the bid-opening," but later that afternoon when "the time was drawing close for me to get my bids together and get over to Elsinore" (from his home in San Juan Capistrano) he received a $6,500 bid for the plumbing. Erroneously thinking he had entered the $9,285 plumbing bid in his total column and had included that sum in his total bid and realizing that the second plumbing bid was nearly $3,000 less than the first, Kastorff then deducted $3,000 from the total amount of his bid and entered the resulting total of $89,994 on the bid form as his bid for the school construction. Thus the total included no allowance whatsoever for the plumbing work.

Kastorff then proceeded to Elsinore and deposited his bid with plaintiff. When the bids were opened shortly after 8 p.m. that evening, it was discovered that of the five bids submitted that of Kastorff was some $11,306 less than the next lowest bid. The school superintendent and the four school board members present thereupon asked Kastorff whether he was sure his figures were correct, Kastorff stepped out in to the hall to check with the person who had assisted in doing the clerical work on the bid, and a few minutes later returned and stated that the figures were correct. He testified that he did not have his worksheets or other papers with him to check against at the time. The board thereupon ... voted to award Kastorff the contract.

The next morning Kastorff checked his worksheets and promptly discovered his error. He immediately drove to the Los Angeles office of the firm of architects which had prepared the plans and specifications for plaintiff, and there saw Mr. Rendon. Mr. Rendon testified that Kastorff "had his maps and estimate work-sheets of the project, and indicated to me that he had failed to carry across the amount of dollars for the plumbing work. It was on the sheet, but not in the total sheet. We examined that evidence, and in our opinion we felt that he had made a clerical error in compiling his bill...." That same morning (August 13) Rendon telephoned the school superintendent and informed him of the error and of its nature and that Kastorff asked to be released from his bid. On August 14 Kastorff wrote a letter to the school board explaining his error and again requesting that he be permitted to withdraw his bid. On August 15, after receiving Kastorff's letter, the board held a special meeting and voted not to grant his request. Thereafter, on August 28, *written notification* was given to Kastorff of award of the contract to him.[1] Subsequently plaintiff submitted to Kastorff a contract to be signed in accordance with his bid, and on September 8, 1952, Kastorff returned the contract to plaintiff with a letter again explaining his error and asking the board to reconsider his request for withdrawal of his bid.

Plaintiff thereafter received additional bids to do the subject construction; let the contract to the lowest bidder, in the amount of $102,900; and

---

1. On the bid form, provided by plaintiff, the bidder agreed "that if he is notified of the acceptance of the proposal within forty-five (45) days from the time set for the opening of bids, he will execute and deliver to you within five (5) days after having received *written notification* a contract as called for in the 'Notice to Contractors.' " (Italics added.)

brought this action seeking to recover from Kastorff the $12,906 difference between that amount and the amount Kastorff had bid.[2] Recovery of $4,499.60 is also sought against Kastorff's surety under the terms of the bond posted with his bid.

Defendants in their answer to the complaint pleaded, among other things, that Kastorff had made an honest error in compiling his bid; that "he thought he was bidding, and intended to bid, $9500.00 more making a total of $99,494.00 as his bid"; that upon discovering his error he had promptly notified plaintiff and rescinded the $89,994 bid. The trial court found that it was true that Kastorff made up a bid sheet, which was introduced in evidence; ... and that Kastorff had neglected to carry over from the left-hand column on the bid sheet to the right-hand column on the sheet a portion of the plumbing (and heating) subcontractor's bid. Despite the uncontradicted evidence related hereinabove, including that of plaintiff's architect and of its school superintendent, both of whom testified as plaintiff's witnesses, the court further found, however, that "it is not true that the right hand column of figures was totaled for the purpose of arriving at the total bid to be submitted by E.J. Kastorff.... It cannot be ascertained from the evidence for what purpose the total of the right hand column of figures on the bid sheet was used nor can it be ascertained from the evidence for what purpose the three bid sheets were used in arriving at the total bid." And although finding that "on or about August 15, 1952," plaintiff received Kastorff's letter of August 14 explaining that he "made an error of omitting from my bid the item of Plumbing," the court also found that "It is not true that plaintiff knew at any time that defendant Kastorff's bid was intended to be other than $89,994.00.... It is not true that the plaintiff knew at the time it requested the execution of the contract by defendant Kastorff that he had withdrawn his bid because of an honest error in the compilation thereof. It is not true that plaintiff had notice of an error in the compilation of the bid by defendant Kastorff and tried nevertheless to take advantage of defendant Kastorff by forcing him to enter a contract on the basis of a bid he had withdrawn.... It is not true that it would be either inequitable or unjust to require defendant Kastorff to perform the contract awarded to him for the sum of $89,994.00, and it is not true that he actually intended to bid for said work the sum of $99,494.00"[3] Judgment was given for plaintiff in the amounts sought, and this appeal by defendants followed.

In reliance upon M.F. Kemper Const. Co. v. City of Los Angeles (1951), 37 Cal.2d 696, 235 P.2d 7, and Lemoge Electric v. County of San Mateo

---

2. Plaintiff's original published call for bids contained the following statement: "No Bidder may withdraw his bid for a period of forty-five (45) days after the date set for the opening thereof." Whether upon Kastorff's rescission for good cause prior to expiration of the 45 day period plaintiff could have accepted the next lowest bid is not an issue before us.

3. Other findings are that Kastorff "in the company of his wife and another couple left San Juan Capistrano for Elsinore ... at 6:00 P.M. on August 12, 1952, a distance of 34 miles by way of California State Highway ... Kastorff had ample time and opportunity after receiving his last subcontractor's bid to extend the figures on his bid sheet from one column to the other, to check and recheck his bid sheet figures and to take his papers to Elsinore and to check them there prior to close of receipt of bids at 8:00 P.M."

(1956), 46 Cal.2d 659, 662, 664, 297 P.2d 638, defendants urged that where, as defendants claim is the situation here, a contractor makes a clerical error in computing a bid on a public work he is entitled to rescind.

In the *Kemper* case one item on a worksheet in the amount of $301,769 was inadvertently omitted by the contractor from the final tabulation sheet and was overlooked in computing the total amount of a bid to do certain construction work for the defendant city. The error was caused by the fact that the men preparing the bid were exhausted after working long hours under pressure. When the bids were opened it was found that plaintiff's bid was $780,305, and the next lowest bid was $1,049,592. Plaintiff discovered its error several hours later and immediately notified a member of defendant's board of public works of its mistake in omitting one item while preparing the final accumulation of figures for its bid. Two days later it explained its mistake to the board and withdrew its bid. A few days later it submitted to the board evidence which showed the unintentional omission of the $301,769 item. The board nevertheless passed a resolution accepting plaintiff's erroneous bid of $780,305, and plaintiff refused to enter into a written contract at that figure. The board then awarded the contract to the next lowest bidder, the city demanded forfeiture of plaintiff's bid bond, and plaintiff brought action to cancel its bid and obtain discharge of the bond. The trial court found that the bid had been submitted as the result of an excusable and honest mistake of a material and fundamental character, that plaintiff company had not been negligent in preparing the proposal, that it had acted promptly to notify the board of the mistake and to rescind the bid, and that the board had accepted the bid with knowledge of the error. The court further found and concluded that it would be unconscionable to require the company to perform for the amount of the bid, that no intervening rights had accrued, and that the city had suffered no damage or prejudice.

On appeal by the city this court affirmed, stating the following applicable rules (at pages 700–703 of 37 Cal.2d, at pages 10, 11 of 235 P.2d):

"Once opened and declared, the company's bid was in the nature of an irrevocable option, a contract right of which the city could not be deprived without its consent unless the requirements for rescission were satisfied. ... [T]he city had actual notice of the error in the estimates before it attempted to accept the bid, and knowledge by one party that the other is acting under mistake is treated as equivalent to mutual mistake for purposes of rescission.... Relief from mistaken bids is consistently allowed where one party knows or has reason to know of the other's error and the requirements for rescission are fulfilled....

"Rescission may be had for mistake of fact if the mistake is material to the contract and was not the result of neglect of a legal duty, if enforcement of the contract as made would be unconscionable, and if the other party can be placed *in statu quo*.... In addition, the party seeking relief must give prompt notice of his election to rescind and must restore or offer to restore to the other party everything of value which he has received under the contract....

"Omission of the $301,769 item from the company's bid was, of course, a material mistake.... [E]ven if we assume that the error was due to some carelessness, it does not follow that the company is without remedy. Civil Code section 1577, which defines mistake of facts for which relief may be allowed, describes it as one not caused by 'the neglect of a legal duty' on the part of the person making the mistake.... It has been recognized numerous times that not all carelessness constitutes a 'neglect of legal duty' within the meaning of the section.... The type of error here involved is one which will sometimes occur in the conduct of reasonable and cautious businessmen, and, under all the circumstances, we cannot say as a matter of law that it constituted a neglect of legal duty such as would bar the right to equitable relief.

"The evidence clearly supports the conclusion that it would be unconscionable to hold the company to its bid at the mistaken figure. The city had knowledge before the bid was accepted that the company had made a clerical error which resulted in the omission of an item amounting to nearly one third of the amount intended to be bid, and, under all the circumstances, it appears that it would be unjust and unfair to permit the city to take advantage of the company's mistake. There is no reason for denying relief on the ground that the city cannot be restored to status quo. It had ample time in which to award the contract without readvertising, the contract was actually awarded to the next lowest bidder, and the city will not be heard to complain that it cannot be placed in statu quo because it will not have the benefit of an inequitable bargain.... Finally, the company gave notice promptly upon discovering the facts entitling it to rescind, and no offer of restoration was necessary because it had received nothing of value which it could restore.... We are satisfied that all the requirements for rescission have been met."

Further, we are persuaded that the trial court's view, as expressed in the finding set forth in the margin,[4] that "Kastorff had ample time and opportunity after receiving his last subcontractor's bid" to complete and check his final bid, does not convict Kastorff of that "neglect of legal duty" which would preclude his being relieved from the inadvertent clerical error of omitting from his bid the cost of the plumbing. (See Civ.Code § 1577; M.F. Kemper Const. Co. v. City of Los Angeles (1951), supra, 37 Cal.2d 696, 702[6], 235 P.2d 7.) Neither should he be denied relief from an unfair, inequitable, and unintended bargain simply because, in response to inquiry from the board when his bid was discovered to be much the lowest submitted, he informed the board, after checking with his clerical assistant, that the bid was correct....

If the situations of the parties were reversed and plaintiff and Kastorff had even executed a formal written contract (by contrast with the preliminary bid offer and acceptance) calling for a fixed sum payment to Kastorff large enough to include a reasonable charge for plumbing but inadvertently through the *district's* clerical error omitting a mutually intended provision requiring Kastorff to furnish and install plumbing, we have no doubt but

---

4. See footnote 3, supra.

that the district would demand and expect reformation or rescission. In the case before us the district expected Kastorff to furnish and install plumbing; surely it must also have understood that he intended to, and that his bid did, include a charge for such plumbing. The omission of any such charge was as unexpected by the board as it was unintended by Kastorff. Under the circumstances the "bargain" for which the board presses (which action we, of course, assume to be impelled by advice of counsel and a strict concept of official duty) appears too sharp for law and equity to sustain.

Plaintiff suggests that in any event the amount of the plumbing bid omitted from the total was immaterial. The bid as submitted was in the sum of $89,994, and whether the sum for the omitted plumbing was $6,500 or $9,285 (the two sub bids), the omission of such a sum is plainly material to the total. In [Lemoge Electric v. County of San Mateo, 46 Cal.2d 659, 661–662, 297 P.2d 638 (1956)] the error which it was declared would have entitled plaintiff to rescind was the listing of the cost of certain materials as $104.52, rather than $10,452, in a total bid of $172,421. Thus the percentage of error here was larger than in *Lemoge*, and was plainly material.

The judgment is reversed.

NOTES

(1) *Knowledge of Mistake.* All courts agree that if an offeree knows or has reason to know, of the offeror's material mistake at the time of acceptance, the offeror is not bound. "One cannot snap up an offer or bid knowing that it was made in mistake." Tyra v. Cheney, 152 N.W. 835 (Minn.1915). Professor Melvin Eisenberg has said that to grant relief for a bidder, in a case like Kastorff's, comports with morality. Eisenberg, Mistake in Contract Law, 91 Calif.L.Rev. 1573, 1586 (2003). On that view, should the size of the party's computational error matter? Is it any more immoral to take advantage of a known thousand-dollar mistake than of a ten-dollar mistake? In Kastorff's case, the court took note of the magnitude of his mistake.

(2) *Revocability.* Ordinarily a general contractor's bid on a construction contract is an offer that is revocable before acceptance. Where, however, the owner is a state or local government, statutes or ordinances usually provide that the general contractor may not withdraw its bid after the bids have been opened. Where the owner is the federal government, the same result has been reached on the basis of federal regulation. See William Keyes, Consideration Reconsidered—The Problem of the Withdrawn Bid, 10 Stan.L.Rev. 441, 448–53 (1958). See the court's footnote 2 on p. 141. Note that Kastoff was not seeking to revoke his offer but rather to rescind the contract.

(3) *Mistakes and Mistakes.* All mistakes are not equal. As noted in the excerpt on subcontractors' bids, p. 138 above, "Mistakes come in a variety of flavors. There may be mistakes in construing the language of the plans and specification, in estimating quantities required, in unit pricing, in multiplying quantities by unit prices, in transferring data from one work-sheet to another, in typing the bid form, and many others." Id. Courts considering bidders' claims for relief for mistake have often distinguished between mistakes that are "clerical" or "computational" from those of "judgment." Consider a dealer in lumber, invited to bid on a sale of shingles required to roof a building. What mistakes might the dealer make that would be certainly ones of judgment? Is it apparent why the courts disfavor giving

relief for mistakes of that kind? Mistakes in bids have been attributable to faulty computer software. See M.A. Mortenson v. Timberline Software Corp., 998 P.2d 305 (Wash.2000).

Does the provision of relief in Kastorff's case tempt bidders to manufacture evidence of mistakes in computation when they have come to regret having bid low because of a misjudgment. Professor Eisenberg has discounted that threat on the ground that typically, when a computational error has been made, "the work papers, surrounding circumstances, or both, clearly demonstrate" the error. See Mistakes ..., cited in Note 1 above, at 1587. It has, however, been argued that "The proof of whether he has made a mistake is so completely within his control and power that the [Owner] is helpless to refute it." Carter, J., dissenting in M.F. Kemper Construction Co. v. City of Los Angeles, 235 P.2d 7, 13 (Cal.1951).

(4) *A Statutory Sequel.* More than a decade after the decision in *Kastorff*, this statute was enacted in California:

A bidder [on a public contract] shall not be relieved of the bid unless by consent of the awarding authority nor shall any change be made in the bid because of mistake, but the bidder may bring an action against the public entity in a court of competent jurisdiction in the county in which the bids were opened for the recovery of the amount forfeited, without interest or costs.

The bidder shall establish to the satisfaction of the court that:

(a) A mistake was made.

(b) He or she gave the public entity written notice within five days after the opening of the bids of the mistake, specifying in the notice in detail how the mistake occurred.

(c) The mistake made the bid materially different than he or she intended it to be.

(d) The mistake was made in filling out the bid and not due to error in judgment or to carelessness in inspecting the site of the work, or in reading the plans or specifications.

Would Kastorff's case have had a different outcome if it had been governed by this statute?

(5) *Knowledge* vs. *Reason to Know.* An offeror who has submitted a mistaken bid may claim that the magnitude of the mistake was such that it should have been apparent from the face of the offer. What sorts of circumstances might warrant suspicion on the part of the offeree?

Heifetz Metal Crafts, Inc. v. Peter Kiewit Sons' Co., 264 F.2d 435 (8th Cir.1959), is a good example. There Kiewit was preparing a bid for the construction of a hospital and Heifetz offered to do the kitchen work for $99,500, $52,000 less than Kiewit's next lowest quotation. Kiewit lowered its bid by $52,000, which made it $17,942,200, the lowest by $9,000. After Kiewit was awarded the contract and had accepted the Heifetz offer, Heifetz discovered that in preparing its quotation it had overlooked some subsidiary kitchen installations required by the plans. It sought rescission and argued that since its quotation was one-third less than the next lowest, Kiewit should have realized that there had been a mistake. The court rejected this contention and held that the contract was enforceable. It relied upon testimony by Kiewit's employees that they were ignorant of the mistake, upon Kiewit's lack of familiarity with the kitchen equipment field, and upon "testimony indicating that at times some contractor would have a special reason for desiring to obtain a particular job and would submit a figure controlled by that consideration." It noted that "the figures submitted by subcontractors on the electrical work for the project has varied from $1,400,000 to $1,850,000 and on the lathing and plastering work from $672,000 to $1,028,000; and the 'mechanical spread' had been between $3,647,000 and $6,000,000."

Is it of any significance that a general contractor will sometimes pass over a low bid to accept one from a subcontractor with which the general contractor has a personal or business connection, and that subcontractors sometimes deliberately make losing bids to break up such combinations? Is it of any significance that subcontractors sometimes bid low in the expectation that changes will later be made to provide for profitable extra work?

(6) *Offers and Errors*. What is a merchant to do when it finds that it has broadcast an ad understating the price for the advertised goods? One solution is to withdraw the ad hastily, before hordes of shoppers have proceeded to checkout, and to conserve good will by honoring the orders received. Another, given a serious understatement, is to dishonor orders from shoppers responding and to depict those shoppers as unscrupulous. Some precautions are also possible. One is for a merchant to buy "typo insurance." Another is to insert protective language in the ad. The legend "One to a customer" would provide some protection. What other protective language comes to mind? See Mark Budnitz, Consumers Surfing for Sales in Cyberspace: What Constitutes Acceptance and What Legal Terms and Conditions Bind the Consumer?, 16 Ga.St.U.L.Rev. 741 (2000). The Toronto Star has reported an instance of goods advertised at a minor fraction of the usual price, for which there were hundreds of takers. "Price Snafu Stings Web Retailer," Nov. 17, 2000.

PROBLEM

Transmission Problems. In the market for a car, Donovan read an advertisement placed by Lexus of Westminster in his local newspaper, the Daily Pilot. The advertisement presented a number of used cars for sale, including a sapphire blue 1995 Jaguar XJ6, VIN 720603, listed for $25,995. Donovan went down to the dealership, took the advertised car for a test drive, and told the sales representative that he would buy it. The sales representative immediately informed Donovan that the advertised price was a mistake. Although Donovan began to write a check for the advertised price, he was informed that the car could only be sold for $37,016. Donovan refused to pay the higher price and sued the dealership for breach of contract. Donovan v. RRL Corp., 88 Cal. Rptr.2d 143 (Cal.App. 1999).

In that case, the appellate court made the following observation: "A first year law student would not be surprised to be called upon to answer the questions we address here. Does an advertisement for a specific used car at a designated price constitute an offer that may be accepted by tendering the purchase price? Does a statute prohibiting an automobile dealer from refusing to sell a vehicle at the advertised price affect the answer? Finally, does the answer change if the erroneous price inserted in the advertisement was the result of an error? We believe the answers are respectively 'possibly,' 'yes,' and 'no.' However, since such cryptic answers would not entitle our hypothetical law student to a passing grade, we must explain these answers below."

Do you agree with the court's answers? As a *real* first year law student, what are your explanations? A few additional facts may help: the newspaper had made a typographical error which caused the 1995 Jaguar to be advertised at the price of a 1994 Jaguar; the dealership failed to proofread the advertising copy received from the Daily Pilot; a California statute makes it unlawful for an automobile dealer to "[f]ail to sell a vehicle to any person at the advertised total price, exclusive of taxes and [certain other specified fees]"; and Donovan did not know the market price of a 1995 Jaguar.

In 2001, the California Supreme Court reversed the appellate court decision. Donovan v. RRL Corp., 27 P.3d 702 (Cal.2001). On what grounds might the lower court have failed to get a passing grade?

SECTION 3. THE ACCEPTANCE

What is an acceptance? Corbin gave this answer: "An acceptance is a voluntary act of the offeree whereby he exercises the power conferred upon him by the offer, and thereby creates the set of legal relations called a contract. What acts are sufficient to serve this purpose? We must look first to the terms in which the offer was expressed, either by words or by other conduct.... The offeror has, in the beginning, full power to determine the acts that are to constitute acceptance." Arthur L. Corbin, Offer and Acceptance, and Some of the Resulting Legal Relations, 26 Yale L.J. 169, 199 (1917).

Assuming that there has been an offer, the offeree by exercising the power of acceptance "thereby creates," as Corbin puts it, "the set of legal relations called a contract." One of the most important consequences of this "set of legal relations" is that the offeror is no longer free to change its mind and withdraw from the relationship without incurring liability. (In Hohfeldian terminology, see Note 2, p. 68, "the offeree has, before the contract is made, a power to create a contract by means of acceptance. A power is the capacity to change a legal relationship.") By what means, then, may the offeree exercise this power of acceptance? If, as Corbin says, the offeror has "full power to determine the acts that are to constitute acceptance," the first step in answering this question is to look at the offer to see what sort of acceptance it invited.

We already know from Chapter 1 that an offeror may bargain either for a performance or for a promise. As suggested at Note 5, pp. 38–39, the more economically significant transactions usually involve the latter sort of bargain, in which the offeror seeks the assurance of another promise in return for its own. When a promise is sought, can it be inferred from conduct of the offeree? Can mere silence ever count? Must the offeree notify the offeror of the acceptance? This section considers these and related questions.

International Filter Co. v. Conroe Gin, Ice & Light Co.

Commission of Appeals of Texas, 1925.
277 S.W. 631.

Action by the International Filter Company against the Conroe Gin, Ice & Light Company. Judgment for defendant was affirmed in 269 S.W. 210, and plaintiff brings error. Reversed and remanded.

■ NICKELS, J. Plaintiff in error, an Illinois corporation, is a manufacturer of machinery, apparatus, etc., for the purification of water in connection with the manufacture of ice, etc., having its principal office in the city of Chicago. Defendant in error is a Texas corporation engaged in the manufacture of ice, etc., having its plant, office, etc., at Conroe, Montgomery

County, Tex. [Hereafter plaintiff in error is referred to as International Filter, and defendant in error as Conroe Gin.]

On February 10, 1920, through its traveling solicitor, Waterman, International Filter, submitted to Conroe Gin, acting through Henry Thompson, its manager, a written instrument, addressed to Conroe Gin, which (with immaterial portions omitted) reads as follows:

"Gentlemen: We propose to furnish, f.o.b. Chicago, one No. two Junior (steel tank) International water softener and filter to purify water of the character shown by sample to be submitted.... Price: Twelve hundred thirty ($1,230.00) dollars.... This proposal is made in duplicate and becomes a contract when accepted by the purchaser and approved by an executive officer of the International Filter Company, at its office in Chicago. Any modification can only be made by duly approved supplementary agreement signed by both parties.

"This proposal is submitted for prompt acceptance, and unless so accepted is subject to change without notice.

> "Respectfully submitted,
> "International Filter Co.
> "W.W. Waterman."

On the same day the "proposal" was accepted by Conroe Gin through notation made on the paper by Thompson reading as follows:

> "Accepted Feb. 10, 1920.
> "Conroe Gin, Ice & Light Co.,
> "By Henry Thompson, Mgr."

The paper as thus submitted and "accepted" contained the notation, "Make shipment by Mar. 10." The paper, in that form, reached the Chicago office of International Filter, and on February 13, 1920, P.N. Engel, its president and vice president, indorsed thereon: "O.K. Feb. 13, 1920, P.N. Engel." February 14, 1920, International Filter wrote and mailed, and in due course Conroe Gin received, the following letter:

> "Feb. 14, 1920.

"Attention of Mr. Henry Thompson, Manager.

"Conroe Gin, Ice & Light Co., Conroe, Texas–Gentlemen: This will acknowledge and thank you for your order given Mr. Waterman for a No. 2 Jr. steel tank International softener and filter, for 110 volt, 60 cycle, single phase current—for shipment March 10th.

"Please make shipment of the sample of water promptly so that we may make the analysis and know the character of the water before shipment of the apparatus. Shipping tag is inclosed, and please note, the instructions to pack to guard against freezing.

> "Yours very truly,
> "International Filter Co.
> "M.B. Johnson."

By letter of February 28, 1920, Conroe Gin undertook to countermand the "order," which countermand was repeated and emphasized by letter of March 4, 1920. By letter of March 2, 1920 (replying to the letter of February 28th), International Filter denied the right of countermand, etc., and insisted upon performance of the "contract." The parties adhered to the respective positions thus indicated, and this suit resulted.

International Filter sued for breach of the contract alleged to have been made in the manner stated above. The defense is that no contract was made because: (1) Neither Engel's indorsement of "O.K.," nor the letter of February 14, 1920, amounted to approval "by an executive officer of the International Filter Company, at its office in Chicago." (2) Notification of such approval, or acceptance, by International Filter was required to be communicated to Conroe Gin; it being insisted that this requirement inhered in the terms of the proposal and in the nature of the transaction and, also, that Thompson, when he indorsed "acceptance" on the paper stated to Waterman, as agent of International Filter, that such notification must be promptly given; it being insisted further that the letter of February 14, 1920, did not constitute such acceptance or notification of approval, and therefore Conroe Gin, on February 28, 1920, etc., had the right to withdraw or countermand, the unaccepted offer. Thompson testified in a manner to support the allegation of his statement to Waterman. There are other matters involved in the suit which must be ultimately determined, but the foregoing presents the issues now here for consideration.

The case was tried without a jury, and the judge found the facts in favor of Conroe Gin on all the issues indicated above, and upon other material issues. The judgment was affirmed by the Court of Civil Appeals, 269 S.W. 210.

We agree with the honorable Court of Civil Appeals upon the proposition that Mr. Engel's indorsement of "O.K." amounted to an approval "by an executive officer of the International Filter Company, at its office in Chicago," within the meaning of the so-called "proposal" of February 10th. The paper then became a "contract," according to its definitely expressed terms, and it became then, and thereafter it remained, an enforceable contract, in legal contemplation, unless the fact of approval by the filter company was required to be communicated to the other party and unless, in that event, the communication was not made.

We are not prepared to assent to the ruling that such communication was essential. There is no disposition to question the justice of the general rules stated in support of that holding, yet the existence of contractual capacity imports the right of the offerer to dispense with notification; and he does dispense with it "if the form of the offer," etc., "shows that this was not to be required." 9 Cyc. 270, 271; Carlill v. Carbolic Smoke Ball Co., 1 Q.B. 256 (and other references in note 6, 9 Cyc. 271)....

The Conroe Gin, Ice & Light Company executed the paper for the purpose of having it transmitted, as its offer, to the filter company at Chicago. It was so transmitted and acted upon. Its terms embrace the offer, and nothing else, and by its terms the question of notification must be judged, since those terms are not ambiguous.

The paper contains two provisions which relate to acceptance by the filter company. One is the declaration that the offer shall "become a contract ... when approved by an executive officer of the International Filter Company, at its Chicago office." The other is thus stated: "This proposal is submitted for prompt acceptance, and unless so accepted is subject to change without notice." The first provision states "a particular mode of acceptance as sufficient to make the bargain binding," and the filter company (as stated above) followed "the indicated method of acceptance." When this was done, so the paper declares, the proposal "became a contract." The other provision does not in any way relate to a different method of acceptance by the filter company. Its sole reference is to the time within which the act of approval must be done; that is to say, there was to be a "prompt acceptance," else the offer might be changed "without notice." The second declaration merely required the approval therein before stipulated for to be done promptly; if the act was so done, there is nothing in the second provision to militate against, or to conflict with, the prior declaration that, thereupon, the paper should become "a contract."

A holding that notification of that approval is to be deduced from the terms of the last-quoted clause is not essential in order to give it meaning or to dissolve ambiguity. On the contrary, such a construction of the two provisions would introduce a conflict, or ambiguity, where none exists in the language itself, and defeat the plainly expressed term wherein it is said that the proposal "becomes a contract ... when approved by an executive officer." There is not anything in the language used to justify a ruling that this declaration must be wrenched from its obvious meaning and given one which would change both the locus and time prescribed for the meeting of the minds. The offerer said that the contract should be complete if approval be promptly given by the executive officer at Chicago; the court cannot properly restate the offer so as to make the offerer declare that a contract shall be made only when the approval shall have been promptly given at Chicago and that fact shall have been communicated to the offerer at Conroe. In our opinion, therefore, notice of the approval was not required.

The letter of February 14th, however, sufficiently communicated notice, if it was required.... Here the fact of acceptance in the particular method prescribed by the offerer is established aliunde the letter—Engel's "O.K." indorsed on the paper at Chicago did that. The form of notice, where notice is required, may be quite a different thing from the acceptance itself; the latter constitutes the meeting of the minds, the former merely relates to that pre-existent fact. The rules requiring such notice, it will be marked, do not make necessary any particular form or manner, unless the parties themselves have so prescribed. Whatever would convey by word or fair implication, notice of the fact would be sufficient. And this letter, we think, would clearly indicate to a reasonably prudent person, situated as was the defendant in error, the fact of previous approval by the filter company. If the Gin, Ice & Light Company had acted to change its position upon it as a notification of that fact, it must be plain that the filter company would have been estopped to deny its sufficiency. . . .

We recommend that the judgment of the Court of Civil Appeals be reversed, and that the cause be remanded to that court for its disposition of all questions not passed upon it by it heretofore and properly before it for determination.

■ CURETON, C.J. Judgment of the Court of Civil Appeals reversed, and cause remanded to the Court of Civil Appeals for further consideration by that court, as recommended by the Commission of Appeals.

NOTES

(1) *Questions.* Which party was the offeror in this case? Who prepared the offer? Which of the following constituted the acceptance: The buyer's notation "Accepted Feb. 10, 1920"? The seller's indorsement "O.K. Feb. 13, 1920"? The seller's Feb. 14, 1920 letter? What function does each of these perform in the formation process?

(2) *Expressions of Acceptance.* The Court of Civil Appeals, had reasoned that International Filter's letter of February 14 "did not constitute an acceptance of appellee's proposal." International Filter Co. v. Conroe Gin, Ice & Light Co., 269 S.W. 210, 215 (1925). It relied on Courtney Shoe Co. v. E.W. Curd & Son, 134 S.W. 146 (Ky.1911). In that case a manufacturer wrote, "Your order . . . is at hand and will receive our prompt and careful attention," but sent a second letter eight days later rejecting the order on the ground that the salesman had made the sale without authority. It was held that the first letter was not an acceptance. Assume, for the moment, that the February 14 letter was the only response to the proposal signed by Conroe Gin. Do you agree with the Court of Civil Appeals?

(3) *Control of Representatives.* When a seller is a large organization with salespersons ("traveling solicitors" in the opinion above) who are expected to use a carefully prepared standard form for all contracts, there is still a risk that the salespersons will make written changes on the form during their negotiations with customers. Does this fact suggest a use for a home-office-approval clause? See Restatement, Second, of Agency § 167 as to the effect of such language as: "No agent of seller has authority to change the terms hereof." What additional benefits or risks might such a clause provide the seller? The buyer?

(4) *Notice.* Can you distinguish the position of International Filter from that of the offeree who merely thinks or mutters "I accept"? See Restatement §§ 54 and 56. For a case holding that the mere signing of the contract by the offeree was not acceptance even though the contract said that it would be binding "when . . . signed by both parties," see Kendel v. Pontious, 261 So.2d 167 (Fla.1972). Why, if notice of acceptance is necessary for an offer that seeks a promise, did the court find that no notice was required in International Filter?

PROBLEM

On May 16, a Seattle retailer ordered men's fall suits on a printed form supplied by the manufacturer's salesman that provided that the manufacturer was not bound until acceptance by one of its officers in New Jersey. On May 23, the manufacturer, by form letter, advised the retailer that, "You may be assured of our very best attention to this order." On July 18, after the time for placing orders for fall suits had passed, and at the instigation of one of the retailer's competitors in Seattle, the manufacturer wrote to "cancel" the order. The retailer sued the manufacturer and had judgment in the trial court, which found that the manufacturer's form letter had been an acceptance. The Supreme Court of Washington affirmed. Are the facts in this case distinguishable from those in *International Filter*, above? Hill's, Inc. v. William B. Kessler, Inc., 246 P.2d 1099 (Wash.1952).

White v. Corlies & Tift
Court of Appeals of New York, 1871.
46 N.Y. 467.

Appeal from judgment of the General Term of the first judicial district, affirming a judgment entered upon a verdict for plaintiff.

The action was for an alleged breach of contract.

The plaintiff was a builder, with his place of business in Fortieth Street, New York City.

The defendants were merchants at 32 Day Street.

In September, 1865, the defendants furnished the plaintiff with specifications for fitting up a suite of offices at 57 Broadway, and requested him to make an estimate of the cost of doing the work.

On September 28th, the plaintiff left his estimate with the defendants, and they were to consider upon it, and inform the plaintiff of their conclusions.

On the same day the defendants made a change in their specifications, and sent a copy of the same, so changed, to the plaintiff for his assent under his estimate, which he assented to by signing the same and returning it to the defendants.

On the day following the defendants' bookkeeper wrote the plaintiff the following note:

"New York, September 29.

"Upon an agreement to finish the fitting up of offices 57 Broadway in two weeks from date, you can begin at once.

"The writer will call again, probably between 5 and 6 this p.m.

"W.H.R.
For J.W. Corlies & Co.,
32 Dey St."

No reply to this note was ever made by the plaintiff; and on the next day the same was countermanded by a second note from the defendants.

Immediately on receipt of the note of September 29th, and before the countermand was forwarded, the plaintiff commenced a performance by the purchase of lumber and beginning work thereon.

And after receiving the countermand, the plaintiff brought this action for damages for a breach of contract.[a]

a. Some additional facts, taken from the record on appeal of White's testimony

may be helpful. Corlies' initial request was to have the office done in black walnut, a hard

The court charged the jury as follows: "From the contents of this note which the plaintiff received, was it his duty to go down to Dey Street (meaning to give notice of assent), before commencing the work?

In my opinion it was not. He had a right to act upon this note and commence the job, and that was a binding contract between the parties."

To this defendants excepted. . . .

■ FOLGER, J. We do not think that the jury found, or that the testimony shows, that there was any agreement between the parties, before the written communication of the defendants of September 30th[b] was received by the plaintiff. This note did not make an agreement. It was a proposition, and must have been accepted by the plaintiff before either party was bound, in contract, to the other. The only overt action which is claimed by the plaintiff as indicating on his part an acceptance of the offer, was the purchase of the stuff necessary for the work, and commencing work, as we understand the testimony, upon that stuff.

We understand the rule to be, that where an offer is made by one party to another when they are not together, the acceptance of it by that other must be manifested by some appropriate act. It does not need that the acceptance shall come to the knowledge of the one making the offer before he shall be bound. But though the manifestation need not be brought to his knowledge before he becomes bound, he is not bound, if that manifestation is not put in a proper way to be in the usual course of events, in some reasonable time communicated to him. Thus a letter received by mail containing a proposal may be answered by letter by mail, containing the acceptance. And in general, as soon as the answering letter is mailed, the contract is concluded. Though one party does not know of the acceptance, the manifestation thereof is put in the proper way of reaching him.

In the case in hand, the plaintiff determined to accept. But a mental determination not indicated by speech, or put in course of indication by act to the other party, is not an acceptance which will bind the other. Nor does an act, which in itself, is no indication of an acceptance, become such, because accompanied by an unevinced mental determination. Where the act uninterpreted by concurrent evidence of the mental purpose accompanying it, is as well referable to one state of facts as another, it is no indication to the other party of an acceptance, and does not operate to hold him to his offer.

Conceding that the testimony shows that the plaintiff did resolve to accept this offer, he did no act which indicated an acceptance of it to the defendants. He, a carpenter and builder, purchased stuff for the work. But

wood, within 21 days. White replied that he could not do the job in a hard wood in that time. Corlies then requested an estimate for white pine, a soft wood. White left the estimate on September 28, but did not indicate the time within which he would finish. Corlies made a change in the specifications to which White assented. There followed the letter of September 29 from Corlies. The countermand from Corlies said that it had decided to do the office in black walnut and requested an estimate for that in place of pine. Record, pp. 7–12.

b. It appears the court meant September 29.

it was stuff as fit for any other like work. He began work upon the stuff, but as he would have done for any other like work. There was nothing in his thought, formed but not uttered, or in his acts that indicated or set in motion an indication to the defendants of his acceptance of their offer, or which could necessarily result therein.

But the charge of the learned judge was fairly to be understood by the jury as laying down the rule to them, that the plaintiff need not indicate to the defendants his acceptance of their offer; and that the purchase of stuff and working on it after receiving the note, made a binding contract between the parties. In this we think the learned judge fell into error.

Judgment reversed, and new trial ordered.

NOTES

(1) *An Ambiguity.* According to Judge Folger's first paragraph, the bookkeeper's note of September 29 was a proposal, and not an acceptance of an offer made by White in the estimate he left with Corlies & Tift. That might be explained in two ways. One is that the estimate was not an offer. Were there any facts that suggest that White's estimate may have constituted an offer? Might "I estimate ..." constitute an offer just as well as "we quote you Mason fruit jars"?

The other explanation is that the opening phrase of the September 29 note—"*Upon an agreement*"—was understood to mean "When we have agreed about finishing the fitting up the offices (and not before)...." The brief on appeal for Corlies & Tift characterized the phrase this way, as one "demanding an agreement." Consider an alternate reading: "With reference to the work of fitting up...." That reading may comport better with 19th-century diction, and with the opinion as a whole.

(2) *Problems of Manifestation.* Assuming that the bookkeeper's note constituted an offer, does the court's opinion imply that White might have accepted it by some kind of activity. If so, what kind of activity might count? Activity at a lumberyard? At his shop? If not, what sense can be made of "... you can begin at once"?

The court stated a familiar rule about contracts created by correspondence: posting a letter sometimes constitutes the acceptance of an offer. (The "mailbox rule" is further considered at p. 185 below. The rule applies only to letters properly stamped and addressed.) In such instances, however, the offeror is at risk, for no more than a few days, of having made a commitment that it is unaware of. Corlies & Tift would have borne that risk if White could have bound it to a contract simply by busying himself with "stuff" suited only for offices at 57 Broadway. On the other hand, Corlies & Tift gave some indication of willingness to bear that risk: "... you can begin at once."

———

EVER–TITE ROOFING CORPORATION v. GREEN, 83 So.2d 449 (La.App.1955). The Greens wished to have Ever–Tite Roofing re-roof their residence, and signed a document that set out the work in detail and the price in monthly installments. This document was also signed by Ever–Tite's sales representative who, however, had no authority to bind Ever–Tite. The document contained a provision that, "This agreement shall become binding only upon written acceptance hereof, by the principal or authorized officer of the Contractor, or upon commencing performance of the work." As the Greens knew, since the work was to be done entirely on credit, it was necessary for Ever–Tite to get credit reports and obtain the approval of the lending institution that was to finance the contract. When this was accomplished, about nine days after execution of the agreement, Ever–Tite loaded two trucks and sent them with its workmen some distance to the Green's residence. Upon their arrival they found that others had been engaged two days before, and they were not permitted to work. Ever–Tite sued the Greens for breach of contract. From a judgment for defendant, plaintiff appealed.

■ AYRES, JUDGE. . . . The basis of the judgment appealed was that defendants had timely notified plaintiff before "commencing performance of work". The trial court held that notice to plaintiff's workmen upon their arrival with the materials that defendants did not desire them to commence the actual work was sufficient and timely to signify their intention to withdraw from the contract. With this conclusion we find ourselves unable to agree. . . . Defendants evidently knew this work was to be processed through plaintiff's Shreveport office. The record discloses no unreasonable delay on plaintiff's part in receiving, processing or accepting the contract or in commencing the work contracted to be done. No time limit was specified in the contract within which it was to be accepted or within which the work was to be begun. It was nevertheless understood between the parties that some delay would ensue before the acceptance of the contract and the commencement of the work, due to the necessity of compliance with the requirements relative to financing the job through a lending agency. The evidence as referred to hereinabove shows that plaintiff proceeded with due diligence. [In an omitted part of the opinion the court set out several articles of the Louisiana Civil Code. Under article 1809, the most relevant here, the offeror "may therefore revoke his offer or proposition before such acceptance, but not without allowing such reasonable time as from the terms of the offer he has given, or from the circumstances of the case he may be supposed to have intended to give to the party to communicate his determination."] [S]ince the contract did not specify the time within which it was to be accepted or within which the work was to have been commenced, a reasonable time must be allowed therefor in accordance with the facts and circumstances and the evident intention of the parties. A reasonable time is contemplated where no time is expressed. What is a reasonable time depends more or less upon the circumstances surrounding each particular case. The delays to process defendants' application were not unusual. The contract was accepted by plaintiff by the commencement of the performance of the work contracted to be done. This commencement began with the loading of the trucks with the necessary materials in Shreveport and transporting such materials and the workmen to defendants' residence. Actual commencement or performance of the work therefore began before any notice of dissent by defendants was given plaintiff. The proposition and its acceptance thus became a completed contract.

[Reversed.]

NOTE

Means of Acceptance. What means of acceptance were authorized by the Greens offer to Ever–Tite? What was the purpose of the words "or upon commencing performance of the work?" Could the court have read this language more favorably to the Greens?

————

THE SIGNIFICANCE OF CONTRACT FORMATION

Whether or not there has been an acceptance may have significance beyond the commercial exchange of goods or services with which contract disputes are usually concerned. The existence of a contract may, for example, determine whether particular statutory protections attach. For example, suppose that as a shopper was lifting a soft drink bottle from the merchant's shelf to place it in a shopping cart, the bottle exploded, seriously injuring the shopper. Was there a "contract for . . . sale," triggering an implied warranty of merchantability, as provided under UCC § 2–314? See Barker v. Allied Supermarket, 596 P.2d 870 (Okla.1979).

Whether a contract has been formed also has significance for purposes of anti-discrimination law. Section 1981 of the Civil Rights Act of 1866 provides that "all persons . . . shall have the same right to make and enforce contracts . . . as is enjoyed by white citizens." 42 U.S.C. § 1981. Against that background, consider these facts. Edith Perry telephoned her hair salon and made an appointment for a "wash and set." When Perry arrived at the salon, she was asked if she would mind seeing another hairdresser as her regular person was sick. Perry agreed. However, when the substitute hairdresser saw Perry, she announced that she did not "do black hair." Perry left the salon distraught and later brought suit under § 1981. The appellate court agreed there had been discriminatory behavior, but remanded the case on the question of whether a contract existed at the time Perry was denied service, as required by § 1981. Do you find an offer and an acceptance in the transaction described? Perry v. Command Performance, 913 F.2d 99 (3d Cir.1990).

Unlike the 1866 Civil Rights Act, which prohibited discrimination in the *making* of contracts, the Civil Rights Act of 1991 makes *post-formation* discriminatory conduct actionable. See Hampton v. Dillard Dept. Stores, 247 F.3d 1091 (10th Cir.2001). Greater exploration of actionable discrimination is left for other courses.

————

NOTIFICATION OF ACCEPTANCE IN UNILATERAL CONTRACTS

As White v. Corlies & Tift suggests, if an offeror proposes a "bilateral" contract and invites acceptance by means of a promise, it is ordinarily understood that the offeree must at least take steps to see that the promise is, in the words of the opinion in that case, "in some reasonable time communicated" to the offeror. The court stressed the fact that White had neither indicated his determination to accept by *speech* nor "put in course of indication" to Corlies & Tift of anything he had *done*. See Restatement § 56. (Can the *International Filter* and *Ever–Tite* cases be reconciled with this rule?)

The necessity of giving notice is less obvious if the offer proposes a "unilateral" contract, inviting acceptance by means of performance and not a promise. A celebrated case is Carlill v. Carbolic Smoke Ball Co., [1893] 1 Q.B. 256 (Court of Appeal 1892). It arose out of the following advertisement: "£ 100 reward will be paid by the Carbolic Smoke Ball Company to any person who contracts the increasing epidemic influenza, colds or any disease caused by taking cold, after having used the ball three times daily for two weeks according to the printed directions supplied with each ball.[a] £ 1000 is deposited with the Alliance Bank, Regent Street shewing our sincerity in the matter. . . ." After buying and using a smokeball as directed, Carlill contracted influenza. When the Company refused to pay, she sued and was awarded £ 100 in damages. The Company argued that Carlille had failed to notify it of her acceptance, but its appeal was dismissed.

As Lindley, L.J., explained, the advertisement was not "a mere puff" but an offer under which "the reward is offered to any person who contracts the epidemic or other disease within a reasonable time after having used the smoke ball." The fact that she had not notified the Company of her acceptance was not fatal to her claim. According to Bowen, L.J., "One cannot doubt that, as an ordinary rule of law, an acceptance of an offer made ought to be notified to the person who makes the offer, in order that the two minds may come together. . . . But there is this clear gloss to be made upon that doctrine, that as notification of acceptance is required for the benefit of the person who makes the offer, the person who makes the offer may dispense with notice to himself, if he thinks it desirable to do so . . . [I]f the person making the offer, expressly or impliedly intimates in his offer that it will be sufficient to act on the proposal without communicating acceptance of it to himself, performance of the condition is a sufficient acceptance without notification. . . ."

How can one tell if the offer has dispensed with notice? Bowen explained: "In many cases you look to the offer itself. In many cases you extract from the character of the transaction. . . . and in the advertisement cases it seems to me to follow as an inference to be drawn from the transaction itself that a person is not to notify his acceptance of the offer before he performs the condition, but that if he performs the condition notification is dispensed with. It seems to me that from the point of view of common sense no other idea could be entertained."

a. The smoke ball was a small compressible hollow ball filled with carbolic acid in powder form, worn around the neck on a cord. When the ball was squeezed, the powder was forced through a small opening in the ball and created a small cloud of smoke. For more on the case, including pictures of the advertisement, facts on the smokeball and the lethality of carbolic acid in more than small amounts, see Simpson, Quackery and Contract Law: The Case of the Carbolic Smoke Ball, 14 J.Legal Stud. 345 (1985), reprinted in A.W.B. Simpson, Leading Cases in the Common Law 259, 262–64 (1995).

NOTES

(1) *Questions*. Was the acceptance of the Carbolic Smoke Ball Company's offer: (a) the purchase of the smoke ball; (b) its use in accordance with directions; (c) the plaintiff's contracting influenza; or (d) all of the above? Which of these acts was bargained for? Recall that a promise may be conditional, so that its performance becomes due only if a specified event occurs. See Note 1, p. 68 above. Was the promise conditional in the Carbolic Smoke Ball case?

(2) *Notice from Afar*. A leading American case on the necessity of notice of acceptance of a unilateral offer is Bishop v. Eaton, 37 N.E. 665, 667 (Mass.1894). In that case Frank Eaton, in Nova Scotia, had written to Bishop, in Illinois, that if Bishop would help Eaton's brother, Harry, to get money, "I will see that it is paid." Bishop did help Harry get money by signing his note as surety when Harry got a loan. When Harry did not repay the loan, Bishop did, and sued Frank on his promise. The court thought that this was a case in which notice of acceptance should have been given, since the loan was made in Illinois and Frank was in Nova Scotia. "Ordinarily there is no occasion to notify the offeror of the acceptance of such an offer, for the doing of the act is a sufficient acceptance, and the promisor knows that he is bound when he sees that action has been taken on the faith of his offer. But if the act is of such a kind that knowledge of it will not quickly come to the promisor, the promisee is bound to give him notice of his acceptance within a reasonable time after doing that which constitutes the acceptance." The court concluded, however, that notice had been given.

INTRODUCTION TO *ALLIED STEEL*

The following case concerns an "indemnity" provision in a purchase order issued by the Ford Motor Company. An indemnity agreement is one whereby a party undertakes contingent liability for a loss threatening another. Agreements of this kind are commonplace. If the loss occurs, the indemnitor pays. See, for example, Bishop v. Eaton, above, and Pacific Gas and Electric v. G.W. Thomas Drayage and Rigging Co., p. 382 below.

Allied Steel and Conveyors, Inc. v. Ford Motor Co.

United States Court of Appeals, Sixth Circuit, 1960.
277 F.2d 907.

[On August 19, 1955, Ford ordered machinery from Allied on Ford's printed form, Purchase Order No. 15145, which provided that if Allied was required to perform work of installation on Ford's premises, Allied would be responsible for all damages caused by the negligence of its own employees. Attached to and made a part of the Purchase Order was another printed form, Form 3618, which included a much broader indemnity provision requiring Allied to assume full responsibility not only for the negligence of its own employees, but also for the negligence of Ford's employees in connection with Allied's work, but this provision was marked "VOID." The Purchase Order was accepted by Allied and the contract performed.

Subsequently, on July 26, 1956, Ford submitted to Allied Amendment No. 2 to Purchase Order 15145, by which Ford proposed to purchase additional machinery. The Amendment provided:

> This purchase order agreement is not binding until accepted. Acceptance should be executed on acknowledgment copy which should be returned to buyer.

The copy of Ford's Form 3618 attached to the Amendment was identical to that attached to Purchase Order No. 15145, but the broad indemnity provision of Form 3618 was not marked "VOID." The acknowledgment copy of the Amendment was executed by Allied on November 10 and reached Ford on November 12, 1956. At that time Allied had already begun installation and on September 5, 1956, Hankins, an employee of Allied, had sustained personal injuries as a result of the negligence of Ford's employees in connection with Allied's work. Hankins later brought suit against Ford and Ford in turn impleaded Allied, relying on the indemnity provision of Form 3618. The trial resulted in a verdict for Hankins against Ford and for Ford against Allied. Allied's motion for judgment notwithstanding the verdict was denied and judgment was entered against it. Allied appealed.]

■ MILLER, DISTRICT JUDGE. . . . Allied first says that the contractual provisions evidenced by Amendment No. 2 were not in effect at the time of the Hankins injury because it had not been accepted at that time by Allied in the formal manner expressly required by the amendment itself. It argues that a binding acceptance of the amendment could be effected only by Allied's execution of the acknowledgment copy of the amendment and its return to Ford.

With this argument we cannot agree. It is true that an offeror may prescribe the manner in which acceptance of his offer shall be indicated by the offeree, and an acceptance of the offer in the manner prescribed will bind the offeror. And it has been held that if the offeror prescribes an exclusive manner of acceptance, an attempt on the part of the offeree to accept the offer in a different manner does not bind the offeror *in the absence of a meeting of the minds on the altered type of acceptance*. Venters v. Stewart, Ky.App., 261 S.W.2d 444, 446; Shortridge v. Ghio, Mo.App., 253 S.W.2d 838, 845. On the other hand, if an offeror merely suggests a permitted method of acceptance, other methods of acceptance are not precluded. Restatement, Contracts, Sec. 61; Williston on Contracts, Third Ed. Secs. 70, 76. Moreover, it is equally well settled that if the offer requests a return promise and the offeree without making the promise actually does or tenders what he was requested to promise to do, there is a contract if such performance is completed or tendered within the time allowable for accepting by making a promise. In such a case a tender operates as a promise to render complete performance. Restatement, Contracts, Sec. 63; Williston on Contracts, Third Ed. Sec. 75.

Applying these principles to the case at bar, we reach the conclusion, first, that execution and return of the acknowledgment copy of Amendment No. 2 was merely a suggested method of acceptance and did not preclude acceptance by some other method; and, second, that the offer was accepted and a binding contract effected when Allied, with Ford's knowledge, consent and acquiescence, undertook performance of the work called for by the amendment. The only significant provision, as we view the amendment, was that it would not be binding until it was accepted by Allied. This provision was obviously for the protection of Ford, Albright v. Stegeman Motorcar Co., 168 Wis. 557, 170 N.W. 951, 952, 19 A.L.R. 463, and its import was that Ford would not be bound by the amendment unless Allied agreed to all of the conditions specified therein. The provision for execution and return of the acknowledgement copy, as we construe the language used, was not to set forth an exclusive method of acceptance but was merely to provide a simple and convenient method by which the assent of Allied to the contractual provisions of the amendment could be indicated. The primary object of Ford was to have the work performed by Allied upon the terms prescribed in the amendment, and the mere signing and return of an acknowledgment copy of the amendment before actually undertaking the work itself cannot be regarded as an essential condition to completion of a binding contract.

It is well settled that acceptance of an offer by part performance in accordance with the terms of the offer is sufficient to complete the contract. . . .

Other authorities are to the effect that the acceptance of a contract may be implied from acts of the parties. Malooly v. York Heating & Vent. Corp., 270 Mich. 240, 253, 258 N.W. 622; and may be shown by proving acts done on the faith of the order, including shipment of the goods ordered, Petroleum Products Distributing Co. v. Alton Tank Line, 165 Iowa 398, 403, 146 N.W. 52. Cf. Texas Co. v. Hudson, 155 La. 966, 971, 99 So. 714, 716. It would seem necessarily to follow that an offeree who has unjustifiably led the offeror to believe that he had acquired a contractual right, should not be allowed to assert an actual intent at variance with the meaning of his acts.

It has been argued on behalf of Allied, by way of analogy, that Ford could have revoked the order when Allied began installing the machinery without first having executed its written acceptance. If this point should be conceded, cf. Venters v. Stewart, supra, it would avail Allied nothing. For, after Allied began performance by installing the machinery called for, and Ford acquiesced in the acts of Allied and accepted the benefits of the performance, Ford was estopped to object and could not thereafter be heard to complain that there was no contract. Sparks v. Mauk, 170 Cal. 122, 148 P. 926. . . .

Affirmed.

NOTES

(1) *Questions.* At what point in time would it be reasonable to say that Ford could not have withdrawn the offer it made to Allied in "Amendment No. 2"? When Allied's truck pulled up at the gate to Ford's plant, and the gate was opened? Before that? After that?

(2) *Case Comparisons.* Can the *Ever–Tite* and *Allied Steel* cases be distinguished from White v. Corlies & Tift? What is the critical language of the offer in each case? What reason did Ford have for putting the clause on its form? Consider, in this connection, the 1970 revision of Ford's purchase order, which reads:

> ACCEPTANCE—Unless otherwise provided herein, it is understood and agreed that the written acceptance by Seller of this purchase order or the

commencement of any work or the performance of any services hereunder by Seller (including the commencement of any work or the performance of any services with respect to samples) shall constitute acceptance by Seller of this purchase order and of all of its terms and conditions, and that such acceptance is expressly limited to such terms and conditions.

Would the result have been different if the court had held that the offer stated the offer had stated the *exclusive* means of acceptance? Had the UCC been enacted at this time, would it have applied to this case? What result under UCC § 2–204(1)(a)?

PROBLEM

Acceptance and Rejection. The Chicago Medical School distributed a bulletin for prospective students stating that it selected applicants "on the basis of scholarship, character, and motivation," in addition to "academic achievement." Robert Steinberg received a bulletin, applied for admission, and paid the School the required $15 fee. Following his rejection, Steinberg learned that candidates were also evaluated on nonacademic criteria, such as their family's ability to make large donations. He argues that by failing to evaluate his application according to the stated criteria, the School is in breach of its contract with him. Can you state a theory of contract liability? Who made the offer? See Steinberg v. Chicago Medical School, 371 N.E.2d 634 (Ill.1977).

SHIPMENT OF GOODS AS ACCEPTANCE

Is a seller's shipment of goods, in response to a buyer's order, an acceptance? The question usually arises when the buyer attempts to revoke an order after the seller has placed the goods on board a carrier in response to the buyer's order. UCC § 2–206(1)(b) provides that an order "for prompt or current shipment shall be construed as inviting acceptance either by a prompt promise to ship or by the prompt or current shipment of conforming or non-conforming goods." Under the Code the buyer's revocation comes too late if the seller has promptly shipped.

The question can arise in another way. Suppose that the seller ships non-conforming goods. Has the seller bound itself to deliver goods that conform to the buyer's order? That question is taken up in the opinion that follows.

Corinthian Pharmaceutical Systems, Inc. v. Lederle Laboratories

United States District Court, S.D. Indiana, Indianapolis Division, 1989.
724 F.Supp. 605.

■ McKINNEY, DISTRICT JUDGE. Defendant Lederle Laboratories is a pharmaceutical manufacturer and distributor that makes a number of drugs, including the DTP vaccine. Plaintiff Corinthian Pharmaceutical is a distributor of drugs that purchases supplies from manufacturers such as Lederle Labs and then resells the product to physicians and other providers. One of the products that Corinthian buys and distributes with some regularity is the DTP vaccine. . . .

Lederle periodically issued a price list to its customers for all of its products. Each price list stated that all orders were subject to acceptance by Lederle at its home office, and indicated that the prices shown "were in effect at the time of publication but are submitted without offer and are subject to change without notice." The price list further stated that changes in price "take immediate effect and unfilled current orders and back orders will be invoiced at the price in effect at the time shipment is made."

From 1985 through early 1986, Corinthian made a number of purchases of the vaccine from Lederle Labs. During this period of time, the largest single order ever placed by Corinthian with Lederle was for 100 vials. When Lederle Labs filled an order it sent an invoice to Corinthian. . . .

During this period of time, product liability lawsuits concerning DTP increased, and insurance became more difficult to procure. As a result, Lederle decided in early 1986 to self-insure against such risks. In order to cover the costs of self-insurance, Lederle concluded that a substantial increase in the price of the vaccine would be necessary.

In order to communicate the price change to its own sales people, Lederle's Price Manager prepared "PRICE LETTER NO. E–48." This document was dated May 19, 1986, and indicated that effective May 20, 1986, the price of the DTP vaccine would be raised from $51.00 to $171.00 per vial. Price letters such as these were routinely sent to Lederle's sales force, but did not go to customers. Corinthian Pharmaceutical did not know of the existence of this internal price letter until a Lederle representative presented it to Corinthian several weeks after May 20, 1986.

Additionally, Lederle Labs also wrote a letter dated May 20, 1986, to its customers announcing the price increase and explaining the liability and insurance problems that brought about the change. Corinthian somehow gained knowledge of this letter on May 19, 1986, the date before the price increase was to take effect. In response to the knowledge of the impending price increase, Corinthian immediately ordered 1000 vials of DTP vaccine from Lederle. Corinthian placed its order on May 19, 1986, by calling Lederle's "Telgo" system. The Telgo system is a telephone computer ordering system that allows customers to place orders over the phone by communicating with a computer. After Corinthian placed its order with the Telgo system, the computer gave Corinthian a tracking number for its order. On the same date, Corinthian sent Lederle two written confirmations of its order. On each form Corinthian stated that this "order is to receive the $64.32 per vial price."

On June 3, 1986, Lederle sent invoice 1771 to Corinthian for 50 vials of DTP vaccine priced at $64.32 per vial. The invoice contained the standard Lederle conditions noted above. The 50 vials were sent to Corinthian and were accepted. At the same time, Lederle sent its customers, including Corinthian, a letter regarding DTP vaccine pricing and orders. This letter stated that the "enclosed represents a partial shipment of the order for DTP vaccine, which you placed with Lederle on May 19, 1986." The letter stated that under Lederle's standard terms and conditions of sale the normal policy would be to invoice the order at the price when shipment was made. However, in light of the magnitude of the price increase, Lederle had decided to make an exception to its terms and conditions and ship a portion of the order at the lower price. The letter further stated that the balance would be priced at $171.00, and that shipment would be made during the week of June 16. The letter closed, "If for any reason you wish to cancel the balance of your order, please contact [us] . . . on or before June 13."

Based on these facts, plaintiff Corinthian Pharmaceutical brings this action seeking specific performance for the 950 vials of DTP vaccine that Lederle Labs chose not to deliver. [Lederle moved for summary judgment urging] a number of alternative grounds for disposing of this claim, including that no contract for the sale of 1000 vials was formed, that if one was formed, it was governed by Lederle's terms and conditions, and that the 50 vials sent to Corinthian were merely an accommodation. . . .

Discussion

Despite the lengthy recitation of facts and summary judgment standards, this is a straightforward sale of goods problem resembling those found in a contracts or sales casebook. The fundamental question is whether Lederle Labs agreed to sell Corinthian Pharmaceuticals 1,000 vials of DTP vaccine at $64.32 per vial. As shown below, the undisputed material facts mandate the conclusion as a matter of law that no such agreement was ever formed. . . .

Initially, it should be noted that this is a sale of goods covered by the Uniform Commercial Code, and that both parties are merchants under the Code. The parties do not discuss which state's laws are to apply to action, but because the Code is substantially the same in all states having any connection to this dispute, the Court will, for ease of reference, refer in general to the U.C.C. with relevant interpretations from Indiana and other states.

The starting point in this analysis is where did the first offer originate. An offer is "the manifestation of willingness to enter into a bargain, so made as to justify another person in understanding that his assent to that bargain is invited and will conclude it." H. Greenberg, Rights and Remedies Under U.C.C. Article 2 § 5.2 at 50 (1987) [hereinafter "Greenberg, U.C.C. Article 2"], (quoting 1 Restatement (Second), Contracts § 4 (1981)). The only possible conclusion in this case is that Corinthian's "order" of May 19, 1986, for 1,000 vials at $64.32 was the first offer. Nothing that the seller had done prior to this point can be interpreted as an offer.

First, the price lists distributed by Lederle to its customers did not constitute offers. It is well settled that quotations are mere invitations to make an offer, particularly where, as here, the price lists specifically stated that prices were subject to change without notice and that all orders were subject to acceptance by Lederle.

Second, neither Lederle's internal price memorandum nor its letter to customers dated May 20, 1986, can be construed as an offer to sell 1,000 vials at the lower price. There is no evidence that Lederle intended Corinthian to receive the internal price memorandum, nor is there anything in the record to support the conclusion that the May 20, 1986, letter was an offer to sell 1,000 vials to Corinthian at the lower price. If anything, the evidence shows that Corinthian was not supposed to receive this letter until after the price increase had taken place. Moreover, the letter, just like the price lists, was a mere quotation (i.e., an invitation to submit an offer) sent to all customers. As such, it did not bestow on Corinthian nor other customers the power to form a binding contract for the sale of one thousand, or, for that matter, one million vials of vaccine.

Thus, as a matter of law, the first offer was made by Corinthian when it phoned in and subsequently confirmed its order for 1,000 vials at the lower price. The next question, then, is whether Lederle ever accepted that offer.

Under the Code, an acceptance need not be the mirror-image of the offer. U.C.C. § 2–207. However, the offeree must still do some act that manifests the intention to accept the offer and make a contract. Under § 2–206, an offer to make a contract shall be construed as inviting acceptance in any manner and by any medium reasonable in the circumstances. The first question regarding acceptance, therefore, is whether Lederle accepted the offer prior to sending the 50 vials of vaccine.

The record is clear that Lederle did not communicate or do any act prior to shipping the 50 vials that could support the finding of an acceptance. When Corinthian placed its order, it merely received a tracking number from the Telgo computer. Such an automated, ministerial act cannot constitute an acceptance. See, e.g., Foremost Pro Color, Inc. v. Eastman Kodak Co., 703 F.2d 534, 539 (9th Cir.1983) (logging purchase orders as received did not manifest acceptance); Southern Spindle & Flyer Co. v. Milliken & Co., 53 N.C.App. 785, 281 S.E.2d 734, 736 (1981) (seller's acknowledgement of receipt of purchase order did not constitute assent to its terms). Thus, there was no acceptance of Corinthian's offer prior to the deliver of 50 vials.

The next question, then, is what is to be made of the shipment of 50 vials and the accompanying letter. Section 2–206(1)(b) of the Code speaks to this issue:

> [A]n order or other offer to buy goods for prompt or current shipment shall be construed as inviting acceptance either by a prompt promise to ship or by the prompt or current shipment of conforming or non-conforming goods, *but such a shipment of non-conforming goods does not constitute an acceptance if the seller seasonally notifies the buyer that the shipment is offered only as an accommodation to the buyer.*

§ 2–206 (emphasis added). Thus, under the Code a seller accepts the offer by shipping goods, whether they are conforming or not, but if the seller ships non-conforming goods and seasonably notifies the buyer that the shipment is a mere accommodation, then the seller has not, in fact, accepted the buyer's offer. See Greenberg, U.C.C. Article 2 § 5.5 at 53.

In this case, the offer made by Corinthian was for 1,000 vials at $64.32. In response, Lederle Labs shipped only 50 vials at $64.32 per vial, and wrote Corinthian indicating that the balance of the order would be priced at $171.00 per vial and would be shipped during the week of June 16. The letter further indicated that the buyer could cancel its order by calling Lederle Labs. Clearly, Lederle's shipment was non-conforming, for it was for only 1/20 th of the quantity desired by the buyer. See § 2–106(2) (goods or conduct are conforming when they are in accordance with the obligations under the contract); Michiana Mack, Inc. v. Allendale Rural Fire Protection, 428 N.E.2d 1367, 1370 (Ind.App.1981) (non-conformity describes goods and conduct). The narrow issue, then, is whether Lederle's response to the offer was a shipment of non-conforming goods not constituting an acceptance because it was offered only as an accommodation under § 2–206.

An accommodation is an arrangement or engagement made as a favor to another. Black's Law Dictionary (5th ed. 1979). The term implies no consideration. Id. In this case, then, even taking all inferences favorably for the buyer, the only possible conclusion is that Lederle Labs' shipment of 50 vials was offered merely as an accommodation; that is to say, Lederle had no obligation to make the partial shipment, and did so only as a favor to the buyer. The accommodation letter, which Corinthian is sure it received, clearly stated that the 50 vials were being sent at the lower price as an exception to Lederle's general policy, and that the balance of the offer would be invoiced at the higher price. The letter further indicated that Lederle's proposal to ship the balance of the order at the higher price could be rejected by the buyer. Moreover, the standard terms of Lederle's invoice stated that acceptance of the order was expressly conditioned upon buyer's assent to the seller's terms.

Under these undisputed facts, § 2–206(1)(b) was satisfied. Where, as here, the notification is properly made, the shipment of nonconforming goods is treated as a counteroffer just as at common law, and the buyer may accept or reject the counteroffer under normal contract rules. 2 W. Hawkland, Uniform Commercial Code Series § 2–206:04 (1987).

Thus, the end result of this analysis is that Lederle Lab's price quotations were mere invitations to make an offer, that by placing its order Corinthian made an offer to buy 1,000 vials at the low price, that by shipping 50 vials at the low price Lederle's response was non-conforming, but the non-conforming response was a mere accommodation and thus constituted a counteroffer. Accordingly, there being no genuine issues of material fact on these issues and the law being in favor of the seller, summary judgment must be granted for Lederle Labs. . . .

For all these reasons, the defendant's motion for summary judgment is granted.

NOTES

(1) *Questions.* What functions does each of the following events play in the process of contract formation: Lederle's letter to customers? Corinthian's telephone order? Telgo's assignment of a tracking number? Lederle's shipment to Corinthian and accompanying letter?

If the seller's shipment is not an acceptance of the buyer's offer but is a counter-offer, what means of acceptance does that counter-offer invite? See UCC § 2–206(1) and Restatement §§ 32 and 62.

The court quickly disposed of the argument that the tracking number was an acceptance by Lederle: "Such an automated, ministerial act cannot constitute an acceptance." Why should that be so? Was the fact of automation or the ministerial purpose that made the computer-generated response legally insignificant in this case?

(2) *Non-conforming.* According to Comment 4 to UCC § 2–206, subsection (1)(b) "deals with the situation where a shipment made following an order is shown by a notification of shipment to be referable to that order but has a defect." If that refers to defective *goods*, the situation in the main case was different. Perhaps, although the statute speaks of non-conforming *goods*, the Comment refers to defective *shipment*. In either case the court's application of the subsection may make good sense. What of an order calling for goods to be "shipped within ten days"? Is a shipment after that a non-conforming one? Observe that the statute speaks of promptness by offerees.

Observe also that, by shipping non-conforming goods, an offeree—one who does not say they are sent as an accommodation—commits itself to supply goods that conform to the order. For example, by shipping wormy apples, a grower might bind itself to ship apples without worms.

To what other situations might the subsection apply? To one in which apples are ordered, and oranges are shipped? Are oranges defective apples?

(3) *Preparation for Shipment of Goods as Acceptance?* What if a buyer attempts to revoke an order after the seller has incurred expense in preparing to ship the goods but has not actually shipped them? In Doll & Smith v. A. & S. Sanitary Dairy Co., 211 N.W. 230 (Iowa 1926), the Dairy Company ordered advertising materials from Doll & Smith ("Doll"), through an agent. Two days after Doll received the order in New York, the Dairy Company wired a cancellation of the order. In an action by Doll it contended that he had incurred expenses in response to the order, having referred it to a factory and paid a commission to the agent. A judgment in favor of the Dairy Company was affirmed on appeal: "No case for damages . . . is made." Can this decision be reconciled with the *Ever–Tite* case, above?

SILENCE NOT ORDINARILY ACCEPTANCE

The general rule is that silence alone is not acceptance. "So fundamental is the tenet . . . that, even as the master of the offer, the offeror is powerless to alter the rule." 1 Farnsworth on Contracts § 3.15 (2d ed. 1998) The offeror who appends to an offer, "Unless I hear from you within 48 hours, you will be deemed to have accepted my offer," cannot hold the offeree who fails to reject. The rule, along with some real or apparent exceptions to it, is stated in Restatement § 69.

In a Massachusetts case from 1893, however, the court concluded that a silent retention amounted to an acceptance. A seller sued for $108.50, the price of 2,350 eelskins that he had sent to the buyer, a manufacturer of whips. Holmes wrote: "The plaintiff was not a stranger to the defendant, even if there was no contract between them. He had sent eelskins in the same way four or five times before, and they had been accepted and paid for.... [S]ending them [imposed] on the defendant a duty to act about them; and silence on its part, coupled with a retention of the skins for an unreasonable time, might be found by the jury to warrant the plaintiff in assuming that they were accepted, and thus to amount to an acceptance." Hobbs v. Massasoit Whip Co., 33 N.E. 495. What, beyond mere silence, was there in this case?

What if the parties are reversed and it is the *buyer* who asserts that the seller has accepted by silent retention of *the buyer's order* ? American Bronze Corp. v. Streamway Products, 456 N.E.2d 1295, 1300 (Ohio App. 1982), is such a case. For over twenty years Streamway had called in orders to American by telephone and followed them up with written purchase orders, at which time American would begin production. When American refused to fill three orders, Streamway claimed damages and, from a denial of its claim, appealed. The Ohio Court of Appeals reversed and remanded, citing UCC § 2–204(1). "The filling of these orders in this manner as a regular practice constituted a valid acceptance and thus created a binding contract.... Absent a notice of rejection Streamway would be justified in believing that American had indeed begun production." What, beyond mere silence, was there in *this* case?

NOTE

Unsolicited Merchandise. A persistent consumer complaint concerns the practice of sending unsolicited merchandise, often coupled with the suggestion that the recipient will be liable for the price if it is not returned. As you might suppose, this suggestion is not the law: the recipient who lays the merchandise on a shelf and does not use it incurs no liability. Nonetheless, the practice is at best irritating and at worst deceptive. A number of states have enacted statutes dealing with it. See, *e.g.,* N.Y.Gen.Bus.L. § 396–2a. Federal laws regulating the mails also restrict such practices.

Marketing programs for book or CD clubs depend on a subscriber's agreement that merchandise not specifically ordered will be paid for in the absence of an instruction to the contrary. Is it significant that these arrangements "typically provide some up-front benefits to the offeree," such as an introductory bonus, and place mailing costs on the offeror? See Avery Katz, The Strategic Structure of Offer and Acceptance: Game Theory and the Law of Contract Formation, 89 Mich.L.Rev. 215, 264–65, 271–72 (1990). Professor Katz suggests an efficiency argument for the offeree's "right to be let alone." More simply, it might be thought that freedom *from* contract is a more important ideal than is freedom *to* contract. See Edwin Patterson, An Apology for Consideration, 58 Colum.L.Rev. 929, 948 (1958).

SECTION 4.   TERMINATION OF THE POWER OF ACCEPTANCE

After a party has made an offer, conferring on another the power of acceptance, that power can be terminated (1) by lapse of the offer, (2) by its revocation by the offeror, (3) by the offeror's death or incapacity, or (4) by the offeree's rejection.

This section begins with lapse—the expiration of the period within which an offer can be accepted. How long does an offer remain "open" when an offeror neglects to state a period for acceptance: When does it become too late for the offeree to accept?

Revocation is considered next. The basic rule in common-law countries is that an offeror can terminate an ordinary offer, at any time before it has been accepted, by revoking it. An exception to this rule occurs when the offeror has made a "firm offer" or option contract. In contrast to ordinary offers, these are offers that are—for a time—not subject to revocation. Irrevocability is the defining characteristic of an option contract.

Attention then briefly turns to a third terminating event: the death or the incapacity of the offeror. While posing interesting conceptual problems (the rule holds whether or not the offeree learns of the death), the practical import of the rule has been greatly reduced since the typical offeror is now often a deathless corporate entity.

The fourth terminating event is rejection, an act by the offeree which puts an end to an ordinary offer. Here we examine what counts as a rejection under the common law "mirror image" rule. The materials also consider the effect of rejecting a firm offer.

One final topic rounds out the Section. When does acceptance, revocation, or rejection that is dispatched become effective: when it is sent, or when it is received? The traditional answers are found in the "mailbox rule," discussed below.

(A) Lapse of an Offer

After some period of time, an offer lapses. If no period is specified in the offer, it lapses after a reasonable time. What is a reasonable time depends, of course, on the circumstances. Take an offer to buy or sell. If the subject matter undergoes rapid fluctuation in price, as is often the case for goods, this will shorten the time. The following cases illustrate some other factors used in determining what is a reasonable time for this purpose.

In Akers v. J.B. Sedberry, Inc., 286 S.W.2d 617 (Tenn.App.1955), Akers, while in a conference with the president of his employer, offered orally to resign. The president ignored the offer and the conference continued. A few days later the president advised Akers by wire that his offer was accepted, and that Akers was to discontinue his association with the Sedberry firm. Akers sued for breach of contract and a decree in his favor was affirmed. "Ordinarily, an offer made by one to another in a face to face conversation is deemed to continue only to the close of their conversation, and cannot be accepted thereafter." Caldwell v. E.F. Spears & Sons, 216 S.W. 83 (Ky.1919).

In Loring v. City of Boston, 48 Mass. 409 (1844), the City of Boston had run in the daily papers an advertisement offering a $1,000 reward for the apprehension and conviction of any person setting fire to any building within the city limits. The advertisements continued for about a week in May, 1837, and did not appear again. In January, 1841, there was a fire in Boston, and Loring, with the reward in mind, pursued the arsonist to New York, arrested him, returned him to Boston, had him indicted and prosecuted, produced evidence that convicted him, and then sued the city for the reward. There was evidence that fire alarms had been frequent before the advertisements but much less so from that time until the end of 1841.

The Supreme Judicial Court of Massachusetts denied recovery. Since the purposes of such an offer are to excite the vigilance of the public and, perhaps, to alarm offenders, the offer of the reward must be notorious in order to be effective. Three years and eight months was not a reasonable time under the circumstances. "In that length of time, the exigency under which it was made having passed, it must be presumed to have been forgotten by most of the officers and citizens of the community, and cannot be presumed to have been before the public as an actuating motive to vigilance and exertion on this subject; nor could it justly and reasonably have been so understood by the plaintiffs." But cf. Carr v. Mahaska County Bankers Ass'n, 269 N.W. 494 (Iowa 1936).

NOTES

(1) *Lapses in Judgment?* A motorist (M) was involved in an accident with C, who suffered an injury and claimed that M's negligence caused it. The attorney (A) for M's insurance company submitted an offer in writing to C's attorney (B). The offer, which did not specify an expiration date, was to pay C $25,000 in full satisfaction of C's claim against M.

Negotiations over this claim continued for many months. After some time, it seemed likely that if C's claim was not filed within a month, C would be barred from suing by a statute of limitations. Six weeks elapsed without a response to the offer. Then B, acting for C, sent a fax to A which purported to accept the offer. What might lead one to think the "acceptance" was too late?

In a contract action based on facts much like these the trial court gave summary judgment for C, the claimant. Appealing, the insurer referred to a two-year period of limitation for bringing personal-injury actions. But the court observed that such a period is not inflexible: excusing circumstances may justify a later suit. The court relied on comment *b* to Restatement § 41: "In general, the question is what time would be thought satisfactory to the offeror by a reasonable man in the position of the offeree." On that basis, what result? See Vaskie v. West American Ins. Co., 556 A.2d 436 (Pa.Super.1989). What suggestions might be made to attorneys A and B about their professional conduct?

(2) *Tardy Acceptances.* What is the effect of an expression of acceptance that arrives too late to operate as an acceptance? Can the offeror choose simply to disregard the delay and treat the message as an acceptance? Or is it a counter-offer, so that no contract results unless the original offeror, in turn, expresses acceptance?

Consider these questions in relation to Note 1. Assume that claimant C's "acceptance" came too late. Assume also that C then sued the motorist for (say) $50,000—somehow overcoming the statute-of-limitations problem. Can M and his insurance company now claim that C's lawsuit is barred by a valid settlement agreement?

(3) *Counting the Offers.* In Newman v. Schiff, 778 F.2d 460, 462 (8th Cir.1985), the plaintiff was a tax lawyer who claimed $100,000 for supplying citations to the Internal Revenue Code in response to a challenge made on a TV call-in show: "If anybody calls this show—I have the Code—and cites any section of this Code that says an individual is required to file a tax return, I will pay them $100,000." The challenge had been made in the evening, on "Nightwatch"; the plaintiff had learned of it from watching a brief segment that was rebroadcast on CBS Morning News. (He called a number at CBS different from the one announced on Nightwatch for call-ins.) Was the plaintiff right in thinking two offers had been made? Under an objective approach, was the plaintiff justified in thinking an offer had been made on the morning program?

PROBLEM

Courtroom Countdown. After falling at a university's ice rink, a claimant sued the university for negligence. A jury trial was held. During a ten minute recess prior to the closing arguments, the university's counsel, Orlando, offered the claimant, through her counsel Haaz, $750,000 to settle the case. At the end of the conversation, Orlando told Haaz, "You've got to get back to me." While making the statement, Orlando looked at the clock and "placed his palms sideward." When the trial resumed, Haaz was granted two minutes to talk to his client. There was no futher communication between counsel. During Orlando's closing argument, the claimant authorized Haaz to accept the settlement offer. Haaz then gave his closing argument. At a sidebar conference following the closings, Haaz stated that his client had accepted the offer, to which Orlando replied, "I don't know if it's still there, judge." Prior to jury deliberations, the claimant moved to enforce the settlement agreement. Had it lapsed? The period between the offer and the statement of acceptance was seventy minutes. What is a reasonable time in such a case? See Yaros v. Trustees of University of Pennsylvania, 742 A.2d 1118 (Pa. 1999). The jury later returned a verdict for the university; does this fact help in deciding the question of lapse? In understanding the timing of the purported acceptance?

(B) REVOCATION OF OFFERS

Grotius, the great seventeenth-century Dutch jurist, favored the rule that prevails at the common law: an offer is freely revocable. But the opposing rule has its adherents. In Germany and some other civil-law countries an offer is irrevocable for a reasonable time unless the offeror expresses a different intention. See 1 Schlesinger (ed.), Formation of *Contracts: A Study of the Common Core of Legal Systems* 780–83 (1968).

Which rule seems preferable? One disadvantage of the German rule is that during the period of irrevocability, the offeree can take advantage of changing economic conditions to speculate at the expense of the offeror. Although Germany and the other countries that have this rule have historically experienced much greater economic upheavals than has the United States, they have been able to live with the rule, at least in part, because it can easily be avoided by expressly reserving the power to revoke or providing that the communication is not an offer at all. The extent to which the offeror in the United States can avoid the common law rule by expressly relinquishing the power to revoke is discussed in connection with "firm offers" under Article 2, p. 176 below.

When is a communication a revocation? In Hoover Motor Express Co. v. Clements Paper Co., 241 S.W.2d 851 (Tenn.1951), Hoover had made an offer to Clements to buy real estate. Although the offer had been made on November 19, and Williams, Clements' vice-president, had been authorized in December to accept it, he had not done so by January 13. On that day Williams telephoned Hoover and "told him that we were ready to go through with it and I would like to discuss it with him." Hoover replied, "Well, I don't know if we are ready. We have not decided, we might not want to go through with it." Clements later sent an acceptance, but the court held that it was too late. Hoover's remark on the telephone "brought home to Williams that Hoover no longer consented to the transaction."

Compare the court's treatment of the claimed revocation in this case with the courts' treatment of the claimed offers in Owen v. Tunison and in Harvey v. Facey, above. Are they consistent?

––––––––

OPTION CONTRACTS

A promise made by an offeror that effectively limits the offeror's power to revoke is called an option or, in the language of the Restatement § 25, an option contract. Usually an option expresses, directly or indirectly, a fixed period within which the offeree must exercise, or "pick up," the option. The following material explores three ways that options may be created: consideration, "firm offers" under the UCC, and reliance by the offeree.

NOTE

Stock Options. While the cases that follow concern short term options for the purchase of real estate, options on stock and other financial instruments for longer periods are increasingly common, whether on the public options markets, the private "over-the-counter" market, or as executive compensation. The prices are volatile. On a day when the market price of a stock increases by only 2%, the price of a short-term option to purchase ("call") the shares might easily double. The stock purchase price named in the contract may be close to the price of the underlying shares when the contract is issued, yet may come to seem very costly, or the reverse, from time to time thereafter. It is known as the "strike price." The reciprocal of a purchase option, which confers the power to sell at a strike price, is a "put." Options relating to frequently traded assets such as securities and commodities are classified in financial markets (along with so-called forward contracts) as "derivatives."

Dickinson v. Dodds

In the Court of Appeal, Chancery Division, 1876.
LR 2 Ch.D. 463.

On Wednesday, the 10th of June, 1874, the defendant John Dodds signed and delivered to the plaintiff, George Dickinson, a memorandum, of which the material part was as follows:

"I hereby agree to sell to Mr. George Dickinson the whole of the dwelling-houses, garden ground, stabling, and outbuildings thereto belonging, situate at Croft, belonging to me, for the sum of £ 800. As witness my hand this tenth day of June, 1874.

£ 800 [Signed] John Dodds."

"P.S.—This offer to be left over until Friday, 9' o'clock a.m. J.D. (The twelfth), 12th June, 1874. [Signed] J. Dodds."

The bill alleged that Dodds understood and intended that the plaintiff should have until Friday, 9 a.m., within which to determine whether he would or would not purchase, and that he should absolutely have until that time the refusal of the property at the price of £ 800, and that the plaintiff in fact determined to accept the offer on the morning of Thursday, the 11th of June, but did not at once signify his acceptance to Dodds, believing that he had the power to accept it until 9 a.m. on Friday.

In the afternoon of the Thursday the plaintiff was informed by a Mr. Berry that Dodds had been offering or agreeing to sell the property to Thomas Allan, the other defendant. Thereupon the plaintiff, at about half past seven in the evening, went to the house of Mrs. Burgess, the mother-in-law of Dodds, where he was then staying, and left with her formal acceptance in writing of the offer to sell the property. According to the evidence of Mrs. Burgess this document never in fact reached Dodds, she having forgotten to give it to him.

On the following (Friday) morning, at about seven o'clock, Berry, who was acting as agent for Dickinson, found Dodds at Darlington Railway station, and handed to him a duplicate of the acceptance by Dickinson, and explained to Dodds its purport. He replied that it was too late, as he had already sold the property. A few minutes later Dickinson himself found Dodds entering a railway carriage, and handed him another duplicate of the notice of acceptance, but Dodds declined to receive it, saying: "You are too late. I have sold the property."

It appeared that on the day before, Thursday, the 11th of June, Dodds had signed a formal contract for the sale of the property to the defendant Allan for £ 800, and received from him a deposit of £ 40.

The bill in this suit prayed that the defendant Dodds might be decreed specifically to perform the contract of the 10th of June, 1874; that he might be restrained from conveying the property to Allan; that Allan might be restrained from taking any such conveyance; that, if any such conveyance had been or should be made, Allan might be declared a trustee of the property for, and might be directed to convey the property to, the plaintiff; and for damages.

Dickenson won a decree of specific performance. Dodds and Allan appealed.

■ JAMES, L.J., after referring to the document of the 10th of June, 1874, continued:

The document, though beginning "I hereby agree to sell," was nothing but an offer, and was only intended to be an offer, for the plaintiff himself tells us that he required time to consider whether he would enter into an agreement or not. Unless both parties had then agreed, there was no concluded agreement then made; it was in effect and substance only an offer to sell. The plaintiff, being minded not to complete the bargain at that time, added this memorandum: "This offer to be left over until Friday, 9 o'clock a.m. 12th June, 1874." That shows it was only an offer. There was no consideration given for the undertaking or promise, to whatever extent it may be considered binding, to keep the property unsold until 9 o'clock on Friday morning; but apparently Dickinson was of opinion, [and probably Dodds was of the same opinion] that he (Dodds) was bound by that promise, and could not in any way withdraw from it, or retract it, until 9 o'clock on Friday morning, and this probably explains a good deal of what afterwards took place. But it is clear settled law, on one of the clearest principles of law, that this promise, being a mere (nudum pactum) was not binding, and that at any moment before a complete acceptance by Dickinson of the offer, Dodds was as free as Dickinson himself. . . .

The plaintiff says in effect that, having heard and knowing that Dodds was no longer minded to sell to him, and that he was selling or sold to some one else, thinking that he could not in point of law withdraw his offer, meaning to fix him to it, and endeavoring to bind him: "I went to the house where he was lodging, and saw his mother-in-law, and left with her an acceptance of the offer, knowing all the while that he had entirely changed his mind. I got an agent to watch for him at 7 o'clock the next morning, and I went to the train just before 9 o'clock, in order that I might catch him and give him my notice of acceptance just before 9 o'clock, and when that occurred he told my agent, and he told me, 'You are too late,' and he then threw back the paper." It is to my mind quite clear that before there was any attempt at acceptance by the plaintiff, he was perfectly well aware that Dodds had changed his mind, and that he had in fact agreed to sell the property to Allan. It is impossible, therefore to say there was ever that existence of the same mind between the two parties which is essential in point of law to the making of an agreement. I am of opinion, therefore, that the plaintiff has failed to prove that there was any binding contract between Dodds and himself.

■ MELLISH, L.J. I am of the same opinion . . . Well, then, this being only an offer, and the law says—and it is clearly rule of law—that, although it is said that the offer is to be left open until Friday morning at 9 o'clock, that did not bind Dodds. . . . Assuming Allan to have known (there is some dispute about it, and Allan does not admit that he knew of it, but I will assume that he did) that Dodds had made the offer to Dickinson, and had given him until Friday morning at 9 o'clock to accept it, still in point of law that could not prevent Alan from making a more favorable offer than Dickinson, and entering at once into a binding agreement with Dodds.

Then Dickinson is informed by Berry that the property has been sold by Dodds to Allan. Berry does not tell us from whom it heard it, but he says that he did hear it, that he knew it, and that he informed Dickinson of it. Now, stopping there, the question which arises is this: If an offer has been made for the sale of the property, and before that offer is accepted the person who has made the offer enters into a binding agreement to sell the property to somebody else, and the person whom the offer was first made receives notice in some way that the property has been sold to another person, can he after that make a binding contract by the acceptance of the offer? I am of opinion that he cannot. The law may be right or wrong in saying that a person who has given to another a certain time within which to accept an offer is not bound by his promise to give that time; but, if he is not bound by that promise, and may still sell the property to some one else, and if it be the law that, on order to make a contract, the two minds must be in agreement at some one time, that is, at the time of the acceptance, how is it possible that when the person to whom the offer has been made the offer has sold the property to someone else, and that, in fact, he has not remained in the same mind to sell it to him, he can be at liberty to accept the offer and thereby make a binding contract? It seems to me that would be simply absurd. If a man makes an offer to sell a particular horse in his stable, and says, "I will give you until the day after to-morrow to accept the offer," and the next day goes and sells the horse to somebody else, and receives the purchase money from him, can the person to whom the offer was originally made then come and say, "I accept," so as to make a binding contract, and so as to be entitled to recover damages for the non-delivery of the horse? If the rule of law is that a mere offer to sell property, which can be withdrawn at any time, and which is made dependent on the acceptance of the person to whom it is made, is a mere nudum pactum, how is it possible that the person to whom the offer has been made can by acceptance make a binding contract after he knows that the person has made the offer has sold the property to some one else? ... I am clearly of opinion that there was no binding contract for the sale of this property by Dodds to Dickinson; and, even if there had been, it seems to me that the sale of the property to Allan was first in point to time. However, it is not necessary to consider, if there had been two binding contracts, which of them would be entitled to priority in equity, because there is no binding contract between Dodds and Dickinson.

NOTES

(1) *Indirect Communication of Revocation.* The opinion gives several versions of what Dickinson knew about what Dodds was doing. What exactly did Berry tell Dickinson? That Dodds had made an *offer* to sell the property or that he had made a *contract* to sell the property? Does it make a difference what Dickinson was told, or by whom? See Restatement § 43.

(2) *All in the Timing.* What can be said in support of a system in which the existence of a contract depends on the exact sequence of "acceptance" and "revocation"? When offeror and offeree meet at a railway station, is it not absurd that their legal relations can depend on who speaks first? See Farnsworth, Mutuality of Obligation in Contract Law, 3 Dayton L.Rev. 271 (1978).

(3) *Revocation of General Offers.* In the case of a general offer, addressed to the general public as reward offers usually are, it is ordinarily impossible for the offeror actually to communicate a revocation to all of the persons who are aware of the offer. Illustrative are the offers in the *Broadnax* case, p. 66 above, and the *Lefkowitz* case, p. 134 above.

The offeror can, of course, be required to give a notice of revocation publicity equal (and usually similar) to that given the offer. But, this being done, is the offeror nevertheless bound by the acceptance of an offeree who was aware of the offer but missed the notice of revocation? The answer is that the offeror is not bound, in spite of the requirement that a revocation be actually communicated to the offeree. See Restatement § 46.

How would one revoke an offer of a reward posted on a bulletin board? Would taking it down be sufficient? When would the revocation take effect? See Carr v. Mahaska County Bankers Ass'n, 269 N.W. 494 (Iowa 1936). In that case, the bank's reward notice has been posted in 1930, taken down in 1931 or 1932, and the reward claimed for the capture of a robber in 1935. Affirming judgment for the claimant who sought the reward, the Supreme Court of Iowa distinguished between the rewards for the discovery of perpetrators of crimes already committed, and those that were "contemplative" and "had to do with ... the robbing of some bank in Mahaska county, should it happen some day." From the nature of the rewards, the court stated "the public could reasonably assume that the offer once made was intended to continue into the future to accomplish [its] evident purpose...."

For an interesting historical example of revocation by publication involving a reward issued by Secretary of War Stanton for Suratt, one of Booth's accomplices in the assassination of President Lincoln, see Shuey v. United States, 92 U.S. 73 (1875).

(4) *Lapse or Revocation?* Consider the following case. In 1911, private land owners dedicated a property to a township for public use. State law required that any such dedication, or offer of public use, be accepted by a formal governmental resolution. (Why might that be?) Raymond and Jean Marx bought the property in the 1970s, and in 1993, they brought a quiet title action seeking to have the land declared theirs and not the township's. The township argued that in 1979 it had passed a resolution accepting all dedicated lands not yet accepted. Had the offer lapsed by 1979? It helps to know that an offer to dedicate land is generally understood as an on-going offer. Nonetheless, in Marx v. Department of Commerce, 558 N.W.2d 460 (Mich.App.1996), the court found that the 68–year delay was too long. But see Ackerman v. Spring Lake Twp., 163 N.W.2d 230 (Mich.App.1968), holding that 28 year delay in accepting dedication was timely. The court in *Marx* also found that the offer had been withdrawn, noting that withdrawal, or revocation, of an offer, differs from lapse in that the "former requires an affirmative act, while the latter stems from inaction." What action constituted the revocation in *Marx*?

PROBLEM

Hedging One's Bets. A offered in writing to sell B Greenacre for $1,000, offer to remain open five days. On the fourth day, B received a report from the county recorder of deeds that the recorder had received for recording a deed of Greenacre from A to C executed that day. Thinking there might be some chance that the recorder was wrong, B notified A of acceptance on the fifth day. The information given by the recorder proved to be erroneous. A denied having a contract with B. Was A right about that? See Restatement § 43, indicating that A is right if the report was "reliable." Might the report have been reliable, although erroneous?

"FIRM OFFERS" UNDER ARTICLE 2

In the early common law an irrevocable offer or option could be created by making the promise under seal. Upon the abolition of the seal, however, the doctrine of consideration became the exclusive means to this end. Decisions such as in Dickinson v. Dodds and its progeny have been subject to some criticism. "Until the nineteenth century was well advanced there seems to have been no serious concern over means for making offers 'firm.' . . . [Then in 1876 in Dickinson v. Dodds] an English court concluded with great confidence that a time limit fixed by the offeror could not prevent revocation before the time limit had expired, for in the absence of consideration any restriction on the power to revoke was simply *nudum pactum.* American decisions have dutifully followed this line ever since and thereby made the consideration test a still more prominent target of public ridicule . . . The difficulties were all manufactured by treating offers as a subordinate form of promise." John P. Dawson, *Gifts and Promises* 211–13 (1980).

The technique of giving a nominal sum in exchange for a promise of irrevocability may be adequate for offers of deals about real property, where the parties might be expected to foresee the possibility of revocation and deal with it in this rather elaborate way. It is less satisfactory for more informal transactions such as those for the sale of goods, where the offeror is less likely to clothe a promise in the trappings of consideration. (compare the circumstances surrounding the typical sale of goods with a sale of real property.)

The Uniform Commercial Code contains an important provision, which, in certain cases, enables an offeree to enforce an offer which, by its terms, states that it will be held open, even though the promise to hold it open was not supported by consideration. See UCC § 2–205 ("Firm Offers"). What conditions must be satisfied in order for the rule to apply? Under the Article 2 rule, how long can a firm offer unsupported by consideration be held open?

NOTES

(1) *Merchants Under Article 2.* Compare the definition of merchant in UCC § 2–104 with language of UCC § 2–205. Can one who does not deal in goods of the kind make a firm offer? Consider, for example, a manufacturer seeking to buy a new piece of factory equipment or to sell a used piece of factory equipment. Would such a manufacturer hold "himself out as having knowledge or skill peculiar to the practices . . . involved in the transaction"? What practices? (According to Comment 2, professional status "may be based upon specialized knowledge as to the goods, specialized knowledge as to business practices, or specialized knowledge as to both and which kind of specialized knowledge may be sufficient . . . is indicated by the nature of the provisions.")

Compare the use of the term "merchant" in UCC § 2–205 with its use in UCC § 2–314(1). Would such a manufacturer impliedly warrant the merchantability of the used piece of factory equipment?

(2) *New York Statute.* In addition to UCC § 2–205, New York has the following comprehensive statute, first enacted in 1941 (along with its statute on "moral obligation" in Note 2, p. 55 above), amended to take account of the Code:

> Except as otherwise provided in section 2–205 with respect to an offer by a merchant to buy or sell goods, when an offer to enter into a contract is made in a writing signed by the offeror, or by his agent, which states that the offer is irrevocable during a period set forth or until a time fixed, the offer shall not be revocable during such period or until such time because of the absence of consideration for the assurance of Irrevocability. When such a writing states that the offer is irrevocable but does not state any period of time of Irrevocability, it shall be construed to state that the offer is irrevocable for a reasonable time. (New York General Obligations Law § 5–1109.)

Is this statute available to a roofer like Ever–Tite, in the case on p. 154 above, if the roofer is doing its business in New York?

(3) *Recitals.* If a sum of money is paid as consideration for an option, this fact is usually recited. What is the effect of such a recital if no payment is made? Some courts have held it to be of no effect. Others have held that it makes the offer irrevocable, either as a binding acknowledgment of payment or as a promise to pay. Restatement § 87 favors the latter view, with the qualifications that the recital be in a signed writing and that the proposed exchange be fair. Comment *b* to that section explains, "The signed writing has vital significance as a formality, while the ceremonial manual delivery of a dollar or a peppercorn is an inconsequential formality."

Ragosta v. Wilder

Supreme Court of Vermont, 1991.
156 Vt. 390, 592 A.2d 367.

■ PECK, JUSTICE. Defendant [Wilder] appeals from a judgment ordering him to convey to plaintiffs [Ragosta] a piece of real property known as "The Fork Shop." Defendant argues that the court improperly found that a binding contract existed and that it misapplied the doctrine of equitable estoppel. He also contends that the ruling cannot be upheld under promissory estoppel principles since the court failed to examine the extent to which enforcement of defendant's promise to sell was required to prevent injustice. Because the trial court's ruling cannot stand on contract or equitable estoppel grounds and because the court's analysis of promissory estoppel is inextricably bound in its contractual analysis, we reverse and remand the cause for further proceedings consistent with the principles expressed herein.

In 1985, plaintiffs became interested in purchasing "The Fork Shop" from defendant, but preliminary negotiations between the parties were fruitless. In 1987, plaintiffs learned that defendant was again considering selling the "The Fork Shop," mailed him a letter offering to purchase the property along with a check for $2,000 and began arrangements to obtain the necessary financing. By letter dated September 28, 1987, defendant returned the $2,000 check explaining that he had two properties "up for sale" and that he would not sign an acceptance to plaintiffs' offer because "that would tie up both these properties until [there was] a closing." In the letter, he also made the following counter-offer:

> I will sell you the Fork Shop and its property as listed in book 35, at page 135 of the Brookfield Land Records on 17 April 1972, for $88,000.00 (Eighty-eight thousand dollars), at anytime up until the 1st of November 1987 that you appear with me at the Randolph National Bank with said sum. At which time they will give you a certified deed to this property or to your agent as directed, providing said property has not been sold.

On October 1st, the date plaintiffs received the letter, they called defendant. The court found that during the conversation plaintiffs told defendant that "the terms and conditions of his offer were acceptable and that they would in fact prepare to accept the offer." Defendant assured plaintiffs that there was no one else currently interested in purchasing "The Fork Shop."

On October 6th, plaintiffs informed defendant that they would not close the sale on October 8th as discussed previously but that they would come to Vermont on October 10th. On October 8th, defendant called plaintiffs and informed them that he was no longer willing to sell "The Fork Shop." The trial court found that, at that time, defendant was aware plaintiffs "had processed their loan application and were prepared to close." Plaintiffs informed defendant that they would be at the Randolph National Bank at 10:00 a.m. on October 15th with the $88,000 purchase price and in fact appeared. Defendant did not. Plaintiffs claim they incurred $7,499.23 in loan closing costs.

Plaintiffs sued for specific performance arguing that defendant had contracted to sell the property to them. They alleged moreover that defendant knew they would have to incur costs to obtain financing for the purchase but assured them that the sale would go through and that they relied on his assurances.

The trial court concluded that defendant "made an offer in writing which could only be accepted by performance prior to the deadline." It concluded further that defendant could not revoke his offer on October 8th because plaintiffs, relying on the offer, had already begun performance and that defendant should be estopped from revoking the offer on a theory of equitable estoppel. It ordered defendant to convey to plaintiffs "The Fork Shop" for $88,000. This appeal followed.

I.

Plaintiffs claim that defendant's letter of September 28, 1987 created a contract to sell "The Fork Shop" to them unless the property was sold to another buyer. Rather, defendant's letter contains an offer to sell the property for $88,000, which the trial court found could only be accepted "by performance prior to the deadline," and a promise to keep the offer open unless the property were sold to another buyer. Defendant received no consideration for either promise. In fact, defendant returned plaintiffs' check for $2,000 which would have constituted consideration for the promise to keep the offer open, presumably because he did not wish to make a firm offer. Thus, the promise to keep the offer to sell open was not enforceable and, absent the operation of equitable estoppel, defendant could revoke the offer to sell the property at any time before plaintiffs accepted it. See Buchannon v. Billings, 127 Vt. 69, 75, 238 A.2d 638, 642 (1968) ("An option is a continuing offer, and *if supported by a consideration,* it cannot be withdrawn before the time limit.") (emphasis added).

Plaintiffs argue that the actions they undertook to obtain financing, which were detrimental to them, could constitute consideration for the promise to keep the offer to sell open. Their argument is unconvincing. Although plaintiffs are correct in stating that a detriment may constitute consideration, they ignore the rule that "[t]o constitute consideration, a performance or a return promise must be bargained for." Restatement (Second) of Contracts § 71(1) (1981). "A performance or return promise is bargained for if it is sought by the promisor in exchange for his promise and is given by the promisee in exchange for that promise." Id. at § 71(2). Plaintiffs began to seek financing even before defendant made a definite offer to sell the property. Whatever detriment they suffered was not in exchange for defendant's promise to keep the offer to sell open.

The trial court ruled that the offer to sell "The Fork Shop" could only be accepted by performance but concluded that in obtaining financing plaintiffs began performance and that therefore defendant could not revoke the offer to sell once plaintiffs incurred the cost of obtaining financing. Section 45 of the Restatement (Second) of Contracts provides that "[w]here an offer invites an offeree to accept by rendering a performance and does not invite a promissory acceptance, an option contract is created when the offeree tenders or begins the invited performance or tenders a beginning of it." However, "[w]hat is begun or tendered must be part of the actual performance invited in order to preclude revocation under this Section." Id. at comment *f.*

Here, plaintiffs were merely engaged in preparation for performance. The court itself found only that "plaintiffs had changed their position in order to tender performance." At most, they obtained financing and assured defendant that they would pay; plaintiffs never tendered to defendant or even began to tender the $88,000 purchase price. Thus, they never accepted defendant's offer and no contract was ever created. See Multicare Medical Center v. State Social & Health Services, 114 Wash.2d 572, 584, 790 P.2d 124, 131 (1990) ("under a unilateral contract, an offer cannot be accepted by promising to perform; rather, the offeree must accept, if at all, by performance, and the contract then becomes executed").[1]

II.

Defendant claims next that the court was not justified in applying equitable estoppel in this case. We agree.

---

1. Because defendant specified that the manner of acceptance would be performance, plaintiffs' argument that they accepted defendant's offer over the telephone must fail. In fact, plaintiffs admitted in their depositions that they were very worried that the property would be sold to someone else prior to closing. Thus, they should have understood that they had no enforceable contract until closing.

One who invokes the doctrine of equitable estoppel has the burden of establishing each of its constituent elements. Four essential elements must be established: first, the party to be estopped must know the facts; second, the party being estopped must intend that his conduct shall be acted upon or the acts must be such that the party asserting the estoppel has a right to believe it is so intended; third, the latter must be ignorant of the true facts; and finally, the party asserting the estoppel must rely on the conduct of the party to be estopped to his detriment.

Fisher v. Poole, 142 Vt. 162, 168, 453 A.2d 408, 411–12 (1982) (citations omitted).

Equitable estoppel is inapplicable here because there were no facts known to defendant but unknown to plaintiffs. Plaintiffs cannot have acted on an understanding that defendant would definitely convey the property to them. On its face, defendant's offer stated only that he would convey the property to plaintiffs if he did not convey it to another party first. The trial court acknowledged that if defendant had sold "The Fork Shop" to another party plaintiffs would not have been entitled to relief. Thus, plaintiffs had no assurance that defendant would definitely convey the property to them even if on October 1st defendant told them that there was no one else interested in buying the property at that time. Moreover, plaintiffs engaged in obtaining financing for the purchase even before defendant made any offer to them whatsoever. They understood, at the time they obtained financing for the transaction, that they were assuming a risk that they would be unable to purchase the property in question. Since the plaintiffs had not tendered performance and did not establish the elements for the application of equitable estoppel, defendant was entitled to withdraw his offer when he did.

III.

[In an omitted part of the opinion, the court held that although the lower court had erred in using a "part performance theory," Wilder's conduct had induced the Ragostas to rely by obtaining financing, and remanded for a determination of the Ragostas' promissory estoppel claim.]

––––––

(C) DEATH OF AN OFFEROR

Restatement § 48 sets out the generally accepted rule in this country that an offeree's power of acceptance is terminated by the offeror's death or supervening incapacity. Corbin said of this rule that there is not "any compelling necessity for its existence," pointing out that if a man contracts to pay debts and then dies, "the law has no difficulty ... in creating legal relations with the dead man's personal representative, and there would be no greater difficulty in declaring the power of acceptance to survive as against the offeror's representative." Corbin, Offer and Acceptance, and Some of the Resulting Legal Relations, 26 Yale L.J. 169, 198 (1917).

Under the original draft of the first Restatement, as written by Professor Williston and his advisers, the unknown death of the offeror did not revoke the offer, but the Council of the American Law Institute changed the rule. Professor Williston concluded that "though the amount of actual authority is not impressive, there is a very general opinion among lawyers that death, even though unknown, does revoke an offer and does revoke an agency," and it was vital that the Restatement rule for contracts coincide with that for agency. 3 Proceedings of the American Law Institute 198 (1925). The Restatement preserves the ALI rule, admitting that it "seems to be a relic of the obsolete view that a contract requires a 'meeting of the minds,' and it is out of harmony with the modern doctrine that a manifestation of assent is effective without regard to actual mental assent." Comment *a* to Restatement § 48. Should the rule be limited to situations in which the offeree has not relied on the assumed contract in ignorance of the fact of the offeror's death?

Death or incapacity of the offeree has the same effect as that of the offeror under Restatement § 48. The death or incapacity of the offeror does not terminate the offeree's power of acceptance under an option contract. The death of a party *after* a contract has been formed may, depending on how pivotal the person's role in the enterprise, affect obligations under the contract and is taken up in Chapter 8.

PROBLEM

In Memoriam. A client, Benjamin Earle, comes to see you with the following story. "About four years ago I had a conversation with my aunt, Mary Dewitt, who lived in Massachusetts, and she said to me something like this, as best I can remember: 'Ben there are few left to come to my funeral. I have thought a great deal of you for coming to your uncle's funeral and bringing that large box of flowers in the terrible snowstorm we had, when our friends could not reach here from Boston, and you coming from Philadelphia. I want you to attend my funeral, Ben, if you outlive me, and I think you will, and I will pay all expenses and I will give you five thousand dollars. I want you to come.' I replied that I would come if I was living and if they informed me in time to get there and if I was able. We talked about it a little more on the occasion of my mother's funeral two years later. Aunt Mary died a few months ago and I went to Massachusetts for her funeral. Soon after the funeral, I received in the mail this paper, bearing the date of our conversation and signed by Aunt Mary." The paper reads, "If Benjamin A. Earle should come to my funeral, I order my executor to pay him the sum of five thousand dollars. Mary Dewitt." The executor has refused to pay and Mr. Earle wants to know whether he has a claim against the estate for $5,000 and his expenses. Advise him. These facts are drawn from Earle v. Angell, 32 N.E. 164 (Mass.1892). See Hamer v. Sidway, p. 34 above.

You may need more facts. What recollections by Earle of events in years past would help to support his claim? In Note 3, p. 125 above, you have been cautioned about prefacing your questions to Earle with an exposition of contract law; according to the Model Rules, a lawyer "shall not ... counsel or assist a witness to testify falsely." Rule 3.4(b). Compare this, from the Freedman book cited in that note.

> It is not the lawyer's function to prejudice his client as a perjurer. He cannot presume that the client will make unlawful use of his advice.... Before [a client] begins to remember essential facts, the client is entitled to know what his own interests are ... To decide otherwise would ... penalize the less well-educated defendant.

Does this mean that in advising Earle you should take account of his level of education?

———

(D) REJECTION AND THE MIRROR IMAGE RULE

The rejection of an offer by the offeree terminates the power of acceptance so that the offeree cannot thereafter accept the offer. The rule raises two questions.

First, can a rejection bar an offeree from subsequently accepting the offer? One argument is that it would be unjust to allow an offeree who has rejected an offer to reconsider and accept if the offeror has already substantially relied on the rejection. But this does not explain the application of the rule where no reliance by the offeror has been shown? Does the discussion of the enforceability of exchanges of promises at p. 67 above suggest an answer?

The second question concerns the kind of response by the offeree that counts as a rejection. The traditional common law answer is that an acceptance must be on the terms proposed by the offer, without the slightest variation. This is called the mirror image rule. A response that does not exactly mirror the terms of the original offer is a rejection, and acts as a counter-offer. The offeror, "as master of the offer," enjoys freedom from contract except on the offeror's own terms.

In Ardente v. Horan, 366 A.2d 162 (R.I.1976), a prospective buyer who had received an offer of residential property signed an agreement, which his lawyer returned with a check and a letter that said: "My clients are concerned that the following items remain with the real estate: a) dining room set and tapestry wall covering in dining room; b) fireplace fixtures throughout; c) the sun parlor furniture. I would appreciate your confirming that these items are a part of the transaction, as they would be difficult to replace." When the offerors refused to convey the property, the offeree sought specific performance. He lost on the ground that an acceptance "must be definite and unequivocal.... An acceptance which is equivocal or upon condition or with a limitation is a counteroffer and requires acceptance by the original offeror before a contractual relationship can exist."

The rigors of the rule that an acceptance must be the mirror image of the offer may be mitigated in practice. First, a court may decide that what seemed to be an additional or different term in the acceptance was really an "implied term" in the offer, so that language at first appearing to vary the terms of the offer did not really do so. An example is the court's treatment of the buyer's addition, "the jars and caps to be strictly first-quality goods," near the end of the opinion in *Fairmount Glass*, p. 130 above. Second, a court may conclude that the language of the acceptance relating to an additional or different term is only suggestive (or precatory, as in begging). Might the court have read the language in Ardente v. Horan, described above, in this manner? This would have resulted in a contract on the terms of the offeror, who could then have decided whether or not to modify that contract by accepting the offeree's additional proposal. Finally, even when neither of these mitigating techniques is available and no contract has been made, parties often act on the assumption that their promises are binding and the transaction is carried out without incident.

Disputes tend to arise in two kinds of cases. In the first, one party claims that a contract was made while the other maintains the contrary. This was the case in *Ardente*, where the sellers seized on the variation to justify their refusal to convey. When the market rises, sellers are tempted to find pretexts for getting out of their bargains; when the market falls, buyers are so tempted. The more rigorous the application of the mirror image rule, the more attractive recourse to such pretexts becomes.

In the second kind of case, some performance has taken place, following an exchange of messages showing that the parties believed they had reached a contract. But the terms proposed by the parties were never an exact match. When a dispute arises with respect to that performance, the parties differ about whose terms control, and each insists on its own. Under the mirror-image rule, the party that sent the last message before performance began usually prevails. This is because each message operated as a rejection of the other's prior message, and as a counter-offer. Performance, or the beginning of performance, by the recipient constituted acceptance of the terms of the final offer in the series. It is advantageous to have fired the "last shot" before that.

We consider the significant changes wrought to the common law approach by UCC § 2–207 in section 5.

NOTES

(1) *Back and Forth Firing.* Under the last-shot rule, a question sometimes arises as to which of the parties was the last to fire before performance. Consider the following long-standing disagreement. MPS, an employment agency, sent the Dresser–Rand company a quotation for labor on a form that included a non-solicitation clause barring Dresser–Rand from hiring MPS employees. Dresser–Rand returned a purchase order, taking specific exception to the non-solicitation clause. Although the parties remained at loggerheads over the clause; over the next five years MPS regularly supplied Dresser–Rand with employees, each time sending a contract with a non-solicitation clause. Dresser–Rand regularly refused to sign, although it always paid MPS for its services. When Dresser–Rand hired MPS employees in violation of the non-solicitation clause, MPS sued for breach of contract. Each party argued that its terms has been accepted by the other. Following summary judgment for Dresser–Rand, MPS appealed. *Held*: Affirmed.

"MPS signified through its course of conduct that it was willing to supply labor to Dresser–Rand despite Dresser–Rand's consistent rejection of any non-solicitation agreement. In effect, MPS accepted Dresser–Rand's counter-offer, which plainly eliminated the non-solicitation clause." In reaching its conclusion, the majority was influenced by "North Carolina's suspicion of direct contractual restraints on employee mobility." Mechanical Plant Services, Inc. v. Dresser Rand Company, 116 F.3d 1474 (4th Cir.1997).

Might one argue on the same facts that Dresser–Rand accepted *MPS's* offer? One judge dissented on the ground that "Our job here is not to pick between these equally plausible conclusions ... Put another way, it is not up to us to determine which party actually 'fired the last shot' and consequently, which party 'accepted' the other party's offer. That is why we have juries, and the question of mutual assent on these facts should not be resolved on summary judgment."

(2) *Flexible Tests of Acceptance.* Negotiations between a landlord and tenant for a long-term lease had arrived at Draft 4, which was submitted to the attorney for the tenant by the landlord's attorney. After a conversation between the attorneys, the tenant's attorney prepared Draft 5, containing some changes, had it executed by the tenant, and sent it to the landlord's attorney. Thereupon the landlord purported to withdraw its offer of a long-term lease. In an eviction action, the trial court concluded that Draft 5 was a counter-offer and that no agreement had been reached. The tenant appealed. *Held:* Reversed and remanded.

Quoting from an earlier Nebraska case, the court stated: "It does not appear to us that the trial court considered whether the new proposals may have constituted an acceptance not dependent on [the landlord's] assent to the added terms, in accordance with Restatement (Second) of Contracts § 61 ..." Distinguishing the earlier case against an expectant tenant who had not been in possession of the premises, the court said, "possession and partial performance render application of flexible tests of acceptance ... all the more appropriate for determining if parties have agreed to a lease even though they have not signed a lease, rather than application of the mirror-image offer-and-acceptance-rule enunciated in [the earlier case]." Stonewood Hotel v. Seven Seas, Inc., 452 N.W.2d 94, 95 (N.D.1990).

————

REJECTION OF AN IRREVOCABLE OFFER

It is doubtful that the holder of a power to accept under an option contract puts an end to the power by rejecting the "offer." See Restatement § 37.

The authorities are sparse. In one of them, Humble Oil held an option contract to acquire some subdivision lots, fixed to expire on June 4. Early in May it wrote to the owner: "Humble ... hereby exercises its option.... The contract of sale is hereby amended to provide that Seller shall extend all utility lines to the property before the date of closing." Twelve days later it wrote again: "The exercise of said option is not qualified and you may disregard the proposed amendment...." Later, Humble sued on a supposed contract of sale. What decision? How different would the case be if Humble had first written: "We have decided not to purchase your property"? Humble Oil & Refining Co. v. Westside Investment Corp., 428 S.W.2d 92 (Tex.1968).

It would be possible to distinguish between the *Humble Oil* case, in which the grantor of the option had received consideration for it, and one in which an offer is irrevocable as a "firm offer" under UCC § 2–205. (Imagine that the Columbus Rolling–Mill had added to its December 8 letter: "Offer firm until then—Dec. 20th.") Is there any reason to make the distinction?

To vary the facts of the iron-rails case, suppose that Railway, holding a firm offer from Rolling–Mill to sell 2,000 tons of rails for March delivery, rejects the offer on December 16th, but purports to accept it on the 18th. On December 17, however, Rolling–Mill has committed all its March output to another customer. How would you explain that Rolling–Mill is under no obligation to Railway?

———

(E) The "Mailbox Rule": Contracts by Correspondence

How do the rules for the bargaining process apply when the parties are at a distance and bargain by correspondence? Suppose, for example, that one party has sent the other an offer and that the offeree has dispatched an acceptance which has not yet been received by the offeror. Is it too late for the offeror to change its mind and revoke the offer? Is it too late for the offeree to change its mind and reject the offer? And is there a contract if the acceptance is somehow lost and is never received by the offeror?

The tendency of the common law has been to answer these questions on the assumption that dispatch of the acceptance is the crucial point at which the contract is made—after which the offeror's power to revoke is terminated, the offeree's power to reject is ended, and the risks of transmission are on the offeror. Because the early cases involved acceptance by post (now "snailmail" to some), this came to be known as the "mailbox rule." A question to be answered in the twenty-first century, when even parties who bargain at a distance frequently do so by near-instantaneous means of communication, is the extent to which the "mailbox rule" will retain significance in contract formation.

The origin of the rule is found in the celebrated case of Adams v. Lindsell, 106 Eng.Rep. 250 (King's Bench 1818), where the Court of King's Bench held that a firm of wool dealers that had made an offer by post to sell "eight hundred tods of wether fleeces" could not revoke the offer after the offeree, a firm of woolen manufacturers, had put a letter of acceptance in the post. The overwhelming weight of authority in the United States supports the "mailbox rule" of Adams v. Lindsell. See Restatement § 63 and Comment *a*, which gives this explanation:

> It is often said that an offeror who makes an offer by mail makes the post office his agent to receive the acceptance, or that the mailing of a letter of acceptance puts it irrevocably out of the offeree's control. Under United States postal regulations, however, the sender of a letter has long had the power to stop delivery and reclaim the letter. A better explanation of the rule that the acceptance takes effect on dispatch is that the offeree needs a dependable basis for his decision whether to accept. In many legal systems such a basis is provided by a general rule that an offer is irrevocable unless it provides otherwise. The common law provides such a basis through the rule that a revocation of an offer is ineffective if received after an acceptance has been properly dispatched.

Restatement Second § 63 makes the mailbox rule applicable only if the acceptance is "made in a manner and by a medium invited by [the] offer." It would not, therefore, ordinarily apply to acceptance by mail of an offer made by telegram, and such an acceptance would be effective only on receipt. A revocation, however, is generally held to be effective only on receipt, not on dispatch. See Restatement § 42.

It has generally been assumed that the "mailbox rule," laid down in connection with the termination of the offeror's power to *revoke*, applies as well in connection with the termination of the offeree's power to *reject*. In other words, once the offeree has dispatched an acceptance, it is too late for the offeree to change its mind and reject the offer. See Restatement § 63. This is, of course, not a necessary result since it would be possible to frame a rule that would deprive the offeror of its power to revoke the offer upon dispatch of the acceptance by the offeree, but leave the offeree free to reject the offer, at least as long as the offeror receives the rejection before receiving the acceptance. The two rules can best be contrasted by considering the case of the *overtaking rejection*.

Suppose that on Monday Buyer receives by mail an offer from Seller of goods. On Tuesday Buyer mails Seller a letter of acceptance which arrives on Friday. On Wednesday Buyer calls Seller to explain that it wants to revoke its acceptance and reject the offer. If the "mailbox rule" is applied, it is too late for Buyer to reconsider and Seller can hold Buyer to a contract. If, on the other hand, acceptance becomes effective on receipt, Buyer remains free to change its mind while the letter is in transit, and Seller cannot hold Buyer to a contract. This rule benefits buyer who, while the letter is in transit is free to watch the market and speculate, having in effect an "option contract" for that period, while Seller is unable to revoke.

Of course, the "mailbox rule" similarly disadvantages one of the parties. Suppose that the rejection does not mention the letter of acceptance, as where Buyer on Wednesday sends an overtaking telegram which is received on Thursday and says simply, "Reject your offer." Under these facts, Seller is prejudiced if it relies on the telegram of rejection, sells the goods to another buyer before receiving the letter of acceptance on Friday, and is then held to a contract with Buyer under the "mailbox rule." Might Buyer be estopped to enforce the contract in such a case? See Comment *c* and Illustration 7 to Restatement § 63.

In addition to fixing when in time acceptance, revocation, and rejection become effective, the mailbox rule has also been called upon to resolve which party should bear the risks of transmission of the acceptance: the offeror or the offeree. On the risk of a mistake in transmission of the offer, see Problem, p. 146 above. Scholars have long differed over the answer. Compare C. Langdell, *Summary of the Law of Contracts* 21 (2d ed. 1880), concluding that the offeree should bear the risk, in part because it is easier for the sender to provide against the possible miscarriage of the letter, with Llewellyn, Our Case–Law of Contract: Offer and Acceptance (pt. 2), 48 Yale L.J. 779, 795 (1939), advocating placing the risk on the offeror, as the party more likely to inquire if no response to an offer is forthcoming. The Restatement takes the view that the offeror should bear the risk, but with some diffidence: "In the interest of simplicity and clarity, the rule has been extended to cases where an acceptance is lost or delayed in the course of transmission. The convenience of the rule is less clear in such cases than in cases of attempted revocation of the offer, however, and the language of the

offer is often properly interpreted as making the offeror's duty of performance conditional upon receipt of the acceptance." Comment *b* to Restatement § 63.

NOTES

(1) *Formation or Performance.* In a leading English case, Bramwell, L.J. put
these questions by way of protest against the mailbox rule: "Suppose a man has
paid his tailor by cheque or bank note [currency], and posts a letter containing a
cheque or bank note to his tailor, which never reaches, is the tailor paid?" Bramwell
added that, if there is a general rule equating the mailing of a letter of acceptance to
communicating with the offeror, "it is equally applicable to all communications that
may be made by post." Household Fire & Carriage Acc. Ins. Co. v. Grant, 4 Ex.D.
216 (Eng.C.A.1879), dissent at 232, 234. And that, Bramwell evidently thought,
would be intolerable.

It is generally understood that while the mailbox rule applies to problems about
the formation of a contract, it does not apply (absent an agreement to the contrary)
to performance. So, if a contract requires payment to a tailor by June 30, the
payment must ordinarily arrive by that date.

(2) *Option Contracts.* Suppose a firm offer by mail to sell goods, under UCC
§ 2–205, in which the offeror writes: "I will give you ten days in which to accept."
If the offer is dated the first day of the month, mailed on the second, and received
on the third, would you expect the final day for informing the offeror of acceptance
to be the 11th? The 12th? The 13th? Other?

The Pennsylvania Academy of Fine Arts (PAFA) held a lease on a parking lot
that was to expire on July 31, 1989. The lease contained an option to purchase, and
this provision: "All notices hereunder shall be in writing and shall be delivered or
mailed by certified mail or registered mail." The option was, according to the lease,
to be exercised at least six months before the expiration of the lease. On January
30, PAFA prepared a letter to the lessor giving notice of its intent to purchase, and
a check for a deposit. The letter, with check enclosed, was sent on the 31st by
certified mail, return receipt requested. The lessor returned the check, saying that
because she did not receive the letter until February 3, she considered the notice
invalid. In an action by PAFA to enforce the lease, it was granted summary
judgment; the lessor appealed. *Held:* Affirmed. Pennsylvania Academy of Fine Arts
v. Grant, 590 A.2d 9 (Pa.Super.1991).

Is this decision consistent with Restatement § 63(b)?

(3) *International Solutions.* In contrast to the common law, the Vienna Convention provides that an acceptance is effective "at the moment the indication of
assent reaches the offeror." CISG art. 18 (2),23. Revocations, however, follow the
"mailbox rule" and are effective only if received before an acceptance has been
dispatched. CISG 16(1). The UNIDROIT Principles are in agreement. See Articles
2.4(2) and 2.6(2).

PROBLEM

Contract? As a result of a dispute regarding the distribution of profits, Ellefson,
one member of the metal band Megadeth, sued the band for fraud. Negotiations
ensued in an effort to settle the case. The parties, through their respective counsel,
drafted a "Settlement and General Release," which was amended several times over
a period of weeks. On May 13, 2004, the defendants informed Ellefson by email that
they were going to "terminate this deal as of 5PM PST on Friday 5/14/04, if we do
not have a signed agreement in hand." The agreement itself was then finalized and

sent to the defendants at 4:45 p.m. on May 14. However, Ellefson's signature page was not faxed to the defendants until 5:16 p.m. On May 20, the defendants' lawyer sent all parties, by regular mail, fully-executed copies of the agreement. On May 24, the Ellefson's lawyer informed the defendants that his client was "withdrawing from these negotiations." The defendants' lawyer responded that "we don't know what you are talking about . . ., there is a signed agreement in place." On June 2, Ellefson received the finalized agreement that had been mailed on May 20.

The defendants filed a motion to enforce the settlement agreement. Should the court grant the motion? See Ellefson v. Megadeth, Inc., 2005 WL 82022 (S.D.N.Y. 2005). In deciding the case, the court noted that "the issue presented by this motion is reminiscent of a first year law school contracts exam." In answering the question, it may help to review Note 2 on Tardy Acceptances, p. 169 above.

SECTION 5. THE BATTLE OF THE FORMS AND THE UNIFORM COMMERCIAL CODE

(A) ACCEPTANCE VARYING OFFER: THE TRADITIONAL VIEW

As we saw in *Fairmount Glass Works*, p. 130 above, a contract for a sale of goods is often the result of an exchange of several messages, rather than a single document signed by both parties. In routine transactions these messages typically consist of standardized printed forms containing several paragraphs of standard terms, with blanks filled in by the parties to fit the particular transaction. A characteristic sequence includes a "request for quotation," answered by a "quotation" form. (Compare the letters exchanged in *Fairmount*.) The ensuing steps are likely to be a "purchase order" followed by a "sales acknowledgment." Note that, typically, it was the buyer that, by its purchase order, made the initial offer and the seller that, by its varying acknowledgment, fired the "last shot," declining to enter into a contract on the buyer's terms (thereby rejecting the buyer's offer) and indicating willingness to enter into a contract on *its* terms (thereby making a counter-offer). When the buyer accepted the goods, it was taken to have accepted the seller's counter-offer and was bound by the seller's terms.

Because each party's form typically contains terms tailored to the benefit of that party, a mismatch of terms is likely. Yet neither the buyer nor the seller may have focused or even noticed the mismatched standard terms. The parties are likely to assume that they have a "deal" in light of their agreement regarding the transaction-specific, or "dickered," terms inserted in the blanks on the forms.

Transactions of this sort often result from what is referred to as a "battle of the forms," and raise an interesting series of questions. Does the exchange of forms create a contract, despite their failure to "mirror" one another? (This question is of particular importance if, before performance, one of the parties abandons the transaction.) If a contract is formed, what are its terms? And what happens if the exchange of forms does not create a contract but the parties nonetheless perform, only to engage in a subsequent dispute about that performance?

As we shall see, the "battle of the forms" arises most often when parties use standardized forms to express offers and acceptances. But it also arises when the parties exchange individualized messages. For example, in 1879 the letters and telegrams below passed between a railway company and a rolling-mill company. The messages of the railway, who initiated the correspondence, are lettered a, c, and e.

(a) Dec. 5: Please quote me prices for 500 to 3,000 tons 50 lb. steel rails, and for 2,000 to 5,000 tons 50 lb. iron rails, March 1880 delivery.

(b) Dec. 8: Your favor of the 5th inst. at hand. We do not make steel rails. For iron rails, we will sell 2,000 to 5,000 tons of 50 lb. rails for fifty-four ($54.00) dollars per gross ton for spot cash, F.O.B. cars at our mill, March delivery. If our offer is accepted, shall expect to be notified of same prior to Dec. 20th.

(c) Dec. 16: PLEASE ENTER OUR ORDER FOR TWELVE HUNDRED TONS RAILS, MARCH DELIVERY, AS PER YOUR FAVOR OF THE EIGHTH. PLEASE REPLY.

(d) Dec. 18: WE CANNOT BOOK YOUR ORDER AT PRESENT AT THAT PRICE.

(e) Dec. 19: PLEASE ENTER AN ORDER FOR TWO THOUSAND TONS RAILS, AS PER YOUR LETTER OF THE EIGHTH. PLEASE FORWARD WRITTEN CONTRACT. REPLY.

At the end of the day the rolling-mill denied the existence of a contract. In an action against it by the railway, judgment was entered for the defendant, on a jury verdict, and the plaintiff appealed. *Held:* Affirmed. "A proposal to accept, or an acceptance, upon terms varying from those offered, is a rejection of the offer, and puts an end to the negotiation, unless the party who made the original offer renews it, or assents to the modification suggested. The other party having once rejected the offer, cannot afterwards revive it by tendering an acceptance of it." Minneapolis & St. Louis Railway Co. v. Columbus Rolling–Mill Co., 119 U.S. 149 (1886).

While the "battle of the forms" often occurs in transactions involving the sale of goods, the problem is not so limited. In Maddox v. Northern Natural Gas Co., 259 F.Supp. 781 (W.D. Okla. 1966), an action to enforce what the plaintiff believed was a contract to settle a personal injury claim, the court stated: "In order that an offer and acceptance may result in a binding contract, the acceptance must be absolute, unconditional, and identical with the terms of the offer, and must in every respect meet and correspond with the offer; and any qualification of or departure from those terms invalidates and rejects the offer. Where a person offers to do a definite thing, and another accepts conditionally, or introduces a new term into the acceptance, his answer is a mere expression of willingness to treat, or it is a counter proposal, and in neither case is there an agreement."

PROBLEM

Consider the sequence of messages in *Minneapolis & St. Louis Railway* above. Using traditional common law rules, how many offers do you identify among the five messages set out above? How many rejections?

Suppose that message (d) had stated: "Cannot reduce quantity. We cannot book your order at present at that price." Can you make an argument that the result in the case should have been different? See Livingstone v. Evans, [1925] 4 D.L.R. 769 (Alberta Sup.Ct.). Can you draft a substitute for message (c) that would have been an offer to buy 1,200 tons of rails but not a rejection of the rolling mill's offer? See Restatement §§ 38 and 39.

―――――――

STANDARD FORMS AND "BATTLE OF THE FORMS"

To understand more fully how standard forms are created and exchanged, here is a more extensive description by Professor Stewart Macaulay based on a study of Wisconsin businesses. In reading the cases that follow, consider what account, if any, should be taken of such findings in formulating the applicable legal rules.

MACAULAY, NON-CONTRACTUAL RELATIONS IN BUSINESS: A PRELIMINARY STUDY, 28 Am.Sociological Rev. 55, 57–59 (1963). A firm will have a set of terms and conditions for purchases, sales, or both printed on the business documents used in these exchanges. Thus the things to be sold and the price may be planned particularly for each transaction, but standard provisions will further elaborate the performances and cover the other subjects of planning. Typically, these terms and conditions are lengthy and printed in small type on the back of the forms. For example, 24 paragraphs in eight point type are printed on the back of the purchase order form used by the Allis Chalmers Manufacturing Company....

In larger firms such "boiler plate" provisions are drafted by the house counsel or the firm's outside lawyer. In smaller firms such provisions may be drafted by the industry trade association, may be copied from a competitor, or may be found on forms purchased from a printer. In any event, salesmen and purchasing agents, the operating personnel, typically are unaware of what is said in the fine print on the back of the forms they use. Yet often the normal business patterns will give effect to this standardized planning. For example, purchasing agents may have to use a purchase order form so that all transactions receive a number under the firm's accounting system. Thus, the required accounting record will carry the necessary planning of the exchange relationship printed on its reverse side. If the seller does not object to this planning and accepts the order, the buyer's "fine print" will control. If the seller does object, differences can be settled by negotiation.

This type of standardized planning is very common.... [However], standardized planning can break down.... [T]he seller may fail to read the buyer's 24 paragraphs of fine print and may accept the buyer's order on the seller's own acknowledgment-of-order form. Typically this form will have ten to 50 paragraphs favoring the seller, and these provisions are likely to be different from or inconsistent with the buyer's provisions. The seller's acknowledgment form may be received by the buyer and checked by a clerk. She will read the *face* of the acknowledgment but not the fine print on the back of it because she has neither the time nor ability to analyze the small print on the 100 to 500 forms she must review each day. The face of the acknowledgment—where the goods and the price are specified—is likely to correspond with the face of the purchase order. If it does, the two forms are filed away. At this point, both buyer and seller are likely to assume they have planned an exchange and made a contract. Yet they have done neither, as they are in disagreement about all that appears on the back of their forms. This practice is common enough to have a name. Law teachers call it "the battle of the forms."

NOTES

(1) *Buyer as Offeror.* In analyzing "the battle of the forms," it is helpful to keep in mind that the most common situation is the one discussed by Professor Macaulay in which the buyer is the offeror and the seller is the offeree. Why is this more common than the situation in the *Fairmount Glass Works* case, p. 130 above, in which the seller was the offeror and the buyer was the offeree?

(2) *Boilerplate.* "Boilerplate" are the standard clauses lifted from formbooks or other agreements on file and inserted permanently into a standard form contract, so it is said, like metal plate is riveted to a boiler. See Sharon Steel Corp. v. Manhattan Bank, 691 F.2d 1039 (2d Cir.1982). As the court stated in that case, boilerplate provisions "do not depend upon particularized intentions of the parties." See Stephen J. Choi and G. Mitu Gulati, Contract as Statute, 104 Mich. L. Rev. 1129 (2006). See generally, Omri Ben–Shahar, Boilerplate: Foundations of Market Contracts Symposium, 104 Mich. L. Rev. 821 *et seq.* (2006).

―――――

(B) TRANSCENDING THE MIRROR IMAGE RULE: UCC § 2–207

Under the logic of the common law mirror image rule, the exchange of non-identical forms did not, by itself, create a contract. Rather, the offeree's form was considered to be a rejection of the offer and a counter-offer on the offeree's terms. The result was often that, even when the parties assumed that they had a contract, they did not and either party could walk away from the transaction with impunity. If the original offeror went ahead and performed the contemplated transaction, even though the writings did not establish a contract under the mirror image rule, courts typically concluded that the offeror's action constituted an acceptance of the offeree's counter-offer. Thus, a contract was formed, and its terms were those sent in the "last shot"—the counter-offer.

In UCC § 2–207 ("Additional Terms in Acceptance or Confirmation"), Article 2 made a marked shift from the common law rules applied to transactions involving a "battle of the forms." Each of the provision's three subsections contains an aspect of this dramatic change, as indicated in the following overview.

To begin, Article 2 abandoned the "mirror image" rule of contract formation in favor of an analysis more attentive to the kinds of commercial practices described above by Professor Macaulay: inconsistent boilerplate passing unheeded between parties that intend to enter into a contractual relationship. This is accomplished through UCC § 2–207(1), which provides that, with certain qualifications discussed in Note 1 below, an "expression of acceptance" may indeed "operate as an acceptance even though it states terms additional to or different from those offered and agreed upon."

When the operation of UCC § 2–207(1) results in a contract being formed, what are its terms? After all, the communications of the parties are not identical; there is no "mirror image." This issue is addressed in UCC § 2–207(2). That section provides an elaborate scheme, explored in the cases below, that determines whether "additional" terms found in the expression of acceptance are part of the contract. The materials that follow also explore the interesting question of the fate of terms that are "different," rather than "additional."

Note that, in separating the determination of formation of the contract in subsection (1) from the determination of the content of the contract in subsection (2), UCC § 2–207 contemplates that the terms of the contract may be determined at a different time than the time at which the contract is formed. There is, for example, the possibility that an "additional term" will become part of the contract later when, after receiving notice of it, the offeror lets a reasonable time elapse without giving "notification of objection" to the additional term. UCC § 2–207(2).

Another innovation is found in subsection (3), which provides that even when the parties' *writings* do not establish a contract under subsection (1), a contract may be found through *conduct* by both parties that recognizes the existence of a contract. In such a case the terms of the contract will be the terms to which both parties have agreed, supplemented by the Code's default rules or "gap fillers." Gap fillers are taken up in Chapter 5.

As courts and commentators have observed, UCC § 2–207 is a challenging exercise in statutory analysis. Almost every phrase of the provision has been the subject of intense debate and substantial litigation. As the court in the next principal case noted, in an omitted part of the opinion, UCC § 2–207 "has been described as a 'murky bit of prose.'" In another case, Judge Easterbrook labeled the section "infamous." See Hill v. Gateway 2000, discussed in Note 2, p. 215 below. UCC § 2–207 therefore provides the opportunity for a close reading of a complicated statute.

The difficulties associated with UCC § 2–207 explain in part why it was one of the provisions addressed in a set of proposed amendments to Article 2 that was developed over an extended period in the 1990s and early 2000s and that was promulgated in 2003. (For more details, see "Revising Article 2," p. 219 below.) No state has enacted the proposed amendments and it is not clear that enactments will be forthcoming in the near future. Nonetheless, in light of the extensive debate and litigation regarding UCC § 2–207, it can be instructive to examine the proposed amendments, which appear in the Selections for Contracts. In considering the materials that follow, note the differences between the amended provisions, which appear in proposed UCC §§ 2–206 and 2–207, and the current text. Would the proposed amendments, if enacted, improve the law?

NOTE

Satisfying Subsection (1). Under UCC § 2–207(1), not all responses to an offer operate as acceptances. Not only must the expression of acceptance be definite, seasonable, and sent within a reasonable time, it must also be sufficiently responsive to the offer to indicate the intent to enter into a contract. A response that differs radically from the offer, particularly with regard to dickered terms, such as price or quantity, may fail as an acceptance and end the inquiry into contract formation then and there. See Koehring Co. v. Glowacki, 253 N.W.2d 64 (Wis.1977).

In addition, under UCC § 2–207(1), the acceptance may, by its own terms, prevent its operation as an acceptance if it is "expressly made conditional on assent to the additional or different terms." This phrase has prompted two much litigated questions, taken up in the cases that follow: (1) Exactly what language or conduct by the offeree makes the acceptance "expressly conditional," and (2) what constitutes "assent" by the offeror?

Dorton v. Collins & Aikman Corp.

United States Court of Appeals, Sixth Circuit, 1972.
453 F.2d 1161.

■ CELEBREZZE, CIRCUIT JUDGE. [Dorton and his partners did business in Tennessee as "The Carpet Mart." Collins & Aikman was a Delaware corporation having its principal place of business in New York. Over a three-year period, in 55 transactions, The Carpet Mart bought carpets from Collins & Aikman. Ultimately, however, The Carpet Mart brought an action against Collins and Aikman in a Tennessee court, claiming damages for fraud and misrepresentation about the quality of the carpets.] The Carpet Mart maintains that in May, 1970, in response to a customer complaint, it learned that not all of the carpets were manufactured from 100% Kodel polyester fiber but rather some were composed of a cheaper and inferior carpet fiber. After the cause was removed to the District Court on the basis of diversity of citizenship, Collins & Aikman moved for a stay pending arbitration, asserting that The Carpet Mart was bound to an arbitration agreement which appeared on the reverse side of Collins & Aikman's printed sales acknowledgment forms. Holding that there existed no binding arbitration agreement between the parties, the District Court denied the stay. For the reasons set out below, we remand the case to the District Court for further findings....

[The court described the dealings between the parties. Upon receiving an order telephoned to the Collins & Aikman order department in Dalton, Georgia, and after a report from its credit department, Collins & Aikman typed the information concerning the particular order on one of its printed acknowledgment forms. One legend or another on the face specified when the order "shall become a contract," *e.g.*,

> (a) when signed and delivered by Buyer to Seller and accepted in writing by Seller or (b) when Buyer has received and retained this order for ten days without objection, or (c) when Buyer has accepted delivery of any part of the merchandise ..., or when Buyer has otherwise indicated acceptance of the terms hereof.

Also:

> ... acceptance (or "order") subject to all of the terms and condi-
> tions on the face and reverse side hereof. ...]

The small print on the reverse side of the forms provided, among other
things, that all claims arising out of the contract would be submitted to
arbitration in New York City.... Absent a delay in the mails ... The
Carpet Mart always received the acknowledgment forms prior to receiving
the carpets. In all cases The Carpet Mart took delivery of and paid for the
carpets without objecting to any terms contained in the acknowledgment
form.

In holding that no binding arbitration agreement was created between
the parties through the transactions above, the District Court relied on
T.C.A. § 47–2–207 [UCC § 2–207]. [The court] found that Subsection 2–
207(3) controlled the instant case ... [and it] concluded that the arbitration clause on the back of Collins & Aikman's sales acknowledgment had
not become a binding term in the 50–odd transactions with The Carpet
Mart.

In reviewing this determination by the District Court, we are aware of
the problems which courts have had in interpreting Section 2–207. Yet
despite the lack of clarity in its language, Section 2–207 manifests definite
objectives which are significant in the present case.

[S]pecifically Subsection 2–207(1) was intended to alter the "ribbon
matching" or "mirror" rule of common law, under which the terms of an
acceptance or confirmation were required to be identical to the terms of the
offer or oral agreement, respectively. 1 W. Hawkland, supra, at 16; R.
Nordstrom, Handbook of the Law of Sales, Sec. 37, at 99–100 (1970). Under
the common law, an acceptance or a confirmation which contained terms
additional to or different from those of the offer or oral agreement constituted a rejection of the offer or agreement and thus became a counter-offer.
The terms of the counter-offer were said to have been accepted by the
original offeror when he proceeded to perform under the contract without
objecting to the counter-offer. Thus, a buyer was deemed to have accepted
the seller's counter-offer if he took receipt of the goods and paid for them
without objection.

Under Section 2–207 the result is different. This section of the Code
recognizes that in current commercial transactions, the terms of the offer
and those of the acceptance will seldom be identical. Rather, under the
current "battle of the forms," each party typically has a printed form
drafted by his attorney and containing as many terms as could be envisioned to favor that party in his sales transactions. Whereas under common
law the disparity between the fineprint terms in the parties' forms would
have prevented the consummation of a contract when these forms are
exchanged, Section 2–207 recognizes that in many, but not all, cases the
parties do not impart such significance to the terms on the printed
forms.... Thus, under Subsection (1), a contract is recognized notwithstanding the fact that an acceptance or confirmation contains terms additional to or different from those of the offer or prior agreement, provided

that the offeree's intent to accept the offer is definitely expressed, see Sections 2–204 and 2–206, and provided that the offeree's acceptance is not expressly conditioned on the offeror's assent to the additional or different terms. When a contract is recognized under Subsection (1), the additional terms are treated as "proposals for addition to the contract" under Subsection (2), which contains special provisions under which such additional terms are deemed to have been accepted when the transaction is between merchants. Conversely, when no contract is recognized under Subsection 2–207(1)—either because no definite expression of acceptance exists or, more specifically, because the offeree's acceptance is expressly conditioned on the offeror's assent to the additional or different terms—the entire transaction aborts at this point. If, however, the subsequent conduct of the parties—particularly, performance by both parties under what they apparently believe to be a contract—recognizes the existence of a contract, under Subsection 2–207(3) such conduct by both parties is sufficient to establish a contract, notwithstanding the fact that no contract would have been recognized on the basis of their writings alone. Subsection 2–207(3) further provides how the terms of contracts recognized thereunder shall be determined.

With the above analysis and purposes of Section 2–207 in mind, we turn to their application in the present case. . . .

[The court considered two possibilities: the defendant's forms were either "acceptances" or they were "confirmations." For resolving this, the court directed the trial court to determine "whether oral agreements were reached between the parties prior to the sending of Collins & Aikman's acknowledgment forms." In an affidavit by a partner in The Carpet Mart there was testimony indicating that they were.

In either event, the court suggested, the plaintiff's oral orders may have embodied an arbitration provision, such that in this respect the defendant's forms were not "additional to or different from" the orders: "we believe that a specific finding on this point will be required on remand."[1]]

[The court next addressed the question whether or not if "additional or different," the defendant's forms were within the proviso of UCC § 2–207(1): "acceptance expressly made conditional on assent to the additional or different terms."] . . . Although Collins & Aikman's use of the words "subject to" suggests that the acceptances were conditional to some extent . . . we believe that [the proviso] was intended to apply only to an acceptance which clearly reveals that the offeree is unwilling to proceed with the transaction unless he is assured of the offeror's assent to the additional or different terms therein. See 1 Hawkland, [A Transactional Guide to the Uniform Commercial Code (1964)] § 1.090303, at 21. That the acceptance is predicated on the offeror's assent must be "directly and distinctly stated

---

1. It is not inconceivable that a buyer might request that all claims be submitted to arbitration, see Universal Oil Products v. S.C.M. Corp., 313 F.Supp. 905 (D.Conn.1970), or that a buyer might orally submit to the seller's known policy of arbitration in order to facilitate acceptance of the offer.

or expressed rather than implied or left to inference." Webster's Third International Dictionary (defining "express").

Although the UCC does not provide a definition of "assent," it is significant that Collins & Aikman's printed acknowledgment forms specified at least seven types of action or inaction on the part of the buyer which—sometimes at Collins & Aikman's option—would be deemed to bind the buyer to the terms therein. These ranged from the buyer's signing and delivering the acknowledgment to the seller—which indeed could have been recognized as the buyer's assent to Collins & Aikman's terms—to the buyer's retention of the acknowledgment for ten days without objection—which could never have been recognized as the buyer's assent to the additional or different terms where acceptance is expressly conditional on that assent.[2]

To recognize Collins & Aikman's acceptances as "expressly conditional on [the buyer's] assent to the additional ... terms" therein, within the proviso of Subsection 2–207(1), would thus require us to ignore the specific language of that provision.[3] Such an interpretation is not justified in view of the fact that Subsection 2–207(1) is clearly designed to give legal recognition to many contracts where the variance between the offer and acceptance would have precluded such recognition at common law.

Because Collins & Aikman's acceptances were not expressly conditional on the buyer's assent to the additional terms within the proviso of Subsection 2–207(1), a contract is recognized under Subsection (1), and the additional terms are treated as "proposals" for addition to the contract under Subsection 2–207(2).[4] Since both Collins & Aikman and The Carpet

---

2. The common law has never recognized silence or inaction as a mode of acceptance. See 1 W. Hawkland, supra, § 1.090301, at 17. Under the counter-offer approach which Section 2–207 was designed to modify, the offeror had to take receipt of and pay for the goods without objection before he was deemed to have accepted the terms of the counter-offer. And although Subsection 2–207(2)(c) provides that certain additional terms can be accepted by the offeror's failure to object, nothing in the Code suggests that silence or inaction can be recognized as an offeror's assent in the present context.

3. We are aware that at least two Courts of Appeals have not chosen to read the Subsection 2–207(1) proviso as strictly as we do here. See Roto–Lith, Ltd. v. F.P. Bartlett & Co., 297 F.2d 497, 499–500 (1st Cir. 1962); Construction Aggregates Corp. v. Hewitt–Robins, Inc., 404 F.2d 505, 509 (5th Cir.1968) (dictum). But see Matter of Doughboy Industries, Inc., and Pantasote Co., 17 A.D.2d 216, 233 N.Y.S.2d 488 (1962). We believe, however, that the approach adopted here is dictated by both the language of the proviso and the purpose of Subsection 2–207(1). [The decision in Roto–Lith was "almost uniformly criticized by the courts and

commentators as an aberration in Article 2 jurisprudence," Gardner Zemke Co. v. Dunham Bush, Inc., 850 P.2d 319, 323 (N.M. 1993), and was finally overturned in Ionics v. Elmwood Sensors, Inc. 110 F.3d 184 (1st Cir.1997). For a thorough discussion, see JOM, Inc. v. Adell Plastics, Inc., 193 F.3d 47 (1st Cir.1999).]

4. Apparently believing that Collins & Aikman's acknowledgments were acceptances "expressly ... conditional on assent to the additional or different terms" under the Subsection 2–207(1) proviso, the District Court recognized contracts between the parties under Subsection 2–207(3) since the subsequent performance by both parties clearly recognized the existence of a contract. Absent our conclusion that Collins & Aikman's acknowledgments do not fall within the Subsection 2–207(1) proviso, we believe that the District Court correctly applied Subsection 2–207(3) to Collins & Aikman's "acceptances" notwithstanding the fact that some of the language of that Subsection appears to refer to the typical situation under Section 2–207 where there exist both a written offer and a written acceptance. Although we recognize the value that writings by both parties serve in sales transactions, where Subsection 2–

Mart are clearly "merchants" as that term is defined in Subsection 2–104(1), the arbitration provision will be deemed to have been accepted by The Carpet Mart under Subsection 2–207(2) unless it materially altered the terms of The Carpet Mart's oral offers. T.C.A. § 47–2–207(2)(b) [UCC § 2–207(2)(b)].[5] We believe that the question of whether the arbitration provision materially altered the oral offer under Subsection 2–207(2)(b) is one which can be resolved only by the District Court on further findings of fact in the present case.[6] If the arbitration provision did in fact materially alter The Carpet Mart's offer, it could not become a part of the contract "unless expressly agreed to" by The Carpet Mart. T.C.A. § 47–2–207 [UCC § 2–207], Comment No. 3.

We therefore conclude that if on remand the District Court finds that Collins & Aikman's acknowledgments were in fact acceptances and that the arbitration provision was additional to the terms of The Carpet Mart's oral orders, contracts will be recognized under Subsection 2–207(1). The arbitration clause will then be viewed as a "proposal" under Subsection 2–207(2) which will be deemed to have been accepted by The Carpet Mart unless it materially altered the oral offers.

[Next the court considered the possibility that the acknowledgment forms were not acceptances but, rather, were confirmations of prior oral agreements between the parties. It said that "an application of Section 2–207 similar to that above will be required."]

. . . Assuming that the District Court finds that the arbitration provision was not a term of the oral agreements between the parties, the arbitration clause will be treated as a "proposal" for addition to the contract under Section 2–207(2). . . . Regardless of whether the District Court finds Collins & Aikman's acknowledgment forms to have been acceptances or confirmations, if the arbitration provision was additional to, and a material alteration of, the offers or prior oral agreements, The Carpet Mart will not be bound to that provision absent a finding that it expressly agreed to be bound thereby. . . .

207(3) is otherwise applicable we do not believe the purposes of that Subsection should be abandoned simply because the offeror chose to rely on his oral offer. In such a case, we believe that the District Court's comparison of the terms of the oral offer and the written acceptance under Subsection (3) would have been correct.

5. The parties do not dispute the fact that The Carpet Mart made no objections to the terms embodied in Collins & Aikman's acknowledgments. Therefore, Subsection 2–207(2)(c) is not relevant in the present case. And although it is not inconceivable that an oral offer could "expressly [limit] acceptance to the terms of the offer" under Subsection 2–207(2)(a), The Carpet Mart has never asserted that this was the nature of its offers to Collins & Aikman. We are therefore concerned with only Subsection 2–207(2)(b).

6. While T.C.A. § 47–2–207 [UCC § 2–207], Official Comment Nos. 4 and 5 provide examples of terms which would and would not materially alter a contract, an arbitration clause is listed under neither. Although we recognize the rule "that the agreement to arbitrate must be direct and the intention made clear, without implication, inveiglement or subtlety," Matter of Doughboy Industries, Inc., and Pantasote Co., 17 A.D.2d 216, 218, 233 N.Y.S.2d 488, 492 (1962) (indicating in dictum that an arbitration clause would materially alter a contract under 2–207(2)(b)), we believe the question of material alteration necessarily rests on the facts of each case. See American Parts Co. v. American Arbitration Ass'n, 8 Mich.App. 156, 171, 154 N.W.2d 5, 14 (1967).

For the reasons set forth above, the case is remanded to the District Court for further findings consistent with this opinion.

NOTES

(1) *Questions.* What is the difference between "an expression of acceptance" and a "written confirmation"? Is there a functional difference between the two under UCC § 2–207(1)? How did the trial court get from subsection (1) to subsection (3)?

(2) *Non-merchants Under Subsection (2).* What result in *Dorton* had the buyer not been Carpet Mart but an individual consumer? What if the buyer had been a business buying carpets not for resale but for use on its own premises?

MATERIALITY

If a response to an offer with "additional" terms operates as an acceptance under UCC § 2–207(1), much then depends on whether or not these terms "materially alter" the contract under UCC § 2–207(2)(b). As explained in Comment 3 to UCC § 2–207, when both parties are merchants, if the additional terms do *not* materially alter the original bargain "they will be incorporated unless notice of objection has already been given or is given within a reasonable time." Useful examples of terms that do and do not amount to material alterations are given in Comments 4 and 5. Comment 4 also suggests the rationale underlying the concept: terms may be found to materially alter if their inclusion would result in "surprise or hardship if incorporated without express awareness by the other party." Comment 5 similarly mentions "the element of unreasonable surprise."

These comments were relied on in Northrop Corporation v. Litronic Industries. In that case an offer was made by Litronic to sell electronic components to Northrop for a weapons system; the offer contained a limited 90–day warranty. Northrop accepted the offer on terms providing for a warranty that was indefinite in duration. In determining whether the buyer's change in the warranty was a material alteration, the court said that, "at least in the absence of some industry custom setting a limit on warranties that do not specify a duration . . ., any limitation on the length of the warranty in the offer would be a materially different term." The case is further presented at p. 202 below.

The question of whether arbitration terms materially alter the terms of a contract has been much litigated. After the decision in *Dorton*, the New York Court of Appeals had occasion to say that they do. Marlene Industries Corp. v. Carnac Textiles, Inc., 380 N.E.2d 239, 242 (N.Y.1978). That decision established that at least in New York "the burden is on the proponent of arbitration to establish that arbitration is not a material alteration." Avedon Engineering, Inc. v. Seatex, 126 F.3d 1279, 1285 n. 15 (10th Cir.1997).

The decision in *Avedon* also serves to remind a reader that even uniformly enacted statutory text does not guarantee uniformity of interpretation and application in courts of the various states. What counts as material—and which party has the corresponding burden of proof—may differ from state to state. As the court explained "It is true that both [New York and Colorado] have adopted identical versions of 2–207, and we agree that choice of law analysis is generally unnecessary if the relevant states have enacted identical controlling statutes." However, because the court believed the two states would analyze the materiality of the arbitration clause differently, it remanded the case for a choice-of-law determination. 126 F.3d at 1284.

NOTES

(1) *Surprise or Hardship?* In an effort to lower its prices by avoiding a local Chicago sales tax, Union Carbide, a supplier of sausage casings, instructed its customers to send their purchase orders to a Union Carbide address outside Chicago. Oscar Mayer Foods entered into several contracts for casings with Union Carbide in this manner. Several years later the relevant tax authorities decided this arrangement was improper and assessed Union Carbide $88,000 in back taxes. Union Carbide paid the sum and then sought to recover it from Oscar Mayer under the terms of an indemnity provision printed on the back of Union Carbide's invoices.[a] Among the issues to be decided by the trial court was whether the indemnity provision materially altered the offer under UCC § 2–207(2). From a summary judgment for the defendants that the alteration was material, Union Carbide appealed. *Held*: Affirmed.

"An alteration is material if consent to it cannot be presumed. That is our gloss; the cases more commonly speak of 'unreasonable surprise' ... But it comes to the same thing. What is expectable, hence unsurprising, is okay. What is unexpected, hence surprising, is not. Not infrequently the test is said to be 'surprise or hardship,' ... but this is a misreading of Official Comment 4 to UCC § 2–207 ... Hardship is a consequence, not a criterion. You cannot walk away from a contract that you can be fairly deemed to have agreed to, merely because your performance turns out to be a hardship for you...." Union Carbide Corp. v. Oscar Mayer Foods Corp., 947 F.2d 1333, 1335 (7th Cir.1991) (Posner, J.).

The court used the facts of the case for a useful review of the applicability of UCC § 2–207: "Every actual purchase of sausage casings involved an exchange of four documents: the standing order, the price book, the release order, the invoice. Such a pattern of sequential exchange of documents governing a single sale is a prototypical situation for the application of UCC § 2–207." 947 F.2d at 1336.

(2) *Battlegrounds of Materiality.* Provisions requiring arbitration and limiting warranties are commonplace occasions for considering whether an additional term would materially alter a contract under Article 2, the issue has also arisen in connection with terms about choice of forum, M.K.C. Equipment Company v. M.A.I.L. Code, Inc., 843 F.Supp. 679 (D.Kan.1994), and time for payment (St. Paul Structural Steel Co. v. ABI Contracting, Inc., 364 N.W.2d 83 (N.D.1985)).

———

C. ITOH & CO. (AMERICA) INC. v. JORDAN INT'L CO., 552 F.2d 1228 (7th Cir.1977). [Itoh sent Jordan a purchase order for steel coils.

---

a. "Buyer shall pay Seller the amount of all governmental taxes ... that Seller may be required to pay with respect to the produc- tion, sale, or transportation of any materials delivered hereunder." 947 F.2d at 1334.

Jordan sent back its acknowledgment form, which contained the following provision:

> Seller's acceptance is, however, expressly conditional on Buyer's assent to the additional or different terms and conditions set forth below and printed on the reverse side. If these terms are not acceptable, Buyer should notify Seller at once.

One of the provisions on the reverse side of Jordan's form was an arbitration clause that had no counterpart in Itoh's purchase order. After the steel had been delivered and paid for, Itoh sued Jordan claiming that the steel was defective and had been delivered late. Jordan moved to stay the proceedings pending arbitration. From a denial of its motion, Jordan appealed.]

■ SPRECHER, CIRCUIT JUDGE. ... The instant case ... involves the classic "battle of the forms".... [Since] it is clear that the statement contained in Jordan's acknowledgment form comes within the Section 2–207(1) proviso ..., the exchange of forms between Jordan and Itoh did not result in the formation of a contract under Section 2–207(1), and Jordan's form became a counteroffer. Thus, "[s]ince ... [Itoh's] purchase order and ... [Jordan's] counter-offer did not in themselves create a contract, Section 2–207(3) would operate to create one because the subsequent performance by both parties constituted 'conduct by both parties which recognizes the existence of a contract.'" Construction Aggregates [Corp. v. Hewitt–Robins, 404 F.2d 505 (7th Cir.1968), cert. denied, 395 U.S. 921 (1969)], at 509.

What are the terms of a contract created by conduct under Section 2–207(3) rather than an exchange of forms under Section 2–207(1)? ... The second sentence of Section 2–207(3) provides that where, as here, a contract has been consummated by the conduct of the parties, "the terms of the particular contract consist of those terms on which the writings of the parties agree, together with any supplementary terms incorporated under any other provisions of this Act." Since it is clear that the Jordan and Itoh forms do not "agree" on arbitration, the only question which remains *under the Code* is whether arbitration may be considered a supplementary term incorporated under some other provision of the Code.

We have been unable to find any case authority shedding light on the question of what constitutes "supplementary terms" within the meaning of Section 2–207(3) and the Official Comments to Section 2–207 provide no guidance in this regard. We are persuaded, however, that the disputed additional terms (i.e., those terms on which the writings of the parties do not agree) which are necessarily excluded from a Subsection (3) contract by the language, "terms on which the writings of the parties agree," cannot be brought back into the contract under the guise of "supplementary terms." ... Accordingly, we find that the "supplementary terms" contemplated by Section 2–207(3) are limited to those supplied by the standardized "gap-filler" provisions of Article Two.... Since provision for arbitration is not a necessary or missing term which would be supplied by one of the Code's "gap-filler" provisions unless agreed upon by the contracting parties, there is no arbitration term in the Section 2–207(3) contract which was created by the conduct of Jordan and Itoh in proceeding to perform even though no contract had been established by their exchange of writings.

We are convinced that this conclusion does not result in any unfair prejudice to a seller who elects to insert in his standard sales acknowledgment form the statement that acceptance is expressly conditional on buyer's assent to additional terms contained therein. Such a seller obtains a substantial benefit under Section 2–207(1) through the inclusion of an "expressly conditional" clause. If he decides after the exchange of forms that the particular transaction is not in his best interest, Subsection (1) permits him to walk away from the transaction without incurring any liability so long as the buyer has not in the interim expressly assented to the additional terms. Moreover, whether or not a seller will be disadvantaged under Subsection (3) as a consequence of inserting an "expressly conditional" clause in his standard form is within his control. If the seller in fact does not intend to close a particular deal unless the additional terms are assented to, he can protect himself by not delivering the goods until such assent is forthcoming. If the seller does intend to close a deal irrespective of whether or not the buyer assents to the additional terms, he can hardly complain when the contract formed under Subsection (3) as a result of the parties' conduct is held not to include those terms. Although a seller who employs such an "expressly conditional" clause in his acknowledgment form would undoubtedly appreciate the dual advantage of not being bound to a contract under Subsection (1) if he elects not to perform and of having his additional terms imposed on the buyer under Subsection (3) in the event that performance is in his best interest, we do not believe such a result is contemplated by Section 2–207. Rather, while a seller may take advantage of an "expressly conditional" clause under Subsection (1) when he elects not to perform, he must accept the potential risk under Subsection (3) of not getting his additional terms when he elects to proceed with performance without first obtaining buyer's assent to those terms. Since the seller injected ambiguity into the transaction by inserting the "expressly conditional" clause in his form, he, and not the buyer, should bear the consequence of that ambiguity under Subsection (3)....

Affirmed.

NOTES

(1) *Conduct as Assent to Conditional Acceptance.* Why did Itoh's acceptance of and payment for the steel not constitute assent to Jordan's "additional or different terms"? (Recall that in Dorton v. Collins & Aikman, above, the court observed that "the UCC does not provide a definition of 'assent.' ")

(2) *Case Comparison.* The transaction in *Itoh* fell into subsection (3) by operation of the "assent made expressly conditional" language in subsection (1). Compare the trial court's decision in *Dorton*, p. 193 above, in which the trial court was reversed for making the same move. What explains the difference in the two decisions?

DIFFERENT TERMS

So far the materials in this section have focused on contracts formed under UCC § 2–207(1) in which the "expression of acceptance" contained terms that were "in addition to" those in the offer. But how does UCC § 2–207 work when the terms in the expression of acceptance *differ* from, rather than add to, the terms in the offer? What has been called the "notorious distinction between 'different' and 'additional' terms" appears upon comparing subsections (1) and (2) of UCC § 2–207. Pace Communs., Inc. v. Moonlight Design, Inc., 31 F.3d 587, 592 (7th Cir.1994).The following case reviews the textual conundrum and competing judicial approaches to a solution. As the trial court in that case observed, "Mischief lurks in the words 'additional to or different from.' " *Id.* at 1174

———

NORTHROP CORP. v. LITRONIC INDUSTRIES, 29 F.3d 1173 (7th Cir.1994). [The facts of Northrop Industries were sketched on p. 198. To review, Litronic offered to sell the Northrop, a giant defense firm, printed wire boards. The offer contained a 90–day warranty stated to be in lieu of any other warranties. Northrop's return invoice contained a warranty period unlimited in duration. After 90 days had passed, Northrop attempted to return some of the wire boards as defective. Litronic refused to accept them, arguing that the 90–day warranty period had lapsed. A preliminary question before the court was how to treat terms that were "different" but not "additional" to those of the offer under subsection (2). From a judgment for Northrup, Litronic appealed.]

■ POSNER, CHIEF JUDGE: [The Code does not explain] what happens if the offeree's response contains different terms (rather than additional ones) within the meaning of section 2–207(1). There is no consensus on that question. See James J. White & Robert S. Summers, Uniform Commercial Code 33–36 (3d ed. 1988); John E. Murray, Jr., "The Chaos of the 'Battle of the Forms': Solutions," 39 Vand.L.Rev. 1307, 1354–65 (1986). We know there is a contract because an acceptance is effective even though it contains different terms; but what are the terms of the contract that is brought into being by the offer and acceptance? One view is that the discrepant terms in both the nonidentical offer and the acceptance drop out, and default terms found elsewhere in the Code fill the resulting gap. Another view is that the offeree's discrepant terms drop out and the offeror's become part of the contract. A third view, possibly the most sensible, equates "different" with "additional" and makes the outcome turn on whether the new terms in the acceptance are materially different from the terms in the offer—in which event they operate as proposals, so that the offeror's terms prevail unless he agrees to the variant terms in the acceptance—or not materially different from the terms in the offer, in which event they become part of the contract. John L. Utz, "More on the Battle of the Forms: The Treatment of 'Different' Terms Under the Uniform Commercial Code," 16 U.C.C.L.J. 103 (1983). This interpretation equating "different" to "additional," bolstered by drafting history which shows that the omission of "or different" from section 2–207(2) was a drafting error, ... substitutes a manageable inquiry into materiality for a hair-splitting inquiry into the difference between "different" and "additional." It is hair-splitting ("metaphysical," "casuistic," "semantic," in the pejorative senses of these words) because all different terms are additional and all additional terms are different.

The majority view is that the discrepant terms fall out and are replaced by a suitable UCC gap-filler. E.g., Daitom, Inc. v. Pennwalt Corp., supra, 741 F.2d at 1578–80; The magistrate judge followed this approach and proceeded to section 2–309, which provides that nonconforming goods may be rejected within a "reasonable" time (see also § 2–601(1)), and she held that the six months that Northrop took to reject Litronic's boards was a reasonable time because of the complexity of the required testing. The leading minority view is that the discrepant terms in the acceptance are to be ignored, Valtrol, Inc. v. General Connectors Corp., 884 F.2d 149, 155 (4th Cir.1989); Reaction Molding Technologies, Inc. v. General Electric Co., 588 F.Supp. 1280, 1289 (E.D.Pa.1984), and that would give the palm to Litronic. Our own preferred view—the view that assimilates "different" to "additional," so that the terms in the offer prevail over the different terms in the acceptance only if the latter are materially different, has as yet been adopted by only one state, California. Steiner v. Mobil Oil Corp., 20 Cal.3d 90, 141 Cal.Rptr. 157, 569 P.2d 751, 759 n. 5 (1977). Under that view, as under what we are calling the "leading" minority view, the warranty in Litronic's offer, the 90–day warranty, was the contractual warranty, because the unlimited warranty contained in Northrop's acceptance was materially different.

Because Illinois in other UCC cases has tended to adopt majority rules, e.g., Rebaque v. Forsythe Racing, Inc., 134 Ill.App.3d 778, 89 Ill.Dec. 595, 598, 480 N.E.2d 1338, 1341 (1985), and because the interest in the uniform nationwide application of the Code—an interest asserted in the Code itself (see § 1–102)—argues for nudging majority views, even if imperfect (but not downright bad), toward unanimity, we start with a presumption that Illinois, whose position we are trying to predict, would adopt the majority view. We do not find the presumption rebutted. The idea behind the majority view is that the presence of different terms in the acceptance suggests that the offeree didn't really accede to the offeror's terms, yet both parties wanted to contract, so why not find a neutral term to govern the dispute that has arisen between them? Of course the offeree may not have had any serious objection to the terms in the offer at the time of contracting; he may have mailed a boilerplated form without giving any thought to its contents or to its suitability for the particular contract in question. But it is just as likely that the discrepant terms in the offer itself were the product of a thoughtless use of a boilerplate form rather than a considered condition of contracting. And if the offeror doesn't want to do business other than on the terms in the offer, he can protect himself by specifying that the offeree must accept all those terms for the parties to have a contract. UCC § 2–207(2)(a).

. . . What we are calling the leading minority view may tempt the offeror to spring a surprise on the offeree, hoping the latter won't read the fine print. Under the majority view, if the offeree tries to spring a surprise (the offeror can't, since his terms won't prevail if the acceptance contains different terms), the parties move to neutral ground; and the offeror can, we have suggested, more easily protect himself against being surprised than the offeree can protect himself against being surprised. The California rule dissolves all these problems, but has too little support to make it a plausible candidate for Illinois, or at least a plausible candidate for our guess as to Illinois's position.

Affirmed.

NOTES

(1) *The Knockout Rule.* The decision in *Northrop* was based on what is commonly called the "knockout rule." Under this approach, when the difference between the seller's terms and the buyer's are material, the two terms cancel each other out, and the contested term is to be supplied by a Code gap-filler. Why did the court in *Northrop* decide to apply to knockout rule despite its preference for a different ("possibly the most sensible") rule? What result with regard to warranties under the view preferred by the court?

A recent empirical study of how firms conduct the battle suggests that "it is difficult for either side to win the battle of the forms with clever drafting, at least if we define 'winning' as making the other side be held to your non-dickered terms. By the same token, it is easy with good drafting never to lose the battle of the forms, at least if 'losing' equals letting your side get stuck with the other party's boilerplate terms." Daniel Keating, Exploring the Battle of the Forms in Action, 98 Mich. L.Rev.2678, 2682 (2000).

(2) *Fairness and the Knockout Doctrine.* According to one court, the overriding goal of Article 2 is "to discern the bargain struck by the contracting parties. However, there are times where the conduct of the parties makes realizing that goal impossible. In such cases, we find guidance in the Code's commitment to fairness, good faith, and conscionable conduct." Gardner Zemke Co. v. Dunham Bush, Inc., fn. 3, p. 196 above. Does the knockout doctrine, by substituting Code gap-fillers for the discordant terms of the parties further the Code's "commitment to fairness"?

Some would argue that it does, in part by enhancing the importance of Code gap-fillers, notably the warranty sections which in most cases work to the general advantage of *buyers*. "Sellers should not be permitted, by surreptitious manipulation of section 2–207, to obtain contract terms that cannot be obtained either through statutory amendment of the U.C.C. gap-filler provisions or by negotiation with the buyer. If warranty, remedy, and arbitration terms are so important to sellers, then those terms are and must be negotiated . . . [I]f the seller 'is not willing to sacrifice the time and effort that this requires, then he should be willing to abide by the rules of Article 2.' " Roszkowski & Wladis, Revised U.C.C. Section 2–207: Analysis and Recommendations, 49 Bus.Law.1065, 1070 (1994). Others contend that sellers are driven to the strategic use of forms exactly to avoid the imposition of gap-fillers such as the warranty of merchantability provided in UCC § 2–314 that, in their view, unreasonably favor buyers.

(3) *Strategies in the "Battle"?* To "win" the battle of the forms, what clauses might a seller insert in its "quotation" or "sales acknowledgment" forms? What

clauses might a buyer insert in its "purchase order" forms? Do those clauses present risks as well as rewards?

When parties have an on-going relationship, one method for avoiding the battle altogether is to negotiate an overriding master agreement to govern all their dealings. Still another is for a trade association to work out standard terms to which its members agree. See, for example, Professor Lisa Bernstein's studies of private codes in the grain and diamond industries, Merchant Law in a Merchant Court, 144 U.Pa.L.Rev.1765 (1996), and Opting Out of the Legal System: Extra Contractual Relations in the Diamond Industry, 21 J.Legal Stud.115 (1992).

Electronic data interchange is another means of reducing sales terms to an agreed "transaction set" to be used between trading partners in all future sales. Professor Keating suggests that these practices may mean the battle of the forms has not been as ferocious as may have been supposed. See Keating, Note 1 above, at 2696–99.

PROBLEM

Misplaced Strategies. Buyer sent Seller a purchase order containing an arbitration clause; Seller returned an invoice silent on arbitration, but stating that "This document is not an Expression of Acceptance or Confirmation document as contemplated in Section 2–207.... The acceptance of any order entered by Buyer is expressly conditional on [Buyer's] assent to any additional or conflicting terms herein." After Seller shipped and Buyer received the goods (bulk nylon fiber or nylon tow), the goods spontaneously combusted, destroying several of Buyer's buildings. (Buyer alleged that a static electric charge in the nylon ignited, causing the fire.) Seller resisted Buyer's lawsuit on the ground that the Buyer was bound to the arbitration clause in its purchase order. What result? See Commerce & Industry Insurance Co. v. Bayer Corp., 742 N.E.2d 567 (Mass.2001).

———

CONTRACT FIRST, TERMS LATER: UCC § 2–207 OR A NEW METHOD OF CONTRACT FORMATION?

An increasingly common transactional scenario is presented when the parties have seemingly entered into a basic contract, but subsequently one party communicates additional terms, sometimes accompanied by language conditioning the contract on acquiescence to those terms. Consider, for example, a disclaimer of warranty included in a package insert, seen only after the product has been purchased and brought home. Does UCC § 2–207 apply to such a transaction? If so, what is the status of the parties' contract and of the additional terms in the package?

The cases that follow investigate the problem of post-agreement terms in three common settings: terms found on box tops, terms found encoded on disks, and terms enclosed in the box containing purchased goods. In reading these cases consider the following question: Are there reasons to distinguish between consumer transactions and commercial transactions?

Step–Saver Data Systems, Inc. v. Wyse Technology

United States Court of Appeals, Third Circuit, 1991.
939 F.2d 91.

■ WISDOM, CIRCUIT JUDGE: The "Limited Use License Agreement" printed on a package containing a copy of a computer program raises the central issue in this appeal. The trial judge held that the terms of the Limited Use License Agreement governed the purchase of the package, and, therefore, granted the software producer, The Software Link, Inc. ("TSL"), a directed verdict on claims of breach of warranty brought by a disgruntled purchaser, Step–Saver Data Systems, Inc. We disagree with the district court's determination of the legal effect of the license, and reverse and remand the warranty claims for further consideration.

[In the spring of 1986 Step–Saver obtained several copies of Wyse Technology's program "Advanced Multilink," which it tested with a view to incorporating it into a multi-user electronic system ("the system"). It decided to do so.] From August of 1986 through March of 1987, Step–Saver purchased and resold 142 copies of the Multilink Advanced program. Step–Saver would typically purchase copies of the program in the following manner. First, Step–Saver would telephone TSL and place an order. (Step–Saver would typically order twenty copies of the program at a time.) TSL would accept the order and promise, while on the telephone, to ship the goods promptly. After the telephone order, Step–Saver would send a purchase order, detailing the items to be purchased, their price, and shipping and payment terms. TSL would ship the order promptly, along with an invoice. The invoice would contain terms essentially identical with those on Step–Saver's purchase order: price, quantity, and shipping and payment terms. No reference was made during the telephone calls, or on either the purchase orders or the invoices with regard to a disclaimer of any warranties.

Printed on the package of each copy of the program, however, would be [form language purporting to express the complete agreement between the parties (the "box-top license"), including] five terms relevant to this action:

(1) The box-top license provides that the customer has not purchased the software itself, but has merely obtained a personal, non-transferable license to use the program.

(2) The box-top license, in detail and at some length, disclaims all express and implied warranties except for a warranty that the disks contained in the box are free from defects.

. . .

(5) The box-top license states: "Opening this package indicates your acceptance of these terms and conditions. If you do not agree with them, you should promptly return the package unopened to the person from whom you purchased it within fifteen days from date of purchase and your money will be refunded to you by that person."

Step–Saver began marketing the system in November of 1986, and sold one hundred forty-two systems mostly to law and medical offices before terminating sales of the system in March of 1987. Almost immediately upon installation of the system, Step–Saver began to receive complaints from some of its customers.[1] At least twelve of Step–Saver's customers filed suit against Step–Saver because of the problems with the multi-user system.

[Efforts by the parties having failed to resolve the problems, Step–Saver brought an action against TSL, charging it with breaches of warranties and seeking indemnity for costs in resolving the customers' suits. Wyse Technology, a manufacturer of terminals, also a defendant, was exonerated in the trial court and on appeal.]

The district court, without much discussion, held, as a matter of law, that the box-top license was the final and complete expression of the terms of the parties' agreement. Because the district court decided the questions of contract formation and interpretation as issues of law, we review the district court's resolution of these questions *de novo*.

Step–Saver contends that the contract for each copy of the program was formed when TSL agreed, on the telephone, to ship the copy at the agreed price.[2] The box-top license, argues Step–Saver, was a material alteration to the parties' contract which did not become a part of the contract under UCC § 2–207. ...

A. *Does UCC § 2–207 Govern the Analysis?*

As a basic principle, we agree with Step–Saver that UCC § 2–207 governs our analysis. We see no need to parse the parties' various actions to decide exactly when the parties formed a contract. TSL has shipped the product, and Step–Saver has accepted and paid for each copy of the program. The parties' performance demonstrates the existence of a contract. The dispute is, therefore, not over the existence of a contract, but the nature of its terms. When the parties' conduct establishes a contract, but the parties have failed to adopt expressly a particular writing as the terms of their agreement, and the writings exchanged by the parties do not agree, UCC § 2–207 determines the terms of the contract.

... Under the common law of sales, and to some extent still for contracts outside the UCC, an acceptance that varied any term of the offer operated as a rejection of the offer, and simultaneously made a counteroffer.... [T]he terms of the party who sent the last form, typically the seller, would become the terms of the parties' contract. This result was known as the "last shot rule".

1. According to the testimony of Jeffrey Worthington, an employee of Step–Saver, twenty to twenty-five of the purchasers of the multi-user system had serious problems with the system that were never resolved.

2. See UCC § 2–206(1)(b) and comment 2. Note that under UCC § 2–201, the oral contract would not be enforceable in the absence of a writing or part performance because each order typically involved more than $500 in goods. However, courts have typically treated the questions of formation and interpretation as separate from the question of when the contract becomes enforceable. See, e.g., C. Itoh & Co. v. Jordan Int'l Co., 552 F.2d 1228, 1232–33 (7th Cir.1977); Southeastern Adhesives Co. v. Funder America, 89 N.C.App. 438, 366 S.E.2d 505, 507–08 (N.C.App.1988)....

The UCC, in § 2–207, rejected this approach. Instead, it recognized that, while a party may desire the terms detailed in its form if a dispute, in fact, arises, most parties do not expect a dispute to arise when they first enter into a contract. As a result, most parties will proceed with the transaction even if they know that the terms of their form would not be enforced.[3] The insight behind the rejection of the last shot rule is that it would be unfair to bind the buyer of goods to the standard terms of the seller, when neither party cared sufficiently to establish expressly the terms of their agreement, simply because the seller sent the last form. . . . In the absence of a party's express assent to the additional or different terms of the writing, section 2–207 provides a default rule that the parties intended, as the terms of their agreement, those terms to which both parties have agreed,[4] along with any terms implied by the provisions of the UCC.

The reasons that led to the rejection of the last shot rule, and the adoption of section 2–207, apply fully in this case. . . .

B.   *Application of § 2–207*

TSL advances two reasons why its box-top license should be considered a conditional acceptance under UCC § 2–207(1). First, TSL argues that the express language of the box-top license, including . . . the phrase "opening this product indicates your acceptance of these terms", made TSL's acceptance "expressly conditional on assent to the additional or different terms". Second, TSL argues that the box-top license, by permitting return of the product within fifteen days if the purchaser[5] does not agree to the terms stated in the license (the "refund offer"), establishes that TSL's acceptance was conditioned on Step–Saver's assent to the terms of the box-top license, citing Monsanto Agricultural Products Co. v. Edenfield.[6] While we are not certain that a conditional acceptance analysis applies when a contract is established by performance,[7] we assume that it does and consider TSL's arguments.

---

3. As Judge Engel has written: "Usually, these standard terms mean little, for a contract looks to its fulfillment and rarely anticipates its breach. Hope springs eternal in the commercial world and expectations are usually, but not always, realized." McJunkin Corp. v. Mechanicals, Inc., 888 F.2d at 481 (6th Cir. 1989).

4. The parties may demonstrate their acceptance of a particular term either "orally or by informal correspondence", UCC 2–207, comment 1, or by placing the term in their respective form.

5. In the remainder of the opinion, we will refer to the transaction as a sale for the sake of simplicity, but, by doing so, do not mean to resolve the sale-license question.

6. 426 So.2d 574 (Fla.Dist.Ct.App. 1982).

7. Even though a writing is sent after performance establishes the existence of a contract, courts have analyzed the effect of such a writing under UCC § 2–207. See Herzog Oil Field Serv. v. Otto Torpedo Co., 391 Pa.Super. 133, 570 A.2d 549, 550 (Pa.Super.Ct.1990); McJunkin Corp. v. Mechanicals, Inc., 888 F.2d at 487. The official comment to UCC 2–207 suggests that, even though a proposed deal has been closed, the conditional acceptance analysis still applies in determining which writing's terms will define the contract.

2. Under this Article a proposed deal which in commercial understanding has in fact been closed is recognized as a contract. Therefore, any additional matter contained in the confirmation or in the acceptance falls within subsection (2) and must be regarded as a proposal for an added term *unless the acceptance is made conditional on the acceptance of the additional or different terms.*

To determine whether a writing constitutes a conditional acceptance, courts have established three tests. [The court described various applications that courts have given to the concluding phrase in subsection (1) of UCC § 2–207, and then recited some further facts about the dealings between the parties.]

Based on these facts, we conclude that TSL did not clearly express its unwillingness to proceed with the transactions unless its additional terms were incorporated into the parties' agreement. The box-top license did not, therefore, constitute a conditional acceptance under UCC § 2–207(1).

3. Did the parties's course of dealing establish that the parties had excluded any express or implied warranties associated with the software program?

TSL argues that because Step–Saver placed its orders for copies of the Multilink Advanced program with notice of the terms of the box-top license, Step–Saver is bound by the terms of the box-top license. Essentially, TSL is arguing that, even if the terms of the box-top license would not become part of the contract if the case involved only a single transaction, the repeated expression of those terms by TSL eventually incorporates them within the contract.

. . . While one court has concluded that terms repeated in a number of written confirmations eventually become part of the contract even though neither party ever takes any action with respect to the issue addressed by those terms, most courts have rejected such reasoning.

. . . [W]e are not convinced that TSL's unilateral act of repeatedly sending copies of the box-top license with its product can establish a course of dealing between TSL and Step–Saver that resulted in the adoption of the terms of the box-top license.

With regard to more specific evidence as to the parties' course of dealing or performance, it appears that the parties have not incorporated the warranty disclaimer into their agreement. First, there is the evidence that TSL tried to obtain Step–Saver's express consent to the disclaimer and limitation of damages provision of the box-top license. Step–Saver refused to sign the proposed agreements. Second, when first notified of the problems with the program, TSL spent considerable time and energy attempting to solve the problems identified by Step–Saver.

Course of conduct is ordinarily a factual issue. But we hold that the actions of TSL in repeatedly sending a writing, whose terms would otherwise be excluded under UCC § 2–207, cannot establish a course of conduct between TSL and Step–Saver that adopted the terms of the writing.

[The court rejected arguments of public policy advanced by TSL.]

C. *The Terms of the Contract*

Under section 2–207, an additional term detailed in the box-top license will not be incorporated into the parties' contract if the term's addition to the contract would materially alter the parties' agreement.[8] Step–Saver

---

8. UCC § 2–207(2)(b).

alleges that several representations made by TSL constitute express warranties, and that valid implied warranties were also a part of the parties' agreement. Because the district court considered the box-top license to exclude all of these warranties, the district court did not consider whether other factors may act to exclude these warranties. The existence and nature of the warranties is primarily a factual question that we leave for the district court,[9] but assuming that these warranties were included within the parties' original agreement, we must conclude that adding the disclaimer of warranty and limitation of remedies provisions from the box-top license would, as a matter of law, substantially alter the distribution of risk between Step–Saver and TSL. Therefore, under UCC § 2–207(2)(b), the disclaimer of warranty and limitation of remedies terms of the box-top license did not become a part of the parties' agreement.

... [T]he box-top license should have been treated as a written confirmation containing additional terms. Because the warranty disclaimer and limitation of remedies terms would materially alter the parties' agreement, these terms did not become a part of the parties' agreement. We remand for further consideration the express and implied warranty claims against TSL.

NOTES

(1) *Questions.* How many "expressions of acceptance" might one find in *Step–Saver*? Why does the court reject TSL's argument that the box-top was a conditional acceptance under subsection (1)? How does the court finally characterize the box-top? On what basis did the court decide that the warranty disclaimer and limitation of remedies provisions were material alterations under subsection (2)?

(2) *Assenting to Material Terms.* In Union Carbide v. Oscar Mayer Foods, discussed at Note 1, p. 199 above, the court stated that "Even if the alteration is material, the other party can, of course, decide to accept it." In that case, involving the materiality of an indemnity clause for taxes, the court thought it important to separate the issue of materiality from that of consent. ("They are close but distinct.") "If the new term does not effect a material alteration, silence is consent, period. If it does effect a material alteration, the party who proposed it must present additional evidence, beyond the term itself, to show that he was reasonable to infer consent to the new term from the other party's failure to object (silence); ordinarily this will be evidence of prior dealings." 947 F.2d at 1336.

The case provides a good workout of this close but distinctive relationship. Union Carbide argued that Oscar Mayer had agreed to the indemnity clause by paying all the sales taxes that appeared on the Union Carbide invoices without complaint. "What difference does it make, asks Union Carbide, if the [tax] increase took the form of an assessment of back taxes? It makes a big difference, amounting to a material alteration to which Oscar Mayer did not consent either explicitly or implicitly.... To assume responsibility for taxes shown on an individual invoice is

---

9. For example, questions exist as to: (1) whether the statements by TSL were representations of fact, or mere statements of opinion; (2) whether the custom in the trade is to exclude warranties and limit remedies in contracts between a software producer and its dealer; (3) whether Step–Saver relied on TSL's alleged representations, or whether these warranties became a basis of the parties' bargain; and (4) whether Step–Saver's testing excluded some or all of these warranties. From the record, it appears that most of these issues are factual determinations that will require a trial, as did the warranty claims against Wyse. But we leave these issues open to the district court on remand.

quite different from assuming an open-ended, indeed, incalculable, liability for back taxes.... [T]his is not a case where consent can be realistically inferred from Oscar Mayer's silence in the face of a succession of acceptances (Union Carbide's invoices) containing the new term." 947 F.2d at 1337.

(3) *Assent and Arbitration.* The fact that arbitration terms are in widespread use sometimes contributes to the conclusion that a particular term was assented to. In Pervel Industries, Inc. v. TM Wallcovering, Inc., 871 F.2d 7 (2d Cir.1989), the court said:

> Where, as here, a manufacturer has a well established custom of sending purchase order confirmations containing an arbitration clause, a buyer who has made numerous purchases over a period of time, receiving in each instance a standard confirmation form which it either signed and returned or retained without objection, is bound by the arbitration provision.... This is particularly true in industries such as fabrics and textiles where the specialized nature of the product has led to the widespread use of arbitration clauses and knowledgeable arbitrators.

Conversely, the fact that a term diverges from trade usage and the like may be a reason to doubt that it was assented to. Business persons, it is said, "do not consider the boilerplate printed on the reverse side of their forms to be part of the deal unless it coincidentally reflects some aspect of custom, usage, course of dealing, or practice that they understand as implicit in the resulting transactional relationship." Thomas J. McCarthy, An Introduction: The Commercial Irrelevancy of the "Battle of the Forms," 49 Bus.Law. 1019, 1026 (1994). If this is correct, how far should the courts consult such practices for indications that a given term was or was not assented to?

The New York Court of Appeals has said that an arbitration term "is a material addition which can become part of a contract only if it is expressly assented to by both parties." Marlene Industries Corp. v. Carnac Textiles, Inc., p. 198 above. Can that statement be reconciled with the excerpt quoted from *Pervel Industries* above? See Diskin v. J.P. Stevens & Co., Inc., 836 F.2d 47 (1st Cir.1987). The problem of mandatory arbitration clauses is discussed in Chapter 6.

(4) *International Solutions.* A provision comparable to UCC § 2–207 appears as Article 19 of the Convention on Contracts for the International Sale of Goods. (Provisions of the Convention, together with an introduction, can be found in Selections for Contracts.) Among the many additional terms considered to alter "materially" the terms of an offer, under that provision are those relating to "the extent of one party's liability to the other or the settlement of disputes." Does this expression embrace all terms that "substantially alter the distribution of risk" between the parties? If so, and if the *Step–Saver* case had been governed by the Convention, would the result have been the same?

In contrast to the approach in the CISG, the UNIDROIT Principles leave the determination of materiality to the "circumstances of each case" and, like the UCC, provides that "surprise to the offerer" is important to that assessment; see UNIDROIT Principles article 2.11 comment 2.

ProCD, Inc. v. Zeidenberg

United States Court of Appeals, Seventh Circuit, 1996.
86 F.3d 1447.

[Every box containing ProCD's software declared that it came with restrictions stated in an enclosed license. This license, encoded on the CD–ROM disks as well as printed in the manual, and which appeared on a user's screen every time the software ran, limited use of the application program and listings to non-commercial purposes. Matthew Zeidenberg bought a consumer package of ProCD's software from a retail outlet but decided to ignore the license. He formed a company to resell the information in ProCD's database at a price less than ProCD charges its commercial customers. ProCD filed suit seeking an injunction against further dissemination that exceeds the rights specified in the licenses.]

■ EASTERBROOK, CIRCUIT JUDGE.[a] The district court held the licenses ineffectual because their terms do not appear on the outside of the packages. The court added that ... a purchaser does not agree to—and cannot be bound by—terms that were secret at the time of purchase. 908 F.Supp. at 654.

Following the district court, we treat the licenses as ordinary contracts accompanying the sale of products, and therefore as governed by the common law of contracts and the Uniform Commercial Code. Whether there are legal differences between "contracts" and "licenses" (which may matter under the copyright doctrine of first sale) is a subject for another day.... Zeidenberg [argues], and the district court held, that placing the package of software on the shelf is an "offer," which the customer "accepts" by paying the asking price and leaving the store with the goods. Peeters v. State, 142 N.W. 181 (1913). In Wisconsin, as elsewhere, a contract includes only the terms on which the parties have agreed. One cannot agree to hidden terms, the judge concluded. So far, so good—but one of the terms to which Zeidenberg agreed by purchasing the software is that the transaction was subject to a license. Zeidenberg's position therefore must be that the printed terms on the outside of a box are the parties' contract—except for printed terms that refer to or incorporate other terms. But why would Wisconsin fetter the parties' choice in this way? Vendors can put the entire terms of a contract on the outside of a box only by using microscopic type, removing other information that buyers might find more useful (such as what the software does, and on which computers it works), or both. The "Read Me" file included with most software, describing system requirements and potential incompatibilities, may be equivalent to ten pages of type; warranties and license restrictions take still more space. Notice on the outside, terms on the inside, and a right to return the software for a refund if the terms are unacceptable (a right that the license expressly extends), may be a means of doing business valuable to buyers and sellers alike. See E. Allan Farnsworth, 1 Farnsworth on Contracts § 4.26 (1990); Restatement (2d) of Contracts § 211 comment *a* (1981) ("Standardization of agreements serves many of the same functions as standardization of goods and services; both are essential to a system of mass production and distribution. Scarce and costly time and skill can be devoted to a class of transactions rather than the details of individual

---

a. Frank Easterbrook (1948–) served for several years in the Department of Justice and then joined the University of Chicago law faculty, where he made important scholarly contributions in the fields of corporate and anti-trust law, and has been an influential proponent of economic analysis to law. In 1985 he was appointed to the United States Court of Appeals, Seventh Circuit.

transactions.''). Doubtless a state could forbid the use of standard contracts in the software business, but we do not think that Wisconsin has done so.

Transactions in which the exchange of money precedes the communication of detailed terms are common. Consider the purchase of insurance. The buyer goes to an agent, who explains the essentials (amount of coverage, number of years) and remits the premium to the home office, which sends back a policy. On the district judge's understanding, the terms of the policy are irrelevant because the insured paid before receiving them. Yet the device of payment, often with a "binder" (so that the insurance takes effect immediately even though the home office reserves the right to withdraw coverage later), in advance of the policy, serves buyers' interests by accelerating effectiveness and reducing transactions costs. Or consider the purchase of an airline ticket. The traveler calls the carrier or an agent, is quoted a price, reserves a seat, pays, and gets a ticket, in that order. The ticket elaborates terms, which the traveler can reject by canceling the reservation. To use the ticket is to accept the terms, even terms that in retrospect are disadvantageous. See Carnival Cruise Lines, Inc. v. Shute, 499 U.S. 585 (1991). Just so with a ticket to a concert. The back of the ticket states that the patron promises not to record the concert; to attend is to agree. A theater that detects a violation will confiscate the tape and escort the violator to the exit. One could arrange things so that every concertgoer signs this promise before forking over the money, but that cumbersome way of doing things not only would lengthen queues and raise prices but also would scotch the sale of tickets by phone or electronic data service.

Consumer goods work the same way. Someone who wants to buy a radio set visits a store, pays, and walks out with a box. Inside the box is a leaflet containing some terms, the most important of which usually is the warranty, read for the first time in the comfort of home. By Zeidenberg's lights, the warranty in the box is irrelevant; every consumer gets the standard warranty implied by the UCC in the event the contract is silent; yet so far as we are aware no state disregards warranties furnished with consumer products. Drugs come with a list of ingredients on the outside and an elaborate package insert on the inside. The package insert describes drug interactions, contraindications, and other vital information—but, if Zeidenberg is right, the purchaser need not read the package insert, because it is not part of the contract.

Next consider the software industry itself. Only a minority of sales take place over the counter, where there are boxes to peruse. A customer may place an order by phone in response to a line item in a catalog or a review in a magazine. Much software is ordered over the Internet by purchasers who have never seen a box. Increasingly software arrives by wire. There is no box; there is only a stream of electrons, a collection of information that includes data, an application program, instructions, many limitations ("MegaPixel 3.14159 cannot be used with BytePusher 2.718"), and the terms of sale. The user purchases a serial number, which activates the software's features. On Zeidenberg's arguments, these unboxed sales are unfettered by terms—so the seller has made a broad warranty and must pay consequential damages for any shortfalls in performance, two "promises" that if taken seriously would drive prices through the ceiling or return transactions to the horse-and-buggy age.

According to the district court, the UCC does not countenance the sequence of money now, terms later. . . . [Yet] only three cases (other than ours) touch on the subject, and none directly addresses it. See Step–Saver Data Systems, Inc. v. Wyse Technology, 939 F.2d 91 (3d Cir.1991); Vault Corp. v. Quaid Software Ltd., 847 F.2d 255, 268–70 (5th Cir.1988); Arizona Retail Systems, Inc. v. Software Link, Inc., 831 F.Supp. 759 (D.Ariz.1993). As their titles suggest, these are not consumer transactions. Step–Saver is a battle-of-the-forms case, in which the parties exchange incompatible forms and a court must decide which prevails. See Northrop Corp. v. Litronic Industries, 29 F.3d 1173 (7th Cir.1994) (Illinois law); Douglas G. Baird & Robert Weisberg, Rules, Standards, and the Battle of the Forms: A Reassessment of § 2–207, 68 Va. L.Rev. 1217, 1227–31 (1982). Our case has only one form; UCC § 2–207 is irrelevant. Vault holds that Louisiana's special shrinkwrap-license statute is preempted by federal law, a question to which we return. And Arizona Retail Systems did not reach the question, because the court found that the buyer knew the terms of the license before purchasing the software.

What then does the current version of the UCC have to say? We think that the place to start is § 2–204(1): "A contract for sale of goods may be made in any manner sufficient to show agreement, including conduct by both parties which recognizes the existence of such a contract." A vendor, as master of the offer, may invite acceptance by conduct, and may propose limitations on the kind of conduct that constitutes acceptance. A buyer may accept by performing the acts the vendor proposes to treat as acceptance. And that is what happened. ProCD proposed a contract that a buyer would accept by using the software after having an opportunity to read the license at leisure. This Zeidenberg did. He had no choice, because the software splashed the license on the screen and would not let him proceed without indicating acceptance. So although the district judge was right to say that a contract can be, and often is, formed simply by paying the price and walking out of the store, the UCC permits contracts to be formed in other ways. ProCD proposed such a different way, and without protest Zeidenberg agreed. Ours is not a case in which a consumer opens a package to find an insert saying "you owe us an extra $10,000" and the seller files suit to collect. Any buyer finding such a demand can prevent formation of the contract by returning the package, as can any consumer who concludes that the terms of the license make the software worth less than the purchase price. Nothing in the UCC requires a seller to maximize the buyer's net gains.

Section 2–606, which defines "acceptance of goods", reinforces this understanding. A buyer accepts goods under § 2–606(1)(b) when, after an opportunity to inspect, he fails to make an effective rejection under § 2–602(1). ProCD extended an opportunity to reject if a buyer should find the license terms unsatisfactory; Zeidenberg inspected the package, tried out the software, learned of the license, and did not reject the goods. We refer to § 2–606 only to show that the opportunity to return goods can be important; acceptance of an offer differs from acceptance of goods after delivery, see Gillen v. Atalanta Systems, Inc., 997 F.2d 280, 284 n. 1 (7th Cir.1993); but the UCC consistently permits the parties to structure their relations so that the buyer has a chance to make a final decision after a detailed review.

Reversed and Remanded.

NOTES

(1) *Case Comparisons.* The court's decision in *ProCD* distinguishes *Step–Saver*, noting that the transaction in that case involved *two* forms, thereby properly triggering a "battle of the forms" analysis. *Does* UCC § 2–207 require two forms? (Review the court's analysis of a possible reading of the facts in *Dorton*, p. 193.) In what ways, if any, is a box-top license different from shrinkwrap terms?

The *ProCD* opinion also noted that unlike *ProCD*, *Step–Saver* was not a consumer transaction. Should the rules of contract formation differ depending on whether the transaction is commercial or consumer in nature? How does UCC § 2–207(2) account for this difference? Assuming that buyer Zeidenberg was not a merchant, what result in *ProCD* if the court had applied UCC § 2–207(2)?

(2) *Case Archeology.* Zeidenberg, a graduate student in computer science at the University of Wisconsin at the time he bought the Select Phone program, consulted with law professor John Kidwell, about his proposed use of the program in light of existing copyright law. Prof. Kidwell told Zeidenberg, that "You're probably legally in the clear, but you'll definitely be sued." For an interview with Zeidenberg, see William Whitford, Freedom from Contract Symposium: Appendix, 2004 Wis. L. Rev. 821. For an analysis and a proposed statutory resolution for *ProCD* and *Hill* (below), see James J. White, Autistic Contracts, 45 Wayne L. Rev. 1693 (2000).

Hill v. Gateway 2000, Inc.

United States Court of Appeals, Seventh Circuit, 1997.
105 F.3d 1147.

■ EASTERBROOK, CIRCUIT JUDGE. A customer picks up the phone, orders a computer, and gives a credit card number. Presently a box arrives, containing the computer and a list of terms, said to govern unless the customer returns the computer within 30 days. Are these terms effective as the parties' contract, or is the contract term-free because the order-taker did not read any terms over the phone and elicit the customer's assent?

One of the terms in the box containing a Gateway 2000 system was an arbitration clause. Rich and Enza Hill, the customers, kept the computer more than 30 days before complaining about its components and performance. They filed suit in federal court arguing, among other things, that the product's shortcomings make Gateway a racketeer (mail and wire fraud are said to be the predicate offenses), leading to treble damages under RICO for the Hills and a class of all other purchasers. Gateway asked the district court to enforce the arbitration clause; the judge refused, writing that "[t]he present record is insufficient to support a finding of a valid arbitration agreement between the parties or that the plaintiffs were given adequate notice of the arbitration clause." Gateway took an immediate appeal, as is its right. 9 U.S.C. § 16(a)(1)(A)....

ProCD, Inc. v. Zeidenberg, 86 F.3d 1447 (7th Cir.1996), holds that terms inside a box of software bind consumers who use the software after an opportunity to read the terms and to reject them by returning the product. Likewise, *Carnival Cruise Lines, Inc. v. Shute,* 499 U.S. 585, 111 S.Ct. 1522, 113 L.Ed.2d 622 (1991), enforces a forum-selection clause that was included among three pages of terms attached to a cruise ship ticket. *ProCD* and *Carnival Cruise Lines* exemplify the many commercial transactions in which people pay for products with terms to follow; *ProCD* discusses others. 86 F.3d at 1451–52. The district court concluded in *ProCD* that the contract is formed when the consumer pays for the software; as a result, the court held, only terms known to the consumer at that moment are part of the contract, and provisos inside the box do not count. Although this is one way a contract could be formed, it is not the only way: "A vendor, as master of the offer, may invite acceptance by conduct, and may propose limitations on the kind of conduct that constitutes acceptance. A buyer may accept by performing the acts the vendor proposes to treat as acceptance." *Id.* at 1452. Gateway shipped computers with the same sort of accept-or-return offer *ProCD* made to users of its software. *ProCD* relied on the Uniform Commercial Code rather than any peculiarities of Wisconsin law; both Illinois and South Dakota, the two states whose law might govern relations between Gateway and the Hills, have adopted the UCC; neither side has pointed us to any atypical doctrines in those states that might be pertinent; *ProCD* therefore applies to this dispute.

Plaintiffs ask us to limit *ProCD* to software, but where's the sense in that? *ProCD* is about the law of contract, not the law of software. Payment preceding the revelation of full terms is common for air transportation, insurance, and many other endeavors. Practical considerations support allowing vendors to enclose the full legal terms with their products. Cashiers cannot be expected to read legal documents to customers before ringing up sales. If the staff at the other end of the phone for direct-sales operations such as Gateway's had to read the four-page statement of terms before taking the buyer's credit card number, the droning voice would anesthetize rather than enlighten many potential buyers. Others would hang up in a rage over the waste of their time. And oral recitation would not avoid customers' assertions (whether true or feigned) that the clerk did not read term X to them, or that they did not remember or understand it. Writing provides benefits for both sides of commercial transactions. Customers as a group are better off when vendors skip costly and ineffectual steps such as telephonic recitation, and use instead a simple approve-or-return device. Competent adults are bound by such documents, read or unread. For what little it is worth, we add that the box from Gateway was crammed with software. The computer came with an operating system, without which it was useful only as a boat anchor. See *Digital Equipment Corp. v. Uniq Digital Technologies, Inc.,* 73 F.3d 756, 761 (7th Cir.1996). Gateway also included many application programs. So the Hills' effort to limit *ProCD* to software would not avail them factually, even if it were sound legally—which it is not.

For their second sally, the Hills contend that *ProCD* should be limited to executory contracts (to licenses in particular), and therefore does not apply because both parties' performance of this contract was complete when the box arrived at their home. This is legally and factually wrong: legally because the question at hand concerns the *formation* of the contract rather than its *performance*, and factually because both contracts were incompletely performed. *ProCD* did not depend on the fact that the seller characterized the transaction as a license rather than as a contract; we treated it as a contract for the sale of goods and reserved the question whether for other purposes a "license" characterization might be preferable. 86 F.3d at 1450. All debates about characterization to one side, the transaction in *ProCD* was no more executory than the one here: Zeidenberg paid for the software and walked out of the store with a box under his arm, so if arrival of the box with the product ends the time for revelation of contractual terms, then the time ended in *ProCD* before Zeidenberg opened the box. But of course ProCD had not completed performance with delivery of the box, and neither had Gateway. One element of the transaction was the warranty, which obliges sellers to fix defects in their products. The Hills have invoked Gateway's warranty and are not satisfied with its response, so they are not well positioned to say that Gateway's obligations were fulfilled when the motor carrier unloaded the box. What is more, both ProCD and Gateway promised to help customers to use their products. Long-term service and information obligations are common in the computer business, on both hardware and software sides. Gateway offers "lifetime service" and has a round-the-clock telephone hotline to fulfill this promise. Some vendors spend more money helping customers use their products than on developing and manufacturing them. The document in Gateway's box includes promises of future performance that some consumers value highly; these promises bind Gateway just as the arbitration clause binds the Hills.

Next the Hills insist that *ProCD* is irrelevant because Zeidenberg was a "merchant" and they are not. Section 2–207(2) of the UCC, the infamous battle-of-the-forms section, states that "additional terms [following acceptance of an offer] are to be construed as proposals for addition to a contract. Between merchants such terms become part of the contract unless ...". Plaintiffs tell us that *ProCD* came out as it did only because Zeidenberg was a "merchant" and the terms inside ProCD's box were not excluded by the "unless" clause. This argument pays scant attention to the opinion in *ProCD,* which concluded that, when there is only one form, "sec. 2–207 is irrelevant." 86 F.3d at 1452. The question in *ProCD* was not whether terms were added to a contract after its formation, but how and when the contract was formed-in particular, whether a vendor may propose that a contract of sale be formed, not in the store (or over the phone) with the payment of money or a general "send me the product," but after the customer has had a chance to inspect both the item and the terms. *ProCD* answers "yes," for merchants and consumers alike. Yet again, for what little it is worth we observe that the Hills misunderstand the setting of *ProCD.* A "merchant" under the UCC "means a person who deals in goods of the kind or otherwise by his occupation holds himself out as having knowledge or skill peculiar to the practices or goods involved in the transaction", § 2–104(1). Zeidenberg bought the product at a retail store, an uncommon place for merchants to acquire inventory. His corporation put ProCD's database on the Internet for anyone to browse, which led to the litigation but did not make Zeidenberg a software merchant.

At oral argument the Hills propounded still another distinction: the box containing ProCD's software displayed a notice that additional terms were within, while the box containing Gateway's computer did not. The difference is functional, not legal. Consumers browsing the aisles of a store can look at the box, and if they are unwilling to deal with the prospect of additional terms can leave the box alone, avoiding the transactions costs of returning the package after reviewing its contents. Gateway's box, by contrast, is just a shipping carton; it is not on display anywhere. Its function is to protect the product during transit, and the information on its sides is for the use of handlers rather than would-be purchasers.

"Fragile!" "This Side Up!"

Perhaps the Hills would have had a better argument if they were first alerted to the bundling of hardware and legal-ware after opening the box and wanted to return the computer in order to avoid disagreeable terms, but were dissuaded by the expense of shipping. What the remedy would be in such a case-could it exceed the shipping charges?-is an interesting question, but one that need not detain us because the Hills knew before they ordered the computer that the carton would include *some* important terms, and they did not seek to discover these in advance. Gateway's ads state that their products come with limited warranties and lifetime support. How limited was the warranty-30 days, with service contingent on shipping the computer back, or five years, with free onsite service? What sort of support was offered? Shoppers have three principal ways to discover these things. First, they can ask the vendor to send a copy before deciding whether to buy. The Magnuson–Moss Warranty Act requires firms to distribute their warranty terms on request, 15 U.S.C. § 2302(b)(1)(A); the Hills do not contend that Gateway would have refused to enclose the remaining terms too. Concealment would be bad for business, scaring some customers away and leading to excess returns from others. Second, shoppers can consult public sources (computer magazines, the Web sites of vendors) that may contain this information. Third, they may inspect the documents after the product's delivery. Like Zeidenberg, the Hills took the third option. By keeping the computer beyond 30 days, the Hills accepted Gateway's offer, including the arbitration clause. . . .

NOTES

(1) *Rolling Contract Formation.* The analysis in *Hill* is sometimes described as recognizing a doctrine of "rolling contract formation." This approach was followed in Brower v. Gateway 2000, 676 N.Y.S.2d 569, 572 (App.Div.1998). "There is no agreement or contract upon the placement of the order or even upon the receipt of the goods. . . . It is only after the consumer has affirmatively retained the merchandise for more than 30 days—within which the consumer has presumably examined

and even used the product(s) and read the agreement—that the contract has been effectuated." In *Brower*, because thirty days had passed, the court found that a contract had been formed on the terms inside the box; however, it declined to enforce the terms on the grounds of unconscionability. The case is discussed further on p. 521 below.

(2) *Rolling Too Far?* In *Hill*, Judge Easterbrook concluded that the contract was created only when the Hills accepted Gateway's offer by keeping the computer beyond 30 days. Suppose that after the Hills had agreed to buy the computer at a particular price and Gateway had charged their credit card, but before delivery of the computer, Gateway refused to sell the computer except at a price higher than that agreed upon. Does Judge Easterbrook mean to say that such refusal would not constitute a breach of contract by Gateway? If so, does that result square with the policy of UCC § 2–207 favoring contract formation?

————

REVISING ARTICLE TWO

In *ProCD*, Judge Easterbrook asked what "the current version" of the UCC had to say about the facts of the case. The phrase anticipated a revision of Article 2 which had been undertaken by the ALI and NCCUSL. Drafters sought to clean up problems and restore uniformity to a code which, over forty years of use and interpretation, had developed its own body of common law.

By summer 1999, the revision process had produced a draft of a substantially revised Article 2 that had been approved by the ALI. However, the revision process collapsed when NCCUSL withdrew the draft from further consideration by its members. (Recall the UCC is a product of both the ALI and NCCUSL; see Note 2, p. 7 above.) For accounts of the collapse, see generally, Symposium, Perspectives on the Uniform Laws Revision Process, 52 Hastings L.J. 603 (2001).

The 1999 collapse was followed by the establishment of a reconstituted drafting committee with a charge to develop a somewhat less ambitious series of amendments to Article 2, focusing on areas in which consensus could easily be achieved. This drafting committee produced a set of proposed amendments to Article 2 that received final approval from ALI and NCCUSL in 2003. Excerpts from those proposed amendments appear in Selections for Contracts. As of 2008, no state had enacted those proposed amendments and the prospects for enactment remain dim.

Nonetheless, the amendments reflect an extensive rethinking of the treatment of such difficult issues as the "battle of the forms," warranties made to remote purchasers, and contracts formed via electronic commerce. A comparison of the proposed amendments with the official text of Article 2 yields greater understanding of the merits and deficiencies in the current law and of the repertoire of potential changes. Take a look at proposed UCC §§ 2–206 and 2–207. How do the rules governing the battle of the forms in the proposed amendments differ from those in current UCC § 2–207?

NOTE

Valuing Uniformity? If a provision of a proposed Article of the UCC is meritorious but seems unlikely to achieve uniform enactment throughout the United States, should the provision be enacted? For a view on balancing the benefits of uniformity against those of law reform that does not achieve uniform enactment, see Neil B. Cohen, Taking Democracy Seriously, 52 Hastings Law Journal 667 (2001).

SECTION 6.   PRECONTRACTUAL LIABILITY

According to orthodox contract doctrine, neither party to contractual negotiations is bound until an offer has been accepted and a contract has been formed. Until then, neither party is safe in acting in reliance on the prospect of a contract. There are, however, some circumstances in which a party may nevertheless incur liability before a contract has been formed.

Consider a notorious hypothetical put by Professor Maurice Wormser nearly a hundred years ago: "Suppose A says to B, 'I will give you $100 if you walk across the Brooklyn Bridge'.... B starts to walk across the Brooklyn Bridge and has gone about one-half of the way across. At that moment A overtakes B and says to him, 'I withdraw my offer.' Has B then any rights against A? Let us now suppose that after A has said, 'I withdraw my offer,' B continues to walk across the Brooklyn Bridge and completes the act of crossing. Under these circumstances, has B any rights against A?" Wormser concluded that he had none. "What A wanted from B, what A asked for, was the act of walking across the bridge. Until that was done, B had not given to A what A had requested. The acceptance by B of A's offer could be nothing but the act on B's part of crossing the bridge. It is elementary that an offeror may withdraw his offer until it has been accepted. It follows logically that A is perfectly within his rights in withdrawing his offer before B has accepted it by walking across the bridge—the act contemplated by the offeror and the offeree as the acceptance of the offer." Wormser, The True Conception of Unilateral Contracts, 26 Yale L.J. 136–37 (1916).

Restatement § 45 states a rule, based on former Restatement § 45 and couched in language of "option contract," that supports a different result. It states that if "an offer invites an offeree to accept by rendering a performance and does not invite a promissory acceptance, an option contract is created when the offeree tenders or *begins* the invited performance ..." (emphasis supplied). In reading this section in its entirety it helps to understand that one cannot "tender" a performance that is to extend over a period of time, such as crossing a bridge.

Indeed, long after Wormser first wrote of the Brooklyn Bridge hypothetical, he admitted: "Since that time I have repented, so that now, clad in sackcloth, I state frankly, that my point of view has changed. I agree, at this time, with the rule set forth in the Restatement...." Book Review, 3 J.Legal Ed. 145 (1950).

Note that the problem posed by the hypothetical and addressed in Restatement § 45 can be avoided if the offer seeks a promise as acceptance and either a promise is given in so many words or one can be inferred from the offeree's conduct. An example of the latter is found in Allied Steel v. Ford Motor Company, p. 158 above, where Ford's offer "was accepted ... when Allied, with Ford's knowledge, consent and acquiescence, undertook performance of the work called for by [Ford's purchase order]." The Restatement allows an offeree to choose the means of acceptance—"either by promising to perform what the offer requests or by rendering the performance"—when the offer itself was unclear about the type of response invited. See Restatement § 32.

NOTE

Objections to Option Contracts. Are there any objections to an option contract? May it not, in a rapidly fluctuating market, give the offeree an unfair chance to speculate during the time when the offeror is bound but the offeree is not? Given this risk, why would an informed offeror enter into an option contract? The traditional answer is that the offeror is compensated for the risk through a higher contract price. We might say that the offeree has paid for the chance to speculate during the time when the offeror is bound. Is it unfair then, if during that period the offeree then decides to take advantage of the fluctuating market? What are the assumptions that underlie the traditional answer? Under what circumstances might those assumptions fail?

Would there be any advantage in limiting recovery by B in the Brooklyn Bridge hypothetical to damages based on B's reliance rather than B's expectation interest? See Fuller and Perdue, The Reliance Interest in Contract Damages: 2, 46 Yale L.J. 373, 410–17 (1937).

PROBLEM

The Move to Maine. Sarah Hodgkin, a widow who lived alone on her farm in Maine, wrote to her daughter and son-in-law, the Brackenburys, in Missouri, offering them the use and income of her farm if they would move to Maine and take care of Mrs. Hodgkin during her life. The letter closed, "you to have the place when I have passed away." The Brackenburys moved to Maine and began performance, but after a few weeks, relations between the parties soured. When Mrs. Hodgkin sought to evict the Brackenburys, they sued to enforce her promise. What result? Brackenbury v. Hodgkin, 102 A. 106 (Me.1917). Would it make a difference if Hodgkin's letter had read: "If you will agree to move to Lewiston and care for me on the home place...." See Davis v. Jacoby, 34 P.2d 1026 (Cal.1934).

What if Hodgkin had died after the Brackenburys had sold their home and business in Missouri and begun the journey to Maine? See the discussion of Death of an Offeror at p. 180 above.

REVOCABILITY AND RELIANCE

Consider a general contractor, such as Kastorff in the case at p. 139 above, that receives bids from subcontractors and uses those bids in making up its own bid. Suppose that Kastorff had properly calculated his bid using the plumbing subcontractor's $6,500 bid, and that after Kastorff had submitted his bid, the plumbing subcontractor had attempted to withdraw the $6,500 bid on the ground that it was the result of a clerical error and should have been $9,500. Could the plumbing subcontractor justify this not on the grounds of mistake but because the offer sought a promise from Kastorff and, no promise having been given, the subcontractors could revoke his offer?

The orthodox response is that found in Judge Learned Hand's opinion in James Baird Co. v. Gimbel Bros., Inc., 64 F.2d 344 (2d Cir.1933). Hand held that promissory estoppel is inapplicable to a bargain promise which occasioned reliance not constituting performance of the consideration sought by the promisor. The subcontractor could withdraw its bid because "an offer for an exchange is not meant to become a promise until a consideration has been received, either a counter-promise or whatever is stipulated. To extend it would be to hold the offeror regardless of the stipulated condition of his offer." The subcontractor's offer could impose a duty to render a performance only when the general contractor "promised to take and pay for it. There is no room in such a situation for the doctrine of 'promissory estoppel.' "

This afforded protection along traditional lines to the offeror, who asks for something (acceptance by the offeree), and is not to be bound until he gets it; the offer is conditional on acceptance. "The element of exchange which marks off the bargain promise also" limits promissory estoppel. Hand's theory is that section 90 of the Restatement was originally intended to cover only the non-bargain situation—the transaction in which no exchange is asked or contemplated—and the drafting history of the section supports this position. Hand also noted that contractors have "a ready escape from their difficulty by insisting upon a contract before they used the figures; and in commercial transactions it does not in the end promote justice to seek strained interpretations in aid of those who do not protect themselves."

As you study the following case, keep in mind that Justice Traynor had to confront Hand's position that in the world of exchange transactions there is no place for section 90, which was intended only to cover the relied-upon gift promise. How does Traynor counter Hand on this?

Drennan v. Star Paving Co.

Supreme Court of California, In Bank, 1958.
51 Cal.2d 409, 333 P.2d 757.

General contractor brought action against paving subcontractor to recover damages because of refusal of subcontractor to perform paving according to bid which subcontractor submitted to general contractor. The Superior Court, Kern County, William L. Bradshaw, J., entered judgment adverse to the subcontractor, and the subcontractor appealed.

■ TRAYNOR, JUSTICE.[a] Defendant appeals from a judgment for plaintiff in an action to recover damages caused by defendant's refusal to perform certain paving work according to a bid it submitted to plaintiff.

On July 28, 1955, plaintiff, a licensed general contractor, was preparing a bid on the "Monte Vista School Job" in the Lancaster school district. Bids had to be submitted before 8:00 p.m. Plaintiff testified that it was customary in that area for general contractors to receive the bids of subcontractors by telephone on the day set for bidding and to rely on them in computing their own bids. Thus on that day plaintiff's secretary, Mrs. Johnson, received by telephone between fifty and seventy-five subcontractors' bids for various parts of the school job. As each bid came in, she wrote it on a special form, which she brought into plaintiff's office. He then posted it on a master cost sheet setting forth the names and bids of all subcontractors. His own bid had to include the names of subcontractors who were to perform one-half of one per cent or more of the construction work, and he had also to provide a bidder's bond of ten per cent of his total bid of $317,385 as a guarantee that he would enter the contract if awarded the work.

Late in the afternoon, Mrs. Johnson had a telephone conversation with Kenneth R. Hoon, an estimator for defendant. He gave his name and telephone number and stated that he was bidding for defendant for the paving work at the Monte Vista School according to plans and specifications and that his bid was $7,131.60. At Mrs. Johnson's request he repeated his bid. Plaintiff listened to the bid over an extension telephone in his office and posted it on the master sheet after receiving the bid form from Mrs. Johnson. Defendant's was the lowest bid for the paving. Plaintiff computed his own bid accordingly and submitted it with the name of defendant as the subcontractor for the paving. When the bids were opened on July 28th, plaintiff's proved to be the lowest, and he was awarded the contract.

On his way to Los Angeles the next morning plaintiff stopped at defendant's office. The first person he met was defendant's construction engineer, Mr. Oppenheimer. Plaintiff testified: "I introduced myself and he immediately told me that they had made a mistake in their bid to me the night before, they couldn't do it for the price they had bid, and I told him I would expect him to carry through with their original bid because I had used it in compiling my bid and the job was being awarded them. And I would have to go and do the job according to my bid and I would expect them to do the same."

Defendant refused to do the paving work for less than $15,000. Plaintiff testified that he "got figures from other people" and after trying for several months to get as low a bid as possible engaged L & H Paving Company, a firm in Lancaster, to do the work for $10,948.60.

a. Roger Traynor (1900–1983) was a member of the law faculty of the University of California at Berkeley from 1930 to 1940 and specialized in tax law. He served from 1940 to 1964 as associate justice of the Supreme Court of California and from 1964 to 1970 as its chief justice. Some of his opinions on contract law are discussed in Macaulay, Mr. Justice Traynor and the Law of Contracts, 13 Stan.L.Rev. 812 (1961).

The trial court found on substantial evidence that defendant made a definite offer to do the paving on the Monte Vista job according to the plans and specifications for $7,131.60, and that plaintiff relied on defendant's bid in computing his own bid for the school job and naming defendant therein as the subcontractor for the paving work. Accordingly, it entered judgment for plaintiff in the amount of $3,817.00 (the difference between defendant's bid and the cost of the paving to plaintiff) plus costs.

Defendant contends that there was no enforceable contract between the parties on the ground that it made a revocable offer and revoked it before plaintiff communicated his acceptance to defendant.

There is no evidence that defendant offered to make its bid irrevocable in exchange for plaintiff's use of its figures in computing his bid. Nor is there evidence that would warrant interpreting plaintiff's use of defendant's bid as the acceptance thereof, binding plaintiff, on condition he received the main contract, to award the subcontract to defendant. In sum, there was neither an option supported by consideration nor a bilateral contract binding on both parties.

Plaintiff contends, however, that he relied to his detriment on defendant's offer and that defendant must therefore answer in damages for its refusal to perform. Thus the question is squarely presented: Did plaintiff's reliance make defendant's offer irrevocable?

Section 90 of the Restatement of Contracts states: "A promise which the promisor should reasonably expect to induce action or forbearance of a definite and substantial character on the part of the promisee and which does induce such action or forbearance is binding if injustice can be avoided only by enforcement of the promise." This rule applies in this state. . . .

Defendant's offer constituted a promise to perform on such conditions as were stated expressly or by implication therein or annexed thereto by operation of law. (See 1 Williston, Contracts [3rd ed.], § 24A, p. 56, § 61, p. 196.) Defendant had reason to expect that if its bid proved the lowest it would be used by plaintiff. It induced "action . . . of a definite and substantial character on the part of the promisee."

Had defendant's bid expressly stated or clearly implied that it was revocable at any time before acceptance we would treat it accordingly. It was silent on revocation, however, and we must therefore determine whether there are conditions to the right of revocation imposed by law or reasonably inferable in fact. In the analogous problem of an offer for a unilateral contract, the theory is now obsolete that the offer is revocable at any time before complete performance. Thus section 45 of the Restatement of Contracts provides: "If an offer for a unilateral contract is made, and part of the consideration requested in the offer is given or tendered by the offeree in response thereto, the offeror is bound by a contract, the duty of immediate performance of which is conditional on the full consideration being given or tendered within the time stated in the offer, or, if no time is stated therein, within a reasonable time." In explanation, comment *b* states that the "main offer includes as a subsidiary promise, necessarily implied, that if part of the requested performance is given, the offeror will not revoke his offer, and that if tender is made it will be accepted. Part performance or tender may thus furnish consideration for the subsidiary promise. Moreover, merely acting in justifiable reliance on an offer may in some cases serve as sufficient reason for making a promise binding (see § 90).''

Whether implied in fact or law, the subsidiary promise serves to preclude the injustice that would result if the offer could be revoked after the offeree had acted in detrimental reliance thereon. Reasonable reliance resulting in a foreseeable prejudicial change in position affords a compelling basis also for implying a subsidiary promise not to revoke an offer for a bilateral contract.

The absence of consideration is not fatal to the enforcement of such a promise. It is true that in the case of unilateral contracts the Restatement finds consideration for the implied subsidiary promise in the part performance of the bargained-for exchange, but its reference to section 90 makes clear that consideration for such a promise is not always necessary. The very purpose of section 90 is to make a promise binding even though there was no consideration "in the sense of something that is bargained for and given in exchange." (See 1 Corbin, Contracts 634 et seq.) Reasonable reliance serves to hold the offeror in lieu of the consideration ordinarily required to make the offer binding. In a case involving similar facts the Supreme Court of South Dakota stated that "we believe that reason and justice demand that the doctrine [of section 90] be applied to the present facts. We cannot believe that by accepting this doctrine as controlling in the state of facts before us we will abolish the requirement of a consideration in contract cases, in any different sense than an ordinary estoppel abolishes some legal requirement in its application. We are of the opinion, therefore, that the defendants in executing the agreement [which was not supported by consideration] made a promise which they should have reasonably expected would induce the plaintiff to submit a bid based thereon to the Government, that such promise did induce this action, and that injustice can be avoided only by enforcement of the promise." Northwestern Engineering Co. v. Ellerman, 10 N.W.2d 879, 884; see also, Robert Gordon, Inc., v. Ingersoll–Rand Co., 7 Cir., 117 F.2d 654, 661; cf. James Baird Co. v. Gimbel Bros., 2 Cir., 64 F.2d 344.

When plaintiff used defendant's offer in computing his own bid, he bound himself to perform in reliance on defendant's terms. Though defendant did not bargain for this use of its bid neither did defendant make it idly, indifferent to whether it would be used or not. On the contrary it is reasonable to suppose that defendant submitted its bid to obtain the subcontract. It was bound to realize the substantial possibility that its bid would be the lowest, and that it would be included by plaintiff in his bid. It was to its own interest that the contractor be awarded the general contract; the lower the subcontract bid, the lower the general contractor's bid was likely to be and the greater its chance of acceptance and hence the greater defendant's chance of getting the paving subcontract. Defendant had reason not only to expect plaintiff to rely on its bid but to want him to. Clearly defendant had a stake in plaintiff's reliance on its bid. Given this interest and the fact that plaintiff is bound by his own bid, it is only fair that plaintiff should have at least an opportunity to accept defendant's bid after the general contract has been awarded to him.

It bears noting that a general contractor is not free to delay acceptance after he has been awarded the general contract in the hope of getting a better price. Nor can he reopen bargaining with the subcontractor and at the same time claim a continuing right to accept the original offer. See, R.J. Daum Const. Co. v. Child, Utah, 247 P.2d 817, 823. In the present case plaintiff promptly informed defendant that plaintiff was being awarded the job and that the subcontract was being awarded to defendant.

Defendant contends, however, that its bid was the result of mistake and that it was therefore entitled to revoke it. It relies on the rescission cases of M.F. Kemper Const. Co. v. City of Los Angeles, 37 Cal.2d 696, 235 P.2d 7, and Brunzell Const. Co. v. G.J. Weisbrod, Inc., 134 Cal.App.2d 278, 285 P.2d 989. See also, Lemoge Electric v. San Mateo County, 46 Cal.2d 659, 662, 297 P.2d 638. In those cases, however, the bidder's mistake was known or should have been known to the offeree, and the offeree could be placed in status quo. Of course, if plaintiff had reason to believe that defendant's bid was in error, he could not justifiably rely on it, and section 90 would afford no basis for enforcing it. Robert Gordon, Inc. v. Ingersoll–Rand, Co., 7 Cir., 117 F.2d 654, 660. Plaintiff, however, had no reason to know that defendant had made a mistake in submitting its bid, since there was usually a variance of 160 per cent between the highest and lowest bids for paving in the desert around Lancaster. He committed himself to performing the main contract in reliance on defendant's figures. Under these circumstances defendant's mistake, far from relieving it of its obligation, constitutes an additional reason for enforcing it, for it misled plaintiff as to the cost of doing the paving. Even had it been clearly understood that defendant's offer was revocable until accepted, it would not necessarily follow that defendant had no duty to exercise reasonable care in preparing its bid. It presented its bid with knowledge of the substantial possibility that it would be used by plaintiff; it could foresee the harm that would ensue from an erroneous underestimate of the cost. Moreover, it was motivated by its own business interest. Whether or not these considerations alone would justify recovery for negligence had the case been tried on that theory (see Biakanja v. Irving, 49 Cal.2d 647, 650, 320 P.2d 16), they are persuasive that defendant's mistake should not defeat recovery under the rule of section 90 of the Restatement of Contracts. As between the subcontractor who made the bid and the general contractor who reasonably relied on it, the loss resulting from the mistake should fall on the party who caused it.

Leo F. Piazza Paving Co. v. Bebek & Brkich, 141 Cal.App.2d 226, 296 P.2d 368, 371, and Bard v. Kent, 19 Cal.2d 449, 122 P.2d 8, 139 A.L.R. 1032, are not to the contrary. In the *Piazza* case the court sustained a finding that defendants intended, not to make a firm bid, but only to give the plaintiff "some kind of an idea to use" in making its bid; there was evidence that the defendants had told plaintiff they were unsure of the significance of the specifications. There was thus no offer, promise, or representation on which the defendants should reasonably have expected the plaintiff to rely. The *Bard* case held that an option not supported by consideration was revoked by the death of the optionor. The issue of recovery under the rule of section 90 was not pleaded at the trial, and it does not appear that the offeree's reliance was "of a definite and substantial character" so that injustice could be avoided "only by the enforcement of the promise." . . .

The judgment is affirmed.

NOTES

(1) *Questions.* Would the decision have been simpler if Drennan had said "I accept" before introducing himself? See Note 2, p. 174 above. Note that the *Kemper* case, which Traynor distinguished in dealing with Star Paving's defense of mistake, was quoted extensively in *Kastorff*. Why was Star Paving denied that defense—one that succeeded in *Kastorff* and *Kemper?*

If, as seems evident, the form of acceptance invited by Star Paving's offer was a promise by Drennan, when did Star Paving expect to receive that promise? Only after Drennan should be awarded the school job? So it seems from the opinion. How soon after? Does the opinion suggest how soon?

Justice Traynor found in Star Paving's offer a promise to hold it open for a time, although he said that the offer was "silent on revocation." He did not find that promise in Restatement § 45. Why not?

(2) *Preparing to Cross the Brooklyn Bridge.* The rationale of the *Drennan* case is reflected in Restatement § 87(2). Would this rule protect B in the Brooklyn Bridge hypothetical if B had spent time and money in preparing to cross the bridge, but had not begun to cross it when A revoked?

(3) *Subcontractor Reliance?* Is a general contractor who uses a subcontractor's bid in its own bid obliged to accept the subcontractor's bid, once the general contractor is awarded the contract? If under *Drennan*, a subcontractor is obliged to hold its bid open because of reliance on it by the general contractor, should not the same be true in reverse? The Supreme Court of Minnesota has answered No, dismissing what it called "a superficial equity notion." In bidding on a municipal project, a general contractor named Madsen had used a bid by the Holman Erection Company to do steel erection. That fact was disclosed in a public record, as was required. The municipality selected Madsen, who engaged another firm to do the steel erection work.

In an action against Madsen, Holman contended that Madsen had accepted Holman's bid by using it and winning the general contract. The court ruled otherwise, affirming a summary judgment in favor of Madsen. Holman Erection Co. v. Orville E. Madsen & Sons, Inc., 330 N.W.2d 693 (Minn. 1983).

The court explained that subcontractors do not rely on a general contractor's use of their bids. A subcontractor is likely to have submitted its bid to a number of general contractors, and the cost of that is "part of the overhead of doing business." (Holman had submitted like bids to six other general contractors bidding against Madsen.) The court said also that the low bidder among competing subcontractors "is not always the one chosen to do the work or the one listed as the potential subcontractor. Reliability, quality of work, and capability to handle the job are all considerations weighted by the general in choosing the subcontractors." Another consideration, apparently operative in *Holman Erection*, is the requirement that a contractor attempt to engage the services of minority-owned firms in certain enterprises.

PROBLEM

Would the result in *Drennan* have been different, given any of the following additional facts?

(1) After being awarded the school job, Drennan went shopping rapidly among other pavers for a price lower than $7,131.60. On hearing that price, none of them would "get under" it. Only then did Drennan try to close with Star Paving. Is anything in the *Drennan* opinion relevant? Anything in Restatement § 87(2)?

(2) Before being awarded the school job, but after receiving Star Paving's bid, Drennan telephoned to ask that Star Paving "shave" its bid a little. Star Paving said it would have to think that over. Without further inquiry, Drennan used Star Paving's bid in making its own.

(3) The conversation just described occurred after the school job was awarded to Drennan. Soon after that conversation Star Paving, having detected its mistake, called Drennan, saying that it would not do the paving for the price it had bid.

LIABILITY WHEN NEGOTIATIONS FAIL

Up to this point we have been concerned with situations in which an offer has been made. Although the law governing contract formation is usually analyzed in terms of the classic rules of offer and acceptance, most major contractual commitments are the product of lengthy negotiations in which it is often difficult later to identify particular messages of offer and acceptance. If the negotiations succeed, a contract will result. But what if the negotiations fail? May a disappointed party have a claim against the other?

If during the course of negotiations one party has conferred a benefit on the other, the recipient may be required to make restitution. To take a clear case, a prospective buyer of land who had made a down payment during negotiations that fail to result in a contract is entitled to repayment.

Claimants seeking recovery for services performed during negotiations have rarely succeeded, however. Songbird Jet Ltd. v. Amax, Inc., 581 F.Supp. 912, 926–27 (S.D.N.Y.1984), illustrates the obstacles faced by such claimants. Amax, the owner of a corporate jet then under construction by Falcon Jet, negotiated with Songbird which sought to purchase the jet as a broker for resale to a third party. When the negotiations fell through, Songbird claimed compensation from Amax for its services. The court denied recovery for Songbird's locating and contracting with French, a Texas oil man, as ultimate buyer: if there was any enrichment of Amax at all, it was not "unjust" because such activities "are regularly engaged in by parties endeavoring to reach a mutual accommodation" and are "the common grist of negotiations." The court also denied recovery for Songbird's suggestion of the idea of an advantageous "tax benefits transaction": this "idea was neither novel nor original" but was instead "a publicized tax saving device known not only to Amax but to the jet industry at large."

The court conceded that Songbird's claim for monitoring services to expedite Falcon Jet's delivery so that the "tax benefit transaction" would not be lost "stands on a somewhat different footing." Nevertheless, in view of Songbird's contract for resale to French, these "services were entirely voluntary and were designed to and had the effect of protecting [its] own interests, . . . even if they incidentally benefited Amax."

The claimant managed to overcome such obstacles in Precision Testing Laboratories, Ltd. v. Kenyon Corp., 644 F.Supp. 1327, 1350–51 (S.D.N.Y. 1986). While Ellis and Kenyon were negotiating a contract to develop emission systems for imported automobiles, Ellis provided substantial labor and technical work in bringing Kenyon's test car to certification level. When the negotiations fell through, Ellis sued Kenyon claiming unjust enrichment. The court held for Ellis, distinguishing *Songbird* on the ground that there Songbird's "services were designed to promote [its] own interests," whereas here "Ellis' services were designed to benefit" Kenyon, and the issuance of a certificate of conformity by the Environmental Protection Administration was clearly such a benefit. The fact that Ellis himself gained knowledge from the experience "does not detract from the lengthy period of time he and his technicians spent working toward bringing Kenyon's car to certification level."

Even when successful, a restitution claim leaves the claimant uncompensated for reliance costs that produced no benefit to the other party. On what ground might a negotiating party recover reliance losses? Misrepresentation is a possibility: a negotiating party may not with impunity misrepresent its intention to come to terms, and liability for misrepresentation includes reliance losses. But rare are the situations in which a party has had a motive for making such a misrepresentation.

Markov v. ABC Transfer & Storage Co., 457 P.2d 535, 537–38, 539 (Wash.1969), involved such a rare situation. The lessor of a warehouse misrepresented to the lessee that it intended to renew the lease for three years, while "it was at the same time quietly negotiating for the sale of its premises." The lessor's motive was to have the premises occupied while negotiating for their sale and to be assured that, should those negotiations fail, the lease could be renewed. When, only a few weeks before the lease expired, the purchaser of the warehouse gave the startled lessee notice to vacate the premises, the lessee claimed damages from the lessor for fraud. The Supreme Court of Washington concluded that the lessor had fraudulently promised "to renew the lease . . . and to negotiate the amount of rentals in good faith," and upheld an award of damages based on the lessee's reliance losses, including not only the extra expense incurred as a result of the precipitous move to another warehouse but also profits lost when the lessee's principal customers left because no preparations had been made for that move.

The next principal case begins our consideration of more fruitful bases of recovery for pre-contractual loss than either restitution or misrepresentation.

———

INTRODUCTION TO *HOFFMAN v. RED OWL*

The next case considers the question of pre-contractual liability in the context of franchising agreements. Franchises have been described as follows: "The franchise system is a method of selling products and services identified by a particular trade name which may be associated with a patent, a trade secret, a particular product design or management expertise. The franchisee usually purchases some products from the franchisor ... and makes royalty payments on the basis of units sold, in exchange for the right to offer products for sale under the trademark. The franchise agreement establishes the relationship between the parties and usually regulates the quality of the product, sales territory, the advertising and other details; and it usually requires that certain supplies be purchased from the franchisor." Kosters v. Seven–Up Co., 595 F.2d 347 (6th Cir. 1979). The nature of the agreement prompts consideration of the relative status and sophistication of two parties, a subject further discussion in Chapter 6 in connection with termination clauses. Here, however, the parties have not reached a bargain, and the question arises: Can there be liability when they fail to do so?

Hoffman v. Red Owl Stores

Supreme Court of Wisconsin, 1965.
26 Wis.2d 683, 133 N.W.2d 267.

[Joseph Hoffman and his wife owned and operated a bakery in Wautoma, Wisconsin. In November, 1959, he contacted Red Owl, which operated a supermarket chain, seeking to obtain a franchise for a Red Owl store in Wautoma. He mentioned that he had only $18,000 to invest and was assured that this would be sufficient. In February, 1961, on the advice of Red Owl's representative, Lukowitz, he acquired a small grocery store as a means of gaining experience. After three months, the store was operating at a profit, and Lukowitz advised him to sell it, assuring him that Red Owl would find him a larger store elsewhere. Hoffman did so in June, 1961, although he was reluctant to lose the summer tourist business. He was again assured that $18,000 would suffice to obtain a franchise. In September, on Lukowitz's advice, Hoffman put $1,000 down on a lot in Chilton selected by Red Owl. Later in September, after meeting with Hoffman to prepare a financial statement, Lukowitz told him, "[E]verything is ready to go. Get your money together and we are set." Lukowitz then told Hoffman to sell his bakery. Hoffman did that in November for $10,000, suffering a loss of $2,000. He then paid $125 a month's rent on a house in Chilton, and then spent $140 in moving his family to Neenah, at Red Owl's suggestion that he get experience by working at a Red Owl store there. When that job did not materialize, Hoffman went to work on the night shift at an Appleton bakery.

By this time, Lukowitz and Hoffman had considered a variety of arrangements under which Red Owl would get some third party to acquire the Chilton lot, build the building, and lease it to Hoffman. They had also agreed on some of the terms of a ten-year lease, with an option in Hoffman to renew the lease or purchase the property. Late in November they met with Red Owl's credit manager and drew up a proposed financing statement showing Hoffman contributing $24,100. $4,600 was an actual cash contribution, and another $7,500 was to be borrowed from his father-in-law. A week or two later, Lukowitz said that according to the home office, if Hoffman could get another $2,000 for promotion, the deal could go through for $26,000. Hoffman got his father-in-law to agree to put up $13,000 if he could come in as a partner. The home office, however, insisted that the father-in-law sign an agreement that the $13,000 was either a gift or a loan subordinate to all general creditors. Early in February, 1962, the negotiations collapsed when Hoffman refused to accede to a proposed financial statement that showed his contribution as $34,000, including $13,000 from his father-in-law as an outright gift. The Hoffmans sued Red Owl and the jury gave a special verdict, assessing damages as $16,735 for the sale of the Wautoma store, $2,000 for the sale of the bakery, $1,000 for taking up the option on the Chilton lot, $140 for moving expenses to Neenah, and $125 for house rental in Chilton. The trial court confirmed the verdict, except for the figure of $16,735 for the sale of the Wautoma store, as to which it ordered a new trial. Red Owl appealed. The Hoffmans also appealed from the order of a new trial.]

■ CURRIE, CHIEF JUSTICE. . . . The record here discloses a number of promises and assurances given to Hoffman by Lukowitz in behalf of Red Owl upon which plaintiffs relied and acted upon to their detriment. . . . There remains for consideration the question of law raised by defendants that agreement was never reached on essential factors necessary to establish a contract between Hoffman and Red Owl. Among these were the size, cost, design, and layout of the store building; and the terms of the lease with respect to rent, maintenance, renewal, and purchase options. This poses the question of whether the promise necessary to sustain a cause of action for promissory estoppel must embrace all essential details of a proposed transaction between promisor and promisee so as to be the equivalent of an offer that would result in a binding contract between the parties if the promisee were to accept the same.

Originally the doctrine of promissory estoppel was invoked as a substitute for consideration rendering a gratuitous promise enforceable as a contract. See Williston, Contracts (1st ed.), p. 307, sec. 139. In other words, the acts of reliance by the promisee to his detriment provided a substitute for consideration. If promissory estoppel were to be limited to only those situations where the promise giving rise to the cause of action must be so definite with respect to all details that a contract would result were the promise supported by consideration, then the defendants' instant promises to Hoffman would not meet this test. However, sec. 90 of Restatement, 1 Contracts, does not impose the requirement that the promise giving rise to the cause of action must be so comprehensive in scope as to meet the requirements of an offer that would ripen into a contract if accepted by the promisee. Rather the conditions imposed are:

(1) Was the promise one which the promisor should reasonably expect to induce action or forbearance of a definite and substantial character on the part of the promisee?

(2) Did the promise induce such action or forbearance?

(3) Can injustice be avoided only by enforcement of the promise?[1]

We deem it would be a mistake to regard an action grounded on promissory estoppel as the equivalent of a breach of contract action. As Dean Boyer points out, it is desirable that fluidity in the application of the concept be maintained. 98 University of Pennsylvania Law Review (1950), 459, at page 497. While the first two of the above listed three requirements of promissory estoppel present issues of fact which ordinarily will be resolved by a jury, the third requirement, that the remedy can only be invoked where necessary to avoid injustice, is one that involves a policy decision by the court. Such a policy decision necessarily embraces an element of discretion.

We conclude that injustice would result here if plaintiffs were not granted some relief because of the failure of defendants to keep their promises which induced plaintiffs to act to their detriment....

[With regard to damages, the court concluded that all those awarded to Hoffman by the trial court had been properly awarded. As noted above, that court had not awarded him the $16,735 claimed for the sale of the Wautoma store.]

We turn now to the damage item with respect to which the trial court granted a new trial, *i.e.*, that arising from the sale of the Wautoma grocery-store fixtures and inventory ... The trial court ruled that [recovery on that account] would be limited to the difference between the sales price received and the fair market value of the assets sold, giving consideration to any goodwill attaching thereto by reason of the transfer of a going business. There was no direct evidence presented as to what this fair market value was on June 6, 1961. The evidence did disclose that Hoffman paid $9,000 for the inventory, added $1,500 to it and sold it for $10,000 or a loss of $500. His 1961 federal income tax return showed that the grocery equipment had been purchased for $7,000 and sold for $7,955.96. Plaintiffs introduced evidence of the buyer that during the first eleven weeks of operation of the grocery store his gross sales were $44,000 and his profit was $6,000 or roughly 15 percent. On cross-examination he admitted that this was gross and not net profit. Plaintiffs contend that in a breach of contract action damages may include loss of profits. However, this is not a breach of contract action.

The only relevancy of evidence relating to profits would be with respect to proving the element of goodwill in establishing the fair market value of the grocery inventory and fixtures sold. Therefore, evidence of profits would be admissible to afford a foundation for expert opinion as to fair market value.

Where damages are awarded in promissory estoppel instead of specifically enforcing the promisor's promise, they should be only such as in the opinion of the court are necessary to prevent injustice. Mechanical or rule of thumb approaches to the damage problem should be avoided....

---

1. See Boyer, 98 University of Pennsylvania Law Review (1950), 459, 460. "Enforcement" of the promise embraces an award of damages for breach as well as decreeing specific performance.

At the time Hoffman bought the equipment and inventory of the small grocery store at Wautoma he did so in order to gain experience in the grocery store business. At that time discussion had already been had with Red Owl representatives that Wautoma might be too small for a Red Owl operation and that a larger city might be more desirable. Thus Hoffman made this purchase more or less as a temporary experiment. Justice does not require that the damages awarded him, because of selling these assets at the behest of defendants, should exceed any actual loss sustained measured by the difference between the sales price and the fair market value.

Since the evidence does not sustain the large award of damages arising from the sale of the Wautoma grocery business, the trial court properly ordered a new trial on this issue.

Order affirmed. . . .

NOTES

(1) *Red Owl Distinguished.* In Gruen Industries, Inc. v. Biller, 608 F.2d 274, 280–81 (7th Cir.1979), Gruen and a subsidiary sought to recover their expenses in reliance on a promise to sell them stock. The expenses were, predominately, substantial attorneys fees incurred for drafting the sales transaction. In upholding summary judgment for the sellers, the court distinguished *Red Owl*. The alleged stock-sale agreement was "not a reasonable basis for reliance" because it "was subject to numerous conditions, some of which were under the control of third parties." Even if the sellers had kept the alleged promises "the sale may very well have failed on the basis of the many contingencies."

(2) *Early Dismissal.* John Grouse, who worked as a pharmacist at Richter Drug in Minneapolis, applied for and was offered a position with Group Health Plan in the same city. Grouse then told Cyrus Elliott, Group Health's Chief Pharmacist, that he had to give Richter two week's notice, which he did. The same day, Grouse received an offer from a Veteran's Administration Hospital in Virginia, but rejected it because of Group Health's offer. Sometime in the next few days, Elliott was told by Donald Shoberg, Group Health's General Manager, that the company required a favorable written reference, a background check, and Shoberg's approval. When references were forthcoming, Shoberg then hired someone else. Grouse had difficulty regaining full time employment and sued for damages. The trial judge dismissed his complaint, and Grouse appealed. *Held:* Reversed and remanded for a trial on the issue of damages. Grouse v. Group Health Plan, Inc., 306 N.W.2d 114 (Minn.1981).

"The parties focus their arguments on whether an employment contract which is terminable at will can give rise to an action for damages if anticipatorily repudiated. . . . Group Health contends that recognition of a cause of action on these facts would result in the anomalous rule that an employee who is told not to report to work the day before he is scheduled to begin has a remedy while an employee who is discharged after the first day does not. We cannot agree since under appropriate circumstances we believe section 90 would apply even after employment has begun. . . . Relief may be limited to damages measured by the promisee's reliance. . . . [T]he appellant had a right to assume he would be given a good faith opportunity to perform his duties to the satisfaction of respondent once he was on the job. He was not only denied that opportunity but resigned the position he already held in reliance on the firm offer which respondent tendered him." Id. (Probably the court's reference to a "firm offer" should be understood to mean "definite offer." It cannot have meant what are described as "firm offers" in UCC § 2–205.) How should Grouse's damages be calculated on a new trial?

(3) *Rough Justice and Public Policy.* Kajima, a general contractor, submitted a bid of some $69 million to the Los Angeles Metropolitan Transportation Authority (MTA) for the construction of a station and tunnel. Despite a California statute requiring the contracts be awarded to the "lowest responsible bidder," the MTA accepted a bid of nearly $1 million more from another firm, under a misapplication of a California statute requiring the use of Disadvantaged Business Enterprises. Kajima itself could have qualified as a Disadvantaged Business Enterprise. Kajima sued the MTA for bid preparation costs of some $45,000 and lost profits on the MTA contract. From a decision for the MTA, Kajima appealed. *Held:* Reversed as to bid preparation costs. Wilson v. Los Angeles County Metropolitan Transportation Authority, 1 P.3d 63, 69 (Cal.2000).

"[W]hen a public entity solicits bids, it represents, consistent with the statutory mandate, that if the contract is awarded, it well be awarded to the lowest responsible bidder.... [If] the contract is awarded to a higher bidder, the elements of a promissory estoppel cause of action appear to be established. ... It is important to note, however, that [promissory estoppel] fits these circumstances imperfectly. Promissory estoppel was developed to do rough justice when a party lacking contractual protection relied on another's promise to its detriment. Here, we use promissory estoppel primarily to further certain public policies by creating a damages remedy for a public entity's statutory violation." The court added however, that the remedy should be limited to what "justice requires." "Allowing recovery of lost profits ... 'could drain the public fisc in response to mere carelessness on the part of low level government officials.' " *Id.* at 69.

Why is the fit with reliance imperfect? On what basis did the court grant relief?

———

Cyberchron Corp. v. Calldata Systems Development, Inc.

United States Court of Appeals, Second Circuit, 1995.
47 F.3d 39.

■ MAHONEY, CIRCUIT JUDGE: [Both parties appeal from a judgment on a claim of promissory estoppel awarding Cyberchron Corporation ("Cyberchron") $162,824.19 for direct labor and materials costs incurred in reliance upon statements and conduct of Calldata Systems Development ("Calldata"). Judge Spatt, the district court judge, denied recovery on Cyberchron's contract and quantum meruit claims.]

BACKGROUND

A.   The Events at Issue....

Cyberchron is engaged in the business of providing customized computer hardware for military and civilian use. Calldata is a subsidiary of Grumman Data Systems Corp. ("Grumman"). Grumman had a contract with the United States Marine Corps to provide a combat command control system for a Marine Corps defense program known as the Advanced Tactical Air Command Central ("ATACC"). The equipment at issue in this case is a "rugged computer work station," consisting of a video processor, a work station, and a color monitor (the "Equipment") that was to be provided for the ATACC program.

During the years 1989 and 1990, the parties were involved in extended negotiations as a result of which Cyberchron attempted to produce the Equipment. Although Cyberchron ultimately produced some Equipment, none was ever delivered to Calldata or Grumman, and no payment for it was ever made to Cyberchron, resulting in this lawsuit. The key problem precluding contractual agreement was the inability of the parties to agree upon the weight of the Equipment, and the penalties to be assessed against Cyberchron for the delivery of Equipment that exceeded the contractually agreed weight . . .

After protracted preliminary negotiations, Grumman delivered a purchase order dated May 15, 1990 to Cyberchron (including subsequent amendments, the "Purchase Order") that set forth a total weight per unit of Equipment (consisting of the three components, video processor, work station, and color monitor) of 145 pounds and specified severe penalties for exceeding that weight.

Cyberchron never agreed to the terms of the Purchase Order, but had previously commenced production of the Equipment despite the absence of any agreement regarding the matter. Grumman and Calldata encouraged Cyberchron in that course. Indeed, in a letter to Cyberchron dated June 26, 1990, Grumman "insisted" that Cyberchron continue to perform its "contractually binding obligations" under the Purchase Order. . . .

The district court made a factual determination, in which we perceive no clear error, that in mid-July 1990 a Grumman representative directed Cyberchron to proceed with production of the Equipment as if there had been agreement on the weight issue, asserting that the terms of the purchase order would be resolved later. In addition, on or about July 30, 1990, Cyberchron submitted a progress payment request in the amount of $495,207.58, representing eighty percent of claimed costs, including overhead charges, incurred by Cyberchron through July 20, 1990. Grumman's business manager, Gerald Glinka, testified that although the purchase order was undefinitized, Grumman would have paid the full amount of this progress payment but for a court order, issued in a suit brought by Digital Equipment Corporation against Grumman and Cyberchron which was eventually dismissed, that barred any payments to Cyberchron by Grumman. The order was subsequently vacated.

Ultimately, agreement between the parties was never achieved. By letter dated September 6, 1990, Calldata directed Cyberchron to show cause within ten days why the Purchase Order should not be terminated. Cyberchron's detailed response dated September 13, 1990 was rejected by Calldata in a letter dated September 25, 1990, in which Calldata "terminated the [Purchase Order] for default effective immediately."

The district court determined, in findings that are not clearly erroneous, that Grumman had commenced negotiations with alternate suppliers of the Equipment in August 1990, and entered into a contract with Codar Technology, Inc. dated September 26, 1990 for equipment "which Grumman conceded was inferior to the Cyberchron equipment and weighed more, according to [a Grumman witness]"....

B. The Ruling of the District Court.

The district court found that no enforceable agreement ever existed because there was no agreement on "two of the most essential, material and substantial terms of the proposed contract, namely, the weights of the three components [of the Equipment] and the weight penalties." ... As a result, Cyberchron's contract claim and Calldata's contractually based counterclaim were dismissed. ... Cyberchron's claim of quantum meruit was also dismissed "in view of the lack of any benefit to the defendant, the failure by the plaintiff to fully perform, and the absence of any unjust enrichment by the defendant." ... Neither party appeals any of these dismissals.

However, the District Court found that because of the mid-July 1990 representations and promises that had been made to Cyberchron, Cyberchron was entitled to reliance damages of $162,824.10 for out-of-pocket labor and materials costs incurred after July 15, 1990 and before the termination of negotiations on September 25, 1990, under a theory of promissory estoppel....

The court denied any recovery for lost profits, or for administrative and general overhead, ... but allowed prejudgment interest from December 18, 1990, the date of the commencement of this litigation. ... The court did not address the issue of "shutdown" expenses occurring after September 25, 1990 ...

DISCUSSION....

A. Recovery on the TLP.

[The court held that the termination liability provision (TLP) of the Purchase Order did not provide a ground for recovery by Cyberchron.]

B. Promissory Estoppel.

"In New York, promissory estoppel has three elements: 'a clear and unambiguous promise; a reasonable and foreseeable reliance by the party to whom the promise is made, and an injury sustained by the party asserting the estoppel by reason of the reliance.'" Arcadian Phosphates, Inc. v. Arcadian Corp., 884 F.2d 69, 73 (2d Cir. 1989) (quoting Esquire Radio & Elecs., Inc. v. Montgomery Ward & Co., 804 F.2d 787, 793 (2d Cir. 1986))....

As noted by Judge Spatt, an unconscionable injury is sometimes required to fulfill the third requirement.... In addition, some courts will apply the doctrine only when enforcement is necessary to avoid injustice. See Werner v. Xerox Corp., 732 F.2d 580, 582–83 (7th Cir.1984) (citing Hoffman v. Red Owl Stores, Inc., 133 N.W.2d 267 (1965)); see also Restatement (Second) of Contracts § 90 (1981). In any event, as will appear, we regard the injury inflicted upon Cyberchron as unconscionable, and believe that injustice can be avoided in this case only by invoking the doctrine of promissory estoppel on Cyberchron's behalf.

Judge Spatt expressly found that Calldata pressured Cyberchron to produce the Equipment, and "assured Cyberchron [in August 1990] that if it did the work, the negotiation problem could be resolved." 831 F.Supp. at 103. The district court also found that in mid-July 1990, Grumman's [manager of procurement, Calvin] Wilhelm directed Cyberchron's Paul "to proceed 'as if the new set of weights was approved . . . and we would work out the definitization of the purchase order later.' " Id. at 102. . . . Later, when Paul asked Wilhelm to put this reassurance in writing, Wilhelm refused. Id. at 114. Paul then stated that: " 'If I have your assurance that we will resolve the issues in the very near future . . .—we will proceed.' " Id. . . . Wilhelm responded: " 'You should proceed.' " Id. . . .

After an August 8, 1990 meeting, Robert C. Drost, Grumman's director of material, took over the Cyberchron negotiations. Id. at 103. Drost assured Paul that " 'everything would be fine' " but insisted that Cyberchron had to " 'keep pushing, keep performing . . . to maintain the schedule.' " Id. at 105. . . . Drost testified that Cyberchron " 'had the responsibility and obligation' " to " 'continue performing,' " and that " 'one can assume' " that Cyberchron would be paid for that continued performance. Id. . . . The district court found that between August 8 and August 28, 1990, Paul was in constant conversation with Grumman personnel, all of whom demanded that Cyberchron continue to manufacture and deliver the Equipment " 'as if the weights were approved.' " Id. at 114. . . . We have no basis to conclude that the trial judge's evaluation of this developing scenario was clearly erroneous. . . .

We accordingly accept the district court's determination that starting in mid-July, there was (1) a clear and unambiguous promise, (2) reasonable and foreseeable reliance thereon, and (3) an unconscionable injury, resulting in injustice that could be remedied only by invoking the doctrine of promissory estoppel. In sum, we agree with Judge Spatt's assessment that:

> Grumman's conduct exerting pressure on Cyberchron to produce the units at great expense, and then abruptly terminating the transaction to purchase heavier, inferior equipment at a later date from another company, was unconscionable. At the same time that Grumman was pressuring Cyberchron to produce, with the promise of payment, it was already negotiating with another company to do the work. 831 F. Supp. at 116.

We reject, however, Cyberchron's argument that promissory estoppel recovery should be extended to the periods prior to mid-July 1990. We are unprepared to conclude that the commitments made at that juncture should be interpreted to validate recovery of the expenses incurred by Cyberchron prior to any promise sufficient to undergird Cyberchron's claim of promissory estoppel. . . .

C. Damages.

Based upon documentary evidence, the district court awarded Cyberchron "reliance damages" for materials purchased in the amount of $53,588.40 and labor costs incurred in the amount of $109,235.79 between July 15 and September 25, 1990, totalling $162,824.19. 831 F. Supp. at 118.

The court specifically declined to provide any award for administrative or engineering overhead on the bases that: (1) these expenses were not proved to have been specifically incurred for the Grumman/Calldata transaction; (2) Cyberchron offered proof of overhead expenses for the six months ended June 30, 1990 rather than the period July 15–September 25, 1990; and (3) the overhead expenses were not proper "reliance damages" but rather were speculative and conjectural. 831 F. Supp. at 117–18. In addition, no award was provided for "shutdown" expenses occurring after September 25, 1990....

Cyberchron does not contend for benefit-of-the-bargain damages on this appeal, but argues that it should have been awarded overhead and "shutdown" expenses. Neither party points to any controlling New York law regarding when overhead costs are recoverable. ... We believe that a ... workable rule would be to allow recovery of reasonable overhead costs when it is shown that there is a demonstrable past history of ongoing business operations, without requiring proof that a specific alternative project would have absorbed the overhead costs at issue. If such a showing can be made in this case, we see no reason for a blanket bar against the recovery of reasonable overhead expenses as long as they are normally allocated to specific projects in accordance with Cyberchron's standard cost accounting practices....

[The court also held that Cyberchron was entitled to recovery of its shutdown costs, even though they were incurred after termination of negotiations and therefore outside the July 15–September 25 time frame, to the extent that these costs were incurred due to reliance upon the Calldata promises.]

CONCLUSION

We affirm the judgment of the district court insofar as it allowed recovery to Cyberchron on a theory of promissory estoppel, but vacate the judgment and remand for a redetermination of damages in accordance with this opinion....

NOTES

(1) *Questions.* What was the scope of the promise that *was* enforceable on the ground of promissory estoppel? In order to show a breach of that promise did Cyberchron have to prove that Grumman/Calldata negotiated in bad faith?

(2) *UNIDROIT Principles.* Might an obligation to negotiate in good faith arise from the mere fact of prolonged negotiations, without such explicit language as that in *Cyberchron*? See UNIDROIT Principles art. 2.15(2), under which "a party who negotiates or breaks off negotiations in bad faith is liable for the losses caused to the other party."

An obligation to negotiate in good faith has found favor in some civil law systems, but American courts have been firm in according parties the freedom to negotiate without risk of precontractual liability imposed by law. This "freedom from contract" is enhanced by the judicial reluctance to read a proposal as an offer in the first place. The assumption is that a party entering negotiations in the hope of the gain that will result from agreement bears the risk of whatever loss results if the other party breaks off the negotiations. See Farnsworth, Precontractual Liability and Preliminary Agreements: Fair Dealing and Failed Negotiations, 87 Colum.L.Rev. 217, 239–43 (1987).

This is not to say, however, that parties willing to undertake the obligation of negotiating in good faith may not do so by express agreement. This is the subject of the next case.

———

PRELIMINARY BINDING AGREEMENTS/PRELIMINARY BINDING COMMITMENTS

To this point, we have been looking at theories of reliance and restitution, advanced when negotiations have failed. In reading the next case, consider the following: May parties undertake an obligation of negotiating in good faith by express agreement?

In Teachers Insurance & Annuity Association v. Tribune Co., 670 F.Supp. 491 (S.D.N.Y.1987), Judge Pierre Leval, later of the Second Circuit, distinguished between two types of binding preliminary agreements, often designated "Tribune I" and "Tribune II." The decision has had wide influence and has been described as follows by the Second Circuit in Adjustrite Systems v. GAB Business Services, 145 F.3d 543, 548 (2d Cir.1998).

A *Tribune* Type I contract "is a fully binding preliminary agreement, which is created when the parties agree on all the points that require negotiation (including whether to be bound) but agree to memorialize their agreement in a more formal document. Such an agreement is fully binding; it is 'preliminary in form—only in the sense that the parties desire a more elaborate formalization of the agreement. ... [I]t binds both sides to their ultimate contractual objective in recognition that, 'despite the anticipation of further formalities,' a contract has been reached...."

A *Tribune* Type II contract, "dubbed a 'binding preliminary commitment' by Judge Leval, ... is created when the parties agree on certain major terms, but leave other terms open for further negotiation. The parties 'accept a mutual commitment to negotiate together in good faith in an effort to reach final agreement.' " In contrast to a Type I agreement, a Type II agreement " 'does not commit the parties to their ultimate contractual objective but rather to the obligation to negotiate the open issues in good faith in an attempt to reach the ... objective within the agreed framework.' ... Indeed if a final contract is not agreed upon, the parties may abandon the transaction as long as they have made a good faith effort to close the deal and have not insisted on conditions that do not conform to the preliminary writing."

Channel Home Centers, Division of Grace Retail Corp. v. Grossman

United States Court of Appeals, Third Circuit, 1986.
795 F.2d 291.

■ BECKER, CIRCUIT JUDGE. This diversity case presents the question whether, under Pennsylvania law, a property owner's promise to a prospective tenant, pursuant to a detailed letter of intent, to negotiate in good faith with the prospective tenant and to withdraw the lease premises from the marketplace during the negotiation, can bind the owner for a reasonable period of time where the prospective tenant has expended significant sums of money in connection with the lease negotiations and preparation and where there was evidence that the letter of intent was of significant value to the property owner. We hold that it may. We therefore vacate and reverse the district court's determination that there was no enforceable agreement, and remand the case for trial. [The district court had made that determination on the view that there was insufficient documentation for enforcement of the owner's letter of intent, a view that was erroneous according to the appellate court.]

Appellant Channel Home Centers ("Channel"), a division of Grace Retail Corporation, operates retail home improvement stores throughout the Northeastern United States, including Philadelphia and its suburbs. Appellee Frank Grossman, a real estate broker and developer, with his sons Bruce and Jeffrey Grossman, either owns or has a controlling interest in appellees Tri–Star Associates ("Tri–Star"), Baker Investment Corporation ("Baker"), and Cedarbrook Associates, a Pennsylvania Limited Partnership ("Cedarbrook").

Between November, 1984 and February, 1985, the Grossmans, through Baker, were in the process of acquiring ownership of Cedarbrook Mall ("the mall") located in Cheltenham Township, Pennsylvania, a northern suburb of Philadelphia. During these months, Baker was the equitable owner of the mall, Tri–Star was acting as the mall's leasing agent, and legal title was in Equitable Life Assurance Society. It was anticipated that, upon closing in February, 1985, Baker would become both legal and equitable owner of the mall. The Grossmans intended to revitalize the mall, which had fallen on hard times prior to their acquisition, through an aggressive rehabilitation and leasing program.

In the third week of November, 1984, Tri–Star wrote to Richard Perkowski, Director of Real Estate for Channel, informing him of the availability of a store location in Cedarbrook Mall which Tri–Star believed Channel would be interested in leasing. Perkowski expressed some interest, and met the Grossmans on November 28, 1984. After Perkowski was given a tour of the premises, the terms of a lease were discussed. Frank Grossman testified that "we discussed various terms, and these terms were, some were loose, some were more or less terms." App. at 364a, 496a–497a.

In a memorandum dated December 7, 1984, to S. Charles Tabak, Channel's senior vice-president for general administration, Perkowski outlined the salient lease terms that he had negotiated with the Grossmans. On or about the same date, Tabak and Leon Burger, President of Channel, visited the mall site with the Grossmans. They indicated that Channel desired to lease the site. Frank Grossman then requested that Channel execute a letter of intent that, as Grossman put it, could be shown to "other people, banks or whatever." Tabak testified that the Grossmans wanted to get Channel into the site because it would give the mall four "anchor" stores. Apparently, Frank Grossman was anxious to get Channel's signature on a letter of intent so that it could be used to help Grossman secure financing for his purchase of the mall.

On December 11, 1984, in response to Grossman's request, Channel prepared, executed, and submitted a detailed letter of intent setting forth a plethora of lease terms which provided, *inter alia,* that

> [t]o induce the Tenant [Channel] to proceed with the leasing of the Store, you [Grossman] will withdraw the Store from the rental market, and only negotiate the above described leasing transaction to completion.
>
> Please acknowledge your intent to proceed with the leasing of the store under the above terms, conditions and understanding by signing the enclosed copy of the letter and returning it to the undersigned within ten (10) days from the date hereof.

App. at 31a.

Frank Grossman promptly signed the letter of intent and returned it to Channel. Grossman contends that Perkowski and Tabak also agreed orally that a draft lease be submitted within thirty (30) days. Perkowski and Tabak denied telling Grossman that a lease would be forthcoming within 30 days or any finite period of time.

Thereafter, both parties initiated procedures directed toward satisfaction of lease contingencies. The letter of intent specified that execution of the lease was expressly subject to each of the following: (1) approval by Channel's parent corporation, W.R. Grace & Company ("Grace"), of the essential business terms of the lease; (2) approval by Channel of the status of title for the site; and (3) Channel's obtaining, with Frank Grossman's cooperation, all necessary permits and zoning variances for the erection of Channel's identification signs. . . .

On December 14, 1984, Channel directed the Grace legal department to prepare a lease for the premises. Channel's real estate committee approved the lease site on December 20, 1984. Channel planning representatives visited the premises on December 21, 1984, to obtain measurements for architectural alterations, renovations and related construction. Detailed marketing plans were developed, building plans drafted, delivery schedules were prepared and materials and equipment deemed necessary for the store were purchased. The Grossmans applied to the Cheltenham Township building and zoning committee for permission to erect commercial signs for Channel and other tenants of the mall.

On January 11, 1985, Frank Shea, Esquire, of the Grace legal department sent to Frank Grossman two copies of a forty-one (41) page draft lease and, in a cover letter, requested copies of several documents to be used as exhibits to the lease. On January 16, 1985, Frank Shea received the following letter from Bruce Grossman:

Dear Mr. Shea:

As you requested, enclosed please find the following documents:

1) A copy of a recent title report for the Cedarbrook Mall (the "Mall"),

2) A legal description of the Mall,

3) A site plan of the Mall, and

4) A description of the Landlord's construction.

As we discussed, we have commenced work on the Channel location at the Mall and would, therefore, appreciate your assistance in expediting the execution of the Channel lease.

I look forward to hearing from you soon.

Very truly yours,

BAKER INVESTMENT CORPORATION

/s/ Bruce S. Grossman,

Executive Vice President

On January 21, 1985, Frank Shea received a copy of a letter from Frank Grossman to Richard Perkowski dated January 17, 1985. It provided:

At Frank Shea's request, enclosed is a site plan for the Cedarbrook Mall and also a copy of the proposed pylon sign design.

We look forward to executing the lease agreement in the very near future. If you have any questions, please feel free to call me.

Bruce Grossman called Shea on January 23, 1985 to discuss the lease. The only item Grossman could recall discussing pertained to the "use" clause in the lease, specifically whether Channel could use the site for warehouse facilities at some future point. Apparently, Grossman then related other areas of concern and Shea suggested that a telephone conference be arranged with all parties the following week. Grossman agreed. According to Grossman, Shea was supposed to initiate the conference call; however, when the call was not forthcoming, Grossman did not attempt to reach Shea or anyone else at Channel. Shea understood that the Grossmans were going to discuss the lease among themselves and get back to him.

On or about January 22, 1985, Stephen Erlbaum, Chairman of the Board of Mr. Good Buys of Pennsylvania, Inc. ("Mr. Good Buys"), contacted Frank Grossman. Like Channel, Mr. Good Buys is a corporation engaged in the business of operating retail home improvement centers; it is a major competitor of Channel in the Philadelphia area. Erlbaum advised Grossman that Mr. Good Buys would be interested in leasing space at Cedarbrook Mall, and sent Grossman printed information about Mr. Good Buys.

On January 24, 1985, construction representatives from Channel met at the mall site to go over building alterations and designs. The next day, January 25, 1985, Erlbaum and other representatives from Mr. Good Buys met with the Grossmans and toured Channel's proposed lease location. When Erlbaum expressed an interest in leasing this site, lease terms were discussed.

On February 6, 1985, Frank Grossman notified Channel that "negotiations terminated as of this date" due to Channel's failure to submit a signed and mutually acceptable lease for the mall site within thirty days of the December 11, 1984 letter of intent. (This was the first and only written evidence of the purported thirty-day time limit. The letter of intent contained no such term....) On February 7, 1985, Mr. Good Buys and Frank Grossman executed a lease for the Cedarbrook Mall. Mr. Good Buys agreed to make base-level annual rental payments which were substantially greater than those agreed to by Channel in the December 11, 1984 letter of intent. Channel's corporate parent, Grace, approved the terms of Channel's proposed lease on February 13, 1985. . . .

Channel argues that the letter, coupled with the surrounding circumstances, constitutes a binding agreement to negotiate in good faith. Appellees rejoin that a promise to negotiate in good faith or to use best efforts to reduce to formal writing an agreement between the parties is enforceable only if the parties have in fact reached agreement on the underlying transaction.... Appellees further argue that even if the agreement were an otherwise enforceable contract, the letter of intent and any promises contained therein are unenforceable by virtue of Channel's lack of consideration.[1] The parties agree that Pennsylvania law applies to the case. . . .

Channel does not contend that the letter of intent is binding as a lease or an agreement to enter into a lease. Rather it is Channel's position that this document is enforceable as a mutually binding obligation *to negotiate in good faith.* By unilaterally terminating negotiations with Channel and precipitously entering into a lease agreement with Mr. Good Buys, Channel argues, Grossman acted in bad faith and breached his promise to "withdraw the Store from the rental market and only negotiate the above-described leasing transaction to completion." . . .

Although no Pennsylvania court has considered whether an agreement to negotiate in good faith may meet [the conditions of enforceability], the jurisdictions that have considered the issue have held that such an agreement, if otherwise meeting the requisites of a contract, is an enforceable contract....[2] We are satisfied that Pennsylvania would follow this rule. Applying Pennsylvania law, then, we must ask (1) whether both parties manifested an intention to be bound by the agreement; (2) whether the terms of the agreement are sufficiently definite to be enforced; and (3) whether there was consideration.

In determining the parties' intentions concerning the letter of intent, we must examine the entire document and the relevant circumstances surrounding its adoption.... The letter of intent, signed by both parties, provides that "[t]o induce the Tenant [Channel] to proceed with the leasing of the Store, you [Grossman] will withdraw the Store from the rental market, and only negotiate the above described leasing transaction to

---

1. The district court also rejected Channel's additional contention that the letter of intent should be enforced under the doctrine of promissory estoppel. In light of our disposition on appeal, we need not reach the propriety of the district court's determinations that neither a unilateral contract analysis nor the doctrine of promissory estoppel is applicable to the instant case. [Footnote transposed.]

2. Good faith in the bargaining or formation stages of the contracting process is distinguishable from the common law duty to perform in good faith. See Restatement of Contracts (Second) § 205 (1979) ("Every contract imposes upon each party a duty of good faith and fair dealing in its performance and its enforcement.")....

completion." . . . The agreement thus contains an unequivocal promise by Grossman to withdraw the store from the rental market and to negotiate the proposed leasing transaction with Channel to completion.

Evidence of record supports the proposition that the parties intended this promise to be binding. After the letter of intent was executed, both Channel and the Grossmans initiated procedures directed toward satisfaction of lease contingencies. Channel directed its parent corporation to prepare a draft lease; Channel planning representatives visited the lease premises to obtain measurements for architectural alterations, renovations, and related construction. Channel developed extensive marketing plans; delivery schedules were prepared and material and equipment deemed necessary for the store were purchased. The Grossmans applied to the township zoning committee for permission to erect Channel signs at various locations on the mall property. Channel submitted a draft lease on January 11, 1985, and the parties, through correspondence and telephone conversations and on-site visits, exhibited an intent to move toward a lease as late as January 23, 1985. . . . Accordingly, the letter of intent and the circumstances surrounding its adoption both support a finding that the parties intended to be bound by an agreement to negotiate in good faith.

We also believe that Grossman's promise to "withdraw the Store from the rental market and only negotiate the above described leasing transaction to completion," viewed in the context of the detailed letter of intent (which covers most significant lease terms . . .), is sufficiently definite to be specifically enforced, provided that Channel submitted sufficient legal consideration in return.

Appellees argue that "[n]o money or thing of value was paid, either at the time of the letter or at any other time that would convert an agreement to negotiate into some enforceable type of contract." Brief of Appellees at 16. We disagree. It seems clear that the execution and tender of the letter of intent by Channel was of substantial value to Frank Grossman. At the time the letter of intent was executed, Grossman was in the process of obtaining financing for his purchase of the mall. When it became apparent to Grossman that Channel—a major corporate tenant—was seriously interested in leasing the mall site, he requested that Channel sign a letter of intent which, as Grossman put it, could be shown to "other people, banks or whatever with a view to getting permanent financing." App. at 366a–367a. Fully aware of Grossman's desire to obtain financing, Channel sought to solidify its bargaining position by requesting that Grossman also sign the letter of intent and promise to "withdraw the store from the rental market and only negotiate the above-described leasing transaction to completion." There being evidence that value passed from each party to the other, we conclude that the record would support a finding that Channel's execution and tender of the letter of intent conferred a bargained for benefit on Grossman which was valid consideration for Grossman's return promise to negotiate in good faith.

In sum, we agree with Channel that the record contains evidence that supports a finding that the parties intended to enter into a binding agreement to negotiate in good faith. We further hold that the agreement had sufficient specificity to make it an enforceable contract if the parties so intended, and that consideration passed between the parties. We will therefore remand this case to the district court for trial.

At least two significant issues must be resolved at trial. First, although our review of the record reveals that there is sufficient evidence to support a finding that the parties intended to be bound by the letter of intent, we do not hold that the evidence requires this conclusion. At trial, evidence will decide this issue.

As noted above, there is also some dispute over whether there was a time limit on the negotiations that was not specified in the letter of intent. Because the district court erroneously concluded that the letter of intent was unenforceable as a matter of law, it made no factual findings with regard to this critical term. If, as appellees suggest, Channel orally agreed to forward a draft lease within 30 days of the date on which the letter of intent was executed, Channel's failure to do so could have terminated the agreement. Alternatively, if, as Channel argues, the parties did not fix a definite time for the duration of negotiations, then a reasonable time would be applicable . . ., and a determination must be made as to what constitutes a reasonable time under all the circumstances.

The judgment of the district court will therefore be reversed, and the case remanded for further proceedings consistent with this opinion.

NOTES

(1) *Measure of Damages.* If the Grossmans were held liable on remand, how would Channel's damages be measured? In terms of its expectation? In terms of its reliance? If Channel could show that it had passed up other opportunities to lease premises in reliance on Grossman's promise to negotiate, would damages based on those lost opportunities be recoverable? Is this one of the relatively rare instances referred to in Note 2, p. 19 above, where courts take account of lost opportunities? Are there reasons why this might be so?

A conventional objection to the recovery of expectation damages when negotiations fail is that a court cannot know what agreement would have been reached and therefore has no way to measure lost expectation. Goodstein Construction Corp. v. City of New York, 604 N.E.2d 1356, 1361 (N.Y.1992). But in Venture Associates Corp. v. Zenith Data Systems Corp., 96 F.3d 275 (7th Cir.1996), Judge Posner said that "if the plaintiff can prove that had it not been for the defendant's bad faith the parties would have made a final contract, then the loss of the benefit of the contract is a consequence of the defendant's bad faith, and, provided that it is a foreseeable consequence, the defendant is liable for that loss—liable, that is, for the plaintiff's consequential damages. . . . The difficulty, which may well be insuperable, is that since by hypothesis the parties had not agreed on *any* of the terms of their contract, it may be impossible to determine what those terms would have been and hence what profit the victim of bad faith would have had. . . . But this goes to the practicality of the remedy, not the principle of it." See 1 Farnsworth on Contracts § 3.26b (2d ed. 1998).

As we will see in *Oglebay Norton*, p. 252 below, a court might even grant specific performance for breach of a promise to negotiate.

(2) *The Meaning of Bad Faith.* What would amount to bad faith in negotiation? In PSI Energy v. Exxon Coal USA, 17 F.3d 969 (7th Cir.1994), Judge Easterbrook

said: "An obligation to negotiate 'in good faith' nixes trickery and certain forms of obduracy, ... but it does not require one side in negotiations to reveal its bargaining strategy or its reservation price, to disclose every tidbit that would be of use to the other side, or to refrain from taking advantage of its opportunities." Would it be bad faith to renege on an agreed term? Recall that a *Tribune* Type II contract requires agreement "on certain major terms." To engage in negotiations with another party (as Grumman did with Codar in *Cyberchron*)? To terminate negotiations without warning in order to make a contract with another party (as Grumman presumably did to make a contract with Codar in *Cyberchron*)? See 1 Farnsworth on Contracts § 3.26b (2d ed. 1998).

SECTION 7.   THE REQUIREMENT OF DEFINITENESS

In *Channel Home Centers*, the court asked first "whether both parties manifested an intention to be bound by the agreement" and second "whether the terms of the agreement are sufficiently definite to be enforced." The preceding sections of this chapter explored the first question: Did both parties assent to be bound? This section explores the second: Is an agreement definite enough to be enforced? Both questions must be answered in the affirmative for there to be a contract.

The requirement of definiteness serves two basic functions. In order for a court to determine whether or not a contract has been broken, it must first know with some certainty what the terms of the contract are. The concept of definiteness is also implicit in the principle that the promisee's expectation interest is to be protected. In calculating the damages that will put a promisee in the position it would have been in had the promise been performed, a court must be able to determine with some precision what the promise was. For requirement of definiteness in Article 2, see UCC § 2–204(3); in the Restatement, see § 33.

The effect of indefiniteness can be seen from Varney v. Ditmars, 111 N.E. 822 (N.Y.1916). Varney, an architectural draftsman, sued Ditmar, his employer, on Ditmar's promise to pay Varney "a fair share of my profits," in addition to a stated salary. The court denied recovery of profits on the ground that the amount was a matter of "pure conjecture" and might be "any amount from a nominal sum to a material part according to the particular views of the person whose guess is considered."

In deciding whether or not an agreement is sufficiently definite, a court may piece together terms from such sources as preliminary negotiations, prior communications, external sources such as governmental regulations and applicable trade usages. A course of dealing between the parties prior to the transaction, or a course of performance between them after their agreement may also provide terms. See UCC § 1–303. Indefiniteness may also be cured, sometimes, by resort to a term implied by law, in the way that the duty to use reasonable efforts was supplied in Wood v. Lucy, p. 83 above.

Terms such as *good faith* and *reasonable efforts* are regarded as sufficiently definite if their content can be determined by reference to some external standard. Probably that would have been done in Wood v. Lucy, had it been necessary to determine what efforts were required of Wood in the circumstances. The processes by which language is interpreted, and terms such as "reasonable efforts" and "good faith" are supplied and construed, are explored in Chapter 5.

It is enough if the agreement provides means for making its terms sufficiently definite by the time performance is called for. Consider, for example, output and requirements contracts; see discussion in Eastern Airlines, p. 76. For another example, in *Fairmount Glass*, p. 130 above, the seller argued "that the contract was indefinite, because the quantity of each size of the jars was not fixed"; but the court held that the agreement was not unenforceable on that ground because the buyer had "the right to name the quantity of each size" before shipment. The same is true when other particulars of performance are to be specified by one of the parties. See UCC § 2–311.

Why are contracting parties sometimes incomplete in setting out the terms of their agreements? Consider the following possibilities:

(a) They do not want to take the time or pay attorneys for their time to work through every eventuality, and are willing to rely on the terms that a court will supply in the event of dispute arises.

(b) They are reluctant to raise difficult issues for fear that the deal may fall through.

(c) They do not foresee the problem that arises.

(d) They choose to withhold business information in order to retain an advantage.

Do other reasons come to mind? Might the reason in a particular case affect the court's willingness to overlook some indefiniteness?

NOTES

(1) *Completely Contingent Contracts and Relational Contracts.* The term "complete contingent contract" is widely used to describe an agreement, surely hypothetical, that provides for *every* possible eventuality or contingency. Contracts that do not provide for all contingencies are called incomplete contracts. The reasons stated in the text above—limited foreseeability, the costs of writing fully contingent agreements, and so on—render all contracts incomplete. Contracts between parties who deal with one another on a regular basis ("repeat players") or who interact over an extended period give rise to what are often called "relational contracts." The expression derives from an influential article by Professor Stewart Macaulay, Non–Contractual Relations in Business: A Preliminary Study, 28 Am.Soc.Rev. 55 (1963). Why might parties in relational parties be less concerned with addressing every contingency, such as the effect of defective performance, than parties to other sorts of parties?

The study of relational contracts, or contracts seen as relational and not merely transactional, was advanced significantly by Professor Ian MacNeil; see MacNeil, Relational Contract Theory: Challenges and Queries, 94 Nw. U. L. Rev. 877 (2000). MacNeil proposed a spectrum on which all contractual behavior lies, ranging from simple, immediate and impersonal exchanges (more "transactional") to complex, extended and personal agreements (more relational).

Taking a more traditional law and economics view, Professors Charles Goetz and Robert Scott offer the following account of relational contracting. "Parties in a bargaining situation are presumed able, at minimal cost, to allocate explicitly the risks that future contingencies may cause one or the other to regret having entered into an executory agreement.... Once the underlying rules policing the bargaining process have been specified, contract rules serve as standard or common risk allocations that can be varied by the individual agreement of particular parties. These rules serve the important purpose of saving most bargainers the cost of negotiating a tailor-made arrangement.... All relevant risks thus can be assigned optimally either by legal rule or through individualized agreement because future contingencies are not only known and understood at the time the bargain is struck, but can also be addressed by efficacious contractual responses." Goetz & Scott, Principles of Relational Contracts, 67 Va.L.Rev. 1089, 1091 (1981).

(2) *Offers of Job Security.* In Sayres v. Bauman, 425 S.E.2d 226 (W.Va.1992), the claimants were employees of a firm whose ownership changed hands. There was evidence that before the buy-out, they were told that "you won't lose your job because a new company is buying us out." The plaintiffs continued in their jobs for more than a year under the new ownership but were then discharged. Might the statement attributed to the former owners be construed as an offer to the employees of job security—one that the employees accepted by continuing on their jobs? In an action by the employees for wrongful discharge, the court reversed a judgment for the plaintiffs, saying: "an oral promise which has as its effect the alteration of an 'at will' employment relationship must contain terms that are both ascertainable and definitive in nature to be enforceable."

Recall that statements of company policy, announced in handbooks or manuals for employees, have often been found to be incorporated in the terms of employment for personnel already in place, as well as for new recruits. The "handbook" cases frequently permit employees to escape the rigors of the doctrine of at-will employment. See the discussion of Employee Handbooks, p. 64 above. In Berube v. Fashion Centre, Ltd., 771 P.2d 1033 (Utah 1989), according to the lead opinion, the defendant employer had "created and distributed a disciplinary action policy which was read and understood by the plaintiff," thereby limiting the grounds on which it could discharge her. The court reversed a judgment for the employer and ordered a retrial on the theory of an implied-in-fact contract. On these facts, was an offer any more evident than in *Sayres*?

(3) *Restitution.* A party who has, in the course of performing an agreement that is unenforceable for indefiniteness conferred a benefit upon the other party is entitled to restitution. For example, in Varney v. Ditmars, above, the court suggested that if the architectural draftsman's work was worth more than his salary, he would have had a right to restitution measured by the difference. Similarly, in Pyeatte v. Pyeatte, p. 113 above, the court refused to enforce the husband's promise to put his wife through a master's degree program, finding the agreement too indefinite as to timing, place, duration, and costs: "Such a loosely worded agreement can hardly be said to have fixed [his] liability with certainty." But although the agreement "failed to meet the requirements of an enforceable contract, [it] still has importance in considering [her] claim for unjust enrichment because it both evidences [her] expectation of compensation and the circumstances which make it unjust to allow [him] to retain the benefits of her extraordinary efforts." The court then awarded the former wife restitution. Why were the Pyeattes not more precise? Which recovery—restitution or expectation—would have been greater?

PROBLEM

Forbearing on a Claim. Review Note 1, p. 71 above. Suppose that Louisa Sheffield had written to Strong: "I will be responsible for my husband's debt if you will not bother him about it for a reasonable time." Would she have been accountable to Strong if he had done nothing about the note for two years? See Baker v. Citizens State Bank of St. Louis Park, 349 N.W.2d 552 (Minn.1984). Farmers Union Oil Co. of New England v. Maixner, 376 N.W.2d 43 (N.D.1985).

———

TOYS, INC. v. F.M. BURLINGTON COMPANY, 582 A.2d 123 (Vt. 1990). [F.M. Burlington Company, a mall owner, entered into a five year lease with Toys, Inc., a retailer. The lease gave Toys an option to renew for an additional five years, requiring Toys to notify Burlington in writing of its intention to exercise the option one year before the lease expired. The lease further provided that "the fixed minimum rental [for the renewal period] shall be renegotiated to the then prevailing rate within the mall." In February, Toys gave timely written notice to Burlington of its intent to renew. Burlington confirmed Toy's exercise of the option and stated the then prevailing rate per square foot in the mall. A week later Toys replied that its renewal had been premised on a "substantially different understanding of the prevailing rate."

For the next ten months, the parties engaged in what the court called "paper jousting" as they attempted to negotiate a rent structure for the renewal period, creating and extending various deadlines for doing so along the way. By November, no agreement had been reached, and Burlington advised Toys that it was listing the location for rent. Toys then left the mall, found alternative space, and sued for breach of contract. Burlington argued, that owing to Toys's failure to accept the prevailing rate stated in February and a second rent proposal made by Burlington in July, the renewal option had lapsed. The trial court granted summary judgment, holding that the lease had created a binding option. Burlington appealed on the ground that the option was too indefinite.]

■ DOOLEY, J. . . . We agree with the trial court that summary judgment for plaintiff was appropriate. . . . The lease provision created a valid option for plaintiff to renew for an additional five years. Defendant characterizes the lease renewal provision as merely an agreement to agree and therefore not enforceable. If defendant's construction were correct, the lease provision would not create an enforceable option. See Reynolds v. Sullivan, 136 Vt. 1, 3, 383 A.2d 609, 611 (1978). In *Reynolds* we held that a preliminary option agreement that was vague and uncertain in its terms "would be an impossibility to enforce." Id. The test is whether the option agreement contains "all material and essential terms to be incorporated in the subsequent document." Id. The agreement in *Reynolds* was labeled as preliminary and specifically provided that the parties "agree to enter an agreement for an option" and that "more specific terms will be stated in the option to purchase." Id. at 2, 383 A.2d at 610.

It is not necessary under *Reynolds* that the option agreement contain all the terms of the contract as long as it contains a practicable, objective method of determining the essential terms. See Krupinsky v. Birsky, 278 A.2d 757, 760 (Vt.1971) (option contract valid even though it "did not fix a price certain" where "it did appoint a mode of determining the price"); Restatement (Second) of Contracts § 33 comment *a*, § 34(1) (1981) ("The terms of a contract may be reasonably certain even though it empowers one or both parties to make a selection of terms in the course of performance."). We must construe the option agreement in a way to give it binding effect if possible. See Agway, Inc. v. Marotti, 540 A.2d 1044, 1046 (Vt.1988) (before voiding a contract for vagueness, indefiniteness or uncertainty of expression, Court must attempt to construe the contract to avoid the defect). We are also mindful that defendant drafted the language of the option clause and that a doubtful provision in a written instrument is construed against the party responsible for drafting it. See Trustees of Net Realty v. AVCO Financial Services, 520 A.2d 981, 983 (Vt.1986).

The option agreement states that "the fixed minimum rental shall be renegotiated to the then prevailing rate within the mall." We believe that this language sets forth a definite, ascertainable method of determining the price term for the lease extension. Within days after plaintiff stated its original intent to exercise its option, defendant replied by quoting the "prevailing rate within the mall" at that time. Neither defendant nor plaintiff have disputed the accuracy of this calculation.

Defendant puts much emphasis on the use of the term "renegotiate" in the renewal clause, as showing an intent to reach a future agreement. While the choice of wording could have been more precise, we agree with the plaintiff that the term means that the then-existing "prevailing rate" would be determined by agreement, and does not mean that the parties would start from a clean slate in renegotiating a rent term. Even if we give defendant the benefit of all inferences and reasonable doubt, we find no genuine issue of fact bearing on whether there was an enforceable option to renew and hold as a matter of law that a valid option existed.

NOTES

(1) *Questions.* What consideration supported the option? What did the exercise of the option require? Could the parties have drafted the rent term more clearly?

(2) *Open Price Term.* Would you expect a similar result if the option provision in *Toys* had been: "Tenant shall be provided one option to extend the lease for five years at annual rentals to be agreed upon"? See Joseph Martin, Jr., Delicatessen, Inc. v. Schumacher, 417 N.E.2d 541 (N.Y.1981). Consider a contract for the sale of goods, which "if [the parties] so intend," can be concluded even though they leave the price term "open." UCC § 2–305. Why might the law be more indulgent of indefiniteness with regard to price in agreements for the sale of goods than in landlord-tenant agreements?

(3) *The Case of the Business Opportunity.* In Lee v. Joseph E. Seagram & Sons, Inc., 552 F.2d 447 (2d Cir.1977), a jury found that when Seagram contracted in writing to buy a wholesale liquor distributorship (Capitol City), it had orally agreed with some of its owners to provide them, within a reasonable time, with a Seagram distributorship in another city, in a location acceptable to them, "whose price would

require roughly an amount equal to the capital obtained by [those owners] for the sale of their interest in Capitol City." In an action by the promisees, a judgment was entered against Seagram and it appealed. It contended in part that the oral agreement was so vague and indefinite as to be unenforceable. *Held:* Affirmed. The plaintiffs had testified about the financial record of Capitol City and produced expert testimony about the industry standard for valuing a liquor distributorship.

Why do you suppose the parties were not more precise in defining their obligations with respect to the new distributorship? What answer can be given to Seagram's further point that the oral agreement was illusory, owing to the promisees' "unbridled discretion" to accept or to reject any new situation that Seagram might proffer? Suppose that the promisee had been an investor negotiating to buy Capitol City, and that Seagram had persuaded the investor to break off negotiations by making a comparable promise. Same result?

FLEXIBLE PRICING

Suppose that over a long term a seller wants to be assured of an outlet for a fixed quantity of a product and that a buyer wants to be assured of a source of supply for the same quantity. Neither party, however, wants to take the risk of a shift in the market: the seller does not want the risk of a rise in prices before delivery, and the buyer does not want the risk of a fall. How can they make an agreement that will be legally enforceable and yet will allow the price of the goods to fluctuate?

One possibility is to leave the price term open; the price will then be "a reasonable price at the time for *delivery*." See UCC § 2–305. Of course this leaves open opportunities for dispute over what is "reasonable."

Would it be useful to designate a third party to fix the price if the parties should disagree? Again, see UCC § 2–305. Another possibility is to use an "escalator clause" under which the price will be fixed according to a formula tied in some way to the market; see *Eastern Airlines*, p. 76 above, and the following case. Would it be easier to draft such an agreement if there were an ascertainable market price for the raw materials required by the seller to produce his product? An ascertainable market price for the product itself? (On ascertainable market price, see UCC §§ 2–723 and 2–724.) Would prices charged by competing sellers or to competing buyers be useful?

Helpful analogies can be found in clauses in leases in which rent is tied to gross profits, in clauses in collective bargaining agreements in which wages are tied to the cost of living, and in clauses in construction contracts in which the price is tied to costs ("cost-plus" contracts). An interesting variant is patterned after the "most favored nation" clause found in treaties. See, for example, Reynolds Metals Co. v. United States, 438 F.2d 983 (Ct.Cl.1971), in which the United States promised Reynolds to amend their contract "if later agreements with the Aluminum Company of America and/or the Kaiser Aluminum and Chemical Company are, in your opinion, more favorable than the agreement which has been executed with you." What standard might a court apply to the term "in your opinion"? An objective one, subjective one, or both?

INTRODUCTION TO *OGLEBAY NORTON*: ASSENT REVISITED

This case returns us to the question of assent, here by parties in a long-term, cooperative contract whose terms became indefinite over the course of the contract's performance. The case raises questions about the vitality of assent when a flexible price mechanism appears to fail. In reading the case, keep the following question in mind: What evidence does the court assemble to assess whether or not the parties intended to remain bound over time?

Oglebay Norton Co. v. Armco, Inc.

Supreme Court of Ohio, 1990.
52 Ohio St.3d 232, 556 N.E.2d 515.

[In 1957, Armco made a long-term contract with Oglebay requiring Oglebay to have adequate shipping capacity available and requiring Armco to use that capacity for the transportation of iron ore on the Great Lakes. The contract provided for a primary and a secondary price mechanism:

> *Armco agrees to pay* ... for all iron ore transported hereunder *the regular net contract rates for the season* in which the ore is transported, *as recognized by the leading iron ore shippers* in such season for the transportation of iron ore.... *If,* in any season of navigation hereunder, *there is no regular net contract rate recognized by the leading iron ore shippers* for such transportation, *the parties shall mutually agree upon a rate* for such transportation, *taking into consideration the contract rate being charged for similar transportation* by the leading independent vessel operators engaged in transportation of iron ore from The Lake Superior District. [Emphasis supplied by the court.

During the next 23 years the parties modified the contract four times, each time extending the time and entailing substantial capital investment by Oglebay to meet Armco's requirements. After the fourth modification, which extended the contract to the year 2010, Oglebay began a $95 million capital improvement program.

From 1957 through 1983 the parties established the contract shipping rate by reference to a rate published in Skillings Mining Review, in accord with the contract's primary price mechanism. After a serious downturn in the iron ore industry in 1983, Armco challenged the rate quoted by Oglebay and the parties negotiated a mutually satisfactory rate for the 1984 season. After that, however, the parties were unable to agree on a rate and, in April of 1986, Oglebay sought a declaratory judgment, asking the court to declare the contract rate to be the correct rate or, in the absence of such a rate, to declare a reasonable rate. Armco denied that the rate sought by Oglebay was the "contract rate" and denied that the court had jurisdiction to declare a rate of its own accord. The parties continued to perform pending resolution of the dispute. In August of 1987, Armco filed a supplementary counterclaim seeking a declaration that the contract was no longer enforceable.

In November of 1987, the trial court issued its declaratory judgment, fixing $6.25 as the rate for the 1986 season and holding that, if the parties were unable to agree on a rate for the upcoming seasons, they must notify the court, which would appoint a mediator and require the parties' chief executive officers to meet and "mutually agree upon a rate." The court of appeals affirmed and a motion was made to certify the record.]

■ PER CURIAM. This case presents three mixed questions of fact and law. First, did the parties intend to be bound by the terms of this contract despite the failure of its primary and secondary pricing mechanisms? Second, if the parties did intend to be bound, may the trial court establish $6.25 per gross ton as a reasonable rate for Armco to pay Oglebay for shipping Armco ore during the 1986 shipping season? Third, may the trial court continue to exercise its equitable jurisdiction over the parties, and may it order the parties to utilize a mediator if they are unable to mutually agree on a shipping rate for each annual shipping season? We answer each of these questions in the affirmative and for the reasons set forth below affirm the decision of the court of appeals.

I

Appellant Armco argues that the complete breakdown of the primary and secondary contract pricing mechanisms renders the 1957 contract unenforceable, because the parties never manifested an intent to be bound in the event of the breakdown of the primary and secondary pricing mechanisms. Armco asserts that it became impossible after 1985 to utilize the first pricing mechanism in the 1957 contract, i.e., examining the published rate for a leading shipper in the "Skillings Mining Review," because after 1985 a new rate was no longer published. Armco asserts as well that it also became impossible to obtain the information necessary to determine and take into consideration the rates charged by leading independent vessel operators in accordance with the secondary pricing mechanism. This is because that information was no longer publicly available after 1985 and because the trial court granted the motions to quash of nonparties, who were subpoenaed to obtain this specific information. Armco argues that since the parties never consented to be bound by a contract whose specific pricing mechanisms had failed, the trial court should have declared the contract to be void and unenforceable.

The trial court recognized the failure of the 1957 contract pricing mechanisms. Yet the trial court had competent, credible evidence before it to conclude that the parties intended to be bound despite the failure of the pricing mechanisms. The evidence demonstrated the long-standing and close business relationship of the parties, including joint ventures, interlocking directorates and Armco's ownership of Oglebay stock. As the trial court pointed out, the parties themselves contractually recognized Armco's vital and unique interest in the combined dedication of Oglebay's bulk vessel fleet, and the parties recognized that Oglebay could be required to ship up to 7.1 million gross tons of Armco iron ore per year.

Whether the parties intended to be bound, even upon the failure of the pricing mechanisms, is a question of fact properly resolved by the trier of fact.... Since the trial court had ample evidence before it to conclude that the parties did so intend, the court of appeals correctly affirmed the trial court regarding the parties' intent. We thus affirm the court of appeals on this question.

II

Armco also argues that the trial court lacked jurisdiction to impose a shipping rate of $6.25 per gross ton when that rate did not conform to the 1957 contract pricing mechanisms. The trial court held that it had the authority to determine a reasonable rate for Oglebay's services, even though the price mechanism of the contract had failed, since the parties intended to be bound by the contract. The court cited 1 Restatement of the Law 2d, Contracts (1981) 92, Section 33, and its relevant comments to support this proposition. Comment *e* to Section 33 explains in part:

"... [Where the parties] intend to conclude a contract for the sale of goods ... and the price is not settled, the price is a reasonable price at the time of delivery if ... (c) the price is to be fixed in terms of some agreed market or other standard as set or recorded by a third person or agency and it is not so set or recorded. Uniform Commercial Code § 2–305(1)." Id. at 94–95....

The court therefore determined that a reasonable rate for Armco to pay to Oglebay for transporting Armco's iron ore during the 1986 shipping season was $6.00 per gross ton with an additional rate of twenty-five cents per gross ton when self-unloading vessels were used. The court based this determination upon the parties' extensive course of dealing, ... "the detriment to the parties respectively, and valid comparisons of market price which reflect [the] economic reality of current depressed conditions in the American steel industry."

The court of appeals concluded that the trial court was justified in setting $6.25 per gross ton as a "reasonable rate" for Armco to pay Oglebay for the 1986 season, given the evidence presented to the trial court concerning various rates charged in the industry and given the intent of the parties to be bound by the agreement....

III

Armco also argues that the trial court lacks equitable jurisdiction to order the parties to negotiate or in the failure of negotiations, to mediate, during each annual shipping season through the year 2010. The court of appeals ruled that the trial court did not exceed its jurisdiction in issuing such an order.

3 Restatement of the Law 2d, Contracts (1981) 179, Section 362, entitled "Effect of Uncertainty of Terms," is similar in effect to Section 33 and states:

"Specific performance or an injunction will not be granted unless the terms of the contract are sufficiently certain to provide a basis for an appropriate order."

Comment *b* to Section 362 explains:

... "Before concluding that the required certainty is lacking, however, a court will avail itself of all of the usual aids in determining the scope of the agreement. ... Expressions that at first appear incomplete may not appear so after resort to usage ... or the addition of a term supplied by law...." Id. at 179.

Ordering specific performance of this contract was necessary, since, as the court of appeals pointed out, ... "the undisputed dramatic changes in the market prices of great lakes shipping rates and the length of the contract would make it impossible for a court to award Oglebay accurate damages due to Armco's breach of the contract." We agree with the court of appeals that the appointment of a mediator upon the breakdown of court-ordered contract negotiations neither added to nor detracted from the parties' significant obligations under the contract.

It is well-settled that a trial court may exercise its equitable jurisdiction and order specific performance if the parties intend to be bound by a contract, where determination of long-term damages would be too speculative. See 3 Restatement of the Law 2d, Contracts, supra, at 171–172, Section 360(a), Comment *b;* Columbus Packing Co. v. State, ex rel. Schlesinger (1919), 126 N.E. 291, 293–294. Indeed, the court of appeals pointed out that under the 1962 amendment, Armco itself had the contractual right to seek a court order compelling Oglebay to specifically perform its contractual duties.

The court of appeals was correct in concluding that ordering the parties to negotiate and mediate during each shipping season for the duration of the contract was proper, given the unique and long-lasting business relationship between the parties, and given their intent to be bound and the difficulty of properly ascertaining damages in this case. The court of appeals was also correct in concluding that ordering the parties to negotiate and mediate with each shipping season would neither add to nor detract from the parties' significant contractual obligations. This is because the order would merely facilitate in the most practical manner the parties' own ability to interact under the contract. Thus we affirm the court of appeals on this question....

Judgment affirmed.

NOTES

(1) *Questions.* What is the significance, if any, of Oglebay's capital improvement plan, and of the four contract modifications? Would the court's assessment of the parties' intent to be bound differ if their inability to agree on a price had occurred at the formation stage?

(2) *Express Default Pricing Mechanisms.* Parties who anticipate the inability to agree on renegotiating a price term in a long-term contract may provide their own default formula, should agreement prove impossible. Consider the following clause

from a contract between a coal supplier and a utility company for the renegotiated price of coal:

> If the parties are unable to reach agreement, BUYER will accept SELLER's last offer or present SELLER with a firm, written offer which it has received from another supplier, which it is willing to accept, for the supply of coal called for under the remaining term of this Agreement (herein referred to as a "competitive offer"). It shall also provide SELLER with documentary proof of such offer, and permit SELLER to examine all supporting data and information submitted with the offer. SELLER shall have the right to meet such competitive offer.

Why did the contract require the competing offer be a firm offer?

The clause is taken from PSI Energy, Inc. v. Exxon Coal USA, Inc., 17 F.3d 969 (7th Cir.1994), mentioned at Note 2, p. 245 above. In that litigation, the seller (Exxon Coal) argued that the firm offer received by the buyer (PSI) from another coal supplier was *not* competitive because delivery and other terms were different from and incommensurate with those in the Exxon–PSI contract. According to Exxon, it was therefore *not* required to meet the offer, and its last offer (of $30 per ton) would be the price. From a trial court ruling for PSI, Exxon appealed. *Held*: Reversed.

"Under the contract, when the parties do not agree and there is no valid competitive offer, the seller's last offer prevails. Not 'the market price' in the abstract, but the seller's last offer. Persons negotiating such a contract would understand that this default rule gives the seller the whip hand; it is simultaneously an element of compensation for taking the risk of developing a new mine (which cost Exxon several hundred million dollars, . . .) and a goad to accommodation. Knowing that it is apt to pay more than the market price if it fails to come up with a competitive offer, PSI had every incentive to be scrupulous in finding a proper bid. We concluded on the prior appeal that it had failed. Now we quantify the price of that failure: $30 per ton." *Id.* at 969 (Easterbrook, J.).

(3) *Remedies*. Generally in those cases where the court orders specific performance or enjoins a threatened breach, it must know the scope of the party's promise with greater precision than when it awards monetary damages, because failure to obey the court's order may subject the promisor to the court's contempt power. Why then in *Oglebay* did the Supreme Court of Ohio approve specific performance with so little apparent hesitation? What exactly did the trial court order the parties to do? Is the remedy *not* so extraordinary under the terms of the particular contract at issue in the case?

CHAPTER 3

STATUTES OF FRAUDS

SECTION 1. OVERVIEW

The film producer Samuel Goldwyn is credited with having said, "An oral contract isn't worth the paper it's written on." Goldwyn may have put his special stamp on the idea, but many people seem to believe that any agreement not in writing is unenforceable. That is an error; some oral agreements are certainly enforceable. Examples given above are those in Hawkins v. McGee and in Sullivan v. O'Connor.

Some contracts must be in writing, however, owing to various "statutes of frauds." That statement prompts several questions, among them these: What agreements are unenforceable if unwritten? And what counts as a writing? In answer to the first question, this chapter lists a number of writing requirements, and provides details about four categories of agreements that require writings. These are agreements requiring more than a year for full performance, those requiring the transfer of an interest in real property, certain sale-of-goods agreements, and suretyship agreements. Another part of the chapter indicates what sorts of documents constitute "writings" that satisfy a statute of frauds.

Hardship and injustice may result when an agreement covered by a statute of frauds—one that must be in writing, that is—is oral. The chapter concludes with a look at rules that ameliorate the operation of statutes of frauds.

(A) STATUTORY TEXTS

Many statutes provide that an agreement of certain types, otherwise enforceable, is not to be enforced if it is not represented by a signed writing. Many of these statutes, though not all, are commonly referred to as "statutes of frauds." Within that category a provision is designated as part of *the* Statute of Frauds—not simply as instances of *a* statute of frauds—if it is traceable to a 1677 act of Parliament, 29 Charles II, c. 3. That statute was titled "An Act for the Prevention of Frauds and Perjuries," and may be called the *classical* Statute of Frauds. Some form of it appears in the statutes of every United States jurisdiction. In this chapter any set of provisions derived from the classical one is identified by capital letters, as in "the Statute of Frauds." In most states these provisions are supplemented by one or more clauses added after the classical clauses were enacted. Moreover, as indicated above, analogous requirements, more or less uniform, are scattered throughout statutes across the United States; these are analogous in that, although not usually called "statutes of frauds," they require that one or another type of agreement be somehow recorded.

In minor part this chapter concerns statutes that speak of the documentation of agreements but are not, in a strict sense, statutes of frauds. An example is this, from Title 9 ("Arbitration") of the United States Code:

> Section 2.   Validity, Irrevocability, and Enforcement of Agreements to Arbitrate
>
> A written provision in any maritime transaction or a contract evidencing a transaction involving commerce to settle by arbitration a controversy thereafter arising out of such contract or transaction, or the refusal to perform the whole or any part thereof, or an agreement in writing to submit to arbitration an existing controversy arising out of such a contract, transaction, or refusal, shall be valid, irrevocable, and enforceable, save upon such grounds as exist at law or in equity for the revocation of any contract.

This provision *validates* documented agreements, rather than *invalidating* undocumented ones as a true statute of frauds does.

In a list below, the entries give general descriptions of nine classes of agreements that, if entirely oral, are made unenforceable by statutes enacted in all or almost all states.

(1) An agreement for any performance that cannot be completed, on one side or the other, within one year from the making of the agreement. ["A contract or modification of a contract for the sale or purchase of a security is enforceable whether or not there is a writing signed or record authenticated by a party against whom enforcement is sought, even if the contract or modification is not capable of performance within one year of its making." UCC § 8–113.]

(2) An agreement for the transfer of an interest in real estate, other than the grant of a lease, and one for the grant of a real-estate lease for a period of one year or more.

(3) An agreement for the sale of goods for a price of $500 or more.

(4) An agreement for the lease of goods providing for rent of $1,000 or more.

(5) An agreement by a person or firm to be "surety" for the debt, or other obligation, of another (typified by this undertaking: "If you will give my brother a few weeks more to pay his bill, I will see that he pays it.").

(6) An agreement by which personal property is to stand as security for an obligation. (The Code section is 9–203(b). Important alternatives to documentation are described there.)

(7) An agreement the performance of which is not to be completed before the end of a lifetime.

(8) An agreement to pay a commission for the services of a real-estate broker.

(9) An agreement by which a person or firm undertakes to extend credit to another. Commonly provisions of this kind affect only agreements of considerable size. But the Georgia Code requires that "[a]ny commitment to lend money" be in writing. Section 13–5–30(7).

The first three entries in the list above, and the fifth, describe agreements about which the current statutes are derived from the prototype Statute of Frauds, 29 Charles II. Entries (3), (4), and (6) represent provisions of the Uniform Commercial Code.

As will be seen, often a promisee can adduce circumstances other than documentation that will lead a court to enforce an agreement within one of these descriptions. For the moment, therefore, it can be said, at most, that the entries above describe agreements that are *prima facie* unenforceable. Even that overstates the situation, for some of the entries are qualified by other statutes. An example is a section of UCC Article 8, set out, in brackets, after the first entry above.

In a Statute of Frauds, a list more or less like the foregoing is likely to follow a pronouncement of unenforceability. Two examples are these:

California Civil Code § 1624(a) (Statute of frauds . . .):

> (a) The following contracts are invalid, unless they, or some note or memorandum thereof, are in writing and subscribed by the party to be charged or by the party's agent. . . .

New York General Obligations Law § 5–701(a) (Agreements required to be in writing):

> (a) Every agreement, promise or undertaking of the following kinds is void, unless it or some note or memorandum thereof be in writing, and subscribed by the party to be charged therewith, or by his lawful agent. . . .

Provisions like these can lead to the disregard of solemn agreements, and to inequitable hardships. As indicated above, these effects are often avoided, or blunted, by mollifying statutes and doctrines. These are now to be mentioned. Some are illustrated by cases in this chapter.

By stating that a promise within the Statute of Frauds is "unenforceable" or "void," the law authorizes a promisor both to admit the existence of a promise and to defend successfully against its enforcement on the grounds of the Statute. This might be called a "rule of effrontery." The Uniform Commercial Code has qualified the "rule of effrontery" with respect to contracts for sale or lease of goods. These qualifications appear in UCC §§ 2–201(3)(b) and 2A–201(4)(b). Apart from statutes, some courts allow an admission to supply a term that is absent from the required documentation. See King v. King, 2007 WL 712050 (R.I.Super.2007). But that position is contested. See Willey v. Willey, 912 A.2d 441 (Vt.2006). One of the parties in that case made an argument that "the doctrine of judicial admissions takes [an] oral settlement agreement outside of the Statute of Frauds." The court answered: "Even if that doctrine had been adopted by this Court, which it has not, it would not apply to admissions made in chambers off the record." *Id.* at 447, n.1.

NOTES

(1) *History*. The following account is an excerpt from C. R. Klewin, Inc. v. Flagship Properties, Inc. more fully set out below at p. 270. The court's opinion referred to 6 W. Holdsworth, *A History of English Law*, 379–84 (1927), and continued as follows.

> The [classical] statute appears to have been enacted in response to developments in the common law arising out of the advent of the writ of assumpsit, which changed the general rule precluding enforcement of oral promises in the King's courts. Thereafter, perjury and the subornation of perjury became a widespread and serious problem. Furthermore, because juries at that time decided cases on their own personal knowledge of the facts, rather than on the evidence introduced at trial, a requirement, in specified transactions, of "some memorandum or note . . . in writing, and signed by the party to be charged" placed a limitation on the uncontrolled discretion of the jury. See 2 A. Corbin, Contracts (1950) § 275, pp. 2–3; 6 W. Holdsworth, *supra*, pp. 387–89; An Act for Prevention of Fraud and Perjuries, 29 Car. 2, c. 3, § 4 (1677), quoted in J. Perillo, "The Statute of Frauds in the Light of the Functions and Dysfunctions of Form," 43 Fordham L. Rev. 39, 39 n.2 (1974). Although the British Parliament [has] repealed most provisions of the statute, [it] nonetheless remains the law virtually everywhere in the United States.

For another concise account see St. Ansgar Mills, Inc. v. Streit, p. 289 below.

(2) *Justifying the Statutes*. A widespread belief that no unwritten agreement is enforceable may be beneficent, even though it is erroneous. It may lead people to document agreements that they would otherwise leave unwritten. Possibly statutes of frauds conduce to that belief. Is that a plausible contemporary justification for statutes of frauds?

More conventional justifications draw on merits ascribed to formalities in general. They prevent the enforcement of many untrustworthy claims; their observance induces caution among people about to make serious undertakings; and they make many transactions familiar, understandable, and easy to replicate by placing them in separate categories. Compare the three functions ascribed to the doctrine of consideration—evidentiary, cautionary, and channeling in Lon Fuller, Consideration and Form, 41 Colum.L.Rev. 799 (1941)—discussed at p. 30 above.

———

(B) EXPLAINING THE LEGISLATIVE CHOICES

Judges and others have speculated for generations about why a particular class of agreements was subjected to a statute of frauds. Informed speculation is not idle, for it may affect the construction of the statute, and may influence a court when it is asked to dispense with the requirement of a writing in the interest of justice. The paragraphs that follow describe explanations that have been given for the principal clauses of the classical

Statute of Frauds. It will be worthwhile to keep them in mind when reading about applications of those clauses.

A major opinion treating the requirement of documentation for an agreement "not to be performed within the space of one year from the making thereof" has this to say:

> The entire Statute was intended to prevent fraud in the proving of certain legal transactions particularly susceptible to deception, mistake and perjury and, with regard specifically to [that requirement], "the design of the statute was, not to trust to the memory of witnesses for a longer time than one year". (Smith v. Westfall, 1 Lord Raymond 316, 317 [1697]). . . .

D & N Boening, Inc. v. Kirsch Beverages, Inc., 472 N.E.2d 992, 993 (N.Y. 1984). See also Goldstick v. ICM Realty, 788 F.2d 456, 464 (7th Cir. 1986), where the court observed that the one-year clause was "apparently founded on a concern with the tendency of evidence to go stale with the passage of time." But in each of the opinions quoted here the court said that the statutory provision was not a good fit with the supposed explanation. "[T]he foundation is weak because the limitation applies even if the promise is broken the day after it is made and suit on it is brought immediately." *Id.* In that event persons who participated in the agreement, or overheard it, would need only short-term memory to describe it.

Perhaps a better reason for the one-year clause is that the consequences of long-term agreements are especially momentous, so that a decision to enter into one should not be made without an opportunity for reflection, or proved without convincing evidence.

A similar ground can be ascribed to the Statute of Frauds provision of UCC Article 2. A contemporary clue is provided by comparing the dollar amount in Section 2–201(1) with the amount in the proposed amendment to that section found in *Selections.* The current text of UCC § 2–201(1) requires a writing only for a sale of goods for the price of $500 or more; the proposed amendment would increase that amount to $5000 or more. In the 19th century, very much the same ground—the significance of the transaction—was ascribed by the Supreme Court of Tennessee to the clause about real property transfers. But in the 21st century, that court disavowed its earlier reasoning, citing changes in social circumstances. See p. 279 below.

A suretyship contract is one that requires one person to answer (in the words of the classical Statute) "for the debts, defaults, and miscarriages" of another. Suretyship contracts are commonly used when a bank or other lender is asked to finance a small corporation; the bank is likely to require that a principal officer or shareholder agree to be liable as "surety"—liable to pay if the borrowing firm fails to repay its loan. A bank is unlikely to overlook the statutory requirement that sureties for its loans have signed papers documenting their undertakings. The reasons for the requirement are more evident when a person asks a friend or relation to stand surety for a hoped-for loan. If a conversation between a lender and a borrower's friend could result in a contract binding on the friend, the two might have different understandings and recollections of what was said. Given a default by the borrower, the lender would have a strong incentive to "remember" an oral commitment by the friend. And a friend or relation of the borrower might well fail, when making an oral commitment, to appreciate and reflect on the risk it entails.

An explanation along that line has been influential in determining the scope of the suretyship provision of a statute of frauds. See Cooper Petroleum Co. v. LaGloria Oil & Gas Co., 436 S.W.2d 889 (Tex. 1969). But it is somewhat infirm. Suppose a case in which a self-professed surety is the one making a claim on a promise, and the sole consideration for the promise is the claimant's undertaking as a surety. The promisor is not liable for breach, it has been held, if the claimant's undertaking was oral. That effect of the suretyship clause is hard to explain by concern for unwary friends and relations.

NOTE

Regulatory Functions. Reflecting at large on the merit of statutes of frauds, one might what to know what classes of persons and firms find the statutes most useful. If, in general, a statute favors entities that have little bargaining power, it might win favor as a consumer-protection measure. Weakness in bargaining is not singular to consumers, of course. In Phillippe v. Shapell Industries, Inc., 743 P.2d 1279 (Cal.1987), an association of realtors argued that a broker's reliance on an oral fee contract should be protected because "disparity of bargaining power is most common in the commercial real estate market." In response, the court cited a survey of firms that showed strong support for the Statute of Frauds. The court also depicted the broker's-fee statute as a protection for parties to sales of homes. Restrictions on oral security agreements, which appear both in Article 9 of the Code and in older statutes, can readily be depicted as a form of consumer protection.

Not all writing requirements protect consumers, however. Some protect providers of medical treatment. For a requirement that distinctly does not protect consumers, see paragraph 7 of Cal.Civ.Code § 1624(a). That paragraph applies to a routine commitment to extend credit in an amount greater than $100,000, if it is made by a vocational lender, and is not made primarily for personal, family, or household purposes. (Commitments to make home-mortgage loans are excepted, generally.) Presumably banks were among the proponents of paragraph 7.

(C) AMELIORATING RULES

If an agreement is "within" a statute of frauds, it is unenforceable unless documented in some way by a "writing" that is "signed." An agreement within a statute may be "taken out" by circumstances accepted as a sufficient reason for enforcing an undocumented agreement. Say, for example, that an opera company were to engage a singer to perform the lead role in *Madama Butterfly* on a number of evenings extending over thirteen months. The agreement being oral, it could not be enforced against her. But if the payments to the singer were made in advance, a court might give effect to the agreement as to the final performances once the final payment had been made. That would be to apply the usual rule that full performance on one side takes an agreement out of the one-year clause. (How the agreement might be enforced against the singer is another matter.) Some courts would insist that the company's final payment be made within a year of the agreement. Even so, it is open to doubt that full payment would constitute full performance on the company's side. As to another clause of the Statute of Frauds, one about selling an interest in real property, an agreement may be taken out of the Statute by *part* performance. That doctrine has applications both for and against a party who has rendered performance.

UCC § 2–201 makes a special case of performance by the parties to a contract for the sale of goods, if the performance takes the form either of the making and acceptance of a payment or the receipt and acceptance of goods. According to subsection UCC § 2–201(3)(c), no matter that further performances are called for by the agreement, and will not be forthcoming, a contract is enforceable against a seller with respect to goods for which payment was received and accepted, and against a buyer with respect to goods that have been received and accepted. (These rules are perceptibly different from one that makes an agreement fully enforceable by reason of part performance. The performance specified in the Code does not "take the agreement out of the statute.")

Part performance of most types of agreement within a statute of frauds may generate a remedy against a recipient of that performance. It is likely to do so when the statute gives immunity to the recipient from an action based on the agreement, and the claimant's performance has conferred a benefit on the recipient that cannot in justice be retained without compensating the claimant for it. That is, the performance generates a claim in restitution—not a claim to counter-performance under the agreement. A rule supporting restitution is stated in the Restatement of Restitution, Section 108(d), and is accommodated in the Restatement of Contracts by Section 375.

The performance by a real-estate broker under an agreement calling for a commission is the subject of an exceptional rule. Agreements of that kind are subject to a clause that supplements the classical Statute in every state. The California statute requires a writing, for example, for an agreement authorizing anyone to find a purchaser of real estate "for compensation or a commission." A broker employed by a would-be seller cannot collect a commission, even if his or her services have resulted in a sale, unless the agreement is documented. Usually the seller is not even accountable in restitution for the reasonable value of the broker's services. See American International Enterprises, Inc. v. F.D.I.C., 3 F.3d 1263, 1270 (9th Cir. 1993). The thought is that rewarding a broker that way would come too close to enforcing the agreement.

It should be evident by now that the courts, and to some extent legislators, have worked hard to ameliorate some of the harsh results that may ensue from applying a statute of frauds. For those that remain, a palliative is found in the doctrine of estoppel. Say that a promisee has relied on the enforceability of an undocumented agreement in a way more or less detrimental to the promisee if enforcement is denied. Add to that fact a callous attitude on the part of the promisor. Add also the fact that the promisor was in a position to take advantage of the promisee. (Perhaps the promisor is an attorney, and the promisee is unlettered in the law.) Add to that a gross misrepresentation by the promisor. (Perhaps the promisor, being asked, had said "Our agreement is not one that need be in writing.") There you have a situation in which a court is sure to act in favor of the promisor.

The claimant supposed above might or might not prevail in an action against the attorney, by way of estoppel, in circumstances less compelling. It has been said that "in cases involving oral contracts the estoppel must be based on misrepresentation or concealment if the Statute of Frauds is to be given effect at all." Ozier v. Haines, 103 N.E.2d 485, 488 (Ill.1952). But the contrary view has impressive support. Also, a client's claim against an attorney, based on an oral agreement between them, has a special appeal if they made the agreement while the two were in a lawyer-client relation—one imposing a high standard of fidelity of lawyer toward client. But estoppels have been applied against persons who had no fiduciary obligation to the claimants. For a generous application of estoppel, see Monarco v. LoGreco, p. 305 below. See also Restatement § 139: "Enforcement by Virtue of Action in Reliance." The section states a rule that is said, in Comment *a*, to be "complementary of § 90." It recites a number of circumstances to be considered in deciding whether or not enforcement is the only way to prevent injustice.

Absent reliance on an undocumented agreement, there remains the possibility that it will be enforced against a promisor who has *waived* the defense of the statute. Unless the waiver occurs in the course of litigation, however, it is a suspect ground for enforcement. Freely applied, the doctrine would amount to overthrowing the statutory requirement.

The doctrinal pattern described above is complex. For several reasons, the reality is even more so. It is more so because of variations, large and small, in the statutes. It is more complex because judges differ among themselves about the deference they owe to those statutes, and in their perceptions of injustice, and because they differ about the relations among the several doctrines alleviating harsh effects of the statutes. A deviation in the pattern is represented by the opinion in Consolidation Services, Inc. v. KeyBank National Ass'n, 185 F.3d 817 (7th Cir.1999). Judge Posner, writing there, spoke of a contract "supposedly barred by the statute of frauds" as being "saved" by restitution "when . . . the promisee's extracontractual remedies would be inadequate." *Id.* at 821. That passage stands in opposition to the more usual view that restitution is an extracontractual remedy, and not one that serves to rescue an agreement.

(D) Ethical Practices and Statutes of Frauds

Using a casebook for the study of contract law may draw attention away from the many agreements that are performed punctiliously by persons who regret having made them. A good number of those persons would think it contemptible to withhold performance of an agreement on no better ground than second thought, even if they knew that a court would condone a breach. Many lawyers would think so.

A lawyer's perspective is different when he is asked to oppose a claim on a "technical" ground. Consider one who is asked to defend a client against the enforcement of an agreement that the client acknowledges having made. Supposing that the lawyer believes that a statute of frauds stands in the way of enforcement, he may have some compunction about invoking it. On the other hand, lawyers are expected to be zealous in representing clients.

Is it unethical of the lawyer to invoke the statute? Unethical *not* to invoke it? The authorities are generally circumspect. The Restatement, Third, of the Law Governing Lawyers speaks of "the general rule that a lawyer may act guided only by the objective of furthering the interests of the lawyer's client." Comment *b* to Section 94. It is careful not to suggest that discipline is in order for trying to exonerate a client from a claim of breach of contract. Dean Robert Stevens thought it a prevailing practice among lawyers, probably, "automatically to plead the Statute of Limitations to a stale claim and the Statute of Frauds when there is known to be no writing signed by the defendant, or his agent, evidencing the contract sued upon." The statutes are there and supply the defenses, he said, "and the attorney would not be giving full and competent service to his client if he did not advise him of them and advance them for him." Stevens, Ethics and the Statute of Frauds, 37 Cornell L.Q. 355 (1952).

But Stevens saw a dilemma for a lawyer asked by a client to repel a claim on an oral agreement that the client privately concedes having made. Almost unanimously the courts approve that practice; but the lawyer's conscience may not. "[W]hat is the lawyer to do? Conscience tells him that the practice is wrong, but the literature from insurance companies reminds him of liability for malpractice." *Id.* at 356. Is admonishing the client a way out? According to the Restatement section last cited, a lawyer counseling a client "... may address nonlegal aspects of a proposed course of conduct, including moral, reputational, economic, social, political, and business aspects." Some might say that admonition is required, and some that it is not enough.

According to the American Bar Association, "a lawyer can be a zealous advocate on behalf of a client and at the same time assume that justice is being done." But this precept is qualified by this introductory phrase: "When an opposing party is well represented...." Preamble to Model Rules of Professional Conduct (2002). One scholar has said that the answer depends on whether or not the lawyer holds "a good faith belief that the assertion of the doctrine or rule in the particular case will further a policy behind the doctrine or rule." Kenney Hegland, Quibbles, 67 Tex.L.Rev. 1491, 1494 (1989). That did not suit Professor John Sutton, who answered that Professor Hegland would leave it to each lawyer on his own "to make the decision concerning fairness and justice." Outlawing Unjust Rules of Law: A Response to *Quibbles,* 67 Tex.L.Rev. 1517, 1522 (1989).

NOTES

(1) *Technicalities.* The want of consideration for a promise appears, sometimes, to be a technical defense. In Mills v. Wyman, p. 50 above, Seth Wyman broke a promise to pay for emergency care given by Mills to his son, and was exonerated of liability because Mills gave no consideration for the promise. The court seems to have disdained the defense, calling the outcome a "strong example of particular injustice." Many attorneys would have qualms about advancing the defense. When a statute of frauds is an effective defense for a self-confessed promise-breaker, is it any more "technical" than the defense that worked for Seth Wyman? Any less so?

(2) *Sanctioning Attorneys.* For a lawyer to present the most technical of defenses is more tolerable than to present to a court a proposition of law that he knows to be untenable. A lawyer is expected, all across the United States, to abstain from doing that. Rules of the courts forbid it; Rule 11 of the Federal Rules of Civil Procedure is one example among many.

A New York rule of judicial administration speaks of frivolity. Conduct is *frivolous* if "it is completely without merit in law and cannot be supported by a reasonable argument for an extension, modification or reversal of existing law." 22 NYCRR § 130–1.1(c)(1). Subject to qualifications, the rule authorizes a court entertaining a civil proceeding to impose costs and other financial sanctions on a party or an attorney engaging in frivolous conduct. An attorney can suffer sanctions for advocating the enforcement of an agreement, as well as for opposing enforcement. See, for example, Yenom Corp. v. 155 Wooster Street Inc., 818 N.Y.S.2d 210 (App.Div.2006). The action was predicated, the court said, on a "part performance argument that was completely without merit in law or fact." *Id.* at 213.

SECTION 2.   WRITING, SIGNING, AND OTHERWISE RECORDING AND AUTHENTICATING

THE CONTENT OF A DOCUMENT

While reading the paragraphs that follow, consider this hypothetical case: Resident posted a sign, "For sale by owner," in front of her condominium on High Street. Soon after that she received a postcard from Seeker containing this legend: "Re Five High Street. My offer is $350,000, subject to an engineer's inspection. Taxes to be prorated." Resident answered with her own postcard, writing on it: "Re condo. I accept your offer. Have your engineer get in touch." Thereafter Seeker's engineer inspected the property and made a report indicating some flaws. Resident regards the report as captious. Together, Resident and Seeker have asked an attorney whether or not either can enforce a sale agreement against the other. The attorney is satisfied that the parties have exchanged promises. She is prepared to get clarification about the supposed flaws. Before doing so, however, she reviewed a few basic precepts of the Statute of Frauds.

First, what constitutes a writing sufficient to satisfy the statutes of frauds? The UCC definition of "writing" provides a helpful start. UCC § 1–201(b)(43) states that writing "includes printing, typewriting, or any other intentional reduction to tangible form." Second, what terms of the contract must appear in the writing? Putting aside for now some important relaxations of this requirement in UCC Article 2, see page 285 below, the requirement of terms is stiff. According to the Restatement, "[t]he 'essential' terms of unperformed promises must be stated." Restatement § 131, Comment *g*. But not all terms are "essential." Comment *g* continues: "What is essential depends on the agreement and its context and also on the subsequent conduct of the parties, including the dispute which arises and the remedy sought." For example, as to a sale of an interest in real property, a memorandum suffices, it seems, although it does not indicate when the transfer is to occur, or when it is to be paid for. The time for performance is not always a dispensable component, however. For the enforcement of some agreements, a period of time must be indicated in the writing. More generally, a description of the transaction or promise (including the price to be paid) and identification of the parties are essential terms.

"The memorandum exacted by the statute does not have to be in one document. It may be pieced together out of separate writings." So said the New York Court of Appeals in Marks v. Cowdin, 123 N.E. 139 (1919), at 141. That court has been less rigorous than some others in requiring a full written expression of the agreement. Even so, it has said this:

> [A]t least one writing, the one establishing a contractual relationship between the parties, must bear the signature of the party to be charged, while the unsigned document must on its face refer to the same transaction as that set forth in the one that was signed.... If [parol] testimony does not convincingly connect the papers, or does not show assent to the unsigned paper, it is within the province of the judge to conclude, as a matter of law, that the statute has not been satisfied.

Crabtree v. Elizabeth Arden Sales Corp., 110 N.E.2d 551, 554 (1953). These requirements can most readily be met by a provision, in a signed writing, that designates and incorporates one or more other writings. For users of e-mail, a commonplace way to stitch two messages together is to *Reply* or to *Reply with history*.

A reference in a signed writing to extrinsic circumstances may suffice to express essential terms of an agreement. So, for example, a long-term employment contract might be enforced although the employee's duties are described in writing only by the job title and the incumbent's name (*e.g.*, "Assistant Treasurer of the Company, replacing Anna Sacks Feinberg upon her retirement"). Compare Marks v. Cowdin, above, in which Cardozo wrote: "the plaintiff does not need the aid of one spoken word of promise to identify his place." Also: "The statute must not be pressed to the extreme of a literal and rigid logic.... The memorandum which it requires, like any other memorandum, must be read in the light of reason."

———

SIGNING

A documented agreement that was signed long after the parties agreed on its terms will satisfy a statute of frauds. Indeed, an agreement made long before any part of it was recorded may be enforced if the subsequent documentation is adequate.

Considerable lenience is shown in deciding what counts as a signature. For an individual, most any scratch may suffice; for any entity, a stamped name and even a letterhead may suffice. What the sponsors of the Code have said about a proposed definition of "Signed," in relation to a sale-of-goods agreement, is generally accurate in relation to other agreements within a statute of frauds:

> [A] complete signature is not necessary. The symbol may be printed, stamped or written; it may be by initials or by thumbprint. It may be on any part of the document and in appropriate cases may be found in a billhead or letterhead. No catalog of possible situations can be complete and the court must use common sense and commercial experience in passing upon these matters. The question always is whether the symbol was executed or adopted by the party with present intention to adopt or accept the writing.

On the other hand, when a claimant asserted an employment contract, and relied, for a writing, on a personnel manual, the court declined to accept the defendant's logo as a signature. It said (quoting) that "a signing consists of both the act of writing a person's name and the intention, in doing this, to execute and authenticate the instrument signed." Falls v. Virginia State Bar, 397 S.E.2d 671, 673 (Va.1990). In the same vein, the New York Court of Appeals has ruled that the "subscribing" of a writing cannot be effected by a fax machine, or by programming the machine to inscribe the sender's name on messages at large. Parma Tile Mosaic & Marble v. Estate of Short, 663 N.E.2d 633 (1996). The court hinted, however, that the sender's name on a cover sheet might serve.

ELECTRONIC DOCUMENTATION

Some years before the end of the 20th century it became apparent that the words "writing," "signed," and "subscribed" in statutes of fraud were threats to electronic commerce. Several statutory responses have emerged in the United States. The character of these responses is illustrated by a proposal to amend the Code. It features, along with changes in Section 2–201, the word *record*, newly defined, and broadening of the definitions of *authenticated* and *sign*. But the sponsors of the Code have had little success in promoting Article 2 as amended.

The Commissioners on Uniform State Laws have had far more success in promoting the Uniform Electronic Transactions Act, commonly known as "UETA." It has been enacted in all but four states. It is the major United States source of validation for electronic agreements not represented in signed writings. That is true even though in 2001 the Congress took action in general accord with UETA. The federal statute is the Electronic Signatures in Global and National Commerce Act, 15 U.S.C. § 7001 *et seq.*, otherwise known as "E–SIGN." The function of that statute is substantially reduced by the fact that, by its own terms, it defers largely to state laws. (Article 2 of the Code, as revised, would take advantage of that deference.)

UETA applies to contracts for the sale of goods that are governed by Article 2 and to most contracts governed by the common law. See Section 3. It provides that "if a law requires a record to be in writing, an *electronic record* satisfies the law," and that "if a law requires a signature, an *electronic signature* satisfies the law." Section 7(c) and (d). The terms italicized here are defined in Section 2. These provisions, taken together, allow the electronic equivalents of signed writings to satisfy a statute of frauds that has not been amended to accommodate electronic commerce. (UETA appears in *Selections*, as well as E-SIGN and the amendments proposed for Article 2.)

Comparable action on the global front is illustrated by a model law on electronic commerce, prepared by the United Nations Commission on International Trade Law.

PROBLEMS

(1) Consider the hypothetical case of the condo sale, at p. 266 above. How should the attorney advise Resident and Seeker?

(2) Consider this change in the hypothetical case: The messages exchanged by Resident and Seeker were not inscribed on postcards, were in the form of e-mails. How might that matter?

Suppose also that on printouts of these messages no person's name appeared, but that each printout bore an e-mail address chosen by its author. What to make of that fact is an obvious question about the law. What answer should a court give?

SECTION 3.   STATUTORY SCOPE

(A) DURATION OF PERFORMANCE: THE ONE–YEAR AND LIFETIME CLAUSES

As indicated above, an agreement that cannot be performed within the year following its making is unenforceable unless circumstances persuade a court otherwise. One circumstance that systematically persuades courts to enforce an agreement within the one-year clause is that, by the time of litigation, the agreement has been performed in full on the part of the claimant. The opinion that follows describes another major principle that limits the application of the clause.

NOTE

Statutory Overlap. A single contract may well fall into more than one class of agreements under the statute of frauds. For example, the contract in Eastern Air Lines v. Gulf Oil Corporation, p. 76 above, was one for a sale of goods, the performance of which required more than a year. It is easy to suppose documentation of that contract which, though it would satisfy UCC § 2–201, would not satisfy the one-year clause. There is authority for suspending the operation of the one-year clause in that situation. Roth Steel Products v. Sharon Steel Corp., 705 F.2d 134 (6th Cir.1983). But the prevailing view is that, with respect to various statute of frauds provisions, an agreement is unenforceable if it is wanting in the documentation required for any class of contracts in which it lies. See Fort Howard Paper Co. v. William D. Witter, Inc., 787 F.2d 784 (2d Cir.1986) (suretyship and finder's-fee provisions).

C. R. Klewin, Inc. v. Flagship Properties, Inc.

Supreme Court of Connecticut, 1991.
220 Conn. 569, 600 A.2d 772.

■ Peters, C. J. The sole question before us in this certified appeal is whether the provision of the statute of frauds, General Statutes § 52–550(a)(5)[1] requiring a writing for an Agreement that is not to be performed within one year from the making thereof, renders unenforceable an oral contract that fails to specify explicitly the time for performance when performance of that contract within one year of its making is exceedingly unlikely. This case comes to this court upon our grant of an application for certification from the United States Court of Appeals for the Second Circuit. . . .

[The facts provided by that court were, abbreviated, as follows. Flagship was the developer of a project, called ConnTech, near the main campus of the University of Connecticut. The master plan called for the construction of housing for hundreds of students and teachers, a hotel and convention center, and twenty industrial buildings. At a meeting, in March of 1986, between Flagship representatives and representatives of C. R. Klewin, the latter named a percentage fee for acting as construction manager for the project. The meeting ended with a handshake and the statement, "We've got a deal."

Construction began on the first phase of the project—"Celeron Square"—in May of 1987. For that phase the parties entered into a written agreement. By the time it was completed, in mid-October, Flagship had become dissatisfied with Klewin's work. In March of 1988 it engaged another firm to do the sitework for Celeron Square II, the next phase. Having been replaced as construction manager, Klewin brought an action against Flagship, charging it with, among other things, breach of a contract for work on the entire project.]

Flagship moved for summary judgment, claiming, *inter alia*, that enforcement of the alleged oral contract was barred by the statute of frauds. The district court granted summary judgment, reasoning that (1) "the contract was not of an indefinite duration or openended" because full performance would take place when all phases of the ConnTech Project were completed, and (2) the contract "as a matter of law" could not possibly have been performed within one year. In drawing this second conclusion, the court focused on the sheer scope of the project and Klewin's

1. General Statutes § 52–550 provides in pertinent part: "(a) No civil action may be maintained in the following cases unless the agreement, or a memorandum of the agreement, is made in writing and signed by the party, or the agent of the party, to be charged . . . (5) upon any agreement that is not to be performed within one year from the making thereof. . . ."

own admission that the entire project was intended to be constructed in three to ten years.

Klewin appealed.... [Wanting for controlling precedent about Connecticut law, the federal appellate court] certified to this court the following questions:

A. Whether under the Connecticut Statute of Frauds, Conn. Gen. Stat. § 52–550(a)(5), an oral contract that fails to specify explicitly the time for performance is a contract of "indefinite duration," as that term has been used in the applicable Connecticut precedent, and therefore outside of the Statute's proscriptions?

B. Whether an oral contract is unenforceable when the method of performance called for by the contract contemplates performance to be completed over a period of time that exceeds one year, yet the contract itself does not explicitly negate the possibility of performance within one year? We answer "yes" to the first question, and "no" to the second....

Modern scholarly commentary has found much to criticize about the continued viability of the statute of frauds. The statute has been found wanting because it serves none of its purported functions very well; see J. Perillo, [The Statute of Frauds in the Light of the Functions and Dysfunctions of Form, 43 Fordham L.Rev. 39 (1974)]; and because it permits or compels economically wasteful behavior; see M. Braunstein, "Remedy, Reason, and the Statute of Frauds: A Critical Economic Analysis," 1989 Utah L. Rev. 383. It is, however, the one-year provision that is at issue in this case that has caused the greatest puzzlement among commentators. As Professor Farnsworth observes, "of all the provisions of the statute, it is the most difficult to rationalize." [At this point the court quoted at some length from the Farnsworth treatise on Contracts. The court followed with "see also" citations as follows.] Goldstick v. ICM Realty, 788 F.2d 456, 464 (7th Cir. 1986); D & N Boening, Inc. v. Kirsch Beverages, Inc., 63 N.Y.2d 449, 454, 472 N.E.2d 992 (1984); 1 Restatement (Second), Contracts (1979) § 130, *comment a*; J. Calamari & J. Perillo, Contracts (3d Ed. 1987) §§ 19–18, p. 807.[2]

Historians have had difficulty accounting for the original inclusion of the one-year provision.[3] Some years after the statute's enactment, one English judge stated that "the design of the statute was, not to trust to the memory of witnesses for a longer time than one year." Smith v. *Westall*, 1 Ld.Raym. 316, 317, 91 Eng.Rep. 1106, 1107 (1697). That explanation is, however, unpersuasive, since, as Farnsworth notes, the language of the statute is ill suited to this purpose. One eminent historian suggested that because such contracts are continuing contracts, it might be very difficult to give evidence of their formation, inasmuch as the rules of evidence of

2. Even the statute's most notable defender chose not to mention the one-year provision when he contended that the statute is "in essence better adapted to our needs than when it was first passed." K. Llewellyn, "What Price Contract? An Essay in Perspective," 40 Yale L.J. 704, 747 (1931).

3. The language of the original English statute was nearly identical to that of the provision we are now considering, including "any agreement that is not to be performed within the space of one year from the making thereof...."

that time prohibited testimony by the parties to an action or any person who had an interest in the litigation. 6 W. Holdsworth, *supra*, p. 392. That argument, however, proves too much, since it would apply equally to all oral contracts regardless of the duration of their performance. The most extensive recent study of the history of English contract law offers plausible explanations for all of the other provisions, but acknowledges that this one is "curious." A. Simpson, A History of the Common Law of Contract (1975) p. 612. More recently, it has been suggested that the provision "may have been intended to prevent oral perjury in actions of assumpsit against customers who had forgotten the details of their purchases." P. Hamburger, "The Conveyancing Purposes of the Statute of Frauds," 27 Am.J.Leg. Hist. 354, 376 n.85 (1983).

In any case, the one-year provision no longer seems to serve any purpose very well, and today its only remaining effect is arbitrarily to forestall the adjudication of possibly meritorious claims. For this reason, the courts have for many years looked on the provision with disfavor, and have sought constructions that limited its application. See, *e.g.*, Landes Construction Co. v. Royal Bank of Canada, 833 F.2d 1365, 1370 (9th Cir. 1987) (noting policy of California courts "of restricting the application of the statute to those situations precisely covered by its language"); Cunningham v. Healthco, Inc., 824 F.2d 1448, 1455 (5th Cir.1987) (one-year provision does not apply if the contract "conceivably" can be performed within one year); Hodge v. Evans Financial Corporation, 823 F.2d 559, 561 (D.C.Cir.1987) (statute of frauds "has long been construed narrowly and literally"); Goldstick v. ICM Realty, *supra*, 464 ("Courts tend to take the concept of 'capable of full performance' quite literally ... because they find the one-year limitation irksome.").

II

Our case law in Connecticut, like that in other jurisdictions, has taken a narrow view of the one-year provision of the statute of frauds now codified as § 52–550(a)(5). In Russell v. Slade, 12 Conn. 455, 460 (1838), this court held that "it has been repeatedly adjudged, that unless it appear *from the agreement itself*, that it is *not* to be performed within a year, the statute does not apply. ... The statute of frauds plainly means an agreement *not* to be performed within the space of a year, and *expressly* and *specifically* so agreed. A *contingency* is not within it; nor any case that *depends upon contingency*. It does *not* extend to cases where the thing only *may* be performed within the year." (Emphases in original; citation and internal quotation marks omitted.)

A few years later, in Clark v. Pendleton, 20 Conn. 495, 508 (1850), the statute was held not to apply to a contract that was to be performed following a voyage that both parties expected to take one and one-half years.... In this century, in Appleby v. Noble, 101 Conn. 54, 57, 124 A. 717 (1924), this court held that "[a] contract is not within this clause of the statute unless *its terms are so drawn* that it cannot by any possibility be performed fully within one year." (Emphasis added.) In Burkle v. Superflow Mfg. Co., 137 Conn. 488, 492–93, 78 A.2d 698 (1951), we delineated the line that separates contracts that are within the one-year provision from those that are excluded from it. "Where *the time for performance is definitely fixed at more than one year*, the contract is, of course, within the statute.... If no time is *definitely fixed* but full performance may occur within one year through the happening of a contingency upon which the contract depends, it is not within the statute." (Emphases added; citations omitted.)

More recently, in Finley v. Aetna Life & Casualty Co., 202 Conn. 190, 197, 520 A.2d 208 (1987), we stated that " '[u]nder the prevailing interpretation, the enforceability of a contract under the one-year provision does not turn on the actual course of subsequent events, nor on the expectations of the parties as to the probabilities. Contracts of uncertain duration are simply excluded; the provision covers *only* those contracts whose performance *cannot possibly* be completed within a year.' (Emphasis added.) 1 Restatement (Second), Contracts, [§ 130, comment *a*]...."

In light of this unbroken line of authority, the legislature's decision repeatedly to reenact the provision in language virtually identical to that of the 1677 statute suggests legislative approval of the restrictive interpretation that this court has given to the one-year provision. "[T]he action of the General Assembly in re-enacting the statute, including the clause in question ... is presumed to have been done in the light of those decisions." Turner v. Scanlon, 146 Conn. 149, 156, 148 A.2d 334 (1959); see also Ralston Purina Co. v. Board of Tax Review, 203 Conn. 425, 439–40, 525 A.2d 91 (1987).

III

Bearing this history in mind, we turn to the questions certified to us by the federal court. Our case law makes no distinction, with respect to exclusion from the statute of frauds, between contracts of uncertain or indefinite duration and contracts that contain no express terms defining the time for performance. The two certified questions therefore raise only one substantive issue. That issue can be framed as follows: in the exclusion from the statute of frauds of all contracts except those "whose performance cannot possibly be completed within a year"; (emphasis omitted) Finley v. Aetna Life & Casualty Co., *supra*, 197; what meaning should be attributed to the word "possibly"? One construction of "possibly" would encompass only contracts whose completion within a year would be inconsistent with the express terms of the contract. An alternate construction would include as well contracts such as the one involved in this case, in which, while no time period is expressly specified, it is (as the district court found) realistically impossible for performance to be completed within a year. We now hold that the former and not the latter is the correct interpretation. "The critical test ... is whether 'by its terms' the agreement is not to be performed within a year," so that the statute will not apply where "the alleged agreement contain[s] [no] provision which directly or indirectly regulated the time for performance." Freedman v. Chemical Construction Corporation, 43 N.Y.2d 260, 265, 372 N.E.2d 12 (1977). "It is the law of this state, as it is elsewhere, that a contract is not within this clause of the statute unless *its terms are so drawn that* it cannot by any possibility be performed fully within one year." (Emphasis added.) Burkle v. Superflow Mfg. Co., *supra*, 492.

Flagship contends, to the contrary, that the possibility to which this court referred in *Burkle* must be a reasonable possibility rather than a theoretical possibility. It is true that in *Burkle* this court rejected the argument that "since all the members of a partnership [that was a party to the contract] may possibly die within a year, the contract is not within the statute." We noted that "[n]o case has come to our attention where the rule that the possibility of death within a year removes a contract from the statute has been extended to apply to the possibility of the death of more than one individual." Id., 494. In *Burkle*, however, we merely refused to extend further yet another of the rules by which the effect of the provision has been limited. *Burkle* did not purport to change the well established rule of narrow construction of the underlying one-year provision.

Most other jurisdictions follow a similar rule requiring an express contractual provision specifying that performance will extend for more than one year. Only "[a] few jurisdictions, contrary to the great weight of authority ... hold that the intention of the parties may put their oral agreement within the operation of the Statute." 3 S. Williston, Contracts (3d Ed. W. Jaeger 1960) § 495, pp. 584–85. In "the leading case on this section of the Statute"; Id., p. 578; the Supreme Court of the United States undertook an extensive survey of the case law up to that time and concluded that "[i]t ... appears to have been the settled construction of this clause of the statute in England, before the Declaration of Independence, that an oral agreement which, according to the intention of the parties, *as shown by the terms of the contract*, might be fully performed within a year from the time it was made, was not within the statute, although the time of its performance was uncertain, and might probably extend, and be expected by the parties to extend, and did in fact extend, beyond the year. The several States of the Union, in reenacting this provision of the statute of frauds in its original words, must be taken to have adopted the known and settled construction which it had received by judicial decisions in England." (Emphasis added.) Warner v. Texas & Pacific R. Co., 164 U.S. 418, 422–23 (1896).... "The parties may well have expected that the contract would continue in force for more than one year; it may have been very improbable that it would not do so; and it did in fact continue in force for a much longer time. But they made no stipulation which in terms, or by reasonable inference, required that result. The question is not what the probable, or expected, or actual performance of the contract was; but whether the contract, according to the reasonable interpretation *of its terms*, required that it should not be performed within the year." (Emphasis added.) Id., 434; see also Walker v. Johnson, 96 U.S. 424, 427 (1877); McPherson v. Cox, 96 U.S. 404, 416–17 (1877).

Because the one-year provision "is an anachronism in modern life ... we are not disposed to expand its destructive force." Farmer v. Arabian

American Oil Co., 277 F.2d 46, 51 (2d Cir.1960).[4] When a contract contains no express terms about the time for performance, no sound reason of policy commends judicial pursuit of a collateral inquiry into whether, at the time of the making of the contract, it was realistically possible that performance of the contract would be completed within a year. Such a collateral inquiry would not only expand the "destructive force" of the statute by extending it to contracts not plainly within its terms, but would also inevitably waste judicial resources on the resolution of an issue that has nothing to do with the merits of the case or the attainment of a just outcome.[5] See 2 A. Corbin, *supra*, § 275, p. 14 (the statute "has been in part the cause of an immense amount of litigation as to whether a promise is within the statute or can by any remote possibility be taken out of it. This latter fact is fully evidenced by the space necessary to be devoted to the subject in this volume and by the vast number of cases to be cited").

We therefore hold that an oral contract that does not say, in express terms, that performance is to have a specific duration beyond one year is, as a matter of law, the functional equivalent of a contract of indefinite duration for the purposes of the statute of frauds. Like a contract of indefinite duration, such a contract is enforceable because it is outside the proscriptive force of the statute regardless of how long completion of performance will actually take.

The first certified question is answered "yes." The second certified question is answered "no."

NOTES

(1) *Questions.* Would the case have been different if the agreement, as alleged, had contained either of the following terms? (a) "Klewin will not be required to do site work for Celeron Square II within twelve months of this agreement." (b) "Klewin's fee is to be, at a minimum, $9 million, payable in full not later than four years from this date."

---

4. In this case, one of the issues before the Second Circuit was whether the oral agreement could have been performed within a year.

5. We recognize, as Flagship observed at oral argument, that comment *a* to § 130 of the Restatement (Second) of Contracts (1979) ... includes an illustration that is inconsistent with the result that we are reaching today. Contrary to illustration 3 (which is drawn from Warner v. Texas & Pacific R. Co., 164 U.S. 418 (1896)), ... which supports our holding, illustration 4 states: "A orally promises B to sell him five crops of potatoes to be grown on a specified farm in Minnesota, and B promises to pay a stated price on delivery. The contract is within the Statute of Frauds. It is impossible in Minnesota for five crops of potatoes to mature in one year." The illustration is adapted from illustration 11 to § 198 of the Restatement (First) of Contracts

(1928), which does not include case citations. The Restatement (Second) supports the illustration by citing Adams v. Big Three Industries, Inc., 549 S.W.2d 411 (Tex.Civ.App. 1977). The *Adams* court held that "when no time for performance has been specified, a 'reasonable time' will be implied, and what is a reasonable time must be determined from all the circumstances, the situation of the parties, and the subject matter of the contract. ... Where an agreement, by its terms or the nature of the performance required, cannot be performed within one year, it necessarily comes within the purview of the statute. ... If, as here, the contract is not a written one and depends upon disputed facts, the determination of what constitutes a reasonable time is a question of fact." (Citations omitted.) Id., 414–15. In our view, illustration 3 more closely represents the law of this state.

(2) *Analogs*. In D & N Boening, Inc. v. Kirsch Beverages, Inc., a New York case cited in *C. R. Klewin*, the court gave the following catalog of earlier New York cases in which oral agreements were upheld as being fully performable within one year:

> [W]here either party had the option to terminate the agreement on seven months' notice; where the agreement merely set the terms of anticipated prospective purchases but did not bind either party to any particular transaction; where defendant had the option to discontinue at any time the activities upon which the agreement was conditioned; where defendant had the option of selling at any time the property on lease to plaintiff for four years; where no provision in the agreement directly or indirectly regulated the time for performance despite the extreme unlikelihood of its completion within one year; where employment was terminable for any just and sufficient cause wherever dismissal was deemed necessary for the welfare of the company.

In *Boening* itself, the alleged agreement was to endure as long as the claimant should perform satisfactorily, exert its best efforts, and act in good faith. (The claimant had been appointed the exclusive distributor, in parts of Long Island, of a chocolate drink called "Yoo–Hoo.") The court said there was no way the performances on either side could be concluded within a year, except by a breach on one side or the other. Compare the paragraph near the end of the foregoing opinion, beginning "We therefore hold...." Is the *Boening* case consistent with that paragraph?

(3) *Opposition*. Opposition to extreme applications of the limiting principle "capable of full performance" is sometimes registered. For example, a judge dissenting in Kitsos v. Mobile Gas Service Corp., 404 So.2d 40, 42 (Ala.1981), spoke disapprovingly of authorities that "grasp for every conceivable exception in order to narrow the Statute's field of operation." This view was partially vindicated in Dean v. Myers, 466 So.2d 952 (Ala.1985), where the court said: "There must be a reasonable possibility of performance within a year.... We see [none], and certainly not within the intention of the parties." According to some precedents, then, when a large-scale development is planned, the agreement may come within the one-year clause even though the work might be completed within a year by extraordinary effort. Is it a good idea for courts to make estimates of what is reasonably possible? When they do, should they take account of the extraordinary capacities of some parties?

(4) *Thwarted Performances*. A long-term contract may be terminated by an event making its performance impossible, or even simply impracticable. An instance is the death of one who has agreed to render personal services. Illness may have the same effect. See Wasserman Theatrical Enterprise v. Harris, 77 A.2d 329 (Conn. 1950), in which Walter Huston, the actor, was excused from appearing on stage because of a minor throat ailment. Excuses of this kind are examined further in Chapter 9.

By common consent, the possibility that a long-term agreement will come to an end owing to supervening impracticability does not prevent the application of the one-year clause to that agreement. See Trovese v. O'Meara, 493 N.W.2d 221 (S.D.1992). There the claimant alleged an agreement to employ her for a year, beginning eight days thereafter. She argued that the agreement would be performed fully if she were to die, as she might do at any time. She was in error: her death would terminate the duties agreed upon as a matter of law, but would not terminate the performance agreed upon.

It is possible to distinguish a case in which a person is hired for five years "if he lives that long." That being done, what of a case in which a person is hired for five years, and the agreement continues: "but if he should die at any time this agreement will come to an end." As to vexing cases like these see Silverman v. Bernot, 239 S.E.2d 118 (Va.1977).

(5) *Performance by Inaction*. Some courts have been more indulgent of non-competition covenants, in relation to the one-year clause, than of employment agreements. See Wyatt v. Dishong, 469 N.E.2d 608, 611 (Ill.App.1984): "a contract containing a covenant not to compete for a period longer than a year does not run afoul of the Statute of Frauds, while a contract containing a term of employment for such a period would do so." What is the difference between the effect of death in the one case and in the other? For a contrary view about covenants not to compete see Reagan Outdoor Advertising, Inc. v. Lundgren, 692 P.2d 776 (Utah 1984).

(6) *Variations*. In a few states the one-year clause has been suppressed. In others the clause is held to apply only when the agreement requires performances *by both parties* extending beyond the one-year period. As to divergent views about that, see Hopper v. Lennen & Mitchell, 146 F.2d 364 (9th Cir. 1944).

———

INFORMAL EXTENSIONS OF EMPLOYMENT

Often a person, having been hired for a term, remains on the job when the term is over. The initial employment agreement is enforceable by either party, even if the term is longer than a year, if it is fully expressed in a writing properly signed. After that, usually there will be a contract for continuing employment, either express or implied. An express agreement was described by witnesses in Rash v. J.V. Intermediate, Ltd. [J.V.], 498 F.3d 1201 (10th Cir.2007). According to them, when Rash's initial employment with J.V. was over the parties "just kept going," and the employer's president said to Rash, "Clayton, as long as you're with J.V., that contract is good 'til the end." In that case and others, problems have arisen about the ensuing relation, absent documentation. A surprising array of views has emerged about it.

One view is that the parties can bind themselves to a term in the written agreement by making an "oral renewal" of the agreement, at least if the renewal is for a period no longer than a year. In re Arbitration (Acadia Company v. Edlitz), 165 N.E.2d 411 (N.Y.1960). At the other extreme is Farone v. Bag'n Baggage, Ltd., 165 S.W.3d 795 (Tex.App.2005). In that case the parties disagreed about Farone's rights long after the close of a term covered by his only written employment agreement. The court said: "there may have been implied agreements to continue the original contract; but, without a further writing during each period of extension of the original two year agreement, any subsequent agreements are not enforceable." *Id.* at 801.

Farone was distinguished in Rash v. J.V. Intermediate, Ltd. (applying Texas law). What *Farone* means, that court thought, is that the parties to an employment contract cannot extend it orally *for a period more than a year*. In Rash's case the trial court had found that the parties had, by implication, extended his employment month to month. *Farone* was therefore distinguishable. "[N]othing [there] precludes parties from impliedly renewing a contract or extending its time period beyond its express terms *indefinitely or for less than one year."* *Id.* at 1214.

LIFETIME AGREEMENTS: *TUCKWILLER'S CASE*

Consider, in light of the statutes referred to at p. 258 above, a transaction addressed in the next chapter of this book. Mrs. Metta Morrison, who suffered from Parkinsonism, discussed the matter of her future care with a younger woman, Ruby Tuckwiller. As a result, Mrs. Tuckwiller wrote as follows: "My offer to Aunt Metta is as follows: I will take care of her for her lifetime.... In exchange she will will me her farm [identifying it] at her death...." Mrs. Morrison assented to that. The question arose, after Mrs. Morrison's death, whether or not the executor of her estate could be compelled to convey the farm to Mrs. Tuckwiller. Apparently Morrison had intended to change her will. But she had failed to do so, and it devised the farm to Davidson College. (Enforceable contracts trump wills in the event of inconsistency.)

It appears that the document expressed an agreement, despite the expression "My offer," that was within two of the categories described at pp. 258–259 above: an agreement for the transfer of real estate, and which was not to be completed before the end of a lifetime. Hence, if the agreement had not been represented in a signed writing or other record, it would have been unenforceable. But the agreement *was* expressed in writing. Also, Morrison had signed it. That might not do, according to the New York and California statutes, unless she *subscribed* it, but the applicable statute required only a signing.

The "lifetime clauses" of the New York and California statutes are not identical. By the former, an agreement is unenforceable if it is entirely oral and if it is one "the performance of which is not to be completed before the end of a lifetime." Contrast the California clause: "by its terms ... not to be performed during the lifetime of the promisor." As to Morrison's promise of the farm, these clauses do not differ; it was not performable within the promisor's lifetime. They differ, however, with respect to the promise of lifetime care. If Tuckwiller had been charged with breach of that promise, she could have answered, in terms of the New York statute, that her promise was not fully performable earlier than Morrison's death. (We are not told that Tuckwiller signed—much less "subscribed"—the paper she wrote.)

The times for full performance (category 1 on the list at pp. 258–259) did not matter in the *Tuckwiller* case for two reasons. For one thing, the applicable law was that of Missouri, and the Missouri statute is satisfied by a writing *signed* by the party to be charged—Morrison's estate, vice

Morrison. Also, the Missouri statute of frauds does not include a "lifetime clause" of any sort.

———

(B) Interests in Real Property

The clause on this subject requires a signed writing for the enforcement of an agreement for the transfer of an interest in real estate (leasing being treated separately). The explanation for the clause has shifted somewhat over time. It is natural to suppose that, in the 17th century and after, divesting a person of an interest in real property appeared to be so grave a matter that a formality should be required. The Tennessee Supreme Court made that assumption. In 1857 it said that the clause in question "was designed to protect the owners of land from being drawn into hasty or inconsiderate agreements in relation to what is deemed the more valuable and important species of property, and to guard against misunderstanding as to the nature and extent of such agreements.... The same policy dictated the enactment that the sale of slaves should be evidenced by writing." Whitby v. Whitby, 36 Tenn. 473, 478. From that assumption the court drew the conclusion that a signed writing is required of sellers only—not of buyers. It held to that conclusion until this century, permitting an oral agreement to be enforced against a buyer. (Technically speaking, the phrase in the statute, "the party to be charged," was taken to signify a seller only.)

In 2006, however, the court reversed itself, saying:

> While we certainly can understand this Court's apparent preference in 1857 for landowners, in modern times where a substantial portion of the population has been involved in some aspect of the transfer of real property, the need for the preference regarding landowners no longer exists. Thus, buyers and sellers should receive equal protection in the process of the sale of land so that neither stands to be unduly benefitted or disproportionately burdened by the fact that the contract has not been reduced to writing.

Blair v. Brownson, 197 S.W.3d 681, 685. Reform came from the legislature at the same time, through the addition of this sentence to the then version of the statute: "In a contract for the sale of lands, tenements, or hereditaments, the party to be charged is the party against whom enforcement of the contract is sought."

These developments leave open the question why a legislature should enact protection for *either* buyers or sellers against oral sale agreements.

NOTES

(1) *A Straddle.* The clause in the Statute of Frauds about real property speaks to the requisite form for transferring an interest, as well as to that for making an enforceable agreement for transfer. Therefore it is a major component of property law, as well as of contract law.

(2) *Stock Sales*. New York courts have held that the clause applies to agreements for the sale of stock in a corporation if its sole asset is an interest in real property. *E.g.,* Yenom Corp. v. 155 Wooster Street Inc., 818 N.Y.S.2d 210 (App.Div. 2006). The opinions in those cases make no reference to the New York version of UCC § 8–113, about sales of securities, set out in brackets at p. 258 above. Presumably the statute did not affect those cases because the shares in question were not "securities" as defined in UCC Article 8 ("Investment Securities"). The New York decisions are at odds, apparently, with Jones v. Adam, 2007 WL 4693280 (Me.Super.2007).

Unlike the Code section, the New York statute requires a note or memorandum, in writing and subscribed, for the sale or purchase of a "cooperative interest"—that being defined so as to include shares in a cooperative housing corporation. It reflects the belief that cooperative interests present issues unique to New York State.

Richard v. Richard

Supreme Court of Rhode Island, 2006.
900 A.2d 1170.

[The Richard family—Norman and his son Gregory, and Gregory's wife Jennifer—were riven twice. Once when the couple separated and later when, in divorce proceedings, the Family Court ordered that Norman convey a residence in Tiverton to Gregory and Jennifer. Norman appealed to this court.

The ground of the Family Court order was an agreement Norman had made to convey the residence to his son and daughter-in-law. The terms of the agreement were not recorded, except for some cryptic ledger entries. The contestants disagreed sharply about those terms. According to Gregory and Jennifer, the price was $70,000, only about a third of the stipulated value of the property. The difference, according to the trial justice, represented family affection. According to Norman, the price was to be much larger; but the trial justice found him to be "quite frankly untruthful".

Before the sale agreement was made, on whatever terms, Jennifer and Gregory had occupied the property as tenants of Norman. Following the agreement, they began making monthly payments to Norman in addition to rent payments. In one way or another, the parties agreed, these amounts were to be used for paying the purchase price. Also, following the agreement, Gregory and Jennifer made some improvements, typified by the renovation of some rooms and the replacement of the front door and of a banister.

On appeal, Norman relied principally on this Rhode Island statute (General Laws 1956 § 9–1–4):

No action shall be brought:

(1) Whereby to charge any person upon any contract for the sale of lands, tenements, or hereditaments, or the making of any lease thereof for a longer time than one year; ... unless the promise or agreement upon which the action shall be brought, or some note or memorandum thereof, shall be in writing, and signed by the party to

be charged therewith, or by some other person by him or her thereunto lawfully authorized.]

■ Williams, Chief Justice ... One exception to this statute is that of part performance: When a party seeking enforcement of an oral contract "has performed to such an extent that repudiation of the contract would lead to an unjust or fraudulent result, the court will disregard the requirement of a writing and enforce an oral agreement." R.W.P. Concessions, Inc. v. Rhode Island Zoological Society, 487 A.2d 129, 131 (R.I.1985). A court generally will enforce an alleged oral contract pursuant to the doctrine of part performance only if a party can adequately demonstrate, in reliance on said agreement, possession of the property, improvements thereon, or payment of a substantial part of the purchase price. Pearl Brewing Co. v. McNaboe, 495 A.2d 238, 242 (R.I.1985) ("[t]aking possession of property ... together with making improvements or paying a substantial part of the purchase price, is generally sufficient to avoid the bar of the statute of frauds"); R.W.P. Concessions, Inc., at 131 ("the terms of the agreement must be clear and the possession or improvements in reliance thereon must be substantial and clearly shown"). "[P]art payment of the purchase price, possession or making improvements severally might not be sufficient to remove the case, yet a combination of all may be." Najarian v. Boyajian, 136 A. 767, 768 (R.I.1927). We note, however, that the statute of frauds is not to be taken lightly, and any partial performance must unequivocally indicate the existence of the purported oral agreement. See Messner Vetere Berger McNamee Schmetterer Euro RSCG, Inc. v. Aegis Group PLC, 711 N.E.2d 953, 956 (N.Y.1999) ("Part performance alone, of course, is not sufficient. The performance must be unequivocally referable to the agreement."); 4 Corbin on Contracts (Statute of Frauds) § 18.11 (rev. ed. 1997).

1. Possession

Norman first argues that the trial justice erred in finding that Jennifer and Gregory satisfied the requisite possession prong of the part performance exception. He claims that Jennifer and Gregory took possession of the Tiverton property pursuant to an oral agreement to *rent* the premises long before the alleged oral promise for conveyance; therefore, Norman suggests, the possession could not have been pursuant to an oral contract to purchase the property.

Although the commencement of a possession contemporaneous to an alleged oral agreement typically might satisfy the possession requirement, a continued or existing possession will not necessarily preclude application of the part performance doctrine. In fact, the authorities are largely in accord that the operative inquiry is whether a possession adequately indicates the existence of an oral contract:

> The continuance in possession by a purchaser who is already in possession may, in a proper case, be sufficiently referable to the parol contract of sale to constitute a part performance thereof. There may be additional acts or peculiar circumstances which sufficiently refer the possession to the contract. So, a prior possession by the purchaser is not an absolute bar to proof of a change in the character of the

possession after the making of a parol contract of sale, although it may cast upon the purchaser the burden of showing that his continued possession is referable to the contract.

Herbstreith v. Walls, 25 N.W.2d 409, 411 (Neb.1946) (quoting 49 Am. Jur. *Statute of Frauds* § 442 at 748); see also [two other cases cited, and] 4 Corbin on Contracts § 18.14 at 538; Restatement (Second) Contracts § 129 (1981).

In the present matter, sufficient competent evidence was presented to support a finding that the continued possession of the Tiverton property by Gregory and Jennifer adequately indicated the existence of the purported oral contract to constitute a part performance thereof. First, the ledger notations made in Norman's own hand begin on June 1, 2001, and indicate receipt of regular $140 payments, and later $100 payments, from Gregory and Jennifer, which were deducted from a $70,000 figure in one ledger. Both Gregory and Jennifer testified that this $70,000 figure represented the negotiated sale price of the Tiverton property. Jennifer testified that the remaining portion of the money paid weekly to Norman was applied to property taxes and insurance. Taken together, this is strong evidence that the nature of the possession of the Tiverton property had changed on or about the dates Jennifer and Gregory claimed as the date of actual contract formation.

Furthermore, many of the improvements were made to the property after the agreement. Norman's own son, Gregory, testified, in the face of contrary evidence from his father, that Norman permitted these improvements because the house rightfully belonged to Gregory and Jennifer. In light of this evidence, we think the possession of the Tiverton property by Gregory and Jennifer satisfied this element of the part performance doctrine.

2. Improvements and Partial Payment

Norman next challenges the trial justice's findings regarding improvements made to the Tiverton property. Under the part performance doctrine, improvements to land purportedly made in reliance upon an oral contract must indicate the existence of the contract in such a way that the improvements "would have been improvident to make in the absence of some such contract, so that they are strong circumstantial evidence of its existence." 4 Corbin on Contracts § 18.15 at 541. Improvements in reliance on an alleged oral contract ordinarily must be permanent. *R.W.P. Concessions, Inc.*, 487 A.2d at 132.

Norman first argues that the trial justice committed reversible error in deeming the improvements made to the Tiverton property to be "substantial" enough to trigger the part performance exception. He contends that the total cost of the improvements made after the agreement—which he values between $2,075 and $2,375—constituted slightly more than 1 percent of the stipulated value of the property, and thus could not be "substantial." Without even reaching whether Norman's assessment of the value of the improvements is factually accurate, we cannot agree with his argument.

First, we note that this Court has never held that the question of whether improvements suffice to constitute part performance turns upon their cost in relation to the total value of the improved property. In *R.W.P. Concessions, Inc.*, 487 A.2d at 131, 132, this Court did recognize that even a substantial expenditure of time and money was insufficient to constitute part performance when improvements to ready a concession stand were easily removable "at the termination of the operating relationship." Yet this is certainly not the case in the present matter, where Jennifer and Gregory imbued the Tiverton property with significant "sweat equity." Specifically, the addition of new doors and a banister, the replacement of floors, and the renovation of bedrooms—all of which Norman concedes took place after the agreement—are improvements not easily removable from the premises, and therefore would have been improvident absent an enforceable contract for the sale of the Tiverton property.

[The court expressed the view that the post-agreement improvements were "sufficient evidence to indicate the existence of an oral agreement."]

Finally, even if the improvements by themselves were insufficient to constitute part performance, some combination of improvements, substantial payment of the purchase price, or possession can be enough. *Najarian* at 768. An independent review of the evidence presented in this case leads us to conclude that the oral contract should be honored. Jennifer and Gregory paid Norman $140 per week from June 1, 2001, until April 12, 2002, when the couple reduced the weekly payments to $100; all these payments were deducted from a $70,000 figure, as evidenced by a ledger kept by Norman. Both Jennifer and Gregory testified that this $70,000 was the negotiated purchase price of the property. The purchase price was later reduced by $22,000 to account for a $30,000 home equity loan taken out by Norman, less an $8,000 private loan from Norman to Gregory and Jennifer. We hold that these payments toward the purchase price of the Tiverton property and the several permanent improvements made thereon, together with the continued possession, sufficiently constitute part performance of the oral contract.

We did not easily or quickly conclude that there was sufficient part performance in this case. This was a close and difficult case for this Court. We would advise bench and bar that we consider the statute of frauds to be as important as it is venerable. We shall continue to look with some degree of skepticism upon the claims of any party who seeks to escape from the statutory mandate by invoking an exception. . . .

Conclusion

For the reasons stated herein, the decision of the Family Court is affirmed. Norman shall convey said property to Jennifer and Gregory for the balance due on the purchase price. [The court directed some monetary adjustments, and remanded to the Family Court.]

NOTES

(1) *Questions.* (a) If an oral purchase agreement is substantiated better by the fact that the purchaser took possession at or after the time of the agreement than

by the fact that the purchaser *remained* in possession, why is it? (b) Apparently Norman knew of the improvements as they were being made. The court made nothing of that fact, however, except in relation to the element of possession. Would the opinion have been more convincing if the court had stressed that fact in part 2 of the opinion? If so, why? (c) Suppose that Norman had received a stream of monthly payments from the claimants, beginning after the leasing agreement. Is it possible to imagine an explanation for those payments, other than an agreement for sale, that is at least equally plausible?

(2) *Part Performance Elsewhere.* In professing that it was serious about the Statute of Frauds, the Rhode Island court echoed others. Writing for the New York Court of Appeals, Judge Cardozo said:

> Not every act of part performance will move a court of equity, though legal remedies are inadequate, to enforce an oral agreement affecting rights in land. There must be performance "unequivocally referable" to the agreement, performance which alone and without the aid of words of promise is unintelligible or at least extraordinary unless as an incident of ownership, assured, if not existing. "An act which admits of explanation without reference to the alleged oral contract or a contract of the same general nature and purpose is not, in general, admitted to constitute part performance" (Woolley v. Stewart, 222 N.Y. 347, 351). What is done must itself supply the key to what is promised. It is not enough that what is promised may give significance to what is done. The housekeeper who abandons other prospects of establishment in life and renders service without pay upon the oral promise of her employer to give her a life estate in land must find her remedy in an action to recover the value of the service.... Her conduct, separated from the promise, is not significant of ownership either present or prospective.... On the other hand, the buyer who not only pays the price, but possesses and improves his acre, may have relief in equity without producing a conveyance.... His conduct is itself the symptom of a promise that a conveyance will be made. Laxer tests may prevail in other jurisdictions [naming one]. We have been consistent here.

Burns v. McCormick, 135 N.E. 273 (1922). The courts of Tennessee are, exceptionally, even less lax. They have "consistently ... refused to enforce an oral contract for the sale of land on the basis of part performance alone. [I]t is now a rule of property in this state that part performance of a parol contract for the sale of land will not take the agreement out of the statute of frauds." Baliles v. Cities Service Co., 578 S.W.2d 621 (Tenn.1979).

New York courts cannot well take that position, for the applicable New York statute on the subject contains this provision: "Nothing contained in this section abridges the powers of courts of equity to compel the specific performance of agreements in cases of part performance." Gen.Oblig.Law 5–703(4).

The passage by Cardozo quoted above indicates that when part performance overrides the statute it does so because it is probative of the making of the alleged agreement. But that was written in 1922. There is some indication that the New York Court of Appeals has shifted its ground, believing that part performance works its magic by weighting the equities in favor of enforcement. In 1999 Judge Robert Smith wrote, for that court, that "the doctrine of part performance is based upon the equitable principle that it would be a fraud to allow one party, insisting on the Statute, to escape performance after permitting the other party, acting in reliance, to substantially perform...." This was said in *Messner Vetere*, cited near the end of first paragraph quoted from Richard v. Richard, at p. 281. That being so, Judge Smith wrote, "the acts of part performance must have been those of the party insisting on the contract, not those of the party insisting on the Statute of Frauds." *Ibid*.

If part performance works its magic because it is probative of the agreement, it is hard to see why conduct of the party insisting on the Statute does not count. On the other hand, the *Messner* opinion cites the Cardozo opinion for the proposition that "The performance must be unequivocally referable to the agreement."

What rationale seems to have informed the opinion in Richard v. Richard?

(3) *Agents without Written Authority*. Employers should be alert to the requirement that real-property sale agreements made by their employees, as agents, should be supported by a written authorization. So should lawyers and their clients. For a rescue operation on behalf of a client, see Halstead v. Murray, 547 A.2d 202 (N.H.1988).

(C) Sales of Goods

This part deals primarily with UCC § 2–201: "Formal Requirements; Statute of Frauds." The section is a descendant of the classical Statute of Frauds, although it is considerably more elaborate. Some other sections of the Code amount to statutes of frauds. One appears in Article 2A ("Leases"; see UCC § 2A–201). According to Article 9 ("Secured Transactions"), the authentication of a security agreement by the debtor is one way of meeting an evidentiary requirement for the enforceability of the agreement, in full, against the debtor and third parties.

UCC § 2–201(1)

UCC § 2–201(1) provides:

(1) Except as otherwise provided in this section a contract for the sale of goods for the price of $500 or more is not enforceable by way of action or defense unless there is some writing sufficient to indicate

that a contract for sale has been made between the parties and signed by the party against whom enforcement is sought or by his authorized agent or broker. A writing is not insufficient because it omits or incorrectly states a term agreed upon but the contract is not enforceable under this paragraph beyond the quantity of goods shown in such writing.

Two phrases in subsection (1) warrant close attention: "contract for the sale of goods," and "sufficient to indicate that a contract for sale has been made." To give a wide sense to the former would tend to amplify the requirement of documentation; to give a wide sense to the latter would tend to diminish it.

PROBLEM

The manager of Alpha Inc. sent an e-mail to Beta Inc., in which the subject line contained this entry: "Re: Steel Scrap for Egypt." In its entirety the body of the message read:

Thanks for your offer per phone earlier today, i.e.:

about 25–30,000 MT HMS1, your option
about 10–5,000 MT P & S, your option
_____

about 30–35,000 MT total, your option
for shipment anytime August, 2006, your option
Price: HMS–USD 300/MT
        P&S–USD 305/MT

As the parties understood, "MT" referred to metric tons, "USD" meant United States dollars, and the other acronyms referred to grades of scrap steel.

Beta has brought an action against Alpha, alleging an agreement to buy steel scrap from it, and a breach of that agreement. Alpha contends that UCC § 2–201 makes any such agreement unenforceable. There is no other documentation. One point made by Alpha is that the e-mail gives no indication whether Alpha is the buyer or the seller. On reading subsection (1), does it appear that this omission is critical? Comment 1 says it is not.

What other ground is there for thinking that the e-mail does not suffice for Beta's purpose? See American Iron & Metal Co. v. U.S. Ferrous ... Tube City Division, 2007 WL 1125682 (D.Conn. 2007). In solving this problem, recall that electronic documentation may satisfy Statute of Frauds requirements; see discussion at p. 268 above.

UCC § 2–201(2)

UCC § 2–201(2) provides:

(2) Between merchants if within a reasonable time a writing in confirmation of the contract and sufficient against the sender is received and the party receiving it has reason to know its contents, it

satisfies the requirements of subsection (1) against such party unless written notice of objection to its contents is given within ten days after it is received.

Although this subsection consists of a single sentence, its application depends on a considerable set of circumstances. Parsing the sentence yields six circumstances. It may help to examine them, as follows, more or less in reverse order:

—The recipient of a message has let ten days go by without having responded to it, or if any response was made within that time it was not a "written notice of objection to [the] contents" of the message.

—The recipient had "reason to know" the contents of the message.

—The message was "a writing in confirmation of the contract."

—It was such that, if the recipient were to bring an action to enforce the contract against the sender, that action would not fail under subsection (1), owing to the fact that the writing is "sufficient . . . and signed . . ." as indicated in that subsection.

—The message was sent "within a reasonable time"; and

—Both the sender and the recipient were "merchants."

Some observations about these elements will be helpful.

Ten days without objection. The ten days referred to begin with the receipt of the message.

What amounts to an objection to the contents of a message is not altogether clear. Comparisons are in order among this array of messages, each beginning "Today we have received your confirmation of the telephone order we placed a week ago for steel scrap to be resold to Egypt," and continuing differently, as follows.

(a) "You are in error. The scrap was to be delivered on April 1, not on May 1."

(b) "We see the price stated as $300 a ton. Although that was the price you named in our conversation, we understood, based on our course of prior dealings, that we would get a discount of 5% for volume."

(c) "We have decided to look elsewhere for this material. Don't ship."

Only the first of these appears to be a clear objection to the *contents* of the confirmation.

(Notice that it may not matter to the seller whether or not the buyer is bound under paragraph (2), owing to a failure to make the kind of objection contemplated there. It will not matter if the buyer has bound itself under paragraph (1). Each one of the three responses above appears to satisfy the requirement of a writing stated there. See Louisville Asphalt Varnish Co. v. Lorick, 8 S.E. 8 (S.C.1888). It will matter, however, if the response in question is unsigned. Also, if a buyer's response were that the confirmation overstated the quantity of goods ordered, paragraph (1) would limit enforcement to the lesser quantity.)

Reason to know. The recipient of a message will rarely lack reason to know its contents. One such reason might be that the message is contained in an envelope suggesting that it contains "junk mail," unrelated to the transaction, that need not be opened before being disposed of.

Sufficient against the sender. This is to say that one must ask, whether the claimant is a buyer or a seller, how the case would stand if the parties were reversed. In an action against a supposed buyer, for example, the question would be whether or not, in an action against the confirming seller the "writing in confirmation" would suffice to bind the seller under subsection (1).

Reasonable time. This expression has been given expansive readings, as shown by St. Ansgar Mills v. Streit, below.

Between merchants. UCC § 2–104 provides definitions of "merchant" and "between merchants." Aside from knowledge or skill imputed to a person or firm by reason of the knowledge of skill of an agent or the like, the key language there indicates that a "merchant" is a person

> who deals in goods of the kind or otherwise by his occupation holds himself out as having knowledge or skill peculiar to the practices or goods involved in the transaction . . .

Whether or not a farmer is a merchant with respect to products that he grows has been litigated considerably, with mixed results. Not so, the Kansas Supreme Court ruled, in an action against a farmer named Urban. The court did not doubt that he had special knowledge or skill in raising wheat. But, it said, "we do not think this factor, coupled with annual sales of a wheat crop and purchases of seed wheat, qualified him as a merchant in that field." Decatur Cooperative Asso. v. Urban, 547 P.2d 323, 328 (1976). The court was influenced by a reference to professionalism in a Comment to § 2–204.

PROBLEM

Cargill Incorporated, a major dealer in agricultural products, brought an action against Jorgenson Farms ("Farms"), alleging breach of a contract to supply it with 80,000 bushels of corn. Part of its evidence was a document titled "Contract #27985." James Jorgenson, a co-owner of Farms, acknowledged he had received that document in October 2003, in a packet of information. But Jorgenson said that he had not noticed the packet until later because October was "harvest time for us and I was busy in the fields." When Jorgenson did notice the document, he protested that there had been no agreement. In the previous July, however, Cargill had mailed to Farms what it called a "confirmation" of an oral sale agreement. Cargill contended that Farms had acquiesced in the supposed contract because it had failed to respond.

On an appeal by Cargill, the court approved a summary judgment against it. Cargill Incorporated v. Jorgenson Farms, 719 N.W.2d 226 (Minn.App.2006). The court said that "under the express terms of the document, no contract was formed." The so-called confirmation indicated that it was to be signed and returned to Cargill. It also said: "Please sign and date the original . . . copy of this contract. The original must be returned to Buyer. . . ."

Neither the trial nor the appellate court made any ruling on Farms's statute of frauds defense. The facts suggest, however, the question whether or not, if an oral agreement had been proved, as Cargill contended, UCC § 2–201 would have permitted its enforcement against Farms. An answer to that might turn on construing subsection (2).

Did either of the papers that Cargill sent Farms amount to what UCC § 2–201(2) calls a *confirmation*? And was either of them "sufficient against the sender [Cargill]"?

St. Ansgar Mills, Inc. v. Streit

Supreme Court of Iowa, 2000.
613 N.W.2d 289.

■ CADY, JUSTICE. A grain dealer appeals from an order by the district court granting summary judgment in an action to enforce an oral contract for the sale of corn based on a written confirmation. The district court held the oral contract was unenforceable because the written confirmation was not delivered within a reasonable time after the oral contract as a matter of law. We reverse the decision of the district court and remand for further proceedings.

I.   Background Facts and Proceedings.

St. Ansgar Mills, Inc. is a family-owned agricultural business located in Mitchell County. As a part of its business, St. Ansgar Mills buys corn from local grain farmers and sells corn to livestock farmers for feed. The price of the corn sold to farmers is established by trades made on the Chicago Board of Trade for delivery with reference to five contract months. The sale of corn for future delivery is hedged by St. Ansgar Mills through an offsetting futures position on the Chicago Board of Trade.

A sale is typically made when a farmer calls St. Ansgar Mills and requests a quote for a cash price of grain for future delivery based on the Chicago Board of Trade price for the delivery.[1] The farmer then accepts or rejects the price. If the price is accepted, St. Ansgar Mills protects the price through a licensed brokerage house by acquiring a hedge position on the Chicago Board of Trade. This hedge position, however, obligates St. Ansgar Mills to purchase the corn at the stated price at the time of delivery. Thus, St. Ansgar Mills relies on the farmer who purchased the grain to accept delivery at the agreed price.

[Duane Streit, the defendant, raised hogs and, assisted by his father, John Streit, operated a "hog finishing operation" which he had acquired from John in 1993.]

Duane and his father have been long-time customers of St. Ansgar Mills. Since 1989, Duane entered into numerous contracts with St. Ansgar Mills for the purchase of large quantities of corn and other grain products. Duane would generally initiate the purchase agreement by calling St. Ansgar Mills on the telephone to obtain a price quote. If an oral contract

---

1. This is not the exclusive method of sale. Another type of sale is based on an order contingent upon the cash price of the corn reaching a specific level. This type of sale, however, was not involved in this case.

was made, an employee of St. Ansgar Mills would prepare a written confirmation of the sale and either mail it to Duane to sign and return, or wait for Duane or John to sign the confirmation when they would stop into the business.

John would regularly stop by St. Ansgar Mills sometime during the first ten days of each month and pay the amount of the open account Duane maintained at St. Ansgar Mills for the purchase of supplies and other materials. On those occasions when St. Ansgar Mills sent the written confirmation to Duane, it was not unusual for Duane to fail to sign the confirmation for a long period of time. He also failed to return contracts sent to him. Nevertheless, Duane had never refused delivery of grain he purchased by telephone prior to the incident which gave rise to this case.

On July 1, 1996, John telephoned St. Ansgar Mills to place two orders for the purchase of 60,000 bushels of corn for delivery in December 1996 and May 1997. This order followed an earlier conversation between Duane and St. Ansgar Mills. After the order was placed, St. Ansgar Mills completed the written confirmation but set it aside for John to sign when he was expected to stop by the business to pay the open account. The agreed price of the December corn was $3.53 per bushel. The price of the May corn was $3.73 per bushel.

John failed to follow his monthly routine of stopping by the business during the month of July. St. Ansgar Mills then asked a local banker who was expected to see John to have John stop into the business.

John did not stop by St. Ansgar Mills until August 10, 1996. On that date, St. Ansgar Mills delivered the written confirmation to him.

Duane later refused delivery of the corn orally purchased on July 1, 1996. The price of corn had started to decline shortly after July 1, and eventually plummeted well below the quoted price on July 1. After Duane refused delivery of the corn, he purchased corn for his hog operations on the open market at prices well below the contract prices of July 1. St. Ansgar Mills later told Duane it should have followed up earlier with the written confirmation and had no excuse for not doing so.

St. Ansgar Mills then brought this action for breach of contract. It sought damages of $152,100, which was the difference between the contract price of the corn and the market price at the time Duane refused delivery.

Duane filed a motion for summary judgment. He claimed the oral contract alleged by St. Ansgar Mills was governed by the provisions of the Uniform Commercial Code, and was unenforceable as a matter of law under the statute of frauds. He claimed the written confirmation delivered to John on August 10, 1996 did not satisfy the statute of frauds for two reasons. First, he was not a merchant. Second, the confirmation was not received within a reasonable time after the alleged oral agreement.

The district court determined a jury question was presented on whether Duane was a merchant under the Uniform Commercial Code. However, the district court found the written confirmation did not satisfy the writing requirements of the statute of frauds because the delivery of the confirmation to John, as Duane's agent, did not occur within a reasonable time after the oral contract as a matter of law. The district court found the size of the order, the volatility of the grain market, and the lack of an explanation by St. Ansgar Mills for failing to send the confirmation to Duane after John failed to stop by the business as expected made the delay between July 1 and August 10 unreasonable as a matter of law.

St. Ansgar Mills appeals. It claims a jury question was presented on the issue of whether a written confirmation was received within a reasonable time.

II. Scope of Review.

We review a ruling for summary judgment for errors at law. Summary judgment is appropriate where the record indicates no genuine issue of material fact exists, therefore the moving party is entitled to judgment as a matter of law. When the facts are not in dispute, we decide whether the district court correctly applied the law to the facts. In doing so, we view the facts in the light most favorable to the party opposing the motion. [Citations in this paragraph omitted.]

III. Statute of Frauds.

The statute of frauds is one of the most well-known and venerable rules applicable to contract law. Generally, it establishes an exception to the proposition that oral contracts are enforceable in a lawsuit if sufficiently proven by requiring certain types of contracts to be in writing and signed by the party against whom enforcement is sought. See Iowa Code § 554.2201(1). [Hereafter in this report, the court's citations to that section are changed to "UCC § 2–201", and corresponding changes are made in the court's citations to other Code provisions.]

[Here the court recounted the history of the Statute of Frauds in England and in the United States at large.]

... Iowa adopted the statute of frauds in 1851.... The statute of frauds also became a part of the Uniform Sales Act in 1906, which Iowa subsequently adopted in 1924.... This statute required all contracts for the sale of goods to be in writing. Over time, the Uniform Sales Act was replaced by the Uniform Commercial Code. The Uniform Commercial Code continued to adhere to the statute of frauds, but was limited in its provisions to the sale of goods in excess of $500. Iowa enacted its version of the Uniform Commercial Code in 1966 including the statute of frauds. [Here the court set out the first sentence of Iowa's statute of frauds for the sale of goods, identical to the first sentence of UCC § 2–201, except that it uses the words "not enforced" in lieu of "not enforceable".]

Although the statute of frauds has been deeply engrained into our law, many of the forces which originally gave rise to the rule are no longer prevalent. J. White & R. Summers, [Uniform Commercial Code § 2–1, at 51 (2d ed. 1980)—hereafter "White & Summers"]. This, in turn, has caused some of the rigid requirements of the rule to be modified.

One statutory exception or modification to the statute of frauds which has surfaced applies to merchants.[2] UCC § 2–201(2). Under [that provision], the writing requirements of UCC § 2–201(1) are considered to be satisfied if, within a reasonable time, a writing in confirmation of the contract which is sufficient against the sender is received and the merchant receiving it has reason to know of its contents, unless written notice of objection of its contents is given within ten days after receipt. Id. Thus, a writing is still required, but it does not need to be signed by the party against whom the contract is sought to be enforced. The purpose of this exception was to put professional buyers and sellers on equal footing by changing the former law under which a party who received a written confirmation of an oral agreement of sale, but who had not signed anything, could hold the other party to a contract without being bound. See White & Summers § 2–3, at 55; Kimball County Grain Coop. v. Yung, 263 N.W.2d 818, 820 (Neb.1978). It also encourages the common, prudent business practice of sending memoranda to confirm oral agreements. White & Summers § 2–3, at 55.

While the written confirmation exception imposes a specific ten-day requirement for a merchant to object to a written confirmation, it employs a flexible standard of reasonableness to establish the time in which the confirmation must be received. . . . The Uniform Commercial Code specifically defines a reasonable time for taking action in relationship to "the nature, purpose and circumstances" of the action. UCC § 2–201(2). Additionally, the declared purpose of the Uniform Commercial Code is to permit the expansion of commercial practices through the custom and practice of the parties. See UCC § 1–102 cmt. 2 (course of dealings, usage of trade or course of performance are material in determining a reasonable time). Furthermore, the Uniform Commercial Code relies upon course of dealings between the parties to help interpret their conduct. UCC § 1–205(1). Thus, all relevant circumstances, including custom and practice of the parties, must be considered in determining what constitutes a reasonable time under UCC § 2–201(2).

Generally, the determination of the reasonableness of particular conduct is a jury question. See Pirelli–Armstrong Tire Co. v. Reynolds, 562 N.W.2d 433, 436 (Iowa 1997); see also Harvey v. Great Atl. & Pac. Tea Co., 388 F.2d 123, 125 (5th Cir. 1968) (passing judgment on the reasonableness of conduct of the parties must be accomplished in light of all the circumstances of the case and should rarely be disposed of by summary judgment). Thus, the reasonableness of time between an oral contract and a subse-

---

2. The Uniform Commercial Code establishes three general exceptions to the writing requirement: (1) goods made specially for the buyer and not suitable for resale to others towards which the seller has made a substantial beginning of their manufacture or commitments for their procurement; (2) where the party against whom enforcement is sought admits the existence of the contract in pleadings, testimony, or before the court; and (3) goods for which payment has been received and goods accepted. See UCC § 2–201(3)(a)–(c). Additionally, a contract "may be made in any manner sufficient to show agreement, including conduct by both parties which recognizes the existence of the contract." Id. § 2–204(1). The agreement which creates the contract qualifies even though the exact moment of its making is undetermined or terms are left open, so long as the parties intended to make a contract. Id. § 2–204(2), (3).

quent written confirmation is ordinarily a question of fact for the jury. MortgageAmerica Corp. v. American Nat'l Bank, 651 S.W.2d 851, 856 (Tex.Ct.App.1983); Schiavi Mobile Homes, Inc. v. Gagne, 510 A.2d 236, 238 (Me.1986) (reasonableness of parties' time for action is a question of fact). It is only in rare cases that a determination of the reasonableness of conduct should be decided by summary adjudication. *Harvey*, 388 F.2d at 125. Summary judgment is appropriate only when the evidence is so one-sided that a party must prevail at trial as a matter of law....

There are a host of cases from other jurisdictions which have considered the question of what constitutes a reasonable time under the written confirmation exception of the Uniform Commercial Code. See Gestetner Corp. v. Case Equip. Co., 815 F.2d 806, 810 (1st Cir.1987) (roughly five month delay reasonable in light of merchants' relationship and parties' immediate action under contract following oral agreement); Serna, Inc. v. Harman, 742 F.2d 186, 189 (5th Cir.1984) (three and one-half month delay reasonable in light of the parties' interaction in the interim, and non-fluctuating prices, thus no prejudice); Cargill, Inc. v. Stafford, 553 F.2d 1222, 1224 (10th Cir.1977) (less than one month delay unreasonable despite misdirection of confirmation due to mistaken addressing); Starry Constr. Co. v. Murphy Oil USA, Inc., 785 F.Supp. 1356, 1362–63 (D. Minn.1992) (six month delay for confirmation of modification order for additional oil unreasonable as a matter of law in light of Persian Gulf War, thus increased prices and demand); Rockland Indus., Inc. v. Frank Kasmir Assoc., 470 F.Supp. 1176, 1179 (N.D.Tex.1979) (letter sent eight months after alleged oral agreement for two-year continuity agreement unreasonable in light of lack of evidence supporting reasonableness of delay); *Yung*, 263 N.W.2d at 820 (six month delay in confirming oral agreement delivered one day prior to last possible day of delivery unreasonable); *Azevedo*, ?? 471 P.2d at 666 (ten week delay reasonable in light of immediate performance by both parties following oral agreement); Lish v. Compton, 547 P.2d 223, 226–27 (Utah 1976) (twelve day delay "outside the ambit which fair-minded persons could conclude to be reasonable" in light of volatile price market and lack of excuse for delay other than casual delay). Most of these cases, however, were decided after a trial on the merits and cannot be used to establish a standard or time period as a matter of law. Only a few courts have decided the question as a matter of law under the facts of the case. *Compare Starry*, 785 F.Supp. at 1362–63 (granting summary judgment), and *Lish*, 547 P.2d at 226–27 (removing claim from jury's consideration), *with* Barron v. Edwards, 206 N.W.2d 508, 511 (Mich.Ct.App.1973) (remanding for further development of facts, summary judgment improper). However, these cases do not establish a strict principle to apply in this case. The resolution of each case depends upon the particular facts and circumstances.

In this case, the district court relied upon the large amount of the sale, volatile market conditions, and lack of an explanation by St. Ansgar Mills for failing to send the written confirmation to Duane in determining St. Ansgar Mills acted unreasonably as a matter of law in delaying delivery of the written confirmation until August 10, 1996. Volatile market conditions, combined with a large sale price, would normally narrow the window of reasonable time under UCC § 2–201(2). However, they are not the only factors to consider. Other relevant factors which must also be considered in this case reveal the parties had developed a custom or practice to delay delivery of the confirmation. The parties also maintained a long-time amicable business relationship and had engaged in many other similar business transactions without incident. There is also evidence to infer St. Ansgar Mills did not suspect John's failure to follow his customary practice in July of stopping by the business was a concern at the time. These factors reveal a genuine dispute over the reasonableness of the delay in delivering the written confirmation, and make the resolution of the issue appropriate for the jury. Moreover, conduct is not rendered unreasonable solely because the acting party had no particular explanation for not pursuing different conduct, or regretted not pursuing different conduct in retrospect. The reasonableness of conduct is determined by the facts and circumstances existing at the time.

Considering our principles governing summary adjudication and the need to resolve the legal issue by considering the particular facts and circumstances of each case, we conclude the trial court erred by granting summary judgment. We reverse and remand the case for further proceedings.

Reversed and remanded.

————

UCC § 2–201(3)

UCC § 2–201(3) is found in *Selections*. In the circumstances stated in UCC § 2–201(3)(a), either party can enforce an oral agreement for the sale of custom goods, once the seller has passed a certain point in their production or procurement. The Comments to Section 2–201 do not mention this provision, on the assumption, apparently, that its merits are obvious. It has this obvious merit: It prevents hardship to a seller who has relied seriously on the agreement before the buyer renounces it, and who would otherwise be uncompensated. Granting that, it does not explain why enforcement *by the buyer* is permitted. Another merit can be ascribed to paragraph (a): It permits enforcement of an agreement when there is evidence to substantiate the testimony of a party that the agreement, although not recorded, was in fact made. In an action by a self-described "seller," that evidence is the claimant's investment in goods having little or no value to anyone other than the supposed buyer. The evidence is probative on the assumption that the claimant's conduct would not make sense, absent an agreement providing her with compensation for it. This line of thought can help to explain why the paragraph permits enforcement *against* a seller, when the claimant is a buyer.

Paragraph (c) lifts the bar of the statute in some situations of performance on both sides: goods tendered by the seller and "received and accepted" by the buyer. It lifts the bar also in some situations of performance on one side only: perhaps the only act of performance was that of the buyer, in paying for some or all of the goods in advance. Unlike paragraph (a), paragraph (c) does not lift the bar with respect to the agreement as a whole, but only with respect to goods paid for, or received and accepted.

Like paragraph (a), paragraph (c) serves, in part, to prevent hardship that might result from a party's reliance on an oral agreement. It may also share with paragraph (a) the merit of permitting the enforcement of agreements to the extent of goods accepted, and payment made, which tend to substantiate the making of the agreement.

Paragraph (b) is about parties who, "in court," would both admit that a contract of sale was made and invoke the statute against its enforcement. With respect to "the quantity of goods admitted," the admission lifts the bar. A proposed amendment would substitute "under oath" for "in court."

ESTOPPEL AND UCC § 2-201

The point has been made, at pp. 263-64 above, that sometimes a person's detrimental reliance on an agreement serves as a reason to enforce it, even though enforcement would otherwise be barred by a statute of frauds. In the context of UCC Article 2, however, some courts have concluded that the text of UCC § 2-201 precludes resort to estoppel. The debate concerns the interaction between two Code provisions, UCC §§ 1-103(b) and 2-201(1).

UCC § 1-103(b) provides (with emphasis added) that

> *Unless displaced by the particular provisions of [the Uniform Commercial Code]*, the principles of law and equity, including ... the law relating to ... estoppel ... shall supplement its provisions.

This provision suggests that, as is the case outside the UCC, estoppel may be used to enforce some contracts whose enforcement would otherwise be barred by a statute of frauds.

But UCC § 1-103(b) may be limited by the opening seven words of UCC § 2-201(1): "Except as otherwise provided *in this section....*" The italicized passage suggests that the only exceptions to the Article 2 statute of frauds must be found in that section, which contains no reference to estoppel.

Opposing views about the interaction of these two provisions are expressed in a number of opinions, including Warder & Lee Elevator, Inc. v. Britten, 274 N.W.2d 339 (Iowa 1979) (divided court), Lige Dickson Co. v. Union Oil Co., 635 P.2d 103 (Wash.1981), and B & W Glass, Inc. v. Weather Shield Mfg., Inc., 829 P.2d 809 (Wyo.1992).

The Supreme Court of Wyoming espoused estoppel in *B & W Glass*, above. In that opinion, the judges said that the "Except" phrase in subsection (1) does not displace general principles of law, such as estoppel:

The effect [of the opening phrase of § 2–201(1)] ... is to alert the reader that the remaining subsections are disjunctive, and it serves to advise the reader of the proposition that the statutory exceptions to the statute of frauds are contained in subsections [(1) and (2) of § 2–201].

The Wyoming court found support in Comment 1 to UCC § 1–103 (as that Comment appeared before the 2001 revision to Article 1), indicating that displacement of general principles is to be found only where another Code provision is explicit on the point. "Neither the text of § 2–201 nor the comments following it specifically refer to estoppel," the court said.

For the view that UCC § 2–201 displaces estoppel see *Lige Dickson* and the dissent by Justice Reynoldson in *Warder & Lee Elevator*. Justice Reynoldson said:

It is a rare case when either promisor in a bilateral contract does not rely on [it]. Most situations in which such an oral contract is breached result in injustice. But [UCC § 2–201] obviously is designed to suffer these injustices in isolated oral contract cases in favor of the general public policy to reduce fraud and perjury, curtail litigation and controversy, and encourage written contracts in sales of goods for a price of $500 or more.... It is significant that by trial time the plaintiff corporation [Elevator] was using written sales contracts with its customers.

Cognizant of the enduring and important debate about the matter, the sponsors of the Code have proposed to resolve it by deleting the opening seven words in UCC § 2–201(1). Explaining the change, in Comment 2 to the proposed amendment, they have said:

[It] was made to provide that the statement of the three statutory exceptions in subsection (3) should not be read as limiting ... the possibility that a promisor will be estopped to raise the statute-of-frauds defense in appropriate cases.

NOTES

(1) *Favoritism?* As indicated above buyers have encountered headwinds in trying to enforce oral sale-of-goods agreements by reason of their prejudicial reliance. The proposed revision of UCC § 2–201 is designed to reverse the direction of the winds. In a case of reliance by a seller, subsection (3)(a) operates in its favor when the goods concerned are custom goods, and the reliance takes one of the forms described there. Otherwise, it may well be that a seller's reliance counts for nothing. When a seller's reliance counts in its favor, it counts also in favor of the buyer; see the discussion of subsection (3)(a) at p. 294 above. Reliance by a buyer does not support enforcement in favor of the seller.

If these arrangements do not exhibit favoritism for buyers, they indicate at least that the relation between UCC § 2–201 and estoppel was not thought through fully by drafters of the section.

(2) *Problem.* Suppose, to change the facts in *B & W Glass*, that Weather had announced, before Glass committed itself to the courthouse job, that it would not supply Glass with windows. Rather, at that time Glass had made a bid to the general contractor, based on Weather's price. Glass could have withdrawn that bid, but the time had passed for it to submit a revised bid. If the actual case was an appropriate one for an estoppel against Weather, is this case a far less appropriate one? See Edward Joy Co. v. Noise Control Products, Inc., 443 N.Y.S.2d 361 (Sup.Ct.1981).

(3) *Restitution and Reliance.* Liability for a benefit received, when required to prevent unjust enrichment, is, like estoppel, a "principle of law," although not one mentioned by name in UCC § 1–103(b). On examining UCC § 2–201, does it appear that this liability is displaced with respect to unenforceable agreements for sales of goods? If so, perhaps removing the "Except" clause from the section would reinstate the liability.

Or perhaps not. Observe that subsection (3)(c) tends to prevent the unjust enrichment of buyers who have taken delivery of goods on credit. Conceivably that is all that UCC § 2–201 contemplates in the way of redress for unjust enrichment. If so, the section is oppressive for buyers who have made prepayments for goods contracted for, and find that their contracts are unenforceable.

———

(D) THE SURETYSHIP CLAUSE

———

SURETYSHIP AGREEMENTS

By the law of every state, an undertaking to be a surety is not enforceable, as a rule, unless it is expressed in a signed writing. The words *surety* and *suretyship* are used to designate agreements within a clause of the Statute of Frauds, although they do not appear in the classical Statute or in statutes that track its language. The usual language is quoted on p. 261 above. The conception of suretyship is touched on there, and is more fully developed here. The Illinois version of the suretyship clause states:

> No action shall be brought ... whereby to charge the defendant upon any special promise to answer for the debt, default or miscarriage of another person ... unless the promise or agreement upon which such action shall be brought, or some memorandum or note thereof, shall be in writing, and signed by the party to be charged therewith, or some other person thereunto by him lawfully authorized.

740 ILCS 80/1. For a catalog of agreements that are and are not "within the Statute of Frauds as a contract to answer for the duty of another," see Restatement, Third, Suretyship & Guaranty § 11.

One reason for the suretyship clause of the Statute of Frauds is that a creditor, or other obligee, may be tempted to fabricate evidence of a suretyship promise when faced with insolvency on the part of an obligor, or when fearing insolvency. "More certain evidence is required when one promises to pay the debt of another because '[t]here is . . . a temptation for a promisee, in a case where the real debtor has proved insolvent or unable to pay, to enlarge the scope of the promise, or to torture mere words of encouragement and confidence into an absolute promise.'" Davis v. Patrick, 141 U.S. 479, 487–88 (1891). The target of abuse of that kind is likely to be a person or firm of substantial means, of course. (When a debt is paid by a surety, the principal debtor is not discharged. The creditor may be quite willing to assign—transfer—to the payor its claim against the debtor; and even if not, the paying surety is entitled to assert that claim by the equitable doctrine of subrogation. But an assignment or subrogation is likely to be cold comfort if the primary obligor is insolvent.)

Another reason for the suretyship clause is concern that, when solicited to become a surety, a person may do so incautiously, not appreciating how serious the consequence may be. To some extent the requirement of a signed writing is a safeguard against that.

An example of a suretyship contract is as follows. Eager wants to enter business by buying an existing shop. He does not have the funds to pay more than a quarter of the owner's asking price. Say that the business is a shoe shop, owned by Founder. Founder will give Eager credit for 3/4ths of the price, but only if it is backed by an assurance of payment, given by a person of means. Eager's father-in-law is well-to-do, believes in the investment, and wants to assist. He therefore promises Founder, when the sale is arranged, to see that, in time, Founder gets payment in full. That promise, not being recorded in any way, is unenforceable.

The term *guaranty* is sometimes conflated with *suretyship contract*, and sometimes distinguished. "A surety's obligation is not conditioned upon another's default. A guarantor, on the other hand, is liable to a creditor only if the debtor does not meet the duties owed to the creditor. . . . The terms surety and guarantor are often confused though they have different meanings." Landover Corp. v. Bellevue Master, LLC, 2006 WL 47662 (W.D.Wash. 2006), *aff'd*, Landover Corp. v. Bellevue Master LLC, 252 Fed.Appx. 800 (9th Cir.2007). Different they may be; but for purposes of the suretyship clause a guarantor is a surety.

What is *not* a suretyship contract requires some attention. A *novation* is not. Broadly speaking, a novation is a change in a contract, substituting one party for another. A narrower use of the word *novation* is common: a substitution of one obligor for another. "A novation is the substitution of parties to a contract with the intent to discharge the initial debtor." *Landover Corp.* on appeal (unpublished). If Beta agrees effectively to pay a debt of Alpha, substituting himself for Alpha as the debtor, that is a novation. The agreement is effective only if the creditor consents to it, and there is consideration running to Beta. The consideration may be no more than the release of Alpha's obligation. (When it is no more than that, it may be supposed that Beta has a benevolent attitude toward Alpha.)

In a situation of suretyship, two persons are bound at some juncture by the same obligation. That is not the effect of a novation. Some agreements having that effect are not suretyship agreements, however. An example would be a promise by Beta, *given to Alpha*, that Beta will pay a debt owed by Alpha. The effectiveness of that agreement would not depend on the creditor's consent. A consideration running to Beta would be a requisite, unless Beta's undertaking were to become binding by reason of reliance on it. (The creditor, learning of Beta's promise, might rely on it by refraining from taking action to collect from Alpha until all of Alpha's assets have been consumed or applied to his other debts.) Beta's promise, as supposed, would not be within the suretyship clause, because it was not directed to the creditor.

An undertaking to make a payment, made to a debtor, is sometimes described as an "original" one, not subject to the suretyship clause, as opposed to a "collateral" one, which is. The opinion that follows illustrates the distinction.

Question. If a promise by Beta to pay Alpha's debt is made both to Alpha and to Alpha's creditor, in a conversation among the three of them, should it be regarded as a promise within the suretyship clause?

———

LANGMAN v. ALUMNI ASSOCIATION OF THE UNIVERSITY OF VIRGINIA, 442 S.E.2d 669 (Va.1994). [The Alumni Association acceded to a "gift" that proved, later, to be burdensome to it. The gift was a deed to a commercial property called "Ferdinand's Arcade." One of the donors was Dr. M.W. Langman. The Association acknowledged the gift and had the deed recorded. When the donors had bought the property, they incurred a debt and granted a lien (mortgage) on the property to secure the debt. Their deed to the Association referred to the debt, and continued:

> The Grantee [Association] does hereby assume payment of such obligation and agrees to hold the Grantors harmless from further liability on such obligation.

Dr. Langman brought this action against the Association a few years later. The loan charges and expenses of operating the Arcade had outrun the income it produced. Langham had had to pay part of the debt that came due following the gift, and she sought reimbursement under the debt-assumption clause quoted above.[a]

The trial court ruled for the Association, finding that it had "no clear understanding of the deed's contents" and that there had been no meeting of the minds with respect to the debt.[b] Langman appealed].

---

a. The other donor, Caleb Stowe, had borne some of the post-transfer charges, writing that off as a gift. Following a business failure, however, he had discontinued payments on the debt.

b. Further findings: The debt-assumption clause was mistakenly placed in the deed by an unknown draftsman; the Association "did not knowingly accept the gift with contractual conditions"; the deed contained provisions contrary to the parties' intentions;

■ BARBARA MILANO KEENAN, JUSTICE. [First, the court rejected some findings by the trial court, saying that the evidence supporting them had been erroneously admitted.]

A grantee who accepts a deed becomes contractually bound by its provisions, and becomes liable to perform any promise or undertaking imposed by the deed on the grantee, including a promise to assume an existing mortgage....

[Next, the court described an argument made by the Association, based on the suretyship clause of the Statute of Frauds, as enacted in Virginia— quoted as in the footnote.[c] From this provision, the Association argued that, because it had not signed a written agreement to assume the mortgage, it was not accountable.] The Alumni Association asserts that, because Langman would remain secondarily liable ... on the mortgage debt even after an effective assumption of the debt, the Alumni Association's agreement to assume the mortgage was a "collateral" promise falling within the scope of Code § 11–2(4). We disagree.

A grantee who assumes an existing mortgage is not a surety. The grantee makes no promise to the mortgagee to pay the debt of another, but promises the grantor to pay to the mortgagee the debt the grantee owes to the grantor. This is an original undertaking. Blanton v. Keneipp, 155 Va. 668, 678, 156 S.E. 413, 416 (1931)....

A collateral undertaking to which Code § 11–2(4) applies is one in which the promisor is merely a surety or guarantor, receives no direct benefit, and is liable only if the debtor defaults. Colonial Ford Truck Sales, Inc. v. Schneider, 325 S.E.2d 91, 93–94 (Va.1985). Here, the Alumni Association received a direct benefit and did not merely act as surety for the grantors. Therefore, we conclude that the trial court did not err in ruling that the statute of frauds does not bar enforcement of the mortgage assumption clause.

NOTE

Corporate Buyouts. A "bilateral agreement to assume a debt" is, as has been said, a common sort of business deal, and can be enforced although it is not recorded. When a new investor acquires control of a business firm, or acquires its principal assets, the cash price may be sharply reduced upon the investor's agreement to undertake some or all of the firm's long-term debt. The following observations apply, taking the investor to be the "promisor" and the seller to be the "original debtor":

and, by disavowing its obligation, the Association had "sufficiently rejected the gift to require a finding ... that the conveyance is ineffective."

The trial court rejected contentions of the Association that the mortgage assumption clause was unenforceable on the basis of actual or constructive fraud, of mutual mistake, or of unilateral mistake induced by inequitable conduct, or by reason of failure of consideration. These rulings were sustained on appeal.

c. Unless a promise, contract, agreement, representation, assurance, or ratification, or some memorandum or note thereof, is in writing and signed by the party to be charged or his agent, no action shall be brought in any of the following cases ...

To charge any person upon a promise to answer for the debt, default, or misdoings of another[.]

[I]f, as between the promisor and the original debtor, the promisor is bound to pay, the debt is his own and not within the statute [of frauds]. "Contrariwise if as between them the original debtor still ought to pay, the debt cannot be the promisor's own and he is undertaking to answer for the debt of another." (Witschard v. Brody & Sons, 257 N.Y. 97, 177 N.E. 385, quoting 1 Williston, Contracts, § 472.) In the latter case the promise is unenforceable in the absence of some memorandum.

Martin Roofing, Inc. v. Goldstein, 457 N.E.2d 700, 701 (N.Y.1983).

CURRENT OBLIGATION

It has sometimes been said that one cannot become a surety by giving an assurance that an *anticipated* debt will be paid—a debt expected to arise in the future. A test case arose when Caterpillar, Inc. made a promise to see that a provider of skilled nursing, Rosewood Care Center, would be paid for giving care to Betty Jo Cook. Cook, an employee of Caterpillar, had suffered a workplace injury, had been hospitalized for some months, and had made a workers' compensation claim against Caterpillar. Rosewood admitted Cook as a patient at the request of Dr. Norma Just, employed by Caterpillar to arrange for medical care in this and like cases. Dr. Just told Rosewood that Cook's care would be "100% covered," and she asked that the bills be sent to Caterpillar's workers' compensation division.

Not being paid in full, Rosewood brought an action against Caterpillar (and Cook). The "facts" just recited are those asserted by Rosewood. The trial court dismissed the action, referring to the suretyship clause of the Statute of Frauds. On a first appeal, the Illinois Appellate Division reversed. It relied on precedents which, it thought, limited the conception of "surety" to one who makes an undertaking with respect to an obligation of another that is already outstanding or that arises concurrently with the undertaking. Caterpillar could not have been a surety for Cook, that court thought, because Cook had no obligation to Rosewood when Caterpillar made its promise.

On a further appeal, Caterpillar had somewhat more success: the court reversed and remanded. As to the supposed limitation, the court said that "[it] is not supported by the statutory language nor is it commensurate with the purposes underlying the statute of frauds." Rosewood Care Center, Inc. v. Caterpillar, Inc., 877 N.E.2d 1091, 1095 (Ill.2007). (The court spoke of the limitation as the *preexisting debt rule*. It is referred to here as the *current-obligation* rule.)

NOTE

Original or Collateral? Following the remand in *Rosewood Care Center* the claimant still faced a statute of frauds problem. The trial court was left free to determine whether Caterpillar's promise was collateral to Cook's liability or was simply its own undertaking. What kinds of evidence might be helpful in this connection? What of testimony by Dr. Just that she meant, on behalf of Caterpillar, to assure Rosewood that it would not suffer from Cook's failure to pay? Or testimony on behalf of Rosewood that it understood Dr. Just to mean "Don't bother Cook; we'll just pay for her care"?

A court might prefer evidence less subjective than testimony about someone's state of mind. What more objective evidence might be introduced?

———

THE MAIN–PURPOSE RULE

Central Ceilings, Inc. v. National Amusements, Inc.

Appeals Court of Massachusetts, 2007.
70 Mass.App.Ct. 172, 873 N.E.2d 754.

[Central Ceilings (Central) was engaged in March of 2000 to do carpentry and other work on a projected theater complex, the owner of which was National Amusements. Central was a subcontractor; the prime contractor was the Old Colony Construction Corporation (Old Colony). By mid-summer all three firms were under some stress. The date for which completion of the complex had been first scheduled had just passed. Completion had been rescheduled for September 3. A delay beyond that seemed likely. The owner cared about delay, partly because it hoped to outstrip competitors. Old Colony had its own problems—unpaid bills and a cash shortage. That led Central to worry about getting payments from Old Colony. Agents of the three firms conferred about their concerns on or about July 1. At the conference, Central's man, McPherson, said to National's man, Brady, "you've got to guarantee me the payment. You've got to guarantee me that I will get funded for this project." Brady said that he would guarantee McPherson.

Central continued work, having been promised that National would pay, in time, what Old Colony owed it on the project. Months later, when National learned that it owed nothing more to Old Colony, it resisted paying Central. Central sued National for breach of contract, and won a verdict and judgment for some $600,000. National appealed. One argument it made was that its guaranty was not supported by a consideration. That was a colorable argument, as will be seen in Chapter 4; but it failed.

First, however, the court addressed another defensive argument. The court said: "The principal issue before us ... is whether enforcement of the oral agreement is barred by the Statute of Frauds." The relevant part of the applicable statute (Massachusetts General Laws chapter 259) is as follows:

§ 1.   Certain Contracts Actionable Only if in Writing.

No action shall be brought: ...

Second, To charge a person upon a special promise to answer for the debt, default or misdoings of another; ...

Unless the promise, contract or agreement upon which such action is brought, or some memorandum or note thereof, is in writing and signed by the party to be charged therewith or by some person thereunto by him lawfully authorized.]

■ PERETTA, JR. ... National argues on appeal that Brady's alleged oral promise to McPherson at the meeting prior to July 4, 2000, was, at best, a promise "to answer for the debt ... of another," G. L. c. 259, § 1, Second, and was unenforceable as it was not in writing....

In ruling on National's posttrial motions, the judge [below] applied the long-recognized exception to the Statute, the so-called "leading object" or "main purpose" exception. In Ames v. Foster, 106 Mass. 400, 403 (1871), the court stated:

> [A] case is not within the statute, where, upon the whole transaction, the fair inference is, that the leading object or purpose and the effect of the transaction was the purchase or acquisition by the promisor from the promisee of some property, lien or benefit which he did not before possess, but which enured to him by reason of his promise, so that the debt for which he is liable may fairly be deemed to be a debt of his own, contracted in such purchase or acquisition.

See Nelson v. Boynton, 3 Met. 396, 44 Mass. 396, 3 Metc. 396, 400 (1841) (cited in *Ames, supra,* and in which "original" and "collateral" promises are distinguished for purposes of Statute); Hayes v. Guy, 348 Mass. 754, 756, 205 N.E.2d 699 (1965) (discussing "main purpose" exception to Statute and citing Williston, Contracts [3rd ed.] § 472); Barboza v. Liberty Contractors Co., 18 Mass.App.Ct. 971, 972, 469 N.E.2d 1303 (1984) (same, citing Restatement [Second] of Contracts § 116 [1979]).

[National contended that the alleged agreement was excepted from the Statute only if it constituted a "novation"—if, that is, it substituted one party for another. The agreement would have been a novation if it had released Old Colony from its obligation to Central, putting National in place as the obligor instead.]

Novation, however, is but one ground on which a promise is removed from the operation of the Statute. The "leading object" exception to the Statute addresses a separate and distinct set of circumstances. They are that (1) a third party is indebted; (2) there is no novation; and (3) the third party's duty to the creditor will be terminated by the performance promised by the defendant. See 4 Corbin, Contracts, *supra* § 16.12 at 362. Under the "leading object" exception to the Statute, an oral agreement that does not effect a novation may nonetheless be enforceable if the facts and circumstances of the transaction show that the promise was given primarily or solely to serve the promisor's own interests....

In another line of decisions, it is recognized that a property owner's promise to pay subcontractors or suppliers may, in appropriate circumstances, come within the "leading object" exception to the Statute. See Hayes v. Guy, 348 Mass. at 756–757; Barboza v. Liberty Contractors Co., 18 Mass.App.Ct. at 971. See also Gegan, Some Exceptions to the Suretyship Statute of Frauds: A Tale of Two Courts, 79 St. John's L. Rev. 319, 353 (2005). Based upon these authorities the question now before us is whether the circumstances presented in the instant case are such as to bring it within the "leading object" exception to the Statute.

There was evidence here to show that (1) National wanted to open the theater at the Project by the end of August so as to capture large audiences over the Labor Day weekend and thereby tap the revenue and business opportunities associated with a movie premier and the Labor Day weekend; (2) as of the beginning of July, the work to be completed for the anticipated opening would have to be completed in a "tight time frame"; (3) Central was one of the "core" subcontractors on the Project and was responsible for significant portions of the work to be completed; (4) Central had completed its preliminary work and was poised to start building; and (5) given the circumstances, Central was one of the few subcontractors in Massachusetts, if not the only one, capable of delivering the necessary work in the time frame desired by National.

Under these circumstances, we conclude that the evidence was sufficient to warrant a finding that National's promise—made through Brady, who was found by the jury to have the apparent authority to make such a promise—was given to secure Central's continued and expedited performance at the Project and that the satisfaction of any obligation on the part of Old Colony was merely incidental to that promise. See *Hayes* at 757; *Barboza* at 971–72.

PROBLEM

The School of Self–Interest. The holder of a mortgage on "Isabella's Arcade" objects to a transfer of the property by the owner (mortgagor), who wishes to convey the property to her college, continuing to pay the mortgage from other assets. In order to obviate the mortgagee's objection, the college gives the mortgagee an oral undertaking that it will satisfy the donor's debt if she fails to do so. The mortgagee withdraws its objection and the gift is made. The donor defaults on the mortgage. Does the suretyship clause bar enforcement of the college's promise? Or does the main-purpose doctrine apply?

OF NURSING CARE AND CATERPILLAR'S MAIN PURPOSE

Refer again to the facts of Rosewood Care Center v. Caterpillar, as stated at p. 301 above, in the Note, "Current Obligation." Rosewood contended that Caterpillar's alleged promise to pay for Cook's care was enforceable, although oral by reason of the main-purpose exception to the statute. Caterpillar denied that the main purpose of its promise, if made, was to promote its own interest, and indeed denied that it had received any benefit from the agreement. Citing authorities, the Illinois court said that most jurisdictions had adopted the exception, and that it had long been a part of Illinois law. The court disposed of the issue in the two following paragraphs:

"Whether the 'main purpose' or 'leading object' of the promisor is to promote a pecuniary or business advantage to it is generally a question for the trier of fact. 9 R. Lord, Williston on Contracts § 22:20, at 308 (4th ed.1999). In making this determination, the following factors may be considered: 'prior default, inability or repudiation of the principal obligor; forbearance of the creditor to enforce a lien on property in which the promisor has an interest or which he intends to use; equivalence between the value of the benefit and the amount promised; lack of participation by the principal obligor in the making of the surety's promise; a larger transaction to which the suretyship is incidental.' Restatement (Second) of Contracts § 116, Comment *b*, at 300 (1981). See also Restatement (Third) of Suretyship & Guaranty § 11, Comment to Subsection (3)(c) (1996); P. Alces, Law of Suretyship & Guaranty, § 4:20 (1996). The crux of this inquiry is the reason the promisor made the promise, *i.e.*, the impetus for the promise. See [Davis v. Patrick], 141 U.S. at 488 ('there is a marked difference between a promise which, without any interest in the subject-matter of the promise in the promisor ... and that which, though operating upon the debt of a third party, is also and mainly for the benefit of the promisor").

"Here, a decision on what was Caterpillar's 'main purpose' or 'leading object' in making the promise cannot be made based on the allegations in the complaint. What is required is evidence from which one can ascertain whether the reason for Caterpillar's promise was in fact or apparently desired by Caterpillar mainly for its own advantage. The determination must be made by the trier of fact based on evidence to be presented by the parties.... [T]his cause must be remanded for further proceedings to determine the 'leading object' or 'main purpose' of Caterpillar's promise."

NOTE

Question: Apart from satisfaction in giving succor to an injured person, what advantage could Caterpillar have expected from inducing Rosewood to care for Cook?

SECTION 4.   RELIANCE AND OTHER EQUITIES

Sometimes reliance by a party on an agreement is a ground for enforcing an agreement that would otherwise be unenforceable owing to a statute of frauds. Enforcement proceeds under the name *estoppel*. In recent times courts have become more receptive to the doctrine as a way to circumvent a statute of frauds. A more restrictive view of estoppel was once prevalent, and still has some currency. For that view see Ozier v. Haines, 103 N.E.2d 485 (Ill.1952): "It is true that harsh results ... may occur where one has changed his position in reliance on the oral promise of another, but it is a result which is invited and risked when the agreement is not reduced to writing in the manner prescribed by law." Otherwise, the court said, the Statute would be rendered "useless and unmeaning."

On p. 295 above, some cases are cited in which buyers of goods succeeded in circumventing UCC § 2–201(1) by reason of their reliance on oral sale agreements. But opposing decisions are cited there also, they being based on the thought that the Code text displaces estoppel with respect to sale-of-goods agreements.

The case that follows is a leading one, indicating a change of attitude about estoppel relation to statutes of frauds. (It did not concern a sale-of-goods agreement.) Restatement § 139, new in the Second Restatement, is a further exemplar of change. It is an adaptation of promissory estoppel in relation to statutes of frauds. According to Comment *a* to the section, it "complements" Restatement § 90.

Monarco v. Lo Greco

Supreme Court of California, 1950.
35 Cal.2d 621, 220 P.2d 737.

■ TRAYNOR, JUSTICE. Natale and Carmela Castiglia were married in 1919 in Colorado. Carmela had three children, John, Rosie and Christie [Lo Greco], by a previous marriage. Rosie was married to Nick Norcia. Natale had one grandchild, plaintiff Carmen Monarco, the son of a deceased daughter by a previous marriage. Natale and Carmela moved to California where they invested their assets, amounting to approximately $4,000, in a half interest in agricultural property. Rosie and Nick Norcia acquired the other half interest. Christie, then in his early teens, moved with the family to California. Plaintiff remained in Colorado. In 1926, Christie, then 18 years old, decided to leave the home of his mother and step-father and seek an independent living. Natale and Carmela, however, wanted him to stay with them and participate in the family venture. They made an oral proposal to Christie that if he stayed home and worked they would keep their property in joint tenancy so that it would pass to the survivor who would leave it to Christie by will except for small devises to John and Rosie. In performance of this agreement Christie remained home and worked diligently in the family venture. He gave up any opportunity for further education or any chance to accumulate property of his own. He received only his room and board and spending money. When he married and suggested the possibility of securing some present interest to support his wife, Natale told him that his wife should move in with the family and that Christie need not worry, for he would receive all the property when Natale and Carmela died. Natale and Carmela placed all of their property in joint tenancy and in 1941 both executed wills leaving all their property to Christie with the exception of small devises to Rosie and John and $500 to plaintiff. Although these wills did not refer to the agreement, their terms were agreed upon by Christie, Natale and Carmela. The venture was successful, so that at the time of Natale's death his and Carmela's interest was worth approximately $100,000. Shortly before his death Natale became dissatisfied with the agreement and determined to leave his half of the joint property to his grandson, the plaintiff. Without informing Christie or Carmela he arranged the necessary conveyances to terminate the joint tenancies and executed a will leaving all of his property to plaintiff. This will was probated and the court entered its decree distributing the property to plaintiff. After the decree of distribution became final, plaintiff brought these actions for partition of the properties and an accounting. By cross-complaint Carmela asked that plaintiff be declared a constructive trustee of the property he received as a result of Natale's breach of his agreement to keep the property in joint tenancy. On the basis of the foregoing facts the trial court gave judgment for defendants and cross-complainant, and plaintiff has appealed.

The controlling question is whether plaintiff is estopped from relying upon the statute of frauds (Civil Code § 1624; Code Civ.Proc. § 1973) to defeat the enforcement of the oral contract. [The provision referred to was, apparently, the California "lifetime clause", paragraph (5) of the Civil Code section cited: "An agreement that by its terms is not to be performed during the lifetime of the promisor." The "real-property clause" of the statute concerns only agreements for leasing realty, and sales of real-property interests.] The doctrine of estoppel to assert the statute of frauds has been consistently applied by the courts of this state to prevent fraud that would result from refusal to enforce oral contracts in certain circumstances. Such fraud may inhere in the unconscionable injury that would result from denying enforcement of the contract after one party has been induced by the other seriously to change his position in reliance on the contract, . . . or in the unjust enrichment that would result if a party who has received the benefits of the other's performance were allowed to rely upon the statute. . . . In many cases both elements are present. Thus, not only may one party have so seriously changed his position in reliance upon, or in performance of, the contract that he would suffer an unconscionable injury if it were not enforced, but the other may have reaped the benefits of the contract so that he would be unjustly enriched if he could escape its obligations. . . .

In this case both elements are present. In reliance on Natale's repeated assurances that he would receive the property when Natale and Carmela died, Christie gave up any opportunity to accumulate property of his own and devoted his life to making the family venture a success. That he would be seriously prejudiced by a refusal to enforce the contract is made clear by a comparison of his position with that of Rosie and Nick Norcia. Because the Norcias were able to make a small investment when the family venture was started, their interest, now worth approximately $100,000, has been protected. Christie, on the other hand, forbore from demanding any present interest in the venture in exchange for his labors on the assurance that Natale's and Carmela's interest would pass to him on their death. Had he invested money instead of labor in the venture on the same oral understanding, a resulting trust would have arisen in his favor. Byers v. Doheny, 105 Cal.App. 484, 493–495, 287 P. 988; see, Restatement, Trusts, § 454, comment *j.* illus. 12. His twenty years of labor should have equal effect. On the other hand, Natale reaped the benefits of the contract. He and his devisees would be unjustly enriched if the statute of frauds could be invoked to relieve him from performance of his own obligations thereunder.

It is contended, however, that an estoppel to plead the statute of frauds can only arise when there have been representations with respect to the requirements of the statute indicating that a writing is not necessary or will be executed or that the statute will not be relied upon as a defense. This element was present in the leading case of Seymour v. Oelrichs, 156 Cal. 782, 106 P. 88, 134 Am.St.Rep. 154, and it is not surprising therefore that it has been listed as a requirement of an estoppel in later cases that have held on their facts that there was or was not an estoppel. . . . Those cases, however, that have refused to find an estoppel have been cases where the court found either that no unconscionable injury would result from refusing to enforce the oral contract, . . . or that the remedy of quantum meruit for services rendered was adequate. . . . In those cases, however, where either an unconscionable injury or unjust enrichment would result from refusal to enforce the contract, the doctrine of estoppel has been applied whether or not plaintiff relied upon representations going to the requirements of the statute itself. . . . Likewise in the case of partly performed oral contracts for the sale of land specific enforcement will be decreed whether or not there have been representations going to the requirements of the statute, because its denial would result in a fraud on the plaintiff who has gone into possession or made improvements in reliance on the contract.... In reality it is not the representation that the contract will be put in writing or that the statute will not be invoked, but the promise that the contract will be performed that a party relies upon when he changes his position because of it. Moreover, a party who has accepted the benefits of an oral contract will be unjustly enriched if the contract is not enforced whether his representations related to the requirements of the statute or were limited to affirmations that the contract would be performed.

It is settled that neither the remedy of an action at law for damages for breach of contract nor the quasi-contractual remedy for the value of services rendered is adequate for the breach of a contract to leave property by will in exchange for services of a peculiar nature involving the assumption or continuation of a close family relationship.... The facts of this case clearly bring it within the foregoing rule....

The judgments are affirmed.

NOTES

(1) *Flexibility.* Comment *b* to Restatement § 139 states: "Like § 90 this Section states a flexible principle, but the requirement of consideration is more easily displaced than the requirement of a writing. The reliance must be foreseeable by the promisor, and enforcement must be necessary to avoid injustice. Subsection (2) lists some of the relevant factors in applying the latter requirement."

One entry in the list of relevant factors is "the extent to which the action or forbearance [on the part of the promisee or a third party] corroborates evidence of the making and terms of the promise." On the facts of *Monarco*, do you see strong corroboration in the conduct of Christie Lo Greco?

(2) *The Case of the Ungrateful Grandfather.* In Estate of Horrigan, 757 So.2d 165 (Miss.1999), it was found that Horrigan's will did not comport with an oral promise he had made to his grandchildren, Ted and Christy. Relying on Horrigan's promise that they would receive, under his will, the dominant interest in his home, these grandchildren had invested most of their savings, some $22,000, in renovating the place. The court of probate awarded the property to Horrigan's widow, according to the will, but charged the property with a lien in favor of Ted and Christy for the amount of their investment, with interest. On review, this disposition was affirmed. Specific performance was not an available remedy, according to the appellate court.

Both in *Horrigan* and in *Monarco*, the courts characterized the relief as a constructive trust. But in *Monarco* the relief granted to Christie Lo Greco amounted to specific performance. According to § 139 of the Restatement, the remedy granted for breach, by reason of reliance, "is to be limited as justice requires." Does this limitation explain the difference between the forms of relief granted in *Monarco* and in *Horrigan*? Is it apparent that justice to the Horrigan grandchildren did not require specific performance?

(3) *Part Performance: Reprise.* Consider *Horrigan* (foregoing Note) as an instance of a contract for a transfer of real property. Is it apparent why part performance by Ted and Christy did not make their contract enforceable? The opinion in the case recites this further fact: Ted and Christy had taken up residence in the house in question. On that account the court directed that they be charged rent for their use of the property. Note, however, that they did not invest in the property as a purchaser usually does, expecting near-term use of the improvements.

(4) *Last Resort?* In some situations of reliance by a promisee on an oral agreement, the promisee might be given a measure of relief without drawing on the doctrine of estoppel and enforcing the agreement. Restitution of benefits conferred on the promisor might be an ample remedy. When it is, the rule of Restatement § 139 does not augment it; so says Comment *d* to the section. The Comment continues: "In some cases it may be appropriate to measure relief by the extent of the promisee's reliance rather than by the terms of the promise." And the black letter contains this sentence: "The remedy granted for breach is to be limited as justice requires." Given these restrictions on estoppel, it might be said that using the doctrine to enforce an oral agreement is the remedy of last resort.

Suppose this rule to be enacted by a legislature: "A promisor who relies on a statute of frauds to prevent the enforcement of a genuine oral agreement is obliged to compensate the claimant for any reasonable reliance on the agreement, assuming that the promisor should have foreseen the possibility of reliance by the claimant of the sort that occurred." How would that differ in practice from a simple rule that, in a proper case, reliance "takes an agreement out of the state"? Is it preferable?

Would the statute supposed have provided an adequate remedy on the facts of *Monarco?* Would it have done so in Richard v. Richard, p. 280 above? (Notice that an affirmative answer to the question about *Richard* might lead to the conclusion that enforcing an oral agreement by reason of part performance ought to be a remedy of last resort.)

(5) *Lawyering and Ethics, Again.* Suppose that you had been asked to represent Carmen Monarco in the action he brought. Would you have had compunctions about doing so, assuming that no doubt existed about the facts stated by the court? (The court's statement of facts rested on findings in the Superior Court for Los Angeles County.)

This might be one answer: "No, because the law of California is not yet settled with respect to estoppels and the Statute." Recall, in this connection, the court's sentence in which it cited Seymour v. Oelrichs, and see again Note 1 above. Another answer might be this: "No, because it is doubtful that a change of position on the part of Christie can constitute an element of estoppel in favor of someone else, and the claimant is Carmen Monarco, not Christie." (Counsel for Monarco made that argument. The court rejected it in a part of the opinion not presented here.)

Consult again the text at p. 264 above, titled "Ethical Practices and Statutes of Frauds." What does it suggest as ways to prevent compunctions from arising, and to quell them if they do?

CHAPTER 4

POLICING THE BARGAINING PROCESS

Although a contract may meet the general requirements for enforceability, such as agreement, consideration and, when relevant, compliance with the statute of frauds, there are cases where the law may refuse nonetheless to enforce the bargain. For example, when a promise is extracted through lawless threat ("Your money or your life!") or through outright fraud, one would not expect the courts to enforce the deal. Of course, bargaining abuses in a commercial society are usually more subtle, and often less egregious, than these. Sometimes the difficulty lies in the particular characteristics of a party to the bargain. Should bargains made where one party is underage or "under the influence" or unsophisticated relative to the other party be enforced? Other times the problem concerns not the bargaining *process* but rather the bargaining *result*: When the old homestead is sold for a song, but there is no proof of anything approaching force or fraud, should law stand content and enforce that bargain?

A variety of mechanisms have been adopted for policing what our society chooses to view as bargaining abuses. In this endeavor, there are three basic types of policing concerns: the *status* of the party seeking relief from a promise, the *behavior* of parties during the bargaining process, and the *substance* of the resulting bargain. While this chapter focuses primarily on the first two, a brief discussion of all three is in order, in part to indicate at the outset the often tangled relation among them.

The first concern attends chiefly to the *status* of the parties. In their strongest form, status-based policing measures disqualify certain classes of persons from committing themselves by contract. Minors, married women, and the mentally infirm have been among the historic classes, and are treated in Section 1. It is useful in considering status-based policing to pay attention to the underlying characteristics and presumptions on which the disqualification, or other form of regulation, is based. Are they innate, as in the case of minors who are understood to be immature and inexperienced, or in any event are deemed to be so; or are they circumstantial, as perhaps in the case of protections placed around consumers?

The second concern focuses on the *behavior* of the parties in the bargaining process. The treatment of duress illustrates the problem, and implicates the difficult issue of how the law should deal with disparities in bargaining power between parties. What sorts of pressure or duress ought the law take into account in refusing to enforce a promise? How do courts distinguish among persuasion, pressure, and duress? What sorts of bargaining inequalities between the parties should the law take into account in policing a bargain? Informational asymmetries? Emotional and economic dependencies? Wealth disparities? In short, what limits or requirements should the law place on how the parties treat one another in the process of striking a deal?

The third concern looks to the *substance* of the bargain. Recall from your study of consideration in Chapter 1 that exchanges of unequal value are commonly enforced: Courts will not inquire into the adequacy of the consideration. Yet the law has introduced a variety of judicial and legislative policing measures that treat particularly lopsided bargains with disfavor. Limits on the substance of a bargain are the principal subject of Chapter 6.

What motivates courts in their policing efforts? To some extent, the answer combines moral conviction with a sense of institutional integrity. In the dramatic phrasing of an older case concerning an agreement to pay a bribe, "no court should be required to serve as the paymaster of thieves." Stone v. Freeman, 298 N.Y. 268, 271 (Ct.App.1948). Put another way, although we accept that contracts are a matter of private ordering—we say that parties can make whatever deal they want and rely on the state for its enforcement—still, contract law must take its place alongside other bodies of law such as criminal law, torts, corporate and family law from which public policies may be drawn. Policing the process or substance of private bargains is a way of coordinating the social and moral values of the broader legal system.

We might also look to one account given by law and economics scholars: courts are reluctant, they say, to enforce agreements involving bargaining failures, such as fraud, for reasons of efficiency. A bargain based on fraud or mistake, when unraveled, might reveal that the parties would not otherwise have entered into the agreement and that their joint welfare would be *reduced* by enforcement.

Whatever the origins of judicial action for policing the bargaining process, other important governmental actors have now entered the arena. The powers of legislatures and administrative agencies are regularly deployed to police both the bargaining process and bargains themselves. As we shall see, many, though not all, legislative and regulatory attempts to set proper conditions for fair and effective bargaining are directed at consumer protection.

This chapter focuses primarily on concerns regarding status and behavior, recognizing that the substance of a deal is sometimes an indication that something has gone awry in the bargaining process. We begin with the question of contractual capacity: What limits does the law place on who can bind themselves contractually? Section 2 turns to the question of pressure and other irregularities in the conduct of the parties leading up the contract. We look first at the issue of duress and the law's attempts to determine how compulsion manifests itself in the twenty-first century. How do courts determine whether a decision to enter, or to modify, a contract is the result of excessive pressure? Section 3 then considers other forms of overreaching, including undue influence and misrepresentation, and the related problem of silence or non-disclosure.

SECTION 1. CAPACITY

What classes of persons are considered by the law to have less than full power to contract? We focus on two important categories of incapacity: minority (traditionally called "infancy") and mental infirmity.

In thinking about contractual incapacity, it is important to consider both the underlying bases and the broader consequences of such a determination. To take an historical example, the common law incapacities of married women were based not on impaired mental faculties but on the legal consequences of marriage. "By marriage, the husband and wife are one person in law; that is, the very being of the woman is suspended during the marriage, or at least is incorporated and consolidated into that of the husband: under whose wing, protection, and *cover*, she performs everything ... [T]herefore all deeds executed, and all acts done, by her during her coverture, are void." 1 Blackstone, Commentaries on the Law of England, 442–443 (1765). Married women's contractual incapacity justified their disqualification from various forms of employment, including the practice of law, for as lawyers they would be unable to contract even with clients. See Bradwell v. Illinois, 83 U.S. 130 (1873). These incapacities were largely removed by "married women's property and earnings statutes" enacted during the middle and late nineteenth century.

Some of those whose capacity was limited under the common law, including married women and sailors, were described as "favorites" of the law. As you read the following cases, consider whether lack of capacity constitutes a benefit or a burden to those so favored.

We begin with minors, recognizing that issues of their incapacity diminished significantly when the age of majority was lowered for most purposes from 21 to 18 in the 1970s in consequence of the Vietnam War. More recently, the capacity problem has been revived as minors increasingly make on-line purchases, including some prohibited for sale to minors, such as alcohol.

Kiefer v. Fred Howe Motors, Inc.

Supreme Court of Wisconsin, 1968.
39 Wis.2d 20, 158 N.W.2d 288.

[Steven Kiefer, a working husband and father, bought a five-year-old Willys station wagon from Fred Howe Motors a few months short of his twenty-first birthday. The contract that he signed stated: "I represent that I am 21 years of age or over and recognize that the dealer sells the above vehicle upon this representation." He had difficulty with the car which he claimed had a cracked block. After becoming of age, he sought to return it, and later sued to recover the price. From judgment for Kiefer, the dealer appealed.]

■ WILKIE, J. ... The law governing agreements made during infancy reaches back over many centuries. The general rule is that "... the contract of a minor, other than for necessaries, is either void or voidable at his option."[a] The only other exceptions to the rule permitting disaffirmance are statutory or involve contracts which deal with duties imposed by law such as a contract of marriage or an agreement to support an illegitimate child. The general rule is not affected by the minor's status as emancipated or unemancipated.

Appellant does not advance any argument that would put this case within one of the exceptions to the general rule, but rather urges that this court, as a matter of public policy, adopt a rule that an emancipated minor over eighteen years of age be made legally responsible for his contracts.

The underpinnings of the general rule allowing the minor to disaffirm his contracts were undoubtedly the protection of the minor. It was thought that the minor was immature in both mind and experience and that, therefore, he should be protected from his own bad judgments as well as from adults who would take advantage of him. The doctrine of the voidability of minors' contracts often seems commendable and just. If the beans that the young naive Jack purchased from the crafty old man in the fairy tale "Jack and the Bean Stalk" had been worthless rather than magical, it would have been only fair to allow Jack to disaffirm the bargain and reclaim his cow. However, in today's modern and sophisticated society the "infancy doctrine" seems to lose some of its gloss.

Paradoxically, we declare the infant mature enough to shoulder arms in the military, but not mature enough to vote; mature enough to marry and be responsible for his torts and crimes, but not mature enough to assume the burden of his own contractual indiscretions. In Wisconsin, the infant is deemed mature enough to use a dangerous instrumentality—a motor vehicle—at sixteen, but not mature enough to purchase it without protection until he is twenty-one.

No one really questions that a line as to age must be drawn somewhere below which a legally defined minor must be able to disaffirm his contracts for nonnecessities. The law over the centuries has considered this age to be twenty-one. Legislatures in other states have lowered the age. We suggest that the appellant might better seek the change it proposes in the legislative halls rather than this court. A recent law review article in the Indiana Law Journal explores the problem of contractual disabilities of minors and points to three different legislative solutions leading to greater freedom to contract. The first approach is one gleaned from the statutes of California and New York, which would allow parties to submit a proposed contract to a court which would remove the infant's right of disaffirmance upon a finding that the particular contract is fair. This suggested approach appears to be extremely impractical in light of the expense and delay that would

---

a. While in many statutes and cases the promise of a person without capacity is said to be "void," it is more accurate to regard it as "voidable."

necessarily accompany the procedure. A second approach would be to establish a rebuttable presumption of incapacity to replace the strict rule. This alternative would be an open invitation to litigation. The third suggestion is a statutory procedure that would allow a minor to petition a court for the removal of disabilities. Under this procedure a minor would only have to go to court once, rather than once for each contract as in the first suggestion.

Undoubtedly, the infancy doctrine is an obstacle when a major purchase is involved. However, we believe that the reasons for allowing that obstacle to remain viable at this point outweigh those for casting it aside. Minors require some protection from the pitfalls of the market place. Reasonable minds will always differ on the extent of the protection that should be afforded. For this court to adopt a rule that the appellant suggests and remove the contractual disabilities from a minor simply because he becomes emancipated, which in most cases would be the result of marriage, would be to suggest that the married minor is somehow vested with more wisdom and maturity than his single counterpart. However, logic would not seem to dictate this result especially when today a youthful marriage is oftentimes indicative of a lack of wisdom and maturity....

[Affirmed.]

■ HALLOWS, CHIEF JUSTICE (dissenting) ... The magical age limit of 21 years as an indication of contractual maturity no longer has a basis in fact or in public policy. [Furthermore,] an automobile to this respondent was a necessity and therefore the contract could not be disaffirmed.... Automobiles for parents under 21 years of age to go to and from work in our current society may well be a necessity, and I think in this case the record shows it is....

NOTES

(1) *Necessaries.* "An infant may bind himselfe to pay for his necessary meat, drinke, apparell, necessary physicke, and such other necessaries, and likewise for his good teaching or instruction, whereby he may profit himselfe afterwards." Coke on Littleton, 13th Ed. (1788), quoted in Gastonia Personnel Corporation v. Rogers, 172 S.E.2d 19 (N.C. 1970). Do you agree with the court in *Kiefer* that under the circumstances of the case, the car was not necessary? What about an educational loan?

What about housing? In Rivera v. Reading Housing Authority, 819 F.Supp. 1323, 1332–34 (E.D.Pa.1993), a teenage mother's application for public housing was rejected:"[I]f a minor is living with a parent or guardian who is able and willing to furnish the minor with housing, housing is not a necessary and a contract entered into by the minor for housing will not be binding.... [For the Housing Authority] to assume the risks of entering into unenforceable contracts would be to jeopardize sound fiscal policy as well as a fair allocation of scarce housing resources."

(2) *Disaffirmance.* A minor may disaffirm a contract not only during minority but also within a reasonable time after reaching the age of majority. In Milicic v. Basketball Marketing Co., Inc. 857 A.2d 689 (Pa. 2004), a 16–year–old Serbian basketball player, relatively unknown in the United States, signed an exclusive endorsement agreement with a sports management company. By his 18th birthday, the player, then a top NBA draft pick, offered to buy out the contract. When the

company refused, the player, Darko Milicic, disaffirmed. Describing him as "a child, living in a foreign country" at the time he signed the agreement, the court upheld the disaffirmance and, quoting from an earlier case reviewed one policy consideration underlying disaffirmance: "minors should not be bound by mistakes resulting from ... the overbearance of unscrupulous adults."

There is "no hard and fast rule as to just what constitutes a 'reasonable' time within which the infant may disaffirm," and courts have permitted disaffirmance months after the minor reached majority. See Keser v. Chagnon, 410 P.2d 637 (Colo.1966). Some states have limited the period of disaffirmance by statute; see Okla.Stat.tit.15 § 19 (one year limit).

On becoming an adult, one who made a contract as a minor may ratify it and so lose the power to disaffirm. The power to disaffirm may also be lost when the contract received judicial approval at the time of its making; see Cal.Fam. Code § 6750–51, governing contracts of minors who contract for "artistic or creative services" or for athletic performances. Disaffirmance may also be lost through parental consent. In 1983, Brooke Shields, an "infant model," sought to disaffirm a contract entered into by her mother, selling the rights to nude photos of Shields taken when she was ten. The court held that a New York statute authorizing parental consent abrogated Shield's common law right to disaffirm. Shields v. Gross, 58 N.Y.2d 338, 350 (1983).

(3) *Restitution.* Upon disaffirming a purchase contract, a minor can get restitution of payments already made to a seller, but must return the goods to the seller. Thus, in *Milicic*, Note 2 above, immediately upon disaffirming, and apparently then well-advised, the player "began returning all monies and products (or their equivalent value)" received under the agreement. The requirement of restoration serves to prevent unjust enrichment of the buyer, but does not necessarily prevent loss to the seller, for the goods may be somewhat worse for wear. In some cases the seller may receive an off-set between the amount of payments to be refunded to the buyer and the value of the goods when returned. See Keser v. Chagnon, Note 2, above.

What are the obligations of restoration if the minor contracted not for goods but for services which have already been received? In Mitchell v. Mizerski, 1995 WL 118429 (Neb.App.1995), a Nebraska court stated: "Due to the nature of the consideration furnished by Mizreski, *i.e.*, paint and body work on the [minor's] ... vehicle, and the ownership of the vehicle, there was nothing that could be returned by Travis.... Although this result appears unjust to Mizreski, Nebraska law imposes such consequence upon adults who enter into contracts with minors, as a means to discourage such contracts." See also, Scott Eden Management v. Kavovit, 563 N.Y.S.2d 1001, 1004 (1990).

(4) *Risky Business.* In another car case, the court observed that "he who deals with a minor does so at his own peril." To reduce the peril, standard form contracts commonly contain a statement above the buyer's signature that the buyer is not below the age of majority. This lays a predicate for an action by the seller for deceit, in the event of disaffirmance. But as *Kiefer*, Note 2 above, suggests, it is not always possible to prove all the elements of deceit, even with the minor's signed statement.

If a seller reasonably believes a minor who has lied about his age, why should the minor be allowed to rely upon his infancy? Does not this clash with the objective standard advanced in Lucy v. Zehmer, p. 117 above? Why was not Kiefer estopped to deny his representation of age?

(5) *Protecting the Elderly.* While the law has traditionally protected *minors,* attention has turned in recent years to protecting older people from objectionable

contracts and bargaining techniques to which they may be particularly vulnerable. These include home solicitation sales and fraudulent telemarketing schemes, particularly for such services as home repair. One mechanism used to police such contracts is a penalty enhancement, typically a civil fine of $10,000, added to a criminal sentence for fraud in cases where the "defendant knew or should have known that the victim of the offense was unusually vulnerable due to age. . . ." See United States v. Williams, 1997 WL 573379 (N.D.Ill.1997), affirming a conviction for Aggravated Home Repair.

Ortelere v. Teachers' Retirement Bd.

New York Court of Appeals, 1969.
25 N.Y.2d 196, 250 N.E.2d 460.

[Grace Ortelere was a 60–year–old New York City schoolteacher who had suffered a nervous breakdown diagnosed as involving "involutional psychosis, melancholia type," and was on leave for mental illness. Her psychiatrist suspected that she also suffered from cerebral arteriosclerosis. Her husband had quit his job as an electrician to stay home and care for her. She had an account of $70,925 in the public retirement system in which she had participated for over 40 years. In 1965, without telling her husband, she obtained a loan from the system in the largest amount possible, $8,760, and made an irrevocable election to take the maximum retirement benefits of $450 a month during her lifetime. This revoked an earlier election under which she would have received only $375 a month but her husband would have taken the unexhausted reserve on her death. The new election left him with no benefits in the event of her death. Two months later she died of cerebral arteriosclerosis. Her husband sued to set aside her election on the ground of mental incompetence. Her psychiatrist testified that she was incapable of making a decision of any kind and that victims of involutional melancholia "can't think rationally. . . . They will even tell you . . . 'I don't know whether I should get up or whether I should stay in bed.' . . . Everything is impossible to decide." From a judgment for Mr. Ortelere, the Board appealed to the Appellate Division, which reversed and dismissed the complaint. The plaintiff appealed.]

■ BREITEL, JUDGE.[a] . . . The particular issue arises on the evidently unwise and foolhardy selection of benefits by a 60–year–old teacher, on leave for mental illness and suffering from cerebral arteriosclerosis . . . The teacher died a little less than two months after making her election of maximum benefits, payable to her during her life, thus causing the entire reserve to fall in. She left her surviving husband of 38 years and two grown children.

. . . Traditionally, in this State and elsewhere, contractual mental capacity has been measured by what is largely a cognitive test. . . . Under this standard the "inquiry" is whether the mind was "so affected as to

---

a. Charles D. Breitel (1908–1991) was appointed to the New York Supreme Court in 1950 after law practice in New York City and service with Thomas E. Dewey, first on his staff when Dewey was district attorney and later as his counsel when Dewey was gover-nor. He was elevated to the Appellate Division in 1952 and to the Court of Appeals in 1967, serving as Chief Judge from 1974 to 1978. He also taught jurisprudence as an adjunct professor at Columbia.

render him wholly and absolutely incompetent to comprehend and understand the nature of the transaction".... A requirement that the party also be able to make a rational judgment concerning the particular transaction qualified the cognitive test.... Conversely, it is also well recognized that contractual ability would be affected by insane delusions intimately related to the particular transaction....

These traditional standards governing competency to contract were formulated when psychiatric knowledge was quite primitive. They fail to account for one who by reason of mental illness is unable to control his conduct even though his cognitive ability seems unimpaired. When these standards were evolving it was thought that all the mental faculties were simultaneously affected by mental illness.... This is no longer the prevailing view....

Of course the greatest movement in revamping legal notions of mental responsibility has occurred in the criminal law. The nineteenth century cognitive test embraced in the *M'Naghten* rules has long been criticized and changed by statute and decision in many jurisdictions (see *M'Naghten's Case,* 10 Clark & Fin. 200; 8 Eng.Rep. 718 [House of Lords, 1843]; Weihofen, Mental Disorder as a Criminal Defense [1954], pp. 65–68)....

It is quite significant that Restatement, 2d, Contracts, states the modern rule on competency to contract.... Thus, the new Restatement section reads: "(1) A person incurs only voidable contractual duties by entering into a transaction if by reason of mental illness or defect ... (b) he is unable to act in a reasonable manner in relation to the transaction and the other party has reason to know of his condition." (Restatement, 2d, Contracts [T.D. No. 1, April 13, 1964], § 18C.) [renumbered 15]....

The system was, or should have been, fully aware of Mrs. Ortelere's condition. They, or the Board of Education, knew of her leave of absence for medical reasons and the resort to staff psychiatrists by the Board of Education. Hence, the other of the conditions for avoidance is satisfied.

Lastly, there are no significant changes of position by the system other than those that flow from the barest actuarial consequences of benefit selection.

Nor should one ignore that in the relationship between retirement system and member, and especially in a public system, there is not involved a commercial, let alone an ordinary commercial, transaction. It is not a sound scheme which would permit 40 years of contribution and participation in the system to be nullified by a one-instant act committed by one known to be mentally ill. This is especially true if there would be no substantial harm to the system if the act were avoided. Of course, nothing less serious than medically classified psychosis should suffice or else few contracts would be invulnerable to some kind of psychological attack. As noted earlier, the trial court's finding and perhaps some of the testimony attempted to fit into the rubrics of the traditional rules. For that reason rather than reinstatement of the judgment at Trial Term there should be a new trial under the proper standards frankly considered and applied.

[Reversed.]

■ JASEN, JUDGE (dissenting). [Judge Jasen set out the full text of a letter from Grace to the Retirement System prior to her election, in which she put eight questions typified by the following (No. 6): "If I take a loan of $5,000 before retiring and select option four-a on both the pension and annuity, what would my allowance be?"] It seems clear that this detailed, explicit and extremely pertinent list of queries reveals a mind fully in command of the salient features of the Teachers' Retirement System. Certainly, it cannot be said the decedent could possess sufficient capacity to compose a letter indicating such a comprehensive understanding of the retirement system, and yet lack the capacity to understand the answers.

As I read the record, the evidence establishes that the decedent's election to receive maximum payments was predicated on the need for a higher income to support two retired persons—her husband and herself. Since the only source of income available to decedent and her husband was decedent's retirement pay, the additional payment of $75 per month which she would receive by electing the maximal payment was a necessity. . . . Under these circumstances, an election of maximal income during decedent's lifetime was not only a rational, but a necessary decision. . . . Moreover, there is nothing in the record to indicate that the decedent had any warning, premonition, knowledge or indication at the time of retirement that her life expectancy was, in any way, reduced by her condition.

The generally accepted test of mental competency to contract which has thus evolved . . . represents a balance struck between policies to protect the security of transactions between individuals and freedom of contract on the one hand, and protection of those mentally handicapped on the other hand. In my opinion, this rule has proven workable in practice and fair in result. . . . As in every situation where the law must draw a line between liability and nonliability, between responsibility and nonresponsibility, there will be borderline cases, and injustices may occur by deciding erroneously that an individual belongs on one side of the line or the other. To minimize the chances of such injustices occurring, the line should be drawn as clearly as possible. . . .

NOTES

(1) *Questions.* Do you agree with Judge Breitel that Grace Ortelere's selection was "evidently unwise and foolhardy"? What additional facts might help in answering that question? At several points in the opinion, the court asserted that no substantial harm to the system would result from setting aside Ortelere's election. Would this be so if the choices made by a large number of participants in a similar pension program proved to be revocable after death? See Kennedy v. New York City Employees' Retirement System, 381 N.Y.S.2d 79 (App.Div.1976).

Is the *Ortelere* rule limited to cases in which the employee has had psychiatric or similar consultation before making an election? How significant was it that "the system was, or should have been, fully aware of Ortelere's condition"? Many employers fund their pension plans through professional insurers, who are not likely to know of an employee's psychosis. Should the knowledge of such an employer be attributed to the insurer? Why should it matter whether or not *either* was aware of the employee's condition? Does it matter under Restatement § 15? See Pentinen v. Retirement System, 401 N.Y.S.2d 587 (App.Div.1978).

(2) *Family Affairs.* Mrs. Ortelere changed her election without telling her husband. Should that fact matter in a determination of her competency? Should she have been required to consult or inform him? When asked at trial whether his wife "handled all the money matters in the house" even during the periods of her breakdown, Mr. Ortelere testified that she did: "She was the businesswoman, yes.... She wouldn't let me have a checkbook. She made out [all] the checks, yes." See Richard Danzig and Geoffrey Watson, *The Capability Problem in Contract Law* 272 (2004). What do you make of Mr. Ortolere's testimony?

Under the Employee Retirement Income Security Act (ERISA), 29 U.S.C. §§ 1001 *et seq.*, a person in Mrs. Ortelere's position could not now, except in some cases of exigency, elect a lifetime annuity and deprive her or his spouse of a survivor's annuity, without the spouse's written consent, given before a witness. (Consent is not required to reduce the survivor's annuity to half the amount payable while both live.)

(3) *Capacities Compared.* Farnum v. Silvano, 540 N.E.2d 202 (Mass.App.1989), was an action by the seller of a home to rescind the sale. The seller was a woman of 90 years, who sometimes exhibited distressing delusions (*e.g.*, that her house had a second story). The purchaser was a young man who had kept up her lawn and who had her confidence. He had paid about 56% of the fair market value of the home, while obtaining a mortgage loan on the property for much more than the fair market value. The trial court concluded that the seller had conveyed her home during a lucid interval and ruled for the defendant. She appealed. *Held:* Reversed, and rescission ordered. The court cited *Ortelere,* and said: "Acting during a lucid interval can be the basis for executing a will.... Competence to enter into a contract presupposes something more than a transient surge of lucidity." What explains the differing measures for capacity with regard to wills and contracts?

Cundick v. Broadbent

United States Court of Appeals, Tenth Circuit, 1967.
383 F.2d 157.

[Darwin Cundick was a 59-year-old sheep rancher who had on occasion sold his lamb crop to J.R. Broadbent. At a meeting between the two men in September, 1963, they signed a one-page contract in longhand by which Cundick agreed to sell all of his ranching properties to Broadbent. Mr. and Mrs. Cundick then took the contract to their lawyer, who refined and amplified it into an eleven-page document, which the parties signed in his office. In October, 1963, the agreement was amended, again with a lawyer's aid, so as to increase the price to Cundick and in another respect favorable to him. Under the amended agreement, more than 2,000 acres of range land went for about $40,000. (An expert later valued it at $89,000.) Also included was Cundick's interest in a development company of which Broadbent was a director, at a price of $46,750. (A witness for Cundick later valued this at $184,000, and one for Broadbent at $73,743.) As late as February, 1964, Cundick was executing documents to carry out the sale. In March, when the price had been paid and the sale was almost completed, Cundick sought to rescind. His wife, who had been appointed his guardian *ad litem* ("for the purpose of suing"), brought an action against Broadbent to set aside the agreement. She asserted that her husband had been mentally incompetent to contract, and that in any event he was mentally infirm and Broadbent had knowingly overreached him. The evidence showed that Cundick had had psychiatric treatment in 1961. Thereafter his family doctor saw him many times about various ailments, but nothing was said or done about a mental condition before the suit was commenced. The court ordered examinations in 1964; they disclosed premature arteriosclerosis. Two neurosurgeons and a psychologist testified that Cundick had been incapable, the previous September, of transacting important business affairs, and that he was a "confused and befuddled man with very poor judgment." There was no medical evidence to the contrary. The trial court nevertheless found: "The acts and conduct of Cundick between September 2, 1963, and the middle of February, 1964, were the acts, conduct and behavior of a person competent to manage his affairs and cognizant of the effect of his actions." It also found that the contract was not unconscionable, unfair or inequitable. From a dismissal of the action, Mrs. Cundick appealed.]

■ MURRAH, CHIEF JUDGE. . . . At one time, in this country and in England, it was the law that since a lunatic or non compos mentis had no mind with which to make an agreement, his contract was wholly void and incapable of ratification. But, if his mind was merely confused or weak so that he knew what he was doing yet was incapable of fully understanding the terms and effect of his agreement, he could indeed contract, but such contract would be voidable at his option. . . . But in recent times courts have tended away from the concept of absolutely void contracts toward the notion that even though a contract be said to be void for lack of capacity to make it, it is nevertheless ratifiable at the instance of the incompetent party. The modern rule, and the weight of authority, seems to be [that] ". . . the contractual act by one claiming to be mentally deficient, but not under guardianship, absent fraud, or knowledge of such asserted incapacity by the other contracting party, is not a void act but at most only voidable at the instance of the deficient party; and then only in accordance with certain equitable principles." Rubenstein v. Dr. Pepper Co., 8 Cir., 228 F.2d 528. . . .

In recognition of different degrees of mental competency the weight of authority seems to hold that mental capacity to contract depends upon whether the allegedly disabled person possessed sufficient reason to enable him to understand the nature and effect of the act in issue. Even average intelligence is not essential to a valid bargain. . . . "Mere weakness of body or mind, or of both, do not constitute what the law regards as mental incompetency sufficient to render a contract voidable. . . . A condition which may be described by a physician as senile dementia may not be insanity in a legal sense." Kaleb v. Modern Woodmen of America, 51 Wyo. 116, 64 P.2d 605, 607. Weakmindedness is, however, highly relevant in determining whether the deficient party was overreached and defrauded. . . .

There was, to be sure, evidence of a change in [Cundick's] personality and attitude toward his business affairs during [the period between his mental examinations in 1961 and 1964]. But the record is conspicuously silent concerning any discussion of his mental condition among his family and friends in the community where he lived and operated his ranch. Certainly, the record is barren of any discussion or comment in Broadbent's presence. It seems incredible that Cundick could have been utterly incapable of transacting his business affairs, yet such condition be unknown on this record to his family and friends, especially his wife who lived and worked with him and participated in the months-long transaction which she now contends was fraudulently conceived and perpetrated. . . .

The narrated facts of this case amply support the trial court's finding to the effect that Broadbent did not deceive or overreach Cundick. . . . [Although] there is positive evidence that the property was worth very much more than what Broadbent paid for it, . . . there was evidence to the effect that after the original contract was signed and some complaint made about the purchase price, the parties agreed to raise the price and the contract was so modified.

[Affirmed.]

■ HILL, CIRCUIT JUDGE (dissenting): . . . . The evidence relied upon by the majority is actually trivial and inconsequential as compared with the undisputed medical testimony. . . . It is inconceivable to me that any mentally competent person, with a lifetime of experience as a successful rancher and stockman, would dispose of his ranch interests at a price equal to less than one-half of the actual value. . . .

NOTES

(1) *Case Comparison.* Are the *Ortelere* and *Cundick* cases distinguishable? To what extent do the differences among the opinions in those cases reflect the different orientations regarding status, behavior, and substance introduced at p. 310 above?

(2) *Supervision.* Guardians or conservators may be appointed for persons of mental debility, as authorized by statutes. California provides for the judicial appointment of conservators for persons who, for specified reasons, are "likely to be deceived or imposed upon by artful or designing persons." See Board of Regents of State University, State of Wisconsin v. Davis, 533 P.2d 1047 (Cal.1975). What virtues and hazards do you see in the process?

(3) *Appearances.* Claims of incapacity raise several issues of proof. In Hakimoglu v. Trump Taj Mahal Associates, 876 F.Supp. 625 (D.N.J.1994), intoxication was raised as a defense to an action by a casino to recover $700,000 in gambling debts. The gambler argued that he had been plied with martinis by the casino; the casino argued that Hakimoglu was not "visibly and obviously drunk." The court said that as the party asserting intoxication, Hakimoglu had "the burden of coming forward with evidence from which a reasonable fact-finder [could] conclude that he was intoxicated." It remanded the case for a jury determination of Hakimoglu's apparent state at the time the credits were extended, as recorded by surveillance cameras and other observers.

(4) *Particularized Incapacities.* Are there other conditions that so impair a person's ability to comprehend a particular transaction as to make a transaction of that kind reversible by that person? What about grief, in connection with buying a coffin for a loved one? Is the example different in kind from the disabling condition in *Ortelere*? Are there disadvantages to using capacity as the policing mechanism in such cases as the purchase of a coffin?

SECTION 2.   OVERREACHING

Under the leadership of equity, the courts have traditionally been insistent that no advantage should be gained through gross unfairness in the *process* of bargaining. The means condemned in classical equity are duress, fraud, and mistake. When a contract is found to result from one of these infirmities, the ordinary remedy is to allow the victim to rescind or avoid it; the contract affected is said to be "avoidable." As the successors to equity powers, courts in which contract litigation is conducted are now competent to avoid a contract without requiring an independent proceeding for rescission.

We begin with duress, or impermissible pressure exerted by one party over another either during pre-contractual bargaining, or, as is often the case, during the attempted renegotiation of an existing deal. We then turn to a second type of misbehavior, one concerning the obligations of one party to make accurate representations to the other in the bargaining context. Not only fraud, in the sense of deliberate trickery or deceit, but even an innocent misrepresentation made in the bargaining process may be a ground for avoiding a contract. Indeed, it is sometimes required that a party possessed of information material to the exchange either disclose it or refrain from exploiting the ignorance of the other. Mistake is taken up in Chapter 9.

What privilege of exploiting superior knowledge for a bargaining advantage should be recognized? How should the risks of inaccuracy in statements and of errors of fact be allocated between the parties? What pressures may be exerted by one party on another to gain assent to a bargain or to the settlement of a dispute? Finally, what role does the doctrine of consideration play in the scheme of policing the bargaining process? These are some of the questions examined here.

(A) PRESSURE IN BARGAINING

When a person has used compulsion on another to obtain a benefit, the victim can sometimes compel restoration: money paid and property transferred under duress may be recovered. Similarly, a promise obtained by duress may not be enforced against the victim. Moses v. Macferlan, 97 Eng.Rep. 676 (King's Bench 1760). In that case Lord Mansfield said that an action for money had and received lies "for money got through imposition (express or implied); or extortion; or oppression; or an undue advantage taken of the plaintiff's situation, contrary to laws made for the protection of persons under those circumstances." In early English cases from which the current doctrine stems, such relief was confined to situations in which coercion took the form of imprisonment or threats of confinement or bodily harm. Later, threats of purely economic injury became a ground for relief when "duress of goods" (a threat to a person's property) was recognized.

The general concept of "economic coercion" has now become a sort of junior partner of duress in redressing oppression.

A number of policy considerations, as well as some surviving technical obstacles, limit the use of duress as a commonplace defense in contract actions. One important limitation is the insistence upon a reasonable degree of temerity in the face of a threat. The requirement of at least some resistance, developed at p. 334 below, restricts relief for duress by denying it to persons who yield to pressure too easily.

A second limitation concerns the substance of the threat. As indicated above, threats to business interests, as well as to life or limb, may now constitute duress. Making someone an offer "they cannot refuse" is not a permissible business practice. Yet not all threats constitute duress. Certainly one who yields to a threat of criminal or tortious injury may be given relief. In contrast, it has also been held that a threat of *lawful* action cannot be wrongful: "It is not duress to threaten to do what there is a legal right to do." Chouinard v. Chouinard, 568 F.2d 430 (5th Cir.1978).

This qualification has particular application to cases in which a dispute is settled under the threat of a lawsuit. As it is not unlawful to institute legal proceedings, a party threatened with suit may not buy its way out and thereafter complain of the bargain. Yet there are limitations even on the threat of suit. As we saw in Fiege v. Boehm, p. 40 above, and Note 3, p. 45 above, on strike suits, one does not have the right to bring a suit without some basis for the underlying claim.

Thus it is not *quite* the rule that one may rightfully threaten any kind of rightful act. "An unjust and inequitable threat is wrongful, although the threatened act would not be a violation of duty in the sense of an independent actionable wrong in the law of crimes, torts, or contracts." McCubbin v. Buss, 144 N.W.2d 175 (Neb.1966). This view is illustrated in cases where an employer exacts a benefit from an employee, under threat of discharge, where the employment is terminable at will. See Gerber v. First Nat. Bank, 332 N.E.2d 615 (Ill.App.1975). As you read the cases in this section consider Lake Land Employment v. Columber, p. 58 above, and whether Lake Land's request in that case that Columber sign a covenant not to compete rose to the level of duress?

NOTES

(1) *Duress by Threat of Suit.* When a party seeks relief from a contract on the ground of coercion, it is not uncommon to find that the complaining party is itself adept at coercive practices. An example is Undersea Eng. & Const. Co. v. International Tel. & Tel. Corp., 429 F.2d 543, 549 (9th Cir.1970). In that case the plaintiff, Undersea, had been a subcontractor on a job for which the defendant, ITT, was the general contractor. Disputes between them led to extended negotiations, and to a settlement which Undersea later sought to void. ITT was depicted as a billion-dollar corporation having elephantine power over Undersea. The court observed, however, that before the settlement "Undersea was using every threat of economic and moral pressure to coerce and force ITT to settle rather than face a law suit with threatened world-wide publicity."

(2) *Duress in Context.* Should the law be concerned with *why* a threat of lawful action was effective against the party complaining of it? Put another way, should the law take account of the social or emotional origins of particular threats, such as the consequences to a young man of being threatened with a paternity suit? Or the humiliation of canceling a wedding the day before unless the bride signs a prenuptial agreement?

What about a wife who is threatened with a divorce by her husband unless she signs a "post-nuptial" property agreement? In Pacelli v. Pacelli, 725 A.2d 56, 58, 61 (N.J.Sup.1999), a wife agreed to a property settlement effective in the case of an eventual divorce, in exchange for her husband's promise not to file for divorce immediately. The court compared the wife's circumstances with that of a fiancé: "[Mrs. Pacelli] faced a more difficult choice than the bride who is presented with a demand for a pre-nuptial agreement. The cost to her would have been the destruction of a family and the stigma of a failed marriage. She testified on several occasions that she signed the agreement to preserve the family and to make sure that her sons were raised in an intact family.... Our point is that the context in which [Mr. Pacelli] made his demand was inherently coercive. [Mrs. Pacelli's] access to eminent counsel is of little relevance because her decision was dictated not by a consideration of her legal rights, but by her desire to preserve the family."

The court held that, while it need not decide if "such agreements are so inherently and unduly coercive that they should not be enforced, ... at the very least, [their content] must be closely scrutinized and carefully evaluated." It concluded that the terms of the Pacelli agreement were "not fair and just."

PROBLEM

Parental Concern. A farm couple mortgaged their property to a bank for the purpose (they said) of preventing their son Glen from going to prison. Glen had been found to have defrauded creditors of his business, a farm-implement dealership. The president of the bank, to which the parents gave a guaranty of Glen's debt, and the mortgage, testified that no threats were made to induce the execution of these papers. But a trial court found otherwise and rescinded the agreement. On the bank's appeal, the court found it incredible that the parents would hazard the fruits of fifty years of toil to try to bail out a business "which was in debt to the extent of $628,000 plus, absent the threat and concern that the son might go to prison."

Before the guaranty was given, Glen's father had consulted a lawyer (whose advice he disregarded) and Glen's mother had berated the bank president for lending him so much money. Should the trial court's decree be reversed? Would it matter that Glen implored his parents to sign? What if the bank had relied on the guaranty by purchasing the claims of other creditors of Glen's business? See Haumont v. Security State Bank, 374 N.W.2d 2 (Neb.1985).

THE PRE–EXISTING DUTY RULE

"Performance of a legal duty owed to a promisor which is neither doubtful nor the subject of honest dispute is not consideration...." Restatement § 73. This is a recent version of an old rule that has given rise to some dissatisfaction. Professor Edwin Patterson observed that it is "on the whole, that adjunct of the doctrine of consideration which has done most to give it a bad name." Patterson, An Apology for Consideration, 58 Colum.L.Rev. 929, 936–38 (1958). On the other hand, as illustrated in the following well-known case, some decisions upholding the rule are generally applauded. The case raises a question often played out on more subtle facts: When is the modification of a contract properly seen as resulting from the genuine assent of the party to whom performance is owed, and when is a renegotiated deal more likely the result of coercion?

Alaska Packers' Ass'n v. Domenico

United States Court of Appeals, Ninth Circuit, 1902.
117 F. 99.

[A group of workmen had individually signed contracts with Alaska Packers to sail from San Francisco to Pyramid Harbor, Alaska "as sailors and fishermen, agreeing to do 'regular ship's duty, both up and down, discharging and loading; and to do any other work whatsoever when requested to do so by the captain or agent of the Alaska Packers' Association." Under the agreement, Alaska Packers was to pay each of the workmen "$50 for the season, and two cents for each red salmon in the catching of which he took part."

Upon arrival at Pyramid Harbor, where Alaska Packers "had about $150,000 invested in a salmon cannery," the workmen "stopped work in a body" and demanded *$100* for their services, stating that "unless they were paid this additional wage they would stop work entirely, and return to San Francisco." Since it was impossible to get substitute workers, the superintendent signed an agreement to pay the larger amount. Upon the return of the men to San Francisco at the end of the season, Alaska Packers paid them in accordance with the first agreement, and the employees sued in admiralty to recover the additional compensation. From judgment for the workmen (the "libelants"), Alaska Packers appealed.]

■ Ross, Circuit Judge. On the trial in the court below, the libelants undertook to show that the fishing nets provided by the respondent were defective, and that it was on that account that they demanded increased wages. On that point, the evidence was substantially conflicting, and the finding of the court was against the libelants the court saying:

> 'The contention of libelants that the nets provided them were rotten and unserviceable is not sustained by the evidence. The defendants' interest required that libelants should be provided with every facility necessary to their success as fishermen, for on such success depended the profits defendant would be able to realize that season from its packing plant, and the large capital invested therein. In view of this self-evident fact, it is highly improbable that the defendant gave libelants rotten and unserviceable nets with which to fish. It follows from this finding that libelants were not justified in refusing performance of their original contract.' 112 Fed. 554.

The evidence being sharply conflicting in respect to these facts, the conclusions of the court, who heard and saw the witnesses, will not be disturbed....

The real questions in the case as brought here are questions of law, and, in the view that we take of the case, it will be necessary to consider but one of those. Assuming that the appellant's superintendent at Pyramid Harbor was authorized to make the alleged contract of May 22d, and that he executed it on behalf of the appellant, was it supported by a sufficient consideration? From the foregoing statement of the case, it will have been seen that the libelants agreed in writing, for certain stated compensation, to render their services to the appellant in remote waters where the season for conducting fishing operations is extremely short, and in which enterprise the appellant had a large amount of money invested; and, after having entered upon the discharge of their contract, and at a time when it was impossible for the appellant to secure other men in their places, the libelants, without any valid cause, absolutely refused to continue the services they were under contract to perform unless the appellant would consent to pay them more money. Consent to such a demand, under such circumstances, if given, was, in our opinion, without consideration, for the reason that it was based solely upon the libelants' agreement to render the exact services, and none other, that they were already under contract to render. The case shows that they willfully and arbitrarily broke that obligation....

Certainly, it cannot be justly held, upon the record in this case, that there was any voluntary waiver on the part of the appellant of the breach of the original contract. The company itself knew nothing of such breach until the expedition returned to San Francisco, and the testimony is uncontradicted that its superintendent at Pyramid Harbor, who, it is claimed, made on its behalf the contract sued on, distinctly informed the libelants that he had no power to alter the original or to make a new contract, and it would, of course, follow that, if he had no power to change the original, he would have no authority to waive any rights thereunder. The circumstances of the present case bring it, we think, directly within the sound and just observations of the Supreme Court of Minnesota in the case of King v. Railway Co., 61 Minn. 482, 63 N.W. 1105:

> 'No astute reasoning can change the plain fact that the party who refuses to perform, and thereby coerces a promise from the other party to the contract to pay him an increased compensation for doing that which he is legally bound to do, takes an unjustifiable advantage of the necessities of the other party. Surely it would be a travesty on justice to hold that the party so making the promise for extra pay was estopped from asserting that the promise was without consideration. A party cannot lay the foundation of an estoppel by his own wrong, where the promise is simply a repetition of a subsisting legal promise. There can be no consideration for the promise of the other party, and there is no warrant for inferring that the parties have voluntarily rescinded or modified their contract. The promise cannot be legally enforced, although the other party has completed his contract in reliance upon it.'

In Lingenfelder v. Brewing Co., 103 Mo. 578, 15 S.W. 844, the court, in holding void a contract by which the owner of a building agreed to pay its architect an additional sum because of his refusal to otherwise proceed with the contract, said:

"It is urged upon us by respondents that this was a new contract. New in what? Jungenfeld was bound by his contract to design and supervise this building. Under the new promise, he was not to do anything more or anything different. What benefit was to accrue to Wainwright? He was to receive the same service from Jungenfeld under the new, that Jungenfeld was bound to tender under the original, contract. What loss, trouble, or inconvenience could result to Jungenfeld that he had not already assumed? No amount of metaphysical reasoning can change the plain fact that Jungenfeld took advantage of Wainwright's necessities, and extorted the promise of five per cent. on the refrigerator plant as the condition of his complying with his contract already entered into. . . .

"To permit plaintiff to recover under such circumstances would be to offer a premium upon bad faith, and invite men to violate their most sacred contracts that they may profit by their own wrong. That a promise to pay a man for doing that which he is already under contract to do is without consideration is conceded by respondents. The rule has been so long imbedded in the common law and decisions of the highest courts of the various states that nothing but the most cogent reasons ought to shake it. (Citing a long list of authorities.) But it is 'carrying coals to Newcastle' to add authorities on a proposition so universally accepted, and so inherently just and right in itself. . . . [W]hen a party merely does what he has already obligated himself to do, he cannot demand an additional compensation therefor; and although, by taking advantage of the necessities of his adversary, he obtains a promise for more, the law will regard it as nudum pactum, and will not lend its process to aid in the wrong." . . .

It results from the views above expressed that the judgment must be reversed. . . .

NOTES

(1) *Questions.* What factors support the court's conclusion? Discussing *Alaska Packers*, Judge Posner concluded that due to the circumstances, the fishermen had a temporary monopoly on labor and that "[t]he exploitation of temporary monopolies is the functional meaning of the legal concept of economic duress." Trompler v. NLRB, 338 F.3d 747, 751–52 (7th Cir. 2003). Is there anything to be said on the fishermen's side? For background on the case, and on the Alaskan salmon canning fishing industry at the turn of the century, see Deborah Threedy, A Fish Story: Alaska Packers' Association v. Domenico, 2000 Utah L.Rev. 185.

(2) *Rejection and Reformation of the Rule.* In some states the pre-existing duty rule has been largely rejected by judicial decision. In Alabama, for example, the rule is that "an executory contract may be modified by the parties without any new consideration other than mutual consent." Winegardner v. Burns, 361 So.2d 1054 (Ala.1978).

Other states have suspended the rule legislatively in certain circumstances. For example, a New York statute provides:

Written agreement for modification or discharge. An agreement, promise or undertaking to change or modify, or to discharge in whole or in part, any contract, obligation, or lease, or any mortgage or other security interest in personal or real property, shall not be invalid because of the absence of consideration, provided that the agreement, promise or undertaking changing, modifying, or discharging such contract, obligation, lease, mortgage or security interest, shall be in writing and signed by the party against whom it is sought to enforce the change, modification or discharge, or by his agent.

N.Y.Gen.Oblig.L., § 5–1103.

How would the Alaska Packers case have been decided under the statute?

Article 2 of the UCC permits the modification of a contract without consideration. See UCC § 2–209(1). How does the Article 2 approach differ from that of the New York statute quoted above? The CISG and the UNIDROIT Principles are in general accord with Article 2. See CISG art. 20(1) and UNIDROIT Principles art. 3.2.

(3) *Duress Nonetheless?* Might a modifying agreement that is within UCC § 2–209(1), or the New York statute quoted above, be voidable for duress if it was induced by one party's threat to break the contract? Comment 2 to UCC § 2–209 states, in part, that "modifications made thereunder must meet the test of good faith imposed by this Act ... and the extortion of a 'modification' without legitimate commercial reason is ineffective as a violation of the duty of good faith." See Farnsworth, Good Faith Purchase and Commercial Reasonableness Under the Uniform Commercial Code, 30 U. Chi. L. Rev. 666, 675–76 (1963). Which part of the UCC definition of good faith might be violated by an extorted modification?

A thoughtful review of the pre-existing duty rule by Professor Robert Hillman concluded that it has been dismissed too summarily in UCC § 2–209. He recommended that a person relying on a concession under certain modifying agreements be put to proof that the concession was not unfairly coerced. Does the rule of Restatement § 89 make a satisfying balance of the opposing considerations? See Hillman, Policing Contract Modifications under the UCC: Good Faith and the Doctrine of Economic Duress, 64 Iowa L.Rev. 849 (1979).

(4) *Pre-existing Statutory Duty?* Michael Borelli and Hilda Borelli were married in 1980. In 1988, Michael suffered a stroke and thereafter required round-the-clock nursing care. Unhappy at being cared for in a rehabilitation center, Michael agreed to transfer certain real property to Hilda upon his death in exchange for her promise to care for him at home for the duration of his illness. Hilda agreed, and took care of Michael until his death, in 1989. Michael's will bequeathed Hilda $100,000; the remainder of his estate, including the promised properties, were left to Michael's daughter by his first marriage. In an action by Hilda for specific performance, the trial court dismissed the complaint on the ground that the agreement was without consideration. Hilda appealed. *Held*: Affirmed. Borelli v. Brusseau, 16 Cal.Rptr.2d 16 (Ct.App.1993).

The court took account of two provisions of the California Civil Code: Section 5100 ("Husband and wife contract toward each other obligations of mutual respect, fidelity, and support"), and Section 5132 ("[A] married person shall support the person's spouse while they are living together ..."). It concluded that "[p]ersonal performance of a personal duty created by the contract of marriage does not constitute a new consideration supporting the indebtedness alleged in this case." The court also found on policy grounds that "deathbed negotiating" was "antithetical to the institution of marriage as the Legislature has defined it." *Id.* at 20.

The dissent noted that "[h]ad there been no marriage and had they been total strangers, there is no doubt Mr. Borelli could have validly contracted to receive [the claimant's] services in exchange for certain of his property. The mere existence of a marriage certificate should not deprive otherwise competent adults of the 'utmost freedom of contract' they would otherwise possess.... In this context, public policy should not be equated with coerced altruism." *Id.* at 23, 25.

(5) *Reliance Redux.* If a promisor is relieved of her promise by virtue of the pre-existing duty rule, might the promisee enforce the promise on a reliance theory?

PROBLEM

Work Reduction. Refer again to Ever–Tite Roofing Corp. v. Green, p. 154 above. Suppose these changes in the facts: Ever–Tite's workmen arrived at the Greens' residence, found no other roofer engaged, and advised the Greens that although new gutters were called for in the signed agreement, Ever–Tite had discontinued gutter work. They persuaded the Greens to initial an amendment to the agreement stating "gutter installation eliminated." Would the Greens be bound by the amendment? See Engle v. Shapert Constr. Co., 443 F.Supp. 1383 (M.D.Pa.1978). Would it matter whether or not Article 2 of the Code applies to a sale and installation of roofing materials?

————

AVOIDING THE PRE–EXISTING DUTY RULE:
RESCISSION AND MODIFICATION

Are parties to a contract ever free to disavow their agreements and bargain with one another anew? Are they always free to do so? In Schwartzreich v. Bauman–Basch, Inc., 131 N.E. 887, 888 (N.Y.1921), Schwartzreich had contracted in writing to work as a clothing designer for Bauman–Basch for one year, beginning several weeks later, at salary of $90 a week. During the period before this employment was to begin, Schwartzreich received an offer of $115 a week to do similar work elsewhere. When he informed Mr. Bauman of this development, Bauman promised to pay him at the weekly rate of $100 if Schwartzreich would reject the other offer. Bauman's testimony about the conversation was as follows:

> "I called him in the office, and I asked him, 'Is that true that you want to leave us?' and he said 'Yes,' and I said, 'Mr. Schwartzreich, how can you do that; you are under contract with us?' He said, 'Somebody offered me more money.' ... I said, 'How much do they offer you?' He said, 'They offered him $115 a week.' ... I said, 'I cannot get a designer now, and, in view of the fact that I have to send my sample line out on the road, I will give you a hundred dollars a week rather than to let you go.' He said, 'If you will give me $100, I will stay.'"

The parties then prepared and signed a new contract just like the earlier one except for the pay rate. At the same time they tore their signatures off the earlier contract. Schwartzreich began work in November, as scheduled, but was discharged soon after. He sued for his wages, which the jury awarded him based on the $100 rate. The trial court set aside the verdict; but it was reinstated on appeal.

According to the appellate court, the situation was one in which "an existing contract is terminated by consent of both parties and a new one executed in its place and stead." The court quoted from Williston:

A rescission followed shortly afterwards by a new agreement in regard to the same subject-matter would create the legal obligations provided in the subsequent agreement.

"Very little difference may appear," the court said, "in a mere change of compensation in an existing and continuing contract and a termination of one contract and the making of a new one for the same time and work, but at an increased compensation. There is, however, a marked difference in principle." Do you see the difference?

NOTES

(1) *Questions.* In *Schwartzreich,* how many contracts did the parties enter into? What was the significance, if any, of the ceremony in which the signatures were torn off the original contract? Would the decision have been different if they had not been torn off until after the parties had signed the new one? If so, is this any way to do business?

The decision in *Schwartzreich* was cited as a source of commercial uncertainty in a study by the New York Law Revision Commission, leading to the enactment of the New York statute on written modifications, set out in Note 2, p. 327 above. There was concern that jury determinations would be unpredictable about whether one contract has been rescinded and replaced by another, or whether the original remained in force with a modification of its terms. N.Y.Law Rev.Com., Second Annual Report 255 (Leg.Doc. No. 65, 1936).

(2) *Lawyers' Roles.* The owners of a farm became dissatisfied with the price they had agreed to accept for it. The buyers agreed to an increase when the sellers' attorney told them that his clients were willing to go to court to get out of the initial agreement, and that they would find litigation expensive. See Recker v. Gustafson, 279 N.W.2d 744 (Iowa 1979).

Are there circumstances in which you, as the lawyer for the sellers, would have declined to negotiate for them in the manner stated? If so, would your decision turn on whether or not the buyers also were advised by counsel? Would it matter that the initial agreement was afflicted (as it was in the case cited) with problems such as definiteness and the statute of frauds?

If an attorney *for the buyers* had advised them to agree to the price increase, would that attorney be at liberty, later, to question the consideration for it? See Rickett v. Doze, 603 P.2d 679 (Mont.1979).

(3) *Restatement.* The two-step process of rescission and modification avoids the pre-existing duty rule as long as the contract is executory, that is, not fully performed on either side. Restatement § 89 provides more directly for the modification of promises "not fully performed on either side." Why is the rule limited to executory contracts?

The Restatement § 89 provides three circumstances in which a promise modifying a contractual duty is binding. The Restatement uses the facts of *Schwartzreich* as an illustration to the section but does not indicate which clause it illustrates. Should the job offer at $115 a week be regarded as a circumstance not anticipated when the contract was made, so that a $10 raise was "fair and equitable" under Restatement § 89(a)? Might subsection (b) or (c) apply?

(4) *The Sheep and the Goats.* It has been urged that the courts should endeavor "to separate the sheep from the goats" by enforcing the new promise in favor of the honest contractor and refusing to enforce it in favor of the dishonest or extortionate contractor. Arthur Corbin, Does a Preexisting Duty Defeat Consideration?, 27 Yale

L.J. 362, 373 (1918). What facts, provable in court, might provide the basis for separating "the sheep from the goats"?

The traditional rationale employed in support of the pre-existing duty doctrine is that it prevents overreaching and blackmail. See Williston, Successive Promises of the Same Performance, 8 Harv.L.Rev. 27 (1894). As Professor Charles Fried notes, however, the modern trend is toward recognition of promises whose legitimacy the strict consideration doctrine placed in doubt, so long as the sincerity of the obligation is clear and the commitment freely made. Charles Fried, *Contract as Promise* (1981) at 39.

Watkins & Son v. Carrig

Supreme Court of New Hampshire, 1941.
91 N.H. 459, 21 A.2d 591, 138 A.L.R. 131.

Assumpsit for work done. By a written contract between the parties the plaintiff agreed to excavate a cellar for the defendant for a stated price. Soon after the work was commenced solid rock was encountered. The plaintiff's manager notified the defendant, a meeting between them was held, and it was orally agreed that the plaintiff should remove the rock at a stipulated unit price about nine times greater than the unit price for excavating upon which the gross amount to be paid according to the written contract was calculated. The rock proved to constitute about two-thirds of the space to be excavated.

A referee found that the oral agreement "superseded" the written contract, and reported a verdict for the plaintiff based on the finding. To the acceptance of the report and an order of judgment thereon the defendant excepted. Further facts appear in the opinion. Transferred by Burque, C.J.

■ ALLEN, CHIEF JUSTICE. When the written contract was entered into, no understanding existed between the parties that no rock would be found in the excavating. The plaintiff's manager made no inquiry or investigation to find out the character of the ground below the surface, no claim is made that the defendant misled him, and the contract contains no reservations for unexpected conditions. It provides that "all material" shall be removed from the site, and its term that the plaintiff is "to excavate" is unqualified. In this situation a defence of mutual mistake is not available. A space of ground to be excavated, whatever its character, was the subject matter of the contract, and the offer of price on that basis was accepted. Leavitt v. Dover, 67 N.H. 94, 32 A. 156, 68 Am.St.Rep. 640. If the plaintiff was unwise in taking chances, it is not relieved, on the ground of mistake, from the burden incurred in being faced with them. The case differs from that of King Co. v. Aldrich, 81 N.H. 42, 121 A. 434, in which the parties did not contract for the property delivered in purported performance of the contract actually made.

The referee's finding that the written contract was "superseded" by an oral contract when the rock was discovered is construed to mean that the parties agreed to rescind the written contract as though it had not been made and entered into an oral one as though it were the sole and original one. The defendant either thought that the contract did not require the excavation of rock on the basis of the contract price or was willing to forego his rights under the contract in respect to rock. It was important to him that the work should not be delayed, and other reasons may have contributed to induce him to the concession he made. In any event, he consented to a special price for excavating rock, whatever his rights under the contract. The plaintiff on the strength of the promise proceeded with the work.

But the defendant contends that the facts do not support a claim of two independent and separate transactions, one in rescission of the written contract as though it were nugatory, and one in full substitution of it. All that is shown, as he urges, is one transaction by which he was to pay more for the excavating than the written contract provided, with that contract otherwise to remain in force. And upon the basis of this position he relies upon the principle of contract law that his promise to pay more was without consideration, as being a promise to pay the plaintiff for performance of its obligation already in force and outstanding. Whether the contract was rescinded with a new one to take its place or whether it remained in force with a modification of its terms, is not important. In the view of a modification, the claim of a promise unsupported by consideration is as tenable as under the view of a rescission. A modification involves a partial rescission.

In the situation presented the plaintiff entered into a contractual obligation. Facts subsequently learned showed the obligation to be burdensome and the contract improvident. On insistent request by the plaintiff, the defendant granted relief from the burden by a promise to pay a special price which overcame the burden. The promise was not an assumption of the burden; the special price was fair and the defendant received reasonable value for it.

The issue whether the grant of relief constituted a valid contract is one of difficulty. The basic rule that a promise without consideration for it is invalid leads to its logical application that a promise to pay for what the promisor already has a right to receive from the promise is invalid. The promisee's performance of an existing duty is no detriment to him, and hence nothing is given by him beyond what is already due the promisor. But the claim is here made that the original contract was rescinded, either in full or in respect to some of its terms, by mutual consent, and since any rescission mutually agreed upon is in itself a contract, the claim of a promise to pay for performance of a subsisting duty is unfounded. The terms of the contract of rescission are of course valid if the rescission is valid. The defendant's answer to this claim is well stated in this quotation from Williston, Contr., 2d Ed., § 130a: "But calling an agreement an agreement for rescission does not do away with the necessity of consideration, and when the agreement for rescission is coupled with a further agreement that the work provided for in the earlier agreement shall be completed and that the other party shall give more than he originally promised, the total effect of the second agreement is that one party promises to do exactly what he had previously bound himself to do, and the other party promises to give an additional compensation therefor.''

With due respect for this eminent authority, the argument appears to clothe consideration with insistence of control beyond its proper demands. With full recognition of the legal worthlessness of a bare promise and of performance of a subsisting duty as a void consideration, a result accomplished by proper means is not necessarily bad because it would be bad if the means were improper or were not employed. . . .

In common understanding there is, importantly, a wide divergence between a bare promise and a promise in adjustment of a contractual promise already outstanding. A promise with no supporting consideration would upset well and long-established human interrelations if the law did not treat it as a vain thing. But parties to a valid contract generally understand that it is subject to any mutual action they may take in its performance. Changes to meet changes in circumstances and conditions should be valid if the law is to carry out its function and service by rules conformable with reasonable practices and understandings in matters of business and commerce. . . . Merger of the rescission and promise into one transaction does not destroy them as elements composing the transaction. . . .

The case is one of a simple relinquishment of a right pertaining to intangible personalty. The defendant intentionally and voluntarily yielded to a demand for a special price for excavating rock. In doing this he yielded his contract right to the price it provided. Whether or not he thought he had the right, he intended, and executed his intent, to make no claim of the right. The promise of a special price for excavating rock necessarily imported a release or waiver of any right by the contract to hold the plaintiff to the lower price the contract stipulated. In mutual understanding the parties agreed that the contract price was not to control. The contract right being freely surrendered, the issue of contract law whether the new promise is valid is not doubtful. If the totality of the transaction was a promise to pay more for less, there was in its inherent makeup a valid discharge of an obligation. Although the transaction was single, the element of discharge was distinct in precedence of the new promise.

The foregoing views are considered to meet the reasonable needs of standard and ethical practices of men in their business dealings with each other. Conceding that the plaintiff threatened to break its contract because it found the contract to be improvident, yet the defendant yielded to the threat without protest, excusing the plaintiff, and making a new arrangement. Not insisting on his rights but relinquishing them, fairly he should be held to the new arrangement. The law is a means to the end. It is not the law because it is the law, but because it is adapted and adaptable to establish and maintain reasonable order. If the phrase justice according to law were transposed into law according to justice, it would perhaps be more accurately expressive. In a case like this, of conflicting rules and authority, a result which is considered better to establish ''fundamental justice and reasonableness'' (Cavanaugh v. Boston & M. Railroad, 76 N.H. 68, 72, 79 A. 694, 696), should be attained. It is not practical that the law should adopt all precepts of moral conduct, but it is desirable that its rules and principles should not run counter to them in the important conduct and transactions of life.

Exceptions overruled.

NOTES

(1) *Questions*. Why was the "insistent request" of the excavator not found to be as coercive as the demands of the fishermen in *Alaska Packers*, p. 325 above? How did the court overcome the rule regarding rescission set out in *Schwartzreich*, p. 329 above? The opinion discusses the importance of "changes [in agreements] to meet changes in circumstances." How good is the argument that circumstances changed in this case? In reflecting about that, consider that the official nickname of New Hampshire is "the Granite State". Is there an argument that Watkins v. Son assumed the risk that performance might be burdensome?

(2) *Transactional Constraints*? What prevents purely opportunistic attempts to renegotiate terms? Economists suggest a number of constraints. "The party demanding modification on threat of breach will need to take account of: the impact of this on future dealings with the other party if repeat transactions are envisaged; the reputation effects on other potential trading partners in the market; ease of substitution by the party from whom the modification is demanded; initial contract terms that may make the latter party unreceptive to a modification (for example, liquidated damage or penalty clauses ...); the possibility of the latter party obtaining specific relief in the form of an injunction or specific performance; exposure to a damages claim in the event that modification is refused and breach occurs." Varouj Aivazian, Michael Trebilcock & Michael Penny, The Law of Contract Modification: The Uncertain Quest for a Bench Mark of Enforceability, 22 Osgoode Hall L.J. 173, 174 (1984). Which of these constraints, if any, might have operated in *Watkins & Son*? In *Alaska Packers*?

YIELDING TO THREAT

How resilient must the pressured party be? And in the face of what degree of impermissible behavior? In Denbow v. Tesch, 278 N.W. 16 (S.D. 1938), a brother threatened his sister that unless she signed an agreement dividing their parents' estate, he would "law and law it" in court and she would get nothing. The sister signed and later sought to have the agreement cancelled. In upholding the agreement, the court stated: "Suffice it to say that if it be assumed that this feeble threat was effective in coercing the signature of the plaintiff, it is not such a threat as will support a conclusion that the consent of the plaintiff was procured through duress and menace."

And what degree of fortitude is required if the threat or pressure is more substantial? The homeowner in *Watkins & Son* seemed to cave quickly. Did he meet the standard of duress and resistance suggested by one court of "restraint or danger, either actually inflicted or impending, which is sufficient in severity or apprehension to overcome the mind of a person of ordinary firmness"? Carrier v. William Penn Broadcasting Co., 233 A.2d 519 (Pa.1967). Other courts imply even stricter tests: duress, as they describe it, must deprive a person of free exercise of will, see

Raymundo v. Hammond Clinic Ass'n, 449 N.E.2d 276 (Ind.1983), or destroy a person's volition, see Konsuvo v. Netzke, 220 A.2d 424 (N.J. 1966). Such expressions, often somewhat metaphorical, appear largely in cases where relief was *granted,* and often in cases where no such total mastery over the innocent party existed.

A classical passage rejecting the "no will" conception of duress is from Holmes: "It always is for the interest of a party under duress to choose the lesser of two evils. But the fact that a choice was made according to interest does not exclude duress. It is the characteristic of duress properly so called." Union Pacific R. Co. v. Public Service Comm., 248 U.S. 67 (1918) (duress by a state agency). On the other hand, it is regularly acknowledged that a perfectly honorable agreement may be made with a person who must either accede to it or face some repugnant alternative. Tidwell v. Critz, 282 S.E.2d 104 (Ga.1981). "The question is one of degree." Hellenic Lines, Ltd. v. Louis Dreyfus Corp., 372 F.2d 753 (2d Cir.1967).

NOTES

(1) *Objective or Subjective?* By what standard is the loss of "free will" measured? As one court has stated, "It was said in the early books that there could not be duress by threats unless the threats were such as 'to put a brave man in fear'; then came the qualified standard of something sufficient to overcome the will of a person of 'ordinary firmness'; but the tendency of more recent cases, and the rules comporting with reason and principle, is that any 'unlawful threats' which do in fact 'overcome the will of the person threatened, and induce him to do an act which he would not otherwise have done ... constitutes duress. The age, sex, capacity, relation of parties and all attendant circumstances must be considered.' " Rubenstein v. Rubenstein, 120 A.2d 11, 14 (N.J.1956). (In that case the threats to a husband from his wife included gang violence and arsenic poisoning.)

How is evidence that a party's will has been overcome to be adduced? In *Rubenstein*, the court said that it may be proved by the party's own testimony.

(2) *Hard Choices.* In considering whether assent has been coerced or whether it simply results from a universe of bleak choices, consider the following case. Nicole, a 17 year old unmarried high school student, executed consent forms surrendering her two day old baby for adoption. Ten days later, and after the statutory period for rescission had passed, she sought to revoke her consent on the ground of duress. She argued that her mother had told her she could not continue to reside in her parents' home if she elected to keep the baby. From a Family Court order vacating Nicole's consent, the adoptive parents appealed. *Held*: Reversed. In re Baby Boy L., 534 N.Y.S.2d 706, 708 (App.Div.1988).

"[S]uggestions, persuasion, arguments or entreaties in favor of adoption do not constitute the 'kind of force' which would sustain a finding of duress.... [M]aternal pressure ... did not necessarily render the circumstances ... coercive nor did the entreaties of her mother impair Nicole's ability to exercise her free will. Instead it appears that Nicole was confronted by an emotionally difficult choice and that she elected to defer to the judgment of her mother." *Id.* at 108.

(3) *Efficient Contracting.* In Selmer Co. v. Blakeslee–Midwest Co., 704 F.2d 924 (7th Cir.1983), the court upheld a settlement agreement between a contractor and a subcontractor, explaining that the financial difficulties of the sub did not present a factual issue of duress. "The fundamental issue in a duress case is ... whether the statement that induced the promise is the kind of offer to deal that we want to discourage, and hence that we call a 'threat.' ... If contractual protections are

illusory, people will be reluctant to make contracts. Allowing contract modifications to be avoided in circumstances such as those in *Alaska Packers* assures prospective contract parties that signing a contract is not stepping into a trap, and by thus encouraging people to make contracts promotes the efficient allocation of resources."

If Alaska Packers had been held chargeable with the higher wage it promised, what measures might it have taken to avoid stepping into the same trap in later fishing seasons? See the excerpt quoted in Note 2 (Transactional Constraints), p. 334 above. Would anything suggested there have served Alaska Packers' purpose?

PROBLEM

Hawaiian Housing. Richards contracted to build housing in Hawaii for the Marine Air Corps, using a subcontractor's bid of $49,000 for the metal work. By error, the subcontractor, Air Conditioning Company (AC), had calculated its bid on the assumption that galvanized sheet metal would be used rather than zinc alloy. When AC informed Richards that it would not do the work for the bid price, Richards "blew up." Over the next two months, hard bargaining ensued, during which Richards insisted that AC was bound by its bid price. At length, Richards and AC executed a contract for the metal work at $62,000. After paying some $50,000 as the work progressed, Richards refused to pay more. In fact, he never intended to pay the higher price. When sued for the remainder, Richards relied on the pre-existing duty rule, and cited the Alaska Packers case. Some additional facts may be useful. AC did not inform Richards of its error for about a month after it had discovered its error and learned of the award of the main contract. The second lowest bid was $83,000. Richards's architect had estimated the cost of the metal work at $16,000. One of the bids it received was for more than $173,000.

What result? Is *Alaska Packers* easily distinguishable? Was Richards in a good position to assert the rule, having retreated from the position that AC was bound by its bid?

AVOIDING THE PRE–EXISTING DUTY RULE: NEW CONSIDERATION

Two problematic aspects of the pre-existing duty rule are presented in two well-known cases: Foakes v. Beer and DiCicco v. Schweitzer. Each involved the court's use of consideration doctrine in determining if the rule applied.

Although the doctrine of consideration underlies the rule, it also offers an escape route. As one court has explained, "any consideration for the new undertaking, however insignificant, satisfies this rule. For instance, an undertaking to pay part of the debt before maturity, or at a place other than that where the obligor was legally bound to pay, or to pay in property, regardless of its value, or to effect a composition with creditors by the payment of less than the sum due, has been held to constitute a consideration sufficient in law." Levine v. Blumenthal, 186 A. 457 (N.J. 1936), aff'd on opinion of Supreme Court, 189 A. 54 (N.J.Err. App.1937). The same thought was expressed much earlier by Lord Coke in Pinnel's Case, decided in 1602, cited as 5 Coke's Rep. 117a (in Vol. 3, Part V), 77 Eng.Rep. 237 (Common Pleas): "by no possibility, a lesser sum can be satisfaction to the plaintiff for a greater sum: but the gift of a horse, hawk or robe, etc. in satisfaction is good."

What modern equivalent of a "horse, hawk or robe" might suitably be used to make a creditor's concession to a debtor binding? Restatement § 73 states that a performance "similar" to that owing "is consideration if it differs from what was required ... in a way which reflects more than a pretense of a bargain." Does the concluding phrase encourage lawyers to concoct trivial new objects of bargaining? Or does this use of consideration enable parties to modify their arrangements in accordance with business practices?

————

PARTIAL PAYMENT

A controversial application of the pre-existing duty rule arises in cases in which *part* of a debt has been paid as part of the creditor's agreement for forgiving the rest. Recall that consideration is only a test of the enforceability of an *executory* promise, one that has not been fully performed. See Note 3, p. 330 above. Does the pre-existing rule prevent enforcement by the debtor of the creditor's forgiveness agreement?

The leading case is Foakes v. Beer, 9 App.Cas. 605 (House of Lords 1884). In that case Mrs. Beer, the creditor, had obtained a judgment against Dr. Foakes, her debtor. She then agreed to forgo interest on her judgment and Dr. Foakes paid the principal amount in installments. Still later, she sued to recover the unpaid interest and prevailed. The law lords found a controlling precedent in Pinnel's Case, above. There it was said that "payment of a lesser sum on the day [*i.e.*, on or after the due date of a money debt] cannot be any satisfaction of the whole." In agreeing to pay the judgment, Dr. Foakes did no more than he was obliged to do in any event.

The rule of Foakes v. Beer has often been doubted or denounced. One eminent judge called it a relic of antique law, and "evidence of the former capacity of lawyers and judges to make the requirement of consideration an overworked shibboleth rather than a logical and just standard of accountability." Rye v. Phillips, 282 N.W. 459 (Minn.1938). Even Lord Blackburn, a concurring judge in Foakes v. Beer, had reservations at the time of the decision. As he explained, "all men of business, whether merchants or tradesmen, do every day recognize and act on the ground that prompt payment of a part of their demand may be more beneficial to them than it would be to insist on their rights and enforce payment of the whole." L.R. 9 A.C. at 617, 622.

Some scholars have gone further and challenged the general rule about pre-existing duty, as it affects the modification of contracts. One thoughtful appraisal is that of Professor Patterson, who observed: "The nineteenth century, striving to bring unity out of diversity, included too many different ideas under the general heading of consideration." An Apology for Consideration, p. 324 above.

A common instance of the Foakes v. Beer problem is a "full satisfaction" or "payment in full" check. Does the tender by a debtor of a payment that the debtor designates as conclusive operate as settlement of the account between the parties? If a creditor accepts the tender, is the debtor discharged from further liability on the account? Suppose, for example, a student mails his landlord a first-month rent check labeled "payment in full," having deducted from the rent owed a sum spent for necessary cleaning before moving in. Such cases prompt two basic questions: Did the creditor by depositing the check assent to the settlement? Did the debtor give consideration for being released from part of the month's rent?

The traditional common law answer is seen in Kibler v. Frank L. Garrett & Sons, Inc., 439 P.2d 416 (Wash.1968). Kibler sent a bill for $826 to Garrett & Sons for harvesting wheat. In return, Kibler received a check for $444. He saw a notation typed on it, "Harvesting Wheat Washington Ranch" but did not notice the additional statement, in fine print, "By endorsement this check when paid is accepted in full payment of the following account." Kibler deposited the check, received payment, and then brought an action for the remaining $382. His action was dismissed, and Kibler appealed. *Held:* Reversed. The court seemed concerned chiefly about the matter of agreement. It said: "while the claim was disputed, there was no showing that the defendant manifested to the plaintiff his intention to pay no more than the amount which he remitted." The fine-print legend was on a "form check, presumably used in the payment of all of the defendant's accounts." Even the attorney for Garrett & Sons was apparently unaware of the fine print until it was called to his attention at the trial.

"Payment in full" cases are now governed by UCC § 3–311 (Accord and Satisfaction by Use of Instrument). Fuller exploration of that provision is left to courses on negotiable instruments.

PRE–EXISTING DUTY TO A THIRD PARTY

A second, less common problem concerning the scope of the pre-existing duty rule is whether the rule applies in cases where a contractual duty "pre-exists," but is owed not to the promisor but to a third party. This was the issue presented in De Cicco v. Schweizer, 117 N.E. 807 (N.Y.1917), and decided by Justice Cardozo. Four days before the wedding of Blanche Schweizer, the groom and the bride's parents entered into an agreement conferring on Blanche an annual payment for as long as she and her fiancee should live. Her father expressed his promise of the annuity in a sentence beginning:

> Whereas, Miss Blanche Josephine Schweizer ... is now affianced to and is to be married to the above said Count Oberto Giacomo Giovanni Francesco Maria Gullinelli: Now in consideration of all that is herein set forth the said Mr. Joseph Schweizer promises....

The first payment ($2,500) was made on the wedding day. After the tenth payment, no more was paid. The couple assigned their rights in the contract to Attilio De Cicco, and he sued the father-in-law, Schweizer. (The court assumed, properly, that De Cicco's right to enforce the contract was as good as that of either Blanche or the Count. Assignment is taken up in Chapter 10 below.)

When the case reached the New York Court of Appeals, Judge Cardozo first stated the defendant's contention "that Count Gulinelli was already affianced to Miss Schweizer, and that the marriage was merely the fulfillment of an existing legal duty." (It is helpful to keep in mind that at this time, a breach of a promise to marry was a viable cause of action; one could not break off an engagement with impunity.) Turning to the law, he accepted the premise of the defendant's argument that "a promise by A. to B. to induce him not to break his contract with C. is void." He then developed a distinction, showing that Schweizer's promise was not of that character. Instead, he reasoned, it was a promise to induce the Count ("B.") not to join with Blanche ("C.") in a voluntary rescission of their engagement. Although neither could rightfully withdraw without the other's consent, *together* they were free to terminate the engagement or postpone the marriage. The consideration, then, for Schweizer's promise was that they did not do so.

The opinion then seeks to make this reading plausible: "It does not seem a far-fetched assumption [in relation to contracts to marry] that one will release where the other has repented . . . one does not commonly apply pressure to coerce the will and action of those who are anxious to proceed. The attempt to sway their conduct by new inducements is an implied admission that both may waver. . . ." And in a final paragraph, Cardozo took higher ground, appealing to "those considerations of public policy which cluster about contracts that touch the marriage relation." Do you find the reasoning in the case plausible, or far-fetched? What was Cardozo trying to accomplish?

In a later opinion, Cardozo cited De Cicco v. Schweizer as a "signpost on the road" toward general acceptance of the doctrine of promissory estoppel. See Allegheny College v. National Chautauqua County Bank, referred to at p. 93 above. Do you see a connection between the case and that doctrine? See also Restatement § 90, Illustration 8.

In Central Ceilings, Inc. v. National Amusements, Inc., p. 302 above, National Amusements made an argument that its promise to Central Ceilings was supported by no consideration other than the latter's performance of its contract with a third party ("Old Colony"). The argument failed. The court rejected, in effect, the rule of New York law stated this way in De Cicco v. Schweizer: "a promise by A. to B. to induce him not to break his contract with C. is void."

NOTE

The Jockey's Case. Mike McDevitt was a jockey who had accepted employment from Shaw to drive a mare named Grace in the Kentucky Futurity. Stokes owned "relatives" of the mare, and stood to gain if she should win. Stokes promised McDevitt a bonus of $1,000 for winning the race. McDevitt won, but Stokes refused to pay, and McDevitt sued him. From judgment for the defendant on a demurrer to the plaintiff's complaint, the plaintiff appealed. *Held:* Affirmed. "To hold that [McDevitt] would not have won the race ... but for the agreement of [Stokes] to pay him the $1,000 ... would be to say that he would have been recreant to the obligation arising out of his employment by Shaw ..." McDevitt v. Stokes, 192 S.W. 681 (Ky.1917). Does this case illustrate (to use Cardozo's words just above) "a promise by A. to B. to induce him not to break his contract with C."?

————

DURESS IN BUSINESS

While coercive behavior may be easier to detect or to condemn when the pressured party is an individual, duress also occurs in commercial dealings between businesses. This form of pressure is known as "economic duress" or "business compulsion." How should courts assess pressure in such cases? What are the requirements of resistance for a business? Do commercial enterprises so regularly anticipate modifications of their arrangements that the pre-existing duty rule can be said to operate anachronistically?

Consider these questions in connection with the following case, which, like *Alaska Packers* and others described above, is about duress. Yet while the court describes the claim of the party subjected to the threat (Loral) as one for damages, it is better understood as a claim to restitution of monies paid under duress. See Restatement § 376.

Austin Instrument, Inc. v. Loral Corporation

Court of Appeals of New York, 1971.
29 N.Y.2d 124, 324 N.Y.S.2d 22, 272 N.E.2d 533.

■ FULD, CHIEF JUDGE.[a] The defendant, Loral Corporation, seeks to recover payment for goods delivered under a contract which it had with the plaintiff Austin Instrument, Inc., on the ground that the evidence establishes, as a matter of law, that it was forced to agree to an increase in price on the items in question under circumstances amounting to economic duress.

In July of 1965, Loral was awarded a $6,000,000 contract by the Navy for the production of radar sets. The contract contained a schedule of deliveries, a liquidated damages clause applying to late deliveries and a cancellation clause in case of default by Loral. The latter thereupon solicited bids for some 40 precision gear components needed to produce the radar sets, and awarded Austin a subcontract to supply 23 such parts. That party commenced delivery in early 1966.

In May, 1966, Loral was awarded a second Navy contract for the production of more radar sets and again went about soliciting bids. Austin bid on all 40 gear components but, on July 15, a representative from Loral

a. Stanley H. Fuld (1903–2003) practiced law in New York City from 1926 to 1935 when he became assistant district attorney. In 1946 he was appointed to the New York Court of Appeals. He became chief judge in 1967 and served until 1974.

informed Austin's president, Mr. Krauss, that his company would be awarded the subcontract only for those items on which it was low bidder. The Austin officer refused to accept an order for less than all 40 of the gear parts and on the next day he told Loral that Austin would cease deliveries of the parts due under the existing subcontract unless Loral consented to substantial increases in the prices provided for by that agreement—both retroactively for parts already delivered and prospectively on those not yet shipped—and placed with Austin the order for all 40 parts needed under Loral's second Navy contract. Shortly thereafter, Austin did, indeed, stop delivery. After contacting 10 manufacturers of precision gears and finding none who could produce the parts in time to meet its commitments to the Navy,[1] Loral acceded to Austin's demands; in a letter dated July 22, Loral wrote to Austin that "We have feverishly surveyed other sources of supply and find that because of the prevailing military exigencies, were they to start from scratch as would have to be the case, they could not even remotely begin to deliver on time to meet the delivery requirements established by the Government.... Accordingly, we are left with no choice or alternative but to meet your conditions."

Loral thereupon consented to the price increases insisted upon by Austin under the first subcontract and the latter was awarded a second subcontract making it the supplier of all 40 gear parts for Loral's second contract with the Navy.[2] Although Austin was granted until September to resume deliveries, Loral did, in fact, receive parts in August and was able to produce the radar sets in time to meet its commitments to the Navy on both contracts. After Austin's last delivery under the second subcontract in July, 1967, Loral notified it of its intention to seek recovery of the price increases.

On September 15, 1967, Austin instituted this action against Loral to recover an amount in excess of $17,750 which was still due on the second subcontract. On the same day, Loral commenced an action against Austin claiming damages of some $22,250—the aggregate of the price increases under the first subcontract—on the ground of economic duress. The two actions were consolidated and, following a trial, Austin was awarded the sum it requested and Loral's complaint against Austin was dismissed on the ground that it was not shown that "it could not have obtained the items in question from other sources in time to meet its commitment to the Navy under the first contract." A closely divided Appellate Division affirmed (316 N.Y.S.2d 528, 532). There was no material disagreement concerning the facts; as Justice Steuer stated in the course of his dissent below, "[t]he facts are virtually undisputed, nor is there any serious question of law. The difficulty lies in the application of the law to these facts." (316 N.Y.S.2d 534.)

The applicable law is clear and, indeed, is not disputed by the parties. A contract is voidable on the ground of duress when it is established that the party making the claim was forced to agree to it by means of a wrongful

---

1. The best reply Loral received was from a vendor who stated he could commence deliveries sometime in October.

2. Loral makes no claim in this action on the second subcontract.

threat precluding the exercise of his free will.... The existence of economic duress or business compulsion is demonstrated by proof that "immediate possession of needful goods is threatened" ... or, more particularly, in cases such as the one before us, by proof that one party to a contract has threatened to breach the agreement by withholding goods unless the other party agrees to some further demand.... However, a mere threat by one party to breach the contract by not delivering the required items, though wrongful, does not in itself constitute economic duress. It must also appear that the threatened party could not obtain the goods from another source of supply and that the ordinary remedy of an action for breach of contract would not be adequate.

We find without any support in the record the conclusion reached by the courts below that Loral failed to establish that it was the victim of economic duress. On the contrary, the evidence makes out a classic case, as a matter of law, of such duress.[3]

It is manifest that Austin's threat—to stop deliveries unless the prices were increased—deprived Loral of its free will. As bearing on this, Loral's relationship with the Government is most significant. As mentioned above, its contract called for staggered monthly deliveries of the radar sets, with clauses calling for liquidated damages and possible cancellation on default. Because of its production schedule, Loral was, in July, 1966, concerned with meeting its delivery requirements in September, October and November, and it was for the sets to be delivered in those months that the withheld gears were needed. Loral had to plan ahead and the substantial liquidated damages for which it would be liable, plus the threat of default, were genuine possibilities. Moreover, Loral did a substantial portion of its business with the Government, and it feared that a failure to deliver as agreed upon would jeopardize its chances for future contracts. These genuine concerns do not merit the label " 'self-imposed, undisclosed and subjective' " which the Appellate Division majority placed upon them. It was perfectly reasonable for Loral, or any other party similarly placed, to consider itself in an emergency, duress situation.

... [T]he parts needed for the October schedule were delivered in late August and early September. Even so, Loral had to "work ... around the clock" to meet its commitments. Considering that the best offer Loral received from the other vendors it contacted was commencement of delivery sometime in October, which, as the record shows, would have made it late in its deliveries to the navy in both September and October, Loral's claim that it had no choice but to accede to Austin's demands is conclusively demonstrated.

We find unconvincing Austin's contention that Loral, in order to meet its burden, should have contacted the Government and asked for an extension of its delivery dates so as to enable it to purchase the parts from

---

3. The suggestion advanced that we are precluded from reaching this determination because the trial court's findings of fact have been affirmed by the Appellate Division ignores the question to be decided. That question, undoubtedly one of law (see Cohen and Karger, Powers of the New York Court of Appeals [1952], § 115, p. 492), is, accepting the facts found, did the courts below properly apply the law to them.

another vendor. Aside from the consideration that Loral was anxious to perform well in the Government's eyes, it could not be sure when it would obtain enough parts from a substitute vendor to meet its commitments. The only promise which it received from the companies it contacted was for *commencement* of deliveries, not full supply, and, with vendor delay common in this field, it would have been nearly impossible to know the length of the extension it should request. It must be remembered that Loral was producing a needed item of military hardware. Moreover, there is authority for Loral's position that nonperformance by a subcontractor is not an excuse for default in the main contract. (See, e.g., McBride & Wachtel, Government Contracts, § 35.10, [11].) In light of all this, Loral's claim should not be held insufficiently supported because it did not request an extension from the Government.

Loral, as indicated above, also had the burden of demonstrating that it could not obtain the parts elsewhere within a reasonable time, and there can be no doubt that it met this burden. The 10 manufacturers whom Loral contacted comprised its entire list of "approved vendors" for precision gears and none was able to commence delivery soon enough.[4] As Loral was producing a highly sophisticated item of military machinery requiring parts made to the strictest engineering standards, it would be unreasonable to hold that Loral should have gone to other vendors, with whom it was either unfamiliar or dissatisfied, to procure the needed parts. As Justice Steuer noted in his dissent, Loral "contacted all the manufacturers whom it believed capable of making these parts" (316 N.Y.S.2d at p. 534), and this was all the law requires.

It is hardly necessary to add that Loral's normal legal remedy of accepting Austin's breach of the contract and then suing for damages would have been inadequate under the circumstances, as Loral would still have had to obtain the gears elsewhere with all the concomitant consequences mentioned above. In other words, Loral actually had no choice, when the prices were raised by Austin, except to take the gears at the "coerced" prices and then sue to get the excess back.

Austin's final argument is that Loral, even if it did enter into the contract under duress, lost any rights it had to a refund of money by waiting, until July, 1967, long after the termination date of the contract, to disaffirm it. It is true that one who would recover moneys allegedly paid under duress must act promptly to make his claim known.... In this case, Loral delayed making its demand for a refund until three days after Austin's last delivery on the second subcontract. Loral's reason—for waiting until that time—is that it feared another stoppage of deliveries which would again put it in an untenable situation. Considering Austin's conduct in the past, this was perfectly reasonable, as the possibility of an application by Austin of further business compulsion still existed until all of the parts were delivered.

---

4. Loral, as do many manufacturers, maintains a list of "approved vendors," that is, vendors whose products, facilities, techniques and performance have been inspected and found satisfactory.

In sum, the record before us demonstrates that Loral agreed to the price increases in consequence of the economic duress employed by Austin. Accordingly, the matter should be remanded to the trial court for a computation of its damages.

The order appealed from should be modified, with costs, by reversing so much thereof as affirms the dismissal of defendant Loral Corporation's claim and, except as so modified, affirmed.

■ BERGAN, JUDGE (dissenting). Whether acts charged as constituting economic duress produce or do not produce the damaging effect attributed to them is normally a routine type of factual issue.

Here the fact question was resolved against Loral both by the Special Term and by the affirmance at the Appellate Division. It should not be open for different resolution here....

When the testimony of the witnesses who actually took part in the negotiations for the two disputing parties is examined, sharp conflicts of fact emerge. Under Austin's version the request for a renegotiation of the existing contract was based on Austin's contention that Loral had failed to carry out an understanding as to the items to be furnished under that contract and this was the source of dissatisfaction which led both to a revision of the existing agreement and to entering into a new one.

This is not necessarily and as a matter of law to be held economic duress. On this appeal it is needful to look at the facts resolved in favor of Austin most favorably to that party. Austin's version of events was that a threat was not made but rather a request to accommodate the closing of its plant for a customary vacation period in accordance with the general understanding of the parties.

Moreover, critical to the issue of economic duress was the availability of alternative suppliers to the purchaser Loral....

Austin asserted and Loral admitted on cross-examination that there were many suppliers listed in a trade registry but that Loral chose to rely only on those who had in the past come to them for orders and with whom they were familiar. It was, therefore, at least a fair issue of fact whether under the circumstances such conduct was reasonable and made what might otherwise have been a commercially understandable renegotiation an exercise of duress.

The order should be affirmed.

■ BURKE, SCILEPPI and GIBSON, JJ., concur with FULD, C.J.

■ BERGAN, J., dissents and votes to affirm in a separate opinion in which BREITEL and JASEN, JJ., concur.

NOTES

(1) *Questions.* Suppose that Loral had renounced its agreement with Austin a year before it did, shortly after acceding to Austin's demands. Laying aside the problem of duress, would it have been justified in renouncing the price increases? Would it have been justified in renouncing the purchase order under the second

Navy contract? What is the answer to these questions under UCC § 2–209(1)? If Loral had consented to Austin's demand for price increases without protesting as it did in the letter of July 22, but had not meant to pay as agreed, would that have been an instance of bad faith on Loral's part? See United States for Use and Benefit of Crane Co. v. Progressive Enterprises, Inc., 418 F.Supp. 662 (E.D.Va.1976).

(2) *Objective Standard?* Did the court apply the test for duress that the danger must have been sufficient to "overcome the mind of a person of ordinary firmness?" See discussion at p. 334 above. Holmes once remarked that to apply a requirement of ordinary courage in duress cases is "an attempt to apply an external standard of conduct in the wrong place." Silsbee v. Webber, 50 N.E. 555 (Mass.1898). And Holmes was usually insistent on objective criteria in the law.

(3) *Threatening Suit.* If the threat is one to sue for a money judgment, one obvious mode of resistance is to defend the suit. Some legal proceedings, however, such as mortgage foreclosure, commonly put the debtor in a situation of some urgency. Even so, the debtor may have recourse to injunctive relief, or to damages for abuse of legal process. To forego such a remedy, in favor of a settlement, is naturally prejudicial to the debtor in making a subsequent complaint of duress. Should the law insist on its preference that wrongful threats be met by resort to the courts? Professor John Dawson observes that if the "freedom to litigate" is prized, to control abuses of it by injunction or tort recoveries impairs that freedom more directly than to do so through relief for duress. "The most that is sought," in the latter form, "is judicial review of a settlement, after surrender to the pressure. The object is neither to transfer nor to prevent losses but to cancel out the gain." Dawson, Duress Through Civil Litigation: I, 45 Mich.L.Rev. 571, 577 (1947).

PROBLEM

Financial Stress. Alyeska Pipeline contracted with Totem Marine, a newly formed corporation, to transport pipe from Houston to Alaska. Impediments were met in loading and sailing, which caused long delays and substantial wrangling between the parties. The goods were finally offloaded in Long Beach California, and the contract was terminated. Totem now presents Alyeska with a $300,000 bill for its services and requests prompt payment as it is likely to go into bankruptcy unless its own creditors are paid. Officials of Alyeska have negotiated with Totem's attorney, and are prepared to offer it $100,000 in full settlement. As counsel to Alyeska, are you confident in advising your client that the settlement with Totem, if accepted, will be upheld? What distinctions are there between this case and Austin Instrument v. Loral Corp.? See Totem Marine Tug & Barge v. Alyeska Pipeline Service Co., 584 P.2d 15 (Alaska, 1978).

UNDUE INFLUENCE

Although this chapter emphasizes the bargaining *process*, the two other policing concerns, substance and status, are often intertwined with judicial determinations about unfairness in bargaining: A bad bargain sometimes indicates that something untoward has happened in the bargaining process, and pressure in bargaining may implicate issues of status.

The materials then focus on the relation between bargaining and the relative status of the parties. What degree of disparity is necessary before the parties are unable to bargain with one another "at arms length"? As we shall see, the disparities that seem to matter are not always monetary, but instead may derive from the degree of influence one party has—and uses—over the other.

———

Odorizzi v. Bloomfield School District

District Court of Appeal, Second District, Division 2, California, 1966.
246 Cal.App.2d 123, 54 Cal.Rptr. 533.

[Donald Odorizzi, an elementary school teacher, was arrested for homosexual activities on June 10. On June 11, he resigned his teaching position, following a visit to his home from the district superintendent and his school principal. The school officials had informed Odorizzi that unless he resigned, he would be dismissed and the charges against him publicized. In July, the criminal charges were dismissed. Odorizzi then sought to rescind his resignation on the grounds that it was obtained by duress and undue influence. From a judgment dismissing Odorizzi's complaint on demurrer, he appealed.]

■ FLEMING, J. Appeal from a judgment dismissing plaintiff's amended complaint on demurrer. Plaintiff Donald Odorizzi was employed during 1964 as an elementary school teacher by defendant Bloomfield School District and was under contract with the district to continue to teach school the following year as a permanent employee. On June 10 he was arrested on criminal charges of homosexual activity, and on June 11 he signed and delivered to his superiors his written resignation as a teacher, a resignation which the district accepted on June 13. In July the criminal charges against Odorizzi were dismissed under Penal Code, section 995, and in September he sought to resume his employment with the district. On the district's refusal to reinstate him he filed suit for declaratory and other relief.

Odorizzi's amended complaint asserts his resignation was invalid because obtained through duress, fraud, mistake, and undue influence and given at a time when he lacked capacity to make a valid contract. Specifically, Odorizzi declares he was under such severe mental and emotional strain at the time he signed his resignation, having just completed the process of arrest, questioning by the police, booking, and release on bail, and having gone for 40 hours without sleep, that he was incapable of rational thought or action. While he was in this condition and unable to think clearly, the superintendent of the district and the principal of his school came to his apartment. They said they were trying to help him and had his best interests at heart, that he should take their advice and immediately resign his position with the district, that there was no time to consult an attorney, that if he did not resign immediately the district would suspend and dismiss him from his position and publicize the proceedings, his "aforedescribed arrest" and cause him "to suffer extreme embarrassment and humiliation"; but that if he resigned at once the incident would not be publicized and would not jeopardize his chances of securing employment as a teacher elsewhere. Odorizzi pleads that because of his faith and confidence in their representations they were able to substitute their will and judgment in place of his own and thus obtain his signature to his purported resignation. A demurrer to his amended complaint was sustained without leave to amend . . .

In our view the facts in the amended complaint are insufficient to state a cause of action for duress, menace, fraud, or mistake, but they do set out sufficient elements to justify rescission of a consent because of undue influence. We summarize our conclusions on each of these points . . .

We agree with respondent's contention that neither duress nor menace was involved in this case, because the action or threat in duress or menace must be unlawful, and a threat to take legal action is not unlawful unless the party making the threat knows the falsity of his claim. The amended complaint shows in substance that the school representatives announced their intention to initiate suspension and dismissal proceedings under Education Code, sections 13403, 13408 et seq. at a time when the filing of such proceedings was not only their legal right but their positive duty as school officials. Although the filing of such proceedings might be extremely damaging to plaintiff's reputation, the injury would remain incidental so long as the school officials acted in good faith in the performance of their duties . . .

[In an omitted part of the decision, the court found that the complaint failed to disclose facts supporting a claim for fraud or for mistake.]

However, the pleading does set out a claim that plaintiff's consent to the transaction had been obtained through the use of undue influence.

Undue influence, in the sense we are concerned with here, is a shorthand legal phrase used to describe persuasion which tends to be coercive in nature, persuasion which overcomes the will without convincing the judgment. (*Estate of Ricks,* 117 P. 539.) The hallmark of such persuasion is high pressure, a pressure which works on mental, moral, or emotional weakness to such an extent that it approaches the boundaries of coercion. In this sense, undue influence has been called overpersuasion. (*Kelly v. McCarthy,* 57 P.2d 118.) Misrepresentations of law or fact are not essential to the charge, for a person's will may be overborne without misrepresentation. By statutory definition undue influence includes "taking an unfair advantage of another's weakness of mind, or . . . taking a grossly oppressive and unfair advantage of another's necessities or distress." (Civ. Code, § 1575.) While most reported cases of undue influence involve persons who bear a confidential relationship to one another, a confidential or authoritative relationship between the parties need not be present when the undue influence involves unfair advantage taken of another's weakness or distress.

We paraphrase the summary of undue influence given the jury by Sir James P. Wilde in *Hall v. Hall,* L.R. 1, P. & D. 481, 482 (1868): To make a good contract a man must be a free agent. Pressure of whatever sort which overpowers the will without convincing the judgment is a species of restraint under which no valid contract can be made. Importunity or threats, if carried to the degree in which the free play of a man's will is overborne, constitute undue influence, although no force is used or threatened. A party may be led but not driven, and his acts must be the offspring of his own volition and not the record of someone else's.

In essence undue influence involves the use of excessive pressure to persuade one vulnerable to such pressure, pressure applied by a dominant subject to a servient object. In combination, the elements of undue susceptibility in the servient person and excessive pressure by the dominating person make the latter's influence undue, for it results in the apparent will of the servient person being in fact the will of the dominant person.

Undue susceptibility may consist of total weakness of mind which leaves a person entirely without understanding (Civ. Code, § 38); or, a lesser weakness which destroys the capacity of a person to make a contract even though he is not totally incapacitated (Civ. Code, § 39; *Peterson v. Ellebrecht,* 23 Cal.Rptr. 349); or, the first element in our equation, a still lesser weakness which provides sufficient grounds to rescind a contract for undue influence (Civ. Code, § 1575; *Faulkner v. Beatty,* 327 P.2d 41; *Stewart v. Marvin,* 294 P.2d 114). Such lesser weakness need not be long-lasting nor wholly incapacitating, but may be merely a lack of full vigor due to age (*Wells Fargo Bank v. Brady,* 254 P.2d 71), physical condition (*Weger v. Rocha,* 32 P.2d 417), emotional anguish (*Moore v. Moore,* 22 P. 589, 874), or a combination of such factors. The reported cases have usually involved elderly, sick, senile persons alleged to have executed wills or deeds under pressure. (*Malone v. Malone,* 317 P.2d 65 [constant importuning of a senile husband]; *Stewart v. Marvin,* 294 P.2d 114 [persistent nagging of elderly spouse].) In some of its aspects this lesser weakness could perhaps be called weakness of spirit. But whatever name we give it, this first element of undue influence resolves itself into a lessened capacity of the object to make a free contract.

In the present case plaintiff has pleaded that such weakness at the time he signed his resignation prevented him from freely and competently applying his judgment to the problem before him. Plaintiff declares he was under severe mental and emotional strain at the time because he had just completed the process of arrest, questioning, booking, and release on bail and had been without sleep for forty hours. It is possible that exhaustion and emotional turmoil may wholly incapacitate a person from exercising his judgment. As an abstract question of pleading, plaintiff has pleaded that possibility and sufficient allegations to state a case for rescission.

Undue influence in its second aspect involves an application of excessive strength by a dominant subject against a servient object. Judicial consideration of this second element in undue influence has been relatively rare, for there are few cases denying persons who persuade but do not misrepresent the benefit of their bargain. Yet logically, the same legal consequences should apply to the results of excessive strength as to the results of undue weakness. Whether from weakness on one side, or strength on the other, or a combination of the two, undue influence occurs whenever there results "that kind of influence or supremacy of one mind over another by which that other is prevented from acting according to his own wish or judgment, and whereby the will of the person is overborne and he is induced to do or forbear to do an act which he would not do, or would do, if left to act freely." (*Webb v. Saunders*, 181 P.2d 43.) Undue influence involves a type of mismatch which our statute calls unfair advantage. (Civ. Code, § 1575.) (20) Whether a person of subnormal capacities has been subjected to ordinary force or a person of normal capacities subjected to extraordinary force, the match is equally out of balance. If will has been overcome against judgment, consent may be rescinded.

The difficulty, of course, lies in determining when the forces of persuasion have overflowed their normal banks and become oppressive flood waters. There are second thoughts to every bargain, and hindsight is still better than foresight. Undue influence cannot be used as a pretext to avoid bad bargains or escape from bargains which refuse to come up to expectations. A woman who buys a dress on impulse, which on critical inspection by her best friend turns out to be less fashionable than she had thought, is not legally entitled to set aside the sale on the ground that the saleswoman used all her wiles to close the sale. A man who buys a tract of desert land in the expectation that it is in the immediate path of the city's growth and will become another Palm Springs, an expectation cultivated in glowing terms by the seller, cannot rescind his bargain when things turn out differently. If we are temporarily persuaded against our better judgment to do something about which we later have second thoughts, we must abide the consequences of the risks inherent in managing our own affairs. (*Estate of Anderson,* 198 P. 407.)

However, overpersuasion is generally accompanied by certain characteristics which tend to create a pattern. The pattern usually involves several of the following elements: (1) discussion of the transaction at an unusual or inappropriate time, (2) consummation of the transaction in an unusual place, (3) insistent demand that the business be finished at once, (4) extreme emphasis on untoward consequences of delay, (5) the use of multiple persuaders by the dominant side against a single servient party, (6) absence of third-party advisers to the servient party, (7) statements that there is no time to consult financial advisers or attorneys. If a number of these elements are simultaneously present, the persuasion may be characterized as excessive. The cases are illustrative:

Moore v. Moore, 22 P. 589, 874. The pregnant wife of a man who had been shot to death on October 30 and buried on November 1 was approached by four members of her husband's family on November 2 or 3 and persuaded to deed her entire interest in her husband's estate to his children by a prior marriage. In finding the use of undue influence on Mrs. Moore, the court commented: "It was the second day after her late husband's funeral. It was at a time when she would naturally feel averse to transacting any business, and she might reasonably presume that her late husband's brothers would not apply to her at such a time to transact any important business, unless it was of a nature that would admit of no delay. And as it would admit of delay, the only reason which we can discover for their unseemly haste is, that they thought that she would be more likely to comply with their wishes then than at some future time, after she had recovered from the shock which she had then so recently experienced. If for that reason they selected that time for the accomplishment of their purpose, it seems to us that they not only took, but that they designed to take, an unfair advantage of her weakness of mind. If they did not, they probably can explain why they selected that inappropriate time for the transaction of business which might have been delayed for weeks without injury to anyone. In the absence of any explanation, it appears to us that the time was selected with reference to just that condition of mind which she alleges that she was then in.

"Taking an unfair advantage of another's weakness of mind is undue influence, and the law will not permit the retention of an advantage thus obtained. (Civ. Code, § 1575.)"

Weger v. Rocha, 32 P.2d 417. Plaintiff, while confined in a cast in a hospital, gave a release of claims for personal injuries for a relatively small sum to an agent who spent two hours persuading her to sign. At the time of signing plaintiff was in a highly nervous and hysterical condition and suffering much pain, and she signed the release in order to terminate the interview. The court held that the release had been secured by the use of undue influence . . .

The difference between legitimate persuasion and excessive pressure . . . rests to a considerable extent in the manner in which the parties go about their business. For example, if a day or two after Odorizzi's release on bail the superintendent of the school district had called him into his office during business hours and directed his attention to those provisions of the Education Code compelling his leave of absence and authorizing his suspension on the filing of written charges, had told him that the district contemplated filing written charges against him, had pointed out the alternative of resignation available to him, had informed him he was free to consult counsel or any adviser he wished and to consider the matter overnight and return with his decision the next day, it is extremely unlikely that any complaint about the use of excessive pressure could ever have been made against the school district.

But, according to the allegations of the complaint, this is not the way it happened, and if it had happened that way, plaintiff would never have resigned. Rather, the representatives of the school board undertook to achieve their objective by overpersuasion and imposition to secure plaintiff's signature but not his consent to his resignation through a high-pressure carrot-and-stick technique-under which they assured plaintiff they were trying to assist him, he should rely on their advice, there wasn't time to consult an attorney, if he didn't resign at once the school district would suspend and dismiss him from his position and publicize the proceedings, but if he did resign the incident wouldn't jeopardize his chances of securing a teaching post elsewhere.

Plaintiff has thus pleaded both subjective and objective elements entering the undue influence equation and stated sufficient facts to put in issue the question whether his free will had been overborne by defendant's agents at a time when he was unable to function in a normal manner. It was sufficient to pose "... the ultimate question ... whether a free and competent judgment was merely influenced, or whether a mind was so dominated as to prevent the exercise of an independent judgment." (Williston on Contracts, § 1625 [rev. ed.]; Rest., Contracts, § 497, com. c.) The question cannot be resolved by an analysis of pleading but requires a finding of fact.

We express no opinion on the merits of plaintiff's case, or the propriety of his continuing to teach school (Ed. Code, § 13403), or the timeliness of his rescission (Civ. Code, § 1691). We do hold that his pleading, liberally construed, states a cause of action for rescission of a transaction to which his apparent consent had been obtained through the use of undue influence.

The judgment is reversed.

NOTES

(1) *Questions.* Why did the court require that a party plead both objective elements of undue influence? What result if the pressured party was a complete pushover?

The court offered a list of seven circumstantial factors that "tend to create a pattern" ripe for the exercise of undue influence. Are there some situations where at least some of these factors—disadvantageous location, timing, absence of advisors—are inherent in the decision-making process? Consider the consent given by a birth mother in placing her child for adoption. See Note 2, p. 335 above. Is a court less likely to find undue influence in, say, a consumer transaction where the buyer can always walk away?

(2) *Confidential Relations.* Although the court found that no confidential relationship existed between Odorizzi and his employers, a finding of a confidential relationship is often the key to success in avoiding a contract on the basis of overreaching. In general, when that finding is made, and the party asserting rights under the contract is the one in whom confidence was reposed, the claimant must show that the bargain was "fair, conscientious, and beyond the reach of suspicion." Young v. Kaye, 279 A.2d 759 (Pa.1971). In that case, representative of many like it, an elderly man was imposed upon by an ex-convict who provided him with services and won his confidence as a "tax consultant." As examples of confidential relations, the court mentioned guardian and ward, principal and agent, attorney and client. Beyond such routine entries, however, the list is not pre-determined. A "confidential relation" does not necessarily attend a friendship, or even a marriage; yet an automobile dealer and a customer have been found to be in that relation, with respect to an arcane feature of their dealings. Browder v. Hanley Dawson Cadillac, 379 N.E.2d 1206 (Ill.App.1978). "It is not restricted to any specific association ... but is deemed to exist whenever the relative position of the parties is such that one has power and means to take advantage of or exert undue influence over the other." Young v. Kaye, above. For a celebrated case in which an heiress alleged that she had been induced, through the abuse of a confidential relation, to support a religious organization over a period of years, and got restitution of assets worth several millions, see In re The Bible Speaks, 869 F.2d 628 (1st Cir.1989), *cert. denied,* 493 U.S. 816 (1989).

(3) *Undue Influence at Home.* Is an agreement between spouses, or one made on behalf of a spouse particularly susceptible to "overpersuasion"? Consider one

spouse's promise to guarantee the debt of the other, either personally, as did Louisa Sheffield, p. 69 above, or by pledging the family home as security for a loan to the other, as in Barclay's Bank v. O'Brien, Note 2, p. 71 above. In the latter case, the law lords noted that "a high proportion of privately owned wealth is invested in the matrimonial home" and that such wealth would become "economically sterile" if suretyship agreements were too easily set aside on the grounds of spousal pressure. But they observed that "[i]n a substantial proportion of marriages it is still the husband who has the business experience and the wife is willing to follow his advice without bringing a truly independent mind and will to bear on financial decisions." 4 All E.R. at 422. In view of these two propositions, the court held that a creditor is "put on inquiry" when a wife offers to stand as surety for her husband in cases when the transaction is on its face not to the financial advantage of the wife *and* there is a substantial risk that "in procuring the wife to act as surety, the husband has committed a legal or equitable wrong that entitles the wife to set aside the transaction." 4 All E.R. at 429. The court further stated that "the underlying risk of one cohabitee exploiting the emotional involvement and trust of the other" is not limited to married couples, and extended the rule announced to any case where "the surety is cohabitating with the principal debtor."

If a creditor is "put on inquiry," what steps might it take to make sure the wife's consent is obtained properly? Should the requirement apply to spouses generally?

———

(B) Concealment and Misrepresentation

According to Chancellor Kent: "Cicero de Officiis, lib. 3. sec. 12–17, states the case of a corn merchant of Alexandria arriving at Rhodes in a time of great scarcity, with a cargo of grain, and with knowledge that a number of other vessels, with similar cargoes, had already sailed from Alexandria for Rhodes, and whom he had passed on the voyage. He then puts the question, whether the Alexandrine merchant was bound in conscience to inform the buyers of that fact, or to keep silence, and sell his wheat for an extravagant price; and he answers it by saying, that, in his opinion, good faith would require of a just and candid man, a frank disclosure of the fact." 2 Kent's Commentaries 491* n. c (3d ed. 1836).

What is the requirement that the law, as opposed to the demand of conscience, makes for disclosing facts in a bargaining context? Many courts have said that they will not insist on the degree of disclosure that a person of exceptional scruple might make. On the other hand, in allowing bargaining advantages to be secured by persons of little scruple, the law may attach a competitive disadvantage to conscientious conduct. See Laidlaw v. Organ, 15 U.S. 178, 195 (1817), in which a buyer, having learned hours before the general population that the British blockade of New Orleans was to be lifted by virtue of the signing of the Treaty of Ghent, bought a huge quantity of tobacco at a most advantageous price from a seller without this information. The seller later sought to have the transaction rescinded for fraud. In dictum, Chief Justice John Marshall stated that the buyer was not bound to communicate the information to the seller because "it would be difficult to circumscribe the contrary doctrine within proper limits." Is there any benefit in the law making an effort to do so?

NOTES

(1) *Investment in Knowledge.* Should there be special rules about information derived from research, training, and experience? It is generally understood that dealers in certain types of merchandise, such as antiques and rare coins, for example, trade on their expertise and experience and are not expected to disclose to their customers all the elements that enter into their evaluations. The expense of acquiring such expertise would not be justified if it did not yield bargaining advantages. To some extent the same consideration affects the degree of disclosure required in most commercial exchanges. Compare the market expertise of middlemen, mentioned in Note 2, p. 463 below.

(2) *The Kidd Creek Strike.* The discovery of an extremely valuable ore deposit near Timmins, Ontario, touched off an immense number of trades. The finder, Texas Gulf Sulphur Company, detected the deposit through aerial searches for electromagnetic "anomalies." Having found one, it purchased mineral rights and options from landowners in the vicinity. When the deposit was verified, but not publicly announced, officers of the firm made purchases of its stock. Some of the officers were successfully charged with violations of the securities laws, for wrongful use of "inside" information. See S.E.C. v. Texas Gulf Sulphur Co., 446 F.2d 1301 (2d Cir.1971). One of the landowners sued the firm for wrongful use of its information in dealing with him: it had failed to disclose "an unusually promising indication of economic mineralization on [his] property."

A justification for enforcing the option is given in Anthony Kronman, Mistake, Disclosure, Information, and the Law of Contracts, 7 J.Leg. Studies 1, 33 (1978). Certain information, Professor Kronman has argued, is "in essence a property right," at least when produced by a "deliberate search for socially useful information." The law tends (he said) to recognize such a right, and "not to recognize it where the information has been casually acquired"—so enhancing efficiency in resource allocation.

Swinton v. Whitinsville Sav. Bank

Supreme Judicial Court of Massachusetts, 1942.
311 Mass. 677, 42 N.E.2d 808.

■ QUA, JUSTICE. The declaration alleges that on or about September 12, 1938, the defendant sold the plaintiff a house in Newton to be occupied by the plaintiff and his family as a dwelling; that at the time of the sale the house "was infested with termites, an insect that is most dangerous and destructive to buildings"; that the defendant knew the house was so infested; that the plaintiff could not readily observe this condition upon inspection; that "knowing the internal destruction that these insects were creating in said house," the defendant falsely and fraudulently concealed from the plaintiff its true condition; that the plaintiff at the time of his purchase had no knowledge of the termites, exercised due care thereafter, and learned of them about August 30, 1940; and that, because of the destruction that was being done and the dangerous condition that was being created by the termites the plaintiff was put to great expense for repairs and for the installation of termite control in order to prevent the loss and destruction of said house.

There is no allegation of any false statement or representation, or of the uttering of a half truth which may be tantamount to a falsehood. There is no intimation that the defendant by any means prevented the plaintiff from acquiring information as to the condition of the house. There is nothing to show any fiduciary relation between the parties, or that the plaintiff stood in a position of confidence toward or dependence upon the defendant. So far as appears the parties made a business deal at arm's length. The charge is concealment and nothing more; and it is concealment in the simple sense of mere failure to reveal, with nothing to show any peculiar duty to speak. The characterization of the concealment as false and fraudulent of course adds nothing in the absence of further allegations of fact. Province Securities Corp. v. Maryland Casualty Co., 269 Mass. 75, 92, 168 S.E. 252.

If this defendant is liable on this declaration every seller is liable who fails to disclose any nonapparent defect known to him in the subject of the sale which materially reduces its value and which the buyer fails to discover. Similarly it would seem that every buyer would be liable who fails to disclose any nonapparent virtue known to him in the subject of the purchase which materially enhances its value and of which the seller is ignorant. See Goodwin v. Agassiz, 283 Mass. 358, 186 N.E. 659. The law has not yet, we believe, reached the point of imposing upon the frailties of human nature a standard so idealistic as this. That the particular case here stated by the plaintiff possesses a certain appeal to the moral sense is scarcely to be denied. Probably the reason is to be found in the facts that the infestation of buildings by termites has not been common in Massachusetts and constitutes a concealed risk against which buyers are off their guard. But the law cannot provide special rules for termites and can hardly attempt to determine liability according to the varying probabilities of the existence and discovery of different possible defects in the subjects of trade. The rule of nonliability for bare nondisclosure has been stated and followed by this court in [seven cases cited]. It is adopted in the American Law Institute's Restatement of Torts, § 551. See Williston on Contracts, Rev. Ed., §§ 1497, 1498, 1499.

The order sustaining the demurrer is affirmed, and judgment is to be entered for the defendant. Keljikian v. Star Brewing Co., 303 Mass. 53, 55–63, 20 N.E.2d 465.

So ordered.

NOTES

(1) *Questions.* Does it follow from this holding that the plaintiff could not have *rescinded* the sale on establishing the facts he alleged? If the decision had been to the contrary, overruling the defendant's demurrer, would it follow that the plaintiff *could* have rescinded the sale? (An answer to this question is suggested by the next main case.) If the sale had not been executed, and the seller had brought an action against the buyer for specific performance, would it have succeeded?

(2) *Latent Defects: Caveat Emptor?* For a statute requiring that sellers of homes disclose defects known to them unless the property is sold "as is," see Va.Code §§ 55–517 *et seq.* (1994). In addition to statutory protection, some courts require that dangerous conditions be disclosed. Some impose a warranty, in cases of sales by builders, that a home is fit for habitation.

In a case like *Swinton,* some courts start with the proposition that a seller of a home should disclose to the buyer a so-called latent defect—a deleterious condition, known to the seller, that is not readily observable. "[W]e are certain," a New Jersey court has said, that *Swinton* "does not represent our sense of justice or fair dealing." Weintraub v. Krobatsch, 317 A.2d 68 (N.J.1974). Another court contrasted the sale of a simple farm home with the sale of a modern residence of complex construction. While the ancient rule of *caveat emptor* "may have had some merit in the agrarian society in which it was applied," the court thought, it is "no longer an expression of American mores." Holcomb v. Zinke, 365 N.W.2d 507 (N.D.1985). But see Boyd, C.J., dissenting, in Johnson v. Davis, 480 So.2d 625 (Fla.1985): although it "sounds progressive, high-minded, and idealistic," a decision to blur the distinction between misrepresentation and nondisclosure can be expected to distort the real-estate market. *Id.* at 629, 631.

What justification might be given for imposing a broad disclosure requirement in connection with the sale of a new home by the builder, but otherwise adhering to the *Swinton* rule? Is the general availability of termite insurance relevant? Compare Compass Point Condominium Owners Ass'n v. First Federal Sav. & Loan Ass'n, 641 So.2d 253 (Ala.1994), with Hill v. Jones, 725 P.2d 1115 (Ariz.App.1986) (seller has duty to disclose the existence of termite damage which materially affects the value of the property). In the case of a builder-vendor, is an implied warranty more suitable, as protection for the buyer, than a disclosure requirement?

(3) *Remedies.* A considerable array of remedies are suggested by the authorities cited in the foregoing note. In *Weintraub,* the buyers were sued initially for specific performance and countered with a rescission claim. In *Johnson,* the sellers were required to repay the amounts they had received from the buyers, with interest. In *Holcomb* (as in *Weintraub*), the court ordered rescission of the contract. It charged the sellers for the buyers' expenses in curing defects, but charged the buyers with the reasonable rental value of the home. In *Compass Point,* the buyers claimed punitive damages. In the Virginia statute, one of the remedies provided for a buyer is recovery of the "actual damages suffered" as a result of an undisclosed defect.

What might a buyer hope to recover in a breach-of-warranty action against the seller? If that action is available to a buyer, should the buyer be permitted to choose rescission instead?

(4) *Career Changes.* A congregation employed a rabbi to provide spiritual leadership on the strength of two services he conducted, a few conversations, and a sparse resume ("references on request"). Thereafter it emerged that he had been convicted for defrauding an insurance company and had been disbarred as an attorney for bribing a police officer. In an action by the employer for rescission of the contract, summary judgment was granted for the plaintiff. See Jewish Center of Sussex County v. Whale, 397 A.2d 712 (N.J. 1978) (concealment), *aff'd,* 432 A.2d 521 (N.J.1981) (misrepresentation).

In another case, an applicant for a teaching position failed to disclose to his Catholic employer at the time he was hired, that years earlier, under a different first name, had been an ordained priest who had left the church and married. When the university learned these facts, it discharged him and he sued for breach of contract. What result under *Swinton?* See Fuller v. De Paul Univ., 12 N.E.2d 213 (Ill. 1938).

PROBLEM

Disclosure and DNA. A variation on Fiege v. Boehm, p. 40 above, has arisen with regard to child support agreements signed by men, typically as part of a divorce settlement with the child's mother. What is the status of such an agreement, entered into on the assumption that the man is the biological father of his children, when DNA testing later shows that he is not? For one such case, see Paternity of Cheryl, 746 N.E.2d 488 (Mass.2001). Does it matter, for purposes of a disclosure analysis, whether the parents are married or not? Should such a contract be set aside on grounds of mistake? Should the father be able to obtain restitution from the mother for monies already paid?

Kannavos v. Annino

Supreme Judicial Court of Massachusetts, 1969.
356 Mass. 42, 247 N.E.2d 708.

[In 1961 or 1962, Mrs. Carrie Annino bought a one-family dwelling in Springfield: No. 11, Ingersoll Grove. She converted it into a multi-family building with eight apartments, without obtaining a building permit, and in knowing violation of the city zoning ordinance. The house was in a "Residence A" district, where multi-family uses were prohibited. In 1965 a real-estate broker was employed to try to sell the property. He placed newspaper ads, of which the following is an example: "Income gross $9,600 yr. in lg. single house, converted to 8 lovely, completely furn. (includ. TV and china) apts. 8 baths, ideal for couple to live free with excellent income. By apt. only. Foote Realty."

Apostolos Kannavos read one of the ads, and got in touch with the broker, Foote. Foote showed him the house, and gave him income and expense figures supplied by Mrs. Annino. Without the aid of a lawyer, Kannavos contracted to buy the property, and did so, borrowing money from a bank for the purpose, and giving it a mortgage. At the closing, attorneys for the seller and for the mortgagee were present, and the latter prepared the papers. Mrs. Annino and Foote knew that Kannavos's reason for buying was to rent the apartments. He was unaware of any zoning or building permit violation, and would not have purchased the property if he had known of any such violation. It was worth substantially less if operated only as a single-family dwelling than it was as an apartment building.

Soon after the sale, the city started legal proceedings to abate the nonconforming use of the building.[a] Kannavos brought a bill in equity against Mrs. Annino to rescind the purchase. The trial court overruled a demurrer, and granted rescission on the basis of findings by a master. Mrs. Annino appealed.

---

a. As to other, similar properties that Kannavos (and an associate) also bought from Mrs. Annino, the city also asserted violations of the building code, but the opinion does not make it clear whether or not No. 11 was in question on this score.

It appeared that Kannavos had immigrated from Greece in 1957, when he was about thirty years old. In this country he had learned English, and become a self-employed hairdresser. It was found that he made no inquiry of anyone about zoning or building permits before or during the closing, and that no statements were made to him on these subjects. Everything that was said to him by or on behalf of the seller was substantially true.]

■ CUTTER, JUSTICE. . . . We assume that, if the vendors had been wholly silent and had made no references whatsoever to the use of the Ingersoll Grove houses, they could not have been found to have made any misrepresentation. See Swinton v. Whitinsville Sav. Bank, 311 Mass. 677, 678–679, 42 N.E.2d 808, 141 A.L.R. 965,[1] where this court affirmed an order sustaining a demurrer to a declaration in an action of tort brought by a purchaser of a house. . . . The court (p. 679) indicated that it was applying a long standing "rule of nonliability for *bare nondisclosure*" (emphasis supplied).

As in the *Swinton* case, the parties here were dealing at arm's length, the vendees were in no way prevented from acquiring information, and the vendors stood in no fiduciary relationship to the vendees. In two aspects, however, the present cases differ from the *Swinton* case: viz. (a) The vendees themselves could have found out about the zoning violations by inquiry through public records, whereas in the *Swinton* case the purchaser would have probably discovered the presence of termites only by retaining expert investigators; and (b) there was something more here than the "bare nondisclosure" of the seller in the *Swinton* case.

(a) We deal first with the affirmative actions by the vendors, their conduct, advertising, and statements. Was enough said and done by the vendors so that they were bound to disclose more to avoid deception of the vendees and reliance by them upon a half truth? In other words, did the statements made by the vendors in their advertising and otherwise take the cases out of the "rule of nonliability for bare nondisclosure" applied in the *Swinton* case?

Although there may be "no duty imposed upon one party to a transaction to speak for the information of the other . . . if he does speak with reference to a given point of information, voluntarily or at the other's request, he is bound to speak honestly and to divulge all the material facts bearing upon the point that lie within his knowledge. Fragmentary information may be as misleading . . . as active misrepresentation, and half-truths may be as actionable as whole lies. . . ." See Harper & James, Torts, § 7.14. See also Restatement: Torts, § 529; Williston, Contracts (2d ed.) §§ 1497–1499. The existence of substantially this principle was assumed in the *Swinton* case, 311 Mass. 677, 678, 42 N.E.2d 808, 141 A.L.R. 965, in the first sentence of the passage from that case quoted above. Massachusetts

---

1. The *Swinton* case may not represent the law elsewhere. See Restatement 2d: Torts, § 551 (Tent. Draft No. 11, April 15, 1965), p. 43; Prosser, Torts (3d ed.), § 101, p. 711. Cf. discussions of situations in landlord and tenant cases like Cutter v. Hamlen, 147 Mass. 471, 474, 18 N.E. 397, 1 L.R.A. 429; Stumpf v. Leland, 242 Mass. 168, 172–174, 136 N.E. 399; Cooper v. Boston Housing Authority, 342 Mass. 38, 40, 172 N.E.2d 117. For general consideration of silence as misrepresentation, see Restatement: Restitution, § 8; Williston, Contracts (2d ed.) § 1497.

decisions have applied this principle. See Kidney v. Stoddard, 7 Metc. 252, 254–255 (a father represented that his son was entitled to credit but failed to disclose that the son was a minor; statement treated as a fraudulent representation); Burns v. Dockray, 156 Mass. 135, 137, 30 N.E. 551 (assertion that title was good [see Lyman v. Romboli, 293 Mass. 373, 374, 199 N.E. 916] but omitting to refer to the possible insanity of one whose incompetence might cloud title); Van Houten v. Morse, 162 Mass. 414, 417–419, 38 N.E. 705, 26 L.R.A. 430 (partial disclosure by a woman to her fiancé about a prior divorce). See also . . . Boston Five Cents Sav. Bank v. Brooks, 309 Mass. 52, 55–56, 34 N.E.2d 435, 437 ("Deception need not be direct. . . . Declarations and conduct calculated to mislead . . . which . . . do mislead one . . . acting reasonably are enough to constitute fraud"). Cf. Wade v. Ford Motor Co., 341 Mass. 596, 597–598, 171 N.E.2d 282.

The master's report provides ample basis for treating the present cases as within the decisions just cited. The original advertisements in effect offered the houses as investment properties and referred to them as single houses converted to apartments. The investment aspect of the houses was emphasized by Foote's action in furnishing income and expense figures. There was an express assertion that 11 Ingersoll Grove was "being rented to the public for multi-family purposes" and that Kannavos and Bellas "could continue to operate . . . [the other properties] as multi-dwelling property." The master's conclusions indicate that this statement applied to all the properties.[2] The buildings were divided into apartments. The sales included refrigerators, stoves, and other furnishings appropriate for apartment use as well as real estate. The vendors knew that the vendees were planning to continue to use the buildings for apartments, and yet the vendors still failed to disclose the zoning and building violations. We conclude that enough was done affirmatively to make the disclosure inadequate and partial, and, in the circumstances, intentionally deceptive and fraudulent.

(b) The second difference between these cases and the *Swinton* case is the character of the defect not disclosed.

In the *Swinton* case, the presence of predatory insects threatened the structure sold. In the absence of any seller's representations whatsoever, there was no duty to disclose this circumstance, even though doubtless it would have been difficult to discover. In the present cases, the defect in the premises related to a matter of public regulation, the zoning and building ordinances. Its applicability to these premises could have been discovered by these vendees or by the vendees' counsel if, acting with prudence, they had retained counsel, which they did not. The bank mortgagee's counsel presumably was looking only to the protection of the bank's security position. Nevertheless, where there is reliance on fraudulent representations or upon statements and action treated as fraudulent, our cases have not barred plaintiffs from recovery merely because they "did not use due diligence . . . [when they] could readily have ascertained from . . . records"

---

2. In any event some discussions with respect to all these properties in the same neighborhood were going on about the same time and the later transaction appears to have been commenced either before or about the time the earlier one was completed.

what the true facts were. See Yorke v. Taylor, 332 Mass. 368, 373, 124 N.E.2d 912. There this court allowed rescission because of the negligent misrepresentation, innocent but false, of the current assessed value of the property being sold. Here the representations made by the advertising and the vendors' conduct and statements in effect were that the property was multi-family housing suitable for investment and that the housing could continue to be used for that purpose. Because the vendors did as much as they did do, they were bound to do more. Failing to do so, they were responsible for misrepresentation. We think the situation is comparable to that in Yorke v. Taylor, 332 Mass. 368, 374, 124 N.E.2d 912, even though there the misrepresentation was "not consciously false" and here it was by half truth.

We hold that the vendors' conduct entitled the vendees to rescind. See Yorke v. Taylor, 332 Mass. 368, 371–372, 374, 124 N.E.2d 912; Restatement: Contracts, §§ 472, 489; Restatement: Restitution, § 28; Williston, Contracts (2d ed.) §§ 1497–1500. There was, in our opinion, much more than "bare nondisclosure" as in the *Swinton* case. Cf. Spencer v. Gabriel, 328 Mass. 1, 2, 101 N.E.2d 369; Donahue v. Stephens, 342 Mass. 89, 92, 172 N.E.2d 101.

[The court affirmed the decree below overruling the demurrer. However, it reversed the final decree so that there might be further consideration of the relief, in view of a fire that had occurred at No. 11 after that decree.]

NOTE

Question. Does it follow from this decision that Kannavos could have maintained an action in deceit against Annino? The requisites of that action, and the remedy it affords, are dealt with in detail in courses on torts. Note, however, that contract remedies are not the only guarantees of minimum decencies in the bargaining process.

PROBLEMS

(1) *Sales Talk.* Consider the following two cases, briefly sketched. How would the Massachusetts court have decided them?

(a) In response to a dealer's advertisement, a shopper bought a used car after a test drive. The salesman had told the shopper it was air-conditioned (repeating a statement in the advertisement), "and that Chrysler was a nice car and all that jazz." The shopper bought the car, and now knows—as the salesman knew earlier—that the knobs marked "air" were for ventilation only. Is the agreement voidable? See Williams v. Rank & Son Buick, Inc., 170 N.W.2d 807 (Wis.1969) (fraud action; 4–3 decision).

(b) A cattleman and a potential buyer discussed with one another sales that had occurred earlier in the day at a local sales barn. (The buyer had attended the earlier sales.) The cattleman contracted to sell 360 head at $60 a hundredweight to that same buyer. Now he knows—as the buyer knew earlier—that some cattle had been sold at the barn for as much as $62 a hundredweight. Is the contract voidable? See Kanzmeier v. McCoppin, 398 N.W.2d 826 (Iowa 1987).

(2) *Handiwork.* John Hand sued his former employer, Dayton–Hudson (D–H), for breach of contract and age discrimination after his job as an attorney was eliminated. D–H moved for summary judgment on the ground that Hand had

released it from these claims. Upon firing Hand, D–H had offered him $38,000 for a general release of any claim he might have against it. The release form was given to Hand for study. He conceived a "clever scheme" for turning the tables (as he put it) on D–H. He retyped the document so as to mimic the original, but inserted the term, "except as to claims of age discrimination and breach of contract." Not suspecting the change, D–H executed the copy and paid Hand $38,000. Assuming that Hand's conduct was fraudulent, and that D–H's failure to read the copy was excusable, should Hand be permitted to return the amount paid him and maintain his claims? Or should he be bound by the release as D–H understood it? For opinions on reformation to conform a writing to an agreement to which one of the parties did not assent, see Hand v. Dayton–Hudson, 775 F.2d 757 (6th Cir.1985).

MISREPRESENTATION

Concealment and nondisclosure are varieties of misrepresentation, a ground for rescinding a contract or for a tort action. As a predicate for a tort action, the plaintiff must establish that the defendant made the misrepresentation knowing it to be false, or at least with reckless disregard for its truth. This element, known as *scienter,* was insisted on in 19th century English cases, and remains influential in many courts today. In contract law it generally has never had the same force, owing partly to the equitable character of rescission. See Halpert v. Rosenthal, 267 A.2d 730 (R.I.1970), a "termite case" making the distinction. As a rule, a party to a contract may avoid it even if the other party obtained its assent by an innocent misrepresentation, *i.e.,* one that the party making it believed to be true. What difference between the functions of tort and contract law might explain this difference in sensitivity to the nature of a falsehood?

In both tort and contract law relief for misrepresentation is restricted in some ways that merit at least a mention. (To the extent that they are distinctive, the principles of tort law will not be pursued here.) It has sometimes been held that a misrepresentation of *law* is innocuous. Yet because the author of a misrepresentation of law is frequently better placed to know the law than the victim of it—a lawyer speaking to a client, an insurance agent to a customer—the inequality of competence succeeds as a ground for giving relief. See *Kannavos,* p. 356 above.

The misrepresentation must be a material one. This requirement is prominent in insurance litigation, where a misrepresentation by a policy buyer relating to health is a commonplace ground for rejecting a claim. Various standards of materiality have been expressed, and while none is applied uniformly, they serve the common function of justifying a certain control by judges over the more volatile behavior of juries.

Some degree of diligence is required of a party who relies on another's statement, though whether a party has been negligent in relying depends partly on the victim's capacities, partly on the nature of the transaction, and partly on the plausibility of the representation. The question of diligence should be distinguished from the question whether any credence was placed in the representation at all. There can be no complaint about a statement by one who heard it and proceeded to investigate its accuracy:

"reliance and verification are incompatible." Hayat Carpet Cleaning Co., Inc. v. Northern Assur. Co., 69 F.2d 805 (2d Cir.1934) (L. Hand, J.). In the currently preferred formulation, the complainant must show not mere reliance, but *justifiable* reliance.

Finally, the traditional rule is that the misrepresentation must be one of fact, and not of opinion. That tradition is rattled by the next principal case, which describes a suspicious representation embedded in an array of other questionable bargaining techniques.

NOTES

(1) *Promissory Fraud.* The law is shot through with the distinction between a promise that is simply broken and one that was made with the intent not to perform. On proving a promisor's intent not to perform, the promisee may get a remedy for a tort. It is essential for the action that " 'the promisor, at the time of making certain representations, lacked any intention to perform them.' " Junk v. Aon Corp., 2007 WL 4292034 (S.D.N.Y. 2007)(citations omitted). In Hoffman v. Red Owl, p. 230 above, would Joseph Hoffman have an action for promissory fraud against Red Owl's representative Lukowitz? Is there a difference between "negligent promising" and promissory fraud? See generally, Ian Ayres and Gregory Klass, *Insincere Promises: The Law of Misrepresented Intent* (2005).

In Junk v. Aon Corp., cited above, Aon had recruited Junk to join its offices in New York. According to Junk, an Aon vice-president had promised that if he accepted Aon's offer, Junk would work exclusively on a revolutionary new software program that Aon was about to "roll out." When Junk expressed concern regarding the delay in development of the product, the vice-president said, "No. no. no. I have guys working on it as we speak and it will be done in three months." Junk accepted the job and moved to New York, but there was no new software to work on. Junk sued for promissory fraud, showing, among other things, that Aon had not started development of the product at the time the vice-president spoke to Junk. Aon moved to dismiss the complaint for Junk's failure to state a claim for promissory fraud. *Held:* Motion denied.

Claims for promissory fraud have also arisen in the academic context. Consider the following: A student brought an action against the administrators of his university, claiming that when the student transferred to the university, the dean had promised him that music courses listed in the school's catalogue would be offered. The student provided proof that at the time of the dean's promise, the dean knew that the school had neither qualified instructors nor the necessary equipment for the courses. What result? See Byrd v. Lamar, 846 So.2d 334 (Ala.,2002).

(2) *What the Document Means.* "A representation as to the legal effect of a document is regarded as a statement of opinion rather than of fact and will not ordinarily support an action for fraud." Fina Supply, Inc. v. Abilene Nat. Bank, 726 S.W.2d 537 (Tex.1987).

In that case a bank (defendant) had given a formal assurance to a customer (plaintiff) that the customer could require the bank to pay certain obligations of a third party. The customer, Fina, dealt in large quantities of oil. The document expressing the bank's assurance had been amended from time to time. In litigation between Fina and the bank about the scope of the bank's assurance, Fina charged that a bank employee had misled it about the effect of the amendments. Fina charged the bank with fraud and sought reformation of the document (letter of credit) expressing the bank's undertaking. From a judgment for Fina, the bank appealed. *Held:* Reversed.

The court stated further that "where the parties are in an equal bargaining position with equal access to legal advice, there is no room for application of the doctrine that misrepresentations of points of law will be considered misrepresentations of fact if they were so intended and understood."

Vokes v. Arthur Murray, Inc.

District Court of Appeal of Florida, Second District, 1968.
212 So.2d 906.

■ PIERCE, JUDGE. . . . Plaintiff Mrs. Audrey E. Vokes, a widow of 51 years and without family, had a yen to be "an accomplished dancer" with the hopes of finding "new interest in life." So, on February 10, 1961, a dubious fate, with the assist of a motivated acquaintance, procured her to attend a "dance party" at Davenport's "School of Dancing" where she whiled away the pleasant hours, sometimes in a private room, absorbing the accomplished sales technique [of J.P. Davenport, the owner of the Arthur Murray franchise], during which her grace and poise were elaborated upon and her rosy future as "an excellent dancer" was painted for her in vivid and glowing colors. As an incident to this interlude, he sold her eight ½-hour dance lessons to be utilized within one calendar month therefrom, for the sum of $14.50 cash in hand paid, obviously a baited "come-on."

Thus she embarked upon an almost endless pursuit of the terpsichorean art during which, over a period of less than sixteen months, she was sold fourteen "dance courses" totalling in the aggregate 2302 hours of dancing lessons for a total cash outlay of $31,090.45, all at Davenport's dance emporium. . . .

These dance lesson contracts and the monetary consideration therefor of over $31,000 were procured from her by means and methods of Davenport and his associates which went beyond the unsavory, yet legally permissible, perimeter of "sales puffing" and intruded well into the forbidden area of undue influence, the suggestion of falsehood, the suppression of truth, and the free exercise of rational judgment, if what plaintiff alleged in her complaint was true. From the time of her first contact with the dancing school in February, 1961, she was influenced unwittingly by a constant and continuous barrage of flattery, false praise, excessive compliments, and panegyric encomiums, to such extent that it would be not only inequitable, but unconscionable, for a Court exercising inherent chancery power to allow such contracts to stand.

She was incessantly subjected to overreaching blandishment and cajolery. She was assured she had "grace and poise"; that she was "rapidly improving and developing in her dancing skill"; that the additional lessons would "make her a beautiful dancer, capable of dancing with the most accomplished dancers"; that she was "rapidly progressing in the development of her dancing skill and gracefulness," etc., etc. She was given "dance aptitude tests" for the ostensible purpose of "determining" the number of remaining hours instructions needed by her from time to time. . . .

[The court described a succession of contracts Vokes signed for more and more lessons to be added onto the hundred of unused lessons she had already purchased, each contract induced by the promise of eligibility for such awards as a "Gold Medal" for achievement.]

All the foregoing sales promotions, illustrative of the entire fourteen separate contracts, were procured by defendant Davenport and Arthur Murray, Inc., by false representations to her that she was improving in her dancing ability, that she had excellent potential, that she was responding to instructions in dancing grace, and that they were developing her into a beautiful dancer, whereas in truth and in fact she did not develop in her dancing ability, she had no "dance aptitude," and in fact had difficulty in "hearing that musical beat." The complaint alleged that such representations to her "were in fact false and known by the defendant to be false and contrary to the plaintiff's true ability, the truth of plaintiff's ability being fully known to the defendants, but withheld from the plaintiff for the sole and specific intent to deceive and defraud the plaintiff and to induce her in the purchasing of additional hours of dance lessons."

[The trial court held that the complaint failed to state a cause of action and dismissed it with prejudice.]

The material allegations of the complaint must, of course, be accepted as true for the purpose of testing its legal sufficiency. Defendants contend that contracts can only be rescinded for fraud or misrepresentation when the alleged misrepresentation is as to a material fact, rather than an opinion, prediction or expectation, and that the statements and representations set forth at length in the complaint were in the category of "trade puffing," within its legal orbit.

It is true that "generally a misrepresentation, to be actionable, must be one of fact rather than of opinion." Tonkovich v. South Florida Citrus Industries, Inc., Fla.App.1966, 185 So.2d 710; Kutner v. Kalish, Fla.App. 1965, 173 So.2d 763. But this rule has significant qualifications, applicable here. It does not apply where there is a fiduciary relationship between the parties, or where there has been some artifice or trick employed by the representor, or where the parties do not in general deal at "arm's length" as we understand the phrase, or where the representee does not have equal opportunity to become apprised of the truth or falsity of the fact represented.... As stated by Judge Allen of this Court in Ramel v. Chasebrook Construction Company, Fla.App.1961, 135 So.2d 876:

> "... A statement of a party having ... superior knowledge may be regarded as a statement of fact although it would be considered as opinion if the parties were dealing on equal terms."

It could be reasonably supposed here that defendants had "superior knowledge" as to whether plaintiff had "dance potential" and as to whether she was noticeably improving in the art of terpsichore....

Even in contractual situations where a party to a transaction owes no duty to disclose facts within his knowledge or to answer inquiries respecting such facts, the law is if he undertakes to do so he must disclose the whole truth. Ramel v. Chasebrook Construction Company, supra; Beagle v. Bagwell, Fla.App.1964, 169 So.2d 43. From the face of the complaint, it should have been reasonably apparent to defendants that her vast outlay of cash for the many hundreds of additional hours of instruction was not justified by her slow and awkward progress, which she would have been made well aware of if they had spoken the "whole truth."

We repeat that where parties are dealing on a contractual basis at arm's length with no inequities or inherently unfair practices employed, the Courts will in general "leave the parties where they find themselves." But in the case sub judice, from the allegations of the unanswered complaint, we cannot say that enough of the accompanying ingredients, as mentioned in the foregoing authorities, were not present which otherwise would have barred the equitable arm of the Court to her. In our view, from the showing made in her complaint, plaintiff is entitled to her day in Court.

It accordingly follows that the order dismissing plaintiff's last amended complaint with prejudice should be and is reversed.

NOTES

(1) *Questions.* How do the representations made to Vokes differ from those made to Kannavos in the previous case? Why did the court not apply the traditional rule limiting misrepresentations to statement of facts?

(2) *Puffing.* The distinction between ordinary puffing ("This property is worth every cent I am asking for it") and representations of fact has lost some of its clarity. Witness a case in which the seller's statement was: "These are good, sound buildings and they will make you a good investment." Maser v. Lind, 148 N.W.2d 831 (Neb.1967). Again, the relative positions of the parties may influence the decision more than the form of words that was used. See, for example, Ward Development Co. v. Ingrao, 493 A.2d 421 (Md.App.1985), in which the court approved a recovery against a seller of homes for negligence in stating an *estimate* of an expense the buyers should expect: "the homeowners relied on Ward ... as knowledgeable in the field of real estate."

(3) *Puttin' on the Ritz.* What exactly is it about the Vokes transaction that is objectionable? That Vokes paid to be flattered? That she paid too much to be flattered? That she bought worthless services? What factors (and language) did the court adduce to support her status as "servient" (to borrow a word from *Odorizzi*)? If Vokes had been employed, and had, at the same time she signed up for the dancing lessons, elected an irrevocable pension option, would grounds exist to set aside her election, should it later prove improvident? See *Ortelere*, p. 316, above.

What mechanisms are appropriate for policing what one scholar has called the "grotesque" bargain in *Vokes*? See Robert Gordon, Unfreezing Legal Realities: Critical Approaches to Law, 15 Fla.St.U.L.Rev. 195 (1987). California, among other states, has enacted a Dance Studio Act providing that any contract for dancing lessons entered into "in reliance upon any willful and false ... or misleading information ... shall be void and unenforceable." Cal.Civ.Code 1812.60. It also requires that "[e]very contract for dance studio lessons ... shall provide that performance of the agreed-upon lessons will begin within six months from the date the contract is entered into." Cal. Civ. Code 1812.54. In People v. Arthur Murray, Inc., 47 Cal.Rptr. 700 (Ct.App. 1965), the court upheld the Act against a constitutional challenge, stating that special regulation was appropriate in a "class of business so habitually fraught with fraud and sharp practices."

CHAPTER 5

Determining the Parties' Obligations under the Contract: Ascertaining, Interpreting, and Supplementing the Agreement

To this point, this book has primarily examined the law governing the creation of enforceable contracts: Has there been agreement? Are the parties' promises supported by consideration? Is the agreement evidenced by a writing or other record, if required by the Statute of Frauds? Has the bargaining process been unobjectionable? Little attention has been paid, however, to the legal system's determination of what obligations the parties have incurred by virtue of their agreement. That subject—determining the obligations of the parties under their contract—is the focus of this chapter.

Not surprisingly, the starting point for determining the obligations of the parties to a contract is their language. One might expect that the words of the parties also would be the ending point, that the obligations of the parties are ascertained by a court simply applying their words. But this puts too much faith in the parties' abilities (or desires) to "put it all in writing" or "get it all down." Even when parties reduce their agreement to writing, they may omit some terms or express others unclearly. How does such imperfection in expressing the deal come about?

Part of the answer concerns the contracting process itself. Transactions come in all shapes and sizes. Some transactions are extensively negotiated and reduced to writing by attorneys who produce draft documents that have been extensively vetted by both sides before being finalized. In such transactions, considerable time and effort is expended in assuring that all matters agreed to during negotiations are reflected in the documents in detail. Sometimes such efforts are imperfectly realized, or the document may be "incomplete" for the reasons considered at p. 247, above. Such efforts are, however, costly and many transactions will not bear the expense of intensive attorney involvement. Often, there is not time for such efforts to take place.

Other transactions are less formally negotiated, with a writing created by the parties themselves, or reduced to writing by use of a form document previously prepared by attorneys for one of the parties.

In either case, when the parties reduce their agreement to writing (for certainty and evidentiary reasons as well as, perhaps, satisfying the Statute of Frauds), it is possible that not everything that was discussed or negotiated between the parties actually appears in the writing. This may go unnoticed, especially if the transaction is fully performed by both parties or if the subject of a subsequent dispute *is* addressed in the writing. But what happens when a dispute arises regarding an aspect of the agreement that is not included in the writing? At that point, the party benefitted by that aspect of the agreement will assert it, but the other party (who may have a strategic incentive to fail to remember such an oral—or parol—agreement) may disagree that such an agreement was ever made. How does the law deal with a dispute about terms allegedly agreed to but not included in the writing?

Before addressing that question, consider a related issue. When parties reach a "meeting of the minds," that agreement is expressed in words. But words are only imperfect proxies for the ideas they represent. Sometimes the words used by the parties admit more than one meaning; sometimes a word will have one meaning in general discourse and a special meaning in a particular business context. What happens when a transaction has been reduced to writing and a dispute arises as to the meaning of what has been written down? Should a court simply do its best to interpret the writing on its own, or may the parties assist the court by providing extrinsic evidence—something outside the writing—regarding the meaning of the terms of the contract?

These distinct problems—whether a writing fully reflects the parties' agreement and what the written terms mean—have one thing in common. In both cases, one or both of the parties may want to use facts outside the written document in order to determine the nature of the full agreement between them.

Over the years, the legal system has channeled this search for truth and meaning into a set of legal rules. The rules addressing the first problem are embodied in the "parol evidence rule," which is the subject of the first section of this chapter. The second problem, often referred to as "contract interpretation," is the subject of a different body of rules that is examined in Sections 2 and 3, with particular emphasis on the use of extrinsic evidence to determine the meaning of contract terms. Other matters addressed in this chapter include the use of extrinsic evidence to supplement or qualify the parties' agreement (Section 4), the limits of interpretation (Section 5), and supplemental contract terms supplied by law (Section 6).

SECTION 1.   THE PAROL EVIDENCE RULE

What does the law do when a party to a contract asserts that there is a term agreed to during the parties' negotiation that does not appear in the writing memorializing their agreement and that the term is part of the contract? The law could treat the problem as it treats most other factual disputes: by hearing the evidence and ascertaining the facts. The evidence in such a case might consist of the writing, testimony of the parties, and other types of evidence such as e-mail or other correspondence. All of that evidence would be before the fact finder, and none of it would have a privileged place in the proof process. The fact finder would decide, based on all the evidence, whether the assertion is true.

For the most part, the law of contract has *not* taken that path. Instead, one of the more complex rules in contract law, the parol evidence rule, has evolved to address this issue. The parol evidence rule may preclude a determination that an agreement made prior to or contemporaneously with the writing, but not reflected in it, is part of the contract.

The parol evidence rule is not aptly named. Although called a rule of "parol" evidence, it is not limited to oral agreements, but operates to exclude writings, such as letters or e-mails, as well. Nor is it, strictly speaking, a rule of "evidence" (such as the hearsay rule) that bars the use of certain types of evidence to prove an ultimate matter of fact, while permitting that fact to be established in a different way. Rather the parol evidence rule is a rule of substantive law that, when it applies, precludes any proof that the terms of the contract are other than as expressed in the writing.

The parol evidence rule is controversial. In England, the Law Commission called it "a technical rule of uncertain ambit which, at best, adds to the complications of litigation without affecting the outcome and, at worst, prevents the courts from getting at the truth." The Law Commission, Law of Contract, The Parol Evidence Rule 25, Working Paper No. 70 (1976). The Commission's provisional recommendation that the rule be abolished was not, however, carried out.

Others have defended the rule. "The parol evidence rule is maligned in some circles as the vestige of an era when judges were hostile to plaintiffs and mistrusted juries, and thus as an arbitrary barrier to getting at the truth. But it has stubbornly refused to die ... and in fact it serves an important social purpose.... Not all parties to contracts want to entrust their fate to the vagaries of juries unversed in the usages of business...." Olympia Hotels Corp. v. Johnson Wax Development Corp., 908 F.2d 1363, 1373 (7th Cir.1990) (Posner, J.).

NOTE

Rule of Substantive Law. Characterizing the parol evidence rule as "substantive" has some important practical consequences. Here are two.

First, in our adversary trial system it is traditionally the responsibility of the party seeking to preclude the admission of evidence to make timely objection to its admission in order to give the trial judge an opportunity to rule before the evidence is admitted. Failure to object is ordinarily a waiver of any ground of complaint against admission, and the evidence becomes part of the proof in the case. By way of contrast, a failure to object to evidence that would establish the existence of an agreement not reflected in the writing does not bar a later assertion of the parol evidence rule. Gajewski v. Bratcher, 221 N.W.2d 614 (N.D.1974).

Second, in our federal court system, under the *Erie* doctrine, federal courts apply state substantive law "to any issue or claim which has its source in state law." C. Wright, A. Miller, & E. Cooper, 19 Federal Practice and Procedure (2d ed.2002) § 4520. Thus, a federal court adjudicating a state law claim must apply the parol evidence rule of the appropriate state. Betz Laboratories, Inc. v. Hines, 647 F.2d 402 (3d Cir.1981).

Gianni v. R. Russell & Co.

Supreme Court of Pennsylvania, 1924.
281 Pa. 320, 126 A. 791.

Action by Frank Gianni against R. Russell & Co., Inc. From judgment for plaintiff, defendant appeals.

Reversed, and judgment entered for defendant.

■ SCHAFFER, J. Plaintiff had been a tenant of a room in an office building in Pittsburgh wherein he conducted a store, selling tobacco, fruit, candy and soft drinks. Defendant acquired the entire property in which the storeroom was located, and its agent negotiated with plaintiff for a further leasing of the room. A lease for three years was signed. It contained a provision that the lessee should "use the premises only for the sale of fruit, candy, soda water," etc., with the further stipulation that "it is expressly understood that the tenant is not allowed to sell tobacco in any form, under penalty of instant forfeiture of this lease." The document was prepared following a discussion about renting the room between the parties and after an agreement to lease had been reached. It was signed after it had been left in plaintiff's hands and admittedly had been read over to him by two persons, one of whom was his daughter.

Plaintiff sets up that in the course of his dealings with defendant's agent it was agreed that, in consideration of his promises not to sell tobacco and to pay an increased rent, and for entering into the agreement as a whole, he should have the exclusive right to sell soft drinks in the building. No such stipulation is contained in the written lease. Shortly after it was signed defendant demised the adjoining room in the building to a drug company without restricting the latter's right to sell soda water and soft drinks. Alleging that this was in violation of the contract which defendant had made with him, and that the sale of these beverages by the drug company had greatly reduced his receipts and profits, plaintiff brought this action for damages for breach of the alleged oral contract, and was permitted to recover. Defendant has appealed.

Plaintiff's evidence was to the effect that the oral agreement had been made at least two days, possibly longer, before the signing of the instrument, and that it was repeated at the time he signed; that, relying upon it, he executed the lease. Plaintiff called one witness who said he heard defendant's agent say to plaintiff at a time admittedly several days before the execution of the lease that he would have the exclusive right to sell soda water and soft drinks, to which the latter replied if that was the case he accepted the tenancy. Plaintiff produced no witness who was present when the contract was executed to corroborate his statement as to what then occurred. Defendant's agent denied that any such agreement was made, either preliminary to or at the time of the execution of the lease.

Appellee's counsel argues this is not a case in which an endeavor is being made to reform a written instrument because of something omitted as a result of fraud, accident, or mistake, but is one involving the breach of an independent oral agreement which does not belong in the writing at all and is not germane to its provisions. We are unable to reach this conclusion.

"Where parties, without any fraud or mistake, have deliberately put their engagements in writing, the law declares the writing to be not only the best, but the only evidence of their agreement." Martin v. Berens, 67 Pa. 459, 463; Irvin v. Irvin, 142 Pa. 271, 287, 21 A. 816.

"All preliminary negotiations, conversations and verbal agreements are merged in and superseded by the subsequent written contract, . . . and 'unless fraud, accident, or mistake be averred, the writing constitutes the agreement between the parties, and its terms cannot be added to nor subtracted from by parol evidence.' " Union Storage Co. v. Speck, 194 Pa. 126, 133, 45 A. 48, 49; Vito v. Birkel, 209 Pa. 206, 208, 58 A. 127.

The writing must be the entire contract between the parties if parol evidence is to be excluded, and to determine whether it is or not the writing will be looked at, and if it appears to be a contract complete within itself, "couched in such terms as import a complete legal obligation without any uncertainty as to the object or extent of the engagement, it is conclusively presumed that the whole engagement of the parties, and the extent and manner of their undertaking, were reduced to writing." Seitz v. Brewers' Refrigerating Machine Co., 141 U.S. 510, 517.

When does the oral agreement come within the field embraced by the written one? This can be answered by comparing the two, and determining whether parties, situated as were the ones to the contract, would naturally and normally include the one in the other if it were made. If they relate to the same subject-matter, and are so interrelated that both would be executed at the same time and in the same contract, the scope of the subsidiary agreement must be taken to be covered by the writing. This question must be determined by the court.

In the case at bar the written contract stipulated for the very sort of thing which plaintiff claims has no place in it. It covers the use to which the storeroom was to be put by plaintiff and what he was and what he was not to sell therein. He was "to use the premises only for the sale of fruit, candy, soda water," etc., and was not "allowed to sell tobacco in any form." Plaintiff claims his agreement not to sell tobacco was part of the consideration for the exclusive right to sell soft drinks. Since his promise to refrain was included in the writing, it would be the natural thing to have included the promise of exclusive rights. Nothing can be imagined more pertinent to these provisions which were included than the one appellee avers.

In cases of this kind, where the cause of action rests entirely on an alleged oral understanding concerning a subject which is dealt with in a written contract it is assumed that the writing was intended to set forth the entire agreement as to that particular subject.

"In deciding upon this intent [as to whether a certain subject was intended to be embodied by the writing], the chief and most satisfactory index ... is found in the circumstance whether or not the particular element of the alleged extrinsic negotiation is dealt with at all in the writing. If it is mentioned, covered, or dealt with in the writing, then presumably the writing was meant to represent all of the transaction on that element, if it is not, then probably the writing was not intended to embody that element of the negotiation." Wigmore on Evidence, 2d Ed., vol. 5, p. 309.

As the written lease is the complete contract of the parties, and since it embraces the field of the alleged oral contract, evidence of the latter is inadmissible under the parol evidence rule.

"The [parol evidence] rule also denies validity to a subsidiary agreement within [the] scope [of the written contract] if sued on as a separate contract, although except for [that rule], the agreement fulfills all the requisites of a valid contract." 2 Williston, Contracts, 1222; Penn Iron Co. v. Diller, 1 Sad., Pa., 82, 1 A. 924; Krueger v. Nicola, 205 Pa. 38, 54 A. 494; Wodock v. Robinson, 148 Pa. 503, 24 A. 73.

There are, of course, certain exceptions to the parol evidence rule, but this case does not fall within any of them. Plaintiff expressly rejects any idea of fraud, accident, or mistake, and they are the foundation upon which any basis for admitting parol evidence to set up an entirely separate agreement within the scope of a written contract must be built. The evidence must be such as would cause a chancellor to reform the instrument, and that would be done only for these reasons (Pioso v. Bitzer, 209 Pa. 503, 58 A. 891) and this holds true where this essentially equitable relief is being given, in our Pennsylvania fashion, through common-law forms.

We have stated on several occasions recently that we propose to stand for the integrity of written contracts. . . . We reiterate our position in this regard.

The judgment of the court below is reversed, and is here entered for defendant.

NOTES

(1) *Rationale.* What are the reasons behind the parol evidence rule? One rationale is that, as Restatement § 213 puts it, the later agreement "discharges prior agreements." Viewed in this way, the rule simply affirms the primacy of a subsequent agreement not only over prior negotiations, which would not be binding in any case, but also over prior agreements, which, though they would be binding, are discharged. See generally Farnsworth on Contracts § 7.2 (4th ed.2004).

Many of the older cases, however, evince a different rationale. As the opinion in the next case explains, Dean Charles McCormick, an expert on the law of evidence, "suggested that the party urging the spoken as against the written word is most often the economic underdog, threatened by severe hardship if the writing is enforced." He argued that the "rule arose to allow the court to control the tendency of the jury to find through sympathy and without a dispassionate assessment of the probability of fraud or faulty memory that the parties made an oral agreement collateral to the written contract, or that the preliminary tentative agreements were not abandoned when omitted from the writing." Does this rationale seem applicable to *Gianni*? Does it explain why the rule bars prior *writings*? Does it explain why the rule does not bar *subsequent* oral agreements?

(2) *"Integrated" Agreements and the Restatement.* Although Professor James Bradley Thayer said of the parol evidence rule that, "Few things are darker than this, or fuller of subtle difficulties," application of the rule is clarified considerably by the scheme adopted by the Restatement. It involves two steps to be followed by the court. See Restatement §§ 209(2), 210(3).

The first step is to see whether a writing has been adopted by the parties as "a *final* expression of one or more terms of an agreement." If there is no such writing, the rule does not apply. If there is such a writing, the agreement is known as an "integrated agreement," with the consequence that "evidence of prior . . . agreements or negotiations is not admissible in evidence to contradict a term of the writing." Restatement §§ 209, 215.

If there is an integrated agreement, so that the rule applies, the second step is to determine whether the writing has been "adopted by the parties as a *complete* and *exclusive* statement of the terms of the agreement." If this is not the case, the agreement is known as a "partially integrated agreement" and the rule has only the effect described in the previous paragraph. If the writing was adopted as a complete and exclusive statement of the terms of the agreement, however, the agreement is referred to as a "completely integrated agreement," with the additional consequence that evidence of "a consistent additional term" is not admissible to supplement the written agreement. Restatement §§ 210, 216. Such evidence is, however, admissible if the writing is only a "partially integrated agreement."

Masterson v. Sine

Supreme Court of California, 1968.
68 Cal.2d 222, 436 P.2d 561.

■ TRAYNOR, CHIEF JUSTICE. Dallas Masterson and his wife Rebecca owned a ranch as tenants in common. On February 25, 1958, they conveyed it to Medora and Lu Sine by a grant deed. "Reserving unto the Grantors herein an option to purchase the above described property on or before February 25, 1968" for the "same consideration as being paid heretofore plus their depreciation value of any improvements Grantees may add to the property from and after two and a half years from this date." Medora is Dallas' sister and Lu's wife. Since the conveyance Dallas has been adjudged bankrupt. His trustee in bankruptcy and Rebecca brought this declaratory relief action to establish their right to enforce the option.

The case was tried without a jury. Over defendants' objection the trial court admitted extrinsic evidence that by "the same consideration as being paid heretofore" both the grantors and the grantees meant the sum of $50,000 and by "depreciation value of any improvements" they meant the depreciation value of improvements to be computed by deducting from the total amount of any capital expenditures made by defendants grantees the amount of depreciation allowable to them under United States income tax regulations as of the time of the exercise of the option.

The court also determined that the parol evidence rule precluded admission of extrinsic evidence offered by defendants to show that the parties wanted the property kept in the Masterson family and that the option was therefore personal to the grantors and could not be exercised by the trustee in bankruptcy.

The court entered judgment for plaintiffs, declaring their right to exercise the option, specifying in some detail how it could be exercised, and reserving jurisdiction to supervise the manner of its exercise and to determine the amount that plaintiffs will be required to pay defendants for their capital expenditures if plaintiffs decide to exercise the option.

Defendants appeal. They contend that the option provision is too uncertain to be enforced and that extrinsic evidence as to its meaning should not have been admitted. The trial court properly refused to frustrate the obviously declared intention of the grantors to reserve an option to repurchase by an overly meticulous insistence on completeness and clarity of written expression. . . . It properly admitted extrinsic evidence to explain the language of the deed . . . to the end that the consideration for the option would appear with sufficient certainty to permit specific enforcement. . . . The trial court erred, however, in excluding the extrinsic evidence that the option was personal to the grantors and therefore nonassignable.

When the parties to a written contract have agreed to it as an "integration"—a complete and final embodiment of the terms of an agreement—parol evidence cannot be used to add to or vary its terms. . . . When only part of the agreement is integrated, the same rule applies to that part, but parol evidence may be used to prove elements of the agreement not reduced to writing. . . .

The crucial issue in determining whether there has been an integration is whether the parties intended their writing to serve as the exclusive embodiment of their agreement. The instrument itself may help to resolve that issue. It may state, for example, that "there are no previous understandings or agreements not contained in the writing," and thus express the parties' "intention to nullify antecedent understandings or agreements." (See 3 Corbin, *Contracts* (1960) § 578, p. 411.) Any such collateral agreement itself must be examined, however, to determine whether the parties intended the subjects of negotiation it deals with to be included in, excluded from, or otherwise affected by the writing. Circumstances at the time of the writing may also aid in the determination of such integration. . . .

California cases have stated that whether there was an integration is to be determined solely from the face of the instrument and that the question for the court is whether it "appears to be a complete . . . agreement. . . ." (See Ferguson v. Koch 268 P. 342, 344 (Cal. 1928); . . .) Neither of these strict formulations of the rule, however, has been consistently applied. The requirement that the writing must appear incomplete on its face has been repudiated in many cases where parol evidence was admitted "to prove the existence of a separate oral agreement as to any matter on which the document is silent and which is not inconsistent with its terms"—even though the instrument appeared to state a complete agreement.... Even under the rule that the writing alone is to be consulted, it was found necessary to examine the alleged collateral agreement before concluding that proof of it was precluded by the writing alone. (See 3 Corbin, Contracts (1960) § 582, pp. 444–446.) It is therefore evident that "The conception of a writing as wholly and intrinsically self-determinative of the parties' intent to make it a sole memorial of one or seven or twenty-seven subjects of negotiation is an impossible one." (9 Wigmore, Evidence (3d ed. 1940) § 2431, p. 103.) For example, a promissory note given by a debtor to his creditor may integrate all their present contractual rights and obligations, or it may be only a minor part of an underlying executory contract that would never be discovered by examining the face of the note.

In formulating the rule governing parol evidence, several policies must be accommodated. One policy is based on the assumption that written evidence is more accurate than human memory.... This policy, however, can be adequately served by excluding parol evidence of agreements that directly contradict the writing. Another policy is based on the fear that fraud or unintentional invention by witnesses interested in the outcome of the litigation will mislead the finder of facts. (... Mitchill v. Lath 160 N.E. 646 (N.Y. 1928)....) ... McCormick has suggested that the party urging the spoken as against the written word is most often the economic underdog, threatened by severe hardship if the writing is enforced. In his view the parol evidence rule arose to allow the court to control the tendency of the jury to find through sympathy and without a dispassionate assessment of the probability of fraud or faulty memory that the parties made an oral agreement collateral to the written contract, or that preliminary tentative agreements were not abandoned when omitted from the writing. (See McCormick, Evidence (1954) § 210.) He recognizes, however, that if this theory were adopted in disregard of all other considerations, it would lead to the exclusion of testimony concerning oral agreements whenever there is a writing and thereby often defeat the true intent of the parties. (See McCormick, op. cit. supra, § 216, p. 441.)

Evidence of oral collateral agreements should be excluded only when the fact finder is likely to be misled. The rule must therefore be based on the credibility of the evidence. One such standard, adopted by section 240(1)(b) of the Restatement of Contracts, permits proof of a collateral agreement if it "is such an agreement as might *naturally* be made as a separate agreement by parties situated as were the parties to the written contract." (Italics added; see McCormick, Evidence (1954) § 216, p. 441; see also 3 Corbin, Contracts (1960) § 583, p. 475, § 594, pp. 568–569; 4 Williston, Contracts (3d ed. 1961) § 638, pp. 1039–1045.) The draftsmen of the Uniform Commercial Code would exclude the evidence in still fewer instances: "If the additional terms are such that, if agreed upon, they would *certainly* have been included in the document in the view of the court, then evidence of their alleged making must be kept from the trier of fact." (Com. 3, § 2–202, italics added.)[1]

---

[1] Corbin suggests that, even in situations where the court concludes that it would not have been natural for the parties to make the alleged collateral oral agreement, parol

The option clause in the deed in the present case does not explicitly provide that it contains the complete agreement, and the deed is silent on the question of assignability. Moreover, the difficulty of accommodating the formalized structure of a deed to the insertion of collateral agreements makes it less likely that all the terms of such an agreement were included.... The statement of the reservation of the option might well have been placed in the recorded deed solely to preserve the grantors' rights against any possible future purchasers and this function could well be served without any mention of the parties' agreement that the option was personal. There is nothing in the record to indicate that the parties to this family transaction, through experience in land transactions or otherwise, had any warning of the disadvantages of failing to put the whole agreement in the deed. This case is one, therefore, in which it can be said that a collateral agreement such as that alleged "might naturally be made as a separate agreement." *A fortiori*, the case is not one in which the parties "would certainly" have included the collateral agreement in the deed.

It is contended, however, that an option agreement is ordinarily presumed to be assignable if it contains no provisions forbidding its transfer or indicating that its performance involves elements personal to the parties.... The fact that there is a written memorandum, however, does not necessarily preclude parol evidence rebutting a term that the law would otherwise presume....

In the present case defendants offered evidence that the parties agreed that the option was not assignable in order to keep the property in the Masterson family. The trial court erred in excluding that evidence.

The judgment is reversed.

■ Peters, Tobriner, Mosk, and Sullivan, JJ., concur.

■ Burke, Justice (dissenting). I dissent. The majority opinion ... [u]ndermines the parol evidence rule as we have known it in this state since at least 1872 by declaring that parol evidence should have been admitted by the trial court to show that a written option, absolute and unrestricted in form, was intended to be limited and nonassignable....

The opinion permits defendants to establish by parol testimony that their grant to their brother (and brother-in-law) of a written option, absolute in terms, was nevertheless agreed to be nonassignable by the grantee (now a bankrupt), and that therefore the right to exercise it did not pass, by operation of the bankruptcy laws, to the trustee for the benefit of the grantee's creditors. And how was this to be shown? By the proffered testimony of the bankrupt optionee himself! Thereby one of his assets (the option to purchase defendants' California ranch) would be withheld from the trustee in bankruptcy and from the bankrupt's creditors....

evidence of such an agreement should nevertheless be permitted if the court is convinced that the unnatural actually happened in the case being adjudicated. (3 Corbin, Contracts, § 485, pp. 478, 480; cf. Murray, The Parol Evidence Rule: A Clarification (1966) 4 Duquesne L.Rev. 337, 341–342.) This suggestion may be based on a belief that judges are not likely to be misled by their sympathies. If the court believes that the parties intended a collateral agreement to be effective, there is no reason to keep the evidence from the jury.

[T]here was nothing ambiguous about the *granting* language of the option and not the slightest suggestion in the document that the option was to be nonassignable. Thus, to permit such words of limitation to be added by parol is to *contradict* the absolute nature of the grant, and to directly violate the parol evidence rule.

Just as it is unnecessary to state in a deed to "lot X" that the house located thereon goes with the land, it is likewise unnecessary to add to "I grant an option to Jones" the words *"and his assigns"* for the option to be assignable. As hereinafter emphasized in more detail, California statutes expressly declare that it *is* assignable, and only if I add language in writing showing my intent to withhold or restrict the right of assignment may the grant be so limited. Thus, to seek to restrict the grant by parol is to *contradict* the written document in violation of the parol evidence rule. . . .

The right of an optionee to transfer his option to purchase property is . . . one of the basic rights which accompanies the option unless limited under the language of the option itself. To allow an optionor to resort to parol evidence to support his assertion that the written option is not transferable is to authorize him to limit the option by attempting to restrict and reclaim rights with which he has already parted. A clearer violation of two substantive and basic rules of law—the parol evidence rule and the right of free transferability of property—would be difficult to conceive. . . .

In an effort to provide justification for applying the newly pronounced "natural" rule to the circumstances of the present case, the majority opinion next attempts to account for the silence of the writing in this case concerning assignability of the option, by asserting that "the difficulty of accommodating the formalized structure of a deed to the insertion of collateral agreements makes it less likely that all the terms of such an agreement were included." What difficulty would have been involved here, to add the words "this option is nonassignable"? The asserted "formalized structure of a deed" is no formidable barrier. . . .

Comment hardly seems necessary on the convenience to a bankrupt of such a device to defeat his creditors. He need only produce parol testimony that any options (or other property, for that matter) which he holds are subject to an oral "collateral agreement" with family members (or with friends) that the property is nontransferable "in order to keep the property in the family" or in the friendly group. In the present case the value of the ranch which the bankrupt and his wife held an option to purchase has doubtless increased substantially during the years since they acquired the option. The initiation of this litigation by the trustee in bankruptcy to establish his right to enforce the option indicates his belief that there is substantial value to be gained for the creditors from this asset of the bankrupt. Yet the majority opinion permits defeat of the trustee and of the creditors through the device of an asserted collateral oral agreement that the option was "personal" to the bankrupt and nonassignable "in order to keep the property in the family"! . . .

I would hold that the trial court ruled correctly on the proffered parol evidence, and would affirm the judgment.

■ McComb, J., concurs.

NOTES

(1) *Questions*. In Restatement terms, how did the agreement in *Masterson* differ from that in *Gianni*? How did the dissenters in *Masterson* differ from the majority? Did Gianni and the Sines seek to introduce extrinsic evidence to show "consistent additional terms"?

(2) *Test of Complete Integration*. To what may a court look in deciding how to characterize a writing under the parol evidence rule? Chief Justice Traynor referred to the "strict formulations of the rule" under which "whether there was an integration is to be determined solely from the face of the instrument and ... the question for the court is whether it 'appears to be a complete ... agreement.' " This view was favored in older cases, of which *Gianni* appears to be an example. The modern view is reflected in Comment *b* to Restatement § 210, which states that "a writing cannot of itself prove its own completeness, and wide latitude must be allowed for inquiry into circumstances bearing on the intention of the parties."

(3) *Merger Clauses*. Chief Justice Traynor observed that the "instrument may help to resolve" the issue of whether the agreement is completely integrated. It is a common practice to include in written contracts a clause known as a "merger," "integration," or "entire agreement" clause, which might read:

> There are no promises, verbal understandings, or agreements of any kind, pertaining to this contract other than specified herein.

Since integration is a matter of the parties' intention, such clauses have usually been given effect, in situations like those in the two preceding cases, to show complete integration.

In L.S. Heath & Son v. AT&T Information Systems, 9 F.3d 561, 569 (7th Cir.1993), the court concluded that an agreement containing a merger clause was nevertheless not completely integrated. The agreement "omits subject matter; it does not identify any prices, products, services, software applications or configurations." The court granted that "the presence of a merger clause is strong evidence that the parties intended the writing to be the complete and exclusive agreement between them, but such a clause is not dispositive.... In order to determine whether the parties intended a writing to be the complete and exclusive agreement between them, a court must compare the writing with the prior negotiations. ... If the allegedly integrated writing does not, without reference to another document or other coordinating information, reveal what the basic transaction entailed, then the writing is not integrated."

As to merger clauses in international commercial contracts, see UNIDROIT Principles art. 2.1.17.

(4) *Unconscionability*. As to whether a merger clause might be held to be unconscionable, see Franklin v. White, 493 N.E.2d 161, 165 (Ind.1986), in which the court said that "there are rules adequately protecting against the unconscionable use of integration clauses."

(5) *"Collateral Agreements."* The fact that the parties have adopted a writing as an integration of one agreement has, of course, no effect on another, entirely separate agreement. Note that Chief Justice Traynor speaks of a "collateral agreement" in Masterson v. Sine. What was that agreement? What was its consideration? Does the notion of a "collateral agreement," as he uses it, differ from that of "partial integration"?

Justice Traynor cites Mitchill v. Lath, 160 N.E. 646, 647 (N.Y.1928). In that case the buyer of land under a written contract attempted to show a prior agreement by the seller to remove an unsightly ice house from a nearby tract. The court held that the parol evidence rule precluded such a showing. For evidence of a contemporaneous oral agreement to be admissible: "(1) The agreement must in form be a collateral one; (2) it must not contradict express or implied provisions of the written contract; (3) it must be one that parties would not ordinarily be expected to embody in the writing." The court thought that "an inspection of this contract shows a full and complete agreement, setting forth in detail the obligations of each party. On reading it, one would conclude that the reciprocal obligations of the parties were fully detailed."

————

Bollinger v. Central Pennsylvania Quarry Stripping and Construction Co.

Supreme Court of Pennsylvania, 1967.
425 Pa. 430, 229 A.2d 741.

■ MUSMANNO, JUSTICE. Mahlon Bollinger and his wife, Vinetta C. Bollinger, filed an action in equity against the Central Pennsylvania Quarry Stripping Construction Company asking that a contract entered into between them be reformed so as to include therein a paragraph alleged to have been omitted by mutual mistake and that the agreement, as reformed, be enforced.

The agreement, as executed, provided that the defendant was to be permitted to deposit on the property of the plaintiffs, construction waste as it engaged in work on the Pennsylvania Turnpike in the immediate vicinity of the plaintiffs' property. The Bollingers claimed that there had been a mutual understanding between them and the defendant that, prior to depositing such waste on the plaintiffs' property, the defendant would remove the topsoil of the plaintiffs' property, pile on it the waste material and then restore the topsoil in a way to cover the deposited waste. The Bollingers averred that they had signed the written agreement without reading it because they assumed that the condition just stated had been incorporated into the writing.

When the defendant first began working in the vicinity of the plaintiffs' property, it did first remove the topsoil, deposited the waste on the bare land, and then replaced the topsoil. After a certain period of time, the defendant ceased doing this and the plaintiffs remonstrated. The defendant answered there was nothing in the written contract which required it to make a sandwich of its refuse between the bare earth and the topsoil. It was at this point that the plaintiffs discovered that that feature of the oral understanding had been omitted from the written contract. The plaintiff husband renewed his protest and the defendant's superintendent replied he could not remove the topsoil because his equipment for that operation had been taken away. When he was reminded of the original understanding, the superintendent said, in effect, he couldn't help that.

The plaintiffs then filed their action for reformation of the contract, the Court granted the requested relief, and the defendant firm appealed. We said in Bugen v. New York Life Insurance Co., 408 Pa. 472, 184 A.2d 499: "A court of equity has the power to reform the written evidence of a contract and make it correspond to the understanding of the parties. . . . However, the mistake must be mutual to the parties to the contract." The fact, however, that one of the parties denies that a mistake was made does not prevent a finding of mutual mistake. Kutsenkow v. Kutsenkow, 414 Pa. 610, 612, 202 A.2d 68.

Once a person enters into a written agreement he builds around himself a stone wall, from which he cannot escape by merely asserting he had not understood what he was signing. However, equity would completely fail in its objectives if it refused to break a hole through the wall when it finds, after proper evidence, that there was a mistake between the parties, that it was real and not feigned, actual and not hypothetical.

The Chancellor, after taking testimony, properly concluded: "We are satisfied that plaintiffs have sustained the heavy burden placed upon them. Their understanding of the agreement is corroborated by the undisputed evidence. The defendant did remove and set aside the topsoil on part of the area before depositing its waste and did replace the topsoil over such waste after such depositing. It follows it would not have done so had it not so agreed. Further corroboration is found in the testimony that it acted similarly in the case of plaintiffs' neighbor Beltzner."

After the Court handed down its Decree Nisi, the defendant petitioned for a rehearing on the ground of after-discovered evidence. Even assuming, without so deciding, that the so-called after-discovered evidence qualified as such, it is not clear that it was sufficiently material or relevant to bring about a change in the result reached by the Chancellor, and he so stated in his Opinion. We are satisfied that the proffered evidence would not be inconsistent with the Chancellor's findings.

Decree affirmed, costs on the appellant.

NOTES

(1) *Questions.* How did the situation of the Bollingers differ from that of Gianni? What would Gianni have had to show in order to bring himself within the rule of *Bollinger*?

(2) *Validity of Agreement.* It is generally held that, since the parol evidence rule proceeds on the assumption that there is a written agreement, it does not bar extrinsic evidence to show that the written agreement is not valid. It does not, for example, preclude the use of extrinsic evidence to show that the writing was a sham, not intended to be enforced, or that a recital of a performance as consideration (*e.g.*, "in consideration of the payment of $10, receipt of which is hereby acknowledged") is false. See Restatement § 214(d).

(3) *Fraud.* For the reason suggested in the preceding note, it is also generally held that the parol evidence rule does not preclude the use of extrinsic evidence to show fraud in the inducement of the contract. It is important in this respect to distinguish a party's fraudulent representation during negotiations, which is not

barred by the rule, from the party's express warranty during negotiations, which is barred.

Is the rule as to fraud the same under UCC § 2–202? For an affirmative answer, see Associated Hardware Supply Co. v. Big Wheel Distributing Co., 355 F.2d 114 (3d Cir.1965). What language in UCC § 2–202 supports such a result? Is UCC § 1–103(b) relevant?

The exception for fraud has been held applicable to promissory fraud, where a promisor makes a promise not intending to perform it. Lovejoy Electronics, Inc. v. O'Berto, 873 F.2d 1001 (7th Cir.1989). But see Alling v. Universal Mfg. Corp., 7 Cal.Rptr.2d 718, 734 (Cal.App.1992) (fraud exception does not apply unless "the false promise is either independent of or consistent with the written instrument").

Would a merger clause preclude the use of extrinsic evidence to show fraud? See Restatement § 214. See also Keller v. A.O. Smith Harvestore Prods., Inc., 819 P.2d 69, 73 (Colo.1991) ("general integration clause does not effect a waiver of a claim of negligent misrepresentation not specifically prohibited by the terms of the agreement").

PROBLEM

Reformation of Bids. Ballard was the successful bidder on the Loving High School job. When the parties signed a written contract, they also executed a change order that modified the contract by deducting the cost of paving parking areas. The parties did not realize that this cost of paving had already been deducted from Ballard's total cost of construction in the contract, so that the result was a double deduction. Has Ballard any remedy? Does the answer depend on whether the mistake is discovered before construction has been begun? See Ballard v. Chavez, 868 P.2d 646 (N.M.1994).

PAROL EVIDENCE AND CONTRACTS FOR THE SALE OF GOODS

For the treatment of parol evidence issues in Article 2 of the UCC, see UCC § 2–202. Note that this section addresses issues in addition to those addressed in the common law parol evidence rule. Which parts of UCC § 2–202 address the parol evidence rule? Is UCC § 2–202 consistent, in concept or results, with the Restatement approach?

PROBLEM

Contract Integration and Sale of Goods. Amy Miller, a local dentist in the market for a new dental chair, went to the Dentco Supply Company ("Dentco") to look at dental chairs. While she was examining a chair known as the "Super Relaxer," the owner of Dentco came over and said "This is our best selling model. It reclines a full 180 degrees." Dr. Miller responded "That's great. My patients will love it; they're always asking if I can tilt them back further." Dr. Miller and Dentco quickly agreed on a price of $9000 for the chair. They then signed a writing that provided, in its entirety:

> Amy Miller ("Miller") and Dentco Supply Company ("Dentco") hereby agree that Miller will buy, and Dentco will sell, one (1) Super Relaxer dental chair for a price of $9000.00. Dentco will deliver and install said chair no later than December 13. Payment in cash is due upon delivery.

> This contract represents a complete and exclusive statement of all of the terms of our transaction.

On December 13, Dentco delivered and installed the Super Relaxer. Dr. Miller asked the installer to sit in the chair so that she could see what it would be like to treat a patient sitting in the chair. Dr. Miller tilted the chair as far back as it could go, and immediately noticed that the chair had not inclined even close to 180 degrees. Dr. Miller would like to sue Dentco for breach of contract because the chair did not recline a full 180 degrees as Dentco's owner had stated that it would. Does she have a cause of action against Dentco?

NO–ORAL–MODIFICATION CLAUSES

Suppose that a party seeks to prove that the provisions of a carefully drafted written contract were varied by a conversation between the parties *after* the contract was made. The parol evidence rule does not speak to this problem (and thus does not preclude this proof), though it is not dissimilar to the problems to which the rule does speak. If one wants to do business on the basis of the written word (preferably one's own), to the exclusion of oral agreements, one has as much interest in excluding subsequent oral agreements as in excluding prior ones. The owner under a construction contract has a particularly strong interest in preventing claims by the builder for extra work allegedly done under oral modifications by the owner's representative on the site. A typical clause, this one taken from Wagner v. Graziano Constr. Co., 136 A.2d 82 (Pa.1957), reads:

> No extra work or changes from plans and specifications under this contract will be recognized or paid for, unless agreed to in writing before the extra work is started or the changes made.

Is such a clause effective?

The traditional answer has been that it is not effective. The reasoning is that any prior agreement, including the no-oral-modification clause itself, can be modified by a later agreement. In the baroque prose of Justice Michael Musmanno, "The most ironclad written contract can always be cut into by the acetylene torch of parol modification supported by adequate proof.... The hand that pens a writing may not gag the mouths of the assenting parties." Wagner v. Graziano Constr. Co., 136 A.2d 82, 83–84 (Pa.1957). The Seventh Circuit, after stating that "an oral modification is enforceable under Texas law even if the contract forbids oral modifications," added that the "Texas approach is by no means idiosyncratic." Autotrol Corp. v. Continental Water Sys. Corp., 918 F.2d 689, 692 (7th Cir.1990).

Moreover, even in those jurisdictions that honor no-oral-modification clauses, a party that seeks to escape the effect of the clause can often do so by showing reliance on the oral modification. As the Supreme Court of Pennsylvania concluded in such a case, "When an owner requests a builder to do extra work, promises to pay for it and watches it performed knowing that it is not authorized in writing, he cannot refuse to pay on the ground that there was no written change order." Universal Builders, Inc. v. Moon Motor Lodge, Inc., 244 A.2d 10, 16 (Pa.1968).

Article 2 of the Uniform Commercial Code applies a rule that is different than the common law rule. Under UCC § 2–209(2), "A signed agreement which excludes modification or rescission except by a signed writing cannot be otherwise modified or rescinded...." Note, however, that under subsection (4) what may fail to be effective as a modification or rescission may nevertheless be effective as a waiver. And under subsection (5) a material change of position in reliance on the waiver may prevent its retraction. Subsection (5) has been the subject of differing interpretations. See the conflicting opinions in Wisconsin Knife Works v. National Metal Crafters, 781 F.2d 1280 (7th Cir.1986) (Posner, J.; Easterbrook, J. dissenting).

On no-oral-modification clauses, see *Farnsworth on Contracts* § 7.6 (4th ed.2004). See also David Snyder, The Law of Contract and the Concept of Change: Public and Private Attempts to Regulate Modification, Waiver, and Estoppel, 1999 Wisconsin L. Rev. 607.

NOTES

(1) *International Solutions.* Article 29(2) of the CISG provides that a written contract "which contains a provision requiring any modification or termination by agreement to be in writing may not be otherwise modified or terminated by agreement." Note that this provision, evidently designed to change the rule in common law countries, makes an exception for cases of reliance. UNIDROIT Principles art. 2.18 contains a similar provision.

(2) *"Private Statutes of Frauds."* It is sometimes suggested that UCC § 2–209(2) allows the parties to set up a "private statute of frauds." The metaphor is, however, misleading. Would UCC § 2–201 necessarily require a writing when a no-oral-modification clause would? Would a writing that satisfies UCC § 2–201 necessarily satisfy a no-oral-modification clause? See Marlowe v. Argentine Naval Commission, 808 F.2d 120 (D.C.Cir.1986).

SECTION 2.   THE USE OF EXTRINSIC EVIDENCE OF THE PARTIES' INTENT

" 'When *I* use a word,' Humpty Dumpty said, in rather a scornful tone, 'it means just what I choose it to mean—neither more nor less.' "

" 'The question is,' said Alice, 'whether you *can* make words mean so many different things.' "

" 'The question is,' said Humpty Dumpty, 'which is to be master—that's all.' " Lewis Carroll, *Through the Looking Glass*, Chapter VI.

As this suggests, the problem of interpretation of language is not peculiar to the law. Scholars less boastful than Humpty Dumpty have urged caution in matters of interpretation. There is no "lawyers' Paradise" where, in Professor Thayer's language, "all words have a fixed, precisely ascertained meaning ... and where, if the writer has been careful, a lawyer, having a document referred to him may sit in his chair, inspect the text, and answer all questions without raising his eyes." As Justice Holmes put it, "A word is not a crystal, transparent and unchanged, it is the skin of a living thought and may vary greatly in color and content according to the circumstances and the time in which it is used." Towne v. Eisner, 245 U.S. 418 (1918).

The admissibility of extrinsic evidence, particularly evidence of the parties' prior negotiations, is one of the most troublesome aspects of contract interpretation. Courts have traditionally employed a two-stage process often referred to as the "plain meaning rule." Because the process is generally used only for completely integrated agreements, it is often regarded as a corollary of the parol evidence rule.

In the first stage, the judge determines whether the language in the written agreement, with respect to the dispute in question, admits of only one plausible meaning or, rather, is ambiguous. If the language is *not* ambiguous, extrinsic evidence as to its meaning will be excluded.

In the second stage, the court determines the meaning of the contract language. If, in the first stage, the language was found to be "ambiguous," extrinsic evidence as to its meaning will be admitted to inform the court's determination of the meaning of the contract language.

Courts disagree about what evidence may be considered in the first stage to determine whether there is ambiguity. The courts of California and New York are often seen as exemplars of opposite approaches. Consider the following cases from courts of those states.

Pacific Gas & Electric Co. v. G.W. Thomas Drayage & Rigging Co.

Supreme Court of California, 1968.
69 Cal.2d 33, 442 P.2d 641.

■ TRAYNOR, CHIEF JUSTICE. Defendant appeals from a judgment for plaintiff in an action for damages for injury to property under an indemnity clause of a contract.

In 1960 defendant entered into a contract with plaintiff to furnish the labor and equipment necessary to remove and replace the upper metal cover of plaintiff's steam turbine. Defendant agreed to perform the work "at [its] own risk and expense" and to "indemnify" plaintiff "against all loss, damage, expense and liability resulting from . . . injury to property, arising out of or in any way connected with the performance of this contract." Defendant also agreed to procure not less than $50,000 insurance to cover liability for injury to property. Plaintiff was to be an additional named insured, but the policy was to contain a cross-liability clause extending the coverage to plaintiff's property.

During the work the cover fell and injured the exposed rotor of the turbine. Plaintiff brought this action to recover $25,144.51, the amount it subsequently spent on repairs. During the trial it dismissed a count based on negligence and thereafter secured judgment on the theory that the indemnity provision covered injury to all property regardless of ownership.

Defendant offered to prove by admissions of plaintiff's agents, by defendant's conduct under similar contracts entered into with plaintiff, and by other proof that in the indemnity clause the parties meant to cover injury to property of third parties only and not to plaintiff's property. Although the trial court observed that the language used was "the classic language for a third party indemnity provision" and that "one could very easily conclude that ... its whole intendment is to indemnify third parties," it nevertheless held that the "plain language" of the agreement also required defendant to indemnify plaintiff for injuries to plaintiff's property. Having determined that the contract had a plain meaning, the court refused to admit any extrinsic evidence that would contradict its interpretation.

When a court interprets a contract on this basis, it determines the meaning of the instrument in accordance with the " ... extrinsic evidence of the judge's own linguistic education and experience." (3 Corbin on Contracts (1960 ed.) [1964 Supp. § 579, p. 225, fn. 56].) The exclusion of testimony that might contradict the linguistic background of the judge reflects a judicial belief in the possibility of perfect verbal expression. (9 Wigmore on Evidence (3d ed. 1940) § 2461, p. 187.) This belief is a remnant of a primitive faith in the inherent potency[1] and inherent meaning of words.[2]

The test of admissibility of extrinsic evidence to explain the meaning of a written instrument is not whether it appears to the court to be plain and unambiguous on its face, but whether the offered evidence is relevant to prove a meaning to which the language of the instrument is reasonably susceptible....

A rule that would limit the determination of the meaning of a written instrument to its four-corners merely because it seems to the court to be clear and unambiguous, would either deny the relevance of the intention of the parties or presuppose a degree of verbal precision and stability our language has not attained.

Some courts have expressed the opinion that contractual obligations are created by the mere use of certain words, whether or not there was any intention to incur such obligations.[3] Under this view, contractual obli-

---

1. E.g., "The elaborate system of taboo and verbal prohibitions in primitive groups; the ancient Egyptian myth of Khern, the apotheosis of the word, and of Thoth, the Scribe of Truth, the Giver of Words and Script, the Master of Incantations; the avoidance of the name of God in Brahmanism, Judaism and Islam; totemistic and protective names in mediaeval Turkish and Finno–Ugrian languages; the misplaced verbal scruples of the 'Precieuses'; the Swedish peasant custom of curing sick cattle smitten by witchcraft, by making them swallow a page torn out of the psalter and put in dough...." from Ullman, The Principles of Semantics (1963 ed.) 43. (See also Ogden and Richards,

The Meaning of Meaning (rev. ed. 1956) pp. 24–47.)

2. " 'Rerum enim vocabula immutabilia sunt, homines mutabilia,' " (Words are unchangeable, men changeable) from Dig. XXXIII, 10, 7 § 2, de sup. leg. as quoted in 9 Wigmore on Evidence, op. cit. supra, § 2461, p. 187.

3. "A contract has, strictly speaking, nothing to do with the personal, or individual, intent of the parties. A contract is an obligation attached by the mere force of law to certain acts of the parties, usually words, which ordinarily accompany and represent a known intent." (Hotchkiss v. National City gations flow, not from the intention of the parties but from the fact that they used certain magic words. Evidence of the parties' intention therefore becomes irrelevant.

In this state, however, the intention of the parties as expressed in the contract is the source of contractual rights and duties. A court must ascertain and give effect to this intention by determining what the parties meant by the words they used. Accordingly, the exclusion of relevant, extrinsic evidence to explain the meaning of a written instrument could be justified only if it were feasible to determine the meaning the parties gave to the words from the instrument alone.

If words had absolute and constant referents, it might be possible to discover contractual intention in the words themselves and in the manner in which they were arranged. Words, however, do not have absolute and constant referents. "A word is a symbol of thought but has no arbitrary and fixed meaning like a symbol of algebra or chemistry, ..." (Pearson v. State Social Welfare Board (1960) 353 P.2d 33, 39.) The meaning of particular words or groups of words varies with the " . . . verbal context and surrounding circumstances and purposes in view of the linguistic education and experience of their users and their hearers or readers (not excluding judges) . . . . A word has no meaning apart from these factors; much less does it have an objective meaning, one true meaning." (Corbin, The Interpretation of Words and the Parol Evidence Rule (1965) 50 Cornell L.Q. 161, 187.) Accordingly, the meaning of a writing " . . . can only be found by interpretation in the light of all the circumstances that reveal the sense in which the writer used the words. The exclusion of parol evidence regarding such circumstances merely because the words do not appear ambiguous to the reader can easily lead to the attribution to a written instrument of a meaning that was never intended. [Citations omitted.]" (Universal Sales Corp. v. Cal. Press Mfg. Co., supra, 20 Cal.2d 751, 776, 128 P.2d 665, 679 (concurring opinion); . . . .)

Although extrinsic evidence is not admissible to add to, detract from, or vary the terms of a written contract, these terms must first be determined before it can be decided whether or not extrinsic evidence is being offered for a prohibited purpose. The fact that the terms of an instrument appear clear to a judge does not preclude the possibility that the parties chose the language of the instrument to express different terms. That possibility is not limited to contracts whose terms have acquired a particular meaning by trade usage, but exists whenever the parties' understanding of the words used may have differed from the judge's understanding.

Accordingly, rational interpretation requires at least a preliminary consideration of all credible evidence offered to prove the intention of the parties.[4] (Civ.Code, § 1647; Code Civ.Proc., § 1860; see also 9 Wigmore on

Bank of New York (S.D.N.Y.1911) 200 F. 287, 293 . . . .)

4. When objection is made to any particular item of evidence offered to prove the intention of the parties, the trial court may not yet be in a position to determine whether in the light of all of the offered evidence, the item objected to will turn out to be admissible as tending to prove a meaning of which the language of the instrument is reasonably susceptible or inadmissible as tending to prove a meaning of which the language is not

Evidence, op. cit. supra, § 2470, fn. 11, p. 227.) Such evidence includes testimony as to the "circumstances surrounding the making of the agreement . . . including the object, nature and subject matter of the writing . . ." so that the court can "place itself in the same situation in which the parties found themselves at the time of contracting." (Universal Sales Corp. v. Cal. Press Mfg. Co., supra, 20 Cal.2d 751, 761, 128 P.2d 665, 671.) If the court decides, after considering this evidence, that the language of a contract, in the light of all the circumstances, is "fairly susceptible of either one of the two interpretations contended for. . . ." (Balfour v. Fresno C. & I. Co. (1895) 109 Cal. 221, 225, 44 P. 876, 877; . . .) extrinsic evidence relevant to prove either of such meanings is admissible.[5]

In the present case the court erroneously refused to consider extrinsic evidence offered to show that the indemnity clause in the contract was not intended to cover injuries to plaintiff's property. Although that evidence was not necessary to show that the indemnity clause was reasonably susceptible of the meaning contended for by defendant, it was nevertheless relevant and admissible on that issue. Moreover, since that clause was reasonably susceptible of that meaning, the offered evidence was also admissible to prove that the clause had that meaning and did not cover injuries to plaintiff's property.[6] Accordingly, the judgment must be reversed. . . .

The judgment is reversed.

■ PETERS, MOSK, BURKE, SULLIVAN, and PEEK, JJ., concur.

■ McComb, J., dissents.

NOTES

(1) *Plain Meaning.* Does California still have a plain meaning rule? Does *Pacific Gas* not require a two stage process (different from that described at p. 382), in which the first stage involves "at least a preliminary consideration of all credible evidence" after which "the court decides" whether the language is "fairly susceptible" of either of the asserted interpretations?

(2) *Ambiguity.* Why do you suppose Justice Traynor included footnote 6, admitting "the existence of an ambiguity" so that the trial court's "exclusion of extrinsic evidence in this case would be error even under a rule that excluded such

reasonably susceptible. In such case the court may admit the evidence conditionally by either reserving its ruling on the objection or by admitting the evidence subject to a motion to strike. (See Evid.Code, § 403.)

5. Extrinsic evidence has often been admitted in such cases on the stated ground that the contract was ambiguous (e.g., Universal Sales Corp. v. Cal.Press Mfg. Co., supra, 128 P.2d 665). This statement of the rule is harmless if it is kept in mind that the ambiguity may be exposed by extrinsic evidence that reveals more than one possible meaning.

6. The court's exclusion of extrinsic evidence in this case would be error even under a rule that excluded such evidence when the instrument appeared to the court to be clear and unambiguous on its face. The controver-sy centers on the meaning of the word "indemnify" and the phrase "all loss, damage, expense and liability." The trial court's recognition of the language as typical of a third party indemnity clause and the double sense in which the word "indemnify" is used in statutes and defined in dictionaries demonstrate the existence of an ambiguity. (Compare Civ.Code, § 2772, "Indemnity is a contract by which one engages to save another from a legal consequence of the conduct of one of the parties, or of some other person," with Civ.Code, § 2527, "Insurance is a contract whereby one undertakes to indemnify another against loss, damage, or liability, arising from an unknown or contingent event.")

evidence when the instrument appeared to the court to be clear and unambiguous on its face'"?

———

DELTA DYNAMICS, INC. v. ARIOTO, 446 P.2d 785 (Cal.1968). [Delta Dynamics and Pixey Distributing made an exclusive distributorship contract under which Delta was to supply trigger locks for firearms to Pixey for five years. Pixey agreed to sell a minimum of 50,000 units during the first year and 100,000 units in each of the following four years. If Pixey failed to meet the minimum, the agreement was "subject to termination." In case of breach by either party, "the party prevailing in any action for damages or enforcement of the terms of this Agreement shall be entitled to reasonable attorneys' fees." When Pixey took only 10,000 locks during the first year, Delta terminated and sued Pixey for damages. Pixey contended that Delta's exclusive remedy for Pixey's failure to meet the minimum was to terminate the contract. The trial court excluded extrinsic evidence offered by Pixey to prove this meaning, and Pixey appealed from a judgment for Delta.]

■ TRAYNOR, CHIEF JUSTICE.... [T]he parties may have included the termination clause to spell out with specificity the condition on which Delta would be excused under the contract, or to set forth the exclusive remedy for a failure to meet the quota in any year, or for both such purposes. That clause is therefore reasonably susceptible of the meaning contended for by Pixey.... There is nothing in the rest of the contract to preclude that interpretation. It does not render meaningless the provision for the recovery of attorney's fees in the event of an action for damages for breach of the contract, for the attorneys' fees provision would still have full effect with respect to other breaches of the contract. Accordingly, the trial court committed prejudicial error by excluding extrinsic evidence offered to prove the meaning of the termination clause contended for by Pixey.

[Reversed.]

NOTE

An "Ominous" Trend. You have been presented with three California cases, decided within less than a year, in which a divided Supreme Court proved receptive to extrinsic evidence: *Masterson*, *PG&E*, and *Delta Dynamics*. In each case Chief Justice Traynor wrote the majority opinion, his support for receptivity declining from case to case. In Delta Dynamics, decided by a 4–3 vote, a dissenter, Justice Stanley Mosk, "confessed" to having supported with misgivings the earlier decisions, which, he said, marked "a course leading toward emasculation of the parol evidence rule. ... Now, however, ... the trend has become so unmistakably ominous that I must urge a halt." 446 P.2d at 789. Do you agree with Justice Mosk?

Greenfield v. Philles Records, Inc.

Court of Appeals of New York, 2002.
98 N.Y.2d 562, 780 N.E.2d 166, 750 N.Y.S.2d 565.

■ GRAFFEO, J. In this contract dispute between a singing group and their record producer, we must determine whether the artists' transfer of full ownership rights to the master recordings of musical performances carried with it the unconditional right of the producer to redistribute those performances in any technological format. In the absence of an explicit contractual reservation of rights by the artists, we conclude that it did.

In the early 1960s, Veronica Bennett (now known as Ronnie Greenfield), her sister Estelle Bennett and their cousin Nedra Talley, formed a singing group known as "The Ronettes." They met defendant Phil Spector, a music producer and composer, in 1963 and signed a five-year "personal services" music recording contract (the Ronettes agreement) with Spector's production company, defendant Philles Records, Inc. The plaintiffs agreed to perform exclusively for Philles Records and in exchange, Philles Records acquired an ownership right to the recordings of the Ronettes' musical performances. The agreement also set forth a royalty schedule to compensate plaintiffs for their services. After signing with Philles Records, plaintiffs received a single collective cash advance of approximately $15,000.

The Ronettes recorded several dozen songs for Philles Records, including "Be My Baby," which sold over a million copies and topped the music charts. Despite their popularity, the group disbanded in 1967 and Philles Records eventually went out of business. Other than their initial advance, plaintiffs received no royalty payments from Philles Records.

Beyond their professional relationship, however, was the story of the personal relationship between Spector and plaintiff Ronnie Greenfield. They married in 1968 but separated after a few years. Greenfield initiated a divorce proceeding against Spector in California and a settlement was reached in 1974. As part of that agreement, Spector and Greenfield executed mutual general releases that purported to resolve all past and future claims and obligations that existed between them, as well as between Greenfield and Spector's companies.

Defendants subsequently began to capitalize on a resurgence of public interest in 1960s music by making use of new recording technologies and licensing master recordings of the Ronettes' vocal performances for use in movie and television productions, a process known in entertainment industry parlance as "synchronization." The most notable example was defendants' licensing of "Be My Baby" in 1987 for use in the motion picture "Dirty Dancing." Defendants also licensed master recordings to third parties for production and distribution in the United States (referred to as domestic redistribution), and sold compilation albums containing performances by the Ronettes. While defendants earned considerable compensation from such licensing and sales, no royalties were paid to any of the plaintiffs.

As a result, plaintiffs commenced this breach of contract action in 1987, alleging that the 1963 agreement did not provide Philles Records with the right to license the master recordings for synchronization and domestic redistribution, and demanded royalties from the sales of compilation albums. Although defendants initially denied the existence of a contract, in 1992 they stipulated that an unexecuted copy of the contract would determine the parties' rights. Defendants thereafter argued that the agreement granted them absolute ownership rights to the master recordings and permitted the use of the recordings in any format, subject only to royalty rights. Following extensive pretrial proceedings . . . , Supreme Court ruled in plaintiffs' favor and awarded approximately $3 million in damages and interest.

The Appellate Division affirmed, concluding that defendants' actions were not authorized by the agreement with plaintiffs because the contract did not specifically transfer the right to issue synchronization and third-party domestic distribution licenses. Permitting plaintiffs to assert a claim for unjust enrichment, the Court found that plaintiffs were entitled to the music recording industry's standard 50% royalty rate for income derived from synchronization and third-party licensing. We granted leave to appeal.

We are asked on this appeal to determine whether defendants, as the owners of the master recordings of plaintiffs' vocal performances, acquired the contractual right to issue licenses to third parties to use the recordings in connection with television, movies and domestic audio distribution. The agreement between the parties consists of a two-page document, which apparently was widely used in the 1960s by music producers signing new artists. Plaintiffs executed the contract without the benefit of counsel. The parties' immediate objective was to record and market the Ronettes' vocal performances and "mak[e] therefrom phonograph records and/or tape recordings and other similar devices (excluding transcriptions)." The ownership rights provision of the contract provides:

"All recordings made hereunder and all records and reproductions made therefrom together with the performances embodied therein, shall be entirely [Philles'] property, free of any claims whatsoever by you or any person deriving any rights of interest from you. Without limitation of the foregoing, [Philles] shall have the right to make phonograph records, tape recordings or other reproductions of the performances embodied in such recordings by any method now or hereafter known, and to sell and deal in the same under any trade mark or trade names or labels designated by us, or we may at our election refrain therefrom."

Plaintiffs concede that the contract unambiguously gives defendants unconditional ownership rights to the master recordings, but contend that the agreement does not bestow the right to exploit those recordings in new markets or mediums since the document is silent on those topics. Defendants counter that the absence of specific references to synchronization and domestic licensing is irrelevant. They argue that where a contract grants full ownership rights to a musical performance or composition, the only restrictions upon the owner's right to use that property are those explicitly enumerated by the grantor/artist.

Despite the technological innovations that continue to revolutionize the recording industry, long-settled common-law contract rules still govern the interpretation of agreements between artists and their record producers. The fundamental, neutral precept of contract interpretation is that agreements are construed in accord with the parties' intent. "The best evidence of what parties to a written agreement intend is what they say in their writing"(*Slamow v. Del Col,* 594 N.E.2d 918 [1992]). Thus, a written agreement that is complete, clear and unambiguous on its face must be enforced according to the plain meaning of its terms (*see e.g. R/S Assoc. v. New York Job Dev. Auth.,* 771 N.E.2d 240 [2002]; *W.W.W. Assoc. v. Giancontieri,* 566 N.E.2d 639 [1990]).

Extrinsic evidence of the parties' intent may be considered only if the agreement is ambiguous, which is an issue of law for the courts to decide (*see W.W.W. Assoc. v. Giancontieri, supra* at 162, 565 N.Y.S.2d 440, 566 N.E.2d 639). A contract is unambiguous if the language it uses has "a definite and precise meaning, unattended by danger of misconception in the purport of the [agreement] itself, and concerning which there is no reasonable basis for a difference of opinion"(*Breed v. Insurance Co. of N. Am.,* 46 385 N.E.2d 1280 [1978]). Thus, if the agreement on its face is reasonably susceptible of only one meaning, a court is not free to alter the contract to reflect its personal notions of fairness and equity (*see e.g. Teichman v. Community Hosp. of W. Suffolk,* 663 N.E.2d 628 [1996]; *First Natl. Stores v. Yellowstone Shopping Ctr.,* 237 N.E.2d 868 [1968]).

The pivotal issue in this case is whether defendants are prohibited from using the master recordings for synchronization, and whatever future formats evolve from new technologies, in the absence of explicit contract language authorizing such uses. Stated another way, does the contract's silence on synchronization and domestic licensing create an ambiguity which opens the door to the admissibility of extrinsic evidence to determine the intent of the parties? We conclude that it does not and, because there is no ambiguity in the terms of the Ronettes agreement, defendants are entitled to exercise complete ownership rights, subject to payment of applicable royalties due plaintiffs. . . .

Defendants further claim that Greenfield is barred from sharing in those royalties because she executed a general release in connection with her divorce from Spector. We look to California law to analyze the scope of Greenfield's release because that is the state where the release was executed and the divorce was finalized. In contrast to the "four corners" rule that New York has long applied, California courts preliminarily consider all credible evidence of the parties' intent in addition to the language of the contract—"[t]he test of admissibility of extrinsic evidence to explain the meaning of a written instrument is not whether it appears to the court to be plain and unambiguous on its face, but whether the offered evidence is relevant to prove a meaning to which the language of the instrument is reasonably susceptible"(*Pacific Gas & Elec. Co. v. G.W. Thomas Drayage & Rigging Co.,* 442 P.2d 641, 644 [1968]).

During proceedings in New York, Supreme Court determined that the extrinsic evidence supported Greenfield's allegation that her right to compensation under the 1963 recording contract was not an intended subject of the release. That finding of fact, affirmed by the Appellate Division, is supported by the record. We find no reason to reverse the Appellate Division's interpretation of California law. Plaintiff Greenfield is therefore entitled to her share of any damages assessed against defendants.

We have reviewed the parties' remaining contentions; they are either academic or meritless.

Accordingly, the order of the Appellate Division should be modified, without costs, and the case remitted to Supreme Court for further proceedings in accordance with this opinion and, as so modified, affirmed.

NOTES

(1) *Only One Interpretation?* Do you agree with the court's conclusion that the recording contract was not ambiguous? Would your answer be the same if the phrase "without limitation of the foregoing" had not been included in the sentence granting Philles the right to make phonograph records, tape recordings or other reproductions of the performances?

(2) *California, Here I Come.* Note that the court's ruling on the second issue in the case was an application of *California* law rather than New York law. Did the court describe California law fairly? How would the first issue in the case have been decided under California law?

————

W.W.W. ASSOCIATES, INC. v. GIANCONTIERI, 77 N.Y.2d 157, 566 N.E.2d 639 (1990), relied on by the court in *Philles*, addressed whether "an unambiguous reciprocal cancellation provision [in a contract to sell real property] should be read in light of extrinsic evidence, as a contingency clause for the sole benefit of the plaintiff purchaser, subject to its unilateral waiver." The court stated:

[Plaintiff's reliance on extrinsic evidence] ignores a vital first step in the analysis: before looking to evidence of what was in the parties' minds, a court must give due weight to what was in their contract.

A familiar and eminently sensible proposition of law is that, when parties set down their agreement in a clear, complete document, their writing should as a rule be enforced according to its terms. Evidence outside the four corners of the document as to what was really intended but unstated or misstated is generally inadmissible to add to or vary the writing.... That rule imparts "stability to commercial transactions by safeguarding against fraudulent claims, perjury, death of witnesses ... infirmity of memory ... [and] the fear that the jury will improperly evaluate the extrinsic evidence." (Fisch, New York Evidence § 42, at 22 [2d ed].) Such considerations are all the more compelling in the context of real property transactions, where commercial certainty is a paramount concern.

Whether or not a writing is ambiguous is a question of law to be resolved by the courts....

The question next raised is whether extrinsic evidence should be considered in order to create an ambiguity in the agreement. That question must be answered in the negative. It is well settled that "extrinsic and parol evidence is not admissible to create an ambiguity in a written agreement which is complete and clear and unambiguous upon its face." (Intercontinental Planning v. Daystrom, Inc., 24 N.Y.2d 372, 379, 248 N.E.2d 576....)

An analysis that begins with consideration of extrinsic evidence of what the parties meant, instead of looking first to what they said and reaching extrinsic evidence only when required to do so because of some identified ambiguity, unnecessarily denigrates the contract and unsettles the law.

NOTES

(1) *Wisdom of the Plain Meaning Rule.* Judge Richard Posner, whose views on the parol evidence rule were quoted earlier at p. 367 above, had this to say in defense of the plain meaning rule: "The older view ... which excludes extrinsic evidence if the contract is clear 'on its face,' is not ridiculous.... The rule tends to cut down on the amount of litigation, in part by reducing the role of the jury; for it is the jury that interprets contracts when interpretation requires consideration of extrinsic evidence. Parties to contracts may prefer, ex ante (that is, when negotiating the contract, and therefore before an interpretive dispute has arisen), to avoid the expense and uncertainty of having a jury resolve a dispute between them, even at the cost of some inflexibility in interpretation." Federal Deposit Ins. Corp. v. W.R. Grace & Co., 877 F.2d 614, 621 (7th Cir.1989).

(2) *International Norms.* UNIDROIT Principles art. 4.3 states that in interpreting contract language "regard shall be had to all the circumstances, including ... preliminary negotiations between the parties." Because article 4.3 does not provide for a first stage in which the admissibility of extrinsic evidence is determined, it is not a plain meaning rule. Is it significant in judging the merit of article 4.3 that the principal application of the Principles is in international commercial arbitrations where the arbitrators are relatively sophisticated and pre-trial discovery is generally very limited? (Does the matter of pre-trial discovery help to distinguish the plain meaning rule as applied to contracts from the plain meaning rule as applied to legislation?)

(3) *Variation by Contract.* Suppose that parties to a contract governed by California law prefer the rule in *Philles* to that in *Pacific Gas,* as Judge Posner predicted they might. Could they, by a provision in their contract, prevent a court from admitting extrinsic evidence that it would otherwise admit in the first stage? Whether the parties could avoid California law altogether by providing for the application of New York law is a question left for a course in conflict of laws.

In Garden State Plaza Corp. v. S.S. Kresge Co., 189 A.2d 448 (N.J.Super.Ct.1963), the court held void as against public policy a clause providing that no "previous negotiations, arrangements, agreements and understandings ... shall be used to interpret or construe this lease." The clause would, the court said, have it construe the contract "wearing judicial blinders. We are requested to conform to a private agreement mandating our performance of a judicial function in a manner which, under our precedents, is not the path to justice in arriving at the binding meaning of a contract." Do you agree? Would it make a difference if the language in question were "plain"?

The United States Court of Appeals for the Ninth Circuit (which includes California) often must apply California law. In the following opinion, this court expressed the view that the California approach to contract interpretation "chips away at the foundation of our legal system."

Trident Center v. Connecticut General Life Ins. Co.

United States Court of Appeals for the Ninth Circuit, 1988.
847 F.2d 564.

■ KOZINSKI, CIRCUIT JUDGE: The parties to this transaction are, by any standard, highly sophisticated business people: Plaintiff is a partnership consisting of an insurance company and two of Los Angeles' largest and most prestigious law firms; defendant is another insurance company. Dealing at arm's length and from positions of roughly equal bargaining strength, they negotiated a commercial loan amounting to more than $56 million. The contract documents are lengthy and detailed; they squarely address the precise issue that is the subject of this dispute; to all who read English, they appear to resolve the issue fully and conclusively.

Plaintiff nevertheless argues here, as it did below, that it is entitled to introduce extrinsic evidence that the contract means something other than what it says. This case therefore presents the question whether parties in California can ever draft a contract that is proof to parol evidence. Somewhat surprisingly, the answer is no.

Facts

The facts are rather simple. Sometime in 1983 Security First Life Insurance Company and the law firms of Mitchell, Silberberg & Knupp and Manatt, Phelps, Rothenberg & Tunney formed a limited partnership for the purpose of constructing an office building complex on Olympic Boulevard in West Los Angeles. The partnership, Trident Center, the plaintiff herein, sought and obtained financing for the project from defendant, Connecticut General Life Insurance Company. The loan documents provide for a loan of $56,500,000 at 12 1/4 percent interest for a term of 15 years, secured by a deed of trust on the project. The promissory note provides that "[m]aker shall not have the right to prepay the principal amount hereof in whole or in part" for the first 12 years. [Promissory] Note at 6. In years 13–15, the loan may be prepaid, subject to a sliding prepayment fee. The note also provides that in case of a default during years 1–12, Connecticut General has the option of accelerating the note and adding a 10 percent prepayment fee.

Everything was copacetic for a few years until interest rates began to drop. The 12 1/4 percent rate that had seemed reasonable in 1983 compared unfavorably with 1987 market rates and Trident started looking for ways of refinancing the loan to take advantage of the lower rates. Connecticut General was unwilling to oblige, insisting that the loan could not be prepaid for the first 12 years of its life, that is, until January 1996.

Trident then brought suit in state court seeking a declaration that it was entitled to prepay the loan now, subject only to a 10 percent prepayment fee. Connecticut General promptly removed to federal court and brought a motion to dismiss, claiming that the loan documents clearly and unambiguously precluded prepayment during the first 12 years. The district court agreed and dismissed Trident's complaint. The court also "*sua sponte,* sanction[ed] the plaintiff for the filing of a frivolous lawsuit." . . . . Trident appeals both aspects of the district court's ruling.

Discussion

I

Trident makes two arguments as to why the district court's ruling is wrong. First, it contends that the language of the contract is ambiguous and proffers a construction that it believes supports its position. Second, Trident argues that, under California law, even seemingly unambiguous contracts are subject to modification by parol or extrinsic evidence. Trident faults the district court for denying it the opportunity to present evidence that the contract language did not accurately reflect the parties' intentions.

A.   The Contract

As noted earlier, the promissory note provides that Trident "shall not have the right to prepay the principal amount hereof in whole or in part before January 1996." [Promissory] Note at 6. It is difficult to imagine language that more clearly or unambiguously expresses the idea that Trident may not unilaterally prepay the loan during its first 12 years. Trident, however, argues that there is an ambiguity because another clause of the note provides that "[i]n the event of a prepayment resulting from a default hereunder or the Deed of Trust prior to January 10, 1996 the prepayment fee will be ten percent (10%)." [Promissory] Note at 6–7. Trident interprets this clause as giving it the option of prepaying the loan if only it is willing to incur the prepayment fee.

We reject Trident's argument out of hand. . . .

B.   Extrinsic Evidence

Trident argues in the alternative that, even if the language of the contract appears to be unambiguous, the deal the parties actually struck is in fact quite different. It wishes to offer extrinsic evidence that the parties had agreed Trident could prepay at any time within the first 12 years by tendering the full amount plus a 10 percent prepayment fee. As discussed above, this is an interpretation to which the contract, as written, is not reasonably susceptible. Under traditional contract principles, extrinsic evidence is inadmissible to interpret, vary or add to the terms of an unambiguous integrated written instrument. *See* 4 S. Williston, *supra* p. 5, § 631, at 948–49; 2 B. Witkin, *California Evidence* § 981, at 926 (3d ed. 1986).

Trident points out, however, that California does not follow the traditional rule. Two decades ago the California Supreme Court in *Pacific Gas & Electric Co. v. G.W. Thomas Drayage & Rigging Co.,* 442 P.2d 641 (1968), turned its back on the notion that a contract can ever have a plain meaning discernible by a court without resort to extrinsic evidence. The court reasoned that contractual obligations flow not from the words of the contract, but from the intention of the parties. "Accordingly," the court stated, "the exclusion of relevant, extrinsic, evidence to explain the meaning of a written instrument could be justified only if it were feasible to determine the meaning the parties gave to the words from the instrument alone." 442 P.2d 641. This, the California Supreme Court concluded, is impossible: "If words had absolute and constant referents, it might be possible to discover contractual intention in the words themselves and in the manner in which they were arranged. Words, however, do not have absolute and constant referents." *Id.* In the same vein, the court noted that "[t]he exclusion of testimony that might contradict the linguistic background of the judge reflects a judicial belief in the possibility of perfect verbal expression. This belief is a remnant of a primitive faith in the inherent potency and inherent meaning of words." *Id.* at 37, 442 P.2d 641, 69 Cal.Rptr. 561 (citation and footnotes omitted).[1]

Under *Pacific Gas,* it matters not how clearly a contract is written, nor how completely it is integrated, nor how carefully it is negotiated, nor how squarely it addresses the issue before the court: the contract cannot be rendered impervious to attack by parol evidence. If one side is willing to claim that the parties intended one thing but the agreement provides for another, the court must consider extrinsic evidence of possible ambiguity. If that evidence raises the specter of ambiguity where there was none before, the contract language is displaced and the intention of the parties must be divined from self-serving testimony offered by partisan witnesses whose recollection is hazy from passage of time and colored by their conflicting interests. *See Delta Dynamics, Inc. v. Arioto,* 69 Cal.2d 525, 532, 446 P.2d 785, 72 Cal.Rptr. 785 (1968) (Mosk, J., dissenting). We question whether this approach is more likely to divulge the original intention of the parties than reliance on the seemingly clear words they agreed upon at the time. *See generally Morta v. Korea Ins. Co.,* 840 F.2d 1452, 1460 (9th Cir.1988).

Pacific Gas casts a long shadow of uncertainty over all transactions negotiated and executed under the law of California. As this case illustrates, even when the transaction is very sizeable, even if it involves only sophisticated parties, even if it was negotiated with the aid of counsel, even if it results in contract language that is devoid of ambiguity, costly and protracted litigation cannot be avoided if one party has a strong enough motive for challenging the contract. While this rule creates much business for lawyers and an occasional windfall to some clients, it leads only to frustration and delay for most litigants and clogs already overburdened courts.

It also chips away at the foundation of our legal system. By giving credence to the idea that words are inadequate to express concepts, *Pacific Gas* undermines the basic principle that language provides a meaningful constraint on public and private conduct. If we are unwilling to say that parties, dealing face to face, can come up with language that binds them, how can we send anyone to jail for violating statutes consisting of mere words lacking "absolute and constant referents"? How can courts ever enforce decrees, not written in language understandable to all, but encoded in a dialect reflecting only the "linguistic background of the judge"? Can lower courts ever be faulted for failing to carry out the mandate of higher courts when "perfect verbal expression" is impossible? Are all attempts to

---

1. In an unusual footnote, the [California Supreme] court compared the belief in the immutable meaning of words with " '[t]he elaborate system of taboo and verbal prohibitions in primitive groups ... [such as] the Swedish peasant custom of curing sick cattle smitten by witchcraft, by making them swallow a page torn out of the psalter and put in dough....' " *Id.* n. 2 (quoting Ullman, *The Principles of Semantics* 43 (1963)). [Footnote by the court] develop the law in a reasoned and principled fashion doomed to failure as "remnant[s] of a primitive faith in the inherent potency and inherent meaning of words"?

Be that as it may. While we have our doubts about the wisdom of *Pacific Gas,* we have no difficulty understanding its meaning, even without extrinsic evidence to guide us. As we read the rule in California, we must reverse and remand to the district court in order to give plaintiff an opportunity to present extrinsic evidence as to the intention of the parties in drafting the contract. It may not be a wise rule we are applying, but it is a rule that binds us. *Erie R.R. Co. v. Tompkins,* 304 U.S. 64, 78, 58 S.Ct. 817, 822, 82 L.Ed. 1188 (1938).

NOTES

(1) *Picking Sides.* This chapter has provided extensive materials about the competing California and New York approaches, providing the reader ample opportunity to assess the claimed advantages and disadvantages of each approach. On balance, which approach do you favor? Why?

(2) *Contracts for the sale of goods.* Under Article 2 of the UCC, must a court find that the words of the agreement are ambiguous before extrinsic evidence of their meaning may be considered? Does UCC § 2–202 provide any guidance?

METHODS OF INTERPRETING AMBIGUOUS CONTRACTS

In analyzing contract language, it is sometimes useful to distinguish *vagueness* from *ambiguity.* A word is vague when its applicability in marginal situations is uncertain, as is the case for the word "green" to describe a color. For another example, if parties contract for the removal of "all the dirt" on a given tract, may sand from a stratum of subsoil be taken? See Highley v. Phillips, 5 A.2d 824 (Md.1939) (held: yes). In contrast, a word is ambiguous when it has two entirely different connotations so that it may be at the same time both appropriate and inappropriate, as is the case for "light" when applied to dark feathers. Since "ambiguous" is often used to comprehend the notion of 'vagueness,' as well as the notion of 'ambiguity' in the narrow sense, some writers prefer to use "ambivalent" or "equivocal" instead. See Oswald v. Allen, p. 424 below. For example, if a contract specifies "tons," are they to be long or short tons? Compare Chemung Iron & Steel Co. v. Mersereau Metal Bed Co., 179 N.Y.S. 577 (N.Y.Sup.1920) (short tons), with Higgins v. California Petroleum & Asphalt Co., 52 P. 1080 (Cal.1898) (long tons). Drafters sometimes find vague terms useful as a means of delegating decisions to a later adjudicator at such time as a dispute on particular facts arises. Think of "a reasonable time," "good faith and fair dealing," and "best efforts." Use of ambiguous terms is simply bad drafting.

NOTES

(1) *Inconsistent Provisions.* One of the most common results of carelessness in drafting is inconsistency between different parts of a written agreement—a lawyer's version of syntactical ambiguity. See Robinhorne Constr. Corp. v. Snyder, 265

N.E.2d 670, 674–75 (Ill.1970) ("This is the kind of case that has been described as 'one where no principle of law is involved, but only the meaning of careless and slovenly documents' ").

(2) *Interpretation in the Agreement Process.* We have already encountered problems of interpretation in the agreement process. See, for example, Owen v. Tunison, p. 127 above, and Harvey v. Facey, p. 129 above. The problems of interpretation there are similar but not identical to the ones we are about to encounter. In United States v. Braunstein, 75 F.Supp. 137, 139 (S.D.N.Y.1947), Judge Harold Medina wrote: "It is true that there is much room for interpretation once the parties are inside the framework of a contract, but it seems that there is less in the field of offer and acceptance. Greater precision of expression may be required, and less help from the court given, when the parties are merely at the threshold of a contract."

(3) *The Role of Punctuation.* Commas are sometimes effective, sometimes not. Consult Overhauser v. United States, 45 F.3d 1085, 1086–87 (7th Cir.1995), rejecting the assumptions "that there is a clear rule of grammar by which the scope of a qualifying phrase can be determined from the placement of commas" and "that the agreement was drafted by a grammarian or at least by someone knowledgeable about obscure rules of grammar." Judge Posner pointed out that even the Supreme Court of the United States "cannot make up its mind whether to be skeptical or credulous about imputing grammatical expertise to drafters of legal documents and using the imputation to decide interpretive questions."

PROBLEMS

(1) *Drafting Exercises.* Try, in each of the following cases: (1) to state the issue in terms of the contract language; and (2) to redraft the contract language, first for one party and then for the other, making as few changes as possible.

(a) A contract for the sale of a photography studio provides that the seller will not compete with the buyer "for the school photography work in any school in Grant County, with the exception of Marion High School and Bennett High School." May the seller compete with the buyer for the photography of Marion College students? See Lawrence v. Cain, 245 N.E.2d 663 (Ind.App.1969).

(b) A lease of premises for a drug store provides for a minimum monthly rental plus a percentage of the "gross sales" of the business. Must the lessee pay a percentage of what it is paid by customers for lottery tickets? Hartig Drug Co. v. Hartig, 602 N.W.2d 794 (Iowa 1999).

(c) A contract between a provider of medical services and a technician employed by it prohibits the technician from competing with the provider for three years "within 50 miles of the Company office." Is the technician prohibited from competing at a location that is a distance of 45 miles, but a 55 mile drive from the Company office? Vantage Technology v. Cross, 17 S.W.3d 637 (Tenn.App.1999).

(d) A construction contract provides that "All domestic water piping and rainwater piping installed above finished ceilings under this specification shall be insulated." Must the contractor insulate domestic water piping installed below finished ceilings? See Paul W. Abbott v. Axel Newman Heating & Plumbing, 166 N.W.2d 323 (Minn.1969).

(2) *A Matter of Taste.* Tastings, Inc. furnishes cafeteria service to business firms. It is about to employ your client as manager of its cafeteria operation at a data processing plant under a two-year contract. The draft contains the following restrictive covenant:

For one year after my employment with you ends, I will not participate in the management of any cafeteria operated by any firm who shall have been your client within the period of one year prior to the termination of my employment or with whom you may have been negotiating during my employment with you if I have participated in such negotiations or had contact with that firm in the course of my employment with you.

Do you see any important ambiguity in this clause? How can it be corrected? (Suppose that your client leaves Tastings at the end of two years and takes a job managing a cafeteria for a firm with which he has had no previous connection but which had been a client of Tastings three months earlier, before deciding to operate its own cafeteria?) See Servomation Mathias, Inc. v. Englert, 333 F.Supp. 9 (M.D.Pa.1971).

(3) *The Ambiguity of "Minerals."* A contract involving the conveyance of land from a railroad to Colorado landowners reserves to the railroad rights to "all coal and other minerals." The landowners claim that the term "minerals" includes oil and gas. Is the term "ambiguous"? If not, who is right? See McCormick v. Union Pacific R.R. Co., 983 P.2d 84 (Colo.App.1998).

(4) *The Ambiguity of "Matriculated."* Raymond Woodcock had student loans from a bank that came due at "the end of the ninth month following the month in which I cease to be matriculated." After graduating from law school and business school, he attended college part-time but not in a degree program and then went into bankruptcy. The bank claims that Raymond was still "matriculated" while he was a part-time student so that the loans did not become due until a statutory period, prior to bankruptcy, when student loans coming due are not dischargeable. Raymond claims that he ceased to be matriculated long before that when he graduated from business school. Is the term "matriculated" ambiguous? If not, who is right? See In re Woodcock, 45 F.3d 363 (10th Cir.1995).

(5) *The Ambiguity of "Exploit."* Emerson granted Orion an exclusive license to "utilize and exploit" Emerson's trademarks in connection with the sale of various consumer electronic items. Emerson claimed that the term "exploit" imposed an express contractual obligation on Orion to use "reasonable efforts" or "due diligence" in selling and marketing Emerson-brand products. Orion argued that the term "exploit" "could as easily be interpreted as granting Orion authority to act in its own self-interest as imposing a duty to act in Emerson's best interests." Is the term "exploit" ambiguous? If not, whose meaning prevails? See Emerson Radio Corp. v. Orion Sales, Inc., 253 F.3d 159 (3rd Cir. 2001).

(6) *An Offer You Can't Refuse?* The Steuarts gave the McChesneys a right of first refusal on a farm under which, if the Steuarts obtained an offer from a third party, the McChesneys had a right to purchase the farm for a price "equivalent to the market value of the premises according to the assessment rolls as maintained by the County of Warren." The agreement was completely integrated.

It is now a decade later, and the assessed value according to the County's tax rolls is $70,000, having been increased by only $8,000 when the farm was reassessed a few years ago. The county's practice is to value real estate for tax purposes at 50% of market value. However, a broker recently appraised the farm at a market value of $500,000 and Lepha Steuart, now a widow, has just received an offer of $350,000 for the farm.

How much must the McChesneys tender in order to exercise their right of first refusal? $500,000? $350,000? $140,000? $70,000? Twice proper assessed value? Would a court admit evidence concerning the county's practice? Would it admit testimony concerning the negotiations from Lepha Steuart and the drafter of the contract? See Steuart v. McChesney, 444 A.2d 659 (Pa.1982).

———

RULES IN AID OF INTERPRETATION

The Statutory Analogy. There is an obvious similarity between the interpretation of contracts and that of statutes. To what extent is the analogy compelling? For example, are the policies for or against the use of legislative history as an aid to statutory interpretation similar to those for or against the use of negotiations ("transactional history") as an aid to contract interpretation?

Purpose Interpretation. Is there an analogy to what is known as "purpose interpretation" in the field of statutory interpretation? According to the formulation in Heydon's Case, 3 Coke 7a, 76 Eng.Rep. 637 (Exchequer 1584), it involves these steps: (1) examination of the law before enactment of the statute; (2) ascertainment of the "mischief or defect" for which the law did not provide; (3) analysis of the remedy provided by the legislature to "cure the disease"; (4) determination of the "true reason of the remedy"; and then (5) application of the statute so as to "suppress the mischief, and advance the remedy." Can you formulate an analogous technique for contract interpretation?

In the case of a statute, purpose interpretation does not depend on the availability of legislative history, and the court may even find a helpful statement of the purpose of enactment set forth in the preamble or purpose clause of the statute itself. Similarly, it is not uncommon for written contracts to begin with a series of recitals of the surrounding circumstances and of the objectives of the parties. Usually prefixed by the word "whereas," contract recitals are not ordinarily drafted as promises or conditions, and their proper role in the interpretation of the main body of the contract has been a source of bafflement to many a judge and lawyer. Courts in this country have frequently repeated with approval Lord Esher's "three rules": "If the recitals are clear and the operative part is ambiguous, the recitals govern the construction. If the recitals are ambiguous, and the operative part is clear, the operative part must prevail. If both the recitals and the operative part are clear, but they are inconsistent with each other, the operative part is to be preferred." Ex parte Dawes, 17 Q.B.D. 275, 286 (1886). But these, like many rules of interpretation, are easier to state than to apply.

Public Interest. In North Gate Corp. v. National Food Stores, Inc., 140 N.W.2d 744 (Wis.1966), a printed shopping center lease prepared by the lessee for use by its retail food stores throughout the country contained a provision that prohibited the owner of the shopping center from leasing to other retail stores. The court observed that "the intent of the provision" was "to restrict trade and the use of land. Such provisions are to be strictly construed." In Chapter 4, we saw that contracts involving performance that would be in violation of some strongly rooted public interest, often expressed in a statute, may be held to be unenforceable. As *North Gate* shows, public interest may also affect the interpretation of contracts.

In State ex rel. Youngman v. Calhoun, 231 S.W. 647 (Mo.App.1921), a physician sold his practice, agreeing not to "establish [himself] as a practicing physician and surgeon within a radius of five miles" of his former office. The court held that he was not precluded from making calls within this area or treating patients from this area who might call at his office outside the area. "The contract in question is clearly one in restraint of trade and personal liberty, and as such should not be construed to extend beyond its fair import." Why? Because of the intention of the parties? See also Sun Oil Co. v. Vickers Refining Co., 414 F.2d 383 (8th Cir.1969), in which the court remarked, in rejecting Sunray's interpretation under which the contract would have been void because of a violation of the antitrust laws: "Sunray's attorneys, experienced in antitrust work, approved the contract without any question of antitrust consequences."

Maxims. Many of the same rules of thumb that are used in the interpretation of statutes are also used in the interpretation of contracts. Maxims such as *ejusdem generis* (of the same kind), *expressio unius est exclusio alterius* (the expression of one thing is the exclusion of another) and *noscitur a sociis* (it is known from its associates) are as popular here as they are there. See J.E. Faltin Motor Transportation, Inc. v. Eazor Express, Inc., 273 F.2d 444 (3d Cir.1959). Their reliability is also as questionable here as it is there.

Some maxims of contract interpretation are not used in statutory interpretation. One of the most time-honored maxims of contract interpretation is that a contract is to be interpreted *contra proferentem* (against its author or profferer). In North Gate Corp. v. National Food Stores, Inc., 140 N.W.2d 744 (Wis.1966), the court applied this to a clause in a printed shopping center lease prepared by the lessee for use by its retail food stores throughout the country. "Where various meanings can be given a term, the term is to be strictly construed against the draftsman of the contract." Why? To carry out the intention of the parties? To penalize sloppy drafters? To encourage careful drafters? (Sir Francis Bacon called the maxim "a schoolmaster of wisdom and diligence in making men watchful in their own business." He conceded, however, that it "is the last to be resorted to." Francis Bacon, A Collection of Some Principal Rules and Maximes of the Common Law 3, 16 (1597).) Has this maxim no statutory analogue? In many instances where the rule has been applied, the party who chose the contract language also had superior bargaining power. Consider in this connection the problems raised in Chapter 4, Policing the Bargain.[a]

Should it make a difference if the party who proffered the contract invited suggestions for change from the other party? See Acme Markets v.

a. That the rule applies to government contracts, see WPC Enterprises, Inc. v. United States, 323 F.2d 874 (Ct.Cl.1963). But see Shedd, Resolving Ambiguities in Interpretation of Government Contracts, 36 Geo. Wash.L.Rev. 1, 21 (1967), where the author concludes, "The rule of interpreting against the drafter, if not discarded entirely, should be relegated to a rule of last resort in contract interpretation...." For dispute in the Supreme Court of the United States over the application of the rule, see United States v. Seckinger, 397 U.S. 203 (1970).

Dawson Enters., 251 A.2d 839 (Md.1969), in which the court noted that the other party had kept the contract for sixty days before signing it, that its president was a member of the bar, and that it had, at least earlier in the negotiations, been represented by "a member of a prominent Washington law firm." The court quoted with approval its suggestion in an earlier case that "perhaps [the *contra proferentem* rule] should have but slight force in a situation where both parties are represented by counsel."

NOTE

"Woe Unto You, Lawyers." Should it make a difference, in interpreting a contract, whether the parties were represented by counsel? In Weiland Tool & Mfg. Co. v. Whitney, 251 N.E.2d 242, 248 (Ill.1969), the court wrote: "In interpreting the letter . . . we have taken into consideration not only that inferences from ambiguous language must be resolved against its author . . . but also that he is a lawyer with a number of years of trial experience and experience as a legal adviser in commercial transactions. He must have had the ability to express [his intention] in concise and clear English . . . if that were his intention. Since he did not do so, we are further persuaded that this was not his intention." See also Gulf Oil Corp. v. American Louisiana Pipe Line Co., 282 F.2d 401 (6th Cir.1960) (fact that both parties were represented by lawyers suggested that difference in language between two sections of contract was not inadvertent).

PROBLEM

On which maxim of interpretation would you rely in each of the following situations?

(a) A lease provides that a tenant can keep "sheep, cows, pigs and other animals" on a farm and you want to argue that a tiger is not included.

(b) A lease provides that a tenant can keep "sheep, cows and pigs" on a farm and you want to argue that a wild boar is not included.

(c) A lease provides that a tenant can keep "cats and dogs" in an apartment and you want to argue that a gerbil is not included.

FUNCTION OF JUDGE AND JURY

A detailed consideration of the respective roles of judge and jury (when trial is by jury) in matters of contract interpretation is best left to a course in evidence or procedure. Nevertheless, a few elementary generalizations may be in order. It is clear that the meaning of language is, strictly speaking, a question of fact. Yet the interpretation of written agreements, as to which there is no dispute over the words used by the parties, has often been withdrawn from the jury by calling it a question of "law" for the judge, rather than a question of "fact" for the jury. One reason for this has been a distrust of unsophisticated, uneducated, and—at least at one time— illiterate jurors. Another reason has been a desire for consistency in interpretation of some kinds of contracts, such as standard insurance policies.

Chief Justice Traynor concluded that it is "solely a judicial function to interpret a written instrument unless the interpretation turns upon the credibility of extrinsic evidence." Parsons v. Bristol Development Co., 402 P.2d 839, 842 (Cal.1965). But Judge Henry Friendly pointed out: "With the courts' growing appreciation of Professor Corbin's lesson that words are seldom so 'plain and clear' as to exclude proof of surrounding circumstances and other extrinsic aids to interpretation ... the exception bids fair largely to swallow the supposed general rule.... Whether determination of meaning be regarded as a question of fact, a question of law, or just itself, reliance on the jury to resolve ambiguities in the light of extrinsic evidence seems quite as it should be, save where the form or subject-matter of a particular contract outruns a jury's competence...." Meyers v. Selznick Co., 373 F.2d 218, 222 (2d Cir.1966).

NOTE

Scope of Review. If a particular question of interpretation is one for the judge and not for the jury, what is the scope of review of the judge's decision on appeal? In Ram Constr. Co., Inc. v. American States Ins. Co., 749 F.2d 1049, 1052–53 (3d Cir.1984), the court reasoned that in matters of interpretation the traditional distribution of functions between judge and jury "rests on outdated common law policy considerations, such as jury illiteracy and lack of respect for writings, as well as such continuing concerns as a judicial desire for uniformity.... In instances of contract interpretation, therefore, assignment to judge or jury does not of itself determine the standard of review to be applied on appeal. Interpretation by a trial court of a factual matter is reviewable on a clearly erroneous basis, rather than as a plenary one."[a]

SECTION 3. THE USE OF EXTRINSIC EVIDENCE FROM COMMERCIAL CONTEXT

Frigaliment Importing Co. v. B.N.S. International Sales Corp.

United States District Court, S.D.N.Y., 1960.
190 F.Supp. 116.

■ FRIENDLY, CIRCUIT JUDGE.[b] The issue is, what is chicken? Plaintiff says "chicken" means a young chicken, suitable for broiling and frying. Defen-

a. Compare Paragon Resources, Inc. v. National Fuel Gas Distribution Corp., 695 F.2d 991, 995 (5th Cir.1983) ("[T]he clearly erroneous rule applies when extrinsic evidence is used to interpret an *ambiguous* contract, and ambiguity is a question of law." Therefore the appellate court "must first review the decision that the contract terms are ambiguous." If it agrees with the trial court that they are, it must "accord 'clearly erroneous' deference to its interpretation of that contract in light of extrinsic evidence.").

b. Henry J. Friendly (1903–1986) clerked for Justice Brandeis and then practiced law in New York for thirty years before becoming a judge, and later chief judge, on the United States Court of Appeals, Second Circuit. He was admired for his keen mind and the breadth of his learning. He advocated a drastic pruning of the diversity jurisdiction of federal courts but would have retained jurisdiction over suits between aliens and United States citizens (as in the principal case) owing to their "possible effect on interdant says "chicken" means any bird of that genus that meets contract specifications on weight and quality, including what it calls "stewing chicken" and plaintiff pejoratively terms "fowl." Dictionaries give both meanings, as well as some others not relevant here. To support its, plaintiff sends a number of volleys over the net; defendant essays to return them and adds a few serves of its own. Assuming that both parties were acting in good faith, the case nicely illustrates Holmes' remark "that the making of a contract depends not on the agreement of two minds in one intention, but on the agreement of two sets of external signs—not on the parties' having *meant* the same thing but on their having *said* the same thing." The Path of the Law, in Collected Legal Papers, p. 178. I have concluded that plaintiff has not sustained its burden of persuasion that the contract used "chicken" in the narrower sense.

The action is for breach of the warranty that goods sold shall correspond to the description, New York Personal Property Law, McKinney's Consol.Laws, c. 41, § 95. Two contracts are in suit. In the first, dated May 2, 1957, defendant, a New York sales corporation, confirmed the sale to plaintiff, a Swiss corporation, of

> "US Fresh Frozen Chicken," Grade A, Government Inspected, Eviscerated
> 2½–3 lbs. and 1½–2 lbs. each
> all chicken individually wrapped in cryovac, packed in secured fiber cartons or wooden boxes, suitable for export
> 75,000 lbs. 2½–3 lbs. $33.00
> 25,000 lbs. 1½–2 lbs. $36.50
> per 100 lbs. FAS New York[c]
> "scheduled May 10, 1957 pursuant to instructions from Penson & Co., New York."

The second contract, also dated May 2, 1957, was identical save that only 50,000 lbs. of the heavier "chicken" were called for, the price of the smaller birds was $37 per 100 lbs., and shipment was scheduled for May 30. The initial shipment under the first contract was short but the balance was shipped on May 17. When the initial shipment arrived in Switzerland, plaintiff found, on May 28, that the 2½–3 lbs. birds were not young chicken suitable for broiling and frying but stewing chicken or "fowl"; indeed, many of the cartons and bags plainly so indicated. Protests ensued. Nevertheless, shipment under the second contract was made on May 29, the 2½–3 lbs. birds again being stewing chicken. Defendant stopped the transportation of these at Rotterdam.

This action followed. Plaintiff says that, notwithstanding that its acceptance was in Switzerland, New York law controls under the principle of Rubin v. Irving Trust Co., 1953, 305 N.Y. 288, 305, 113 N.E.2d 424, 431; defendant does not dispute this, and relies on New York decisions. I shall follow the apparent agreement of the parties as to the applicable law.

national relations." H. Friendly, Federal Jurisdiction: A General View at 150 n. 42 (1973).

    c. F.A.S. is a common trade term that means, in this context, that for the stated price the seller will place the chicken "free alongside" a ship at the named port, here New York.

Since the word "chicken" standing alone is ambiguous, I turn first to see whether the contract itself offers any aid to its interpretation. Plaintiff says the 1½–2 lbs. birds necessarily had to be young chicken since the older birds do not come in that size, hence the 2½–3 lbs. birds must likewise be young. This is unpersuasive—a contract for "apples" of two different sizes could be filled with different kinds of apples even though only one species came in both sizes. Defendant notes that the contract called not simply for chicken but for "US Fresh Frozen Chicken, Grade A, Government Inspected." It says the contract thereby incorporated by reference the Department of Agriculture's regulations, which favor its interpretation; I shall return to this after reviewing plaintiff's other contentions.

The first hinges on an exchange of cablegrams which preceded execution of the formal contracts. The negotiations leading up to the contracts were conducted in New York between defendant's secretary, Ernest R. Bauer, and a Mr. Stovicek, who was in New York for the Czechoslovak government at the World Trade Fair. A few days after meeting Bauer at the fair, Stovicek telephoned and inquired whether defendant would be interested in exporting poultry to Switzerland. Bauer then met with Stovicek, who showed him a cable from plaintiff dated April 26, 1957, announcing that they "are buyer" of 25,000 lbs. of chicken 2½–3 lbs. weight, Cryovac packed, grade A Government inspected, at a price up to 33 cents per pound, for shipment on May 10, to be confirmed by the following morning, and were interested in further offerings. After testing the market for price, Bauer accepted, and Stovicek sent a confirmation that evening. Plaintiff stresses that, although these and subsequent cables between plaintiff and defendant, which laid the basis for the additional quantities under the first and for all of the second contract, were predominantly in German, they used the English word "chicken"; it claims this was done because it understood "chicken" meant young chicken whereas the German word, "Huhn," included both "Brathuhn" (broilers) and "Suppenhuhn" (stewing chicken), and that defendant, whose officers were thoroughly conversant with German, should have realized this. Whatever force this argument might otherwise have is largely drained away by Bauer's testimony that he asked Stovicek what kind of chickens were wanted, received the answer "any kind of chickens," and then, in German, asked whether the cable meant "Huhn" and received an affirmative response. . . .

Plaintiff's next contention is that there was a definite trade usage that "chicken" meant "young chicken." Defendant showed that it was only beginning in the poultry trade in 1957, thereby bringing itself within the principle that "when one of the parties is not a member of the trade or other circle, his acceptance of the standard must be made to appear" by proving either that he had actual knowledge of the usage or that the usage is "so generally known in the community that his actual individual knowledge of it may be inferred." 9 Wigmore, Evidence (3d ed. 1940) § 2464. Here there was no proof of actual knowledge of the alleged usage; indeed, it is quite plain that defendant's belief was to the contrary. In order to meet the alternative requirement, the law of New York demands a showing that "the usage is of so long continuance, so well established, so notorious, so universal and so reasonable in itself, as that the presumption is violent that the parties contracted with reference to it, and made it a part of their agreement." Walls v. Bailey, 1872, 49 N.Y. 464, 472–473.

Plaintiff endeavored to establish such a usage by the testimony of three witnesses and certain other evidence. Strasser, resident buyer in New York for a large chain of Swiss cooperatives, testified that "on chicken I would definitely understand a broiler." However, the force of this testimony was considerably weakened by the fact that in his own transactions the witness, a careful businessman, protected himself by using "broiler" when that was what he wanted and "fowl" when he wished older birds. Indeed, there are some indications, dating back to a remark of Lord Mansfield, Edie v. East India Co., 2 Burr. 1216, 1222 (1761), that no credit should be given "witnesses to usage, who could not adduce instances in verification." 7 Wigmore, Evidence (3d ed. 1940) § 1954; see McDonald v. Acker, Merrall & Condit Co., 2d Dept.1920, 192 App.Div. 123, 126, 182 N.Y.S. 607. While Wigmore thinks this goes too far, a witness' consistent failure to rely on the alleged usage deprives his opinion testimony of much of its effect. Niesielowski, an officer of one of the companies that had furnished the stewing chicken to defendant, testified that "chicken" meant "the male species of the poultry industry. That could be a broiler, a fryer or a roaster," but not a stewing chicken; however, he also testified that upon receiving defendant's inquiry for "chickens," he asked whether the desire was for "fowl or frying chickens" and, in fact, supplied fowl, although taking the precaution of asking defendant, a day or two after plaintiff's acceptance of the contracts in suit, to change its confirmation of its order from "chickens," as defendant had originally prepared it, to "stewing chickens." Dates, an employee of Urner–Barry Company, which publishes a daily market report on the poultry trade, gave it as his view that the trade meaning of "chicken" was "broilers and fryers." In addition to this opinion testimony, plaintiff relied on the fact that the Urner–Barry service, the Journal of Commerce, and Weinberg Bros. & Co. of Chicago, a large supplier of poultry, published quotations in a manner which, in one way or another, distinguish between "chicken," comprising broilers, fryers and certain other categories, and "fowl," which, Bauer acknowledged, included stewing chickens. This material would be impressive if there were nothing to the contrary. However, there was, as will now be seen.

Defendant's witness Weininger, who operates a chicken eviscerating plant in New Jersey, testified "Chicken is everything except a goose, a duck, and a turkey. Everything is a chicken, but then you have to say, you have to specify which category you want or that you are talking about." Its witness Fox said that in the trade "chicken" would encompass all the various classifications. Sadina, who conducts a food inspection service, testified that he would consider any bird coming within the classes of "chicken" in the Department of Agriculture's regulations to be a chicken. The specifications approved by the General Services Administration include fowl as well as broilers and fryers under the classification "chickens." Statistics of the Institute of American Poultry Industries use the phrases "Young chickens" and "Mature chickens," under the general heading

"Total chickens." and the Department of Agriculture's daily and weekly price reports avoid use of the word "chicken" without specification.

Defendant advances several other points which it claims affirmatively support its construction. Primary among these is the regulation of the Department of Agriculture, 7 C.F.R. §§ 70.300–70.370, entitled, "Grading and Inspection of Poultry and Edible Products Thereof." and in particular § 70.301 which recited:

Chickens. The following are the various classes of chickens:

    (a) Broiler or fryer . . .

    (b) Roaster . . .

    (c) Capon . . .

    (d) Stag . . .

    (e) Hen or stewing chicken or fowl . . .

    (f) Cock or old rooster . . .

Defendant argues, as previously noted, that the contract incorporated these regulations by reference. Plaintiff answers that the contract provision related simply to grade and Government inspection and did not incorporate the Government definition of "chicken," and also that the definition in the Regulations is ignored in the trade. However, the latter contention was contradicted by Weininger and Sadina; and there is force in defendant's argument that the contract made the regulations a dictionary, particularly since the reference to Government grading was already in plaintiff's initial cable to Stovicek.

Defendant makes a further argument based on the impossibility of its obtaining broilers and fryers at the 33 cents price offered by plaintiff for the 2½–3 lbs. birds. There is no substantial dispute that, in late April, 1957, the price for 2½–3 lbs. broilers was between 35 and 37 cents per pound, and that when defendant entered into the contracts, it was well aware of this and intended to fill them by supplying fowl in these weights. It claims that plaintiff must likewise have known the market since plaintiff had reserved shipping space on April 23, three days before plaintiff's cable to Stovicek, or, at least, that Stovicek was chargeable with such knowledge. It is scarcely an answer to say, as plaintiff does in its brief, that the 33 cents price offered for the 2½–3 lbs. "chickens" was closer to the prevailing 35 cents price for broilers than to the 30 cents at which defendant procured fowl. Plaintiff must have expected defendant to make some profit—certainly it could not have expected defendant deliberately to incur a loss.

Finally, defendant relies on conduct by the plaintiff after the first shipment had been received. On May 28 plaintiff sent two cables complaining that the larger birds in the first shipment constituted "fowl." Defendant answered with a cable refusing to recognize plaintiff's objection and announcing "We have today ready for shipment 50,000 lbs. chicken 2½–3 lbs. 25,000 lbs. broilers 1½–2 lbs.," these being the goods procured for shipment under the second contract, and asked immediate answer "whether we are to ship this merchandise to you and whether you will accept the merchandise." After several other cable exchanges, plaintiff replied on May

29 "Confirm again that merchandise is to be shipped since resold by us if not enough pursuant to contract chickens are shipped the missing quantity is to be shipped within ten days stop we resold to our customers pursuant to your contract chickens grade A you have to deliver us said merchandise we again state that we shall make you fully responsible for all resulting costs." Defendant argues that if plaintiff was sincere in thinking it was entitled to young chickens, plaintiff would not have allowed the shipment under the second contract to go forward, since the distinction between broilers and chickens drawn in defendant's cablegram must have made it clear that the larger birds would not be broilers. However, plaintiff answers that the cables show plaintiff was insisting on delivery of young chickens and that defendant shipped old ones at its peril. Defendant's point would be highly relevant on another disputed issue—whether if liability were established, the measure of damages should be the difference in market value of broilers and stewing chicken in New York or the larger difference in Europe, but I cannot give it weight on the issue of interpretation. Defendant points out also that plaintiff proceeded to deliver some of the larger birds in Europe, describing them as "poulets"; defendant argues that it was only when plaintiff's customers complained about this that plaintiff developed the idea that "chicken" meant "young chicken." There is little force in this in view of plaintiff's immediate and consistent protests.

When all the evidence is reviewed, it is clear that defendant believed it could comply with the contracts by delivering stewing chicken in the 2½–3 lbs. size. Defendant's subjective intent would not be significant if this did not coincide with an objective meaning of "chicken." Here it did coincide with one of the dictionary meanings, with the definition in the Department of Agriculture Regulations to which the contract made at least oblique reference, with at least some usage in the trade, with the realities of the market, and with what plaintiff's spokesman had said. Plaintiff asserts it to be equally plain that plaintiff's own subjective intent was to obtain broilers and fryers; the only evidence against this is the material as to market prices and this may not have been sufficiently brought home. In any event it is unnecessary to determine that issue. For plaintiff has the burden of showing that "chicken" was used in the narrower rather than in the broader sense, and this it has not sustained.

This opinion constitutes the Court's findings of fact and conclusions of law. Judgment shall be entered dismissing the complaint with costs.

NOTES

(1) *"What is Chicken"*? Judge Friendly says that "The issue is, what is chicken?" Is this the issue that the court had to decide? He also says that the case "nicely illustrates Holmes' remark 'that the making of a contract depends ... not on the parties' having *meant* the same thing but on their having *said* the same thing.'" Does it? Would the result have been the same if *both* parties had *meant* broilers although they had *said* "chicken"? Is there any reason to hold the parties to a meaning that *neither* attached to their language?

See also Shrum v. Zeltwanger, 559 P.2d 1384 (Wyo.1977) (what is a cow?); Johnson v. Calvert, 5 Cal.4th 84 (1993) (what is a mother?).

(2) *Corporate Intent.* Since both parties in *Frigaliment* were corporations, the notion that either "meant" anything or had any "intention" may seem somewhat strained. It would seem even more strained if other persons, including lawyers, had participated in the negotiations along with Bauer and Stovicek. Courts have not been greatly troubled by the problems of finding a collective "intention" in such cases. (For example, Judge Friendly states that B.N.S. "was only beginning in the poultry trade." Would it have been significant if Bauer had been hired by B.N.S. because of his long experience in that trade?) For a rare instance where such a problem was raised, see Franklin Life Ins. Co. v. Mast, 435 F.2d 1038 (9th Cir.1970), where the court said, "Whatever may have been the secret intent of Mast, it is clear that the intent of his attorney in fact . . . was to enter into a bona fide agreement."

(3) *Incorporation by Reference.* Are there any special problems that arise in the interpretation of terms, such as the regulations of the Department of Agriculture, that have been incorporated in a contract by reference? Cf. Wilcox v. Wilcox, 406 S.W.2d 152 (Ky.1966), involving a divorce settlement in which the husband agreed to make maintenance payments until his daughter reached "the age of majority." The court held that the husband's obligation continued until the child reached 21, the statutory age of majority at the time of the agreement, even though the statutory age had subsequently been lowered to 18.

If you wanted to incorporate the UNIDROIT Principles, would it suffice to say, "This contract incorporates the UNIDROIT Principles"? Is it significant that the Principles are in the process of revision?

(4) *Usage.* Judge Friendly observes that Frigaliment's evidence of trade usage "would be impressive if there were nothing to the contrary"—but "there was." Usage will be taken up later in this chapter. How did the parties attempt to show usage? See UCC § 1–303.

PROBLEM

Is Silence Golden? Fredrick Hamann, who taught at the Garden City Community Junior College, wanted a year's leave to take a teacher training course. The college regulations incorporated by reference in his contract of employment provided:

> Professional employees granted leaves will, if possible, be reinstated in positions that are similar to the position held when granted the leave.

When he was offered a leave, he knew that the college interpreted this to mean that it would not be required to re-hire him unless there was a similar position open when he re-applied. However, he consulted a lawyer, who advised that in his judgment the provision should be interpreted to mean that the college was required to re-hire him even though a similar position might not be open. Secure in this knowledge, Hamann said nothing and accepted the leave. When he sought to return, the college told him that he could not do so because there was no similar position available. What do you think of the lawyer's advice? See Hamann v. Crouch, 508 P.2d 968 (Kan.1973).

————

HURST v. W.J. LAKE & CO., 16 P.2d 627 (Or.1932). [Hurst contracted to sell Lake 350 tons of horse meat scraps at $50 a ton. The specifications stated "minimum 50% protein" and the contract provided that if any of the scraps "analyzes less than 50% of protein" Lake was to have a discount of

$5.00 a ton. Lake paid only $45 a ton for 140 tons that contained protein varying from 49.53 to 49.96 per cent. Hurst sued to recover the balance of $5 a ton, alleging that both parties were members of a group of traders in horse meat scraps and that the defendant was aware of a usage, prevalent among that group, under which the terms "minimum 50% protein" and "less than 50% protein" required the buyer to accept all scraps containing 49.5 per cent protein or more and pay for them at the rate provided for scraps containing 50% protein. The trial court entered judgment on the pleadings for the defendant and the plaintiff appealed.]

■ ROSMAN, J. . . . [T]he language of the dictionaries is not the only language spoken in America. For instance, the word "thousand" as commonly used has a very specific meaning . . ., but the language of the various trades and localities has assigned to it meanings quite different from that just mentioned. Thus in the bricklaying trade a contract which fixes the bricklayer's compensation at "$5.25 a thousand" does not contemplate that he need lay actually 1,000 bricks in order to earn $5.25, but that he should build a wall of a certain size. Brunold v. Glasser, 25 Misc. 285, 53 N.Y.S. 1021; Walker v. Syms, 118 Mich. 183, 76 N.W. 320. In the lumber industry a contract requiring the delivery of 4,000 shingles will be fulfilled by the delivery of only 2,500 when it appears that by trade custom two packs of a certain size are regarded as 1,000 shingles, and that hence the delivery of eight packs fulfills the contract, even though they contain only 2,500 shingles by actual count. Soutier v. Kellerman, 18 Mo. 509. And, where the custom of a locality considers 100 dozen as constituting a thousand, one who has 19,200 rabbits upon a warren under an agreement for their sale at the price of 60 pounds for each thousand rabbits will be paid for only 16,000 rabbits. Smith v. Wilson, 3 Barn. & Adol. 728. Numerous other instances could readily be cited showing the manner in which the meaning of words has been contracted, expanded, or otherwise altered by local usage, trade custom, dialect influence, code agreement, etc. . . .

The defendant cites numerous cases in many of which the courts held that, when a contract is expressed in language which is not ambiguous upon its face the court will receive no evidence of usage, but will place upon the words of the parties their common meaning; in other words, in those decisions the courts ran the words of the parties through a judicial sieve whose meshes were incapable of retaining anything but the common meaning of the words, and which permitted the meaning which the parties had placed upon them to run away as waste material. Surely those courts did not believe that words are always used in their orthodox sense. The rulings must have been persuaded by other considerations. The rule which rejects evidence of custom has the advantage of simplicity; it protects the writing from attack by some occasional individual who will seek to employ perjured testimony in proof of alleged custom; and, if one can believe that the parol evidence rule is violated when common meaning is rejected in favor of special meaning, then the above rule serves the purpose of the parol evidence rule. Without setting forth the manner in which we came to our conclusion, we state that none of these reasons appeals to us as sufficient to exclude evidence of custom and assign to the words their common meaning only, even though the instrument is nonambiguous upon its face....

[Reversed.]

NOTES

(1) *Questions.* State the issue in Hurst v. Lake in terms of the contract language. How will trade usage help to resolve that issue at the trial? See Holmes, The Theory of Legal Interpretation, 12 Harv. L. Rev. 417, 420 (1899). Even Holmes endorsed trade usage, as distinguished from private codes or conventions: "when you have the security of a local or class custom or habit of speech, it may be presumed that the writer conforms to the usage of his place or class when that is what a normal person in his situation would do." How can Hurst prove usage? Why did the buyer fail in its attempt to prove usage in *Frigaliment*?

(2) *Commercial Context in the UCC.* Note that the UCC has two provisions relating to the use of commercial context: §§ 1–303 and 2–202. Would the buyer in *Frigaliment* have succeeded under the UCC? See UCC § 1–303. Under the UCC, what is the difference between a usage of trade and a course of dealing? How would a party like Hurst prove a course of dealing? What impact does UCC § 2–202 have on the admissibility of usage? What impact does UCC § 1–303(e) have? How does the rule in UCC § 1–303(e) differ from a plain meaning rule?

For a critical view of the Code provisions on usage, see Lisa Bernstein, The Questionable Empirical Basis of Article 2's Incorporation Strategy: A Preliminary Study, 66 U.Chi.L.Rev. 710 (1999).

(3) *Knowledge of Usage.* Under UCC § 1–303, would the buyer have been bound by the usage if the buyer had been unaware of it? Recall that in *Frigaliment* the seller had no knowledge of the usage claimed by the buyer. If the buyer had succeeded in proving that usage, would the seller, who "was only beginning in the poultry trade," have been bound by it? Compare Foxco Industries, Ltd. v. Fabric World, Inc., 595 F.2d 976 (5th Cir.1979) (buyer bound by usage of trade association as to meaning of "first quality," though it was not a member and did not know of industry usage), with Flower City Painting Contractors, Inc. v. Gumina Constr. Co., 591 F.2d 162 (2d Cir.1979) ("neophyte minority painting contractor" with first substantial subcontract did not have reason to know of trade usage).

In Martin Rispens & Son v. Hall Farms, Inc., 621 N.E.2d 1078, 1084 (Ind.1993), a seller argued that its implied warranty of merchantability under a contract for the sale of seeds from Rispens to Hall Farms had been excluded by a usage of trade under UCC § 2–316(3)(c). The problem, thought the court, is that "Rispens and Hall Farms are not in the same trade; Rispens is in the business of selling seeds while Hall Farms is in the business of planting seeds and producing crops. Thus, Rispens can effectively negate the implied warranty of merchantability only by establishing that Hall Farms was or should have been aware of the asserted usage of trade." But was not Hall Farms in the business of buying seeds? Suppose that in *Frigaliment*, the buyer had been the operator of a large chain of fried chicken restaurants?

PROBLEM

What is "Slaw"? Williams, a Georgian, contracted to sell "slaw cabbage" to Curtin, a New Yorker, who buys cabbage for processing into cole slaw. Both parties had federal licenses to buy and sell perishable agricultural commodities in interstate commerce. Curtin was to send trucks for the cabbage. Because of the weather, most of the cabbage did not grow to the desired size and the market price for cabbage increased dramatically. Williams, claiming that according to a usage of trade in Georgia "slaw cabbage" meant large cabbage, delivered only the large cabbage to Curtin and sold the rest on the risen market. Curtin, claiming that according to a usage of trade in the interstate cole slaw market, "slaw cabbage" meant all cabbage suitable for making cole slaw, seeks damages for breach of contract. If both usages can be established, which applies? See Williams v. Curtin, 807 F.2d 1046 (D.C.Cir. 1986).

Section 4. The Use of Extrinsic Evidence to Supplement or Qualify the Agreement: Course of Dealing, Usage of Trade, and Course of Performance

UCC § 1–303(d) provides that a course of dealing, usage of trade, and course of performance may not only "give particular meaning to . . . terms of an agreement," but may also "supplement or qualify" those terms. In *Frigaliment*, p. 401 above, and *Hurst*, p. 407 above, we saw how usage can give meaning to contract language. The two cases that follow are concerned with how usage and course of dealing may *supplement* or *qualify* contract language.

Nanakuli Paving & Rock Co. v. Shell Oil Co.

United States Court of Appeals, Ninth Circuit, 1981.
664 F.2d 772.

■ Hoffman, District Judge. . . . Nanakuli, the second largest asphaltic paving contractor in Hawaii, had bought all its asphalt requirements from 1963 to 1974 from Shell under two long-term supply contracts; its suit charged Shell with breach of the later 1969 contract. The jury returned a verdict of $220,800 for Nanakuli on its first claim, which is that Shell breached the 1969 contract in January, 1974, by failing to price protect Nanakuli on 7200 tons of asphalt at the time Shell raised the price for asphalt from $44 to $76. Nanakuli's theory is that price-protection, as a usage of the asphaltic paving trade in Hawaii, was incorporated into the 1969 agreement between the parties, as demonstrated by the routine use of price protection by suppliers to that trade, and reinforced by the way in which Shell actually performed the 1969 contract up until 1974. Price protection, appellant claims, required that Shell hold the price on the tonnage Nanakuli had already committed because Nanakuli had incorporated that price into bids put out to or contracts awarded by general contractors and government agencies. The District Judge set aside the verdict and granted Shell's motion for judgment n.o.v., which decision we vacate. We reinstate the jury verdict because we find that, viewing the evidence as a whole, there was substantial evidence to support a finding by reasonable jurors that Shell breached its contract by failing to provide protection for Nanakuli in 1974. Quichocho v. Kelvinator Corp., 546 F.2d 812, 813 (9th Cir.1976). We do not believe the evidence in this case was such that, giving Nanakuli the benefit of all inferences fairly supported by the evidence and without weighing the credibility of the witnesses, only one reasonable conclusion could have been reached by the jury. Cockrum v. Whitney, 479 F.2d 84, 85–86 (9th Cir.1973).

Nanakuli offers two theories for why Shell's failure to offer price protection in 1974 was a breach of the 1969 contract. First, it argues, all material suppliers to the asphaltic paving trade in Hawaii followed the trade usage of price protection and thus it should be assumed, under the U.C.C., that the parties intended to incorporate price protection into their 1969 agreement. This is so, Nanakuli continues, even though the written contract provided for price to be "Shell's Posted Price at time of delivery," F.O.B. Honolulu.... The U.C.C. looks to the actual performance of a contract as the best indication of what the parties intended those terms to mean. Nanakuli points out that Shell had price protected it on the two occasions of price increases under the 1969 contract other than the 1974 increase. In 1970 and 1971 Shell extended the old price for four and three months, respectively, after an announced increase....[1]

Nanakuli's second theory for price protection is that Shell was obliged to price protect Nanakuli, even if price protection was not incorporated into their contract, because price protection was the commercially reasonable standard for fair dealing in the asphaltic paving trade in Hawaii in 1974....

Shell presents three arguments for upholding the judgment n.o.v. or, on cross appeal, urging that the District Judge erred in admitting certain evidence. First, it says, the District Court should not have denied Shell's motion *in limine* to define trade, for purposes of trade usage evidence, as the sale and purchase of asphalt in Hawaii, rather than expanding the definition of trade to include other suppliers of materials to the asphaltic paving trade. Asphalt, its argument runs, was the subject matter of the disputed contract and the only product Shell supplied to the asphaltic paving trade. Shell protests that the judge, by expanding the definition of trade to include the other major suppliers to the asphaltic paving trade, allowed the admission of highly prejudicial evidence of routine price protection by all suppliers of aggregate. Asphaltic concrete paving is formed by mixing paving asphalt with crushed rock, or aggregate, in a "hot-mix" plant and then pouring the mixture onto the surface to be paved. Shell's second complaint is that the two prior occasions on which it price protected Nanakuli, although representing the only other instances of price increases under the 1969 contract, constituted mere waivers of the contract's price term, not a course of performance of the contract. A course of performance of the contract, in contrast to a waiver, demonstrates how the parties understand the terms of their agreement.... Shell's final argument is that, even assuming its prior price protection constituted a course of perform-ance and that the broad trade definition was correct and evidence of trade usages by aggregate suppliers was admissible, price protection could not be

---

1. Price protection was practiced in the asphaltic paving trade by either extending the old price for a period of time after a new one went into effect or charging the old price for a specified tonnage, which represented work committed at the old price. In addition, several months' advance notice was given of price increases.

construed as reasonably consistent with the express price term in the contract, in which case the Code provides that the express term controls.

We hold that the judge did not abuse his discretion in defining the applicable trade, for purposes of trade usages, as the asphaltic paving trade in Hawaii, rather than the purchase and sale of asphalt alone.... Additionally, we hold that, under the facts of this case, a jury could reasonably have found that Shell's acts on two occasions to price protect Nanakuli were not ambiguous and therefore indicated Shell's understanding of the terms of the agreement with Nanakuli rather than being a waiver by Shell of those terms.

Lastly we hold that, although the express price terms of Shell's posted price of delivery may seem, at first glance, inconsistent with a trade usage of price protection at time of increases in price, a closer reading shows that the jury could have reasonably construed price protection as consistent with the express term....

Trade Usage Before and After 1969

The key to price protection being so prevalent in 1969 that both parties would intend to incorporate it into their contract is found in one reality of the Oahu asphaltic paving market: the largest paving contracts were let by government agencies and none of the three levels of government—local, state, or federal—allowed escalation clauses for paving materials. If a paver bid at one price and another went into effect before the award was made, the paving company would lose a great deal of money, since it could not pass on increases to any government agency or to most general contractors. Extensive evidence was presented that, as a consequence, aggregate suppliers routinely price protected paving contractors in the 1960's and 1970's, as did the largest asphaltic supplier in Oahu, Chevron. Nanakuli presented documentary evidence of routine price protection by aggregate suppliers as well as two witnesses.... Both testified that price protection to their knowledge had always been practiced.... Such protection consisted of advance notices of increases, coupled with charging the old price for work committed at that price or for enough time to order the tonnage committed. The smallness of the Oahu market led to complete trust among suppliers and pavers.... None of the aggregate companies had a contract with Nanakuli expressly stating price protection would be given....

Shell's Course Of Performance Of The 1969 Contract

The Code considers actual performance of a contract as the most relevant evidence of how the parties interpreted the terms of that contract. In 1970 and 1971, the only points at which Shell raised prices between 1969 and 1974, it price protected Nanakuli by holding its old price for four and three months, respectively, after announcing a price increase....

Scope Of Trade Usage

The validity of the jury verdict in this case depends on four legal questions. First, how broad was the trade to whose usages Shell was bound under its 1969 agreement with Nanakuli: did it extend to the Hawaiian asphaltic paving trade or was it limited merely to the purchase and sale of asphalt, which would only include evidence of practices by Shell and Chevron? Second, were the two instances of price protection of Nanakuli by Shell in 1970 and 1971 waivers of the 1969 contract as a matter of law or was the jury entitled to find that they constituted a course of performance of the contract? Third, could the jury have construed an express contract term of Shell's posted price at delivery as reasonably consistent with a trade usage and Shell's course of performance of the 1969 contract of price protection, which consisted of charging the old price at times of price increases, either for a period of time or for specific tonnage committed at a fixed price in non-escalating contracts? Fourth, could the jury have found that good faith obliged Shell to at least give advance notice of a $32 increase in 1974, that is, could they have found that the commercially reasonable standards of fair dealing in the trade in Hawaii in 1974 were to give some form of price protection? . . .

The Code defines usage of trade as "any practice or method of dealing having such regularity of observance in a *place, vocation or trade* as to justify an expectation that it will be observed with respect to the transaction in question." Id. § 490:1–205(2) (emphasis supplied). . . . [A] usage need not necessarily be one practiced by members of the party's own trade or vocation to be binding *if* it is so commonly practiced in a locality that a party should be aware of it. . . . A party is always held to conduct generally observed by members of his chosen trade because the other party is justified in so assuming unless he indicates otherwise. He is held to more general business practices to the extent of his actual knowledge of those practices or to the degree his ignorance of those practices is not excusable: they were so generally practiced he should have been aware of them.

No U.C.C. cases have been found on this point, but the court's reading of the Code language is similar to that of two of the best-known commentators on the U.C.C.:

> Under pre-Code law, a trade usage was not operative against a party who *was not a member of the trade unless* he actually knew of it or *the other party could reasonably believe he knew of it.*

J. White & R. Summers, Uniform Commercial Code, § 12–6 at 371 (1972) (emphasis supplied). . . . White and Summers add (emphasis supplied):

> This view has been carried forward by 1–205(3). . . . [U]sage of the trade is only binding on *members of the trade* involved *or persons* who know or *should know about it.* Persons who should be aware of the trade usage doubtless *include those who regularly deal with members of the relevant trade,* and also members of a second trade that commonly deals with members of a relevant trade (for example, farmers should know something of seed selling).

White & Summers, supra, § 12–6 at 371. Using that analogy, even if Shell did not "regularly deal" with aggregate supplies, it did deal constantly and almost exclusively on Oahu with one asphalt paver. It therefore should have been aware of the usage of Nanakuli and other asphaltic pavers to bid at fixed prices and therefore receive price protection from their materials suppliers due to the refusal by government agencies to accept escalation clauses. Therefore, we do not find the lower court abused its discretion or misread the Code as applied to the peculiar facts of this case in ruling that the applicable trade was the asphaltic paving trade in Hawaii. An asphalt seller should be held to the usages of trade in general as well as those of asphalt sellers and common usages of those to whom they sell. Certainly, under the unusual facts of this case it was not unreasonable for the judge to extend trade usages to include practices of other material suppliers toward Shell's primary and perhaps only customer on Oahu. He did exclude, on Shell's motion *in limine,* evidence of cement suppliers. He only held Shell to routine practices in Hawaii by the suppliers of the two major ingredients of asphaltic paving, that is, asphalt and aggregate. Those usages were only practiced towards two major pavers. It was not unreasonable to expect Shell to be knowledgeable about so small a market. In so ruling, the judge undoubtedly took into account Shell's half-million dollar investment in Oahu strictly because of a long-term commitment by Nanakuli, its actions as partner in promoting Nanakuli's expansion on Oahu, and the fact that its sales on Oahu were almost exclusively to Nanakuli for use in asphaltic paving. The wisdom of the pre-trial ruling was demonstrated by evidence at trial that Shell's agent in Hawaii stayed in close contact with Nanakuli and was knowledgeable about both the asphaltic paving market in general and Nanakuli's bidding procedures and economics in particular.

Shell argued not only that the definition of trade was too broad, but also that the practice itself was not sufficiently regular to reach the level of a usage and that Nanakuli failed to show with enough precision how the usage was carried out in order for a jury to calculate damages. The extent of a usage is ultimately a jury question. The Code provides, "The existence and scope of such a usage are to be proved as facts." Haw.Rev.Stat. § 490:1–205(2). The practice must have "such regularity of observance . . . as to justify an expectation that it will be observed. . . ." Id. The Comment explains:

> The ancient English tests for "custom" are abandoned in this connection. Therefore, it is not required that a usage of trade be "ancient or immemorial," "universal" or the like. . . . [F]ull recognition is thus available for new usages and for usages currently observed by the great majority of decent dealers, even though dissidents ready to cut corners do not agree.

Id., Comment 5. The Comment's demand that "not universality but only the described 'regularity of observance' " is required reinforces the provision only giving "effect to usages of which the parties 'are or should be aware'. . . ." Id., Comment 7. A "regularly observed" practice of protection, of which Shell "should have been aware," was enough to constitute a usage that Nanakuli had reason to believe was incorporated into the agreement.

Nanakuli went beyond proof of a regular observance. It proved and offered to prove that price protection was probably a universal practice by suppliers to the asphaltic paving trade in 1969. . . . Shell did not point in rebuttal to one instance of failure to price protect by any supplier to an asphalt paver in Hawaii before its own 1974 refusal to price protect Nanakuli. Thus, there clearly was enough proof for a jury to find that the practice of price protection in the asphaltic paving trade existed in Hawaii in 1969 and was regular enough in its observance to rise to the level of a usage that would be binding on Nanakuli and Shell. . . .

Waiver or Course of Performance

Course of performance under the Code is the action of the parties in carrying out the contract at issue, whereas course of dealing consists of relations between the parties prior to signing that contract. Evidence of the latter was excluded by the District Judge; evidence of the former consisted of Shell's price protection of Nanakuli in 1970 and 1971. Shell protested that the jury could not have found that those two instances of price protection amounted to a course of performance of its 1969 contract, relying on two Code comments. First, one instance does not constitute a course of performance. "A single occasion of conduct does not fall within the language of this section. . . ." Haw.Rev.Stat. § 490:2–208, Comment 4. Although the Comment rules out one instance, it does not further delineate how many acts are needed to form a course of performance. The prior occasions here were only two, but they constituted the only occasions before 1974 that would call for such conduct. In addition, the language used by a top asphalt official of Shell in connection with the first price protection of Nanakuli indicated that Shell felt that Nanakuli was entitled to some form of price protection. On that occasion in 1970 Blee, who had negotiated the contract with Nanakuli and was familiar with exactly what terms Shell was bound to by that agreement, wrote of the need to "bargain" with Nanakuli over the extent of price protection to be given, indicating that some price protection was a legal right of Nanakuli's under the 1969 agreement.

Shell's second defense is that the Comment expresses a preference for an interpretation of waiver.

> 3. Where it is difficult to determine whether a particular act merely sheds light on the meaning of the agreement or represents a waiver of a term of the agreement, the preference is in favor of "waiver" whenever such construction, plus the application of the provisions on the reinstatement of rights waived . . ., is needed to preserve the flexible character of commercial contracts and to prevent surprise or other hardship.

Id., Comment 3. The preference for waiver only applies, however, where acts are ambiguous. It was within the province of the jury to determine whether those acts were ambiguous, and if not, whether they constituted waivers or a course of performance of the contract. The jury's interpretation of those acts as a course of performance was bolstered by evidence offered by Shell that it again price protected Nanakuli on the only two occasions of post–1974 price increases, in 1977 and 1978.

Express Terms as Reasonably Consistent With Usage in Course of Performance

Perhaps one of the most fundamental departures of the Code from prior contract law is found in the parol evidence rule and the definition of an agreement between two parties. Under the U.C.C., an agreement goes beyond the written words on a piece of paper. " 'Agreement' means the bargain of the parties in fact as found in their language or by implication from other circumstances including course of dealing or usage of trade or course of performance as provided in this chapter (sections 490:1–205 and 490:2–208)." Id. § 490:1–201(3). Express terms, then, do not constitute the entire agreement, which must be sought also in evidence of usages, dealings, and performance of the contract itself. . . . Course of dealings is more important than usages of the trade, being specific usages between the two parties to the contract. "[C]ourse of dealing controls usage of trade." Id. § 490:1–205(4). . . .

A commercial agreement, then, is broader than the written paper and its meaning is to be determined not just by the language used by them in the written contract but "by their action; read and interpreted in the light of commercial practices and other surrounding circumstances. The measure and background for interpretation are set by the commercial context, which may explain and supplement even the language of a formal or final writing." Id., Comment 1. Performance, usages, and prior dealings are important enough to be admitted always, even for a final and complete agreement; only if they cannot be reasonably reconciled with the express terms of the contract are they not binding on the parties. "The express terms of an agreement and an applicable course of dealing or usage of trade shall be construed wherever reasonable as consistent with each other; but when such construction is unreasonable express terms control both course of dealing and usage of trade and course of dealing controls usage of trade." Id. § 490:1–205(4). . . .

Our study of the Code provisions and Comments, then, form the first basis of our holding that a trade usage to price protect pavers at times of price increases for work committed on nonescalating contracts could reasonably be construed as consistent with an express term of seller's posted price at delivery. Since the agreement of the parties is broader than the express terms and includes usages, which may even add terms to the agreement, and since the commercial background provided by those usages is vital to an understanding of the agreement, we follow the Code's mandate to proceed on the assumption that the parties have included those usages unless they cannot reasonably be construed as consistent with the express terms. . . .

Some guidelines can be offered as to how usage evidence can be allowed to modify a contract. First, the court must allow a check on usage evidence by demanding that it be sufficiently definite and widespread to prevent unilateral post-hoc revision of contract terms by one party. The Code's intent is to put usage evidence on an objective basis. . . .

Although the Code abandoned the traditional common law test of nonconsensual custom and views usage as a way of determining the parties' probable intent, . . . thus abolishing the requirement that common law custom be universally practiced, trade usages still must be well settled. . . . Here the evidence was overwhelming that all suppliers to the asphaltic paving trade price protected customers under the same types of circumstances. Chevron's contract with H.B. was a similar long-term supply contract between a buyer and seller with very close relations, on a form supplied by the seller, covering sales of asphalt, and setting the price at seller's posted price, with no mention of price protection. . . .

[In addition, here] the express price term was "Shell's Posted Price at time of delivery." A total negation of that term would be that the buyer was to set the price. It is a less than complete negation of the term that an unstated exception exists at times of price increases, at which times the old price is to be charged, for a certain period or for a specified tonnage, on work already committed at the lower price on nonescalating contracts. Such a usage forms a broad and important exception to the express term, but does not swallow it entirely. Therefore, we hold that, under these particular facts, a reasonable jury could have found that price protection was incorporated into the 1969 agreement between Nanakuli and Shell and that price protection was reasonably consistent with the express term of seller's posted price at delivery.

Good Faith in Setting Price

Nanakuli offers an alternative theory why Shell should have offered price protection at the time of the price increases of 1974. Even if price protection was not a term of the agreement, Shell could not have exercised good faith in carrying out its 1969 contract with Nanakuli when it raised its price by $32 effective January 1 in a letter written December 31st and only received on January 4, given the universal practice of advance notice of such an increase in the asphaltic paving trade. The Code provides, "A price to be fixed by the seller or by the buyer means a price for him to fix in good faith," Haw.Rev.Stat. § 490:2–305(2). For a merchant good faith means "the observance of reasonable commercial standards of fair dealing in the trade." Id. 490:2–103(1)(b). The comment to Section 2–305 explains, "[I]n the normal case a 'posted price' . . . satisfies the good faith requirement." Id., Comment 3. However, the words "in the normal case" mean that, although a posted price will usually be satisfactory, it will not be so under all circumstances. In addition, the dispute here was not over the amount of the increase—that is, the price that the seller fixed—but over the manner in which that increase was put into effect. It is true that Shell, in order to observe the good faith standards of the trade in 1974, was not bound by the practices of aggregate companies, which did not labor under the same disabilities as did asphalt suppliers in 1974. However, Nanakuli presented evidence that Chevron, in raising its price to $76, gave at least six weeks' advance notice, in accord with the long-time usage of the asphaltic paving trade. Shell, on the other hand, gave absolutely no notice, from which the jury could have concluded that Shell's manner of carrying out the price increase of 1974 did not conform to commercially reasonable standards. In both the timing of the announcement and its refusal to protect work already bid at the old price, Shell could be found to have breached the obligation of good faith imposed by the Code on all merchants. "Every contract or duty within this chapter imposes an obligation of good faith in its performance or enforcement," id. § 490:1–203, which for merchants entails the observance of commercially reasonable standards of fair dealing in the trade. The Comment to 1–203 reads:

> This section sets forth a basic principle running throughout this Act. The principle involved is that in commercial transactions good faith is required in the performance and enforcement of all agreements or duties. Particular applications of this general principle appear in specific provisions of the Act.... It is further implemented by Section 1–205 on course of dealing and usage of trade.

Id. § 490:1–203, Comment. Chevron's conduct in 1974 offered enough relevant evidence of commercially reasonable standards of fair dealing in the asphalt trade in Hawaii in 1974 for the jury to find that Shell's failure to give sufficient advance notice and price protect Nanakuli after the imposition of the new price did not conform to good faith dealings in Hawaii at that time.

Because the jury could have found for Nanakuli on its price protection claim under either theory, we reverse the judgment of the District Court and reinstate the jury verdict for Nanakuli in the amount of $220,800, plus interest according to law.

■ KENNEDY, CIRCUIT JUDGE, concurring specially: ... Our opinion should not be interpreted to permit juries to import price protection or a similarly specific contract term from a concept of good faith that is not based on well-established custom and usage or other objective standards of which the parties had clear notice. Here, evidence of custom and usage regarding price protection in the asphaltic paving trade was not contradicted in major respects, and the jury could find that the parties knew or should have known of the practice at the time of making the contract. In my view, these are necessary predicates for either theory of the case, namely, interpretation of the contract based on the course of its performance or a finding that good faith required the seller to hold the price....

NOTES

(1) *Questions.* Is this a case in which usage was employed, in the words of UCC § 1–303(d), to "give particular meaning to ... terms of an agreement"? To "supplement" those terms? To "qualify" them? (If the purpose was interpretation, what language was being interpreted?)

Recall that in *Naval Institute*, p. 9 above, the trial court had dismissed Naval Institute's complaint for breach of Berkley's agreement to publish the paperback "not sooner than October" on the ground that Berkley "was entitled, in accordance with industry custom, to ship prior to the agreed publication date." The Second Circuit concluded that if the quoted language "had any meaning whatever, it meant at least that Berkley was not allowed to cause such voluminous paperback retail sales prior to that date." Did Berkley seek to use "industry custom" to interpret the language of the agreement? To supplement it? To qualify it? (If the purpose was interpretation, what language was being interpreted?)

In discussing waiver or course of performance, the court states that there were two prior occasions of price protection before 1974, as well as two after 1974. Would it be useful to know if the increases on those occasions were comparable to the jump from $44 to $76 in 1974?

(2) *At What Time?* Should a court apply a usage of trade as of the time of the making of the contract, or as of the time of its performance? In answer to Shell's objection to the trial court's admission of evidence of usage after 1969, the Court of Appeals, in an omitted footnote, said that it did "not need to decide whether usage evidence after a contract was signed is admissible to show that a party's reliance on a given usage was justifiable, given its continuation, because part of that evidence dealing with asphalt prices was admissible to show the reasonable commercial standards of fair dealing prevalent in the trade in 1974 and the part dealing with the continuation of price protection by aggregate suppliers, after 1969 was not so extensive as to be prejudicial to Shell."

(3) *Usage and Omitted Cases.* Look back at *Drennan,* p. 222 above. Could a general contractor use usage of trade to show that a subcontractor's bid, which was silent as to revocability, was irrevocable? What facts would be sufficient to establish such a usage? See Albert v. R.P. Farnsworth & Co., 176 F.2d 198 (5th Cir.1949); cf. Industrial Electric–Seattle v. Bosko, 410 P.2d 10 (Wash.1966).

Columbia Nitrogen Corp. v. Royster Co.

United States Court of Appeals, Fourth Circuit, 1971.
451 F.2d 3.

[Royster manufactured and sold mixed fertilizers, the principal components of which are nitrogen, phosphate, and potash. Columbia was primarily a producer of nitrogen, although it also manufactured some mixed fertilizer for several years. Royster had been a major buyer from Columbia, but Columbia had never been a significant buyer from Royster. In the fall of 1966, Royster built a phosphate production facility and, to dispose of what it did not need, negotiated a contract to sell to Columbia a minimum of 31,000 tons of phosphate a year for three years, with an option to extend. The contract stated the price per ton subject to an escalation clause dependent on production costs. It set the quantities under the heading "Products Supplied Under Contract Minimum Tonnage Per Year" and contained a merger clause.

When phosphate prices plunged precipitously, Columbia was unable to resell competitively and ordered less than one tenth of the scheduled tonnage during the first contract year. Royster sold the unaccepted phosphate below the contract price and sued for damages. Columbia sought to show by witnesses with long experience in the trade that because of uncertain crop and weather conditions, farming practices and government agricultural programs, express price and quantity terms in the mixed fertilizer industry are mere projections to be adjusted according to market forces. Columbia also sought to show that in its business dealings with Royster during the previous six years—mainly nitrogen sales to Royster—there was repeated and substantial deviation from stated amount or price. The district court excluded this evidence on the ground that "custom and usage or course of dealing are not admissible to contradict the express, plain, unambiguous language of a valid written contract, which by virtue of its detail negates the proposition that the contract is open to variances in its terms." From a $750,000 judgment for Royster, Columbia appealed on the ground that the proffered evidence was improperly excluded.]

■ BUTZNER, CIRCUIT JUDGE. . . . There can be no doubt that the Uniform Commercial Code restates the well established rule that evidence of usage of trade and course of dealing should be excluded whenever it cannot be reasonably construed as consistent with the terms of the contract. . . . Royster argues that the evidence should be excluded as inconsistent because the contract contains detailed provisions regarding the base price, escalation, minimum tonnage, and delivery schedules. The argument is based on the premise that because a contract appears on its face to be complete, evidence of course of dealing and usage of trade should be excluded. We believe, however, that neither the language nor the policy of the Code supports such a broad exclusionary rule. Section 8.2–202 expressly allows evidence of course of dealing or usage of trade to explain or supplement terms intended by the parties as a final expression of their agreement. When this section is read in light of Va.Code Ann. § 8.1–205(4), it is clear that the test of admissibility is not whether the contract appears on its face to be complete in every detail, but whether the proffered evidence of course of dealing and trade usage reasonably can be construed as consistent with the express terms of the agreement. . . .

For the following reasons it is reasonable to construe this evidence as consistent with the express terms of the contract:

The contract does not expressly state that course of dealing and usage of trade cannot be used to explain or supplement the written contract.

The contract is silent about adjusting prices and quantities to reflect a declining market. It neither permits nor prohibits adjustment, and this neutrality provides a fitting occasion for recourse to usage of trade and prior dealing to supplement the contract and explain its terms.

Minimum tonnages and additional quantities are expressed in terms of "Products Supplied Under Contract." Significantly, they are not expressed as just "Products" or as "Products Purchased Under Contract." The description used by the parties is consistent with the proffered testimony.

Finally, the default clause of the contract refers only to the failure of the buyer to pay for delivered phosphate.[a] During the contract negotiations, Columbia rejected a Royster proposal for liquidated damages of $10 for each ton Columbia declined to accept. On the other hand, Royster rejected a Columbia proposal for a clause that tied the price to the market by obligating Royster to conform its price to offers Columbia received from other phosphate producers. The parties, having rejected both proposals, failed to state any consequences of Columbia's refusal to take delivery—the kind of default Royster alleges in this case. Royster insists that we span this hiatus by applying the general law of contracts permitting recovery of

---

a. A footnote in the court's opinion contained excerpts from the contract, including the following default clause: "*Default*—If Buyer fails to pay for any delivery under this contract within 30 days after Seller's invoice to Buyer and then if such invoice is not paid within an additional 30 days after the Seller notifies the Buyer of such default, then after that time the Seller may at his option defer further deliveries hereunder or take such action as in their judgment they may decide including cancellation of this contract. Any balances carried beyond 30 days will carry a service fee of ¾ of 1% per month."

damages upon the buyer's refusal to take delivery according to the written provisions of the contract. This solution is not what the Uniform Commercial Code prescribes. Before allowing damages, a court must first determine whether the buyer has in fact defaulted. It must do this by supplementing and explaining the agreement with evidence of trade usage and course of dealing that is consistent with the contract's express terms. Va.Code Ann. §§ 8.1–205(4), 8.2–202. Faithful adherence to this mandate reflects the reality of the marketplace and avoids the overly legalistic interpretations which the Code seeks to abolish. . . .

Nor can we accept Royster's contention that the testimony should be excluded under the contract clause: "No verbal understanding will be recognized by either party hereto; this contract expresses all the terms and conditions of the agreement, shall be signed in duplicate, and shall not become operative until approved in writing by the Seller." Course of dealing and trade usage are not synonymous with verbal understandings, terms and conditions. Section 8.2–202 draws a distinction between supplementing a written contract by consistent additional terms and supplementing it by course of dealing or usage of trade. Evidence of additional terms must be excluded when "the court finds the writing to have been intended also as a complete and exclusive statement of the terms of the agreement." Significantly, no similar limitation is placed on the introduction of evidence of course of dealing or usage of trade. Indeed the official comment notes that course of dealing and usage of trade, unless carefully negated, are admissible to supplement the terms of any writing, and that contracts are to be read on the assumption that these elements were taken for granted when the document was phrased.[b] Since the Code assigns course of dealing and trade usage unique and important roles, they should not be conclusively rejected by reading them into stereotyped language that makes no specific reference to them. . . .

[Judgment vacated and case remanded.]

NOTE

Specific Reference to Usage. Would the result have been different if the merger clause had begun with general language such as this: "No verbal understanding, usage of trade or course of dealing will be recognized by either party hereto. . . ."?

SECTION 5. OBJECTIVE INTERPRETATION AND ITS LIMITS

Just as objective and subjective theories have influenced the law of contract formation, they have also influenced the law of contract interpre-

---

b. Va.Code Ann. § 8.2–202, Comment 2 states:

"Paragraph (a) [of § 8.202] makes admissible evidence of course of dealing, usage of trade and course of performance to explain or supplement the terms of any writing stating the agreement of the parties in order that the true understanding of the parties as to the agreement may be reached. Such writings are to be read on the assumption that the course of prior dealings between the parties and the usages of trade were taken for granted when the document was phrased. Unless carefully negated they have become an element of the meaning of the words used. Similarly, the course of actual performance by the parties is considered the best indication of what they intended the writing to mean."

tation. There would be little disagreement with the proposition that, where the parties have in fact attached different meanings to their language, an objective standard should determine which meaning will prevail. But the objectivists argue that, even where the parties have in fact attached the same meaning to their language, an objective standard should determine the meaning, which might be different from their shared meaning. Judge Learned Hand, for example, said: "It is quite true that we commonly speak of a contract as a question of intent, and for most purposes it is a convenient paraphrase, accurate enough, but, strictly speaking, untrue. It makes not the least difference whether a promisor actually intends that meaning which the law will impose upon his words. The whole House of Bishops might satisfy us that he had intended something else, and it would make not a particle of difference in his obligation. That obligation the law attaches to his act of using certain words, provided, of course, the actor be under no disability." Eustis Mining Co. v. Beer, Sondheimer & Co., 239 F. 976, 984 (S.D.N.Y.1917). The currency of this view can be judged from the following cases. See Restatement § 201.

INTRODUCTION TO *RAFFLES v. WICHELHAUS*

The next case has been characterized as "one of the best known old chestnuts of the common law.... No student of the law of contract could regard his education as complete without ... reading the case...." At least some of the case's fascination is due to the circumstances that "the judges ... thought the solution to the problem presented to them to be so obvious that they gave judgment for the defendants without troubling to give any reasons for their decision." A.W.B. Simpson, Contracts for Cotton to Arrive: The Case of the Two Ships Peerless, 11 Cardozo L. Rev. 287, 287–88 (1989).

Raffles v. Wichelhaus

Court of Exchequer, 1864.
2 H.&C. 906, 159 Eng.Rep. 375.

Declaration. For that it was agreed between the plaintiff and the defendants, to wit, at Liverpool, that the plaintiff should sell to the defendants, and the defendants buy of the plaintiff, certain goods, to wit, 125 bales of Surat cotton, guaranteed middling fair merchant's Dhollorah, to arrive ex Peerless from Bombay; and that the cotton should be taken from the quay, and that the defendants would pay the plaintiff for the same at a certain rate, to wit, at the rate of 17¼d. per pound, within a certain time then agreed upon after the arrival of the said goods in England. Averments: that the said goods did arrive by the said ship from Bombay in England, to wit, at Liverpool, and the plaintiff was then and there ready and willing and offered to deliver the said goods to the defendants, etc. Breach: that the defendants refused to accept the said goods or pay the plaintiff for them.

Plea. That the said ship mentioned in the said agreement was meant and intended by the defendants to be the ship called the Peerless, which sailed from Bombay, to wit, in October; and that the plaintiff was not ready and willing, and did not offer, to deliver to the defendants any bales of cotton which arrived by the last-mentioned ship, but instead thereof was only ready and willing, and offered to deliver to the defendants 125 bales of Surat cotton which arrived by another and different ship, which was also called the Peerless, and which sailed from Bombay, to wit, in December.

Demurrer, and joinder therein.

MILWARD in support of the demurrer. The contract was for the sale of a number of bales of cotton of a particular description, which the plaintiff was ready to deliver. It is immaterial by what ship the cotton was to arrive, so that it was a ship called the Peerless. The words "to arrive ex Peerless," only mean that if the vessel is lost on the voyage, the contract is to be at an end. [Pollock, C.B. It would be a question for the jury whether both parties meant the same ship called the Peerless.] That would be so if the contract was for the sale of a ship called the Peerless; but it is for the sale of cotton on board a ship of that name. [Pollock, C.B. The defendant only bought that cotton which was to arrive by a particular ship. It may as well be said that if there is a contract for the purchase of certain goods in warehouse A that is satisfied by the delivery of goods of the same description in warehouse B.] In that case there would be goods in both warehouses; here it does not appear that the plaintiff had any goods on board the other Peerless. [Martin, B. It is imposing on the defendant a contract different from that which he entered into. Pollock, C.B. It is like a contract for the purchase of wine coming from a particular estate in France or Spain, where there are two estates of that name.] The defendant has no right to contradict by parol evidence a written contract good upon the face of it. He does not impute misrepresentation or fraud, but only says that he fancied the ship was a different one. Intention is of no avail, unless stated at the time of the contract. [Pollock, C.B. One vessel sailed in October and the other in December.] The time of sailing is no part of the contract.

MELLISH (Cohen with him) in support of the plea. There is nothing on the face of the contract to show that any particular ship called the Peerless was meant; but the moment it appears that two ships called the Peerless were about to sail from Bombay there is a latent ambiguity, and parol evidence may be given for the purpose of showing that the defendant meant one Peerless and the plaintiff another. That being so, there was no consensus ad litem, and therefore no binding contract. He was then stopped by the court.

■ PER CURIAM. There must be judgment for the defendants.

Judgment for the defendants.

NOTES

(1) *Gilmore on "Peerless."* Professor Grant Gilmore wrote that "the celebrated case of Raffles v. Wichelhaus . . . is to the ordinary run of case law as the recently popular theater of the absurd is to the ordinary run of theater." He noted that if the ship which sailed first had also arrived first and if the market price had broken between the two arrival dates, the buyer would presumably have pleaded these facts, and since he did not "we may . . . safely assume that there was no such issue to be raised." There was therefore merit to Milward's argument that it was "immaterial by what ship the cotton was to arrive, so [long as] it was a ship called

the Peerless." According to Gilmore, this "meant only that 'if the vessel is lost on the voyage, the contract is to be at an end' (that is, the seller would bear the loss but the buyer would have no claim for damages for non delivery)." But "the judges, no doubt mistakenly, believed that the identity of the carrying ship was important." Grant Gilmore, *The Death of Contract* 35–39 (1974).

(2) *Simpson on Gilmore.* Professor Brian Simpson concluded otherwise in a detailed examination of the background of the contract, which was made in 1862 at the time of the cotton shortage created by the blockade of the southern states during the Civil War. The shortage made cotton prices high and volatile and caused English spinners to look to India. Speculators were attracted to "arrival" contracts, under which the buyer purchased cotton in transit for forward delivery. Although the time of arrival was of paramount importance to the buyer, it was not common for the contract to specify this time because of the uncertainties involved. One technique that made it possible for the buyer to at least estimate the approximate date of arrival was to name the ship and sometimes the port of departure. The contract in the principal case was such a "ship named" and "port named" contract.

Simpson concludes that Gilmore's "speculations as to the background are inevitably misconceived, being unrelated to evidence," and that "it is perfectly plain that in arrival contracts where ship and port were named, the identity of the carrying vessel was of central importance" because "that fixed the time of arrival and delivery." A.W.B. Simpson, Contracts for Cotton to Arrive: The Case of the Two Ships *Peerless,* 11 Cardozo L.Rev. 287, 324 (1989).

How might the outcome of this debate affect the value of the case as a precedent?

(3) *CISG.* In MCC–Marble Ceramic Center, Inc. v. Ceramica Nuova d'Agostino, S.P.A., 144 F.3d 1384 (11th Cir.1998), the court stated that, "Contrary to what is familiar practice in United States courts, the CISG appears to permit a substantial inquiry into the parties' subjective intent. . . ." Does the court's statement accord with Restatement § 201, which says that a term to which "the parties have attached the same meaning . . . is interpreted in accordance with that meaning." Is it clear that the parol evidence rule (or the plain meaning rule) applies to testimony of a party, or its representative, as to the party's "subjective intent"?

PROBLEM

Wichelhaus v. Raffles. Suppose that Raffles had not shipped cotton on either ship and that Wichelhaus had sued Raffles for breach of contract. What result? Suppose that Wichelhaus, having found no cotton on the October Peerless, had learned for the first time of the December Peerless and decided to wait for it. If the price of cotton had continued to rise, could he have held Raffles to a contract to deliver cotton on the December Peerless?

———

OSWALD v. **ALLEN,** 417 F.2d 43 (2d Cir.1969). [Dr. Oswald, a coin collector from Switzerland, arranged to see Mrs. Allen's collection of Swiss coins in Newburgh, New York, where two of her collections, referred to as the "Swiss Coin Collection" and the "Rarity Coin Collection," were located in separate bank vaults. After examining the coins in the Swiss Coin Collection, he was shown several valuable Swiss coins from the Rarity Coin Collection, although he later testified that he did not know that they were in a separate "collection." During the drive back to New York City, Dr.

Oswald, who spoke very little English, arranged with the help of his brother to buy for $50,000 what Mrs. Allen thought was her Swiss coin collection and what Dr. Oswald thought were all her Swiss coins. He later wrote her to "confirm my purchase of all your Swiss coins (gold, silver and copper) at the price of $50,000," and she wrote back that she had arranged to go to Newburgh with Dr. Oswald's agent. When Dr. Oswald was informed that she would not go through with the sale because of her children's wishes, he sued for specific performance. From a judgment dismissing his complaint after trial, he appealed.]

■ MOORE, CIRCUIT JUDGE.... In such a factual situation the law is settled that no contract exists. The Restatement of Contracts [First] in section 71(a) adopts the rule of Raffles v. Wichelhaus, 2 Hurl. & C. 906, 159 Eng.Rep. 375 (Ex.1864). Professor Young states that rule as follows: "when any of the terms used to express an agreement is ambivalent, and the parties understand it in different ways, there cannot be a contract unless one of them should have been aware of the other's understanding." Young, Equivocation in Agreements, 64 Colum.L.Rev. 619, 621 (1964). Even though the mental assent of the parties is not requisite for the formation of a contract (see Comment to Restatement of Contracts § 71 (1932)), the facts found by the trial judge clearly place this case within the small group of exceptional cases in which there is "no sensible basis for choosing between conflicting understandings." Young, at 647. The rule of Raffles v. Wichelhaus is applicable here.

[The court also held that the exchange of letters did not satisfy the Statute of Frauds.]

Affirmed.

NOTES

(1) *Holmes and Young on Peerless.* Here is Holmes's analysis of *Raffles*: "[W]hile other words may mean different things, a proper name means one person or thing and no other.... In theory of speech your name means you and my name means me, and the two names are different. They are different words.... [H]ere the parties have said different things and never have expressed a contract." Holmes, The Theory of Legal Interpretation, 12 Harv.L.Rev. 417, 418 (1899).

In the article quoted by Judge Moore in *Oswald*, Professor William Young wrote: "Roughly speaking, the rule is restricted to differences of understanding which have their source in the ambivalence or 'double meaning' of an expression. . . . Holmes's formulation would have limited the application of the Peerless rule too narrowly. The Restatement test [now stated in Restatement Second § 20] is too broad." Young, Equivocation in the Making of Agreements, 64 Colum.L.Rev. 619, 646–47 (1964).

(2) *"What is Chicken"? (Reprise).* Is the Restatement test too broad? At the end of the *Frigaliment* opinion, Judge Friendly said that "the burden of showing that 'chicken' was used in the narrower rather than in the broader sense" was on the buyer. Its action for breach of warranty therefore failed. See UCC § 2–607(4). Recall that in *Frigaliment* the seller stopped shipment under the second contract at Rotterdam as a result of the buyer's protests. Does it follow from the dismissal of the buyer's complaint that the seller would necessarily have prevailed in an action against the buyer for breach of this contract? Would not the seller have had the

burden of showing that "chicken" was used in the broader sense? Is it possible that the seller might have failed to sustain this burden?

In a case like Raffles v. Wichelhaus, is it possible that the seller might fail to meet the burden of showing that "Peerless" was used in the sense of the ship sailing in December, and that the buyer might also fail to meet the burden of showing that "Peerless" was used in the sense of the ship sailing in October?

Colfax Envelope Corp. v. Local No. 458–3M

United States Court of Appeals for the Seventh Circuit, 1994.
20 F.3d 750.

■ POSNER, CHIEF JUDGE: This appeal in a suit over a collective bargaining agreement presents a fundamental issue of contract law, that of drawing the line between an ambiguous contract, requiring interpretation, and a contract that, because it cannot be said to represent the agreement of the parties at all, cannot be interpreted, can only be rescinded and the parties left to go their own ways. Colfax, the plaintiff, is a manufacturer of envelopes. It does some printing of its envelopes, and the seventeen employees who do the printing are represented by the defendant union. Colfax has two printing presses. One prints 78–inch–wide sheets in four colors. The other prints 78–inch–wide sheets in five colors, but most of the time Colfax prints only four-color sheets on it.

Colfax has so few printing employees that it does not bother to participate in the collective bargaining negotiations between the union and the Chicago Lithographers Association, an association for collective bargaining of the other Chicago printing companies whose employees are represented by this union. Instead, whenever the union and the CLA sign a new collective bargaining agreement, the union sends Colfax a summary of the changes that the new agreement has made in the old one. If Colfax is content with the changes, the union sends it a copy of the complete new agreement, which Colfax signs and returns. If Colfax doesn't like the terms negotiated by the CLA, it is free to do its own bargaining with the union.

The collective bargaining agreements specify minimum manning requirements for each type of press used by the printers. The agreement in force between 1987 and 1991 fixed those minima as three men for four-color presses printing sheets 45 to 50 inches wide and four men for four-color presses printing sheets wider than 50 inches. Five-color presses printing sheets more than 55 inches wide required five men unless only four colors were printed, in which event only four men were required. The upshot was that under these agreements, all of which Colfax had signed, Colfax had to man each of its presses (which were 78–inch presses) with four men except on the rare occasions when it printed five-color sheets on its second press, and then it had to add a man.

In 1991 the union negotiated a new agreement with the CLA and sent a summary of the changes to Colfax. The letter enclosing the summary asked Colfax to indicate whether it agreed to the terms in the summary.

(This may have been a departure from past practice, in which Colfax signed the complete agreement rather than the summary, but if so neither party makes anything of it.) In a section on manning requirements, the summary lists "4C 60 Press–3 Men" and "5C 78 Press–4 Men." Believing (in part because union members who claimed to be familiar with the new agreement had told Colfax that Colfax would really like the changes in it) that this meant that all presses operated as four-color presses would now require only three men to man them, Colfax's president and majority shareholder, Charles Patten, signed the union's letter, indicating acceptance of the terms in the summary. Later a copy of the actual agreement arrived, but it contained a crucial typo, which supported Patten's understanding of the summary. When a corrected copy of the agreement finally arrived, the manning requirements stated in it were different from what Patten had understood from the summary. Four-color presses between 45 and 60 inches required three men, but all four-color presses over 60 inches required four men. The changes had not benefited Colfax at all, and because it was under competitive pressure, it would have liked to negotiate better terms. Patten refused to sign the agreement but the union took the position that Colfax was bound to it by its acceptance of the summary.

Colfax brought this suit under section 301 of the Taft–Hartley Act, 29 U.S.C. § 185, for a declaration that it has no collective bargaining contract with the union because the parties never agreed on an essential term—the manning requirements for Colfax's printing presses. The union counterclaimed for an order to arbitrate. The union's position was that Colfax had accepted the new agreement, which requires arbitration of all disputes "arising out of the application or interpretation of this contract." The district judge granted summary judgment for the union, concluding that the reference to the new manning requirement for a four-color 60–inch press in the summary of changes that Colfax had accepted referred unambiguously to 60–inch presses and had no application to any other presses, such as Colfax's 78–inch presses. Colfax has appealed.

One way to describe the issue that divides the parties is that they disagree about the meaning of the term "4C 60 Press–3 Men." Colfax believes that it means four-color presses printing sheets 60 inches and over, while the union believes that it means four-color presses 60 inches and under (down to 45 inches). Remember that the previous agreement had allowed the use of three-man crews on four-color presses between 45 and 50 inches. The union interprets the change as extending the upper bound of the three-man range to 60 inches. Ordinarily a dispute over the meaning of a contractual term is, if the contract contains an arbitration clause, for the arbitrator to decide. But sometimes the difference between the parties goes so deep that it is impossible to say that they ever agreed—that they even *have* a contract that a court or arbitrator might interpret. In the famous though enigmatic and possibly misunderstood case of *Raffles v. Wichelhaus*, 2 H.&C. 906, 159 Eng.Rep. 375 (Ex. 1864), the parties made a contract for the delivery of a shipment of cotton from Bombay to England on the ship *Peerless*. Unbeknownst to either party, there were two ships of that name sailing from Bombay on different dates. One party thought the contract referred to one of the ships, and the other to the other. The court held that there was no contract; there had been no "meeting of the minds." See generally A.W. Brian Simpson, "Contracts for Cotton to Arrive: The Case of the Two Ships *Peerless*," 11 *Cardozo L.Rev.* 287 (1989).

The premise—that a "meeting of the minds" is required for a binding contract—obviously is strained. 2 E. Allan Farnsworth, *Contracts* § 7.9, at p. 251 (1990). Most contract disputes arise because the parties did not foresee and provide for some contingency that has now materialized—so there was no meeting of minds on the matter at issue—yet such disputes are treated as disputes over contractual meaning, not as grounds for rescinding the contract and thus putting the parties back where they were before they signed it. So a literal meeting of the minds is not required for an enforceable contract, which is fortunate, since courts are not renowned as mind readers. Let us set the concept to one side, therefore, and ask how (else) to explain *Raffles v. Wichelhaus* and cases like it. It seems to us as it has to other courts that a contract ought to be terminable without liability and the parties thus allowed to go their own ways when there is "no sensible basis for choosing between conflicting understandings" of the contractual language, as the court said in an American *Raffles*-like case, *Oswald v. Allen,* 417 F.2d 43, 45 (2d Cir.1969), quoting William F. Young, Jr., "Equivocation in the Making of Agreements," 64 *Colum.L.Rev.* 619, 647 (1964). In *Oswald* the misunderstanding arose because the parties did not speak the same language (literally). In *Balistreri v. Nevada Livestock Production Credit Association,* 262 Cal.Rptr. 862 (1989), the parents of an aspiring farmer thought they had pledged property they owned in Sebastopol to secure a loan to their son, and indeed the lender's cover letter described the property as "your Sebastopol residence." But the actual deed of trust listed the parents' home in Petaluma as the collateral. The court held that there had been no meeting of the minds.

Raffles and *Oswald* were cases in which neither party was blameable for the mistake; *Balistreri* a case in which both were equally blameable, the parents for having failed to read the deed of trust, the lender for having drafted a misleading cover letter. It is all the same. *Restatement (Second) of Contracts* §§ 20(1)(a), (b) (1981). If neither party can be assigned the greater blame for the misunderstanding, there is no nonarbitrary basis for deciding which party's understanding to enforce, so the parties are allowed to abandon the contract without liability. *Neel v. Lang,* 236 Mass. 61, 127 N.E. 512 (1920); *Konic International Corp. v. Spokane Computer Services, Inc.,* 109 Idaho 527, 529, 708 P.2d 932, 934 (App.1985). These are not cases in which one party's understanding is more reasonable than the other's. Compare *Restatement, supra,* § 20(2)(b). If rescission were permitted in *that* kind of case, the enforcement of every contract would be at the mercy of a jury, which might be persuaded that one of the parties had genuinely held an idiosyncratic idea of its meaning, so that there had been, in fact, no meeting of the minds. Cf. Young, *supra,* at 646. Intersubjectivity is not the test of an enforceable contract.

The clearest cases for rescission on the ground that there was "no meeting of the minds" (or, better, that there was a "latent ambiguity" in the sense that neither party knew that the contract was ambiguous) are ones in which an offer is garbled in transmission. The cases we have cited are all of that character, if "transmission" is broadly construed. *Vickery v. Ritchie*, 202 Mass. 247, 88 N.E. 835 (1909), provides a further illustration. A landowner and a contractor signed what they believed to be duplicate copies of a contract for the construction of a Turkish bath house. Because of a fraud by the architect for which neither the contractor nor the landowner could be blamed, the copy signed by the landowner stated the price as $23,000 and the copy signed by the contractor stated it as $34,000. Through no fault of their own, the parties had signed different contracts. Or consider *Konic International Corp. v. Spokane Computer Services, Inc., supra*. The seller quoted a price of "fifty-six twenty," which the buyer thought meant $56.20. In fact the seller had meant $5,620. In both cases rescission was permitted, the first being a case in which neither party was at fault, the second one in which both were equally at fault, being careless in their utterance and interpretation, respectively, of an ambiguous oral formula.

Our case is superficially similar. The actual terms of the 1991 agreement were muddied in the summary that the union gave Colfax and that Colfax signed, making it possible that the parties had different understandings. The difference between this case and the others is that Colfax, unlike the hapless promisors in the cases we have cited, should have realized that the contract was unclear. The buyer in *Konic* thought—*really* thought—that he was being quoted a price of $56.20, and no doubt fell off his stool when he discovered that the price was a hundred times greater than he thought. But the expression "4C 60 Press" does not on its face speak to the minimum manning requirement for a 4C 78 Press. The union's interpretation, that the phrase merely extended the upper bound of the old range for three-man four-color presses from 50 to 60 inches, may or may not be correct. The fact that the union restated and clarified the interpretation in the corrected agreement that it sent Colfax is not decisive on the question, because it is the summary rather than the corrected full agreement that is the contract between these parties. But Colfax, if reasonable, could not have doubted from reading the summary that interpretations of the kind that the union and the district judge later placed upon it would be entirely plausible. Colfax had a right to *hope* that its interpretation would prevail but it had no right to accept the offer constituted by the summary on the premise that either its interpretation was correct or it could walk away from the contract. "Heads I win, tails you lose," is not the spirit that animates the principle that latent ambiguity is a ground for rescission of a contract.

It is common for contracting parties to agree—that is, to *signify* agreement—to a term to which each party attaches a different meaning. It is just a gamble on a favorable interpretation by the authorized tribunal should a dispute arise. Parties often prefer to gamble in this way rather than to take the time to try to iron out all their possible disagreements, most of which may never have any consequence. Colfax gambled on persuading an arbitrator that the reference in the summary to the four-color 60–inch press meant what Colfax believes it means. The union gambled on the arbitrator's adopting the meaning that the union later made clear in the full agreement—but, to repeat, if there is a contract it is (the parties agree) the summary, read in light of the collective bargaining agreement that was being modified, that is the contract between these parties.

When parties agree to a patently ambiguous term, they submit to have any dispute over it resolved by interpretation. That is what courts and arbitrators are *for* in contract cases—to resolve interpretive questions founded on ambiguity. It is when parties agree to terms that reasonably appear to each of them to be unequivocal but are not, cases like that of the ship *Peerless* where the ambiguity is buried, that the possibility of rescission on grounds of mutual misunderstanding, or, the term we prefer, latent ambiguity, arises. A reasonable person in Colfax's position would have realized that its interpretation of the term "4C 60 Press–3 Men" might not coincide with that of the other party or of the tribunal to which a dispute over the meaning of the term would be submitted. It threw the dice, and lost, and that is the end of the case. It cannot gamble on a favorable interpretation and, if that fails, repudiate the contract with no liability. Cf. *Prudential Ins. Co. v. Miller Brewing Co.,* 789 F.2d 1269, 1278 (7th Cir.1986).

[In the remainder of the opinion, the court held that the arbitrator, rather than a court, should determine whether, "under a proper interpretation of the contract, there really was no meeting of the minds over the manning requirements and therefore that the contract should be rescinded after all."]

NOTES

(1) *A Matter of Terminology?* In *Oswald,* the court concluded that "no contract exists." In *Colfax,* the court phrased the question as one of whether the contract should be rescinded. Is there a difference in meaning between these formulations?

(2) *A Matter of Timing?* Eleven years after the *Colfax* decision, its author qualified his views a bit. Judge Posner wrote, "When neither party is blamable, or both parties are equally blamable, for an incurable uncertainty in their contract, it makes economic sense to allow the contract to be rescinded. For in such a case there is no presumption that one party was trying to repudiate a value-maximizing transaction. But the qualification 'equally blamable' is important, because one function of contract enforcement, as we will see, is to penalize a party who negligently creates interpretive uncertainty." In a footnote, though, he added, "But this is in general rather than in every case. As Scott Hemphill has pointed out to me, rescission should not be ordered if the consequence is a windfall to one of the parties, even if the party was blameless for the mistake giving rise to the claim for rescission. In Raffles, the contract was a losing one for the buyers whichever date the cotton was shipped on, so that by rescinding the contract they were able to shift to the seller a loss unrelated to the mutual mistake." Richard Posner, The Law and Economics of Contract Interpretation, 83 Texas L. Rev. 1581, 1591 & n.20 (2005)

SECTION 6. SUPPLEMENTING THE AGREEMENT WITH TERMS SUPPLIED BY LAW: GAP FILLERS, WARRANTIES, AND MANDATORY TERMS

Until now, this chapter has focused on determining the terms of parties' obligations to each other by ascertaining and interpreting their agreement in fact. As we have seen, though, parties do not enter into "complete contingent contracts" in which every eventuality is the subject of an explicit (or even implicit) agreement. Rather, the agreement of the parties is, of necessity, incomplete. Although major issues are resolved by bargaining and, in many cases, issues that recur with some frequency are covered by boilerplate terms, other issues that may give rise to dispute may not be the subject of agreement between the parties.

Why is this the case? For one thing, "if all terms were expressly agreed to, even the simplest contracts would become intolerably long." Farnsworth, Contracts § 7.15 at 495 (4th ed. 2004). Moreover, "businessmen pay more attention to describing the performance in an exchange than to planning for contingencies or defective performance . . ." Stuart Macaulay, Non–Contractual Relations in Business: A Preliminary Study, 28 Am. Soc. Rev. 55, 60 (1963).

(A) FILLING CONTRACTUAL GAPS—GENERALLY

What happens when a dispute arises about which there has been no agreement between the parties, either explicit or implicit (*e.g.*, via course of dealing, usage of trade, etc.)? In such a case, the process of ascertaining and interpreting the parties' agreement that has been the subject of this chapter will not yield an answer to the dispute. Accordingly, the court may need to supply a term to deal with the dispute. This process is usually referred to as "implication."

The process of implication may have one of two bases. The first basis for implication may be the actual expectations of the parties. "If the court is persuaded that the parties shared a common expectation with respect to the omitted case, the court will give effect to that expectation, even though the parties did not reduce it to words." Farnsworth, Contracts § 7.16 at 499 (4th ed. 2004). In the absence of a common expectation, matters are more difficult and courts are faced with a number of theories. Jeremy Bentham argued that the court should implement the bargain the parties would have made had they considered the matter, thus remedying "the shortsightedness of individuals, by doing for them what they would have done for themselves if their imagination had anticipated the march of nature." *A General View of a Complete Code of Laws, in 3 Works of Jeremy Bentham* 191 (J. Bowring ed. 1843). Others have argued against that view, suggesting a different basis for implication. "It might seem that the parties themselves have become so far disembodied spirits that their actual persons should be allowed to rest in peace. In their place there rises the figure of the fair and reasonable man . . . the anthropomorphic conception of justice." Davis Contractors v. Fareham Urban Dist. Council, [1956] A.C. 696, 728 (1956). This is the view generally adopted by the Restatement. See Restatement § 204. More recently, the debate has been augmented by a focus on law and economics. See, *e.g.*, Ian Ayres and Robert Gertner, Filling Gaps in Incomplete Contracts: An Economic Theory of Default Rules, 99 Yale L.J. 87 (1989). Among the other possibilities noted by Ayres and

Gertner is the "penalty default rule . . . designed to give at least one party to the contract an incentive to contract around the default rule and therefore to choose affirmatively the contract provision they prefer." *Id.* at 91.

————

(B) FILLING COMMON CONTRACTUAL GAPS BY STATUTE

Some issues with respect to which parties tend to omit agreement occur with such frequency that the law has developed "off-the-rack" default terms—terms that courts imply in the absence of agreement between the parties—to address those issues. This practice is extensively developed in Article 2 of the Uniform Commercial Code.

Consider the following example: Brown and Silver, located some distance away from each other, have entered into a contract pursuant to which Brown has agreed to buy 1000 grommets from Silver for $100. All the basic terms of the contract have been specified except for the location at which the grommets will be tendered to Brown. On the date for performance under the agreement, each party awaits performance by the other; Brown assumes that Silver will deliver the grommets to Brown, while Silver assumes that Brown will come to Silver's plant to pick up the grommets. When Silver does not deliver, and Brown does not pick up the grommets at Silver's plant, each believes the other is in breach.

Who is right—Brown or Silver? In the absence of actual agreement as to where tender will take place, and of any course of dealing or usage of trade relevant to the issue, the process of ascertaining and interpreting the parties' agreement does not yield an answer as to the location of tender. Because issues of this sort arise with some frequency, the drafters of UCC Article 2 provided "gap fillers" to resolve this and several other gaps as a matter of law.

How does UCC Article 2 resolve the gap in the contract between Brown and Silver described above? See UCC § 2–308. When must Brown pay? See UCC § 2–310.

Avoiding the Gaps. Assume that Buyer and Seller are aware of the resolution of the "tender gap" provided in UCC § 2–308, but would prefer to resolve the matter differently. Are they nonetheless constrained by the rule in that section? Would your answer be different if UCC § 2–308 did not contain the phrase "unless otherwise agreed"? See UCC §§ 1–302(a) and 1–302(c).

How Wide the Gaps? As noted above, major issues in a transaction tend to be resolved by negotiation between the parties leading to an explicit term. Can the law supply a key term when the parties have not bargained with respect to it? For example, assume that Seller and Buyer have agreed to a sale of goods but have failed to reach agreement as to the price of the goods. (Why might they fail to agree with respect to such a key term?) Will the law enforce such an agreement as a contract? If so, what is the contract price? See UCC § 2–305(1).

––––––

(C) GAP FILLING WITH RESPECT TO PRODUCT QUALITY— IMPLIED WARRANTIES IN ARTICLE 2

In contracts for the sale of goods, it is common for the agreement to be silent about whether the goods must meet any particular standard of quality in order to fulfill the seller's obligation under the contract. One way of dealing with such omissions is through the well-known maxim of *caveat emptor*, or "buyer beware." In other words, if the agreement is silent as to product quality, the contract does not impose any minimum standard; if a buyer wishes to contract only for goods that meet a particular standard, he or she must contract for that result. See, *e.g.*, Seixas v. Woods, 2 Cai. R. 48, 2 Am.Dec. 215 (Supreme Court of N.Y. 1804). See generally Walton Hamilton, The Ancient Maxim Caveat Emptor, 40 Yale L.J. 1133 (1931).

More recently, the law has taken a different path. In certain circumstances, the law supplies a default term with respect to the standards that a contacting party's performance must fulfill, even when the parties' agreement could easily be interpreted and enforced without such a term. Such implied terms are default terms in the sense that the parties can contract to the contrary. The term "gap fillers" does not adequately describe them, though, since the agreement could be understood and applied even in the absence of the supplied terms.

Such contract terms implied by law usually are referred to as "implied warranties." While implied warranties are sometimes utilized in a number of different contexts, their most common use appears to be in sale of goods contracts governed by UCC Article 2.

Implied warranties are dealt with extensively in UCC Article 2. The two most important rules are those that provide for an implied warranty of merchantability (UCC § 2–314) and an implied warranty of fitness for particular purpose (UCC § 2–315). In addition, UCC § 2–312 provides for a warranty of title and a warranty against infringement. This following material focuses on the implied warranties of merchantability and fitness.

For each of the Article 2 implied warranties, three questions must be addressed. First, in what circumstances does Article 2 make the warranty part of the contract? Second, what is the content of the warranty? Third, may the parties, if they so desire, conclude a contract that does not contain the warranty?

––––––

THE IMPLIED WARRANTY OF MERCHANTABILITY

When does the implied warranty of merchantability come into existence? According to UCC § 2–314(1), "a warranty that the goods shall be merchantable is implied in a contract for their sale if the seller is a merchant with respect to goods of the kind." This is not the only time that Article 2 applies a special rule for merchants. Indeed, the term appears fourteen times in Article 2. We have already encountered one use of the term in there: Recall that, pursuant to UCC § 2–205, a promise by a merchant to hold an offer open is sometimes irrevocable even when not supported by consideration.

Who qualifies as a merchant? The term "merchant" is defined in UCC § 2–104. Section 2–314 qualifies the term by requiring that the seller be a merchant with respect to goods of the kind that are being sold. Does this mean that a seller of goods can be a merchant without triggering the implied warranty of merchantability?

Problems. Consider the definition of "merchant" in deciding whether a contract to sell goods by each of the following sellers would contain an implied warranty of merchantability:

(1) A retired lawyer no longer has use for her late-model automobile. She enters into a contract to sell the automobile to her next-door neighbor.

(2) A used-car dealer enters into a contract to a sell a used car from his lot to a buyer.

(3) A used-car dealer has just bought a new desk for his office. He has no use for the old desk, so he enters into a contract to sell it to a visitor to his showroom who admired it and asked to buy it.

What is Merchantability? If the seller is a merchant with respect to goods of the kind, the contract for their sale contains a warranty that the goods shall be merchantable. What does it mean for goods to be merchantable? Read UCC § 2–314(2), noting each of the criteria of merchantability. What is the significance of the phrase "at least"?

Most litigation under UCC § 2–314(2) has concerned the second ("fair average quality") and third ("fit for the ordinary purpose for which such goods are used") criteria of merchantability. As courts have frequently noted, "fair average quality" and "fit" set standards that are short of perfection. See, *e.g.*, *In re First Hartford Corp.*, 63 B.R. 479 (Bankr. S.D.N.Y. 1986) ("Satisfaction of this implied warranty entails a finding 'that the article is reasonably fit for the ordinary uses for which it was manufactured and [it] need only be of 'medium quality or goodness' ' . . . In addition, under a section 2–314 analysis, all we need find is that the [item sold] be reasonably fit for its ordinary uses, not that it be perfect.")

A recurring issue is whether the buyer's use of the goods is "ordinary," as illustrated by the next case.

Koken v. Black & Veatch Construction, Inc.

United States Court of Appeals, First Circuit, 2005.
426 F.3d 39.

■ DYK, CIRCUIT JUDGE. On May 17, 1999, a fire occurred during a torch-cutting operation performed as part of a construction project in Maine. A fire blanket had been used to protect the area beneath the welding. The project was owned by Androscoggin Energy LLC ("Androscoggin") and insured by appellant Reliance Insurance Company ("Reliance"). Appellant Black & Veatch Construction, Inc. ("B&V") was the general contractor. Appellees Redco, Inc. ("Redco") and O'Connor Constructors, Inc. ("O'Connor") were subcontractors.

Although the fire was quickly put out through the use of a fire extinguisher, the chemicals in the fire extinguisher caused damage to the generator. The damage to the generator caused an estimated $9 million in repair and delay costs. This incident led to the claims and cross-claims at issue in this case.

At the heart of the case are allegations that appellee Auburn Manufacturing, Inc. ("Auburn") manufactured the fire blanket and appellee Inpro, Inc. ("Inpro") distributed it ... and that the blanket was unfit for its ordinary purpose....

The appellants also brought breach of warranty claims against Auburn and Inpro. Presumably, this refers to the implied warranty of merchantability, though in the four lines in its brief addressing the breach of warranty claim, B&V did not bother to say so. This, in itself, would furnish a basis for rejecting B&V's claim.... Moreover, even were we inclined to overlook the cursory briefing, we would nonetheless affirm the entry of summary judgment. We explain briefly.

Under the Maine version of the Uniform Commercial Code, "a warranty that the goods shall be merchantable is implied in a contract for their sale if the seller is a merchant with respect to goods of that kind." 11 Me.Rev.Stat. Ann. § 2–314(1) (2004). There is no dispute that both Auburn and Inpro are merchants of fire blankets. To be "merchantable," a good must be "fit for the ordinary purposes for which such goods are used." 11 Me.Rev.Stat. Ann. § 2–314(2)(c) (2004).

The first step of the analysis is whether the good was being used for its ordinary purposes. The plaintiff bears the burden of establishing the ordinary purposes of a good. *Binks Mfg. Co. v. Nat'l Presto Indus.*, 709 F.2d 1109, 1121 (7th Cir.1983). "[T]he ordinary purposes for which goods are used ... go to uses which are customarily made of the goods in question." U.C.C. § 2–315 cmt. 2 (2004). Examining the record, it is far from clear that Austin was using the fire blanket for its "ordinary purposes." Although there is no evidence that a fire blanket was inappropriate for cutting operations or horizontal capture generally, there also appears to be no evidence that the fire blanket was appropriate for such use. However, Auburn and Inpro appear to have waived this issue below, when they represented that they do "not contend that the wrong blanket was used for the application described by Perry Austin." Therefore, we must address whether the appellants have carried their burden of producing evidence sufficient to support a finding that the blanket was "unfit" for this purpose.

In *Lorfano* [*v. Dura Stone Steps, Inc.*, 569 A.2d 195 (Me. 1990)], the Supreme Judicial Court held that steps outside a building were fit for their ordinary purpose because they "performed as expected." 569 A.2d at 197. The district court held there was no breach of warranty here because the fire blanket likewise "performed as expected" and was thus fit for its ordinary use. *Recommended Decision* at 25 (citing *Lorfano*, 569 A.2d at 197). B&V responds that since Austin was surprised that the blanket melted,[1] it obviously did not perform as Austin expected. That is true but not on point. The question is not the subjective expectations of the particular user, but the reasonable expectations of an ordinary user or purchaser. *See Venezia v. Miller Brewing Co.*, 626 F.2d 188, 190 (1st Cir.1980) ("Under Massachusetts law the question of fitness for ordinary purposes is largely one centering around reasonable consumer expectations."). For example, in *Alevromagiros v. Hechinger Co.*, 993 F.2d 417 (4th Cir.1993), the Fourth Circuit, applying Virginia law in a product liability and breach of warranty case, held that the standard was objective rather than subjective. An expert witness testified that, "tragically," the industry standards used in the manufacture of the allegedly unfit ladder "did not require triangular braces on the rear portion of a ladder." *Id.* at 420. The court held that this testimony was not sufficient to take the issue of the reasonableness of the standards to the jury, because the expert testified to no customs of the trade, referred to no literature in the field, and did not identify the reasonable expectations of consumers. His comment that the advisory industry standards "tragically" did not require the use of triangular braces does not constitute proof that industry standards are inadequate. It is merely another example of his own subjective opinion.

Id. at 421.

As the district court concluded, there is no testimony in the summary judgment record here (for example, by experts in the field) that the ordinary user reasonably expected a fire blanket to prevent the type of melting that Austin observed. Indeed, there is testimony by others, for example, the foreman Paul Gagnon, that while he expected the blanket to contain sparks and small fires, he thought the blanket performed as they expected and that burn-through holes in blankets were not uncommon.

Because B&V failed to produce evidence establishing the expectations of ordinary users beyond the subjective views of a single individual, summary judgment on the breach of warranty claim was properly granted.

NOTES

(1) *You Get What You Pay For.* This case emphasizes that the question of whether goods are merchantable focuses on their "ordinary" use rather than the

---

1. Austin's testimony may fairly be described as occasionally self-contradictory and lacking in clarity. Viewing the record in the light most favorable to the appellants, the pertinent testimony was as follows:

> Q: So, what you're saying is you were mistaken in your assumption that the blanket would stop a fire?
>
> A: Yes.
>
> Q: But you don't think there's anything wrong with the blanket?

A: Other than the fact that it started melting on me, no.

. . .

> Q: Did the blanket actually start melting?
>
> A: It was bubbling up, black.

. . .

> Q: So, were you pretty surprised to see that?
>
> A: Oh, yes. Very surprised.

use to which a buyer has put them. Why should the warranty be limited in this way? What would be the effect on the price of goods if there were an implied warranty that the goods be fit for whatever purpose to which the buyer puts them? Would buyers who use the goods for their ordinary purposes be happy about that result? As you learn, in the pages that follow, about the implied warranty of fitness for particular purpose and about express warranties, consider how those warranties may help a buyer who intends to use the goods atypically.

(2) *Implied Warranty for Services?* Should there be an implied warranty of merchantability for contracts outside the scope of UCC Article 2? For example, what about situations in which a party is in the business of performing services (*e.g.*, house painting, dentistry, or tutoring) rather than selling goods. Article 2 does not govern contracts entered into by those parties, who might be considered "merchants" with respect to the services they offer. In contracts for the provision of services by such a merchant of services, is there an implied warranty analogous to the implied warranty of merchantability, requiring that the services will be provided in such a way that meets minimum standards and that would pass without objection in that business? Surprisingly, this area is not well-developed, and the cases vary from state to state.

THE IMPLIED WARRANTY OF FITNESS
FOR PARTICULAR PURPOSE

While the implied warranty of merchantability relates to the ordinary use of the goods in question, the law in some circumstances provides protection for a buyer who intends to put goods to non-standard use. This protection, termed the implied warranty of fitness for particular purpose, is found in UCC § 2–315. That section both describes the situations in which the implied warranty of fitness for particular purpose arises and indicates the content of that warranty. With respect to those issues, can you identify the differences between this warranty and the implied warranty of merchantability? Keep those differences in mind as you read the following case.

Lewis v. Mobil Oil Corporation

United States Court of Appeals, Eighth Circuit, 1971.
438 F.2d 500.

■ GIBSON, CIRCUIT JUDGE. In this diversity case the defendant appeals from a judgment entered on a jury verdict in favor of the plaintiff in the amount of $89,250 for damages alleged to be caused by use of defendant's oil.

Plaintiff Lewis has been doing business as a sawmill operator in Cove, Arkansas, since 1956. In 1963, in order to meet competition, Lewis decided to convert his power equipment to hydraulic equipment. He purchased a hydraulic system in May 1963, from a competitor who was installing a new system. The used system was in good operating condition at the time Lewis purchased it. It was stored at his plant until November 1964, while a new mill building was being built, at which time it was installed. Following the installation, Lewis requested from Frank Rowe, a local Mobil oil dealer, the proper hydraulic fluid to operate his machinery. The prior owner of the hydraulic system had used Pacemaker oil supplied by Cities Service, but plaintiff had been a customer of Mobil's for many years and desired to continue with Mobil. Rowe said he didn't know what the proper lubricant for Lewis' machinery was, but would find out. The only information given to Rowe by Lewis was that the machinery was operated by a gear-type pump; Rowe did not request any further information. He apparently contacted a Mobil representative for a recommendation, though this is not entirely clear, and sold plaintiff a product known as Ambrex 810. This is a straight mineral oil with no chemical additives.

Within a few days after operation of the new equipment commenced, plaintiff began experiencing difficulty with its operation. The oil changed color, foamed over, and got hot. The oil was changed a number of times, with no improvement. By late April 1965, approximately six months after operations with the equipment had begun, the system broke down, and a complete new system was installed. The cause of the breakdown was undetermined, but apparently by this time there was some suspicion of the oil being used. Plaintiff Lewis requested Rowe to be sure he was supplying the right kind of oil. Ambrex 810 continued to be supplied.

From April 1965 until April 1967, plaintiff continued to have trouble with the system, principally with the pumps which supplied the pressure. Six new pumps were required during this period, as they continually broke down. During this period, the kind of pump used was a Commercial pump which was specified by the designer of the hydraulic system. The filtration of oil for this pump was by means of a metal strainer, which was cleaned daily by the plaintiff in accordance with the instruction given with the equipment.

In April 1967, the plaintiff changed the brand of pump from a Commercial to a Tyrone pump. The Tyrone pump, instead of using the metal strainer filtration alone, used a disposable filter element in addition. Ambrex 810 oil was also recommended by Mobil and used with this pump, which completely broke down three weeks later. At this point, plaintiff was visited for the first time by a representative of Mobil Oil Corporation, as well as a representative of the Tyrone pump manufacturer.

On the occasion of this visit, May 9, 1967, plaintiff's system was completely flushed and cleaned, a new Tyrone pump installed, and on the pump manufacturer's and Mobil's representative's recommendation, a new oil was used which contained certain chemical additives, principally a "defoamant." Following these changes, plaintiff's system worked satisfactorily up until the time of trial, some two and one-half years later.

Briefly stated, plaintiff's theory of his case is that Mobil supplied him with an oil which was warranted fit for use in his hydraulic system, that the oil was not suitable for such use because it did not contain certain additives, and that it was the improper oil which caused the mechanical breakdowns, with consequent loss to his business. The defendant contends that there was no warranty of fitness, that the breakdowns were caused not by the oil but by improper filtration, and that in any event there can be no recovery of loss of profits in this case.

I. THE EXISTENCE OF WARRANTIES

Defendant maintains that there was no warranty of fitness in this case, that at most there was only a warranty of merchantability and that there was no proof of breach of this warranty, since there was no proof that Ambrex 810 is unfit for use in hydraulic systems generally. We find it unnecessary to consider whether the warranty of merchantability was breached, although there is some proof in the record to that effect, since we conclude that there was a warranty of fitness.

Plaintiff Lewis testified that he had been a longtime customer of Mobil Oil, and that his only source of contact with the company was through Frank Rowe, Mobil's local dealer, with whom he did almost all his business. It was common knowledge in the community that Lewis was converting his sawmill operation into a hydraulic system, Rowe knew this, and in fact had visited his mill on business matters several times during the course of the changeover. When operations with the new machinery were about to commence, Lewis asked Rowe to get him the proper hydraulic fluid. Rowe asked him what kind of a system he had, and Lewis replied it was a Commercial pump type. This was all the information asked or given. Neither Lewis nor Rowe knew what the oil requirements for the system were, and Rowe knew that Lewis knew nothing more specific about his requirements. Lewis also testified that after he began having trouble with his operations, while there were several possible sources of the difficulty the oil was one suspected source, and he several times asked Rowe to be sure he was furnishing him with the right kind.

Rowe's testimony for the most part confirmed Lewis'. It may be noted here that Mobil does not contest Rowe's authority to represent it in this transaction, and therefore whatever warranties may be implied because of the dealings between Rowe and Lewis are attributable to Mobil. Rowe admitted knowing Lewis was converting to a hydraulic system and that Lewis asked him to supply the fluid. He testified that he did not know what should be used and relayed the request to a superior in the Mobil organization, who recommended Ambrex 810. This is what was supplied.

When the first Tyrone pump was installed in April 1967, Rowe referred the request for a proper oil recommendation to Ted Klock, a Mobil engineer. Klock recommended Ambrex 810. When this pump failed a few weeks later, Klock visited the Lewis plant to inspect the equipment. The system was flushed out completely and the oil was changed to DTE–23 and Del Vac Special containing several additives. After this, no further trouble was experienced.

This evidence adequately establishes an implied warranty of fitness. Arkansas has adopted the Uniform Commercial Code's provision for an implied warranty of fitness. . . .

Under this provision of the Code, there are two requirements for an implied warranty of fitness: (1) that the seller have "reason to know" of the use for which the goods are purchased, and (2) that the buyer relies on the seller's expertise in supplying the proper product. Both of these requirements are amply met by the proof in this case. Lewis' testimony, as confirmed by that of Rowe and Klock. shows that the oil was purchased specifically for his hydraulic system, not for just a hydraulic system in general, and that Mobil certainly knew of this specific purpose. It is also clear that Lewis was relying on Mobil to supply him with the proper oil for the system, since at the time of his purchases, he made clear that he didn't know what kind was necessary.

Mobil contends that there was no warranty of fitness for use in his particular system because he didn't specify that he needed an oil with additives, and alternatively that he didn't give them enough information for them to determine that an additive oil was required. However, it seems that the circumstances of this case come directly within that situation described in the first comment to this provision of the Uniform Commercial Code:

'§ 1. Whether or not this warranty arises in any individual case is basically a question of fact to be determined by the circumstances of the contracting. Under this section the buyer need not bring home to the seller actual knowledge of the particular purpose for which the goods are intended or of his reliance on the seller's skill and judgment, if the circumstances are such that the seller has reason to realize the purpose intended or that the reliance exists.' [UCC § 2–315], Comment 1 (1961).

Here Lewis made it clear that the oil was purchased for his system, that he didn't know what oil should be used, and that he was relying on Mobil to supply the proper product. If any further information was needed, it was incumbent upon Mobil to get it before making its recommendation. That it could have easily gotten the necessary information is evidenced by the fact that after plaintiff's continuing complaints, Mobil's engineer visited the plant, and, upon inspection, changed the recommendation that had previously been made.

Additionally, Mobil contends that even if there were an implied warranty of fitness, it does not cover the circumstances of this case because of the abnormal features which the plaintiff's system contained, namely an inadequate filtration system and a capacity to entrain excessive air. There are several answers to this contention. First of all, the contention goes essentially to the question of causation—i.e., whether the damage was caused by a breach of warranty or by some other cause—and not to the existence of a warranty of fitness in the first place. Secondly, assuming that certain peculiarities in the plaintiff's system did exist, the whole point of an implied warranty of fitness is that a product be suitable for a specific purpose, and that a seller should not supply a product which is not so suited. Thirdly, there is no evidence in the record that the plaintiff's system was unique or abnormal in these respects. It operated satisfactorily under the prior owner, and the new system has operated satisfactorily after it was adequately cleaned and an additive type oil used.

NOTES

(1) *Non-Merchant Warrantors?* Must a seller of goods be a merchant for the implied warranty of fitness to become part of the contract? Can you imagine a situation in which a non-merchant is the seller and this warranty arises?

(2) *These Shoes are Made for Walking*. Comment 2 to UCC § 2–315 provides the following guidance for distinguishing the warranty of fitness for *particular* purpose from the warranty of merchantability, which relates to the *ordinary* purposes for which such goods are used: "A 'particular' purpose differs from the ordinary purpose for which the goods are used in that it envisages a specific use by the buyer which is peculiar to the nature of his business whereas the ordinary purposes for which goods are used are those envisaged in the concept of merchantability and go to uses which are customarily made of the goods in question. For example, shoes are generally used for the purpose of walking upon ordinary ground, but a seller may know that a particular pair was selected to be used for climbing mountains."

EXCLUDING IMPLIED WARRANTIES FROM THE CONTRACT

While Article 2 contains detailed rules that determine when an implied warranty is part of a contract, they do not make implied warranties mandatory. Rather, both UCC § 2–314 and UCC § 2–315 refer to UCC § 2–316 for detailed rules that indicate how a contract for sale of goods can be concluded *without* those warranties. Thus, while implied warranties may be considered to be a type of default rule, UCC § 2–316 provides that it takes more than simple agreement to the contrary to prevent them from becoming part of the contract. It is obvious why a seller would prefer that a contract not contain implied warranties, but why might a buyer agree to a contract without them?

UCC Sections 2–316(2) and 2–316(3) contain several routes by which implied warranties can be kept out of a contract. Focus first on UCC § 2–316(2). For each of the implied warranty of merchantability and the implied warranty of fitness, consider whether particular words must be used to exclude the warranty and whether the words of exclusion may be oral or must be in a writing or other record. If the exclusion is accomplished by a writing, is it effective if the words of exclusion are in the "fine print?"

Note that the opening phrases of both UCC § 2–316(2) and UCC § 2–316(3) subordinate the former section to the latter. In what ways does UCC § 2–316(3)(a) qualify or override UCC § 2–316(2)? If the seller states orally that the goods are offered "as is" and the buyer agrees to that, is this sufficient to exclude the implied warranty of fitness? If the "as is" term appears in writing, but is buried in fine print on page 72 of a 96–page agreement, does it suffice to exclude the implied warranty of merchantability?

South Carolina Electric and Gas Co. v. Combustion Engineering, Inc.

Court of Appeals of South Carolina, 1984.
283 S.C. 182, 322 S.E.2d 453.

■ GOOLSBY, JUDGE. The appellant South Carolina Electric and Gas Company (SCE&G) seeks to recover damages in excess of $350,000 that SCE&G

alleges it sustained as a result of a fire that occurred when a flexible metal hose ruptured and sprayed heated fuel oil across the surface of a steam generating boiler at the Arthur Williams Station, a power generating plant owned by SCE&G. The circuit court granted summary judgment in favor of the respondent Combustion Engineering, Inc. (Combustion), which manufactured and sold the boiler and its ancillary equipment to SCE&G, and the respondent Daniel International Corporation (Daniel), which constructed the power plant and installed the boiler as well as the pipes and hoses that connected to it.

SCE&G appeals the grant of summary judgment in favor of Combustion on causes of action for (1) breach of an implied warranty that the boiler unit was fit for a particular purpose, (2) breach of an implied warranty that the boiler unit was merchantable, and (3) negligence in the design of the fuel piping. . . .

I.   Case Against Combustion

A.   Implied Warranties

SCE&G entered into the contract with Combustion for the sale of the boiler unit in early 1970. The sales contract contains an item labeled "WARRANTY," that expressly warrants the equipment to be free "from defects in material and workmanship for a period of one year." Because the boiler became operational on March 18, 1973, and the fire that brought on this litigation occurred over two years later on May 19, 1975, the one-year warranty provision had expired at the time of the fire.

The warranty item also contains a disclaimer of warranties provision. It states that "[t]here are no other warranties, whether expressed or implied, other than title."

The circuit court, in granting Combustion summary judgment on each cause of action alleging a breach of an implied warranty, ruled that the disclaimer excludes an implied warranty of merchantability as well as an implied warranty of fitness for a particular purpose.

SCE&G, however, maintains that Combustion was not entitled to summary judgment. It argues that the disclaimer, as a matter of law, does not exclude the implied warranties alleged in its complaint because the disclaimer does not meet the requirements of Subsection (2) of Section 36–2–316 of the South Carolina Code of Laws (1976) and that a question of fact exists as to whether the disclaimer can come within the exceptions to Subsection (2) permitted by Subsection (3) of that statute.

We agree with SCE&G that the disclaimer does not satisfy the requirements of Subsection (2). First of all, the disclaimer nowhere mentions the word "merchantability," as it must do under Subsection (2) to exclude an implied warranty of merchantability.

Further, the written language of disclaimer, as a matter of law, is not "conspicuous," as Subsection (2) requires it to be to exclude an implied warranty of fitness for a particular purpose as well as an implied warranty of merchantability. Indeed, the written agreement is twenty-two typewritten pages in length and is mostly single-spaced. The disclaimer itself appears on page 17 of the agreement in the last sentence of a two-paragraph item. It is indistinctive both as to color and as to type. *See* S.C.Code of Laws § 36–1–210(10) (1976) ("A ... clause is conspicuous when it is so written that a reasonable person against whom it is to operate ought to have noticed it.... Language in the body of a form is 'conspicuous' if it is in larger or other contrasting type or color"); *Billings v. Joseph Harris Company, Inc.,* 220 S.E.2d 361 (1975); *Chrysler Corp. v. Wilson Plumbing Company, Inc.,* 208 S.E.2d 321 (1974).

Moreover, the item containing the disclaimer is misleading in that it is suggestive of "a grant of a warranty rather than a disclaimer" because the heading of the item, printed in underlined capital letters, simply reads "*WARRANTY.*" *Hartman v. Jensen's Inc.,* 289 S.E.2d 648 (1982).

But the question remains concerning whether a genuine issue of material fact exists as to whether the disclaimer, as the circuit court found, falls within the exception prescribed by Subsection (3)(a). Subsection (3)(a) permits, as do Subsections (3)(b) and (c), the exclusion of implied warranties when "the circumstances surrounding the transaction are in themselves sufficient to call the buyer's attention to the fact that no implied warranties are made or that a certain implied warranty is excluded." S.C.Code of Laws § 36–2–316 official comment 6 (1976).

In support of its motion for summary judgment, Combustion submitted the affidavit of Kurt W. Johnson that identified several documents exchanged between Combustion and SCE&G relative to the purchase by SCE&G of the boiler from Combustion. The first document, dated August 15, 1968 and entitled "Proposal No. 16268–E," originated with Combustion. It included the disclaimer at issue here. Five months later on January 31, 1969, SCE&G wrote Combustion stating that its August 1968 proposal was unacceptable in certain respects. SCE&G advised Combustion that it required that any purchase order filled by Combustion be subject to certain prescribed conditions. One condition was that Combustion agree "to be bound in relation to [its] equipment by the ... warranties implied by the laws of the State of South Carolina."

Combustion responded to SCE&G's letter on February 19, 1969, and informed SCE&G that it could not accept the condition relating to implied warranties. Combustion insisted that it "have a limitation on the warranty period and a limitation on the remedy for breach of any warranty, expressed or implied." On February 21, 1969, SCE&G replied to Combustion's letter of two days before and advised Combustion that it agreed that the "warranties implied by [the] laws of the State of South Carolina shall be limited" to the warranty item included in the original proposal.

The parties differ concerning whether the correspondence mentioned above forms part of the contract and whether it constitutes evidence extrinsic to the contract. SCE&G maintains that the correspondence is not part of the contract and that consideration of it by the circuit court to determine whether the disclaimer is effective demonstrates conclusively that the disclaimer is ambiguous. SCE&G relies on the settled rule that the intention of the parties to an ambiguous contract is a question of fact for the jury to determine and is not a question that a court should decide on summary judgment. *See Wheeler v. Globe & Rutgers Fire Insurance Co.*, 118 S.E. 609 (1923) ("where a contract is not clear, or is ambiguous and capable of one or more constructions, what the parties really intended, as a matter of fact, should be submitted to a jury").

We need not decide whether the correspondence forms part of the contract because we think that the language of the disclaimer itself is unambiguous. In plain language, the disclaimer excludes all warranties other than the express one-year warranty and the warranty of title.

Although we do not use the correspondence to resolve an ambiguity in the language employed by the disclaimer, we do consider the correspondence to determine whether the language of disclaimer was unbargained for and unexpected by SCE&G, the buyer. If the evidentiary material presented in connection with Combustion's motion for summary judgment shows that no genuine issue of fact exists as to whether the language of disclaimer was unbargained for and unexpected and that, as a matter of fact, the language was bargained for and expected, SCE & G could not rightly claim, irrespective of the requirements of Subsection (2), that the language does not exclude the two implied warranties asserted by Combustion. *See* S.C.Code of Laws § 36–2–316 official comment 1 (1976) (Subsections (2) and (3) designed to protect the buyer from "unexpected and unbargained language of disclaimer"). In such a case, summary judgment for Combustion would be entirely proper.

As we view the record, Combustion was entitled to summary judgment as a matter of law on the causes of action alleging breaches of implied warranties of merchantability and fitness for a particular purpose....

The correspondence exchanged between Combustion and SCE&G relating to the warranty item and submitted in support of Combustion's motion for summary judgment discloses that the language of disclaimer included in the warranty item came as no surprise to SCE&G and that SCE&G in fact bargained with Combustion over a period of seven months concerning it. SCE&G makes no factual showing to the contrary. As the correspondence indicates, the disclaimer, which is written in simple language, was subjected to detailed review by SCE&G and was agreed upon by SCE&G only after Combustion refused to accept SCE&G's condition that Combustion be bound by the "warranties implied by the laws of the State of South Carolina."

In addition, both corporations are commercially sophisticated and possess relatively equal bargaining strength. The sheer size of the transaction itself ($12,139,786.00) and the length of the negotiations (approximately nineteen months) suggest as much. As in *AMF Incorporated v. Computer Automation, Inc.*, 573 F.Supp. 924, 930 (S.D. Ohio 1983), which also involved "commercially sophisticated businesses," it would strain "credulity to hold that a business like [SCE&G] was not, or should not have been, aware of the language disclaiming implied warranties."

We therefore hold that an effective disclaimer of implied warranties under Subsection (3)(a) was shown; thus, the language of the disclaimer at issue here was effective notwithstanding its failure to satisfy the requirements of Subsection (2). *See Tennessee Carolina Transportation Inc. v. Strick Corp.*, 196 S.E.2d 711 (1973) (*dictum* that actual awareness by a nonconsumer buyer of a disclaimer prior to entering into a sales contract and possession of substantially equivalent bargaining power satisfies purpose of "conspicuous" requirement); *cf. Country Clubs, Inc. v. Allis-Chalmers Manufacturing Co.*, 430 F.2d 1394, 1397 (6th Cir.1970) (exclusion of implied warranty of merchantability upheld under Subsection 3(c) where course of dealing indicated buyer "had acquiesced in the limited warranty provision" and sale involved experienced businessmen dealing at arm's length).

NOTE

Inspection. Note that UCC § 2–316(3)(b) provides an additional circumstance in which implied warranties do not become part of the contract—when a buyer has inspected goods before entering into a contract, there are no implied warranties with respect to defects that ought to have been revealed by inspection. Why do you think that the statute contains this rule?

PROBLEM

Latent Defect. NAK sold Garlock industrial oil seal products that caused significant oil leakage problems in Garlock's equipment. It is uncontested that such oil seal products were not merchantable. Before entering into the contract, NAK sent samples of the oil seal products and Garlock tested them to ensure that they were the proper configuration and dimension, and otherwise met specification requirements. Garlock did the normal tests designated by the American Society for Testing and Materials (ASTM) to check the basic physical properties of the compound of which the seals were made. The seals met specifications and passed the standard ASTM tests. Garlock did not do any functional testing of the samples. If the defect in NAK's products was one that would not be detected by the ASTM tests, is there a warranty of merchantability with respect to that defect? See Garlock Sealing Technologies, LLC v. NAK Sealing Technologies Corp., 56 Cal. Rptr.3d 177 (Cal. App. 2007).

OTHER LIMITS ON EXCLUDING IMPLIED WARRANTIES

Courts and legislatures have, in certain circumstances, limited the ability of sellers to limit or exclude implied warranties, even when the requirements of UCC § 2–316 have been fulfilled. Consider the following materials.

Henningsen v. Bloomfield Motors, Inc.

Supreme Court of New Jersey, 1960.
32 N.J. 358, 161 A.2d 69.

[Claus Henningsen purchased a new Plymouth automobile from Bloomfield Motors. His wife Helen was injured when the steering mechanism failed ten days after it had been delivered. They both sued Bloomfield Motors and the manufacturer, Chrysler Corporation, for breach of an implied warranty of merchantability imposed by the Uniform Sales Act. The defendants contended that the warranty had been disclaimed, as permitted by the Act, and relied upon a provision contained on the back of the purchase contract, among eight and a half inches of fine print, which purported to limit liability for breach of warranty to replacement of defective parts for the period of 90 days after delivery or 4,000 miles of driving, whichever was shorter.[a] The provisions on the back of the purchase contract were referred to on the front, above the signature lines, in language printed in six point type, as follows, although most of the language on the front was in twelve point type:[b]

"The front and back of this Order comprise the entire agreement affecting this purchase and no other agreement or understanding of any nature concerning same has been made or entered into, or will be recognized. I hereby certify that no credit has been extended to me for the purchase of this motor vehicle except as appears in writing on the face of this agreement.

"I have read the matter printed on the back hereof and agree to it as a part of this order the same as if it were printed above my signature. I certify that I am 21 years of age, or older, and hereby acknowledge receipt of a copy of this order."

From judgment for the plaintiffs the defendant appealed.][c]

■ Francis, J. ... In assessing [the disclaimer's] significance we must keep in mind the general principle that, in the absence of fraud, one who does not choose to read a contract before signing it, cannot later relieve himself of his burdens.... And in applying that principle, the basic tenet of freedom of competent parties to contract is a factor of importance.... The traditional contract is the result of free bargaining of parties who are brought together by the play of the market, and who meet each other on a footing of approximate economic equality. In such a society there is no danger that freedom of contract will be a threat to the social order as a

---

a. "It is expressly agreed that there are no warranties, express or implied, made by either the dealer or the manufacturer on the motor vehicle, chassis, or parts furnished hereunder except as follows:

The manufacturer warrants each new motor vehicle (including original equipment placed thereon by the manufacturer except tires), chassis or parts manufactured by it to be free from defects in material or workmanship under normal use and service. Its obligation under this warranty being limited to making good at its factory any part or parts thereof which shall, within ninety (90) days after delivery of such vehicle to the original purchaser or before such vehicle has been driven 4,000 miles, whichever event shall first occur, be returned to it with transportation charges prepaid and which its examination shall disclose to its satisfaction to have been thus defective; this warranty being expressly in lieu of all other warranties expressed or implied, and all other obligations or liabilities on its part, and it neither assumes nor authorizes any other person to assume for it any other liability in connection with the sale of its vehicles...."

b. The cases in this book are set in 10 point type, the notes in 9 point type, and the footnotes in 8 point type. To a considerable extent, however, the readability of type depends not only on its size but also upon the width of the column.

c. The case is severely edited; the official report fills sixty pages.

whole. But in present-day commercial life the standardized mass contract has appeared. It is used primarily by enterprises with strong bargaining power and position. "The weaker party, in need of the goods or services, is frequently not in a position to shop around for better terms, either because the author of the standard contract has a monopoly (natural or artificial) or because all competitors use the same clauses. His contractual intention is but a subjection more or less voluntary to terms dictated by the stronger party, terms whose consequences are often understood in a vague way, if at all." Kessler, "Contracts of Adhesion—Some Thoughts About Freedom of Contract," 43 Colum.L.Rev. 629, 632 (1943).... Such standardized contracts have been described as those in which one predominant party will dictate its law to an undetermined multiple rather than to an individual. They are said to resemble a law rather than a meeting of the minds. Siegelman v. Cunard White Star, 221 F.2d 189, 206 (2 Cir.1955)....

The warranty before us is a standardized form designed for mass use. It is imposed upon the automobile consumer. He takes it or leaves it, and he must take it to buy an automobile. No bargaining is engaged in with respect to it. In fact, the dealer through whom it comes to the buyer is without authority to alter it; his function is ministerial—simply to deliver it. The form warranty is not only standard with Chrysler but, as mentioned above, it is the uniform warranty of the Automobile Manufacturers Association. Members of the Association are: General Motors, Inc., Ford, Chrysler, Studebaker–Packard, American Motors (Rambler), Willys Motors, Checker Motors Corp., and International Harvester Company. Automobile Facts and Figures (1958 Ed., Automobile Manufacturers Association) 69. Of these companies, the "Big Three" (General Motors, Ford, and Chrysler) represented 93.5% of the passenger-car production for 1958 and the independents 6.5%. Standard & Poor (Industrial Surveys, Autos, Basic Analysis, June 25, 1959) 4109. And for the same year the "Big Three" had 86.72% of the total passenger vehicle registrations. Automotive News, 1959 Almanac (Slocum Publishing Co., Inc.) p. 25.

The gross inequality of bargaining position occupied by the consumer in the automobile industry is thus apparent. There is no competition among the car makers in the area of the express warranty. Where can the buyer go to negotiate for better protection? Such control and limitation of his remedies are inimical to the public welfare and, at the very least, call for great care by the courts to avoid injustice through application of strict common-law principles of freedom of contract....

Although the courts, with few exceptions, have been most sensitive to problems presented by contracts resulting from gross disparity in buyer-seller bargaining positions, they have not articulated a general principle condemning, as opposed to public policy, the imposition on the buyer of a skeleton warranty as a means of limiting the responsibility of the manufacturer. They have endeavored thus far to avoid a drastic departure from age-old tenets of freedom of contract by adopting doctrines of strict construction, and notice and knowledgeable assent by the buyer to the attempted exculpation of the seller.... Accordingly to be found in the cases are statements that disclaimers and the consequent limitation of liability will not be given effect if "unfairly procured," . . .; if not brought to the buyer's attention and he was not made understandingly aware of it . . . or if not clear and explicit. . . .

The rigid scrutiny which the courts give to attempted limitations of warranties and of the liability that would normally flow from a transaction is not limited to the field of sales of goods. Clauses on baggage checks restricting the liability of common carriers for loss or damage in transit are not enforceable unless the limitation is fairly and honestly negotiated and understandingly entered into. . . . The same holds true in cases of such limitations on parcel check room tickets . . . and on storage warehouse receipts . . .; on automobile parking lot or garage tickets or claim checks . . .; as to exculpatory clauses in leases releasing a landlord of apartments in a multiple dwelling house from all liability for negligence where inequality of bargaining exists. . . .

It is true that the rule governing the limitation of liability cases last referred to is generally applied in situations said to involve services of a public or semi-public nature. Typical, of course, are the public carrier or storage or parking lot cases. . . . But in recent times the books have not been barren of instances of its application in private contract controversies. . . .

Basically, the reason a contracting party offering services of a public or *quasi*-public nature has been held to the requirements of fair dealing, and, when it attempts to limit its liability, of securing the understanding consent of the patron or consumer, is because members of the public generally have no other means of fulfilling the specific need represented by the contract. Having in mind the situation in the automobile industry as detailed above, and particularly the fact that the limited warranty extended by the manufacturers is a uniform one, there would appear to be no just reason why the principles of all of the cases set forth should not chart the course to be taken here.

It is undisputed that the president of the dealer with whom Henningsen dealt did not specifically call attention to the warranty on the back of the purchase order. . . . The words "warranty" or "limited warranty" did not even appear in the fine print above the place for signature, and a jury might well find that the type of print itself was such as to promote lack of attention rather than sharp scrutiny. . . .

But there is more than this. Assuming that a jury might find that the fine print referred to reasonably served the objective of directing a buyer's attention to the warranty on the reverse side, and, therefore, that he should be charged with awareness of its language, can it be said that an ordinary layman would realize what he was relinquishing in return for what he was being granted? . . . Any ordinary layman of reasonable intelligence, looking at the phraseology, might well conclude that Chrysler was agreeing to replace defective parts and perhaps replace anything that went wrong because of defective workmanship during the first 90 days or 4,000 miles of operation, but that he would not be entitled to a new car. It is not unreasonable to believe that the entire scheme being conveyed was a proposed remedy for physical deficiencies in the car.

In the context of this warranty, only the abandonment of all sense of justice would permit us to hold that, as a matter of law, the phrase "its obligation under this warranty being limited to making good at its factory any part or parts thereof" signifies to an ordinary reasonable person that he is relinquishing any personal injury claim that might flow from the use of a defective automobile. Such claims are nowhere mentioned. The draftsmanship is reflective of the care and skill of the Automobile Manufacturers Association in undertaking to avoid warranty obligations without drawing too much attention to its effort in that regard....

The task of the judiciary is to administer the spirit as well as the letter of the law. On issues such as the present one, part of that burden is to protect the ordinary man against the loss of important rights through what, in effect, is the unilateral act of the manufacturer. The status of the automobile industry is unique. Manufacturers are few in number and strong in bargaining position. In the matter of warranties on the sale of their products, the Automobile Manufacturers Association has enabled them to present a united front. From the standpoint of the purchaser, there can be no arms length negotiating on the subject. Because his capacity for bargaining is so grossly unequal, the inexorable conclusion which follows is that he is not permitted to bargain at all. He must take or leave the automobile on the warranty terms dictated by the maker. He cannot turn to a competitor for better security.

Public policy is a term not easily defined. Its significance varies as the habits and needs of a people may vary. It is not static and the field of application is an ever increasing one. A contract, or a particular provision therein, valid in one era may be wholly opposed to the public policy of another.... Courts keep in mind the principle that the best interests of society demand that persons should not be unnecessarily restricted in their freedom to contract. But they do not hesitate to declare void as against public policy contractual provisions which clearly tend to the injury of the public in some way....

[Affirmed.]

NOTES

(1) *Warranties under Article 2.* The UCC became effective in New Jersey in 1963. If Henningsen had bought his Plymouth in 1964, what result under the Code? See UCC § 2–316(2). See Matthews v. Ford Motor Co., 479 F.2d 399 (4th Cir.1973). See also UCC § 2–719(2), which provides that "where circumstances cause an exclusive or limited remedy to fail of its essential purpose, remedy may be had as provided in [the UCC]."

(2) *Protection and Overprotection.* Within a few years after *Henningsen*, manufacturers began to jockey for competitive advantage by extending and advertising their warranties. "The experience proved beyond doubt that consumers do care enough about warranties to make their selections felt competitively *if they are sufficiently informed to do so.*" David Slawson, Standard Form Contracts, 84 Harv.L.Rev. 529, 548 (1971). More recently, car buyers have been offered still further protection against defects in the form of term contracts for repair sold for a separate price. Do such market developments undercut the court's reasoning in *Henningsen*?

Do consumers ever buy too much protection against risk? For some period of time, car-rental companies required their customers to purchase expensive "supplemental liability protection" ("SLP") which typically duplicated the insurance coverage most renters had under their existing car, home, life or health insurance policies. In 2003, the New York Attorney General's Office settled a suit brought against the nation's largest car rental company for "deceptive insurance charges." The company agreed to pay $2,000,000 in restitution to tens of thousands of customers who purchased unnecessary liability insurance. See Office of Attorney General Press Release, http://www.oag.state.ny.us/press/2003/jul/jul21b_03.html[a]. A New York statute now requires rental vehicle and wireless communications counters to "make readily available to the prospective customer" information disclosing that SLP policies may provide a duplication of coverage the customer already has under other policies. See NY C.L.S. Ins. § 2131(e)(2)(B).

(3) *Federal Protection for Consumers.* In the case of contracts to sell goods to consumers, federal law limits the ability of sellers to disclaim implied warranties. Section 108 of the Magnuson–Moss Warranty Act (15 U.S.C. §§ 2301–2312) provides, in relevant part, that:

> (a) No supplier [of consumer products] may disclaim or modify (except as provided in subsection (b) of this section) any implied warranty to a consumer with respect to such consumer product if (1) such supplier makes any written warranty to the consumer with respect to such consumer product or (2) at the time of sale, or within 90 days thereafter, such supplier enters into a service contract with the consumer which applies to such consumer product.

> (b) For purposes of this [Act] . . . implied warranties may be limited in duration to the duration of a written warranty of reasonable duration, if such limitation is conscionable and is set forth in clear and unmistakable language and prominently displayed on the face of the warranty.

> (c) A disclaimer, modification, or limitation made in violation of this section shall be ineffective for purposes of . . . State law.

(D) EXPRESS WARRANTIES

Recall the *Bayliner* case at page 4 above, which introduced the concept of express warranties governed by UCC § 2–313. Conceptually, express warranties differ from implied warranties in that they are the product of bargaining between the parties rather than implication by law. Comment 1 to UCC § 2–313 states that express warranties "rest on 'dickered' aspects of the individual bargain." As such, express warranties may be considered to be merely terms of the agreement between the parties, not worthy of extensive discussion. Nonetheless, UCC § 2–313 contains detailed provisions about how such terms become part of the contract.

Under UCC § 2–313(1), an express warranty may be created in any of three ways. First, an affirmation of fact or promise made by the seller with respect to the goods creates a warranty that they will conform to that affirmation or promise. UCC § 2–313(1)(a). Second, a description of the

a.   Last visited June 4, 2008.

goods creates a warranty that they will conform to the description. UCC § 2–313(1)(b). Third, a sample or model of the goods creates a warranty that the "whole of the goods" will conform to the sample or model. UCC § 2–313(1)(c).

Three aspects of UCC § 2–313 are noteworthy. First, there is no requirement that the buyer have relied on the affirmation of fact, promise, description, sample, or model in order for it to be part of the contract, but it must have been part of the "basis of the bargain." That phrase has been the subject of extensive litigation. See cases collected at 1 Hawkland UCC Series § 2–313:5 (2008).

Second, "it is not necessary to the creation of an express warranty that the seller use formal words such as 'warrant' or 'guarantee' or that he have a specific intention to make a warranty ..." UCC § 2–313(2). Thus, a seller who has made an affirmation of fact, promise, or the like with respect to the goods cannot escape the conclusion that there is an express warranty merely by claiming that he did not intend to incur that obligation.

Third, "an affirmation merely of the value of the goods or a statement purporting to be merely the seller's opinion or commendation of the goods does not create a warranty." UCC § 2–313(2). This rule, sometimes known as the "puffing" exception or the "sales talk" exception, is attributed to "common experience [that] discloses that some statements or predictions cannot fairly be viewed as entering into the bargain." We have encountered this rule already in the *Bayliner* case in Chapter One.

_____

(E) SUPPLEMENTING THE CONTRACT WITH MANDATORY TERMS—GOOD FAITH

It is now well-established in American law that virtually all contracts contain an obligation of good faith (or "good faith and fair dealing") in their performance and enforcement. For example, UCC § 1–304 provides that "Every contract or duty within [the Uniform Commercial Code] imposes an obligation of good faith in its performance and enforcement." Similarly, Restatement § 205 provides that "Every contract imposes upon each party a duty of good faith and fair dealing in its performance and its enforcement."

What is "good faith"? The Uniform Commercial Code defines the term as "honesty in fact and the observance of reasonable commercial standards of fair dealing." UCC § 1–201(b)(20). The first portion of that definition is sometimes referred to as the "subjective test" of good faith, while the second portion is sometimes referred to as the "objective test." It should be noted that until the recent revision of UCC Article 1, the definition of "good faith" in that Article referred only to "honesty in fact." See former UCC § 1–201(19). Former UCC § 2–103(1)(b), however, imposed the higher standard, including observance of reasonable commercial standards of fair dealing, on merchants.

The obligation to perform and enforce in good faith is present even if the parties have not bargained for it. Moreover, unlike gap fillers and other default terms, the parties cannot, by agreement, prevent the obligation from becoming part of their contract. See UCC § 1–302(b). Thus, the obligation of good faith is said to be a mandatory term of a contract. In contracts governed by the Uniform Commercial Code, however, there is explicit authorization for the parties to determine by agreement "the standards by which the performance of [the obligation of good faith in the performance and enforcement of the contract] is to be measured if those standards are not manifestly unreasonable." *Id.*

Because the obligation of good faith is one that relates to performance and enforcement of a contract, consideration of the content of that obligation is deferred until the next chapter, which addresses legal doctrines that police the performance of contracts by the parties.

CHAPTER 6

LIMITS ON THE BARGAIN AND ITS PERFORMANCE

Let us now assume that two parties have successfully bargained with one another, and a deal has been struck. Are there circumstances where the law may still refuse to enforce the deal not out of concern about the bargaining process but rather about its content? Are there limits to the now familiar rule that "[p]arties of sufficient mental capacity for the management of their own business have the right to make their own bargains?" Hardesty v. Smith, 3 Ind. 39 (1851). To answer the question, we return to the matter of policing and look at three areas in which the law has found it appropriate to place limits on the *substance* of a bargain and, through the obligation of "good faith," also on its *performance*.

The first limitation treats unfairness in the terms of a bargain under the common law. That there are limiting principles to prevent the routine enforcement of unequal bargains might come as something of a surprise. The core idea of consideration is the *fact* of a bargain, not its content. "If the requirement of a consideration is met, there is no additional requirement of ... equivalence in the values exchanged." Restatement § 79(b). Yet although the law contains an implicit judgment that a promise should be enforced whether or not something of equal value was given for it, courts have developed a variety of common law policing measures, or "conventional controls," as we have called them, to limit certain bargains marked by an inequality of exchange. These are explored in Section 1.

The second limiting principle is the relatively modern doctrine of unconscionability, which denies enforcement to a contract, or to a particular term within a contract, that is found to be oppressive. Unconscionability encompasses some of the same procedural concerns about the bargaining process considered in Chapter 4 on Policing, but it also has a substantive dimension directed at the inequality of the exchange. Section 2 considers the types of contracts in which oppressive terms sometimes, though not always, manifest themselves—standard form contracts and adhesion contracts. What factors do courts consider in determining whether a contract is procedurally or substantively unconscionable? Does one (or more) unconscionable term taint the entire agreement? The materials in Section 3 explore these and other questions and others in relation to commercial, consumer, and employment agreements.

In addition to limits imposed on the content of a bargain, the law insists on certain decencies in how the parties carry out their contractual obligations. These derive from an obligation developed in the common law that parties must perform in good faith. The Restatement asserts a "duty of good faith and fair dealing" in contract performance and enforcement. See Restatement § 205. The Uniform Commercial Code imposes a similar "obligation of good faith." See UCC § 1–304. Section 4 takes a closer look at how the concept of good faith has been defined and applied.

The final section of this chapter, Public Policy, deals with bargains challenged not because they threaten the interests of individual parties, but because they threaten the interests of the public at large. Here courts are concerned with contracts that violate specific laws, like murder or corruption, and also with those that contravene the more amorphous category of "public policy." This section addresses these specific examples and it also reflects on more general questions of public policy. To some extent, of course, the topic has already been introduced. Impositions on the terms of performance of a contract based, for example, on concerns about good faith are themselves expressions of public policy. How do courts determine what counts as "public policy"? What sources do they look to in order to refuse enforcement of a contract with which the parties themselves may be perfectly content? As with other policing measures, here too hard questions arise about coordinating judicial and legislative functions in defining and giving effect to public policy.

SECTION 1.   UNFAIRNESS

The function of policing bargains was traditionally a specialty of equity courts, which were empowered to grant specific relief. See the discussion at pp. 583–584 above. A decree of specific performance was not a matter of right in the same sense as was an award of damages, and was therefore often denied in cases when the bargain was procured by sharp practice, or when the exchange appeared highly disproportionate. Enforceability was also regularly denied when the bargain was affected by mistake, a subject considered in Chapter 8.

By contrast, in cases "at law" courts lacked the inherent discretion to weigh equities, and resorted to more established methods of policing, such as finding that a particularly overbearing provision conflicts with an established public policy. Courts have also manipulated the doctrine of consideration to serve the ideal of fairness, including determinations about whether or not there was any "bargain" at all.

In reading the three cases that follow, consider whether certainty regarding the enforcement of promises in commercial affairs has been overvalued or undervalued. Keep in mind the suggestion that "There does come a point where the additional costs of having personalized transactions may be too great; a little injustice may be a social good." Arthur Leff, Injury, Ignorance and Spite—The Dynamics of Coercive Collection, 80 Yale L.J. 1, 42 (1970). See if you agree. Undoubtedly Leff meant not that injustice is a good in itself, but that in the context of contract law, it might be an acceptable price to pay for such values as certainty.

McKinnon v. Benedict

Supreme Court of Wisconsin, 1968.
38 Wis.2d 607, 157 N.W.2d 665.

[In 1960 Roderick McKinnon, the owner of a thousand acre property on Mamie Lake, Wisconsin, assisted Mr. and Mrs. Roy Benedict in buying a resort known as Bent's Camp. The camp consisted of a lodge and some cabins on about 80 acres that were enclosed by the lake and by McKinnon's property. McKinnon promised some help in getting business and in other minor respects, but his principal contribution was in making a loan of $5,000. The Benedicts used the advance as part of a down payment on a land purchase contract with the previous owners of the camp. In exchange, the Benedicts promised McKinnon to cut no trees between their camp and his property, and to make no improvements "closer to [his] property than the present buildings." The term of these restrictions was 25 years. They did not affect all the resort tract, but did affect all the most desirable portion.

The Benedicts' resort business did not prosper although they repaid the loan to McKinnon in about seven months. In 1964 they decided to add a trailer park and tent camp, and in the fall and following spring they invested some $9,000 in bulldozing and installing utilities. The summer of 1965 brought McKinnon from Arizona, where he spent the winters, and also brought a suit by McKinnon against the Benedicts seeking to enjoin them from continuing with their projected improvements. The trial court granted the injunction and the Benedicts appealed.]

■ HEFFERNAN, JUSTICE. . . . No action at law has been commenced for damages by virtue of the breach of the restrictions; and, in fact, the plaintiffs in their complaint claim that they have no adequate remedy at law. [The court expounded some "ancient principles of equity," and quoted the Restatement of Contracts § 367.ᵃ]

Coupled with the general equitable principle that contracts that are oppressive will not be enforced in equity is the principle of public policy that restrictions on the use of land "are not favored in the law" (Mueller v. Schier (1926), 189 Wis. 70, 82, 205 N.W. 912, 916), and that restrictions and prohibitions as to the use of real estate should be resolved, if a doubt exists, in favor of the free use of the property. Stein v. Endres Home Builders, Inc. (1938) 228 Wis. 620, 629, 280 N.W. 316. . . .

The great hardship sought to be imposed upon the Benedicts is apparent. What was the consideration in exchange for this deprivation of use? The only monetary consideration was the granting of a $5,000 loan, interest free, for a period of seven months. The value of this money for that period of time, if taken at the same interest rate as the 5 percent used on the balance of the land contract, is approximately $145; and it should be

---

a. Specific enforcement of a contract may be refused if

(a) The consideration for it is grossly inadequate or its terms are otherwise unfair, or

(b) its enforcement will cause unreasonable or disproportionate hardship or loss to the defendant or to third persons, or

(c) it was induced by some sharp practice, misrepresentation, or mistake.

noted that this was not an unsecured loan, since McKinnon took a mortgage on the cottage property of the Benedicts in Michigan. In addition, McKinnon stated that he would "help you try" to reach a solution of the problem posed by Mrs. Vair's occupancy of one of the cottages on a fifty-year lease at $5 per year. His one attempt, as stated above, was a failure; and McKinnon's promise to generate business resulted in an occupancy by only one group for less than a week. For this pittance and these feeble attempts to help with the operational problems of the camp, the Benedicts have sacrificed their right to make lawful and reasonable use of their property.

In oral argument it was pointed out that the value of the $5,000 loan could not be measured in terms of the interest value of the money, since, without this advance, Benedict would have been unable to purchase the camp at all. To our mind, this is evidence of the fact that Benedict was not able to deal at arm's length with McKinnon, for his need for these funds was obviously so great that he was willing to enter into a contract that results in gross inequities. Lord Chancellor Northington said "necessitous men are not, truly speaking, free men." Vernon v. Bethell (1762), 2 Eden 110, 113.

We find that the inadequacy of consideration is so gross as to be unconscionable and a bar to the plaintiffs' invocation of the extraordinary equitable powers of the court.

While there is no doubt that there are benefits from this agreement to McKinnon, they are more than outweighed by the oppressive terms that would be imposed upon the Benedicts. McKinnon testified that he and his wife spend only the summer months on their property. Undoubtedly, these are the months when it is most important that there be no disruption of the natural beauty or the quiet and pleasant enjoyment of the property, nevertheless, there was testimony that the trailer camp could not be seen from the McKinnon home, nor could the campsite be seen during the summer months of the year, when the leaves were on the trees. Thus, the detriment of which the McKinnons complain, that would be cognizable in an equity action, is minimal,[1] while the damage done to the Benedicts is severe.

Considering all the factors—the inadequacy of the consideration, the small benefit that would be accorded the McKinnons, and the oppressive conditions imposed upon the Benedicts—we conclude that this contract failed to meet the test of reasonableness that is the *sine qua non* of the enforcement of rights in an action in equity.

5A Corbin, *Contracts*, sec. 1164, p. 219, points out that, although a contract is harsh, oppressive, and unconscionable, it may nevertheless be enforceable at law; but, in the discretion of the court, equitable remedies will not be enforced against one who suffers from such harshness and oppression.

---

1. McKinnon testified that the value of his property had depreciated in the amount of $50,000. That testimony was properly admissible, but its probative value was slight, especially since plaintiff's expert real estate witness stated that he was unable to testify to the amount of the depreciated value.

A fair reading of the transcript indicates no sharp practice, dishonesty, or overreaching on the part of McKinnon. However, there was a wide disparity between the business experience of the parties. McKinnon was a man of stature in the legal field, an investment counsellor, a former officer of a major corporation, and had held posts of responsibility with the United States government, while, insofar as the record shows, Benedict was a retail jeweler and a man of limited financial ability. He no doubt overvalued the promises of McKinnon to assist in getting the operation "well organized" and to solve the lease problem and to "generate business." These factors, in view of Benedict's financial inability to enter into an armslength transaction, may be explanatory of the reason for the agreement, but the agreement viewed even as of the time of its execution was unfair and based upon inadequate consideration. We, therefore, have no hesitancy in denying the plaintiffs the equitable remedy of injunction. . . .

[Reversed.]

NOTES

(1) *Questions.* If the Benedicts had begun their new business immediately after making the agreement of 1960, would the court have given McKinnon the relief that he sought? May the Benedicts now bulldoze on their property and make improvements wherever they please?

In denying the plaintiffs relief, the court took note of a public policy disfavoring restrictions on the use of land, citing a 1926 case. Are there counterveiling public policies that might be invoked today?

(2) *Damages at Law.* In denying specific performance to a claimant, the courts sometimes take comfort in the thought that the decision does not deprive the claimant of *all* remedies but only remits it the more perfunctory one of damages. Is that an empty justification in a case like McKinnon v. Benedict? Was there an effective remedy available to McKinnon other than specific performance? Remedies are dealt with in more detail in the following chapter.

(3) *The Contours of Equitable Discretion.* "Within the ambit of those factors of contract-producing behavior which would result in a denial of specific performance, a bewildering number of permutations work to inform the chancellor's discretion. In these cases one runs continually into the old, the young, the ignorant, the necessitous, the illiterate, the improvident, the drunken, the naive and the sick, all on one side of the transaction, with the sharp and hard on the other. Language of quasi-fraud and quasi-duress abounds. Certain whole classes of presumptive sillies like sailors and heirs and farmers and women continually wander on and off stage. Those not certifiably crazy, but nonetheless pretty peculiar, are often to be found. And in most of the cases, of course, several of these factors appear in combination. . . . Almost without exception, actions for specific performance were (and are) brought with respect to transactions involving real property." Arthur Leff, Unconscionability and the Code—the Emperor's New Clause, 115 U.Pa.L.Rev. 485, 531–34 (1967).

(4) *Class and Contract.* The court in *McKinnon* suggested that "necessitous men are not, truly speaking, free men." The question of comparative wealth arises in cases throughout this chapter. Consider as you proceed how courts and legislatures take account of wealth and other disparities between parties in policing bargains. Is class, like minority, a status to which the law should attend, perhaps creating a presumption of vulnerability?

Tuckwiller v. Tuckwiller

Supreme Court of Missouri, 1967.
413 S.W.2d 274.

[John and Ruby Tuckwiller lived on the family farm in Missouri, which John farmed as a renter. Almost half of the 160 acre farm was owned by Mrs. Metta Hudson Morrison, John's aunt. When she was about 70 years of age, Mrs. Morrison contracted Parkinson's disease. At about the same time she gave up her residence in New York and returned to the Hudson farm, where some rooms were reserved for her use. In April she was hospitalized for about a week, as a result of dizziness and falling. She was thought then to have had a stroke, and showed some mental confusion. But at the first of May her doctor and a friend found her "clear as a bell." She knew, the doctor said, that Parkinsonism is a progressive disease, leaving the victim ultimately dependent entirely on outside care.

Before the April incident, Mrs. Tuckwiller had been urged by Mrs. Morrison to quit a job she held and care for her for the rest of her life, and the subject was discussed again after Mrs. Morrison's release from the hospital. The two were quite congenial. On May 3, Mrs. Morrison signed the following paper, written by Mrs. Tuckwiller:

My offer to Aunt Metta is as follows

I will take care of her for her lifetime; by that I mean provide her 3 meals per day—a good bed—do any possible act of nursing and provide her every pleasure possible.

In exchange she will will me her (Corum) farm at her death keeping all money made from it during her life. She will maintain expense of her medicine.

On May 6 Mrs. Tuckwiller resigned her job, and Mrs. Morrison made an appointment with a lawyer to change her will. Later that day, however, she fainted and fell. She was taken to the hospital, where, except for four days, she remained until her death on June 14. She was 73 at that time. Mrs. Tuckwiller spent much time at the hospital during Mrs. Morrison's final illness, assisting as she could, but Mrs. Morrison was attended by special nurses.

Before leaving for the hospital on May 6, Mrs. Morrison had the date put on the paper set out above, and obtained the signatures of the two ambulance attendants as witnesses. Her will, dated in 1961, was never changed. It provided for the sale of the farm, the proceeds to be used for a student loan fund at Davidson College. The farm had an "inventory value" of $34,400.

Mrs. Tuckwiller brought a bill for specific performance of the contract, which was resisted by the College and Mrs. Morrison's executor, Marion Tuckwiller. The trial court granted the relief, and the defendants appealed.]

■ Welborn, Commissioner. . . . [I]n determining whether or not a contract is so unfair or inequitable or is unconscionable so as to deny its specific performance, the transaction must be viewed prospectively, not retrospectively. The same rule applies with respect to sufficiency of consideration.... Viewed in this light, we find that plaintiff gave up her employment with which she was well satisfied and undertook what was at the time of the contract an obligation of unknown and uncertain duration, involving duties which, in the usual course of the disease from which Mrs. Morrison suffered, would have become increasingly onerous.... Viewed from the standpoint of Mrs. Morrison, the contract cannot be considered unfair. She was appreciative of the care and attention which plaintiff had given her prior to the agreement. Although, as defendants suggest, such prior services cannot provide the consideration essential to a binding contract, such prior services and the past relation of the parties may properly be considered in connection with the fairness of the contract and adequacy of the consideration. 5A Corbin on Contracts, § 1165, p. 227. Aware of her future outlook and having no immediate family to care for her, Mrs. Morrison was understandably appreciative of the personal care and attention of plaintiff and concerned with the possibility of routine impersonal care over a long period of time in a nursing home or similar institution. Having no immediate family which might be the object of her bounty, she undoubtedly felt more free to agree to dispose of the farm without insisting upon an exact quid pro quo. Her insistence that the contract be witnessed prior to her hospitalization is clear evidence of her satisfaction with the bargain as was her unsuccessful effort to change her will to carry out her agreement....

Properly viewed from the standpoint of the parties at the time of the agreement, we find that the contract was fair, not unconscionable, and supported by an adequate consideration. Although not conceding that such conclusion is correct, defendants argue, in effect, that in view of the obviously brief duration of plaintiff's services and their value in comparison with the value of the farm, plaintiff should be obliged to accept the offered payment of the reasonable value of her services and denied the relief of specific performance. Defendants point out that the trial court found that valuing the services which plaintiff rendered might be "possible." That conclusion is undoubtedly correct and unquestionably the monetary value of plaintiff's services would have been a quite small proportion (perhaps one percent) of the value of the farm. Once, however, the essential fairness of the contract and the adequacy of the consideration are found, the fact that the subject of the contract is real estate answers any question of adequacy of the legal remedy of monetary damages. "Whenever a contract concerning real property is in its nature and incidents entirely unobjectionable—that is, when it possesses none of those features which ... appeal to the discretion of the court—it is as much a matter of course for a court of equity to decree a specific performance of it, as it is for a court of law to give damages for the breach of it." Pomeroy's Specific Performance of Contracts (3d ed.), § 10, p. 23.

[Affirmed.]

NOTES

(1) *Questions.* The defendants agree that Ruby Tuckwiller should get *something.* How would they have calculated her damages? What risks did Ruby assume

in this agreement? What risks did each of the parties in McKinnon v. Benedict assume? How is the question of relative risk implicated in the two decisions?

(2) *Professional Services.* In Gladding v. Langrall, Muir & Noppinger, 401 A.2d 662 (Md.1979), the court rejected a claim of unconscionability in reliance on the principle that a bargain is to be evaluated by reference to the situation existing at the time it was struck. Is this principle of special importance to lawyers who spend many billable hours on claims of questionable value? See Cetenko v. United California Bank, 638 P.2d 1299 (Cal.1982). Compare Brobeck, Phleger & Harrison v. Telex Corp., 602 F.2d 866 (9th Cir.1979), in which a law firm recovered a million dollars for filing a petition for certiorari.

What about lawyers who contract for contingent fees? What risk do clients and lawyers take in making such an arrangement? Would you expect the principle to be equally reliable for an attorney and for an accountant, each working for a contingent fee? In *Gladding* the court spoke of "the broader judicial interest in attorney-client contracts, which exist only because of the attorney's status as an officer of the court." The claimant was an accounting firm. It recovered a fee of more than $30,000 (in addition to a retainer of $10,000) for seventeen hours of professional services. The fee was a percentage of tax savings effected for the firm's clients through a settlement with the Internal Revenue Service.

Black Industries, Inc. v. Bush

United States District Court, D. New Jersey, 1953.
110 F.Supp. 801.

[Black Industries ("Black"), a manufacturer of machine parts, was asked to bid on contracts with The Hoover Company for anvils, holder primers and plunger supports, and with Standby Products for two of the same items. Black contracted to buy the same items to be included in the Hoover bid from a supplier, George F. Bush, doing business as G.F. Bush Associates ("Bush"). Bush agreed to manufacture anvils at a price of $4.40 per thousand; holder primers at $11.50 per thousand and plunger supports at a price of $12 per thousand, all in accordance with government specifications provided by Black.

The terms of the contract were set out in a letter from Black to Bush, and signed "as agreed to" by Bush. The letter stated that Black Industries had "spent considerable time, effort and money in developing the contract" to the point where The Hoover Company issued a purchase order. The letter further stated: "The purchase order [from Hoover], when received, will run directly to George F. Bush and Associates ... Your company is to ship the material directly to The Hoover Co. ... Your company, however, is not to bill The Hoover Co. All shipping invoices, documents of transfer and title are to be forwarded to me, and I shall have the exclusive right to bill, upon (your) billing forms and receive payment therefor in your behalf.... It is understood that I shall have the right to receive payment, cash checks made payable to your company under The Hoover Co. contract; and to remit to you (retaining sums) as compensation due me." The letter stated that Black's compensation was to be the difference between Bush's price to Black and Black's price to Hoover. A similar arrangement was in place between Black and Standby products.

The Hoover Company agreed to purchase the parts from Black at a rate of $8.10 per thousand anvils, $16 per thousand holder primers and $21.20 per thousand plunger supports. After beginning performance of the contract, Bush failed to complete the order, and Black sued for damages of $14,625 for the Hoover contract and $4,460.95 for the Standby contract. Black was to receive a "profit" of 84.09% on anvils, 39.13% on holder primers, and 68.33% on plunger supports under the Hoover contract, and similar percentages under the Standby contract.

In its decision the court noted that the items purchased by Hoover and Standby were to be used to fulfill contracts with United States government in aid of "the defense effort," *i.e.*, the Korean War of 1950–53. Bush moved for summary judgment on the ground that the contract was void against public policy because Black's "profits" were passed on to the government and the public in the form of increased prices. In support of his motion, Bush cited two federal laws intended to prevent excessive profits on war contracts: Renegotiation Act, 50 U.S.C.A. Appendix, § 1211, and 41 U.S.C.A. § 51.

■ FORMAN, CHIEF JUDGE. . . . In order to declare a contract, entered by the parties freely and without evidence of fraud, void as against public policy, the contract must be invalid on the basis of recognized legal principles. [In an omitted passage, the court quotes from Muschany v. United States, 324 U.S. 49, 66–67 (1945), as follows: "It is a matter of public importance that good faith contracts of the United States should not be lightly invalidated." Then it discusses three types of illegal contracts, as indicated in the following paragraph.]

The contract in the present case, however, does not fall in any of these categories. It is not a contract by the defendant to pay the plaintiff for inducing a public official to act in a certain manner; it is not a contract to do an illegal act; and it is not a contract which contemplates collusive bidding on a public contract. It should be noted that the first and third categories of cases, upon which the defendant relies most heavily, involve agreements which directly impinge upon government activities. In the case at hand, the contract's only effect on the government was that ultimately the government was to buy the product of which defendant's goods were to be a component. Neither the defendant nor the plaintiff had any dealings with the United States on account of this contract, and therefore the profit accruing to the plaintiff was not to have been earned as a result of either inducing government action or interfering with the system of competitive bidding. This contract cannot, therefore, be declared void as against public policy on the basis of the precedents cited by the defendant.

It is quite possible that the plaintiff was to have received a very high profit on the sale of the parts, either because The Hoover Company agreed to pay too high a price or because the defendant quoted too low a price. Further proof would be required to establish this as a fact. Even if it were proved that the plaintiff was to have received a far greater profit than the defendants for a much smaller contribution, the defendant would neverthe- less be bound by his agreement by the familiar rule that relative values of the consideration in a contract between business men dealing at arm's length without fraud will not affect the validity of the contract. The Coast National Bank v. Bloom, 113 N.J.L. 597, 174 A. 576, 95 A.L.R. 528 (E. & A. 1934); Restatement of the Law of Contracts § 81 (1932).

The fact that the government is the ultimate purchaser of the product in which defendant's parts are used is cited by the defendant as a reason to hold that this contract is void as against public policy. To so hold would necessitate either ruling that all contracts are void if they provide for compensation for middlemen, such as Black Industries, between producer and purchaser of goods which ultimately are incorporated in products sold to the government, a result which is not supported by precedent and which would defy the realities of our economic life, or deciding in every case involving such a contract whether the compensation paid a middleman such as the plaintiff here who locates purchasers and assists the producer in other ways, is reasonable. This latter course would, in effect, impose price regulatory functions on the court. There are other and more effective methods of insuring that the government does not pay an unreasonable price for its supplies. The manufacturer selling directly to the United States must conform to procedures such as bidding designed to protect the government, and which should, in conjunction with the ordinary consider- ations of profits and loss, insure that prime contractors do not pay outlandish prices for the products they buy in order to fulfill a government contract. The contract may be subject to renegotiation. 50 U.S.C.A. Appen- dix, § 1211 et seq. I do not believe that it is the function of the court to interfere by determining the validity of a contract between ordinary busi- ness men on the basis of its beliefs as to the adequacy of the consideration. Consequently, I hold that, assuming the facts to be as stated by the defendant, the contract sued on in this case is not void as against public policy and the defendant's motion for a summary judgment will, therefore, be denied.

Let an order be submitted in accordance with this opinion.

NOTES

(1) *Price Regulation.* The arguments against courts' inquiring into the "rela- tive value of the consideration in a contract between business men dealing at arm's length without fraud" have been summarized as follows: "(1) The efficient adminis- tration of the law of contracts requires that courts shall not be required to prescribe prices. (2) The test of enforceability should be certain and should not be beclouded by such vague terms as 'fair' or 'reasonable' as tests of validity. (3) There is still the somewhat old-fashioned theory that persons of maturity and sound mind should be free to contract imprudently as well as prudently." Edward Patterson, An Apology for Consideration, 58 Colum.L.Rev. 929 (1958).

Does it appear that courts, in specific performance actions, undertake price regulatory functions? Does the equitable power exercised in McKinnon v. Benedict invite litigation in a large proportion of contracts about land? If so, it may tend to impair the value of such contracts as the Tuckwillers made with Mrs. Morrison, in

Tuckwiller v. Tuckwiller. Should the courts be cautious, on that account, in attempting supervision over the values exchanged?

(2) *Intermediaries or "Middlemen".* The court acknowledges that Black might have stood to receive a "far greater profit" than Bush "for a much smaller contribution." What was the nature of Black's contribution in this transaction?

Intermediaries typically perform an "informational" or "search" function by bringing together buyers and sellers who would otherwise be ignorant of one another's needs or existence. They may also perform "risk-shifting" functions, by taking on themselves the risks of market fluctuations that would otherwise be borne by buyers or sellers. Both of these functions are highly developed in well organized markets.

Does it appear that Black's "contribution" involved either an informational or a risk-shifting function? If it involved the former, did Black supply Hoover with enough information about available suppliers to merit the compensation it received? Why did Hoover not contact Bush directly? Why did Bush not contact Hoover directly? Would Bush have been able to charge Black more if he had known how much Hoover was paying Black?

PUBLIC POLICIES, EXCESSIVE PROFITS, AND GOVERNMENT CONTRACTS

One of Bush's arguments in the case above was that Black's profits were passed on to the government and the public in the form of excessive prices, contrary to "public policy." Referring to existing and "more effective methods," the court suggested that the government is able to take care of itself in this regard, citing the Federal Renegotiation Act of 1942.

Since that time, additional statutory measures have been enacted to protect the government (and taxpayers) from profiteering. The Competition in Contracting Act of 1984 requires that subject to certain exceptions, federal contracts are to be awarded on the basis of "full and open competition." 31 U.S.C. § 3729 *et seq.* Exceptions, which authorize noncompetitive or "no-bid" contracts, include cases in which only one responsible source can provide the goods or services required, and emergency circumstances which require immediate contract awards. For example, a sizable number of contracts awarded in the aftermath of Hurricane Katrina (for roofing, trailers, debris removal) fell under the emergency exception, and were awarded without competitive bidding; see Presidential's Council on Integrity and Efficiency, Oversight of Gulf Coast Hurricane Recovery: A Semiannual Report to Congress at 9 (October 2006), available at http://www.dhs.gov/xoig/assets/katovrsght/OIG_pcie_sept06.pdf.

Other mechanisms for avoiding excessive profits are limitations placed on awarding various forms of "cost reimbursement" contracts, rather than fixed price contracts. See Federal Acquisition Regulation (FAR), 48 C.F.R. § 16.301. Might the government ever prefer a cost-plus contract? Under what circumstances? See John Cibinic and Ralph Nash, *Formation of Government Contracts,* 1061 *et seq.* (3rd ed., 1998). FAR provides the framework for all government procurement contracts. Such contracts are explored in depth in the Cibinic and Nash treatise.

Excessive profits may also result when a party acts egregiously in the performance of a contract, say, by submitting claims for work not actually done. To protect against such practices Congress enacted the False Claims Act (FCA). Originally enacted in 1863 in response to fraudulent claims submitted to the government during the Civil War, the current version was passed in 1986; see 31 U.S.C. § 3729 *et seq.* It provides that "any person who knowingly presents, or causes to be presented, to an officer or employer of the United States Government a false or fraudulent claim for payment is liable to the United States" for a civil penalty of not more than $10,000 and three times the amount of damages which the government sustains, or treble damages. 31 U.S.C. § 3729(a)(1). Proceedings under the Act may be brought by a private person (called a "relator"), acting in the public interest. Actions brought by private persons are called *qui tam* actions, the phrase short for *"qui tam pro domino rege quam pro se ipso in hac parte sequitur"* (who pursues this action on our Lord the King's behalf as well as his own), Rockwell International Corp. v. United States, 549 U.S. ___, 127 S.Ct. 1397 (2007) n. 2. The United States may choose to intervene in a *qui tam* action, also as a relator. For a *qui tam* action brought in the aftermath of Hurricane Katrina and involving the unethical behavior of counsel, see United States v. State Farm Insurance Company, 2008 WL 2130314 (S.D.Miss.).

Claims under the FCA are subject to a number of requirements—the false claim must be presented "knowingly," for example—and are often difficult to prove. In a 2006 case, the United States claimed that a private U.S. contractor had submitted inflated invoices to the Coalition Provisional Authority in Iraq for reimbursement of $3,000,000 in costs not actually expended in performing its duties under a $20,000,000 contract to provide machinery and security for the Iraqi Currency Exchange. After a 12–day trial, the jury found for the government. The contractor appealed on the ground that it had not presented a false claim to the United States government. Held: *Reversed.* United States v. Custer Battles LLC, 444 F.Supp.2d 678 (E.D.Va.2006).

The court found that although Custer Battles had knowingly presented inflated invoices, and although the Coalition Provisional Authority was "principally controlled and funded by the U.S., this degree of control did not rise to the level of executive control required to qualify as an instrumentality of the U.S. government."

Overseeing government contracts—their formation, performance completion, billing, and so on—is a vast task, headed in the first instance at the federal level by the Comptroller General of the U.S., and the General Accounting Office. See, for example, Rebuilding Iraq: Status of Competition for Iraq Construction Contracts, Report to Congressional Committees, U.S. Government Accounting Office (2006). The Inspector General is also charged with various oversight functions; see 5 U.S.C. App. § 2. See, for example, Special Inspector General for Iraq Reconstruction, Iraq Reconstruction: Lessons Learned in Contracting and Procurement (2006), available at http://www.sigir.mil/reports/pdf/Lessons_Learned_July21.pdf.

Do government contracts raise policy concerns in addition to those concerning excessive profits? What policies, if any, are supported by the court's observation in Black v. Bush, above, that "good faith contracts of the United States should not be lightly invalidated?"

SECTION 2. STANDARD FORM AND ADHESION CONTRACTS

The preceding section explored traditional common law principles concerned with the equality of exchange. Just as the policing measures were "conventional," so in a sense, were the contracts: *individualized* agreements, tailored to the specifics of the particular deal by the parties themselves. This section focuses on a now ubiquitous type of contract that emerged some two hundred years ago—the *standard form contract*.

Like the mass production of goods, the mass production of contracts may serve the interests of both courts and parties. Among the advantages claimed for their use are the following: they take advantage of the lessons of experience and enable a judicial interpretation of one contract to serve as an interpretation of all contracts; they reduce uncertainty and save time and trouble; they simplify planning and administration and make superior drafting skills more widely available; and they make risks calculable and "[increase] that real security which is the necessary basis of initiative and the assumption of foreseeable risks." Morris Cohen, The Basis of Contract, 46 Harv.L.Rev. 553, 558 (1933).

Professor Friedrich Kessler elaborated the matter of risk: "It has been noted that uniformity of terms of contracts typically recurring in a business enterprise is an important factor in the exact calculation of risks. Risks which are difficult to calculate can be excluded altogether. Unforeseeable contingencies affecting performance, such as strikes, fire, and transportation difficulties can be taken care of. The standard clauses in insurance policies are the most striking illustrations of successful attempts on the part of business enterprises to select and control risks assumed under a contract. The insurance business probably deserves credit also for having first realized the full importance of the so-called 'juridical risk', the danger that a court or jury may be swayed by 'irrational factors' to decide against a powerful defendant.... Standardized ... contracts have thus become an important means of excluding or controlling the 'irrational factor' in litigation. In this respect they are a true reflection of the spirit of our time with its hostility to irrational factors in the judicial process, and they belong in the same category as codifications and restatements." Kessler, Contracts of Adhesion—Some Thoughts About Freedom of Contract, 43 Colum.L.Rev. 629, 631–32 (1943).

On the other hand, standard form contracts, often referred to as "contracts of adhesion," offer the means by which one party may impose its will upon another. How does this come about? There are several means of imposition, which often appear in combination. First, an enterprise may have such disproportionately strong economic power that it can dictate its terms to the weaker party. Second, there may be no opportunity to bargain over terms at all; the standardized contract is often a take-it-or-leave-it proposition. Finally, standardized contracts are often used by a party who has had the advantage of time and expert advice in preparing it while the other party may have no real opportunity to scrutinize, and often no real means to understand, the contract. This difficulty may be compounded by the use of fine print and obfuscating clauses.

The cases in this section present types of standard form contracts probably familiar to readers who have rented an apartment, checked a coat or backpack, bought a car, or purchased travel tickets. In each case, the court is concerned with whether a party to a standardized contract can reasonably be held to have seen, understood, and assented to its unfavorable terms, and accordingly, to be bound by them. The following questions provide a framework for thinking about policing bargains in an impersonal market where the "individuality of the parties which so frequently gave color to the old type of contract has disappeared." Kessler, Contracts of Adhesion—Some Thoughts About Freedom of Contract, 43 Colum.L.Rev. 629, 631–32 (1943). Should it matter whether a party is a firm in a commercial deal, or an individual in a consumer agreement? How do courts determine public policy, a concept often invoked in deciding whether or not a particular term should be enforced? Finally, how should lawmakers evaluate attempts to ensure fairness in a particular case by means of a rule that may complicate, burden, or increase the expense of contracting, sometimes for those the law seeks to protect?

Before turning to these issues, we take a moment to consider standard form contracts within a larger social framework.

NOTES

(1) *From Status to Contract, and Back.* One of the great generalizations about social history is the thesis of Sir Henry Maine that the history of progressive societies may be described as a movement from status to contract. In *Ancient Law* (1865), Maine stated: "The movement of the progressive societies has been uniform in one respect. Through all its course it has been distinguished by the gradual dissolution of family dependency and the growth of individual obligation in its place. The individual is steadily substituted for the Family, as the unit of which civil laws take account.... Nor is it difficult to see what is the tie between man and man which replaces by degrees those forms of reciprocity in rights and duties which have their origin in the Family. It is Contract.... All the forms of Status taken notice of in the Law of Persons were derived from, and to some extent are still coloured by, the powers and privileges anciently residing in the Family. If then we employ Status, agreeably with the usage of the best writers, to signify these personal conditions only, and avoid applying the term to such conditions as are the immediate or remote result of agreement, we may say that the movement of the progressive societies has hitherto been a movement *from Status to Contract.*"

Over a century later, some scholars detected a reverse tendency in the law. They suggested that standard form contracts may be conducive to a regressive regime of status: "With the decline of the free enterprise system due to the innate trend of competitive capitalism towards monopoly, the meaning of contract has changed radically. Society, when granting freedom of contract, does not guarantee that all members of the community will be able to make use of it to the same extent. On the contrary, the law, by protecting the unequal distribution of property, does nothing to prevent freedom of contract from becoming a one-sided privilege.... Freedom of contract enables enterprisers to legislate by contract and, what is even more important, to legislate in a substantially authoritarian manner without using the appearance of authoritarian forms. Standard contracts in particular could thus become effective instruments in the hands of powerful industrial and commercial overlords enabling them to impose a new feudal order of their own making upon a vast host of vassals.... Thus the return back from contract to status which we experience today was greatly facilitated by the fact that the belief in freedom of contract has remained one of the firmest axioms in the whole fabric of the social philosophy of our culture." Friedrich Kessler, Contracts of Adhesion—Some Thoughts About Freedom of Contract, 43 Colum.L.Rev. 629, 640 (1943).

Consider as you read further, whether the law's efforts at policing have thwarted or facilitated the new "feudal order."

(2) *Distinctions.* The term "contract of adhesion" was first used in the United States by Professor Patterson, The Delivery of a Life–Insurance Policy, 33 Harv. L.Rev. 198, 222 (1919). It was coined by Raymond Saleilles as "contrat d'adhésion" to describe contracts "in which one predominant unilateral will dictates its law to an undetermined multitude rather than to an individual ... as in all employment contracts of big industry, transportation contracts of big railroad companies and all those contracts which, as the Romans said, resemble a law much more than a meeting of the minds." Saleilles, *De la Declaration de Volonté* 229 (1901).

Are all standard form contracts contracts of adhesion? In Oblix, Inc. v. Winiecki, 374 F.3d 488 (7th Cir. 2004), the court upheld an employment agreement "offered on a take-it-or-leave-it" basis against the claim that the agreement and an arbitration clause within were "adhesive." Returning to the fundamentals of consideration, Judge Easterbrook stated that the claimant "does not deny the arbitration clause is supported by consideration—her salary. Oblix paid [her] to do a number of things; one of the things it paid her to do was agree to non-judicial dispute resolution."

O'Callaghan v. Waller & Beckwith Realty Co.

Supreme Court of Illinois, 1958.
15 Ill.2d 436, 155 N.E.2d 545.

■ SCHAEFER, JUSTICE.[a] This is an action to recover for injuries allegedly caused by the defendant's negligence in maintaining and operating a large apartment building. Mrs. Ella O'Callaghan, a tenant in the building, was injured when she fell while crossing the paved courtyard on her way from the garage to her apartment. She instituted this action to recover for her injuries, alleging that they were caused by defective pavement in the courtyard. Before the case was tried, Mrs. O'Callaghan died and her administrator was substituted as plaintiff. The jury returned a verdict for the plaintiff in the sum of $14,000, and judgment was entered on the verdict. Defendant appealed. The Appellate Court held that the action was

a. Walter V. Schaefer (1904–1986) practiced law and served in a variety of governmental posts in Chicago between 1928 and 1940, when he became a professor of law at Northwestern University. From 1951 to 1976 he was a member of the Illinois Supreme Court, serving as Chief Judge. He was one of the Advisers for the Restatement Second.

barred by an exculpatory clause in the lease that Mrs. O'Callaghan had signed, and that a verdict should have been directed for the defendant. 146 N.E.2d 198. It therefore reversed the judgment and remanded the cause with directions to enter judgment for the defendant. We granted leave to appeal.

In reaching its conclusion the Appellate Court relied upon our recent decision in Jackson v. First National Bank, 114 N.E.2d 721. There we considered the validity of such an exculpatory clause in a lease of property for business purposes. We pointed out that contracts by which one seeks to relieve himself from the consequences of his own negligence are generally enforced "unless (1) it would be against the settled public policy of the State to do so, or (2) there is something in the social relationship of the parties militating against upholding the agreement." 114 N.E.2d at page 725. And we held that there was nothing in the public policy of the State or in the social relationship of the parties to forbid enforcement of the exculpatory clause there involved.

The exculpatory clause in the lease now before us clearly purports to relieve the lessor and its agents from any liability to the lessee for personal injuries or property damage caused by any act or neglect of the lessor or its agents. It does not appear to be amenable to the strict construction to which such clauses are frequently subjected. See 175 A.L.R. 8, 89. The plaintiff does not question its applicability, and she concedes that if it is valid it bars her recovery. She argues vigorously, however, that such a clause is contrary to public policy, and so invalid, in a lease of residential property.

Freedom of contract is basic to our law. But when that freedom expresses itself in a provision designed to absolve one of the parties from the consequences of his own negligence, there is danger that the standards of conduct which the law has developed for the protection of others may be diluted. These competing considerations have produced results that are not completely consistent. This court has refused to enforce contracts exculpating or limiting liability for negligence between common carriers and shippers of freight or paying passengers (Chicago and Northwestern Railway Co. v. Chapman, 24 N.E. 417, 8 L.R.A. 508), between telegraph companies and those sending messages (Tyler, Ullman & Co. v. Western Union Telegraph Co., 60 Ill. 421), and between masters and servants (Campbell v. Chicago, Rock Island and Pacific Railway Co., 90 N.E. 1106). The obvious public interest in these relationships, coupled with the dominant position of those seeking exculpation, were compelling considerations in these decisions, which are in accord with similar results in other jurisdictions. See 175 A.L.R. 8.

On the other hand, as pointed out in the *Jackson* case, the relation of lessor and lessee has been considered a matter of private concern. Clauses that exculpate the landlord from the consequences of his negligence have been sustained in residential as well as commercial leases.... There are intimations in other jurisdictions that run counter to the current authority. See Kuzmiak v. Brookchester, Inc., 1955, 111 A.2d 425; Kay v. Cain, 1946, 81 U.S.App.D.C. 24. The New Hampshire court applies to exculpatory clauses in all leases its uniform rule that any attempt to contract against liability for negligence is contrary to public policy. Papakalos v. Shaka, 1941, 18 A.2d 377. But apart from the Papakalos case we know of no court of last resort that has held such clauses invalid in the absence of a statute so requiring.

A contract shifting the risk of liability for negligence may benefit a tenant as well as a landlord. See Cerny–Pickas & Co. v. C.R. Jahn Co., 131 N.E.2d 100. Such an agreement transfers the risk of a possible financial burden and so lessens the impact of the sanctions that induce adherence to the required standard of care. But this consideration is applicable as well to contracts for insurance that indemnify against liability for one's own negligence. Such contracts are accepted, and even encouraged. See Ill.Rev. Stat.1957, chap. 95½, pars. 7–202(1) and 7–315.

The plaintiff contends that due to a shortage of housing there is a disparity of bargaining power between lessors of residential property and their lessees that gives landlords an unconscionable advantage over tenants. And upon this ground it is said that exculpatory clauses in residential leases must be held to be contrary to public policy. No attempt was made upon the trial to show that Mrs. O'Callaghan was at all concerned about the exculpatory clause, that she tried to negotiate with the defendant about its modification or elimination, or that she made any effort to rent an apartment elsewhere. To establish the existence of a widespread housing shortage the plaintiff points to numerous statutes designed to alleviate the shortage (see Ill.Rev.Stat.1957, chap. 67½, *passim*) and to the existence of rent control during the period of the lease. 65 Stat. 145 (1947), 50 U.S.C.A. Appendix, § 1894.

Unquestionably there has been a housing shortage. That shortage has produced an active and varied legislative response. Since legislative attention has been so sharply focused upon housing problems in recent years, it might be assumed that the legislature has taken all of the remedial action that it thought necessary or desirable. One of the major legislative responses was the adoption of rent controls which placed ceilings upon the amount of rent that landlords could charge. But the very existence of that control made it impossible for a lessor to negotiate for an increased rental in exchange for the elimination of an exculpatory clause. We are asked to assume, however, that the legislative response to the housing shortage has been inadequate and incomplete, and to augment it judicially.

The relationship of landlord and tenant does not have the monopolistic characteristics that have characterized some other relations with respect to which exculpatory clauses have been held invalid. There are literally thousands of landlords who are in competition with one another. The rental market affords a variety of competing types of housing accommodations, from simple farm house to luxurious apartment. The use of a form contract does not of itself establish disparity of bargaining power. That there is a shortage of housing at one particular time or place does not indicate that such shortages have always and everywhere existed, or that there will be shortages in the future. Judicial determinations of public policy cannot readily take account of sporadic and transitory circumstances.

They should rather, we think, rest upon a durable moral basis. Other jurisdictions have dealt with this problem by legislation. McKinney's Consol.Laws of N.Y.Ann., Real Property Laws, sec. 234, Vol. 49, Part I; Ann.Laws of Mass., Vol. 6, c. 186, sec. 15. In our opinion the subject is one that is appropriate for legislative rather than judicial action.

The judgment of the Appellate Court is affirmed.

■ BRISTOW, JUSTICE, and DAILY, CHIEF JUSTICE (dissenting). We cannot accept the conclusions and analysis of the majority opinion, which in our judgment not only arbitrarily eliminates the concept of negligence in the landlord and tenant relationship, but creates anomalies in the law, and will produce grievous social consequences for hundreds of thousands of persons in this State.

According to the undisputed facts in the instant case, this form lease with its exculpatory clause, was executed in a metropolitan area in 1947, when housing shortages were so acute that "waiting lists" were the order of the day, and gratuities to landlords to procure shelter were common. (U.S.Sen.Rep.1780, Committee on Banking & Currency, vol. II, 81st Cong., 2nd Sess. (1950), p. 2565 et seq.; Cremer v. Peoria Housing Authority, 78 N.E.2d 276.) While plaintiff admittedly did not negotiate about the exculpatory clause, as the majority opinion notes, the record shows unequivocally that the apartment would not have been rented to her if she had quibbled about any clause in the form lease. According to the uncontroverted testimony, "If a person refused to sign a [form] lease in the form it was in, the apartment would not be rented to him."

Apparently, the majority opinion has chosen to ignore those facts and prevailing circumstances, and finds instead that there were thousands of landlords competing with each other with a variety of rental units. Not only was the element of competition purely theoretical—and judges need not be more naive than other men—but there wasn't even theoretical competition, as far as the exculpatory clauses were concerned, since these clauses were included in all form leases used by practically all landlords in urban areas. Simmons v. Columbus Venetian Stevens Building, Inc., Ill.App., 155 N.E.2d 372; 1952 Ill.L.Forum, 321, 328. . . .

Thus, we are *not* construing merely an isolated provision of a contract specifically bargained for by one landlord and one tenant, "a matter of private concern," as the majority opinion myoptically [sic] views the issue in order to sustain its conclusion. We are construing, instead, a provision affecting thousands of tenants now bound by such provisions, which were foisted upon them at a time when it would be pure fiction to state that they had anything but a Hobson's choice in the matter. Can landlords, by that technique, immunize themselves from liability for negligence, and have the blessings of this court as they destroy the concept of negligence and standards of law painstakingly evolved in the case law? That is the issue in this case, and the majority opinion at no time realistically faces it. . . .

In the instant case we must determine whether the exculpatory clause in the lease offends the public policy of this State. We realize that there is no precise definition of "public policy" or rule to test whether a contract is contrary to public policy, so that each case must be judged according to its own peculiar circumstances. First Trust & Savings Bank of Kankakee v. Powers, 65 N.E.2d 377. None would dispute, however, that there is a recognized policy of discouraging negligence and protecting those in need of goods or services from being overreached by those with power to drive unconscionable bargains.

. . . In determining whether such clauses should be deemed void, the courts have weighed such factors as the importance which the subject has for the physical and economic well-being of the group agreeing to the release; their bargaining power; the amount of free choice actually exercised in agreeing to the exemption; and the existence of competition among the group to be exempted. (Williston, Contracts, vol. 6, p. 4968; "The Significance of Bargaining Power in the Law of Exculpation," 37 Col.L.Rev. 248; 15 Univ.Pitt.L.Rev. 493.) Adjudged by such criteria, it is evident that the subject matter of the exculpatory clause herein—shelter—is indispensable for the physical well being of tenants; that they have nothing even approaching equality of bargaining power with landlords and no free choice whatever in agreeing to the exemption, since they will be confronted with the same clause in other form leases if they seek shelter elsewhere. Although the majority opinion claims that such clauses may also benefit tenants, it is hard for us to envisage a tenant on a waiting list for an apartment, insisting that the lease include a provision relieving him from liability for his negligence in the maintenance of the premises. Consequently, in our judgment, every material ground for voiding the exculpatory clause exists in the lease involved in the instant case. . . .

NOTES

(1) *Questions.* What fact, authorities, and public policies did the majority array to support its conclusion that the liability disclaimer did not violate public policy? The dissent? Which do you find more persuasive?

What factors distinguish *Henningsen* from *O'Callaghan,* p. 445 above? Is there any indication that the Henningsens were concerned about their warranty protection? Was there an agreement among American automobile manufacturers at the time of the case to follow the language proposed by the Association? Is a standard-form apartment lease any less a contract of adhesion than a new car purchase contract?

(2) *Current Law.* Most states now provide by statute that provisions in residential leases exculpating the landlord from liability to the tenant for negligence are ineffective. In a few states, variant rules prevail. In Maine, for example, a tenant may accept in writing "specified conditions which may violate the warranty of fitness for human habitation in return for a stated reduction in rent or other specified fair consideration." Me.Rev.Stat.Ann.Tit. 14 §§ 6021(4)(B), (5) and 6026(5). In Texas, waivers by a tenant of a landlord's responsibilities must be made "knowingly, voluntarily, and for consideration." Tex.Prop.Code § 92.006(e)(4)(D). Are there situations in which a residential tenant might prefer, with full information, to exculpate a landlord from liability for negligence?

In several states, including Illinois, there are statutory limitations on exculpatory provisions in commercial leases as well. 765 ILCS 705/1. What differences between residential and commercial leasing might justify a difference in treatment?

(3) *Strict Construction.* Courts sometimes rely on "rules of construction" to bypass claims of contractual unfairness. Consider Galligan v. Arovitch, 219 A.2d 463 (Pa.1966), in which a tenant in an apartment building suffered injury in a fall on the lawn. She sued the owner for negligence in maintenance. The plaintiff's lease, like Mrs. O'Callaghan's, excluded liability of the owner for injury arising from her use of the hallways and six other common areas, including sidewalks. Judgment was given for the defendant on the pleadings. On appeal, the judgment was reversed. The opinion of the court was based on the location of the injury—the lawn was not mentioned in the lease. "A lawn and a sidewalk are clearly different locations."

Consider the view of Professor Llewellyn: "A court can 'construe' language into patently not meaning what the language is patently trying to say. It can find inconsistencies between clauses and throw out the troublesome one. It can even reject a clause as counter to the whole purpose of the transaction.... The difficulty with these techniques of ours is threefold. First, since they all rest on the admission that the clauses in question are permissible in purpose and content, they invite the draftsman to recur to the attack. Give him time, and he will make the grade. Second, since they do not face the issue, they fail to accumulate either experience or authority in the needed direction: that of marking out for any given type of transaction what the *minimum decencies* are which a court will insist upon as essential to an enforceable bargain of a given type, or as being inherent in a bargain of that type. Third, since they purport to construe, and do not really construe, nor are intended to, but are instead tools of intentional and creative misconstruction, they seriously embarrass later efforts at true construction, later efforts to get at the true meaning of those wholly legitimate contracts and clauses which call for their meaning to be got at instead of avoided. The net effect is unnecessary confusion and unpredictability, together with inadequate remedy, and evil persisting that calls for remedy. Covert tools are never reliable tools." Llewellyn, Book Review, 52 Harv. L.Rev. 700, 702 (1939).

PROBLEM

Abusive Drafting. A landlord, believing that tenants often give credence to lease provisions even if they are unenforceable, asks his attorney to prepare a waiver of tenants' rights that the attorney knows to be unenforceable. How should the attorney respond? See generally, Bailey Kuklin, On the Knowing Inclusion of Unenforceable Contract and Lease Terms, 6 U.Cin.L.Rev.845 (1988).

What if the attorney does not know, but only suspects, that the suggested provision is unenforceable? Consider the following Opinion from the Ethics Committee of the Alaska Bar Association: "Disciplinary Rule 7–102(A)(7) states that a lawyer shall not 'counsel or assist his client in conduct that the lawyer knows to be illegal or fraudulent'. Thus, if the lawyer determines that the contract is illegal, then the lawyer must refuse to participate in drafting the contract.... The Code of Professional Responsibility does not prohibit an attorney from drafting a contract which might be held voidable or unenforceable, provided that the attorney advises the client of the particular risks involved in the particular contract that is being drafted." AK. Eth. Op. 84–4, 1984 WL 270979 (Alaska Bar.Assn.Eth.Comm.1984). The New York State Bar is in agreement; see NY Eth. Op. 584, 1987 WL 109300 (N.Y.St.Bar.Assn.Comm.Prof.Eth.,1987). For the problems of leasing apartments in college towns, and a model lease enacted in Davis, California in response to those problems, see Daniel E. Wenner, Renting in Collegetown, 84 Corn.L.Rev.543 (1999).

AGREEING TO BOILERPLATE

In *O'Callahan*, the issue was whether the disclaimer of liability in a standard form lease violated public policy. Both the majority and the dissent agreed that O'Callahan neither "tried to negotiate" nor "quibbled" about the clause with her landlord. She apparently understood that she had signed a lengthy agreement with many provisions, and that if the disclaimer term was valid, she was bound.

It is common, however, to find disclaimers on "contracts" of a much less formal nature, such as the tickets, stubs, and passes that are regularly issued to customers by laundries, parking lots, coat checks, and the like. To what extent are exculpatory clauses, printed on unsigned papers incident to everyday transactions, effective? Has the holder assented to the terms of the stub?

In a well-known case involving a claim check, reproduced here, a "parcel room" purported to limit its liability for checked items that were lost or damaged.

H. & M. PARCEL ROOM, INC.
BROADWAY & 33rd ST., HUDSON TUNNELS
OPEN 7:00 A. M. - CLOSE 1:00 A. M.
(E. S. Time Except When Another Time Is In Effect)

■ CONTRACT ■

THIS CONTRACT IS MADE ON THE FOLLOWING CONDITIONS AND IN CONSIDERATION OF THE LOW RATE AT WHICH THE SERVICE IS PERFORMED, AND ITS ACCEPTANCE BY THE DEPOSITOR, EXPRESSLY BINDS BOTH PARTIES TO THE CONTRACT.
CHARGE—10 CENTS FOR EVERY 24 HOURS OR FRACTION THEREOF, FOR EACH PIECE COVERED BY THIS CONTRACT.
LOSS OR DAMAGE—NO CLAIM SHALL BE MADE IN EXCESS OF $25.00 FOR LOSS OR DAMAGE TO ANY PIECE.
UNCLAIMED ARTICLES REMAINING AFTER 90 DAYS MAY BE SOLD AT PUBLIC OR PRIVATE SALE TO SATISFY ACCRUED CHARGES.
PHONE PEnnsylvania 6-2467 H. & M. PARCEL ROOM, INC.

34--971

[C1224]

A patron left a package at the parcel room and received but did not read the claim check. When another person holding the ticket later returned to reclaim the package, he was told that it had been delivered to someone else by mistake. He sued the parcel room for the alleged value of the contents, $1,000, and the trial court gave judgment for nearly that amount. On successive appeals, the judges were in disagreement, some arguing that recovery should be limited to $25, the maximum provided by the terms of the claim check. In the words of one judge: "The parcel check . . . had conspicuously printed the word 'Contract' on the face thereof near the top in bold face type, clearly legible in red ink. . . . The whole form was exceptionally brief. . . . Plaintiffs . . . had ample opportunity to read the notice on the check stub . . . The package, alleged to contain valuable furs, was tied up with a piece of cord in a brown paper parcel. The charge for checking was the trivial sum of ten cents."[a]

a. An explanation for these facts is suggested by the following report: "Public lockers in Penn Station. Locked trunks in parked cars. This is where the contraband is hidden,

Nonetheless, the court affirmed the trial court's judgment, holding that " 'The coupon was presumptively intended as between the parties to serve the special purpose of affording a means of identifying the parcel left by the bailor. In the mind of the bailor the little piece of cardboard ... did not arise to the dignity of a contract by which he agreed that in the event of the loss of the parcel, even through the negligence of the bailee itself, he would accept therefor a sum which, perhaps, would be but a small fraction of its actual value.' ... While the defendant bailee should be protected in its legal right to limit its responsibility, the public should also be safeguarded against imposition. If the bailee wishes to limit its liability for negligence, it must at least show that it has given adequate notice of the special contract and that it has received the assent thereto of those with whom it transacts business." Klar v. H. & M. Parcel Room, Inc., 61 N.Y.S.2d 285 (App.Div.1946), aff'd mem., 73 N.E.2d 912 (N.Y.1947).

NOTES

(1) *Questions.* What competing principles does the court in *Klar* attempt to reconcile? Do you think the solution is a good one? In *Klar* and similar cases, it may be said that courts have policed against overreaching by manipulating the principles of contract formation. What are the limits of this method?

(2) *Assenting to Boilerplate.* In connection with the bargaining process, consider Professor Llewellyn's influential commentary on boilerplate: "Instead of thinking about 'assent' to boiler-plate clauses, we can recognize that so far as concerns the specific, there is no assent at all. What has in fact been assented to, specifically, are the few dickered terms, and the broad type of the transaction, and but one thing more. That one thing more is a blanket assent (not a specific assent) to any not unreasonable or indecent terms the seller may have on his form, which do not alter or eviscerate the reasonable meaning of the dickered terms." Llewellyn, *The Common Law Tradition: Deciding Appeals* 370–71 (1960). For discussions of boilerplate in commercial and electronic commerce, see Omri Ben–Shahar, ed., *Boilerplate: The Foundation of Market Contracts* (2007).

Restatement § 211(3) provides that where a party effectively manifests assent to a standardized expression of agreement, and the other party has reason to believe that he would not have done so if he had known that it contained a particular term, "the term is not part of the agreement." How would the parcel room case be decided under this provision?

(3) *Insurance Contracts.* Insurance contracts have provided a rich source for the regulation of adhesion contracts. In Darner Motor Sales v. Universal Underwriters, 682 P.2d 388, 399 (Ariz.1984), the court applied the Restatement provision to the terms of an "umbrella" insurance policy favorably to the insured. It characterized the policy as one which, "because of the nature of the enterprise, customers

deposited there surreptitiously by one party and picked up quietly by another. Is it narcotics, jewels, gold bullion? No, it is furs, or, more accurately, parts of fur garments, awaiting sewing so that the complete garment can be made available for sale. The lined skins are placed in lockers or car-trunks by fur-garment producers willing to use non-union contractors, usually a one-man sewing shop or a shop with a few workers. After picking up the garments at their convenience, the contractors sew them for 50 per cent less than a unionized shop would. They then return the garments via the same conduits to their unionized clients. Although outlawed in labor-management contracts, the increasing use of such contractors has produced consternation in an already-troubled industry." The New York Times, March 26, 1972, Business Section, p. 1.

will not be expected to read and over which they have no real power of negotiation." Another technique used to overcome terms that have literally been disclosed, but that would likely come as a surprise to the insured is the "doctrine of reasonable expectations." It holds that when insurance is sold in circumstances that discourage detailed inquiries, the reasonable expectations of the buyer should be honored even though the policy terms do not support them. See Robert Keeton & Alan Widiss, *Insurance Law § 6.3* (prac. ed. 1988). "In general, courts will protect the reasonable expectations of applicants, insureds, and intended beneficiaries regarding the coverage afforded ... even though a careful examination of the policy provisions indicates that such expectations are contrary to the expressed intention of the insurer." For a discussion of *Darner*, see Jean Braucher, Cowboy Contracts: The Arizona Supreme Court's Grand Tradition of Transactional Fairness, 50 Ariz. L. Rev. 191, 213–18 (2008).

Should a buyer of automobile insurance get coverage according to an ordinary buyer's reasonable expectations, notwithstanding a policy exclusion? See Powers v. Detroit Auto. Inter–Insurance Exchange, 398 N.W.2d 411 (Mich.1986) ("It is fatuous to suppose the policy owner had any part in the language of the policy besides filling in the blanks.... The common wisdom is that very few insurance policy purchasers read all or even substantially all of the purchased contract, and it is not guaranteeable that they would understand it if they did"). See also Sparks v. St. Paul Ins. Co., 495 A.2d 406 (N.J.1985): "... courts have a special responsibility to prevent the marketing of policies that provide unrealistic and inadequate coverage." Why might courts be particularly concerned about hidden or unsuspected limitations in insurance contracts?

Are adhesion contracts always unenforceable? The question is considered in the next case, featuring a rock concert promoter.

————

GRAHAM v. SCISSOR–TAIL, INC., 171 Cal.Rptr. 604 (1981). [Bill Graham, "an experienced promoter and producer of musical concerts," entered into a contract with Scissor–Tail, Inc., a corporation representing recording artist Leon Russell. In 1973, Graham and Scissor–Tail agreed to a multi-city concert tour by Russell. Graham signed four contracts, all prepared on an identical form known in the industry as an "American Federation of Musicians (A.F.of M.) Form B Contract." The contract provided that any disputes would be arbitrated by the union's International Executive Board. Russell's concerts met with mixed success and a dispute arose concerning whether losses from one concert could be off-set against profits from another. The parties were unable to resolve the issue, and Graham filed an action for breach of contract. Scissor–Tail moved to compel arbitration and won. After the International Executive Board ruled in Scissor–Tail's favor, Graham appealed from a judgment confirming the arbitrator's award on the grounds that the entire contract was unenforceable as a contract of adhesion, and that the arbitration provision was unconscionable.]

■ THE COURT: The term "contract of adhesion," now long a part of our legal vocabulary, has been variously defined in the cases and other legal literature. The serviceable general definition first suggested by Justice Tobriner in 1961, however, has well stood the test of time and will bear little improvement: "The term signifies a standardized contract, which, imposed and drafted by the party of superior bargaining strength, relegates to the subscribing party only the opportunity to adhere to the contract or reject it." (Neal v. State Farm Ins. Cos. (1961) 188 Cal.App.2d 690, 694 [10 Cal.Rptr. 781].)

Such contracts are, of course, a familiar part of the modern legal landscape, in which the classical model of "free" contracting by parties of equal or near-equal bargaining strength is often found to be unresponsive to the realities brought about by increasing concentrations of economic and other power. They are also an inevitable fact of life for all citizens—businessman and consumer alike....

We believe that the contract here in question, in light of all of the circumstances presented, may be fairly described as adhesive. Although defendant and its supporting amicus curiae are strenuous in their insistence that Graham's prominence and success in the promotion of popular music concerts afforded him considerable bargaining strength in the subject negotiations, the record before us fairly establishes that he, for all his asserted stature in the industry, was here reduced to the humble role of "adherent." It appears that all concert artists and groups of any significance or prominence are members of the A.F. of M.; [and] that pursuant to express provision of the A.F. of M.'s constitution and bylaws members are not permitted to sign any form of contract other than that issued by the union.... In these circumstances it must be concluded that Graham, whatever his asserted prominence in the industry, was required by the realities of his business as a concert promoter to sign A.F. of M. form contracts with *any* concert artist with whom he wished to do business....

To describe a contract as adhesive in character is not to indicate its legal effect. It is, rather, "the beginning and not the end of the analysis insofar as enforceability of its terms is concerned." (Wheeler v. St. Joseph Hospital, supra, 63 Cal.App.3d 345, 357.) Thus, a contract of adhesion is fully enforceable according to its terms, unless certain other factors are present which, under established legal rules—legislative or judicial—operate to render it otherwise.

Generally speaking, there are two judicially imposed limitations on the enforcement of adhesion contracts or provisions thereof. The first is that such a contract or provision which does not fall within the reasonable expectations of the weaker or "adhering" party will not be enforced against him. (See, e.g., Gray v. Zurich Insurance Co. (1966) 419 P.2d 168; Steven v. Fidelity & Casualty Co. (1962) 377 P.2d 284). The second—a principle of equity applicable to all contracts generally—is that a contract or provision, even if consistent with the reasonable expectations of the parties, will be denied enforcement if, considered in its context, it is unduly oppressive or "unconscionable." We proceed to examine whether the instant contract, and especially that provision thereof requiring the arbitration of disputes before the A.F. of M., should have been denied enforcement under either of these two principles.

We cannot conclude on the record before us that the contractual provision requiring arbitration of disputes before the A.F. of M. was in any way contrary to the reasonable expectations of plaintiff Graham. By his own declarations and testimony, he had been a party to literally thousands of A.F. of M. contracts containing a similar provision; indeed it appears that during the 3 years preceding the instant contracts he had promoted 15 or more concerts with Scissor–Tail, on each occasion signing a contract containing arbitration provisions similar to those here in question. It also appears that he had been involved in prior proceedings before the A.F. of M. regarding disputes with other musical groups arising under prior contracts. Finally, the discussions taking place following the Oakland concert, together with his telegram indicating that he himself would file charges with the A.F. of M. if the matter were not settled to his satisfaction ..., all strongly suggest an abiding awareness on his part that all disputes arising under the contracts were to be resolved by arbitration before the A.F. of M. For all of these reasons it must be concluded that the provisions requiring such arbitration ... were wholly consistent with Graham's reasonable expectations upon entering into the contract.

[The court concluded, however, that "[b]ecause [the A.F.M. arbitration provision] designates an arbitrator who, by reason of its status and identity, is presumptively biased in favor of one party," it was unconscionable. This aspect of the case is discussed at Note 4, p. 515 below.]

NOTE

Refining Expectations. What factors made the contract Graham signed one of adhesion? Why, according to the court in this portion of the opinion, was it nonetheless enforceable against Graham?

THE DUTY TO READ AND THE DUTY TO DISCLOSE

In *Henningsen*, the court was concerned not only with whether the purchasers had agreed to Chrysler's disclaimer, but whether at a more fundamental level, they had seen and understood it. What are the obligations of a party to understand the terms of a standardized agreement? What are the obligations, if any, of the imposing party to facilitate such understanding?

The starting point is the common law rule that "in the absence of fraud, one who signs a written agreement is bound by its terms whether he read and understood it or not, or whether he can read or not." Cohen v. Santoianni, 112 N.E.2d 267, 271 (Mass.1953).

In Washington Mutual Finance Group, LLC v. Bailey, 364 F.3d 260, 264–265 (5th Cir. 2004), a group of Mississippi borrowers sought to set aside an agreement with their bank, arguing, in part, that although the borrowers had signed the agreement, they had not read or understood it because they were illiterate. The trial court found the agreement was unenforceable, and the bank appealed. *Held*: Reversed. "The Mississippi Supreme Court has held that, as a matter of law, an individual's inability to understand a contract is not a sufficient basis for concluding a contract is unenforceable." The court quoted earlier Mississippi cases stating that "the suggestion of illiteracy cannot prevail, for the manifest reason that there cannot be two separate departments in the law of contracts, one for the educated and another for those who are not" and that "a person who cannot read had a duty to find someone to read the contract to him."

Yet while there is a general duty to read the contract one signs—or at least there is no relief for those who fail to do so—courts have fashioned various exceptions to relieve a party who has signed a standard form contract that is unintelligible. In one older case, the typography of an insurance policy, long a source of impenetrable documents, was held to present a triable issue of a "fraudulent plot" on the part of the insurer. De Lancey v. Rockingham Farmers' Mut. Fire Insurance Co., 52 N.H. 581 (1873) ("Seldom has the art of typography been so successfully diverted from the diffusion of knowledge to the suppression of it.") Over a hundred years later, in McCarthy Well Co. v. St. Peter Creamery, Inc., 410 N.W.2d 312 (Minn.1987), the court described the contract at issue as "difficult, exceedingly tedious, and even physically painful" to read: "This is not a case of unconscionability as that concept is usually understood.... Rather, this is a case where a party is not able to know what the contract terms are because they are unreadable. As a matter of law, the exculpatory clause will not be enforced."

Legislatures have also sought to make parties aware of terms. For example, a New York statute regulating retail installment sales requires contracts to include the following admonition to buyers: "Do not sign this agreement until you read it." N.Y.Pers.Prop.L. § 402. To ensure that parties can literally see what they are expected to read, the use of red ink for certain terms is sometimes required, as are suitable font sizes and the placement of captions. Other statutes require only that particular information be "conspicuous." The Code, for example, requires that any curtailment of the implied fitness warranty must be "conspicuous," see UCC § 2–316(2), and defines the term with reference to what "a reasonable person against which it is to operate ought to have noticed." See UCC § 1–201(b)(10).

To ensure that terms are not only visible, but intelligible as well, a number of states have enacted "plain language statutes." The New York version requires that agreements affected be

    1. Written in a clear and coherent manner using words with common and every day meanings;

    2. Appropriately divided and captioned by its various sections.

The statute covers written residential leases, and written agreements "to which a consumer is a party and the money, property or service which is the subject of the transaction is primarily for personal, family or household purposes." A qualification is made for agreements "involving amounts in excess of fifty thousand dollars." Gen.Oblig.L. § 5–702.

Still other statutes require that information particularly relevant to the transaction be included, primarily in industries whose contracts have tended to be obscure and one-sided. Thus the Truth in Lending Act (Title I of the Consumer Credit Protection Act) requires early disclosure by financers of an annual percentage rate (APR), which expresses a ratio between the "finance charge" and the "amount financed"—interest and principal in common parlance.

Does the requirement presuppose some level of financial sophistication on the part of those who may borrow money? Are there intrinsic limitations on the utility of disclosure requirements? Are consumers up to the task?

NOTES

(1) *Plain Language in Application.* If the contract in the *Henningsen* case had been subject to a plain-language statute, might the decision have been based on the statute? A characteristic remedy provided for the violation of such a statute is a modest monetary claim, perhaps augmented by an attorney's fee. The New York statute allows recovery of "any actual damages sustained," but it also provides that a violation does not affect the enforceability of an agreement.

Suppose that the contract in *Henningsen* had complied with an applicable plain-language statute. Would that have required the court to modify its opinion in any way?

(2) *Prominent Entities and Average Joes.* In Avenell v. Westinghouse Electric Corp., 324 N.E.2d 583 (Ohio App.1974), a finding of conspicuousness was made—and approved on appeal—for the reason, among others, that the buyer, the Toledo Edison Company, was a "prominent, sophisticated entity." Is there a difference between this case and one in which the buyer is an "average Joe" (or Jane) but happens to know of the disclaimer? What reason might there be for refusing to recognize a distinction?

A similar issue arose regarding the duty to read. In Fraass Surgical Mfg. Co., Inc. v. United States, 571 F.2d 34 (Ct.Cl.1978), an Air Force procurement contract assigned a risk to the supplier which, in previous contracts between the same parties, had been assigned to the government. If the government had known that the supplier was unaware of the change, an appropriate remedy would have been to reform the document so as to assign the risks as before. That knowledge was not proved, however. The supplier's president testified that he did not read the contract "because contracts that he had signed in 1963 and 1960 had contained the other clause." The court found this testimony unacceptable: "He is an experienced businessman and should know better."

(3) *On–Line Disclosures.* In 2000, the Federal Trade Commission published Dot Com Disclosure guidelines which require any disclosure covered by FTC regulations to be "clear and conspicuous." The guidelines advise advertisers with regard to the placement and prominence of disclosures ("Don't be coy"; "Don't be subtle"), as well as the physical proximity of the disclaimer to the claim being qualified. For example, advertisers are encouraged to "Use text or visual cues to encourage consumers to scroll" and to place hyperlinks to disclaimers near the relevant information. What techniques, if any, might encourage on-line purchasers not to "click through" automatically?

––––––

INTRODUCTION TO *CARNIVAL CRUISE LINES*

In the following case, sometimes studied in civil procedure courses, the Court considered the enforceability of a "forum selection" clause in Carnival Cruise Line's contracts with customers. The clause purported to restrict the customers, in bringing suits on their contracts, to actions in the courts of Florida. There is, however, a threshold question about the enforceability of *any* choice-of-forum provision. Courts have traditionally expressed hostility to such a provision, by saying that the parties cannot "oust" a court of jurisdiction over a dispute properly presented to it. A shift of attitude is reflected in the Restatement, Second, of Conflict of Laws § 80, which provides that a choice-of-forum provision "will be given effect unless it is unfair and unreasonable," and in a case on which *Carnival Cruise Lines* relies, The Bremen v. Zapata Off–Shore Co., 407 U.S. 1 (1972). The question may be further considered in a course on the conflict of laws.

Carnival Cruise Lines, Inc. v. Shute

Supreme Court of the United States, 1991.
499 U.S. 585, 111 S.Ct. 1522, 113 L.Ed.2d 622.

■ JUSTICE BLACKMUN delivered the opinion of the Court.

In this admiralty case we primarily consider whether the United States Court of Appeals for the Ninth Circuit correctly refused to enforce a forum-selection clause contained in tickets issued by petitioner Carnival Cruise Lines, Inc., to respondents Eulala and Russel Shute.

I

The Shutes, through an Arlington, Wash., travel agent, purchased passage for a 7–day cruise on petitioner's ship, the *Tropicale*. Respondents paid the fare to the agent who forwarded the payment to petitioner's headquarters in Miami, Fla. Petitioner then prepared the tickets and sent them to respondents in the State of Washington. The face of each ticket, at its left-hand lower corner, contained this admonition:

"SUBJECT TO CONDITIONS OF CONTRACT ON LAST PAGES IMPORTANT! PLEASE READ CONTRACT—ON LAST PAGES 1, 2, 3"

The following appeared on "contract page 1" of each ticket:

"*TERMS AND CONDITIONS OF PASSAGE CONTRACT TICKET*

"3. (a) The acceptance of this ticket by the person or persons named hereon as passengers shall be deemed to be an acceptance and agreement by each of them of all of the terms and conditions of this Passage Contract Ticket.

"8. It is agreed by and between the passenger and the Carrier that all disputes and matters whatsoever arising under, in connection with or incident to this Contract shall be litigated, if at all, in and before a Court located in the State of Florida, U.S.A., to the exclusion of the Courts of any other state or country."

The last quoted paragraph is the forum-selection clause at issue.

II

Respondents boarded the *Tropicale* in Los Angeles, Cal. The ship sailed to Puerto Vallarta, Mexico, and then returned to Los Angeles. While the ship was in international waters off the Mexican coast, respondent Eulala Shute was injured when she slipped on a deck mat during a guided tour of the ship's galley. Respondents filed suit against petitioner in the United

States District Court for the Western District of Washington, claiming that Mrs. Shute's injuries had been caused by the negligence of Carnival Cruise Lines and its employees.

Petitioner moved for summary judgment, contending that the forum clause in respondents' tickets required the Shutes to bring their suit against petitioner in a court in the State of Florida. Petitioner contended, alternatively, that the District Court lacked personal jurisdiction over petitioner because petitioner's contacts with the State of Washington were insubstantial. The District Court granted the motion, holding that petitioner's contacts with Washington were constitutionally insufficient to support the exercise of personal jurisdiction.

The Court of Appeals reversed. Reasoning that "but for" petitioner's solicitation of business in Washington, respondents would not have taken the cruise and Mrs. Shute would not have been injured, the court concluded that petitioner had sufficient contacts with Washington to justify the District Court's exercise of personal jurisdiction. 897 F.2d 377, 385–386 (C.A.9 1990).

Turning to the forum-selection clause, the Court of Appeals acknowledged that a court concerned with the enforceability of such a clause must begin its analysis with The Bremen v. Zapata Off–Shore Co., 407 U.S. 1 (1972), where this Court held that forum-selection clauses, although not "historically . . . favored," are "prima facie valid." Id., at 9–10. See 897 F.2d, at 388. The appellate court concluded that the forum clause should not be enforced because it "was not freely bargained for." Id., at 389. As an "independent justification" for refusing to enforce the clause, the Court of Appeals noted that there was evidence in the record to indicate that "the Shutes are physically and financially incapable of pursuing this litigation in Florida" and that the enforcement of the clause would operate to deprive them of their day in court and thereby contravene this Court's holding in *The Bremen*. 897 F.2d, at 389.

We granted certiorari to address the question whether the Court of Appeals was correct in holding that the District Court should hear respondents' tort claim against petitioner. 498 U.S. 807–808 (1990). Because we find the forum-selection clause to be dispositive of this question, we need not consider petitioner's constitutional argument as to personal jurisdiction. . . .

III

We begin by noting the boundaries of our inquiry. First, this is a case in admiralty, and federal law governs the enforceability of the forum-selection clause we scrutinize. . . . Second, we do not address the question whether respondents had sufficient notice of the forum clause before entering the contract for passage. Respondents essentially have conceded that they had notice of the forum-selection provision. Brief for Respondents 26. . . .

Within this context, respondents urge that the forum clause should not be enforced because, contrary to this Court's teachings in *The Bremen,* the clause was not the product of negotiation, and enforcement effectively would deprive respondents of their day in court. . . .

IV

Both petitioner and respondents argue vigorously that the Court's opinion in *The Bremen* governs this case, and each side purports to find ample support for its position in that opinion's broad-ranging language. This seeming paradox derives in large part from key factual differences between this case and *The Bremen,* differences that preclude an automatic and simple application of *The Bremen*'s general principles to the facts here.

In *The Bremen,* this Court addressed the enforceability of a forum-selection clause in a contract between two business corporations. An American corporation, Zapata, made a contract with Unterweser, a German corporation, for the towage of Zapata's oceangoing drilling rig from Louisiana to a point in the Adriatic Sea off the coast of Italy. The agreement provided that any dispute arising under the contract was to be resolved in the London Court of Justice. After a storm in the Gulf of Mexico seriously damaged the rig, Zapata ordered Unterweser's ship to tow the rig to Tampa, Fla., the nearest point of refuge. Thereafter, Zapata sued Unterweser in admiralty in federal court at Tampa. Citing the forum clause, Unterweser moved to dismiss. The District Court denied Unterweser's motion, and the Court of Appeals for the Fifth Circuit, sitting en banc on rehearing, and by a sharply divided vote, affirmed. In re Complaint of Unterweser Reederei, GmBH, 446 F.2d 907 (1971).

This Court vacated and remanded, stating that, in general, "a freely negotiated private international agreement, unaffected by fraud, undue influence, or overweening bargaining power, such as that involved here, should be given full effect." 407 U.S., at 12–13 (footnote omitted). The Court further generalized that "in the light of present-day commercial realities and expanding international trade we conclude that the forum clause should control absent a strong showing that it should be set aside." Id., at 15. The Court did not define precisely the circumstances that would make it unreasonable for a court to enforce a forum clause. Instead, the Court discussed a number of factors that made it reasonable to enforce the clause at issue in *The Bremen* and that, presumably, would be pertinent in any determination whether to enforce a similar clause.

In this respect, the Court noted that there was "strong evidence that the forum clause was a vital part of the agreement, and [that] it would be unrealistic to think that the parties did not conduct their negotiations, including fixing the monetary terms, with the consequences of the forum clause figuring prominently in their calculations." Id., at 14 (footnote omitted). Further, the Court observed that it was not "dealing with an agreement between two Americans to resolve their essentially local disputes in a remote alien forum," and that in such a case, "the serious inconvenience of the contractual forum to one or both of the parties might carry greater weight in determining the reasonableness of the forum clause." Id., at 17. The Court stated that even where the forum clause establishes a remote forum for resolution of conflicts, "the party claiming [unfairness] should bear a heavy burden of proof." Ibid.

In applying *The Bremen,* the Court of Appeals in the present litigation took note of the foregoing "reasonableness" factors and rather automatically decided that the forum-selection clause was unenforceable because, unlike the parties in *The Bremen,* respondents are not business persons and did not negotiate the terms of the clause with petitioner. Alternatively, the Court of Appeals ruled that the clause should not be enforced because enforcement effectively would deprive respondents of an opportunity to litigate their claim against petitioner.

The Bremen concerned a "far from routine transaction between companies of two different nations contemplating the tow of an extremely costly piece of equipment from Louisiana across the Gulf of Mexico and the Atlantic Ocean, through the Mediterranean Sea to its final destination in the Adriatic Sea." Id., at 13. These facts suggest that, even apart from the evidence of negotiation regarding the forum clause, it was entirely reasonable for the Court in *The Bremen* to have expected Unterweser and Zapata to have negotiated with care in selecting a forum for the resolution of disputes arising from their special towing contract.

In contrast, respondents' passage contract was purely routine and doubtless nearly identical to every commercial passage contract issued by petitioner and most other cruise lines. See, e.g., Hodes v. S.N.C. Achille Lauro ed Altri–Gestione, 858 F.2d 905, 910 (C.A.3 1988), cert. dism'd, 490 U.S. 1001 (1989). In this context, it would be entirely unreasonable for us to assume that respondents—or any other cruise passenger—would negotiate with petitioner the terms of a forum-selection clause in an ordinary commercial cruise ticket. Common sense dictates that a ticket of this kind will be a form contract the terms of which are not subject to negotiation, and that an individual purchasing the ticket will not have bargaining parity with the cruise line. But by ignoring the crucial differences in the business contexts in which the respective contracts were executed, the Court of Appeals' analysis seems to us to have distorted somewhat this Court's holding in *The Bremen.*

In evaluating the reasonableness of the forum clause at issue in this case, we must refine the analysis of *The Bremen* to account for the realities of form passage contracts. As an initial matter, we do not adopt the Court of Appeals' determination that a nonnegotiated forum-selection clause in a form ticket contract is never enforceable simply because it is not the subject of bargaining. Including a reasonable forum clause in a form contract of this kind well may be permissible for several reasons: First, a cruise line has a special interest in limiting the fora in which it potentially could be subject to suit. Because a cruise ship typically carries passengers from many locales, it is not unlikely that a mishap on a cruise could subject the cruise line to litigation in several different fora. See *The Bremen,* 407 U.S., at 13, and n. 15; *Hodes,* 858 F.2d, at 913. Additionally, a clause establishing ex ante the forum for dispute resolution has the salutary effect of dispelling any confusion about where suits arising from the contract must be brought and defended, sparing litigants the time and expense of pretrial motions to determine the correct forum and conserving judicial resources that otherwise would be devoted to deciding those motions. See Stewart Organization, [Inc. v. Ricoh Corp., 487 U.S. 22 (1988)] 487 U.S., at 33 (concurring opinion). Finally, it stands to reason that passengers who purchase tickets containing a forum clause like that at issue in this case benefit in the form of reduced fares reflecting the savings that the cruise line enjoys by limiting the fora in which it may be sued. Cf. Northwestern Nat. Ins. Co. v. Donovan, 916 F.2d 372, 378 (C.A.7 1990).

[The Court also rejected the Court of Appeal's determination that Florida was so inconvenient for the Shutes as to contribute to the unreasonableness of the forum clause.] In the present case, Florida is not a "remote alien forum," nor—given the fact that Mrs. Shute's accident occurred off the coast of Mexico—is this dispute an essentially local one inherently more suited to resolution in the State of Washington than in Florida. In light of these distinctions, and because respondents do not claim lack of notice of the forum clause, we conclude that they have not satisfied the "heavy burden of proof," [407 U.S., at 17] required to set aside the clause on grounds of inconvenience.

It bears emphasis that forum-selection clauses contained in form passage contracts are subject to judicial scrutiny for fundamental fairness. In this case, there is no indication that petitioner set Florida as the forum in which disputes were to be resolved as a means of discouraging cruise passengers from pursuing legitimate claims. Any suggestion of such a bad-faith motive is belied by two facts: Petitioner has its principal place of business in Florida, and many of its cruises depart from and return to Florida ports. Similarly, there is no evidence that petitioner obtained respondents' accession to the forum clause by fraud or overreaching. Finally, respondents have conceded that they were given notice of the forum provision and, therefore, presumably retained the option of rejecting the contract with impunity. In the case before us, therefore, we conclude that the Court of Appeals erred in refusing to enforce the forum-selection clause. . . .

The judgment of the Court of Appeals is reversed.

■ JUSTICE STEVENS, with whom JUSTICE MARSHALL joins, dissenting. The Court prefaces its legal analysis with a factual statement that implies that a purchaser of a Carnival Cruise Lines passenger ticket is fully and fairly notified about the existence of the choice of forum clause in the fine print on the back of the ticket. Even if this implication were accurate, I would disagree with the Court's analysis. But, given the Court's preface, I begin my dissent by noting that only the most meticulous passenger is likely to become aware of the forum-selection provision. I have therefore appended to this opinion a facsimile of the relevant text, using the type size that actually appears in the ticket itself. A careful reader will find the forum-selection clause in the 8th of the 25 numbered paragraphs.

Of course, many passengers, like the respondents in this case, will not have an opportunity to read paragraph 8 until they have actually purchased their tickets. By this point, the passengers will already have accepted the condition set forth in paragraph 16(a), which provides that "the Carrier shall not be liable to make any refund to passengers in respect of . . . tickets wholly or partly not used by a passenger." Not knowing whether or not that provision is legally enforceable, I assume that the average passenger would accept the risk of having to file suit in Florida in the event of an injury, rather than canceling—without a refund—a planned vacation at the last minute. The fact that the cruise line can reduce its litigation costs, and therefore its liability insurance premiums, by forcing this choice on its passengers does not, in my opinion, suffice to render the provision reasonable. Cf. Steven v. Fidelity & Casualty Co. of New York, 58 Cal.2d 862, 883, 377 P.2d 284, 298 (1962) (refusing to enforce limitation on liability in insurance policy because insured "must purchase the policy before he even knows its provisions").

Even if passengers received prominent notice of the forum-selection clause before they committed the cost of the cruise, I would remain persuaded that the clause was unenforceable under traditional principles of federal admiralty law and is "null and void" under the terms of Limitation of Vessel Owner's Liability Act, ch. 521, 49 Stat. 1480, 46 U.S.C.App. § 183c, which was enacted in 1936 to invalidate expressly stipulations limiting shipowners' liability for negligence. . . .

Clauses limiting a carrier's liability or weakening the passenger's right to recover for the negligence of the carrier's employees come in a variety of forms. Complete exemptions from liability for negligence or limitations on the amount of the potential damage recovery, requirements that notice of claims be filed within an unreasonably short period of time, provisions mandating a choice of law that is favorable to the defendant in negligence cases, and forum-selection clauses are all similarly designed to put a thumb on the carrier's side of the scale of justice.

Forum-selection clauses in passenger tickets involve the intersection of two strands of traditional contract law that qualify the general rule that courts will enforce the terms of a contract as written. Pursuant to the first strand, courts traditionally have reviewed with heightened scrutiny the terms of contracts of adhesion, form contracts offered on a take-or-leave basis by a party with stronger bargaining power to a party with weaker power. Some commentators have questioned whether contracts of adhesion can justifiably be enforced at all under traditional contract theory because the adhering party generally enters into them without manifesting knowing and voluntary consent to all their terms. See, e.g., Rakoff, Contracts of Adhesion: An Essay in Reconstruction, 96 Harv.L.Rev. 1173, 1179–1180 (1983); Slawson, Mass Contracts: Lawful Fraud in California, 48 S.Cal. L.Rev. 1, 12–13 (1974); K. Llewellyn, The Common Law Tradition 370–371 (1960).

The common law, recognizing that standardized form contracts account for a significant portion of all commercial agreements, has taken a less extreme position and instead subjects terms in contracts of adhesion to scrutiny for reasonableness. [Mr. Justice Stevens then quotes Judge Skelly Wright's decision in Williams v. Walker–Thomas Furniture Co., p. 403 below, that "when a party of little bargaining power, and hence little real choice, signs a commercially unreasonable contract with little or no knowledge of its terms, it is hardly likely that his consent, or even an objective manifestation of his consent, was ever given to all of the terms. In such a case ... the court should consider whether the terms of the contract are so unfair that enforcement should be withheld."]

The second doctrinal principle implicated by forum-selection clauses is the traditional rule that "contractual provisions, which seek to limit the place or court in which an action may ... be brought, are invalid as contrary to public policy." See Dougherty, Validity of Contractual Provision Limiting Place or Court in Which Action May Be Brought, 31 A.L.R.4th 404, 409, § 3 (1984).... A forum-selection clause in a standardized passenger ticket would clearly have been unenforceable under the common law before our decision in *The Bremen,* see 407 U.S., at 9, and n. 10, and, in my opinion, remains unenforceable under the prevailing rule today.

[Mr. Justice Stevens discussed the Court's decision in *The Bremen,* and gave reasons for a "liberal reading" of the statute relied on by the Shutes.]

The Courts of Appeals, construing an analogous provision of the Carriage of Goods by Sea Act, 46 U.S.C.App. § 1300 et seq., have unanimously held invalid as limitations on liability forum-selection clauses requiring suit in foreign jurisdictions.... The forum-selection clause here does not mandate suit in a foreign jurisdiction, and therefore arguably might have less of an impact on a plaintiff's ability to recover. See Fireman's Fund American Ins. Cos. v. Puerto Rican Forwarding Co., 492 F.2d 1294 (C.A.1 1974). However, the plaintiffs in this case are not large corporations but individuals, and the added burden on them of conducting a trial at the opposite end of the country is likely proportional to the additional cost to a large corporation of conducting a trial overseas.

Under these circumstances, the general prohibition against stipulations purporting "to lessen, weaken, or avoid" the passenger's right to a trial certainly should be construed to apply to the manifestly unreasonable stipulation in these passengers' tickets. Even without the benefit of the statute, I would continue to apply the general rule that prevailed prior to our decision in *The Bremen* to forum-selection clauses in passenger tickets.

I respectfully dissent.

NOTES

(1) *Innocents Abroad.* How would the Shutes have fared if (a) they had contracted for their cruise with a Greek ship owner, (b) their travel agent had dealt with a New York firm as the ship's agent, (c) the contract had restricted actions to the courts of Athens, and (d) the Shutes had brought the action in New York? See Effron v. Sun Line Cruises, Inc., 67 F.3d 7 (2d Cir.1995).

(2) *Legislative Amendment.* In 1992, Congress responded to *Carnival Cruise Lines* by amending a federal statute that the Court, in an omitted part of the opinion, had held inapplicable to the forum-selection clause at issue.

(3) *Scrolling.* Subscribers to an on-line computer service (MSN) challenged the validity of a forum-selection clause included in the MSN membership agreement. The clause stated: "This agreement is governed by the laws of the State of Washington, USA, and you consent to the exclusive jurisdiction and venue of the courts in King County, Washington in all disputes arising out of or relating to your

use of MSN or your MSN membership." Unlike the plaintiffs in *Carnival Cruise Lines*, the subscribers argued that they had *not* received adequate notice of the clause, and therefore it had not become part of the contract. From a New Jersey trial court judgment dismissing the action on the basis of the forum selection clause, the subscribers appealed. *Held*: Affirmed.

The court held that although the medium used to convey the terms was electronic and not printed, "there is no significant difference." "The plaintiffs in this case were free to scroll through the various computer screens that presented the terms of their contract before clicking their agreement.... [T]here was nothing extraordinary about the size or placement of the forum selection clause text.... It was the first item in the last paragraph of the electronic document. We note that a few paragraphs of the contract were presented in upper face typeface, presumably for emphasis, but most provisions, including the forum selection clause, were presented in lower face typeface. We discern nothing about the style or mode of presentation, or the placement of the provision, that can be taken as a basis for concluding that the [clause] was proffered unfairly, or with a design to conceal or de-emphasize its provisions." Caspi v. Microsoft, 732 A.2d 528, 531–32 (N.J.1999).

(4) *Distributive Justice as a Limiting Factor?* Professor Anthony Kronman has argued that "[t]he attack on contracts of adhesion rests upon an unstated conception of distributive fairness; though often overlooked, it is this conception that gives the attack its appeal." Kronman, Paternalism and the Law of Contracts, 92 Yale L.J. 763, 771–72 (1983). Kronman offers the example of the owner of a much coveted oil painting, who dictates the terms of sale, including price and a disclaimer regarding the painting's authenticity, to an eager buyer (Kronman): "Clearly, the fact that I lack bargaining power and must adhere to the terms he proposes does not by itself justify a judicial or legislative effort to tip the balance in my favor. The imbalance in this case, which stems from the fact that he owns the painting and I do not, is unobjectionable because we do not care how control over the painting is distributed.

"We feel differently about the distribution of control over society's available housing stock.... The distribution of housing matters more to us than the distribution of paintings: Only the first is likely to seem important from the standpoint of most theories of distributive justice. Those contracts of adhesion that disturb us do so, then, because they reflect an underlying distribution of power or resources that offends our conception of distributive fairness; when distributive concerns are weak or nonexistent, contracts of adhesion are less troubling and the concept of adhesion itself loses meaning."

Do you agree? Can there be a contract of adhesion for the purchase of cruise tickets?

SOURCES OF POLICING: COURTS, LEGISLATURES, AND AGENCIES

What combination of judicial, legislative, and administrative remedies promise the best result for policing the use of standard form contracts? The following materials review the respective merits and limitations of each. In evaluating the remedies, consider also the competencies of the different state actors to produce and to enforce them.

Judicial Measures. Professor Llewellyn thought that the courts had the solution to problems of standard form contracts ready at hand. As discussed in Note 2, p. 474 above, it is to recognize a distinction between "dickered" terms and boiler-plate clauses. Building on that distinction, he wrote, "the true answer to the whole problem seems, amusingly, to be one which could occur to any court or any lawyer, at any time...." Yet, another thoughtful scholar has countered that "the courts have neither the equipment nor the materials for resolving the basic conflicts of modern society over ... the limits to be set to the use, or misuse, of economic power." John Dawson, Economic Duress—An Essay in Perspective, 45 Mich.L.Rev. 253, 289 (1947). See also Robert Hale, Bargaining, Duress, and Economic Liberty, 43 Colum.L.Rev. 603 (1943).

In like vein, the doctrine of unconscionability, at least in some formulations, has been criticized as a cover for smuggling notions of distributive justice into the judicial process. Schwartz, Seller Unequal Bargaining Power and the Judicial Process, 49 Ind.L.J. 367, 396 (1974) ("The unequal bargaining power concept should be abandoned"); see also Note 4, p. 487 above. Still other scholars have urged the courts to take wide liberties with the terms of standard form contracts and have proposed models of judicial activity more elaborate than anything Llewellyn suggested. See Charles Oldfather Jr., Toward a Usable Method of Judicial Review of the Adhesion Contractor's Lawmaking, 16 U.Kan.L.Rev. 303 (1968); David Slawson, Standard Form Contracts and Democratic Control of Lawmaking Power, 84 Harv.L.Rev. 529 (1971). Automobile manufacturers, Professor Slawson observes, "make more warranty law in a day than most legislatures or courts make in a year." *Id.* at 530.

Statutory Measures. Legislation has been the traditional means of constraining the use of economic power in the imposition of contract terms. Congress has addressed imbalances in bargaining power, for example, in laws that permit collective bargaining by workers, through statutes and administrative rules regulating quasi-public industries such as common carriers and utilities, and more generally through anti-trust laws aimed at preserving a party's opportunity to choose among firms. Other statutes, such as the Consumer Credit Protection Act of 1968, 15 U.S.C. § 1601 et seq., the Magnuson–Moss Warranty Act, Note 3, p. 450 above, and various state laws have focused more directly on consumer protection.

Protective legislation can be grouped loosely into three types. The first, prompted by concern about the fairness of particular terms or of the exchange as a whole, seeks to control the terms of exchange. A second type of measure proceeds from the assumption that consumers can best improve their position through well-informed shopping, facilitated by various disclosure requirements. The third type of control, premised on the belief that consumers suffer systemic handicaps in the effective enforcement of their rights, focuses on remedies. These measures, and others, are exemplified by a New York law regulating the dating service industry, and are the subject of the next principal case.

Administrative Measures. The statutory mandate for many administrative agencies often has more to do with setting the price that a given firm (a public utility, say) may charge than with language in the firm's contracts. Yet agencies have on occasion used their powers to exert control over contract language as well as rates. In many business areas—notably insurance—regulating contract terms is a central part of an agency's mandate.

Sometimes an agency acts in a quasi-judicial way, as when the Federal Trade Commission charges a merchant with a deceptive practice. As the FTC has explained:

> Normally we expect the marketplace to be self-correcting, and we rely on consumer choice—the ability of individual consumers to make their own private purchasing decisions without regulatory intervention—to govern the markets.... However, it has long been recognized that certain types of sales techniques may prevent consumers from effectively making their own decisions and that corrective action may then be necessary. Most of the Commission's unfairness matters are brought ... not to second guess the wisdom of particular consumer decisions, but rather to halt some form of seller behavior that unreasonably creates or takes advantage of an obstacle to the free exercise of consumer decisionmaking. F.T.C. v. IFC Credit Corp., 543 F.Supp.2d 925 (N.D.Ill.2008).

For example, in F.T.C. v. QT, Inc., 448 F.Supp.2d 908 (N.D.Ill.2006), the court enjoined the sale of the "Q–Ray Ionized Bracelet" which the defendants had advertised in print and through infomercials as providing "immediate," "significant," and "medically proven" pain relief. During a seven day trial, the court heard testimony from a number of physicians and scientific researchers. The court ordered the defendants to refund the purchase price to buyers and also to disgorge the $22,500,000 in profits it made during the period the infomercials had been broadcast.

What advantages do you see for consumers in agency supervision?

Doe v. Great Expectations

Civil Court of the City of New York, New York County, 2005.
809 N.Y.S.2d 819.

■ LEBEDEFF, D. Two claimants sue to recover, respectively, $1,000 and $3,790 paid under a contract for defendant's services, which offer to expand a client's social horizons primarily through posting a client's video and profile on an Internet site on which other clients can review them and thereafter, as desired, approach a selected client for actual social interaction. Because of the similarities of these two cases, a consolidated decision is issued.[1]

---

1. The boilerplate printed form contracts has standard terms, reciting that plaintiff would receive a "photo shoot, video, workbook on dating, counseling, background checks, [and] dating etiquette" (para. 2 [a]), and that the defendant "will provide zero number of social referrals" and "is not promising to furnish the Member with any social referrals and the Member does not desire or expect the Company to furnish social referrals" (para. 6; capitalization in original contract removed). The text of the personal shopper membership paragraph does not identify what additional services would be provided nor set forth any assurances regarding introductions (para. 2[a]).

Upon the basis of the contract and testimony, the court determines that the transactions were subject to the Dating Services Law, which regulates defined "social referral services" falling within the scope of General Business Obligations Law § 394–c (Gen. Bus. § 394–c[1][a], " 'social referral service' shall include any service for a fee providing matching of members of the opposite sex, by use of computer or any other means, for the purpose of dating and general social contact"). In relation to the application of the Dating Services Law, more than a decade ago, it was judicially determined that the Law did cover services which match members by creating a location and mechanism for members to assess each other by reviewing another member's video, photograph and profile a substantially similar service to the one defined by the written contract terms here (*Great Expectations Creative Management, Inc. v. Attorney–General of the State of New York*, 616 N.Y.S.2d 917 [Sup.Ct. N.Y. Co.1994] member profile, photos and video maintained at company's center for perusal by other members, such services were covered by statute because "It does not matter whether defendant actually matches its members. It is sufficient if defendant made available the matching of members . . . or supplied the means for matching the members") [citations omitted].

The mere fact that the basic social introduction process was to be conducted on the Internet in this case does not place the dating service outside the scope of the law. The statute specifically includes services which utilize computers (Gen. Bus. § 394–c[1][a], " 'social referral service' shall include any service for a fee providing matching of members . . . by use of computer . . . for the purpose of dating and general social contact"). . . .

Because the Dating Service Law is found applicable, the court will review the contract and the service's operation for compliance with the statute. Two types of departures are found. First, there was a massive overcharge by the dating service. Where, as here, the dating service does not assure it will furnish a client with a specified number of social referrals per month, the service may charge no more than twenty-five dollars (Gen. Bus. § 394–c [3], "Every contract for social referral service which requires payment by the purchaser of such service of a total amount in excess of twenty-five dollars shall provide that the seller of such service must furnish to the purchaser a specified certain number of social referrals per month"). The subject dating service contracts assured that there would be no referrals and, even as the oral assurances given to claimant Roe of twelve introductions to be provided over the course of 36 months, failed to commit to any number of introductions in any given month. Accordingly, $25 was the maximum lawful charge for each contract.

Claimant Doe signed a $1,000 contract for a term of six months. Claimant Roe signed a $3,790 contract for a term of 36 months, which was eventually extended to a total duration of 54 months. Although the printed text of both contracts were identical, Ms. Roe's contract bears the additional handwritten notations of "Marriage Program" and "Platinum Shopper" which indicated that the program orally assured her she would be introduced to twelve people through the program and, in Ms. Doe's contract, the personal shopper membership paragraph is stricken. Ms. Roe testified that she was introduced to no prospective suitors and met only one person who approached her after seeing her posted information; Ms. Doe met no one through the service but, at some point, stopped checking with the service to see if any other clients had reached out to her . . .

Second, in both cases, the defendant's form contract violated every mandate of the Dating Service Law, with the single exception that each contract did contain notice of a three day "cooling off" right to cancel (Gen. Bus. § 394–c[7][a] to [d]). The required provisions omitted from the contracts establish a failure to comply with Gen. Bus. § 394–c subdivision 3 (contracts above twenty-five dollars to state "specified certain number of social referrals per month"), subdivision 4 (contracts above twenty-five dollars to set forth client has "option to cancel the contract and to receive a refund" if minimum referrals not made), subdivision 5 (undertaking service provider will not reveal "any information and material of a personal or private nature" without client's written consent), subdivision 5–a. (granting client "unilateral right to place his or her membership on hold for a period of up to one year"), subdivision 6 (commitment of return to client of "all information and material of a personal or private nature acquired from a purchaser directly or indirectly including but not limited to answers to tests and questionnaires, photographs or background information . . . by certified mail" after conclusion of contract), subdivision 8 (specification of the maximum distance for any face-to-face meeting), and subdivision 8–a (requirement to set forth a policy to be applied if the client "moves to permanently reside at a location outside the service area"). The posture that defendant's services were not governed by the law in any respect also is demonstrated by the failure to provide to the clients written notice of the mandatory "Dating Service Consumer Bill of Rights" (Gen. Bus. § 394–c[7][e], "In every social referral service sale or renewal, the seller shall provide each purchaser with a clear and conspicuous, separate written notice, to be known as the 'Dating Service Consumer Bill of Rights', which shall contain . . . [specified] information", including notice that if the fee exceeded twenty-five dollars, a minimum number of social referrals must be set out as required by Gen. Bus. § 394–c[e][3]).

Turning to the issue of damages, the Dating Service Law states that "[a]ny person who has been injured by reason of a violation of this section may bring . . . an action to recover his or her actual damages or fifty dollars whichever is greater" (Gen. Bus. § 394–c[9][b]). The court is fully satisfied that "actual damages" includes the difference between each contract price and the $25 fee which is the maximum fee permitted under the Dating Service Law for these contracts.

Both claimants seek a return of the full balance paid, which raises the question of whether they establish damages justifying a return of the additional $25 each. This court had its opportunity to "view the witnesses, hear the testimony and observe demeanor." Issues of credibility, as well as the weight to be given to the evidence presented, are primarily questions to be determined by the court in a non-jury trial.

In this case, each claimant, both appearing to be intelligent, well spoken and attractive professional women, carefully negotiated the services to be provided. Defendant had the obligation to assure that each client of the dating service was made aware of statutory rights by providing each with the "Dating Service Consumer Bill of Rights" (Gen. Bus. § 394–c[7][e]). Based upon the testimony, the court determines that each claimant would not have signed a contract containing terms violating applicable law, had she known of her rights and, accordingly, each claimant is entitled to a refund of the final $25.00 balance at issue, which finding achieves substantial justice in these Small Claims matters (N.Y.C.C.A. § 1805[a]).

Given the foregoing, it is determined that the claimants are entitled to a full refund as restitutionary damages. The statute's reference to "actual damages" was added to the Dating Service law in 1992 (L. 1992, c. 348, § 1, adding subdivision 9(b) to Gen. Bus. § 394–c), and as a part of the same legislation newly authorized the Attorney General to bring enforcement actions and to seek civil penalties of up to $1,000 for each violation (Gen. Bus. § 394–c [9][a]; *see*, for example, *People by Vacco v. Introductions Inc.*, 252 A.D.2d 631, 632, [3d Dept.1998], suit against dating service sought restitution for 521 customer complaints in the amount of $204,287.10 and penalties of $150,000).

Logic indicates that the 1992 amendment "evened the playing field" by offering a single remedy of restitution to a consumer, which could be achieved by the alternate routes of commencing an individual suit or filing a complaint with the Attorney General. It then follows that the legislature, by adding the "actual damage" language to the statute in 1992 did not erode New York State's commitment to protect consumers from price gouging by dating services. However, such contracts may no longer simply be set aside as contrary to public policy, as was done in the 1991 decision based upon an earlier version of the Dating Service Law (*Chassman v. People Resources, supra,* 151 Misc.2d at 528–529, 573 N.Y.S.2d 589, given the then existing "statute's silence as to the penalty for non-compliance . . . public policy demands . . . non-complying contracts be deemed void and unenforceable. If such contracts were to be enforced . . . social referral services would continue to violate the statute with impunity, secure in the knowledge that the only penalty they face will be a reduction in their fee to the statutory limit").

Based upon the foregoing, the court awards actual damages of the face amount of the contract to each claimant, with interest to commence on the date of the contract payment. Because claimant Doe's contract has expired and claimant Roe's contract is terminated by reason of this determination, defendant may wish to return personal material to each claimant, notwithstanding that such obligation does not appear in this contract (Gen. Bus. § 394–c[6], quoted above). A failure to return personal materials could well lead to adverse consequences outside the scope of this litigation.

Finally, the court considers whether it should exercise its judicial discretion to report the activity found to violate applicable law to appropriate governmental authorities, which in this case would be to the New York State Attorney General's Consumer Fraud Unit, as well as the New York City Department of Consumer Affairs (Gen. Bus. § 394–c[9][c], "In cities having a population over one million, the provisions of this section may be enforced concurrently with the attorney general by the director of a local or municipal consumer affairs office").

Although "[n]o . . . rule has been adopted as to what is required if a judge receives information indicating that a litigant or witness appears to be guilty of unlawful conduct", it has been recognized that "as a general rule judges are granted the discretion, under the proper circumstances, ... to report instances of illegal conduct revealed in the course of proceedings before the judge" (New York State Office of Court Administration's Advisory Committee on Judicial Ethics Opinion 03–110, August 13, 2004). As to the exercise of such discretion, in a 1988 opinion, the Advisory Committee wrote (1) that the "desirability or appropriateness ... depends on all the circumstances, such as the nature of the [offense], the effect of such report on the administration of justice, and, in particular, on the court's truth determining function, and whether it was revealed by the perpetrator's voluntary testimony," (2) that a report could be "undesirable" if it "would dissuade witnesses on trial from telling the whole truth or encourage the threat of possible criminal proceedings as a means of pressure, for settlement purposes or otherwise, by one litigant against another" and (3) a judicial decision to report would be proper if the judge concluded "reporting such a revealed [offense] is in the public interest" (Joint Opinion 88–85 and 88–103, December 8, 1988).

The court considers the following factors: (1) that reporting the wrongful activity found impacts upon the public interest, given that the acts violated rules governing a regulated industry and appear to reflect a continuing pattern and practice on the part of the defendant as indicated by, among other things, the use of a printed boilerplate form found not to be in accordance with applicable laws; (2) the court's past and future truth determining function in each matter has not been, and will not be, impacted by a potential or actual report because no threat of future reporting was posed during the course of these proceedings, and these matters are now disposed; and (3) a question touching upon the administration of justice and the integrity of a court order may be posed in that a similar course of conduct by the same or a related defendant was previously litigated (*Great Expectations Creative Management, Inc. v. Attorney–General of the State of New York, supra*). As to the manner of the report, it shall be accomplished by forwarding a copy of this decision to the appropriate public officials.

Prior to the issuance of a judgment, the name of the defendant in each case is amended to reflect that the defendant Great Expectations is also known as GE Management Group of NY, Inc., as indicated in the written contracts.

This decision constitutes the order of the court.

NOTES

(1) *Questions.* What exactly had Great Expectations promised Roe and Doe?

What result if Roe and Doe had received the Dating Service Bill of Rights when they signed their contracts? What measure of damages did Roe and Doe receive? How does a civil penalty differ from punitive damages, discussed in White v. Benkowski, p. 23 above?

Great Expectations had argued, unsuccessfully, that because it merely provided its clients with access to one another's profiles, it was not a social referral service and not covered by the statute; see also Grossman v. MatchNet, 10 A.D.3d 577 (2004).

The court found the claimants were "intelligent" and careful negotiators. What result in a similar case had the claimants been found to be of average ability and nonchalant when signing up for dating services?

(2) *Remedies in Practice Reprised.* The claimants brought their suit in New York Civil Court, which has jurisdiction over civil matters not exceeding $25,000. As stated on the court's website: "Our court is where everyday people come to resolve their everyday legal problems. Whether you are a local merchant, a consumer, a debtor, or a creditor, the Civil Court is dedicated to providing access to fair and efficient justice." http://www.courts.state.ny.us/courts/nyc/smallclaims/index.shtml. Small claims courts, like the New York Civil Court, facilitate the appearance of pro se litigants like Roe and Doe, who represented themselves in the case and appeared without the formal assistance of counsel.

(3) *Scope of Protection.* What factors may have contributed to the decision by the New York legislature to enact, and then to amend, its dating services law?

The Dating Service Law appears to apply only to opposite-sex couples. Does this raise an issue of discrimination? See Note 2 on p. 560 below. The topic is left for consideration in courses on constitutional law.

SECTION 3.   UNCONSCIONABILITY

In McKinnon v. Benedict, p. 455 above, the court found the inadequacy of consideration "so gross as to be unconscionable and a bar to the plaintiff's invocation of the extraordinary equitable powers of the court." But although the concept of unconscionability itself is by no means new, its embodiment in the Uniform Commercial Code in the early 1960's focused new attention on the doctrine. No longer limited to actions in equity, the doctrine is now a defense in its own right. As with conventional controls, the elements of status, behavior, and substance, in their various combinations, remain a focus of concern.

The statutory starting point is UCC § 2–302, one of the most widely debated sections of the Code. The section authorizes a court to refuse enforcement or to limit the application of a contract or clause that it determines to have been "unconscionable." Comment 1 to that section reads in part:

"This section is intended to make it possible for the courts to police explicitly against the contracts or clauses which they find to be unconscionable. In the past such policing has been accomplished by adverse construction of language, by manipulation of the rules of offer and acceptance or by determinations that the clause is contrary to public policy or to the dominant purpose of the contract.... The principle is one of the prevention of oppression and unfair surprise (Cf. Campbell Soup Co. v. Wentz, 172 F.2d 80, 3d Cir.1948) and not of disturbance of allocation of risks because of superior bargaining power."

Campbell Soup Co. v. Wentz, found at p. 584 below, concerned a standard form canner-grower contract. Wentz, a farmer, had committed his entire crop of carrots to Campbell for a price of not to exceed $30 a ton. By the time for delivery a scarcity had developed. Carrots were virtually unobtainable, and their price had risen to at least $90 a ton. When

Campbell's suppliers, including Wentz, began to sell some of their committed crops to others, it brought an action for specific performance. The court of appeals found several provisions of the contracts to be objectionable and refused to grant equitable relief. For example, the growers were not permitted to sell even those carrots rejected by Campbell to anyone else without Campbell's written permission. As to this provision, the court stated that "This is the kind of provision which the late Francis H. Bohlen would call 'carrying a good joke too far.'" In refusing to enforce the contract on the ground of unconscionability, the court stated that "we are not suggesting that the contract is illegal. Nor are we suggesting any excuse for the grower in this case who has deliberately broken an agreement." Nonetheless, noting that the contract was obviously "drawn by skillful draftsmen with the buyer's interests in mind," the court found it was "too hard a bargain to entitle the plaintiff to relief in a court of conscience."

Campbell Soup, like most of the other cases used by the drafters to illustrate the application of unconscionability, involved commercial sales between businesses. Since the Code's enactment, however, unconscionability has made its mark primarily in the area of consumer contracts. In addition, state codes now regularly include provisions authorizing courts to deny enforcement to all types of contracts, whether in part or in their entirety, on ground of unconscionability. See Cal. Civ. Code § 1670.5; Tex.Bus. & Com.Code Ann. § 17.45(5).

NOTES

(1) *Questions.* Does the *Campbell Soup* decision, cited in Comment 1 to UCC § 2–302, support the Code rule? *Campbell Soup* is the basis for Illustration 1 to Restatement § 208, which states a rule in virtually the same terms as UCC § 2–302(1). The section is without parallel in the original Restatement.

(2) *Overservice by the Profession.* Professor Llewellyn, the Chief Reporter of the Code, defended the section at the hearings of the New York Law Revision Commission in 1954 in these words:

"Business lawyers tend to draft to the edge of the possible. Any engineer makes his construction within a margin of safety, and a wide margin of safety, so that he knows for sure that he is getting what he is gunning for. The practice of business lawyers has been, however—it has grown to be so in the course of time—to draft, as I said before, to the edge of the possible.

"Let me rapidly state that I do not find that this is desired by the business lawyers' clients.... The only doubt that comes up in regard to unconscionability is, if you start drafting to the absolute limit of what the law can conceivably bear. At that point you run into what they run into now, and what you run into now is, the court kicks it over." Report of the New York State Law Revision Commission for 1954, N.Y.Leg.Doc. (1954) No. 65, pp. 177–78.

Note that under UCC § 2–302 the issue of unconscionability is not to be submitted to a jury. What do you think explains this reservation by the Code drafters?

UNCONSCIONABILITY: TWO VIEWS

The following excerpts from two wide-ranging essays indicating the differing degrees of welcome the doctrine of unconscionability has received. Each author is concerned with the relation of unconscionability to classic common law concepts. The first offers a defense and explication of the doctrine; the second raises a fundamental objection.

(a) *An Explication.* "When the concept of unconscionability was first made explicit by the Uniform Commercial Code, the initial effort was to reconcile it with the bargain principle. A major step in this direction was a distinction, drawn in 1967 by Professor Arthur Leff, between 'procedural' and 'substantive' unconscionability. Leff defined procedural unconscionability as fault or unfairness in the bargaining *process;* substantive unconscionability as fault or unfairness in the bargaining *outcome*—that is, unfairness of terms. The effect (if not the purpose) of this distinction, which influenced much of the later analysis, was to domesticate unconscionability by accepting the concept insofar as it could be made harmonious with the bargain principle (that is, insofar as it was 'procedural'), while rejecting its wider implication that in appropriate cases the courts might review bargains for fairness of terms. Correspondingly, much of the scholarly literature and case law concerning unconscionability has emphasized the element of unfair surprise, in which a major underpinning of the bargain principle—knowing assent—is absent by hypothesis."

"Over the last fifteen years, however, there have been strong indications that the principle of unconscionability authorizes a review of elements well beyond unfair surprise, including, in appropriate cases, fairness of terms. For example, Comment *c* to section 208 of the Restatement (Second) of Contracts states that '[t]heoretically it is possible for a contract to be oppressive taken as a whole, even though there is no weakness in the bargaining process and no single term which is in itself unconscionable.' . . . [A] basic thesis of this Article is that unconscionability is a paradigmatic concept that can never be exhaustively described. It is, however, a major purpose [here] to suggest a methodology by which specific unconscionability norms should be developed. Three general propositions underlie the methodology, and should be stated at the outset: (1) Since the bargain principle rests on arguments of fairness and efficiency, it is appropriate to develop and apply a specific unconscionability norm whenever a class of cases can be identified in which neither fairness nor efficiency support the bargain principle's application. (2) The development and application of specific unconscionability norms is closely related to the manner in which the relevant market deviates from a perfectly competitive market. (3) The distinction between procedural and substantive unconscionability is too rigid to provide significant help in either the development or the application of such norms." Melvin Eisenberg, The Bargain Principle and Its Limits, 95 Harv.L.Rev. 741, 752–54 (1982).

(b) *A Fundamental Objection.* "[This paper offers a defense] against modern attacks [on] the principle of freedom of contract which was central to the classical common law. Properly understood, that position does not require a court to enforce every contract brought before it. It does, however, demand that the reasons invoked for not enforcing the contract be of one of two sorts. Either there must be proof of some defect in the process of contract formation (be it duress, fraud or undue influence); or there must be, but only within narrow limits, some incompetence of the party against whom the agreement is to be enforced. The doctrine of unconscionability is important in both these respects because it can, if wisely applied, allow the courts to police these two types of problems, and thereby improve the general administration of the contract law. Yet when the doctrine of unconscionability is used in its substantive dimension, be it in a commercial or consumer context, it serves only to undercut the private right of contract in a manner that is apt to do more social harm than good. The result of the analysis is the same even if we view the question of unconscionability from the lofty perspective of public policy. '[I]f there is one thing which more than another public policy requires, it is that men of full age and competent understanding shall have the utmost liberty of contracting, and that their contracts when entered into freely and voluntarily shall be held sacred and shall be enforced by Courts of justice.' "[1] Richard Epstein, Unconscionability: A Critical Reappraisal, 18 J.Law & Econ. 293, 315 (1975).

Williams v. Walker–Thomas Furniture Co.

United States Court of Appeals, District of Columbia Circuit, 1965.
350 F.2d 445.

■ J. Skelly Wright, Circuit Judge. Appellee, Walker–Thomas Furniture Company, operates a retail furniture store in the District of Columbia. During the period from 1957 to 1962 each appellant in these cases purchased a number of household items from Walker–Thomas, for which payment was to be made in installments. The terms of each purchase were contained in a printed form contract which set forth the value of the purchased item and purported to lease the item to appellant for a stipulated monthly rent payment. The contract then provided, in substance, that title would remain in Walker–Thomas until the total of all the monthly payments made equaled the stated value of the item, at which time appellants could take title. In the event of a default in the payment of any monthly installment, Walker–Thomas could repossess the item.

The contract further provided that "the amount of each periodical installment payment to be made by (purchaser) to the Company under this present lease shall be inclusive of and not in addition to the amount of each installment payment to be made by (purchaser) under such prior leases, bills or accounts; *and all payments now and hereafter made by (purchaser) shall be credited pro rata on all outstanding leases, bills and accounts* due the Company by (purchaser) at the time each such payment is made." (Emphasis added.) The effect of this rather obscure provision was to keep a balance due on every item purchased until the balance due on all items, whenever purchased, was liquidated. As a result, the debt incurred at the time of purchase of each item was secured by the right to repossess all the

---

1. Printing and Numerical Registering
Co. v. Sampson, L.R. 19 Eq. 462, 465 (1875).

items previously purchased by the same purchaser, and each new item purchased automatically became subject to a security interest arising out of the previous dealings.

On May 12, 1962, appellant Thorne purchased an item described as a Daveno, three tables, and two lamps, having total stated value of $391.10. Shortly thereafter, he defaulted on his monthly payments and appellee sought to replevy all the items purchased since the first transaction in 1958. Similarly, on April 17, 1962, appellant Williams bought a stereo set of stated value of $514.95.[1] She too defaulted shortly thereafter, and appellee sought to replevy all the items purchased since December, 1957.[a] The Court of General Sessions granted judgment for appellee. The District of Columbia Court of Appeals affirmed, and we granted appellants' motion for leave to appeal to this court.

Appellants' principal contention, rejected by both the trial and the appellate courts below, is that these contracts, or at least some of them, are unconscionable and, hence, not enforceable. In its opinion in Williams v. Walker–Thomas Furniture Company, 198 A.2d 914, 916 (1964), the District of Columbia Court of Appeals explained its rejection of this contention as follows:

"Appellant's second argument presents a more serious question. The record reveals that prior to the last purchase appellant had reduced the balance in her account to $164. The last purchase, a stereo set, raised the balance due to $678. Significantly, at the time of this and the preceding purchases, appellee was aware of appellant's financial position. The reverse side of the stereo contract listed the name of appellant's social worker and her $218 monthly stipend from the government. Nevertheless, with full knowledge that appellant had to feed, clothe and support both herself and seven children on this amount, appellee sold her a $514 stereo set.

"We cannot condemn too strongly appellee's conduct. It raises serious questions of sharp practice and irresponsible business dealings. A review of the legislation in the District of Columbia affecting retail sales and the pertinent decisions of the highest court in this jurisdiction disclose, however, no ground upon which this court can declare the contracts in question contrary to public policy. We note that were the Maryland Retail Installment Sales Act, Art. 83 §§ 128–153, or its equivalent, in force in the District of Columbia, we could grant appellant appropriate relief. We think Congress should consider corrective legislation to protect the public from such exploitive contracts as were utilized in the case at bar."

We do not agree that the court lacked the power to refuse enforcement to contracts found to be unconscionable. In other jurisdictions, it has been

---

1. At the time of this purchase her account showed a balance of $164 still owing from her prior purchases. The total of all the purchases made over the years in question came to $1,800. The total payments amounted to $1,400.

a. "The store's records showed that of a combined total claim of $444 as of December 26, 1962, Ora still owed 25¢ on item 1, purchased December 23, 1957 (price $45.65); 3on item 2, purchased December 31, 1957 (price $13.21); ... and similarly for subsequent purchases...." Skilton & Helstad, Protection of the Installment Buyer of Goods under the UCC, 65 Mich.L.Rev. 1465 (1967) held as a matter of common law that unconscionable contracts are not enforceable.[2] While no decision of this court so holding has been found, the notion that an unconscionable bargain should not be given full enforcement is by no means novel. In Scott v. United States, 79 U.S. (12 Wall.) 443, 445, 20 L.Ed. 438 (1870), the Supreme Court stated:

> "... If a contract be unreasonable and unconscionable, but not void for fraud, a court of law will give to the party who sues for its breach damages, not according to its letter, but only such as he is equitably entitled to...."

Since we have never adopted or rejected such a rule, the question here presented is actually one of first impression.

Congress has recently enacted the Uniform Commercial Code, which specifically provides that the court may refuse to enforce a contract which it finds to be unconscionable at the time it was made. [Section 2–302] The enactment of this section, which occurred subsequent to the contracts here in suit, does not mean that the common law of the District of Columbia was otherwise at the time of enactment, nor does it preclude the court from adopting a similar rule in the exercise of its powers to develop the common law for the District of Columbia. In fact, in view of the absence of prior authority on the point, we consider the congressional adopting of Section 2–302 persuasive authority for following the rationale of the cases, from which the section is explicitly derived.[3] Accordingly, we hold that where the element of unconscionability is present at the time a contract is made, the contract should not be enforced.

Unconscionability has generally been recognized to include an absence of meaningful choice on the part of one of the parties together with contract terms which are unreasonably favorable to the other party. Whether a meaningful choice is present in a particular case can only be determined by consideration of all the circumstances surrounding the transaction. In many cases the meaningfulness of the choice is negated by a gross inequality of bargaining power.[4] The manner in which the contract was entered is also relevant to this consideration. Did each party to the

---

2. Campbell Soup Co. v. Wentz, 172 F.2d 80 (3d Cir.1948); Indianapolis Morris Plan Corp. v. Sparks, 132 Ind.App. 145, 172 N.E.2d 899 (1961); Henningsen v. Bloomfield Motors, Inc., 32 N.J. 358, 161 A.2d 69, 84–96 (1960). Cf. 1 Corbin, Contracts Section 128 (1963).

3. See Comment, Sec. 2–302, Uniform Commercial Code (1962). Compare Note, 45 Va.L.Rev. 583, 590 (1959), where it is predicted that the rule of Sec. 2–302 will be followed by analogy in cases which involve contracts not specifically covered by the section. Cf. 1 State of New York Law Revision Commission, Report and Record of Hearings on the Uniform Commercial Code 108–110 (1954) (remarks of Professor Llewellyn).

4. See Henningsen v. Bloomfield Motors, Inc., supra Note 2, 161 A.2d 69 at 86,

and authorities there cited. Inquiry into the relative bargaining power of the two parties is not an inquiry wholly divorced from the general question of unconscionability, since a one-sided bargain is itself evidence of the inequality of the bargaining parties. This fact was vaguely recognized in the common law doctrine of intrinsic fraud, that is, fraud which can be presumed from the grossly unfair nature of the terms of the contract. See the oft-quoted statement of Lord Hardwicke in Earl of Chesterfield v. Janssen, 28 Eng. Rep. 82, 100 (1751):

> "... (Fraud) may be apparent from the intrinsic nature and subject of the bargain itself; such as no man in his senses and not under delusion would make ..."

contract, considering his obvious education or lack of it, have a reasonable opportunity to understand the terms of the contract, or were the important terms hidden in a maze of fine print and minimized by deceptive sales practices? Ordinarily, one who signs an agreement without full knowledge of its terms might be held to assume the risk that he has entered a one-sided bargain.[5] But when a party of little bargaining power, and hence little real choice, signs a commercially unreasonable contract with little or no knowledge of its terms, it is hardly likely that his consent, or even an objective manifestation of his consent, was ever given to all the terms. In such a case the usual rule that the terms of the agreement are not to be questioned[6] should be abandoned and the court should consider whether the terms of the contract are so unfair that enforcement should be withheld.[7]

In determining reasonableness or fairness, the primary concern must be with the terms of the contract considered in light of the circumstances existing when the contract was made. The test is not simple, nor can it be mechanically applied. The terms are to be considered "in the light of the general commercial background and the commercial needs of the particular trade or case."[8] Corbin suggests the test as being whether the terms are "so extreme as to appear unconscionable according to the mores and business practices of the time and place." 1 Corbin, op. cit. supra Note 2.[9] We think this formulation correctly states the test to be applied in those cases where no meaningful choice was exercised upon entering the contract.

Because the trial court and the appellate court did not feel that enforcement could be refused, no findings were made on the possible unconscionability of the contracts in these cases. Since the record is not sufficient for our deciding the issue as a matter of law, the cases must be remanded to the trial court for further proceedings.

So ordered.

■ DANAHER, CIRCUIT JUDGE (dissenting): The District of Columbia Court of Appeals obviously was as unhappy about the situation here presented as

---

5. See Restatement, Contracts Sec. 70 (1932); Note, 63 Harv.L.Rev. 494 (1950). See also Daley v. People's Building, Loan & Savings Ass'n, 178 Mass. 13, 59 N.E. 452, 453 (1901), in which Mr. Justice Holmes, while sitting on the Supreme Judicial Court of Massachusetts, made this observation:

"... Courts are less and less disposed to interfere with parties making such contracts as they choose, so long as they interfere with no one's welfare but their own.... It will be understood that we are speaking of parties standing in an equal position where neither has any oppressive advantage or power...."

6. This rule has never been without exception. In cases involving merely the transfer of unequal amounts of the same commodity, the courts have held the bargain unenforceable for the reason that "in such a case, it is clear, that the law cannot indulge in the presumption of equivalence between the consideration and the promise." 1 Williston, Contracts Sec. 115 (3d ed. 1957).

7. See the general discussion of "Boiler–Plate Agreements" in Llewellyn, The Common Law Tradition 362–371 (1960).

8. Comment, Uniform Commercial Code Sec. 2–307.

9. See Henningsen v. Bloomfield Motors, Inc., supra Note 2; Mandel v. Liebman, 303 N.Y. 88, 100 N.E.2d 149 (1951). The traditional test as stated in Greer v. Tweed ..., 13 Abb.Pr., N.S. (N.Y.1872), at 429, is "such as no man in his senses and not under delusion would make on the one hand, and as no honest or fair man would accept, on the other."

any of us can possibly be. Its opinion in the *Williams* case, quoted in the majority text, concludes: "We think Congress should consider corrective legislation to protect the public from such exploitive contracts as were utilized in the case at bar."

My view is thus summed up by an able court which made no finding that there had actually been sharp practice. Rather the appellant seems to have known precisely where she stood.

There are many aspects of public policy here involved. What is a luxury to some may seem an outright necessity to others. Is public oversight to be required of the expenditures of relief funds? A washing machine, e.g., in the hands of a relief client might become a fruitful source of income. Many relief clients may well need credit, and certain business establishments will take long chances on the sale of items, expecting their pricing policies will afford a degree of protection commensurate with the risk. Perhaps a remedy when necessary will be found within the provisions of the "Loan Shark" law, D.C.Code Sections 26–601 et seq. (1961).

I mention such matters only to emphasize the desirability of a cautious approach to any such problem, particularly since the law for so long has allowed parties such great latitude in making their own contracts. I dare say there must annually be thousands upon thousands of installment credit transactions in this jurisdiction, and one can only speculate as to the effect the decision in these cases will have.[10]

I join the District of Columbia Court of Appeals in its disposition of the issues.

NOTES

(1) *Questions.* What exactly did the court hold? What should the trial court do on remand?

What is offensive about the allocation of payment provision? It may help to know that another way to apportion a payment is in relation to the *original* debt for each item. If the store had applied Mrs. Williams' payments that way, she would evidently have paid in full for about a dozen of the 16 items she bought from the store. Could the store have been compelled to reallocate her payments in that manner, as a plausible reading of the contract?

What is offensive about the cross-collateral or "dragnet" clause? Under this provision the seller is entitled to repossess one item for the buyer's failure to pay for another. If the repossessed items are resold for less than the buyer's indebtedness, the seller is generally entitled to a deficiency judgment for the difference. If they are resold for more than is due, the seller must account to the buyer for the surplus. What is the likelihood of a surplus on the resale of second-hand consumer goods? If it is unlikely that the seller will recoup by repossessing the goods, what functions might the seller's right to repossess serve?

If the seller had pointed out and explained the allocation and cross-collateral clauses to Mrs. Williams, would that have made a difference to the holding? Is the court concerned with the terms of the deal, the bargaining process, or characteris-

10. However the provision ultimately may be applied or in what circumstances, D.C.Code Sec. 28–2–302 (Supp. IV, 1965) did not become effective until January 1, 1965.

tics (or assumptions about characteristics) of Mrs. Williams in relation to the transaction?

(2) *Case in Context.* In evaluating the *Williams* decision, consider the following description of the Walker–Thomas store and its customers in the 1970s:

The primary need of Walker–Thomas customers is installment credit. Whereas downtown and suburban "name" stores turn away almost all unemployed and benefit-receiving credit applicants, Walker–Thomas abounds with easy credit.... In fact, credit is not merely available at Walker–Thomas, it is required. The company often tells customers that for purchases above $100, credit is the only acceptable means of payment.

The shopping radius of poor people is often quite narrow.... [Walker–Thomas'] 30–odd traveling representatives ... widen this shopping area so that [it] often become the only accessible merchant of credit. The sales representative system also allows the extension of credit to people who could not otherwise qualify under normal circumstances. Most stores require customers to bring payments to the store or mail them; the burden is theirs. Walker–Thomas, in contrast, brings collection to its clientele.... Since its customers' prime source of income is the monthly benefit checks, salespeople can schedule collection for days when checks are likely to arrive.... The salespeople and the postman therefore tend to arrive simultaneously; the salesperson then cashes the check, taking out the amount of the monthly payment....

Besides goods and services, the salespeople also provide intangible, psychological rewards for their customers. Many people are making their first major purchase on credit, and ... it is the salesperson who is providing the previously unattainable product. ... Like the cashing of benefits checks, [arranging credit and delivering goods quickly] must be understood in the context of the treatment these customers usually receive in retail stores. They are often abused and misunderstood because of language difficulties [and] watched suspiciously by security guards ... In contrast, the Walker–Thomas sales representative ... takes orders and produces goods without any effort on the customer's part, seems to understand payment difficulties, explains contractual arrangements in simple language, even keeps track of accounts in his or her notebook.... Their treatment of their low-income constituency encourages the transformation of a professional relationship into one of a highly personal, highly informal, mutually beneficial nature. Or so it would appear." Daniel Greenberg, Easy Terms, Hard Times: Complaint Handling in the Ghetto 379, 381–84, in *No Access to Law: Alternatives to the American Judicial System*, Laura Nader, ed. (1980) "(quoting 1968 report by the National Advisory Commission on Civil Disorders)".

(3) *The Lawyer's Role.* Mrs. Williams was represented by the Legal Assistance Office of the bar association. That office "was willing to concede that the store could repossess the stereo record player for nonpayment, but what stirred them to action was that the seller sought to scoop up all that it had ever sold to Ora." Skilton & Helstad, fn. a, p. 498, above. As a legal precedent, the court's ruling on unconscionability is more significant for consumers generally than any victory Mrs. Williams could have won on the basis of interpretation of her contract. Legal-aid lawyers report that they can often settle complaints of individual consumer debtors on favorable terms. In such a situation, what is the duty of the lawyer? Should they urge such a client to forgo settlement on a narrow claim in the hope of obtaining a landmark ruling on a broader principle like unconscionability? What are the ethical considerations?

(4) *Unconscionability and Incapacity.* Is the *Williams* case good for consumers? Professor Leff drew an analogy between unconscionability and incapacity, discussed in Note 2, p. 457 above, arguing that both illustrate a tendency toward stereotyping

of parties. Leff wrote: "One can see it enshrined in the old English equity courts' jolly treatment of English seamen as members of a happy, fun-loving race . . ., but certainly not to be trusted to take care of themselves. What effect, if any, this had upon the sailors is hidden behind the judicial chuckles as they protected their loyal sailor boys, but one cannot help wondering how many sailors managed to get credit at any reasonable price. In other words, the benevolent have a tendency to colonize, whether geographically or legally." Leff, Unconscionability and the Code—The Emperor's New Clause, 115 U.Pa.L.Rev. 485, 556–58 (1967).

Is this fair criticism of the *Williams* case? *Is* the lower court's decision paternalistic? Should the application of the principle of unconscionability be regarded as defining a new class of persons—"the poor" or "the vulnerable"—lacking the capacity to contract fully? Should the focus remain on the characteristics of the *transaction* rather than the characteristics of the subservient party?

(5) *Rent-to-Own.* One way sellers have gotten around regulations attempting to protect consumers in credit sales is to *lease,* rather than sell, household goods. As described by one court, "the rent-to-own contract is styled as a lease renewal from week-to-week or month-to-month. Upon renewal for the stipulated number of weeks or months, the 'lessee' obtains ownership of the personal property. The 'lessee' had the option to terminate the lease at any time in this fashion, and can eliminate a financial burden at anytime. In return, the consumer ordinarily pays considerably more for the item than the retail price and loses any equity that may have accrued before termination of the agreement if less than all the specified renewals are made." Green v. Continental Rentals, 678 A.2d 759 (N.J.Super.1994). In that case the court found that the "rent" was really interest in disguise and therefore constituted an unconscionable practice under New Jersey's Consumer Fraud Act. Federal Reserve Board regulations, however, exclude rent-to-own contracts from the definition of "credit sales" under the Federal Truth in Lending Act. See Ortiz v. Rental Management Inc., 65 F.3d 335 (3d Cir.1995).

———

PRICE UNCONSCIONABILITY

May a court determine that the price charged for goods is so high that the contract is unconscionable on that ground alone? Must the court be prepared to say what the "intrinsic" value of the goods is? Must it be prepared to say what costs of doing business the seller may reasonably incur? Or what would be a reasonable profit? Is it a valid defense to a claim of price unconscionability that the seller proves no greater profit than a similarly situated seller would receive? The following case and notes suggest the parameters of answers to these questions.

Jones v. Star Credit Corp.

N.Y.Supreme Court, 1969.
298 N.Y.S.2d 264.

■ WACHTLER, J. On August 30, 1965 the plaintiffs, who are welfare recipients, agreed to purchase a home freezer unit for $900 as the result of a visit from a salesman representing Your Shop At Home Service, Inc. With the addition of the time credit charges, credit life insurance, credit property insurance, and sales tax, the purchase price totalled $1,234.80. Thus far the plaintiffs have paid $619.88 toward their purchase. The defendant claims that with various added credit charges paid for an extension of time there is a balance of $819.81 still due from the plaintiffs. The uncontroverted proof at the trial established that the freezer unit, when purchased, had a maximum retail value of approximately $300. The question is whether this transaction and the resulting contract could be considered unconscionable within the meaning of Section 2–302 of the Uniform Commercial Code....

[The court mentioned a concern for "the uneducated and often illiterate individual who is the victim of gross inequality of bargaining power, usually the poorest members of the community."]

Concern for the protection of these consumers against overreaching by the small but hardy breed of merchants who would prey on them is not novel. The dangers of inequality of bargaining power were vaguely recognized in the early English common law when Lord Hardwicke wrote of a fraud, "which may be apparent from the intrinsic nature and subject of the bargain itself; such as no man in his senses and not under delusion would make." The English authorities on this subject were discussed in Hume v. United States, 132 U.S. 406, 10 S.Ct. 134, 33 L.Ed. 393 (1889) where the United States Supreme Court characterized these as "cases in which one party took advantage of the other's ignorance of arithmetic to impose upon him, and the fraud was apparent from the face of the contracts."

The law is beginning to fight back against those who once took advantage of the poor and illiterate without risk of either exposure or interference. From the common law doctrine of intrinsic fraud we have over the years, developed common and statutory law which tells not only the buyer but also the seller to beware. This body of laws recognizes the importance of a free enterprise system but at the same time will provide the legal armor to protect and safeguard the prospective victim from the harshness of an unconscionable contract.

Section 2–302 of the Uniform Commercial Code enacts the moral sense of the community into the law of commercial transactions.... It permits a court to accomplish directly what heretofore was often accomplished by construction of language, manipulations of fluid rules of contract law and determinations based upon a presumed public policy.

There is no reason to doubt, moreover, that this section is intended to encompass the price term of an agreement. In addition to the fact that it has already been so applied ... the statutory language itself makes it clear that not only a clause of the contract, but the contract in toto, may be found unconscionable as a matter of law. Indeed, no other provision of an agreement more intimately touches upon the question of unconscionability than does the term regarding price.

Fraud, in the instant case, is not present; nor is it necessary under the statute. The question which presents itself is whether or not, under the circumstances of this case, the sale of a freezer unit having a retail value of $300 for $900 ($1,439.69 including credit charges and $18 sales tax) is unconscionable as a matter of law. The court believes it is.

Concededly, deciding the issue is substantially easier than explaining it. No doubt, the mathematical disparity between $300, which presumably includes a reasonable profit margin, and $900, which is exorbitant on its face, carries the greatest weight. Credit charges alone exceed by more than $100 the retail value of the freezer. These alone, may be sufficient to sustain the decision. Yet, a caveat is warranted lest we reduce the import of Section 2–302 solely to a mathematical ratio formula. It may, at times, be that; yet it may also be much more. The very limited financial resources of the purchaser, known to the sellers at the time of the sale, is entitled to weight in the balance. Indeed, the value disparity itself leads inevitably to the felt conclusion that knowing advantage was taken of the plaintiffs. In addition, the meaningfulness of choice essential to the making of a contract, can be negated by a gross inequality of bargaining power. (Williams v. Walker–Thomas Furniture Co., 121 U.S.App.D.C. 315, 350 F.2d 445.)

There is no question about the necessity and even the desirability of instalment sales and the extension of credit. Indeed, there are many, including welfare recipients, who would be deprived of even the most basic conveniences without the use of these devices. Similarly, the retail merchant selling on instalment or extending credit is expected to establish a pricing factor which will afford a degree of protection commensurate with the risk of selling to those who might be default prone. However, neither of these accepted premises can clothe the sale of this freezer with respectability.

Support for the court's conclusion will be found in a number of other cases already decided.... [I]n Frostifresh Corp. v. Reynoso [274 N.Y.S.2d 757, aff'd, 281 N.Y.S.2d 964], the sale of a refrigerator costing the seller $348 for $900 plus credit charges of $245.88 was unconscionable as a matter of law....

Having already paid more than $600 toward the purchase of this $300 freezer unit, it is apparent that the defendant has already been amply compensated. In accordance with the statute, the application of the payment provision should be limited to amounts already paid by the plaintiffs and the contract be reformed and amended by changing the payments called for therein to equal the amount of payment actually so paid by the plaintiffs.

NOTES

(1) *The Question of Remedies.* If the Jones family had paid $1,000 before complaining of the contract, would the court have permitted them to recover a part of it? If they had paid only $300, would the court have required them to pay more? What is the rationale of stopping the payments at $619.88?

In Frostifresh Corp. v. Reynoso, mentioned in the case above, the seller of a freezer sued the Reynosos for the unpaid balance of the price. The Reynosos had made only one payment of $32 on a purchase price of $348. The trial court made a simple deduction, and gave judgment for $316. On appeal, the judgment was reversed, and the trial court was directed to give judgment for the "net cost for the refrigerator-freezer, plus a reasonable profit, in addition to trucking and service charges necessarily incurred and reasonable finance charges." Two comments on the case follow:

"This case means that sellers can charge the most exorbitant rates, secure in the knowledge that at the worst they will be able to recover a reasonable profit plus all their expenses." Ray Narral, Interview, in *The Law and the Low Income Consumer* 330 (Carol H. Katz, ed., 1968).

"It must be recognized that even in the poverty situations, putting aside the cases of fraud and high pressure in home sales, the buyers do want the goods. Even in the famous *Frostifresh* case, the question of remedies was complicated by the fact that the Spanish-speaking people deceived into buying a home freezer at a high price *chose to keep the freezer*. Thus we cannot adopt restrictions on remedies so punitive as to put the credit sellers in the poverty areas, and their financers, out of business. Despite the present high social cost, they serve a social purpose." Homer Kripke, Consumer Credit Regulation: A Creditor–Oriented Viewpoint, 68 Colum.L.Rev. 455, 478 (1968).

For an alternative method of calculating profit, see The Uniform Consumer Credit Code, adopted in 11 states, which focuses on what is too much for the buyer to pay, rather than on what is too much for the seller to charge. It directs that a comparison be made between the for-credit price and the value "measured by the price at which similar property or services are readily obtainable in credit transactions by like consumers. . . ." Gross disparity between the two is one of the factors to be considered in determining whether or not an agreement is unconscionable.

(2) Price Justification? In an FTC survey of retailing in the District of Columbia, sellers catering primarily to low-income customers were found to use comparatively high markups and prices, although their "net profit on sales . . . was only slightly higher and net profit return on net worth was considerably lower when compared to general market retailers." Federal Trade Commission, Economic Report on Installment Credit and Retail Sales Practices of District of Columbia Retailers (1968). Should this be a defense to a claim of price unconscionability? It has been suggested that a price exceeding the "average" by 100% be deemed prima facie unconscionable. Richard Speidel, Unconscionability, Assent and Consumer Protection, 31 U.Pitt.L.Rev. 359, 372–73 (1970). Would it be better to focus attention on the mark-up of an item than on its price? Should a seller be compelled to produce information regarding costs, profits, and mark-ups? See Patterson v. Walker–Thomas Furniture Co., 277 A.2d 111 (D.C.App.1971). Does such disclosure have special difficulties in disputes regarding lawyers' fees? See Note 2, below.

(3) Payday Lending. Over the past two decades, payday lending has gone from a relatively modest industry to one now processing billions in loans each year. Payday loans work like this: For a fee of $15, a person seeking to borrow $100 for a two-week period, for example, writes a check for the loan amount, forward-dating the check to the borrower's next payday. While a $15 fee may seem modest, when calculated as an interest rate, $15 for a two-week $100 loan translates to an annual percentage rate of 390%. Many borrowers "roll over" their loans, paying an additional $15 every two weeks to stop the lender from depositing the check. Are such rates an unconscionable price for a loan, or does the industry provide a valuable service to those who would otherwise lack collateral to borrow from more traditional sources?

For analyses of some of the complexities of payday lending, see Richard Brooks, Credit Past Due, 106 Colum.L.Rev. 994 (2006) and Ronald Mann and Jim Hawkins, Just Until Payday, 54 UCLA L.Rev. 855 (2007).

Concerned about the impact of payday lending on military personnel, in 2006 Congress enacted legislation capping annual interest rates on credit extended to military personnel at 36%. See 10 U.S.C.A. § 987. For background, see the Department of Defense, *Report On Predatory Lending Practices Directed at Members of the*

Armed Forces and Their Dependents (2006), available at http://www.defense.gov/pubs/pdfs/Report_to_Congress_final.pdf.

PROBLEMS

(1) *Historical Price Unconscionability.* The Indian Claims Commission Act of 1946 authorized tribes to bring claims against the United States resulting from treaties, contracts, or agreements revisable on the basis of fraud, duress, or unconscionable consideration. The Nez Perce Tribe claimed compensation under the Act for 549,559 acres of farm and timberland it ceded to the U.S. in 1894 for $2.97 per acre. (Under the terms of the sale, the purchase price was put into a trust account for the Tribe at interest for a period of years.) The Tribe claimed the true market value was over $12. The Commission found that the market value at the time of the sale was $4, and that the differential between $4 and $2.97 was not unconscionable. The Tribe appealed. What result? See Nez Perce Tribe of Indians v. United States, 176 Ct.Cl. 815, 828–29 (Ct.Cl.1966).

(2) *Billable Hours.* Over an 18–month period a law firm billed a client something over $2,000,000 in legal fees for work done on a matter by a lawyer working under contract for the firm. The client later sued the firm for malpractice, claiming also that the firm's fees were unconscionable. To prove the latter, the client sought to discover the firm's profits on his matter. From a judgment denying his motion to produce this information, client appealed. The Rules of Professional Conduct of the State Bar prohibit attorneys from charging unconscionable fees and set out specific guidelines for making that determination. What result on appeal? Is a law firm's profit margin irrelevant to the inquiry? Are profit margins for law firms different from profit margins for freezer sales? See Shaffer v. Superior Court, 39 Cal.Rptr.2d 506 (Ct.App.1995).

———

UNCONSCIONABILITY IN FRANCHISES

While much of the commentary on unconscionability has focused on its role in consumer cases, the doctrine applies in commercial agreements as well; recall the discussion of *Campbell Soup*, p. 494 above. It is not surprising, however, that courts have been less willing to find unconscionability in agreements where the bargaining position of the parties is more likely to be equal, and where experienced traders are less likely to be confronted with "unfair surprise" in terms. For example, in an action by Continental Airlines against Goodyear Rubber, the Ninth Circuit refused to accept Continental's claim of unconscionability: the doctrine "cannot be invoked by so sophisticated a party as Continental in reference to a contract so laboriously negotiated." Continental Airlines v. Goodyear Tire & Rubber Co., 819 F.2d 1519, 1527 (9th Cir.1987).

Of course, not all businesses have equal clout. A Michigan court upheld a trial court ruling that a cancellation clause was unconscionable in light of the fact that " 'big sharks' in the garment industry were able to impose these clauses [on] small independent manufacturers." Gianni Sport Ltd. v. Gantos, Inc., 391 N.W.2d 760, 762 (Mich.App.1986).

One area where the imbalance in positions between commercial parties is sometimes found involves franchise agreements. We have already seen the problems of Hoffman in his efforts to obtain a franchise from Red Owl. And even when the deal is struck, the relationship between franchisor and franchisee remains complex. The franchisor may contend that the franchisee has provided substandard service, damaging the reputation of the product or the services on which royalties and consumer loyalty depend. Diverting from the reputation of the franchise may also injure other franchisees whose interests the franchisor represents. The franchisee may object that the franchisor has skimped on advertising or has siphoned off revenues through a competing franchisee. On the complexities of franchise relationships generally, see Gillian Hadfield, Problematic Relations: Franchising and the Law of Incomplete Contracts, 42 Stan.L.Rev. 927 (1990).

Disputes also arise with regard to the basic terms of the underlying contract. Franchise agreements typically take the form of a standardized agreement prepared by the franchisor, containing terms that are not open to negotiation and are strikingly favorable to the franchisor. In particular, a franchisor may reserve the power of termination on short notice, "at any time for any reason." See Corenswet, Inc. v. Amana Refrigeration, Inc., 594 F.2d 129 (5th Cir.1979). The power is defended on the ground that it serves to discipline a slack franchisee tempted by free-rider possibilities to piggyback on the general quality of franchise.

Might a termination power, or another provision harsh on a franchisee, be regarded as unconscionable, and so unenforceable? In a case involving a lease between the Shell Oil Company and a service station operator, a New Jersey court held that it was. Shell had terminated the franchise on ten days notice, as provided for in the parties' contracts. Among the facts deemed "significant" by the trial court were "the gross disparity in bargaining power between Shell and Marinello, resulting in Shell's ability to dictate the terms of the agreements; the grossly unfair contractual provisions at issue; and the clear tendency to injure the public."

The New Jersey Supreme Court expressed full agreement with the "basic determination ... that Shell had no legal right to terminate its relationship with Marinello except for good cause...." Shell Oil Co. v. Marinello, 307 A.2d 598 (N.J.1973).

In contrast, Dairy Mart's termination of one of its franchises on 90 days notice and without cause was found *not* to be unconscionable. In Zapatha v. Dairy Mart, Inc., 408 N.E.2d 1370, 1377 (Mass.1980), the court stated that:

> We find no potential for unfair surprise to the Zapathas.... The termination provision was neither obscurely worded, nor buried in fine print in the contract. Contrast Williams v. Walker–Thomas, [p. 497 above]. The provision was specifically pointed out to Mr. Zapatha before it was signed; Mr. Zapatha testified that he thought the provision was "straightforward," and that he declined the opportunity to take the agreement to a lawyer for advice.

The court also rejected the argument that the termination clause was oppressive. "As an investment, the Zapathas had only to purchase the inventory of goods to be sold but as Dairy Mart concedes, on termination by it without cause Dairy Mart was obliged to repurchase all the Zapathas' saleable merchandise inventory, including items not purchased from Dairy Mart, at 80% of its retail value. There was no potential for forfeiture or loss of investment."

NOTE

Legislation. A number of state and federal fair-practices acts are directed at franchising. For example, the Automobile Dealers' Day in Court Act of 1956, imposed on the automobile manufacturers a duty of good faith "in performing or complying with any of the terms or provisions of [a dealer's] franchise, or in terminating, canceling, or not renewing the franchise." 15 U.S.C. §§ 1221 et seq. The subject of good faith is taken up later in this chapter.

See also The Petroleum Marketing Practices Act of 1978, which substantially preempted state regulation of the termination and renewal of franchise relationships between motor-fuel dispensers and their suppliers, in an attempt to "level the playing field." 15 U.S.C. §§ 2801–2806. See Simmons v. Mobil Oil Corp., 29 F.3d 505 (9th Cir.1994). In 1979, by rule, the FTC established a minimum federal standard of disclosure applicable to all "franchise and business opportunity offerings." 16 C.F.R. § 436. A number of state disclosure requirements are also operative.

————

UNCONSCIONABILITY: ARBITRATION CLAUSES

A question that arises with increasing frequency is the enforceability of mandatory arbitration clauses. The cases that follow consider mandatory arbitration clauses in two contexts: employment agreements, where such clauses are often included as a condition of employment, and consumer transactions.

In an important 2001 case, the Supreme Court held that mandatory arbitration agreements in employment agreements are generally enforceable under the Federal Arbitration Act (FAA), "save for upon such grounds as exist at law or in equity for the revocation of any contract." Circuit City Stores, Inc. v. Adams, 532 U.S. 105, 112 (2001). The case below considers the latter qualification. Under what circumstances might an arbitration clause be unenforceable on the ground of unconscionability?

Armendariz v. Foundation Health Psychcare Services, Inc.

Supreme Court of California, 2000.
24 Cal.4th 83, 6 P.3d 669.

■ Mosk, J. [In 1995, Foundation Health Psychcare Services ("employer") hired Marybeth Armendariz and Dolores Olague–Rodgers ("employees") in the "Provider Relations Group." Both employees had filled out and signed employment application forms, which included an arbitration clause pertaining to any future claim of wrongful termination. Later, they executed a separate employment arbitration agreement, containing the same arbitration clause.[a] A year later, the employees were informed that their positions were "being eliminated" and that they were "being terminated." They claimed that during their year of employment, their supervisors and coworkers engaged in sexually-based harassment and discrimination and that they were "terminated . . . because of their perceived and/or actual sexual orientation (heterosexual)."

When the employees sued for violations of California's Fair Employment and Housing Act (FEHA) and for wrongful termination, the employer sought to compel arbitration. The employees argued they could not be compelled to arbitrate antidiscrimination claims under the FEHA, that several provisions of the arbitration agreement they had signed were unconscionable, and that these unconscionable terms rendered the entire arbitration agreement unenforceable.

The trial court declared the arbitration clause unconscionable and, "given the overall unfairness" of the provision, invalidated the entire agreement. The Court of Appeal reversed as to severability, holding that while the damages provision was unconscionable and contrary to public policy, the rest of the arbitration agreement should be enforced. The employer appealed.

With regard to the arbitrability of statutory claims, the Supreme Court held that employees can be compelled, under an arbitration agreement, to arbitrate such claims so long as the arbitration procedures permit the employees to vindicate their statutory rights. For such vindication to occur, "the arbitration must meet certain minimum requirements, including the neutrality of the arbitrator, the provision of adequate discovery, a written decision that will permit a limited form of judicial review, and limitations on the cost of arbitration." The court then turned to the employees' claims of unconscionability of the arbitration agreement.]

1.   General Principles of Unconscionability

. . . In this section, we will consider objections to arbitration that apply more generally to any type of arbitration imposed on the employee by the employer as a condition of employment, regardless of the type of claim being arbitrated. These objections fall under the rubric of "unconscionability."

---

a. The clause states in full: "I agree as a condition of my employment, that in the event my employment is terminated, and I contend that such termination was wrongful or otherwise in violation of the conditions of employment or was in violation of any express or implied condition, term or covenant of employment, whether founded in fact or in law, including but not limited to the covenant of good faith and fair dealing, or otherwise in violation of any of my rights, I and Employer agree to submit any such matter to binding arbitration pursuant to the provisions of title 9 of Part III of the California Code of Civil Procedure, commencing at section 1280 et seq. or any successor or replacement statutes. I and Employer further expressly agree that in any such arbitration, my exclusive remedies for violation of the terms, conditions or covenants of employment shall be limited to a sum equal to the wages I would have earned from the date of any discharge until the date of the arbitration award. I understand that I shall not be entitled to any other remedy, at law or in equity, including but not limited to reinstatement and/or injunctive relief."

We explained the judicially created doctrine of unconscionability in *Scissor-Tail, supra*, 28 Cal.3d 807, 171 Cal.Rptr. 604, 623 P.2d 165.... If the contract is adhesive, the court must then determine whether "other factors are present which, under established legal rules—legislative or judicial—operate to render it [unenforceable]." (*Scissor-Tail, supra*, at p. 820, fn. omitted.) "Generally speaking, there are two judicially imposed limitations on the enforcement of adhesion contracts or provisions thereof. The first is that such a contract or provision which does not fall within the reasonable expectations of the weaker or 'adhering' party will not be enforced against him.... The second—a principle of equity applicable to all contracts generally—is that a contract or provision, even if consistent with the reasonable expectations of the parties, will be denied enforcement if, considered in its context, it is unduly oppressive or 'unconscionable.' " (*Ibid.*) Subsequent cases have referred to both the "reasonable expectations" and the "oppressive" limitations as being aspects of unconscionability. [Citations omitted.]

In 1979, the Legislature enacted Civil Code section 1670.5, which codified the principle that a court can refuse to enforce an unconscionable provision in a contract.... Because unconscionability is a reason for refusing to enforce contracts generally, it is also a valid reason for refusing to enforce an arbitration agreement under Code of Civil Procedure section 1281, [which] provides that arbitration agreements are "valid, enforceable and irrevocable, save upon such grounds as exist [at law or in equity] for the revocation of any contract." ...

As explained in *A & M Produce Co., supra*, 135 Cal.App.3d 473, 186 Cal.Rptr. 114, "unconscionability has both a 'procedural' and a 'substantive' element," the former focusing on "oppression" or "surprise" due to unequal bargaining power, the latter on "overly harsh" or "one-sided" results. (*Id.* at pp. 486–487,) "The prevailing view is that [procedural and substantive unconscionability] must both be present in order for a court to exercise its discretion to refuse to enforce a contract or clause under the doctrine of unconscionability." (Stirlen v. Supercuts, Inc., 51 Cal.App.4th [1519, 1533], 60 Cal.Rptr.2d 138 [(1997)] (*Stirlen*).) But they need not be present in the same degree. "Essentially a sliding scale is invoked which disregards the regularity of the procedural process of the contract formation, that creates the terms, in proportion to the greater harshness or unreasonableness of the substantive terms themselves." (15 Williston on Contracts (3d ed. 1972) § 1763A, pp. 226–227; see also *A & M Produce Co., supra*, 135 Cal.App.3d at p. 487.) In other words, the more substantively oppressive the contract term, the less evidence of procedural unconscionability is required to come to the conclusion that the term is unenforceable, and vice versa.

2. Unconscionability and Mandatory Employment Arbitration

Applying the above principles to this case, we first determine whether the arbitration agreement is adhesive. There is little dispute that it is. It was imposed on employees as a condition of employment and there was no opportunity to negotiate.

Moreover, in the case of preemployment arbitration contracts, the economic pressure exerted by employers on all but the most sought-after employees may be particularly acute, for the arbitration agreement stands between the employee and necessary employment, and few employees are in a position to refuse a job because of an arbitration requirement. While arbitration may have its advantages in terms of greater expedition, informality, and lower cost, it also has, from the employee's point of view, potential disadvantages: waiver of a right to a jury trial, limited discovery, and limited judicial review. Various studies show that arbitration is advantageous to employers not only because it reduces the costs of litigation, but also because it reduces the size of the award that an employee is likely to get, particularly if the employer is a "repeat player" in the arbitration system. (Bingham, *Employment Arbitration: The Repeat Player Effect* (1997) 1 Employee Rts. & Employment Policy J. 189 . . .) It is perhaps for this reason that it is almost invariably the employer who seeks to compel arbitration.

Arbitration is favored in this state as a voluntary means of resolving disputes, and this voluntariness has been its bedrock justification. . . . Given the lack of choice and the potential disadvantages that even a fair arbitration system can harbor for employees, we must be particularly attuned to claims that employers with superior bargaining power have imposed one-sided, substantively unconscionable terms as part of an arbitration agreement. . . . With this in mind, we turn to the employees' specific unconscionability claims.

. . . [T]he employees contend that the agreement is substantively unconscionable because it requires only employees to arbitrate their wrongful termination claims against the employer, but does not require the employer to arbitrate claims it may have against the employees. In asserting that this lack of mutuality is unconscionable, they rely primarily on the opinion of the Court of Appeal in *Stirlen, supra.* [Reviewing that case, the court found in it support for the employees' case.] The *Stirlen* court did not hold that all lack of mutuality in a contract of adhesion was invalid, [but only required a] "modicum of bilaterality" in an arbitration agreement. . . . We conclude that [*Stirlen* is] correct in requiring this "modicum of bilaterality" in an arbitration agreement. Given the disadvantages that may exist for plaintiffs arbitrating disputes, it is unfairly one-sided for an employer with superior bargaining power to impose arbitration on the employee as plaintiff but not to accept such limitations when it seeks to prosecute a claim against the employee, without at least some reasonable justification for such one-sidedness based on "business realities."

The employer cites a number of cases that have held that a lack of mutuality in an arbitration agreement does not render the contract illusory as long as the employer agrees to be bound by the arbitration of employment disputes. . . . We agree that such lack of mutuality does not render the contract illusory, *i.e.,* lacking in mutual consideration. We conclude, rather, that in the context of an arbitration agreement imposed by the employer on the employee, such a one-sided term is unconscionable. Although parties are free to contract for asymmetrical remedies and arbitration clauses of varying scope, *Stirlen* [is] correct that the doctrine of unconscionability limits the extent to which a stronger party may, through a contract of adhesion, impose the arbitration forum on the weaker party without accepting that forum for itself.

We disagree that enforcing "a modicum of bilaterality" in arbitration agreements singles out arbitration for suspect status.... We agree with the *Stirlen* court that the ordinary principles of unconscionability may manifest themselves in forms peculiar to the arbitration context. One such form is an agreement requiring arbitration only for the claims of the weaker party but a choice of forums for the claims of the stronger party. The application of this principle to arbitration does not disfavor arbitration. It is no disparagement of arbitration to acknowledge that it has, as noted, both advantages and disadvantages. The perceived advantages of the judicial forum for plaintiffs include the availability of discovery and the fact that courts and juries are viewed as more likely to adhere to the law and less likely than arbitrators to "split the difference" between the two sides, thereby lowering damages awards for plaintiffs.... An employer may accordingly consider courts to be a forum superior to arbitration when it comes to vindicating its own contractual and statutory rights, or may consider it advantageous to have a choice of arbitration or litigation when determining how best to pursue a claim against an employee. It does not disfavor arbitration to hold that an employer may not impose a system of arbitration on an employee that seeks to maximize the advantages and minimize the disadvantages of arbitration for itself at the employee's expense.... We emphasize that if an employer does have reasonable justification for the arrangement—i.e., a justification grounded in something other than the employer's desire to maximize its advantage based on the perceived superiority of the judicial forum—such an agreement would not be unconscionable. Without such justification, we must assume that it is.

Applying these principles to the present case, we note the arbitration agreement was limited in scope to employee claims regarding wrongful termination. Although it did not expressly authorize litigation of the employer's claims against the employee, as was the case in *Stirlen* ... such was the clear implication of the agreement....

This is not to say that an arbitration clause must mandate the arbitration of all claims between employer and employee in order to avoid invalidation on grounds of unconscionability. Indeed, as the employer points out, the present arbitration agreement does not require arbitration of all conceivable claims that an employee might have against an employer, only wrongful termination claims. But an arbitration agreement imposed in an adhesive context lacks basic fairness and mutuality if it requires one contracting party, but not the other, to arbitrate all claims arising out of the same transaction or occurrence or series of transactions or occurrences. The arbitration agreement in this case lacks mutuality in this sense because it requires the arbitration of employee—but not employer—claims arising out of a wrongful termination. An employee terminated for stealing trade secrets, for example, must arbitrate his or her wrongful termination claim under the agreement while the employer has no corresponding obligation to arbitrate its trade secrets claim against the employee.

The unconscionable one-sidedness of the arbitration agreement is compounded in this case by the fact that it does not permit the full recovery of damages for employees, while placing no such restriction on the employer. Even if the limitation on FEHA damages is severed as contrary to public policy, the arbitration clause in the present case still does not permit full recovery of ordinary contract damages. The arbitration agreement specifies that damages are to be limited to the amount of backpay lost up until the time of arbitration. This provision excludes damages for prospective future earnings, so-called "front pay," a common and often substantial component of contractual damages in a wrongful termination case.... The employer, on the other hand, is bound by no comparable limitation should it pursue a claim against its employees.

[The court rejected the argument that the wording of the agreement resulted from the position of the employees within the organization, which made an employment suit against them unlikely, and might reflect the fact that the parties did not foresee the possibility of any dispute arising from employment that was not initiated by the employee.] The fact that it is unlikely an employer will bring claims against a particular type of employee is not, ultimately, a justification for a unilateral arbitration agreement. It provides no reason for categorically exempting employer claims, however rare, from mandatory arbitration. Although an employer may be able, in a future case, to justify a unilateral arbitration agreement, the employer in the present case has not done so.

[The court found no abuse of discretion in the trial court's ruling that, because the arbitration was permeated by an unlawful purpose, it was not severable.]

Reversed.

NOTES

(1) *Post–Armendariz.* In 2004, the 7th Circuit Court of Appeals came to the opposite conclusion to that in *Armendariz*. In Oblix v. Winiecki, 374 F.3d 488 (7th Cir.2004), the employment agreement at issue contained a broad, one-sided arbitration clause, which, like the one in Armendariz, did not require the employer to arbitrate all potential claims against its employees. With regard to the latter issue, Judge Easterbrook said that the absence of mutuality was "neither here nor there." Reversing the lower court, which had relied on *Armendariz* in refusing to enforce the arbitration clause, he stated: "Standard-form agreements are a fact of life, and given [FAA preference for arbitration], arbitration agreements in [employment contracts] must be enforced unless the states would refuse to enforce all off-the-shelf package deals."

In California, *Armendariz* has spawned a great deal of litigation as courts attempt to locate the contours of unconscionability as applied to mandatory arbitration in employment agreements. Cases finding unconscionability include Pinedo v. Premium Tobacco, 102 Cal.Rptr.2d 435 (Ct.App.2000) ("multiple defects") and Villa Milano Homeowner's Association v. Il Davorge, 102 Cal.Rptr.2d 1 (Ct.App.2000), extending *Armendariz* analysis to arbitration provision in the Covenants, Conditions, and Restrictions between a developer and homeowners. Cases finding *no* unconscionability include Pichly v. Nortech Waste LLC, 105 Cal.Rptr.2d 21 (Ct.App. 2001) (arbitration provision in a trucker's employment contract "neither one-sided nor overly harsh") and Baker v. Osborne Development Corp., 71 Cal.Rptr.3d 854 (Ct.App.2008).

In Shubin v. William Lyon Homes, Inc., 101 Cal.Rptr.2d 390, 402 (Ct.App. 2000), the court addressed the question of whether the circumstances under which the employee signs the arbitration provision may create *procedural* unconscionability. The court found that the office manager "said and did things to hurry or pressure Shubin into signing documents placed before her, without having the time to carefully read their contents ... [and with] no realistic opportunity to suggest modifications," procedural unconscionability was established.

(2) *Severability*. The California Civil Code, modeled after UCC § 2–302, applies the doctrine of unconscionability to *all* contracts, and provides that in cases of unconscionability a court may refuse to enforce the entire contract, may sever the unconscionable provisions and enforce the remainder, or may "so limit the application of any unconscionable clause as that avoid any unconscionable result." Cal. Civil Code § 1670.5(a). In *Armendariz*, the employer argued that only those provisions to violate public policy should be held unenforceable and that the remainder of the arbitration agreement should be upheld. The court was guided by Comment 2 to § 1670, which states that a court may decline to sever when "the contract as a whole is permeated by the unconscionability." In an omitted portion of the opinion, the court found that because the unconscionability went to the scope of the arbitration requirement, there *was* no single provision whose severance could "remove the unconscionable taint from agreement." 99 Cal.Rptr.2d at 776.

Compare Bolter v. Superior Court of Orange County, 104 Cal.Rptr.2d 888, 895 (Ct.App.2001), in which the court found unconscionable a provision requiring "mom-and-pop" carpet cleaning franchisees in California to arbitrate all disputes in Utah, but held that "[i]t is not necessary to throw the baby out with the bath water, i.e., the unconscionable provisions can be severed and the rest of the [arbitration] agreement enforced."

Severability, or divisibility, is discussed further in Chapter 8, below.

(3) *Geese and Ganders*. In dismissing the employee's argument in Oblix, Note 1 above, Judge Easterbrook stated: "Businesses regularly agree to arbitrate their disputes with each other; giving employees the same terms and forum (the AAA) that a firm deems satisfactory for commercial dispute resolution is not suspect." 374 F.3d at 491.

But a recent study of the use of arbitration clauses by firms in their contracts with one another suggests that "large corporate actors do not systematically embrace arbitration." Theodore Eisenberg and Geoffrey Miller, The Flight from Arbitration: An Empirical Study of Ex Ante Arbitration Clauses in the Contracts of Publicly Held Companies, 56 DePaul L. Rev. 335 (2007). The authors examined 2800 contracts filed by public firms with the Securities and Exchange Commission in 2002 and found that only 11% included arbitration clauses. Eisenberg and Miller conclude that notwithstanding the factors often advanced for including arbitration clauses in consumer contracts—cost savings, simpler procedure—from an economic perspective, it appears that "corporate representatives believe that litigation can add value over arbitration."

(4) *Scissor–Tail Revisited*. In Graham v. Scissor–Tail, cited in *Armendariz* and at p. 475 above, the California Supreme Court found unconscionable a clause in an entertainment industry contract requiring all arbitrations to be heard by the union of one of the parties. "Although our review of the record has disclosed nothing

which would indicate that A.F. of M. procedures operate to deny any party a fair opportunity to present his position prior to decision, we are of the view that the 'minimum levels of integrity' which are requisite to a contractual arrangement for the nonjudicial resolution of disputes are not achieved by an arrangement which designates the union of one of the parties as the arbitrator of disputes arising out of employment—especially when, as here, the arrangement is the product of circumstances indicative of adhesion." 623 P.2d at 177. Recognizing the state's strong public policy of favoring arbitration as a method of dispute resolution, the court severed the objectionable provision appointing the less than neutral arbitrator and remanded the case for the selection of a "suitable" arbitrator by the parties, or as a default, by the court.

Scott v. Cingular Wireless

Supreme Court of Washington, En Banc, 2007.
160 Wash.2d 843.

■ CHAMBERS, J. Plaintiffs Doug Scott, Loren and Sandra Tabasinske, and Patrick and Janet Oishi (plaintiffs) purchased cellular telephones and calling plans from Cingular. The contracts they all signed were standard preprinted agreements that included a clause requiring mandatory arbitration. That arbitration clause, in turn, contained a provision prohibiting consolidation of cases, class actions, and class arbitration. Cingular also retained the right to unilaterally revise the agreement and, in July 2003, did so. Customers were informed via a monthly "bill stuffer" titled in bold print, "IMPORTANT INFORMATION CONCERNING YOUR CONTRACT." The revised arbitration clause still prohibited class actions.[1] It also specified that arbitration would be conducted according to American Arbitration Association (AAA) rules; that Cingular would pay the filing, administrator, and arbitration fees unless the customer's claim was found to be frivolous; that Cingular would reimburse the customer for reasonable attorney fees and expenses incurred for the arbitration (provided that the customer recovered at least the demand amount); and that the arbitration would take place in the county of the customer's billing address. It also removed limitations on punitive damages.

The plaintiffs' underlying suit asserts that they were improperly billed for long distance and/or out-of network "roaming" calls[2] and that as a result of these improper billing practices, individual customers were overcharged up to around $45 a month. Plaintiffs filed a class action suit to challenge the legality of these additional charges. While the plaintiffs admit no individual consumer suffered a significant loss, they claim that in the

---

1. The modified arbitration clause provides in part:

You agree that, by entering into this Agreement, you and Cingular are waiving the right to a trial by jury .... You and Cingular agree that YOU AND CINGULAR MAY BRING CLAIMS AGAINST THE OTHER ONLY IN YOUR OR ITS INDIVIDUAL CAPACITY, and not as a plaintiff or class member in any purported class or repre-

sentative proceeding.... if this specific proviso is found to be unenforceable, then the entirety of this arbitration clause shall be null and void.

CP at 356. [emphases in original]. We do not consider whether the bill stuffer was an effective way to modify the contract.

2. "Roaming" occurs when a subscriber of one wireless service provider uses another provider's facilities.

aggregate, Cingular unilaterally overcharged the public by very large sums of money.

Cingular moved to compel individual arbitration. Plaintiffs resisted, arguing that the class action waiver is substantively and procedurally unconscionable and thus unenforceable. . . .

The trial court granted Cingular's motion, concluding that although Cingular's contract is a contract of adhesion, it is not sufficiently complex, illegible, or misleading to be deemed procedurally unconscionable. The court also found no substantive unconscionability. We accepted review, and received helpful amicus curiae briefs from the American Association of Retired Persons and the National Association of Consumer Advocates; from Amazon.com, Inc., Intel Corporation, Microsoft Corporation, and RealNetworks, Inc.; from the Association of Washington Business; from the Chamber of Commerce of the United States of America; from the Attorney General of Washington; from CTIA—The Wireless Association; and from the Washington State Trial Lawyers Association Foundation.

In essence, plaintiffs and their supporting amici argue Cingular's class action waiver is substantively and procedurally unconscionable. They contend it both denies consumers a meaningful opportunity to prove their cases and undermines the protections of Washington's CPA.

Cingular and its supporting amici argue, however, that the majority of courts (at least at the time they made the argument) addressing the question have found class action waivers enforceable. *E.g.,* [citing cases from the 11th, 5th, and 4th Circuit Courts of Appeals, and three other cases.] Plaintiffs respond that an increasing number of courts have found class action waivers in arbitration clauses substantively unconscionable. *E.g., Ting v. AT&T,* 319 F.3d 1126 (9th Cir.2003); . . . *Discover Bank v. Superior Court of Los Angeles,* 113 P.3d 1100 (2005) [and 14 other cases cited]. There is a clear split of authority. . . .

This case is somewhat unusual in our experience because it is not the arbitration clause itself the plaintiffs challenge. Instead, it is the class action waiver embedded within it. We begin by considering whether that waiver itself is unconscionable and unenforceable under Washington law.

B. PUBLIC POLICY

I. CLASS ACTIONS AND THE WASHINGTON CPA

An agreement that has a tendency " 'to be against the public good, or to be injurious to the public' " violates public policy. *King v. Riveland,* 886 P.2d 160 (1994) (quoting *Marshall v. Higginson,* 813 P.2d 1275 (1991)). An agreement that violates public policy may be void and unenforceable. RESTATEMENT (SECOND) OF CONTRACTS 178 (1981). Washington's CR 23 authorizes class actions and demonstrates a state policy favoring aggregation of small claims for purposes of efficiency, deterrence, and access to justice . . . As we have noted before, when consumer claims are small but numerous, a class-based remedy is the only effective method to vindicate the public's rights. . . . Class remedies not only resolve the claims of the individual class members but can also strongly deter future similar wrongful conduct, which benefits the community as a whole. Judge Mosk understood this over 30 years ago:

> Frequently numerous consumers are exposed to the same dubious practice by the same seller so that proof of the prevalence of the practice as to one consumer would provide proof for all. Individual actions by each of the defrauded consumers is often impracticable because the amount of individual recovery would be insufficient to justify bringing a separate action; thus an unscrupulous seller retains the benefits of its wrongful conduct. A class action by consumers produces several salutary byproducts, including a therapeutic effect upon those sellers who indulge in fraudulent practices, aid to legitimate business enterprises by curtailing illegitimate competition, and avoidance to the judicial process of the burden of multiple litigation involving identical claims. The benefit to the parties and the courts would, in many circumstances, be substantial.

Vasquez v. Superior Court of San Joaquin County, 4 Cal.3d 800, 808, 94 Cal.Rptr. 796, 484 P.2d 964 (1971). Class actions exist because too many are injured to name. *Weiss v. Regal Collections*, 385 F.3d 337 (3d Cir.2004). That said, class action waivers have been found permissible in some contexts ... *See generally Discover Bank,* 30 Cal.Rptr.3d 76, 113 P.3d 1100....

We turn to whether this class action waiver is unconscionable because it undermines Washington's CPA to the extent that it is "injurious to the public." *See* [*King v. Riveland,* 886 P.2d 160 (Wash. 1994)]....

Private enforcement of the CPA was not possible until 1971, when the legislature created the private right of action to encourage it.... Private citizens act as private attorneys general in protecting the public's interest against unfair and deceptive acts and practices in trade and commerce. *Lightfoot v. MacDonald*, 544 P.2d 88 (1976). Consumers bringing actions under the CPA do not merely vindicate their own rights; they represent the public interest and may seek injunctive relief even when the injunction would not directly affect their own private interests....

Courts have previously held that class actions are a critical piece of the enforcement of consumer protection law. The reason is clear. Without class actions, many meritorious claims would never be brought.... Class actions are vital where the damage to any individual consumer is nominal and that vital piece is exactly what the plaintiffs claim the class action waiver before us seeks to eviscerate.

Thus we conclude that without class actions, consumers would have far less ability to vindicate the CPA *See Carnegie v. Household Int'l, Inc.,* 376 F.3d 656, 661 (7th Cir. 2004). Again, the CPA contemplates that individual consumers will act as "private attorneys general," harnessing individual interests in order to promote the public good. *See Wash. State Physicians Ins. Exch. & Ass'n v. Fisions Corp.,* 858 P.2d 1054 (1993)....

Without class action suits the public's ability to perform this function is drastically diminished. We agree with plaintiffs and the Washington attorney general and conclude the class action waiver clause before us is an unconscionable violation of this State's policy to "protect the public and foster fair and honest competition," RCW 19.86.920, because it drastically forestalls attempts to vindicate consumer rights. To the extent that this clause prevents CPA cases, it is substantively unconscionable.[3]

II.   EXCULPATION

We turn now to whether this class action waiver is unconscionable for effectively exculpating its drafter from liability for a large class of wrongful conduct. Contract provisions that exculpate the author for wrongdoing, especially intentional wrongdoing, undermine the public good. *Adler v. Fred Lind Manor,* 103 P.3d 773 (2004).... Exculpation from any potential liability for unfair or deceptive acts or practices in commerce clearly violates public policy. RCW 19.86.920; *cf. Discover Bank,* 113 P.3d 1100. As our sister court said, " '[a] company which wrongfully extracts a dollar from each of millions of customers will reap a handsome profit; the class action is often the only effective way to halt and redress such exploitation.' " *Discover Bank,* 113 P.3d 1100 (quoting *Blue Chip Stamps v. Superior Court,* 556 P.2d 755 (1976) (Tobriner, J., concurring)).

Of course, on its face, the class action waiver does not exculpate Cingular from anything; it merely channels dispute resolution into individual arbitration proceedings or small claims court. But in effect, this exculpates Cingular from legal liability for any wrong where the cost of pursuit outweighs the potential amount of recovery. As the ever inimitable Judge Posner has aptly noted, "[t]he *realistic* alternative to a class action is not 17 million individual suits, but zero individual suits, as only a lunatic or a fanatic sues for $30." [*Carnegie v. Household Int'l, Inc.,* 376 F.3d 656, 661 (7th Cir.2004)].

In such cases, the ability to proceed as a class transforms a merely theoretically possible remedy into a real one.... It is often the only meaningful type of redress available for small but widespread injuries. *See, e.g., Discover Bank,* 113 P.3d 1100; *Gilman,* 692 A.2d 454. Without it, many consumers may not even realize that they have a claim.... The class action provides a mechanism to alert them to this fact. Second, again, claims as small as those in this case are impracticable to pursue on an individual basis even in small claims court, and particularly in arbitration. Shifting the cost of arbitration to Cingular does not seem likely to make it worth the time, energy, and stress to pursue such individually small claims. The plaintiffs also presented evidence that the prohibitive cost actually does prevent claims. In addition to the declarations discussed above, it appears that no claims from Washington customers have been brought to arbitration against Cingular in the past six years.

Cingular contends that it has cured any concerns about access to a remedy by promising to pay all AAA filing, administrative, and arbitrator fees unless the arbitrator finds the claim frivolous, and by promising to pay the attorneys fees under certain circumstances. While laudable, it appears

---

3. Because we find the class action waiver substantively unconscionable, we find it unnecessary to address plaintiffs' claims of procedural unconscionability.

to us that these provisions do not ensure that a remedy is practically available. First, the attorney fees are awarded only if the plaintiffs recover at least the full amount of their demand.[4] A plaintiff could recover 99 percent of a claim and still not be awarded any attorney fees.... Even if all of the contingencies are met and attorney fees are awarded, the arbitrator may consider the amount in controversy in awarding fees. While technically the plaintiffs are not prevented from hiring an attorney, practically, attorneys are generally unwilling to take on individual arbitrations to recover trivial amounts of money. This is of course, precisely why class actions were created in the first place....

... [T]his class action waiver effectively prevents one party to the contract, the consumer, from pursuing valid claims, effectively exculpating the drafter from potential liability for small claims, no matter how widespread.... A clause that unilaterally and severely limits the remedies of only one side is substantively unconscionable under Washington law for denying any meaningful remedy. [Citations omitted.]

... Since Cingular's class action waiver states that if it "is found to be unenforceable, then the entirety of this arbitration clause shall be null and void," there remains no basis to compel arbitration. We do not reach plaintiffs' remaining claims. We reverse and remand to the trial court for further proceedings consistent with this opinion.[5]

■ MADSEN, J. (dissenting). The public policy that the majority says is violated by the class action waiver at issue is a public policy created by the majority itself. If there is to be state policy forbidding class action waivers in consumer agreements, it should come from our legislature, not this court.

Perhaps more troubling, though, is that the majority's new policy disfavors arbitration, contradicting the strong legislative public policy favoring arbitration of disputes embodied in the Federal Arbitration Act (FAA), Title 9 U.S.C. Under the act, every presumption must be resolved in favor of an arbitration agreement. This policy of presuming validity of an arbitration agreement is of particular force where, as here, the arbitration agreement includes significant financial protection for consumers, belying the majority's claim that, because small claims are at issue, recovery is effectively unattainable and the class action waiver acts as an exculpatory clause. If this arbitration clause violates "public policy," then I cannot imagine any in the consumer context that would not.

Finally, without justification the majority departs from the usual case-by-case analysis for determining contract unconscionability in favor of a

---

4. The provision reads: "[I]f the arbitrator grants relief to you that is equal to or greater than the value of your Demand, Cingular shall reimburse you for your reasonable attorneys' fees and expenses incurred for the arbitration." CP at 356.

5. We respectfully disagree with our learned colleague in dissent that this opinion presumes the CPA invalidates all class action waivers. We mean to say only that class action waivers that *prevent* vindication of rights secured by the CPA are invalid. We agree with our dissenting colleague that whether any particular class action waiver is unenforceable will turn on the facts of the particular case. We can certainly conceive of situations where a class action waiver would not prevent a consumer from vindicating his or her substantive rights under the CPA and would thus be enforceable....

sweeping rule that will invalidate thousands of arbitration contracts without regard to the specific terms of those agreements.

Because the majority takes on the legislative prerogative of making public policy and contravenes federal law requiring that arbitration agreements be accorded the same consideration as other contracts, I dissent. . . .

I would reject the argument that plaintiffs will be unable to obtain legal representation and therefore the arbitration agreement's class action waiver is unconscionable. Instead, because Cingular has promised to pay the costs of arbitration plus attorneys' fees and costs if the plaintiffs are successful in obtaining the relief they seek, plaintiffs are able to pursue their small value claims and the class action waiver does not effectively act as an exculpatory clause relieving Cingular of liability. The plaintiffs' important goal of vindicating the public interest under the CPA can be accomplished on an individual basis. I would hold that the plaintiffs have failed to show that the class action waiver is substantively unconscionable because it is one-sided in effect, as they have not shown an undue burden to one side or unfair advantage or benefit to the other. I would affirm the superior court's order compelling arbitration.

NOTES

(1) *Access to Adjudication.* What provision had Cingular made for customer arbitration? Compare this to the proposed arbitration in *Scissor–Tail, Inc.,* p. 475 above, or to the concerns expressed by the dissent in *Carnival Cruise Lines,* p. 484 above, regarding the Shutes' ability to litigate in Florida under the choice of forum clause. Is the problem in this case access to arbitration, something else, or both?

(2) *Gateway Again.* In Brower v. Gateway, Note 1, p. 218 above, consumers sought to avoid an arbitration clause included among the "Standard Terms and Conditions" that arrived with their mail-order computer, on the grounds that the term was unconscionable "due to the unduly burdensome procedure and cost for the individual consumer." The disputed clause required the New York buyers to arbitrate in Chicago. From an order granting Gateway's motion to dismiss, the consumers appealed. *Held*: Modified in part. Brower v. Gateway 2000, 676 N.Y.S.2d 569, 574 (App.Div.1998).

Noting that the contract was not one of adhesion ("if any term of the agreement is unacceptable to the consumer, he or she can easily buy a competitor's product instead [and] reject Gateway's agreement by returning the merchandise"), the court found no procedural unconscionability: "any purchaser has 30 days within which to thoroughly examine the contents of their shipment, including the terms of the Agreement. . . ." As to the substantive aspect of the claim, the court found that the inconvenience of arbitrating before the International Chamber of Commerce in Chicago was not sufficiently burdensome, but that the *cost* of doing so was. "Barred from resorting to the courts by the arbitration clause in the first instance, the designation of a financially prohibitive forum effectively bars consumers from this forum as well; consumers are thus left with no forum at all in which to resolve a dispute."

The court then noted a new arbitration agreement that Gateway "claims has been extended to all customers, past, present, and future (apparently through publication in a quarterly magazine sent to anyone who has ever purchased a Gateway product)." The new agreement provides for the consumer's choice of arbitration with either the ICC or the American Arbitration Association at any location agreed to by the parties. (The new terms further state that agreement as to location "shall not be unreasonably withheld.") The court remanded the case for the parties to seek appropriate substitution of the arbitrator.

(3) *Amici.* The court in *Cingular* acknowledges the contribution of various *amici curiae*, or friends of the court, who submitted briefs in the case. For the history of participation of non-litigants in the briefing process, see Samuel Krislov, The Amicus Curiae Brief: From Friendship to Advocacy, 72 Yale L. J. 694 (1963).

PROBLEM

Add-on Arbitration Agreements. A bank decides that it prefers arbitration, rather than trial, as the mode of resolving potential disputes with its customers. It mails an announcement so stating to holders of accounts in the bank on the subject along with the bank's regular monthly statements. Each depositor has signed a signature card, upon opening an account, which incorporates the bank's rules and charges as set out in a booklet handed at that time to the depositor. According to the booklet, the bank may from time to time alter its rules upon giving notice to customers. The arbitration announcement refers to that provision, specifies an arbitration procedure, and states that either party to a dispute thereafter arising about charges and credits to an account may demand arbitration. In a class action by depositors brought against the bank for a declaratory judgment that the rule change is ineffective, what result? See Bank One v. Coates, 125 F.Supp.2d 819 (S.D.Miss.2001).

SECTION 4. PERFORMING IN GOOD FAITH

In Chapter 5, we examined terms, such as gap fillers and warranties, that the law sometimes adds to the parties' actual agreement in determining the full extent of their contractual obligations. The implied duty of good faith in performance and enforcement of a contract—also known as the implied duty of good faith and fair dealing in performance and enforcement—is another such term, added to the parties' agreement both by the common law and the UCC. See Restatement § 205 and UCC § 1–304. The duty governs the performance and enforcement of a contract, and not its negotiation and formation. In reading the materials that follow, think about (i) what sorts of contracts include a duty of good faith; (ii) how courts determine the content of the duty; and (iii) the consequences of a party's failure to act in good faith.

Dalton v. Educational Testing Service

Court of Appeals of New York, 1995.
87 N.Y.2d 384, 663 N.E.2d 289.

[In May 1991, Brian Dalton took the Scholastic Aptitude Test (SAT), administered by Educational Testing Service (ETS). In November he took the test a second time and his combined score increased 410 points.[a] Because the increase was more than 350 points, his test results fell within the ETS category of "Large Score Differences" or "discrepant scores," and

---

a. Out of a maximum of 1600 points.

members of the ETS Test Security Office reviewed his sheets. On finding disparate handwriting, they submitted the answer sheets to a document examiner, who opined that they were completed by different individuals. Dalton's case was then forwarded to the Board of Review, which preliminarily decided that substantial evidence supported cancelling his November score.

When he registered for the November SAT, Dalton had signed a statement agreeing to the conditions in the New York State edition of the Registration Bulletin, which reserved to ETS "the right to cancel any test score ... if ETS believes that there is reason to question the score's validity." The Registration Bulletin further provided that, if "the validity of a test score is questioned because it may have been obtained unfairly, ETS [will] notif[y] the test taker of the reasons for questioning the score" and offer the test-taker five options: (1) the opportunity to provide additional information, (2) confirmation of the score by taking a free retest, (3) authorization for ETS to cancel the score and refund all fees, (4) third-party review by any institution receiving the test score or (5) arbitration.

ETS notified Dalton of its preliminary decision to cancel his November SAT score in a letter informing him that the handwriting disparity and the difference in his scores suggested that someone else may have completed his answer sheet and advising him that he could supply additional information or elect one of the other options. Dalton opted to present additional information, including verification that he was suffering from mononucleosis during the May examination, diagnostic test results from a preparatory course he took prior to the November examination (he had taken no similar course prior to the May SAT) that were consistent with his performance on that test, a statement from an ETS proctor who remembered his presence in November, statements from two students—one previously unacquainted with Dalton—that he had been in the room during the test, and a report from a document examiner obtained by his family who concluded that Dalton was the author of both answer sheets.

After several Board of Review meetings, ETS submitted the handwriting exemplars to a second document examiner who, like its first, opined that the tests were not completed by the same individual. ETS continued to question the validity of Dalton's November score, and Dalton's father commenced an action on his son's behalf to prevent ETS from cancelling the November score and to compel its immediate release.

Following a 12–day nonjury trial, the trial judge found that ETS failed "to make even rudimentary efforts to evaluate or investigate the information" furnished by Dalton. The Board of Review members believed that the sole issue was the disparate handwriting and that evidence regarding Dalton's health or his presence was irrelevant. The judge concluded that ETS had failed to act in good faith as required by its contract and ordered ETS to release the November score. The Appellate Division affirmed.]

■ KAYE, CHIEF JUDGE.... [W]e agree that ETS breached its contract with Dalton but differ as to the scope of the relief. By accepting ETS' standardized form agreement when he registered for the November SAT, Dalton entered into a contract with ETS. . . . Implicit in all contracts is a covenant of good faith and fair dealing in the course of contract performance. . . .

Encompassed within the implied obligation of each promisor to exercise good faith [is] a pledge that "neither party shall do anything which will have the effect of destroying or injuring the right of the other party to receive the fruits of the contract" (Kirks La Shelle Co. v. Armstrong Co., 263 N.Y. 79, 87, 188 N.E. 163). Where the contract contemplates the exercise of discretion, this pledge includes a promise not to act arbitrarily or irrationally in exercising that discretion . . . The duty of good faith and fair dealing, however, is not without limits, and no obligation can be implied that "would be inconsistent with other terms of the contractual relationship" (Murphy v. American Home Prods. Corp., 58 N.Y.2d 293, 304, 448 N.E.2d 86).

The parties here agreed to the provisions in the Registration Bulletin, which expressly permit cancellation of a test score so long as ETS found "reason to question" its validity after offering the test-taker the five specified options. Nothing in the contract compelled ETS to prove that the test-taker cheated. Nor did the invitation to the test-taker to furnish ETS with relevant information reasonably and realistically translate into any requirement that ETS conduct a field investigation or gather evidence to verify or counter the test-taker's documentation. Indeed, such an obligation would be inconsistent with the contractual language placing the burden squarely on the test-taker to overcome the ETS finding of score invalidity. ETS, therefore, was under no duty, express or implied, to initiate an external investigation into a questioned score.

The contract, however, did require that ETS consider any relevant material that Dalton supplied to the Board of Review. . . . Dalton triggered this . . . obligation on the part of ETS by exercising his contractual option to provide ETS with information. . . . Nevertheless, with the exception of the document examiner's report, ETS disputes the relevancy of this information. . . . [However,] ETS expressly framed the dispositive question as one of suspected impersonation. Because the statements from the classroom proctor and November test-takers corroborated Dalton's contention that he was present at and in fact took the November examination, they were relevant to this issue. Likewise, inasmuch as the medical documentation concerning Dalton's health at the time of the May SAT provided an explanation for his poor performance on that examination, and the consistent diagnostic test results demonstrated his ability to achieve such a dramatic score increase, these items were also germane to the question whether it was Dalton or an imposter who completed the November examination. . . .

When ETS fulfills its contractual obligation to consider relevant material provided by the test-taker and otherwise acts in good faith, the testing service—not the courts—must be the final arbiter of both the appropriate weight to accord that material and the validity of the test score. This Court will not interfere with that discretionary determination unless it is performed arbitrarily or irrationally. Where, however, ETS refuses to exercise its discretion in the first instance by declining even to consider relevant material submitted by the test-taker, the legal question is whether this refusal breached an express or implied term of the contract, not whether it was arbitrary or irrational. Here, the courts below agreed that ETS did not consider the relevant information furnished by Dalton. By doing so, ETS failed to comply in good faith with its own test security procedures, thereby breaching its contract with Dalton. . . .

We agree with the trial court and Appellate Division that Dalton is entitled to specific performance of the contract. Dalton is not, however, entitled to release of his score as though fully validated. The goal of specific performance is to produce "as nearly as is practicable, the same effect as if the contract had been performed" (Farnsworth, Contracts § 12.5, at 823 [1982]). Had the contract here been performed, ETS would have considered the information provided by Dalton in reaching a final decision. ETS never promised to release a score believed to be invalid, and the validity of Dalton's November SAT score has yet to be determined. Indeed, the trial court specifically noted that it was not resolving the question whether Dalton in fact took the November test. . . .

Dalton is entitled to relief that comports with ETS' contractual promise—good-faith consideration of the material he submitted to ETS. We cannot agree with Dalton's assumption that ETS will merely rubber-stamp its prior determination without good-faith attention to his documentation and that reconsideration by ETS will be an empty exercise. Our conclusion that the contract affords Dalton a meaningful remedy rests also on the provision in the Procedures for Questioned Scores allowing Dalton to utilize one or more of the remaining four options in combination with renewed consideration by the Board of Review. Those options—including third-party review by any institution receiving the test score as well as arbitration—remain available should ETS determine that the information submitted fails to resolve its concerns about the validity of the November score.

Accordingly, the Appellate Division Order should be modified in accordance with this opinion and, as so modified, affirmed, without costs.

NOTES

(1) *Questions.* The court explains that ETS and not the courts must be the final arbiter when ETS "fulfills its contractual obligation to consider relevant material provided by the test-taker and otherwise acts in good faith." It therefore orders "good-faith consideration of the material he submitted to ETS." The court rejects Dalton's contention "that ETS will merely rubber-stamp its prior determination without good-faith attention to his documentation." What criteria would the court use to define "good faith" if it were asked to hold ETS in contempt for failure to comply with the court's order? Two judges dissented on the ground that "ETS acted within its discretion in continuing the security process rather than releasing the score after considering and rejecting Dalton's evidence" and there was "no evidence that ETS acted arbitrarily in its decision-making process." 663 N.E.2d at 297 (Levine, J. dissenting).

(2) *The Case of the "Dynamic Duo."* Fight promoters Butch Lewis and Don King, doing business as the Dynamic Duo, Inc., made a contract with Hilton Hotels to stage at the Las Vegas Hilton the final four fights in the Unification Series, so

called because it was designed to select a single champion from those recognized by three world boxing organizations. Hilton claimed that it was understood that Michael Spinks, the IBF champion, would be available for these events, though the contract was silent as to this. Spinks forfeited his title before the time for the events, and Hilton, claiming that the Dynamic Duo had deliberately induced the forfeiture, sued Dynamic Duo. From judgment for the defendant, plaintiff appealed. *Held:* Reversed and remanded.

"Even though Dynamic Duo did not have a contractual duty to furnish Spinks as a contestant in the Hilton events, it did have a legal duty not to interfere with Spinks' capacity to be a contestant and effectively prevent Spinks from participating in the Hilton events.... If ... Lewis ... had Spinks stripped of the IBF title in order to undermine the Unification Series and permit Lewis and Dynamic Duo to make more money outside the series, this conduct could be seen as a breach of the covenant of good faith and fair dealing implied in the parties' contract." It was therefore error to exclude the testimony of the Chair of the Nevada Athletic Commission that he had "heard Lewis say that he was going to pull Spinks out of the Unification Series in order to make 'big money' elsewhere." Hilton Hotels Corp. v. Butch Lewis Productions, 808 P.2d 919 (Nev.1991).

Eastern Air Lines, Inc. v. Gulf Oil Corporation

United States District Court, Southern District of Florida, 1975.
415 F.Supp. 429.

[The facts and part of the opinion in this case are at p. 76 above.]

■ JAMES LAWRENCE KING, DISTRICT COURT JUDGE.... Gulf suggests that Eastern violated the contract between the parties by manipulating its requirements through a practice known as "fuel freighting" in the airline industry. Requirements can vary from city to city depending on whether or not it is economically profitable to freight fuel. This fuel freighting practice in accordance with price could affect lifting from Gulf stations by either raising such liftings or lowering them. If the price was higher at a Gulf station, the practice could have reduced liftings there by lifting fuel in excess of its actual operating requirements at a prior station, and thereby not loading fuel at the succeeding high price Gulf station. Similarly where the Gulf station was comparatively cheaper, an aircraft might load more heavily at the Gulf station and not load at other succeeding non-Gulf stations.

The court however, finds that Eastern's performance under the contract does not constitute a breach of its agreement with Gulf and is consistent with good faith and established commercial practices as required by U.C.C. § 2–306.

"Good faith" means "honesty in fact in the conduct or transaction concerned" [former] U.C.C. § 1–201(19). Between merchants, "good faith" means "honesty in fact and the observance of reasonable commercial standards of fair dealing in the trade"; [former] U.C.C. § 2–103(1)(b) and Official Comment 2 of U.C.C. § 2–306.[a] The relevant commercial practices are "courses of performance," "courses of dealing" and "usages of trade."[b]

---

a. The current Official Text of the UCC contains the broader standard in the Article 1 definition; see UCC § 1–201(b)(20).

b. U.C.C. § 1–303(a) defines "course of performance" as "a sequence of conduct between the parties to a particular transaction

Throughout the history of commercial aviation, including 30 years of dealing between Gulf and Eastern, airlines' liftings of fuel by nature have been subject to substantial daily, weekly, monthly and seasonal variations, as they are affected by weather, schedule changes, size of aircraft, aircraft load, local airport conditions, ground time, availability of fueling facilities, whether the flight is on time or late, passenger convenience, economy and efficiency of operation, fuel taxes, into-plane fuel service charges, fuel price, and, ultimately, the judgment of the flight captain as to how much fuel he wants to take.

All these factors are, and for years have been, known to oil companies, including Gulf, and taken into account by them in their fuel contracts. Gulf's witnesses at trial pointed to certain examples of numerically large "swings" in monthly liftings by Eastern at various Gulf stations. Gulf never complained of this practice and apparently accepted it as normal procedure. Some of the "swings" were explained by the fueling of a single aircraft for one flight, or by the addition of one schedule in mid-month. The evidence establishes that Eastern, on one occasion, requested 500,000 additional gallons for one month at one station, without protest from Gulf, and that Eastern increased its requirements at another station more than 50 percent year to year, from less than 2,000,000 to more than 3,000,000 gallons, again, without Gulf objection.

The court concludes that fuel freighting is an established industry practice, inherent in the nature of the business. The evidence clearly demonstrated that the practice has long been part of the established courses of performance and dealing between Eastern and Gulf. As the practice of "freighting" or "tankering" has gone on unchanged and unchallenged for many years accepted as a fact of life by Gulf without complaint, the court is reminded of Official Comment 1 to U.C.C. § 2–208:

> "The parties themselves know best what they have meant by their words of agreement and their action under that agreement is the best indication of what that meaning was."

that exists if: (1) the agreement of the parties with respect to the transaction involves repeated occasions for performance by a party; and (2) the other party, with knowledge of the nature of the performance and opportunity for objection to it, accepts the performance or acquiesces in it without objection." At the time this case was decided, the substance of what is now UCC § 1–303(a) was found in former UCC § 2–208.

U.C.C. § 1–303(b) defines "course of dealing" as "a sequence of conduct concerning previous transactions between the parties to a particular transaction that is fairly to be regarded as establishing a common basis of understanding for interpreting their expressions and other conduct."

U.C.C. § 1–303(c) defines "usage of trade" as "any practice or method of dealing having such regularity of observance in a place, vocation or trade as to justify an expectation that it will be observed with respect to the transaction in question."

U.C.C. § 1–303(e) provides that "(1) express terms prevail over course of performance, course of dealing, and usage of trade; (2) course of performance prevails over course of dealing and usage of trade; and (3) course of dealing prevails over usage of trade."

From a practical point of view, "freighting" opportunities are very few, according to the uncontradicted testimony, as the airline must perform its schedules in consideration of operating realities. There is no suggestion here that Eastern is operating at certain Gulf stations but taking no fuel at all. The very reason Eastern initially desired a fuel contract was because the airline planned to take on fuel, and had to have an assured source of supply.

If a customer's demands under a requirements contract become excessive, U.C.C. § 2–306 protects the seller and, in the appropriate case, would allow him to refuse to deliver unreasonable amounts demanded (but without eliminating his basic contract obligation); similarly, in an appropriate case, if a customer repeatedly had no requirements at all, the seller might be excused from performance if the buyer suddenly and without warning should descend upon him and demand his entire inventory, but the court is not called upon to decide those cases here.

Rather, the case here is one where the established courses of performance and dealing between the parties, the established usages of the trade, and the basic contract itself all show that the matters complained of for the first time by Gulf after commencement of this litigation are the fundamental given ingredients of the aviation fuel trade to which the parties have accommodated themselves successfully and without dispute over the years.

> "The practical interpretation given to their contracts by the parties to them while they are engaged in their performance, and before any controversy has arisen concerning them, is one of the best indications of their true intent, and courts that adopt and enforce such a construction are not likely to commit serious error."

Manhattan Life Ins. Co. of New York v. Wright, 126 F. 82, 87 (8th Cir.1903). Accord, Spindler v. Kushner, 284 So.2d 481, 484 (Fla.App.1973).

The court concludes that Eastern has not violated the contract.

NOTES

(1) *Obligation of Good Faith.* UCC § 1–304 provides that "Every contract or duty within [the Uniform Commercial Code] imposes an obligation of good faith in its performance and enforcement." Originally, "good faith" was generally defined to mean only "honesty in fact in the conduct or transaction concerned," a purely subjective test. See former UCC § 1–201(19). But, as noted in *Eastern Air Lines,* Article 2 also contained a special definition of "good faith" for merchants: "honesty in fact and the observance of reasonable commercial standards of fair dealing in the trade." Former UCC § 2–103(1)(b). When UCC Article 1 was revised in 2001, the heightened "merchant standard" of good faith in Article 2 was incorporated into the general definition of "good faith" in Article 1 and made applicable to all parties, whether or not they are merchants. See UCC § 1–201(b)(20).

What sort of evidence might parties adduce with respect to "honesty in fact"? What sort of evidence might parties adduce with respect to the observance of reasonable commercial standards of fair dealing? What does *Eastern Air Lines* suggest?

(2) *Good Faith as "Independent Duty"?* In 1994, the Uniform Commercial Code's Permanent Editorial Board issued its Commentary No. 10 on UCC 1–203.[a] It resulted in the addition of language to the Official Comment stating that the section "does not support an independent cause of action for failure to perform or enforce in good faith" and seeks to make clear "that the doctrine of good faith merely directs a court towards interpreting contracts within the commercial context in which they are created, performed and enforced, and does not create a separate duty of fairness and reasonableness which can be independently breached."

Is this consistent with Comment 8 to UCC § 2–309(3), which states that the subsection "recognizes that the application of principles of good faith and sound commercial practice normally call for [reasonable] notification of the termination of a going contract relationship as will give the other party reasonable time to seek a substitute relationship"?

(3) *A Comparative Approach.* The notion of an obligation of good faith in the performance of contract duties is a familiar one to civil law systems, most notably the German. Article 242 of the German Civil Code imposes an obligation of "performance according to the requirements of good faith [*Treu and Glauben*], common habits being duly taken into consideration." It is not a familiar notion to the common law, and the Code provisions occasioned considerable discussion. See Steven Burton, Breach of Contract and the Common Law Duty to Perform in Good Faith, 94 Harv.L.Rev. 369 (1980); Farnsworth, Good Faith Performance and Commercial Reasonableness under the Uniform Commercial Code, 30 U.Chi.L.Rev. 666 (1963); Robert Summers, "Good Faith" in General Contract Law and the Sales Provisions of the Uniform Commercial Code, 54 Va.L.Rev. 195 (1968).

(4) *International Solutions.* Although article 1.7 of the UNIDROIT Principles requires that a party "act in accordance with good faith and fair dealing in international trade," the Vienna Convention contains no comparable provision. Article 7(1) of the Convention provides that in "the *interpretation* of this Convention, regard is to be had to ... the observance of good faith in international trade," but this does not speak of a duty of *performance* by a contracting party.

"At a late stage in the preparation of the Sales Convention this language was adopted as a compromise between two divergent views: (a) Some delegations supported a general rule that ... the parties must observe principles of 'fair dealing' and must act in 'good faith'; Others resisted this step on the ground that 'fair dealing' and 'good faith' had no fixed meaning and would lead to uncertainty." Ultimately it was "decided that an obligation of 'good faith' should not be imposed loosely and at large, but should be restricted to a principle for interpreting the provisions of the Convention." John Honnold, *Uniform Law for International Sales under the 1980 United Nations Convention* 99 (3d ed. 1999).

———

MARKET STREET ASSOCIATES v. FREY, 941 F.2d 588 (7th Cir. 1991). [J.C. Penney, the retail chain, entered into a sale and leaseback arrangement with General Electric Pension Trust in order to finance Penney's growth. Under paragraph 34, the pension trust agreed to give reasonable consideration to requests by Penney for the financing of additional improvements. It went on to provide, in effect, that if the average annual appreciation in the property exceeded 6 percent, a breakdown in the

---

a. This section was subsequently re-numbered UCC § 1–304.

negotiations over the financing of improvements would entitle Penney to buy back the property for less than its market value.

Twenty years later, Market Street Associates, Penney's successor under one of the leases, sought to buy back the property it leased from the pension trust in order to use the property to get financing elsewhere. When Erb of the pension trust, who was responsible for the property, was slow in responding, Orenstein of Market Street Associates then sent two letters to Erb formally requesting $4 million financing but not mentioning paragraph 34. (Orenstein later stated in his deposition that it had occurred to him that Erb might not know about paragraph 34.) Erb responded to the first by saying that the amount requested was below the pension trust's $7 million minimum. Over a month later, Orenstein wrote Erb that Market Street was exercising its option under paragraph 34, which had evidently become advantageous to it.

When the pension trust refused to sell, Market Street Associates sought specific performance. The district judge granted summary judgment for the pension trust, holding that Market Street Associates had violated the duty of good faith. Market Street Associates appealed.]

■ POSNER, J. . . . [T]he judge emphasized a statement by Orenstein in his deposition that it had occurred to him that Erb mightn't know about paragraph 34, though this was unlikely (Orenstein testified) because Erb or someone else at the pension trust would probably check the file and discover the paragraph and realize that if the trust refused to negotiate over the request for financing, Market Street Associates, as Penney's assignee, would be entitled to walk off with the property for (perhaps) a song. The judge inferred that Market Street Associates didn't want financing from the pension trust—that it just wanted an opportunity to buy the property at a bargain price and hoped that the pension trust wouldn't realize the implications of turning down the request for financing. Market Street Associates should, the judge opined, have advised the pension trust that it was requesting financing pursuant to paragraph 34, so that the trust would understand the penalty for refusing to negotiate. . . .

So we must consider the meaning of the contract duty of "good faith." The Wisconsin cases are cryptic as to its meaning though emphatic about its existence, so we must cast our net wider. . . . The particular confusion to which the vaguely moralistic overtones of "good faith" give rise is the belief that every contract establishes a fiduciary relationship. A fiduciary is required to treat his principal as if the principal were he, and therefore he may not take advantage of the principal's incapacity, ignorance, inexperience, or even naiveté. . . .

But it is unlikely that Wisconsin wishes, in the name of good faith, to make every contract signatory his brother's keeper, especially when the brother is the immense and sophisticated General Electric Pension Trust, whose lofty indifference to small (= < $7 million) transactions is the signifier of its grandeur. In fact the law contemplates that people frequently will take advantage of the ignorance of those with whom they contract, without thereby incurring liability. . . . The duty of honesty, of good faith even expansively conceived, is not a duty of candor. You can make a binding contract to purchase something you know your seller undervalues. . . . That of course is a question about formation, not performance, and the particular duty of good faith under examination here relates to the latter rather than to the former. But even after you have signed a contract, you are not obliged to become an altruist toward the other party and relax the terms if he gets into trouble in performing his side of the bargain. . . . Otherwise mere difficulty of performance would excuse a contracting party—which it does not. . . .

But it is one thing to say that you can exploit your superior knowledge of the market—for if you cannot, you will not be able to recoup the investment you made in obtaining that knowledge—or that you are not required to spend money bailing out a contract partner who has gotten into trouble. It is another thing to say that you can take deliberate advantage of an oversight by your contract partner concerning his rights under the contract. Such taking advantage is not the exploitation of superior knowledge or the avoidance of unbargained-for expense; it is sharp dealing. . . .

The essential issue bearing on Market Street Associates' good faith was Orenstein's state of mind, a type of inquiry that ordinarily cannot be concluded on summary judgment, and could not be here. If Orenstein believed that Erb knew or would surely find out about paragraph 34, it was not dishonest or opportunistic to fail to flag that paragraph, or even to fail to mention the lease, in his correspondence and (rare) conversations with Erb, especially given the uninterest in dealing with Market Street Associates that Erb fairly radiated. To decide what Orenstein believed, a trial is necessary. . . .

Reversed and remanded.

NOTES

(1) *Opinion on Remand.* After a trial on remand, the district judge held that Market Street Associates was not entitled to specific performance. "While Orenstein initially assumed that the Trust would review the lease and make its determination as to whether it should provide financing to Market Street in light of paragraph 34, he subsequently recognized that the Trust was not operating under paragraph 34. While Orenstein knew this fact, he did not bring the matter to the Trust's attention, and continued to write ambiguous letters, until he wished to utilize the purchase option, thereby purchasing the property at a discounted cost. By so doing, this court concludes that Orenstein breached his duty to use good faith in his dealings with the Trust, and Market Street is not entitled to specific performance." Market Street Associates v. Frey, 817 F.Supp. 784, 788 (E.D.Wis.1993).

(2) *Opportunism.* Note that Judge Posner says that a trial is necessary to determine whether Orenstein was "dishonest or opportunistic." Five years later, Judge Posner's colleague, Judge Easterbrook, discussed opportunism in Industrial Representatives, Inc. v. CP Clare Corp., 74 F.3d 128, 129–30, 132 (7th Cir.1996). " 'Opportunism' in the law of contracts usually signifies one of two situations. First, there is effort to wring some advantage from the fact that the party who performs first sinks costs, which the other party may hold hostage by demanding greater compensation in exchange for its own performance. The movie star who sulks (in the hope of being offered more money) when production is 90% complete, and reshooting the picture without him would be exceedingly expensive, is behaving

opportunistically in this sense. [citing Alaska Packers' Ass'n v. Domenico, p. 325 above.] ... Second, there is an effort to take advantage of one's contracting partner in a way that could not have been contemplated at the time of drafting, and which therefore was not resolved explicitly by the parties. [citing *Market Street Associates*.] ... Contract law does not require parties to be fair, or kind, or reasonable, or to share gains or losses equitably.... It does require parties to avoid taking advantage of the opportunities that arise from sequential performance, when the contract does not cover a particular subject."

Bloor v. Falstaff Brewing Corp.

United States Court of Appeals, Second Circuit, 1979.
601 F.2d 609.

■ FRIENDLY, CIRCUIT JUDGE: This action, wherein federal jurisdiction is predicated on diversity of citizenship, 28 U.S.C. § 1332, was brought in the District Court for the Southern District of New York, by James Bloor, Reorganization Trustee of Balco Properties Corporation, formerly named P. Ballantine & Sons (Ballantine), a venerable and once successful brewery based in Newark, N.J. He sought to recover from Falstaff Brewing Corporation (Falstaff) for breach of a contract dated March 31, 1972, wherein Falstaff bought the Ballantine brewing labels, trademarks, accounts receivable, distribution systems and other property except the brewery. The price was $4,000,000 plus a royalty of fifty cents on each barrel of the Ballantine brands sold between April 1, 1972 and March 31, 1978. Although other issues were tried, the appeals concern only two provisions of the contract. These are:

8. *Certain Other Covenants of Buyer.*

(a) After the Closing Date the [Buyer] will use its best efforts to promote and maintain a high volume of sales under the Proprietary Rights.

2(a)(v) [The Buyer will pay a royalty of $.50 per barrel for a period of 6 years], provided, however, that if during the Royalty Period the Buyer substantially discontinues the distribution of beer under the brand name "Ballantine" (except as the result of a restraining order in effect for 30 days issued by a court of competent jurisdiction at the request of a governmental authority), it will pay to the Seller a cash sum equal to the years and fraction thereof remaining in the Royalty Period times $1,100,000, payable in equal monthly installments on the first day of each month commencing with the first month following the month in which such discontinuation occurs....

Bloor claimed that Falstaff had breached the best efforts clause, 8(a), and indeed that its default amounted to the substantial discontinuance that would trigger the liquidated damage clause, 2(a)(v). In an opinion that interestingly traces the history of beer back to Domesday Book and beyond, Judge Brieant upheld the first claim and awarded damages but dismissed the second. Falstaff appeals from the former ruling, Bloor from the latter. Both sides also dispute the court's measurement of damages for breach of the best efforts clause.

We shall assume familiarity with Judge Brieant's excellent opinion, 454 F.Supp. 258 (S.D.N.Y.1978), from which we have drawn heavily, and will state only the essentials. Ballantine had been a family owned business, producing low-priced beers primarily for the northeast market, particularly New York, New Jersey, Connecticut and Pennsylvania. Its sales began to decline in 1961, and it lost money from 1965 on. On June 1, 1969, Investors Funding Corporation (IFC), a real estate conglomerate with no experience in brewing, acquired substantially all the stock of Ballantine for $16,290,000. IFC increased advertising expenditures, levelling off in 1971 at $1 million a year. This and other promotional practices, some of dubious legality, led to steady growth in Ballantine's sales despite the increased activities in the northeast of the "nationals"[1] which have greatly augmented their market shares at the expense of smaller brewers. However, this was a profitless prosperity; there was no month in which Ballantine had earnings and the total loss was $15,500,000 for the 33 months of IFC ownership.

After its acquisition of Ballantine, Falstaff continued the $1 million a year advertising program, IFC's pricing policies, and also its policy of serving smaller accounts not solely through sales to independent distributors, the usual practice in the industry, but by use of its own warehouses and trucks—the only change being a shift of the retail distribution system from Newark to North Bergen, N.J., when brewing was concentrated at Falstaff's Rhode Island brewery. However, sales declined and Falstaff claims to have lost $22 million in its Ballantine brand operations from March 31, 1972 to June 1975. Its other activities were also performing indifferently, although with no such losses as were being incurred in the sale of Ballantine products, and it was facing inability to meet payrolls and other debts. In March and April 1975 control of Falstaff passed to Paul Kalmanovitz, a businessman with 40 years experience in the brewing industry. After having first advanced $3 million to enable Falstaff to meet its payrolls and other pressing debts, he later supplied an additional $10 million and made loan guarantees, in return for which he received convertible preferred shares in an amount that endowed him with 35% of the voting power and became the beneficiary of a voting trust that gave him control of the board of directors.

Mr. Kalmanovitz determined to concentrate on making beer and cutting sales costs. He decreased advertising, with the result that the Ballantine advertising budget shrank from $1 million to $115,000 a year.[2] In late 1975 he closed four of Falstaff's six retail distribution centers, including the North Bergen, N.J. depot, which was ultimately replaced by two distributors servicing substantially fewer accounts. He also discontinued various illegal practices that had been used in selling Ballantine products.[3] What

---

1. Miller's, Schlitz, Anheuser–Busch, Coors and Pabst.

2. This was for cooperative advertising with purchasers.

3. There were two kinds of illegal practices, the testimony on both of which is, unsurprisingly, rather vague. Certain "national accounts", i.e. large draught beer buyers, were gotten or retained by "black bag-

ging", the trade term for commercial bribery. On a smaller scale, sales to taverns were facilitated by the salesman's offering a free round for the house of Ballantine if it was available ("retention"), or the customer's choice ("solicitation"). Both practices seem to have been indulged in by many brewers, including Falstaff before Kalmanovitz took control.

happened in terms of sales volume is shown in plaintiff's exhibit 114 J, a chart which we reproduce in the margin.[4] With 1974 as a base, Ballantine declined, 29.72% in 1975 and 45.81% in 1976 as compared with a 1975 gain of 2.24% and a 1976 loss of 13.08% for all brewers excluding the top 15. Other comparisons are similarly devastating, at least for 1976.[5] Despite the decline in the sale of its own labels as well as Ballantine's, Falstaff, however, made a substantial financial recovery. In 1976 it had net income of $8.7 million and its year-end working capital had increased from $8.6 million to $20.2 million and its cash and certificates of deposit from $2.2 million to $12.1 million.

Seizing upon remarks made by the judge during the trial that Falstaff's financial standing in 1975 and thereafter "is probably not relevant" and a footnote in the opinion, 454 F.Supp. at 267 n. 7,[6] appellate counsel for Falstaff contend that the judge read the best efforts clause as requiring Falstaff to maintain Ballantine's volume by any sales methods having a good prospect of increasing or maintaining sales or, at least, to continue lawful methods in use at the time of purchase, no matter what losses they would cause. Starting from this premise, counsel reason that the judge's conclusion was at odds with New York law, stipulated by the contract to be controlling, as last expressed by the Court of Appeals in Feld v. Henry S. Levy & Sons, Inc., 37 N.Y.2d 466, 373 N.Y.S.2d 102, 335 N.E.2d 320 (1975). The court was there dealing with a contract whereby defendant agreed to sell and plaintiff to purchase all bread crumbs produced by defendant at a certain factory. During the term of the agreement defendant ceased producing bread crumbs because production with existing facilities was "very uneconomical," and the plaintiff sued for breach. This case was governed by § 2–306 of the Uniform Commercial Code [which the opinion quoted].

4. Percentage Increase or Decline in Sales Volume of Ballantine Beer, Falstaff Beer and Comparable Brewers for Years Ending December 31, 1972–1976.

1 Ballantine Beer
2 Falstaff Beer
3 All brewers except top 10
4 All brewers except top 15
5 All brewers except top 20
6 Eastern Brewers
7 Comparably sized brewers, adjusted

1972. 1973. 1974 1975. 1976. 1977.

5. Falstaff argues that a trend line projecting the declining volume of Ballantine's sales since 1966, before IFC's purchase, would show an even worse picture. We agree with plaintiff that the percentage figures since 1974 are more significant; at least the judge was entitled to think so.

6. "Even if Falstaff's financial position had been worse in mid–1975 than it actually was, and even if Falstaff had continued in that state of impecuniosity during the term of the contract, performance of the contract is not excused where the difficulty of performance arises from financial difficulty or economic hardship." As the New York Court of Appeals stated in 407 E. 61st Garage, Inc. v. Savoy Corp., 23 N.Y.2d 275, 281, 296 N.Y.S.2d 338, 344, 244 N.E.2d 37, 41 (1968):

"[W]here impossibility or difficulty of performance is occasioned only by finan-

Affirming the denial of cross-motions for summary judgment, the court said that, absent a cancellation on six months' notice for which the contract provided:

> defendant was expected to continue to perform in good faith and could cease production of the bread crumbs, a single facet of its operation, only in good faith. Obviously, a bankruptcy or genuine imperiling of the very existence of its entire business caused by the production of the crumbs would warrant cessation of production of that item; the yield of less profit from its sale than expected would not. Since bread crumbs were but a part of defendant's enterprise and since there was a contractual right of cancellation, good faith required continued production until cancellation, even if there be no profit. In circumstances such as these and without more, defendant would be justified, in good faith, in ceasing production of the single item prior to cancellation only if its losses from continuance would be more than trivial, which, overall, is a question of fact.

37 N.Y.2d 471–72, 373 N.Y.S.2d 106, 335 N.E.2d 323.[7] Falstaff argues from this that it was not bound to do anything to market Ballantine products that would cause "more than trivial" losses.

---

cial difficulty or economic hardship, even to the extent of insolvency or bankruptcy, performance of a contract is not excused. (Citations omitted.)"

7. The text of the Feld opinion did not refer to the case cited by Judge Brieant in the preceding footnote, 407 East 61st Garage, Inc. v. Savoy Fifth Avenue Corporation, 23 N.Y.2d 275, 296 N.Y.S.2d 338, 244 N.E.2d 37 (1968), which might suggest a more onerous obligation here. The Court of Appeals there reversed a summary judgment in favor of the defendant, which had discontinued operating the Savoy Hilton Hotel because of substantial financial losses, in alleged breach of a five-year contract with plaintiff wherein the defendant had agreed to use all reasonable efforts to provide the garage with exclusive opportunity for storage of the motor vehicles of hotel guests. Although the court did use the language quoted by Judge Brieant, the actual holding was simply that "an issue of fact is presented whether the agreement did import an implied promise by Savoy to fulfill its obligations for an entire five-year period." 23 N.Y.2d at 281, 296 N.Y.S.2d at 343, 244 N.E.2d at 41.

Other cases suggest that under New York law a "best efforts" clause imposes an obligation to act with good faith in light of one's own capabilities. In Van Valkenburgh v. Hayden Publishing Co., 30 N.Y.2d 34, 330 N.Y.S.2d 329, 281 N.E.2d 142 (1972), the court held a publisher liable to an author when, in clear bad faith after a contract dispute, he hired another to produce a book very similar to plaintiff's and then promoted it to those who had been buying the latter. On the other hand, a defendant having the exclusive right to sell the plaintiff's product may sell a similar product if necessary to meet outside competition, so long as he accounts for any resulting losses the plaintiff can show in the sales of the licensed product. Parev Products Co. v. I. Rokeach & Sons, 124 F.2d 147 (2d Cir.1941). A summary definition of the best efforts obligation, cited by Judge Brieant, 454 F.Supp. at 266, is given in Arnold Productions, Inc. v. Favorite Films Corp., 176 F.Supp. 862, 866 (S.D.N.Y.1959), aff'd 298 F.2d 540 (2d Cir.1962), to wit, performing as well as "the average prudent comparable" brewer.

The net of all this is that the New York law is far from clear and it is unfortunate that a federal court must have to apply it.

We do not think the judge imposed on Falstaff a standard as demanding as its appellate counsel argues that he did. Despite his footnote 7, see note 6 supra, he did not in fact proceed on the basis that the best efforts clause required Falstaff to bankrupt itself in promoting Ballantine products or even to sell those products at a substantial loss. He relied rather on the fact that Falstaff's obligation to "use its best efforts to promote and maintain a high volume of sales" of Ballantine products was not fulfilled by a policy summarized by Mr. Kalmanovitz as being:

We sell beer and you pay for it. . . .

We sell beer, F.O.B. the brewery. You come and get it.

—however sensible such a policy may have been with respect to Falstaff's other products. Once the peril of insolvency had been averted, the drastic percentage reductions in Ballantine sales as related to any possible basis of comparison, see fn. 5, required Falstaff at least to explore whether steps not involving substantial losses could have been taken to stop or at least lessen the rate of decline. The judge found that, instead of doing this, Falstaff had engaged in a number of misfeasances and nonfeasances which could have accounted in substantial measure for the catastrophic drop in Ballantine sales shown in the chart, see 454 F.Supp. at 267–72. These included the closing of the North Bergen depot which had serviced "Mom and Pop" stores and bars in the New York metropolitan area; Falstaff's choices of distributors for Ballantine products in the New Jersey and particularly the New York areas, where the chosen distributor was the owner of a competing brand; its failure to take advantage of a proffer from Guinness–Harp Corporation to distribute Ballantine products in New York City through its Metrobeer Division; Falstaff's incentive to put more effort into sales of its own brands which sold at higher prices despite identity of the ingredients and were free from the $.50 a barrel royalty burden; its failure to treat Ballantine products evenhandedly with Falstaff's; its discontinuing the practice of setting goals for salesmen; and the general Kalmanovitz policy of stressing profit at the expense of volume. In the court's judgment, these misfeasances and nonfeasances warranted a conclusion that, even taking account of Falstaff's right to give reasonable consideration to its own interests, Falstaff had breached its duty to use best efforts as stated in the *Van Valkenburgh* decision, supra, 30 N.Y.2d at 46, 330 N.Y.S.2d at 334, 281 N.E.2d at 145.

Falstaff levels a barrage on these findings. The only attack which merits discussion is its criticism of the judge's conclusion that Falstaff did not treat its Ballantine brands evenhandedly with those under the Falstaff name. We agree that the subsidiary findings "that Falstaff but not Ballantine had been advertised extensively in Texas and Missouri" and that "[i]n these same areas Falstaff, although a 'premium' beer, was sold for extended periods below the price of Ballantine," while literally true, did not warrant the inference drawn from them. Texas was Falstaff territory and, with advertising on a cooperative basis, it was natural that advertising expenditures on Falstaff would exceed those on Ballantine. The lower price for Falstaff was a particular promotion of a bicentennial can in Texas, intended to meet a particular competitor.

However, we do not regard this error as undermining the judge's ultimate conclusion of breach of the best efforts clause. While that clause clearly required Falstaff to treat the Ballantine brands as well as its own, it does not follow that it required no more. With respect to its own brands, management was entirely free to exercise its business judgment as to how to maximize profit even if this meant serious loss in volume. Because of the obligation it had assumed under the sales contract, its situation with respect to the Ballantine brands was quite different. The royalty of $.50 a barrel on sales was an essential part of the purchase price. Even without the best efforts clause Falstaff would have been bound to make a good faith effort to see that substantial sales of Ballantine products were made, unless it discontinued under clause 2(a)(v) with consequent liability for liquidated damages. Cf. Wood v. Duff–Gordon, 222 N.Y. 88, 118 N.E. 214 (1917) (Cardozo, J.). Clause 8 imposed an added obligation to use "best efforts to promote and maintain a *high* volume of sales...." (emphasis supplied). Although we agree that even this did not require Falstaff to spend itself into bankruptcy to promote the sales of Ballantine products, it did prevent the application to them of Kalmanovitz' philosophy of emphasizing profit *über alles* without fair consideration of the effect on Ballantine volume. Plaintiff was not obliged to show just what steps Falstaff could reasonably have taken to maintain a high volume for Ballantine products. It was sufficient to show that Falstaff simply didn't care about Ballantine's volume and was content to allow this to plummet so long as that course was best for Falstaff's overall profit picture, an inference which the judge permissibly drew. The burden then shifted to Falstaff to prove there was nothing significant it could have done to promote Ballantine sales that would not have been financially disastrous.

Having correctly concluded that Falstaff had breached its best efforts covenant, the judge was faced with a difficult problem in computing what the royalties on the lost sales would have been. There is no need to rehearse the many decisions that, in a situation like this, certainty is not required; "[t]he plaintiff need only show a 'stable foundation for a reasonable estimate of royalties he would have earned had defendant not breached.'" Contemporary Mission, Inc. v. Famous Music Corp., 557 F.2d 918, 926 (2 Cir.1977), quoting Freund v. Washington Square Press, Inc., 34 N.Y.2d 379, 383, 357 N.Y.S.2d 857, 861, 314 N.E.2d 419, 421 (1974). After carefully considering other possible bases, the court arrived at the seemingly sensible conclusion that the most nearly accurate comparison was with the combined sales of Rheingold and Schaefer beers, both, like Ballantine, being "price" beers sold primarily in the northeast, and computed what Ballantine sales would have been if its brands had suffered only the same decline as a composite of Rheingold and Schaefer....

We also reject plaintiff's complaint on his cross-appeal that the court erred in not taking as its standard for comparison the grouping of all but the top 15 brewers, Ballantine having ranked 16th in 1971. The judge was entirely warranted in believing that the Rheingold–Schaefer combination afforded a better standard of comparison. [Finally, the court rejected plaintiff's contention that Falstaff's actions triggered the liquidated damage clause.]

The judgment is affirmed. Plaintiff may recover two-thirds of his costs.

NOTES

(1) *Best Efforts.* This case involves interpretation and application of a "best efforts" clause in the parties' agreement. Is there a connection between interpretation and application of a best efforts clause and the duty of good faith? Would Falstaff's duties under the contract be any different if the best efforts clause had not appeared in the contract?

(2) *What Efforts are "Best"?* How can a court determine what a duty of best efforts requires in a particular case? Courts have often looked to the behavior of others engaged in like activities. See the court's reference near the end of footnote 7 to the performance of " 'the average prudent comparable' brewer." UNIDROIT Principles art. 5.1.4(2) requires "such efforts as would be made by a reasonable person of the same kind in the same circumstances."

The question is of interest to lawyers. In Lucas v. Hamm, 364 P.2d 685, 690 (Cal.1961), the court took a tolerant view of the efforts of a lawyer who, in drafting a will for a client, had failed to apply correctly the rule against perpetuities and restraints on alienation and was sued by the disappointed beneficiaries named in the will. The court, noting that these were subjects that "have long perplexed the courts and the bar," thought "it would not be proper to hold that defendant failed to use such skill, prudence and diligence as lawyers of ordinary skill and capacity ordinarily exercise."

For another test, see Olympia Hotels Corp. v. Johnson Wax Dev. Corp., 908 F.2d 1363, 1373 (7th Cir.1990), in which Judge Posner said that if a hotel-management firm "worked as hard for [this customer] as it did for its other, but noncomplaining, customers, then it was using best efforts."

(3) *As If a Single Firm.* Professors Goetz and Scott propose a more sophisticated test. They note that "best efforts" contracts are often used instead of vertical integration in a single firm and argue that such contracts "can most sensibly be construed as requiring the level of effort necessary to maximize the joint net product flowing from the contractual relationship. This joint-maximization criterion . . . produces the largest possible net product for ultimate division between the parties." They admit, however, that it is hard to tell from damage computations in cases like *Bloor* what standard of performance has been applied. In *Bloor*, damages were "projected from the behavior of 'comparable' brands that were marketed by integrated non-royalty-paying firms. Thus, the 'comparable brand' volume behavior could be regarded as a good proxy for the joint-maximization outcome for the Ballantine–Falstaff contractual combination. There is, however, no real indication in the decision that the use of integrated firms as comparable entities was understood or intended in this way." Charles Goetz & Robert Scott, Principles of Relational Contracts, 67 Va.L.Rev. 1089, 1149–50, 1123 (1981). See also Mark Gergen, The Use of Open Terms in Contracts, 92 Colum.L.Rev. 997 (1992).

For support, see Tigg Corp. v. Dow Corning Corp., 962 F.2d 1119, 1125 (3d Cir.1992), in which the court said that a duty of best efforts requires a buyer under an exclusive dealing agreement "to consider the best interests of the seller and itself as if they were one firm."

(4) *Exclusivity.* Would Otis Wood have broken his contract with Lady Duff Gordon if he had handled the fashions of another designer at the same time? Does a promise to use best efforts imply exclusivity?

In Van Valkenburgh, Nooger & Neville, Inc. v. Hayden Publishing Co., 281 N.E.2d 142 (N.Y.1972), cited by Judge Friendly, the court concluded that a publisher's undertaking to use efforts to promote an author's works "does not close off the right of a publisher to issue books on the same subject, to negotiate with and pay authors to write such books and to promote them fully according to the publisher's economic interests, even though those later publications adversely affect the contracting author's sales.... Although a publisher has a general right to act on its own interests in a way that may incidentally lessen an author's royalties, there may be a point where that activity is so manifestly harmful to the author, and must have been seen by the publisher to be so harmful, as to justify the court in saying there was a breach of the covenant to promote the author's work."

This qualification of a party's "general right to act on its own interests" is illustrated by Joyce Beverages of N.Y., Inc. v. Royal Crown Cola Co., 555 F.Supp. 271 (S.D.N.Y.1983), in which Joyce had agreed to "devote its best efforts ... so as to achieve maximum distribution and sale [of Royal Crown] beverages within the territory." The court held that undertaking to distribute Seven–Up beverages was a breach. "A best efforts clause is not *per se* breached by a mere undertaking of a competitive product line ...; it depends on the circumstances.... [But here the] entire pattern of industry practice since the beginning of the soft drink industry has been for distributors to distribute only one cola. This best efforts clause is properly read in terms of the trade practice and usage." In addition, "Seven–Up's national advertising campaign denigrates the content of Royal Crown cola products. Seven–Up's slogan is 'You don't need caffeine and neither does your cola.' "

PERCENTAGE LEASES

An example of flexible pricing (see discussion on p. 251 above), that is especially favored by retailers is a lease which fixes the rent as a stated percentage of the lessee's receipts or profits. Under such a lease the lessor has a hedge against inflation and also shares to some extent the lessee's risk of success or failure. Although a wide variety of formulas is possible, the most common one is based, for reasons of accounting convenience, on the lessee's gross receipts. Under such a formula, it is in the lessor's interest that the lessee maximize its gross receipts, while it is in the lessee's interest that it maximize its net profit. The extreme case arises when the lessee finds that it is operating at a loss and wants to go out of business.

If the situation is viewed through the optic of Wood v. Lucy, p. 83 above, it would appear that, since the lessor has given the lessee the exclusive use of the land in return for a percentage of gross receipts, the lessee would be under a duty to use reasonable efforts. Consider these facts: A physical therapist who, when the business turned unprofitable, abandoned her business percentage lease and paid no rent. In holding that this was a breach, the court said: "The lessee obligated herself to pay rent at the rate of 5% of the gross receipts of the business. No minimum rent was reserved. Under these circumstances we are of the opinion that the lease must be construed as including an implied covenant to continue the business.... Any other construction would excuse the plaintiff from the obligation to pay any rent to the defendants and would, therefore, defeat the defendants' purpose in entering into the lease." Prins v. Van Der Vlugt, 337 P.2d 787, 796 (Or.1959).

By inserting a provision for a minimum rental in a percentage lease, the lessor can eliminate some of the risk that it would otherwise face. If the lessor chooses this kind of protection is the lessee still under a duty to use best efforts? In Dickey v. Philadelphia Minit–Man Corp, the Supreme Court of Pennsylvania said that it was not. "If an implied covenant, as claimed by the [lessor], should be held to arise in such cases, what would be the extent of the restriction thereby imposed on the lessee? Would it extend to each and every act on his part that might serve to reduce the extent of his business and thereby the percentage rental based thereon? ... It would obviously be quite unreasonable and wholly undesirable to imply an obligation that would necessarily be vague, uncertain, and generally impracticable." 105 A.2d 580 (Pa.1954).

GOOD FAITH IN TERMINATION

Distributorship and franchise agreements are usually explicit as to duration and termination. When they are not, courts have generally held that they are terminable at will by either party. The following materials consider the treatment of the at-will rule in cases where the distributor or franchisee has not had an opportunity to recoup its initial investment or has not been given time to arrange a substitute relationship.

LOCKEWILL, INC. v. UNITED STATES SHOE CORP., 547 F.2d 1024 (8th Cir.1976). [In 1965, Grant Williams, a man experienced in the shoe business, made an oral agreement with Pappagallo, Inc., a distributor of fashionable women's shoes that then sold only through small stores, each known as "The Shop for Pappagallo." Under the agreement, Williams was to open such a shop in the St. Louis area and purchase shoes in reasonable volume, in return for the exclusive right to market Pappagallo products in that area. Nothing was said about duration or termination. When Williams asked about the propriety of a written contract, Maurice Bandler, the sole owner of Pappagallo and a lawyer, said that none was necessary and that their handclasp was sufficient. Williams organized a corporation to run the shop, invested about $100,000 in the venture and sold Pappagallo products for years. During this time, however, United States Shoe Corp. bought out Bandler's interest in Pappagallo, and in the summer of 1973 an arrangement was made under which Stix, Baer & Fuller, a large St. Louis department store, would be allowed to sell Pappagallo shoes in competition with Williams' shop. In 1974, when Stix, Baer & Fuller began selling Pappagallo shoes, Williams sued Pappagallo and United States Shoe for breach of the exclusivity provision of the 1965 distributorship agreement. From a judgment awarding the plaintiff $150,000 in damages, the defendants appealed.]

■ HENLEY, CIRCUIT JUDGE. . . . The law of Missouri, which we are undertaking to apply in this case, appears to be that where the parties to a franchise or exclusive agency or distributorship agreement which is silent as to duration and which does not deal specifically with termination begin to perform thereunder, the agreement is construed to be terminable at the will of either party. See ... Beebe v. Columbia Axle Co., 233 Mo.App. 212, 117 S.W.2d 624 (1938).

That general rule, however, is subject to an important limitation which was expressed in *Beebe,* supra, in the following language (117 S.W.2d at 629): "The limitation is that, in any case of an indefinite agency where it is revoked by the principal, if it appears that the agent, induced by his appointment, has in good faith incurred expense and devoted time and labor in the matter of the agency without having had a sufficient opportunity to recoup such from the undertaking, the principal will be required to compensate him in that behalf; for the law will not permit one thus to deprive another of value without awarding just compensation. The just principle acted upon by the courts in the circumstances suggested requires no more than that, in every instance, the agent shall be afforded a reasonable opportunity to avail himself of the primary expenditures and efforts put forth to the end of executing the authority conferred upon him and that, if such opportunity is denied him, the principal shall compensate him accordingly. (Citations omitted.)" In a case to which the limitation of the general rule is applicable, the agent is entitled to recoupment or to compensation on a quantum meruit basis rather than by way of ordinary damages for breach of contract.... Applying to this case the principles of Missouri law that have been mentioned, we hold that apart from any question of the statute of frauds, which was pleaded by the defendants, the agreement between plaintiff and Pappagallo was binding, at least quasi-contractually, on Pappagallo and later on U.S. Shoe for a reasonable time after plaintiff had opened its shop in May, 1965, to the end that plaintiff might have a reasonable opportunity to recover its initial investment and expenses. During that period of time Pappagallo and U.S. Shoe were required to supply goods to the plaintiff and to refrain from interfering with his exclusive distributorship in the St. Louis area.

However, we are convinced that reasonable men could not differ on the proposition that by late 1973 and early 1974 such a reasonable time or period had expired, and that U.S. Shoe and Pappagallo had the right to terminate their contractual relations with plaintiff entirely, which they did not do, or to cancel the exclusivity feature of plaintiff's distributorship, which they did do when they permitted SBF to open Shops for Pappagallo in its stores.

And, we are convinced that plaintiff suffered no legal wrong when U.S. Shoe and Pappagallo finally implemented a change in marketing policy which had evidently been in contemplation for some years.

It is true that plaintiff was not given any formal or written notice of what the defendants intended to do. However, it is evident that at least by late September, 1973 plaintiff had received actual notice of what was in the wind, and there is nothing to indicate that plaintiff sustained any loss or damage by the fact that it was not given formal notice. It will be remembered that the contract said nothing about termination and naturally there was no requirement of formal notice of cancellation.... [Reversed.]

NOTES

(1) *Agreements Without End.* What result when an agreement for continuing performance fails to specify an end date? Consider two examples. Tanner supplied promotional materials to radio stations, taking in part payment advertising air time, or "spots," that he then sold to advertisers. His contracts with the stations provided that the spots were "valid until used." In William B. Tanner Co., Inc. v. Sparta–Tomah Broad. Co., Inc., 716 F.2d 1155 (7th Cir.1983), the court observed that similar contracts with such language had "turned out to be a significant boon to the legal profession," prompting "a raft of cases across the country where courts have struggled to discern exactly what was intended" by "words of somewhat astonishing imprecision." The court noted the reluctance of courts "to interpret contracts providing for some perpetual or unlimited contractual right unless the contract clearly states that that is the intention of the parties." It found that the contract was "incomplete with respect to the duration of the validity of the spots" and remanded the case for a determination of a "reasonable time" to limit validity. The court also mentioned that the "compelling policy reasons" that applied to employment contracts "do not obtain here." What are those reasons?

But see Warner–Lambert Pharmaceutical v. John J. Reynolds, Inc., 178 F.Supp. 655 (S.D.N.Y.1959), in which the court upheld the provision of an 1881 contract "to pay monthly to [the inventor of Listerine], his heirs, executors or assigns, the sum of twenty dollars for each and every gross of said Listerine hereafter sold by myself, my heirs, executors or assigns." The court refused "gratuitously to rewrite the contract" and held that Warner–Lambert "is obligated to make the periodic payments called for ... as long as it continues to sell the preparation described ... as Listerine," even though the secret formula had become a matter of public knowledge and could, by the mid-1950s, be produced by anyone.

(2) *Reliance as Fall-back?* Prince, an established beer distributor, undertook a Miller High Life distributorship, knowing that it would be two or three years before he would realize a profit. The contract provided, "Either of us can terminate this relationship at any time without incurring liability to the other." Less than two years later, Miller terminated the distributorship because it had become involved in a lawsuit with a corporation controlled by Prince. Prince had just begun to make a profit, after having sustained losses of over $20,000, not including his time and effort. Miller then appointed another distributor, whose operation showed a substantial increase in sales. Prince sued Miller for what he had spent in preparation for and operation of the distributorship and for reasonable compensation for his services. The trial court directed a verdict for the defendant and the plaintiff appealed. *Held:* Affirmed.

"It is appellant's contention that where a manufacturer and a distributor enter into an arrangement whereby the distributor is to develop a market for and sell the manufacturer's products, and it is contemplated by both parties that expenditures of time and money by the distributor are necessary to build up his distributorship, though the relationship be one terminable at will, the law will not allow the manufacturer to exercise its rights of cancellation with impunity, but will imply an obligation on its part to respond in damages sufficient to compensate the distributor for his expenditures made and losses incurred in reliance upon the agreement if the manufacturer terminates the distributorship before the distributor is afforded a reasonable time to recoup his losses.... This statement of the law is supported by respectable authority.... [In those cases, however, there] was no specific written agreement authorizing cancellation without liability. . . . Appellant cannot disregard the contract and sue for his reliance damage. Because of the valid contract the theory of promissory estoppel is not applicable." Prince v. Miller Brewing Co., 434 S.W.2d 232 (Tex.App.1968).

What result if Prince had been able to show that Miller had terminated the contract in order to let a close personal friend of one of its officers have a profitable franchise? Suppose that Miller had granted Prince a franchise and then terminated it immediately? What if the wording of the termination clause read simply, "Either of us can terminate this relationship at any time"?

(3) *Unconditional Right to Terminate.* In Sons of Thunder v. Borden, Inc., 690 A.2d 575, 588 (N.J.1997), the Supreme Court of New Jersey upheld the proposition that "a party to a contract may breach the implied covenant of good faith and fair dealing in performing its obligations even when it exercises an express and unconditional right to terminate. Other courts have stated that a party can violate the implied covenant of good faith and fair dealing without violating an express term of a contract. . . . Legal scholars have also commented on the independence of the implied duty to act in good faith and the express terms of the contract." See also Bak–A–Lum Corp. of America v. Alcoa Building Products, Inc., 351 A.2d 349 (N.J. 1976).

Compare the quotation from *Sons of Thunder* with the following by Judge Easterbrook in Kham & Nate's Shoes v. First Bank of Whiting, 908 F.2d 1351, 1357 (7th Cir.1990). "Firms that have negotiated contracts are entitled to enforce them to the letter, even to the great discomfort of their trading partners, without being mulcted for lack of 'good faith.' Although courts often refer to the obligation of good faith that exists in every contractual relation, . . . this is not an invitation to the court to decide whether one party ought to have exercised privileges expressly reserved in the document. . . . When the contract is silent, principles of good faith . . . fill the gap. They do not block use of terms that actually appear in the contract." Is there tension between these views?

Many courts have expressed the same view as Judge Easterbrook, that "principles of good faith . . . do not block use of terms that actually appear in the contract." Is this consistent with the view of the Permanent Editorial Board for the Uniform Commercial Code, noted at p. 529, *supra*, that "the doctrine of good faith merely directs a court towards interpreting contracts within the commercial context in which they are created, performed and enforced, and does not create a separate duty of fairness and reasonableness which can be independently breached"?

(4) *Have It Your Way?* Do statutes that restrict a franchisor's power to terminate only for good cause, or for particular causes, tend to enhance or to reduce efficiencies in marketing? Does your answer depend on whether or not the statute permits the franchisor to terminate a franchise in order to maintain its competitive position in the market?

SECTION 5. PUBLIC POLICY

In the preceding sections the law's concern has been with protecting one party to an agreement against imposition by the other party. In this section the concern shifts to the protection of the public at large against imposition by *both* parties. When will a court refuse to enforce an agreement, fairly and freely entered into, on the ground that to enforce it would contravene "public policy"?

Such agreements fall into two general categories. First are contracts that violate specific laws; these are commonly called "illegal contracts." A court will not generally enforce a private agreement—say, a hit contract—to do what the law explicitly prohibits. The enactment of a criminal code is understood as a clear expression of policy, even though statutes proscribing conduct rarely speak to the enforceability of contracts involving the conduct. (Two exceptions are usury and gambling statutes which characteristically state that contracts in violation of them are "void.")

What if there is no explicit prohibition against a particular act, product, or type of agreement? When no statute is quite "on point," how do courts determine whether the enforcement of a contract violates public policy? In this second category of cases, courts often detect or derive policy from legislation *related* to the subject of the agreement, again, even when the statutes themselves are silent on contractual enforceability. In other cases, courts have formulated policies from their own sense of social or legal norms. And sometimes, despite entreaties from one or the other party, courts have found insufficient authority to apply the doctrine of public policy, so that performance will not be excused.

In addition to guiding courts in their decisions whether or not to enforce contracts, public policy is also implemented positively through contract. Government procurement contracts provide a clear example of how policies can be advanced through choices about contracting partners or by the terms of the contract itself. See generally William Leimkuhler, Enforcing Social and Economic Policy Through Government Contracts, 1980 Annual Survey of American Law 539. For example, non-discrimination has been a policy goal of the Minority Business Enterprise provision of the Public Works Employment Act of 1977; for a case involving this provision, see Note 3 p. 227 above. Other examples include purchasing regulations that favor domestic products, or regional industries, or that require the use of "green," or ecologically friendly, materials in construction, manufacture, or the provision of services. See also Christopher Yukins, Making Federal Information Technology Accessible: A Case Study in Social Policy and Procurement, 33 Pub. Contract L. J. 667 (2004) (discussing Section 508 of the Federal Rehabilitation Act, requiring that all information technology bought the United States be accessible to persons with disabilities).

The possibility of promoting public policies through procurement or other government contracts has been given increased attention in the last several years as a growing number of public functions—schools, prisons, security—are contracted to private parties, or "outsourced," in the general turn to market competition known as privatization. Privatization is itself an instance of public policy. See Jody Freeman, Extending Public Norms Through Privatization, 116 Harv. L.Rev. 1285 (2003). For thoughtful explorations, see John Donahue, *The Privatization Decision: Public Ends,*

Private Means (1989), and Martha Minow and Jody Freeman, eds., *Government by Contract* (forthcoming 2009).

NOTE

Finding Policy. The Arizona Supreme Court directly considered the question of "where 'public policy' may be found and how it may be recognized and articulated." In Wagenseller v. Scottsdale Memorial Hosp., 710 P.2d 1025, 1033 (Ariz.1985), the court stated:

> As the expressions of our founders and those we have elected to our legislature, our state's constitution and statutes embody the public conscience of the people of this state. It is thus in furtherance of their interests to hold that an employer may not with impunity violate the dictates of public policy found in the provisions of our statutory and constitutional law.
>
> We do not believe, however, that expressions of public policy are contained only in the statutory and constitutional law, nor do we believe that all statements made in either a statute or the constitution are expressions of public policy. Turning first to the identification of other sources, we note our agreement with the following:
>
> Public policy is usually defined by the political branches of government. Something "against public policy" is something that the Legislature has forbidden. But the Legislature is not the only source of such policy. In common-law jurisdictions the courts too have been sources of law, always subject to legislative correction, and with progressively less freedom as legislation occupies a given field. Lucas v. Brown & Root, 736 F.2d 1202, 1205 (8th Cir.1984).

(A) ILLEGAL CONTRACTS

Even in the case of criminal prohibition on conduct, there are subtleties in application. If, for example, the performance of a contract *contributes* to an illegal act, but is not itself prohibited, should the disappointed party be able to sue for damages? Should a contract that is the *product* of an illegal act, such as bribery or an anti-trust conspiracy, be enforced? Should it matter if the statute mandates other specific penalties?

As you read the following materials, consider two contrasting positions on these questions. In 1692, Lord Holt expressed the influential view that "every contract made for or about any matter or thing which is prohibited and made unlawful by any statute, is a void contract, though the statute itself doth not mention that it shall be so, but only inflicts a penalty on the offender, because a penalty implies a prohibition, though there are no prohibitory words in the statute." Bartlett v. Vinor, 90 Eng.Rep. 750 (King's Bench). In 1936, Professor Walter Gellhorn wrote: "The judges are not bound to regard as void every contract which seems in some way to fall within the general aura of the criminal law, but only those whose enforcement, they are persuaded, after respectfully studying the 'public policy' involved, will disserve the general interest as it has been indicated by the legislature." Gellhorn, Contracts and Public Policy, 35 Colum.L.Rev. 679, 686 (1936).

Bovard v. American Horse Enterprises, Inc.

Court of Appeal, Third District, California, 1988.
201 Cal.App.3d 832, 247 Cal.Rptr. 340.

■ PUGLIA, PRESIDING JUSTICE. [In 1978, James Ralph agreed to purchase American Horse Enterprises, Inc. from Robert Bovard. In connection with the purchase, Ralph signed several promissory notes. When Ralph failed to pay on the notes, Bovard sued. At the trial, testimony revealed that the corporation was in the business of manufacturing jewelry and drug paraphernalia, primarily bongs and roach clips, used to smoke marijuana and tobacco. The trial court excused the jury in order to determine whether the contract for sale of the corporation was illegal and void.

The court held that although the manufacture of drug paraphernalia was not itself illegal at the time the contract was entered into,[a] a public policy against the manufacture of drug paraphernalia was implicit in a state statute making the possession, use and transfer of marijuana unlawful. The court held that the consideration was therefore "contrary to the policy of express law" and declared the contract illegal and void.[b] Bovard appealed.]

. . . Whether a contract is contrary to public policy is a question of law to be determined from the circumstances of the particular case. (Kallen v. Delug (1984) 203 Cal.Rptr. 879; Russell v. Soldinger (1976) 131 Cal.Rptr. 145.) Here, the critical facts are not in dispute. Whenever a court becomes aware that a contract is illegal, it has a duty to refrain from entertaining an action to enforce the contract. . . . Furthermore the court will not permit the parties to maintain an action to settle or compromise a claim based on an illegal contract. (Union Collection Co. v. Buckman (1907) 150 Cal. 159, 165,; see also First Nat. Bk. v. Thompson (1931) 212 Cal. 388, 405.)

The question whether a contract violates public policy necessarily involves a degree of subjectivity. Therefore, ". . . courts have been cautious in blithely applying public policy reasons to nullify otherwise enforceable contracts. This concern has been graphically articulated by the California Supreme Court as follows: 'It has been well said that public policy is an unruly horse, astride of which you are carried into unknown and uncertain paths,[c] . . . While contracts opposed to morality or law should not be allowed to show themselves in courts of justice, yet public policy requires and encourages the making of contracts by competent parties upon all valid and lawful considerations, and courts so recognizing have allowed parties the widest latitude in this regard; and, unless it is entirely plain that a contract is violative of sound public policy, a court will never so declare. "The power of the courts to declare a contract void for being in contraven-

---

a. The court noted that "the manufacture of drug paraphernalia, including bongs and roach clips, was made criminal effective January 1, 1983, . . . by Health and Safety Code sections 11014.5 and 11364.7."

b. Under California Civ. Code § 1667, consideration is not lawful if it is: 1. Contrary to an express provision of law; 2. Contrary to

the policy of express law, though not expressly prohibited; or, 3. Otherwise contrary to good morals. If part of a single consideration for one or more objects is unlawful, "the entire contract is void." Civ.Code, § 1608.

c. The phrase originated in Richard v. Mellish, 130 Eng.Rep. 294, 303 (Common Pleas, 1824) (Burrough, J.).

tion of sound public policy is a very delicate and undefined power, and, like the power to declare a statute unconstitutional, should be exercised only in cases free from doubt." [Citation.] ... "No court ought to refuse its aid to enforce a contract on doubtful and uncertain grounds. The burden is on the defendant to show that its enforcement would be in violation of the settled public policy of this state, or injurious to the morals of its people." [Citation.]'" (Moran v. Harris, quoting Stephens v. Southern Pacific Co. (1895) 109 Cal. 86, 89–90.)

Bovard places great reliance on Moran v. Harris, [(1982) 182 Cal.Rptr. 519], to support his argument the trial court erred in finding the contract violative of public policy. In Moran, two lawyers entered into a fee splitting agreement relative to a case referred by one to the other. The agreement was made in 1972, ten months before the adoption of a rule of professional conduct prohibiting such agreements. In 1975, the attorney to whom the case had been referred settled the case, but then refused to split the attorney's fees with the referring attorney. (Id., 182 Cal.Rptr. 519.) The trial court held the fee splitting contract violated public policy. The appellate court reversed, noting the rule of professional conduct had been amended effective January 1, 1979, to permit fee splitting agreements; thus there was no statute or rule prohibiting fee splitting agreements either at the time the attorneys' contract was formed or after January 1, 1979, during the pendency of the action to enforce the fee splitting contract.... Here, in contrast to Moran, there is positive law on which to premise a finding of public policy ... on a statute prohibiting the possession, use and transfer of marijuana which long antedated the parties' contract.

Moran suggests factors to consider in analyzing whether a contract violates public policy: "Before labeling a contract as being contrary to public policy, courts must carefully inquire into the nature of the conduct, the extent of public harm which may be involved, and the moral quality of the conduct of the parties in light of the prevailing standards of the community...." (Id., 182 Cal.Rptr. 519.)

[The court then set out Restatement 2d § 178.] Applying the Restatement test to the present circumstances, we conclude the interest in enforcing this contract is very tenuous. Neither party was reasonably justified in expecting the government would not eventually act to geld American Horse Enterprises, a business harnessed to the production of paraphernalia used to facilitate the use of an illegal drug. Moreover, although voidance of the contract imposed a forfeiture on Bovard, he did recover the corporate machinery, the only assets of the business which could be used for lawful purposes, i.e., to manufacture jewelry. Bovard recovered the machinery through "self-help." Thus, the forfeiture was significantly mitigated if not negligible. Finally, there is no special public interest in the enforcement of this contract, only the general interest in preventing a party to a contract from avoiding a debt.

On the other hand, the Restatement factors favoring a public policy against enforcement of this contract are very strong. As we have explained, the public policy against manufacturing paraphernalia to facilitate the use of marijuana is strongly implied in the statutory prohibition against the possession, use, etc., of marijuana, a prohibition which dates back at least to 1929. (See Stats.1929, ch. 216, § 1, p. 380.) Obviously, refusal to enforce the instant contract will further that public policy not only in the present circumstances but by serving notice on manufacturers of drug paraphernalia that they may not resort to the judicial system to protect or advance their business interests. Moreover, it is immaterial that the business conducted by American Horse Enterprises was not expressly prohibited by law when Bovard and Ralph made their agreement since both parties knew that the corporation's products would be used primarily for purposes which were expressly illegal. We conclude the trial court correctly declared the contract contrary to the policy of express law and therefore illegal and void.

NOTES

(1) *In Pari Delicto.* In an omitted part of the opinion, the court found that because the parties were *in pari delicto* with regard to their contractual dispute they should be left as the court found them. The doctrine is this: In circumstances of equal fault, the position of the defendant is the more compelling (*in pari delicto potior est conditio defendantis*). "While it may not always seem an honorable thing to do, a party to an illegal agreement is permitted to set up the illegality as a defense even though the party may be alleging his or her own turpitude." Early Detection Center, Inc. v. Wilson, 811 P.2d 860, 867 (Kan.1991). Of course, many a claimant has contended that the parties are *not* equally culpable, though the trial court would have none of it in *Bovard*.

In some exceptional cases, a party *in pari delicto* may obtain restitutionary relief, alleviating the harshness that would result if parties to an illegal contract were always "left where they are found, to stew in their own juice." *Id.* According to the Restatement, restitution is available to a party "who would otherwise suffer a forfeiture that is disproportionate in relation to the contravention of public policy involved." See § 197, Comment *b.*

(2) *Clean Hands.* Suits for equitable remedies such as specific performance and rescission are sometimes disposed of on the maxim, "He who comes into equity must come with clean hands." Application of the doctrine poses several questions: How clean must hands be? Is cleanliness a relative matter? Must there be a relation between the bad behavior and the suit itself? Consider this case: A lumber wholesaler sought to enforce a non-compete clause against a former employee who had gone on his own in violation of the terms of the covenant. The employee argued that by engaging in unethical practices—eavesdropping on clients' in a scheme involving telephone calls and making improper profits on customer claims—the employer had unclean hands and equitable relief should be denied. The wholesaler responded that the employee had engaged in some of the very practices complained about. The trial court dismissed the complaint and awarded the employee his attorney's fees. Both sides appealed. *Held:* Affirmed in part; reversed in part. North Pacific Lumber Co. v. Oliver, 596 P.2d 931, 943 (Or.1979).

Noting that "[e]ven equity does not require saintliness," the Supreme Court of Oregon stated that "the misconduct must bear a certain kind of relationship to the subject matter of the suit before a court will consider it." *Id.* at 939. The court held that the eavesdropping, while perhaps a violation of a state statute, was in this case unconnected with the employee's work and therefore did not implicate the clean hands doctrine. The improper profit scheme was another matter: "A court of equity should not lend its aid to an employer who attempts to enforce a contract of employment the performance of which involves participation by the employee in such wrongdoing." *Id.* at 944. Because the employee had knowingly "participated in the ill-gotten gains," the court reversed the trial court's award of attorney's fees.

X.L.O. Concrete Corp. v. Rivergate Corp.

New York Court of Appeals, 1994.
83 N.Y.2d 513, 611 N.Y.S.2d 786, 634 N.E.2d 158.

■ CIPARICK, J. The question presented in this action for breach of contract, account stated, and unjust enrichment is whether interposition of an antitrust illegality defense under the Donnelly Act (General Business Law §§ 340 et seq.) prevents enforcement of the contract between these parties as a matter of law. . . .

The parties, plaintiff X.L.O. Concrete Corp., as subcontractor, and defendant Rivergate Corporation, as general contractor, entered into a written contract on May 12, 1983 for construction of the concrete super-structure and fills of a project located in Manhattan. Plaintiff fully performed its obligations under the contract and sought payment of $844,125.07, the balance due and owing. Defendant refused to pay on the ground that the contract was an integral feature of an extortion and labor bribery operation known as the "Club." [The trial court dismissed the complaint and Rivergate appealed.]

The "Club" was an arrangement between the "Commission" of La Cosa Nostra, a ruling body comprised of four of the five New York City organized crime family bosses, and seven concrete construction companies operating in New York City, and the District Council of Cement and Concrete Workers, Laborers International Union of North America (see United States v. Salerno, 868 F.2d 524, 528–529, [describing the Club and its workings in fuller detail]). The Commission decided which concrete companies would be permitted to undertake construction jobs in New York City worth more than two million dollars; contractors who took jobs over two million were required to pay the Commission two percent of the contract price for guaranteed "labor peace." The Commission not only approved which companies got which jobs, but also rigged the bidding to ensure that the designated company would submit the lowest bid. The Commission enforced compliance through threatened or actual labor unrest or violence. In May 1981, plaintiff became the last concrete contractor doing business in New York City to join the Club.

[The Commission allocated the Rivergate project to X.L.O. who paid the 2% "labor peace" fee. X.L.O. then negotiated a contract with Rivergate for $16,544,125. Since the contract was so large, X.L.O. also gave a representative from the Commission, who was also the president of the District Council of Cement and Concrete Workers, a $50,000 "gift."]

The record indicates that defendant negotiated the contract with full knowledge of the Club and its rules. Plaintiff completed the work agreed upon under the contract and, upon defendant's refusal to pay, commenced this action. [The Supreme Court dismissed the complaint, and certain counterclaims; the Appellate Division modified the judgment to the extent of reinstating the complaint, and in certain other respects.]

The interposition of antitrust defenses in contract actions is not favored (see Kelly v. Kosuga, 358 U.S. 516, 518, 3 L.Ed.2d 475, 79 S.Ct. 429). The concern is that "successful interposition of antitrust defenses is too likely to enrich parties who reap the benefits of a contract and then seek to avoid the corresponding burdens" (Viacom International, Inc. v. Tandem, 526 F.2d 593, 599). Nevertheless, antitrust defenses will be upheld in cases where a court's judgment would result in enforcement of the "precise conduct made unlawful by the Act" (Kelly v. Kosuga, 358 U.S. 516, 520, 3 L.Ed.2d 475, 79 S.Ct. 429 ...). Beyond that point, however, "courts are to be guided by the overriding general policy ... 'of preventing people from getting other people's property for nothing when they purport to be buying it' " (id. at 520–521 [quoting Continental Wall Paper Co. v. Louis Voight & Sons Co., 212 U.S. 227, 271, 53 L.Ed. 486, 29 S.Ct. 280] [Holmes, J., dissenting]). Thus, a contract which is legal on its face and does not call for unlawful conduct in its performance is not voidable simply because it resulted from an antitrust conspiracy (see, *Kelly,* supra ... but see *Continental Wall Paper,* supra ...)

... [T]he critical question is whether the contract is so integrally related to the agreement, arrangement or combination in restraint of competition that its enforcement would result in compelling performance of the precise conduct made unlawful by the antitrust laws (id. at 520). This question we cannot answer on the record before us. Whether the contract was an indivisible, effectuating component of an illegal arrangement that would be consummated by granting the judgment sought in this action is a question that requires further development at trial.

The extent to which the contract price is excessive and discriminatory and fails to reflect fair market value at the contract date because of an unlawful attempt to stifle competition is an important issue requiring development. The unlawful use of market power to inflate the contract price, and the resulting anti-competitive effects, must be assessed in determining whether granting the judgment sought "would be to make the courts a party to the carrying out of one of the very restraints forbidden by the [antitrust laws]" (*Kelly,* 358 U.S., at 520).

Additionally, the equities of the parties must be examined. Courts should avoid upholding antitrust defenses in contract cases where doing so would work a substantial forfeiture on one party while unjustly enriching the other.... A relevant consideration is whether sustaining the illegality defense would render the contract void in its entirety or whether recovery could still be had on a quantum meruit basis. Additionally, the relative culpability, bargaining power, and knowledge of the parties to the contract should also be considered in assessing the possibility of unjust enrichment.

Finally, the public policy in favor of frustrating or discouraging unlawful schemes such as the Club must not be deprecated. However, such a danger is reduced where statutory remedies exist and the State Attorney General can directly attack the alleged antitrust violations.

In light of our analysis, the Court rejects defendant's remaining contention that the contract should be held per se illegal under the Donnelly Act....

Order affirmed, with costs, and certified question answered in the affirmative.

NOTES

(1) *Questions.* Were the parties *in pari delicto?* Did the court decide that further findings in the trial court might warrant a recovery for unjust enrichment, but not of the balance due under the contract? That they might warrant a recovery in excess of the defendant's enrichment? The Attorney General of New York State filed a brief as amicus curiae *opposing* the result in this case. How did the court take account of statutory remedies available to the Attorney General?

(2) *Degrees of Involvement.* Justice Holmes indicated that in selling goods, a merchant may safely exhibit an "understood indifference" to the buyer's intended use of the goods. Graves v. Johnson, 60 N.E. 383 (Mass.1901). "[A] sale otherwise lawful is not connected with subsequent unlawful conduct by the mere fact that the seller correctly divines the buyer's unlawful intent, closely enough to make the sale unlawful.... Of course the [buyer-defendant] was free to change his mind, and there was no communicated desire of the plaintiffs to co-operate with the defendant's present intent.... [T]he decisions tend more and more to agree that the connection with the unlawful act in cases like the present is too remote."

The principle was applied in Fineman v. Faulkner, 93 S.E. 384, 385 (N.C.1917), in which the plaintiff had made a credit sale of a phonograph to a buyer known "by general reputation" to be a prostitute. The defendant, administrator of the buyer's estate, sought to avoid payment on that ground. The court held that "[t]he sale of an Edison talking machine was a legitimate transaction ... The seller had no control over the use to which it should be put, and did not sell to aid in any illegal purpose, and cannot be held responsible therefor from the simple fact that he knew that the purchaser was carrying on an illegal business." For a case involving the attempted rescission of an real estate sale transacted in North Carolina during the Civil War, see Phillips v. Hooker, 62 N.C. 193 (1867) (buying property with Confederate notes did not "have tendency to aid the rebellion").

(3) *Public Policing of Illegal Contracts.* Although in *X.L.O.* the contracts were between private parties, the problem of illegal contracts is of special interest to city and state governments. Consider the following:

> New York City is one of the biggest contracting entities in the world. Each year City agencies enter into approximately 40,000 contracts worth almost $6.5 billion. These contracts cover everything from pencils to legal services for indigent criminal defendants, from methadone treatment to architectural consultants, from external auditing to massive public works projects. Awarding and monitoring these contracts is one of the city government's great responsibilities.

Frank Anechiarico and James Jacobs, Purging Corruption from Public Contracting, 40 N.Y.L.Sch.L.Rev.143 (1995). The authors describe efforts by the City Comptroller's Office to clean up a system marked by kickbacks and racketeering through competitive bidding and awards to the "lowest responsible bidder."

———

We now look briefly at three specific types of illegalities, inducing official action, commercial bribery, and violations of licensing laws.

———

INDUCING OFFICIAL ACTION

Recall that in Black v. Bush, p. 460 above, the court found that the profits received by Black were not the result of impermissible "dealings with government," such as inducing governmental action. Influence peddling is a common subject of judicial denunciation, although not all efforts to procure favorable official action are condemned as such. Consider the role of lobbyists. The proper line has been stated as follows: "The authorities very generally hold that a contract to pay for services to be performed in the endeavor to obtain or defeat legislation by other means than the use of argument addressed to the reason of the legislators, such as, for example, for the exertion of personal or political influence apart from the appeal to reason as applied to the consideration of the merits or demerits of the legislation in question, is an illegal contract." Campbell County v. Howard & Lee, 112 S.E. 876 (Va.1922).

There have also been statutory enactments aimed at reducing various forms of official corruption. In addition to the *qui tam* actions discussed above at p. 464, these include the Anti–Kickback Act of 1986, 41 U.S.C. §§ 51–58, and the False Statements Act, 18 U.S.C. § 1001.

NOTES

(1) *Chutzpah Defined and Illustrated.* A judge was offered a bribe and consulted the state's attorney, who advised the judge to accept the money. It became evidence in criminal proceedings against the payor, who was convicted and imprisoned. The payor then moved for the return of the money by the state, and that was ordered (by another judge). The state appealed. The court considered the case under the aspect of failure of consideration, or breach by the "bribed" judge. *Held:* Reversed. The court opened its opinion with a definition of "chutzpah." (According to the court, the term refers to a person who has "gall, moxie, nerve and audacity compounded with brazen assertiveness.") It went on to say that "Any attempt to bribe a member of the judiciary, or one of the satellites of the judiciary, is a reprehensible, odious act striking at the heart of the judicial system. For the bribe then to be repaid to the briber, on order of a court, erodes the public's confidence in the court's common sense and judgment."

The convicted briber could not recover damages for breach of a contract to commit a crime. "Parties of that ilk are left where they are found, to stew in their own juice." State v. Strickland, 400 A.2d 451, 454–55 (Md.App.1979).

(2) *Undoing Official Corruption.* In 2004, Darlene Druyun, for nine years the Air Force's top civilian acquisition official, pleaded guilty for conspiring to violate a federal statute prohibiting certain government employees from participating in the award of government contracts to firms in which the employee, or the employee's spouse or child, has a financial interest. See 18 U.S.C. § 208(a). Druyun had over a period of years favored the Boeing Corporation in awarding contracts; she admitted that her decisions were influenced by Boeing having hired her future son-in-law and her daughter in 2000, and "her own desire to be employed by Boeing."

Following the exposure of Druyun's malfeasance in 2006, L–3 Communication Integrated Systems, a firm whose bid had been rejected in one of Druyun's deals, filed a "post-award bid protest" alleging that the Air Force had breached its obligation to fairly consider its offer. It sought as damages its bid and proposal preparation costs. The government moved to dismiss that claim on the grounds that claimants must provide "clear and convincing evidence" to overcome the presumption that contracting officers act in "good faith." *Held*: For claimant. L–3 Communications Integrated Systems v. United States, 79 Fed. Cl. 453 (Fed.Cl.2007).

Acknowledging the "heavy burden" required to overcome the presumption, the court held that L–3 had stated claim upon which relief could be granted. The court observed that most post-bid protests seek to undo the contract award and secure a recompetition, re-evaluation, or, in rare instances, the "award itself." Here, however, is was "too late for injunctive relief" as the contract had been largely performed, leaving L–3 with the possibility only of its bid and preparation costs.

If L–3 were successful in its claim, might it recover more by receiving its bid preparation costs than by securing a recompetition or re-evalution of its bid?

COMMERCIAL BRIBERY

Is a contract that is induced by bribery unenforceable on ground of public policy? We have already seen that "[I]t is well settled both in law and in equity that the court will not aid either party to an illegal agreement.... While it may not always seem an honorable thing to do, a party to an illegal agreement is permitted to set up the illegality as a defense even though the party may be alleging his or her own turpitude." Early Detection Center, Inc. v. Wilson, 811 P.2d 860, 867 (Kan.1991).

The following pattern is typical of commercial bribery: a seller bribes a buyer's purchasing agent to buy goods from the seller. After the goods are delivered, the buyer then refuses to pay on grounds of public policy. In a New York case, Sirkin v. Fourteenth Street Store, 108 N.Y.S. 830, 833–834 (App.Div.1908), the court refused to enforce such a contract, stating that "nothing will be more effective in stopping the growth and spread of this corrupting and now criminal custom...." It denied recovery to the seller, taking guidance from a state statute which made it a misdemeanor for a seller to offer a commission, discount, or bonus to a purchasing agent, and for the agent to receive it. The statute provided for a fine of not more than $500 and imprisonment of not more than a year. (The contract for the bribe itself is unenforceable as a promise inducing violation of an agent's fiduciary duty; see Restatement § 193 and Illustration 12 to Restatement § 178, the latter taken from *Sirkin*.) "Two judges dissented, saying that [i]t is not part of our duty to assume legislative power and prescribe an additional punishment...."

One problem with denying recovery is that the buyer retains the goods without paying for them. This was the result in a later New York case, McConnell v. Commonwealth Pictures Corp., 166 N.E.2d 494 (N.Y.1960). A movie distributor agreed to pay McConnell $10,000 (plus a percentage of gross receipts) if McConnell negotiated a contract between the distributor and a certain movie producer. McConnell negotiated the contract by paying the producer's agent a $10,000 bribe. When the distributor found out about the bribe, it refused to pay McConnell his percentage of gross receipts on the ground of public policy. McConnell sued, arguing that there was nothing improper about his contract with the distributor, who had known nothing about McConnell's negotiation techniques. Unlike *Sirkin*, he argued, the contract being sued upon had not been obtained by bribery.

The court held that "It is beside the point that the present plaintiff ... might be able to prove a prima facie case without the bribery being exposed":

> It is argued that [denying enforcement] here means that the doing of any small illegality in the performance of an otherwise lawful contract will deprive the doer of all rights, with the result that the other party will get a windfall.... Our ruling does not go as far as that. It is not every minor wrongdoing in the course of contract performance that will insulate the other party from liability for work done or good furnished. There must at least be a direct connection between the illegal transaction and the obligation sued upon.

What, if any, public policies are advanced by permitting recovery on a contract that is itself not illegal?

NOTE

Beneficiary of the Bribe. What becomes of the bribe? It appears, as in *McConnell,* that some "surplus" maybe realized by persons not parties to the contract—those who took the bribe. In *Sirkin*, the court said: "The servant would be accountable to his master or employer for any moneys thus received...." Presumably the employer could have gotten that relief *in addition* to retaining the goods without paying for them.

Might not the bribe be disgorged and applied elsewhere? Such dispositions have been proposed, though not as yet adopted in the United States. See Harold Berman, *Justice in the U.S.S.R.* 141 (1963) (forfeit to the state), and Warren Seavey, Problems in Restitution, 7 Okla.L.Rev. 257, 259 (1954). See also Catherine Sharkey, Punitive Damages as Social Damages, 113 Yale L.J. 347, 402 (2003) (suggesting in the context of torts that "[i]t is not difficult to imagine [a court-administered scheme] that would attempt to provide redress or compensation for more diffuse harms to individuals or groups caused by the same, or similar, wrong-doing on the part of the defendant").

———

LICENSING LAWS

In Sirkin v. Fourteenth St. Store, discussed in Commercial Bribery, above, the court said that "one who is required by law to procure a license to conduct any trade, calling, or profession may not recover for services rendered or property sold, without first obtaining such license." The statement goes too far. When the purpose of a licensing requirement is ascertained to be raising public revenue, and not the protection of the public's welfare—health, morals or the like—a claimant's want of a license is generally not a bar.

If a person whose vocation is related to the construction industry, such as an architect or a mechanical engineer, performs services without having a mandated license or certification, should the services go uncompensated?

Consider the following. In September, 2005, Trade–Winds Environmental Restoration, Inc. (Trade–Winds) entered into a contract with Stewart Development (Stewart) to perform mold remediation on Stewart's building, which had sustained water damage as a result of Hurricane Katrina. The contract price was to be based on a "rate-sheet" provided by Trade–Winds and estimated at $750,000. At the time the contract was signed, Trade–Winds did not hold a license as a mold remediation contractor. After Trade–Winds completed the work, it submitted an invoice to Stewart for $9,000,000. Stewart paid $7,500,000, but when Trade–Winds failed to provide documentation to support its invoice, Stewart refused further payment, and Trade–Winds sued for the balance. Stewart sued for summary judgment, on the ground that the contract was null and void because Trade–Winds had been unlicensed. *Held*: For Stewart. Trade–Winds Environmental Restoration, Inc. v. Stewart, 2008 WL 236891 (E.D.La.) Trade–Winds argued that "to void this contract would be against the public policy of facilitating clean-up after [disasters]" and would "cause a chilling effect on the willingness of remediation specialists to perform work in Louisiana." The court noted "the competing policy interest of protecting the public from the unlawful acts of contractors" and pointed to the language of the licensing statute itself: the "purpose of [the mold remediation licensing laws] is to require qualifying criteria in a professional field in which unqualified individuals may injure or mislead the public...." The court observed that "the policy decisions made by the legislature are expressly stated in the statutes.... [It] is not the place of this court to second guess such decisions." The court rejected Trade-winds argument that the Governor had suspended licensing laws with regard to debris removal in the aftermath of other disasters, noting that "while the Executive Branch does have the power to temper legislative intent in times of emergency, no such order was given in this case." Why might Stewart have paid so much of the invoice when it so greatly exceeded the estimate?

NOTES

(1) *Recovery and Restitution?* As a general rule, illegality precludes not only the enforcement of an agreement but also any restitutionary claims. This can produce what appear to be striking injustices in individual cases. Note that Restatement § 178 provides that in weighing the enforcement of a term, account should be taken of "any forfeiture that would result if enforcement were denied."

(2) *Line Drawing.* In Town Planning & Engineering Associates, Inc. v. Amesbury Specialty Co., 342 N.E.2d 706 (Mass.1976), concerning the plaintiff's want of a certification as an engineer, the court considered the possibility of confining the plaintiff's recovery to "a quantum meruit less than the contract price." It concluded, however, that a "vector of considerations" pointed toward recovery of the contract price. One consideration was whether or not "the characteristics which gave the plaintiff's act its value to the defendant [were] the same as those which made it a violation" of law (quoting from George Gardner, An Inquiry into the Principles of the Law of Contracts, 46 Harv.L.Rev. 1, 37 (1932)). Contrast Kansas City Community Center v. Heritage Industries, Inc., 972 F.2d 185 (8th Cir.1992) (architect). For a useful distinction between a claim made by an unlicensed contractor in its capacity as a contractor and one made by an unlicensed contractor

in its capacity as a joint venturer, see In re Lake Providence Properties, Inc., 168 B.R. 876 (W.D.N.C.1994).

(B) JUDICIALLY CREATED PUBLIC POLICY

How should courts police bargains on policy grounds when there is no clear statutory prohibition against a particular kind of agreement? In such cases, the court must be satisfied nonetheless that a strong public policy can be articulated. The guiding principle is one of protecting "some aspect of the public welfare." See Restatement § 179. That provision identifies two such areas "now rooted in precedents collected over the centuries." They are polices against the restraint of trade and against the impairment of family relations.

Of course, precedents from which policies derive do not always remain rooted over the centuries. As we saw with regard to the disclaimers in standard form contracts, policies may change over time. What sort of facts might lead a court to recognize a change in public policy? An example is found in the instance of cohabitation agreements between unmarried persons. Until the 1970s, such agreements were generally unenforceable on the ground that enforcement would "weaken marriage as the foundation of our family-based society." Hewitt v. Hewitt, Note 3, p. 115. Over time, however, courts have begun to uphold cohabitation contracts, so long as "the business part of a contract between cohabiting or romantically attached partners can be separated from the personal part." Thomas v. LaRosa, 400 S.E.2d 809, 813 (W.Va.1990).

At moments of possible cultural change, courts may be particularly sensitive about sources of policy guidance. Thus in *Hewitt*, decided in 1979, the court invoked policies *about* policy to deny enforcement to a cohabitation agreement:

"If resolution of this issue rests ultimately on the grounds of public policy, by what body should that policy be determined? [In Marvin v. Marvin, the California court], viewing the issue as governed solely by contract law, found judicial policy-making appropriate. Its decision was facilitated by California precedent and that State's no-fault divorce law. In our view, however, ... [t]he question whether change is needed in the law governing the rights of parties in this delicate area of marriage-like relationships involves evaluations of sociological data and alternatives we believe best suited to the superior investigative and fact-finding facilities of the legislative branch in the exercise of its traditional authority to declare public policy in the domestic relations field." 394 N.E.2d at 1209.

Are legislatures generally better at fact-finding of this kind than courts? Recall the recourse to sources of fact-finding by judges in both opinions in *O'Callaghan*, p. 467 above.

RESTRAINTS OF TRADE

Hopper v. All Pet Animal Clinic

Supreme Court of Wyoming, 1993.
861 P.2d 531.

■ TAYLOR, JUSTICE. [For three years following her education as a veterinarian, Dr. Glenna Hopper worked—part-time at first—at the All Pet Animal Clinic, Inc., in Laramie, Wyoming. She and her employer executed an agreement, effective in March of 1989, containing this provision:

> This agreement may be terminated by either party upon 30 days' notice to the other party. Upon termination, Dr. Hopper agrees that she will not practice small animal medicine for a period of three years from the date of termination within 5 miles of the corporate limits of the City of Laramie, Wyoming. Dr. Hopper agrees that the duration and geographic scope of that limitation is reasonable.[a]

Later the president of All Pet, Dr. R.B. Johnson, heard a rumor that Dr. Hopper was investigating the purchase of a competing practice and suggested that she buy her way out of the covenant about competition. In her response she said that she could do anything she wanted. Thereupon she was discharged. In July, 1991, having purchased the other practice, she began operating the Gem City Veterinary Clinic. In November, All Pet sued for an injunction, claiming also damages. (An additional plaintiff was the Alpine Animal Clinic, Inc., in which Dr. Hopper and Dr. Johnson had also been associated.) The case came to trial in the following year, more than two years after Hopper was discharged. The plaintiffs did not seek a temporary injunction.]

It appeared that slightly more than half of Hopper's gross income was derived from small-animal practice, and the evidence showed a substantial overlap of clientele in her former and current practices. The trial court granted an injunction, but concluded that the amount of the plaintiff's damages was too speculative to be allowed. Both parties appealed.]

A. *The Enforceability of a Covenant Not to Compete*

The common law policy against contracts in restraint of trade is one of the oldest and most firmly established. Restatement (Second) of Contracts §§ 185–188 (1981) (Introductory Note at 35). See Dutch Maid Bakeries v. Schleicher, 58 Wyo. 374, 131 P.2d 630, 634 (1942). The traditional disfavor of such restraints means covenants not to compete are construed against the party seeking to enforce them. . . . The initial burden is on the employer to prove the covenant is reasonable and has a fair relation to, and is necessary for, the business interests for which protection is sought. Tench v. Weaver, 374 P.2d 27, 29 (Wyo.1962).

Two principles, the freedom to contract and the freedom to work, conflict when courts test the enforceability of covenants not to compete.

---

a. This term was part of the first written agreement between Hopper and the Clinic, executed in December, 1989, but was antedated to the preceding March, when Hopper had begun work.

Ridley v. Krout, 180 P.2d 124, 128 (Wyo. 1947). There is general recognition that while an employer may seek protection from improper and unfair competition of a former employee, the employer is not entitled to protection against ordinary competition. See, e.g. Duffner v. Alberty, 718 S.W.2d 111, 112 (Ark. 1986) and American Sec. Services, Inc. v. Vodra, 385 N.W.2d 73, 78 (Neb. 1986). The enforceability of a covenant not to compete depends upon a finding that the proper balance exists between the competing interests of the employer and the employee. See Restatement (Second) of Agency § 393 cmt. e (1958) (noting that without a covenant not to compete, an agent, employee, can compete with a principal despite past employment and can begin preparations for future competition, such as purchasing a competitive business, before leaving present employment).

Wyoming adopted a rule of reason inquiry from the Restatement of Contracts testing the validity of a covenant not to compete. *Dutch Maid Bakeries*, 131 P.2d 634 (citing Restatement of Contracts §§ 513–515 (1932)); *Ridley*, 180 P.2d at 127. The present formulation of the rule of reason is contained in Restatement (Second) of Contracts, supra § 188: ... See also Restatement (Second) of Contracts, supra, §§ 186–187.[b] An often quoted reformulation of the rule of reason inquiry states that "[a] restraint is reasonable only if it (1) is no greater than is required for the protection of the employer, (2) does not impose undue hardship on the employee, and (3) is not injurious to the public." Harlan M. Blake, Employee Agreements Not to Compete, 73 Harv.L.Rev. 625, 648–49 (1960).... [W]e turn to the rule of reason inquiry....

The special interests of All Pet and Alpine identified by the district court as findings of fact are not clearly erroneous. Dr. Hopper moved to Laramie upon completion of her degree prior to any significant professional contact with the community. Her introduction to All Pet's and Alpine's clients, client files, pricing policies, and practice development techniques provided information which exceeded the skills she brought to her employment. While she was a licensed and trained veterinarian when she accepted employment, the additional exposure to clients and knowledge of clinic operations her employers shared with her had a monetary value for which the employers are entitled to reasonable protection from irreparable harm. See Reddy [v. Community Health Foundation of Man, 298 S.E.2d 906 (1982)] at 912–14 (discussing the economic analysis applied to restrictive covenants). The proven loss of 187 of All Pet's and Alpine's clients to Dr. Hopper's new practice sufficiently demonstrated actual harm from unfair competition.

---

b. According to § 187, "A promise to refrain from competition that imposes a restraint that is not ancillary to an otherwise valid transaction or relationship is unreasonably in restraint of trade."

Comment *b* to the section contains these observations: "The promisee's interest ... may arise out of a relation between himself as employer or principal and the promisor as employee or agent.... In order for a restraint to be ancillary to a transaction or relationship the promise that imposes it must be made as part of that transaction or relationship. A promise made subsequent to the transaction or relationship is not ancillary to it. In the case of an ongoing transaction or relationship, however, it is enough if the promise is made before its termination, as long as it is supported by consideration and meets the other requirements of enforceability."

The reasonableness, in a given fact situation, of the limitations placed on a former employee by a covenant not to compete are determinations made by the court as a matter of law. See, e.g. Jarrett v. Hamilton, 346 S.E.2d 875, 876 (Ga. 1986). Therefore, the district court's conclusions of law about the reasonableness of the type of activity, geographic, and durational limits contained in the covenant are subject to *de novo* review.

... [I]n Cukjati [v. Burkett, 772 S.W.2d 215 (Tex. 1989)] at 216, 218, the Court of Appeals of Texas held a covenant not to compete was unreasonable because it limited a veterinarian from practicing within twelve miles of his former employer's clinic in North Irving, a community within the Dallas–Fort Worth metropolitan area. Because evidence from that proceeding disclosed that Dallas area residents are unlikely to travel more than a few miles for pet care, the court found the restriction unreasonable. Id. at 218. The number of veterinarians and the demands upon their services obviously varies between Laramie, Wyoming and metropolitan Dallas, Texas, creating a different usage pattern. We believe the reasonableness of individual limitations contained in a specific covenant not to compete must be assessed based upon the facts of that proceeding. *Ridley*, 180 P.2d at 131.

Enforcement of the practice restrictions Dr. Hopper accepted as part of her covenant not to compete does not create an unreasonable restraint of trade. While the specific terms of the covenant failed to define the practice of small animal medicine the parties' trade usage provided a conforming standard of domesticated dogs and cats along with exotic animals maintained as household pets. As a veterinarian licensed to practice in Wyoming, Dr. Hopper was therefore permitted to earn a living in her chosen profession without relocating by practicing large animal medicine, a significant area of practice in this state. The restriction on the type of activity contained in the covenant was sufficiently limited to avoid undue hardship to Dr. Hopper while protecting the special interests of All Pet and Alpine. ...

The public will not suffer injury from enforcement of the covenant. ...

The geographical limit contained in the covenant not to compete restricts Dr. Hopper from practicing within a five mile radius of the corporate limits of Laramie. As a matter of law, this limit is reasonable in this circumstance. The evidence presented at trial indicated that the clients of All Pet and Alpine were located throughout the county. Despite Wyoming's rural character, the five mile restriction effectively limited unfair competition without presenting an undue hardship. Dr. Hopper could, for example, have opened a practice at other locations within the county.

A durational limitation should be reasonably related to the legitimate interest which the employer is seeking to protect. Restatement (Second) of Contracts, supra, § 188 cmt. b. ...

A one year durational limit sufficiently secures All Pet's and Alpine's interest in pricing policies and practice development information. Pricing policies at All Pet and Alpine were changed yearly, according to Dr. Johnson, to reflect changes in material and service costs provided by the clinics as well as new procedures. Practice development information, especially in a learned profession, loses its value quickly as technological change occurs and new reference material become [sic] available. We hold, as a matter of law, that enforcement of a one year durational limit is reasonable and sufficiently protects the interest of All Pet and Alpine without violating public policy. . . . Because we hold that the covenant's three year durational term imposed a partially unreasonable restraint of trade, we remand for a modification of the judgment to enjoin Dr. Hopper from unfair competition for a duration of one year from the date of termination.

B. *Damages for Violation of a Covenant Not to Compete*

[The court rejected the calculations of damages suggested by the plaintiffs, all of which were "based on figures for gross profits."]

The finding of the district court that the amount of damages suffered was speculative and unproven by a preponderance of the evidence is not clearly erroneous. . . .

■ CARDINE, JUSTICE, dissenting. Glenna Hopper has beaten the system. Just prior to being terminated, Dr. Hopper informed Dr. Johnson that "the [covenant] isn't worth the paper it's written on." And she was right. . . .

The court has now decided as a matter of law that a one-year non-competition restriction is reasonable, and a longer period is unreasonable. . . .

I would require that appellant be enjoined from that part of the practice of veterinary medicine specified in the covenant not to compete from the date the trial court, on remand, enters its modified judgment for at least the one-year period which this court now finds reasonable.

NOTES

(1) *Question.* How might Dr. Johnson's lawyer have drafted the clause to provide his client better protection?

(2) *Policy Sources and Limitations.* In 1985, accountant Daniel Miller signed an employment contract with Donald DeMuth. The contract contained a non-competition clause which provided that "if Employer terminates the Agreement for cause, and Employee [engages in accounting work] within a 50–mile radius of any of Employer's current or former clients, [Employee] agrees to pay the Employer 125% of the previous 12 months charges [received from any former client]." Cause was defined to include "moral turpitude, being charged with a felony, . . . intentionally losing clients, engaging in sexual activities in the office, and homosexuality." In 1990, DeMuth fired Miller for cause for appearing on a local television station representing a gay and lesbian coalition. Miller then opened a competing firm and solicited DeMuth's clients, 17 of whom became Miller's clients. DeMuth sought compensation under the non-competition clause. Miller argued that enforcement of the penalty provision would violate his rights to be free from workplace discrimination on the basis of sexual preference. From a judgment for DeMuth, Miller appealed. *Held*: Affirmed.

"[Appellant's] claim [of discrimination] is not actionable under any Pennsylvania statute or its constitution and is certainly not in violation of the doctrines of due process and equal protection in the Fourteenth Amendment to the U.S. Constitution.... It surely follows that, because the defendant agreed to the terms of his contract for a period of five years without objection or renegotiation, he must be held to adhere to its (non-competition) terms, absent any evidence of a clear violation of public policy which we have detected here." The court commented in a footnote that "appellant's arguments of discrimination in the workplace, directed at gays and lesbians, would be better directed toward the Legislature (the real body politic) to effectuate a change in the treatment of those whose sexual preferences impact upon their work environment." DeMuth v. Miller, 652 A.2d 891 (Pa.Super.1995).

(3) *Practicing Law: A Special Case?* "Should an attorney who leaves a law firm be free to compete with that firm?" That was the question in Howard v. Babcock, 863 P.2d 150, 161 (Cal.1993) (Justice Kennard, dissenting).

In that case partners in a law firm had agreed that anyone withdrawing from the partnership would receive a share of the firm's net profit for a period following the withdrawal. If, however, that person engaged in a designated type of competitive practice, any profit-sharing would be at the discretion of the remaining partners. Three partners withdrew and the limitation was invoked against them. They sought a declaration that the limitation was unenforceable. From a judgment favoring the defendants, the plaintiffs appealed once, with limited success, and sought further review. *Held:* Reversed.

Citing changes in "law firm culture," the court said that "the general rules and habits of commerce have permeated the legal profession." Many other courts have "interpreted the rules of professional conduct of their states ... as prohibiting all agreements restricting competition among lawyers, including those that merely assess a cost for competition.... Upon reflection [however], we have determined that these courts' steadfast concern to assure the theoretical freedom of each lawyer to choose whom to represent and what kind of work to undertake, and the theoretical freedom of any client to select his or her attorney of choice is inconsistent with the reality that both freedoms are actually circumscribed." Howard v. Babcock, 863 P.2d 150 (Cal.1993).

(4) *Rejection or Reformation?* If a non-compete clause is found to be unreasonably broad, what becomes of it? Formerly, most courts employed the "all or nothing at all" rule, under which the court either enforced the clause as written or rejected it altogether. See Ehlers v. Iowa Warehouse Co., 188 N.W.2d 368 (Iowa 1971). *Partial* enforcement, as in *Hopper,* was criticized, as by the dissent in that case, as empowering courts to remake the parties' agreement on the court's terms. The trend, however, has been toward *some* form of judicial modification, and courts have taken two approaches.

The first is the "blue pencil" rule under which courts cross out, or "blue pencil," words "to the extent that a grammatically meaningful reasonable restriction remains after the words making the restriction unreasonable are stricken." Central Adjustment Bureau, Inc. v. Ingram, 678 S.W.2d 28 (Tenn. 1984) (explaining that in a restriction on soliciting business clients in "Toledo, Ohio, and the United States," the court could "blue pencil" "Ohio, and the United States" leaving the covenant enforceable in Toledo). While the blue pencil rule prevents courts from rewriting private agreements in a literal sense, it has been criticized as emphasizing form over substance.

The second approach, employed in *Hopper* above, is the rule of reasonableness, under which the covenant will be enforced only to the extent reasonably necessary to protect the employer's interest. As both Williston and Corbin stated:

"This is not making a new contract for the parties; it is a choice among the possible effects of the one that they made, establishing the one that is the most desirable for the contractors and the public at large." Williston and Corbin, On the Doctrine of Beit v. Beit, 23 Conn. B.J. 40, 49–50 (1949).

The Restatement follows this approach. See Restatement § 184. One objection to the rule is that employers can draft oppressive restrictions knowing that at worst a court will enforce the covenant on reasonable terms. Does the Restatement rule also invite abuses by drafters of non-compete clauses?

————

PUBLIC POLICY AND TERMINATION OF AT–WILL EMPLOYEES

Since the late nineteenth century, courts have shown a strong preference for termination at will in employment agreements; see Employment Agreements, p. 58 above. Courts resolutely ignored contrary indications such as description of the employment as "permanent" or "lifetime." Thus the statement that "so long as you do your job you can be here until you're a hundred" was held "insufficient as a matter of law" to vary the at-will rule. Mursch v. Van Dorn Co., 851 F.2d 990, 996 (7th Cir.1988).

In the mid–1970's, however, a revolution began with decisions that qualified the employer's power to terminate under employment agreements. The seminal case was Monge v. Beebe Rubber Co., 316 A.2d 549 (N.H.1974), involving a worker fired because she resisted her foreman's sexual advances. There is now general agreement that a plainly opportunistic discharge is actionable. Thus, if an employee is discharged without good cause "the obligation of good faith and fair dealing imposed on an employer requires that the employer be liable for the loss in compensation that is ... clearly related to an employee's past service," such as commissions earned by that service. Gram v. Liberty Mut. Ins. Co., 429 N.E.2d 21, 29 (Mass. 1981).

But in addition to the demands of good faith, most courts, like that in the following case, have fashioned a public policy exception to an employer's right to terminate at-will employees.

Sheets v. Teddy's Frosted Foods

Supreme Court of Connecticut, 1980.
179 Conn. 471, 427 A.2d 385.

■ PETERS, ASSOCIATE JUSTICE.[a] The issue in this case is whether an employer has a completely unlimited right to terminate the services of an employee whom it has hired for an indefinite term. The plaintiff, Emard H. Sheets, filed a complaint that as amended alleged that he had been wrongfully

---

a. Ellen Ash Peters (1930–) was a member of the faculty of the Yale Law School for over two decades, teaching and writing in the fields of contracts and commercial law and serving as an Adviser for the Restatement Second of Contracts. In 1978 she was appointed an associate justice of the Connecticut Supreme Court, serving as Chief Justice from 1984 to 1996. For discussion of her decisions involving the Uniform Commercial Code, see Comment, 21 Conn.L.Rev. 753 (1989).

discharged from his employment as quality control director and operations manager of the defendant, Teddy's Frosted Foods, Inc. The defendant responded with a motion to strike the complaint as legally insufficient. The plaintiff declined to plead further when that motion was granted. From the consequent rendering of judgment for the defendant, the plaintiff has appealed to this court.

. . . The complaint alleges that for a four year period, from November 1973 to November 1977, the plaintiff was employed by the defendant, a producer of frozen food products, as its quality control director and subsequently also as operations manager. In the course of his employment, the plaintiff received periodic raises and bonuses. In his capacity as quality control director and operations manager, the plaintiff began to notice deviations from the specifications contained in the defendant's standards and labels, in that some vegetables were substandard and some meat components underweight. These deviations meant that the defendant's products violated the express representations contained in the defendant's labeling; false or misleading labels in turn violate the provisions of General Statutes § 19–222, the Connecticut Uniform Food, Drug and Cosmetic Act. In May of 1977, the plaintiff communicated in writing to the defendant concerning the use of substandard raw materials and underweight components in the defendant's finished products. His recommendations for more selective purchasing and conforming components were ignored. On November 3, 1977, his employment with the defendant was terminated. Although the stated reason for his discharge was unsatisfactory performance of his duties, he was actually dismissed in retaliation for his efforts to ensure that the defendant's products would comply with the applicable law relating to labeling and licensing.

The plaintiff's complaint alleges that his dismissal by his employer was wrongful in three respects. He claims that there was a violation of an implied contract of employment, a violation of public policy, and a malicious discharge. On this appeal, the claim of malice has not been separately pursued, and we are asked to consider only whether he has stated a cause of action for breach of contract or for intentionally tortious conduct. On oral argument, it was the tort claim that was most vigorously pressed, and it is upon the basis of tort that we have concluded that the motion to strike was granted in error.

The issue before us is whether to recognize an exception to the traditional rules governing employment at will so as to permit a cause of action for wrongful discharge where the discharge contravenes a clear mandate of public policy. In addressing that claim, we must clarify what is not at stake in this litigation. The plaintiff does not challenge the general proposition that contracts of permanent employment, or for an indefinite term, are terminable at will. . . . Nor does he argue that contracts terminable at will permit termination only upon a showing of just cause for dismissal. Some statutes, such as the Connecticut Franchise Act, General Statutes § 42–133e through 42–133h, do impose limitations of just cause upon the power to terminate some contracts; see § 42–133f; but the legislature has recently refused to interpolate such a requirement into contracts of employment. See H.B. No. 5179, 1974 Sess. There is a significant distinction between a criterion of just cause and what the plaintiff is seeking. "Just cause" substantially limits employer discretion to terminate, by requiring the employer, in all instances, to proffer a proper reason for dismissal, by forbidding the employer to act arbitrarily or capriciously.... By contrast, the plaintiff asks only that the employer be responsible in damages if the former employee can prove a demonstrably improper reason for dismissal, a reason whose impropriety is derived from some important violation of public policy.

The argument that contract rights which are inherently legitimate may yet give rise to liability in tort if they are exercised improperly is not a novel one. Although private persons have the right not to enter into contracts, failure to contract under circumstances in which others are seriously misled gives rise to a variety of claims sounding in tort. See Kessler & Fine, "Culpa in Contrahendo," 77 Harv.L.Rev. 401 (1964). The development of liability in contract for action induced by reliance upon a promise, despite the absence of common law consideration normally required to bind a promisor; see Restatement (Second), Contracts '90 (1973); rests upon principles derived at least in part from the law of tort. See Gilmore, The Death of Contract 8–90 (1974). By way of analogy, we have long recognized abuse of process as a cause of action in tort whose gravamen is the misuse or misapplication of process, its use "in an improper manner or to accomplish a purpose for which it was not designed." Varga v. Pareles, 137 Conn. 663, 667, 81 A.2d 112, 115 (1951); Schaefer v. O.K. Tool Co., 110 Conn. 528, 532–33, 148 A. 330 (1930); Restatement (Second), Torts § 682 (1977); Wright & Fitzgerald, Connecticut Law of Torts § 163 (1968); Prosser, Torts § 121 (1971).

It would be difficult to maintain that the right to discharge an employee hired at will is so fundamentally different from other contract rights that its exercise is never subject to judicial scrutiny regardless of how outrageous, how violative of public policy, the employer's conduct may be. Cf. General Statutes § 31–126 (unfair employment practices). The defendant does not seriously contest the propriety of cases in other jurisdictions that have found wrongful and actionable a discharge in retaliation for the exercise of an employee's right to: (1) refuse to commit perjury; ... (2) file a workmen's compensation claim; ... (3) engage in union activity; ... (4) perform jury duty.... While it may be true that these cases are supported by mandates of public policy derived directly from the applicable state statutes and constitutions, it is equally true that they serve at a minimum to establish the principle that public policy imposes some limits on unbridled discretion to terminate the employment of someone hired at will.... No case has been called to our attention in which, despite egregiously outrageous circumstances, the employer's contract rights have been permitted to override competing claims of public policy, although there are numerous cases in which the facts were found not to support the employee's claim....

The issue then becomes the familiar common law problem of deciding where and how to draw the line between claims that genuinely involve the mandates of public policy and are actionable, and ordinary disputes between employee and employer that are not. We are mindful that courts should not lightly intervene to impair the exercise of managerial discretion or to foment unwarranted litigation. We are, however, equally mindful that the myriad of employees without the bargaining power to command employment contracts for a definite term are entitled to a modicum of judicial protection when their conduct as good citizens is punished by their employers.

The central allegation of the plaintiff's complaint is that he was discharged because of his conduct in calling to his employer's attention repeated violations of the Connecticut Uniform Food, Drug and Cosmetic Act. This act prohibits the sale of mislabeled food. General Statutes §§ 19–213, 19–222. The act, in § 19–215, imposes criminal penalties upon anyone who violates § 19–213; subsection (b) of § 19–215 makes it clear that criminal sanctions do not depend upon proof of intent to defraud or mislead, since special sanctions are imposed for intentional misconduct. The plaintiff's position as quality control director and operations manager might have exposed him to the possibility of criminal prosecution under this act. The act was intended to "safeguard the public health and promote the public welfare by protecting the consuming public from injury by product use and the purchasing public from injury by merchandising deceit...." General Statutes § 19–211.

It is useful to compare the factual allegations of this complaint with those of other recent cases in which recovery was sought for retaliatory discharge. In Geary v. United States Steel Corporation, [456 Pa. 171, 319 A.2d 174 (1974)], in which the plaintiff had disputed the safety of tubular steel casings, he was denied recovery because, as a company salesman, he had neither the expertise nor the corporate responsibility to "exercise independent, expert judgment in matters of product safety." Id., 319 A.2d 178. By contrast, this plaintiff, unless his title is meaningless, did have responsibility for product quality control. Three other recent cases in which the plaintiff's claim survived demurrer closely approximate the claim before us....

In the light of these recent cases, which evidence a growing judicial receptivity to the recognition of a tort claim for wrongful discharge, the trial court was in error in granting the defendant's motion to strike. The plaintiff alleged that he had been dismissed in retaliation for his insistence that the defendant comply with the requirements of a state statute, the Food, Drug and Cosmetic Act. We need not decide whether violation of a state statute is invariably a prerequisite to the conclusion that a challenged discharge violates public policy. Certainly when there is a relevant state statute we should not ignore the statement of public policy that it represents. For today, it is enough to decide that an employee should not be put to an election whether to risk criminal sanction or to jeopardize his continued employment.

There is error and the case is remanded for further proceedings.

■ In this opinion BOGDANSKI and HEALEY, JJ., concurred.

■ COTTER, CHIEF JUSTICE (dissenting).... The majority by seeking to extend a "modicum" of judicial protection to shield employees from retaliatory discharges instead offers them a sword with which to coerce employers to retain them in their employ. In recognizing an exception to the traditional rules governing employment at will and basing a new cause of action for retaliatory discharge on the facts of this case, the majority is necessarily led to the creation of an overly broad new cause of action whose nuisance value alone may impair employers' ability to hire and retain employees who are best suited to their requirements. Other jurisdictions which have recognized a cause of action for retaliatory discharge have done so on the basis of a much clearer and more direct contravention of a mandate of public policy.

... [T]he purposes of the statute the majority would rely on, ... can only be considered as, at most, marginally affected by an allegedly retaliatory discharge of an employee who observed the supposed sale of shortweight frozen entrees and the use of U.S. Government Certified "Grade B" rather than "Grade A" vegetables. A retaliatory discharge in the present case would not necessarily thwart or inhibit the Connecticut Uniform Food, Drug and Cosmetic Act's purpose of protecting the consumer. The plaintiff, if he desired to protect the consumer, could have communicated, even anonymously, to the commissioner of consumer affairs his concerns that his employer was violating the Food, Drug and Cosmetic Act so as to invoke the statute's enforcement mechanisms. See General Statutes §§ 19–214 through 19–217. To further and comply with the public policy expressed in Connecticut's Uniform Food, Drug and Cosmetic Act and to avoid the exceedingly remote possibility of criminal sanctions, the plaintiff need not have jeopardized his continued employment. There is no indication that the plaintiff has either, before or after his discharge, informed or even attempted to inform the commissioner of consumer protection of violations the plaintiff claims to have first noted in his fourth year as the defendant's quality control director and fourth month as its operations manager. Unlike those cases where an employer allegedly discharged employees for engaging in union activities or filing workmen's compensation claims and the discharge itself contravened a statutory mandate, in the present case the discharge itself at most only indirectly impinged on the statutory mandate.

Consequently, the majority seemingly invites the unrestricted use of an allegation of almost any statutory or even regulatory violation by an employer as the basis for a cause of action by a discharged employee hired for an indefinite term....

■ In this opinion LOISELLE, J., concurred.

NOTES

(1) *Discharge for Cause.* Justice Peters explains: "There is a significant distinction between a criterion of just cause and what the plaintiff is seeking. 'Just cause' substantially limits employer discretion to terminate, by requiring the employer, in all instances, to proffer a proper reason for dismissal, by forbidding the employer to act arbitrarily or capriciously." Courts have generally been unwilling to hold that an employer is under a duty of good faith and fair dealing that allows discharge only

for good cause. If a duty of good faith and fair dealing is implied in every contract, is an at-will employment agreement a "contract" for this purpose?

Justice Peters cautions, "We need not decide whether violation of a state statute is invariably a prerequisite to the conclusion that a challenged discharge violates public policy." Courts differ as to whether the public policy must be reflected in some form of legislation. In Johnson v. McDonnell Douglas Corp., 745 S.W.2d 661, 663 (Mo.1988), for example, the Supreme Court of Missouri took the extreme view that the public policy exception applied only where the employee has "the benefit of a constitutional provision, a statute, or a regulation based on a statute."

(2) *Absence of a Statute.* Chief Justice Cotter, dissenting, protested that "the majority seemingly invites the unrestricted use of an allegation of almost any statutory or even regulatory violation by an employer as the basis for a cause of action by a discharged employee hired for an indefinite term." About two decades later, the Connecticut court revisited the breadth of the exception.

Virginia Daley, who was responsible for design development in Aetna's field offices, gave birth to a son in July 1991. She requested an alternative schedule permitting her to work at home one day a week and was turned down. There were complaints about her inadequate performance, and she was on and off probation. In November 1991, prompted by an award Aetna received for its model family leave programs, Daley drafted an interoffice memo expressing dissatisfaction with her experience and that of unidentified co-workers. After more complaints about her performance, she was fired in February 1993. She sued for wrongful discharge citing, among other sources of public policy, Connecticut and federal employment and child welfare statutes. From a directed verdict for Aetna, Daley appealed. Held: Affirmed.

"[T]he public policy exception to the at will doctrine is a narrow one, and ... we do not 'lightly intervene to impair the exercise of managerial discretion or to foment unwarranted litigation.' ... Absent unusual circumstances, we will interfere with a personnel decision only if it implicates an explicit statutory or constitutional provision, or judicially conceived notion of public policy.... [W]e are mindful that we should not ignore the statement of public policy that is represented by a relevant statute.... [But to] impute a statement of public policy beyond that which is represented ... would subject the employer who maintains compliance with express statutory obligations to unwarranted litigation for failure to comply with a heretofore unrecognized public policy mandate." Daley v. Aetna Life & Cas. Co., 734 A.2d 112, 133 (Conn.1999).

(3) *Presence of a Statute.* Carole Burnham, office manager in a dental office, filed an anonymous complaint with the Connecticut State Dental Association alleging that the dentists engaged in unsanitary practices in violation of the federal Occupational and Health Act. When she was fired two weeks later, she sued for wrongful termination, relying on Connecticut's "whistleblower statute," enacted in 1982 (two years after the decision in Sheets). From summary judgment for defendants, she appealed. *Held:* Affirmed.

Connecticut's whistleblower statute "prohibits employers from retaliating against employees who report 'a violation or a suspected violation of any state or federal law ... to a public body.'" Plaintiff does not dispute the trial court's conclusion that the Dental Association is not a "public body" within the definition in the whistleblower statute. "Alternatively, ... plaintiff's claim is precluded by virtue of the existence of a statutory remedy under that statute.... The existence of this statutory remedy [of a civil action after exhaustion of administrative remedies] precludes the plaintiff from bringing a common law wrongful discharge action based on an alleged violation" of the statute. (The court also concluded that the plaintiff's claim was precluded by the existence of a statutory administrative remedy under federal law.) Burnham v. Karl & Gelb, 745 A.2d 178, 182–183 (Conn.2000).

(4) *Empirical Effects.* What are the economic effects of judicial modification of the at-will doctrine? A study by Professor Thomas Miles found that wrongful-discharge laws had "no statistically significant effects on either employment or unemployment." Miles, Common Law Exceptions to Employment at Will and U.S. Labor Markets, 16 J. of Law, Econ., and Org. 74 (2000); see also David Autor, John Donohue, Stewart Schwab, The Employment Consequences of Wrongful–Discharge Laws: Large, Small, or None at All? 94 Am. Econ. Rev. 440 (2004).

Consider, in this connection, the arguments of Judge Easterbrook, in dissent, for the importance of giving employers the ability to decide who shall work for them. "It is easy for a jury to mistake a pest, a busybody, for a champion of the law. Firms need to prune their work forces of persons who create more trouble than they are worth; time diverted from business means lower efficiency and higher prices for consumers, undermining still another public policy. Employers fearing litigation—with high legal fees and the risk of punitive damages—will keep troublesome and inefficient employees on the payroll. Everyone loses when that happens." Belline v. K–Mart Corp., 940 F.2d 184, 191 (7th Cir.1991).

Should judges take account of the effects of common law decisions on workplace practices? If your answer is Yes, what data or other sources of information should judges consider in deciding what those effects are?

PROBLEM

Suppose that an at-will employee is asked by his employer to sign an unreasonable covenant not to compete, and that upon his refusal to do so, he is fired. Would the employee have a claim for wrongful discharge under *Sheets*? D'sa v. Playhut, Inc., 102 Cal.Rptr.2d 495 (Ct.App.2000).

———

BALLA v. GAMBRO, INC., 584 N.E.2d 104 (Ill.1991). [Roger Balla, a member of the Illinois bar, was in house counsel at Gambro, Inc., a distributor of kidney dialysis equipment. In addition to being "responsible for all legal matters" he had non-legal responsibilities including duties as "manager of regulatory affairs." When Balla told the president of Gambro to reject a shipment of dialyzers from its parent corporation in Germany because they did not comply with FDA regulations, the president ignored him and told the parent that they would sell the dialyzers to "a customer who buys only on price." On discovering this, Balla told the president that he would do whatever was necessary to stop their sale. Shortly thereafter the president fired Balla, who then reported the shipment to the FDA, which seized it and determined that it was adulterated. Balla sued Gambro for $22 million in tort for retaliatory discharge. The trial judge granted Gambro's motion for summary judgment, stating that since Balla's decision involved "applying law to fact," the duties that led to his discharge were "clearly within the attorney client relationship" and Gambro had the "absolute right" to discharge its attorney. On appeal by Balla, the Illinois

Court of Appeals remanded, holding that Balla's right to sue for retaliatory discharge depended on facts to be determined at a trial. Gambro appealed.]

■ CLARK, JUSTICE.... [G]enerally, in house counsel do not have a claim under the tort of retaliatory discharge.... Appellee is and was subject to the Illinois Code of Professional Responsibility ... adopted by this court. The tort of retaliatory discharge is a limited and narrow exception to the general rule of at will employment....

In this case, the public policy to be protected, that of protecting the lives and property of citizens, is adequately safeguarded without extending the tort of retaliatory discharge to in house counsel. Appellee was required under the Rules of Professional Conduct to report Gambro's intention to sell the "misbranded and/or adulterated" dialyzers.

A lawyer *shall* reveal information about a client to the extent it appears necessary to prevent the client from committing an act that would result in death or serious bodily injury. (Emphasis added.) ...

Appellee alleges, and the FDA's seizure of the dialyzers indicates, that the use of the dialyzers would cause death or serious bodily injury. Thus, under the above cited rule, appellee was under the mandate of this court to report the sale of these dialyzers.

In his brief to this court, appellee argues that not extending the tort of retaliatory discharge to in house counsel would present attorneys with a "Hobson's choice." According to appellee, in house counsel would face two alternatives: either comply with the client/employer wishes and risk both the loss of a professional license and exposure to criminal sanctions, or decline to comply with client/employer's wishes and risk the loss of a full time job with the attendant benefits. We disagree.... [I]n house counsel plainly are not confronted with such a dilemma. In house counsel do not have a choice of whether to follow their ethical obligations as attorneys licensed to practice law, or follow the illegal and unethical demands of their clients. In house counsel must abide by the Rules of Professional Conduct. Appellee had no choice but to report to the FDA Gambro's intention to sell or distribute these dialyzers, and consequently protect the aforementioned public policy.

In addition, we believe that extending the tort of retaliatory discharge to in house counsel would have an undesirable effect on the attorney client relationship that exists between these employers and their in house counsel. Generally, a client may discharge his attorney at any time, with or without cause.... This rule applies equally to in house counsel as it does to outside counsel.... We believe that if in house counsel are granted the right to sue their employers for retaliatory discharge, employers might be less willing to be forthright and candid with their in house counsel for advice regarding potentially questionable corporate conduct, knowing that their in house counsel could use this information in a retaliatory discharge suit.... If extending the tort of retaliatory discharge might have a chilling effect on the communications between the employer/client and the in house counsel, we believe that it is more wise to refrain from doing so....

We also believe that it would be inappropriate for the employer/client to bear the economic costs and burdens of their in house counsel's adhering to their ethical obligations under the Rules of Professional Conduct.... The employer/client would be forced to pay damages to its former in house counsel to essentially mitigate the harm the attorney suffered for having to abide by Rules of Professional Conduct. This, we believe, is impermissible for all attorneys know or should know in their professional career that at certain times they will have to forgo economic gains in order to protect the integrity of the legal profession....

Appellee argues that, if he did learn of Gambro's alleged violation of FDA regulations as manager of regulatory affairs, and acted pursuant to his duties as manager of regulatory affairs, he is merely an "employee" at Gambro and therefore should be entitled to bring a cause of action for retaliatory discharge.... [A]lthough appellee may have been the manager of regulatory affairs for Gambro, his discharge resulted from information he learned as general counsel, and from conduct he performed as general counsel.

For the foregoing reasons the decision of the appellate court is reversed and the decision of the trial court is affirmed.

NOTES

(1) *Questions.* Did Balla's discharge contravene, in the words of Sheets, "a clear mandate of public policy"? Do you agree that the policy was, in the words of the court, "adequately safeguarded without extending the tort of retaliatory discharge" to Balla? Do you agree with the court that Balla was not put to a "Hobson's Choice"? Is there any way that in house counsel can protect themselves from discharge in Balla's circumstances?

(2) *Balla Extended.* In Jacobson v. Knepper & Moga, 706 N.E.2d 491, 494 (Ill.1998), the Supreme Court of Illinois extended Balla to a claim by a lawyer that he had been discharged by the law firm that had employed him in retaliation for his reporting the firm's illegal practices to a principal partner of the firm. "[P]laintiff, as a licensed attorney employed as such by the defendant law firm, cannot maintain a cause of action for retaliatory discharge because the ethical obligations imposed by the Rules of Professional Conduct provide adequate safeguards to the public policy implicated in this case."

(3) *Balla Rejected.* The reasoning in Balla was rejected by the Supreme Court of California in General Dynamics Corp. v. Superior Court, 876 P.2d 487, 500 (Cal.1994), a retaliatory discharge suit by an in house counsel. The court admitted that the Illinois courts had "grappled conscientiously with the conflicting values presented," but added that "one searches in vain for a principled link between the ethical duties of the in house attorney and the court's refusal to grant such an employee a tort remedy under conditions that directly implicate those professional obligations.... Granted the priest like license to receive the most intimate and damning disclosures of the client, granted the sanctity of the professional privilege, granted the uniquely influential position attorneys occupy in our society, it is precisely because of that role that attorneys should be accorded a retaliatory discharge remedy in those instances in which mandatory ethical norms embodied in the Rules of Professional Conduct collide with illegitimate demands of the employer and the attorney insists on adhering to his or her clear professional duty. It is, after

all, the office of the retaliatory discharge tort to vindicate fundamental public policies by encouraging employees to act in ways that advance them.''

In GTE Products Corp. v. Stewart, 653 N.E.2d 161, 166 (Mass.1995), the Supreme Judicial Court of Massachusetts found the California approach ''more persuasive. We would be reluctant to conclude that an employee, solely by reason of his or her status as an attorney, must be denied protection from wrongful discharge arising from the performance of an action compelled by a clearly defined public policy of the Commonwealth.''

(4) *Tort or Contract?* Note that in *Sheets,* Justice Peters says that ''it is upon the basis of tort that we have concluded that the motion to strike was granted in error'' and that Balla discusses ''the tort of retaliatory discharge.'' What are the advantages to an employee of a remedy in tort as distinguished from one in contract and what are the disadvantages?

Consider also the issue raised in Corl v. Huron Castings, 544 N.W.2d 278, 286, 291 (Mich.1996). There the court held, in a 4–3 decision, that where an employee sued for breach of a just cause employment contract, his ''damage award should be reduced by the amount he received in unemployment compensation benefits'' because the ''collateral source rule, [discussed in Note 3, p. 617 below], does not apply in cases of common law contract.'' A dissenting judge protested that the ''doctrinal foundation of the ... claim is neither fish nor fowl'' and the answer ''cannot be found in the rote application of the distinction between contract and tort.''

(5) *Emotional Distress.* Claims of emotional distress may also be made in the context of at-will agreements. Some courts have recognized that even where the discharge itself may not have been wrongful, the conduct surrounding the discharge may have been tortious. In Dzinglski v. Weirton Steel Corp., 445 S.E.2d 219, 224, 226, 227 (W.Va.1994), the court said that it had recognized ''the tort of outrage or intentional infliction of emotional distress,'' even though it had ''yet to decide a case where a defendant's conduct was found to be sufficiently outrageous to satisfy the requirements'' for that tort. However, though ''not unsympathetic to the distress doubtless suffered'' by the employee, the court concluded ''that the distress stemmed from the discharge itself and not from the investigatory process coincident with the discharge,'' and it was therefore error to find that the investigation constituted the tort. For a discussion of emotional distress in the context of employment contracts, see Note 2, p. 671 below.

(6) *North of the Border.* In Wallace v. United Grain Growers Ltd., 152 D.L.R.4th 1 (Sup.Ct.Can.1997), the Supreme Court of Canada upheld an award of 24 months' salary in lieu of notice when an employer discharged its top salesman at the age of 59 after 14 years with the company. What reasons might explain the refusal of American courts to impose in employment cases a notice requirement analogous to that imposed in franchise cases?

FAMILY RELATIONS

Simeone v. Simeone

Supreme Court of Pennsylvania, 1990.
581 A.2d 162.

■ FLAHERTY, J. [In 1975, Catherine Walsh, a twenty-three year old unemployed nurse, was engaged to Frederick Simeone, a thirty-nine year old neurosurgeon. On the eve of their wedding, Frederick's attorney presented

Catherine with a prenuptial agreement. Among other provisions, the agreement limited Catherine in the event of a separation or divorce to a maximum total payment from Frederick of $25,000. Without seeking her own counsel and without explanation from Frederick's attorney regarding the legal rights surrendered, Catherine signed the agreement. The parties were married the next day, separated in 1982, and began divorce proceedings in 1984. In 1985, Catherine filed a claim for alimony *pendente lite*. Frederick resisted such payment arguing that between 1982 and 1984, he had made payments to Catherine satisfying the $25,000 limit. The master upheld the prenuptial agreement; that finding was affirmed on appeal. Catherine appealed to the Supreme Court.

In its decision, the court noted a rule established in Estate of Geyer, 533 A.2d 423 (1987), that a prenuptial agreement is valid "if it *either* made a reasonable provision for the spouse *or* was entered after a full and fair disclosure of the general financial positions of the parties and the statutory rights being relinquished." The court stated that "there is need for a reexamination of the foundations upon which *Geyer* and earlier cases rested, and a need for clarification of the standards by which the validity of prenuptial agreements will be judged."]

There is no longer validity in the implicit presumption that supplied the basis for *Geyer* and similar earlier decisions. Such decisions rested upon a belief that spouses are of unequal status and that women are not knowledgeable enough to understand the nature of contracts that they enter. Society has advanced, however, to the point where women are no longer regarded as the "weaker" party in marriage, or in society generally. Indeed, the stereotype that women serve as homemakers while men work as breadwinners is no longer viable. Quite often today both spouses are income earners. Nor is there viability in the presumption that women are uninformed, uneducated, and readily subjected to unfair advantage in marital agreements. Indeed, women nowadays quite often have substantial education, financial awareness, income, and assets.

Accordingly, the law has advanced to recognize the equal status of men and women in our society. See, e.g., Pa. Const. art. 1, § 28 (constitutional prohibition of sex discrimination in laws of the Commonwealth). Paternalistic presumptions and protections that arose to shelter women from the inferiorities and incapacities which they were perceived as having in earlier times have, appropriately, been discarded. . . . It would be inconsistent, therefore, to perpetuate the standards governing prenuptial agreements that were described in *Geyer* and similar decisions, as these reflected a paternalistic approach that is now insupportable.

Further, *Geyer* and its predecessors embodied substantial departures from traditional rules of contract law, to the extent that they allowed consideration of the knowledge of the contracting parties and reasonableness of their bargain as factors governing whether to uphold an agreement. Traditional principles of contract law provide perfectly adequate remedies where contracts are procured through fraud, misrepresentation, or duress. Consideration of other factors, such as the knowledge of the parties and the reasonableness of their bargain, is inappropriate. See *Geyer,* 533 A.2d at

434–35 (Flaherty, J. dissenting). Prenuptial agreements are contracts, and, as such, should be evaluated under the same criteria as are applicable to other types of contracts....

Contracting parties are normally bound by their agreements, without regard to whether the terms thereof were read and fully understood and irrespective of whether the agreements embodied reasonable or good bargains. See ... *Bollinger v. Central Pennsylvania Quarry Stripping & Construction Co.,* 229 A.2d 741, 742 (1967) ... Based upon these principles, the terms of the present prenuptial agreement must be regarded as binding, without regard to whether the terms were fully understood by appellant. *Ignorantia non excusat.*

Accordingly, we find no merit in a contention raised by appellant that the agreement should be declared void on the ground that she did not consult with independent legal counsel. To impose a *per se* requirement that parties entering a prenuptial agreement must obtain independent legal counsel would be contrary to traditional principles of contract law, and would constitute a paternalistic and unwarranted interference with the parties' freedom to enter contracts....

By invoking inquiries into reasonableness, ... the functioning and reliability of prenuptial agreements is severely undermined. Parties would not have entered such agreements, and, indeed, might not have entered their marriages, if they did not expect their agreements to be strictly enforced. If parties viewed an agreement as reasonable at the time of its inception, as evidenced by their having signed the agreement, they should be foreclosed from later trying to evade its terms by asserting that it was not in fact reasonable. Pertinently, the present agreement contained a clause reciting that "each of the parties considers this agreement fair, just and reasonable...."

We are reluctant to interfere with the power of persons contemplating marriage to agree upon, and to act in reliance upon, what *they* regard as an acceptable distribution scheme for their property. A court should not ignore the parties' expressed intent by proceeding to determine whether a prenuptial agreement was, in the court's view, reasonable at the time of its inception or the time of divorce. These are exactly the sorts of judicial determinations that such agreements are designed to avoid....

In discarding the approach of *Geyer* ... , we do not depart from the longstanding principle that a full and fair disclosure of the financial positions of the parties is required. Absent this disclosure, a material misrepresentation in the inducement for entering a prenuptial agreement may be asserted. *Hillegass Estate,* 244 A.2d 672, 676–77 (Pa.1968). Parties to these agreements do not quite deal at arm's length, but rather at the time the contract is entered into stand in a relation of mutual confidence and trust that calls for disclosure of their financial resources. *Id.* at 149 ... It is well settled that this disclosure need not be exact, so long as it is "full and fair." *Kaufmann Estate,* 171 A.2d 48, 51 n. 8 (1961). In essence therefore, the duty of disclosure under these circumstances is consistent with traditional principles of contract law....

Appellant's final contention is that the agreement was executed under conditions of duress in that it was presented to her at 5 p.m. on the eve of her wedding, a time when she could not seek counsel without the trauma, expense, and embarrassment of postponing the wedding. The master found this claim not credible. The courts below affirmed that finding, upon an ample evidentiary basis. Appellee testified that, although the final version of the agreement was indeed presented to appellant on the eve of the wedding, he had engaged in several discussions with appellant regarding the contents of the agreement during the six month period preceding that date.... Yet another witness confirmed that, during the months preceding the wedding, appellant participated in several discussions of prenuptial agreements. And the legal counsel who prepared the agreement for appellee testified that ... he was present when the agreement was signed and that appellant expressed absolutely no reluctance about signing. It should be noted, too, that during the months when the agreement was being discussed appellant had more than sufficient time to consult with independent legal counsel if she had so desired.... Under these circumstances, there was plainly no error in finding that appellant failed to prove duress.

Order affirmed.

■ PAPADAKOS, J., concurring. ... I cannot join the opinion authored by Mr. Justice Flaherty, because, it must be clear to all readers, it contains a number of unnecessary and unwarranted declarations regarding the "equality" of women. Mr. Justice Flaherty believes that, with the hard-fought victory of the Equal Rights Amendment in Pennsylvania, all vestiges of inequality between the sexes have been erased and women are now treated equally under the law. I fear my colleague does not live in the real world. If I did not know him better I would think that his statements smack of male chauvinism, an attitude that "you women asked for it, now live with it." If you want to know about equality of women, just ask them about comparable wages for comparable work. Just ask them about sexual harassment in the workplace. Just ask them about the sexual discrimination in the Executive Suites of big business. And the list of discrimination based on sex goes on and on.

I view prenuptial agreements as being in the nature of contracts of adhesion with one party generally having greater authority than the other who deals in a subservient role. I believe the law protects the subservient party, regardless of that party's sex, to insure equal protection and treatment under the law.

The present case does not involve the broader issues to which the gratuitous declarations in question are addressed, and it is injudicious to offer declarations in a case which does not involve those issues. Especially when those declarations are inconsistent with reality.

■ McDERMOTT, J., dissenting. ... Were a contract of marriage, the most intimate relationship between two people, not the surrender of freedom, an offering of self in love, sacrifice, hope for better or for worse, the begetting of children and the offer of effort, labor, precious time and care for the safety and prosperity of their union, then the majority would find me among them.

At the time of dissolution of the marriage, a spouse should be able to avoid the operation of a pre-nuptial agreement upon clear and convincing proof that, despite the existence of full and fair disclosure at the time of the execution of the agreement, the agreement is nevertheless so inequitable and unfair that it should not be enforced in a court of this state. Although the spouse attempting to avoid the operation of the agreement will admittedly have a difficult burden given the standard of proof, and the fact of full and fair disclosure, we must not close our courts to relief where to enforce an agreement will result in unfairness and inequity. The majority holds to the view, without waiver, that parties, having contracted with full and fair disclosure, should be made to suffer the consequences of their bargains. In so holding, the majority has given no weight to the other side of the scales: the state's paramount interest in the preservation of marriage and the family relationship, and the protection of parties to a marriage who may be rendered wards of the state, unable to provide for their own reasonable needs. Our sister states have found such treatment too short a shrift for so fundamental a unit of society.

NOTE

Questions. What competing public policies are invoked by Justices Flaherty, Papadakos, and McDermott?

In the Matter of BABY M

Supreme Court of New Jersey, 1988.
537 A.2d 1227.

■ WILENTZ, C.J. [William Stern and Mary Beth Whitehead entered into a written agreement that, in exchange for $10,000, Whitehead would be inseminated with Stern's sperm, give any resulting baby to Stern, and terminate her own parental rights. In March, 1986, Whitehead delivered a baby girl. When she refused to turn over the baby permanently, Stern sought specific enforcement of the contract. (Stern also obtained an order awarding him custody of the baby until the case was decided.)

Following a lengthy trial, the court upheld the validity of contract, and ordered that Whitehead's parental rights be terminated. Mrs. Whitehead appealed.]

In this matter the Court is asked to determine the validity of a contract that purports to provide a new way of bringing children into a family. For a fee of $10,000, a woman agrees to be artificially inseminated with the semen of another woman's husband; she is to conceive a child, carry it to term, and after its birth surrender it to the natural father and his wife. The intent of the contract is that the child's natural mother will thereafter be forever separated from her child. The wife is to adopt the child, and she and the natural father are to be regarded as its parents for all purposes. The contract providing for this is called a "surrogacy contract," the natural mother inappropriately called the "surrogate mother."

We invalidate the surrogacy contract because it conflicts with the law and public policy of this State. While we recognize the depth of the yearning of infertile couples to have their own children, we find the payment of money to a "surrogate" mother illegal, perhaps criminal, and potentially degrading to women. Although in this case we grant custody to the natural father, the evidence having clearly proved such custody to be in the best interests of the infant, we void both the termination of the surrogate mother's parental rights and the adoption of the child by the wife/stepparent. We thus restore the "surrogate" as the mother of the child. We remand the issue of the natural mother's visitation rights to the trial court, since that issue was not reached below and the record before us is not sufficient to permit us to decide it *de novo*.

We find no offense to our present laws where a woman voluntarily and without payment agrees to act as a "surrogate" mother, provided that she is not subject to a binding agreement to surrender her child. Moreover, our holding today does not preclude the Legislature from altering the current statutory scheme, within constitutional limits, so as to permit surrogacy contracts. Under current law, however, the surrogacy agreement before us is illegal and invalid. . . .

II.

INVALIDITY AND UNENFORCEABILITY OF SURROGACY CONTRACT

We have concluded that this surrogacy contract is invalid. Our conclusion has two bases: direct conflict with existing statutes and conflict with the public policies of this State, as expressed in its statutory and decisional law.

One of the surrogacy contract's basic purposes, to achieve the adoption of a child through private placement, though permitted in New Jersey "is very much disfavored." *Sees v. Baber*, 377 A.2d 628 (1977). Its use of money for this purpose—and we have no doubt whatsoever that the money is being paid to obtain an adoption and not, as the Sterns argue, for the personal services of Mary Beth Whitehead—is illegal and perhaps criminal. *N.J.S.A.* 9:3–54. In addition to the inducement of money, there is the coercion of contract: the natural mother's irrevocable agreement, prior to birth, even prior to conception, to surrender the child to the adoptive couple. Such an agreement is totally unenforceable in private placement adoption. *Sees,* 377 A.2d 628. Even where the adoption is through an approved agency, the formal agreement to surrender occurs only *after* birth (as we read *N.J.S.A.* 9:2–16 and –17, and similar statutes), and then, by regulation, only after the birth mother has been offered counseling. *N.J.A.C.* 10:121A–5.4(c). Integral to these invalid provisions of the surrogacy contract is the related agreement, equally invalid, on the part of the natural mother to cooperate with, and not to contest, proceedings to terminate her parental rights, as well as her contractual concession, in aid of the adoption, that the child's best interests would be served by awarding custody to the natural father and his wife-all of this before she has even conceived, and, in some cases, before she has the slightest idea of what the natural father and adoptive mother are like.

The foregoing provisions not only directly conflict with New Jersey statutes, but also offend long-established State policies. These critical terms, which are at the heart of the contract, are invalid and unenforceable; the conclusion therefore follows, without more, that the entire contract is unenforceable.

A. Conflict with Statutory Provisions

The surrogacy contract conflicts with: (1) laws prohibiting the use of money in connection with adoptions; (2) laws requiring proof of parental unfitness or abandonment before termination of parental rights is ordered or an adoption is granted; and (3) laws that make surrender of custody and consent to adoption revocable in private placement adoptions.

(1) Our law prohibits paying or accepting money in connection with any placement of a child for adoption. *N.J.S.A.* 9:3–54a. Violation is a high misdemeanor. Excepted are fees of an approved agency (which must be a non-profit entity), and certain expenses in connection with childbirth. *N.J.S.A.* 9:3–54b.[1]

Considerable care was taken in this case to structure the surrogacy arrangement so as not to violate this prohibition.... Nevertheless, it seems clear that the money was paid and accepted in connection with an adoption....

The prohibition of our statute is strong. Violation constitutes a high misdemeanor ... carrying a penalty of three to five years imprisonment. *N.J.S.A.* 2C:43–6a(3). The evils inherent in baby-bartering are loathsome for a myriad of reasons. The child is sold without regard for whether the purchasers will be suitable parents. N. Baker, *Baby Selling: The Scandal of Black Market Adoption* 7 (1978). The natural mother does not receive the benefit of counseling and guidance to assist her in making a decision that may affect her for a lifetime. In fact, the monetary incentive to sell her child may, depending on her financial circumstances, make her decision less voluntary. *Id.* at 44....

The provision in the surrogacy contract, agreed to before conception, requiring the natural mother to surrender custody of the child without any

---

1. *N.J.S.A.* 9:3–54 reads as follows:

a. No person, firm, partnership, corporation, association or agency shall make, offer to make or assist or participate in any placement for adoption and in connection therewith

(1) Pay, give or agree to give any money or any valuable consideration, or assume or discharge any financial obligation; or

(2) Take, receive, accept or agree to accept any money or any valuable consideration.

b. The prohibition of subsection a. shall not apply to the fees or services of any approved agency in connection with a placement for adoption, nor shall such prohibition apply to the payment or reimbursement of medical, hospital or other similar expenses incurred in connection with the birth or any illness of the child, or to the acceptance of such reimbursement by a parent of the child.

c. Any person, firm, partnership, corporation, association or agency violating this section shall be guilty of a high misdemeanor.

right of revocation is one more indication of the essential nature of this transaction: the creation of a contractual system of termination and adoption designed to circumvent our statutes.

B. Public Policy Considerations

The surrogacy contract's invalidity, resulting from its direct conflict with the above statutory provisions, is further underlined when its goals and means are measured against New Jersey's public policy. The contract's basic premise, that the natural parents can decide in advance of birth which one is to have custody of the child, bears no relationship to the settled law that the child's best interests shall determine custody....

Under the contract, the natural mother is irrevocably committed before she knows the strength of her bond with her child. She never makes a totally voluntary, informed decision, for quite clearly any decision prior to the baby's birth is, in the most important sense, uninformed, and any decision after that, compelled by a pre-existing contractual commitment, the threat of a lawsuit, and the inducement of a $10,000 payment, is less than totally voluntary. Her interests are of little concern to those who controlled this transaction....

Worst of all, however, is the contract's total disregard of the best interests of the child. There is not the slightest suggestion that any inquiry will be made at any time to determine the fitness of the Sterns as custodial parents, of Mrs. Stern as an adoptive parent, their superiority to Mrs. Whitehead, or the effect on the child of not living with her natural mother.

This is the sale of a child, or, at the very least, the sale of a mother's right to her child, the only mitigating factor being that one of the purchasers is the father. Almost every evil that prompted the prohibition on the payment of money in connection with adoptions exists here....

First, and perhaps most important, all parties concede that it is unlikely that surrogacy will survive without money. Despite the alleged selfless motivation of surrogate mothers, if there is no payment, there will be no surrogates, or very few. That conclusion contrasts with adoption; for obvious reasons, there remains a steady supply, albeit insufficient, despite the prohibitions against payment. The adoption itself, relieving the natural mother of the financial burden of supporting an infant, is in some sense the equivalent of payment.

Second, the use of money in adoptions does not *produce* the problem-conception occurs, and usually the birth itself, before illicit funds are offered. With surrogacy, the "problem," if one views it as such, consisting of the purchase of a woman's procreative capacity, at the risk of her life, is caused by and originates with the offer of money.

Third, with the law prohibiting the use of money in connection with adoptions, the built-in financial pressure of the unwanted pregnancy and the consequent support obligation do not lead the mother to the highest paying, ill-suited, adoptive parents. She is just as well-off surrendering the child to an approved agency. In surrogacy, the highest bidders will presumably become the adoptive parents regardless of suitability, so long as payment of money is permitted.

Fourth, the mother's consent to surrender her child in adoptions is revocable, even after surrender of the child, unless it be to an approved agency, where by regulation there are protections against an ill-advised surrender. In surrogacy, consent occurs so early that no amount of advice would satisfy the potential mother's need, yet the consent is irrevocable. . . .

In the scheme contemplated by the surrogacy contract in this case, a middle man, propelled by profit, promotes the sale. Whatever idealism may have motivated any of the participants, the profit motive predominates, permeates, and ultimately governs the transaction. The demand for children is great and the supply small. The availability of contraception, abortion, and the greater willingness of single mothers to bring up their children has led to a shortage of babies offered for adoption. [citations omitted] The situation is ripe for the entry of the middleman who will bring some equilibrium into the market by increasing the supply through the use of money. . . .

The point is made that Mrs. Whitehead *agreed* to the surrogacy arrangement, supposedly fully understanding the consequences. Putting aside the issue of how compelling her need for money may have been, and how significant her understanding of the consequences, we suggest that her consent is irrelevant. There are, in a civilized society, some things that money cannot buy. In America, we decided long ago that merely because conduct purchased by money was "voluntary" did not mean that it was good or beyond regulation and prohibition. *West Coast Hotel Co. v. Parrish*, 300 *U.S.* 379 (1937). Employers can no longer buy labor at the lowest price they can bargain for, even though that labor is "voluntary," 29 *U.S.C.* § 206 (1982), . . . or purchase the agreement of workers to subject themselves to unsafe or unhealthful working conditions, 29 *U.S.C.* §§ 651 to 678. (Occupational Safety and Health Act of 1970). There are, in short, values that society deems more important than granting to wealth whatever it can buy, be it labor, love, or life. Whether this principle recommends prohibition of surrogacy, which presumably sometimes results in great satisfaction to all of the parties, is not for us to say. We note here only that, under existing law, the fact that Mrs. Whitehead "agreed" to the arrangement is not dispositive. . . .

The surrogacy contract is based on, principles that are directly contrary to the objectives of our laws. It guarantees the separation of a child from its mother; it looks to adoption regardless of suitability; it totally ignores the child; it takes the child from the mother regardless of her wishes and her maternal fitness; and it does all of this, it accomplishes all of its goals, through the use of money.

Beyond that is the potential degradation of some women that may result from this arrangement. In many cases, of course, surrogacy may bring satisfaction, not only to the infertile couple, but to the surrogate mother herself. The fact, however, that many women may not perceive surrogacy negatively but rather see it as an opportunity does not diminish its potential for devastation to other women.

In sum, the harmful consequences of this surrogacy arrangement appear to us all too palpable. In New Jersey the surrogate mother's agreement to sell her child is void.[2] Its irrevocability infects the entire contract, as does the money that purports to buy it....

CONCLUSION

This case affords some insight into a new reproductive arrangement: the artificial insemination of a surrogate mother. The unfortunate events that have unfolded illustrate that its unregulated use can bring suffering to all involved. Potential victims include the surrogate mother and her family, the natural father and his wife, and most importantly, the child. Although surrogacy has apparently provided positive results for some infertile couples, it can also, as this case demonstrates, cause suffering to participants, here essentially innocent and well-intended.

We have found that our present laws do not permit the surrogacy contract used in this case. Nowhere, however, do we find any legal prohibition against surrogacy when the surrogate mother volunteers, without any payment, to act as a surrogate and is given the right to change her mind and to assert her parental rights. Moreover, the Legislature remains free to deal with this most sensitive issue as it sees fit, subject only to constitutional constraints.

If the Legislature decides to address surrogacy, consideration of this case will highlight many of its potential harms. We do not underestimate the difficulties of legislating on this subject. In addition to the inevitable confrontation with the ethical and moral issues involved, there is the question of the wisdom and effectiveness of regulating a matter so private, yet of such public interest. Legislative consideration of surrogacy may also

---

2. Michigan courts have also found that these arrangements conflict with various aspects of their law. *See Doe v. Kelley,* 307 *N.W.*2d 438 (1981), *cert.*den., 459 *U.S.* 1183 (1983) (application of sections of Michigan Adoption Law prohibiting the exchange of money to surrogacy is constitutional)....

The Supreme Court of Kentucky has taken a somewhat different approach to surrogate arrangements. In *Surrogate Parenting Assocs. v. Commonwealth ex. rel. Armstrong,* 704 *S.W.*2d 209 (Ky.1986), the court held that the "fundamental differences" between surrogate arrangements and baby-selling placed the surrogate parenting agreement beyond the reach of Kentucky's baby-selling statute. *Id.* at 211....

Concomitant with this pro-surrogacy conclusion, however, the court held that a "surrogate" mother has the right to void the contract if she changes her mind during pregnancy or immediately after birth. *Id.* at 212-13. The court relied on statutes providing

that consent to adoption or to the termination of parental rights prior to five days after the birth of the child is invalid, and concluded that consent before conception must also be unenforceable. *Id.* at 212-13....

In contrast to the law in the United States, the law in the United Kingdom concerning surrogate parenting is fairly well-settled. Parliament passed the Surrogacy Arrangements Act, 1985, ch. 49, which made initiating or taking part in any negotiations with a view to making or arranging a surrogacy contract a criminal offense. The criminal sanction, however, does not apply to the "surrogate" mother or to the natural father, but rather applies to other persons engaged in arranging surrogacy contracts on a commercial basis.... It should be noted, however, that certain surrogacy arrangements, *i.e.,* those arranged without brokers and revocable by the natural mother, are not prohibited under current law in the United Kingdom.

provide the opportunity to begin to focus on the overall implications of the new reproductive biotechnology-*in vitro* fertilization, preservation of sperm and eggs, embryo implantation and the like. The problem is how to enjoy the benefits of the technology-especially for infertile couples-while minimizing the risk of abuse. The problem can be addressed only when society decides what its values and objectives are in this troubling, yet promising, area.

[The court remanded the case for a custody determination based on the best interests of the child].

NOTES

(1) *Questions.* What sources did the court use to inform its decision that the contract is unenforceable? What is the status of an unpaid surrogacy agreement in New Jersey after *Baby M*?

A copy of the contract between Stern and Whitehead is found in *Selections.* Do you think all of its terms would be enforceable even if the court had found no public policy violation?

In reading the decision above, when did you first get a sense of how the court might rule? Note 2, p. 85, above describes Judge Cardozo's skill in persuading us to see Lady Duff–Gordon and the transaction in a particular way. What, if any, rhetorical devices does the New Jersey court use to depict paid surrogacy as "against public policy"?

(2) *Case Comparison.* Would the court in *Simeone* enforce Whitehead's promise to Stern? Should women be permitted to consent to surrogacy agreements? If so, should their consent be subject to any conditions?

(3) *Middlemen and Money.* The importance of middlemen, or intermediaries, in facilitating transactions was discussed in Note 2, p. 463. In *Baby M,* the court took a less laudatory view, characterizing the middleman as "propelled by profit" to "promot[e] the sale." Is that not the very function middlemen serve? Is the problem in *Baby M* that profit was diverted from Whitehead to the middleman? Or was the middleman chastised for performing the search function too well and bringing parties together in a market for reproductive services that itself offends public policy in New Jersey?

Since *Baby M,* a number of surrogate mothers have opened their own surrogacy agencies, becoming their own brokers. See Carol Sanger, Developing Markets in Babymaking: In the Matter of Baby M, 30 Harvard J. Law & Gender 67 (2007). See also, Deborah Spar, *The Baby Business: How Money, Science, and Politics Drive the Commerce of Conception* (2006). Note that brokering surrogacy in the United Kingdom, fn. 2 above, is a criminal act. What effect is this likely to have on a market for surrogacy? Might commercial surrogacy disappear?

(4) *Markets and Legal Regimes.* In *Baby M.,* the court noted that the state legislature remained free to deal with surrogacy ("this troubling yet promising area") "as it sees fit." A number of legislatures have done just that. See Va. Code Ann. §§ 20–156 to 20–165 (Michie 2000) (Assisted Conception).

What is the relation between the background legal regime and markets? Certainly law provides a system of property rights against which exchanges take place: Parties want to know with certainty what is theirs to sell and what interests they acquire when they buy something. But as Professor Willard Hurst wrote in his study of the lumber industry in nineteenth-century Wisconsin, "it was the law of *contract* which supplied the assurances and the procedures and the tools necessary for the immediate operation and steadily expanding energy of the [lumber industry].... For the timber industry as for other business, contract law provided a framework of reasonably assured expectations within which men might plan and venture. The availability of the forms and procedures of contract thus helped the expansion of the market." *Law and Economic Growth: The Legal History of the Lumber Industry in Wisconsin 1836–1915*, 285 *et. seq.* (1964) (emphasis added).

"Reasonably assured expectations" may also be at stake in family agreements. As the court noted in *Simeone*, p. 571 above, parties to prenuptial agreements might "not have entered such agreements, and, indeed, might not have entered their marriages, if they did not expect their agreements to be strictly enforced." The certainty of enforcement may be particularly important in developing markets, such as those for reproductive parts and services, where there is significant emotional investment in the transaction, and where "lost opportunities" may be significant. For example, in California, surrogacy contracts are enforceable as a matter of common law, see Johnson v. Calvert, 851 P.2d 776 (Cal.1993). Surrogacy organizations commonly emphasize this point to would-be clients: "Infertile couples around the world have found California to be a favorable legal forum.... Prospective parents, surrogates, and egg donors can be reasonably certain that their intentions, as expressed by their agreement, will be upheld in California." http://www.surrogacy.com/Articles/news_view.asp?ID=99.

CHAPTER 7

REMEDIES FOR BREACH

The remedy for breach of contract is presumptively compensatory, or *substitutional* relief, in the form of a judgment awarding money damages to be paid to the aggrieved promisee, rather than *specific* relief, in the form of a court order directing the promisor to perform its promise. The following excerpt gives some historical background for this presumption.

"The common law courts did not generally grant specific relief for breach of contract. The usual form of relief at common law was substitutional, and the typical judgment declared that the plaintiff recover from the defendant a sum of money. . . . If the sum was not paid, a writ of execution was issued, empowering the sheriff to seize and sell so much of the defendant's property as was required to pay the plaintiff. . . .

"Promises were enforced in equity in a very different way. . . . Under the influence of canon law—for the early chancellors were usually clerics—decrees in equity came to take the form of the chancellor's personal command to the defendant to do or not to do something. The defendant that disobeyed could be punished not only for criminal contempt, at the instance of the court, but also for civil contempt, at the instance of the plaintiff. This put into the plaintiff's hands the extreme sanction of imprisonment, which might be supplemented by fines payable to the plaintiff and by sequestration of the defendant's goods. So it was said that equity acted *in personam,* against the person of the defendant, while the law acted *in rem,* against the defendant's property. But it did not follow that the chancellor stood ready to order every defaulting promisor to perform its promise. Equitable relief was confined to special cases by both historical and practical limitations.

"The most important historical limitation grew out of the circumstance that the chancellor had originally granted equitable relief in order to supply the deficiencies of the common law. Equitable remedies were therefore readily characterized as 'extraordinary.' When, during the long jurisdictional struggle between the two systems of courts, some means of accommodation was needed, an adequacy test was developed to prevent the chancellor from encroaching on the powers of the common law judges. Equity would stay its hand if the remedy of an award of damages at law was 'adequate.' To this test was added the gloss that damages were ordinarily adequate—a gloss encouraged by the philosophy of free enterprise with its confidence that a market economy ought to enable the injured party to arrange a substitute transaction. . . . So English courts came to regard money damages as the norm and specific relief as the deviation. Only for land, which English courts regarded with particular esteem, was a general exception made, on the ground that each parcel of land was 'unique' so money damages were inadequate. This strong preference of English courts for substitutional relief stands in sharp contrast to the preference of civil law systems, those derived from the Roman law, for specific relief.

"A second historical limitation, or group of limitations, is based on the concept that equitable relief is discretionary. Since the chancellor was to act according to 'conscience' (which prompted the notorious charge that his conscience might vary with the length of his foot), he might withhold relief if considerations of fairness or morality dictated. Gradually these equitable restrictions became more precise and hardened into rules. Some of the most renowned are embodied in equity's colorful maxims: 'one who seeks equity must do equity'; 'one who comes into equity must come with clean hands'; and 'equity aids the vigilant.' One of the most troublesome of these rules was the now discredited 'mutuality of remedy' rule, under which the injured party's right to specific relief depended on whether it would have been available to the other party, had the breach been on the other side. . . .

"Thus it came to be that, although the injured party can always claim damages for breach of contract, that party's right to specific relief as an alternative is much more limited. The historical development of parallel systems of law and equity may afford an adequate explanation for the reluctance of our courts to grant specific relief more widely, but it is scant justification for it. A more rational basis can today be found in the severity of the sanctions available for enforcement of equitable orders. Nevertheless, the modern trend is clearly in favor of the extension of specific relief at the expense of the traditional primacy of damages." See 3 *Farnsworth on Contracts* § 12.4 (2d ed. 1998).

We begin our discussion of modern remedies with specific relief. The initial case, *Campbell Soup*, was first encountered on p. 494 in the materials on unconscionability. The excerpt of the opinion below addresses Campbell's demand for specific performance of a contract for carrots from Wentz.

SECTION 1. SPECIFIC RELIEF

Campbell Soup Co. v. Wentz

United States Court of Appeals, Third Circuit, 1948.
172 F.2d 80.

■ GOODRICH, CIRCUIT JUDGE.[a] These are appeals from judgments of the District Court denying equitable relief to the buyer under a contract for the sale of carrots. The defendants in No. 9648 are the contract sellers. The

---

a. Herbert F. Goodrich (1889–1962) taught law for twenty-five years at Iowa, Michigan and Pennsylvania, where he also served as dean. Beginning in 1940 he served as judge on the United States Court of Appeals for the Third Circuit, and beginning in 1947 he served as director of the American Law Institute. His best-known book is a text on the conflict of laws.

defendant in No. 9649 is the second purchaser of part of the carrots which are the subject matter of the contract.

The transactions which raise the issues may be briefly summarized. On June 21, 1947, Campbell Soup Company (Campbell), a New Jersey corporation, entered into a written contract with George B. Wentz and Harry T. Wentz, who are Pennsylvania farmers, for delivery by the Wentzes to Campbell of all the Chantenay red cored carrots to be grown on fifteen acres of the Wentz farm during the 1947 season.

Where the contract was entered into does not appear. The contract provides, however, for delivery of the carrots at the Campbell plant in Camden, New Jersey. The prices specified in the contract ranged from $23 to $30 per ton according to the time of delivery. The contract price for January, 1948 was $30 a ton.

The Wentzes harvested approximately 100 tons of carrots from the fifteen acres covered by the contract. Early in January, 1948, they told a Campbell representative that they would not deliver their carrots at the contract price. The market price at that time was at least $90 per ton, and Chantenay red cored carrots were virtually unobtainable. The Wentzes then sold approximately 62 tons of their carrots to the defendant Lojeski, a neighboring farmer. Lojeski resold about 58 tons on the open market, approximately half to Campbell and the balance to other purchasers.

On January 9, 1948, Campbell, suspecting that Lojeski was selling it "contract carrots," refused to purchase any more, and instituted these suits against the Wentz brothers and Lojeski to enjoin further sale of the contract carrots to others, and to compel specific performance of the contract. The trial court denied equitable relief. We agree with the result reached, but on a different ground from that relied upon by the District Court.

[The court said that the form of relief was for it to decide, as a federal court. Yet it noted that the federal rule on the point did not appear to differ from that of either state whose law might be applied—New Jersey or Pennsylvania.] A party may have specific performance of a contract for the sale of chattels if the legal remedy is inadequate. Inadequacy of the legal remedy is necessarily a matter to be determined by an examination of the facts in each particular instance.

We think that on the question of adequacy of the legal remedy the case is one appropriate for specific performance. It was expressly found that at the time of the trial it was "virtually impossible to obtain Chantenay carrots in the open market." This Chantenay carrot is one which the plaintiff uses in large quantities, furnishing the seed to the growers with whom it makes contracts. It was not claimed that in nutritive value it is any better than other types of carrots. Its blunt shape makes it easier to handle in processing. And its color and texture differ from other varieties. The color is brighter than other carrots. The trial court found that the plaintiff failed to establish what proportion of its carrots is used for the production of soup stock and what proportion is used as identifiable physical ingredients in its soups. We do not think lack of proof on that point is material. It did appear that the plaintiff uses carrots in fifteen of its twenty-one soups. It also appeared that it uses these Chantenay carrots diced in some of them and that the appearance is uniform. The preservation of uniformity in appearance in a food article marketed throughout the country and sold under the manufacturer's name is a matter of considerable commercial significance and one which is properly considered in determining whether a substitute ingredient is just as good as the original.

The trial court concluded that the plaintiff had failed to establish that the carrots, "judged by objective standards," are unique goods. This we think is not a pure fact conclusion like a finding that Chantenay carrots are of uniform color. It is either a conclusion of law or of mixed fact and law and we are bound to exercise our independent judgment upon it. That the test for specific performance is not necessarily "objective" is shown by the many cases in which equity has given it to enforce contracts for articles— family heirlooms and the like—the value of which was personal to the plaintiff.

Judged by the general standards applicable to determining the adequacy of the legal remedy we think that on this point the case is a proper one for equitable relief. There is considerable authority, old and new, showing liberality in the granting of an equitable remedy. We see no reason why a court should be reluctant to grant specific relief when it can be given without supervision of the court or other time-consuming processes against one who has deliberately broken his agreement. Here the goods of the special type contracted for were unavailable on the open market, the plaintiff had contracted for them long ahead in anticipation of its needs, and had built up a general reputation for its products as part of which reputation uniform appearance was important. We think if this were all that was involved in the case specific performance should have been granted....

The judgments will be affirmed.

NOTES

(1) *Inadequacy of Money Damages.* Why was a money damage award an inadequate remedy for Campbell? Campbell brought the action for specific performance after suspecting that it was buying from Lojeski "contract carrots" (that is, those very carrots that Wentz agreed to sell to Campbell) at an inflated price. But if it was getting the specific carrots for which it contracted, albeit at an inflated price, why wouldn't a monetary award equivalent to the excess of what was paid by Campbell suffice?

(2) *Incommensurability and Uncertainty.* The inadequacy of money damages is sometimes grounded in the belief that money offers no substitute for the promised performance, as when breach leads to the deprivation of a loved one's companionship or the loss of a firm's goodwill. Claimants also sometimes speak of money as being incommensurable with a specified performance, but more often the issue of inadequacy turns on uncertainty. When the performance would provide a "peculiar and unique value," money damages are often viewed as too speculative and therefore not compensatory. Again, Campbell's damages do not seem to have been beyond measure by reason of incommensurability or uncertainty. Its loss appears to have been simply the extra amount it had to pay for the very carrots for which it

contracted. Invoices and the contract could establish this difference with near certainty.

Professor Victor Goldberg has suggested that the uncertainty in the case was not the kind that relates to calculation of damages. Rather, the uncertainty revolved around Campbell not knowing in fact whether it was buying contract carrots or other carrots. Suspecting is not the same as knowing. Because it is difficult for buyers like Campbell to know whether Wentz and other growers report their output truthfully, Campbell may get fewer carrots or carrots of a lower quality than it contracted for with Wentz. Goldberg, *Framing Contract Law*, 217 (2006). How does injunctive relief—an order of specific performance—address this concern?

(3) *Cotton Crisis*. In 1973 there was a spectacular rise in the price of cotton on the American market. The causes were said to include large shipments to China, high water and flood conditions in the cotton belt, late plantings forced by heavy rains, and the devaluation of the dollar. In the early months of the year, before planting, a cotton farmer will make a "forward" sale contract for delivery to the buyer of all cotton to be raised and harvested on a specified tract at a fixed price per pound, without guarantee of quantity or quality. The farmer can then use this contract to finance the raising of the crop. Early in 1973, cotton farmers made such contracts to sell at a price roughly equal to the price on the market at that time, some 30 cents a pound. By the time the cotton had been raised and was ready for delivery, however, the market price had risen to about 80 cents a pound. The farmers felt, as one judge later put it, "sick as an old hound dog who ate a rotten skunk." Many refused to perform the forward contracts that they had made at the lower price, and scores of lawsuits resulted throughout the cotton belt.[a]

If buyers of cotton asked you what remedies they have against recalcitrant farmers under enforceable contracts like that described at p. 1 above, what advice would you give about specific performance? Since buying substitute cotton on a risen market would simply cost more money, would not an award of damages be "adequate to protect [their] expectation interest"? Cases denying specific performance of cotton contracts include Weathersby v. Gore, 556 F.2d 1247 (5th Cir.1977), and Duval & Co. v. Malcom, 214 S.E.2d 356 (Ga.1975).

But see Mitchell–Huntley Cotton Co., Inc. v. Waldrep, 377 F.Supp. 1215, 1219 (N.D.Ala.1974), where the court granted a declaratory judgment that a buyer who was "in the business of buying cotton from producers and others and selling and delivering same to textile mills and others" was entitled to specific performance of its contracts with farmers and enjoined the farmers from violating them. "The cotton in question is unique and irreplaceable because of the scarcity of cotton.... The majority of all cotton to be produced in the United States in the 1973 crop year has been sold under contracts similar to those here at issue. There is no substantial carry-over of merchantable grades and classes of cotton from prior years in storage in the United States and there will be very little cotton available for purchase in the open market through the 1973 cotton season." Does it appear that the buyer's damage remedy was inadequate if, as the court found, "a drastic shortage of cotton developed and the price for same on the open market had increased [from an original contract price of $.30 per pound] to an amount in excess of $.80 per pound"?

(4) *Question*. The contract in *Campbell* was governed by the Uniform Sales Act, the predecessor of Article 2 of the UCC. What are the standards for specific performance in Article 2? See UCC § 2–716.

---

a. This summary is taken largely from one of the cotton cases, Bolin Farms v. American Cotton Shippers Ass'n, 370 F.Supp. 1353 (W.D.La.1974).

Klein v. PepsiCo, Inc.

United States Court of Appeals, Fourth Circuit, 1988.
845 F.2d 76.

■ ERVIN, CIRCUIT JUDGE: This case turns on whether a contract was formed between Universal Jet Sales, Inc. ("UJS") and PepsiCo, Inc., ("PepsiCo") for the sale of a Gulfstream G–II corporate jet to UJS for resale to one Eugene V. Klein. If a contract was formed, the question remains whether the district court acted within his discretion by ordering specific performance of the contract. We believe the district court properly found that a contract was formed; however, we conclude that the remedy of specific performance is inappropriate. Accordingly, we affirm in part, reverse and remand in part.

I.

In March 1986, Klein began looking for a used corporate jet; specifically, he wanted a G–II. He contacted Patrick Janas, President of UJS, who provided information to Klein about several aircraft including the PepsiCo aircraft. Klein's pilot and mechanic, Mr. Sherman and Mr. Quaid, inspected the PepsiCo jet in New York. Mr. James Welsch served as the jet broker for PepsiCo.

Klein asked that the jet be flown to Arkansas for his personal inspection. On March 29, 1986, he inspected the jet. Mr. Rashid, PepsiCo Vice President for Asset Management and Corporate Service, accompanied the jet to Arkansas and met Mr. Klein. Janas also went to Arkansas. Klein gave Janas $200,000 as a deposit on the jet, and told Janas to offer $4.4 million for the aircraft.

On March 31, 1986, Janas telexed the $4.4 million offer to Welsch. The telex said the offer was subject to a factory inspection satisfactory to the purchaser, and a definitive contract. On April 1, PepsiCo counteroffered with a $4.7 million asking price. After some dickering, Welsch offered the jet for $4.6 million. Janas accepted the offer by telex on April 3. Janas then planned to sell the aircraft to Klein for $4.75 million. In Finding of Fact number 18 Judge Williams declared that a contract had been formed at this point.

Judge Williams ruled that a contract was evidenced by Janas' confirming telex which "accepted" PepsiCo's offer to sell the jet, and noted that a $100,000 down payment would be wired. The telex also asked for the proper name of the company selling the aircraft. See Finding of Fact number 22.

On April 3, Janas sent out copies of the Klein/UJS agreement and the UJS–PepsiCo agreement to the respective parties. Janas also sent a bill of sale to the escrow agent handling the deal on April 8. Mr. Rochoff, PepsiCo's corporate counsel, spoke with Janas about the standard contract sent by Janas to PepsiCo. He noted only that the delivery date should be changed.

On Monday, April 7, the aircraft was flown to Savannah, Georgia for the pre-purchase inspection. Quaid was present at the inspection for Klein.

Archie Walker, PepsiCo's chief of maintenance, was present for the seller. Walker and Quaid discussed a list of repairs to be made to the jet. Most of the problems were cured during the inspection. However, one cosmetic problem was to be corrected in New York, and there were cracks in the engine blades of the right engine.

On April 8, a boroscopic examination conducted by Aviall revealed eight to eleven cracks on the turbine blades. Walker told Rashid that the cost of repairing the blades would be between $25,000 to $28,000. Judge Williams found in Finding of Fact numbers 34 through 37 that PepsiCo, through Walker and Rashid, agreed to pay for the repair to the engine.

On April 9, the plane was returned to New York. Rashid wanted the plane grounded; however, it was sent to retrieve the stranded PepsiCo Chairman of the Board from Dulles airport that same evening. Donald Kendall, the Chairman, on April 10, called Rashid and asked that the jet be withdrawn from the market. Rashid called Welsch who effected the withdrawal. On the 11th Janas told Klein that PepsiCo refused to tender the aircraft. The deal was supposed to close on Friday, April 11.

On April 14, Klein telexed UJS demanding delivery of the aircraft. That same day, UJS telexed PepsiCo demanding delivery and expressing satisfaction with the pre-purchase inspection. On April 15, PepsiCo responded with a telex to UJS saying that it refused to negotiate further because discussions had not reached the point of agreement; in particular, Klein was not prepared to go forward with the deal.

Judge Williams, in a lengthy opinion, made numerous findings of fact. Such findings are reviewed only for clear error. Davis v. Food Lion, 792 F.2d 1274, 1277 (4th Cir.1986). If the findings are based on determinations of witness credibility, are consistent, and are corroborated by extrinsic evidence, they are virtually never clearly erroneous. Brown v. Baltimore and Ohio R. Co., 805 F.2d 1133, 1140 (4th Cir.1986).

Judge Williams' decision to grant specific performance is reviewed only for an abuse of discretion. Haythe v. May, 223 Va. 359, 288 S.E.2d 487 (1982); Horner v. Bourland, 724 F.2d 1142, 1144–45 (5th Cir.1984). Keeping these standards in mind, we now turn to the first issue, whether the district court clearly erred in finding that a contract arose between PepsiCo and UJS.

II.

PepsiCo argues forcefully that no contract was formed between it and UJS. The soft drink dealer argues first that the parties did not intend to be bound until a complete integration was written in final form. Until that definitive written contract existed, PepsiCo maintains that no contract existed. The company argues that the March 31 and April 1 telexes explicitly stated that no contract would exist until a written agreement was executed. Because no written agreement had been executed (PepsiCo had not signed the sales agreement sent by Janas to PepsiCo) the company argues that it had the right to withdraw from the negotiations. PepsiCo cites Reprosystem, B.V. v. SCM Corp., 727 F.2d 257, 262 (2d Cir.1984), cert.

denied, 469 U.S. 828 (1984) and Skycom Corp. v. Telstar Corp., 813 F.2d 810, 815–16 (7th Cir.1987) for the general proposition that either party can withdraw from negotiations for any reason.

Upon reviewing the facts, Judge Williams ruled that a contract was formed between the parties. He explains:

> A contract was formed between UJS and PepsiCo for the sale of the GII aircraft, Serial No. 170, for $4.6 million. The contract formation is based upon (1) UJS's April 3rd confirming telex; (2) the conduct of the parties, e.g., (a) PepsiCo's failure to communicate any objection to the terms of the April 3rd telex confirming the agreement reached between Welsch and Janas; (b) PepsiCo's directive to UJS to wire transfer a One Hundred Thousand Dollar ($100,000.00) down payment, which money was received by PepsiCo; (c) PepsiCo's communication with UJS that the Sales Agreement, which served to memorialize the contract, appeared "fine"; (d) PepsiCo's execution of the Bill of Sale for the aircraft and its sending of the Bill of Sale to the escrow agent, as called for by Janas and in the Sales Agreement; (e) PepsiCo's sending the aircraft to Savannah, Georgia, for a prepurchase inspection as called for in both the April 3rd confirming telex and the Sales Agreement; and (f) admissions of PepsiCo, through Rashid, that UJS's offer to purchase the airplane was accepted.

Conclusion of Law number 6. Finally, Judge Williams expressly held that the intent to memorialize the contract in writing was not necessarily a condition to the existence of the contract itself. (Conclusion of Law number 8).

PepsiCo offers no reason as to why Judge Williams' findings on this issue are clearly erroneous. They merely disagree with his characterizations of the facts. This court may disagree with his characterization too, but that does not amount to a firm and definite conviction that a mistake has been committed. Anderson v. City of Bessemer City, N.C., 470 U.S. 564 (1985).

PepsiCo argues secondly, that no contract was formed because the condition of inspection satisfactory to the buyer had not been met. PepsiCo urges strongly that neither UJS nor Klein were willing to accept the aircraft "as is," so the condition was unsatisfied. Judge Williams ruled that when PepsiCo agreed to make the repairs, the condition was satisfied. Furthermore, the court below ruled that the condition was excused by PepsiCo's refusal to tender the aircraft so that the buyer could express his dissatisfaction. [Conditions are discussed in Chapter 8 below.]

The district court's first ruling, that the condition was satisfied by PepsiCo's offers to pay for the repairs, resolves this issue. Judge Williams ruled that based on the conversations between Walker and Rashid, the seller had agreed to make the necessary repairs to market the plane. See Finding of Fact 34–37 at JA 89–90. Again, PepsiCo offers no suggestion that Judge Williams committed any error, much less clear error. Rather, PepsiCo urges its version of the facts on this court. Without more, the company loses.

Ultimately, then, a contract exists between PepsiCo and UJS for the sale of one G–II Gulfstream aircraft. Because PepsiCo failed to deliver the aircraft, the district court ordered relief in the form of specific performance. We now consider the appropriateness of the relief ordered.

III.

The Virginia Code § 8.2–716 [UCC § 2–716, as enacted in Virginia] permits a jilted buyer of goods to seek specific performance of the contract if the goods sought are unique, or in other proper circumstances. Judge Williams ruled that: 1) the G–II aircraft involved in this case is unique and 2) Klein's inability to cover with a comparable aircraft is strong evidence of "other proper circumstances." Conclusions of Law No. 31 and No. 32. These conclusions are not supported in the record.

We note first that Virginia's adoption of the Uniform Commercial Code does not abrogate the maxim that specific performance is inappropriate where damages are recoverable and adequate. Griscom v. Childress, 183 Va. 42, 31 S.E.2d 309, 311 (1944). In this case Judge Williams repeatedly stated that money damages would make Klein whole. Klein argued that he wanted the plane to resell it for a profit. Finally, an increase in the cost of a replacement does not merit the remedy of specific performance. Hilmor Sales Co. v. Helen Neuschaefer Division of Supronics Corp., 6 U.C.C.Rep. Serv. 325 (N.Y.Sup.Ct.1969). There is no room in this case for the equitable remedy of specific performance.

Turning now to the specific rulings of the court below, Judge Williams explained that the aircraft was unique because only three comparable aircraft existed on the market. Therefore, Klein would have to go through considerable expense to find a replacement. Klein's expert testified that there were twenty-one other G–II's on the market, three of which were roughly comparable. Klein's chief pilot said that other G–II's could be purchased. Finally, we should note that UJS bought two G–II's which they offered to Klein after this deal fell through, and Klein made bids on two other G–II's after PepsiCo withdrew its aircraft from the market. Given these facts, we find it very difficult to support a ruling that the aircraft was so unique as to merit an order of specific performance.

Judge Williams ruled further that Klein's inability to cover his loss is an "other proper circumstance" favoring specific performance. Klein testi-fied himself that he didn't purchase another G–II because prices had started to rise. Because of the price increase, he decided to purchase a G–III aircraft. As noted earlier, price increases alone are no reason to order specific performance. Because money damages would clearly be adequate in this case, and because the aircraft is not unique within the meaning of the Virginia Commercial Code, we reverse the grant of specific performance and remand the case to the district court for a trial on damages.

Affirmed in Part, Reserved and Remanded in Part.

NOTES

(1) In King Aircraft Sales v. Lane, 846 P.2d 550 (Wash.App.1993), the court upheld a decree of specific performance of a contract to sell two airplanes "even

though the legal remedy of damages may have been available." The court distinguished *Klein* on the ground that prior to the adoption of the Code, Washington courts "did not always require the absence of a legal remedy" or that the goods be "absolutely 'unique.'" See also In re Bullett Jet Charter, 177 B.R. 593, 599 (Bankr.N.D.Ill.1995) (expert "testified persuasively that there was no similar aircraft like it on the market").

(2) *The Automobile Cases.* After the Second World War, a number of disappointed buyers sought specific performance of their contracts to buy scarce new automobiles from automobile dealers. Most buyers lost. A typical case is McCallister v. Patton, 215 S.W.2d 701 (Ark.1948), in which the buyer sought specific performance of a contract made on or about September 15, 1945, to buy a Ford super deluxe tudor sedan. (The war with Japan had ended on September 2, 1945.) The buyer alleged that "new Ford automobiles have been hard to obtain" and that he had been "unable to purchase an automobile at any other place or upon the open market of the description named." The Supreme Court of Arkansas held that his complaint was properly dismissed, taking "judicial notice of the fact that large numbers of cars of the type mentioned in the alleged contract have been produced since 1945, and sold through both new and used car dealers in the open market. It is neither alleged nor contended that the car ordered has any special or peculiar qualities not commonly possessed by others of the same make so as to make it practically impossible to replace it in the market."

For a rare case allowing specific performance, see Boeving v. Vandover, 218 S.W.2d 175 (Mo.App.1949), in which the dealer had attempted to impose the additional requirement of a trade-in upon the buyer. The trial court found that "if [the buyer] lost his priority with [the seller] he would be forced to place his order with some other Buick Agency and await his turn, which might take from one to two years." Might the Arkansas court have reached a different decision if additional facts had been alleged? What facts?

Would UCC § 2–716 have changed the result in the *McCallister* case? For a Code case allowing specific performance of a contract for the sale of a Corvette Pace Car, produced in a limited edition of 6,000, see Sedmak v. Charlie's Chevrolet, Inc., 622 S.W.2d 694 (Mo.App.1981).

(3) *International Rules.* The common law's preference for damages over specific performance is not found in civil law countries. This difference resulted in an important compromise in the CISG. Article 46(1), which provides that a buyer "may *require* performance by the seller of his obligations," embodies the civil law approach. But this provision is undercut by article 28, which was added at the insistence of common law countries. It provides that even if a buyer is entitled to require performance, "a court is not bound to enter judgment for specific performance unless the court would do so under its own law in respect of similar contracts of sale not governed by the Convention." The significance of article 28 in an action brought in the United States was stated in Magellan International Corp. v. Salzgitter Handel, 76 F.Supp.2d 919 (N.D.Ill.1999) at 926: "Simply put, that looks to the availability of such relief under the UCC," citing UCC § 2–716(1). What decision in *Klein* under the Convention? Can you think of any disadvantages of a rule that makes the availability of specific performance depend on where the action is brought? See generally J. Honnold, *Uniform Law for International Sales under the 1980 United Nations Convention* 218–28 (3d ed. 1999).

Compare UNIDROIT Principles art. 7.2.2: "Where a party who owes an obligation other than one to pay money does not perform, the other party may require performance unless ... the party entitled to performance may reasonably obtain performance from another source." What decision in *Klein* under the UNIDROIT Principles?

Morris v. Sparrow

Supreme Court of Arkansas, 1956.
225 Ark. 1019, 287 S.W.2d 583.

■ ROBINSON, JUSTICE. Appellee Archie Sparrow filed this suit for specific performance, seeking to compel appellant Morris to deliver possession of a certain horse, which Sparrow claims Morris agreed to give him as part consideration for work done by Sparrow. The appeal is from a decree requiring the delivery of the horse.

Morris owns a cattle ranch near Mountain View, Arkansas, and he also participates in rodeos. Sparrow is a cowboy, and is experienced in training horses; occasionally he takes part in rodeos. He lives in Florida; while at a rodeo in that state, he and Morris made an agreement that they would go to Morris' ranch in Arkansas and, later, the two would go to Canada. After arriving at the Morris ranch, they changed their plans and decided that, while Morris went to Canada, Sparrow would stay at the ranch and do the necessary work. The parties are in accord that Sparrow was to work 16 weeks for a money consideration of $400. But, Sparrow says that as an additional consideration he was to receive a brown horse called Keno, owned by Morris. However, Morris states that Sparrow was to get the horse only on condition that his work at the ranch was satisfactory, and that Sparrow failed to do a good job. Morris paid Sparrow the amount of money they agreed was due, but did not deliver the horse.

At the time Sparrow went to Morris' ranch, the horse in question was practically unbroken; but during his spare time, Sparrow trained the horse and, with a little additional training, he will be a first class roping horse.

First there is the issue of whether Sparrow can maintain, in equity, a suit to enforce, by specific performance, a contract for the delivery of personal property. Although it has been held that equity will not ordinarily enforce, by specific performance, a contract for the sale of chattels, it will do so where special and peculiar reasons exist which render it impossible for the injured party to obtain relief by way of damages in an action at law.... Certainly when one has made a roping horse out of a green, unbroken pony, such a horse would have a peculiar and unique value; if Sparrow is entitled to prevail, he has a right to the horse instead of its market value in dollars and cents.

Morris claims that the part of the agreement whereby Sparrow was to receive the horse was conditional, depending on Sparrow doing a good job, and that he did not do such a job. Both parties were in Chancery Court and the Chancellor had a better opportunity than this court to evaluate the testimony of the witnesses; we cannot say the Chancellor's finding in favor of Sparrow is against the preponderance of the evidence....

Affirmed.

SPECIFIC PERFORMANCE AND INVESTMENT

Archie Sparrow spent his spare time training Keno to make it a first class roping horse. Surely he invested his time and effort in this way based on his expectation of receiving the horse at the end of the 16 week contract period. Would he have invested as much of his time and effort if he knew that instead of getting Keno he would only get money damages in the event that Chip Morris should break the contract? The answer depends on the *measure* of money damages, the topic of the next section. However, if he was assured of getting Keno through an award of specific performance he would have every reason to invest his energies as he did.

How does the availability of various remedies for breach affect the willingness of parties to invest resources in reliance on contracts? This question has been the central focus of an extensive literature over the past thirty years.[a] The standard conclusion is that parties will not invest sufficiently unless they expect to receive the full return of those investments. For example, if Morris can breach his contract with Sparrow and pay only a pittance then Sparrow will have greatly reduced incentives to invest in the horse. But if Morris is required specifically to perform (or pay money damages that take into account the value of Sparrow's investment) then Sparrow's incentive to underinvest goes away.

But is it possible to invest *too much*? When Sparrow invests as though he will get performance with certainty he takes no account of the possibility that performance may not be forthcoming. This issue returns us to the concept of efficient breach discussed in Chapter 1. There we observed that when a breaching promisor can fully compensate the promisee, breach may be Pareto efficient: the promisee can be left no worse off and the promisor better off by the breach. A failure to account for the likelihood of efficient breach when making investment decisions can lead parties to invest too much. After all, they may not get the goods, or other performance, they had counted on. Specific performance can encourage exactly this kind of disregard of the possibility of breach, leading parties to invest as though they are certain to receive performance: either the promisor will perform or the court will order specific performance.[b]

NOTES

(1) *Bargaining Around Court Orders.* As we shall see shortly, in our discussion of the Coase Theorem at p. 604, an order of specific performance does not necessarily imply that parties will actually perform. Disputants commonly reach

---

a. See Oliver Williamson, *Markets and Hierarchies* (1975); Benjamin Klein, Robert Crawford & Armen Alchian, Vertical Integration, Appropriable Rents, and the Competitive Contracting Process, 21 J. L. & Econ. 297 (1978); Oliver Hart & John Moore, Foundations of Incomplete Contracts, 66 Rev. Econ. Stud. 115 (1999).

b. The same is true for money damages that compensate promisees fully for their investments.

private settlements, even after receiving a court order. What does this suggest about the likelihood of overinvestment given specific performance?

(2) *Canned Tomatoes.* The Curtice Brothers Company, operator of a tomato canning business, sued James Catts and others for breach of contract and sought specific performance of Catts's promise to deliver "the entire product of certain land planted with tomatoes." In granting specific performance, the court emphasized the importance of Curtice Brothers' planning and investment.

"Complainants' factory has a capacity of about one million cans of tomatoes. The season for packing lasts about six weeks. The preparations made for this six weeks of active work must be carried out in all features to enable the business to succeed. These preparations are primarily based upon the capacity of the plant. Cans and other necessary equipments, including labor, must be provided and secured in advance with reference to the capacity of the plant during the packing period.... The condition which arises from the breach of the contracts is not merely a question of the factory being compelled to pay a higher price for the product. Losses sustained in that manner could, with some degree of accuracy, be estimated. The condition which occasions the irreparable injury by reason of the breaches of the contracts is the inability to procure at any price at the time needed and of the quality needed the necessary tomatoes to insure the successful operation of the plant.... The business and its needs are extraordinary in that the maintenance of all of the conditions prearranged to secure the pack are a necessity to insure the successful operation of the plant." Curtice Bros. Co. v. Catts, 66 A. 935, 936 (N.J.Ch. 1907).

What relationship might there be, if any, between the short packing season of only six weeks and protecting the investments of the business? Recall Alaska Packers' Ass'n v. Domenico at p. 325, where the court similarly made reference to the shortness of the packing season and the firm's investments.

(3) *Personal Service Contracts and Moral Hazard.* A court will not order specific performance of a contract to provide a service that is personal in nature. One concern is the difficulty of passing judgment on the quality of performance. A second concern is the undesirability of compelling the continuance of personal relations after disputes have arisen and confidence and loyalty have been shaken (and, in some instances, of imposing what might seem like involuntary servitude).

Catts, in the case above, sought to avoid specific performance by claiming that specific performance would amount to compelling personal services. The court held that Catts "may be restrained from selling the crop to others, and, if necessary, a receiver can be appointed to harvest the crop." The difficulties courts face in monitoring performance, along with the concern that a party compelled to perform by a judicial order may not have the best incentives to perform well, create the risk that individuals will take less than ideal actions knowing that they will not be made fully accountable for their actions, so-called "moral hazard." Appointing a receiver to perform the task may help, but is not a complete solution to the moral hazard problem. Can you see why?

(4) *Negative Injunctions.* Though courts are reluctant to compel performance of contracts to provide services that are personal in nature, they are quite willing to enjoin parties from other performances in appropriate circumstances. The classic case is Lumley v. Wagner, 42 Eng. Rep. 687, 693 (Ch. 1852), which arose out of a contract in which Johanna Wagner, an opera singer from the court of Prussia, agreed to sing exclusively for Benjamin Lumley, proprietor of Her Majesty's Theatre in London, for a period of three months. When Frederick Gye, proprietor of the Royal Italian Opera in London, persuaded Wagner to break her contract and sing at his theater, Lumley obtained an injunction restraining her from doing so. On

appeal, the Lord Chancellor upheld the injunction. "It is true that I have not the means of compelling her to sing, but she has no cause of complaint if I compel her to abstain from the commission of an act which she has bound herself not to do, and thus possibly cause her to fulfil her engagement."

As indicated above, a court will not grant an injunction unless the remedy in damages would be inadequate. This requirement is met if the employee's services are unique or extraordinary, either because of special skill that the employee possesses, as in Wagner's case, or because of special knowledge that the employee has acquired of the employer's business.

Injunctions are especially common in the world of sports, where the availability of such relief is enhanced by the belief that the requirement "that the player be an athlete of exceptional talent ... is met prima facie in cases involving professional athletes." Nassau Sports v. Peters, 352 F.Supp. 870, 876 (E.D.N.Y.1972).

(5) *Clean Hands on the Playing Field.* The requirement that "one who comes into equity must come with clean hands" has come under special scrutiny in cases involving professional athletes. Thus in New York Football Giants, Inc. v. Los Angeles Chargers Football Club, Inc., 291 F.2d 471 (5th Cir.1961), it was held that the Giants, who had kept a contract with Charles Flowers secret so he could play as an amateur in the Sugar Bowl, lacked "clean hands" and could not have Flowers enjoined from playing with the Chargers. But see Houston Oilers v. Neely, 361 F.2d 36 (10th Cir.1966), in which the court said that "if the rule announced in [the *Flowers*] case was intended to apply to every instance in which a contract is entered into with a college football player before a post-season game with an understanding that it will be kept secret to permit that player to compete in the game, then we must respectfully disagree."

Laclede Gas Co. v. Amoco Oil Co.

United States Court of Appeals, Eighth Circuit, 1975.
522 F.2d 33.

■ ROSS, CIRCUIT JUDGE. The Laclede Gas Company (Laclede), a Missouri corporation, brought this diversity action alleging breach of contract against the Amoco Oil Company (Amoco), a Delaware corporation. It sought relief in the form of a mandatory injunction prohibiting the continuing breach or, in the alternative, damages. The district court held a bench trial on the issues of whether there was a valid, binding contract between the parties and whether, if there was such a contract, Amoco should be enjoined from breaching it. It then ruled that the "contract is invalid due to lack of mutuality" and denied the prayer for injunctive relief. The court made no decision regarding the requested damages. Laclede Gas Co. v. Amoco Oil Co., 385 F.Supp. 1332, 1336 (E.D.Mo.1974). This appeal followed, and we reverse the district court's judgment.

On September 21, 1970, Midwest Missouri Gas Company (now Laclede), and American Oil Company (now Amoco), the predecessors of the parties to this litigation, entered into a written agreement which was designed to provide central propane gas distribution systems to various residential developments in Jefferson County, Missouri, until such time as natural gas mains were extended into these areas. The agreement contemplated that as individual developments were planned the owners or developers would apply to Laclede for central propane gas systems. If Laclede determined that such a system was appropriate in any given development, it could request Amoco to supply the propane to that specific development. This request was made in the form of a supplemental form letter, as provided in the September 21 agreement; and if Amoco decided to supply the propane, it bound itself to do so by signing this supplemental form.

Once this supplemental form was signed the agreement placed certain duties on both Laclede and Amoco. Basically, Amoco was to "[i]nstall, own, maintain and operate ... storage and vaporization facilities and any other facilities necessary to provide [it] with the capability of delivering to [Laclede] commercial propane gas suitable ... for delivery by [Laclede] to its customers' facilities." Amoco's facilities were to be "adequate to provide a continuous supply of commercial propane gas at such times and in such volumes commensurate with [Laclede's] requirements for meeting the demands reasonably to be anticipated in each Development while this Agreement is in force." Amoco was deemed to be "the supplier," while Laclede was "the distributing utility."

For its part Laclede agreed to "[i]nstall, own, maintain and operate all distribution facilities" from a "point of delivery" which was defined to be "the outlet of [Amoco] header piping." Laclede also promised to pay Amoco "the Wood River Area Posted Price for propane plus four cents per gallon for all amounts of commercial propane gas delivered" to it under the agreement.

Since it was contemplated that the individual propane systems would eventually be converted to natural gas, one paragraph of the agreement provided that Laclede should give Amoco 30 days written notice of this event, after which the agreement would no longer be binding for the converted development.

Another paragraph gave Laclede the right to cancel the agreement. However, this right was expressed in the following language:

> This Agreement shall remain in effect for one (1) year following the first delivery of gas by [Amoco] to [Laclede] hereunder. Subject to termination as provided in Paragraph 11 hereof [dealing with conversions to natural gas], this Agreement shall automatically continue in effect for additional periods of one (1) year each unless [Laclede] shall, not less than 30 days prior to the expiration of the initial one (1) year period or any subsequent one (1) year period, give [Amoco] written notice of termination.

There was no provision under which Amoco could cancel the agreement.

For a time the parties operated satisfactorily under this agreement, and some 17 residential subdivisions were brought within it by supplemental letters. However, for various reasons, including conversion to natural gas, the number of developments under the agreement had shrunk to eight by the time of trial. These were all mobile home parks.

During the winter of 1972–73 Amoco experienced a shortage of propane and voluntarily placed all of its customers, including Laclede, on an 80% allocation basis, meaning that Laclede would receive only up to 80% of its previous requirements. Laclede objected to this and pushed Amoco to give it 100% of what the developments needed. Some conflict arose over this before the temporary shortage was alleviated.

Then, on April 3, 1973, Amoco notified Laclede that its Wood River Area Posted Price of propane had been increased by three cents per gallon. Laclede objected to this increase also and demanded a full explanation. None was forthcoming. Instead Amoco merely sent a letter dated May 14, 1973, informing Laclede that it was "terminating" the September 21, 1970, agreement effective May 31, 1973. It claimed it had the right to do this because "the Agreement lacks 'mutuality.' "[1]

The district court felt that the entire controversy turned on whether or not Laclede's right to "arbitrarily cancel the Agreement" without Amoco having a similar right rendered the contract void "for lack of mutuality" and it resolved this question in the affirmative. We disagree with this conclusion and hold that settled principles of contract law require a reversal.

I.

[The court held that Laclede's power to terminate did not make its promise illusory and that the agreement was an enforceable contract for Laclede's requirements for the subdivision. The district court, therefore, erred in holding that there was no binding contract.]

II.

Since he found that there was no binding contract, the district judge did not have to deal with the question of whether or not to grant the injunction prayed for by Laclede. He simply denied this relief because there was no contract. Laclede Gas Co. v. Amoco Oil Co., supra, 385 F.Supp. at 1336.

Generally the determination of whether or not to order specific performance of a contract lies within the sound discretion of the trial court. Landau v. St. Louis Public Service Co., 364 Mo. 1134, 273 S.W.2d 255, 259 (1954). However, this discretion is, in fact, quite limited; and it is said that when certain equitable rules have been met and the contract is fair and plain "specific performance goes as a matter of right." Miller v. Coffeen, 365 Mo. 204, 280 S.W.2d 100, 102 (1955), quoting, Berberet v. Myers, 240 Mo. 58, 77, 144 S.W. 824, 830 (1912). (Emphasis omitted.)

With this in mind we have carefully reviewed the very complete record on appeal and conclude that the trial court should grant the injunctive relief prayed. We are satisfied that this case falls within that category in which specific performance should be ordered as a matter of right....

Amoco contends that four of the requirements for specific performance have not been met. Its claims are: (1) there is no mutuality of remedy in

---

1. While Amoco sought to repudiate the agreement, it resumed supplying propane to the subdivisions on February 1, 1974, under the mandatory allocation guidelines promul- gated by the Federal Energy Administration under the Federal Mandatory Allocation Program for propane. It is agreed that this is now being done under the contract.

the contract; (2) the remedy of specific performance would be difficult for the court to administer without constant and long-continued supervision; (3) the contract is indefinite and uncertain; and (4) the remedy at law available to Laclede is adequate. The first three contentions have little or no merit and do not detain us for long.

There is simply no requirement in the law that both parties be mutually entitled to the remedy of specific performance in order that one of them be given that remedy by the court. . . .

While a court may refuse to grant specific performance where such a decree would require constant and long-continued court supervision, this is merely a discretionary rule of decision which is frequently ignored when the public interest is involved. . . .

Here the public interest in providing propane to the retail customers is manifest, while any supervision required will be far from onerous.

Section 370 of the Second Restatement of Contracts (1932) provides:

> Specific enforcement will not be decreed unless the terms of the contract are so expressed that the court can determine with reasonable certainty what is the duty of each party and the conditions under which performance is due.

We believe these criteria have been satisfied here. As discussed in part I of this opinion, as to all developments for which a supplemental agreement has been signed, Amoco is to supply all the propane which is reasonably foreseeably required, while Laclede is to purchase the required propane from Amoco and pay the contract price therefor. The parties have disagreed over what is meant by "Wood River Area Posted Price" in the agreement, but the district court can and should determine with reasonable certainty what the parties intended by this term and should mold its decree, if necessary accordingly.[2] Likewise, the fact that the agreement does not have a definite time of duration is not fatal since the evidence established that the last subdivision should be converted to natural gas in 10 to 15 years. This sets a reasonable time limit on performance and the district court can and should mold the final decree to reflect this testimony.

It is axiomatic that specific performance will not be ordered when the party claiming breach of contract has an adequate remedy at law. Jamison Coal & Coke Co. v. Goltra, 143 F.2d 889, 894 (8th Cir.), cert. denied, 323 U.S. 769 (1944). This is especially true when the contract involves personal property as distinguished from real estate.

However, in Missouri, as elsewhere, specific performance may be ordered even though personalty is involved in the "proper circumstances." Mo.Rev.Stat. § 400.2–716(1); Restatement of Contracts, supra, § 361. And a remedy at law adequate to defeat the grant of specific performance "must be as certain, prompt, complete, and efficient to attain the ends of justice as a decree of specific performance." National Marking Mach. Co. v. Triumph

---

2. The record indicates that Laclede has now accepted Amoco's interpretation and has agreed that "Wood River Area Posted Price" means Amoco's posted price for propane at its Wood River refinery.

Mfg. Co., 13 F.2d 6, 9 (8th Cir.1926). Accord, Snip v. City of Lamar, 239 Mo.App. 824, 201 S.W.2d 790, 798 (1947).

One of the leading Missouri cases allowing specific performance of a contract relating to personalty because the remedy at law was inadequate is Boeving v. Vandover, 240 Mo.App. 117, 218 S.W.2d 175, 178 (1949). In that case the plaintiff sought specific performance of a contract in which the defendant had promised to sell him an automobile. At that time (near the end of and shortly after World War II) new cars were hard to come by, and the court held that specific performance was a proper remedy since a new car "could not be obtained elsewhere except at considerable expense, trouble or loss, which cannot be estimated in advance."

We are satisfied that Laclede has brought itself within this practical approach taken by the Missouri courts. As Amoco points out, Laclede has propane immediately available to it under other contracts with other suppliers. And the evidence indicates that at the present time propane is readily available on the open market. However, this analysis ignores the fact that the contract involved in this lawsuit is for a long-term supply of propane to these subdivisions. The other two contracts under which Laclede obtains the gas will remain in force only until March 31, 1977, and April 1, 1981, respectively; and there is no assurance that Laclede will be able to receive any propane under them after that time. Also it is unclear as to whether or not Laclede can use the propane obtained under these contracts to supply the Jefferson County subdivisions, since they were originally entered into to provide Laclede with propane with which to "shave" its natural gas supply during peak demand periods.[3] Additionally, there was uncontradicted expert testimony that Laclede probably could not find another supplier of propane willing to enter into a long-term contract such as the Amoco agreement, given the uncertain future of worldwide energy supplies. And, even if Laclede could obtain supplies of propane for the affected developments through its present contracts or newly negotiated ones, it would still face considerable expense and trouble which cannot be estimated in advance in making arrangements for its distribution to the subdivisions.

Specific performance is the proper remedy in this situation, and it should be granted by the district court.[4] . . .

[Reversed and remanded.]

NOTES

(1) *The Code and Specific Performance.* Comments 1 and 2 to UCC § 2–716 say: "[W]ithout intending to impair in any way the exercise of the court's sound discretion in the matter, this Article seeks to further a more liberal attitude than some courts have shown in connection with the specific performance of contracts of

---

3. During periods of cold weather, when demand is high, Laclede does not receive enough natural gas to meet all this demand. It, therefore, adds propane to the natural gas it places in its distribution system. This practice is called "peak shaving."

4. In fashioning its decree the district court must take into account any relevant rules and regulations promulgated under the Federal Mandatory Allocation Program.

sale.... In view of this Article's emphasis on the commercial feasibility of replacement, a new concept of what are 'unique' goods is introduced under this section. Specific performance is no longer limited to goods which are already specific or ascertained at the time of contracting. The test of uniqueness under this section must be made in terms of the total situation which characterizes the contract. Output and requirements contracts involving a particular or peculiarly available source or market present today the typical commercial specific performance situation, as contrasted with contracts for the sale of heirlooms or priceless works of art which were usually involved in the older cases. However, uniqueness is not the sole basis of the remedy under this section for the relief may also be granted 'in other proper circumstances'...."

In the case of a long-term output or requirements contract, might the difficulty of proving damages amount to "other proper circumstances" even if there is no "particular or peculiarly available source or market"? If Laclede were limited to damages, how would its damages be calculated under the Code? In Eastern Rolling Mill Co. v. Michlovitz, 145 A. 378 (Md.1929), a five-year output contract for scrap steel was broken by the seller in the first year. Part of the court's justification for ordering specific performance was that any estimate of damages "would be speculative and conjectured, and not, therefore, compensatory.... To substitute damages by guess for due performance of contract could only be because 'there's no equity stirring.' "

(2) *Another Form of Specific Relief.* In addition to the possibility of specific relief in the form of a decree of specific performance under UCC § 2–716(1), a buyer of goods may in some circumstances also obtain specific relief through an action to replevy the goods under UCC § 2–716(3).

A seller may in some circumstances obtain what amounts to specific relief through an action for the price under UCC § 2–709(1)(b). Can the seller do so if it can resell? What would you advise an aggrieved seller to do following breach in order to lay the foundation for a possible action for the price under this section?

———

NORTHERN DELAWARE INDUSTRIAL DEVELOPMENT CORP. v. E.W. BLISS CO., 245 A.2d 431 (Del.Ch.1968). Bliss, a general contractor, contracted to modernize the plant of the Phoenix Steel Corporation, for $27,500,000. [Phoenix was, along with Northern Delaware, a party to the contract and a plaintiff in the case.] The plant was spread over a 60–acre site. Work did not progress as rapidly as contemplated in the contract, and Phoenix sought an order to have Bliss put 300 more workers on the job, as required by the contract, to make up a full second shift during the period that one of Phoenix's mills had to be shut down because of the work. The court denied specific performance.

■ MARVEL, VICE CHANCELLOR.... It is not that a court of equity is without jurisdiction in a proper case to order the completion of an expressly designed and largely completed construction contract, particularly where the undertaking is tied in with a contract for the sale of land and the construction in question is largely finished.... The point is that a court of equity should not order specific performance of any building contract in a situation in which it would be impractical to carry out such an order, ... unless there are special circumstances or the public interest is directly involved.... I conclude that to grant specific performance ... would be inappropriate in view of the imprecision of the contract provision relied upon and the impracticability if not impossibility of effective enforcement by the Court of a mandatory order designed to keep a specific number of men on the job at the site of a steel mill which is undergoing extensive modernization and expansion. If plaintiffs have sustained loss as a result of actionable building delays ..., they may, at an appropriate time, resort to law for a fixing of their claimed damages. [On a motion for reargument, Phoenix argued that it sought only an order "directing the performance of a ministerial act, namely the hiring by defendant of more workers." The court denied the motion, relying on "the well established principle that performance of a contract for personal services, even of a unique nature, will not be affirmatively and directly enforced."]

NOTES

(1) *Distinctions.* Consider the remark of Chancellor Walworth in denying a decree of specific performance against an opera singer: "I am not aware that any officer of this court has that perfect knowledge of the Italian language, or possesses that exquisite sensibility in the auricular nerve, which is necessary to understand and to enjoy with a proper zest the peculiar beauties of the Italian opera, so fascinating to the fashionable world." De Rivafinoli v. Corsetti, 4 Paige Ch. 264, 270 (N.Y.1833). Is this point distinguishable from that in *Northern Delaware*?

Courts have shown increasing willingness to order specific performance of construction contracts. In most of these cases, however, the construction was to take place on the defendant's land with a conveyance or lease to follow. See, *e.g.*, Floyd v. Watson, 254 S.E.2d 687, 690 (W.Va.1979), where the court noted that the agreement "includes a provision for conveyance of land, and therefore specific performance is proper." Cf. City Stores Co. v. Ammerman, 266 F.Supp. 766 (D.D.C.1967), aff'd, 394 F.2d 950 (D.C.Cir.1968).

(2) *Specific Performance in Arbitration.* Suppose that Bliss and Phoenix had included in the construction contract the American Arbitration Association's arbitration clause, incorporating § R–45(a), quoted in Note 2, p. 28 above. Would the court have enforced an arbitral award granting the relief that it refused in the actual case? The New York Court of Appeals held that such an award was enforceable in Grayson–Robinson Stores, Inc. v. Iris Construction Corp., 168 N.E.2d 377 (N.Y.1960) (a 4–3 decision).

Walgreen Co. v. Sara Creek Property Co.

United States Court of Appeals, Seventh Circuit, 1992.
966 F.2d 273.

[For decades, Walgreen, a "discount" chain, had operated a pharmacy in the Southgate Mall in Milwaukee. Under its lease, the landlord, Sara Creek, promised not to lease space in the mall to another store operating a pharmacy. In 1990, fearful that its "anchor [largest] tenant" was about to close its store, Sara Creek informed Walgreen that it intended to buy out that tenant and install in its place a store operated by Phar–Mor, a "deep discount" chain that would contain a pharmacy. Its entrance was to be within a couple of hundred feet of Walgreen's. Walgreen sought an injunction against Sara Creek. After a hearing, the trial judge entered a permanent injunction against Sara Creek's letting the premises to Phar–Mor until Walgreen's lease expired. At the hearing Sara Creek's expert witnesses had testified that Walgreen's damages could be readily estimated, whereas Walgreen's employees had testified to the contrary, asserting among other reasons that those damages included intangibles such as good will. Sara Creek appealed.]

■ POSNER, CIRCUIT JUDGE. . . . Sara Creek reminds us that damages are the norm in breach of contract as in other cases. Many breaches, it points out, are "efficient" in the sense that they allow resources to be moved into a more valuable use. . . . Perhaps this is one—the value of Phar–Mor's occupancy of the anchor premises may exceed the cost to Walgreen of facing increased competition. If so, society will be better off if Walgreen is paid its damages, equal to that cost, and Phar–Mor is allowed to move in rather than being kept out by an injunction. That is why injunctions are not granted as a matter of course, but only when the plaintiff's damages remedy is inadequate. Northern Indiana Public Service Co. v. Carbon County Coal Co., 799 F.2d 265, 279 (7th Cir.1986). Walgreen's is not, Sara Creek argues; the projection of business losses due to increased competition is a routine exercise in calculation. Damages representing either the present value of lost future profits or (what should be the equivalent, . . . the diminution in the value of the leasehold) have either been awarded or deemed the proper remedy in a number of reported cases for breach of an exclusivity clause in a shopping-center lease. . . . Why, Sara Creek asks, should they not be adequate here?

The benefits of substituting an injunction for damages are twofold. First, it shifts the burden of determining the cost of the defendant's conduct from the court to the parties. If it is true that Walgreen's damages are smaller than the gain to Sara Creek from allowing a second pharmacy into the shopping mall, then there must be a price for dissolving the injunction that will make both parties better off. Thus, the effect of upholding the injunction would be to substitute for the costly processes of forensic fact determination the less costly processes of private negotiation. Second, a premise of our free-market system, and the lesson of experience here and abroad as well, is that prices and costs are more accurately determined by the market than by government. A battle of experts is a less reliable method of determining the actual cost to Walgreen of facing new competition than negotiations between Walgreen and Sara Creek over the price at which Walgreen would feel adequately compensated for having to face that competition.

That is the benefit side of injunctive relief but there is a cost side as well. Many injunctions require continuing supervision by the court, and that is costly. . . . Some injunctions are problematic because they impose costs on third parties. . . . A more subtle cost of injunctive relief arises from the situation that economists call "bilateral monopoly," in which two parties can deal only with each other: the situation that an injunction creates. . . . The sole seller of widgets selling to the sole buyer of that product would be an example. But so will be the situation confronting

Walgreen and Sara Creek if the injunction is upheld. Walgreen can "sell" its injunctive right only to Sara Creek, and Sara Creek can "buy" Walgreen's surrender of its right to enjoin the leasing of the anchor tenant's space to Phar–Mor only from Walgreen. The lack of alternatives in bilateral monopoly creates a bargaining range, and the costs of negotiating to a point within that range may be high. Suppose the cost to Walgreen of facing the competition of Phar–Mor at the Southgate Mall would be $1 million, and the benefit to Sara Creek of leasing to Phar–Mor would be $2 million. Then at any price between those figures for a waiver of Walgreen's injunctive right both parties would be better off, and we expect parties to bargain around a judicial assignment of legal rights if the assignment is inefficient. R.H. Coase, "The Problem of Social Cost," 3 J. Law & Econ. 1 (1960). But each of the parties would like to engross as much of the bargaining range as possible—Walgreen to press the price toward $2 million, Sara Creek to depress it toward $1 million. With so much at stake, both parties will have an incentive to devote substantial resources of time and money to the negotiation process. The process may even break down, if one or both parties want to create for future use a reputation as a hard bargainer; and if it does break down, the injunction will have brought about an inefficient result. All these are in one form or another costs of the injunctive process that can be avoided by substituting damages.

The costs and benefits of the damages remedy are the mirror of those of the injunctive remedy. The damages remedy avoids the cost of continuing supervision and third-party effects, and the cost of bilateral monopoly as well. It imposes costs of its own, however, in the form of diminished accuracy in the determination of value, on the one hand, and of the parties' expenditures on preparing and presenting evidence of damages, and the time of the court in evaluating the evidence, on the other.

The weighing up of all these costs and benefits is the analytical procedure that is or at least should be employed by a judge asked to enter a permanent injunction, with the understanding that if the balance is even the injunction should be withheld. The judge is not required to explicate every detail of the analysis and he did not do so here, but as long as we are satisfied that his approach is broadly consistent with a proper analysis we shall affirm; and we are satisfied here. The determination of Walgreen's damages would have been costly in forensic resources and inescapably inaccurate. . . . The lease had ten years to run. So Walgreen would have had to project its sales revenues and costs over the next ten years, and then project the impact on those figures of Phar–Mor's competition, and then discount that impact to present value. All but the last step would have been fraught with uncertainty. . . .

Affirmed.

SPECIFIC PERFORMANCE, EFFICIENCY, AND THE COASE THEOREM

In the light of earlier discussions on efficient breach, p. 21 above, is specific performance an efficient remedy? Suppose that PepsiCo, after contracting to sell its jet to Klein for $4.75 million, gets an offer of $100,000 more from Gross, who has been searching for just such a jet. If Klein can compel PepsiCo to deliver the jet, it might be supposed that Gross, who values it more than Klein, would not end up with it. This, however, ignores two possibilities—resale and renegotiation.

If Klein compels PepsiCo to deliver the jet, Gross can still end up with the jet by buying it from Klein. If Klein sells the jet to Gross for $4.85 million, it will then be Klein who realizes the $100,000. If Klein cannot compel PepsiCo to deliver the jet, it will be PepsiCo that realizes the $100,000, less any liability to Klein. In both instances the jet goes to Gross, who values it most. In the rhetoric of modern economic theory this is known as an *allocatively efficient* outcome, which means simply that resources end up in the hands of those who value them most. In the first instance the cash surplus of the sale goes to Klein. In the second instance it goes to Pepsico. This movement of cash is normally treated as having no (allocative) efficiency consequences because parties are assumed to value cash in exactly the same way. Unlike the jet, the cash is no more valuable in Klein's hands than it is in Gross's hands or on PepsiCo's balance sheet. Klein is enriched in one case and PepsiCo in the other, and since the jet in either case goes to its highest-value user (Gross), it makes no difference from the point of view of efficiency whether it is Klein or PepsiCo who is made better off from the transaction, all else equal.

All else is seldom equal, of course. The cost of the transaction between Klein and Gross is unlikely to be exactly the same as the cost of the transaction between Pepsico and Gross. The costs include the costs to the parties of finding each other (search costs), negotiating over the terms (bargaining costs) and writing up their agreement ("ink" costs). These "transaction costs" may prohibit a direct exchange between Klein and Gross. If the transaction costs to Klein and Gross of completing a new contract are greater than the $100,000 surplus available from trading, then a trade between them will not happen.

Gross may yet end up with the jet even if Klein receives an order of specific performance. This is because it may be to the mutual advantage of Klein and PepsiCo to negotiate around the order of specific performance rather than for Klein to compel PepsiCo to perform. If Klein compels PepsiCo to perform and then does not find Gross, neither PepsiCo nor Klein will realize any of the $100,000 surplus. But if Klein negotiates with PepsiCo to release it from the contract so that PepsiCo can sell the jet to Gross, PepsiCo and Klein can share the $100,000. (Observe that, on this assumption, a rule of specific performance results in a sharing of the $100,000. The negotiations will determine the share that each gets, but since Gross gets the jet in any case, the efficiency of the rule does not turn on this.) There is, however, a cost to negotiating, and if it is assumed that PepsiCo and Klein would not think it worth their while to negotiate a release where only $100,000 is at stake, Gross will not end up with the jet in this way.

But if we assume that there are no costs to PepsiCo and Klein for bargaining with each other, then neither a specific performance rule nor a money damage rule—*any* money damage rule—is more efficient with regard to the allocation of resources. This provocative result is known as the Coase Theorem. The Coase Theorem states that when transaction costs are absent (or sufficiently small) and legal entitlements well-defined, parties will bargain to an allocatively efficient outcome under any remedy. That is, bargaining will result in the goods going to the party who values them the most, irrespective of the remedy provided by the court.

The Coase Theorem is often misread as suggesting that the remedies themselves have no efficiency implications. Nothing could be further from the truth. Professor Coase did not believe that transaction costs are typically absent.[a] He argued just the opposite: since transaction costs are always present, the remedy may indeed affect the allocation of goods. With regard to efficiency, then, much turns on the transaction costs associated with various remedial regimes. This insight has sparked a large literature attempting to characterize the circumstances wherein a transaction costs analysis would favor one type of remedy over another. These analyses focus on the costs of bargaining, search costs, the legal costs of determining damages, the monitoring costs of specific performance, etc., as well as the psychological costs and biases related to certain remedies. No general efficiency argument has been put forth in favor of a singly preferred remedy. Nor is one is not likely to appear. Perhaps this is as it should be. The value of Coase's insight is that it focuses our attention on the transaction costs of contracting and asks us to think about the desirability of particular remedies given these constraints.[b]

SECTION 2.   MEASURING EXPECTATION

The usual remedy for breach of contract is an award of damages, typically based on the *expectation interest*. Recall from Chapter 1 that an award of expectation damages is a sum of money that will, to the extent that money can, put the promisee in the position he would have been in had the promise been performed. The promisee is then said to have received "the benefit of the bargain" or to have been "made whole."

Although this is an intuitive and simple principle, its practical implementation can be challenging. Unlike restitution damages (based on the *actual* benefit the promisee has conferred on the promisor) or reliance damages (based on the *actual* amount the promisee has expended in reliance on the promise), expectation damages poses a counterfactual

a. Ronald H. Coase, (1910–), professor emeritus at the University of Chicago Law School, first observed the salience of transaction costs in his early work on industrial organization. In "The Nature of the Firm," 4 *Economica* 386 (1937), Coase introduced transaction costs to explain why some firms contract for their needs in the market, while other firms expand their internal operations to satisfy their own needs, so-called "vertical integration." Later, he again used the idea of transaction costs to describe certain efficiency effects of legal rules in his famous article, "The Problem of Social Costs," 3 J.L. & Econ. 1 (1960). In 1991 Coase received the Nobel Prize in Economics principally for these two bodies of work.

b. The Coase Theorem makes no claims about distributive fairness, investment efficiency, or wealth effects that result from distinct assignments of legal entitlements.

difficulty: What value would the promisee have received had the breach not occurred? Finding a monetary equivalent to this value is straightforward in some instances, "as, for example, where the injured party has simply had to pay an additional amount to arrange a substitute transaction and can be adequately compensated by damages based on the amount." Restatement § 347, comment *a*. Similarly, where the promisee's expected advantage consists largely or exclusively of the realization of profit, as is the case for most commercially significant exchanges, the expectation interest can be expressed in money with some assurance. This is particularly true in well-defined or "thick" markets, where there are many buyers and sellers trading over particular goods.

In principle the expectation interest is based on that of the particular promisee at hand, quite without regard to that of the hypothetical reasonable promisee, and depends on the particular promisee's unique circumstances or those of its enterprise. Markets merely facilitate the identification of a promisee's expectation interest, either because the market approximates the promisee's interests well or because it allows the promisee to realize that interest through a substitute transaction.

More generally, Restatement § 347 looks to three broad factors in measuring a party's expectation interest:

"(a) the loss in the value to him of the other party's performance caused by its failure or deficiency, plus

(b) any other loss, including incidental or consequential loss, caused by the breach, *less*

(c) any cost or other loss that he has avoided by not having to perform."

Consider these factors in turn. First, the breach may cause the injured party a loss by limiting or eliminating the expected return, or value, of performance itself. The difference between the value to the injured party of the performance that should have been received and the value to that party of what, if anything, was actually received is the injured party's *loss in value* (a).

Second, the breach may cause the injured party loss other than *loss in value,* such as physical harm to that party's person or property or expenses incurred in an attempt to salvage the transaction after breach. This residual category is the injured party's *other loss* (b).

Any breach, regardless of its seriousness, may result in *loss in value* (a) and in *other loss* (b). A serious breach may give the injured party a choice between continuing performance and stopping performance and treating the contract as terminated.

If the injured party chooses to stop performance and treat the contract as terminated, the breach may affect it in a third way. The breach may have a beneficial effect on the injured party by saving that party further expense that would have been incurred had performance continued. Moreover, the breach may have an additional effect on the injured party by allowing that party to avoid some loss by salvaging and reallocating some or all of the resources that it otherwise would have had to devote to performance of the contract. These savings are the injured party's *costs and other loss avoided* (c) and should be subtracted from any expectation damage award that a breaching promisor would have to pay.[a] Hence the general measure of damages is the sum of these factors, which can be expressed as a simple formula:

> *Damages* = (a) *loss in value* + (b) *other loss* – (c) *cost and loss avoided*.

Hold aside *other loss* (b) for a moment and focus on the two remaining factors in the equation above—*loss in value* (a) and *cost and loss avoided* (c). Estimation of *loss in value* and *cost and loss avoided* pose different challenges depending on which party is in breach. In most agreements, one of the parties (say, a buyer) is simply required to pay money while the other party (say, a seller) is required to furnish goods, land, or services in return for a money payment. When the seller is the injured party, and the breach consists of the buyer's failure to pay, the difficulty largely lies in the determination of the seller's *cost and loss avoided,* since its *loss in value* is simply the amount of money that the buyer has failed to pay. When the seller is in breach, the difficulty lies in the determination of the buyer's *loss in value,* since its *cost and loss avoided* is simply the amount of money that it has not yet paid.

Now consider the *other loss* category, which consists mainly of incidental and consequential losses. "Incidental losses include costs incurred in a reasonable effort, whether successful or not, to avoid loss, as where a party [*e.g.,* a buyer] pays brokerage fees in arranging or attempting to arrange a substitute transaction." Restatement § 347, comment *c.* Typically, for a seller of goods, they include costs incurred in halting delivery and in transporting, housing and caring for goods after breach by the recipient. See, *e.g.,* UCC § 2–710 (Seller's Incidental Damages). Consequential losses encompass, but are not limited to, harm to persons or property as a result of breach. As between the buyer and the seller, one might expect consequential losses to be suffered more likely by the former. The cases that follow illustrate these basic factors in practical application.

INTRODUCTION TO *VITEX*: LOST PROFITS AND FIXED COSTS

The venerated British economist John Maynard Keynes once famously quipped that "in the long run we are all dead." *A Tract on Monetary Reform* (1923). The more prosaic distinction economists typically draw between the long run and the short run involves the variability of inputs used by firms in producing goods and services. Inputs, also called factors of production, include such things as raw materials, machinery, and labor.

---

a. It may help in understanding the distinction between *cost avoided* and *loss avoided* to imagine a contract for the sale of two products to be manufactured by the seller. Suppose that the buyer repudiates after the seller has manufactured one of the products. The saving that results when the seller stops production of the second product is the seller's *cost avoided.* The saving that results when the seller sells the first product to another buyer is the seller's *loss avoided.*

The short run is defined by economists as the period during which at least one input is fixed—that is, not variable. A factory is a common example of a short run fixed input. With enough time, or in the long run, new factories may be built and existing ones modified, but in the short run a factory is not variable.

The costs associated with fixed inputs are called, uninspiringly, fixed costs. Those costs must be borne before any goods can be produced. For example, a factory must be established before any goods can be manufactured. How then do these fixed costs relate to the profits expected from subsequent agreements to produce goods? This question is thoughtfully taken up in the next case. The opinion introduces the lost-profits measure of expectation damages. Lost profits are simply the profits that a firm would have earned had the breach not occurred. In commercial transactions, where parties are largely motivated by expected profits, lost profits are excellent approximations of the *expectation interest;* the connection between profits and expectancy is simple and direct. But there's often a devil in the details. Recall the observation above that when a seller is the injured party, the difficulty in determining damages lies largely in the estimation of its *cost and loss avoided* (c). How do fixed costs figure in this calculation?

Vitex Manufacturing Corp. v. Caribtex Corp.

United States Court of Appeals, Third Circuit, 1967.
377 F.2d 795.

■ STALEY, CHIEF JUDGE. This is an appeal by Caribtex Corporation from a judgment of the District Court of the Virgin Islands finding Caribtex in breach of a contract entered into with Vitex Manufacturing Company, Ltd., and awarding $21,114 plus interest to Vitex for loss of profits. The only substantial question raised by Caribtex is whether it was error for the district court, sitting without a jury, not to consider overhead as part of Vitex's costs in determining the amount of profits lost. We conclude that under the facts presented, the district court was not compelled to consider Vitex's overhead costs, and we will affirm the judgment.

Before discussing the details of the controversy between the parties, it will be helpful to briefly describe the peculiar legal setting in which this suit arose. At the time of the events in question, there were high tariff barriers to the importation of foreign wool products. However, under § 301 of the Tariff Act of 1930, 19 U.S.C.A. § 1301a, repealed but the provision continued under Revised Tariff Schedules, 19 U.S.C.A. § 1202, note 3(a)(i)(ii) (1965), if such goods were imported into the Virgin Islands and were processed in some manner so that their finished value exceeded their importation value by at least 50%, then the high tariffs to importation into the continental United States would be avoided. Even after the processing, the foreign wool enjoyed a price advantage over domestic products so that the business flourished. However, to keep the volume of this business at such levels that Congress would not be stirred to change the law, the Virgin Islands Legislature imposed "quotas" on persons engaging in processing, limiting their output. 33 V.I.C. § 504 (Supp.1966).

Vitex was engaged in the business of chemically shower-proofing imported cloth so that it could be imported duty-free into the United States. For this purpose, Vitex maintained a plant in the Virgin Islands and was entitled to process a specific quantity of material under the Virgin Islands quota system. Caribtex was in the business of importing cloth into the islands, securing its processing, and exporting it to the United States.

In the fall of 1963, Vitex found itself with an unused portion of its quota but no customers, and Vitex closed its plant. Caribtex acquired some Italian wool and subsequently negotiations for a processing contract were conducted between the principals of the respective companies in New York City. Though the record below is clouded with differing versions of the negotiations and the alleged final terms, the trial court found upon substantial evidence in the record that the parties did enter into a contract in which Vitex agreed to process 125,000 yards of Caribtex's woolen material at a price of 26 [25?] cents per yard.

Vitex proceeded to re-open its Virgin Islands plant, ordered the necessary chemicals, recalled its work force and made all the necessary preparations to perform its end of the bargain. However, no goods were forthcoming from Caribtex, despite repeated demands by Vitex, apparently because Caribtex was unsure that the processed wool would be entitled to duty-free treatment by the customs officials. Vitex subsequently brought this suit to recover the profits lost through Caribtex's breach.

Vitex alleged, and the trial court found, that its gross profits for processing said material under the contract would have been $31,250 and that its costs would have been $10,136, leaving Vitex's damages for loss of profits at $21,114. On appeal, Caribtex asserted numerous objections to the detailed computation of lost profits. While the record below is sometimes confusing, we conclude that the trial court had substantial evidence to support its findings on damages. It must be remembered that the difficulty in exactly ascertaining Vitex's costs is due to Caribtex's wrongful conduct in repudiating the contract before performance by Vitex. Caribtex will not be permitted to benefit by the uncertainty it has caused. Thus, since there was a sufficient basis in the record to support the trial court's determination of substantial damages, we will not set aside its judgment. Stentor Elec. Mfg. Co. v. Klaxon Co., 115 F.2d 268 (C.A.3, 1940), rev'd other grounds 313 U.S. 487 (1941); 5 Williston, Contracts § 1345 (rev. ed. 1937).

Caribtex first raised the issue at the oral argument of this appeal that the trial court erred by disregarding Vitex's overhead expenses in determining lost profits. In general, overhead "... may be said to include broadly the continuous expenses of the business, irrespective of the outlay on a particular contract." Grand Trunk W.R.R. Co. v. H.W. Nelson Co., 116 F.2d 823, 839 (C.A.6, 1941). Such expenses would include executive and clerical salaries, property taxes, general administration expenses, etc.[1] Although Vitex did not expressly seek recovery for overhead, if a portion of these fixed expenses should be allocated as costs to the Caribtex contract, then under the judgment of the district court Vitex tacitly recovered these expenses as part of its damages for lost profits, and the damages should be

---

1. Caribtex could not be referring to overhead expenses as including labor costs and the like, because the trial judge did charge as costs all the expenses directly associated with the reactivation of Vitex's plant, and the actual processing of Caribtex's goods according to the terms of the contract.

reduced accordingly. Presumably, the portion to be allocated to costs would be a pro rata share of Vitex's annual overhead according to the volume of business Vitex would have done over the year if Caribtex had not breached the contract.

Although there is authority to the contrary, we feel that the better view is that normally, in a claim for lost profits, overhead should be treated as a part of gross profits and recoverable as damages, and should not be considered as part of the seller's costs. A number of cases hold that since overhead expenses are not affected by the performance of the particular contract, there should be no need to deduct them in computing lost profits. E.g., Oakland California Towel Co. v. Sivils, 52 Cal.App.2d 517, 520, 126 P.2d 651, 652 (1942); Jessup & Moore Paper Co. v. Bryant Paper Co., 297 Pa. 483, 147 A. 519, 524 (1929); Annot., 3 A.L.R.3d 689 (1965) (collecting cases on both sides of the controversy). The theory of these cases is that the seller is entitled to recover losses incurred and gains prevented in excess of savings made possible, Restatement, Contracts § 329 (made part of the law of the Virgin Islands, 1 V.I.C. § 4); since overhead is fixed and nonperformance of the contract produced no overhead cost savings, no deduction from profits should result.

The soundness of the rule is exemplified by this case. Before negotiations began between Vitex and Caribtex, Vitex had reached a lull in business activity and had closed its plant. If Vitex had entered into no other contracts for the rest of the year, the profitability of its operations would have been determined by deducting its production costs and overhead from gross receipts yielded in previous transactions. When this opportunity arose to process Caribtex's wool, the only additional expenses Vitex would incur would be those of re-opening its plant and the direct costs of processing, such as labor, chemicals and fuel oil. Overhead would have remained the same whether or not Vitex and Caribtex entered their contract and whether or not Vitex actually processed Caribtex's goods. Since this overhead remained constant, in no way attributable-to or affected-by the Caribtex contract, it would be improper to consider it as a cost of Vitex's performance to be deducted from the gross proceeds of the Caribtex contract.

However, Caribtex may argue that this view ignores modern accounting principles, and that overhead is as much a cost of production as other expenses. It is true that successful businessmen must set their prices at sufficient levels to recoup all their expenses, including overhead, and to gain profits. Thus, the price the businessman should charge on each transaction could be thought of as that price necessary to yield a pro rata portion of the company's fixed overhead, the direct costs associated with production, and a "clear" profit. Doubtless this type of calculation is used by businessmen and their accountants. Pacific Portland Cement Co. v. Food Mach. & Chem. Corp., 178 F.2d 541 (C.A.9, 1949). However, because it is useful for planning purposes to allocate a portion of overhead to each transaction, it does not follow that this allocate share of fixed overhead should be considered a cost factor in the computation of lost profits on individual transactions.

First, it must be recognized that the pro rata allocation of overhead costs is only an analytical construct. In a similar manner one could allocate a pro rata share of the company's advertising cost, taxes and/or charitable gifts. The point is that while these items all are paid from the proceeds of the business, they do not normally bear such a direct relationship to any individual transaction to be considered a cost in ascertaining lost profits.

Secondly, even were we to recognize the allocation of overhead as proper in this case, we should uphold the tacit award of overhead expense to Vitex as a "loss incurred." Conditioned Air Corp. v. Rock Island Motor Transit Co., 253 Iowa 961, 114 N.W.2d 304, cert. denied, 371 U.S. 825 (1962). By the very nature of this allocation process, as the number of transactions over which overhead can be spread becomes smaller, each transaction must bear a greater portion or allocate share of the fixed overhead cost. Suppose a company has fixed overhead of $10,000 and engages in five similar transactions; then the receipts of each transaction would bear $2000 of overhead expense. If the company is now forced to spread this $10,000 over only four transactions, then the overhead expense per transaction will rise to $2500, significantly reducing the profitability of the four remaining transactions. Thus, where the contract is between businessmen familiar with commercial practices, as here, the breaching party should reasonably foresee that his breach will not only cause a loss of "clear" profit, but also a loss in that the profitability of other transactions will be reduced. Resolute Ins. Co. v. Percy Jones, Inc., 198 F.2d 309 (C.A.10, 1952); Cf. In re Kellett Aircraft Corp., 191 F.2d 231 (C.A.3, 1951). Therefore, this loss is within the contemplation of "losses caused and gains prevented," and overhead should be considered to a compensable item of damage.

Significantly, the Uniform Commercial Code, adopted in the Virgin Islands, 11A V.I.C. § 1–101 et seq., and in virtually every state today, provides for the recovery of overhead in circumstances similar to those presented here. Under 11A V.I.C. § 2–708, the seller's measure of damage for non-acceptance or repudiation is the difference between the contract price and the market price, but if this relief is inadequate to put the seller in as good position as if the contract had been fully performed, "... then the measure of damages is the *profit (including reasonable overhead)* which the seller would have made from full performance by the buyer...." 11A V.I.C. § 2–708(2). (Emphasis added.) While this contract is not controlled by the Code, the Code is persuasive here because it embodies the foremost modern legal thought concerning commercial transactions. Indeed, it may overrule some of the cases denying recovery for overhead. E.g., Wilhelm Lubrication Co. v. Brattrud, 197 Minn. 626, 632, 268 N.W. 634, 636, 106 A.L.R. 1279 (1936).

Caribtex also argued that the contract should not be enforced because it was unconscionable. While Vitex was to make a large profit on the processing and Caribtex did bear the risk of failure to meet customs standards, the contract was freely entered-into, after much negotiation, between parties of apparently equal bargaining strength. This was not a contract of adhesion—Vitex was not the only processor in the Virgin

Islands and Caribtex's bargaining strength was evidenced by the successive and substantial price reductions it wrested from Vitex during the negotiations. Compare, Campbell Soup Co. v. Wentz, 172 F.2d 80 (C.A.3, 1948); Henningsen v. Bloomfield Motors, Inc., 32 N.J. 358, 161 A.2d 69, 75 A.L.R.2d 1 (1960).

The judgment of the district court will be affirmed.

NOTES

(1) *Cost and Loss Avoided.* In *Vitex*, the court observed that "since overhead is fixed and nonperformance of the contract produced no overhead cost savings, no deduction from profits should result." In terms of the damages formula above (*Damages* = (a) *loss in value* + (b) *other loss* − (c) *cost and loss avoided*), this means that the overhead to which the court referred was not a part of the third component. Are all overhead expenses fixed and unavoidable?

(2) *Profit at the Margin.* Profit is the difference between revenue earned and all expenditures required to generate that revenue. These expenditures include fixed and non-fixed costs. But to determine the lost profit from a particular contract, as the court sought to do in *Vitex*, one would look to *marginal* revenue and *marginal* cost—not to total revenue and total cost, or average revenue and average cost. The marginal revenue a party receives from a contract is the additional revenue resulting from that contract. (Often, but not always, that amount is the contract price.) The marginal cost of a contract is the cost of completing performance of that contract. Therefore, so far as the fixed costs of performing have been expended already, they are not part of the marginal cost of performing. Only the further expenditures required to perform the contract enter into marginal cost.

(3) *Overhead Costs.* The *Vitex* court relied on the marginal-cost logic above in reaching its conclusions regarding Vitex's overhead costs in the lost-profit calculation. But the court also said that "even were we to recognize the allocation of overhead as proper in this case, we should uphold the tacit award of overhead expense to Vitex as a 'loss incurred.'" Under which loss category—*i.e.*, *loss in value* (a), or *other loss* (b)—would this loss fall? Note that UCC § 2–708 gives little guidance as to how overhead is to be taken into account.

(4) *Sunk Costs.* Suppose that a firm leases a fleet of trucks for $500,000 in order to make delivery of goods as required by a large sale contract. If, following a breach by the buyer, the firm sublets the fleet for $400,000, then only $100,000 of this expenditure is "sunk." Sunk costs are those that cannot be avoided or recouped once they have been made. How much effort should a court require of an injured party to limit its losses to sunk costs alone?

Laredo Hides Co., Inc. v. H & H Meat Products Co., Inc.

Court of Civil Appeals of Texas, 1974.
513 S.W.2d 210.

■ BISSETT, JUSTICE. This is a breach of contract case. Laredo Hides Company, Inc., the buyer, sued H & H Meat Products Company, Inc., the seller, to recover damages for breach of a written contract for the sale of cattle hides. Trial was to the court without a jury. A take nothing judgment in favor of defendant was rendered. Plaintiff has appealed.

The controlling facts of the case are undisputed. H & H Meat Products Company, Inc. (H & H) is a meat processing and packing corporation, located in Mercedes, Texas. It sells cattle hides as a by-product of its business. Laredo Hides Company, Inc. (Laredo Hides) is a corporation, located in Laredo, Texas. It purchases cattle hides from various meat packers in the United States and ships them to tanneries in Mexico.

A written contract dated February 29, 1972, was executed whereby Laredo Hides agreed to buy H & H's entire cattle hide production during the period March through December, 1972.... [After two deliveries of hides, a $9,000 check sent by Laredo Hides to H & H in payment for the second shipment was delayed in the mail. Before it arrived, H & H gave Laredo Hides an ultimatum demanding payment within a few hours. When the demand was not met, H & H notified Laredo Hides on March 30, 1972, that H & H regarded this as a breach justifying cancellation of the contract and that it would deliver no more hides. In an omitted part of the opinion, the court held that H & H's precipitous action was unjustified, that its refusal to deliver more hides was itself a breach by repudiation of the contract that relieved Laredo Hides of tendering performance during the remaining months of the contract, and that the trial court's disposition of the case was error.]

Laredo Hides, on March 3, 1972, had contracted with a Mexican tannery for the sale of all the hides which it expected to purchase from H & H under the February 29, 1972, contract. Following the cancellation by H & H of the contract, Laredo Hides, in order to meet the requirements of its contract with the tannery, was forced to purchase hides on the open market in substitution for the hides which were to have been delivered to it under the contract with H & H.

H & H's total production during the months April through December, 1972, was 17,218 hides. Under the contract with H & H, the price was $9.75 per hide for bull, steer and heifer hides, and $9.75 per hide for cow hides if the shipment was under 5% cow hides. In the event the shipment was more than 5% cow hides, the price on the excess of cow hides over 5% was reduced to $7.50 per cow hide. The market price for hides steadily increased following the execution of the contract in question. By December 31, 1972, the average cost of bull hides was about $33.00 each and the average cost of cow, heifer and steer hides was about $22.00 each. The total additional cost to Laredo Hides of purchasing substitute hides from other suppliers was $142,254.48. The additional costs (transportation and handling charges) to Laredo Hides which resulted because of the purchases from third parties amounted to $3,448.95....

Since this case must be reversed, we now confront the issue of damages. The guidelines for determining a buyer's remedies in a case where there is a breach of a contract for the sale of goods by a seller are found in Chapter 2 of the Texas Business and Commerce Code [the Uniform Commercial Code, as enacted in Texas]. Among other remedies afforded by the Code, when there is a repudiation of the contract by the seller or a failure to make delivery of the goods under contract, the buyer may cover under § 2.711. He may have damages under § 2.712 "by making in good faith and without unreasonable delay any reasonable purchase of or contract to purchase goods in substitution for those due from the seller", and "may recover from the seller as damages the difference between the cost of cover and the contract price together with any incidental or consequential damages" provided by the chapter; or, he may, under § 2.713, have damages measured by "the difference between the market price at the time when the buyer learned of the breach and the contract price together with any incidental and consequential damages" provided by the chapter.

Laredo Hides instituted suit in May, 1972, and filed its amended petition (its trial pleading) on October 24, 1972, when performance was still due by H & H under the contract. It prayed for specific performance, or in the alternative "... damages at least in the amount of one hundred thousand dollars ($100,000), the same being the damages proximately caused by defendant's breach of the contract ..." There was never a trial amendment of this petition. There were no exceptions by H & H to Laredo Hides' pleadings. Trial commenced on February 28, 1973, was recessed on March 2, 1973, resumed on May 15, 1973, and ended May 16, 1973. Judgment was signed and rendered on August 6, 1973.

Laredo Hides offered uncontroverted evidence of the hide production of H & H from April to December, 1972. It also established the price for the same number of hides which it was forced to buy elsewhere. There was testimony that purchases had to be made periodically throughout 1972 since Laredo Hides had no storage facilities, and the hides would decompose if allowed to age. Furthermore, White, a C.P.A., testified as to statistical summaries which he made showing the cost of buying substitute hides. These summaries were made from invoices which are also in evidence. All of this evidence was admitted without objection. Clearly, Laredo Hides elected to pursue the remedy provided by § 2.712 of the Code, and by its pleadings and evidence brought itself within the purview of the "cover" provisions contained therein.

It is not necessary under § 2.712 that the buyer establish market price. Duesenberg and King, Sales and Bulk Transfers under the U.C.C. § 14.04 Matthew Bender (1974). Where the buyer complies with the requirements of § 2.712, his purchase is presumed proper and the burden of proof is on the seller to show that "cover" was not properly obtained. Spies, Sales, Performance and Remedies, 44 Tex.L.Rev. 629, 638 (1966). There was no evidence offered by H & H to negate this presumption or to "establish expenses saved in consequence of the seller's breach", as permitted by § 2.712.

The difference between the cover price and the contract price is shown to be $134,252.82 for steer hides and $8,001.66 for bull hides, or a total of $142,254.48. In addition, Laredo Hides offered evidence of increased transportation costs of $1,435.77, and increased handling charges of $2,013.18. These are clearly recoverable as incidental damages where the buyer elects to "cover". §§ 2.715(a); 2.712(b)....

There is no evidence that Laredo Hides, in any manner, endeavored to increase its damages sustained when H & H refused to deliver any more hides to it. Laredo Hides, in purchasing the hides in substitution of the hides which should have been delivered under the contract, acted promptly and in a reasonable manner. The facts of this case regarding the issue of liability of H & H and the issues pertaining to damages suffered by Laredo Hides, have been fully and completely developed in the court below. The facts upon which judgment should have been rendered for Laredo Hides by the trial court are conclusively established. It, therefore, becomes the duty of this Court to render judgment which the trial court should have rendered. . . .

Applying the rules announced by the above cited cases and authorities to the instant case, we hold that the record does not support the findings of fact made by the trial judge and there is no legal justification for the conclusion of law reached by the court. Accordingly, the judgment of the trial court is reversed, and judgment is here rendered for Laredo Hides in the amount of $152,960.04, together with interest thereon at the rate of 6% per annum from August 6, 1973, the date judgment was rendered by the trial court, until paid.

Reversed and rendered.

NOTES

(1) *What Is Cover?* Note that although Laredo Hides' contract with H & H was for a term of ten months, its substitute purchases were on the "spot" market. What statutory language justified the court in treating these purchases as cover? Compare McGinnis v. Wentworth Chevrolet Co., 668 P.2d 365 (Or.1983) (rental of car in lieu of purchase), and Cives Corp. v. Callier Steel Pipe & Tube, Inc., 482 A.2d 852 (Me.1984) (manufacture of goods in lieu of purchase). What result if the hides purchased on the spot market had been of a better quality than those that H & H had contracted to supply? See Martella v. Woods, 715 F.2d 410 (8th Cir.1983) (heifer buyer's purchase of better heifers), and Handicapped Children's Education Board v. Lukaszewski, 332 N.W.2d 774 (Wis.1983) (Board's hire of better-qualified teacher).

Would it make a difference if other hides of the quality contracted for were available on the spot market?

If Laredo Hides had been denied recovery under UCC § 2–712 (because the goods in the second transaction were held not to be "in substitution for those due from the seller"), then to what relief would it have been entitled?

(2) *Substitute Transactions: Goods.* Often, following breach, the injured party arranges a substitute transaction and claims damages based on that transaction rather than on one of the damage formulas set out earlier. Laredo Hides did that by arranging substitute purchases of hides and basing its damages on the cover price in those transactions under UCC § 2–712. The rule of that section is a Code innovation. It has no antecedent in prior law. (For comparable provisions, see CISG art. 75 and UNIDROIT Principles art. 7.4.5.) Had this case arisen before the enactment of the Code, Laredo Hides would have had to prove damages based on the difference between market price and contract price under the common law rule of Texas that was the antecedent of UCC § 2–713. What disadvantages would that have had for Laredo Hides?

In connection with the foregoing question, consider what the Supreme Court of Maine said in Williams v. Ubaldo, 670 A.2d 913 (Me.1996), a case involving the sale of a home. "The reports of professional appraisers have been accepted as evidence of the fair market value of real estate.... Evidence of the price resulting from a subsequent sale is also probative of a property's fair market value." *Id.* at 917.

(3) *Substitute Transactions: Services.* If an employee is fired in breach of a contract and does other work as a result of being freed from that contract, the employee's damages are based on the salary that would have been earned under the broken contract less that earned by doing the other work. In State ex rel. Schilling v. Baird, 222 N.W.2d 666, 670 (Wis.1974), Schilling, a deputy sheriff who was wrongfully suspended, argued that he was not required to deduct his earnings from other work because they were not made between midnight and eight in the morning, the shift to which he was assigned as a deputy. "With this conclusion the Court cannot agree. It lends itself to an almost absurd result. Under this interpretation all Schilling had to do was to refrain from getting a third shift job and could then earn as much as he wanted or was fortunate enough to earn and would not be required to deduct any of it."

Under the "collateral source" rule that prevails in some states, an employee's recovery in tort is reduced by sums received from a collateral source, such as unemployment compensation and similar benefits, in order to avoid double recovery. Courts in states with the rule have divided over whether an employee who sues in contract must deduct such sums. See 3 Farnsworth on Contracts § 12.9 n. 14 (2d ed.1998).

Sometimes it is no simple matter to decide whether another comparable opportunity accepted by the injured party after breach should be treated as a "substitute" in calculating damages. Often a seller or other supplier claims that a subsequent transaction *was not* a substitute in order to have not only the benefit of that transaction but also damages based on profits lost on the original transaction.

A person fired from a full-time job cannot expect to make gainful use of the released time and to have the gain disregarded in an action based on wrongful firing. That is so whether or not the old and new jobs are in the same line. Recall the wrongfully suspended deputy sheriff in Schilling, above.

Unlike sheriffs, schoolteachers, and stars of the stage, persons in the building trades commonly apply their personal services to the simultaneous performance of multiple contracts; and firms in those trades may not apply the personal service of any specified individual to a contract. Hence it is generally assumed that a person or firm can undertake a new repair or construction job while continuing work on jobs already booked, adding as necessary to the work force and the stock of tools and materials. On that assumption, earnings on a new job are not credited against a builder's claim for having been dismissed, wrongfully, from an "old" one. The breach has resulted in "lost volume" for the builder.

(4) *Covering, the UCC.* Recall that in Klein's case he had bought a G–III jet after declining, on the ground of price, offers by UJS to sell him two G–IIs. Suppose that, instead, he had made a prompt purchase of another G–II, and had paid more than the contract price—say $250,000 more. Under UCC § 2–712 his "reasonable purchase of ... goods in substitution for those due from the seller" would have been "cover," entitling Klein to damages based on "the difference between the cost of cover and the contract price" (here $250,000).

Section 2–712 would have afforded Klein two advantages over UCC § 2–713. First, he would not have to prove market price, which would probably require expert witnesses, but could simply use his cover contract to show the cover price. Second, he could recover his actual additional cost of a substitute (here $250,000) rather than the hypothetical cost of a substitute (here $200,000) if he had obtained it on the market.

If the seller is the injured party, the Code accords a remedy analogous to that of cover for a buyer. Given that the goods concerned have been identified to the contract, Section 2–706 permits the seller to make a resale of the goods and to base damages on the resale price.

(5) *An "Alternative Product" Rule.* On occasion a seller of goods, in breach, has contested the buyer's claim of loss by contending that, aside from the contract in question, nothing would have averted the loss. The argument amounts to saying that a recovery of a claimant's lost expectation cannot be justified if, when the contract was made, that party could not have accomplished its purpose by dealing with someone else, and so lost no opportunity. One court has subscribed to that rule. Overstreet v. Norden Laboratories, 669 F.2d 1286 (6th Cir.1982). Norden Labs had supplied Dr. Overstreet with a vaccine for horses, said by him to have been ineffective. In an appeal by Norden, one issue was the trial court's instruction to a jury about damages. Norden persuaded two of the judges that it could limit its liability by showing that no effective vaccine had been available to Overstreet. One judge opposed that limitation, ascribing it to what he called an "alternative product" rule. A contrasting decision is that in Chatlos Systems v. National Cash Register [NCR] Corp., 670 F.2d 1304 (3d Cir.1982). NCR, having warranted the performance of its computer system, contended, in effect, that no other computer system in the same price range could have achieved the performance expected by the buyer of its system. The buyer presented testimony of the high value of a system that would serve the buyer as NCR had warranted that its system would. NCR sought to counter that valuation. It had gotten the witness to concede that the price of the high-value system would exceed by far the price paid to NCR for its system. Given that fact, NCR said, the testimony was like substituting a Rolls Royce for a Ford. The analogy did not move a majority of the court.

In Overstreet's case the court drew a different analogy. It said:

> "Let us assume, as appears to be the case, that nothing will reverse or prevent baldness.... Suppose a warrantor, in good faith, represents to a man who is beginning to go bald that use of the warrantor's product will prevent the loss of his hair. The product fails to work and the man goes bald.... If in reliance on the warranty he gave away his assortment of wigs he could recover from the warrantor the cost of replacing them.... However, he could not recover for the loss of his hair. The breach simply had no effect on the presence or absence of the hair."

Id. at 1296–97. Should the bald man recover for his lost expectation? The court thought not. It called its ruling a straightforward application of the requirement of causation.

PROBLEM

A Lucky Star. Star Paving subcontracted with Drennan to do for $15,000 the paving required under Drennan's contract to build a school for the Lancaster School District. Drennan wrongfully ordered Star to stop work at a time when it would have cost Star $5,000 to complete it. Luckily for Star, it was able at once to make a contract with the School District to finish the job at a price of $7,000. Star demands $10,000 ($15,000 minus $5,000) from Drennan. Drennan offers to pay $8,000 ($15,000 minus $7,000). Who is right? See Olds v. Mapes–Reeves Constr. Co., 58 N.E. 478 (Mass.1900). Would it make a difference if one or more terms of the second contract (*e.g.*, one about liability in the event of breach) were significantly different from those of the first?

R.E. Davis Chemical Corp. v. Diasonics, Inc.

United States Court of Appeals, Seventh Circuit, 1987.
826 F.2d 678.

■ CUDAHY, CIRCUIT JUDGE. Diasonics, Inc. appeals from the orders of the district court denying its motion for summary judgment and granting R.E. Davis Chemical Corp.'s summary judgment motion. Diasonics also appeals from the order dismissing its third-party complaint against Dr. Glen D. Dobbin and Dr. Galdino Valvassori. We affirm the dismissal of the third-party complaint, reverse the grant of summary judgment in favor of Davis and remand for further proceedings.

I.

Diasonics is a California corporation engaged in the business of manu-facturing and selling medical diagnostic equipment. Davis is an Illinois corporation that contracted to purchase a piece of medical diagnostic equipment from Diasonics. On or about February 23, 1984, Davis and Diasonics entered into a written contract under which Davis agreed to purchase the equipment. Pursuant to this agreement, Davis paid Diasonics a $300,000 deposit on February 29, 1984. Prior to entering into its agreement with Diasonics, Davis had contracted with Dobbin and Valvasso-ri to establish a medical facility where the equipment was to be used. Dobbin and Valvassori subsequently breached their contract with Davis. Davis then breached its contract with Diasonics; it refused to take delivery of the equipment or to pay the balance due under the agreement. Diasonics later resold the equipment to a third party for the same price at which it was to be sold to Davis.

Davis sued Diasonics, asking for restitution of its $300,000 down payment under section 2–718(2) of the Uniform Commercial Code (the "UCC" or the "Code").... Diasonics counterclaimed. Diasonics did not deny that Davis was entitled to recover its $300,000 deposit less $500 as provided in section 2–718(2)(b). However, Diasonics claimed that it was entitled to an offset under section 2–718(3). Diasonics alleged that it was a "lost volume seller," and, as such, it lost the profit from one sale when Davis breached its contract. Diasonics' position was that, in order to be put in as good a position as it would have been in had Davis performed, it was entitled to recover its lost profit on its contract with Davis under section 2–708(2) of the UCC....

Diasonics subsequently filed a third-party complaint against Dobbin and Valvassori, alleging that they tortiously interfered with its contract with Davis. Diasonics claimed that the doctors knew of the contract between Davis and Diasonics and also knew that, if they breached their contract with Davis, Davis would have no use for the equipment it had agreed to buy from Diasonics.

The district court dismissed Diasonics' third-party complaint for failure to state a claim upon which relief could be granted, finding that the complaint did not allege that the doctors intended to induce Davis to breach its contract with Diasonics. The court also entered summary judgment for Davis. The court held that lost volume sellers were not entitled to recover damages under 2–708(2) but rather were limited to recovering the difference between the resale price and the contract price along with incidental damages under section 2–706(1).... Davis was awarded $322,656, which represented Davis' down payment plus prejudgment interest less Diasonics' incidental damages. Diasonics appeals the district court's decision respecting its measure of damages as well as the dismissal of its third-party complaint.

II.

We consider first Diasonics' claim that the district court erred in holding that Diasonics was limited to the measure of damages provided in 2–706 and could not recover lost profits as a lost volume seller under 2–708(2). Surprisingly, given its importance, this issue has never been addressed by an Illinois court, nor, apparently, by any other court construing Illinois law. Thus, we must attempt to predict how the Illinois Supreme Court would resolve this issue if it were presented to it. Courts applying the laws of other states have unanimously adopted the position that a lost volume seller can recover its lost profits under 2–708(2). Contrary to the result reached by the district court, we conclude that the Illinois Supreme Court would follow these other cases and would allow a lost volume seller to recover its lost profit under 2–708(2).

We begin our analysis with 2–718(2) and (3). Under 2–718(2)(b), Davis is entitled to the return of its down payment less $500. Davis' right to restitution, however, is qualified under 2–718(3)(a) to the extent that Diasonics can establish a right to recover damages under any other provision of Article 2 of the UCC. Article 2 contains four provisions that concern the recovery of a seller's general damages (as opposed to its incidental or consequential damages): 2–706 (contract price less resale price); 2–708(1) (contract price less market price); 2–708(2) (profit); and 2–709 (price). The problem we face here is determining whether Diasonics' damages should be measured under 2–706 or 2–708(2). To answer this question, we need to engage in a detailed look at the language and structure of these various damage provisions.

The Code does not provide a great deal of guidance as to when a particular damage remedy is appropriate. The damage remedies provided under the Code are catalogued in section 2–703, but this section does not indicate that there is any hierarchy among the remedies. One method of approaching the damage sections is to conclude that 2–708 is relegated to a role inferior to that of 2–706 and 2–709 and that one can turn to 2–708 only after one has concluded that neither 2–706 nor 2–709 is applicable.[1] Under

---

1. Evidence to support this approach can be found in the language of the various damage sections and of the official comments to the UCC. See § 2–709(3) ("a seller who is held not entitled to the price under this Section shall nevertheless be awarded damages this interpretation of the relationship between 2–706 and 2–708, if the goods have been resold, the seller can sue to recover damages measured by the difference between the contract price and the resale price under 2–706. The seller can turn to 2–708 only if it resells in a commercially unreasonable manner or if it cannot resell but an action for the price is inappropriate under 2–709. The district court adopted this reading of the Code's damage remedies and, accordingly, limited Diasonics to the measure of damages provided in 2–706 because it resold the equipment in a commercially reasonable manner.

The district court's interpretation of 2–706 and 2–708, however, creates its own problems of statutory construction. There is some suggestion in the Code that the "fact that plaintiff resold the goods [in a commercially reasonable manner] does *not* compel him to use the resale remedy of § 2–706 rather than the damage remedy of § 2–708." Harris, A Radical Restatement of the Law of Seller's Damages: Sales Act and Commercial Code Results Compared, 18 Stan.L.Rev. 66, 101 n. 174 (1965) (emphasis in original). Official Comment 1 to 2–703, which catalogues the remedies available to a seller, states that these "remedies are essentially cumulative in nature" and that "[w]hether the pursuit of one remedy bars another depends entirely on the facts of the individual case." See also State of New York, Report of the Law Revision Comm'n for 1956, 396–97 (1956).[2]

for non-acceptance under the preceding section [§ 2–708]"); UCC Comment 7 to § 2–709 ("[i]f the action for the price fails, the seller may nonetheless have proved a case entitling him to damages for non-acceptance [under § 2–708]"); UCC Comment 2 to § 2–706 ("[f]ailure to act properly under this section deprives the seller of the measure of damages here provided and relegates him to that provided in Section 2–708"); UCC Comment 1 to § 2–704 (describes § 2–706 as the "primary remedy" available to a seller upon breach by the buyer); see also Commonwealth Edison Co. v. Decker Coal Co., 653 F.Supp. 841, 844 (N.D.Ill.1987) (statutory language and case law suggest that "§ 2–708 remedies are available only to a seller who is not entitled to the contract price" under § 2–709); Childres & Burgess, Seller's Remedies: The Primacy of UCC § 2–708(2), 48 N.Y.U.L.Rev. 833, 863–64 (1973). As one commentator has noted, 2–706 is the Code section drafted specifically to define the damage rights of aggrieved reselling sellers, and there is no suggestion within it that the profit formula of section 2–708(2) is in any way intended to qualify or be superior to it." Shanker, The Case for a Literal Reading of UCC Section 2–708(2) (One Profit for the Reseller), 24 Case W.Res. 697, 699 (1973).

2. UCC Comment 2 to 2–708(2) also suggests that 2–708 has broader applicability than suggested by the district court. UCC Comment 2 provides:

This section permits the recovery of lost profits in all appropriate cases, which would include all standard priced goods. The normal measure there would be list price less cost to the dealer or list price less manufacturing cost to the manufacturer.

The district court's restrictive interpretation of 2–708(2) was based in part on UCC Comment 1 to 2–704 which describes 2–706 as the aggrieved seller's primary remedy. The district court concluded that, if a lost volume seller could recover its lost profit under 2–708(2), every seller would attempt to recover damages under 2–708(2) and 2–706 would become the aggrieved seller's residuary remedy. This argument ignores the fact that to recover under 2–708(2), a seller must first establish its status as a lost volume seller....

The district court also concluded that a lost volume seller cannot recover its lost profit under 2–708(2) because such a result would negate a seller's duty to mitigate damages. This position fails to recognize the fact that, by definition, a lost volume seller cannot mitigate damages through resale. Resale does not reduce a lost volume seller's damages because the breach has still resulted in its losing one sale and a corresponding profit. See Autonumerics, 144 Ariz. at 192, 696 P.2d at 1341.

Those courts that found that a lost volume seller can recover its lost profits under 2–708(2) implicitly rejected the position adopted by the district court; those courts started with the assumption that 2–708 applied to a lost volume seller without considering whether the seller was limited to the remedy provided under 2–706. None of those courts even suggested that a seller who resold goods in a commercially reasonable manner was limited to the damage formula provided under 2–706. We conclude that the Illinois Supreme Court, if presented with this question, would adopt the position of these other jurisdictions and would conclude that a reselling seller, such as Diasonics, is free to reject the damage formula prescribed in 2–706 and choose to proceed under 2–708.

Concluding that Diasonics is entitled to seek damages under 2–708, however, does not automatically result in Diasonics being awarded its lost profit. Two different measures of damages are provided in 2–708. Subsection 2–708(1) provides for a measure of damages calculated by subtracting the market price at the time and place for tender from the contract price.[3] The profit measure of damages, for which Diasonics is asking, is contained in 2–708(2). However, one applies 2–708(2) only if "the measure of damages provided in subsection (1) is inadequate to put the seller in as good a position as performance would have done...." ... Diasonics claims that 2–708(1) does not provide an adequate measure of damages when the seller is a lost volume seller.[4] To understand Diasonics' argument, we need to define the concept of the lost volume seller. Those cases that have addressed this issue have defined a lost volume seller as one that has a predictable and finite number of customers and that has the capacity either to sell to all new buyers or to make the one additional sale represented by the resale after the breach. According to a number of courts and commentators, if the seller would have made the sale represented by the resale whether or not the breach occurred, damages measured by the difference between the contract price and market price cannot put the lost volume seller in as good a position as it would have been in had the buyer performed.[5] The breach effectively cost the seller a "profit," and the seller can only be made whole by awarding it damages in the amount of its "lost profit" under 2–708(2).

We agree with Diasonics' position that, under some circumstances, the measure of damages provided under 2–708(1) will not put a reselling seller in as good a position as it would have been in had the buyer performed

---

3. There is some debate in the commentaries about whether a seller who has resold the goods may ignore the measure of damages provided in 2–706 and elect to proceed under 2–708(1). Under some circumstances the contract-market price differential will result in overcompensating such a seller. See J. White & R. Summers, Handbook of the Law under the Uniform Commercial Code § 7–7, at 271–73 (2d ed. 1980); Sebert, Remedies under Article Two of the Uniform Commercial Code: An Agenda for Review, 130 U.Pa.L.Rev. 360, 380–83 (1981). We need not struggle with this question here because Diasonics has not sought to recover damages under 2–708(1).

4. This is also the position adopted by those courts that have held that a lost volume seller can recover its lost profits under 2–708(2)....

5. According to one commentator,

Resale results in loss of volume only if three conditions are met: (1) the person who bought the resold entity would have been solicited by plaintiff had there been no breach and resale; (2) the solicitation would have been successful; and (3) the plaintiff could have performed that additional contract.

Harris, supra, at 82 (footnotes omitted).

because the breach resulted in the seller losing sales volume. However, we disagree with the definition of "lost volume seller" adopted by other courts. Courts awarding lost profits to a lost volume seller have focused on whether the seller had the capacity to supply the breached units in addition to what it actually sold. In reality, however, the relevant questions include, not only whether the seller could have produced the breached units in addition to its actual volume, but also whether it would have been profitable for the seller to produce both units. Goetz & Scott, Measuring Sellers' Damages: The Lost–Profits Puzzle, 31 Stan.L.Rev. 323, 332–33, 346–47 (1979). As one commentator has noted, under

> the economic law of diminishing returns or increasing marginal costs[,] ... as a seller's volume increases, then a point will inevitably be reached where the cost of selling each additional item diminishes the incremental return to the seller and eventually makes it entirely unprofitable to conclude the next sale.

Shanker, supra n. 1, at 705. Thus, under some conditions, awarding a lost volume seller its presumed lost profit will result in overcompensating the seller, and 2–708(2) would not take effect because the damage formula provided in 2–708(1) does place the seller in as good a position as if the buyer had performed. Therefore, on remand, Diasonics must establish, not only that it had the capacity to produce the breached unit in addition to the unit resold, but also that it would have been profitable for it to have produced and sold both. Diasonics carries the burden of establishing these facts because the burden of proof is generally on the party claiming injury to establish the amount of its damages; especially in a case such as this, the plaintiff has easiest access to the relevant data....[6]

One final problem with awarding a lost volume seller its lost profits was raised by the district court. This problem stems from the formulation of the measure of damages provided under 2–708(2) which is "the profit (including reasonable overhead) which the seller would have made from full performance by the buyer, together with any incidental damages provided in this Article (Section 2–710), due allowance for costs reasonably incurred and due credit for payments or *proceeds of resale*." ... (emphasis added). The literal language of 2–708(2) requires that the proceeds from resale be credited against the amount of damages awarded which, in most cases, would result in the seller recovering nominal damages. In those cases in which the lost volume seller was awarded its lost profit as damages, the courts have circumvented this problem by concluding that this language only applies to proceeds realized from the resale of uncompleted goods for scrap. See, e.g., Neri [v. Retail Marine Corp., 30 N.Y.2d 393, 399 & n. 2, 334 N.Y.S.2d 165, 169 & n. 2, 285 N.E.2d 311, 314 & n. 2 (1972)]; *see also* J. White & R. Summers, Handbook of the Law under the Uniform Commercial Code § 7–13, at 285 ("courts should simply ignore the 'due credit' language in lost volume cases") (footnote omitted). Although neither the

---

6. As some commentators have pointed out, the cost of calculating a loss of profit may be very high. Goetz & Scott, supra, at 353 ("the complexity of the lost-volume prob-lem suggests that the information costs of exposing an overcompensatory rule are rela-tively high").

text of 2–708(2) nor the official comments limit its application to resale of goods for scrap, there is evidence that the drafters of 2–708 seemed to have had this more limited application in mind when they proposed amending 2–708 to include the phrase "due credit for payments or proceeds of resale."[7] We conclude that the Illinois Supreme Court would adopt this more restrictive interpretation of this phrase rendering it inapplicable to this case.

We therefore reverse the grant of summary judgment in favor of Davis and remand with instructions that the district court calculate Diasonics' damages under 2–708(2) if Diasonics can establish, not only that it had the capacity to make the sale to Davis as well as the sale to the resale buyer, but also that it would have been profitable for it to make both sales. Of course, Diasonics, in addition, must show that it probably would have made the second sale absent the breach.

[In an omitted part of the opinion, the court went on to uphold dismissal of the third-party complaint.]

NOTES

(1) *Appeal after Remand.* On remand, after a three-day bench trial, the district judge concluded that Diasonics had adequately established damages for lost profits amounting to $453,050 and entered judgment for that sum less the $300,000 deposit retained by Diasonics. On appeal by Davis, the Court of Appeals upheld this conclusion as not clearly erroneous. "The evidence is undisputed that Diasonics possessed the capacity to manufacture one more MRI. Diasonics also demonstrated that it was ... 'beating the bushes for all possible sales.' ... Diasonics was still a young company struggling to acquire business in an extremely competitive market.... The mere fact that Diasonics was unable to specify the particular unit Davis contracted to buy and trace the exact resale buyer for that unit ... should not foreclose it from recovering lost profits." R.E. Davis Chemical Corp. v. Diasonics, Inc., 924 F.2d 709, 711–12 (7th Cir.1991).

(2) *Lost Volume.* Many hundreds of pages of economic analysis have been devoted to the subject of sellers' claims of lost volume resulting from buyers' breaches. Two helpful sources are Robert Cooter & Melvin Eisenberg, Damages for Breach of Contract, 73 Cal.L.Rev. 1432, 1444–77 (1985); Goldberg, *Framing Contract Law* (2006).

In practice, the outcome may turn on who has the burden of proof on the issue of lost volume. Courts have generally placed the burden of proof on the seller. See Famous Knitwear Corp. v. Drug Fair, Inc., 493 F.2d 251 (4th Cir.1974). But in Islamic Republic of Iran v. Boeing Co., 771 F.2d 1279 (9th Cir.1985), the court rejected the argument that to take advantage of UCC § 2–708(2) a seller must prove that the market is one "in which supply exceeds demand." "We will not ... impose rigid and complex burdens of proof on this section.... Most other jurisdictions have held that to qualify as a 'lost volume' seller under section 2–708(2), the seller needs to show only that it *could have* supplied both the breaching purchaser and the resale purchaser."

7. In explaining its recommendation that 2–708 be amended to include the requirement that due credit be given for resale, the Enlarged Editorial Board stated that its purpose was "to clarify the privilege of the seller to realize junk value when it is manifestly useless to complete the operation of manufacture." Supplement No. 1 to the 1952 Official Draft (1955), quoted in Harris, supra, at 98.

PROBLEM

A Paradox. How do you explain the following paradox? In order to justify allowing recovery for breach of a contract on which neither party appears to have relied, a court reasons that the injured party might have passed up the opportunity of making a similar alternative contract but should not be required to prove this. Then in calculating the injured party's damages, the court reasons that the injured party lost volume because it would not have passed up the opportunity of making a similar alternative contract but would have made both contracts. Judicial inconsistency?

————

LOSING CONTRACTS

If a lottery operator failed to deliver a purchased ticket, the purchaser could "get his money back whether or not he eventually would have won the lottery." Does this mean that an aggrieved party is generally entitled to restitution under a "losing contract"—even though that party would have sustained a loss had that contract been performed?

Consider the following as a possible solution. "In cases where the venture would have proved profitable to the promisee, there is no reason why he should not recover his expenses. On the other hand, on those occasions in which the performance would not have covered the promisee's outlay, such a result imposes the risk of the promisee's contract upon the promisor. We cannot agree that the promisor's default in performance should under this guise make him an insurer of the promisee's venture; yet it does not follow that the breach should not throw upon him the duty of showing that the value of the performance would in fact have been less than the promisee's outlay. It is often very hard to learn what the value of the performance would have been; and it is a common expedient, and a just one, in such situations to put the peril of the answer upon that party who by his wrong has made the issue relevant to the rights of the other. On principle therefore the proper solution would seem to be that the promisee may recover his outlay in preparation for the performance, subject to the privilege of the promisor to reduce it by as much as he can show that the promisee would have lost, if the contract had been performed." Learned Hand in L. Albert & Son v. Armstrong Rubber Co., 178 F.2d 182, 189 (2d Cir.1949).

The case just quoted from involved material delay by a seller of machines to be used by the buyer to reclaim old rubber during World War II. The buyer did not ask for loss of profits when the delay caused this speculative venture to fall through, but did claim expenses in reliance on the seller's promise to deliver on time, including the cost of laying foundations for the machines. It was this claim to which Hand spoke. For a defense of expectation-based recovery in such cases, see Andrew Kull, Restitution as a Remedy for Breach of Contract, 67 S. Cal.L.Rev. 1465 (1994); Henry Mather, Restitution as a Remedy for Breach of Contract: The Case of the Partially Performing Seller, 92 Yale L.J. 14 (1982).

UCC § 2–718(2) provides for some restitution when a party has prepaid. Notice that this section applies to pre-paying buyers. What about a pre-delivering seller? See UCC § 2–709.

PROBLEM

Flour Markets. Buyer made a $500,000 payment on a contract for the sale of flour for a total price of $1,400,000. Seller broke the contract by failing to deliver the flour, although the market price of the flour had dropped to $1,100,000 by the time of delivery. Is Buyer entitled to restitution of $500,000 from Seller? See Bush v. Canfield, 2 Conn. 485 (1818).

United States v. Algernon Blair, Inc.

United States Court of Appeals, Fourth Circuit, 1973.
479 F.2d 638.

■ CRAVEN, CIRCUIT JUDGE. May a subcontractor, who justifiably ceases work under a contract because of the prime contractor's breach, recover in quantum meruit the value of labor and equipment already furnished pursuant to the contract irrespective of whether he would have been entitled to recover in a suit on the contract? We think so, and, for reasons to be stated, the decision of the district court will be reversed.

The subcontractor, Coastal Steel Erectors, Inc., brought this action under the provisions of the Miller Act, 40 U.S.C.A. § 270a et seq., in the name of the United States against Algernon Blair, Inc., and its surety, United States Fidelity and Guaranty Company. Blair had entered a contract with the United States for the construction of a naval hospital in Charleston County, South Carolina. Blair had then contracted with Coastal to perform certain steel erection and supply certain equipment in conjunction with Blair's contract with the United States. Coastal commenced performance of its obligations, supplying its own cranes for handling and placing steel. Blair refused to pay for crane rental, maintaining that it was not obligated to do so under the subcontract. Because of Blair's failure to make payments for crane rental, and after completion of approximately 28 percent of the subcontract, Coastal terminated its performance. Blair then proceeded to complete the job with a new subcontractor. Coastal brought this action to recover for labor and equipment furnished.

The district court found that the subcontract required Blair to pay for crane use and that Blair's refusal to do so was such a material breach as to justify Coastal's terminating performance. This finding is not questioned on appeal. The court then found that under the contract the amount due Coastal, less what had already been paid, totaled approximately $37,000. Additionally, the court found Coastal would have lost more than $37,000 if it had completed performance. Holding that any amount due Coastal must be reduced by any loss it would have incurred by complete performance of the contract, the court denied recovery to Coastal. While the district court correctly stated the " 'normal' rule of contract damages," we think Coastal is entitled to recover in quantum meruit.

In United States for Use of Susi Contracting Co. v. Zara Contracting Co., 146 F.2d 606 (2d Cir.1944), a Miller Act action, the court was faced with a situation similar to that involved here—the prime contractor had unjustifiably breached a subcontract after partial performance by the subcontractor. The court stated:

> For it is an accepted principle of contract law, often applied in the case of construction contracts, that the promisee upon breach has the option to forego any suit on the contract and claim only the reasonable value of his performance.

146 F.2d at 610. . . . Quantum meruit recovery is not limited to an action against the prime contractor but may also be brought against the Miller Act surety, as in this case. Further, that the complaint is not clear in regard to the theory of a plaintiff's recovery does not preclude recovery under quantum meruit. Narragansett Improvement Co. v. United States, 290 F.2d 577 (1st Cir.1961). A plaintiff may join a claim for quantum meruit with a claim for damages from breach of contract.

In the present case, Coastal has, at its own expense, provided Blair with labor and the use of equipment. Blair, who breached the subcontract, has retained these benefits without having fully paid for them. On these facts, Coastal is entitled to restitution in quantum meruit.

> The "restitution interest," involving a combination of unjust impoverishment with unjust gain, presents the strongest case for relief. If, following Aristotle, we regard the purpose of justice as the maintenance of an equilibrium of goods among members of society, the restitution interest presents twice as strong a claim to judicial intervention as the reliance interest, since if A not only causes B to lose one unit but appropriates that unit to himself, the resulting discrepancy between A and B is not one unit but two.

Fuller & Perdue, The Reliance Interest in Contract Damages, 46 Yale L.J. 52, 56 (1936).

The impact of quantum meruit is to allow a promisee to recover the value of services he gave to the defendant irrespective of whether he would have lost money on the contract and been unable to recover in a suit on the contract. Scaduto v. Orlando, 381 F.2d 587, 595 (2d Cir.1967). The measure of recovery for quantum meruit is the reasonable value of the performance, Restatement of Contracts § 347 (1932); and recovery is undiminished by any loss which would have been incurred by complete performance. 12 Williston on Contracts § 1485, at 312 (3d ed. 1970). While the contract price may be evidence of reasonable value of the services, it does not measure the value of the performance or limit recovery. Rather, the standard for measuring the reasonable value of the services rendered is the amount for which such services could have been purchased from one in the plaintiff's position at the time and place the services were rendered.

Since the district court has not yet accurately determined the reasonable value of the labor and equipment use furnished by Coastal to Blair, the case must be remanded for those findings.[1] When the amount has been determined, judgment will be entered in favor of Coastal, less payments already made under the contract. Accordingly, for the reasons stated above, the decision of the district court is

Reversed and remanded with instructions.

NOTES

(1) *Measure of Restitution Interest.* What recovery for Builder under the losing contract according to *Algernon Blair?* What is the court's justification for measuring Coastal's restitution interest by "the reasonable value of the performance"? Is this a proper measure of the "benefits" that Blair "retained without having fully paid for"? How does it differ from Coastal's reliance interest? See Restatement § 371. The conclusion that "the property owner is enriched by each stroke of the hammer or the paint brush" is characterized as "Pickwickian" in Edwin Patterson, The Scope of Restitution and Unjust Enrichment, 1 Mo.L.Rev. 223, 230 (1936).

For a case allowing recovery for expenditures prior to the making of the contract, see Anglia Television Ltd. v. Reed, 3 All.E.R. 690 (Court of Appeal 1971). When an actor repudiated his contract to play the lead role for a studio, the studio abandoned the film and sued for expenditures including those incurred before contracting with him. Lord Denning explained that this sum was recoverable since "it was such as would reasonably be in the contemplation of the parties as likely to be wasted if the contract was broken." Can such recovery be justified?

Of course a claimant that, like Coastal, asks for restitution must account for any benefits that it has received. In Coastal's case its benefits were "what had already been paid," its progress payments. Accounting for a claimant's benefits is not always so simple. In EarthInfo v. Hydrosphere Resource Consultants, 900 P.2d 113, 120–21 (Colo.1995), Hydrosphere sought restitution, having "rescinded" its software development contracts with Earthinfo because of the latter's "substantial" breach in suspending royalty payments. The court allowed restitution based on Earthinfo's profits during time the contract was in effect and then turned to Earthinfo's claim to the benefit it had conferred on Hydrosphere during that time. The Supreme Court of Colorado said that on remand the trial court "must determine which part of the profit results from [Earthinfo's] own independent efforts and which part results from the benefits provided by [Hydrosphere].... The allocation ... may be affected by such factors as the seriousness of [Earthinfo's] wrongdoing and the extent to which [Hydrosphere's] contribution was at risk in the profit making enterprise." The burden of establishing the parties' relative contributions was on Earthinfo.

(2) *Contract Price as a Ceiling.* An injured party who has fully performed and then been refused payment can not recover more than the contract price. Should an injured party who has not fully performed be allowed to recover "the reasonable value of the performance" even if it exceeds the contract price? Using the contract price as a ceiling on recovery in such a case will not entirely avoid problems of measurement of the benefit conferred on the party in breach, since that benefit must, at least in principle, be measured before it can be known whether the ceiling has been reached. On the other hand, not using the contract price as a ceiling on

---

1. Under the view of the case taken by the district court it was unnecessary to precisely appraise the value of services and materials rendered; an approximation was thought to suffice because the hypothetical loss had the contract been fully performed was greater in amount.

recovery may result in a more generous recovery for part performance than would have been allowed for full performance.

For authority that the contract price is a ceiling, see Johnson v. Bovee, 574 P.2d 513 (Colo.App.1978). Cf. John T. Brady & Co. v. City of Stamford, 599 A.2d 370, 377 (Conn.1991), in which the court, through Peters, C.J., held that where "work on the project was 99 percent complete," restitution was precluded by the rule that after "full performance ... the appropriate measure of the value of the benefit conferred ... is the value that the parties themselves, in their contract, have assigned to that performance." For authority that it is not, see Southern Painting Co. v. United States, 222 F.2d 431 (10th Cir.1955).

PROBLEM

Kansas City to Atlantic City and Back. Security Stove in Kansas City had developed a furnace which it was anxious to exhibit at a trade association convention in Atlantic City, although it was not yet on the market. Since it was too late to ship it by freight, Security Stove made a contract for its shipment with Express Company, explaining its need, asking that it be shipped to arrive by October 8, and reminding Express Company of the urgency shortly before the date for shipment. Express Company picked up the shipment of 21 numbered packages, but the package containing the gas manifold, the most important part of the exhibit, was mislaid and did not arrive until the convention closed. Security Stove sues to recover from Express Company for express charges to Atlantic City, freight charges back to Kansas City, travel and hotel expenses and salaries for its employees who went to the convention to exhibit the furnace, and rental for the booth. What decision? See Security Stove & Mfg. Co. v. American Railway Express Co., 51 S.W.2d 572 (Mo.App.1932).

SECTION 3. LIMITATIONS ON DAMAGES

(A) AVOIDABILITY

In Virtue v. Bird, 84 Eng.Rep. 1000, 86 Eng.Rep. 200 (King's Bench 1678), a quaint case from three centuries ago, the plaintiff contracted to carry goods to Ipswich and to deliver them to a place to be appointed by the defendant. When the plaintiff arrived in Ipswich, however, "the defendant delayed by the space of six hours the appointment of the place; insomuch that his horses being so hot ... and standing in aperto aere, they died soon after." The court denied him recovery of this loss on the ground that "it was the plaintiff's folly to let the horses stand," for he "might have taken his horses out of the cart, or have laid down the [goods] any where in Ipswich."

Under an important limitation on expectation, an aggrieved promisee is not allowed to recover loss that it could reasonably have avoided. See Restatement § 350. Although it is sometimes said that the injured party is under a "duty" to mitigate damages, the injured party incurs no liability to the party in breach for a failure to mitigate. Recovery is the same regardless of whether the injured party takes steps in mitigation or not.

The injured party is simply precluded from recovering for loss that it could reasonably have avoided.

Where there is a market for goods, a buyer's damages are based on the assumption that the buyer could reasonably have avoided greater loss by obtaining substitute goods on the market. See UCC § 2–713, under which "the measure of damages ... is the difference between the market price ... and the contract price." See also CISG arts. 76(1), 77; UNIDROIT Principles arts. 7.4.6, 7.4.8.

For an example, recall that in *Klein,* p. 588 above, the court said that "money damages would clearly be adequate in this case" and remanded the case for a trial on damages. How should damages be calculated in such a trial? Recall that Klein "argued that he wanted the plane to resell it for a profit." Should Klein be allowed to recover the profit (say $500,000) he lost on that resale? This, along with return of his payments, would seem to give Klein his expectation by putting him in the position he would have been in had PepsiCo delivered the G–II jet. But if Klein could have realized the resale profit by obtaining a substitute G–II jet on the market for a somewhat enhanced price (say $200,000 more than the $4.75 million he was to pay PepsiCo), he could have put himself in that position for only $200,000.

Rockingham County v. Luten Bridge Co.

United States Circuit Court of Appeals, Fourth Circuit, 1929.
35 F.2d 301, 66 A.L.R. 735.

[Action at law, instituted in the district court, to recover an amount alleged to be due under a contract for the construction of a bridge in North Carolina. The contract was entered into by the Board of County Commissioners on January 7, 1924; but there was considerable public opposition to the building of the bridge, and on February 21, 1924, the board notified the plaintiff not to proceed any further under the contract, which it refused (unjustifiably, as the court found) to recognize as valid.[a] At that time plaintiff had expended about $1900 for labor done and material on the ground. Despite this notice from the county commissioners, plaintiff continued to build the bridge in accordance with the terms of the contract. The present action is brought to recover $18,301.07, the amount alleged to be due plaintiff for work done before November 3, 1924. The trial court directed a verdict for plaintiff for this sum. Defendant appealed.]

a. The vote of the commissioners had been three to two in favor of the contract, but on February 11 one of the commissioners who had voted in favor sent his resignation to the clerk, who immediately accepted it. Later the same day this commissioner attempted to withdraw his resignation, but the clerk ignored this and appointed another person to succeed him. The three commissioners who had voted in favor attended no further meetings, but the new commissioner together with the two who had voted against met frequently and, on February 21, unanimously adopted a resolution asserting that the contract was not valid and directing the clerk to so notify Luten, which he did. On April 7, the board passed a resolution reciting that it had been informed that one of its members was privately insisting that the bridge be built and repudiating this action by the member. In September it passed a resolution stating that it would pay no bills for the bridge.

■ PARKER, CIRCUIT JUDGE. . . . Coming, then, to the third question—i.e., as to the measure of plaintiff's recovery—we do not think that, after the county had given notice, while the contract was still executory, that it did not desire the bridge built and would not pay for it, plaintiff could proceed to build it and recover the contract price. It is true that the county had no right to rescind the contract, and the notice given plaintiff amounted to a breach on its part; but, after plaintiff had received notice of the breach, it was its duty to do nothing to increase the damages flowing therefrom. If A enters into a binding contract to build a house for B, B, of course, has no right to rescind the contract without A's consent. But if, before the house is built, he decides that he does not want it, and notifies A to that effect, A has no right to proceed with the building and thus pile up damages. His remedy is to treat the contract as broken when he receives the notice, and sue for the recovery of such damages as he may have sustained from the breach, including any profit which he would have realized upon perform-ance, as well as any other losses which may have resulted to him. In the case at bar, the county decided not to build the road of which the bridge was to be a part, and did not build it. The bridge, built in the midst of the forest, is of no value to the county because of this change of circumstances. When, therefore, the county gave notice to the plaintiff that it would not proceed with the project, plaintiff should have desisted from further work. It had no right thus to pile up damages by proceeding with the erection of a useless bridge.

The contrary view was expressed by Lord Cockburn in Frost v. Knight, L.R. 7 Ex. 111, but, as pointed out by Prof. Williston (Williston on Contracts, vol. 3, p. 2347), it is not in harmony with the decisions in this country. The American rule and the reasons supporting it are well stated by Prof. Williston as follows:

"There is a line of cases running back to 1845 which holds that, after an absolute repudiation or refusal to perform by one party to a contract, the other party cannot continue to perform and recover damages based on full performance. This rule is only a particular application of the general rule of damages that a plaintiff cannot hold a defendant liable for damages which need not have been incurred; or, as it is often stated, the plaintiff must, so far as he can without loss to himself, mitigate the damages caused by the defendant's wrongful act. The application of this rule to the matter in question is obvious. If a man engages to have work done, and afterwards repudiates his contract before the work has been begun or when it has been only partially done, it is inflicting damage on the defendant without benefit to the plaintiff to allow the latter to insist on proceeding with the contract. The work may be useless to the defendant, and yet he would be forced to pay the full contract price. On the other hand, the plaintiff is interested only in the profit he will make out of the contract. If he receives this it is equally advantageous for him to use his time otherwise." . . .

Judgment reversed.

NOTE

The Code. Under UCC § 2–704(2), a seller that is to manufacture goods may proceed to complete their manufacture upon the buyer's repudiation, instead of halting manufacture and salvaging them while in process, "in the exercise of reasonable commercial judgment for the purposes of avoiding loss and of effective realization." The seller that does so may then base recovery on the goods as completed, even if the "reasonable commercial judgment" turned out to be wrong. Is the manufacturer's situation in any way distinguishable from that of the Luten Bridge Co.?

PROBLEM

Walking Across the Brooklyn Bridge. In the Brooklyn Bridge hypothetical (p. 220 above), assume that on finishing the walk across the bridge B will have to spend $10 to take a taxi back to where A is waiting. If A attempts to revoke the $100 offer after B has taken only a few steps, can B recover $100 after continuing to walk across the bridge and spending the $10 on a taxi? See Restatement § 45(2). What do you think B should do when A attempts to revoke? What answer if A's offer had been to pay B $100 in return for B's *promise* to walk across the bridge? Is § 45(2) consistent with the principle of avoidability?

––––––––

AVOIDABILITY UNDER CONTRACTS FOR THE SALE OF GOODS

It is one thing to say, as the court did in the *Luten Bridge* case, that the injured party cannot recover for cost that could have been avoided by simply *stopping performance*. It is another to take a second step and say that the injured party cannot recover for loss that could have been avoided by taking *affirmative steps* to arrange a substitute transaction. This second step is the basis for some of the most important rules governing damages for breach of contract for the sale of goods.

In a market economy, it is assumed that the injured party can generally arrange a substitute transaction and, under the principle of avoidability, is expected to do so. If the seller fails to deliver goods, the buyer can go into the market and "cover" by obtaining substitute goods, so that the buyer's damages should be based on the difference between a presumably greater price that the buyer will have to pay on the market and the lesser contract price. See UCC § 2–712. If the buyer fails to take and pay for goods, the seller can go into the market and resell to a substitute buyer, so that the seller's damages should be based on the difference between the presumably greater contract price and a lesser price it will receive on the market. See UCC § 2–706.

For the injured party that fails to take advantage of the availability of a substitute transaction on the market, the limitation of avoidability results in a formula based on the difference between the contract price and the market price at which it could have arranged a hypothetical substitute transaction. If, when the seller fails to deliver goods, the buyer fails to go into the market and "cover," its damages are based on "the difference between the market price ... and the contract price." UCC § 2–713. If, when the buyer fails to take and pay for goods, the seller fails to go into the market and resell, its damages are based on "the difference between the market price ... and the unpaid contract price." UCC § 2–708. On proof of market price, see UCC §§ 2–723, 2–724.

NOTE

Windfalls? The Code rules in this area have occasioned criticism on the ground that they sometimes seem to give the injured party a "windfall" by allowing that party to recover more than its actual loss, in disregard of the goal stated in UCC § 1–305(a) of putting that party "in as good a position as if the other party had fully performed."

Suppose, for example, that the injured party has arranged an actual substitute transaction for a price *more* favorable than the market price. Can the injured party recover damages based on market price even though those damages exceed that party's actual loss? Comment 5 to UCC § 2–713 suggests that a buyer cannot do so by explaining that the section "provides a remedy which is completely alternative to cover ... and applies only when and to the extent that the buyer has not covered." See also UCC §§ 2–703, 2–711. But the Code nowhere suggests that a seller is subject to a similar restriction after a resale for more than market price. Should the Code be read as giving a "windfall" to a seller but not to a buyer? To neither? To both?

PROBLEMS

(1) *Klein Revisited.* In *Klein*, p. 588 above, suppose that Klein could have resold the G–II jet for $500,000 and that he could have bought one of the other similar G–II jets for $200,000 more than the contract price with PepsiCo.

If he promptly bought a G–III jet for $400,000 more than the contract price, how much could he recover?

If, after several inquiries, he promptly bought another G–II jet for $250,000 more than the contract price, how much could he recover?

If, after several inquiries, he promptly bought another G–II jet for $150,000 more than the contract price, how much could he recover?

(2) *Waiting for a Windfall?* Seller contracts to sell Buyer goods for $100,000. Buyer then makes a contract to resell the goods to another purchaser at $125,000. Seller fails to deliver. The market price of similar goods at and immediately after the delivery date is $110,000. Since Buyer's resale contract does not require delivery for six months, Buyer waits and does not go into the market for six months, by which time the market price has dropped to $90,000. How much should Buyer recover? Would $10,000 give Buyer a "windfall"? (Suppose that the market price had *risen* to $120,000 during Buyer's delay. How much should Buyer recover?) Is the applicable section UCC § 2–712 or 2–713?

Tongish v. Thomas

Supreme Court of Kansas, 1992.
840 P.2d 471.

[Dennis Tongish, a farmer, made a contract with the Decatur Coop Association under which he was to grow 116.8 acres of sunflower seeds, to be purchased by Coop at $13 per hundredweight for large seeds and $8 per hundredweight for small seeds, delivery to be in thirds by December 31, 1988, March 31, 1989, and May 31, 1989. Coop had a contract to deliver the seeds to Bambino Bean & Seed for the same price it paid Tongish plus a 55 cent per hundredweight handling fee, Coop's only anticipated profit. Owing to a short crop, bad weather, and other factors, the market price of sunflower seeds in January 1989 had risen to double that in the Tongish contract. Tongish notified Coop that he would make no more deliveries and sold the balance of his crop to Danny Thomas for about $20 per hundred-weight or $14,714, which was $5,153 more than the Coop contract price. Coop sued Tongish and recovered $455 in damages, based on its loss of handling charges. Coop appealed and the Court of Appeals reversed for determination of damages based on market price under UCC § 2–713. Tongish appealed, arguing that under UCC § 1–106 the trial court was correct.]

■ McFarland, Justice: This case presents the narrow issue of whether damages arising from the nondelivery of contracted-for sunflower seeds should be computed on the basis of K.S.A. 84–1–106 or K.S.A. 84–2–713. . . . The analyses and rationale of the Court of Appeals utilized in resolving the issue are sound and we adopt the following portion thereof: . . .

"There is authority for appellee's position that K.S.A. 84–2–713 should not be applied in certain circumstances. In Allied Canners & Packers, Inc. v. Victor Packing Co., 162 Cal.App.3d 905, 209 Cal.Rptr. 60 (1984), Allied contracted to purchase 375,000 pounds of raisins from Victor for 29.75 cents per pound with a 4% discount. Allied then contracted to sell the raisins for 29.75 cents per pound expecting a profit of $4,462.50 from the 4% discount it received from Victor. 162 Cal.App.3d at 907–08 [209 Cal. Rptr. 60].

"Heavy rains damaged the raisin crop and Victor breached its contract, being unable to fulfill the requirement. The market price of raisins had risen to about 80 cents per pound. Allied's buyers agreed to rescind their contracts so Allied was not bound to supply them with raisins at a severe loss. Therefore, the actual loss to Allied was the $4,462.50 profit it expected, while the difference between the market price and the contract price was about $150,000. 162 Cal.App.3d at 908–09 [209 Cal.Rptr. 60].

"The California appellate court, in writing an exception, stated: 'It has been recognized that the use of the market-price contract-price formula under section 2–713 does not, absent pure accident, result in a damage award reflecting the buyer's actual loss. [Citations omitted.]' 162 Cal. App.3d at 912 [209 Cal.Rptr. 60]. The court indicated that section 2–713 may be more of a statutory liquidated damages clause and, therefore, conflicts with the goal of section 1–106. The court discussed that in situations where the buyer has made a resale contract for the goods, which the seller knows about, it may be appropriate to limit 2–713 damages to actual loss. However, the court cited a concern that a seller not be rewarded for a bad faith breach of contract. 162 Cal.App.3d at 912–14 [209 Cal.Rptr. 60].

"In Allied, the court determined that if the seller knew the buyer had a resale contract for the goods, and the seller did not breach the contract in bad faith, the buyer was limited to actual loss of damages under section 1–106. 162 Cal.App.3d at 915 [209 Cal.Rptr. 60].

"The similarities between the present case and *Allied* are that the buyer made a resale contract which the seller knew about. (Tongish knew the seeds eventually went to Bambino, although he may not have known the details of the deal.) However, in examining the breach itself, Victor could not deliver the raisins because its crop had been destroyed. . . . Victor had no raisins to sell to any buyer, while Tongish took advantage of the doubling price of sunflower seeds and sold to Danny Thomas. Although the trial court had no need to find whether Tongish breached the contract in bad faith, it did find there was no valid reason for the breach. Therefore, the nature of Tongish's breach was much different than Victor's in *Allied*.

"Section 2–713 and the theories behind it have a lengthy and somewhat controversial history. In 1963, it was suggested that 2–713 was a statutory liquidated damages clause and not really an effort to try and accurately predict what actual damages would be. Peters, Remedies for Breach of Contracts Relating to the Sale of Goods Under the Uniform Commercial Code: A Roadmap for Article Two, 73 Yale L.J. 199, 259 (1963).

"In 1978, Robert Childres called for the repeal of section 2–713. Childres, Buyer's Remedies: The Danger of Section 2–713, 72 Nw.U.L.Rev. 837 (1978). Childres reflected that because the market price/contract price remedy 'has been the cornerstone of Anglo–American damages' that it has been so hard to see that this remedy 'makes no sense whatever when applied to real life situations.' 72 Nw.U.L.Rev. at 841–42.

"In 1979, David Simon and Gerald A. Novack wrote a fairly objective analysis of the two arguments about section 2–713 and stated:

'For over sixty years our courts have divided on the question of which measure of damages is appropriate for the supplier's breach of his delivery obligations. The majority view, reinforced by applicable codes, would award market damages even though in excess of plaintiff's loss. A persistent minority would reduce market damages to the plaintiff's loss, without regard to whether this creates a windfall for the defendant. Strangely enough, each view has generally tended to disregard the arguments, and even the existence, of the opposing view.' Simon and Novack, Limiting the Buyer's Market Damages to Lost Profits: A Challenge to the Enforceability of Market Contracts, 92 Harv.L.Rev. 1395, 1397 (1979).

"Although the article discussed both sides of the issue, the authors came down on the side of market price/contract price as the preferred damages theory. The authors admit that market damages fly in the face 'of the familiar maxim that the purpose of contract damages is to make the injured party whole, not penalize the breaching party.' 92 Harv.L.Rev. at 1437. However, they argue that the market damages rule discourages the breach of contracts and encourages a more efficient market. 92 Harv.L.Rev. at 1437.

"The *Allied* decision in 1984, which relied on the articles cited above for its analysis to reject market price/contract price damages, has been sharply criticized. In Schneider, UCC § Section 2–713: A Defense of Buyers' Expectancy Damages, 22 Cal.W.L.Rev. 233, 266 (1986), the author stated that *Allied* 'adopted the most restrictive [position] on buyer's damages. This Article is intended to reverse that trend.' Schneider argued that by following section 1–106, 'the court ignored the clear language of section 2–713's compensation scheme to award expectation damages in accordance with the parties' allocation of risk as measured by the difference between contract price and market price on the date set for performance.' 22 Cal.W.L.Rev. at 264.

"Recently in Scott, The Case for Market Damages: Revisiting the Lost Profits Puzzle, 57 U.Chi.L.Rev. 1155, 1200 (1990), the *Allied* result was called 'unfortunate.' Scott argues that section 1–106 is 'entirely consistent' with the market damages remedy of 2–713. 57 U.Chi.L.Rev. at 1201. According to Scott, it is possible to harmonize sections 1–106 and 2–713. Scott states, 'Market damages measure the expectancy ex ante, and thus reflect the value of the option; lost profits, on the other hand, measure losses ex post, and thus only reflect the value of the completed exchange.' 57 U.Chi.L.Rev. at 1174. The author argues that if the nonbreaching party has laid off part of the market risk (like Coop did) the lost profits rule creates instability because the other party is now encouraged to breach the contract if the market fluctuates to its advantage. 57 U.Chi.L.Rev. at 1178.

"We are not persuaded that the lost profits view under *Allied* should be embraced. It is a minority rule that has received only nominal support. We believe the majority rule or the market damages remedy as contained in K.S.A. 84–2–713 is more reasoned and should be followed as the preferred measure of damages. While application of the rule may not reflect the actual loss to a buyer, it encourages a more efficient market and discourages the breach of contracts." Tongish v. Thomas, 16 Kan.App.2d at 811–17 [829 P.2d 916].

At first blush, the result reached herein appears unfair. However, closer scrutiny dissipates this impression. By the terms of the contract Coop was obligated to buy Tongish's large sunflower seeds at $13 per hundredweight whether or not it had a market for them. Had the price of sunflower seeds plummeted by delivery time, Coop's obligation to purchase at the agreed price was fixed. If loss of actual profit pursuant to K.S.A. 84–1–106(1) would be the measure of damages to be applied herein, it would enable Tongish to consider the Coop contract price of $13 per hundredweight plus 55 cents per hundredweight handling fee as the "floor" price for his seeds, take advantage of rapidly escalating prices, ignore his contractual obligation, and profitably sell to the highest bidder. Damages computed under K.S.A. 84–2–713 encourage the honoring of contracts and market stability. . . .

[Judgment of the Court of Appeals affirmed.]

NOTES

(1) *Questions.* If Coop had gone into the market after Tongish's repudiation and bought seeds to deliver to Bambino for $14,714, could it have recovered $5,153 from Tongish under UCC § 2–712? If Coop bought no seeds to deliver to Bambino and therefore had to pay damages to Bambino, could Coop recover those damages from Tongish? Note that Allied's buyers had agreed to rescind their contracts. Should the result in *Tongish* be different if Bambino had agreed to rescind its contract with Coop? Compare Iron Trade Products v. Wilkoff, p. 759 below, with H–W–H Cattle Co. v. Schroeder, 767 F.2d 437 (8th Cir.1985). Should the result in *Tongish* be different if Coop had protected itself by reserving the power to

cancel the contract with Bambino on breach by Tongish? See Farnsworth, Legal Remedies for Breach of Contract, 70 Colum.L.Rev. 1145, 1190 n. 189 (1970).

(2) *A Cautionary Note on Efficient Breach.* Recall the discussion of The Economics of Remedies at p. 20 above. It would be a mistake to assume that a seller like Tongish, who deals with a commodity that has a market, can often commit such a breach when there is a rise in the market.

If Tongish had not made his contract with Coop, he would, of course, have been free to take advantage of the risen market for sunflower seeks and sell his crop on the market, as he did to Thomas. But he had a contract with Coop. If we suppose that the contract price was $13 per hundred-weight and that the risen market price was $20 per hundredweight, he would have gained an additional $7 per hundredweight by breaking his contract with Coop and selling on the risen market.

How much of that gain would be left after paying damages to Coop under the decision in *Tongish* to apply UCC § 2–713? How much of the gain would be left after paying damages to Coop under the decision in *Allied*? Can the difference in your answers be justified on the ground, noted by the court in *Tongish,* that "the nature of Tongish's breach" was much different than Victor's in *Allied*?

How can one explain the difference between a case such as *Naval Institute*, which seems to invite thoughts of efficient breach, and *Tongish*, which seems to discourage such thoughts?

(3) *More Middlemen.* Coop acted like a middleman between Tongish and Bambino Bean & Seed. Coop's expected profit for this service was 55 cent per hundredweight handling fee, or about $455. But recall that there were two separate contracts: one between Coop and Tongish; the other between Coop and Bambino Bean & Seed. If Bambino Bean & Seed breached or renegotiated its contract with Coop, then Coop's damages from Tongish's breach would not have been $455. Should the damages available to Coop depend on what might have happened to Bambino? See Goldberg's *Framing Contract Law* 225 (2006) on the middleman's damages.

PROBLEM

Tongish Topsy–Turvy? Seller contracts to sell Buyer goods for $100,000. Seller then makes a contract to purchase the goods from a supplier for $90,000. The market price for similar goods then falls to $75,000, and Buyer repudiates the contract. (The market price then remains constant through the delivery date.) Seller has neither received the goods from its supplier nor resold them to another buyer. How much should Seller recover? Would $25,000 give Seller a "windfall"? Does UCC § 2–708(2) apply if a seller will be overcompensated by UCC § 2–708(1)? Compare Nobs Chemical, U.S.A., Inc. v. Koppers Co., Inc., 616 F.2d 212 (5th Cir.1980), with Trans World Metals, Inc. v. Southwire Co., 769 F.2d 902 (2d Cir.1985), and see Robert Scott, The Case for Market Damages: Revisiting the Lost Profits Puzzle, 57 U.Chi.L.Rev. 1155, 1175–79 (1990).

———

INTRODUCTION TO *PARKER v. TWENTIETH CENTURY FOX*

The application of the principle of avoidability to contracts of employ-ment has proved particularly troublesome. In Gandell v. Pontigny, 171

Eng.Rep. 119 (1816), the court simply refused to apply the principle. A merchant was sued by his clerk, whom he had wrongfully discharged in the middle of a quarter. The clerk was allowed to recover the agreed compensation for the entire quarter, including the part when he had not worked, on Lord Ellenborough's reasoning that:

> Having served a part of the quarter and being willing to serve the residue, in contemplation of law he may be considered to have served the whole.

In Howard v. Daly, 61 N.Y. 362 (1875), a leading American case, Theodore W. Dwight[a] rejected this doctrine of "constructive service" as

> so wholly irreconcilable to that great and beneficent rule of law, that a person discharged from service must not remain idle, but must accept employment elsewhere if offered, that we cannot accept it.... The doctrine of "constructive service" is not only at war with principle but with the rules of political economy, as it encourages idleness and gives compensation to men who fold their arms and decline service, equal to those who perform with willing hands their stipulated amount of labor.

The case that follows is premised on rejection of the doctrine of constructive service and on applicability of the principle of avoidability.

Parker v. Twentieth Century–Fox Film Corp.

Supreme Court of California, 1970.
3 Cal.3d 176, 474 P.2d 689.

■ BURKE, JUSTICE. Defendant Twentieth Century–Fox Film Corporation appeals from a summary judgment granting to plaintiff the recovery of agreed compensation under a written contract for her services as an actress in a motion picture. As will appear, we have concluded that the trial court correctly ruled in plaintiff's favor and that the judgment should be affirmed.

Plaintiff is well known as an actress,[b] and in the contract between plaintiff and defendant is sometimes referred to as the "Artist." Under the contract, dated August 6, 1965, plaintiff was to play the female lead in defendant's contemplated production of a motion picture entitled "Bloomer Girl." The contract provided that defendant would pay plaintiff a minimum "guaranteed compensation" of $53,571.42 per week for 14 weeks commencing May 23, 1966, for a total of $750,000.[c] Prior to May 1966 defendant

---

a. Theodore W. Dwight (1822–1892) served as professor of law at Hamilton College, and then as professor of law and later as warden of the law school at Columbia from 1858 to 1891. His principal field was contracts. His method of teaching involved interrogation of his students on an assigned text, and it is reported that, "He could so cross-examine a dunce that the dunce would come off amazed at his own unconscious cerebration." From 1873 to 1875 he was a member of the New York Commission of Appeals, which had been created to help the Court of Appeals dispose of its backlog of undecided cases. It was said that his sixty-eight opinions were "monographs, exhausting the particular subject," and it was doubted "whether in any

reports a greater amount of learning is anywhere condensed into an equal number of pages."

b. Mrs. Parker may be better known to the reader under her professional name, Shirley MacLaine.

c. According to the opinion in the Court of Appeal, "It is admitted that, under the contract ... the defendant was entitled to cancel the production, or to dispense with plaintiff's services, so long as it paid her the guaranteed compensation. Plaintiff's cause of action, therefore, is not actually for a breach of her employment contract by an unlawful discharge; rather it is for a recovery under the contract according to its terms. The par-decided not to produce the picture and by a letter dated April 4, 1966, it notified plaintiff of that decision and that it would not "comply with our obligations to you under" the written contract.

By the same letter and with the professed purpose "to avoid any damage to you," defendant instead offered to employ plaintiff as the leading actress in another film tentatively entitled "Big Country, Big Man" (hereinafter, "Big Country"). The compensation offered was identical, as were 31 of the 34 numbered provisions or articles of the original contract.[1] Unlike "Bloomer Girl," however, which was to have been a musical production, "Big Country" was a dramatic "western type" movie. "Bloomer Girl" was to have been filmed in California; "Big Country" was to be produced in Australia. Also, certain terms in the proffered contract varied from those of the original.[2] Plaintiff was given one week within which to accept; she did not and the offer lapsed. Plaintiff then commenced this action seeking recovery of the agreed guaranteed compensation.

The complaint sets forth two causes of action. The first is for money due under the contract; the second, based upon the same allegations as the

ties also are in agreement that defendant's alternative obligation to pay plaintiff $750,000 if it did not utilize her services in 'Bloomer Girl' was subject to an implied condition that she mitigate defendant's obligations by accepting other suitable employment." 81 Cal. Rptr. 221, 222 (Ct.App.1969). This agreement is consistent with the rule that if the party in breach has "the option of choosing between two alternatives at the time of breach, 'the measure of damages is the loss caused by reason of the promisor failing to perform the promise with the lesser value.'" Liberty Bank v. Talman Home Mortgage Corp., 877 F.2d 400, 407 (8th Cir. 1989). Under the "play or pay" contract, the studio could therefore choose liability under the "play" branch as to which the mitigation principle applied. For criticism of the case, see Goldberg, Bloomer Girl Revisited or How to Frame an Unmade Picture, 1998 Wis. L.Rev. 1051.

1. Among the identical provisions was the following found in the last paragraph of Article 2 of the original contract: "We [defendant] shall not be obligated to utilize your [plaintiff's] services in or in connection with the Photoplay hereunder, our sole obligation, subject to the terms and conditions of this Agreement, being to pay you the guaranteed compensation herein provided for."

2. Article 29 of the original contract specified that plaintiff approved the director already chosen for "Bloomer Girl" and that in case he failed to act as director plaintiff was to have approval rights of any substitute director. Article 31 provided that plaintiff was to have the right of approval of the "Bloomer Girl" dance director, and Article 32 gave her the right of approval of the screenplay.

Defendant's letter of April 4 to plaintiff, which contained both defendant's notice of breach of the "Bloomer Girl" contract and offer of the lead in "Big Country," eliminated or impaired each of those rights. It read in part as follows: The terms and conditions of our offer of employment are identical to those set forth in the "BLOOMER GIRL" Agreement, Articles 1 through 34 and Exhibit A to the Agreement, except as follows:

"1. Article 31 of said Agreement will not be included in any contract of employment regarding 'BIG COUNTRY, BIG MAN' as it is not a musical and it thus will not need a dance director.

"2. In the 'BLOOMER GIRL' agreement, in Articles 29 and 32, you were given certain director and screenplay approvals and you had preapproved certain matters. Since there simply is insufficient time to negotiate with you regarding your choice of director and regarding the screenplay and since you already expressed an interest in performing the role in 'BIG COUNTRY, BIG MAN,' we must exclude from our offer of employment in 'BIG COUNTRY, BIG MAN' any approval rights as are contained in said Articles 29 and 32; however, we shall consult with you respecting the director to be selected to direct the photoplay and will further consult with you with respect to the screenplay and any revisions or changes therein, provided, however, that if we fail to agree ... the decision of ... [defendant] with respect to the selection of a director and to revisions and changes in the said screenplay shall be binding upon the parties to said agreement."

first, is for damages resulting from defendant's breach of contract. Defendant in its answer admits the existence and validity of the contract, that plaintiff complied with all the conditions, covenants and promises and stood ready to complete the performance, and that defendant breached and "anticipatorily repudiated" the contract. It denies, however, that any money is due to plaintiff either under the contract or as a result of its breach, and pleads as an affirmative defense to both causes of action plaintiff's allegedly deliberate failure to mitigate damages, asserting that she unreasonably refused to accept its offer of the leading role in "Big Country."

Plaintiff moved for summary judgment under Code of Civil Procedure section 437c, the motion was granted, and summary judgment for $750,000 plus interest was entered in plaintiff's favor. This appeal by defendant followed. . . .

The general rule is that the measure of recovery by a wrongfully discharged employee is the amount of salary agreed upon for the period of service, less the amount which the employer affirmatively proves the employee has earned or with reasonable effort might have earned from other employment. . . . However, before projected earnings from other employment opportunities not sought or accepted by the discharged employee can be applied in mitigation, the employer must show that the other employment was comparable, or substantially similar, to that of which the employee has been deprived; the employee's rejection of or failure to seek other available employment of a different or inferior kind may not be resorted to in order to mitigate damages. . . .

In the present case defendant has raised no issue of *reasonableness of efforts* by plaintiff to obtain other employment; the sole issue is whether plaintiff's refusal of defendant's substitute offer of "Big Country" may be used in mitigation. Nor, if the "Big Country" offer was of employment different or inferior when compared with the original "Bloomer Girl" employment, is there an issue as to whether or not plaintiff acted reasonably in refusing the substitute offer. Despite defendant's arguments to the contrary, no case cited or which our research has discovered holds or suggests that reasonableness is an element of a wrongfully discharged employee's option to reject, or fail to seek different or inferior employment lest the possible earnings therefrom be charged against him in mitigation of damages.[3]

---

3. Instead, in each case the reasonableness referred to was that of the *efforts* of the employee to obtain other employment that was not different or inferior; his right to reject the latter was declared as an unqualified rule of law. Thus, Gonzales v. Internat. Assn. of Machinists, supra, 213 Cal.App.2d 817, 823–824, 29 Cal.Rptr. 190, 194, holds that the trial court correctly instructed the jury that plaintiff union member, a machinist, was required to make "such *efforts* as the average [member of his union] desiring employment would make at that particular time and place" (italics added); but, further, that the court *properly rejected* defendant's *offer of proof* of the *availability of other kinds of employment* at the same or higher pay than plaintiff usually received and all outside the jurisdiction of his union, as plaintiff could not be required to accept different employment or a nonunion job.

In Harris v. Nat. Union, etc., Cooks and Stewards, supra, 116 Cal.App.2d 759, 761, 254 P.2d 673, 676, the issues were stated to be, inter alia, whether comparable employment was open to each plaintiff employee,

Applying the foregoing rules to the record in the present case, with all intendments in favor of the party opposing the summary judgment motion—here, defendant—it is clear that the trial court correctly ruled that plaintiff's failure to accept defendant's tendered substitute employment could not be applied in mitigation of damages because the offer of the "Big Country" lead was of employment both different and inferior, and that no factual dispute was presented on that issue. The mere circumstance that "Bloomer Girl" was to be a musical review calling upon plaintiff's talents as a dancer as well as an actress, and was to be produced in the City of Los Angeles, whereas "Big Country" was a straight dramatic role in a "Western Type" story taking place in an opal mine in Australia, demonstrates the difference in kind between the two employments; the female lead as a dramatic actress in a western style motion picture can by no stretch of imagination be considered the equivalent of or substantially similar to the lead in a song-and-dance production. Additionally, the substitute "Big Country" offer proposed to eliminate or impair the director and screenplay approvals accorded to plaintiff under the original "Bloomer Girl" contract (see fn. 2, ante), and thus constituted an offer of inferior employment. No expertise or judicial notice is required in order to hold that the deprivation or infringement of an employee's rights held under an original employment contract converts the available "other employment" relied upon by the employer to mitigate damages, into inferior employment which the employee need not seek or accept. (See Gonzales v. Internat. Assn. of Machinists, supra, 213 Cal.App.2d 817, 823–824, 29 Cal.Rptr. 190; and fn. 3, ante.) . . .

In view of the determination that defendant failed to present any facts showing the existence of a factual issue with respect to its sole defense—plaintiff's rejection of its substitute employment offer in mitigation of damages—we need not consider plaintiff's further contention that for various reasons, including the provisions of the original contract set forth in footnote 1, ante, plaintiff was excused from attempting to mitigate damages.

The judgment is affirmed.

■ SULLIVAN, ACTING CHIEF JUSTICE (dissenting). . . . Over the years the courts have employed various phrases to define the type of employment which the employee, upon his wrongful discharge, is under an obligation to accept. Thus in California alone it has been held that he must accept employment which is "substantially similar" . . .; "comparable employment" . . .; employment "in the same general line of the first employment" . . .; "equivalent to his prior position" . . .; "employment in a similar capacity" . . .; employment which is "not . . . of a different or inferior kind". . . .

For reasons which are unexplained, the majority . . . select from among the various judicial formulations which contain one particular phrase, "Not of a different or inferior kind," with which to analyze this case. I have

and if so whether each plaintiff made a *reasonable effort* to secure such employment. It was held that the trial court *properly sustained an objection to an offer to prove a custom of accepting a job in a lower rank* when work in the higher rank was not available, as "The duty of mitigation of damages . . . does not require the plaintiff 'to seek or to accept other employment of a different or inferior kind.'" (p. 764[5], 254 P.2d p. 676.)

discovered no historical or theoretical reason to adopt this phrase, which is simply a negative restatement of the affirmative standards set out in the above cases, as the exclusive standard. Indeed, its emergence is an example of the dubious phenomenon of the law responding not to rational judicial choice or changing social conditions, but to unrecognized changes in the language of opinions or legal treatises. However, the phrase is a serviceable one and my concern is not with its use as the standard but rather with what I consider its distortion.

The relevant language excuses acceptance only of employment which is of a *different kind . . . .* It has never been the law that the mere existence of *differences between two jobs in the same field* is sufficient, as a matter of law, to excuse an employee wrongfully discharged from one from accepting the other in order to mitigate damages. Such an approach would effectively eliminate any obligation of an employee to attempt to minimize damage arising from a wrongful discharge. The only alternative job offer an employee would be required to accept would be an offer of his former job by his former employer.

Although the majority appear to hold that there was a difference "in kind" between the employment offered plaintiff in "Bloomer Girl" and that offered in "Big Country", an examination of the opinion makes crystal clear that the majority merely point out differences between the two *films* (an obvious circumstance) and then apodictically assert that these constitute a difference in the *kind of employment.* The entire rationale of the majority boils down to this: that the *"mere circumstances"* that "Bloomer Girl" was to be a musical review while "Big Country" was a straight drama "demonstrates the difference in kind" since a female lead in a western is not "the equivalent of or substantially similar to" a lead in a musical. This is merely attempting to prove the proposition by repeating it. It shows that the vehicles for the display of the star's talents are different but it does not prove that her employment as a star in such vehicles is of necessity different *in kind* and either inferior or superior.

I believe that the approach taken by the majority (a superficial listing of differences with no attempt to assess their significance) may subvert a valuable legal doctrine.[4] The inquiry in cases such as this should not be whether differences between the two jobs exist (there will always be differences) but whether the differences which are present are substantial enough to constitute differences in the *kind* of employment or, alternatively, whether they render the substitute work employment of an *inferior kind . . . .*

I remain convinced that the relevant question in such cases is whether or not a particular contract provision is so significant that its omission creates employment of an inferior kind. This question is, of course, inti-

---

4. The values of the doctrine of mitigation of damages in this context are that it minimizes the unnecessary personal and social (e.g., nonproductive use of labor, litigation) costs of contractual failure. If a wrongfully discharged employee can, through his own action and without suffering financial or psychological loss in the process, reduce the damages accruing from the breach of contract, the most sensible policy is to require him to do so. I fear the majority opinion will encourage precisely opposite conduct.

mately bound up in what I consider the ultimate issue: whether or not the employee acted reasonably. This will generally involve a factual inquiry to ascertain the importance of the particular contract term and a process of weighing the absence of that term against the countervailing advantages of the alternate employment. In the typical case, this will mean that summary judgment must be withheld. . . .

NOTES

(1) *Questions.* Would it have made a difference if the studio's offer of substitute employment had been conditioned on MacLaine's surrender of her rights under the old contract?

Who should bear the burden of proof on the issue of avoidability? In Delliponti v. DeAngelis, 681 A.2d 1261, 1265 (Pa.1996), the court placed the burden on the defendant employer and held that it had failed to meet that burden. Although the plaintiff, a municipal employee, testified only "that she made telephone inquiries regarding three job openings she read about in the newspaper but did not pursue any other jobs," the court concluded that the municipality's "assertion that there were unquestionably comparable jobs available does not establish that there were actual vacant positions available" to the employee.

(2) *"Honor and Respect."* Personal service contracts often involve considerations not common in the case of other kinds of contracts. "If the general counsel of a large corporation is wrongfully discharged, he is not required, in order to mitigate his damages, to take a job as a dishwasher. . . . Our case involves a contract to build a sewer. There is no suggestion that the contractor, a corporation rather than an individual, would have lost 'honor and respect' by taking steps to mitigate its damages. And we cannot imagine how any such steps could be thought to degrade or humiliate the corporation." S.A. Healy Co. v. Milwaukee Metropolitan Sewerage District, 50 F.3d 476, 481 (7th Cir.1995) (Posner, C.J.).

The court in *Parker* laid no stress on the fact that the offer of substitute employment came from the employer that had broken the contract in suit. Might this circumstance call "honor and respect" into question? Might the answer depend on the circumstances of the breach? In Voorhees v. Guyan Machinery Co., 446 S.E.2d 672, 679 (W.Va.1994), the court explained that "an offer of reemployment by an employer will not diminish the employee's recovery if the offer is not accepted if circumstances are such as to render further association between the parties offensive or degrading to the employee." The court went on to observe that the former employer's offer of reemployment came after it had caused the employee to lose his job with his new employer and after he had sued his former employer, and concluded that expecting him to return to work for his former employer "in such circumstances would be tantamount to expecting that Sulla and Gaius Marius might form a productive working relationship after Sulla's march on Rome."

(3) *An Equal–Opportunity Exception?* Does the avoidability principle apply even if the party in breach has an equal opportunity to reduce the damages by the same act? In Shea–S&M Ball v. Massman–Kiewit–Early, 606 F.2d 1245, 1249–50 (D.C.Cir.1979), one contractor sued another for damage caused by the other's failure to control groundwater and prevent a sewer from overflowing.[a] The Court of Appeals held that it was error for the trial court to conclude that the plaintiff "had not properly mitigated its damages by failing to build a dike. . . . 'The duty to

a. The first contractor was an intended beneficiary of the second contractor's con- tract with the owner, the Washington Metropolitan Area Transit Authority.

mitigate damages is not applicable where the party whose duty it is primarily to perform a contract has equal opportunity for performance and equal knowledge of the consequences of nonperformance.'" Here the defendant "had the primary responsibility for controlling its water runoff and had the same opportunity as [the plaintiff] to build a dike that would have prevented the damages." A few courts have taken a similar position, severely criticized in Cates v. Morgan Portable Building Corp., 780 F.2d 683, 689 (7th Cir.1985) (Posner, C.J.: position is "discordant with common law principles" by not preserving injured party's "incentive to consider a wide range of possible methods of mitigation of damages").

PROBLEMS

(1) *A Classic Problem.* First Bank repossessed a collection of classic automobiles together with thousands of rare parts no longer manufactured. It contracted to sell them to Frederick Simeone, a private collector of vintage automobiles, for $400,000. Because of legal problems arising from the repossession, First Bank refused Simeone's tender of the price and later, mistakenly thinking it was relieved of its obligation to Simeone because of a provision in their contract, sold the cars and parts to SMB, Inc., which resold them for $1,000,000. Simeone sued First Bank and recovered $2,600,000, based on expert testimony that the cars and parts were worth $3,000,000. First Bank appealed on the ground that Simeone "could have mitigated his damages by purchasing the vehicles and parts from SMB, Inc. at the increased price." What result on appeal? See Simeone v. First Bank National Assn., 73 F.3d 184 (8th Cir.1996).

(2) *Diasonics (Reprise).* Suppose that in *Diasonics*, p. 619 above, a company affiliated with Davis had offered to buy the equipment if Davis did not, so that Davis would not lose its deposit. What result if Diasonics had ignored the offer? See Schiavi Mobile Homes, Inc. v. Gironda, 463 A.2d 722 (Me.1983).

AVOIDABILITY AND THE COST OF REMEDY DEFECT

Cases of defective, as distinguished from merely incomplete, performance may raise difficult problems of avoidability. If the breach consists merely of incomplete performance, the injured party can usually arrange to have someone else complete the work at less than the loss in value to the injured party. The limitation of avoidability then has the effect of restricting the injured party to damages based on that lesser cost to complete the work rather than on the loss in value. Suppose, for example, that a builder breaks a contract to construct a factory by failing to finish the roof, making the factory, unusable. The owner cannot recover the relatively enormous loss resulting from the inability to use the factory but is relegated to the relatively small amount that it will cost to get another builder to finish the roof.

If the performance is defective rather than merely incomplete, however, trouble may arise. In that case, part of the cost to remedy the defect and complete performance as agreed will probably be the cost of undoing some of the work already done. The total cost to remedy the defect may then exceed the loss in value to the injured party so that an award based on that cost would to that extent be a windfall. The following case involves this situation.

Jacob & Youngs v. Kent

Court of Appeals of New York, 1921.
230 N.Y. 239, 129 N.E. 889, 23 A.L.R. 1429.

■ CARDOZO, J. The plaintiff built a country residence for the defendant at a cost of upwards of $77,000, and now sues to recover a balance of $3,483.46, remaining unpaid. The work of construction ceased in June, 1914, and the defendant then began to occupy the dwelling. There was no complaint of defective performance until March, 1915. One of the specifications for the plumbing work provides that "all wrought iron pipe must be well galvanized, lap welded pipe of the grade known as 'standard pipe' of Reading manufacture." The defendant learned in March, 1915, that some of the pipe, instead of being made in Reading, was the product of other factories. The plaintiff was accordingly directed by the architect to do the work anew. The plumbing was then encased within the walls except in a few places where it had to be exposed. Obedience to the order meant more than the substitution of other pipe. It meant the demolition at great expense of substantial parts of the completed structure. The plaintiff left the work untouched, and asked for a certificate that the final payment was due. Refusal of the certificate was followed by this suit.[a]

The evidence sustains a finding that the omission of the prescribed brand of pipe was neither fraudulent nor willful. It was the result of the oversight and inattention of the plaintiff's sub-contractor. Reading pipe is distinguished from Cohoes pipe and other brands only by the name of the manufacturer stamped upon it at intervals of between six and seven feet. Even the defendant's architect, though he inspected the pipe upon arrival, failed to notice the discrepancy. The plaintiff tried to show that the brands installed, though made by other manufacturers, were the same in quality, in appearance, in market value and in cost as the brand stated in the contract—that they were, indeed, the same thing, though manufactured in another place. The evidence was excluded, and a verdict directed for the defendant. The Appellate Division reversed, and granted a new trial ...

[In a portion of the opinion presented on p. 724, the court concluded that Kent was required to pay Jacob and Youngs the contract price, subject to an allowance for the damages resulting from the breach.]

In the circumstances of this case, we think the measure of the allowance is not the cost of replacement, which would be great, but the difference in value, which would be either nominal or nothing. Some of the

---

a. The record on appeal indicates that, under the contract, payments were to be made monthly as the work progressed, on the certificate of the architect in an amount which "in his judgment" represented the amount due less 15% to be withheld. The specifications attached to the contract provided that where "any particular brand of manufactured article is specified, it is to be considered as a standard," and that a contractor "desiring to use another shall first make application in writing to the Architect ... and obtain their written approval of the change." The specifications made the architect's decision "as to the character of any material or labor furnished by the Contractor ... final and conclusive." Furthermore, "Any work furnished by the Contractor, the material or workmanship of which is defective or which is not fully in accordance with the drawings and specifications, in every respect, will be rejected and is to be immediately torn down, removed and remade or replaced in accordance with the drawings and specifications, whenever discovered.... The Owner will have the option at all times to allow the defective or improper work to stand and to receive from the Contractor a sum of money equivalent to the difference in value of the work as performed and as herein specified." Record p. 98–108. For the contract terms and much useful background, see Danzig, *The Capability Problem in Contract Law* 108–28 (1978).

exposed sections might perhaps have been replaced at moderate expense. The defendant did not limit his demand to them, but treated the plumbing as a unit to be corrected from cellar to roof.[b] In point of fact, the plaintiff never reached the stage at which evidence of the extent of the allowance became necessary. The trial court had excluded evidence that the defect was unsubstantial, and in view of that ruling there was no occasion for the plaintiff to go farther with an offer of proof. We think, however, that the offer, if it had been made, would not of necessity have been defective because directed to difference in value. It is true that in most cases the cost of replacement is the measure (Spence v. Ham, supra). The owner is entitled to the money which will permit him to complete, unless the cost of completion is grossly and unfairly out of proportion to the good to be attained. When that is true, the measure is the difference in value. Specifications call, let us say, for a foundation built of granite quarried in Vermont. On the completion of the building, the owner learns that through the blunder of a subcontractor part of the foundation has been built of granite of the same quality quarried in New Hampshire. The measure of allowance is not the cost of reconstruction. "There may be omissions of that which could not afterwards be supplied exactly as called for by the contract without taking down the building to its foundations and at the same time the omission may not affect the value of the building for use or otherwise, except so slightly as to be hardly appreciable" (Handy v. Bliss, 204 Mass. 513, 519, 90 N.E. 864. Cf. Foeller v. Heintz, 137 Wis. 169, 178, 118 N.W. 543; Oberlies v. Bullinger, 132 N.Y. 598, 601, 30 N.E. 999; 2 Williston on Contracts, sec. 805, p. 1541). The rule that gives a remedy in cases of substantial performance with compensation for defects of trivial or inappreciable importance, has been developed by the courts as an instrument of justice. The measure of the allowance must be shaped to the same end.

The order should be affirmed, and judgment absolute directed in favor of the plaintiff upon the stipulation, with costs in all courts.

NOTES

(1) *Substantial Performance.* Kent promised to pay Jacob & Youngs if it built him a house as specified. Building the house as specified was therefore a condition of Jacob & Youngs' right to recover from Kent on that promise. In an omitted part of the opinion, Cardozo explains that Jacob & Youngs can recover from Kent on that promise in spite of the fact that it did not strictly fulfill that requirement. As to this, three judges dissent. This notion of substantial, as opposed to strict, performance, and the law of conditions in general, are taken up in Chapter 8. For present purposes, we are concerned only with the part of Cardozo's opinion in which he considers how much, if anything, should be deducted from that recovery as Kent's damages. (To remove the problem of substantial performance from the picture, assume that Kent had paid Jacob & Youngs in full and was suing for damages.)

b. In a brief per curiam opinion on a motion for reargument, the Court of Appeals later said that it "did not overlook the specification which provides that defective work shall be replaced" (see footnote a above). But for the promise to replace, as for the promise to install, the law "restricts the remedy to damages." 130 N.E. 933 (1921).

(2) *Relevance of Diminution in Value.* Diminution in market price is useful in fixing a lower limit for recovery, since the value of property to its owner is usually no less than the net price at which the owner could sell it. Similarly, cost to remedy the defect is useful in fixing an upper limit for recovery since, even if that cost is less than the loss in value to the owner, the lesser sum will enable the owner to complete and avoid any loss in value.

"An owner's recovery is not necessarily limited to diminution in value whenever that figure is less than the cost of repair. It is true that in a case where the cost of repair exceeds the damages under the value formula, an award under the cost of repair measure may place the owner in a better economic position than if the contract had been fully performed, since he could pocket the award and then sell the defective structure. On the other hand, it is possible that the owner will use the damage award for its intended purpose and turn the structure into the one originally envisioned. He may do this for a number of reasons, including personal esthetics or a hope for increased value in the future. If he does this his economic position will equal the one he would have been in had the contractor fully performed. The fact finder is the one in the best position to determine whether the owner will actually complete performance, or whether he is only interested in obtaining the best immediate economic position he can. In some cases, such as where the property is held solely for investment, the court may conclude as a matter of law that the damage award can not exceed the diminution in value. Where, however, the property has special significance to the owner and repair seems likely, the cost of repair may be appropriate even if it exceeds the diminution in value." Advanced, Inc. v. Wilks, 711 P.2d 524, 527 (Alaska 1985).

(3) *Proving Diminution in Value.* Do you agree that the "difference in value" to *Kent* "would be either nominal or nothing"? It may be that the difference between the *market price* of a house with Reading pipe and one with Cohoes pipe is zero, because buyers of houses consider the two kinds of pipe to be of equal value *to them.* But why should *Kent's* recovery be limited by this? "If a proud householder, who plans to live out his days in the home of his dreams, orders a new roof of red barrel tile and the roofer instead installs a purple one, money damages for the reduced value of his house may not be enough to offset the strident offense to aesthetic sensibilities, continuing over the life of the roof." Gory Associated Industries v. Jupiter Roofing & Sheet Metal, 358 So.2d 93, 95 (Fla.Ct.App.1978).

The problem of determining loss in value is most acute when, as in the principal case, there is great disparity between the minimum of diminution in market price and the maximum of cost to remedy the defect. Which better approximates loss in value? Although the opinion gives us no insight into why Kent might have specified Reading rather than some other brand of pipe, it does suggest one reason for the disparity between the maximum and minimum. Does that reason suggest which better approximates loss in value? (If a very large fraction of the disparity represents the cost of undoing and redoing the work, how large a fraction represents the loss in value to Kent?) Who should have the burden with respect to diminution in value?

One court has said that if the builder "thought that the cost of repairs was an unreasonable measure of damages given what it believed to be the relatively small decrease in value resulting from the breach, it clearly had the burden to present evidence from which the jury could find the diminution in value." Advanced, Inc. v. Wilks, at 526 (quoted in Note 2 above). But the builder could do this simply by presenting evidence of market price.

Another court has said that, as plaintiff, the owner "had the burden of producing evidence that afforded the jury a reasonable basis to measure" the owner's loss. But that court went on to say, "It is undisputed that homeowners are qualified to testify as to their personal opinion regarding the value, or diminution in value, of their properties." This is so even though the homeowner may rely in part on the cost of repairs in forming that opinion. The appropriate vehicle for challenging such an opinion is cross-examination. Tessmann v. Tiger Lee Constr. Co., 634 A.2d 870, 873 (Conn.1993).

Could Kent's lawyer have done more?

PROBLEMS

(1) *The Deep End.* Stephen Forsyth made a contract with Ruxley for a swimming pool on his estate. The price was $100,000, and the contract specified that the depth of the pool was to be 7 feet 9 inches at the deep end. However, Ruxley encountered unexpected rock and, after Forsyth had paid the price in full, he discovered that the pool was only 6 feet 6 inches deep at the deep end. (A depth of 5 feet 6 inches is considered safe for diving and, in any case, Forsyth had no plans to install a diving board.) To increase the depth to that required by the contract would involve demolishing and replacing the pool, with additional excavation, at a cost of $180,000, and Forsyth testified that he had no intention of having this done. Forsyth sued for damages based on the $180,000 cost. The jury awarded him $10,000 on an instruction that they could award damages for "loss of pleasure and amenity." Both parties appealed. What result? Ruxley Electronics & Construction, Ltd. v. Forsyth, [1995] 3 W.L.R. 118 (House of Lords).

Would your answer be affected if Forsyth had testified that he planned to demolish and rebuild the pool if he recovered the $180,000? Would it be affected if it had been proved that Ruxley saved $50,000 by building the shallower pool?

(2) *The Thinned Blue Line.* Security Services contracted with Engulf & Devour, Inc., a multinational corporation, to provide twenty plainclothed guards for a price of $18,000, paid in advance, in order to prevent disruption by protestors at its annual meeting of shareholders. Because no protestors appeared at the meeting, the guards were not needed. However, Engulf & Devour later learned that Security Services provided only fourteen guards. Does Engulf & Devour have a claim for damages against Security Services?

Groves v. John Wunder Co.

Supreme Court of Minnesota, 1939.
205 Minn. 163, 286 N.W. 235.

■ STONE, J. Action for breach of contract. Plaintiff got judgment for a little over $15,000. Sorely disappointed by that sum, he appeals.

In August, 1927 S.J. Groves & Sons Company, a corporation (hereinafter mentioned simply as Groves), owned a tract of 24 acres of Minneapolis suburban real estate. It was served or easily could be reached by railroad trackage. It is zoned as heavy industrial property. But for lack of development of the neighborhood its principal value thus far may have been in the deposit of sand and gravel which it carried. The Groves company had a plant on the premises for excavating and screening the gravel. Nearby defendant owned and was operating a similar plant.

In August, 1927, Groves and defendant made the involved contract. For the most part it was a lease from Groves, as lessor, to defendant, as lessee; its term seven years. Defendant agreed to remove the sand and gravel and to leave the property "at a uniform grade, substantially the same as the grade now existing at the roadway . . . on said premises, and that in stripping the overburden . . . it will use said overburden for the purpose of maintaining and establishing said grade."

Under the contract defendant got the Groves screening plant. The transfer thereof and the right to remove the sand and gravel made the consideration moving from Groves to defendant, except that defendant incidentally got rid of Groves as a competitor. On defendant's part it paid Groves $105,000. So that from the outset, on Groves' part the contract was executed except for defendant's right to continue using the property for the stated term. (Defendant had a right to renewal which it did not exercise.)

Defendant breached the contract deliberately. It removed from the premises only "the richest and best of the gravel" and wholly failed, according to the findings, "to perform and comply with the terms, conditions, and provisions of said lease . . . with respect to the condition in which the surface of the demised premises was required to be left." Defendant surrendered the premises, not substantially at the grade required by the contract "nor at any uniform grade." Instead, the ground was "broken, rugged and uneven." Plaintiff sues as assignee and successor in right of Groves.

As the contract was construed below, the finding is that to complete its performance 288,495 cubic yards of overburden would need to be excavated, taken from the premises, and deposited elsewhere. The reasonable cost of doing that was found to be upwards of $60,000. But, if defendant had left the premises at the uniform grade required by the lease, the reasonable value of the property on the determinative date would have been only $12,160. The judgment was for that sum,[a] including interest, thereby nullifying plaintiff's claim that cost of completing the contract rather than difference in value of the land was the measure of damages. The gauge of damage adopted by the decision was the difference between the market value of plaintiff's land in the condition it was [in] when the contract was made and what it would have been if defendant had performed. The one question for us arises upon plaintiff's assertion that he was entitled, not to that difference in value, but to the reasonable cost to him of doing the work called for by the contract which defendant left undone.

1. Defendant's breach of contract was wilful. There was nothing of good faith about it. Hence, that the decision below handsomely rewards bad faith and deliberate breach of contract is obvious. That is not allowable. Here the rule is well settled, and has been since Elliott v. Caldwell, 43 Minn. 357, 45 N.W. 845, 9 L.R.A. 52, that, where the contractor wilfully and fraudulently varies from the terms of a construction contract, he cannot sue thereon and have the benefit of the equitable doctrine of

---

a. This was on the assumption that the land as it was left could not have been sold on the market.

substantial performance. That is the rule generally. See Annotation, "Wilful or intentional variation by contractor from terms of contract in regard to material or work as affecting measure of damages," 6 A.L.R. 137.

Jacob & Youngs, Inc. v. Kent, 230 N.Y. 239, 243, 244, 129 N.E. 889, 891, 23 A.L.R. 1429, is typical. It was a case of substantial performance of a building contract. (This case is distinctly the opposite.) Mr. Justice Cardozo, in the course of his opinion, stressed the distinguishing features. "Nowhere," he said, "will change be tolerated, however, if it is so dominant or pervasive as in any real or substantial measure to frustrate the purpose of the contract." Again, "the willful transgressor must accept the penalty of his transgression."

2. In reckoning damages for breach of a building or construction contract, the law aims to give the disappointed promisee, so far as money will do it, what he was promised. 9 Am.Jur. Building and Construction Contracts, sec. 152. It is so ruled by a long line of decisions in this state beginning with Carli v. Seymour, Sabin & Co., 26 Minn. 276, 3 N.W. 348, where the contract was for building a road. There was a breach. Plaintiff was held entitled to recover what it would cost to complete the grading as contemplated by the contract. For our other similar cases, see 2 Dunnell, Minn.Dig., 2 Ed. & Supp., secs. 2561, 2565.

Never before, so far as our decisions show, has it even been suggested that lack of value in the land furnished to the contractor who had bound himself to improve it [gave] any escape from the ordinary consequences of a breach of the contract. . . .

Even in case of substantial performance in good faith, the resulting defects being remediable, it is error to instruct that the measure of damage is "the difference in value between the house as it was and as it would have been if constructed according to contract." The "correct doctrine" is that the cost of remedying the defect is the "proper" measure of damages. Snider v. Peters Home Building Co., 139 Minn. 413, 414, 416, 167 N.W. 108.

Value of the land (as distinguished from the value of the intended product of the contract, which ordinarily will be equivalent to its reasonable cost) is no proper part of any measure of damages for wilful breach of a building contract. The reason is plain.

The summit from which to reckon damages from trespass to real estate is its actual value at the moment. The owner's only right is to be compensated for the deterioration in value caused by the tort. That is all he has lost.[b] But not so if a contract to improve the same land has been breached by the contractor who refuses to do the work, especially where, as here, he has been paid in advance. The summit from which to reckon damages for that wrong is the hypothetical peak of accomplishment (not value) which would have been reached had the work been done as demanded by the contract.

---

b. So also in condemnation cases, where the owner loses nothing of promised contractual performance.

The owner's right to improve his property is not trammeled by its small value. It is his right to erect thereon structures which will reduce its value. If that be the result, it can be of no aid to any contractor who declines performance. As said long ago in Chamberlain v. Parker, 45 N.Y. 569, 572: "A man may do what he will with his own, . . . and if he chooses to erect a monument to his caprice or folly on his premises, and employs and pays another to do it, it does not lie with a defendant who has been so employed and paid for building it, to say that his own performance would not be beneficial to the plaintiff." To the same effect is Restatement, Contracts, sec. 346, p. 576, Illustrations of Subsection (1), par. 4.

Suppose a contractor were suing the owner for breach of a grading contract such as this. Would any element of value, or lack of it, in the land have any relevance in reckoning damages? Of course not. The contractor would be compensated for what he had lost, i.e., his profit. Conversely, in such a case as this, the owner is entitled to compensation for what he has lost, that is, the work or structure which he has been promised, for which he has paid, and of which he has been deprived by the contractor's breach.

To diminish damages recoverable against him in proportion as there is presently small value in the land would favor the faithless contractor. It would also ignore and so defeat plaintiff's right to contract and build for the future. To justify such a course would require more of the prophetic vision than judges possess. This factor is important when the subject matter is trackage property in the margin of such an area of population and industry as that of the Twin Cities. . . .

The genealogy of the error pervading the argument contra is easy to trace. It begins with Seely v. Alden, 61 Pa. 302, 100 Am.Dec. 642, a tort case for pollution of a stream. Resulting depreciation in value of plaintiff's premises, of course, was the measure of damages. About 40 years later, in Bigham v. Wabash–Pittsburg T. Ry., 223 Pa. 106, 72 A. 318, the measure of damages of the earlier tort case was used in one for breach of contract, without comment or explanation to show why. . . .

It is at least interesting to note Morgan v. Gamble, 230 Pa. 165, 79 A. 410, decided two years after the *Bigham* case. The doctrine of substantial performance is there correctly stated, but plaintiff was denied its benefit because he had deliberately breached his building contract. It was held that: "Where a building contractor agrees to lay an extra strong lead water pipe, and he substitutes therefor an iron pipe, he will be required to allow to the owners in a suit upon the contract, not the difference [in value] between the iron and lead pipes, but the cost of laying a lead pipe as provided in the agreement."

To show how remote any factors of value were considered, it was also held that: "Where a contractor of a building agrees to construct two gas lines, one for natural gas, and one for artificial gas, he will not be relieved from constructing both lines, because artificial gas was not in use in the town in which the building was being constructed."

The objective of this contract of present importance was the improvement of real estate. That makes irrelevant the rules peculiar to damages to chattels, arising from tort or breach of contract.... In tort, the thing lost is money value, nothing more. But under a construction contract, the thing lost by a breach such as we have here is a physical structure or accomplishment, a promised and paid for alteration in land. That is the "injury" for which the law gives him compensation. Its only appropriate measure is the cost of performance.

It is suggested that because of little or no value in his land the owner may be unconscionably enriched by such a reckoning. The answer is that there can be no unconscionable enrichment, no advantage upon which the law will frown, when the result is but to give one party to a contract only what the other has promised; particularly where, as here, the delinquent has had full payment for the promised performance.

3.   It is said by the Restatement, Contracts, sec. 346, Comment *b*: "Sometimes defects in a completed structure cannot be physically remedied without tearing down and rebuilding, at a cost that would be imprudent and unreasonable. The law does not require damages to be measured by a method requiring such economic waste. If no such waste is involved, the cost of remedying the defect is the amount awarded as compensation for failure to render the promised performance."

The "economic waste" declaimed against by the decisions applying that rule has nothing to do with the value in money of the real estate, or even with the product of the contract. The waste avoided is only that which would come from wrecking a physical structure, completed, or nearly so, under the contract. The cases applying that rule go no further. Illustrative are Buchholz v. Rosenberg, 163 Wis. 312, 156 N.W. 946; Burmeister v. Wolfgram, 175 Wis. 506, 185 N.W. 517. Absent such waste, as it is in this case, the rule of the Restatement, Contracts, sec. 346, is that "the cost of remedying the defect is the amount awarded as compensation for failure to render the promised performance." That means that defendants here are liable to plaintiff for the reasonable cost of doing what defendants promised to do and have wilfully declined to do.

It follows that there must be a new trial. The initial question will be as to the proper construction of the contract. Thus far the case has been considered from the standpoint of the construction adopted by plaintiff and acquiesced in, very likely for strategic reasons, by defendants. The question has not been argued here, so we intimate no opinion concerning it, but we put the question whether the contract required removal from the premises of any overburden. The requirement in that respect was that the overburden should be used for the purpose of "establishing and maintaining" the grade. A uniform slope and grade were doubtless required. But whether, if it could not be accomplished without removal and deposit elsewhere of large amounts of overburden, the contract required as a condition that the grade everywhere should be as low as the one recited as "now existing at the roadway" is a question for initial consideration below.

The judgment must be reversed with a new trial to follow.

So ordered.

■ [JUSTICE OLSON, dissenting in an opinion in which JUSTICE HOLT joined, urged that the diminished value rule be applied in the absence of evidence to show that the completed product was to satisfy the personal taste of the promisee, and denied that the wilfulness of the breach should affect the measure of damages.]

NOTES

(1) *Explanation.* In 1927, when the parties were bargaining over the terms of their contract, they would surely not knowingly have agreed to have Wunder assume such a burdensome task if it would have been of so slight a benefit to Groves. What is the explanation for the circumstances that, after seven years, Wunder's task was so burdensome and Groves's benefit was apparently so slight? That Wunder had underestimated the burden? That Groves had overestimated the benefit? That the cost of Wunder's performance had risen? That the amount of the benefit to Groves had fallen? That Wunder's performance would not have been so burdensome if it had done the restoration as the work progressed? That the actual benefit to Groves would have been greater than that reflected in the market price of the land? Some combination of these? Which of these possible explanations would justify the court's decision?

According to one critic, "not enforcing the contract would have given the defendant a windfall. But enforcing the contract gave the plaintiff an equal and opposite windfall, in the form of a cushion, which almost certainly the parties had not intended, against the impact of the Depression on land values." R. Posner, Economic Analysis of Law 121 (7th ed. 2007).

After the decision in Groves, Wunder paid Groves $55,000 to settle the claim. The land was left until 1951, when some grading was done on a portion at a cost of $6,000, and in 1953 this portion was sold for $45,000 to a buyer who planned to use it for a factory. Does this suggest anything about the proper measure of recovery?

(2) *"Wilfulness."* The court says that Wunder's "breach of contract was wilful." In H.P. Droher & Sons v. Toushin, 85 N.W.2d 273 (Minn.1957), the court distinguished *Groves* on the ground that, "The majority opinion is based, at least in part, on the fact that the breach of the contract was wilful and in bad faith". What does "wilful" mean in this context? Holmes said that for breach of contract "the measure of damages generally is the same, whatever the cause of the breach." Globe Refining Co. v. Landa Cotton Oil Co., 190 U.S. 540, 544 (1903). Is the *Groves* case an exception? If Wunder must pay over $47,000 more in damages if its breach is "wilful," is this not a penalty for "wilfulness"? Is that consistent with the goals of contract remedies?

PROBLEM

Advising Wunder. If you had been counsel for Wunder and had been asked by your client whether it should perform its promise to do the grading at a cost of $60,000 if the benefit to Groves would be under $13,000, what advice would you have given? If Wunder then refused to perform, would its breach be "wilful"?

Peevyhouse v. Garland Coal & Mining Co.

Supreme Court of Oklahoma, 1963.
1962 OK 267, 382 P.2d 109.

[In 1954 Willie and Lucille Peevyhouse leased their farm for five years to Garland Coal & Mining Co. to strip mine coal. In addition to the usual covenants, Garland agreed to perform specified restorative and remedial work at the end of the lease. It failed to do this work, which would have involved the moving of many thousands of cubic yards of dirt at a cost of about $29,000. Had the work been done, the market price of the farm would have been increased by only $300. The Peevyhouses sued for $25,000 in damages. The trial court gave judgment on a verdict for $5,000. Both parties appealed.]

■ JACKSON, JUSTICE. . . . On appeal, the issue is sharply drawn. Plaintiffs contend that the true measure of damages in this case is what it will cost plaintiffs to obtain performance of the work that was not done because of defendant's default. Defendant argues that the measure of damages is the cost of performance "limited, however, to the total difference in the market value before and after the work was performed". It appears that this precise question has not heretofore been presented to this court. . . .

Plaintiffs rely on Groves v. John Wunder Co., 205 Minn. 163, 286 N.W. 235, 123 A.L.R. 502. In that case, the Minnesota court, in a substantially similar situation, adopted the "cost of performance" rule as opposed to the "value" rule. The result was to authorize a jury to give plaintiff damages in the amount of $60,000, where the real estate concerned would have been worth only $12,160, even if the work contracted for had been done.

It may be observed that Groves v. John Wunder Co., supra, is the only case which has come to our attention in which the cost of performance rule has been followed under circumstances where the cost of performance greatly exceeded the diminution in value resulting from the breach of contract. Incidentally, it appears that this case was decided by a plurality rather than a majority of the members of the court. . . .

We do not think [that] either [the] analogy [of a "building and construction" or a "grading and excavation" contract] is strictly applicable to the case now before us. The primary purpose of the lease contract between plaintiffs and defendant was neither "building and construction" nor "grading and excavation". It was merely to accomplish the economical recovery and marketing of coal from the premises, to the profit of all parties. The special provisions of the lease contract pertaining to remedial work were incidental to the main object involved.

Even in the case of contracts that are unquestionably building and construction contracts, the authorities are not in agreement as to the factors to be considered in determining whether the cost of performance rule or the value rule should be applied. The American Law Institute's Restatement of the Law, Contracts, Volume 1, Sections 346(1)(a)(i) and (ii) submits the proposition that the cost of performance is the proper measure of damages "if this is possible and does not involve *unreasonable economic waste*"; and that the diminution in value caused by the breach is the proper measure "if construction and completion in accordance with the contract would involve *unreasonable economic waste*". (Emphasis supplied.) In an explanatory comment immediately following the text, the Restatement makes it clear that the "economic waste" referred to consists of the destruction of a substantially completed building or other structure. Of course no such destruction is involved in the case now before us.

On the other hand, in McCormick, Damages, Section 168, it is said with regard to building and construction contracts that "... in cases where the defect is one that can be repaired or cured without *undue expense*" the cost of performance is the proper measure of damages, but where "... the defect in material or construction is one that cannot be remedied without *an expenditure for reconstruction disproportionate to the end to be attained*" (emphasis supplied) the value rule should be followed. The same idea was expressed in Jacob & Youngs, Inc. v. Kent, 230 N.Y. 239, 129 N.E. 889, 23 A.L.R. 1429, as follows: "The owner is entitled to the money which will permit him to complete, unless the cost of completion is grossly and unfairly out of proportion to the good to be attained. When that is true, the measure is the difference in value."

It thus appears that the prime consideration in the Restatement was "economic waste"; and that the prime consideration in McCormick, Damages, and in Jacob & Youngs, Inc. v. Kent, supra, was the relationship between the expense involved and the "end to be attained"—in other words, the "relative economic benefit"....

We ... hold that where, in a coal mining lease, lessee agrees to perform certain remedial work on the premises concerned at the end of the lease period, and thereafter the contract is fully performed by both parties except that the remedial work is not done, the measure of damages in an action by lessor against lessee for damages for breach of contract is ordinarily the reasonable cost of performance of the work; however, where the contract provision breached was merely incidental to the main purpose in view, and where the economic benefit which would result to lessor by full performance of the work is grossly disproportionate to the cost of performance, the damages which lessor may recover are limited to the diminution in value resulting to the premises because of the non-performance....

[Judgment reduced to $300 and affirmed (4–3).]

■ IRWIN, JUSTICE (dissenting).... Although the contract speaks for itself, there were several negotiations between the plaintiffs and defendant before the contract was executed. Defendant admitted in the trial of the action, that plaintiffs insisted that the above provisions be included in the contract and that they would not agree to the coal mining lease unless the above provisions were included....

[I]n my opinion, the plaintiffs were entitled to specific performance of the contract and since defendant has failed to perform, the proper measure of damages should be the cost of performance. Any other measure of damage would be holding for naught the express provisions of the contract; would be taking from the plaintiffs the benefits of the contract and placing those benefits in defendant which has failed to perform its obligations; would be granting benefits to defendant without a resulting obligation; and would be completely rescinding the solemn obligation of the contract for the benefit of the defendant to the detriment of the plaintiffs by making an entirely new contract for the parties....

NOTES

(1) Groves *and* Peevyhouse. Are *Groves* and *Peevyhouse* distinguishable? Is it clear that the loss in value to the Peevyhouses was not $5,000? Did Garland get a "windfall"? See E. Allan Farnsworth, Your Loss or My Gain? The Dilemma of the Disgorgement Principle in Breach of Contract, 94 Yale L.J. 1339 (1985). What result in these cases under Restatement § 348(2)? For the background of *Peevyhouse*, see Judith Maute, *Peevyhouse v. Garland Coal Co.* Revisited: The Ballad of Willie and Lucille, 89 Nw.U.L.Rev. 1341 (1995).

Peevyhouse was reconsidered in Schneberger v. Apache Corp., 890 P.2d 847, 850, 854, 855 (Okl.1994), an action for breach of a contract to reduce water pollution that had been caused during the defendant's drilling operations. The plaintiffs argued "that recent statutory enactments and federal case law reflect a change in Oklahoma policy regarding protecting the environment from pollution caused by oil and gas drilling operations," and that this policy change "clearly indicates that the diminution in value rule established in *Peevyhouse* is outdated and ... that the cost of remediation is the proper measure of damages for pollution caused by oil and gas operations." The Supreme Court of Oklahoma, however, adhered to *Peevyhouse*, noting that the parties to the contract "were free to specify in the contract what the measure of damages would be in the event of a breach," and that even if the court were to use the more generous measure, nothing would require "a plaintiff to apply the award to reclaiming the land."

(2) *"Economic Waste."* The first Restatement, we are told by the court in *Peevyhouse*, speaks of "economic waste" in the sense of destruction of a substantially completed structure. If Kent had been awarded damages measured by the cost to replace the pipe with Reading pipe, would he then have been required to replace it? Does it seem likely that he would have done so? In what sense is there "economic waste" if he is awarded damages measured by the cost to complete? See Comment *c* to Restatement § 348.

PROBLEM

Threatening Inefficient Performance. Suppose that the value to the Peevyhouses of having the land graded is $8,000, that the cost to Garland of grading it is $30,000, and that the parties are confident that a court will award $30,000 as damages for breach of contract by Garland. If Garland has not decided whether or not to grade the land and offers to split the $22,000 difference and pay the Peevyhouses $19,000 ($8,000 + $11,000), should the Peevyhouses accept? Suppose that Garland threatens to grade the land if they do not accept? Does this call into question the wisdom of a rule that would result in an award of $30,000 as damages? See Ian Ayres and Kristin Madison, Threatening Inefficient Performance of Injunctions and Contracts, 148 U.Pa.L.Rev. 45, 52–53 (1999) (noting that, as compared to litigation, "actual performance potentially saves attorney fees").

(B) FORESEEABILITY

Until the nineteenth century, judges left the assessment of damages for breach of contract largely to the discretion of the jury. It was no accident that the development of rules to curb this discretion, and the "outrageous and excessive" verdicts that resulted, coincided with the end of the industrial revolution and with a consequent solicitude for burgeoning enterprise. Hadley v. Baxendale is the leading case in this development.

Hadley v. Baxendale

Court of Exchequer, 1854.
9 Ex. 341, 156 Eng.Rep. 145.

[Plaintiffs, who operated a mill at Gloucester, sued defendants, who were common carriers, for damages for breach of a contract of carriage. The declaration contained two counts, but prior to the trial plaintiffs entered a *nolle prosequi* as to the first. In the second count plaintiffs alleged that they were forced to shut their mill down because the crank shaft of the steam engine, by which their mill was operated, became broken; that they arranged with W. Joyce & Co., of Greenwich, the manufacturers of the engine, to make a new shaft from the pattern of the old one; that they delivered the broken shaft to defendants who, in consideration of the payment of their charges, promised to use due care to deliver it to W. Joyce & Co. within a reasonable time but that defendants failed to do so; that by reason of defendants' negligence the completion of the new shaft and the reopening of plaintiffs' mill were delayed five days longer than would otherwise have been the case; and that during that period plaintiffs were compelled to pay wages and lost profits aggregating 300£ for which amount plaintiffs sought judgment. Defendants pleaded that they had paid 25£ into court in satisfaction of plaintiffs' claim; plaintiffs replied that this sum was insufficient for that purpose; and issue was joined upon this replication.]

At the trial before Crompton, J., at the last Gloucester Assizes, it appeared that the plaintiffs carried on an extensive business as millers at Gloucester; and that, on the 11th of May, their mill was stopped by a breakage of the crank shaft by which the mill was worked. The steam-engine was manufactured by Messrs. Joyce & Co., the engineers at Greenwich, and it became necessary to send the shaft as a pattern for a new one to Greenwich. The fracture was discovered on the 12th, and on the 13th the plaintiffs sent one of their servants to the office of the defendants, who are the well known carriers trading under the name of Pickford & Co., for the purpose of having the shaft carried to Greenwich. The plaintiffs' servant told the clerk that the mill was stopped, and that the shaft must be sent immediately; and in answer to the inquiry when the shaft would be taken, the answer was, that if it was sent up by twelve o'clock any day, it would be delivered at Greenwich on the following day. On the following day the shaft was taken by the defendants, before noon, for the purpose of being conveyed to Greenwich, and the sum of 2£ 4s. was paid for its carriage for the whole distance; at the same time the defendants' clerk was told that a special entry, if required, should be made to hasten its delivery. The delivery of the shaft at Greenwich was delayed by some neglect; and the consequence was, that the plaintiffs did not receive the new shaft for several days after they would otherwise have done, and the working of their mill was thereby delayed, and they thereby lost the profits they would otherwise have received.

On the part of the defendants, it was objected that these damages were too remote, and that the defendants were not liable with respect to them. The learned Judge left the case generally to the jury, who found a verdict with 25£ damages beyond the amount paid into Court.

Whateley, [for defendants], in last Michaelmas Term, obtained a rule nisi for a new trial, on the ground of misdirection. * * *

■ ALDERSON, B. We think that there ought to be a new trial in this case; but, in so doing, we deem it to be expedient and necessary to state explicitly the rule which the Judge, at the next trial, ought, in our opinion, to direct the jury to be governed by when they estimate the damages.

It is, indeed, of the last importance that we should do this; for, if the jury are left without any definite rule to guide them, it will, in such cases as these, manifestly lead to the greatest injustice. The Courts have done this on several occasions; and, in Blake v. Midland Railway Company, 21 L.J., Q.B. 237, the Court granted a new trial on this very ground, that the rule had not been definitely laid down to the jury by the learned judge at Nisi Prius.

"There are certain established rules," this Court says, in Alder v. Keighley, 15 M. & W. 117, "according to which the jury ought to find." And the Court, in that case, adds: "and here there is a clear rule, that the amount which would have been received if the contract had been kept is the measure of damages if the contract is broken."

Now we think the proper rule in such a case as the present is this: Where two parties have made a contract which one of them has broken, the damages which the other party ought to receive in respect of such breach of contract should be such as may fairly and reasonably be considered either arising naturally, i.e., according to the usual course of things, from such breach of contract itself, or such as may reasonably be supposed to have been in the contemplation of both parties, at the time they made the contract, as the probable result of the breach of it. Now, if the special circumstances under which the contract was actually made were communicated by the plaintiffs to the defendants, and thus known to both parties, the damages resulting from the breach of such a contract, which they would reasonably contemplate, would be the amount of injury which would ordinarily follow from a breach of contract under these special circumstances so known and communicated. But, on the other hand, if these special circumstances were wholly unknown to the party breaking the contract, he, at the most, could only be supposed to have had in his contemplation the amount of injury which would arise generally, and in the great multitude of cases not affected by any special circumstances, from such a breach of contract. For, had the special circumstances been known, the parties might have specially provided for the breach of contract by special terms as to the damages in that case; and of this advantage it would be very unjust to deprive them.

Now the above principles are those by which we think the jury ought to be guided in estimating the damages arising out of any breach of contract. It is said, that other cases, such as breaches of contract in the nonpayment of money, or in the not making a good title to land, are to be treated as exceptions from this, and as governed by a conventional rule. But as, in such cases, both parties must be supposed to be cognizant of that well-known rule, these cases may, we think, be more properly classed under the rule above enunciated as to cases under known special circumstances, because there both parties may reasonably be presumed to contemplate the estimation of the amount of damages according to the conventional rule.

Now, in the present case if we are to apply the principles above laid down, we find that the only circumstances here communicated by the plaintiffs to the defendants at the time the contract was made, were, that the article to be carried was the broken shaft of a mill, and that the plaintiffs were the millers of that mill. But how do these circumstances show reasonably that the profits of the mill must be stopped by an unreasonable delay in the delivery of the broken shaft by the carrier to the third person? Suppose the plaintiffs had another shaft in their possession put up or putting up at the time, and that they only wished to send back the broken shaft to the engineer who made it; it is clear that this would be quite consistent with the above circumstances, and yet the unreasonable delay in the delivery would have no effect upon the intermediate profits of the mill. Or, again, suppose that, at the time of the delivery to the carrier, the machinery of the mill had been in other respects defective, then, also, the same results would follow. Here it is true that the shaft was actually sent back to serve as a model for a new one, and that the want of a new one was the only cause of the stoppage of the mill, and that the loss of profits really arose from not sending down the new shaft in proper time, and that this arose from the delay in delivering the broken one to serve as a model. But it is obvious that, in the great multitude of cases of millers sending off broken shafts to third persons by a carrier under ordinary circumstances, such consequences would not, in all probability, have occurred; and these special circumstances were here never communicated by the plaintiffs to the defendants.

It follows, therefore, that the loss of profits here cannot reasonably be considered such a consequence of the breach of contract as could have been fairly and reasonably contemplated by both the parties when they made this contract. For such loss would neither have flowed naturally from the breach of this contract in the great multitude of such cases occurring under ordinary circumstances, nor were the special circumstances, which, perhaps, would have made it a reasonable and natural consequence of such breach of contract, communicated to or known by the defendants. The Judge ought, therefore, to have told the jury that, upon the facts then before him, they ought not to take the loss of profits into consideration at all in estimating the damages. There must therefore be a new trial in this case.

Rule absolute.

NOTES

(1) *Rule of* Hadley v. Baxendale. Do you think that in Hadley v. Baxendale the court applied the rule that it formulated correctly or incorrectly? Cf. Victoria

Laundry (Windsor) Ltd. v. Newman Industries Ltd., 2 K.B. 528, 537 (1949): "In considering the meaning and application of these rules, it is essential to bear clearly in mind the facts on which Hadley v. Baxendale proceeded. The head-note is definitely misleading in so far as it says that the defendant's clerk, who attended at the office, was told that the mill was stopped and that the shaft must be delivered immediately. The same allegation figures in the statement of facts which are said ... to have 'appeared' at the trial before Crompton J. If the Court of Exchequer had accepted these facts as established, the court must, one would suppose, have decided the case the other way round.... But it is reasonably plain from Baron Alderson's judgment that the court rejected this evidence, for ... he says: 'We find that the only circumstances here communicated by the plaintiffs to the defendants at the time when the contract was made were that the article to be carried was the broken shaft of a mill and that the plaintiffs were the millers of that mill.' ...''

Hadley v. Baxendale has prompted much discussion. For criticism of the rule, see Barry Adler, The Questionable Ascent of *Hadley v. Baxendale,*, 51 Stan.L.Rev. 1547 (1999); Eisenberg, The Principle of *Hadley v. Baxendale,* 80 Calif.L.Rev. 563 (1992). For a thorough discussion of the background of the case, see Richard Danzig, *Hadley v. Baxendale:* A Study in the Industrialization of the Law, 4 J.Legal Stud. 249 (1975).

The common law rule laid down in Hadley v. Baxendale may be usefully contrasted with other the formulations of foreseeability in contracts, see Restatement § 351 and UCC § 2–715(2), as well as torts, see Restatement, Second, of Torts § 435.

(2) *Limitation of Risk.* "The rule of Hadley v. Baxendale is an attempt to restrict the promisor's liability for breach of promise to those consequences, the risk of which he knew about, or must be taken to have known about, when he made the contract. The scope of damage for breach of contract is much narrower than the 'proximate consequence' rule which prevails in actions to recover for a tort. If we may assume that the defaulting promisor is usually an *entrepreneur,* a business man who has undertaken a risky enterprise, the law here manifests a policy to encourage the *entrepreneur* by reducing the extent of his risk below that amount of damage which, it might be plausibly argued, the promisee has actually been caused to suffer." Edwin Patterson, The Apportionment of Business Risks Through Legal Devices, 24 Colum.L.Rev. 335, 342 (1924).

In British Columbia Saw Mill Co. v. Nettleship, L.R. 3 C.P. 499 (1868), Willes, J., criticized the result reached in an old case "said to have been decided two centuries ago where a man going to be married to an heiress, his horse having cast a shoe on the journey, employed a blacksmith to replace it, who did the work so unskilfully that the horse was lamed, and the rider not arriving in time, the lady married another; and the blacksmith was held liable for the loss of the marriage." But cf. Coppola v. Kraushaar, 92 N.Y.S. 436 (App.Div.1905), in which a disappointed suitor whose betrothed broke their engagement after their wedding was delayed sued to recover five hundred dollars, expended uselessly on the wedding, from the defendant, whose failure to deliver two gowns, ordered for the bride, had caused the postponement of the wedding. "Before the defendant can be held to these alleged damages ... I think that the parties must have had in contemplation that the wedding would never occur if the defendant failed to furnish the 'two dresses' on the day before the appointed time.... While such a disappointment would naturally be keen to any prospective bride, it was hardly to be contemplated, in the absence of specific warning, that she would forever refuse to wed if those 'two dresses' were not forthcoming before the day set for the ceremony. The damages are too remote."

(3) *Allocation of Risk.* Restatement § 351(3) confronts the problem of risk by stating that a court may limit damages even for foreseeable loss "if it concludes that in the circumstances justice so requires in order to avoid disproportionate compensation." In Sundance Cruises Corp. v. American Bureau of Shipping, 7 F.3d 1077, 1084 (2d Cir.1993), the court held that a shipowner was "not entitled to rely on a classification certificate as a guarantee to the owner that the vessel is soundly constructed." The court reasoned that "the great disparity between the fee charged ($85,000) by ABS for its services and the damages sought by Sundance ($264,000,-000) is strong evidence that such a result was not intended by the parties. Citing Restatement § 351, the court concluded 'that the small fees charged could not have been intended to cover the risk of such liability; the ship classification industry could not continue to exist under such terms.' " See Larry Garvin, Disproportionality and the Law of Consequential Damages: Default Theory and Cognitive Reality, 59 Ohio St. L.J. 339 (1998).

(4) *Consequential Damages.* Damages that, in Baron Alderson's words, would not be considered as "arising naturally," but only as a result of "the special circumstances under which the contract was actually made," are often called "consequential" damages. The Code has given special significance to this term by providing in UCC § 2–712(2) for buyer's recovery of "any incidental or consequential damages" while providing in UCC § 2–708(1) for seller's recovery of only "any incidental damages." In addition, UCC § 2–715 refers to both "incidental" and "consequential" damages "resulting from seller's breach," while UCC § 2–710 speaks only of "incidental damages to an aggrieved seller." Can you justify such a distinction between buyers and sellers?

Courts have read the Code as precluding recovery by sellers of consequential damages, a reading that has resulted in attempts by sellers to characterize claims such as those for additional interest costs resulting from breach as "incidental" rather than "consequential" and therefore allowable under UCC § 2–710. In St. Paul Structural Steel Co. v. ABI Contracting, Inc., 364 N.W.2d 83 (N.D.1985), the court accepted a seller's argument that "interest payments incurred as a result of a buyer's breach of a sales agreement do constitute incidental damages."

Disputes over the meaning of "consequential" also arise when the contract contains a provision precluding recovery of "consequential damages." For a case involving such a clause, see Reynolds Metals Co. v. Westinghouse Electric Corp., 758 F.2d 1073 (5th Cir.1985) (where seller of transformer failed to provide competent engineer to install it, buyer was limited to "difference-in-value losses" based on fee that competent engineer would have charged and could not recover consequential damages for cost of repairing damage to transformer caused by breach).

(5) *Availability of Cover.* Courts have often assumed that in our market economy there is ordinarily a market on which an injured buyer can cover. They have therefore concluded that losses resulting from the buyer's inability to cover do not follow from the breach in the ordinary course and are foreseeable by the seller only if the seller was aware of facts making the buyer's inability to cover foreseeable. See Marcus & Co. v. K.L.G. Baking Co., 3 A.2d 627 (N.J.1939). Does UCC § 2–715(2)(a) dispense with the requirement that the buyer's inability to cover be foreseeable?

————

DELCHI CARRIER SPA v. ROTOREX CORP., 71 F.3d 1024 (2d Cir.1995). [Rotorex, a New York corporation, agreed to supply compressors to Delchi, an Italian manufacturer of air conditioners, in three shipments.

While the second shipment was en route, Delchi discovered that the first shipment had both higher power consumption and lower cooling capacity than the contract required. Delchi asked Rotorex to supply conforming compressors and, when Rotorex refused, Delchi cancelled the contract and sought another source. Delchi sued Rotorex seeking incidental and consequential damages. From a $1,248,332 judgment for Delchi, both parties appealed.]

■ WINTER, CIRCUIT JUDGE. . . . [T]he instant matter is governed by the CISG, . . . a self-executing agreement between the United States and other signatories, including Italy. Because there is virtually no caselaw under the Convention, we look to its language and to "the general principles" upon which it is based. See CISG art. 7(2). The Convention directs that its interpretation be informed by its "international character and . . . the need to promote uniformity in its application and the observance of good faith in international trade." See CISG art. 7(1). . . . Caselaw interpreting analogous provisions of Article 2 of the Uniform Commercial Code ("UCC") may also inform a court where the language of the relevant CISG provisions tracks that of the UCC. . . .

The CISG [art. 74] provides

Damages for breach of contract . . . may not exceed the loss which the party in breach foresaw or ought to have foreseen at the time of the conclusion of the contract, in the light of the facts and matters of which he then knew or ought to have known, as a possible consequence of the breach of contract.

Rotorex contends . . . that the district court improperly awarded lost profits for unfilled orders from Delchi affiliates in Europe and from sales agents within Italy. We disagree. The CISG requires that damages by limited by the familiar principle of foreseeability established in Hadley v. Baxendale. . . . However, it was objectively foreseeable that Delchi would take orders for . . . sales based on the number of compressors it had ordered and expected to have ready for the season. . . .

On its cross-appeal, Delchi challenges the district court's denial of various consequential and incidental damages . . . on the ground that . . . an award would constitute a double recovery for Delchi. We disagree. . . . The expenses incurred by Delchi for shipping, customs, and related matters for the two returned shipments of Rotorex compressors, including storage expenses for the second shipment at Genoa, [along with the] unreimbursed tooling expenses and the cost of useless insulation and tubing materials . . . are legitimate [incidental and] consequential damages that in no way duplicate lost profits damages.

The labor expense incurred as a result of the production line shutdown . . . is also a reasonably foreseeable result of delivering nonconforming compressors for installation in air conditioners. . . . Whether Delchi's labor costs during this four-day period are variable or fixed costs is in large measure a fact question that we cannot answer because we lack factual findings by the district court. We therefore remand to the district court on this issue. . . .

[Affirmed in part and reversed and remanded in part.]

NOTES

(1) *"Possible" or "Probable"?* Judge Winter explains that cases under the Code may "inform a court where the language of the relevant CISG provisions tracks that of the UCC." The relevant CISG provision speaks of "a *possible* consequence of the breach." Do you find this language in the Code? Recall that in Hadley v. Baxendale Baron Alderson spoke of "the *probable* result of the breach," language that has been carried over into Restatement § 351(1), which speaks of "a *probable* result of the breach." Is the difference between "possible" and "probable" significant? See also UNIDROIT Principles 7.4.4 ("likely").

(2) *Buyer for Resale.* The court's decision on Delchi's "lost profits for unfilled orders" is not surprising. If a seller knows it is selling to a buyer for resale, loss of such profits is generally regarded as foreseeable. Loss of profits on future contracts is another matter.

Nevertheless, Hendricks, an import agent, overcame this obstacle under a contract to buy garments from Daewoo, a Korean manufacturer. As Daewoo knew, Hendricks needed the garments for resale to Champion, a wholesaler of sporting apparel, with whom Hendricks had developed a continuing relationship. The garments had serious defects ("too risky to market"), and Champion terminated its relationship with Hendricks. Hendricks sued Daewoo for damages including its loss of future Champion contracts and had judgment based on a $375,000 jury verdict. Daewoo appealed. As to foreseeability, the court said: "We think that a rational jury could conclude in these circumstances that Daewoo could have foreseen that a nonconforming tender, as severe and pervasive as the present evidence demonstrates, probably would cause Hendricks, in the ordinary course of events, to lose future Champion contracts." Hendricks & Associates v. Daewoo Corp., 923 F.2d 209, 215 (1st Cir.1991). For the court's disposition of the case, see Note 1, p. 673 below.

PROBLEM

Sweetening a Damage Claim. Federal contracted to sell 75,000 tons of sugar to Czarnikow, to be delivered directly to Czarnikow's customers. In the contracts that Czarnikow then made in turn with its customers, it provided that the sugar was to be "Federal" brand, but this provision was not known to Federal. (Recall that in *Tongish*, p. 633 above, the court noted that "Tongish knew the seeds eventually went to Bambino, although he may not have known the details of the deal.") When the sugar delivered by Federal turned out to be defective, Czarnikow spent $340,000 in the settlement of claims and the defense of law suits brought by its customers, an amount that was inflated because Czarnikow's obligations to them could not be met by delivery of sugar from other suppliers, which it might have obtained on the market. Is Federal liable for $340,000? Czarnikow–Rionda Co. v. Federal Sugar Refining Co., 173 N.E. 913 (N.Y.1930).

Assuming that Federal is liable for $340,000, could Czarnikow recover an additional $100,000 by showing that it had lost this much in profits when its volume dropped because it was deprived of $340,000 in capital? See Lewis v. Mobil Oil Corp., 438 F.2d 500 (8th Cir.1971).

Might these questions be answered differently under Article 2 of the UCC and the CISG?

Kenford Co. v. County of Erie

Court of Appeals of New York, 1989.
73 N.Y.2d 312, 537 N.E.2d 176.

■ MOLLEN, JUDGE. This appeal arises out of breach of contract litigation spanning 18 years and involving the proposed construction and operation of a domed stadium facility in the County of Erie. The issue is whether the plaintiff Kenford Company, Inc. (Kenford) is entitled to recover damages against the defendant County of Erie (County) for the loss of anticipated appreciation in the value of the land which Kenford owned in the periphery of the proposed stadium site. Under the circumstances of this case, we conclude that Kenford is not entitled to recovery on this claim since there is no evidence to support a determination that the parties contemplated, prior to or at the time of the contract, assumption by the County of liability for these damages.

By way of background, the County of Erie adopted enabling legislation in May 1968 authorizing it to finance and construct a domed sports stadium in the vicinity of the City of Buffalo. The County, simultaneously, adopted a resolution authorizing a $50 million bond resolution for the purpose of financing the construction of the proposed stadium.... Kenford, through its president and sole shareholder, Edward H. Cottrell, submitted an offer ... to donate to the County the land upon which the stadium was to be built, in exchange for which the County was to permit ... the management company of Dome Stadium, Inc. (DSI), to lease or manage the proposed stadium facility.

In June 1969, the County adopted a resolution accepting Kenford's ... offer, after which the parties engaged in contract negotiations. During this period of time, Cottrell, as agent for Kenford, exercised his options on several parcels of land located in the Town of Lancaster. On August 8, 1969, the County, Kenford and DSI executed a contract which provided, in pertinent part, that Kenford would donate 178 acres of land located in the Town of Lancaster to the County for use in construction of the stadium and necessary access roadways. In consideration therefor, the County agreed to commence construction of the stadium within 12 months. The County also agreed to negotiate a 40–year lease with DSI for the operation of the facility which was to provide, inter alia, that the County would receive, as its consideration, lease revenues of not less than $63.75 million over the 40–year term to be comprised of (1) all tax revenues received by the County generated by the operation of the stadium site area; (2) rental payments from DSI; and (3) increased real property taxes resulting from increased assessments and other tax revenues received from or generated by "the peripheral lands and development thereof". The term "peripheral lands" was defined as "those lands presently owned, contracted for or hereinafter acquired by Edward H. Cottrell or Kenford, and located within the area of the Town of Lancaster". If a mutually satisfactory lease could not be agreed upon within three months of the contract signing, the County and DSI were to execute a 20–year management agreement which was annexed to the contract.[1]

[When the County learned] that the proposed project would cost approximately $72 million which was $22 million in excess of the County's prior bond resolution [it terminated the contract and] Kenford and DSI instituted the instant breach of contract action and sought specific performance thereof, or, in the alternative, damages in the amount of $90 million.[2] ... [A damage trial] resulted in a jury award to Kenford in the sum of $18 million for its lost appreciation in the value on its property located on the periphery of the proposed stadium site and an award of over $6 million in out-of-pocket expenses. DSI was awarded $25.6 million in lost profits under the parties' 20–year management contract.

On appeal, the Appellate Division, while affirming the major portion of the $6 million jury award for Kenford's mitigation and reliance damages, reversed the award to DSI for loss of profits as well as a portion of the award to Kenford for out-of-pocket expenses and directed a new trial on the damage award for loss of anticipated appreciation in the value of Kenford's peripheral lands.... On this latter point, the majority of the Appellate Division determined that Kenford's loss of land appreciation was both a foreseeable and certain damage for which it was entitled to recover. The majority, however, found that the award was based upon improper appraisal evidence [and remanded].... Two Justices dissented ... and took the position that these damages were not foreseeable and, in any event, were inherently speculative and, therefore, not recoverable.

DSI subsequently sought review of the Appellate Division's dismissal of its breach of contract claim against the County. This court, addressing itself solely to the denial of DSI's right to recover its loss of profits under the 20–year management contract, affirmed that portion of the Appellate Division's decision. Therein, we determined that those damages were not recoverable on the twofold basis that the County's liability for DSI's loss of profits was not in the contemplation of the parties at the time of the execution of the contract and, secondly, the damages were too speculative and, thus, did not satisfy the legal requirements of proof with reasonable certainty....

[On retrial on the issue of damages for Kenford's loss of anticipated land appreciation, the jury awarded Kenford the sum of $6.5 million. The Appellate Division affirmed, and the County appealed, raising the issue whether Kenford was entitled to recover damages for lost anticipated appreciation in the value of its peripheral lands.]

It is well established that in actions for breach of contract, the nonbreaching party may recover general damages which are the natural and probable consequence of the breach. "[In] order to impose on the defaulting party a further liability than for damages [which] naturally and directly [flow from the breach], i.e., in the ordinary course of things, arising from a breach of contract, such unusual or extraordinary damages must

---

1. Despite extensive negotiations, the County and DSI never agreed upon a satisfactory 40–year lease agreement.

2. The plaintiffs were later granted permission to increase the ad damnum clause to $495 million....

have been brought within the contemplation of the parties as the probable result of a breach at the time of or prior to contracting" (Chapman v. Fargo, 223 N.Y. 32, 36, 119 N.E.76); see also Czarnikow Rionda Co. v. Federal Sugar Ref. Co., 255 N.Y 33, 173 N.E. 913; . . . Hadley v. Baxendale, 9 Exch. 341, 156 Eng. Rep. 145. . . . In determining the reasonable contemplation of the parties, the nature, purpose and particular circumstances of the contract known by the parties should be considered . . . as well as "what liability the defendant fairly may be supposed to have assumed consciously, or to have warranted the plaintiff reasonably to suppose that it assumed, when the contract was made" (Globe Ref. Co. v. Landa Cotton Oil Co., 190 U.S. 540, 544 [Holmes, J.]). . . .

In the case before us, it is beyond dispute that at the time the contract was executed, all parties thereto harbored an expectation and anticipation that the proposed domed stadium facility would bring about an economic boom in the County and would result in increased land values and increased property taxes. This expectation is evidenced by the terms of the provision of the parties' contract requiring the County and DSI to undertake negotiations of a lease which would provide for specified revenues to be derived from, inter alia, the increased taxes on the peripheral lands. We cannot conclude, however, that this hope or expectation of increased property values and taxes necessarily or logically leads to the conclusion that the parties contemplated that the County would assume liability for Kenford's loss of anticipated appreciation in the value of its peripheral lands if the stadium were not built. On this point, our decision in the prior appeal regarding DSI's right to recover damages for lost profits under the 20–year management contract is particularly instructive: "Initially, the proof does not satisfy the requirement that liability for loss of profits over a 20–year period was in the contemplation of the parties at the time of the execution of the basic contract or at the time of its breach. . . . Indeed, the provisions in the contract providing remedy for a default do not suggest or provide for such a heavy responsibility on the part of the County. In the absence of any provision for such an eventuality, *the commonsense rule to apply is to consider what the parties would have concluded had they considered the subject.* The evidence here fails to demonstrate that liability for loss of profits over the length of the contract would have been in the contemplation of the parties at the relevant time" ([Kenford Co. v. County of Erie,] 67 N.Y.2d 257, 262, 493 N.E.2d 234 [emphasis added]).

Similarly, there is no provision in the contract between Kenford and the County, nor is there any evidence in the record to demonstrate that the parties, at any relevant time, reasonably contemplated or would have contemplated that the County was undertaking a contractual responsibility for the lack of appreciation in the value of Kenford's peripheral lands in the event the stadium was not built. This conclusion is buttressed by the fact that Kenford was under no contractual obligation to the County to acquire or maintain ownership of any land surrounding the 178 acres it was required to donate to the County. Although the County was aware that Kenford had acquired and intended to further acquire peripheral lands, this knowledge, in and of itself, is insufficient, as a matter of law, to impose liability on the County for the loss of anticipated appreciation in the value of those lands since the County never contemplated at the time of the contract's execution that it assumed legal responsibility for these damages upon a breach of the contract.... [In] Hadley v. Baxendale, 9 Exch. 341, 156 Eng. Rep. 145, supra [the common carrier was not liable for the loss of profits at the plaintiffs' flour mill since the carrier, who knew that the mill was closed, was not aware that the mill's continued operation was dependent solely on prompt delivery of the mill's broken shaft].

Undoubtedly, Kenford purchased the peripheral lands in question with the hope of benefiting from the expected appreciation in the value of those lands once the stadium was completed and became operational. In doing so, Kenford voluntarily and knowingly assumed the risk that, if the stadium were not built, its expectations of financial gain would be unrealized. There is no indication that either Kenford or the County reasonably contemplated at the time of the contract that this risk was assumed, either wholly or partially, by the County. To hold otherwise would lead to the irrational conclusion that the County, in addition to promising to build the domed stadium, provided a guarantee that if for any reason the stadium were not built, Kenford would still receive all the hoped for financial benefits from the peripheral lands it anticipated to receive upon the completion of the stadium. According to Kenford's version of the facts, Kenford was to realize all of its anticipated gains with or without the stadium. Clearly, such a result is illogical and without any basis whatsoever in the record.

Thus, the constant refrain which flows throughout the legion of breach of contract cases dating back to the leading case of Hadley v. Baxendale (9 Exch. 341, 156 Eng. Rep. 145, supra) provides that damages which may be recovered by a party for breach of contract are restricted to those damages which were reasonably foreseen or contemplated by the parties during their negotiations or at the time the contract was executed. The evident purpose of this well-accepted principle of contract law is to limit the liability for unassumed risks of one entering into a contract and, thus, diminish the risk of business enterprise.... In the case before us, although Kenford obviously anticipated and expected that it would reap financial benefits from an anticipated dramatic increase in the value of its peripheral lands upon the completion of the proposed domed stadium facility, these expectations did not ripen or translate into cognizable breach of contract damages since there is no indication whatsoever that the County reasonably contemplated at any relevant time that it was to assume liability for Kenford's unfulfilled land appreciation expectations in the event that the stadium was not built. Thus, under the principles set forth in Hadley v. Baxendale (supra) and its progeny of cases in this State ... Kenford is not entitled to recovery, as a matter of law, for its lost appreciation in the value of its peripheral lands caused by the County's breach of the parties' contract.

[Reversed and] award for loss of anticipated profits from appreciation in the value of peripheral lands stricken.

NOTES

(1) *Limitation of Risk (Reprise)*. Note the court's quotation from Globe Refining Co. v. Landa Cotton Oil Co. In that case Holmes laid down a "tacit agreement"

test, declaring that "the extent of liability ... should be worked out on terms which it fairly may be presumed he would have assented to if they had been presented to his mind.... [It] depends on what liability the defendant fairly may be supposed to have assumed consciously, or to have warranted the plaintiff reasonably to suppose that it assumed, when the contract was made.... [M]ere notice to a seller of some interest or probable action of the buyer is not enough."

This test has not generally found favor. According to Comment 2 to UCC § 2–715, "The 'tacit agreement' test for the recovery of consequential damages is rejected." What does *Kenford's* use of the test show about the attitude of the New York Court of Appeals toward limitation of risk?

(2) *Jury Instructions.* Because the issue of foreseeability is often one for the jury, it is of interest to see how judges instruct juries on the issue. In Redgrave v. Boston Symphony Orchestra, Inc., 602 F.Supp. 1189 (D.Mass.1985), the actress Vanessa Redgrave sued the Boston Symphony Orchestra for breach of a contract under which she was to appear as narrator in the Orchestra's centenary performances of Stravinsky's opera-oratorio Oedipus Rex, claiming, among other things, damages for harm to her professional career. She alleged that the Orchestra had cancelled the performances in retaliation for her public expressions on political issues, and the Orchestra argued that it had done so because Redgrave's statements in support for the Palestine Liberation Organization caused it to fear a disruption of the performances. Here is the judge's instruction on the issue of foreseeability.[a]

Damages are allowed for consequential harm to her professional career only if the harm was a foreseeable consequence within the contemplation of the parties to the contract when it was made.

By the phrase "harm that is a foreseeable consequence within the contemplation of the parties" we mean harm of a kind within one or more of the following groups:

(1) harm of a kind that was referred to in communications between the parties while they were negotiating at or before the time the contract was made; (2) any other harm of a kind foreseeable as sufficiently likely to result from cancellation that it would have been taken into account in the exercise of reasonable care in assessing the possible costs and benefits of the proposed contract and in deciding whether or not to enter into the contract. The test of foreseeable harm is an objective one based on what a party to the contract, at the time of making the contract, knew or had reason to foresee or had reason to know or ought to have known would be harm which could result from the breach of the contract. To be within the contemplation of the parties, the harm must be of a kind that either was foreseen or else was foreseeable by a reasonable person in the position of the party now being sued, taking into account the facts and circumstances that party or its agents knew, as well other facts and circumstances, if any, which a reasonable person in that position would have known through the exercise of reasonable care. Thus, in order to find that consequential harm was within the contemplation of both parties in this case, you must find that BSO's agents knew or should have known, when the contract was made, that there was a substantial likelihood that a cancellation would be likely to cause Vanessa Redgrave to lose other professional work.

a. The judge was Robert E. Keeton, an author of a leading textbook on insurance, R. Keeton & A. Widiss, *Insurance Law* (1988).

The plaintiffs have the burden of proving by a preponderance of the evidence that the harm was a foreseeable consequence within the contemplation of the parties. You are not allowed to speculate on this question.

The jury found that harm to Redgrave's professional career was foreseeable and awarded $100,000 in consequential damages. The trial judge concluded that this award was supported by the evidence but that, on principles analogous to the law of defamation, Redgrave could not recover for such harm on the facts of the case. Therefore, he limited Redgrave's recovery to $27,500, the amount she was to be paid for the performances less expenses that she would have incurred to perform the contract. The Court of Appeals held that it was error so to limit damages but concluded that, though the quoted instruction was "appropriate," Redgrave's evidence was sufficient to support only some $12,000 in consequential damages. Redgrave v. Boston Symphony Orchestra, Inc., 855 F.2d 888 (1st Cir.1988).

PROBLEM

Cold Steel. In September, Torrington, the successful bidder with the New York State Department of Transportation on a highway reconstruction job in northern New York, made a subcontract with Fort Pitt for the structural steel to be used for a bridge, "Delivery to be mutually agreed upon." In November, Torrington advised that it would need the steel the following June, and Fort Pitt replied that it was tentatively scheduling delivery accordingly. In January, however, Fort Pitt advised that it could not meet the June date. When most of the steel did not arrive until mid-September, this delayed the pouring of the concrete until the end of October when there was danger of freezing. To mitigate damages, Torrington had the concrete poured on a crash basis in a single day, which entailed additional costs including overtime pay and extra equipment. Torrington sued Fort Pitt for damages based on these additional costs.

Fort Pitt argued that when it made the contract in September it was advised that the total work was to be completed in two years and could not reasonably have anticipated that Torrington would so expedite the work that steel delivery would be called for within a year. It claimed that, under Hadley v. Baxendale, whatever knowledge it received after the contract was made cannot expand its liability. Torrington, on the other hand, argued that Fort Pitt should be charged with whatever knowledge it had in November when the June delivery date was agreed upon, and Fort Pitt, as an experienced bridge fabricator, must have then realized that any delay beyond August would jeopardize the pouring of the concrete and force postponement of the work until spring.

Is Fort Pitt or Torrington right? See Spang Industries, Inc. v. Aetna Casualty & Surety Co., 512 F.2d 365 (2d Cir.1975).

SENTIMENTAL VALUE

In Mieske v. Bartell Drug Co., 593 P.2d 1308 (Wash.1979), the court said this in connection with a claim for damages caused by the loss of a home-movie record of a couple's wedding and later family life. "The fact that damages are difficult to ascertain and measure does not diminish the loss to the person whose property has been destroyed. . . . The problem is to establish the value to the owner. . . . Recognizing that value to the owner encompasses a subjective element, the rule has been established that compensation for sentimental or fanciful values will not be allowed....

"What is sentimental value? The broad dictionary definition is that sentimental refers to being 'governed by feeling, sensibility or emotional idealism....' Webster's Third New International Dictionary (1963). Obviously that is not the exclusion contemplated by the statement that sentimental value is not to be compensated. If it were, no one would recover for the wrongful death of a spouse or a child. Rather, the type of sentiment which is not compensable is that which relates to 'indulging in feeling to an unwarranted extent' or being 'affectedly or mawkishly emotional ...' Webster's Third New International Dictionary (1963).

"Under these rules, the court's damages instruction was correct. In essence it allowed recovery for the actual or intrinsic value to the plaintiffs but denied recovery for any unusual sentimental value of the film to the plaintiffs or a fanciful price which plaintiffs, for their own special reasons, might place thereon."

Was the value of Keno to Archie Sparrow in Morris v. Sparrow, p. 593 above, sentimental or something else?

———

EMOTIONAL DISTRESS

Courts have been reluctant to allow damages for emotional distress resulting from breach of contract. See Restatement § 353. Sometimes emotional distress is not foreseeable, and, even if it is foreseeable, the resulting damages are often particularly difficult to establish and to measure. See Goldberg, Emotional Distress Damages and Breach of Contract: A New Approach, 20 U.C.Davis L.Rev. 57 (1986).

Furthermore, some courts have likened the award of damages for emotional distress to the award of punitive damages. In Brown v. Fritz, 699 P.2d 1371, 1374–75 (Idaho 1985), for example, the court overturned an award of $15,000 for the emotional distress of a home buyer when she discovered that the sellers had fraudulently represented the property. When the buyer learned that the sellers had previously sold part of the property to another and that the sewage system malfunctioned, causing raw sewage to accumulate beneath the house, she resold the property and "suffered severe emotional distress which manifested itself in physical symptoms, including the need for substantial hospitalization."

The court noted that in a decision five years earlier it had said that "the commercial nature of the contract" was relevant but not decisive, indicating a distinction between commercial contracts and " 'non-commercial' contracts, such as to perform a caesarean section, to bury a body, or to deliver a bride's trousseau." The court also noted that in a decision two years earlier it had said that punitive damages "should be awarded only in the most unusual and compelling circumstances" and "will be sustained on appeal only when it is shown that the defendant acted in a manner that was 'an extreme deviation from reasonable standards of conduct, and that the act was performed by the defendant with an understanding of or disregard for its likely consequences.' "

The home buyer's emotional distress "resulted from the negotiations for and the consummation of a contract to convey real property" and not "from an 'independent' tort involving a physical or a constructive contact between two parties who were not in a contractual relationship." Observing "the close parallel between allowable damages for breach of contract under the terminology of 'emotional distress' and for punitive damages," the court held that "when damages are sought for breach of a contractual relationship, there can be no recovery for emotional distress suffered by the plaintiff. If the conduct of a defendant has been sufficiently outrageous, we view the proper remedy to be in the realm of punitive damages."

NOTES

(1) *The Case of the "Whole Damned Business."* Blummer Lamm employed the Shingletons, undertakers, to inter her husband in a vault guaranteed to be watertight. About three months later, during a heavy rain, the vault rose above the ground, and the Shingletons undertook to reinter the body. They raised the vault in Lamm's presence and found that the casket was wet. The sight "caused her considerable shock and made her extremely nervous as a result of which she became a nervous wreck." One of the Shingletons said he would not get the mud out of the vault and "to hell with the whole damned business, it's no concern of mine." This made Lamm "so nervous she could hardly stand up." She sued for breach of contract and, from judgment that she take nothing, she appealed. *Held:* Reversed.

Although "as a general rule," damages for mental anguish are not recoverable in a contract action, the law is "in a state of flux. . . . Where the contract is personal in nature and the contractual duty or obligation is so coupled with matters of mental concern or solicitude, or with the sensibilities of the party to whom the duty is owed, that a breach of that duty will necessarily or reasonably result in mental anguish or suffering, and it should be known to the parties from the nature of the contract that such suffering will result from its breach, compensatory damages therefor may be recovered. . . . The contract was predominantly personal in nature and no substantial pecuniary loss would follow its breach." Lamm v. Shingleton, 55 S.E.2d 810, 813 (N.C.1949).

For an unusual case granting recovery for "mental anguish" resulting from the defective construction of a new home, see B & M Homes v. Hogan, 376 So.2d 667 (Ala.1979). The court noted that the "largest single investment the average American family will make is the purchase of a home" and concluded that "any reasonable builder could easily foresee that an individual would undergo extreme mental anguish if their newly constructed house contained defects as severe as those shown to exist in this case." For a contrary and more traditional view, see Ostrowe v. Darensbourg, 377 So.2d 1201 (La.1979).

(2) *Employment Contracts.* Claims of damages for emotional distress are common in actions for breach of employment contracts. In Francis v. Lee Enterprises, 971 P.2d 707, 713 (Haw.1999), the court held that though "damages for emotional distress . . . are generally not recoverable in contract," they may be awarded where "the contract is of such a kind that serious emotional disturbance is a particularly foreseeable result if a breach occurs. . . . [I]n deciding whether such damages are recoverable, we shift the focus of the inquiry away from the *manner* of the breach and to the *nature* of the contract."

Courts have, however, generally found reasons to refuse such damages for breach of employment contracts. For example, in Saporoso v. Aetna Life & Cas. Co., 603 A.2d 1160, 1166–67 (Conn.1992), the Supreme Court of Connecticut concluded that there "is no reasonable basis in the evidence for a jury to have found that . . . when the plaintiff resumed her employment with Aetna, it was reasonably foreseeable that if the plaintiff's employment should be terminated, with or without cause, she would suffer a continuing disability from a psychiatric disorder related to her employment or the circumstances of her discharge." See also Gaglidari v. Denny's Restaurants, 815 P.2d 1362, 1370, 1373 (Wash.1991), where the court said that its research had found only one state, Colorado, that rejects the "traditional common law doctrine . . . that tort damages for emotional distress caused by breach of an employment contract are not recoverable" and added that "the overwhelming majority of courts deny recovery for mental distress damages even though they might be foreseeable within the rule stated in Hadley v. Baxendale."

(3) *The Case of the Designer Dress.* The purchaser of a custom-made wedding dress sued "the high fashion designer . . . known to the cognoscenti simply as Halston" for "mental anguish" caused because the dress was allegedly improperly made and could not be worn by the purchaser's daughter at her wedding. *Held:* Cause of action dismissed. Levin v. Halston Ltd., 398 N.Y.S.2d 339 (N.Y.City Ct.1977).

(C) CERTAINTY

In an omitted part of the opinion you just read in *Kenford*, the court discussed its earlier decision in Kenford Co. v. County of Erie, 493 N.E.2d 234 (N.Y.1986). It recalled that in that decision it had reviewed DSI's award of $25.6 million in lost profits under its 20–year management contract and had "determined that those damages were not recoverable on the twofold basis that the County's liability for DSI's profits was not in the contemplation of the parties at the time of the execution of the contract and, secondly, the damages were too speculative and, thus, did not satisfy the legal requirement of proof with reasonable certainty."

You may remember that the term "speculative" also appeared in the opinion in *Naval Institute*, p. 9 above. There Berkley challenged as "speculative" the premise "that, but for the breach by Berkley, Naval would have sold in September the same number of hardcover copies it sold in August." In that case the court rejected the challenge, saying that "it is not error to lay the normal uncertainty in such hypotheses at the door of the wrongdoer who altered the proper course of events."

These two cases point up an important limitation on the disappointed promisee's right to contract damages. As put in a seminal New York case decided in 1858, damages for breach of contract must "be shown, by clear and satisfactory evidence, to have been actually sustained" and "be shown with certainty, and not left to speculation or conjecture." Griffin v. Colver, 16 N.Y. 489, 491 (1858).

Contemporary formulations, however, insist only on "reasonable certainty" rather than on "certainty" itself. Restatement § 352, for example, precludes recovery "for loss beyond an amount that the evidence permits to be established with reasonable certainty." Comment 1 to UCC § 1–106 explains that damages need not "be calculable with mathematical accuracy," are "at best approximate," and "have to be proved with whatever definiteness and accuracy the facts permit, but no more." And UNIDROIT Principles art. 7.4.3 requires only "a reasonable degree of certainty." Nevertheless, it is clear that in this regard the injured party has a more onerous burden than that imposed by the ordinary requirement to make its case by the "preponderance of evidence."

NOTES

(1) *Buyer for Resale (Reprise)*. Recall that in Note 2, p. 663 above, the Court of Appeals upheld Hendricks' damage award against Daewoo in the face of a challenge based on Hadley v. Baxendale. As to certainty of proof of lost profits, however, Hendricks did not fare as well. *Held:* Affirmed conditioned on a remittitur of damages in excess of $45,000, otherwise Daewoo's motion for new trial to be granted.

"We can only conclude that no loss of prospective profits in an amount even approaching the $375,000 consequential damages award was proven in the manner required by Massachusetts law.... With no evidence of *past* profits, future profit margins, future business revenues or expenses, beyond [the year of the breach], and no formula or method for divining any other element in a rational projection or calculation of prospective profits, the jury was left entirely to guesswork ... The jury could have found, without impermissible resort to surmise and speculation, that Hendricks was entitled to recover no more than $45,000 for loss of prospective profits...." Hendricks & Associates v. Daewoo Corp., 923 F.2d 209, 217, 220, 221 (1st Cir.1991).

(2) *The Value of a Chance*. In Collatz v. Fox Wisconsin Amusement Corp., 239 Wis. 156, 300 N.W. 162 (1941), the plaintiff, one of two finalists in a quiz contest held at the defendant's theater, claimed a half interest in the automobile offered as a prize, on the ground that it had been arbitrarily awarded to the other finalist before completion of the contest. The court held for the defendant. The plaintiff "suffered no damage because of the defendant's breach of the contract, for it cannot be assumed nor is it susceptible of proof that had the contest proceeded to a proper finish he would have become the winner." The classic case to the contrary is Chaplin v. Hicks, [1911] 2 K.B. 786, in which the winner of a preliminary round in a beauty contest prevailed. Accord: Wachtel v. National Alfalfa Journal Co., 176 N.W. 801 (Iowa 1920). See Restatement § 348(3); UNIDROIT Principles art. 7.4.3(2).

(3) *The Right to Work*. In *Parker*, could Shirley MacLaine have recovered more than $750,000? Would not starring in "Bloomer Girl" have enhanced her reputation as an actress? A few courts have favored recovery for lost reputation. See Herbert Clayton & Jack Waller, Ltd. v. Oliver [1930] A.C. 209, in which the court said: "Here both parties knew that as flowing from the contract the plaintiff would be billed and advertised as appearing at the Hippodrome, and in the theatrical profession this is a valuable right."

See also Malik v. Bank of Credit & Commerce Intl., [1997] 3 All E.R. 1, 11 (House of Lords) (Lord Steyn: "there is no good reason why in the field of employment law recovery of financial loss in respect of damage to reputation caused by breach of contract is necessarily excluded"). Compare the discussion of sentimental value, p. 669–70 above.

American courts, however, have generally denied recovery for lost reputation on grounds of either uncertainty or unforeseeability. Cases are discussed in Redgrave v. Boston Symphony Orchestra, Note 2, p. 668 above. The court there noted that she did not claim that "her general reputation as a professional actress has been tarnished" but rather "that a number of specific movie and theater performances that would have been offered to her in the usual course of events were not offered to her." How did Redgrave's situation differ from MacLaine's?

Fera v. Village Plaza, Inc.

Supreme Court of Michigan, 1976.
396 Mich. 639, 242 N.W.2d 372.

■ T.G. KAVANAGH, CHIEF JUSTICE. Plaintiffs received a jury award of $200,000 for loss of anticipated profits in their proposed new business as a result of defendants' breach of a lease. The Court of Appeals reversed.... We reverse and reinstate the jury's award.

On August 20, 1965 plaintiffs and agents of Fairborn–Village Plaza executed a ten-year lease for a "book and bottle" shop in defendants' proposed shopping center. This lease provided for occupancy of a specific location at a rental of $1,000 minimum monthly rent plus 5% of annual receipts in excess of $240,000. A $1,000 deposit was paid by plaintiffs.

After this lease was executed, plaintiffs gave up approximately 600 square feet of their leased space so that it could be leased to another tenant. In exchange, it was agreed that liquor sales would be excluded from the percentage rent override provision of the lease.

Complications arose, including numerous work stoppages. Bank of the Commonwealth received a deed in lieu of foreclosure after default by Fairborn and Village Plaza. Schostak Brothers managed the property for the bank.

When the space was finally ready for occupancy, plaintiffs were refused the space for which they had contracted because the lease had been misplaced, and the space rented to other tenants. Alternative space was offered but refused by plaintiffs as unsuitable for their planned business venture.

Plaintiffs initiated suit in Wayne Circuit Court, alleging *inter alia* a claim for anticipated lost profits. The jury returned a verdict for plaintiffs against all defendants for $200,000.

The Court of Appeals reversed and remanded for new trial on the issue of damages only, holding that the trial court "erroneously permitted lost profits as the measure of damages for breach of the lease." 52 Mich.App. 532, 542, 218 N.W.2d 155, 160.

In Jarrait v. Peters, 145 Mich. 29, 31–32, 108 N.W. 432 (1906), plaintiff was prevented from taking possession of the leased premises. The jury gave plaintiff a judgment which included damages for lost profits. This Court reversed:

"It is well settled upon authority that the measure of damages when a lessor fails to give possession of the leased premises is the difference between the actual rental value and the rent reserved. 1 Sedgwick on Damages (8th Ed.) par. 185. Mr. Sedgwick says:

" 'If the business were a new one, since there could be no basis on which to estimate profits, the plaintiff must be content to recover according to the general rule.'

"The rule is different where the business of the lessee has been interrupted. . . .

"The evidence admitted tending to show the prospective profits plaintiff might have made for the ensuing two years should therefore have been excluded under the objections made by defendant, and the jury should have been instructed that the plaintiff's damages, if any, would be the difference between the actual rental value of the premises and the rent reserved in the lease."

Six years later, in Isbell v. Anderson Carriage Co., 170 Mich. 304, 318, 136 N.W. 457, 462 (1912), the Court wrote:

"It has sometimes been stated as a rule of law that prospective profits are so speculative and uncertain that they cannot be recognized in the measure of damages. This is not because they are profits, but because they are so often not susceptible of proof to a reasonable degree of certainty. Where the proof is available, prospective profits may be recovered, when proven, as other damages. But the jury cannot be asked to guess. They are to try the case upon evidence, not upon conjecture."

These cases and others since should not be read as stating a rule of law which prevents every new business from recovering anticipated lost profits for breach of contract. The rule is merely an application of the doctrine that "[i]n order to be entitled to a verdict, or a judgment, for damages for breach of contract, the plaintiff must lay a basis for a reasonable estimate of the extent of his harm, measured in money". 5 Corbin on Contracts, § 1020, p. 124. The issue becomes one of sufficiency of proof. "The jury should not [be] allowed to speculate or guess upon this question of the amount of loss of profits." Kezeli v. River Rouge Lodge IOOF, 195 Mich. 181, 188, 161 N.W. 838, 840 (1917). . . .

The rule was succinctly stated in Shropshire v. Adams, 40 Tex.Civ.App. 339, 344, 89 S.W. 448, 450 (1905):

"Future profits as an element of damage are in no case excluded merely because they are profits but because they are uncertain. In any case when by reason of the nature of the situation they may be established with reasonable certainty they are allowed."

It is from these principles that the "new business"/"interrupted business" distinction has arisen.

"If a business is one that has already been established a reasonable prediction can often be made as to its future on the basis of its past history. * * * If the business * * * has not had such a history as to make it possible to prove with reasonable accuracy what its profits have been in fact, the profits prevented are often but not necessarily too uncertain for recovery." 5 Corbin on Contracts, § 1023, pp. 147, 150–151. Cf. Jarrait v. Peters, supra.

The Court of Appeals based its opinion reversing the jury's award on two grounds: First, that a new business cannot recover damages for lost profits for breach of a lease. We have expressed our disapproval of that rule. Secondly, the Court of Appeals held plaintiffs barred from recovery because the proof of lost profits was entirely speculative. We disagree.

The trial judge in a thorough opinion made the following observations upon completion of the trial.

"On the issue of lost profits, there were days and days of testimony. The defendants called experts from the Michigan Liquor Control Commission and from Cunningham Drug Stores, who have a store in the area, and a man who ran many other stores. The plaintiffs called experts and they, themselves, had experience in the liquor sales business, in the book sales business and had been representatives of liquor distribution firms in the area.

"The issue of the speculative, conjectural nature of future profits was probably the most completely tried issue in the whole case. Both sides covered this point for days on direct and cross-examination. The proofs ranged from no lost profits to two hundred and seventy thousand dollars over a ten-year period as the highest in the testimony. A witness for the defendants, an expert from Cunningham Drug Company, testified the plaintiffs probably would lose money. Mr. Fera, an expert in his own right, testified the profits would probably be two hundred and seventy thousand dollars. The jury found two hundred thousand dollars. This is well within the limits of the high and the low testimony presented by both sides, and a judgment was granted by the jury.

"The Court cannot invade the finding of fact by the jury, unless there is no testimony to support the jury's finding. There is testimony to support the jury's finding. We must realize that witness Stein is an interested party in this case, personally. He is an officer or owner in Schostak Brothers. He may personally lose money as a result of this case. The jury had to weigh this in determining his credibility. How much credibility they gave his testimony was up to them. How much weight they gave to counter-evidence was up to them. . . .

"The Court must decide whether or not the jury had enough testimony to take this fact from the speculative-conjecture category and find enough facts to be able to make a legal finding of fact. This issue [damages for lost profits] was the most completely tried issue in the whole case. Both sides put in testimony that took up days and encompassed experts on both sides. This fact was adequately taken from the category of speculation and conjecture by the testimony and placed in the position of those cases that hold that even though loss of profits is hard to prove, if proven they should be awarded by the jury. In this case, the jury had ample testimony to make this decision from both sides. . . ."

As Judge Wickens observed, the jury was instructed on the law concerning speculative damages. The case was thoroughly tried by all the parties. Apparently, the jury believed the plaintiffs. That is its prerogative.

The testimony presented during the trial was conflicting. The weaknesses of plaintiffs' specially prepared budget were thoroughly explored on cross-examination. Defendants' witnesses testified concerning the likelihood that plaintiffs would not have made profits if the contract had been performed. There was conflicting testimony concerning the availability of a liquor license. All this was spread before the jury. The jury weighed the conflicting testimony and determined that plaintiffs were entitled to damages of $200,000.

As we stated in Anderson v. Conterio, 303 Mich. 75, 79, 5 N.W.2d 572, 574 (1942):

> "The testimony ... is in direct conflict, and that of plaintiff ... was impeached to some extent. However, it cannot be said as a matter of law that the testimony thus impeached was deprived of all probative value or that the jury could not believe it. The credibility of witnesses is for the jury, and it is not for us to determine who is to be believed."

The trial judge, who also listened to all of the conflicting testimony, denied defendants' motion for a new trial, finding that the verdict was justified by the evidence. We find no abuse of discretion in that decision....

While we might have found plaintiffs' proofs lacking had we been members of the jury, that is not the standard of review we employ. "As a reviewing court we will not invade the fact finding of the jury or remand for entry of judgment unless the factual record is so clear that reasonable minds may not disagree." Hall v. Detroit, 383 Mich. 571, 574, 177 N.W.2d 161, 163 (1970). This is not the situation here.

The Court of Appeals is reversed and the trial court's judgment on the verdict is reinstated....

■ COLEMAN, JUSTICE (concurring in part, dissenting in part). Although anticipated profits from a new business may be determined with a reasonable degree of certainty such was not the situation regarding loss of profits from liquor sales as proposed by plaintiffs.

First, plaintiffs had no license and a Liquor Control Commission regional supervisor and a former commissioner testified that the described book and bottle store could not obtain a license. Further, the proofs of possible profits from possible liquor sales—if a license could have been obtained—were too speculative. The speculation of possible licensing plus the speculation of profits in this case combine to cause my opinion that profits from liquor sales should not have been submitted to the jury.

I ... would have allowed proof of loss from the bookstore operation to go to the jury, but not proof of loss from liquor sales. ... I would affirm the trial court judgment conditioned upon plaintiffs' consenting within 30 days following the release of this opinion, to "remitting that portion of the judgment in excess of $60,000. Otherwise, the judgment should be reversed and a new trial had.'' Plaintiffs are also entitled to the $1,000 deposit.

NOTES

(1) *New Businesses.* For a stricter view, see Evergreen Amusement Corp. v. Milstead, 112 A.2d 901 (Md.1955), an action against a contractor for damages for delay in the opening of a drive-in theater from June 1 to mid-August. The operator of the theater proffered a witness who had built a majority of the drive-in theaters in the area and who would have testified as to reasonably anticipated profits for the months in question by comparison with the theater's profits for the same months of the following year. The court held that it was not error to refuse to hear the witness. "[T]he general rule clearly is that loss of profit is a definite element of damages in an action for breach of contract or in an action for harming an established business which has been operating for a sufficient length of time to afford a basis of estimation with some degree of certainty as to the probable loss of profits, but that, on the other hand, loss of profits from a business which has not gone into operation may not be recovered because they are merely speculative and incapable of being ascertained with the requisite degree of certainty.... While this Court has not laid down a flat rule (and does not hereby do so), nevertheless, no case has permitted recovery of lost profits under comparable circumstances.''

(2) *Royalties from Artistic Creations.* The requirement of reasonable certainty has plagued plaintiffs whose claims are based on lost royalties from artistic creations. In Contemporary Mission, Inc. v. Famous Music Corp., 557 F.2d 918, 926, 927 (2d Cir.1977), a generous result was reached under New York law. The plaintiffs, a group of Roman Catholic priests who wrote musical compositions and recordings, sued Famous Music for breach of its contract to make and sell records on a royalty basis from the master tape recording of the priests' rock opera "Virgin.''

The Court of Appeals held that the trial court erred in excluding a statistical analysis, together with expert testimony, in order to prove how successful the most successful of the opera's single recordings, "Fear No Evil,'' would have been. The court acknowledged that the requirement of certainty "operates with particular severity in cases involving artistic creations such as books, ... movies, ... and, by analogy, records.'' Nevertheless, at the time of the breach, "the record was real, the price was fixed, the market was buying and the record's success, while modest, was increasing. Even after the promotional efforts ended, the record was withdrawn from the marketplace, it was carried, as a result of its own momentum, to an additional 10,000 sales and to a rise from approximately number 80 on the 'Hot Soul Singles' chart of Billboard magazine to number 61.'' The court, however, rejected the plaintiff's "domino theory'' of projected damages under which, if "Fear No Evil'' had become a "hit,'' it would have generated opportunities for concert and theatrical tours and similar benefits, on the ground that "these additional benefits are too dependent upon taste or fancy to be considered anything other than speculative and uncertain.''

(3) *Good Will.* The requirement of certainty is likely to be particularly troublesome to a claimant that seeks to recover for loss of business reputation, or what is commonly termed "good will.'' For many years, Pennsylvania refused to allow recovery for loss of good will on the ground that "damages of this nature would be entirely too speculative''. Harry Rubin & Sons v. Consolidated Pipe Co., 153 A.2d 472, 476 (Pa.1959) (wholesaler's loss of good will due to manufacturer's failure to deliver hula hoops). In 1990, however, Pennsylvania joined the overwhelming majority of states by overruling such cases "to the extent they prohibit a plaintiff from alleging a claim for damage to good will as a matter of law.'' AM/PM Franchise

Ass'n v. Atlantic Richfield Co., 584 A.2d 915, 926 (Pa.1990) (gasoline franchisee's loss of good will due to franchisor's breach of warranty).

SECTION 4.   "LIQUIDATED DAMAGES" AND "PENALTIES"

At the beginning of this book, it was pointed out that the law's concern is directed at relief of promisees to redress breach rather than at punishment of promisors to compel performance, and that for this reason punitive damages are not ordinarily awarded for breach of contract. The *promisee,* however, may be concerned with compulsion of the promisor. Consider the following explanation, given by a bridge engineer for the California Division of Highways, of the completion assessment—the per-day assessment for each day the contractor overruns the specified contract time. "The sole purpose of a completion assessment is to assure that the contract work will be done within the time specified, ... to threaten the Contractor with sufficient monetary loss so that he will find it advantageous to apply sufficient men and equipment to the work to get it done on time. Whereas moderate liquidated damages such as $100 per day may well be used to insure the completion of a normal project having no special urgency, higher amounts are used to force faster work on jobs which must be finished in less than a normal construction time. High assessments may be used to emphasize the need for haste and should be of sufficient size to make it economically desirable that the contractor expedite his work by the use of multiple shifts or additional equipment." A. Elliott, A Study of Liquidated Damages on Highway Contracts 5 (Cal.Div.Hwys.1956). Should courts lend their aid to the enforcement of such penalties where the parties have bargained for and agreed to them?

NOTES

(1) *Penalties and Reliance Investments.* Sometimes a promisee can encourage the promisor's timely performance by stipulating liquidated damages. Of course, the promisor must agree to the stipulated damages and will likely demand compensation for being accountable for an award greater than the legal default. If the promisor agrees to the stipulated award, the promisee may feel more confident when relying on the contract because the promisor's commitments are more credible, given the heightened remedy. Consider the effect of such confidence on the incentives of parties to invest. If two sophisticated parties contract to provide efficient incentives to invest using a liquidated clause, should the court refuse to enforce the clause even if it appears punitive?

(2) *Paying for Nothing?* As suggested in the note above, promisors should be expected to demand compensation for facing a risk of paying high liquidated damages in the even of breach. If, following a breach by the promisor, the court refuses to enforce the liquidated clause, has the promisor been unjustly enriched?

Consider again the study of liquidated damages in California highway contracts mentioned above: "High liquidated damages have a tendency to make the contractors jittery. A fear of the high cost of delay will cause an involuntary rise in bid prices. All of the bidders' thinking on prices must inevitably be colored by the specter of the high damages lurking in the background. This only emphasizes the need to use this specialized treatment and high liquidated damages only on those projects where the urgency really exists. Otherwise the State will be paying extra for expediting jobs which do not need the hurry and will not justify the higher cost. High liquidated damages make a contractor susceptible to considerable labor pressure. When a contractor is working under high liquidated damages, it gives the unions a powerful lever to force compliance with demands which may or may not be justified. The contractor is forced to give in because he cannot afford a delaying argument or strike. This pressure also may have a widespread effect. When labor unions make an advance by this sort of a squeeze play against the contractor working under high liquidated damages, other contractors in the area find that they too must give the same benefits or face considerable trouble." A. Elliott, A Study of Liquidated Damages on Highway Contracts 21–22 (Cal.Div.Hwys.1956).

(3) *Penalties in Other Legal Systems.* What concerns might justify a limitation on freedom of contract with respect to penalties? Are terms providing for penalties more onerous than other terms? Some insights may be gained from a look at other legal systems.

According to article 1152 of the French Civil Code: "When the agreement provides that the party who fails to carry it out shall pay a certain sum as damages, no larger or smaller amount can be awarded to the other party." In 1975, however, following a recommendation that there be judicial control over penal clauses in leases, this article was amended by adding: "However, the judge may reduce or increase the penalty that has been agreed upon if it is plainly excessive or ridiculously low. No effect will be given to an agreement to the contrary." What might have prompted these changes?

No attempt was made in the CISG to draft a rule on stipulated damages. But see UNIDROIT Principles art. 7.4.13.

(4) *Penalties in California.* In 1977 California enacted a statute under which "a provision in a contract liquidating the damages for the breach of the contract is valid unless the party seeking to invalidate the provision establishes that the provision was unreasonable under the circumstances existing at the time the contract was made." Cal.Civil Code § 1671. The statute does not apply against a consumer and in certain other situations.

Wasserman's Inc. v. Township of Middletown

Supreme Court of New Jersey, 1994.
137 N.J. 238, 645 A.2d 100.

■ POLLOCK, J. Pursuant to a public advertisement for bids, plaintiff Wasserman's Inc. (Wasserman's) and defendant, Township of Middletown (the Township or Middletown), entered into a commercial lease for a tract of municipally-owned property. The agreement contained a clause providing that if the Township cancelled the lease, it would pay the lessee, Wasserman's, a pro-rata reimbursement for any improvement costs and damages of twenty-five percent of the lessee's average gross receipts for one year. In 1989, the Township cancelled the lease and sold the property, but refused to pay the agreed damages.

[Wasserman's and a man doing business as "Jo–Ro" sued for damages according to the terms of the lease. (Jo–Ro was a plaintiff because Wasserman's had ceased doing business, apparently, and had sublet the store to Jo–Ro. The sublease provided that the parties to it would share any payments made by the Township under the cancellation provision.) The

Township answered, and sought a declaration that part of the cancellation provision was invalid—the part about paying Wassermans' 25% of its average yearly gross receipts.]

On cross-motions for summary judgment, the Law Division held that the lease and the cancellation clause were enforceable. It subsequently required the Township to pay damages in the amount of $346,058.44 plus interest. [On a first appeal, that was affirmed. This court granted certification.] We conclude that the lease is enforceable. We affirm the award of renovation costs and remand to the Law Division the issue of the enforceability of the stipulated damages clause.

I

[Wasserman's had won the lease by bidding for it. It provided for a monthly rental of $458.33 throughout a thirty-year term. Wasserman's object was to run a general store. The Township set the value of the property at $47,500. Initially the store comprised 3,200 square feet. During its occupancy, Wasserman's enlarged it. It sublet the premises to Jo–Ro not much more than two years after beginning its occupancy, charging Jo–Ro a monthly rent of $1,850.]

[The Township's cancellation of the lease was effective on the last day of 1988. Some six months later the Township sold the property at public auction for $610,000.]

At the center of the dispute is the cancellation clause in the lease. [The clause provided that, if the Township should cancel the lease, it would pay some of the cost of any improvements made by Wasserman's. (For any improvement, the amount was to be calculated by reference to the period of the tenancy remaining when the improvement was made, in relation to the entire term of the lease.] More controversial is the second half of the clause.... That provision requires the Township to pay "twenty-five percent of the lessee[']s average gross receipts for one year (to be computed by + (adding) the lessee[']s total gross receipts for the lessee[']s three full fiscal years immediately preceding the time of cancellation of the lease and ÷ (dividing by) 12 (twelve) ...." ...

II

The Law Division initially granted plaintiffs a partial summary judgment according "full force and effect" to the lease and the cancellation clause. On a subsequent motion, the court awarded plaintiffs damages of $346,058.44 plus ten-percent prejudgment interest. The trial court calculated damages as follows:

$142,336.01 (construction costs) multiplied by 11.75 (remaining years) divided by 30 years (term of lease) for a total of $55,748.27.

$3,483,722.25 (Jo–Ro's gross receipts for the years 1985, 1986, 1987) divided by 12 equalling $290,310.18.

Construction compensation	$ 55,748.27
Gross receipts compensation	+ 290,310.18
Total amount due	$346,058.45

III

[In a part of the opinion omitted here, the court rejected the Township's argument that the lease did not meet the requirements for a valid public contract.]

IV

The provision in the termination clause providing for damages based on the lessee's gross receipts presents a more difficult issue. The issue is whether that provision is an enforceable liquidated damages provision or is an unenforceable penalty clause.

Disapproval of penalty clauses originated at early common law when debtors bound themselves through sealed penalty bonds for twice the amount of their actual debts. Charles J. Goetz & Robert E. Scott, Liquidated Damages, Penalties and the Just Compensation Principle: Some Notes on an Enforcement Model and a Theory of Efficient Breach, 77 Colum.L.Rev. 554, 554 (1977) (hereinafter Goetz & Scott). Because clauses in penalty bonds "carried an unusual danger of oppression and extortion," equity courts refused to enforce them. Id. at 555. "This equitable rule, designed to prevent overreaching and to give relief from unconscionable bargains, was later adopted by courts of law." John D. Calamari & Joseph M. Perillo, The Law of Contracts, § 14–31 at 639 (3d ed. 1987) (hereinafter Calamari & Perillo). In a sense, judicial reluctance to enforce penalty clauses is a product of history.

For more than five centuries, courts have scrutinized contractual provisions that specify damages payable in the event of breach. Wassenaar v. Panos, 331 N.W.2d 357 (Wis.1983) . . . [Hereafter, references to this case give page numbers only.] The validity of these "stipulated damage clauses" has depended on a judicial assessment of the clauses as an unenforceable penalty or as an enforceable provision for "liquidated damage." Thus, " '[l]iquidated damages' and 'penalties' are terms used to reflect legal conclusions as to the enforceability or nonenforceability, respectively, of stipulated damage clauses." Kenneth W. Clarkson et al., Liquidated Damages v. Penalties: Sense or Nonsense?, 1978 Wis.L.Rev. 351, 351 n. 1 (hereinafter Clarkson).

Thirty years ago, the Appellate Division distinguished liquidated damages and penalty clauses:

> *Liquidated damages* is the sum a party to a contract agrees to pay if he breaks some promise, and which, having been arrived at by a good faith effort to estimate in advance the actual damages that will probably ensue from the breach, is legally recoverable as agreed damages if the breach occurs. A *penalty* is the sum a party agrees to pay in the event of a breach, but which is fixed, not as a pre-estimate of probable actual damages, but as a punishment, the threat of which is

designed to prevent the breach. Parties to a contract may not fix a penalty for its breach. The settled rule in this State is that such a contract is unlawful.

[Westmount Country Club v. Kameny, 82 N.J.Super. 200, 205, 197 A.2d 379 (1964) (citations omitted).]

Stating the distinction, however, has been easier than describing its underlying rationale. " '[T]he ablest judges have declared that they felt themselves embarrassed in ascertaining the principle on which the decisions [distinguishing penalties from liquidated damages] were founded.' " E. Allan Farnsworth, Contracts § 12.18 at 937 (2d ed. 1990) (alterations in original) (quoting Cotheal v. Talmage, 9 N.Y. 551, 553 (1854))....

As the law has evolved, a stipulated damage clause "must constitute a reasonable forecast of the provable injury resulting from breach; otherwise, the clause will be unenforceable as a penalty and the non-breaching party will be limited to conventional damage measures." Goetz & Scott, supra, 77 Colum.L.Rev. at 554. So viewed, "reasonableness" emerges as the standard for deciding the validity of stipulated damages clauses. See *Wassenaar* at 361 (noting that "[t]he overall single test of validity is whether the clause is reasonable under the totality of circumstances").

The reasonableness test has developed as a compromise between two competing viewpoints concerning stipulated damages clauses. The Wisconsin Supreme Court has described the policy considerations underlying these viewpoints:

> Enforcement of stipulated damages clauses is urged because the clauses serve several purposes. The clauses allow the parties to control their exposure to risk by setting the payment for breach in advance. They avoid the uncertainty, delay, and expense of using the judicial process to determine actual damages. They allow the parties to fashion a remedy consistent with economic efficiency in a competitive market, and they enable the parties to correct what the parties perceive to be inadequate judicial remedies by agreeing upon a formula which may include damage elements too uncertain or remote to be recovered under rules of damages applied by the courts. In addition to these policies specifically relating to stipulated damages clauses, considerations of judicial economy and freedom of contract favor enforcement of stipulated damages clauses.

> A competing set of policies disfavors stipulated damages clauses, and thus courts have not been willing to enforce stipulated damages clauses blindly without carefully scrutinizing them. Public law, not private law, ordinarily defines the remedies of the parties. Stipulated damages are an exception to this rule. Stipulated damages allow private parties to perform the judicial function of providing the remedy in breach of contract cases, namely, compensation of the nonbreaching party, and courts must ensure that the private remedy does not stray too far from the legal principle of allowing compensatory damages. Stipulated damages substantially in excess of injury may justify an inference of unfairness in bargaining or an objectionable *in terrorem*

agreement to deter a party from breaching the contract, to secure performance, and to punish the breaching party if the deterrent is ineffective.

[*Wassenaar* at 362.]

Consistent with the principle of reasonableness, New Jersey courts have viewed enforceability of stipulated damages clauses as depending on whether the set amount "is a reasonable forecast of just compensation for the harm that is caused by the breach" and whether that harm "is incapable or very difficult of accurate estimate." Westmount Country Club, supra, 82 N.J.Super. at 206, 197 A.2d 379. . . .

Uncertainty or difficulty in assessing damages is best viewed not as an independent test, Calamari and Perillo, *supra*, § 14–31 at 641; Goetz & Scott, *supra*, 77 Colum.L.Rev. at 559 (stating, "liquidated damages provisions have seldom been voided solely because the damages were easy to estimate"), but rather as an element of assessing the reasonableness of a liquidated damages clause, *Wassenaar* at 363. Thus, "[t]he greater the difficulty of estimating or proving damages, the more likely the stipulated damages will appear reasonable." *Ibid.*

Some courts in other jurisdictions have also considered whether the parties intended the clause to be one for liquidated damages. Clarkson, *supra*, 1978 Wis.L.Rev. at 353. Even those courts recognize that "subjective intent has little bearing on whether the clause is objectively reasonable." *Wassenaar* at 363. . . .

Although the Appellate Division has indicated that courts should determine the enforceability of a stipulated damages clause as of the time of the making of the contract. *Westmount Country Club, supra*, 82 N.J.Super. at 206, 197 A.2d 379, the modern trend is towards assessing reasonableness either at the time of contract formation or at the time of the breach. Calamari & Perillo, *supra*, § 14–31 at 642 (stating, "there are two moments at which the liquidated damages clause may be judged rather than just one").

Actual damages, moreover, reflect on the reasonableness of the parties' prediction of damages. "If the damages provided for in the contract are grossly disproportionate to the actual harm sustained, the courts usually conclude that the parties' original expectations were unreasonable." *Wassenaar* at 364; see 5A Corbin on Contracts § 1063 (1951) (Corbin) ("It is to be observed that hindsight is frequently better than foresight, and that, in passing judgment upon the honesty and genuineness of the pre-estimate made by the parties, the court cannot help but be influenced by its knowledge of subsequent events."). Determining enforceability at the time either when the contract is made or when it is breached encourages more frequent enforcement of stipulated damages clauses. Calamari & Perillo, supra, § 14–31 at 642.

Two of the most authoritative statements concerning liquidated damages are contained in the Uniform Commercial Code and the Restatement (Second) of Contracts, both of which emphasize reasonableness as the touchstone. Farnsworth, *supra*, § 12.18 at 938. [Here the court set out UCC § 2–718(1) and Restatement § 356(1).]

Consistent with the trend toward enforcing stipulated damages clauses, the Appellate Division has recognized that such clauses should be deemed presumptively reasonable and that the party challenging such a clause should bear the burden of proving its unreasonableness. . . . Similarly, most courts today place the burden on the party challenging a stipulated damages clause. . . .

In commercial transactions between parties with comparable bargaining power, stipulated damage provisions can provide a useful and efficient remedy. See Priebe & Sons v. United States, 332 U.S. 407, 411–13 (1947). . . . Sophisticated parties acting under the advice of counsel often negotiate stipulated damages clauses to avoid the cost and uncertainty of litigation. Such parties can be better situated than courts to provide a fair and efficient remedy. Absent concerns about unconscionability, courts frequently need ask no more than whether the clause is reasonable. We do not reach the issue of the enforceability of liquidated damage clauses in consumer contracts. Notwithstanding the presumptive reasonableness of stipulated damage clauses, we are sensitive to the possibility that, as their history discloses, such clauses may be unconscionable and unjust. . . .

V

The purpose of a stipulated damages clause is not to compel the promisor to perform, but to compensate the promisee for non-performance. Farnsworth, supra, § 12.18 at 936 . . . Thus, the subject cancellation clause is unreasonable if it does more than compensate plaintiffs for their approximate actual damages caused by the breach.

Whether measured from the time of execution of the contract or from the termination of the lease, . . . damages based on gross receipts run the risk of being found unreasonable. Generally speaking, gross receipts do not reflect actual losses incurred because of the cancellation. Gross receipts, unlike net profits, do not account for ordinary expenses; nor do they account for the expenses specifically attributable to the breach. Here, we cannot determine whether the stipulated amount was based on damages that would likely flow from a breach or whether it is an arbitrary figure unrelated to any such damages. . . .

Courts also have disapproved the use of gross receipts as a measure of damages apart from stipulated damages clauses. . . . Evaluating damages based on gross income is problematic partly because such damages would be too speculative or uncertain. Furthermore, basing damages on gross profits could award the plaintiff a windfall. . . .

We cannot determine from plaintiffs' gross receipts the losses they sustained because of the Township's cancellation of the lease. The subject clause requires the Township to pay damages of twenty-five percent of the lessee's average gross receipts for one year. Under the lease, average gross receipts are calculated by taking an average of the lessee's total gross receipts for three fiscal years immediately preceding the cancellation. So calculated, Jo–Ro's average yearly gross was $1,161,240.75. Twenty-five percent of this figure amounts to $290,310.18.

This amount, however, does not necessarily reflect plaintiffs' actual losses on considering operating expenses or relocation costs and other expenses attributable to defendant's breach. As reflected in Jo–Ro's income-tax returns, Jo–Ro earned a net profit of $3,649 in 1985, $414 in 1986, and sustained a loss of $323 in 1987. We recognize the difference between tax losses and actual losses. Yet, to the extent that tax returns reflect actual profit or loss, they demonstrate the unreasonableness of damages exceeding $290,000, which were calculated on the basis of gross receipts.

The decision whether a stipulated damages clause is enforceable is a question of law for the court. . . . Although the question is one of law, it may require resolution of underlying factual issues. . . .

On balance, we believe we should remand this matter to the trial court to consider the reasonableness of the clause in light of this opinion. In resolving that issue, the court should consider, among other relevant considerations, the reasonableness of the use of gross receipts as the measure of damages no matter when the cancellation occurs; the significance of the award of damages based on twenty-five percent of one year's average gross receipts, rather than on some other basis such as total gross receipts computed for each year remaining under the lease; the reasoning of the parties that supported the calculation of the stipulated damages; the lessee's duty to mitigate damages; and the fair market rent and availability of replacement space. We leave to the sound discretion of the trial court the extent to which additional proof is necessary on the reasonableness of the clause. Because stipulated damages clauses are presumptively reasonable, . . . the burden of production and of persuasion rests on the Township.

To summarize, we affirm the judgment of the Appellate Division that the Township is liable to plaintiffs for terminating the lease. . . . We also affirm the judgment of the Appellate Division awarding plaintiffs damages of $55,748.27 for renovation costs. We remand to the Law Division the issue whether the clause requiring payment of stipulated damages based on the lessee's gross receipts is a valid liquidated damages clause.

NOTES

(1) *Arguments on Remand.* If you were the lawyer for the defendant Township on remand, what arguments and evidence would you use to meet the "burden" of challenging the clause? If you were the lawyer for the plaintiffs, Wasserman's and Jo–Ro, how would you counteract Justice Pollock's critical remarks on gross receipts as a standard? Is it relevant that on termination the plaintiffs lost the use for twelve more years, at an annual rental of only $5,500, of property then worth some $600,000? Does their unproductive use of the property affect your answer?

(2) *A "Second Look"?* Note that Justice Pollock reports that "the modern trend is towards assessing reasonableness either at the time of contract formation or at the time of the breach." This echoes the language of UCC § 2–718, which speaks of the "anticipated or actual harm." But Article 2A of the Code, dealing with

leases of goods, departs from the language of Article 2 and speaks of only the "anticipated harm." UCC § 2A–504(1).

In Kelly v. Marx, 705 N.E.2d 1114, 1117 (Mass.1999), the court, in allowing the seller of a house to keep the purchaser's 5% deposit as liquidated damages, rejected the "second look" approach described by Justice Pollock in favor of a "single look" approach. "In addition to meeting the parties' expectations, the 'single look' approach helps resolve disputes efficiently by making it unnecessary to wait until actual damages from a breach are proved.... The 'second look,' by contrast, undermines the 'peace of mind and certainty of result' ... the parties sought when they contracted for liquidated damages. It increases the potential for litigation by inviting the aggrieved party to attempt to show ... evidence of damage flowing from the breach...." The court rejected the argument that the " 'second look' approach would allow the court to guard against undue windfalls, such as the one the defendants would receive here, ... because the defendants suffered no loss from the breach."

(3) *Subterfuge?* Can a party by the use of subterfuge accomplish the same purpose that a penalty would accomplish? Instead of providing a penalty of $10,000 a day for each day's delay in construction beyond June 1, up to a maximum of $100,000, an owner might adjust the price and provide a *bonus* of $10,000 a day for each day's early completion before June 10, up to a maximum of $100,000.

The proscription of penalties might not extend to alternative performances. Instead of having an employee promise not to compete or pay a penalty of $100,000, an employer might have the employee promise either not to compete or, in the alternative, pay $100,000. Is this a "subterfuge" or a different sort of agreement? Is it arguable that the provision in *Wasserman's* was such an agreement?

(4) *Arbitration and Liquidated Damages.* Suppose that Wasserman's lease had included the arbitration clause recommended by the American Arbitration Association. See Note 2, p. 28 above. Would the court have enforced an arbitration award granting damages under the clause even if the court had considered it a penalty clause? In Matter of Associated General Contractors, 335 N.E.2d 859, 859 (N.Y. 1975), New York's highest court concluded that a party, having "chosen the arbitration forum for the resolution of disputes," was bound by the arbitrators' determination "that the damages clause was not a penalty and was therefore enforceable."

PROBLEMS

(1) *A Corvette Stalled.* Jim Steinke contracted with Circle B to restore its vintage Corvette car. Circle B paid $2,000 down, leaving a balance of $10,000. For delay, the contract provided for "a penalty of $100 per day assessed and deducted from the amount of $10,000." When Steinke finished the work 160 days late, Circle B refused to pay the $10,000 balance and claimed an additional $6,000. What result? How would you have drafted the clause on behalf of Circle B? Circle B Enterprises v. Steinke, 584 N.W.2d 97 (N.D.1998).

(2) *Paradise Lost.* A travel bureau offers a kosher Passover vacation at a resort hotel in Puerto Rico, including two complete Seders. Its contract includes a provision for "liquidated damages" based on a sliding scale and culminating in forfeiture of 100% of the price for cancellations made within 14 days of departure. Is

the provision enforceable against a client who cancels 13 days before departure? See Turner–Schraeter v. Brighton Travel Bureau, 685 N.Y.S.2d 692 (App.Div.1999).

————

DAVE GUSTAFSON & CO. v. STATE, 156 N.W.2d 185 (S.D.1968) [Gustafson surfaced a new state highway that paralleled an older road that remained open during and after the construction. From the $530,724.14 due for the work, the state withheld $14,070 that it claimed as liquidated damages for a delay of 67 days. The contract provided a graduated scale of "liquidated damages per day" under which damages of $210 per day were fixed for a contract in an amount of over $500,000 but not more than $1,000,000. This daily damage multiplied by 67 gave $14,070. When Gustafson sued, the trial court upheld the state's claim and Gustafson appealed.]

■ HANSON, PRESIDING JUDGE. . . . [As this court said in an earlier case,] "A provision for payment of a stipulated sum as a liquidation of damages will ordinarily be sustained if it appears that at the time the contract was made the damages in the event of a breach will be incapable or very difficult of accurate estimation, that there was a reasonable endeavor by the parties as stated to fix fair compensation, and that the amount stipulated bears a reasonable relation to probable damages and not disproportionate to any damages reasonably to be anticipated."

This case reflects the modern tendency not to "look with disfavor upon 'liquidated damages' provisions in contracts. When they are fair and reasonable attempts to fix just compensation for anticipated loss caused by breach of contract, they are enforced . . . They serve a particularly useful function when damages are uncertain in nature or amount or are unmeasurable, as is the case in many government contracts." Priebe & Sons v. United States, 332 U.S. 407. . . .

Judged in this light and by the standards established in Anderson v. Cactus Heights Country Club, 80 S.D. 417, 125 N.W.2d 491, the provision in question must be considered to be one for liquidated damages rather than a penalty for the following reasons: I. Damages for delay in constructing a new highway are impossible of measurement. II. The amount stated in the contract as liquidated damages indicates an endeavor to fix fair compensation for the loss, inconvenience, added costs, and deprivation of use caused by delay. Daily damage is graduated according to total amount of work to be performed. It may be assumed that a large project involves more loss than a small one and each day of delay adds to the loss, inconvenience, cost and deprivation of use. . . . For the same reasons we must conclude the amount stipulated in the contract bears a reasonable relation to probable damages and is not, as a matter of law, disproportionate to any and all damage reasonably to be anticipated from the unexcused delay in performance.

Affirmed.

NOTES

(1) *Take-or-Pay.* Contracts in the petroleum industry sometimes contain what are known as "take-or-pay" clauses, which have been attacked as penalty provi-

sions. Here is one court's analysis. "Under a take-and-pay clause, the pipeline is required annually to take and pay for a minimum contract quantity of gas. A take-and-pay clause benefits the producer by maximizing revenue through the steady depletion of gas reserves.... Under a take-or-pay clause, the pipeline is required annually to take and pay for a minimum contract quantity of gas *or* pay for a specified quantity. A take-or-pay clause differs from a take-and-pay clause in that it assures the producer a constant cash flow rather than the actual purchase of the contract quantity of gas over the term of the contract.... In addition, a take-or-pay clause adds some measure of flexibility in a long-term gas purchase contract by allowing the pipeline to pay for a specified quantity in lieu of taking the contract quantity without endangering its long-term source of supply.... Because one of the alternative performances in a take-or-pay contract is the payment of money, courts have distinguished the 'pay' provision from a liquidated damage provision." Prenalta Corp. v. Colorado Interstate Gas Co., 944 F.2d 677, 680, 689 (10th Cir.1991).

(2) *Questionable Categories.* As this chapter has suggested, an injured party may have difficulty in recovering for loss that falls in a variety of categories. These include sentimental value, value of a chance, emotional distress, lost volume, loss of reputation, and loss of good will. To what extent will loss in these categories, if not recoverable in the absence of agreement, serve to support the enforceability of a clause stipulating damages? See Wassenaar v. Panos, 331 N.W.2d 357 (Wis.1983), discussed in *Wasserman's.* Recall that in Schneberger v. Apache Co., Note 1, p. 656 above, the Supreme Court of Oklahoma, in adhering to *Peevyhouse,* noted that the parties to the contract "were free to specify in the contract what the measure of damages would be in the event of a breach."

(3) *Equitable Relief.* Should a valid liquidated damages clause bar equitable relief that would otherwise be available? See Karpinski v. Ingrasci, Note 1, p. 440 above; Bowen v. Carlsbad Ins. & Real Estate, Inc., 724 P.2d 223 (N.M.1986).

Can parties by explicit provision bar equitable relief that would otherwise be available? Can parties by explicit provision make equitable relief available where it would not be otherwise? For a case holding that specific performance was available against farmers who had contracted to sell the cotton that they produced where at trial "the parties stipulated that the cotton involved was unique," see R.L. Kimsey Cotton Co., Inc. v. Ferguson, 214 S.E.2d 360 (Ga.1975). See Note 3, p. 587 above.

PROBLEMS

(1) Suppose that in the Dave Gustafson case the state highway had connected with a bridge that was also under construction, but by a different contractor. Would the result have been the same if, because of a delay by that contract, the bridge had also been closed for 67 days, so that the highway could not have been used even if it had been completed on time?

Would it affect your answer if the contractor responsible for the bridge had had a similar clause stipulating damages and had argued that it was invalid because the delay in the highway would have prevented the use of the bridge even if it had been completed on time?

Compare Massman Constr. Co. v. City Council of Greenville, 147 F.2d 925 (5th Cir.1945), with California & Hawaiian Sugar Co. v. Sun Ship, Inc., 794 F.2d 1433 (9th Cir.1986), and Southwest Engineering Co. v. United States, 341 F.2d 998 (8th Cir.1965).

(2) Seller contracts to deliver to Buyer a machine that is readily available on the market for $1,000 more than the contract price. If Seller fails to deliver, what are the rights of the parties under each of the following provisions?

(a) In the event of Seller's failure to deliver, Seller shall pay Buyer a penalty of $10,000.

(b) In the event of Seller's failure to deliver, Seller shall be liable to Buyer for $10,000 in liquidated damages.

(c) Seller hereby agrees, at Seller's option, to either deliver the machine to Buyer or to pay Buyer $10,000.

CHAPTER 8

PERFORMANCE AND BREACH

An exchange of promises will lead to an exchange of performances in the ordinary course of affairs. One who has committed oneself in exchange for a return performance is entitled, as stated in Comment 1 to UCC § 2–609, to "a continuing sense of reliance and security that the promised performance will be forthcoming when due." Much detail in the law of contract is understandable only with reference to this principle that a party's fair expectation of return performance deserves protection.

One means of protection is to afford an immediate remedy for breach. But there are other means of at least equal importance for assuring a party's expectations, such as permitting the party to defer or withhold its own performance in the face of a threat that it will not receive what was promised in exchange. Protection in this form is generally described in the language of conditions. Another means of assuring one's expectation is the right to demand assurance of performance from the other party. That right, recognized in Article 2 of the Uniform Commercial Code and the Restatement, is discussed later in this chapter.

Section 1 considers what a party may do to establish a condition by language in the agreement. It shows that the parties have wide liberty both to shape their commitments and to protect their expectations through suitable use of the language of conditions. Section 2 introduces the idea of constructive (implied) conditions of exchange. It shows how constructive conditions in a contract are determined according to the order of the performances required by the contract, and how this may afford one party some assurance that the other will perform as agreed. Section 3 examines three ways that courts mitigate the sometimes harsh results of constructive conditions: substantial performance, divisibility, and restitution. Section 4 deals with the right to suspend performance and terminate the contract when breach occurs during the course of performance. Finally, Section 5 concerns prospective, as distinguished from actual, nonperformance. Here we consider repudiation and the right to demand assurance of a promised performance.

SECTION 1. CONDITIONS

———

(A) EFFECTS OF CONDITIONS

Thus far, this book has been largely concerned with the imposition and enforcement of *duties*. What follows deals mainly with how duties are qualified by being subjected to the occurrence of *conditions*. According to Restatement § 224, "A condition is an event, not certain to occur, which must occur, unless its nonoccurrence is excused, before performance under a contract becomes due." The event may or may not be within the control of the parties. If it is not, if it is fortuitous, the promise is sometimes said to be "aleatory." Our present interest is with the interpretation of language relating to such events.

NOTE

Conditions "Precedent" and "Subsequent." "Parties sometimes provide that the occurrence of an event, such as the failure of one of them to commence an action within a prescribed time, will extinguish a duty after performance has become due, along with any claim for breach. Such an event has often been called a 'condition subsequent' while an event of the kind defined in this section has been called a 'condition precedent.'" Comment *e* to Restatement § 224. The Restatement abandons the term "condition subsequent" and calls a "condition precedent" simply a "condition."

The terms "condition precedent" and "condition subsequent" have a significance in the law of procedure that is independent of their significance, or lack of it, in the law of contracts. This significance is best left for the treatment of burdens of pleading and burdens of proof in a course in civil procedure.

Luttinger v. Rosen

Supreme Court of Connecticut, 1972.
164 Conn. 45, 316 A.2d 757.

■ LOISELLE, ASSOCIATE JUSTICE. The plaintiffs contracted to purchase for $85,000 premises in the city of Stamford owned by the defendants and paid a deposit of $8500. The contract was "subject to and conditional upon the buyers obtaining first mortgage financing on said premises from a bank or other lending institution in an amount of $45,000 for a term of not less than twenty (20) years and at an interest rate which does not exceed 8½ per cent per annum." The plaintiffs agreed to use due diligence in attempting to obtain such financing. The parties further agreed that if the plaintiffs were unsuccessful in obtaining financing as provided in the contract, and notified the seller within a specific time, all sums paid on the contract would be refunded and the contract terminated without further obligation of either party.

In applying for a mortgage which would satisfy the contingency clause in the contract, the plaintiffs relied on their attorney who applied at a New Haven lending institution for a $45,000 loan at 8¼ percent per annum interest over a period of twenty-five years. The plaintiffs' attorney knew that this lending institution was the only one which at that time would lend as much as $45,000 on a mortgage for a single-family dwelling. A mortgage commitment was obtained for $45,000 with "interest at the prevailing rate at the time of closing but not less than 8¾%." Since this commitment failed to meet the contract requirement, timely notice was given to the defendants and demand was made for the return of the down payment. The defendants' counsel thereafter offered to make up the difference between the interest rate offered by the bank and the 8½ percent rate provided in the contract for the entire twenty-five years by a funding arrangement, the exact terms of which were not defined. The plaintiffs did not accept this offer and on the defendants' refusal to return the deposit an action was brought. From a judgment rendered in favor of the plaintiffs the defendants have appealed.

The defendants claim that the plaintiffs did not use due diligence in seeking a mortgage within the terms specified in the contract. The unattacked findings by the court establish that the plaintiffs' attorney was fully informed as to the conditions and terms of mortgages being granted by various banks and lending institutions in and out of the area and that the application was made to the only bank which might satisfy the mortgage conditions of the contingency clause at that time. These findings adequately support the court's conclusion that due diligence was used in seeking mortgage financing in accordance with the contract provisions. Brauer v. Freccia, 159 Conn. 289, 293, 268 A.2d 645. The defendants assert that notwithstanding the plaintiffs' reliance on their counsel's knowledge of lending practices, applications should have been made to other lending institutions. This claim is not well taken. The law does not require the performance of a futile act. Vachon v. Tomascak, 155 Conn. 52, 57, 230 A.2d 5; Tracy v. O'Neill, 103 Conn. 693, 699, 131 A. 417; Janulewycz v. Quagliano, 88 Conn. 60, 64, 89 A. 897.

The remaining assignment of error briefed by the defendants is that the court erred in concluding that the mortgage contingency clause of the contract, a condition precedent, was not met and, therefore, the plaintiffs were entitled to recover their deposit. "A condition precedent is a fact or event which the parties intend must exist or take place before there is a right to performance." Lach v. Cahill, 138 Conn. 418, 421, 85 A.2d 481, 482. Lach v. Cahill, supra; Bialeck v. Hartford, 135 Conn. 551, 556, 66 A.2d 610. In this case the language of the contract is unambiguous and clearly indicates that the parties intended that the purchase of the defendants' premises be conditioned on the obtaining by the plaintiffs of a mortgage as specified in the contract. From the subordinate facts found the court could reasonably conclude that since the plaintiffs were unable to obtain a $45,000 mortgage at no more than 8½ percent per annum interest "from a bank or other lending institution" the condition precedent to performance of the contract was not met and the plaintiffs were entitled to the refund of their deposit. Any additional offer by the defendants to fund the difference in interest payments could be rejected by the plaintiffs. See Lach v. Cahill, supra, 138 Conn. 420, 85 A.2d 481. There was no error in the court's exclusion of testimony relating to the additional offer since the offer was obviously irrelevant.

There is no error.

NOTES

(1) *Whose Performance Conditional?* Recall the definition of condition in Restatement § 224. What was the *event* that was the condition in *Luttinger*? Whose *performance* did not become due if the event did not occur? If the Luttingers had

won the Connecticut lottery and chose to proceed without a mortgage, would the Rosens have been justified in refusing on the ground that the Luttingers had not obtained a mortgage with the specified terms?

(2) *Allocation of Risk.* Why was the promise of the Luttingers made conditional? Because an event that is a condition must, according to the Restatement definition, be "not certain to occur," making an event a condition involves an allocation of the risk of the nonoccurrence of the event. Who took that risk and how great was it? Why did the mortgage commitment at 8¾%, together with the offer of the Rosens to make up the difference in interest rates, not amount to an occurrence of the stipulated event?

Homebuyers today often secure pre-approval letters from banks even before they have identified a property to purchase. Does any financing risk between the parties remain when pre-approval letters are used? If so, to whom is the risk allocated?

(3) *Why Not?* Assuming that the Rosens' offer to make up the difference in interest rate would have had the same financial consequences as a mortgage with the specified terms from a "bank or other lending institution," what reasons might have induced the Luttingers not to proceed? "Whatever may be the subjective intention of a buyer in any particular case, one can readily think of reasons why a buyer may make an offer contingent upon financing by a specific lending institution or through a particular type of loan. Examples of such reasons are: That the buyer will feel more confident of his own judgment of the price he is to pay if a lending institution is willing to make a loan; That the buyer would rather have the matter, in the event of default, in the hands of an established lending institution than in the hands of an individual who might be less able, if not less willing, to adjust matters reasonably." Fairchild, J., dissenting in Kovarik v. Vesely, 89 N.W.2d 279, 285–86 (Wis.1958).

(4) *Financing Conditions.* Conditions like that in *Luttinger* are widespread and often give rise to disputes. How long did the Luttingers have to try to get a mortgage with the specified terms? How hard did they have to try to get one? In Informed Physician Services v. Blue Cross, 711 A.2d 1330, 1343 (Md.1998), the court said that though " 'standing idly by' and falling on one's sword" will not suffice, a party need not "incur extraordinary expense simply to establish reasonableness or good faith." Which standard did the Luttingers have to meet, reasonable efforts or only good faith?

In Barber v. Jacobs, 753 A.2d 430, 434 (Conn.App.2000), with facts "analogous to those in Luttinger v. Rosen," the only bank to which the purchasers applied for a loan turned them down because the property failed to comply with wetlands agency standards. The court held that the purchasers had made a sufficient effort to obtain a loan because, "as the attorney in *Luttinger* knew that other loans were not available," here the purchaser's lawyer "drew on his experience to conclude that the wetlands problem could not be easily overcome."

Did the Luttingers in effect have an option to buy the house? Note that the parties had agreed that if the Luttingers could not obtain a mortgage as specified, the contract would be terminated and all sums paid on the contract would be refunded. Do you think that the result would have been different without such a provision? What inference do you draw with respect to the right of the Luttingers to a refund if they had not tried hard enough to get a mortgage with the specified terms? Would the nonoccurrence of the condition then be "excused," to use the Restatement's terminology?

INTRODUCTION TO *INTERNATIO–ROTTERDAM*

Comment *b* to Restatement § 224 explains that because "there is inherent in the concept of condition some degree of uncertainty as to the occurrence of the event. . . . [T]he mere passage of time, as to which there is no uncertainty, is not a condition." But the occurrence of an event *within some period of time* is a common kind of condition. Whether contract language dealing with time is sufficient to impose such a condition is often a disputed question, as in the next case.

Internatio–Rotterdam, Inc. v. River Brand Rice Mills, Inc.

United States Court of Appeals, Second Circuit, 1958.
259 F.2d 137.

■ HINCKS, CIRCUIT JUDGE. Appeal from the United States District Court, Southern District of New York, Walsh, Judge, upon the dismissal of the complaint after plaintiff's case was in.

The defendant-appellee, a processor of rice, in July 1952 entered into an agreement with the plaintiff-appellant, an exporter, for the sale of 95,600 pockets of rice. The terms of the agreement, evidenced by a purchase memorandum, indicated that the price per pocket was to be "$8.25 F.A.S. Lake Charles and/or Houston, Texas"; that shipment was to be "December, 1952, with two weeks call from buyer" and that payment was to be by "irrevocable letter of credit to be opened immediately payable against" dock receipts and other specified documents. In the fall, the appellant, which had already committed itself to supplying this rice to a Japanese buyer, was unexpectedly confronted with United States export restrictions upon its December shipments and was attempting to get an export license from the government. December is a peak month in the rice and cotton seasons in Louisiana and Texas, and the appellee became concerned about shipping instructions under the contract, since congested conditions prevailed at both the mills and the docks. The appellee season-ably elected to deliver 50,000 pockets at Lake Charles and on December 10 it received from the appellant instructions for the Lake Charles shipments. Thereupon it promptly began shipments to Lake Charles which continued until December 23, the last car at Lake Charles being unloaded on December 31. December 17 was the last date in December which would allow appellee the two week period provided in the contract for delivery of the rice to the ports and ships designated. Prior thereto, the appellant had been having difficulty obtaining either a ship or a dock in this busy season in Houston. On December 17, the appellee had still received no shipping instructions for the 45,600 pockets destined for Houston. On the morning of the 18th, the appellee rescinded the contract for the Houston shipments, although continuing to make the Lake Charles deliveries. It is clear that one of the reasons for the prompt cancellation of the contract was the rise in market price of rice from $8.25 per pocket, the contract price, to $9.75. The appellant brought this suit for refusal to deliver the Houston quota.

The trial court, in a reasoned but unreported opinion which dealt with all phases of the case, held that New York would apply Texas law. Auten v.

Auten, 308 N.Y. 155, 124 N.E.2d 99, 50 A.L.R.2d 246. We think this ruling right, but will not discuss the point because it is conceded that no different result would follow from the choice of Louisiana law.

The area of contest is also considerably reduced by the appellant's candid concession that the appellee's duty to ship, by virtue of the two-week notice provision, did not arise until two weeks after complete shipping instructions had been given by the appellant. Thus on brief the appellant says: "[w]e concede (as we have done from the beginning) that on a fair interpretation of the contract appellant had a duty to instruct appellee by December 17, 1952 as to the place to which it desired appellee to ship—at both ports, and that, being late with its instructions in this respect, appellant could not have demanded delivery (at either port) until sometime after December 31, 1952." This position was taken, of course, with a view to the contract provision for shipment "December, 1952": a two-week period ending December 31 would begin to run on December 17. But although appellant concedes that the two weeks' notice to which appellee was entitled could not be shortened by the failure to give shipping instructions on or before December 17, it stoutly insists that upon receipt of shipping instructions subsequent to December 17 the appellee thereupon became obligated to deliver within two weeks thereafter. We do not agree.

It is plain that a giving of the notice by the appellant was a condition precedent to the appellee's duty to ship. Corbin on Contracts, Vol. 3, § 640. Id. § 724. Obviously, the appellee could not deliver free alongside ship, as the contract required, until the appellant identified its ship and its location. Jacksboro Stone Co. v. Fairbanks Co., 48 Tex.Civ.App. 639, 107 S.W. 567; Fortson Grocery Co. v. Pritchard Rice Milling Co., Tex.Civ.App., 220 S.W. 1116. Thus the giving of shipping instructions was what Professor Corbin would classify as a "promissory condition": the appellant promised to give the notice and the appellee's duty to ship was conditioned on the receipt of the notice. Op. cit. § 633, p. 523, § 634, footnote 38. The crucial question is whether that condition was performed. And that depends on whether the appellee's duty of shipment was conditioned on notice *on or before December 17,* so that the appellee would have two weeks wholly within December within which to perform, or whether, as we understand the appellant to contend, the appellant could perform the condition by giving the notice later in December, in which case the appellee would be under a duty to ship within two weeks thereafter. The answer depends upon the proper interpretation of the contract: if the contract properly interpreted made shipment *in December* of the essence then the failure to give the notice on or before December 17 was nonperformance by the appellant of a condition upon which the appellee's duty to ship in December depended.

In the setting of this case, we hold that the provision for December delivery went to the essence of the contract. In support of the plainly stated provision of the contract there was evidence that the appellee's mills and the facilities appurtenant thereto were working at full capacity in December when the rice market was at peak activity and that appellee had numerous other contracts in January as well as in December to fill. It is reasonable to infer that in July, when the contract was made, each party wanted the protection of the specified delivery period; the appellee so that it could schedule its production without undue congestion of its storage facilities and the appellant so that it could surely meet commitments which it in turn should make to its customers. There was also evidence that prices on the rice market were fluctuating. In view of this factor it is not reasonable to infer that when the contract was made in July for December delivery, the parties intended that the appellant should have an option exercisable subsequent to December 17 to postpone delivery until January. United Irr. Co. v. Carson Petroleum Co., Tex.Civ.App., 283 S.W. 692; Steiner v. United States, D.C., 36 F.Supp. 496. That in effect would have given the appellant an option to postpone its breach of the contract, if one should then be in prospect, to a time when, so far as could have been foreseen when the contract was made, the price of rice might be falling. A postponement in such circumstances would inure to the disadvantage of the appellee who was given no reciprocal option. Further indication that December delivery was of the essence is found in the letter of credit which was provided for in the contract and established by the appellant. Under this letter, the bank was authorized to pay appellee only for deliveries "during December, 1952." It thus appears that the appellant's interpretation of the contract, under which the appellee would be obligated, upon receipt of shipping instructions subsequent to December 17, to deliver in January, would deprive the appellee of the security for payment of the purchase price for which it had contracted.

Since, as we hold, December delivery was of the essence, notice of shipping instructions *on or before December 17* was not merely a "duty" of the appellant—as it concedes: it was a condition precedent to the performance which might be required of the appellee. The nonoccurrence of that condition entitled the appellee to rescind or to treat its contractual obligations as discharged. Corbin on Contracts, §§ 640, 724 and 1252; Williston on Sales, §§ 452, 457; Restatement, Contracts, § 262.... On December 18th the appellant [appellee?] unequivocally exercised its right to rescind. Having done so, its obligations as to the Houston deliveries under the contract were at an end. And of course its obligations would not revive thereafter when the appellant finally succeeded in obtaining an export permit, a ship and a dock and then gave shipping instructions; when it expressed willingness to accept deliveries in January; or when it accomplished a "liberalization" of the outstanding letter of credit whereby payments might be made against simple forwarder's receipts instead of dock receipts.[1]

The appellant urges that by reason of substantial part performance on its part prior to December 17th, it may not be held to have been in default for its failure sooner to give shipping instructions. The contention has no basis on the facts. As to the Houston shipments the appellant's activities prior to December 17th were not in performance of its contract: they were merely preparatory to its expectation to perform at a later time. The mere

---

1. The appellee was not informed that the letter of credit had "liberalized" until after it had rescinded. Moreover, even the liberalized letter did not call for payment of deliveries not made until January.

establishment of the letter of credit was not an act of performance: it was merely an arrangement made by the appellant for future performance which as to the Houston deliveries because of appellant's failure to give shipping instructions were never made. From these preparatory activities the appellee had no benefit whatever.

The appellant also maintains that the contract was single and "indivisible" and that consequently appellee's continuing shipments to Lake Charles after December 17 constituted an election to reaffirm its total obligation under the contract. This position also, we hold untenable. Under the contract, the appellee concededly had an option to split the deliveries betwixt Lake Charles and Houston. The price had been fixed on a per pocket basis, and payment, under the letter of credit, was to be made upon the presentation of dock receipts which normally would be issued both at Lake Charles or Houston at different times. The fact that there was a world market for rice and that in December the market price substantially exceeded the contract price suggests that it would be more to the appellants' advantage to obtain the Lake Charles delivery than to obtain no delivery at all. The same considerations suggest that by continuing with the Lake Charles delivery the appellee did not deliberately intend to waive its right to cancel the Houston deliveries. Conclusions to the contrary would be so greatly against self-interest as to be completely unrealistic. The only reasonable inference from the totality of the facts is that the duties of the parties as to the Lake Charles shipment were not at all dependent on the Houston shipments. We conclude their duties as to shipments at each port were paired and reciprocal and that performance by the parties as to Lake Charles did not preclude the appellee's right of cancellation as to Houston. Cf. Corbin on Contracts §§ 688, 695; Simms–Wylie Co. v. City of Ranger, Tex.Civ.App., 224 S.W.2d 265.

Finally, we hold that the appellant's claims of estoppel and waiver have no basis in fact or in law.

Affirmed.

NOTES

(1) *Letters of Credit.* A seller may, as a means of assuring payment for goods, require a buyer to obtain a letter of credit from a bank. The bank, by issuing its letter of credit at the buyer's request, undertakes with the seller that it will pay against the seller's orders in an amount equal to the purchase price, on condition that the orders, known as "drafts" or "bills of exchange," are accompanied by documents affording control over the goods. The documents specified are commonly bills of lading, issued by a carrier. Less commonly they may be documents of other sorts, such as the dock receipts in *Internatio–Rotterdam*, that also carry with them power over the goods. When the seller ships the goods, it forwards to the issuing bank its draft together with the specified document covering the goods. The bank then pays the draft and takes up the document. As soon as the buyer reimburses the bank, the buyer may have the document and use it to obtain the goods from the carrier. Letters of credit reallocate risk of nonpayment away from sellers. Recall the discussion of homebuyer's pre-approval letters, Note 2, p. 694 above, which served a similar function. What consideration supports these credit agreements?

(2) *Questions.* What was the event that was the condition in *Internatio–Rotterdam?* Was the event also the subject of a promise? What did Internatio–Rotterdam argue? What did River Brand argue? What did the court conclude?

(3) *When Time Is of the Essence.* What did the court mean when it said that delivery in December "was of the essence"? Why did the court conclude that this was so? "The importance of prompt delivery by a seller of goods generally derives from the circumstance that goods, as contrasted with land, are particularly likely to be subject to rapid fluctuations in market price." Restatement § 242, Comment *c.* Were there other reasons in *Internatio–Rotterdam?* In a case involving the sale of timber on a wooded lot the Supreme Court of New Hampshire said, "Time is generally not of the essence in contract, unless the contract specifically so states, even if a particular time schedule is specified." Fitz v. Coutinho, 622 A.2d 1220, 1223 (N.H.1993).

Of course it is "open to the parties to make performance or tender by a stated date a condition by their agreement." (Such a date is sometimes called a "drop dead" date.) However, "stock phrases [such] as 'time is of the essence' do not necessarily have this effect." Restatement Second, § 242 Comment *d.* And "a specific date for performance does not necessarily mean that performance by that date is of the essence of the contract." Arkla Energy Resources v. Roye Realty & Developing, 9 F.3d 855, 863 (10th Cir.1993).

———

SEPARATE CONTRACTS

A party's breach of a contract does not allow the other party to terminate a different contract subsisting between the two, or even to suspend performance of the other contract, unless the parties have otherwise agreed. "Neither the Uniform Commercial Code nor general contract law gives either party to a contract the right to refuse performance because the other has breached a separate contract between them." Northwest Lumber Sales, Inc. v. Continental Forest Products, Inc., 495 P.2d 744, 749 (Or.1972). That rule would have made a difference in the foregoing case if the parties there had entered into one contract for "Houston rice" and another for "Lake Charles rice." The authorities do not lay down a rule or standard, it has been said, for "deciding whether a series of transactions constitutes one contract or two." The cases are not numerous and "have not crystallized an identifiable doctrine, though the term 'divisibility' is sometimes used to name the issue." Coplay Cement Company, Inc. v. Willis & Paul Group, 983 F.2d 1435, 1439 (7th Cir.1993). In that case the judges said

> "The simplest and best rule that we can think of is that if the transactions are embodied in separate documents, each complete in itself, in the sense that ascertaining the terms does not require consulting the document for the other transaction, they are separate contracts."

Id. Does an alternate test come to mind?

One who breaks a contract may anticipate that the other party will, for that reason, lose confidence in the performance of a separate contract between them. If that should happen, the promise breaker might be required to give an assurance of that performance upon demand by the other party, see p. 975 below. The right to demand assurance tends to tie together separate contracts that would otherwise operate independently of one another.

(B) PROBLEMS OF INTERPRETATION

CONDITION, DUTY, OR BOTH?

A party seeking a particular performance from another party might ask the other party to undertake a duty to render that performance, might make its own performance conditional on the other party rendering that performance, or might do both. As *Internatio–Rotterdam* shows, determining which has been done may pose a difficult question of interpretation from which important consequences follow. Here is an example based on the venerable case Constable v. Cloberie, 81 Eng.Rep. 1141 (King's Bench 1626).

Cargo Owner desires Ship Owner to sail from England to Cadiz and back carrying Cargo Owner's goods. Ship Owner agrees to do so in return for Cargo Owner's promise to pay. In addition, Cargo Owner wants to encourage Ship Owner to sail with the next wind and for this is willing to pay, in addition to the freight, a premium equal to 10% of the freight. Cargo Owner might ask Ship Owner to undertake a duty to sail with the next wind, or might make sailing with the next wind a condition of Cargo Owner's own duty to pay a 10% premium, or might do both. The consequences will be different in each case.

Suppose that Cargo Owner has Ship Owner undertake a duty to sail with the next wind. Sailing with the next wind will discharge Ship Owner's duty. If Ship Owner delays in sailing, however, Cargo Owner will be entitled to any damages caused by Ship Owner's delay. (This ignores the impact of the doctrine of "constructive conditions of exchange," which is taken up in the next section.)

Suppose that Cargo Owner makes sailing with the next wind a condition of the Cargo Owner's duty to pay a 10% premium. Sailing with the next wind will satisfy the condition of Cargo Owner's duty. If Ship Owner delays in sailing, however, Cargo Owner, though not entitled to damages, will not have to pay the premium.

Suppose that Cargo Owner has Ship Owner undertake a duty to sail with the next wind *and* makes sailing with the next wind a condition of Cargo Owner's duty to pay a 10% premium. As was pointed out in *Internatio–Rotterdam*, Corbin used the term "promissory condition" to describe this case. Sailing with the next wind will discharge Ship Owner's duty *and* will satisfy the condition of Cargo Owner's duty. If Ship Owner delays in sailing, however, Cargo Owner will be entitled to any damages caused Ship Owner's delay *and* in addition will not have to pay the premium.

NOTE

Preference in Interpretation. If language is unclear, a court will prefer an interpretation that imposes a duty rather than a condition. As Comment *c* to Restatement § 227(1) puts it, "The preferred interpretation avoids the harsh results that might otherwise result from the non-occurrence of a condition and still gives adequate protection to the obligor under the rules ... relating to promises for an exchange of performances." In the next section, we examine those rules.

PROBLEM

Drafting. Assume that the contract begins: "In consideration of Ship Owner's promise to sail to Cadiz and return with cargo, Cargo Owner promises to pay freight at [a specified rate]." Draft clauses to follow which would make sailing with the next wind: (1) a duty of Ship Owner; (2) a condition of Cargo Owner's duty to pay a 10% premium; (3) both a duty of Ship Owner and a condition of Cargo Owner's duty to pay a 10% premium.

Peacock Construction Co. v. Modern Air Conditioning, Inc.

Supreme Court of Florida, 1977.
353 So.2d 840.

■ BOYD, ACTING CHIEF JUSTICE. We issued an order allowing certiorari in these two causes because the decisions in them of the District Court of Appeal, Second District, conflict with the decision in Edward J. Gerrits, Inc. v. Astor Electric Service, Inc., 328 So.2d 522 (Fla. 3d DCA 1976). The two causes have been consolidated for all appellate purposes in this Court because they involve the same issue. That issue is whether the plaintiffs, Modern Air Conditioning and Overly Manufacturing, were entitled to summary judgments against Peacock Construction Company in actions for breaches of identical contractual provisions.

Peacock Construction was the builder of a condominium project. Modern Air Conditioning subcontracted with Peacock to do the heating and air conditioning work and Overly Manufacturing subcontracted with Peacock to do the "rooftop swimming pool" work. Both written subcontracts provided that Peacock would make final payment to the subcontractors,

> "within 30 days after the completion of the work included in this sub-contract, written acceptance by the Architect and full payment therefor by the Owner."

Modern Air Conditioning and Overly Manufacturing completed the work specified in their contracts and requested final payment. When Peacock refused to make the final payments the two subcontractors separately brought actions in the Lee County Circuit Court for breach of contract. In both actions it was established that no deficiencies had been found in the completed work. But Peacock established that it had not received from the owner[1] full payment for the subcontractors' work. And it defended on the basis that such payment was a condition which, by express term of the final payment provision, had to be fulfilled before it was obligated to perform under the contract. On motions by the plaintiffs, the trial judges granted summary judgments in their favor. The orders of judgment implicitly interpreted the contract not to require payment by the owner as a condition precedent to Peacock's duty to perform.

The Second District Court of Appeal affirmed the lower court's judgment in the appeal brought by Peacock Construction Company. In so doing it adopted the view of the majority of jurisdictions in this country that provisions of the kind disputed here do not set conditions precedent but rather constitute absolute promises to pay, fixing payment by the owner as a reasonable time for when payment to the subcontractor is to be made. When the judgment in the *Overly Manufacturing* case reached the Second District Court, *Modern Air Conditioning* had been decided and the judgment, therefore, was affirmed on the authority of the latter decision. These two decisions plainly conflict with *Gerrits,* supra.

In *Gerrits,* the Court had summarily ordered judgment for the plaintiff/subcontractor against the defendant/general contractor on a contractual provision for payment to the subcontractor which read,

> The money to be paid in current funds and at such times as the General Contractor receives it from the Owner. Id. at 523.

In its review of the judgment, the Third District Court of Appeal referred to the fundamental rule of interpretation of contracts that it be done in accordance with the intention of the parties. Since the defendant had introduced below the issue of intention, a material issue, and since the issue was one that could be resolved through a factual determination by the jury, the Third District reversed the summary judgment and remanded for trial.

Peacock urges us to adopt *Gerrits* as the controlling law in this State. It concedes that the Second District's decisions are backed by the weight of authority. But it argues that they are incorrect because the issue of intention is a factual one which should be resolved after the parties have had an opportunity to present evidence on it. Peacock urges, therefore, that the causes be remanded for trial. If there is produced no evidence that the parties intended there be condition precedents, only then, says Peacock, should the judge, by way of a directed verdict for the subcontractors, be allowed to take the issue of intention from the jury.

The contractual provisions in dispute here are susceptible to two interpretations. They may be interpreted as setting a condition precedent or as fixing a reasonable time for payment. The provision disputed in *Gerrits* is susceptible to the same two interpretations. The questions presented by the conflict between these decisions, then, are whether ambiguous contractual provisions of the kind disputed here may be interpreted only by the factfinder, usually the jury, or if they should be

---

1. The owner, a corporation, had entered proceedings in bankruptcy.

interpreted as a matter of law by the court, and if so what interpretation they should be given.

Although it must be admitted that the meaning of language is a factual question, the general rule is that interpretation of a document is a question of law rather than of fact. 4 Williston on Contracts, 3rd Ed., § 616. If an issue of contract interpretation concerns the intention of parties, that intention may be determined from the written contract, as a matter of law, when the nature of the transaction lends itself to judicial interpretation. A number of courts, with whom we agree, have recognized that contracts between small subcontractors and general contractors on large construction projects are such transactions. Cf. Thos. J. Dyer Co. v. Bishop International Engineering Co., 6 Cir., 303 F.2d 655 (1965). The reason is that the relationship between the parties is a common one and usually their intent will not differ from transaction to transaction, although it may be differently expressed.

That intent in most cases is that payment by the owner to the general contractor is not a condition precedent to the general contractor's duty to pay the subcontractors. This is because small subcontractors, who must have payment for their work in order to remain in business, will not ordinarily assume the risk of the owner's failure to pay the general contractor. And this is the reason for the majority view in this country, which we now join.

Our decision to require judicial interpretation of ambiguous provisions for final payment in subcontracts in favor of subcontractors should not be regarded as anti-general contractor. It is simply a recognition that this is the fairest way to deal with the problem. There is nothing in this opinion, however, to prevent parties to these contracts from shifting the risk of payment failure by the owner to the subcontractor. But in order to make such a shift the contract must unambiguously express that intention. And the burden of clear expression is on the general contractor.

The decisions of the Second District Court of Appeal to affirm the summary judgments were correct. We adopt, therefore, these two decisions as the controlling law in Florida and we overrule *Gerrits*, to the extent it is inconsistent with this opinion.

The orders allowing certiorari in these two causes are discharged. It is so ordered.

NOTES

(1) *Fact or Law?* As to the decision of the court in *Peacock* to treat the question of interpretation as "a matter of law," recall the discussion at p. 400 above. Thirteen years later, in DEC Electric, Inc. v. Raphael Construction Corp., 558 So.2d 427 (Fla.1990), the same court had certified to it a question "of great public importance":

> Must all payment provisions in contracts between contractors and subcontractors or suppliers that concern a condition or time of payment provision be construed as a matter of law?

Answering in the affirmative, the court explained that if the provision "is clear and unambiguous, it is interpreted as setting a condition precedent," but if it "is ambiguous it is interpreted as fixing a reasonable time for the general contractor to pay.... Once a judge decides that a provision is ambiguous there is nothing for the jury to decide or interpret." How does this differ from a traditional plain meaning rule?

(2) *Public Policy.* In Wm. R. Clarke Corp. v. Safeco Insurance Co., 938 P.2d 372, 376 (Cal.1997), a "pay if paid" provision was held to be unenforceable as contrary to the public policy evidenced by provisions of the California Constitution and the California Civil Code dealing with mechanic's liens. Under the Civil Code, "a subcontractor may not waive its mechanic's lien rights except under certain specified circumstances ... and a pay if paid provision is in substance a waiver of mechanic's lien rights because it has the same practical effect as an express waiver of those rights."

(3) *Brokers and Conditions.* In Harding Realty, Inc. v. Turnberry Towers Corp., 436 So.2d 983, 984 (Fla.App.1983), the owner of a condominium development made an agreement with a real estate broker providing that the broker "shall be entitled to a commission of 3%, at time of closing," on the sale of units to purchasers brought by the broker. When two such purchasers defaulted and the owner kept their deposits, the broker sued for its 3% commission. The court affirmed an award of summary judgment to the owner, noting that "the great weight of authority holds that contractual provisions for payment of a brokerage commission at the time of sale, closing, or settlement render such occurrence a condition precedent of payment."

In what ways is the situation of the broker distinguishable from that of the subcontractor?

PROBLEM

Pay If *Paid or Pay* When *Paid?* Redraft the clause in *Peacock* so that it would "unambiguously" shift to the subcontractors the risk of the owner's failure to pay.

Gibson v. Cranage

Supreme Court of Michigan, 1878.
39 Mich. 49.

■ Marston, J. Plaintiff in error brought assumpsit to recover the contract price for the making and execution of a portrait of the deceased daughter of defendant. It appeared from the testimony of the plaintiff that he at a certain time called upon the defendant and solicited the privilege of making an enlarged picture of his deceased daughter. He says "I was to make an enlarged picture that he would like, a large one from a small one, and one that he would like and recognize as a good picture of his little girl, and he was to pay me."

The defendant testified that the plaintiff was to take the small photograph and send it away to be finished, "and when returned if it was not perfectly satisfactory to me in every particular, I need not take it or pay for it. I still objected and he urged me to do so. There was no risk about it; if it was not perfectly satisfactory to me I need not take it or pay for it."

There was little if any dispute as to what the agreement was. After the picture was finished it was shown to defendant who was dissatisfied with it and refused to accept it. Plaintiff endeavored to ascertain what the objections were, but says he was unable to ascertain clearly, and he then sent the picture away to the artist to have it changed.

On the next day he received a letter from defendant reciting the original agreement, stating that the picture shown him the previous day was not satisfactory and that he declined to take it or any other similar picture, and countermanded the order. A further correspondence was had, but it was not very material and did not change the aspect of the case. When the picture was afterwards received by the plaintiff from the artist, he went to see defendant and to have him examine it. This defendant declined to do, or to look at it, and did not until during the trial, when he examined and found the same objections still existing.

We do not consider it necessary to examine the charge in detail, as we are satisfied it was as favorable to plaintiff as the agreement would warrant.

The contract (if it can be considered such) was an express one. The plaintiff agreed that the picture when finished should be satisfactory to the defendant, and his own evidence showed that the contract in this important particular had not been performed. It may be that the picture was an excellent one and that the defendant ought to have been satisfied with it and accepted it, but under the agreement the defendant was the only person who had the right to decide this question. Where parties thus deliberately enter into an agreement which violates no rule of public policy, and which is free from all taint of fraud or mistake, there is no hardship whatever in holding them bound by it.

Artists or third parties might consider a portrait an excellent one, and yet it prove very unsatisfactory to the person who had ordered it and who might be unable to point out with clearness or certainty the defects or objections. And if the person giving the order stipulates that the portrait when finished must be satisfactory to him or else he will not accept or pay for it, and this is agreed to, he may insist upon his right as given him by the contract. McCarren v. McNulty, 7 Gray, 141; Brown v. Foster, 113 Mass., 136; 18 Amer., 465.

The judgment must be affirmed with costs.

NOTES

(1) *Questions.* Would the result have been the same if Cranage had refused to look at the portrait at all?

Would the result have been the same if Gibson's promise had been to paint the exterior of Cranage's barn? Does a satisfaction clause impose different risks on a seller of land, a painter of a portrait, and a painter of a barn?

Note that if Gibson had painted Cranage's barn, a question of unjust enrichment might arise. Such questions are taken up in Section 3(c) below.

Observe that the court said that Gibson "agreed that the picture when finished should be satisfactory" to Cranage. Did the court hold that Gibson was under a duty to furnish a picture satisfactory to Cranage? Could Cranage have recovered damages from Gibson for his failure to do so?

(2) *Effect of Forfeiture.* It should be apparent that the law of conditions has a draconian quality. If Gibson's portrait does not satisfy Cranage, Gibson gets nothing for his efforts and is left with a painting that is of no value to him. (Should we assume that Gibson was himself the artist? If not, what should we assume about his agreement with the artist?) Comment *b* to Restatement § 227 explains that "forfeiture" is used in that Restatement to refer to "the denial of compensation" that results if the non-occurrence of a condition causes the obligee "to lose his right to the agreed exchange after he has relied substantially on the expectation of that exchange, as by preparation or performance." Gibson's risk of forfeiture if Cranage was not satisfied may thus have been greater than Hopper's risk of forfeiture in *Mattei v. Hopper*, p. 72 above, if Mattei was not satisfied.

(3) *Satisfaction in Real Estate Transactions.* Provisions like that in *Mattei* play an important role in real estate transactions. Suppose that Mattei, the developer, had refused to go through with the purchase of the tract on the ground that the leases were not satisfactory to him and that Hopper had sued Mattei. Would the issue of "satisfaction" be more likely to go to a jury under the standard of "an exercise of judgment in good faith" used by the Supreme Court of California or under "the standard of a reasonable person" rejected by that court? See Note 4 below.

(4) *The Case of the Cheaper Chips.* Potato farmers contracted to sell twelve loads of potatoes that "chipt to buyer satisfaction," at $4.25 per hundredweight. When the market price declined to $2.00 per hundredweight, the buyer rejected the last nine loads claiming that the potatoes would not chip satisfactorily. The farmers had samples tested by an expert who found them entirely satisfactory. After unsuccessful negotiations—during which the buyer's agent said "I can buy potatoes all day for $2.00"—the farmers sued. From a judgment for the farmers on a jury verdict, the buyer appealed. *Held:* Affirmed.

> "The law requires such a claim of dissatisfaction to be made in good faith, rather than in an effort to escape a bad bargain." As a "merchant" under UCC § 2–104(1), the buyer was held to the objective standard of UCC § 2–103, which requires "honesty in fact and the observance of reasonable commercial standards of fair dealing in the trade." "Because there was evidence that the potatoes would 'chip' satisfactorily, the jury was not required to accept Buyer's subjective claim to the contrary." Neumiller Farms, Inc. v. Cornett, 368 So.2d 272 (Ala.1979). Note that under the revised Article 1 of the Code, one no longer has to be a merchant for the heightened definition of good faith to be applicable. See UCC § 1–203.

Would the farmers necessarily have lost under the standard of good faith used in *Mattei*?

PROBLEM

Drafting. Can you draft language that would make an objective test applicable to the painting of a portrait? That would make a subjective test applicable to the painting of a barn?

In Morin Building Products Co., Inc. v. Baystone Construction, Inc., 717 F.2d 413 (7th Cir.1983), Judge Richard Posner posed the example of a manager of a steel plant who rejected a shipment of pig iron "because he did not think the pigs had a pretty shape." He concluded that the "reasonable-man standard would be applied even if the contract had an 'acceptability shall rest strictly with the [buyer]' clause, for it would be fantastic to think that the iron supplier would have subjected his contract rights to the whimsy of the buyer's agent." Do you understand Judge Posner to be saying that the "reasonable-man standard" would be applied in the case of painting a barn no matter what you drafted? If so, do you agree?

It might not be necessary to apply a reasonableness standard in the case of the pigs to avoid rejection for their want of "a pretty shape". It has been pointed out that "it is only the decision contracted for that is final" and a decision "not on the question submitted ... is outside of the contract and is given no effect by it." Devoine Co. v. International Co., 136 A. 37, 38 (Md.1927).

As to mixed motives, as where a buyer rejects goods both because of dissatisfaction and because of finding a cheaper source of supply, see Columbia Christian Coll. v. Commonwealth Props., 594 P.2d 401, 407–08 (Or.1979) ("the party's dissatisfaction must relate to the specific subject matter of the condition," but as long as "one of the sources of dissatisfaction gives him a right under the contract to repudiate, the fact that there are other sources of dissatisfaction is immaterial").

THIRD–PARTY SATISFACTION

Some of the risk inherent in making the other party's duty conditional on its own satisfaction can be eliminated by making its duty conditional instead on the satisfaction of an independent third party, perhaps an expert of some kind. Widespread use is made of such terms in construction contracts, where the owner's duty to pay the contractor is often conditional on satisfaction of the architect. It is also possible to make the architect's approval conclusive on the owner, that is, to make approval the sole condition of the owner's duty. As to such provisions see Note 3, p. 727 below.

The architect judging the work of a builder is regarded as a professional of sufficient independence, though the representative of the owner, that his or her decisions are generally considered "final" if rendered "in good faith." The usual test is one of honest, not reasonable, satisfaction. (Actual provisions are often more complex, as can be seen from the Standard Construction Agreement in the Selections.) Provisions requiring certificates of engineers are usually interpreted in the same way, though the engineer, unlike an architect, is commonly a salaried employee of the owner.

What if the architect exercises honest but egregiously bad judgment? In RaDec Construction v. School District No. 17, 535 N.W.2d 408, 409 (Neb.1995), the trial court disregarded the architect's determination of the reduction in price under a revised earthworking plan. The architect had, among other things, used the grading subcontractor's figures without verifying them and had ignored the contractor's figures that accurately represented the cost. The Nebraska Supreme Court affirmed on the ground that the architect's determination "constituted a gross mistake" and "was patently erroneous and therefore legally equivalent to bad faith for the purposes of deciding the instant case." Is this consistent with the meaning of "bad faith" in cases you have read? Is it unjustified?

NOTES

(1) *Satisfaction in New York.* Recall that the lawsuit in Jacob & Youngs v. Kent, p. 645, above, began after the builder, having refused to replace the Cohoes pipe, asked for an architect's certificate for the final payment and the architect refused. Why did the architect's good-faith refusal not bar the builder from recovery of the final payment? New York courts have taken the peculiar position that even when it comes to third party satisfaction the test is one of reasonable rather than honest satisfaction.

In Nolan v. Whitney, 88 N.Y. 648 (1882), a contractor, who had agreed to do masonry work to the satisfaction of the architect, sued for a $2,700 final payment on the total price of $11,700, although the architect had refused—as in Jacob & Youngs v. Kent—to give a certificate for that payment. The Court of Appeals affirmed a judgment for the contractor for the $2,700 less a $200 deduction for trivial defects in the plastering. When the contractor "had substantially performed his contract, the architect was bound to give him the certificate, and his refusal to give it was unreasonable, and it is held that an unreasonable refusal on the part of an architect in such a case to give the certificate dispenses with its necessity."

(2) *The Case of the Refusal Without Reason.* A contractor sued an owner, who defended on the ground that the contractor had not procured an architect's certificate. The contractor's complaint alleged "fraud on the part of the architect." A judgment of the trial court for the contractor was reversed on appeal, and the contractor appealed. *Held:* Reversed and judgment of trial court affirmed.

"It is inferable from the architect's own testimony that he was ready to issue the certificate, but that the defendants wished to cut down the final payment by several hundred dollars on account of a counterclaim which the architect refused to recognize or support except for a much smaller sum; that he advised the plaintiff to 'get after them and get his money'; and that when plaintiff asked for the certificate, it was on the day before suit was begun, after plaintiff had retained counsel, and that he then refused it because he 'did not want it to appear that he was issuing a certificate for a case.' ... [H]is refusal under such circumstances was fraudulent.... [Otherwise] a corrupt architect would be greatly aided in extorting money from the contractor as a condition of awarding a certificate that was fully earned." Rizzolo v. Poysher, 99 A. 390 (N.J.1916).

PROBLEMS

(1) *Drafting for Kent.* If you had represented Kent, could you have redrafted the provision requiring architect's certificates to have protected your client? How?

(2) *Slap Shot.* Randy Giunto was selected as a contestant at a Florida Panthers hockey game. He was to shoot a puck at a small slot 118 feet away and if the puck passed "completely through" the slot he would win $1 million. According to the rules the contest judges' decisions were "final in all matters." On Giunto's shot the puck hit the corner, rebounded from side to side, and stopped just slightly within the slot. Giunto insisted that it had passed "completely through," but the contest judge disagreed. Is Giunto entitled to the $1 million? See Giunto v. Florida Coca–Cola Bottling Co., 745 So.2d 1020 (Fla.App.1999).

(C) MITIGATING DOCTRINES

We now turn to three ways in which courts mitigate the harsh effect that the non-occurrence of a condition may otherwise have. They involve:

first, prevention; second, a set of doctrines including waiver, estoppel, and election; and third, interpretation and avoidance of forfeiture.

———

PREVENTION

One who prevents the occurrence of a condition of one's own duty may be precluded from later asserting the non-occurrence of that condition. The duty of good faith performance that is usually imposed requires at least that one do nothing to prevent the occurrence of such a condition.

Questions of prevention often arise in cases involving real-estate brokers. Recall Note 3, p. 704 above, which dealt with the right of a broker whose commission was payable "at time of closing." If a broker's right is so conditioned, can the broker nevertheless recover the commission if the sale is not consummated because the *seller,* rather than the *buyer,* backs out? For an affirmative answer, see Drake v. Hosley, 713 P.2d 1203 (Alaska 1986), in which the court held that the condition was excused by the seller's "frustrating conduct" in selling the property to a third party.

NOTES

(1) *A Coup at the NRA.* At an annual meeting of the National Rifle Association (NRA), the organization was "taken over" by dissident members. Earlier, the decision had been made to sell its headquarters in the District of Columbia and move to Colorado, and the president had signed a contract of sale to a purchaser procured by Shear, as broker, and selected by the Management Committee, "subject to the approval of the Board." His $150,000 commission was confirmed before the takeover, under an agreement making it "contingent on settlement." After the takeover, the Management Committee declined to recommend the sale to the Board, and the NRA by-laws were amended to prohibit changing the headquarters and to strip the Board of power to approve the sale. Shear sued the NRA and, from dismissal of his complaint, he appealed. *Held:* Reversed.

The court discussed an "assumption of risk" exception to the prevention doctrine, to the effect that the doctrine does not apply if the contract authorizes prevention. But it ruled that the doctrine of prevention and not the exception applied. The court thought it "somewhat inaccurate to call the assumption of risk rule ... an 'exception' to the prevention doctrine." Since prevention is a breach of contract, it is a corollary "that there is no prevention when the contract authorizes a party to prevent a condition from occurring.... Shear did not assume the risk that the Management Committee would refuse to recommend the contract, or that the Board would be deprived ... of authority to approve the contract." Shear v. National Rifle Association, 606 F.2d 1251 (D.C.Cir.1979).

The court also rejected the Association's contention that "nothing but abject speculation could show that 'the condition [settlement] would have occurred.'" Shear also alleged that when he signed his contingent-on-settlement agreement the NRA official who signed for it knew of the impending coup, and that he (Shear) would not have signed if he had known of it. What sort of claim does this allegation support?

(2) *The Case of the School Board's Lesson.* The New York City Board of Education let a contract for work on a school building, containing a condition that

the agreement should be binding only if "the comptroller shall indorse hereon his certificate" that appropriated and unexpended funds were on hand to meet the estimated expense. After the contractor had done some preliminary work, the Board "rescinded" the contract. Although it did not question that the required funds were available, it justified its action by the comptroller's failure to certify the contract. He had withheld certification at the Board's request. The contractor sued the Board. From a judgment for the defendant, the plaintiff appealed. *Held:* Reversed.

The Board's action could not be justified by the comptroller's failure to certify the contract. "The general rule is, as it has been frequently stated, that a party to a contract cannot rely on the failure of another to perform a condition precedent where he has frustrated or prevented the occurrence of the condition." Kooleraire Service & Installation Corp. v. Board of Education, 268 N.E.2d 782 (N.Y.1971).

WAIVER, ESTOPPEL, AND ELECTION

A requirement that a condition occur may of course be eliminated by agreement between the parties. Furthermore, after a contract is made, an obligor whose duty is conditional may promise to perform despite the nonoccurrence of a condition or despite a delay in its occurrence. See Restatement § 84. Such a promise is commonly termed a *waiver*. Although it is often said that a waiver is "the intentional relinquishment of a known right," this is misleading. What is involved is not the relinquishment of a right and the termination of the reciprocal duty, but rather the excuse of the nonoccurrence of a condition of a duty. The creditor who discharges a debt by release or renunciation does not "waive" the debt in the strict sense of that word. However, as Corbin said, the word is one "of indefinite connotation" that, "like a cloak, . . . covers a multitude of sins." Corbin, Conditions in the Law of Contracts, 28 Yale L.J. 739, 754 (1919).

A party that, without consideration, has waived a condition that is within the other party's control *before* the time for occurrence of the condition can retract the waiver and reinstate the requirement that the condition occur unless the other party has relied to such an extent that retraction would be unjust. See Restatement § 84(2); UCC § 2–209(5). If there has been such reliance, *estoppel* will preclude retraction. However, a party that has waived a condition *after* the time for occurrence of the condition is subject to a dramatically different rule under which the waiver cannot be retracted, even in the absence of reliance. See Restatement § 84(1). Such waivers smack of election.

The word *election* signifies a choice, one that is binding on the party that makes it, even without reliance by the other party. When the time for occurrence of a condition has expired, the party whose duty is conditional has a choice between, on the one hand, taking advantage of the nonoccurrence of the condition and treating the duty as discharged or, on the other hand, disregarding the nonoccurrence of the condition and treating the duty as unconditional. Under the rule just stated, a party that chooses to disregard the nonoccurrence of a condition is bound by an election to treat the duty as unconditional. The parties that have most often been bound by such elections are insurers.

NOTES

(1) *Anti–Waiver Clauses.* A party may have a better chance to fend off a claim of waiver if the contract contains an anti-waiver clause. Such a clause typically states that no action or inaction by that party shall amount to a waiver of any condition of any duty of that party. However, such clauses are not always honored by courts. See Connecticut Fire Insurance Co. v. Fox, 361 F.2d 1 (10th Cir.1966), holding that a "non-waiver" agreement providing that the insurer's investigation would not waive any conditions of the policy did not prevent waiver of the proof of loss requirement by an adjuster on whom the insureds relied "to know what they must do to recover their loss."

(2) *Waiver or Course of Performance.* It is often argued that conduct results in a waiver. Recall that in *Eastern Air Lines*, p. 76 above, conduct resulted in a course of performance under UCC § 2–208. How do these two effects of conduct differ? As one court has pointed out, in contrast to course of dealings, "the conduct of the parties in *performing* an agreement may be relevant to show a modification or waiver of a provision inconsistent with their conduct in the performance of that agreement." J.R. Hale Contracting Co. v. United New Mexico Bank, 799 P.2d 581, 587 (N.M.1990). According to Comment 3 to UCC § 2–208, "Where it is difficult to determine whether a particular act merely sheds light on the meaning of the agreement or represents a waiver of a term of the agreement, the preference is in favor of 'waiver' whenever such construction, plus the application of the provisions on the reinstatement of rights waived (see Section 2–209), is needed to preserve the flexible character of commercial contracts and to prevent surprise or other hardship."

(3) *Prevention and Waiver.* Prevention is sometimes coupled with waiver. In McCarthy v. Tobin, 706 N.E.2d 629 (Mass.1999), the court concluded that the vendor had waived the deadline for the execution of a more formal purchase and sale agreement for real estate. The vendor's lawyer, "acting as her agent, voluntarily undertook the task of drafting the purchase and sale agreement. He did not produce the final draft until it was impossible for [the purchaser] to sign it before the deadline. He also did not object to the passage of the deadline in the telephone calls and facsimile transmissions that followed. Instead he continued to deal with [the purchaser's] lawyer in an effort to craft a mutually satisfactory agreement."

McKENNA v. VERNON, 101 A. 919 (Pa.1917). [McKenna undertook to build a moving picture theatre in Philadelphia for Vernon. The contract price, $8,750, was to be paid in installments for the first 80% of the work, and the final installment within 30 days after completion of the work. The work was to be done under the direction of an architect, whose certificate of work done was to be the condition of each payment by Vernon. McKenna received several payments, amounting in all to $6,000, and brought this action for the remainder of the contract price. Vernon asserted that the work was defective, but the architect testified that there were no unauthorized departures from the specifications, and McKenna had judgment for $2,500. Vernon appealed on the theory that no right of action existed in the absence of a certificate from the architect of final completion of the building. *Held:* Affirmed.]

■ STEWART, JUSTICE. . . . All payments were to be made only on certificate of the architect, and yet with a single exception each of the seven payments made as the work progressed was made without a certificate being asked for. With such constant and repeated disregard on the part of the owner to exact compliance with this provision in the contract, it is too late now for him to insist that failure on the part of the plaintiff to secure such certificate before suit defeats his right of action. . . . If he waived it repeatedly, as he did here, during the progress of the work, he cannot complain if he be held to have waived it when he seeks to defend against a final payment for work shown to have been honestly and substantially performed, especially when almost daily he has had the work under his own observation, without remonstrance or complaint at any time with respect to either the work done or materials employed. . . .

NOTE

The Benefits of Lenience. In Sethness–Greenleaf v. Green River Corp., 65 F.3d 64, 67 (7th Cir.1995), involving a soft drink manufacturer's claim for delayed payments from buyers of concentrate for Green River Soda, Judge Easterbrook wrote that "a vendor who cuts the buyer some slack—even 14 months worth of slack—does not thereby 'agree' to forbear indefinitely. The buyer may enjoy the extra breathing room, but when the vendor's patience runs out the buyer must pay up or face the consequences. . . . Were it otherwise, vendors would be inclined to cut off supplies at the first sign of trouble, and buyers as a whole would lose the benefits of lenience."

After giving McKenna "the benefits of lenience" by making several payments without certificates, could Vernon have insisted on certificates for subsequent payments? How? If McKenna had asked for and received, early in the course of performance, Vernon's promise that he would not insist on compliance with the condition, enforcement of the promise would present an obvious problem of consideration. Was there no problem of consideration in McKenna v. Vernon?

PROBLEMS

(1) *A Change of Mind.* Suppose that in *Luttinger*, after the Luttingers had failed to get a mortgage, a relative offered to provide the financing and they assured the Rosens that they would proceed with the transaction. What would be the legal position of the Luttingers if the relative then reneged and they told the Rosens that they had changed their mind and did not want to buy the house? Would it make a difference if the Rosens could prove that they had relied on the assurance? Loda v. H.K. Sargeant & Associates, 448 A.2d 812 (Conn.1982); Williams v. Ubaldo, 670 A.2d 913 (Me.1996).

(2) *Another Change of Mind.* Suppose that in *Mattei,* p. 72 above, Mattei had told Hopper that he was not satisfied with the leases obtained but the next day, still within the 120–day period, had changed his mind and said he was satisfied. Would Hopper have been bound? Is the discussion of Rejection of an Irrevocable Offer, p. 184 above, helpful in answering this question? See Beverly Way Associates v. Barham, 276 Cal.Rptr. 240 (Ct.App.1990).

———

INTERPRETATION AND AVOIDANCE OF FORFEITURE

As we have seen, courts have traditionally preferred interpretations of contract language that avoid forfeiture. Language making a promise conditional may be interpreted in such a way that the condition has occurred, as where a condition of satisfaction is taken to be reasonable satisfaction. Language that does not clearly make a promise conditional may be interpreted as not imposing a condition at all, as when a clause is read as a pay-when-paid rather than a pay-if-paid provision.

Interpretation cannot prevent forfeiture, however, if the drafter of the contract has taken pains to make clear that forfeiture is intended. Even in such a case, the Restatement asserts that a condition may sometimes be excused to avoid "disproportionate forfeiture." Restatement § 229. See Hoosier Energy Rural Elec. Coop. v. Amoco Tax Leasing IV Corp., 34 F.3d 1310, 1320 (7th Cir.1994) (explaining that though it is unclear whether New York would follow § 229, "New York recognizes equity's abhorrence of a forfeiture"). However, courts have often preferred more traditional methods, some bordering on subterfuge, to avoid forfeiture.

NOTE

The Case of Constructive Fraud. A contract for the construction of low-rent housing required the Housing Authority to extend the time for completing the work "when in its judgment the findings of fact of the [Authority's] Contracting Officer justify such an extension, and his findings of fact thereon shall be final and conclusive upon the parties." The contractor gave notice of a delay resulting from a shortage of plumbers, and the Officer found that a delay of only 15 days was justified. The contractor sued the Authority, complaining that the Officer had arrived at the figure of 15 days by taking 8% of the actual delay of 182 days because the plumbing cost was only that percentage of the cost of the entire contract. The Authority moved for summary judgment. *Held:* Summary judgment denied. The Officer's finding may be set aside, and the issue of allowable delay presented to a jury.

"It is unfortunate that a finding of constructive fraud must be made in so many words when, in fact, we are actually dealing with serious errors in calculations. However, the decisions refer to such miscalculations as constructive fraud and I find it necessary to pin that label upon the contracting officer's erroneous findings here although, actually, there is no hint of bad faith, dishonesty or deliberate wrongful conduct upon the part of the contracting officer or the Authority. I am sure that these errors were the product of inexperience and mistaken judgment." Anthony P. Miller, Inc. v. Wilmington Housing Authority, 179 F.Supp. 199 (D.Del.1959). Is a contracting officer the same sort of third party as an architect?

———

HICKS v. BUSH, 180 N.E.2d 425 (N.Y.1962). [Frederick Hicks executed a completely integrated written agreement with shareholders of the Clinton G. Bush Company under which the parties were to merge their corporate interests into a single "holding" company, Bush–Hicks Enterprises. Each party was to subscribe to a specified number of shares of this new company, transferring to it shares representing his existing corporate interest. Hicks transferred his stock, but the others did not, and the merger did not take place. When Hicks sued the others for specific performance, they set up as an affirmative defense that the written agreement was executed "upon a parol condition" that it "was not to operate" as a contract and that the merger was not "to become effective" until "equity expansion funds" of $672,500 were first raised, and they had not been raised. At the trial, the evidence showed that this sum was essential to the successful operation of the merger, and that the parties had agreed that the entire merger deal was subject to the condition that the sum be raised, the writing not to become effective as a binding contract until the specified equity expansion funds were obtained. As one witness said, the understanding was "Get the money or no deal." The Court noted that "Hicks, however, testified that he was 'absolutely positive' that nothing was said about such a condition at the time of the signing and that 'to the best of my knowledge no such language was ever used at any time let alone on the day of the signing.'" Record at pp. 410, 434. From an adverse judgment, Hicks appealed.]

■ FULD, JUDGE. . . . The applicable law is clear, the relevant principles settled. Parol testimony is admissible to prove a condition precedent to the legal effectiveness of a written agreement . . . if the condition does not contradict the express terms of such written agreement. . . . A certain disparity is inevitable, of course, whenever a written promise is, by oral agreement of the parties, made conditional upon an event not expressed in the writing. Quite obviously, though, the parol evidence rule does not bar proof of every orally established condition precedent, but only of those which in a real sense contradict the terms of the written agreement. . . . Upon the present appeal, our problem is to determine whether there is such a contradiction. . . .

There is here no direct or explicit contradiction between the oral condition and the writing; in fact, the parol agreement deals with a matter on which the written agreement, as in some of the cases cited . . . , is silent. The plaintiff, however, contends that, since the written agreement provides in terms that the obligations of the parties were to be terminated if the merged corporation failed to accept any of their stock subscriptions within 25 days, the additional oral condition—that the writing "was [not] to become operative" and that the merger was "not to become effective" until the expansion funds had been raised—is irreconcilable with the written agreement.

As already indicated, and analysis confirms it, the two conditions may stand side by side. The oral requirement that the writing was not to take effect as a contract until the equity expansion funds were obtained is simply a further condition—a condition added to that requiring the acceptance of stock subscriptions within 25 days—and not one which is contradictory. If both provisions had been contained in the written agreement, it is clear that the defendants would not have been under immediate legal duty to transfer the stock in their companies to Bush–Hicks Enterprises until both conditions had been fulfilled and satisfied. And it is equally clear that evidence of an oral condition is not to be excluded as contradictory or "inconsistent" merely because the written agreement contains other conditions precedent. . . .

In short, the parties in the case before us intended that their respective rights and duties with respect to the contemplated transfers of stock in the operating companies to the holding company be subject to two conditions, each independent of the other—the acceptance of the stock subscription within a specified period and the procuring of expansion funds of $672,500. As the courts below found, the parties did not contemplate performance of the written agreement until such funds were first received. In other words, it was their desire and understanding that the merger was to be one of proposal only and that, even though the formal preliminary steps were to be taken, the writing was not to become operative as a contract or the merger effective until $672,500 was raised. It is certainly not improbable that parties contracting in these circumstances would make the asserted oral agreement; the condition precedent at hand is the sort of condition which parties would not be inclined to incorporate into a written agreement intended for public consumption. The challenged evidence was, therefore, admissible and, since there was ample proof attesting to the making of the oral agreement, the trial court was fully warranted in holding that no operative or binding contract ever came into existence. . . .

[Affirmed.]

NOTES

(1) *Questions.* Were the defendants attempting to show that no obligations were to arise under the writing until the funds were procured, or that the obligations that had arisen under the writing were conditional on the procurement of the funds? Is the decision consistent with *W.W.W. Associates*, p. 390 above?

(2) *The Code.* What would have been the result in Hicks v. Bush if UCC § 2-202 had been applicable? See Hunt Foods & Industries v. Doliner, 270 N.Y.S.2d 937 (App.Div.1966).

(3) *Merger Clauses and Conditions.* In Kryl v. Mechalson, 47 N.W.2d 899 (Wis.1951), the court held that an oral condition to the contract could be established in spite of the following language: "It is understood that this contract is complete in itself, and that the party of the first part is not bound by any other terms or agreements other than are herein contained." See Edward T. Kelly Co. v. Von Zakobiel, 171 N.W. 75 (Wis.1919).

(4) *Big MACs.* In *Hicks v. Bush* the contemplated merger of two corporations was made contingent on the realization of "equity expansion funds" in the amount of $672,500. This was a relatively simple transaction with a clearly stipulated contingency. More complicated mergers and acquisitions typically contain "material adverse change" (MAC) or "material adverse effect" (MAE) clauses that condition the parties' commitments to each other on the non-occurrence of events that would have a material adverse effect on a business, its assets or liabilities, or that would otherwise substantially affect the value of the contemplated deal. What constitutes "material" is often not specified in these clauses, leaving courts to struggle to find the parties' intent. See In re IBP, Inc. v. Tyson Foods, Inc., 789 A.2d 14 (Del.Ch. 2001).

PROBLEMS

(1) *Drafting (Reprise).* Review the clause that you drafted in response to the Problem, p. 710 above. Can you improve it in the light of Hicks v. Bush? Be sure to take account of Note 3, p. 715 above.

(2) *Conditions Compared.* Suppose that in *Luttinger,* the agreement had contained a merger clause but had not contained a financing condition. Would the Luttingers have been permitted to testify that the parties had orally agreed on a financing condition as part of their contract? See Luria Bros. & Co. v. Pielet Bros. Scrap Iron & Metal, Inc., 600 F.2d 103 (7th Cir.1979).

Section 2. Constructive Conditions of Exchange

This section introduces problems of performance and non-performance that do not turn on express conditions. Two main instruments of the law's development in this regard are the conceptions of "constructive conditions" and "material breach." A party's failure to *render* a performance—or in some cases its failure to *offer* a performance—is a possible excuse for the non-performance of a duty undertaken by the other party. Moreover, a *prospective* failure to perform may have the same effect. A traditional way of affirming these effects is to say that the commitments exchanged by the parties are "dependent covenants." (And a way of denying these effects is to speak of "independent covenants.") The first case in the section, Kingston v. Preston, is a cornerstone of the law of constructive conditions, reasoned in terms of such dependency.

Kingston v. Preston was regarded in its own time as a notable advance in the doctrine of dependency of covenants, and has been so referred to ever since. To speak in current terms, it is regarded as the chief inspiration for constructive conditions. The views expressed by Lord Mansfield have been commonly seen as modifying an attitude of the common law that was centuries old. Although the dependency of promises was neither invented nor finally resolved in that case, it is the most celebrated of a long series on the subject.

The impact of Kingston v. Preston is suggested by a hypothetical case stated in 1500 concerning a father who covenants to transfer an estate to his daughter and her husband-to-be, as part of a marriage settlement between the two men. According to the old text, even if the prospective husband is faithless—"if I marry another woman"—the father can be compelled to convey. The father's remedy would be a separate action for damages for breach of contract. The result represents in an extreme degree the principle that mutual covenants are independent unless expressed to be otherwise; in current terms we might say that the marriage is not a constructive condition of the father's promise. The result is otherwise, says the note, if the father's covenant refers to the marriage promise as being made "for the same cause." Y.B.Trin. 15 Hen. 7, f. 10, pl. 17 (1500).

The defendant in Kingston v. Preston was in business as a silk mercer, and the plaintiff had entered his business as a "covenant servant," or apprentice. The articles of indenture provided that after a year and a quarter the mercer would retire from the business. Thereafter it was to be carried on by the apprentice and a partner—either a nephew of the mercer or someone else nominated by the defendant. The apprentice was to pay for his share of the business in monthly installments of £250. To assure these payments, the apprentice agreed to give the mercer "good and sufficient security," approved of by him, "at and before the sealing and delivery of the deeds" conveying the business.

The apprentice sued the mercer, alleging that he had refused to surrender the business at the appointed time. The defendant pleaded that the plaintiff had not given sufficient security for the payments. To this the plaintiff demurred, and arguments ensued as reported below.

Kingston v. Preston

King's Bench, 1773.
Lofft 194, 2 Doug. 689, 99 Eng.Rep. 437.

On the part of the plaintiff, the case was argued by Mr. Buller, who contended that the covenants were mutual and independent, and therefore a plea of the breach of one of the covenants to be performed by the plaintiff was no bar to an action for a breach by the defendant of one which he had bound himself to perform, but that the defendant might have his remedy for the breach by the plaintiff in a separate action. On the other side, Mr. Gross insisted that the covenants were dependent in their nature, and therefore performance must be alleged: the security to be given for the money was manifestly the chief object of the transaction, and it would be highly unreasonable to construe the agreement so as to oblige the defendant to give up a beneficial business, and valuable stock-in-trade, and trust to the plaintiff's personal security (who might, and, indeed was admitted to be worth nothing), for the performance of his part.

In delivering the judgment of the Court, Lord Mansfield expressed himself to the following effect: There are three kinds of covenants: 1. Such as are called mutual and independent, where either party may recover damages from the other for the injury he may have received by a breach of the covenants in his favor, and where it is no excuse for the defendant to allege a breach of the covenants on the part of the plaintiff. 2. There are covenants which are conditions and dependent, in which the performance of one depends on the prior performance of another, and, therefore, till this prior condition is performed, the other party is not liable to an action on his covenant. 3. There is also a third sort of covenants, which are mutual conditions to be performed at the same time; and in these, if one party was ready and offered to perform his part, and the other neglected or refused to perform his, he who was ready and offered has fulfilled his engagement, and may maintain an action for the default of the other; though it is not certain that either is obliged to do the first act. His Lordship then proceeded to say, that the dependence or independence of covenants was to be collected from the evident sense and meaning of the parties, and that, however transposed they might be in the deed, their precedency must depend on the order of time in which the intent of the transaction requires their performance. That, in the case before the Court, it would be the greatest injustice if the plaintiff should prevail: the essence of the agreement was, that the defendant should not trust to the personal security of the plaintiff, but, before he delivered up his stock and business, should have good security for the payment of the money. The giving such security, therefore, must necessarily be a condition precedent. Judgment was accordingly given for the defendant, because the part to be performed by the plaintiff was clearly a condition precedent.

NOTE

An Example. In Eastern Air Lines v. Gulf, p. 76, 526 above, Gulf's defense was descended from Kingston v. Preston. Gulf argued that it was relieved of its duty to furnish jet fuel to Eastern Air Lines because of the latter's breach of its duty of good faith and fair dealing. Implicit in this defense was the proposition that Gulf's promise was dependent upon Eastern Air Lines' promise, that is, that performance by Eastern Air Lines was a constructive condition of Gulf's duty to furnish jet fuel. According to Restatement § 232, the existence of this relation is presumed to exist when a contract includes an exchange of promises, "unless a contrary intention is clearly manifested."

PROBLEM

Drafting (Reprise). Refer again to the Drafting Problem, p. 701 above, especially the direction to draft a clause making "sailing with the next wind" the subject of a duty alone. Do you see a difficulty in doing this, not apparent till now? How would you redraft the clause in the light of Kingston v. Preston?

————

TIME FOR PERFORMANCE

Because of the doctrine of constructive conditions, fixing the time for performance under a contract has the important effect of allocating the risk that one party will perform but will not receive the other party's return performance. Recall Judge Easterbrook's description, in Note 2, p. 531 above, of an opportunistic situation in which "there is effort to wring some advantage from the fact that the party who performs first sinks costs, which the other party may hold hostage by demanding greater compensation in exchange for its own performance." This situation of opportunism is sometimes referred to a the "holdup problem," and it may lead parties to underinvest in otherwise desirable contracts or not enter into an agreement at all.

The parties themselves can, of course, fix the times for performance in their contract, as the mercer did in Kingston v. Preston by providing that the apprentice was to give security "at and before the sealing and delivery of the deeds." If the contract is silent, default rules may fix the times for performance. One of the most common is that "When the performance of a contract consists in doing (faciendo) on one side, and in giving (dando) on the other side, the doing must take place before the giving." Coletti v. Knox Hat Co., Inc., 169 N.E. 648, 649–650 (N.Y.1930).

"Centuries ago, the principle became settled that where work is to be done by one party and payment is to be made by the other, the performance of the work must precede payment, in the absence of a showing of a contrary intention. It is sometimes supposed, that this principle grew out of employment contracts, and reflects a conviction that employers as a class are more likely to be responsible than are workmen paid in advance. Whether or not the explanation is correct, most parties today contract with reference to the principle, and unless they have evidenced a contrary intention it is at least as fair as the opposite rule would be." Restatement § 234, Comment *e*.

Stewart v. Newbury

Court of Appeals of New York, 1917.
220 N.Y. 379, 115 N.E. 984.

■ CRANE, J. [Stewart, a builder, offered to do the excavation work for Newbury's new foundry building at 65 cents per cubic yard, to furnish labor and forms for the concrete work at $2.05 per cubic yard, and to furnish labor to put in re-enforcing (of the concrete) at $4.00 per ton. Newbury accepted this offer. As a result of a dispute, described in the opinion, over payment, Stewart sued Newbury. From judgment upon a verdict for Stewart, Newbury appealed, the Appellate Division affirmed, and Newbury appealed again.]

Nothing was said in writing about the time or manner of payment. The plaintiff, however, claims that after sending his letter and before receiving that of the defendant he had a telephone communication with Mr. Newbury and said: "I will expect my payments in the usual manner," and Newbury said, "All right, we have got the money to pay for the building." This conversation over the telephone was denied by the defendants.

The custom, the plaintiff testified, was to pay 85 per cent every thirty days or at the end of each month, 15 per cent being retained till the work was completed.

In July the plaintiff commenced work and continued until September 29th, at which time he had progressed with the construction as far as the first floor. He then sent a bill for the work done up to that date for $896.35. The defendants refused to pay the bill and work was discontinued.

The plaintiff claims that the defendants refused to permit him to perform the rest of his contract, they insisting that the work already done was not in accordance with the specifications. The defendants claimed upon the trial that the plaintiff voluntarily abandoned the work after their refusal to pay his bill.

On October 5, 1911, the defendants wrote the plaintiff a letter containing the following: "Notwithstanding you promised to let us know on Monday whether you would complete the job or throw up the contract, you have not up to this time advised us of your intention.... Under the circumstances we are compelled to accept your action as being an abandonment of your contract and of every effort upon your part to complete your work on our building. As you know, the bill which you sent us and which we declined to pay is not correct, either in items or amount, nor is there anything due you under our contract as we understand it until you have completed your work on our building."

To this letter the plaintiff replied the following day. In it he makes no reference to the telephone communication agreeing, as he testified, to make "the usual payments," but does say this: "There is nothing in our agreement which says that I shall wait until the job is completed before any payment is due, nor can this be reasonably implied. . . . As to having given you positive date as to when I should let you know what I proposed doing, I did not do so; on the contrary I told you that I would not tell you positively what I would do until I had visited the job, and I promised that I would do this at my earliest convenience. . . ."

The defendant Herbert Newbury testified that the plaintiff "ran away and left the whole thing." And the defendant F.E. Newbury testified that he was told by Mr. Stewart's man that Stewart was going to abandon the job; that he thereupon telephoned Mr. Stewart, who replied that he would let him know about it the next day, but did not.

In this action, which is brought to recover the amount of the bill presented as the agreed price and $95.68 damages for breach of contract, the plaintiff had a verdict for the amount stated in the bill, but not for the other damages claimed, and the judgment entered thereon has been affirmed by the Appellate Division.

The appeal to us is upon exceptions to the judge's charge. The court charged the jury as follows: "Plaintiff says that he was excused from completely performing the contract by the defendant's unreasonable failure to pay him for the work he had done during the months of August and September. . . . Was it understood that the payments were to be made monthly? If it was not so understood the defendant's only obligation was to make payments at reasonable periods, in view of the character of the work, the amount of work being done and the value of it. In other words, if there was no agreement between the parties respecting the payments, the defendants' obligation was to make payments at reasonable times. . . . But whether there was such an agreement or not, you may consider whether it was reasonable or unreasonable for him to exact payment at that time and in that amount."

The court further said, in reply to a request to charge:

"I will say in that connection, if there was no agreement respecting the time of payment, and if there was no custom that was understood by both parties, and with respect to which they made the contract, then the plaintiff was entitled to payments at reasonable times."

The defendants' counsel thereupon made the following request, which was refused: "I ask your Honor to instruct the jury that if the circumstances existed as your Honor stated in your last instruction, then the plaintiff was not entitled to any payment until the contract was completed."

The jury was plainly told that if there were no agreement as to payments, yet the plaintiff would be entitled to part payment at reasonable times as the work progressed, and if such payments were refused he could abandon the work and recover the amount due for the work performed.

This is not the law. Counsel for the plaintiff omits to call our attention to any authority sustaining such a proposition and our search reveals none. In fact the law is very well settled to the contrary. This was an entire contract. (Ming v. Corbin, 142 N.Y. 334, 340, 341, 37 N.E. 105.) Where a contract is made to perform work and no agreement is made as to payment, the work must be substantially performed before payment can be demanded. . . .

This case was also submitted to the jury upon the ground that there may have been a breach of contract by the defendants in their refusal to permit the plaintiff to continue with his work, claiming that he had departed from the specifications, and there was some evidence justifying this view of the case, but it is impossible to say upon which of these two theories the jury arrived at its conclusion. The above errors, therefore, cannot be considered as harmless and immaterial. . . . As the verdict was for the amount of the bill presented and did not include the damages for a breach of contract, which would be the loss of profits, it may well be presumed that the jury adopted the first ground of recovery charged by the court as above quoted and decided that the plaintiff was justified in abandoning work for nonpayment of the installment.

The judgment should be reversed, and a new trial ordered, costs to abide the event.

NOTES

(1) *Questions.* If the jury believed Stewart's evidence about the telephone conversation with Newbury, does it follow that he was justified in abandoning the work? Would it matter whether this conversation occurred before or after the contract was concluded? If it occurred before, how might Stewart's case be affected by the parol evidence rule? If it occurred afterward, what was the consideration for Newbury's promise to pay "in the usual manner"? Might it make a difference if the contract contained a merger clause? A no-oral-modification clause?

(2) *Progress Payments.* For repair work on buildings and chattels, and similar modest jobs, payment is often withheld until completion. But for sizable construction work it is well-nigh universal practice to agree upon periodic progress payments in favor of the contractor. As security for completion, the owner retains a fraction (usually 10–20%) of the amount earned each month by the contractor, and the sums withheld (sometimes called the "retainage") are payable only upon completion. Does this practice indicate that contractors are dissatisfied with the rule in Stewart v. Newbury? Is it a reason for discarding the rule?

————

CONCURRENT CONDITIONS AND TENDER

In Kingston v. Preston, Mansfield spoke of promises "which are mutual conditions to be performed at the same time; and in these, if one party was ready and offered to perform his part, and the other neglected or refused to perform his, he who was ready and offered has fulfilled his engagement, and may maintain an action for the default of the other; though it is not certain that either is obliged to do the first act."

The Court of Kings Bench applied this analysis in Morton v. Lamb, 101 Eng.Rep. 890 (Kings Bench 1797), several years after Mansfield's death. When a buyer of grain alleged that the seller had failed to deliver the grain, although the buyer was ready to receive it, the court upheld the seller's objection that the buyer had failed to allege that he was ready to pay for the grain. "[W]here two concurrent acts are to be done, the party who sues the other for non-performance must aver that he has performed, or was ready to perform, his part of the contract."

Courts still apply this rule to contracts for the sale of goods where there is no provision for credit or other means of payment. Courts express the mutual dependency of the parties' promises by saying that tender of the goods by the seller and tender of the price by the buyer are "concurrent conditions." "Tender of delivery is a condition to the buyer's duty to accept the goods and ... to pay for them" (UCC § 2–507(1)), and "tender of payment is a condition to the seller's duty to tender and complete any delivery" (UCC § 2–511(1)).

"A formal tender is seldom made in business transactions," it is said, "except to lay the foundation for subsequent assertion in a court of justice of rights which spring from refusal of the tender."[a] Courts are not often called on to say what is or is not a formal tender of performance under a contract. Partly for that reason, as the word "tender" is commonly used it suggests a degree of punctilio in conduct that is seldom achieved. Paradoxically, the strict sense of the word is supported by a set of rules dispensing with the necessity of tender in ordinary contract litigation.

The Code states the requisites, under contracts for the sale of goods, for a seller's tender of delivery (UCC § 2–507) and for a buyer's tender of payment (UCC § 2–511). A comment after the former section identifies two senses of the word "tender." In the stricter sense, it "contemplates an offer coupled with a present ability to fulfill all the conditions resting on the tendering party and must be followed by actual performance if the other party shows himself ready to proceed." But the comment indicates that something less than this will suffice to put the other party in default "if he fails to proceed in some manner."

If a buyer has not made an arrangement with the seller for credit, must the buyer proffer payment in money—i.e., "legal tender"? The Code recognizes that it is commercially normal to accept a check from a "seemingly solvent party," and states a rule designed to avoid "commercial surprise." Tendering a check is commonly sufficient under this rule, "unless the seller demands payment in legal tender and gives any extension of time reasonably necessary to procure it." UCC § 2–511(2).

a. Lehman, J., dissenting, in Petterson v. Pattberg, 161 N.E. 428 (N.Y.1928).

NOTE

Specific Performance. In actions for specific performance, and especially those based on land-sale contracts, constructive conditions of exchange sometimes do not operate with the same effect as in ordinary damage actions. Because the remedy takes the form of an *order,* a court can insert a condition that effectively secures the receipt by the defendant of the plaintiff's promised performance.

In McMillan v. Smith, 363 S.W.2d 437, 442 (Tex.1962), the plaintiffs, purchasers of a ranch, were uncertain what the per-acre price amounted to, in the aggregate. Upon making a deposit into court, they alleged their ability and willingness to pay "such further sum as the Court may order." The court accepted this invitation, saying: "Historically, in a suit for specific performance, the question as to the necessity for a tender of performance by a purchaser has been determined according to equitable rules rather than to those applicable to an action at law. The latter requires the purchaser, as a condition precedent, to tender performance. Courts of equity, on the other hand, have not been bound by strict and inflexible rules."

SECTION 3.   MITIGATING DOCTRINES

(A) SUBSTANTIAL PERFORMANCE

In *Luttinger* the court required strict compliance with the express financing condition, saying simply that if the condition "is not fulfilled the contract is not enforceable." Where constructive rather than express conditions are concerned, however, the rule is often one of substantial performance. The origin of the rule has been traced to another decision by Mansfield, one about the sale of a plantation in the West Indies. Boone v. Eyre, 126 Eng.Rep. 160, Note (Kings Bench 1777).

The rule has found its chief proving ground in suits on construction contracts. Why should this be so? Several considerations suggest the answer. Leases of real property have traditionally been regarded as exempt from the usual contract rules of constructive conditions. As for employment contracts, it is usual for an employer to pay wages at short intervals, and to reserve the power of termination at will. As for contracts for the sale of goods, the seller who is denied a remedy can usually dispose of the goods elsewhere and will not suffer a loss comparable to that of the builder who cannot enforce the contract. As for land sale contracts, enforcement is regularly sought in a court of equity, in which there are specialized rules serving some of the same objects as the doctrine of substantial performance. But neither party to a construction contract ordinarily has access to the remedy of specific performance.

"Through the doctrine of substantial performance," it is said, "the judges installed themselves as administrators of the execution and discharge of contracts. They freed themselves from rigid rules and adopted a broad standard under which they could apply a policy of making contract effective." J. Corry, Law and Policy 41–43 (1959). This must not be understood to mean that the courts will directly administer the performance of a contract, but it means that practical judgments about performance figure in their decisions about money claims. Should courts undertake a more active role as to construction contracts? Having become "administrators of the execution" of such contracts, would judges find it a short and easy next step to order the correction of defective work?

The following case was first presented in Chapter 7, p. 645. There we focused on the part of Judge Cardozo's opinion going to "the measure of the allowance." The excerpts below of Judge Cardozo's opinion and the dissent relate to the operation of conditions.

Jacob & Youngs v. Kent
Court of Appeals of New York, 1921.
230 N.Y. 239, 129 N.E. 889, 23 A.L.R. 1429.

[The facts and part of the opinion in this case are presented at p. 645 above.]

■ CARDOZO, J. The plaintiff built a country residence for the defendant at a cost of upwards of $77,000, and now sues to recover a balance of $3,483.46, remaining unpaid.... One of the specifications for the plumbing work provides that "all wrought iron pipe must be well galvanized, lap welded pipe of the grade known as 'standard pipe' of Reading manufacture." The defendant learned in March, 1915, that some of the pipe, instead of being made in Reading, was the product of other factories....

The evidence sustains a finding that the omission of the prescribed brand of pipe was neither fraudulent nor willful. It was the result of the oversight and inattention of the plaintiff's sub-contractor.... The plaintiff tried to show that the brands installed, though made by other manufacturers, were the same in quality, in appearance, in market value and in cost as the brand stated in the contract—that they were, indeed, the same thing, though manufactured in another place. The evidence was excluded, and a verdict directed for the defendant. The Appellate Division reversed, and granted a new trial.

We think the evidence, if admitted, would have supplied some basis for the inference that the defect was insignificant in its relation to the project. The courts never say that one who makes a contract fills the measure of his duty by less than full performance. They do say, however, that an omission, both trivial and innocent, will sometimes be atoned for by allowance of the resulting damage, and will not always be the breach of a condition to be followed by a forfeiture (Spence v. Ham, 163 N.Y. 220, 57 N.E. 412; Woodward v. Fuller, 80 N.Y. 312; Glacius v. Black, 67 N.Y. 563, 566; Bowen v. Kimbell, 203 Mass. 364, 370, 89 N.E. 542.) The distinction is akin to that between dependent and independent promises, or between promises and conditions (Anson on Contracts, Corbin's Ed., sec. 367: 2 Williston on Contracts, sec. 842). Some promises are so plainly independent that they can never by fair construction be conditions of one another. (Rosenthal Paper Co. v. Nat. Folding Box & Paper Co., 226 N.Y. 313, 123 N.E. 766; Bogardus v. N.Y. Life Ins. Co., 101 N.Y. 328, 4 N.E. 522.) Others are so plainly dependent that they must always be conditions. Others, though dependent and thus conditions when there is departure in point of substance, will be viewed as independent and collateral when the departure is insignificant (2 Williston on Contracts, secs. 841, 842; Eastern Forge Co. v. Corbin, 182 Mass. 590, 592, 66 N.E. 419; Robinson v. Mollett, L.R., 7 Eng. & Ir.App. 802, 814; Miller v. Benjamin, 142 N.Y. 613, 37 N.E. 631). Considerations partly of justice and partly of presumable intention are to tell us whether this or that promise shall be placed in one class or another. The simple and the uniform will call for different remedies from the multifarious and the intricate. The margin of departure within the range of normal expectation upon a sale of common chattels will vary from the margin to be expected upon a contract for the construction of a mansion or a "skyscraper." There will be harshness sometimes and oppression in the implication of a condition when the thing upon which labor has been expended is incapable of surrender because united to the land, and equity and reason in the implication of a like condition when the subject-matter, if defective, is in shape to be returned. From the conclusions that promises may not be treated as dependent to the extent of their uttermost minutiae without a sacrifice of justice, the progress is a short one to the conclusion that they may not be so treated without a perversion of intention. Intention not otherwise revealed may be presumed to hold in contemplation the reasonable and probable. If something else is in view, it must not be left to implication. There will be no assumption of a purpose to visit venial faults with oppressive retribution.

Those who think more of symmetry and logic in the development of legal rules than of practical adaptation to the attainment of a just result will be troubled by a classification where the lines of division are so wavering and blurred. Something, doubtless, may be said on the score of consistency and certainty in favor of a stricter standard. The courts have balanced such considerations against those of equity and fairness, and found the latter to be the weightier. The decisions in this state commit us to the liberal view, which is making its way, nowadays, in jurisdictions slow to welcome it (Dakin & Co. v. Lee, 1916, 1 K.B. 566, 579). Where the line is to be drawn between the important and the trivial cannot be settled by a formula. "In the nature of the case precise boundaries are impossible" (2 Williston on Contracts, sec. 841). The same omission may take on one aspect or another according to its setting. Substitution of equivalents may not have the same significance in fields of art on the one side and in those of mere utility on the other. Nowhere will change be tolerated, however, if it is so dominant or pervasive as in any real or substantial measure to frustrate the purpose of the contract (Crouch v. Gutmann, 134 N.Y. 45, 51, 31 N.E. 271). There is no general license to install whatever, in the builder's judgment, may be regarded as "just as good" (Easthampton L. & C., Ltd. v. Worthington, 186 N.Y. 407, 412, 79 N.E. 323). The question is one of degree, to be answered, if there is doubt, by the triers of the facts (Crouch v. Gutmann; Woodward v. Fuller, supra), and, if the inferences are certain, by the judges of the law (Easthampton L. & C. Co., Ltd. v. Worthington, supra). We must weigh the purpose to be served, the desire to be gratified, the excuse for deviation from the letter, the cruelty of enforced adherence. Then only can we tell whether literal fulfillment is to be implied by law as a condition. This is not to say that the parties are not free by apt and certain words to effectuate a purpose that performance of every term shall be a condition of recovery. That question is not here. This is merely to say that the law will be slow to impute the purpose, in the silence of the parties, where the significance of the default is grievously out of proportion to the oppression of the forfeiture. The willful transgressor must accept the penalty of his transgression (Schultze v. Goodstein, 180 N.Y. 248, 251, 73 N.E. 21; Desmond–Dunne Co. v. Friedman–Doscher Co., 162 N.Y. 486, 490, 56 N.E. 995). For him there is no occasion to mitigate the rigor of implied conditions. The transgressor whose default is unintentional and trivial may hope for mercy if he will offer atonement for his wrong (Spence v. Ham, supra). . . .

The order should be affirmed, and judgment absolute directed in favor of the plaintiff upon the stipulation, with costs in all courts.

■ McLAUGHLIN, J. (dissenting). I dissent. The plaintiff did not perform its contract. Its failure to do so was either intentional or due to gross neglect which, under the uncontradicted facts, amounted to the same thing, nor did it make any proof of the cost of compliance, where compliance was possible. . . .[a]

The plaintiff agreed that all the pipe used should be of the Reading Manufacturing Company . . . It installed between 2,000 and 2,500 feet of pipe, of which only 1,000 feet at most complied with the contract. No explanation was given why pipe called for by the contract was not used, nor was any effort made to show what it would cost to remove the pipe of other manufacturers and install that of the Reading Manufacturing Company. The defendant had a right to contract for what he wanted. He had a right before making payment to get what the contract called for. It is no answer to this suggestion to say that the pipe put in was just as good as that made by the Reading Manufacturing Company, or that the difference in value between such pipe and the pipe made by the Reading Manufacturing Company would be either "nominal or nothing." Defendant contracted for pipe made by the Reading Manufacturing Company. What his reason was for requiring this kind of pipe is of no importance. He wanted that and was entitled to it. . . . The rule, therefore, of substantial performance, with damages for unsubstantial omissions, has no application. . . .

■ HISCOCK, CH. J., HOGAN and CRANE, JJ., concur with CARDOZO, J.; POUND and ANDREWS, JJ., concur with McLAUGHLIN, J.

NOTE

(1) *Preference in Interpretation (Reprise)*. How does the doctrine of substantial performance, which applies only to constructive and not express conditions, relate to the preference in interpretation mentioned in the Note, p. 701 above?

(2) *"Willful" Breach*. Cardozo says that Jacob & Youngs' breach was not "willful." It is generally said that a "willful" deviation from the terms of the

---

a. An omitted part of the dissent explains that on the first delivery of pipe Jacob & Youngs's superintendent examined the pipe to make certain it was of Reading manufacture, the subcontractor's foreman simply left word at its shop that he wanted a certain number of feet without specifying the manufacture, and there was no examination before installation.

contract always precludes a finding of substantial performance. (This is often said when the facts seem to show a breach that would prevent substantial performance in any case.)

What kinds of breach by a builder should be regarded as "willful"? Substitution of inferior materials to make a profit? Substitution of equivalent materials to make a profit? What if the builder departs from the plans to meet unforeseen construction problems? What if it is impossible to follow the plans literally?

Is there a better term than "willful" to describe conduct that will bar a builder from claiming substantial performance? Restatement § 241 avoids that word, taking the view that the pertinent inquiry is not simply whether the breach was "willful" but whether the behavior of the party in default "comports with standards of good faith and fair dealing." Even an adverse conclusion on this point is not decisive but is to be weighed with other factors, such as the extent to which the owner will be deprived of a reasonably expected benefit and the extent to which the builder may suffer forfeiture, in deciding whether there has been substantial performance.

(3) *Producing Evidence.* If there is substantial performance, who has the burden of showing how much should be allowed as damages? Some courts require the owner to produce evidence of damages resulting from defects in the builder's work. But see Vance v. My Apartment Steak House, 677 S.W.2d 480 (Tex.1984), requiring the builder, as plaintiff, to establish the cost of remedying defects. A minority of the justices here thought it "anomalous" to require that the plaintiff provide support for the defendant's position.

Who is in a better position to establish the loss to the defendant? Does the answer depend on the question how that loss is measured?

PROBLEMS

(1) *Credit for Unpaid Price?* Contractor installed a heating system in an office building and did such poor work as to be liable to Owner for $250,000. Owner has withheld $150,000 of the contract price. How much does Contractor owe Owner? $250,000 or only $100,000? See Kirk Reid Company v. Fine, 139 S.E.2d 829 (Va.1965).

(2) *Drafting.* If you had represented Kent when he made his contract, could you have drafted a provision that would have barred recovery by Jacob & Youngs? Recall Cardozo's dictum in Jacob & Youngs v. Kent: "This is not to say that the parties are not free by apt and certain words to effectuate a purpose that performance of every term shall be a condition of recovery." In Oppenheimer & Co. v. Oppenheim, Appel, Dixon & Co., 660 N.E.2d 415, 420 (N.Y. 1995), the court quoted this dictum when rejecting the "proposition that the substantial performance doctrine applies universally, including when the language of the agreement leaves no doubt that an express condition precedent was intended."

Consider the contract provisions set out in footnote a, p. 645 above. How could they have been improved?

(3) *Conclusiveness of Certificate.* A contractor who agrees to procure the certificate of an architect or an engineer as a condition of payment may want to take care lest the provision on the subject be read as leaving the certificate inconclusive when it is issued, so that the contractor remains exposed to a claim that its performance was defective. The other party may wish, naturally, to retain such a claim notwithstanding the issuance of a certificate. What language would you suggest to avert the risk for the contractor? What language to have the opposite effect? How would you interpret the language in footnote a, p. 645?

Plante v. Jacobs

Supreme Court of Wisconsin, 1960.
10 Wis.2d 567, 103 N.W.2d 296.

[Eugene Plante contracted with Frank and Carol Jacobs to furnish the materials and construct a house upon their lot in Brookfield, in accordance with plans and specifications, for the sum of $26,765. During the course of construction Plante was paid $20,000. Disputes arose between the parties, the Jacobs refused to continue payment, and Plante did not complete the house. He sued to establish a lien on the property as a way of recovering the unpaid balance of the contract price, plus extras. The owners—who are the appellants—answered with allegations of faulty workmanship and incomplete construction.]

■ HALLOWS, JUSTICE. The defendants argue the plaintiff cannot recover any amount because he has failed to substantially perform the contract. The plaintiff conceded he failed to furnish the kitchen cabinets, gutters and downspouts, sidewalk, closet clothes poles, and entrance seat amounting to $1,601.95. This amount was allowed to the defendants. The defendants claim some 20 other items of incomplete or faulty performance by the plaintiff and no substantial performance because the cost of completing the house in strict compliance with the plans and specifications would amount to 25 or 30 per cent of the contract price. The defendants especially stress the misplacing of the wall between the living room and the kitchen, which narrowed the living room in excess of one foot. The cost of tearing down this wall and rebuilding it would be approximately $4,000. The record is not clear why and when this wall was misplaced, but the wall is completely built and the house decorated and the defendants are living therein. Real estate experts testified that the smaller width of the living room would not affect the market price of the house.

The defendants rely on Manitowoc Steam Boiler Works v. Manitowoc Glue Co., 1903, 120 Wis. 1, 97 N.W. 515, for the proposition there can be no recovery on the contract as distinguished from *quantum meruit* unless there is substantial performance. This is undoubtedly the correct rule at common law. For recovery on *quantum meruit*, see Valentine v. Patrick Warren Construction Co., 1953, 263 Wis. 143, 56 N.W.2d 860. The question here is whether there has been substantial performance. The test of what amounts to substantial performance seems to be whether the performance meets the essential purpose of the contract. In the Manitowoc case the contract called for a boiler having a capacity of 150 per cent of the existing boiler. The court held there was no substantial performance because the boiler furnished had a capacity of only 82 per cent of the old boiler and only approximately one-half of the boiler capacity contemplated by the contract. In Houlahan v. Clark, 1901, 110 Wis. 43, 85 N.W. 676, the contract provided the plaintiff was to drive pilings in the lake and place a boat house thereon parallel and in line with a neighbor's dock. This was not done and the contractor so positioned the boat house that it was practically useless to the owner. Manthey v. Stock, 1907, 133 Wis. 107, 113 N.W. 443, involved a contract to paint a house and to do a good job, including the removal of the old paint where necessary. The plaintiff did not remove the old paint, and blistering and roughness of the new paint resulted. The court held that the plaintiff failed to show substantial performance. The defendants also cite Manning v. School District No. 6, 1905, 124 Wis. 84, 102 N.W. 356. However, this case involved a contract to install a heating and ventilating plant in the school building which would meet certain tests which the heating apparatus failed to do. The heating plant was practically a total failure to accomplish the purposes of the contract. See also Nees v. Weaver, 1936, 222 Wis. 492, 269 N.W. 266, 107 A.L.R. 1405 (roof on a garage).

Substantial performance as applied to construction of a house does not mean that every detail must be in strict compliance with the specifications and the plans. Something less than perfection is the test of specific [substantial?] performance unless all details are made the essence of the contract. This was not done here. There may be situations in which features or details of construction of special or of great personal importance, if not performed, would prevent a finding of substantial performance of the contract. In this case the plan was a stock floor plan. No detailed construction of the house was shown on the plan. There were no blueprints. The specifications were standard printed forms with some modifications and additions written in by the parties. Many of the problems that arose during the construction had to be solved on the basis of practical experience. No mathematical rule relating to the percentage of the price, of cost of completion, or of completeness can be laid down to determine substantial performance of a building contract. Although the defendants received a house with which they are dissatisfied in many respects, the trial court was not in error in finding the contract was substantially performed.

The next question is what is the amount of recovery when the plaintiff has substantially, but incompletely, performed. For substantial performance the plaintiff should recover the contract price less the damages caused the defendant by the incomplete performance. Both parties agree. Venzke v. Magdanz, 1943, 243 Wis. 155, 9 N.W.2d 604, states the correct rule for damages due to faulty construction amounting to such incomplete performance, which is the difference between the value of the house as it stands with faulty and incomplete construction and the value of the house if it had been constructed in strict accordance with the plans and specifications. This is the diminished-value rule. The cost of replacement or repair is not the measure of such damage, but is an element to take into consideration in arriving at value under some circumstances. The cost of replacement or the cost to make whole the omissions may equal or be less than the difference in value in some cases and, likewise, the cost to rectify a defect may greatly exceed the added value to the structure as corrected. The defendants argue that under the Venzke rule their damages are $10,000. The plaintiff on review argues the defendants' damages are only $650. Both parties agree the trial court applied the wrong rule to the facts.

The trial court applied the cost-of-repair or replacement rule as to several items, relying on Stern v. Schlafer, 1943, 244 Wis. 183, 11 N.W.2d 640, 12 N.W.2d 678, wherein it was stated that when there are a number of small items of defect or omission which can be remedied without the reconstruction of a substantial part of the building or a great sacrifice of work or material already wrought in the building, the reasonable cost of correcting the defect should be allowed. However, in Mohs v. Quarton, 1950, 257 Wis. 544, 44 N.W.2d 580, the court held when the separation of defects would lead to confusion, the rule of diminished value could apply to all defects.

In this case no such confusion arises in separating the defects. The trial court disallowed certain claimed defects because they were not proven. This finding was not against the great weight and clear preponderance of the evidence and will not be disturbed on appeal. Of the remaining defects claimed by the defendants, the court allowed the cost of replacement or repair except as to the misplacement of the living-room wall. Whether a defect should fall under the cost-of-replacement rule or be considered under the diminished-value rule depends upon the nature and magnitude of the defect. This court has not allowed items of such magnitude under the cost-of-repair rule as the trial court did. Viewing the construction of the house as a whole and its cost we cannot say, however, that the trial court was in error in allowing the cost of repairing the plaster cracks in the ceilings, the cost of mud jacking and repairing the patio floor, and the cost of reconstructing the non-weight-bearing and nonstructural patio wall. Such reconstruction did not involve an unreasonable economic waste.

The item of misplacing the living-room wall under the facts of this case was clearly under the diminished-value rule. There is no evidence that defendants requested or demanded the replacement of the wall in the place called for by the specifications during the course of construction. To tear down the wall now and rebuild it in its proper place would involve a substantial destruction of the work, if not all of it, which was put into the wall and would cause additional damage to other parts of the house and require replastering and redecorating the walls and ceilings of at least two rooms. Such economic waste is unreasonable and unjustified. The rule of diminished value contemplates the wall is not going to be moved. Expert witnesses for both parties, testifying as to the value of the house, agreed that the misplacement of the wall had no effect on the market price. The trial court properly found that the defendants suffered no legal damage, although the defendants' particular desire for specified room size was not satisfied. For a discussion of these rules of damages for defective or unfinished construction and their application see Restatement, 1 Contracts, pp. 572–573, sec. 346(1)(a) and illustrations. . . .

Judgment affirmed.

NOTES

(1) *Question.* Was the failure "to furnish the kitchen cabinets, gutters and downspouts, sidewalk, closet poles, and entrance seat" not a "willful" breach? Is Wisconsin's test of substantial performance less exacting than New York's?

(2) *Variations on the Rule.* Courts have sometimes made arbitrary distinctions in an attempt to give more precision to the vague notion of "substantial performance."

It is sometimes said that there can be no substantial performance if there are "structural defects." Where the size and placement of girders was faulty, affecting the solidity of the building, these were "deviations from the general plan of so essential a character that they cannot be remedied without partially reconstructing the building, and hence do not come within the rule of substantial performance." Spence v. Ham, 57 N.E. 412, 414 (N.Y.1900). But see Kizziar v. Dollar, 268 F.2d 914, 917 (10th Cir.1959), in which the court concluded that "the foundation, although not equal to that specified, was standard and adequate for that type of building." Was the misplacement of the wall in Plante v. Jacobs a "structural defect"?

It is sometimes said that there is no substantial performance if the defects exceed a certain percent of the contract price. "Under ordinary circumstances ... a failure to perform 10 percent of the contract price will not admit of the claim of substantial performance." Rochkind v. Jacobson, 110 N.Y.S. 583, 584 (App.Div. 1908). But see Jardine Estates v. Donna Brook Corp., 126 A.2d 372 (N.J.Super.1956) where the court said, "The matter is not to be determined on a percentage basis, for the cost of remedying defects may sometimes even exceed the outlay for original construction."

(3) *Seriatim Objections.* A builder has put up a dwelling, under contract with the owner of the lot, and considers that all the specifications have been met. If, however, the owner disagrees, the builder means to do corrective work. The builder wishes to do all such work at one time, before moving its crew and equipment away. How can the builder elicit a definitive list of the owner's objections?

In Cawley v. Weiner, 140 N.E. 724 (N.Y.1923), the owners of a new bungalow moved in before the builder had stopped work, and handed him a list of 17 items that they considered necessary by way of change in or addition to the structure. For about a week after that, apparently, the builder continued work. Not being paid in full, he brought suit against the owners for the price. At the trial, they offered to prove three particulars, not specified in the earlier list, in which the plaintiff had failed of performance. The trial court excluded the evidence on grounds of waiver and estoppel, and gave the plaintiff judgment for virtually the whole amount he claimed. The owners appealed. *Held:* Reversed.

"Unless the plaintiff were in some way harmed by the action of these defendants in furnishing him with a list of the defects, how are they estopped from showing the departures from the plans and specifications?" Can you reconcile this decision with that in McKenna v. Vernon, p. 711 above?

———

THE PERFECT TENDER RULE

During the nineteenth century a rule developed that a buyer was entitled to reject goods unless the seller made a "perfect tender." The requirement of perfection covered not only the quantity and quality of the goods but also the details of shipment. In the words of Learned Hand, "There is no room in commercial contracts for the doctrine of substantial performance." Mitsubishi Goshi Kaisha v. J. Aron & Co., 16 F.2d 185, 186 (2d Cir.1926). This rule of strict performance remained unchallenged during the first half of the twentieth century. In its terms, it applied even though it was not practical for the seller to resell the rejected goods as, for example, if the goods were perishable or specially manufactured. Because the buyer's right to reject did not depend on the buyer's having been harmed by the breach, the rule offered an inviting pretext for buyers that sought to escape their contract obligations on discovering that they no longer needed the goods or that the market price had fallen. The shortcomings of the rule did not escape criticism.

The drafters of the Uniform Commercial Code gave the following reasons for retaining the perfect tender rule in UCC § 2–601: "first, . . . the buyer should not be required to guess at his peril whether a breach is material; second, . . . proof of materiality would sometimes require disclosure of the buyer's private affairs such as secret formulas or processes."

However, the Code softens the rule in several ways. First, UCC § 2–508 gives a seller the power to cure a defective tender "if the time for performance has not yet expired"—and, in some situations, even if that time has expired. Note that under the Code the decision to attempt to cure is within the seller's discretion. Article 46(2)(3) of the Vienna Convention, however, gives the buyer a right to *require* the seller to cure. Second, UCC § 2–608 allows a buyer who has already accepted goods to revoke that acceptance (and return the goods to the seller) only if the "non-conformity substantially impairs [their] value to him." Third, UCC § 2–612 similarly allows a buyer under a contract for delivery of goods in installments to reject an installment only if a non-conformity as to the goods "substantially impairs the value of that installment" and to claim a breach of the whole contract only for a breach that "substantially impairs the value of the whole contract."

NOTES

(1) *International Solutions.* The Vienna Convention abandons the perfect tender rule in favor of a rule of "fundamental breach." Article 25 defines that term as a breach that "results in such detriment to the other party as substantially to deprive him of what he is entitled to expect under the contract, unless the party in breach did not foresee, and a reasonable person of the same kind in the same circumstances would not have foreseen, such a result."

In *Delchi Carrier*, p. 661 above, the court quoted article 25 and said, "Because the cooling power and energy consumption of an air conditioning compressor are important determinants of the product's value, the district court's conclusion that Rotorex was liable for a fundamental breach of contract under the Convention was proper."

Is the Convention's rule of fundamental breach an improvement on the rule in UCC § 2–601? Is the Convention's formulation better than that in UCC §§ 2–608 and 2–612?

See UNIDROIT Principles art. 7.3.1, which speaks of "fundamental non-performance" and gives a list of factors to be used in determining whether a non-performance is fundamental.

(2) *The Case of the Off–Color Books.* The Supermind Publishing Company paid a deposit to a printing firm under a contract for the production of a book. In an action to recover the deposit, a witness for Supermind, as plaintiff, testified that the books tendered were gray, whereas the defendant's newsprint sample was white; there was also evidence of other defects. On a jury finding that the books failed to conform to the contract, the plaintiff got judgment for the deposit, and the defendant appealed. *Held:* Affirmed.

In dictum the court said that if the printing firm had carried the burden of showing that "the buyer's motivation in rejecting the goods was to escape the bargain," this would have established a breach of the duty of good faith. But there was no evidence that "its primary motivation in rejection of the books was to escape a bad bargain." Such a finding, the court said, might be warranted by evidence of rejection on account of a minor defect, in a falling market. The court cited UCC §§ 1–203 and 2–103(1)(b). Printing Center of Texas, Inc. v. Supermind Publishing Co., Inc., 669 S.W.2d 779 (Tex.Ct.App.1984). Although the court relied on the Code, it expressed grave doubt that the contract was governed by Article 2. Good faith under UCC § 1–202(b)(20) applies to all parties, not just merchants.

Was the court's dictum consistent with UCC § 2–601? How would the court's reasoning have been different if the contract had required that the quality of the books be satisfactory to the plaintiff?

(B) DIVISIBILITY

Gill v. Johnstown Lumber Co.

Supreme Court of Pennsylvania, 1892.
151 Pa. 534, 25 A. 120.

[Assumpsit for driving logs under a written contract, the terms of which are set forth in the opinion. John L. Gill agreed to drive some four million feet of logs, and to begin driving at once, "if sufficient natural water, or by the use of splash dams." The trial court directed a verdict for the Johnstown Lumber Co. on the ground that the contract was "entire" and that Gill defaulted when a flood carried a considerable proportion of the logs past the Johnstown Lumber Co.'s boom.[a] Gill appealed.]

■ HEYDRICK, J. The single question in this cause is whether the contract upon which the plaintiff sued is entire or severable. If it is entire it is conceded that the learned court below properly directed a verdict for the defendant; if severable, it is not denied that the cause ought to have been submitted to the jury. The criterion by which it is to be determined to which class any particular contract shall be assigned is thus stated in 1 Parsons on Contracts, 29–31: "If the part to be performed by one party consists of several and distinct items, and the price to be paid by the other is (1) apportioned to each item to be performed, or (2) is left to be implied by law, such a contract will generally be held to be severable.... But if the consideration to be paid is single and entire the contract must be held to be entire, although the subject of the contract may consist of several distinct and wholly independent items." The rule thus laid down was ... applied in Ritchie v. Atkinson, 10 East, 295, a case not unlike the present. There the master and freighter of a vessel of four hundred tons mutually agreed that

---

a. On May 31, 1889, ten days after the date of the contract, the then-largest earthen dam, above Johnstown, broke. More than 2,000 lives were lost. That and other flooding in the area, caused by a great rain, carried log booms estimated at many millions of feet of timber into the Potomac River and the Chesapeake Bay. R. O'Connor, Johnstown— The Day the Dam Broke (1957).

the ship should proceed to St. Petersburg, and there load from the freighter's factors a complete cargo of hemp and iron and deliver the same to the freighter at London on being paid freight for hemp £5 per ton, for iron 5s. per ton, and certain other charges, one half to be paid on delivery and the other at three months. The vessel proceeded to St. Petersburg, and when about half loaded was compelled by the imminence of a Russian embargo upon British vessels to leave, and returning to London deliver to the freighter so much of the stipulated cargo as had been taken on board. The freighter, conceiving that the contract was entire and the delivery of a complete cargo a condition precedent to a recovery of any compensation, refused to pay at the stipulated rate for so much as was delivered. Lord Ellenborough said: "The delivery of the cargo is in its nature, divisible, and therefore I think it is not a condition precedent; but the plaintiff is entitled to recover freight in proportion to the extent of such delivery; leaving the defendant to his remedy in damages for the short delivery."

Applying the test of an apportionable or apportioned consideration to the contract in question, it will be seen at once that it is severable. The work undertaken to be done by the plaintiff consisted of several items, viz., driving logs, first, of oak, and second of various other kinds of timber, from points upon Stony creek and its tributaries above Johnstown to the defendant's boom at Johnstown, and also driving cross-ties from some undesignated point or points, presumably understood by the parties, to Bethel in Somerset county, and to some other point or points below Bethel. For this work the consideration to be paid was not an entire sum, but was apportioned among the several items at the rate of one dollar per thousand feet for the oak logs; seventy-five cents per thousand feet for all other logs; three cents each for cross-ties driven to Bethel, and five cents each for cross-ties driven to points below Bethel. But while the contract is severable, and the plaintiff entitled to compensation at the stipulated rate for all logs and ties delivered at the specified points, there is neither reason nor authority for the claim for compensation in respect to logs that were swept by the flood to and through the defendant's boom, whether they had been driven part of the way by the plaintiff or remained untouched by him at the coming of the flood. In respect to each particular log the contract in this case is like a contract of common carriage, which is dependent upon the delivery of the goods at the designated place, and if by *casus* the delivery is prevented the carrier cannot recover pro tanto for freight for part of the route over which the goods were taken: Wharton, Law of Contracts, sec. 714. Indeed this is but an application of the rule already stated. The consideration to be paid for driving each log is an entire sum per thousand feet for the whole distance and is not apportioned or apportionable to parts of the drive.

The judgment is reversed and a venire facias de novo is awarded.

NOTES

(1) *Questions.* If some of the oak logs had been driven halfway, might the plaintiff have recovered at the rate of 50¢ per thousand feet for them? Why was the contract not divisible by distances?

(2) *The Case of the Magic Tees.* The Army Signal Corps made an "Industrial Preparedness Contract" with Lerner under which Lerner was to equip itself for the production, in volume, of an item called a microwave magic tee. The work was to be done in four steps, the first three of which involved a pilot run and the acquisition of equipment. Step IV was to be taken on Government order only in case of a national emergency and required volume production of the magic tees. Lerner was obligated to maintain a status of readiness for this over a six-year period. When the first three steps had been substantially completed and the Government had paid Lerner about $128,000, Lerner transferred all its assets to assignees for the benefit of creditors, as an alternative to bankruptcy. The assignees sued the Government for about $45,000, the sum owed for completing the first three steps. The Government counterclaimed for damages and moved for summary judgment. *Held:* Summary judgment granted.

The court considered the purpose of the contract and concluded that the first three steps were "merely incidental to Step IV, which was the ultimate objective. . . . The duty to stand by and be ready to perform Step IV was the essential element of the bargain. The contract was not divisible." The assignment for the benefit of creditors operated as a total breach, for it is an implied condition in every contract that the promisor will not permit itself to be disabled from performing. Pennsylvania Exchange Bank v. United States, 170 F.Supp. 629 (Ct.Cl.1959).

(3) *Uses of Divisibility.* Reconsider the "rice" case, *Internatio–Rotterdam,* p. 695 above. What argument did the buyer try to combat by maintaining that the contract was not divisible? Compare the plaintiff's claim in that case and the defendant's contention in Gill v. Johnstown Lumber Co. Does it seem that the doctrine of divisibility has various uses?

In the rice case, would the seller have been *justified* in withholding further shipments to Lake Charles after December 17th? If it had done so, how would you compare the merits of the buyer's claim with that in Gill v. Johnstown Lumber Company? With the claim in Pennsylvania Exchange Bank v. United States?

(C) RESTITUTION

We have seen a variety of situations in which restitution may be available. In many of these situations there is no agreement that can be enforced. The parties may not have dealt with one another (Chapter 1) , or they may have engaged in negotiations that fell short of a contract (Chapter 2), or they may have made an agreement that proved to be unenforceable for some reason such as the statute of frauds (Chapter 3), or a contravention of public policy (Chapter 4). Restitution was also introduced in our discussions of remedies (Chapter 7), and the nonoccurrence of a condition (Chapter 8). As we will see in Chapter 9, restitution may also be available when an agreement has become unenforceable by reason of mistake, impracticability of performance, or frustration of purpose.

As we saw in cases of losing contracts, even when there is a breach of an enforceable agreement, the *aggrieved* party may prefer restitution to other forms of relief, and it is commonly available (see Note 3, p. 19 above and *Algernon Blair,* p. 626 above). But what of restitution for a party *in breach* of an enforceable agreement? If that party has performed in part, and is unable to enforce the contract because it has failed to complete performance, may it nevertheless get restitution? Such claims have met serious resistance, especially when the plaintiff's breach may be characterized as "willful." The remarks of the court in the venerable case of Lawrence v. Miller 86 N.Y. 131, 140 (1881), represent the traditional response. "To allow a recovery of this money would be to sustain an action by a party on his own breach of his own contract, which the law does not allow.... That would be ill doctrine."

Some other responses are shown in this section. The following case is a watershed.

Britton v. Turner

Supreme Court of Judicature of New Hampshire, 1834.
6 N.H. 481.

Assumpsit, for work and labor, performed by the plaintiff, in the service of the defendant, from March 9, 1831, to December 27, 1831.

The declaration contained the common counts, and among them a count in quantum meruit, for the labor, averring it to be worth $100.

At the trial in the C.C. Pleas, the plaintiff proved the performance of the labor as set forth in the declaration.

The defense was that it was performed under a special contract; that the plaintiff agreed to work one year, from some time in March, 1831, to March, 1832, and that the defendant was to pay him for said year's labor the sum of $120; and the defendant offered evidence tending to show that such was the contract under which the work was done. Evidence was also offered to show that the plaintiff left the defendant's service without his consent, and it was contended by the defendant that the plaintiff had no good cause for not continuing in his employment. There was no evidence offered of any damage arising from the plaintiff's departure, farther than was to be inferred from his nonfulfillment of the entire contract.

The court instructed the jury that, if they were satisfied from the evidence that the labor was performed under a contract to labor a year, for the sum of $120, and if they were satisfied that the plaintiff labored only the time specified in the declaration, and then left the defendant's service, against his consent, and without any good cause, yet the plaintiff was entitled to recover, under his quantum meruit count, as much as the labor he performed was reasonably worth, and under this direction the jury gave a verdict for the plaintiff for the sum of $95.

The defendant excepted to the instructions thus given to the jury.

■ PARKER, J., delivered the opinion of the court. It may be assumed that the labor performed by the plaintiff, and for which he seeks to recover a compensation in this action, was commenced under a special contract to labor for the defendant the term of one year, for the sum of $120, and that the plaintiff has labored but a portion of that time, and has voluntarily failed to complete the entire contract.

It is clear, then, that he is not entitled to recover upon the contract itself, because the service, which was to entitle him to the sum agreed upon, has never been performed.

But the question arises: Can the plaintiff, under these circumstances, recover a reasonable sum for the service he has actually performed, under the count in quantum meruit? Upon this, and questions of a similar nature, the decisions to be found in the books are not easily reconciled.

It has been held, upon contracts of this kind for labor to be performed at a specified price, that the party who voluntarily fails to fulfill the contract by performing the whole labor contracted for, is not entitled to recover anything for the labor actually performed, however much he may have done towards the performance, and this has been considered the settled rule of law upon this subject. [Citations of Massachusetts, New York and English cases omitted.]

That such rule in its operation may be very unequal, not to say unjust, is apparent. A party who contracts to perform certain specified labor, and who breaks his contract in the first instance, without any attempt to perform it, can only be made liable to pay the damages which the other party has sustained by reason of such non-performance, which in many instances may be trifling; whereas a party who in good faith has entered upon the performance of his contract, and nearly completed it, and then abandoned the further performance, although the other party has had the full benefit of all that has been done, and has perhaps sustained no actual damage, is in fact subjected to a loss of all which has been performed, in the nature of damages for the non-fulfillment of the remainder, upon the technical rule, that the contract must be fully performed in order to [sustain] a recovery of any part of the compensation.

By the operation of this rule, then, the party who attempts performance may be placed in a much worse situation than he who wholly disregards his contract, and the other party may receive much more, by the breach of the contract, than the injury which he has sustained by such breach, and more than he could be entitled to were he seeking to recover damages by an action.

The case before us presents an illustration. Had the plaintiff in this case never entered upon the performance of his contract, the damage could not probably have been greater than some small expense and trouble incurred in procuring another to do the labor which he had contracted to perform. But having entered upon the performance, and labored nine and a half months, the value of which labor to the defendant as found by the jury is $95, if the defendant can succeed in this defense, he in fact receives nearly five-sixths of the value of a whole year's labor, by reason of the breach of contract by the plaintiff, a sum not only utterly disproportionate to any probable, not to say possible damage which could have resulted from the neglect of the plaintiff to continue the remaining two and a half months, but altogether beyond any damage which could have been recovered by the defendant, had the plaintiff done nothing towards the fulfillment of his contract.

Another illustration is furnished in Lantry v. Parks, 8 Cow., N.Y., 63. There the defendant hired the plaintiff for a year, at ten dollars per month. The plaintiff worked ten and a half months, and then left saying he would work no more for him. This was on Saturday—on Monday the plaintiff returned, and offered to resume his work, but the defendant said he would employ him no longer. The court held that the refusal of the defendant [plaintiff?] on Saturday was a violation of his contract, and that he could recover nothing for the labor performed.

There are other cases, however, in which principles have been adopted leading to a different result.

It is said, that where a party contracts to perform certain work, and to furnish materials, as, for instance, to build a house, and the work is done, but with some variations from the mode prescribed by the contract, yet if the other party has the benefit of the labor and materials he should be bound to pay so much as they are reasonably worth. 2 Stark.Ev. 97, 98; Hayward v. Leonard, 7 Pick., Mass., 181. . . .

A different doctrine seems to have been holden in Ellis v. Hamlen, 3 Taunt. 52, and it is apparent, in such cases, that if the house has not been built in the manner specified in the contract, the work has not been done. The party has no more performed what he contracted to perform, than he who has contracted to labor for a certain period, and failed to complete the time.

It is in truth virtually conceded in such cases that the work has not been done, for, if it had been, the party performing it would be entitled to recover upon the contract itself, which it is held he cannot do.

Those cases are not to be distinguished, in principle, from the present, unless it be in the circumstance, that where the party has contracted to furnish materials, and do certain labor, as to build a house in a specified manner, if it is not done according to the contract, the party for whom it is built may refuse to receive it—elect to take no benefit from what has been performed—and therefore, if he does receive, he shall be bound to pay the value; whereas in a contract for labor, merely, from day to day, the party is continually receiving the benefit of the contract under an expectation that it will be fulfilled, and cannot, upon the breach of it, have an election to refuse to receive what has been done, and thus discharge himself from payment.

But we think this difference in the nature of the contracts does not justify the application of a different rule in relation to them. The party who contracts for labor merely, for a certain period, does so with full knowledge that he must, from the nature of the case, be accepting part performance from day to day, if the other party commences the performance, and with knowledge also that the other may eventually fail of completing the entire term. If under such circumstances he actually receives a benefit from the labor performed, over and above the damage occasioned by the failure to complete, there is as much reason why he should pay the reasonable worth of what has thus been done for his benefit, as there is when he enters and occupies the house which has been built for him, but not according to the stipulations of the contract, and which he perhaps enters, not because he is satisfied with what has been done, but because circumstances compel him to accept it such as it is, that he should pay for the value of the house.

Where goods are sold upon a special contract as to their nature, quality, and price, and have been used before their inferiority has been discovered, or other circumstances have concurred which have rendered it impracticable or inconvenient for the vendee to rescind the contract in toto, it seems to have been the practice formerly to allow the vendor to recover the stipulated price, and the vendee recovered by a cross-action damages for the breach of the contract. "But according to the later and more convenient practice, the vendee in such case is allowed, in an action for the price, to give evidence of the inferiority of the goods in reduction of damages, and the plaintiff who has broken his contract is not entitled to recover more than the value of the benefits which the defendant has actually derived from the goods; and where the latter has derived no benefit, the plaintiff cannot recover at all." 2 Stark.Ev. 640, 642; Okell v. Smith, 1 Starkie's Rep. 107. . . .

There is a close analogy between all these classes of cases, in which such diverse decisions have been made.

If the party who has contracted to receive merchandise takes a part and uses it, in expectation that the whole will be delivered, which is never done, there seems to be no greater reason that he should pay for what he has received than there is that the party who has received labor in part, under similar circumstances, should pay the value of what has been done for his benefit.

It is said that in those cases where the plaintiff has been permitted to recover there was an acceptance of what had been done. The answer is that where the contract is to labor from day to day, for a certain period, the party for whom the labor is done in truth stipulates to receive it from day to day, as it is performed, and although the other may not eventually do all he has contracted to do, there has been, necessarily, an acceptance of what has been done in pursuance of the contract, and the party must have understood when he made the contract that there was to be such acceptance.

If, then, the party stipulates in the outset to receive part performance from time to time, with a knowledge that the whole may not be completed, we see no reason why he should not equally be holden to pay for the amount of value received, as where he afterwards takes the benefit of what has been done, with a knowledge that the whole which was contracted for has not been performed. In neither case has the contract been performed. In neither can an action be sustained on the original contract. In both the party has assented to receive what is done. The only difference is that in the one case the assent is prior, with a knowledge that all may not be performed; in the other it is subsequent, with a knowledge that the whole has not been accomplished.

We have no hesitation in holding that the same rule should be applied to both classes of cases, especially as the operation of the rule will be to make the party who has failed to fulfill his contract liable to such amount of damages as the other party has sustained, instead of subjecting him to an entire loss for a partial failure, and thus making the amount received in many cases wholly disproportionate to the injury. 1 Saund. 320, c; 2 Stark.Ev. 643. It is as "hard upon the plaintiff to preclude him from recovering at all, because he has failed as to part of his entire undertaking," where his contract is to labor for a certain period, as it can be in any other description of contract, provided the defendant has received a benefit and value from the labor actually performed.

We hold, then, that where a party undertakes to pay upon a special contract for the performance of labor, or the furnishing of materials, he is not to be charged upon such special agreement until the money is earned according to the terms of it, and where the parties have made an express contract the law will not imply and raise a contract different from that which the parties have entered into, except upon some farther transaction between the parties.

In case of a failure to perform such special contract, by the default of the party contracting to do the service, if the money is not due by the terms of the special agreement he is not entitled to recover for his labor, or for the materials furnished, unless the other party receives what has been done, or furnished, and upon the whole case derives a benefit from it. Taft v. Montague, 14 Mass. 282; 2 Stark.Ev. 644.

But if, where a contract is made of such a character, a party actually receives labor, or materials, and thereby derives a benefit and advantage, over and above the damage which has resulted from the breach of the contract by the other party, the labor actually done, and the value received, furnish a new consideration, and the law thereupon raises a promise to pay to the extent of the reasonable worth of such excess. This may be considered as making a new case, one not within the original agreement, and the party is entitled to "recover on his new case, for the work done, not as agreed, but yet accepted by the defendant." 1 Dane's Abr. 224.

If on such failure to perform the whole, the nature of the contract be such that the employer can reject what has been done, and refuse to receive any benefit from the part performance, he is entitled so to do, and in such case is not liable to be charged, unless he has before assented to and accepted of what has been done, however much the other party may have done towards the performance. He has in such case received nothing, and having contracted to receive nothing but the entire matter contracted for, he is not bound to pay, because his express promise was only to pay on receiving the whole, and having actually received nothing the law cannot and ought not to raise an implied promise to pay. But where the party receives value—takes and uses the materials, or has advantage from the labor, he is liable to pay the reasonable worth of what he has received. Farnsworth v. Garrard, 1 Camp. 38. And the rule is the same whether it was received and accepted by the assent of the party prior to the breach, under a contract by which, from its nature, he was to receive labor, from time to time until the completion of the whole contract, or whether it was received and accepted by an assent subsequent to the performance of all which was in fact done. If he received it under such circumstances as precluded him from rejecting it afterwards, that does not alter the case—it has still been received by his assent.

In fact, we think the technical reasoning—that the performance of the whole labor is a condition precedent, and the right to recover anything dependent upon it; that, the contract being entire, there can be no apportionment; and that, there being an express contract, no other can be implied, even upon the subsequent performance of service—is not properly applicable to this species of contract, where a beneficial service has been actually performed; for we have abundant reason to believe, that the general understanding of the community is that the hired laborer shall be entitled to compensation for the service actually performed, though he do not continue the entire term contracted for, and such contracts must be presumed to be made with reference to that understanding, unless an express stipulation shows the contrary. . . .

It is easy, if parties so choose, to provide by an express agreement that nothing shall be earned, if the laborer leaves his employer without having performed the whole service contemplated, and then there can be no pretense for a recovery if he voluntarily deserts the service before the expiration of the time.

The amount, however, for which the employer ought to be charged, where the laborer abandons his contract, is only the reasonable worth, or the amount of advantage he receives upon the whole transaction (Wadleigh v. Sutton, 6 N.H. 15), and, in estimating the value of the labor, the contract price for the service cannot be exceeded. . . .

If a person makes a contract fairly, he is entitled to have it fully performed; and, if this is not done, he is entitled to damages. He may maintain a suit to recover the amount of damage sustained by the non-performance. The benefit and advantage which the party takes by the labor, therefore, is the amount of value which he receives, if any, after deducting the amount of damage; and if he elects to put this in defense he is entitled so to do, and the implied promise which the law will raise, in such case, is to pay such amount of the stipulated price for the whole labor, as remains after deducting what it would cost to procure a completion of the residue of the service and also any damage which has been sustained by reason of the nonfulfillment of the contract. If in such case it be found that the damages are equal to or greater than the amount of the labor performed, so that the employer, having a right to the full performance of the contract, has not upon the whole case received a beneficial service, the plaintiff cannot recover. . . .

Applying the principles thus laid down, to this case, the plaintiff is entitled to judgment on the verdict. The defendant sets up a mere breach of the contract in defense of the action, but this cannot avail him. He does not appear to have offered evidence to show that he was damnified by such breach, or to have asked that a deduction should be made upon that account. The direction to the jury was therefore correct, that the plaintiff was entitled to recover as much as the labor performed was reasonably worth, and the jury appear to have allowed a pro rata compensation, for the time which the plaintiff labored in the defendant's service.

As the defendant has not claimed or had any adjustment of damages, for the breach of the contract, in this action, if he has actually sustained damage he is still entitled to a suit to recover the amount.....

Judgment on the verdict.

NOTES

(1) *Pay Periods.* Was the contract divisible by months? How much would Britton have recovered if it were?

Employee claims, based either on divisibility or restitution, are of little importance today because statutes generally require that employees be paid no less frequently than monthly.

(2) *Trend.* In 1978, Professor George Palmer reported that the doctrine of Britton v. Turner was still a minority position. 1 G. Palmer, Law of Restitution § 5.13 (1978). Thirty years later, Professor Robert Gordon observed that "legislation mandating regular wage payments has rendered the doctrine of the case mostly irrelevant." Robert W. Gordon, Britton v. Turner: A signpost on the Crooked Road to "Freedom" in the Employment Contract, in Contract Stories (Douglas G. Baird, ed.) 2007, p. 187. The trend, however, is plainly in its favor. Both the UCC § 2–718(2) and Restatement § 374 state rules in accord with the doctrine from the case.

PROBLEM

Lawyer–Client Relations. Begovich, who was charged with murder, retained Murphy to defend him and paid him a total of $6,500. Murphy consulted with his client and made two appearances in his behalf, these services not being worth more than $2,500. At that point Begovich committed suicide. The administrator of the estate sued Murphy for $4,000, and Murphy demurred. What decision? See Begovich v. Murphy, 101 N.W.2d 278 (Mich.1960).

Kirkland v. Archbold

Court of Appeals of Ohio, Cuyahoga County, 1953.
113 N.E.2d 496.

[The plaintiff contracted to make alterations and repairs on a dwelling house owned by the defendant. Paragraph 20 of the contract provided: "The Owner agrees to pay the Contractor, as follows: $1,000 when satisfactory work has been done for ten days; an additional $1,000 when twenty days work has been completed; an additional $1,000 when thirty days work has been completed, and $1,000 on completion of the contract. $2,000 shall be paid within thirty days after the completion of the contract." After the plaintiff had worked for two months on the job he was prevented from proceeding further. He claims that he and his sub-contractors had reasonably expended $2,985 at that point. He has been paid only $800, and he sues for damages in the amount of the difference.

The trial court found that the plaintiff was in default in attempting to plaster the house over wood lath instead of rock lath, and without the use of rock wool. Paragraph 4 of the contract provided: "All outside walls are to be lined with rock wool and rock lathe, superimposed thereon." Thus the defendant was within her rights in preventing the plaintiff from proceeding. However, the court held that her payment of $800 was an admission that the first installment of the price was earned, and gave the plaintiff judgment for $200. The plaintiff appealed.]

■ Skeel, Presiding Judge. . . . The court committed error prejudicial to the rights of plaintiff in holding that the provisions of the contract were severable. The plaintiff agreed to make certain repairs and improvements on the defendant's property for which he was to be paid $6,000. The total consideration was to be paid for the total work specified in the contract. The fact that a schedule of payments was set up based on the progress of the work does not change the character of the agreement. Newman Lumber Co. v. Purdum, 41 Ohio St. 373.

The court found that the plaintiff and not the defendant breached the agreement, leaving the job without just cause, when the work agreed upon was far from completed. In fact, the plaintiff by his pleadings and evidence does not attempt to claim substantial performance on his part. The question is, therefore, clearly presented on the facts as the court found them to be, as to whether or not the plaintiff being found in default can maintain a cause of action for only part performance of his contract.

The earlier case law of Ohio has refused to permit a plaintiff to found an action on the provisions of a contract where he himself is in default. The only exception to the rule recognized is where the plaintiff has substantially performed his part of the agreement. . . .

The result of decisions which deny a defaulting contractor all right of recovery even though his work has enriched the estate of the other party to the contract is to penalize the defaulting contractor to the extent of the value of all benefit conferred by his work and materials upon the property of the other party. This result comes from unduly emphasizing the technical unity and entirety of contracts. Some decisions permit such result only when the defaulting contractor's conduct was willful or malicious.

An ever-increasing number of decisions of courts of last resort now modify the severity of this rule and permit defaulting contractors, where their work has contributed substantial value to the other contracting party's property, to recover the value of the work and materials expended on a quantum meruit basis, the recovery being diminished, however, to the extent of such damage as the contractor's breach causes the other party. These decisions are based on the theory of unjust enrichment. The action is not founded on the broken contract but on a quasi-contract to pay for the benefits received, which cannot be returned, diminished by the damages sustained because of the contractor's breach of his contract.

The leading case supporting this theory of the law is Britton v. Turner, 6 N.H. 481, 26 Am.Dec. 713. . . .

Williston on Contracts, Vol. 5, p. 4123, par. 1475, says: "The element of forfeiture in wholly denying recovery to a plaintiff who is materially in default is most strikingly exemplified in building contracts. It has already been seen how, under the name of substantial performance, many courts have gone beyond the usual principles governing contracts in allowing relief in an action on the contract. But many cases of hardship cannot be brought within the doctrine of substantial performance, even if it is liberally interpreted; and the weight of authority strongly supports the statement that a builder, whose breach of contract is merely negligent, can recover the value of his work less the damages caused by his default; but that one who has wilfully abandoned or broken his contract cannot recover. The classical English doctrine, it is true, has denied recovery altogether where there has been a material breach even though it was due to negligence rather than wilfulness; and a few decisions in the United States follow this rule, where the builder has not substantially performed. But the English court has itself abandoned it and now holds that where a builder has supplied work and labor for the erection or repair of a house under a lump sum contract, but has departed from the terms of the contract, he is entitled to recover for his services and materials, unless (1) the work that he has done has been of no benefit to the owner; (2) the work he has done is entirely different from the work which he has contracted to do; or (3) he has abandoned the work and left it unfinished. The courts often do not discuss the question whether one who has intentionally abandoned the contract did so merely to get out of a bad bargain or whether he acted in a mistaken belief that a just cause existed for the abandonment. Where the latter situation exists, however, it would seem that the defaulter might properly be given recovery for his part performance. It seems probable that the tendency of decisions will favor a builder who has not been guilty of conscious moral fault in abandoning the contract or in its performance."

The drastic rule of forfeiture against a defaulting contractor who has by his labor and materials materially enriched the estate of the other party should in natural justice, be afforded relief to the reasonable value of the work done, less whatever damage the other party has suffered. . . .

We conclude, therefore, that the judgment is contrary to law as to the method by which the right to judgment was determined. . . .

For the foregoing reasons the judgment is reversed and the cause is remanded for further proceedings.

NOTES

(1) *Divisibility.* Can the court's holding that the contract was not divisible because the "total consideration was to be paid for the total work" be reconciled with the decision in *Internatio–Rotterdam,* p. 695 above? Would the trial court's treatment of the contract in *Kirkland* as divisible have been justified if the *defendant* had broken the contract rather than the plaintiff?

(2) *Sales of Goods.* UCC § 2–718(2), which gives a defaulting buyer a right to restitution, follows the trend set by Britton v. Turner. The Code provision was examined in *Diasonics,* p. 619 above, where the court explained that absent proof of Diasonics' damages as a lost volume seller, Davis would have been entitled to the return of all but $500 of its $300,000 down payment.

If a seller delivers part of the goods contracted for, and defaults as to the rest, having received no payment, is the seller entitled to the price fixed by the contract for the goods delivered, or to the amount by which the buyer is enriched? See UCC § 2–607(1).

(3) *Sales of Land.* The traditional rule that denies restitution to a party in breach has been particularly tenacious in connection with down payments by purchasers of land.

In 1986, the New York Court of Appeals declined to overrule its century-old decision in Lawrence v. Miller, quoted at p. 736 above. "The rule permitting a party in default to seek restitution for part performance has much to commend it in its general applications. But as applied to real estate down payments approximating 10% it does not appear to offer a better or more workable rule than the long-established 'usage' in this State with respect to the seller's right to retain a down payment upon default." In a footnote, however, the court emphasized that it expressed no view as to payments in excess of 10%. Maxton Builders, Inc. v. Lo Galbo, 502 N.E.2d 184, 188–89 (N.Y.1986).

In 1980, the Supreme Court of Connecticut arrived at a similar result from the opposite direction. In Vines v. Orchard Hills, Inc., 435 A.2d 1022, 1027, 1029 (Conn.1980), the court began by explaining "that a purchaser whose breach is not willful has a restitutionary claim to recover moneys that unjustly enrich his seller." But it concluded that the seller was entitled to retain the buyer's down payment of 10%, which had been designated in the contract as liquidated damages, because a "liquidated damages clause allowing the seller to retain 10 percent of the contract price as earnest money is presumptively a reasonable allocation of the risks associated with default." The presumption is a rebuttable one.

In 1991, the Supreme Court of New Jersey overruled cases adhering to the common law rule and adopted "the modern approach" of Restatement § 374(1). In Kutzin v. Pirnie, 591 A.2d 932, 941 (N.J.1991), the court held that the defaulting purchasers were entitled "to restitution for any benefit that they conferred by way of part performance or reliance in excess of the loss that they caused by their own breach," but noted that they had the burden of proving unjust enrichment. The holding was "not affected by the fact that the $36,000 deposit was less than ten percent of the $365,000 purchase price." However, the contract said nothing about liquidated damages.

PROBLEM

Variations on a Theme. Suppose that in *Luttinger*, p. 692 above, the Luttingers had not made any attempt to get a mortgage. Could the Rosens have retained the $8,500 or any part of it? Would the answer be different if the amount had been $12,750 instead of $8,500? Would the answers be different if the house had been in New York? In New Jersey? Would it make a difference if the contract had provided that in case of default by the Luttingers the Rosens could retain the $8,500 "as liquidated damages"? Suppose it had provided that they could retain the $8,500 "as liquidated damages at their option"?

SECTION 4.   SUSPENDING PERFORMANCE AND TERMINATING THE CONTRACT

Courts developed the doctrine of substantial performance to deal with the relatively simple case in which the party in breach has finished performing and the injured party refuses to pay the price because the performance is defective or incomplete. Often the dispute arises at a much earlier stage of performance, however, and the question is whether a breach justifies the injured party in exercising a right to self-help by suspending performance or by refusing to render performance and terminating the contract. Sometimes the injured party is the defendant, seeking merely to justify its nonperformance in an action that has been brought by the other party. Sometimes the injured party is the plaintiff, seeking to justify its nonperformance in an action that it has brought against the other party for damages for total breach. These cases of breach in the course of performance pose particularly thorny problems of counseling.

It may be useful at this point to have an idea of the analysis used in the Restatement to deal with these problems that arise when an aggrieved party seeks to suspend performance or to refuse to render performance and terminate the contract.

At the outset, one asks whether there is an uncured breach by the other party, since the problems we are addressing arise only if there is a breach. Next one asks whether it is a breach of a duty of performance that was to be exchanged under an exchange of promises (as opposed to a duty under a promise on which the injured party's promise does not depend). Under the Restatement analysis it is presumed that this is the case unless "a contrary intention is clearly manifested." Comment *a* to Restatement § 232. Then one asks whether the breach went to a performance that was to be rendered at an earlier time than that of the aggrieved party. See Restatement § 237.

The next question is the one that often occasions dispute. Assuming that there is an uncured breach by the other party with respect to a performance due at an earlier time under an exchange of promises, is the breach serious enough to justify self-help in the form of suspension or termination? Is it what is called a *material* breach? See Restatement § 241. If the breach is *not* a material breach, the aggrieved party has no choice but to continue performance and treat the breach as a *partial* breach, which gives a right to damages but not a right to suspend or terminate. If the breach *is* a material breach, however, the aggrieved party has a choice: either continue performance and treat the breach as a partial breach or stop performing and treat the breach as a *total* breach. (It may help to realize that in the Restatement vernacular, whether a breach is to be characterized as *material* or *not material* is not within the control of the aggrieved party, but whether to treat a material breach as *partial* or *total* is a matter for decision by the aggrieved party.) Treating the breach as a total breach has drastic consequences: "it discharges the injured party's remaining duties" and it "gives rise to a claim for damages for total breach."

If the circumstances make it appropriate for the aggrieved party to suspend performance and give the other party a chance to cure, the aggrieved party is expected to do so before treating the breach as total. Circumstances that are significant in determining how long an aggrieved party, having suspended, must wait before terminating are listed in Restatement § 242.

For an analysis in Restatement terms, see 2 Farnsworth on Contracts §§ 8.16, 8.17, 8.18 (2d ed.1998).

AFTER–ACQUIRED EVIDENCE

Suppose that a party terminates a contract without justification, but later discovers facts that, had they been known, would have justified termination. Can the party use those facts to avoid liability? The prevailing view is that it can use those facts even though it was ignorant of them at the time of termination. This view that after-acquired evidence can provide a complete defense has been called into question, however, in connection with employment agreements.

Johnson v. Honeywell Info. Sys., Inc., 955 F.2d 409, 413 (6th Cir.1992), arose out of a suit by an employee for breach of a just-cause employment contract. The court concluded that under the prevailing view, "the Michigan Supreme Court would hold that just cause for termination of employment may include facts unknown to an employer at the time of dismissal, though obviously such facts would be neither the actual nor inducing cause for the discharge." On this reasoning, after-acquired evidence may enable an employer to entirely escape liability. In Lewis v. Fisher Service Co., 495 S.E.2d 440, 445 (S.C.1998), the court reached a similar conclusion in a handbook case, adding the requirement that "by clear and convincing evidence it [be] proven that the employee's wrongdoing was of such severity that the employee in fact would have been terminated on these grounds alone if the employer had known of it at the time of the discharge."

Courts have, however, recognized "that the use of after-acquired evidence in connection with employment agreements presents some policy concerns." These include fears "that employers and their lawyers will scour the employee's work record and interview co-workers in an attempt to dig up on-the-job misconduct," that "an employer might ignore employee wrongdoing, but tuck away that knowledge for the day that a charge of discrimination is made," or that "an employee might endure repeated harassment or discrimination without complaint because she knows her work record is not spotless." Noting these fears, the Supreme Court of Arizona adhered "to the traditional contract approach" for claims based on an employment contract, but took a different approach for claims in tort, like that in Sheets v. Teddy's Frosted Foods, p. 562 above, for wrongful termination in violation of public policy.[a] As to these claims, the court concluded that an employer can use after-acquired evidence if it "can demonstrate that it would have fired an employee had it known of prior

a. An important employment agreement case is McKennon v. Nashville Banner Publ'g Co., 513 U.S. 352, 358, 362 (1995) (Kennedy, J.). Unlike the employee in *Sheets*, the employee in *McKennon* claimed that her discharge was explicitly prohibited by a federal statute, the Age Discrimination in Employment Act. After observing that the objectives of that statute "are furthered when even a single employee establishes that an employer has discriminated," the Court concluded that "the beginning point in the trial court's formulation of a remedy should be calculation of backpay from the date of the unlawful discharge to the date the new information was discovered."

misconduct," but even then the employee can recover for lost earnings "for the period between the time of discharge and the time the employer discovers the misconduct." O'Day v. McDonnell Douglas Helicopter Co., 959 P.2d 792, 796–97, 799 (Ariz.1998). The court added that "after-acquired evidence does not affect other compensatory damages attributable to the employer's wrongful conduct, including any decrease in earning capacity, and punitive damages, if they are otherwise warranted by the evidence."

Walker & Co. v. Harrison

Supreme Court of Michigan, 1957.
347 Mich. 630, 81 N.W.2d 352.

■ SMITH, JUSTICE. This is a suit on a written contract. The defendants are in the dry-cleaning business. Walker & Company, plaintiff, sells, rents, and services advertising signs and billboards. These parties entered into an agreement pertaining to a sign. The agreement is in writing and is termed a "rental agreement." It specifies in part that:

"The lessor agrees to construct and install, at its own cost, one 18′ 9″ high × 8′ 8″ wide pylon type d.f. neon sign with electric clock and flashing lamps. . . . The lessor agrees to and does hereby lease or rent unto the said lessee the said SIGN for the term, use and rental and under the conditions, hereinafter set out, and the lessee agrees to pay said rental. . . .

"(a) The term of this lease shall be 36 months. . . .

"(b) The rental to be paid by lessee shall be $148.50 per month for each and every calendar month during the term of this lease; . . . .

"(d) Maintenance. Lessor at its expense agrees to maintain and service the sign together with such equipment as supplied and installed by the lessor to operate in conjunction with said sign under the terms of this lease; this service is to include cleaning and repainting of sign in original color scheme as often as deemed necessary by lessor to keep sign in first class advertising condition and make all necessary repairs to sign and equipment installed by lessor. . . ."

At the "expiration of this agreement," it was also provided, "title to this sign reverts to lessee." This clause is in addition to the printed form of agreement and was apparently added as a result of defendants' concern over title, they having expressed a desire "to buy for cash" and the salesman, at one time, having "quoted a cash price."

The sign was completed and installed in the latter part of July, 1953. The first billing of the monthly payment of $148.50 was made August 1, 1953, with payment thereof by defendants on September 3, 1953. The first payment was also the last. Shortly after the sign was installed, someone hit it with a tomato. Rust, also, was visible on the chrome, complained defendants, and in its corners were "little spider cobwebs." In addition, there were "some children's sayings written down in here." Defendant Herbert Harrison called Walker for the maintenance he believed himself entitled to under subparagraph (d) above. It was not forthcoming. He called again and again. "I was getting, you might say, sorer and sorer.... Occasionally, when I started calling up, I would walk around where the tomato was and get mad again. Then I would call up on the phone again." Finally, on October 8, 1953, plaintiff not having responded to his repeated calls, he telegraphed Walker that:

"You Have Continually Voided Our Rental Contract By Not Maintaining Signs As Agreed As We No Longer Have A Contract With You Do Not Expect Any Further Remuneration."

[Walker answered by letter, pointing out that the telegram did not "make any specific allegations as to what the failure of maintenance comprises," and concluding:]

"We would like to call your attention to paragraph G in our rental contract, which covers procedures in the event of a Breach of Agreement. In the event that you carry out your threat to make no future monthly payments in accordance with the agreement, it is our intention to enforce the conditions outlined under paragraph G[a].... Unless we receive both the September and October payments by October 25th, this entire matter will be placed in the hands of our attorney for collection in accordance with paragraph G which stipulates that the entire amount is forthwith due and payable."

No additional payments were made and Walker sued in assumpsit for the entire balance due under the contract, $5,197.50, invoking paragraph (g) of the agreement. Defendants filed answer and claim of recoupment, asserting that plaintiff's failure to perform certain maintenance services constituted a prior material breach of the agreement, thus justifying their repudiation of the contract and grounding their claim for damages. The case was tried to the court without a jury and resulted in a judgment for the plaintiff. The case is before us on a general appeal.

---

a. "(g) Breach of Agreement. Lessee shall be deemed to have breached this agreement by default in payment of any installment of the rental herein provided for; abandonment of the sign or vacating premises where the sign is located; termination or transfer of lessee's interest in the premises by insolvency, appointment of a receiver for lessee's business; filing of a voluntary or involuntary petition in bankruptcy with respect to lessee or the violation of any of the other terms or conditions hereof. In the event of such default, the lessor may, upon notice to the lessee, which notice shall conclusively be deemed sufficient if mailed or delivered to the premises where the sign was or is located, take possession of the sign and declare the balance of the rental herein provided for to be forthwith due and payable, and lessee hereby agrees to pay such balance upon any such contingencies. Lessor may terminate this lease and without notice, remove and repossess said sign and recover from the lessee such amounts as may be unpaid for the remaining unexpired term of this agreement. Time is of the essence of this lease with respect to the payment of rentals herein provided for. Should lessee after lessor has declared the balance of rentals due and payable, pay the full amount of rental herein provided, he shall then be entitled to the use of sign, under all the terms and provisions hereof, for the balance of the term of this lease. No waiver by either party hereto of the nonperformance of any term, condition or obligation hereof shall be a waiver of any subsequent breach of, or failure to perform the same, or any other term, condition or obligation hereof. It is understood and agreed that the sign is especially constructed for the lessee and for use at the premises now occupied by the lessee for the term herein provided; that it is of no value unless so used and that it is a material consideration to the lessor in entering into this agreement that the lessee shall continue to use the sign for the period of time provided herein and for the payment of the full rental for such term."

Defendants urge upon us again and again, in various forms, the proposition that Walker's failure to service the sign, in response to repeated requests, constituted a material breach of the contract and justified repudiation by them. The legal proposition is undoubtedly correct. Repudiation is one of the weapons available to an injured party in event the other contractor has committed a material breach. But the injured party's determination that there has been a material breach, justifying his own repudiation, is fraught with peril, for should such determination, as viewed by a later court in the calm of its contemplation, be unwarranted, the repudiator himself will have been guilty of material breach and himself have become the aggressor, not an innocent victim.

What is our criterion for determining whether or not a breach of contract is so fatal to the undertaking of the parties that it is to be classed as "material"? There is no single touchstone. Many factors are involved. They are well stated in section 275 of Restatement [first] of Contracts in the following terms:

"In determining the materiality of a failure fully to perform a promise the following circumstances are influential:

"(a) The extent to which the injured party will obtain the substantial benefit which he could have reasonably anticipated;

"(b) The extent to which the injured party may be adequately compensated in damages for lack of complete performance;

"(c) The extent to which the party failing to perform has already partly performed or made preparations for performance;

"(d) The greater or less hardship on the party failing to perform in terminating the contract;

"(e) The wilful, negligent or innocent behavior of the party failing to perform;

"(f) The greater or less uncertainty that the party failing to perform will perform the remainder of the contract."

We will not set forth in detail the testimony offered concerning the need for servicing. Granting that Walker's delay (about a week after defendant Herbert Harrison sent his telegram of repudiation Walker sent out a crew and took care of things) in rendering the service requested was irritating, we are constrained to agree with the trial court that it was not of such materiality as to justify repudiation of the contract, and we are particularly mindful of the lack of preponderant evidence contrary to his determination. Jones v. Eastern Michigan Motorbuses, 287 Mich. 619, 283 N.W. 710. The trial court, on this phase of the case, held as follows:

"Now Mr. Harrison phoned in, so he testified, a number of times. He isn't sure of the dates but he sets the first call at about the 7th of August and he complained then of the tomato and of some rust and some cobwebs. The tomato, according to the testimony, was up on the clock; that would be outside of his reach, without a stepladder or something. The cobwebs are within easy reach of Mr. Harrison and so would the rust be. I think that Mr. Bueche's argument that these were not materially a breach would clearly be true as to the cobwebs and I really can't believe in the face of all the testimony that there was a great deal of rust seven days after the installation of this sign. And that really brings it down to the tomato. And, of course, when a tomato has been splashed all other (sic) your clock, you don't like it. But he says he kept calling their attention to it, although the rain probably washed some of the tomato off. But the stain remained, and they didn't come. I really can't find that that was such a material breach of the contract as to justify rescission. I really don't think so."

Nor, we conclude, do we. There was no valid ground for defendants' repudiation and their failure thereafter to comply with the terms of the contract was itself a material breach, entitling Walker, upon this record, to judgment.

The question of damages remains. [The court concluded that it need not address the question "whether this contract is one of sale or of lease" because the parties have agreed that the remedy sought is "acceleration of 'rentals' due."] The trial court cut down such sum by the amount that service would have cost Walker during the unexpired portion of the agreement (Restatement, Contracts, § 335) and as to such diminution Walker does not complain or cross-appeal. Judgment was, therefore, rendered for the cash price of the sign, for such services and maintenance as were extended and accepted, and interest upon the amount in default. There was no error.

Affirmed. Costs to appellee.

NOTES

(1) *Counseling.* If Harrison had consulted you before he sent the telegram, what would you have advised him to do?

It would have been safe for Harrison to have hired someone to clean off the sign and then sue Walker for partial breach, claiming what he paid. Would it have been safe for Harrison to have deducted that amount from the amount due under paragraph (b)? (The right of a party to withhold payment due on this ground is taken up later in connection with the next case.)

(2) *Condition v. Promise.* Maintenance of the sign by Walker with some diligence, and in some degree of respectability, was of course a constructive condition of Harrison's duty to keep up the rental payments. Walker's duty of maintenance, as stated in paragraph (d), would not be met by anything less than punctilious performance. But the condition of performance by Harrison need not be so stringent. Obviously there is some softening effect, or "play," in the process of deriving a condition from a promise. Compare the effect the paragraph might have had if it had been written in terms of an express condition.

Recall that in *Delta Dynamics,* p. 386 above, Pixey was required to sell a minimum of 50,000 units in its first year but sold only 10,000. When you read that case you were asked what remedies would have been available to Delta if the agreement had not contained a provision allowing Delta to terminate if Pixey did not meet the minimum. What would be your answer now? What remedies would have been available if Pixey had taken only 49,999 locks? At what point would Pixey's breach have been *material*?

(3) *Question of Law or Fact?* Did the court make its own judgment whether or not Walker's conduct amounted to a material breach? Or did it accept the trial

judge's determination as a permissible finding on the evidence? Should the issue of materiality of a breach ever be submitted to a jury? And if so, should they be directed to balance the factors mentioned in Restatement § 241, or in some similar list? What merit or demerit do you find in treating the issue as a "question of law"?

(4) *Irrelevance of Good Faith.* Good faith will not prevent a statement from being a repudiation. In United California Bank v. Prudential Ins. Co., 681 P.2d 390, 431 (Ariz.App.1983), the court declined to "engraft a vague fault principle onto one branch of settled contract doctrine. If a 'good faith' contract interpretation is made as a defense to a claim of breach by anticipatory repudiation, then it should be a defense where the repudiating party believes wrongly but in 'good faith' that there is no contract at all or that the contract has been terminated, modified, or rescinded."

(5) *Delay Under the CISG.* Recall that the CISG abandons the "perfect tender" rule in favor of a rule of "fundamental breach" (Note 1, p. 732 above). If a seller delays delivery of the goods under a contract that does not make time "of the essence," how can the buyer know how much delay will make the seller's breach "fundamental"?

Article 47(1) empowers the buyer to "fix an additional period of time of reasonable length for performance by the seller of his obligations." If the seller fails to deliver the goods within this additional period, article 49(1)(b) provides that the buyer may declare the contract avoided, regardless of whether the failure amounts to a "fundamental breach." Articles 63(1) and 64(1)(b) set out comparable rules for the seller in the event of a breach by the buyer.

These provisions of the CISG were inspired by the *Nachfrist* provisions of German law. Under German law, however, failure to give a *Nachfrist* notice may preclude termination, whereas under the Convention it gives an alternative ground for avoidance. See J. Honnold, Uniform Law for International Sales under the 1980 United Nations Convention ¶¶ 27, 289, 305 (3d ed. 1999).

PROBLEMS

(1) *Drafting.* How might Harrison's telegram have been drafted to put pressure on Walker without risk to Harrison? Would it have been safe for Harrison to have demanded Walker's assurance of proper maintenance in the future? (The right of a party that has become insecure about the other party's performance to demand assurance of due performance is dealt with in Section 5(B) below.)

If Harrison had consulted you before signing the agreement, what proposals would you have made for changes in its terms? Do the provisions of the Vienna Convention described above give you any ideas for changes?

(2) *Liquidated Damages or Penalty?* Is the provision providing for recovery of unpaid amounts in the third sentence of paragraph (g), see footnote a above, p. 749 above, enforceable?

K & G Construction Co. v. Harris

Court of Appeals of Maryland, 1960.
223 Md. 305, 164 A.2d 451.

[A case was stated for appeal in an action by a Contractor against a Subcontractor, and the following facts were given. K & G Construction Company was the owner and general contractor for a housing subdivision project. Harris and Brooks contracted with it to do excavating and earth-moving work on the project. Certain provisions of the agreement were as follows:

"Section 4. (b) Progress payments will be made each month during the performance of the work. Subcontractor will submit to Contractor, by the 25th of each month, a requisition for work performed during the preceding month. Contractor will pay these requisitions, less a retainer equal to ten per cent (10%), by the 10th of the months in which such requisitions are received.[a]

"(c) No payments will be made under this contract until the insurance requirements of Sec. 9 hereof have been complied with.

"Section 8. . . . All work shall be performed in a workmanlike manner, and in accordance with the best practices.

"Section 9. Subcontractor agrees to carry, during the progress of the work, . . . liability insurance against . . . property damage, in such amounts and with such companies as may be satisfactory to Contractor and shall provide Contractor with certificates showing the same to be in force."

While in the course of his employment by the Subcontractor on the project, a bulldozer operator drove his machine too close to Contractor's house while grading the yard, causing the immediate collapse of a wall and other damage to the house. Contractor was generally satisfied with Subcontractor's work and progress as required by the contract until September 12, 1958, with the exception of the bulldozer accident which occurred on August 9. The Subcontractor and its insurance carrier refused to repair damage or compensate Contractor for damage to the house, claiming that there was no liability on the part of the Subcontractor.

For work done prior to July 25, the Subcontractor submitted a requisition payable under the terms of the contract on or before August 10. Contractor refused to pay it because the bulldozer damage had not been repaired or paid for. Subcontractor continued to work on the project until September 12, when it discontinued work because of Contractor's refusal to pay the said requisition, but notified Contractor by registered letter of its willingness to return to the job upon payment. Contractor later requested it to return and complete work, which Subcontractor refused to do because of nonpayment of work requisitions of July 25 and thereafter. Contractor had another excavating concern complete the work, for which it paid $450 above the contract price.

Contractor's suit against Subcontractor contained two counts: (1) for the bulldozer damage, alleging negligence, and (2) for $450 as damages for breach of contract. Subcontractor filed a counterclaim for work done and not paid for and for profit it lost by not being permitted to finish the job, totalling $2,824.50. The bulldozer damage claim was submitted to a jury, who found in favor of Contractor in the amount of $3,400, and that judgment has been paid. The other claims were submitted to the trial judge, who allowed the Subcontractor's claim in full. Contractor appealed from this determination.]

---

a. This section is not a model for clarity.

■ PRESCOTT, JUDGE. . . . The vital question, more tersely stated, remains: Did the contractor have a right, under the circumstances, to refuse to make the progress payment due on August 10, 1958?

The answer involves interesting and important principles of contract law. Promises and counter-promises made by the respective parties to a contract have certain relations to one another, which determine many of the rights and liabilities of the parties. Broadly speaking, they are (1) independent of each other, or (2) mutually dependent, one upon the other. They are independent of each other if the parties intend that *performance* by each of them is in no way conditioned upon *performance* by the other. 5 Page, The Law of Contracts, ¶ 2971. In other words, the parties exchange promises for promises, not the *performance* of promises for the *performance* of promises. 3 Williston, Contracts (Rev.Ed.), ¶ 813, n.6. A failure to perform an independent promise does not excuse non-performance on the part of the adversary party, but each is required to perform his promise, and, if one does not perform, he is liable to the adversary party for such non-performance. (Of course, if litigation ensues questions of set-off or recoupment frequently arise.) Promises are mutually dependent if the parties intend *performance* by one to be conditioned upon *performance* by the other, and, if they be mutually dependent, they may be (a) precedent, i.e., a promise that is to be performed before a corresponding promise on the part of the adversary party is to be performed, (b) subsequent, i.e., a corresponding promise that is not to be performed until the other party to the contract has performed a precedent covenant, or (c) concurrent, i.e., promises that are to be performed at the same time by each of the parties, who are respectively bound to perform each. Page, op. cit., ¶¶ 2941, 2951, 2961. . . .

In the early days, it was settled law that covenants and mutual promises in a contract were *prima facie* independent, and that they were to be so construed in the absence of language in the contract clearly showing that they were intended to be dependent. Williston, op. cit., ¶816; Page, op. cit., ¶¶ 2944, 2945. In the case of Kingston v. Preston, 2 Doug. 689, decided in 1774, Lord Mansfield, contrary to three centuries of opposing precedents, changed the rule, and decided that performance of one covenant might be dependent on prior performance of another, although the contract contained no express condition to that effect. Page, op. cit., ¶946; Williston, op. cit., ¶817. The modern rule, which seems to be of almost universal application, is that there is a presumption that mutual promises in a contract are dependent and are to be so regarded, whenever possible. Page, op. cit., ¶2946; Restatement, Contracts, § 266. Cf. Williston, op. cit., ¶812. . . .

. . . It would, indeed present an unusual situation if we were to hold that a building contractor, who has obtained someone to do work for him and has agreed to pay each month for the work performed in the previous month, has to continue the monthly payments, irrespective of the degree of skill and care displayed in the performance of work, and his only recourse is by way of suit for ill-performance. If this were the law, it is conceivable, in fact, probable, that many contractors would become insolvent before they were able to complete their contracts. As was stated by the Court in Measures Brothers Ltd. v. Measures, 2 Ch. 248: "Covenants are to be construed as dependent or independent according to the intention of the parties and the good sense of the case."

We hold that when the subcontractor's employee negligently damaged the contractor's wall, this constituted a breach of the subcontractor's promise to perform his work in a "workmanlike manner, and in accordance with the best practices." Gaybis v. Palm, 201 Md. 78, 85, 93 A.2d 269; Johnson v. Metcalfe, 209 Md. 537, 544, 121 A.2d 825; 17 C.J.S. Contracts § 515; Weiss v. Sheet Metal Fabricators, 206 Md. 195, 203, 110 A.2d 671. And there can be little doubt that the breach was material: the damage to the wall amounted to more than double the payment due on August 10. Speed v. Bailey, 153 Md. 655, 661, 662, 139 A. 534. 3A Corbin, Contracts, § 708, says: "The failure of a contractor's [in our case, the subcontractor's] performance to constitute 'substantial' performance may justify the owner [in our case, the contractor] in refusing to make a progress payment.... If the refusal to pay an installment is justified on the owner's [contractor's] part, the contractor [subcontractor] is not justified in abandoning work by reason of that refusal. His abandonment of the work will itself be a wrongful repudiation that goes to the essence, even if the defects in performance did not." See also Restatement, Contracts, § 274; ... and compare Williston, op. cit., §§ 805, 841 and 842. Professor Corbin, in § 954, states further: "The unexcused failure of a contractor to render a promised performance when it is due is always a breach of contract.... Such failure may be of such great importance as to constitute what has been called herein a 'total' breach.... For a failure of performance constituting such a 'total' breach, an action for remedies that are appropriate thereto is at once maintainable. Yet the injured party is not required to bring such action. He has the option of treating the nonperformance as a 'partial' breach only...." In permitting the subcontractor to proceed with work on the project after August 9, the contractor, obviously, treated the breach by the subcontractor as a partial one. As the promises were mutually dependent and the subcontractor had made a material breach in his performance, this justified the contractor in refusing to make the August 10 payment; hence, as the contractor was not in default, the subcontractor again breached the contract when he, on September 12, discontinued work on the project, which rendered him liable (by the express terms of the contract) to the contractor for his increased cost in having the excavating done—a stipulated amount of $450. Cf. Keystone Engineering Corp. v. Sutter, 196 Md. 620, 628, 78 A.2d 191....

[Defendant also contended] that the contractor had no right to refuse the August 10 payment, because the subcontractor had furnished the insurance against property damage, as called for in the contract. There is little, or no, merit in this suggestion. The subcontractor and his insurance company denied liability. The furnishing of the insurance by him did not constitute a license to perform his work in a careless, negligent, or unworkmanlike manner; and its acceptance by the contractor did not preclude his assertion of a claim for unworkmanlike performance directly against the subcontractor.

Judgment against the appellant reversed; and judgment entered in favor of the appellant against the appellees for $450, the appellees to pay the costs.

NOTES

(1) *Exercise in Restatement Analysis.* It may be useful to try out on the *K & G* case the Restatement analysis suggested at p. 746 above. First, was there an uncured breach by Harris? (How was the answer to this question determined?) Second, was the breach by Harris a breach of a duty of performance that was to be exchanged under an exchange of promises (as opposed to a duty under a promise on which the injured party's promise did not depend)? (Is it arguable that this is a case in which "a contrary intention is clearly manifested" by language in the contract [§§ 4(c) and 9] supporting the inference that the contractor's duty to pay was *independent* of isolated acts of carelessness by the subcontractor?) Third, did the breach by Harris go to a performance that was to be rendered at an earlier time than that of K & G?

The fourth question, and the one that often occasions dispute, is whether the breach by Harris a material breach. As to this the court thought there could be "little doubt." Is that because Harris "did his work in a careless, negligent or unworkmanlike manner"? Or because the insurer denied liability? (It is a customary condition in liability insurance policies that the insured shall not assume any obligation in connection with an accident, except at its own cost.) If the subcontractor and its insurer had conceded liability at once, reserving only the question of how much damage was done, would the contractor have been justified in withholding the August payment? What if the subcontractor had promised at once to repair the damage?

(2) *Election of Remedies.* Under the Restatement analysis, if the breach was a material breach, K & G had a choice: either continue performance and treat the breach as a partial breach, or stop performing and treat the breach as a total breach. This choice may have grave consequences.

"When a party materially breaches a contract, the non-breaching party must choose between two remedies—he can elect to terminate the contract and recover ... damages or he can continue the contract and recover damages solely for the breach.... A party can indicate that he has chosen to continue the contract by continuing to perform under the contract or by accepting the performance of the breaching party.... Once a party elects to continue the contract, he can never thereafter elect to terminate the contract based on that breach." Bigda v. Fischbach Corp., 898 F.Supp. 1004, 1011 (S.D.N.Y.1995).

The court in *K & G* says that by "permitting the subcontractor to proceed," K & G "obviously, treated the breach by the subcontractor as a partial one." Why, then, was not K & G barred by its election from treating Harris's breach as a total breach?

(3) *An Alternate Ground.* Would the court's reasoning have been simpler if it had said that the contractor was entitled to set off the bulldozer damage against the requisition payable August 10th? Would it have been sound? With respect to the sale of goods, see UCC § 2–717.

In Andersen, A New Look at Material Breach in the Law of Contracts, 21 U.C.Davis L.Rev. 1073, 1122 fn.149 (1988), the author states that withholding "appears to have been allowed" in *K & G*, where the court "said that the general contractor was justified in both requiring the subcontractor to continue performance and in withholding the next two progress payments, which amounted to something less than the cost of repairing the damage.... It is unclear to what extent *K & G* is sound authority for the victim's right to withhold in the absence of cancellation, however. The court justified the withholding with a dubious reading of a passage from Corbin, which refers to temporary withholding of performance by the victim of a material breach during a period in which cure by the other is possible." See also Note, 62 Fordham L.Rev. 163 (1993).

At common law, however, there was scant support for a right to withhold comparable to that in UCC § 2–717. Still, in J.C. Patel v. Telerent Leasing Corp., 574 So.2d 3, 8 (Miss.1990), the court upheld a motel owner's right to withhold payment from the lessor of television sets, describing the right as "general law." In ARP Films v. Marvel Entertainment Group, 952 F.2d 643, 649 (2d Cir.1991), the court declined to approve withholding by a licensee under a license agreement covering rights to Spiderman and other cartoon characters. It rejected the licensee's contention that "withholding the payments and reports was a self-help measure designed to force [the licensor] to repent" and concluded that the licensee had only "two options: (1) it could have stopped performance and sued for total breach; or (2) it could have affirmed the contract by continuing to perform while suing in partial breach."

(4) *Wrongful Refusal to Make Progress Payments*. When a dispute arises under a construction contract, it is not uncommon for the owner to withhold the amount due as a progress payment. If the withholding is wrongful, what is the builder entitled to do? Is it safe for the builder to discontinue work? To walk off the job?

In one case where the builder walked off and sued for damages, the trial judge instructed the jury that if the defendant failed to make payments as called for by the contract—"a substantial failure, amounting substantially to the withholding of the whole payment, not necessarily the whole payment, but the bulk of the payment"—such failure constituted a breach on the part of defendant justifying plaintiff in stopping work and entitling it to recover damages (including lost profits) from defendant. A judgment for the builder was affirmed by the Supreme Court of the United States, which thought that in a construction contract a stipulation for progress payments "must be deemed so material that a substantial failure to pay would justify the contractor in declining to proceed.... As is usually the case with building contracts, it evidently was in the contemplation of the parties that the contractor could not be expected to finance the operation to completion without receiving the stipulated payments on account as the work progressed. In such cases a substantial compliance as to advance payments is a condition precedent to the contractor's obligation to proceed." Guerini Stone Co. v. P.J. Carlin Constr. Co., 248 U.S. 334, 344–45 (1919). But see Stewart v. C & C Excavating & Constr. Co., 877 F.2d 711, 714 (8th Cir.1989), holding that there was no material breach where the deficiency was "an insignificant portion of the total contract price" and "not a substantial portion of the gross progress payment earned for that pay period."

Note that in *Guerini* the Court used the words "declining to proceed." It will be recalled that under the Restatement analysis if the circumstances make it appropriate for the builder to suspend performance—by "declining to proceed"—and give the owner a chance to cure, the builder is expected to do so before terminating and treating the breach as total. How long would a builder, having suspended, have to wait before terminating?

HINDRANCE AND PREVENTION

Recall Gulf's contention, in *Eastern Air Lines* (pp. 76, 526 above), that "fuel freighting" by Eastern was a breach of its duty of good faith performance. If Gulf had prevailed, it might have been justified in terminating the contract. (Would this have been so if the breach was not material?)

As Gulf's contention suggests, a party's breach of the duty of good faith performance may have the same effect as any other breach under the doctrine of constructive conditions. Moreover, a party's interference with the other party's performance may well be such a breach.

Consider United States v. Peck, 102 U.S. 64 (1880), described this way in the case that follows: "Peck contracted to sell the government a certain quantity of hay for the Tongue River station, and the trial court found it was mutually understood the hay was to be cut on government lands called 'the Big Meadows,' in the Yellowstone valley, which was the only available source of supply, also that thereafter the government caused all of that hay to be cut for it by other parties, in view of which Peck was relieved from his contract." The Supreme Court of the United States held that "the conduct of one party to a contract which prevents the other from performing his part is an excuse for nonperformance."[a]

When will hindrance short of prevention have the same effect? Compare the effect of prevention in the case of express conditions, discussed in Prevention, p. 709 above.

NOTES

(1) *Cooperation.* In many situations a contracting party is responsible for taking affirmative steps to cooperate with the other party, even though the parties have not troubled to express such a duty in their agreement. This is likely to be so if it can be shown that such cooperative effort is essential to the other party's performance.

This principle is frequently applied in construction cases. Under building contracts it is understood that a contractor, or subcontractor, cannot proceed effectively until a site is provided and prepared in a way appropriate for the work. See R.G. Pope Constr. Co., Inc. v. Guard Rail of Roanoke, Inc., 244 S.E.2d 774 (Va.1978) (subcontractor's "performance of the duty to install guardrail was subject to certain conditions, the most important of which was the implied condition that a site would be available for such installation").

Similar reasoning was applied in Kehm Corp. v. United States, 93 F.Supp. 620 (Ct.Cl.1950), in which the Government was held accountable for a supplier's delays

---

a. "The older common law did not uniformly require the promisor to refrain from actively preventing the promisee from performing the condition of the promise. In one early case the defendant had given his penal bond to pay the plaintiff eighty pounds unless the defendant should procure a marriage to take place between the plaintiff and one Bridget Palmer, before a certain day. The defendant pleaded that before that day the plaintiff addressed Bridget in such vile and insulting language that the defendant could not bring about the marriage. The plea was adjudged bad on the ground that the defendant should show that he used due diligence to bring about the marriage. [Blandford v. Andrews, 78 Eng.Rep. 930 (King's Bench 1599).] ... These decisions show that the implication of a condition of non-prevention was by no means inevitable." Patterson, Constructive Conditions in Contracts, 42 Colum.L.Rev. 903, 931–32 (1942).

in producing concrete bombs for practice in the Navy. When the Navy lost interest in the concrete bomb program, the Government delayed in providing tail assemblies, and Kehm's casting work became extended, sporadic, and costly. Speaking of Kehm's obligation, the court said: "The promisor's undertaking normally gives rise to an implied complementary obligation on the part of the promisee: He must not only not hinder his promisor's performance, he must do whatever is necessary to enable him to perform.... The implied obligation is as binding as if it were spelled out. Wood v. Lucy [p. 83 above]."

Naturally there are contracting parties who, in a spirit of self-pity or worse, demand more than their fair share of cooperation. There is a countervailing principle that "enthusiasm is not required in performing contractual obligations." Esmieu v. Hsieh, 580 P.2d 1105, 1109 (Wash.App.1978).

(2) *Influences in Cooperation Cases*. "While not every act or omission by the obligor which may expedite performance by the obligee (of his promise or of a condition) is required, the acts or omissions which are clearly within the obligor's control and which are the normal or obvious means of the obligee's performance, are presumably required of the obligor, or he assumes the risk of their non-occurrence. The justifiable reliance by the obligee, the usages of the trade or activity, the mores of the community, are obviously influential in determining what co-operation is required in a particular transaction. Judicial opinions reveal these influences. The moral notions of carelessness or diligence, malice or inadvertence, have sporadic influence. The avoidance of unjust enrichment seems also influential." Patterson, Constructive Conditions in Contracts, 42 Colum.L.Rev. 903, 937–38 (1942).

Iron Trade Products Co. v. Wilkoff Co.

Supreme Court of Pennsylvania, 1922.
272 Pa. 172, 116 A. 150.

■ WALLING, J. In July, 1919, plaintiff entered into a written contract with defendant for the purchase of 2,600 tons of section relaying rails, to be delivered in New York harbor at times therein specified for $41 a ton. Defendant failed to deliver any of the rails, and plaintiff brought this suit, averring, by reason of such default, it had been compelled to purchase the rails elsewhere (2,000 tons thereof at $49.20 per ton and 600 tons at $49 per ton), also that the market or current price of the rails at the time and place of delivery was approximately $50 per ton, and claiming as damages the difference between what it had been compelled to pay and the contract price. Defendant filed an affidavit of defense and a supplement thereto, both of which the court below held insufficient and entered judgment for plaintiff, from which defendant brought this appeal.

In effect, the affidavit of defense avers the supply of such rails was very limited, there being only two places in the United States (one in Georgia and one in West Virginia) where they could be obtained in quantities to fill the contract, and that pending the time for delivery defendant was negotiating for the required rails when plaintiff announced to the trade its urgent desire to purchase a similar quantity of like rails, and in fact bought 887 tons and agreed to purchase a much larger quantity from the parties with whom defendant had been negotiating, further averring this conduct on behalf of plaintiff reduced the available supply of relaying rails and enhanced the price to an exorbitant sum, rendering performance by defendant impossible. The affidavit, however, fails to aver knowledge on part of plaintiff that the supply of rails was limited or any intent on its part to prevent, interfere with, or embarrass defendant in the performance of the contract; and there is no suggestion of any understanding, express or implied, that defendant was to secure the rails from any particular source, or that plaintiff was to refrain from purchasing other rails; hence it was not required to do so. The true rule is stated in Williston on Contracts, p. 1308, as quoted by the trial court, viz.:

"If a party seeking to secure all the merchandise of a certain character which he could entered into a contract for a quantity of the required goods, and subsequently made performance of the contract by the seller more difficult by making other purchases which increased the scarcity of the available supply, his conduct would furnish no excuse for refusal to perform the prior contract."

Mere difficulty of performance will not excuse a breach of contract. Corona C. & C. Co. v. Dickinson, 261 Pa. 589, 104 A. 741; Janes v. Scott, 59 Pa. 178, 98 Am.Dec. 328; 35 Cyc. 245. Defendant relies upon the rule stated in United States v. Peck, 102 U.S. 64, 26 L.Ed. 46, that—

"The conduct of one party to a contract which prevents the other from performing his part is an excuse for nonperformance."

The cases are not parallel. Here plaintiff's conduct did not prevent performance by defendant, although it may have added to the difficulty and expense thereof. There is no averment that plaintiff's purchases exhausted the supply of rails, and the advance in price caused thereby is no excuse. The *Peck* Case stands on different ground. . . .

The affidavit "denies that there was any market or market price or current price for such relaying rails" at any time from the date of the contract to the beginning of this suit, but other statements therein amount to an admission of a market price. For example, it speaks of "the trade in Pittsburgh, New York, and other centers of such trade"; also of "the very small quantity of such rails in the market." The affidavit further states that—

"After making the said contract with the plaintiff the defendant began negotiations with the persons from whom the said rails in Georgia and West Virginia might be purchased; and in each of the two cases referred to such negotiations had proceeded so far that defendant could have purchased 2,600 tons of such rails either in Georgia or West Virginia at some such price as that contracted to the plaintiff, or less, or not greatly in excess thereof.

"In fact, the plaintiff bought a quantity of such rails, to wit, 887 tons, and at one time had contracted for the purchase of a much larger quantity thereof, from the same persons with whom the defendant had been negotiating for the same, and at higher prices than had been offered to the defendant by the same persons within the terms of the said contract.

"And affiant, while denying, as aforesaid, that the plaintiff was compelled to purchase the said rails or any of them, avers that, if the plaintiff was so compelled, it was only as the result of plaintiff's own interference with the defendant's performance of the said contract, and avers that but for the said interference the defendant would have made full performance of its said contract."

The above and the admitted facts that plaintiff actually bought the 2,600 tons and had previously resold the same indicate a market value, and the specific averment thereof, in the statement of claim is not sufficiently denied in the affidavit. An affidavit of defense must be considered as a whole, and therein a general denial is of no avail against an admission of the same fact. An affidavit that is contradictory or equivocal is insufficient. See Noll v. Royal Exchange Assurance Corp., 76 Pa.Super.Ct. 510.

The supplemental affidavit avers that when the contract in suit was made plaintiff, to the knowledge of defendant, had resold the 2,600 tons of rails at $42.25 per ton, and, furthermore, that the purchaser at such resale released plaintiff from all claim for damages under the contract.... The fact that a vendee has resold the goods contracted for is of no moment unless made a part of the contract; for, if not, he is entitled to the benefit of his bargain, regardless of the disposition he may intend to make of the property involved. To hold otherwise would inject collateral issues in trials for breaches of such contracts.

The assignments of error are overruled, and the judgment is affirmed.

NOTE

(1) *The Case of the Overbidding Buyer.* Anna Meyerhofer was interested in some houses in Brooklyn that were to be offered at a foreclosure sale. Since Benjamin Patterson was in a favorable position to buy them, they entered into a contract of sale under which Meyerhofer agreed to pay Patterson $23,000 for the houses, no mention being made of the fact that he did not own them. When Patterson attended the foreclosure sale, Meyerhofer was also there, and whenever he made a bid she bid higher. The houses were struck down to her for $22,380. Patterson sued for $620 damages and, from a judgment for Meyerhofer, he appealed. *Held:* Reversed and remanded.

"In the case of every contract there is an implied undertaking on the part of each party that he will not intentionally and purposely do anything to prevent the other party from carrying out the agreement on his part." Patterson v. Meyerhofer, 97 N.E. 472 (N.Y.1912).

What distinguishes this case from *Iron Trade Products*?

(2) *Questions.* In Note 1, p. 636 above, which dealt with Buyer's damages against Seller, you were asked about the effect if Buyer's purchaser on resale released Buyer. Note that the court in *Iron Trade Products* declines to consider the assertion "that the purchaser at such resale released plaintiff from all claim for damages under the contract." If one takes the contract price as $41 per ton, the price under Iron Trade Products' contract for resale as $42.25 per ton, the price at which Iron Trade Products purchased other rails as $49 per ton, and the market price as $50 per ton, what should Iron Trade Products' damages be? (Is it clear that there was a market price?)

New England Structures, Inc. v. Loranger

Supreme Judicial Court of Massachusetts, 1968.
354 Mass. 62, 234 N.E.2d 888.

■ CUTTER, JUSTICE. In one case the plaintiffs, doing business as Theodore Loranger & Sons (Loranger), the general contractor on a school project, seeks to recover from New England Structures, Inc., a subcontractor (New England), damages caused by an alleged breach of the subcontract. Loranger avers that the breach made it necessary for Loranger at greater expense to engage another subcontractor to complete work on a roof deck. In a cross action, New England seeks to recover for breach of the subcontract by Loranger alleged to have taken place when Loranger terminated New England's right to proceed. The actions were consolidated for trial. A jury returned a verdict for New England in the action brought by Loranger, and a verdict for New England in the sum of $16,860.25 in the action brought by New England against Loranger. The cases are before us on Loranger's exceptions to the judge's charge.

Loranger, under date of July 11, 1961, entered into a subcontract with New England by which New England undertook to install a gypsum roof deck in a school, then being built by Loranger. New England began work on November 24, 1961. On December 18, 1961, New England received a telegram from Loranger which read, "Because of your . . . repeated refusal . . . or inability to provide enough properly skilled workmen to maintain satisfactory progress, we . . . terminate your right to proceed with work at the . . . school as of December 26, 1961, in accordance with Article . . . 5 of our contract. We intend to complete the work . . . with other forces and charge its costs and any additional damages resulting from your repeated delays to your account." New England replied, "Failure on your [Loranger's] part to provide . . . approved drawings is the cause of the delay." The telegram also referred to various allegedly inappropriate changes in instructions.

The pertinent portions of art. 5 of the subcontract are set out in the margin.[1] Article 5 stated grounds on which Loranger might terminate New England's right to proceed with the subcontract.

There was conflicting evidence concerning (a) how New England had done certain work; (b) whether certain metal cross pieces (called bulb tees) had been properly "staggered" and whether joints had been welded on both sides by certified welders, as called for by the specifications; (c) whether

---

1. "The Subcontractor agrees to furnish sufficient labor, materials, tools and equipment to maintain its work in accordance with the progress of the general construction work by the General Contractor. Should the Subcontractor fail to keep up with . . . [such] progress . . . then he shall work overtime with no additional compensation, if directed to do so by the General Contractor. If the Subcontractor should be adjudged a bankrupt . . . or *if he should persistently . . . fail to supply enough properly skilled workmen* . . . or . . . disregard instructions of the General Contractor or fail to observe or perform the provisions of the Contract, then the General Contractor may, by *at least five . . . days prior written notice to the Subcontractor* without prejudice to any other rights or remedies, *terminate the Subcontractor's right to proceed with the work.* In such event, the General Contractor may . . . prosecute the work to completion . . . and the Subcontractor shall be liable to the General Contractor for any excess cost occasioned . . . thereby . . ." (emphasis supplied).

New England had supplied an adequate number of certified welders on certain days; (d) whether and to what extent Loranger had waived certain specifications; and (e) whether New England had complied with good trade practices. The architect testified that on December 14, 1961, he had made certain complaints to New England's president. The work was completed by another company at a cost in excess of New England's bid. There was also testimony (1) that Loranger's job foreman told one of New England's welders "to do no work at the job site during the five day period following the date of Loranger's termination telegram," and (2) that, "if New England had been permitted to continue its work, it could have completed the entire subcontract ... within five days following the date of the termination telegram."

The trial judge ruled, as matter of law, that Loranger, by its termination telegram confined the justification for its notice of termination to New England's "repeated refusal ... or inability to provide enough properly skilled workmen to maintain satisfactory progress." He then gave the following instructions: "If you should find that New England ... did not furnish a sufficient number of men to perform the required work under the contract within a reasonable time ... then you would be warranted in finding that Loranger was justified in terminating its contract; and it may recover in its suit against New England.... [T]he termination ... cannot, as ... matter of law, be justified for any ... reason not stated in the telegram of December 18 ... including failure to stagger the joints of the bulb tees or failure to weld properly ... or any other reason, unless you find that inherent in the reasons stated in the telegram, namely, failure to provide enough skilled workmen to maintain satisfactory progress, are these aspects. Nevertheless, these allegations by Loranger of deficiency of work on the part of New England Structures may be considered by you, if you find that Loranger was justified in terminating the contract for the reason enumerated in the telegram. You may consider it or them as an element of damages sustained by Loranger...."[2] Counsel for Loranger claimed exceptions to the portion of the judge's charge quoted above in the body of this opinion.[3]

1. Some authority supports the judge's ruling, in effect, that Loranger, having specified in its telegram one ground for termination of the subcontract, cannot rely in litigation upon other grounds, except to the extent that the other grounds may directly affect the first ground asserted. See Railway Co. v. McCarthy, 96 U.S. 258, 267–268, 24 L.Ed. 693 ("Where

---

2. The judge also instructed, "[I]f you find that on the day following the sending of this telegram ... employees of New England ... were refused permission to continue that work, then you may consider that as a breach of the contract by Loranger, for Loranger's telegram terminated the contract ... as of December 26th [by] the giving of five days notice.... [I]f you find that [employees of] New England ... reported for work and were only informed that they were to call their office and were not prevented from working then ... you would be warranted in finding that this was not a refusal on the part of Loranger to permit them to work for the period between the receipt of the telegram and the date of the termination, December 26th."

3. No exception appears to have been claimed to the portion of the charge (see fn. 2) relating to whether Loranger prevented New England from performing work on the subcontract during the period from December 19 to December 26.

a party gives a reason for his conduct and decision touching ... a contro-versy, he cannot, after litigation has begun, change his ground, and put his conduct upon ... a different consideration. He is not permitted thus to mend his hold. He is *estopped* from doing it by a settled principle of law" [emphasis supplied]).... In each of these cases, there is reference to estoppel or "waiver" as the legal ground behind the principle.

Our cases somewhat more definitely require reliance or change of position based upon the assertion of the particular reason or defence before treating a person, giving one reason for his action, as estopped later to give a different reason. See Bates v. Cashman, 230 Mass. 167, 168–169, 119 N.E. 663, 664. There it was said, "The defendant is not prevented from setting up this defense. Although he wrote respecting other reasons for declining to perform the contract, he expressly reserved different grounds for his refusal.[4] While of course one cannot fail in good faith in presenting his reasons as to his conduct touching a controversy he is not prevented from relying upon one good defense among others urged simply because he has not always put it forward, when it does not appear that he has acted dishonestly or that the other party has been misled to his harm, or that he is estopped on any other ground." See Brown v. Henry, 172 Mass. 559, 567, 52 N.E. 1073; Moss v. Old Colony Trust Co., 246 Mass. 139, 150, 140 N.E. 803; Sheehan v. Commercial Travelers Mut. Acc. Assn. of America, 283 Mass. 543, 551–553, 186 N.E. 627, 88 A.L.R. 975; Restatement: Contracts, § 304; Williston, Contracts (3d ed.) § 742 (and also §§ 678, 679, 691); Corbin, Contracts, §§ 762, 1218, 1266 (and also §§ 265, 721, 727, 744, 756). See also Randall v. Peerless Motor Car Co., 212 Mass. 352, 376, 99 N.E. 221.

We think Loranger is not barred from asserting grounds not mentioned in its telegram unless New England establishes that, in some manner, it relied to its detriment upon the circumstance that only one ground was so asserted. Even if some evidence tended to show such reliance, the jury did not have to believe this evidence. They should have received instructions that they might consider grounds for termination of the subcontract and defences to New England's claim (that Loranger by the telegram had committed a breach of the subcontract), other than the ground raised in the telegram, unless they found as a fact that New England had relied to its detriment upon the fact that only one particular ground for termination was mentioned in the telegram.

2. [In an omitted part of the opinion, the court concluded that art. 5 of the subcontract (see fn. 1) did not give New England a right during the five-day notice period to attempt to cure its default and, in doing so, to rely on the particular ground stated in the telegram. That provision merely entitled New England to be told when it must quit the premises, and after receipt of the notice it had no further opportunity to cure defaults.]

Exceptions sustained.

---

4. The original papers show (record, p. 22) that the reservation was, "The statement of the foregoing [reason] is not to be taken as waiving any other reason for ... Cashman's refusal to proceed further with the agree-ment." This distinction from the present case, in our opinion, does not affect the prin-ciple that any estoppel to assert a different reason must rest on actual reliance.

NOTES

(1) *Golden Silence.* "When a party believes it is entitled to terminate a contract at will, it often will refrain from stating its reasons. The party may also refrain from undertaking a complete (and possibly costly) investigation of possible grounds for termination. Should it turn out that the contract was not terminable at will, it would be unfair, without some additional showing, to preclude the party from asserting legitimate grounds for termination." First Commodity Traders, Inc. v. Heinold Commodities, Inc., 591 F.Supp. 812, 822 (N.D.Ill.1984), aff'd, 766 F.2d 1007 (7th Cir.1985).

If this is good policy, does it follow that it is wise for a land-purchaser, believing there is a defect in the seller's title, to withdraw without giving a reason? For a buyer of goods to reject a tender without giving a reason? See UCC § 2–605(1).

(2) *Anti–Waiver Clauses (Reprise).* Recall the discussion of anti-waiver clauses in the context of express conditions, Note 1, p. 711 above. Such clauses are also frequently invoked in the context of constructive conditions of exchange. But, again, courts have not always honored such clauses. See Dillingham Commercial Co. v. Spears, 641 P.2d 1 (Alaska 1982), in which the court held that, despite an anti-waiver clause, a landlord's "long acquiescence" in late rental payments "constituted a waiver of her right to claim a default for [her tenant's] late payments."

SECTION 5.   PROSPECTIVE NONPERFORMANCE

———

(A) ANTICIPATORY REPUDIATION

In Walker & Co. v. Harrison, the court referred to Harrison's telegram as one "of repudiation." What is a repudiation? "[I]t should be shown that the announcement of an intention not to perform was positive and un-equivocal." Tenavision, Inc. v. Neuman, 379 N.E.2d 1166, 1168 (N.Y.1978). "In order to constitute a repudiation, a party's language must be sufficiently positive to be reasonably interpreted to mean that the party will not or cannot perform.... [L]anguage that under a fair reading 'amounts to a statement of intention not to perform except on conditions which go beyond the contract' constitutes a repudiation. Comment 2 to Uniform Commercial Code § 2–610." Restatement § 250, Comment *b.*

The "announcement of an intention not to perform" need not be in words. When, in Stewart v. Newbury, Stewart "voluntarily abandoned the work," his conduct without more amounted to a repudiation. See Wholesale Sand & Gravel v. Decker, 630 A.2d 710, 711 (Me.1993) (after second weekend of work, contractor "removed its equipment and did not return").

What are the consequences of a repudiation? If the repudiation is accompanied by a breach by nonperformance, it "gives rise to a claim for damages for total breach" (with an exception to be considered shortly). Thus Harrison's repudiation in Walker & Co. v. Harrison, coupled with his breach by nonpayment of rent, would have given Walker a claim for damages for total breach quite without regard to whether Harrison's breach was material. Our concern is with the consequences of a repudiation when it is not accompanied by a breach by nonperformance. Such a repudiation is often called an "anticipatory repudiation" because it occurs before the time for performance has arrived.[a]

We will consider five questions relating to the consequences of an anticipatory repudiation. First, is the recipient of a repudiation free to make other arrangements? Second, can the recipient of a repudiation go to court immediately, even before the time for performance has arrived? Third, can the recipient of a repudiation ignore the repudiation and await performance? Fourth, what are the consequences if the recipient of a repudiation urges retraction of the repudiation? Fifth, can a party that has repudiated withdraw the repudiation?

NOTE

Repudiation by Conduct. Claims of repudiation by conduct are sometimes troublesome in real estate transactions. In Neves v. Wright, 638 P.2d 1195, 1198 (Utah 1981), the court explained: "The rule that a seller of real estate need not have title at all times during the executory period of a contract, is not designed to favor sellers over buyers; rather, the purpose is to enhance the alienability of real estate by providing necessary flexibility in real estate transactions. Nevertheless, it is essential that in every case there be a close scrutiny of the facts, and the rule must be carefully applied to avoid unfairness, sharp practice, and outright dishonesty. If it plainly appears that a seller has lost or encumbered his ownership so that he will not be able to fulfill his contract, he cannot insist that a buyer continue to make payments." Suppose that in *Mattei,* p. 72 above, Hopper had given an option to another prospective buyer during the 120–day period. Would this have been a repudiation?

PROBLEM

You Know Quite as Well as We Do. When a buyer of iron rails complained that the first two shipments were short, and expressed the wish to be relieved from the contract, the seller, in England, asked "to know definitely what is your intention." The buyer, in New York, replied: "You ask us to determine whether we will or will not object to receive further shipments because of past defaults. We tell you we will if we are entitled to do so, and will not if we are not entitled to do so. We do not think you have the right to compel us to decide a disputed question of law to relieve you from the risk of deciding it yourself. You know quite as well as we do what is the rule and its uncertainty of application." Has the buyer repudiated? See Norrington v. Wright, 115 U.S. 188 (1885).

Hochster v. De La Tour
Queen's Bench, 1853.
2 E. & B. 678, 118 Eng.Rep. 922.

[Action of assumpsit.] Declaration: "for that, heretofore, to wit, on 12th April 1852, in consideration that plaintiff, at the request of defendant

---

a. The term "anticipatory breach" is sometimes used in place of "anticipatory repudiation." Comment *a* to Restatement § 253 calls the term "anticipatory breach" an elliptical expression for a "breach by anticipatory repudiation, because it occurs before there is any breach by non-performance."

would agree with the defendant to enter into the service and employ of the defendant in capacity of a courier, on a certain day then to come, to wit, the 1st day of June, 1852, and to serve the defendant in that capacity, and travel with him on the continent of Europe as a courier for three months certain from the day and year last aforesaid, and to be ready to start with the defendant on such travels on the day and year last aforesaid, at and for certain wages or salary, to wit," £10 per month of such service, "the defendant then agreed with the plaintiff, and then promised him, that he, the defendant, would engage and employ the plaintiff in the capacity of a courier on and from the said 1st day of June, 1852, for three months" on these terms; "and to start on such travels with the plaintiff on the day and year last aforesaid, and to pay the plaintiff" on these terms. [Further averments of the plaintiff were that he did make the agreement, "confiding in" the defendant's promise, and that—as the defendant always knew— from that time until the defendant broke his promise the plaintiff was "always ready and willing" to start travels with the defendant on the day aforesaid, and would have entered the defendant's service on that day but for the defendant's breach. "(Y)et the defendant, not regarding the said agreement ... before the said 1st June, 1852, wrongfully wholly refused" to employ the plaintiff for the three months agreed upon, or for any other time, and then "absolved" the plaintiff from performance of the agreement and from "being ready and willing to perform," and put an end to the engagement, to the plaintiff's damage.] The writ was dated on the 22d of May, 1852.

Pleas: 1. That defendant did not agree or promise in manner, and form, & c.: conclusion to the country. Issue thereon.

2. That plaintiff did not agree with defendant in manner and form, & c.: conclusion to the country. Issue thereon.

3. That plaintiff was not ready and willing, nor did defendant absolve, exonerate, or discharge plaintiff from being ready and willing, in manner and form, & c.: conclusion to the country. Issue thereon.

4. That defendant did not refuse or decline, nor wrongfully absolve, exonerate, or discharge, nor wrongfully break, put an end to or determine, in manner and form, & c.: conclusion to the country. Issue thereon.

On the trial before Erle, J., at the London sittings in last Easter term, it appeared that plaintiff was a courier, who in April, 1852, was engaged by defendant to accompany him on a tour, to commence on 1st June, 1852, on the terms mentioned in the declaration. On the 11th May, 1852, defendant wrote to plaintiff that he had changed his mind, and declined his services. He refused to make him any compensation. The action was commenced on 22d May. The plaintiff, between the commencement of the action and the 1st of June, obtained an engagement with Lord Ashburton, on equally good terms, but not commencing till 4th July. The defendant's counsel objected that there could be no breach of the contract before the 1st of June. The learned judge was of contrary opinion, but reserved leave to enter a nonsuit on this objection. The other questions were left to the jury, who found for plaintiff.

■ LORD CAMPBELL, C.J.,[a] now delivered the judgment of the court:

On this motion in arrest of judgment, the question arises whether if there be an engagement between A. and B. whereby B. engages to employ A. on and from a future day for a given period of time, to travel with him into a foreign country as a courier, and to start with him in that capacity on that day, A. being to receive a monthly salary during the continuance of such service, B. may, before the day, refuse to perform the agreement and break and renounce it, so as to entitle A. before the day to commence an action against B. to recover damages for breach of the agreement, A. having been ready and willing to perform it, till it was broken and renounced by B.

The defendant's counsel very powerfully contended that, if the plaintiff was not contented to dissolve the contract, and to abandon all remedy upon it, he was bound to remain ready and willing to perform it till the day when the actual employment as courier in the service of the defendant was to begin; and that there could be no breach of the agreement, before that day, to give a right of action. But it cannot be laid down as a universal rule that, where by agreement an act is to be done on a future day, no action can be brought for a breach of the agreement till the day for doing the act has arrived. If a man promises to marry a woman on a future day, and before that day marries another woman, he is instantly liable to an action for breach of promise of marriage. Short v. Stone, 8 Q.B. 358. If a man contracts to execute a lease on and from a future day for a certain term, and, before that day, executes a lease to another for the same term, he may be immediately sued for breaking the contract. Ford v. Tiley, 6 B. & C. 325. So if a man contracts to sell and deliver specific goods on a future day, and before the day he sells and delivers them to another he is immediately liable to an action at the suit of the person with whom he first contracted to sell and deliver them. Bowdell v. Parsons, 10 East, 359.

One reason alleged in support of such an action is, that the defendant has, before the day, rendered it impossible for him to perform the contract at the day; but this does not necessarily follow; for, prior to the day fixed for doing the act, the first wife may have died, a surrender of the lease executed might be obtained, and the defendant might have repurchased the goods so as to be in a situation to sell and deliver them to the plaintiff. Another reason may be that, where there is a contract to do an act on a future day, there is a relation constituted between the parties in the meantime by the contract, and that they impliedly promise that in the meantime neither will do anything to the prejudice of the other inconsistent with that relation. As an example, a man and woman engaged to

a. John Campbell (1779–1861), a Scot of ancient lineage, matriculated at St. Andrews University at the age of eleven. Upon entering the English bar he predicted that he would become Lord Chancellor. His name is associated with a number of law reform statutes which he pressed as a member of Parliament, as Attorney General, and in the House of Lords. As a reward for his services to the government, he was made the first Baron Campbell. He won literary fame with his "Lives of the Lord Chancellors," followed by the "Lives of the Chief Justices." These works are full of good stories, inaccuracies, and harsh judgments; it was said that they had added a new sting to death. He held judicial office briefly as Lord Chancellor of Ireland, where he was not popular, and as Chief Justice of England from 1850 to 1859. He became Lord Chancellor of England at the age of eighty.

marry are affianced to one another during the period between the time of the engagement and the celebration of the marriage. In this very case of traveller and courier, from the day of the hiring till the day when the employment was to begin, they were engaged to each other; and it seems to be a breach of an implied contract if either of them renounced the engagement. This reasoning seems in accordance with the unanimous decisions of the Exchequer Chamber in Elderton v. Emmens, 6 C.B. 160, which we have followed in subsequent cases in this court.

The declaration in the present case, in alleging a breach, states a great deal more than a passing intention on the part of the defendant which he may repent of, and could only be proved by evidence that he had utterly renounced the contract, or done some act which rendered it impossible for him to perform it. If the plaintiff has no remedy for breach of the contract unless he treats the contract as in force, and acts upon it down to the 1st June, 1852, it follows that, till then, he must enter into no employment which will interfere with his promise "to start with the defendant on such travels on the day and year," and that he must then be properly equipped in all respects as a courier for a three months' tour on the continent of Europe. But it is surely much more rational, and more for the benefit of both parties, that, after the renunciation of the agreement by the defendant, the plaintiff should be at liberty to consider himself absolved from any future performance of it, retaining his right to sue for any damage he has suffered from the breach of it. Thus, instead of remaining idle and laying out money in preparations which must be useless, he is at liberty to seek service under another employer, which would go in mitigation of the damages to which he would otherwise be entitled for a breach of the contract. It seems strange that the defendant, after renouncing the contract, and absolutely declaring that he will never act under it, should be permitted to object that faith is given to his assertion, and that an opportunity is not left to him of changing his mind. If the plaintiff is barred of any remedy by entering into an engagement inconsistent with starting as a courier with the defendant on the 1st June, he is prejudiced by putting faith in the defendant's assertion; and it would be more consistent with principle if the defendant were precluded from saying that he had not broken the contract when he declared that he entirely renounced it. Suppose that the defendant, at the time of his renunciation, had embarked on a voyage for Australia, so as to render it physically impossible for him to employ the plaintiff as a courier on the continent of Europe in the months of June, July and August, 1852; according to decided cases, the action might have been brought before the 1st June; but the renunciation may have been founded on other facts, to be given in evidence, which would equally have rendered the defendant's performance of the contract impossible. The man who wrongfully renounces a contract into which he has deliberately entered cannot justly complain if he is immediately sued for a compensation in damages by the man whom he has injured; and it seems reasonable to allow an option to the injured party, either to sue immediately, or to wait till the time when the act was to be done, still holding it as prospectively binding for the exercise of this option, which may be advantageous to the innocent party, and cannot be prejudicial to the wrongdoer.

An argument against the action before the 1st of June is urged from the difficulty of calculating the damages; but this argument is equally strong against an action before the 1st of September, when the three months would expire. In either case, the jury in assessing the damages would be justified in looking to all that happened, or was likely to happen, to increase or mitigate the loss of the plaintiff down to the day of trial. We do not find any decision contrary to the view we are taking of this case. Leigh v. Paterson, 8 Taunt, 540, only shows that upon a sale of goods to be delivered at a certain time, if the vendor before the time gives information to the vendee that he cannot deliver them, having sold them, the vendee may calculate the damages according to the state of the market when they ought to have been delivered. . . .

If it should be held that, upon a contract to do an act on a future day, a renunciation of the contract by one party dispenses with a condition to be performed in the meantime by the other, there seems no reason for requiring that other to wait till the day arrives before seeking his remedy by action; and the only ground on which the condition can be dispensed with seems to be, that the renunciation may be treated as a breach of contract.

Upon the whole, we think that the declaration in this case is sufficient. It gives us great satisfaction to reflect that, the question being on the record, our opinion may be reviewed in a Court of Error. In the meantime, we must give judgment for the plaintiff.

Judgment for plaintiff.

NOTES

(1) *A Non Sequitur.* According to Lord Campbell, if Hochster "has no remedy for breach of the contract unless he treats the contract as in force, and acts upon it down to the 1st June, 1852, it follows that, till then, he must enter into no employment which will interfere with his promise." Does this statement not conflate the first and second of the five questions listed above relating to the consequences of an anticipatory repudiation? Why does it follow that if Hochster could not have gone to court until June 1 he would not have been free to make another arrangement with Lord Ashburton before then?

Whatever the logic of Lord Campbell's opinion, Hochster v. De La Tour has generally been followed in the United States. See Restatement § 253; UCC § 2–610. Massachusetts is a notable exception. See Cavanagh v. Cavanagh, 598 N.E.2d 677, 679 (Mass.App.1992) (aside from UCC § 2–610, "Massachusetts has not generally recognized the doctrine of anticipatory repudiation").

(2) *Exception for One–Sided Contracts.* It was mentioned earlier, p. 765 above, that there was an exception to the rule that a repudiation accompanied by a breach by nonperformance gives rise to a claim for damages for total breach. It is generally accepted that if, at the time of the breach, the aggrieved party has fully performed and the only remaining duty of performance of the party in breach is to pay money in independent installments, the failure to pay one or more installments, whether or not coupled with a repudiation, will not give rise to a claim for damages for total breach. Nor will a repudiation alone give rise to such a claim. The breach will not, in other words, accelerate the time for payment of the balance of the debt, and therefore suit must be brought for the installments as they come due.

The exception can be found in Restatement §§ 243(3), 253. Note that while the former section is limited to obligations "for the payment of money in installments," the latter section is not so limited. What might be the reason for this difference?

(3) *Acceleration Clauses.* The exception just described is almost invariably avoided by the inclusion of an acceleration clause. A typical clause might read, "On any default in payment of principal or interest, the creditor may declare all amounts remaining payable immediately due and payable." UCC § 1–309 imposes limits on a party's right to accelerate payment "at will" or "when he deems himself insecure," but not in the event of a default.

(4) *The Rose Bowl Affair.* The University of Southern California advertised "economy" season tickets to its football games, promising that if its team went to the Rose Bowl each holder of such a season ticket would be given an option to buy a Rose Bowl ticket. Roger Diamond, a lawyer and Trojan football fan, bought an "economy" season ticket, but when the Trojans were selected for the Rose Bowl the University wrote Diamond that, for reasons beyond its control, first-time economy season ticket holders could not be given the promised options. Diamond brought a class action on behalf of economy season ticket holders. From summary judgment for the University, Diamond appealed. *Held:* Affirmed.

"[P]laintiff forgets that, logically or not, it is the general rule, recognized in this state, that the doctrine of breach by anticipatory repudiation does not apply to contracts which are unilateral in their inception or have become so by complete performance by one party." Diamond v. University of Southern California, 89 Cal.Rptr. 302, 305 (Ct.App.1970).

Kanavos v. Hancock Bank & Trust Co.

Supreme Judicial Court of Massachusetts, 1985.
395 Mass. 199, 479 N.E.2d 168.

■ WILKINS, JUSTICE. This appeal presents two basic questions. First, if, for valid consideration, the owner of stock in a corporation has agreed to give A the opportunity to purchase that stock at the price at which the owner intends to sell it to another in the future (a right of first refusal) but the owner instead sells the stock to a third party without giving A the opportunity to match the third party's offer and thus acquire the stock, does A's right to recover in an action for breach of contract in any way depend on whether A had the financial ability to purchase the stock during the relevant time? Second, if A's right does so depend, as we conclude it does, does A have the burden of proving his financial ability to perform or is the burden on the repudiating former stockholder to prove A's inability to perform?

The plaintiff Harold J. Kanavos (Kanavos) is A in the example given, an individual to whom the defendant Hancock Bank & Trust Company (bank) gave the right to acquire all the stock of 1025 Hancock, Inc., before the bank sold the stock to anyone else on the same terms. This corporation owned a fourteen-story apartment building, known as Executive House, on Hancock Street in Quincy. The corporation was a G.L. c. 121A limited dividend corporation, and the first mortgage was guaranteed by the Federal Housing Administration of the Department of Housing and Urban Development. On July 16, 1976, James M. Brown, then executive vice president of the bank, gave Kanavos a letter in which the bank agreed to pay him $40,000 for surrendering an option to purchase the stock and further gave Kanavos "the option to match the price of sale of said property to extend for a 60 day period from the time our offer is received." In November, 1976, the bank entered into a purchase and sale agreement to sell the stock for $760,000 to a third person and, early in December, the bank sold the stock accordingly without giving Kanavos notice and the opportunity to purchase the stock.

For the purpose of determining Kanavos's contract damages, apart from the $40,000 to be paid for the surrender of his option, the parties and the trial judge treated the value of the stock as equal to the value of the equity in the apartment building. The balance on the first mortgage was $2,500,000 at the relevant times. When the jury, in response to a special verdict question, concluded that the apartment complex was worth $4,000,000, contract damages were determined by subtracting from $4,000,000 the balance due on the mortgage ($2,500,000) and the sale price of the stock ($760,000). That damage figure ($740,000) equaled the amount by which the fair market value of the stock exceeded the price at which it was sold. The $40,000 option surrender payment was then added to arrive at a final judgment of $780,000.

The judge presented the case to the jury seeking a special verdict.... The bank's only challenge to the special verdict and resulting judgment is that the judge failed to instruct the jury (and give them an associated special verdict question) that the plaintiff had to be ready, willing, and able, pursuant to the letter creating the right of first refusal, to pay the bank $760,000 (i.e., within the sixty days, to match the offer the bank received and accepted).

The judge ruled, over objection, that Kanavos's ability to pay $760,000 was not material to this case. This is the first issue we stated above in the abstract. We conclude that Kanavos's financial ability was material because he should not recover contract damages, even from a repudiating promisor, under an agreement to sell stock unless he could have complied with his concurrent obligation to pay for the stock (or, as is not the case here, unless the bank's conduct substantially prevented Kanavos from being able to meet his obligation).

When the bank received an offer for the stock that it was prepared to accept, the bank was obliged to give Kanavos the right to match that offer. At that point, Kanavos had an option to purchase the stock on the same terms, although, of course, in this case he was unaware that such an offer (and hence the option) existed. He could have exercised his option by tendering the purchase price, and the bank would have been obliged to deliver the shares of stock. In the circumstances of this case, Kanavos was not obliged to make a meaningless tender of the purchase price. The stock had already been sold. However, one party's repudiation of a bilateral contract containing simultaneous obligations does not normally make immaterial the question whether the other party could perform his obligation. "It is the general rule 'that when performance under a contract is concurrent, one party cannot put the other in default unless he is ready, able, and willing to perform and has manifested this by some offer of performance' although a tender of performance is not necessary 'if the other party has shown that he cannot or will not perform.' " Mayer v. Boston Metropolitan Airport, Inc., 355 Mass. 344, 354, 244 N.E.2d 568 (1969), quoting Leigh v. Rule, 331 Mass. 664, 668, 121 N.E.2d 854 (1954).

The weight of authority in this country is that the financial ability of a prospective buyer of property is a material issue in his action for damages against a repudiating defendant for breach of an agreement to sell that property for an established price. See 5 S. Williston, Contracts § 699, at 352–353 (Jaeger ed. 1961), and 6 S. Williston, Contracts § 882, at 394 (Jaeger ed. 1962); 4 A. Corbin, Contracts § 978, at 924–925 (1951); Restatement (Second) of Contracts § 254, Comment *a* (1981) (the duty of a repudiating party "to pay damages is discharged if it subsequently appears that there would have been a total failure of performance by the injured party"); Farnsworth, The Problems of Nonperformance in Contract, 17 New Eng.L.Rev. 249, 306 (1982) (If a seller repudiates an option to sell land, "[a]lthough the holder of the option is under no duty to pay the price of the land, his payment of the price is a condition of the seller's repudiated duty"); Taylor, The Impact of Article 2 of the U.C.C. on the Doctrine of Anticipatory Repudiation, 9 B.C.Indus. & Com.L.Rev. 917, 927 (1967)[1].... We have taken the view that, even where promises were not concurrent, a plaintiff could only recover nominal or small damages against a defendant who repudiated a contract, where it would have been impossible for the plaintiff to perform a contractual obligation arising shortly after the defendant's breach. See Randall v. Peerless Motor Car Co., 212 Mass. 352, 382, 99 N.E. 221 (1912).

Here, the bank's obligation to sell the shares and Kanavos's obligation to pay for them were concurrent obligations. If neither could perform, even if the bank repudiated the contract, neither could recover. 6 S. Williston, supra § 882, at 389–391. Kanavos did not have to show that he was ready, willing, and able to purchase the stock on the day the bank repudiated its agreement with him by selling the stock. Thomas v. Christensen, 12 Mass.App.Ct. 169, 177, 422 N.E.2d 472 (1981). That principle does not mean, however, that his ability to purchase the stock during the option period is irrelevant.

Kanavos relies, as the trial judge apparently did, on a statement in Lowe v. Harwood, 139 Mass. 133, 135, 29 N.E. 538 (1885), that, when a seller repudiates a purchase and sale agreement by selling land to a third person, the inability of the plaintiff to pay the purchase price according to the contract terms is unimportant in an action for breach of contract.[2] The

---

1. "Under general contract law there was, however, a twist: If the nonrepudiating party was not in a position to perform either at the time of repudiation or at sometime thereafter prior to the date for performance, he had no remedy. The fact that the repudiation may have been unjustified did not change this result, and the burden of proving the necessary ability to perform was on the nonrepudiating plaintiff." Id.

2. The relevant language of the opinion is as follows: "It is suggested that it does not appear that the plaintiff was able to pay the money which he was to pay. But he was personally bound for it, and the degree of his ability at any moment before he was called on to pay was no concern of the defendant's.

Lowe opinion cites no relevant authority for the proposition that a repudiating seller is liable in damages to a buyer who could not have carried out his end of the bargain. That principle ... appears now to be extinct.... There is no compelling reason to adopt such a rule at this time.[3]

If, as we have concluded, Kanavos's ability to match the offer which the bank accepted is material to his right to recover, the question then is whether the burden of proof should be placed on Kanavos to show his ability or on the bank to show his lack of ability. The general rule is that the plaintiff must prove his ability to perform his obligations under a contract of the type involved here. See Wolbarsht v. Donnelly, 302 Mass. 568, 570–571, 20 N.E.2d 415 (1939); 5 S. Williston, supra § 699, at 352–353; 4 A. Corbin, supra § 978, at 925; Taylor, 9 B.C.Indus. & Com.L.Rev. supra at 927 ("the burden of proving the necessary ability to perform was on the nonrepudiating plaintiff"). Cf. Restatement (Second) of Contracts § 245, Comment *b* (1981) (where an express condition of the defendant's liability has not occurred but the defendant has already repudiated the contract, the repudiating defendant has the burden of proving that the condition would not have occurred). There is not, however, a unanimity of view in this country on the placing of the burden of proof in such a case....

The burden was on Kanavos to prove his ability to finance the purchase of the stock. The fact of his ability to do so was an essential part of establishing the defendant's liability. Circumstances concerning his ability to raise $760,000 for the stock were far better known to him than to the bank. It is, of course, true that the bank created the problem by selling the stock to another in violation of its contractual obligation, and one could argue that, therefore, it should take the risk of failing to establish Kanavos's inability to purchase the stock. Such an argument, however, has not been generally accepted, for to do so would in effect place on the defendant the burden of disproving a fact essential to the plaintiff's case.

There was evidence from which the jury would have been warranted in finding that Kanavos had the ability to finance the purchase of the stock. Although he admitted that he was in financial difficulty during the relevant times, he had connections with people who might have assisted him. He testified that he could have purchased the stock if the bank had given him timely notice of his rights. Moreover, the jury found that the apartment complex was worth $1,500,000 more than the principal balance of the first

---

The way for the defendant to test that was to tender performance on his side conditionally upon the plaintiff's performing his part of the agreement. See Brown v. Davis, 138 Mass. 458."

3. We perceive no reason why Kanavos's ability to purchase the stock should be any less significant than the ability of a person who had the right to buy property under a purchase and sale agreement or of a person who held an option to purchase property. Once the bank determined that it would sell the property to a third person, Kanavos's rights were substantially equivalent to an option to buy. Once the bank repudiated its obligation to Kanavos by selling the stock to a third person, Kanavos's rights and his burden of proof were the same as they would have been if he had been a buyer under a repudiated purchase and sale or option agreement. The bank's repudiation of the agreement giving Kanavos a right of first refusal did not estop the bank from arguing that Kanavos lacked the ability to pay for the stock.

mortgage, and thus $780,000 more than Kanavos would have had to have paid the bank for the stock (the sale price of $760,000 less the $40,000 the bank owed him). This differential suggests that financing was not an impossibility for Kanavos. Considering Kanavos's admitted financial difficulties at that time, the question of his ability to purchase the stock (or to sell his rights to another) may depend on whether the earnings of the apartment complex were sufficient to support some arrangement to finance the acquisition within the various limitations applicable under the federally guaranteed first mortgage (assuming it were not to be discharged in the process).

The question of Kanavos's ability to purchase the stock should have been submitted to the jury. We see no reason, however, for a retrial of those issues already decided by the jury. We remand the case for a retrial on the question whether, if he had had proper notice of his right to purchase the stock, Kanavos would have been ready, willing, and able to do so during the option period.

So ordered.

NOTES

(1) *Analogy to Express Conditions.* The first question addressed by the court is analogous to one that arises in the case of an express condition. In Shear v. National Rifle Association, discussed in Note 1, p. 709 above, the NRA argued that, even if the Management Committee had recommended the sale and even if the by-laws had not been amended, "nothing but abject speculation could show that 'the condition [settlement] would have occurred.'" The court rejected this argument, noting that "almost all cases in which prevention is alleged will involve speculation as to what would have happened had the defendant's conduct not taken place." 606 F.2d at 1257.

In American List Corp. v. U.S. News & World Report, 549 N.E.2d 1161, 1165 (N.Y.1989), the court rejected the argument "that in discounting the total amount due under the contract to its present value, the court may factor in the risk that the nonrepudiating party will be unable to perform the contract in the future" since such a rule "would require the nonrepudiating party to prove its ability to perform in the future, despite the fact that the doctrine [of anticipatory breach] is intended to operate to relieve the nonrepudiating party of that very performance." Is this consistent with the decision in *Kanavos*?

(2) *Tender Excused.* Laredo Hides Co. v. H & H Meat Products Co., p. 613 above, reports that H & H, the seller of cattle hides, gave an "ultimatum" to Laredo Hides, the buyer, about payment for hides that had been delivered. Liborio Hinojosa, acting for H & H, set March 21 as a deadline for payment. It passed without action satisfactory to him, and he refused payment when it was later tendered. The next delivery of hides was scheduled under the contract for Saturday, April 1. On the Thursday before that, March 30, an agent for Laredo Hides telephoned Hinojosa to ask if Saturday's shipment would be ready for pickup. "Hinojosa unequivocally told him that he was not going to sell him any more hides, and further advised that it was useless for him to send a truck for the hides, since at 4:30 p.m., Tuesday, March 21st, he had made up his mind to terminate the contract." The suit by Laredo Hides followed. On appeal by H & H, the point seems to have been made, on behalf of H & H, that Laredo Hides had taken no further action in performance of the contract.

Before confronting the issue of damages, the court disposed of that point. "Where one of the parties repudiates the contract and absolutely refuses to perform the duties and obligations required of him, the other party need not go through the useless act of tendering performance. Under the record before us, H & H repudiated the contract with Laredo Hides on March 30, 1972. That repudiation relieved Laredo Hides of itself tendering performance during the remaining months covered by the contract. It would have been useless and futile for Laredo Hides to have made such a tender twice in each of the months remaining."

That mere doubts are not enough to excuse tender, see Swiss Bank Corp. v. Dresser Industries, 141 F.3d 689, 692 (7th Cir.1998) (Posner, C.J.: "[W]hen a performing party is not told and does not know that his tender of performance will be refused, he must tender, rather than force a court to decide years later what would have happened had he tendered").

McCloskey & Co. v. Minweld Steel Co.

United States Court of Appeals, Third Circuit, 1955.
220 F.2d 101.

Suit by contractor against subcontractor alleging anticipatory breach of three contracts entered into by parties. The United States District Court for the Western District of Pennsylvania, Joseph P. Willson, J., granted defendant's motion for judgment on ground that plaintiff had not made out prima facie case, and entered order denying plaintiff's motion for findings of fact, to vacate judgments and for new trial, and plaintiff appealed....

Order affirmed.

■ McLAUGHLIN, CIRCUIT JUDGE. Plaintiff-appellant, a general contractor, sued on three contracts alleging an anticipatory breach as to each. At the close of the plaintiff's case the district judge granted the defense motions for judgment on the ground that plaintiff had not made out a cause of action.

By the contracts involved the ... defendant, a fabricator and erector of steel, agreed to furnish and erect all of the structural steel required on two buildings to be built on the grounds of the Hollidaysburg State Hospital, Hollidaysburg, Pa. and to furnish all of the long span steel joists required in the construction of one of the two buildings. Two of the contracts were dated May 1, 1950 and the third May 26, 1950. By Article V of each of the contracts "Should the Sub–Contractor [the defendant herein] ... at any time refuse or neglect to supply a sufficiency ... of materials of the proper quality, ... in and about the performance of the work required to be done pursuant to the provisions of this agreement ..., or fail, in the performance of any of the agreements herein contained, the Contractor shall be at liberty, without prejudice, to any other right or remedy, on two days' written notice to the Sub–Contractor, either to provide any such ... materials and to deduct the cost thereof from any payments then or thereafter due the Sub–Contractor, or to terminate the employment of the Sub–Contractor for the said work and to enter upon the premises.... "

There was no stated date in the contracts for performance by the defendant subcontractor. Article VI provided for completion by the subcontractor of its contract work "by and at the time or times hereafter stated to-wit:

"Samples, Shop Drawings and Schedules are to be submitted in the quantities and manner required by the Specifications, for the approval of the Architects, immediately upon receipt by the Sub–Contractor of the contract drawings, or as may be directed by the Contractor. All expense involved in the submission and approval of these Samples, Shop Drawings and Schedules shall be borne by the Sub–Contractor.

"All labor, materials and equipment required under this contract are to be furnished at such times as may be directed by the Contractor, and in such a manner so as to at no time delay the final completion of the building.

"It being mutually understood and agreed that prompt delivery and installation of all materials required to be furnished under this contract is to be the essence of this Agreement."

Appellee Minweld Steel Co., Inc., the subcontractor, received contract drawings and specifications for both buildings in May, 1950. On June 8, 1950, plaintiff McCloskey & Co. wrote appellee asking when it might "expect delivery of the structural steel" for the buildings and "also the time estimated to complete erection." Minweld replied on June 13, 1950, submitting a schedule estimate of expecting to begin delivery of the steel by September 1, and to complete erection approximately November 15. On July 20, 1950 plaintiff wrote Minweld threatening to terminate the contracts unless the latter gave unqualified assurances that it had effected definite arrangements for the procurement, fabrication and delivery within thirty days of the required materials. On July 24, 1950 Minweld wrote McCloskey & Co. explaining its difficulty in obtaining the necessary steel. It asked McCloskey's assistance in procuring it and stated that "We are as anxious as you are that there be no delay in the final completion of the buildings or in the performance of our contract,...."[1]

---

1. This letter in full is as follows:

Minweld Steel Company
Incorporated
Shaler and Wabash Streets
Pittsburgh 20, Pa.

July 24, 1950.

McClosky & Company
1620 Thompson Street
Philadelphia 21, Penna.

In re: New Hospital Buildings
Hollidaysburg State Hospital
Hollidaysburg, Pennsylvania

Attention of J.C. McCloskey,
Vice President

Dear Sir:

This will acknowledge receipt of your letter of July 20th, 1950, which was received by us today.

Upon receipt of the architect's specifications, we completed the engineering and erection plans on the said specifications. Immediately after those details were available, we attempted to place orders for the steel with the Bethlehem Steel Company. Our order was held in the offices of the Bethlehem Steel Company for two weeks before we were notified that it could not be supplied. Since that time, we have tried the U.S. Steel Corporation and Carnegie Illinois, both companies informing us that they were under contract for approximately one year and could not fulfill the order.

The recent directive by the President of the United States, with which we assume you are familiar, has further tightened up the steel market so that at the present writing we cannot give you any positive promise as to our ability to obtain the steel or delivery dates.

Plaintiff-appellant claims that by this last letter, read against the relevant facts, defendant gave notice of its positive intention not to perform its contracts and thereby violated same.[2] Some reference has already been made to the background of the July 24th letter. It concerned Minweld's trouble in securing the steel essential for performance of its contract. Minweld had tried unsuccessfully to purchase this from Bethlehem Steel, U.S. Steel and Carnegie–Illinois. It is true as appellant urges that Minweld knew and was concerned about the tightening up of the steel market.[3] And as is evident from the letter it, being a fabricator and not a producer, realized that without the help of the general contractor on this hospital project particularly by it enlisting the assistance of the General State Authority,[4] Minweld was in a bad way for the needed steel. However, the letter conveys no idea of contract repudiation by Minweld. That company admittedly was in a desperate situation. Perhaps if it had moved earlier to seek the steel its effort might have been successful. But that is mere speculation for there is no showing that the mentioned producers had they been solicited sooner would have been willing to provide the material.

Minweld from its written statement did, we think, realistically face the problem confronting it. As a result it asked its general contractor for the aid which the latter, by the nature of the construction, should have been willing to give. Despite the circumstances there is no indication in the letter that Minweld had definitely abandoned all hope of otherwise receiving the steel and so finishing its undertaking. One of the mentioned producers might have relented. Some other supplier might have turned up. It was McCloskey & Co. who eliminated whatever chance there was. That concern instead of aiding Minweld by urging its plea for the hospital construction materials to the State Authority which represented the Commonwealth of Pennsylvania took the position that the subcontractor had repudiated its agreement and then moved quickly to have the work completed. Shortly thereafter, and without the slightest trouble as far as

In view of the directive from Washington and the tightening up of the entire steel industry, we solicit your help and that of the General State Authority in aiding us to obtain the steel for these contracts.

We are as anxious as you are that there be no delay in the final completion of the buildings or in the performance of our contract, but we have nowhere else to turn at the present time for the supply of steel necessary under said contracts, unless through your aid and assistance, and that of the General State Authority, a supplier can be induced to give us the materials needed.

The U.S. Steel Corporation informs us that you have discussed this matter with them and are presently aware of our present difficulties.

If steel is to be supplied to these hospital buildings by governmental directive, we feel that the steel should be supplied to us for completion under our contract.

Very truly yours,

Minweld Steel Company, Inc.
   J.A. Roberts
     Sales Manager

JAR/fs

c/c Travelers Indemnity Co.,
    Hartford, Conn.
   General State Authority,
    Harrisburg, Penna.

2. Plaintiff cancelled the contracts on July 26, 1950 on the ground that the July 24th letter constituted an admission of defendant's inability to perform the required work.

3. The Korean War broke out on June 24, 1950.

4. The Pennsylvania state agency which represented and owned the Hollidaysburg State Hospital.

appears, McCloskey & Co. procured the steel from Bethlehem[5] and brought in new subcontractors to do the work contemplated by the agreement with Minweld.

Under the applicable law Minweld's letter was not a breach of the agreement. The suit is in the federal court by reason of diversity of citizenship of the parties. Though there is no express statement to that effect the contracts between the parties would seem to have been executed in Pennsylvania with the law of that state applicable. In McClelland v. New Amsterdam Cas. Co., 1936, 322 Pa. 429, 433, 185 A. 198, 200, the Pennsylvania Supreme Court held in a case where the subcontractor had asked for assistance in obtaining credit, "In order to give rise to a renunciation amounting to a breach of contract there must be an absolute and unequivocal refusal to perform or a distinct and positive statement of an inability to do so." Minweld's conduct is plainly not that of a contract breaker under that test. See also Dingley v. Oler, 1886, 117 U.S. 490. Restatement of Contracts, Comment (i) to Sec. 318 (1932) speaks clearly on the point saying:

"Though where affirmative action is promised mere failure to act, at the time when action has been promised, is a breach, failure to take preparatory action before the time when any performance is promised is not an anticipatory breach, even though such failure makes it impossible that performance shall take place, and though the promisor at the time of the failure intends not to perform his promise." See Williston on Contracts, Vol. 5, Sec. 1324 (1937), Corbin on Contracts, Vol. 4, Sec. 973 (1951).

Appellant contends that its letter of July 20, requiring assurances of arrangements which would enable appellee to complete delivery in thirty days, constituted a fixing of a date under Article VI of the contracts. The short answer to this is that the thirty day date, if fixed, was never repudiated. Appellee merely stated that it was unable to give assurances as to the preparatory arrangements. There is nothing in the contracts which authorized appellant to demand or receive such assurances.

The district court acted properly in dismissing the actions as a matter of law on the ground that plaintiff had not made out a prima facie case.

The order of the district court of July 14, 1954 denying the plaintiff's motion for findings of facts, to vacate the judgments and for new trials will be affirmed.

NOTES

(1) *What is a Repudiation (Reprise)?* If the test for determining what is a repudiation is an objective one, it is surely no better to say "I cannot perform the contract" than to say "I will not perform it." Is it any better to say, "I will try to perform, though I see no prospect of succeeding"? How does that differ from what Minweld wrote to McCloskey in the main case?

---

5. Bethlehem had originally submitted a bid in competition with Minweld. Its new proposals were dated July 28, 1950 and were finally accepted by McCloskey & Co. on Au-gust 7, 1950. The long span steel joists required by the third contract were procured from the Frederick Grundy Iron Works.

A party who is delinquent in performance, or threatened with inability, can surely plead with the other for leniency without being guilty of a repudiation. If pressed, one may hope to skirt a repudiation with cautiously written letters, perhaps drafted with the aid of counsel. How may the other party force the issue? Would it be easier to do so in a face-to-face encounter than by correspondence? Which party is likely to call for a conference? See Plunkett v. Comstock–Cheney Co., 208 N.Y.S. 93 (App.Div.1925).

In formulating tests for repudiation, what bearing might it have if a party having grounds to expect a breach by the other had a right to demand assurance of due performance?

(2) *Counseling (Reprise)*. If McCloskey had asked for your help in drafting its letter of July 20, what would you have advised? What were the risks of a badly drafted letter? Might a face-to-face encounter have been preferable for McCloskey? If McCloskey had asked you how it should respond to Minweld's letter of July 24, what would you have advised? Could McCloskey have made use of Article V, which allowed McCloskey to either provide the materials itself and deduct the cost or terminate the contract if Minweld should "at any time refuse or neglect to supply a sufficiency . . . of materials"?

If Minweld had asked for your help in drafting its letter of July 24, what would you have advised? What were the risks of a badly drafted letter? Might a face-to-face encounter have been preferable for Minweld?

––––––––

C.L. MADDOX, INC. v. COALFIELD SERVICES, INC., 51 F.3d 76 (7th Cir.1995). [Maddox, who had a contract with Old Ben Coal Company to demolish and replace a loading facility in one of the company's mines, decided to subcontract everything except the fabrication of the new facility. In February, Maddox met with the president of Coalfield, who offered to do the job for $230,000 in the three weeks that Maddox wished because of his commitments to Old Ben.

Coalfield's crew traveled to the mine on March 19. On the same day Coalfield faxed a proposed contract to Maddox, specifying a price of $230,000, completion within three weeks, and biweekly progress payments. Maddox called Coalfield the same day and said that he would sign the proposal, but he never did. Coalfield's crew began work the next day, March 20. Progress was slower than expected. On April 8, after Maddox had failed to reply to repeated requests to sign the proposal, Coalfield ordered its crew to stop work and come to the surface with its tools and equipment. It faxed Maddox that it would not proceed unless Maddox accepted the proposed contract and paid an invoice for $103,500, which was 45 percent of the contract price, the percentage of the job that Coalfield claimed it had completed.

Maddox replied by fax the same day, apologizing for not having responded sooner, and saying that though, from information received from the project superintendent, "your 45 percent completion is a little high, . . . we shall in good faith accept the 45 percent completion figure and pay accordingly less 10 percent retention." But Maddox appeared to condition this promise on Coalfield's signing an enclosed "acceptance letter" extending the deadline for completion of the work from three weeks to four and adding a liquidated-damages clause requiring Coalfield to pay $1,000 for each day's delay beyond the four-week deadline. Coalfield balked. It had been working for three weeks and estimated that completion might take another five weeks beyond this new deadline, with a potential liability of $35,000 if it agreed to liquidated damages.

Coalfield faxed Maddox the same day, rejecting the acceptance letter and refusing to complete the project unless Maddox paid the $103,500 invoice and accepted Coalfield's May 19 offer, with an exception for the date of completion. It added, "if you decide to accept the above conditions, we will proceed with work starting April 16," eight days from the date of the fax. Maddox replied that if Coalfield did not resume work by April 9, it would be in breach. Coalfield never resumed work.

Maddox sued for damages based on the cost of paying another contractor to finish the job in time to avoid a breach of its contract with Old Ben. Coalfield counterclaimed for $103,500 based on the percentage of the job that it claimed it had completed. The parties consented to a trial before a magistrate judge, who found for Coalfield. Maddox appealed.]

■ POSNER, CHIEF JUDGE. [The court concluded that there was a contract even though the parties had not reduced their oral agreement to writing.] By suspending work on April 8, before the job was finished, Coalfield broke the contract—unless the suspension was a legitimate self-help response to a breach or threatened breach by Maddox. The magistrate judge thought it was, thought that Maddox had committed a breach that consisted of failing to make any of the biweekly progress payments required by the proposal that Mr. Maddox had promised to sign. Yet Coalfield's first invoice was sent to Maddox after Coalfield stopped work, and since the progress payments were based on the percentage of work completed Maddox could hardly be expected to pay before Coalfield informed it of the progress of the work. (Anyway Coalfield had been working for barely two weeks when it invoiced Maddox.) The same timing problem afflicts Coalfield's argument that the stoppage was also justified by Maddox's insistence on a liquidated-damages clause. It would have been justified had the insistence preceded the stoppage. . . . But the sequence was reversed.

To get around the issue of timing, Coalfield argues that there was no stoppage on April 8. It had merely brought its crew to the surface. It could have put them back to work. Stopping work for just a few hours was not a breach of its duty to perform; abandonment came later, after Maddox's bombshell. Yet Coalfield's second fax announced that even if Maddox accepted all its demands it would not resume work for eight days. We infer that bringing the crew and all its tools and equipment to the surface was a substantial interruption in Coalfield's work and probably, since Coalfield knew that Maddox was in a hurry for the job to be completed, a substantial enough interruption to constitute a breach of contract, unless excused by Maddox's own breach or anticipatory repudiation.

We think the stoppage was excused. Maddox's refusal for three weeks to sign Coalfield's proposal, or even to send an acceptance with noncon- forming terms, or even just to respond somehow to Coalfield's repeated demands rather than simply ignore them, gave Coalfield substantial grounds for interrupting its work in order to avoid running up additional costs without any assurance of payment. We must remember that Coalfield was working under an oral contract with many omitted terms, because Mr. Maddox might deny that he had phoned his acceptance of the terms in Coalfield's written proposal. Every day that Coalfield continued working, it put itself further in Maddox's power. Had it finished the job it would have found itself owed $230,000 with no leverage over Maddox to extract the money short of a suit to enforce what, depending on Mr. Maddox's testimony and its reception by a jury, might be merely a vague oral contract. Coalfield's good judgment in pausing—the reasonableness of its suspicion that Maddox had no intention of complying with the oral agreement—was shortly vindicated by Maddox's demand for a liquidated-damages clause. So unlikely was the clause to be accepted, given the virtual certainty that Coalfield would not be able to finish the job in four weeks, that the most plausible interpretation of Maddox's action is that it was seeking excuses for not paying Coalfield anything. Our reaction might be different if liquidated damages clauses were standard in the industry, but there is no evidence that they are.

We do not suggest that the proposal of a liquidated damages clause was itself a breach of contract. Even the written proposal was sketchy; there were many open terms. Maddox was free to ask for whatever terms it liked even though, since the parties already had a contract, Coalfield was not obligated to accept any of Maddox's proposals. Nor do we suggest that Coalfield could justify the stoppage on the basis of events that happened later. It is merely that those events are evidence that the earlier suspicions that precipitated the stoppage were indeed reasonable. . . .

Maddox hints at an argument that Coalfield broke the contract by failing to complete performance within three weeks. The implication is that Coalfield used Maddox's failure to sign the proposal as a pretext to walk off a job that it could not complete at a profit because it had underestimated the difficulties. It is not a bad argument, . . . but it is insufficiently developed to justify a reversal. We do not know whether the agreement required completion within three weeks or merely estimated completion within that time. . . .

[Affirmed in part but remanded for redetermination of Coalfield's damages.]

NOTE

Questions. If the "substantial interruption in Coalfield's work" on April 8 would have justified termination by Maddox "unless excused by Maddox's own breach or anticipatory repudiation," what was the excuse for the interruption? Was the silence of Maddox in the face of Coalfield's repeated requests to sign the contract a breach by nonperformance? A repudiation?

PERMISSIBLE RESPONSES TO REPUDIATION

Recall Lord Campbell's statement in Hochster v. De La Tour, p. 776, "that the renunciation may be treated as a breach of contract." His use of "may" suggests that the recipient of a repudiation can choose to treat the repudiation as a breach or not, much as the recipient of an offer can choose to accept the offer or not. However, the temptation to analogize a repudiation to an offer leads to unsatisfactory results when the recipient of the repudiation disregards it.

If the recipient disregards the repudiation, will the rights of the parties be determined as if the repudiation had never occurred, as would be the case if the recipient of an offer disregarded it? Lord Cockburn seemed to think so when he said, in Frost v. Knight, L.R. 7 Ex. 111, 112 (1872), that the aggrieved party, "if he pleases, may treat the notice of intention as inoperative . . . but in that case he keeps the contact alive for the benefit of the other party as well as his own." But the court in Rockingham County v. Luten Bridge Co., p. 630 above, dismissed Lord Cockburn's view as "not in harmony with the decisions in this country." Would not Lord Cockburn's view have allowed the Luten Bridge Co. "to pile up damages by proceeding with the erection of a useless bridge"? Where, however, the recipient's disregard of a repudiation involves nothing more than waiting for the other party to perform despite the repudiation, Lord Cockburn's view has had more appeal.

That was the situation in Phillpotts v. Evans, 151 Eng.Rep. 200, 201 (Exchequer 1839), a suit by a seller on a contract for the sale of wheat. The market having fallen, the buyer repudiated before the time for delivery. The market price continued to fall between the day of the repudiation and the last day when the seller could have delivered. The question was whether the damages should be calculated with reference to the market price at the time of the buyer's repudiation, or to the price at the later time. Naturally, the buyer preferred the earlier date. The seller, however, prevailed for, according the Lord Abinger, the seller was not bound at the time of the repudiation "to sell in order to reduce damages." The Supreme Court of the United States took the same approach in Roehm v. Horst, 178 U.S. 1 (1900), a leading American case on anticipatory breach of contract.

The following case wrestles with the problem under the Uniform Commercial Code.

Cosden Oil & Chemical Co. v. Karl O. Helm Aktiengesellschaft

United States Court of Appeals, Fifth Circuit, 1984.
736 F.2d 1064.

■ REAVLEY, CIRCUIT JUDGE: We must address one of the most difficult interpretive problems of the Uniform Commercial Code—the appropriate time to measure buyer's damages where the seller anticipatorily repudiates a contract and the buyer does not cover. The district court applied the Texas version of Article 2 and measured buyer's damages at a commercially reasonable time after seller's repudiation. We affirm, but remand for modification of damages on another point.

Case History

This contractual dispute arose out of events and transactions occurring in the first three months of 1979, when the market in polystyrene, a petroleum derivative used to make molded products, was steadily rising. During this time Iran, a major petroleum producer, was undergoing political turmoil. Karl O. Helm Aktiengesellschaft (Helm or Helm Hamburg), an international trading company based in Hamburg, West Germany, anticipated a tightening in the world petrochemical supply and decided to purchase a large amount of polystyrene. Acting on orders from Helm Hamburg, Helm Houston, a wholly-owned subsidiary, initiated negotiations with Cosden Oil & Chemical Company (Cosden), a Texas-based producer of chemical products, including polystyrene.

. . . Negotiating over the telephone and by telex, the parties agreed to the purchase and sale of 1250 metric tons[1] of high impact polystyrene at $.2825 per pound and 250 metric tons of general purpose polystyrene at $.265 per pound. [The confirmations of these contracts gave Helm options for additional amounts of each type of polystyrene. Upon the proper exercise of these options, Helms held four confirmations, numbered 04 through 07. Numbers 04 and 06 represented the "high impact" product.

[On or about January 26 Cosden shipped 90,000 pounds of this product. After encountering difficulties described in the note,[2] Cosden notified Helm in late January that delivery under the 04 contract might be delayed. On February 6, Cosden informed Helm that it "was cancelling orders 05, 06, and 07 because two plants were 'down' and it did not have sufficient product to fill the orders." In mid-February Cosden shipped some 1,260,000 pounds under order 04. It refused, as "not possible," a request to make the final delivery under 04 by March 16; and near the end of March it cancelled the remainder of 04. Meanwhile, Cosden remained unpaid for product it had delivered.[3]]

---

1.   One metric ton equals approximately 2,204.5 pounds.

2.   "As Helm had expected, polystyrene prices began to rise in late January, and continued upward during February and March. Cosden also experienced problems at two of its plants in late January. Normally, Cosden supplied its Calumet City, Illinois, production plant with styrene monomer, the 'feed stock' or main ingredient of polystyrene, by barges that traveled from Louisiana up the Mississippi and Illinois Rivers to a canal that extended to Cosden's plant. Due to the extremely cold winter of 1978–79, however, the Illinois River and the canal froze, suspending barge traffic for a few weeks. A different problem beset Cosden's Windsor, New Jersey, production plant. A new reactor, used in the polystyrene manufacturing process, had recently been installed at the Windsor plant. A manufacturing defect soon became apparent, however, and Cosden returned the reactor to the manufacturer for repair, which took several weeks. At the time of the reactor breakdown, Cosden was manufacturing only general purpose at the Windsor plant. Cosden had planned on supplying Helm's high impact orders from the Calumet City plant." 736 F.2d at 1068.

3.   After Helm Hamburg learned of Cosden's cancellation, apparently in February, "Wolfgang Gordian, a member of Helm's executive board, sent an internal memorandum to Helm Houston outlining a strategy. Helm would urge that Cosden continue to perform under 04 and, after receiving the high impact polystyrene, would offset amounts owing under 04 against Helm's damages for nondelivery of the balance of polystyrene."

Cosden sued Helm, seeking damages for Helm's failure to pay for delivered polystyrene. Helm counterclaimed for Cosden's failure to deliver polystyrene as agreed. The jury found on special verdict that Cosden had agreed to sell polystyrene to Helm under all four orders.[a] The jury also found that Cosden anticipatorily repudiated orders 05, 06, and 07 and that Cosden cancelled order 04 before Helm's failure to pay for the second 04 delivery constituted a repudiation. The jury fixed the per pound market prices for polystyrene under each of the four orders at three different times: when Helm learned of the cancellation, at a commercially reasonable time thereafter, and at the time for delivery.

The district court ... determined that Helm was entitled to recover $628,676 in damages representing the difference between the contract price and the market price at a commercially reasonable time after Cosden repudiated its polystyrene delivery obligations and that Cosden was entitled to an offset of $355,950 against those damages for polystyrene delivered, but not paid for, under order 04.

Time for Measuring Buyer's Damages

Both parties find fault with the time at which the district court measured Helm's damages for Cosden's anticipatory repudiation of orders 05, 06, and 07.[4] Cosden argues that damages should be measured when Helm learned of the repudiation. Helm contends that market price as of the last day for delivery—or the time of performance—should be used to compute its damages under the contract-market differential. We reject both views, and hold that the district court correctly measured damages at a commercially reasonable point after Cosden informed Helm that it was cancelling the three orders.

Article 2 of the Code has generally been hailed as a success for its comprehensiveness, its deference to mercantile reality, and its clarity. Nevertheless, certain aspects of the Code's overall scheme have proved troublesome in application. The interplay among sections 2.610, 2.711, 2.712, 2.713, and 2.723, Tex.Bus. & Com.Code Ann. (Vernon 1968), represents one of those areas, and has been described as "an impossible legal thicket." J. White & R. Summers, Uniform Commercial Code § 6-7 at 242 (2d ed. 1980). The aggrieved buyer seeking damages for seller's anticipatory repudiation presents the most difficult interpretive problem.[5] Section 2.713 describes the buyer's damages remedy:

Buyer's Damages for Non–Delivery or Repudiation

(a) Subject to the provisions of this chapter with respect to proof of market price (Section 2.723), the measure of damages for non-

---

a. It found also that the four orders comprised one contract, and, according to a stipulation, Cosden was not in breach prior to March 19.

4. The damages measurement problem does not apply to Cosden's breach of order 04, which was not anticipatorily repudiated. The time Helm learned of Cosden's intent to deliver no more polystyrene under 04 was the same time as the last date of performance, which had been extended to the end of March.

5. The only area of unanimous agreement among those that have studied the Code provisions relevant to this problem is that they are not consistent, present problems in interpretation, and invite amendment.

delivery or repudiation by the seller is the difference between the market price *at the time when the buyer learned of the breach* and the contract price together with any incidental and consequential damages provided in this chapter (Section 2.715), but less expenses saved in consequence of the seller's breach.

(emphasis added).

Courts and commentators have identified three possible interpretations of the phrase "learned of the breach." If seller anticipatorily repudiates, buyer learns of the breach:

(1) When he learns of the repudiation;

(2) When he learns of the repudiation plus a commercially reasonable time; or

(3) When performance is due under the contract.

We would not be free to decide the question if there were a Texas case on point.... [But] no Texas case has addressed the Code question of buyer's damages in an anticipatory repudiation context....[6]

We do not doubt, and Texas law is clear, that market price at the time buyer learns of the breach is the appropriate measure of section 2.713 damages in cases where buyer learns of the breach at or after the time for performance. This will be the common case, for which section 2.713 was designed. See Peters, Remedies for Breach of Contracts Relating to the Sale of Goods Under the Uniform Commercial Code: A Roadmap for Article Two, 73 Yale L.J. 199, 264 (1963). In the relatively rare case where seller anticipatorily repudiates and buyer does not cover, see Anderson, supra, at 318, the specific provision for anticipatory repudiation cases, section 2.610, authorizes the aggrieved party to await performance for a commercially reasonable time before resorting to his remedies of cover or damages.

In the anticipatory repudiation context, the buyer's specific right to wait for a commercially reasonable time before choosing his remedy must be read together with the general damages provision of section 2.713 to extend the time for measurement beyond when buyer learns of the breach. Comment 1 to section 2.610 states that if an aggrieved party "awaits performance beyond a commercially reasonable time he cannot recover resulting damages which he should have avoided." This suggests that an aggrieved buyer can recover damages where the market rises during the commercially reasonable time he awaits performance. To interpret 2.713's "learned of the breach" language to mean the time at which seller first communicates his anticipatory repudiation would undercut the time that 2.610 gives the aggrieved buyer to await performance.

The buyer's option to wait a commercially reasonable time also interacts with section 2.611, which allows the seller an opportunity to retract his

6. Before Texas adopted the Code, its courts applied the traditional time-of-performance measure of damages in repudiation cases. See, e.g., Henderson v. Otto Goedecke, Inc., 430 S.W.2d 120, 123–24 (Tex.Civ.App.— Tyler 1968, writ ref'd n.r.e.); Anderson, Learning of Breaches Under Section 2–713 of the Code, 40 Tex.B.J. 317, 318 & n. 7 (1977). By interpreting the time buyer learns of the breach to mean a commercially reasonable time after buyer learns of the repudiation, we depart from pre-Code law....

repudiation. Thus, an aggrieved buyer "learns of the breach" a commercially reasonable time after he learns of the seller's anticipatory repudiation. The weight of scholarly commentary supports this interpretation. See J. Calamari & J. Perillo, Contracts § 14–20 (2d ed. 1977); Sebert, Remedies Under Article Two of the Uniform Commercial Code: An Agenda for Review, 130 U.Pa.L.Rev. 360, 372–80 (1981); Wallach, Anticipatory Repudiation and the UCC, 13 U.C.C.L.J. 48 (1980); Peters, supra, at 263–68.

Typically, our question will arise where parties to an executory contract are in the midst of a rising market. To the extent that market decisions are influenced by a damages rule, measuring market price at the time of seller's repudiation gives seller the ability to fix buyer's damages and may induce seller to repudiate, rather than abide by the contract. By contrast, measuring buyer's damages at the time of performance will tend to dissuade the buyer from covering, in hopes that market price will continue upward until performance time.

Allowing the aggrieved buyer a commercially reasonable time, however, provides him with an opportunity to investigate his cover possibilities in a rising market without fear that, if he is unsuccessful in obtaining cover, he will be relegated to a market-contract damage remedy measured at the time of repudiation. The Code supports this view. While cover is the preferred remedy, the Code clearly provides the option to seek damages. See § 2.712(c) & comment 3. If "[t]he buyer is always free to choose between cover and damages for non-delivery," and if 2.712 "is not intended to limit the time necessary for [buyer] to look around and decide as to how he may best effect cover," it would be anomalous, if the buyer chooses to seek damages, to fix his damages at a time before he investigated cover possibilities and before he elected his remedy. See id. comment 2 & 3; Dura–Wood Treating Co. v. Century Forest Industries, Inc., 675 F.2d 745, 754 (5th Cir.1982) ("buyer has some time in which to evaluate the situation"). Moreover, comment 1 to section 2.713 states, "The general baseline adopted in this section uses as a yardstick the market in which the buyer would have obtained cover had he sought that relief." See § 2.610 comment 1. When a buyer chooses not to cover, but to seek damages, the market is measured at the time he could have covered—a reasonable time after repudiation. See §§ 2.711 & 2.713.

Persuasive arguments exist for interpreting "learned of the breach" to mean "time of performance," consistent with the pre-Code rule. See J. White & R. Summers, supra, § 6–7; Anderson, supra. If this was the intention of the Code's drafters, however, phrases in section 2.610 and 2.712 lose their meaning. If buyer is entitled to market-contract damages measured at the time of performance, it is difficult to explain why the anticipatory repudiation section limits him to a commercially reasonable time to await performance. See § 2.610 comment 1. Similarly, in a rising market, no reason would exist for requiring the buyer to act "without unreasonable delay" when he seeks to cover following an anticipatory repudiation. See § 2.712(a).

The interplay among the relevant Code sections does not permit, in this context, an interpretation that harmonizes all and leaves no loose ends.

We therefore acknowledge that our interpretation fails to explain the language of section 2.723(a) insofar as it relates to aggrieved buyers. We note, however, that the section has limited applicability—cases that come to trial before the time of performance will be rare. Moreover, the comment to section 2.723 states that the "section is not intended to exclude the use of any other reasonable method of determining market price or of measuring damages. . . ." In light of the Code's persistent theme of commercial reasonableness, the prominence of cover as a remedy, and the time given an aggrieved buyer to await performance and to investigate cover before selecting his remedy, we agree with the district court that "learned of the breach" incorporates section 2.610's commercially reasonable time.[7]

"Cover" as a Ceiling

At trial Cosden argued that Helm's purchases of polystyrene from other sources in early February constituted cover. Helm argued that those purchases were not intended to substitute for polystyrene sales cancelled by Cosden. Helm, however, contended that it did cover by purchasing large amounts of high impact polystyrene from other sources late in February and around the first of March. Cosden claimed that these purchases were not made reasonably and that they should not qualify as cover. The jury found that none of Helm's purchases of polystyrene from other sources were cover purchases.

---

7. We note that two circuits arrived at a similar conclusion by different routes. In Cargill, Inc. v. Stafford, 553 F.2d 1222 (10th Cir.1977), the court began its discussion of damages by embracing the "time of performance" interpretation urged by Professors White and Summers. Id. at 1226. Indeed, the court stated that "damages normally should be measured from the time when performance is due and not from the time when the buyer learns of repudiation." Id. Nevertheless, the court conclude[d] that under § 4–2–713 a buyer may urge continued performance for a reasonable time. At the end of a reasonable period he should cover if substitute goods are readily available. If substitution is readily available and buyer does not cover within a reasonable time, damages should be based on the price at the end of that reasonable time rather than on the price when performance is due. Id. at 1227. The Cargill court would employ the time of performance measure only if buyer had a valid reason for not covering.

In First Nat'l Bank of Chicago v. Jefferson Mortgage Co., 576 F.2d 479 (3d Cir. 1978), the court initially quoted with approval legislative history that supports a literal or "plain meaning" interpretation of New Jersey's section 2–713. Nevertheless, the court hedged by interpreting that section "to measure damages within a commercially reasonable time after learning of the repudiation." Id. at 492. In light of the unequivocal repudiation and because cover was "easily and immediately . . . available . . . in the well-organized and easily accessible market," id. at 493 (quoting Oloffson v. Coomer, 11 Ill. App.3d 918, 296 N.E.2d 871 (1973)), a commercially reasonable time did not extend beyond the date of repudiation.

We agree with the First National court that "the circumstances of the particular market involved should determine the duration of a 'commercially reasonable time.' " 576 F.2d at 492; see Tex.Bus. & Com.Code § 1.204(b). In this case, however, there was no showing that cover was easily and immediately available in an organized and accessible market and that a commercially reasonable time expired on the day of Cosden's cancellation. We recognize that § 2.610's "commercially reasonable time" and § 2.712's "without unreasonable delay" are distinct concepts. Often, however, the two time periods will overlap, since the buyer can investigate cover possibilities while he awaits performance. See Sebert, supra, at 376–77 & n. 80.

Although the jury in the present case did not fix the exact duration of a commercially reasonable time, we assume that the jury determined market price at a time commercially reasonable under all the circumstances, in light of the absence of objection to the form of the special issue.

Now Cosden argues that the prices of polystyrene for the purchases that Helm claimed were cover should act as a ceiling for fixing market price under section 2.713. We refuse to accept this novel argument. Although a buyer who has truly covered may not be allowed to seek higher damages under section 2.713 than he is granted by section 2.712, see § 2.713 comment 5; J. White & R. Summers, supra, § 6–4 at 233–34, in this case the jury found that Helm did not cover. We cannot isolate a reason to explain the jury's finding: it might have concluded that Helm would have made the purchases regardless of Cosden's nonperformance or that the transactions did not qualify as cover for other reasons. Because of the jury's finding, we cannot use those other transactions to determine Helm's damages.

[The jury found that Cosden was excused by commercial impracticability—UCC § 2–615—from performing under orders 05 and 07, but that Cosden had failed to allocate its production as that section requires. At the trial court's direction, the jury therefore assessed damages based on the amount of general purpose polystyrene that Cosden should have allocated to Helm. On appeal, this was held to be error: owing to the misallocation, Cosden should have been allowed no credit for commercial impracticability.]

Affirmed, but, in part, reversed and remanded.

NOTES

(1) *The Reverse Case.* Suppose that the market price of polystyrene had dropped rather than risen after Cosden made its sale agreements with Helm, and that Helm, the buyer, rather than Cosden, the seller, had repudiated in February, 1979. For that case UCC § 2–708(1) provides for damages based on the difference between the unpaid contract price and the market price *"at the time and place for tender."* UCC § 2–708(1). If that rule were different, the decision in the main case would be easier to accept, would it not? What might account for the difference?

If Helm had repudiated the contract, might Cosden have recovered under UCC § 2–706?

(2) *Retraction.* The court observes that the "buyer's option to wait a commercially reasonable time" interacts with UCC § 2–611, "which allows the seller an opportunity to retract his repudiation." An offer and an anticipatory repudiation have virtually nothing in common except that each may be withdrawn, an offer by revocation and a repudiation by retraction. An anticipatory repudiation thus differs from a breach by nonperformance, since in the case of the latter there is nothing that the defaulting party can do to deprive the other of a claim for damages, at least nominal. See Restatement § 256.

When is it too late to retract a repudiation? This is the subject of the next case.

(3) *Urging Retraction.* The modern view is that the recipient of a repudiation may urge its retraction without becoming committed to further performance if it is not retracted. See UCC § 2–610(b), Restatement § 257.

PROBLEMS

(1) *Repudiation and Arbitration.* If Cosden had succeeded in getting Helm to agree to the inclusion of the AAA Standard Arbitration Clause in Note 2, p. 28 above, with arbitration in Texas, where Cosden's headquarters were located, would

Cosden's repudiation disable it from insisting on that clause? See Kulukundis Shipping Co. v. Amtorg Trading Corp., 126 F.2d 978 (2d Cir.1942). What answer if the clause, instead of providing for arbitration, provided that "all disputes and matters ... shall be litigated ... before a Court located in the State of Texas, to the exclusion of the Courts of any other state or country"? See the clause in *Carnival Cruise Lines v. Shute*, p. 480 above; see Marra v. Papandreou, 216 F.3d 1119 (D.C.Cir. 2000).

If you represented Cosden, what arguments could you muster for your client?

(2) *A Matter of an Option.* Charles Hermanowski, former president of Acton Corporation, was given a five year non-cancelable stock option to purchase 50,000 shares of Acton's common stock at $2 per share. One year later, when the market price of the stock was $3 per share, Acton, in the mistaken belief that the option was cancelable, notified Hermanowski that it had cancelled it. At the end of three years the price had risen to $5 per share. At the end of four years the price stood at $4 per share, and Hermanowski notified Acton that he exercised the option. When Acton reiterated that it had cancelled the option, Hermanowski sued. How much should Hermanowski recover? $50,000? $100,000? $150,000? See Hermanowski v. Acton Corp., 580 F.Supp. 140 (E.D.N.Y.1983), aff'd per curiam, 729 F.2d 921 (2d Cir.1984).

Does Hermanowski's right to enforce the option depend on whether he objected to Acton's initial notification of cancellation? On whether he tendered $100,000 when he notified Acton that he exercised the option?

United States v. Seacoast Gas Co.

United States Court of Appeals, Fifth Circuit, 1953.
204 F.2d 709.

Suit against gas company and its surety on gas company's performance bond, for damages alleged to have resulted from an anticipatory breach of contract in nature of notice of intent to cancel contract as of November 15, 1947. The United States District Court for the Southern District of Georgia entered judgment in favor of gas company and surety, and plaintiff appealed....

Judgment reversed, cause remanded with directions.

■ HUTCHESON, CHIEF JUDGE. Brought against Seacoast Gas Company and the surety on its performance bond, the suit was for damages alleged to have resulted from the anticipatory breach by the Gas Company of its contract with plaintiff to supply gas to a federal housing project during the period from April 15, 1947, to June 15, 1948. The claim was: that on October 7, 1947, while performance of the contract was in progress, Seacoast anticipatorily breached the contract by writing plaintiff unequivocally that, because of plaintiff's breach of the contract, Seacoast intended to cancel same as of November 15, 1947; that the plaintiff immediately notified Seacoast that it did not recognize any right in it to cease performance and that it proposed to advertise for bids to insure a continued supply of gas if Seacoast's breach persisted; that, thereafter, having advertised for bids and on November 6th, having received the low bid from Trion Company, it on that date notified Seacoast by letter that unless it retracted its repudiation of the contract within three days from the letter date, Trion's bid would be accepted and

Seacoast and its surety would be held liable for breach of contract; and that thereafter Seacoast not having retracted within the time fixed, plaintiff on November 10, accepted Trion's bid, and, pursuant thereto, began its preparations to execute with Trion a contract for a price in excess of that provided in the Seacoast contract, and Seacoast is liable to plaintiff for this excess.

Defendant Seacoast, admitting in its pleading and its testimony that the facts were substantially as claimed by plaintiff, defended on the ground: that it had retracted its notice of repudiation and given assurance of its intention to continue to perform before the plaintiff had actually signed the new contract; and that, since, as it claimed, plaintiff had not then substantially changed its position or suffered any damages as a result of Seacoast's notice to terminate the contract and cease performance under it, the retraction was timely and healed the breach.

Upon the issue thus joined, the cause was tried to the court without a jury, and the court stating the question for decision thus, "The question in this case is as to whether Seacoast Gas Company, Inc. withdrew its notice of cancellation of its contract prior to the rendering of the contract to the Trion Gas Company," found that it had done so. On the basis of this finding and a further finding that on November 13, two days before the termination date which Seacoast had fixed in its notice, Zell, who was president both of Seacoast and of Trion Company, to whom the new contract was awarded, notified the regional counsel for the Public Housing Authority that Seacoast admitted it had no right to cancel the contract and was rescinding its notice, the court held that the anticipatory breach had been healed and plaintiff could not recover.[a]

Appealing from this judgment, plaintiff is here insisting that under the settled law governing anticipatory breaches not only as it is laid down in Georgia but generally, Seacoast's retraction came too late to heal the breach, and the judgment must be reversed.

Appellees, on their part, insist that the judgment appealed from was soundly based in law and in fact and must be affirmed.

We do not think so. The undisputed facts establish: that Zell, president of both companies, was present at the opening of the new bids on November 6, 1947, and upon being asked to withdraw Seacoast's notice that it would cease performing the contract, refused to do so; that on that date the Public Housing Administration regional counsel wrote Seacoast by registered mail, addressed "Attention Zell," advising of the steps the government had taken and stating that unless Seacoast retracted its repudiation within three days from the date of the letter, Trion's bid would be accepted and Seacoast and its sureties would be held liable for breach of contract; and that having received no response from Seacoast within the three days specified, and Zell again asked on November 10th, to retract the notice of repudiation having refused to do so, the government accepted Trion's bid

---

a. Your editors are not prepared to speculate on Zell's motives for the behavior of his two companies.

and proceeded with the execution of the contract. The record standing thus, under settled law not only of Georgia but generally elsewhere, the breach was not healed, the judgment was wrong, and it must be reversed.

A comparison of the briefs and arguments of appellant and appellees will show that the case is in quite small compass. Both agree that Seacoast's letter of October 24th [sic] operated as an anticipatory breach and that unless effectively withdrawn during the *locus poenitentiae* it operated to put Seacoast in default and to render it liable for the loss to the government of the difference in price between the old and the new contract.

Appellees, after quoting from Anson on Contracts, 6th Ed., Sec. 385, p. 444:

"The repudiator has the power of retraction prior to any change of position by the other party, but not afterwards."

go on to say:

"So we see that the authorities seem to be unanimous that a person who gives notice of his intention not to perform a contract may withdraw such notice and offer to perform prior to the time the other party acted or relied thereon."

Based upon these premises, they insist that "the undisputed evidence is that appellant did not 'accept the bid of Trion Gas' until November 17th, which was after the notice of cancellation had been withdrawn in writing."

We think: that this statement is erroneous; that it represents the crucial difference between the parties; and that the error of the statement lies in the fact that it confuses the acceptance of the bid with the signing of the contract.

It is true that the contract was not signed until the 17th, after Seacoast had retracted its notice and if appellees were correct in its position that the date of the signing of the new contract was determinative of this case, they would be correct in their conclusion that the judgment should be affirmed.

But that position is not correct. In fact and in law, when the government took bids and notified Seacoast that unless it retracted within three days it would proceed to accept the Trion bid and award the contract to it, the *locus poenitentiae* ended with these three days. The fact that Seacoast claims that it did not receive the notice is completely immaterial both because it was not necessary for the government to give any notice or fix any time and because Zell, on November 10th, repeated to the Regional Counsel his refusal to retract.

All that is required to close the door to repentance is definite action indicating that the anticipatory breach has been accepted as final, and this requisite can be supplied either by the filing of a suit or a firm declaration, as here, that unless within a fixed time the breach is repudiated, it will be accepted.

Here, in addition to this firm declaration, the record shows the taking of bids and the awarding of the contract to the lowest bidder. The error of the district judge lies, we think, in holding that the *locus poenitentiae* was extended until the 17th, when the contract was signed, and that Seacoast having repented before the signing of the contract, had healed the breach and restored the contract to its original vitality.

Whatever of doubt there may be, and we have none with respect to this view, as a matter of strict law, there can be none with respect to the justice or equity of this determination when it is considered; that Zell, the president and practically sole owner of Seacoast, was the organizer, the president and practically sole owner of Trion; that he organized Trion for the sole purpose of the bidding; and that on the date the bids were opened and later on the date the contract was awarded, he, though requested to do so, refused to withdraw Seacoast's repudiation and continued in that refusal until a day or two before the contract was signed.

The evidence showing, as it does, without contradiction, that the signing of the contract was not delayed because of a purpose on the part of the government to extend the time for Seacoast's repentance, but because until that date Trion had not furnished his bond, we think it clear that, in entering judgment for the defendants, the court erred. The judgment is, therefore, reversed and the cause is remanded with directions to enter judgment for plaintiff for the loss Seacoast's breach of contract has caused it.

NOTES

(1) *The Door to Repentance.* What did the government have to do to "close the door to repentance"? The government's "firm declaration" took effect on November 9. Would such "definite action indicating that the anticipatory breach has been accepted as final" have been enough if there had been no change of position by the government? What result if Seacoast had attempted to retract its repudiation on November 10, just before the government accepted Trion's bid? If such definite action would have been enough, did it make any difference whether the government was bound when it accepted Trion's bid on November 10 or only when the contract was signed on November 17?

Under UCC § 2–611 it is enough that the aggrieved party "has indicated that he considers the repudiation final," and Restatement § 256 adopts the same formula as the Code. But why, *without any step in reliance,* should a mere firm declaration "close the door to repentance"? Is this because the repudiation is treated as an offer that can be accepted?

Comment *c* to Restatement § 256 explains that though it is the aggrieved party's material change of position in reliance on the repudiation that makes it unjust for the repudiating party to retract the repudiation, "it is undesirable to make the injured party's rights turn exclusively on such a vague criterion," and in the interest of certainty that party "may therefore prevent subsequent nullification by indicating to the other party that he considers the repudiation final." For discussion of this reasoning, see E. Farnsworth, Changing Your Mind: The Law of Regretted Decisions 62–63 (1998).

(2) *The Rose Bowl Affair (Reprise).* After the class action was brought in the case discussed in Note 4, p. 771 above, the University had what the trial court called a "sudden affluence in the matter of tickets" and offered tickets to members of the plaintiff's class. The Court of Appeals decided the case on the assumption, "at least for the sake of argument, that the filing of an action is a sufficient change in

position to destroy the power to retract an anticipatory repudiation." What does *Seacoast* say about the correctness of this assumption?

PROBLEMS

(1) *Speculation by Repudiation.* Seller contracts to sell Buyer goods for $100,000. A week later, when the market price of the goods has risen to $110,000, Seller repudiates and Buyer does nothing in response. A week later when the market price of the goods has fallen to $90,000, Seller retracts its repudiation. Is the retraction effective?

(2) *Repudiation Plus More.* On June 1, seller and buyer contracted for the sale of a house, closing to be on June 30, "time is of the essence." On June 20, the buyer repudiated and the seller urged performance. Nothing further happened until September 1 when the buyer sent a letter of retraction and sought to perform. The seller refused. Need the seller prove reliance? Glass v. Anderson, 596 S.W.2d 507 (Tex.1980).

(3) *Jarbeau's Case.* The Jarbeau Comedy Company arranged to appear at the Buffalo Academy of Music for three days in December under a contract calling for equal division of gross receipts. In August the Company's impresario sent the Academy a draft contract increasing his share, explaining that he could not think of playing for less than 60%. The Academy returned the contract unsigned "for the reason that we have a contract signed by you and do not need any other for the appearance of Verona Jarbeau and company at our Academy." On November 17 the impresario wrote again, sending advertising material and saying, "Please keep Miss Jarbeau before the public as much as possible. I want to see her turn them away in your town." Owing to the itinerant habits of both parties, the plaintiff did not receive the defendants' response for about a month. It expressed surprise that Miss Jarbeau intended to play the Academy and explained that the Academy was booked to other performers. The Company sued the Academy for damages based on its expenses. What result? Bernstein v. Meech, 29 N.E. 255 (N.Y.1891).

(B) ASSURANCE OF DUE PERFORMANCE

We have seen several examples of parties that might have wished, as things developed, to have some assurance that the other party would perform as agreed. The common law, however, gave no right to such assurance. "A party does not contract for oral assurances of performance, but for performance of the contract." BAII Banking Corp. v. UPG, Inc., 985 F.2d 685, 903 (2d Cir.1993).

The drafters of the Code saw the need for an exception, and this exception was carried over into the Restatement Second. "Ordinarily an obligee has no right to demand reassurance by the obligor that the latter will perform when his performance is due. However, a contract 'imposes an obligation on each party that the other's expectation of receiving due performance will not be impaired.' Uniform Commercial Code § 2–609(1). When, therefore, an obligee reasonably believes that the obligor will commit a breach by nonperformance that would of itself give him a claim for damages for total breach (§ 243), he may, under the rule stated in this Section, be entitled to demand assurance of performance." Restatement

§ 251, Comment *a*. Section 251 had no counterpart in the first Restatement. It is a generalization from UCC § 2–609, which was itself a legislative innovation.

The sort of case that chiefly inspired the Code section was one in which a seller committed itself to supply goods for payment thereafter, and received signals before making delivery that the buyer was in financial distress. In an extreme case, the court held that a seller "obviously" had grounds for insecurity after learning these facts: the buyer was in arrears in payment for goods already delivered; it had a bad credit reputation; its "Fifth Avenue Showroom" turned out to be a telephone answering service; and its "factory" turned out to be someone else's premises, to which the buyer did not have a key. Turntables, Inc. v. Gestetner, 382 N.Y.S.2d 798 (App.Div.1976).

NOTE

(1) *Opportunism*. It was pointed out in the discussion of "Time for Performance," p. 718 above, that one answer to opportunism is to insist that the other party go first, so as to have the protection afforded by the doctrine of constructive conditions. Another is to require the other party to furnish a guarantee of performance by a reliable third party. The right to demand assurances is yet another answer.

(2) *Breach of a Separate Contract (Reprise)*. Recall that the doctrine of constructive conditions cannot be invoked where there has been a breach of a separate contract. This is so even if the separate contract has been repudiated. UCC § 2–610 applies only when a party "repudiates *the* contract." But might UCC § 2–609 help an apprehensive party in such a situation? According to Comment 3 to UCC § 2–609, "under commercial standards and in accord with commercial practice, a ground for insecurity need not arise from or be directly related to the contract in question."

PROBLEM

You Know Quite as Well as We Do (Reprise). Review the letter in the Problem at p. 766 above. Would the seller be justified in demanding assurance of due performance under UCC § 2–609?

Pittsburgh–Des Moines Steel Co. v. Brookhaven Manor Water Co.

United States Court of Appeals, Seventh Circuit, 1976.
532 F.2d 572.

[At the request of the Water Company (Brookhaven), Pittsburgh–Des Moines Steel Company (PDM) submitted a revised proposal to build an elevated tank for $175,000. The original proposal called for progress payments to PDM; the revised offer called for no payment until the tank had been built and tested. After Brookhaven's acceptance, PDM heard something about a loan that Brookhaven was negotiating for. The credit manager for PDM wrote the prospective lender (copy to Brookhaven) asking for a notice that $175,000 had been put in escrow for the job, and adding: "As a matter of good business we are holding this matter in abeyance until receipt of such notification." The loan did not go through. Then the credit manager wrote the president of Brookhaven asking for his personal guarantee of payment, "to protect us between now and the time your loan is completed." The letter mentioned the escrow again, this time as a requirement. The president sent a statement of his personal worth. PDM stopped fabricating parts, and the tank was never built.

PDM sued Brookhaven, charging repudiation of the contract, and Brookhaven entered a counterclaim. A jury returned a verdict for PDM, but the trial court entered a judgment notwithstanding the verdict, in Brookhaven's favor. PDM appealed.]

■ PELL, CIRCUIT JUDGE. . . . PDM argues that its position was in accordance with Section 2–609 of the Uniform Commercial Code. [The court concluded that though "the finished tank was scarcely one to be taken off the shelf," it "was a 'movable' 'thing' 'specially manufactured'" so that the contract was one for the sale of goods and Article 2 of the Code applied.] The question remaining is whether PDM's actions subsequent to the execution of the contract were within the protection provided by § 2–609. We hold that they were not.

The performance to which PDM was entitled was the full payment of the purchase price within a specified time after the completion of the tank. While we have a substantial question as to whether PDM made a written demand as required by the statute, in keeping with our concept that the UCC should be liberally construed, we do not desire to rest our decision on a formalistic approach. Letters were written which conveyed what PDM wanted done before they would pursue their obligations under the contract. The fundamental problem is that these letters, if they be deemed to be in the nature of a demand, demanded more than that to which PDM was entitled and the demand was not founded upon what in our opinion was an actuating basis for the statute's applicability.

We do not construe § 2–609 as being a vehicle without more for an implied term being inserted in a contract when a substantially equivalent term was expressly waived in the contract. The something more to trigger applicability of the statute is that the expectation of due performance on the part of the other party entertained at contracting time no longer exists because of "reasonable grounds for insecurity" arising. We find that PDM's actions in demanding either the escrowing of the purchase price or a personal guarantee lacked the necessary predicate of reasonable grounds for insecurity having arisen. The contract negates the existence of any basis for insecurity at the time of the contract when PDM was willing to wait 30 days beyond completion for payment. The fact that Brookhaven had not completed its loan negotiations does not constitute reasonable grounds for insecurity when the money in question was not to be needed for some months. Reasonable business men prefer in the absence of some compulsive reason not to commence paying interest on borrowed money until the time for the use for that money is at hand. The credit manager's January letter that the order was being held in abeyance until receipt of notification of escrowing was based upon a "matter of good business," but not upon any change of condition bearing upon Brookhaven's ability to discharge its payment obligation under the contract. With regard to the later request for a personal guarantee, it is not uncommon for an individual to decline assuming obligations of a corporation in which he is a shareholder. Indeed, the use of the corporate device frequently has as a principal purpose the limitation on individual exposure to liability. If an unfavorable risk in dealing with a corporation exists at contracting time, good business judgment may well indicate that an assurance be secured before contracting that there will be individual shareholder backup. None of this occurred and the record is silent as to any reasonable grounds for insecurity arising thereafter. . . .

We, of course, would not deprive PDM of resort to § 2–609 if there had been a demonstration that reasonable grounds for insecurity had arisen. The proof in that respect was lacking. The comptroller and supervisor of PDM's credit department testified that he had access to all of the credit information that the company had regarding Brookhaven, that he had reviewed that information, and that he was unaware of any change in the financial condition of Brookhaven between November of 1968 and the end of 1969.[a] . . . The fact, if it were a fact, that Brookhaven may not have had a large amount of cash lying in the bank in a checking account, not an unusual situation for a real estate developer, does not support the belief that it, as a company with substantial assets, would fail to meet its obligations as they fell due. Section 2–609 is a protective device when reasonable grounds for insecurity arise; it is not a pen for rewriting a contract in the absence of those reasonable grounds having arisen, particularly when the proposed rewriting involves the very factors which had been waived by the one now attempting to wield the pen. The situation is made no more persuasive for PDM when it is recalled that that company was the original scrivener.

Brookhaven's request to put off the contract for a year clearly came after PDM's repudiation of the contract and was indicative of nothing more than that Brookhaven was willing to undertake a new arrangement with PDM a year hence. Pursuant to § 2–610 of the UCC, Brookhaven was entitled to suspend its own performance by virtue of the anticipatory repudiation by PDM and to resort to available remedies, including damages pursuant to § 2–711 of the Code.[1] . . .

Affirmed.

■ CUMMINGS, CIRCUIT JUDGE (concurring). Although I agree with the result reached in the majority opinion, I differ with the reasoning. Reasonable

a. In omitted part of the opinion, the court wrote: "The district court apparently regarded the matter as being the not entirely unfamiliar situation of a corporate credit department not viewing a contract of sale with the same *joie de vivre* as did the sales department; but the court thought that the sales department had legally committed the firm and that the credit department had gone beyond the grounds for actuating the assurance provided by the statute."

1. We have not attempted to determine whether the parties were merchants within the meaning of subsection 2 of § 2–609 in which case the determination of the reasonableness of grounds for insecurity would be in accordance with commercial standards. There being no evidence as to what commercial standards might be applicable, we have attempted to construe the controlling phrase in accordance with what appears to us to be its plain meaning.

men could certainly conclude that PDM had legitimate grounds to question Brookhaven's ability to pay for the water tank. When the contract was signed, the parties understood that Brookhaven would obtain a loan to help pay for the project. When the loan failed to materialize, a prudent business-man would have "reasonable grounds for insecurity." I disagree that there must be a fundamental change in the financial position of the buyer before the seller can invoke the protection of UCC § 2–609. Rather, I believe that the Section was designed to cover instances where an underlying condition of the contract, even if not expressly incorporated into the written docu-ment, fails to occur. See Comment 3 to UCC § 2–609. Whether, in a specific case, the breach of the condition gives a party "reasonable grounds for insecurity" is a question of fact for the jury.

UCC § 2–609, however, does not give the alarmed party a right to redraft the contract. . . . The district court could properly conclude as a matter of law that these requests by PDM demanded more than a commer-cially "adequate assurance of due performance."

NOTES

(1) *Questions.* How many ill-advised things did PDM do? To whom should a demand for assurances be directed? Who should be asked to furnish the assurances? How specific should the demand be? Is the recipient justified in demanding to know what specific form of assurance would be satisfactory? If a demand is made for a specific form of assurance (*e.g.*, a bank guarantee) that is inconvenient or impossible for the recipient to give, but another form would serve the purpose equally well, is the demand effective? For the proposition that "the mere fact that the [insecure party] demanded performance beyond that required by the contract did not trans-form its demand into a repudiation as a matter of law," see Top of Iowa Co-op. v. Sime Farms, Inc., 608 N.W.2d 454, 469 (Iowa 2000).

For more on UCC § 2–609, see Richard Craswell, Insecurity, Repudiation, and Cure, 19 J.Legal Stud. 399 (1990); Gregory Crespi, The Adequate Assurances Doctrine after U.C.C. § 2–609: A Test of the Efficiency of the Common Law, 38 Vill.L.Rev. 179 (1993); Larry Garvin, Adequate Assurance of Performance: Of Risk, Duress, and Cognition, 69 U.Colo.L.Rev. 71 (1998).

(2) *Oral Demand.* It has been held that an oral demand may suffice under UCC § 2–609 "as long as the demand provides a 'clear understanding' of the insecure party's intent to suspend performance until receipt of adequate assurances from the other party." See Atwood–Kellogg, Inc. v. Nickeson Farms, 602 N.W.2d 749, 753 (S.D.1999). Is there any reason for requiring a writing?

(3) *Scope of the Code.* The scope of Article 2 is often called into question in contracts, like that in *PDM*, involving both services and goods. Article 2 would plainly not apply, for example, to a contract to paint a house, even though a small amount of goods will be transferred, but where is the dividing line?

Courts have often answered this question by looking for the "predominant factor" of the contract. In reaching its conclusion in PDM, the court relied on the leading case of Bonebrake v. Cox, 499 F.2d 951, 960 (8th Cir.1974), in which the court held that Article 2 applied to a contract for the sale and installation of used bowling equipment for a lump sum, even though the contract involved substantial amounts of labor. The court described the test as whether the "predominant factor . . . is the rendition of service, with goods incidentally involved (*e.g.*, contract with artist for painting) or is a transaction of sale, with labor incidentally involved (*e.g.*, installation of a water heater in a bathroom)." In Kirkpatrick v. Introspect

Healthcare Corp., 845 P.2d 800 (N.M.1992), however, the court applied the *Boneb-rake* test to conclude that a contract to create the interior design for a health care facility did not come within Article 2 even though it required the interior designer to sell furnishings to complete the designs.

What was the "predominant factor" in McCloskey v. Minweld, p. 776 above?

(4) *International Solutions.* Article 71 of the CSIG allows a party "to suspend the performance of his obligations if, after the conclusion of the contract, it becomes apparent that the other party will not perform a substantial part of his obligations," but the party "must continue with performance if the other party provides adequate assurance of his performance." How does this provision differ from UCC § 2–609?

UNIDROIT Principles art. 7.3.4 follows the language of UCC § 2–609 more closely. How does this provision differ from UCC § 2–609?

PROBLEMS

(1) *Drafting for the Textile Trade.* Suppose that you have been asked by the Associations that have promulgated the Standard Textile Salesnote ("Worth Street Rules"), widely used in the textile trade, to review these Rules under the Uniform Commercial Code. The Rules provide that on Buyer's breach of any term "of this or any other contract with Seller, all sums owing under this or any other contract between Buyer and Seller, shall at the option of Seller ... at once become due." This paragraph also requires payments by Buyer in the event that net balances under all their contracts exceed Buyer's established credit limit, and provides that on Buyer's failure "to make any such payment within five (5) days after demand in writing, Seller shall have the option to cancel this and other contracts between Buyer and Seller."

Under UCC § 1–302(b), is this a "manifestly unreasonable" standard of performance of a seller's non-disclaimable duty of reasonableness prescribed in the Code? Is it a permissible variation of UCC § 2–609? How would you advise the Associations?

(2) *Drafting for the Lumber Business.* Suppose that you have been asked by a trade association of lumber dealers for your opinion on the following provision.

> The seller shall have the right to cancel on account of any arbitrary deductions made by the buyer with respect to, or failure to comply with, contract terms in respect to any prior shipment, or on account of any transfer of or change in the buyer's business, its insolvency, suit by other creditors, failure of buyer to meet financial obligations to seller, impairment of buyer's credit information, or for unfavorable credit reports made to seller through usual channels of credit information unless the buyer shall promptly furnish to the seller's satisfaction guaranty of full payment for any shipment made or to be made. Notice of such cancellation shall be given in writing.

Recall the discussion of acceleration clauses in Note 3, p. 771 above. Is UCC § 1–309 applicable to the term quoted above? Is there any other reason to expect that that term would not be effective? See UCC § 1–302(b). How would you advise the trade association?

Norcon Power Partners v. Niagara Mohawk Power Corp.

New York Court of Appeals, 1998.
92 N.Y.2d 458, 705 N.E.2d 656.

■ BELLACOSA. J. The doctrine, known as demand for adequate assurance of future performance, is at the heart of a Federal lawsuit that stems from a

1989 contract between Norcon Power Partners, L.P., an independent power producer, and Niagara Mohawk Power Corporation, a public utility provider. Niagara Mohawk undertook to purchase electricity generated at Norcon's Pennsylvania facility. The contract was for 25 years, but the differences emerged during the early years of the arrangement.

The case arrives on this Court's docket by certification of the substantive law question from the United States Court of Appeals for the Second Circuit. Our Court is presented with an open issue that should be settled within the framework of New York's common-law development. We accepted the responsibility to address this question involving New York contract law:

"Does a party have the right to demand adequate assurance of future performance when reasonable grounds arise to believe that the other party will commit a breach by non-performance of a contract governed by New York law, where the other party is solvent and the contract is not governed by the U.C.C.?" . . .

As framed by the particular dispute, we answer the law question in the affirmative with an appreciation of this Court's traditional common-law developmental method, and as proportioned to the precedential sweep of our rulings.

I.

The Second Circuit Court of Appeals describes the three pricing periods, structure and details as follows:

"In the first period, Niagara Mohawk pays Norcon six cents per kilowatt-hour for electricity. In the second and third periods, the price paid by Niagara Mohawk is based on its 'avoided cost.' The avoided cost reflects the cost that Niagara Mohawk would incur to generate electricity itself or purchase it from other sources. In the second period, if the avoided cost falls below a certain floor price (calculated according to a formula), Niagara Mohawk is obligated to pay the floor price. By the same token, if the avoided cost rises above a certain amount (calculated according to a formula), Niagara Mohawk's payments are capped by a ceiling price. An 'adjustment account' tracks the difference between payments actually made by Niagara Mohawk in the second period and what those payments would have been if based solely on Niagara Mohawk's avoided cost.

"In the third period, the price paid by Niagara Mohawk is based on its avoided cost without any ceiling or floor price. Payments made by Niagara Mohawk in the third period are adjusted to account for any balance existing in the adjustment account that operated in the second period. If the adjustment account contains a balance in favor of Niagara Mohawk—that is, the payments actually made by Niagara Mohawk in the second period exceeded what those payments would have been if based solely on Niagara Mohawk's avoided cost—then the rate paid by Niagara Mohawk will be reduced to reflect the credit. If the adjustment account contains a balance in favor of Norcon, Niagara

Mohawk must make increased payments to Norcon. If a balance exists in the adjustment account at the end of the third period, the party owing the balance must pay the balance in full within thirty days of the termination of the third period"....

In February 1994, Niagara Mohawk presented Norcon with a letter stating its belief, based on revised avoided cost estimates, that substantial credits in Niagara Mohawk's favor would accrue in the adjustment account during the second pricing period. "[A]nalysis shows that the Cumulative Avoided Cost Account ... will reach over $610 million by the end of the second period." Anticipating that Norcon would not be able to satisfy the daily escalating credits in the third period, Niagara Mohawk demanded that "Norcon provide adequate assurance to Niagara Mohawk that Norcon will duly perform all of its future repayment obligations."

Norcon promptly sued Niagara Mohawk in the United States District Court, Southern District of New York. It sought a declaration that Niagara Mohawk had no contractual right under New York State law to demand adequate assurance, beyond security provisions negotiated and expressed in the agreement. Norcon also sought a permanent injunction to stop Niagara Mohawk from anticipatorily terminating the contract based on the reasons described in the demand letter. Niagara Mohawk counterclaimed. It sought a counter declaration that it properly invoked a right to demand adequate assurance of Norcon's future payment performance of the contract.

The District Court granted Norcon's motion for summary judgment. It reasoned that New York common law recognizes the exceptional doctrine of demand for adequate assurance only when a promisor becomes insolvent, and also when the statutory sale of goods provision under UCC 2–609, is involved. Thus, the District Court ruled in Norcon's favor because neither exception applied, in fact or by analogy to the particular dispute....

The Second Circuit Court of Appeals preliminarily agrees ... with the District Court that, except in the case of insolvency, no common-law or statutory right to demand adequate assurance exists under New York law which would affect non-UCC contracts, like the instant one. Because of the uncertainty concerning this substantive law question the Second Circuit certified the question to our Court as an aid to its correct application of New York law, and with an eye toward settlement of the important precedential impact on existing and future non-UCC commercial law matters and disputes.

II.

Our analysis should reference a brief review of the evolution of the doctrine of demands for adequate assurance. Its roots spring from the doctrine of anticipatory repudiation (see Garvin, Adequate Assurance of Performance: Of Risk, Duress, and Cognition, 69 U.Colo.L.Rev. 71, 77 [1998]). Under that familiar precept, when a party repudiates contractual duties "prior to the time designated for performance and before" all of the consideration has been fulfilled, the "repudiation entitles the nonrepudiating party to claim damages for total breach" (Long Is. R.R. Co. v. Northville Indus. Corp., 41 N.Y.2d 455, 463; see II Farnsworth, Contracts § 8.20;

Restatement [Second] of Contracts § 253; UCC 2–610). A repudiation can be either "a statement by the obligor to the obligee indicating that the obligor will commit a breach that would of itself give the obligee a claim for damages for total breach" or "a voluntary affirmative act which renders the obligor unable or apparently unable to perform without such a breach" (Restatement [Second] of Contracts § 250; see II Farnsworth, Contracts § 8.21; UCC 2–610, Comment 1).

That switch in performance expectation and burden is readily available, applied and justified when a breaching party's words or deeds are unequivocal. Such a discernible line in the sand clears the way for the nonbreaching party to broach some responsive action. When, however, the apparently breaching party's actions are equivocal or less certain, then the nonbreaching party who senses an approaching storm cloud, affecting the contractual performance, is presented with a dilemma, and must weigh hard choices and serious consequences. One commentator has described the forecast options in this way:

> "If the promisee regards the apparent repudiation as an anticipatory repudiation, terminates his or her own performance and sues for breach, the promisee is placed in jeopardy of being found to have breached if the court determines that the apparent repudiation was not sufficiently clear and unequivocal to constitute an anticipatory repudiation justifying nonperformance. If, on the other hand, the promisee continues to perform after perceiving an apparent repudiation, and it is subsequently determined that an anticipatory repudiation took place, the promisee may be denied recovery for post-repudiation expenditures because of his or her failure to avoid those expenses as part of a reasonable effort to mitigate damages after the repudiation" (Crespi, The Adequate Assurances Doctrine after U.C.C. § 2–609: A Test of the Efficiency of the Common Law, 38 Vill.L.Rev. 179, 183 [1993] . . .).

III.

The Uniform Commercial Code settled on a mechanism for relieving some of this uncertainty. It allows a party to a contract for the sale of goods to demand assurance of future performance from the other party when reasonable grounds for insecurity exist (see UCC 2–609; II Farnsworth, Contracts § 8.23). When adequate assurance is not forthcoming, repudiation is deemed confirmed, and the nonbreaching party is allowed to take reasonable actions as though a repudiation had occurred (see 4 Anderson, Uniform Commercial Code § 2–609:3 [3d ed.1997 rev.]).

UCC 2–609 provides, in relevant part:

> "(1) A contract for sale imposes an obligation on each party that the other's expectation of receiving due performance will not be impaired. When reasonable grounds for insecurity arise with respect to the performance of either party the other may in writing demand adequate assurance of due performance and until he receives such assurance may if commercially reasonable suspend any performance for which he has not already received the agreed return . . . .

"(4) After receipt of a justified demand failure to provide within a reasonable time not exceeding thirty days such assurance of due performance as is adequate under the circumstances of the particular case is a repudiation of the contract."

In theory, this UCC relief valve recognizes that "the essential purpose of a contract between commercial [parties] is actual performance … and that a continuing sense of reliance and security that the promised performance will be forthcoming when due, is an important feature of the bargain" (UCC 2–609, Comment 1). In application, section 2–609 successfully implements the laudatory objectives of quieting the doubt a party fearing repudiation may have, mitigating the dilemma flowing from that doubt, and offering the nonbreaching party the opportunity to interpose timely action to deal with the unusual development. . . .

Indeed, UCC 2–609 has been considered so effective in bridging the doctrinal, exceptional and operational gap related to the doctrine of anticipatory breach that some States have imported the complementary regimen of demand for adequate assurance to common-law categories of contract law, using UCC 2–609 as the synapse (see, e.g., Lo Re v. Tel–Air Communications, 200 N.J.Super. 59, 490 A.2d 344 [finding support in UCC 2–609 and Restatement (Second) of Contracts § 251 for applying doctrine of adequate assurance to contract to purchase radio station]; Conference Ctr. v. TRC—The Research Corp. of New England, 189 Conn. 212, 455 A.2d 857 [analogizing to UCC 2–609, as supported by Restatement (Second) of Contracts § 251, in context of constructive eviction]).

Commentators have helped nudge this development along. They have noted that the problems redressed by UCC 2–609 are not unique to contracts for sale of goods, regulated under a purely statutory regime. Thus, they have cogently identified the need for the doctrine to be available in exceptional and qualifying common-law contractual settings and disputes because of similar practical, theoretical and salutary objectives (e.g., predictability, definiteness, and stability in commercial dealings and expectations). . . .

The American Law Institute through its Restatement (Second) of Contracts has also recognized and collected the authorities supporting this modern development. Its process and work settled upon this black letter language:

"(1) Where reasonable grounds arise to believe that the obligor will commit a breach by non-performance that would of itself give the obligee a claim for damages for total breach under § 243, the obligee may demand adequate assurance of due performance and may, if reasonable, suspend any performance for which he has not already received the agreed exchange until he receives such assurance.

"(2) The obligee may treat as a repudiation the obligor's failure to provide within a reasonable time such assurance of due performance as is adequate in the circumstances of the particular case" (Restatement [Second] of Contracts § 251).

Modeled on UCC 2–609, Restatement § 251 tracks "the principle that the parties to a contract look to actual performance 'and that a continuing sense of reliance and security that the promised performance will be forthcoming when due, is an important feature of the bargain'" (Restatement [Second] of Contracts § 251, Comment *a*, quoting UCC 2–609, Comment 1). The duty of good faith and fair dealing in the performance of the contract is also reflected in section 251 (see Restatement [Second] of Contracts § 251, Comment *a*).

Some States have adopted Restatement § 251 as their common law of contracts, in varying degrees and classifications (see, e.g., Carfield & Sons v. Cowling, 616 P.2d 1008 [Colo.] [construction contract]; Spitzer Co. v. Barron, 581 P.2d 213 [Alaska] [construction contract]; Drinkwater v. Patten Realty Corp., 563 A.2d 772 [Me.] [sale of real estate]; Jonnet Dev. Corp. v. Dietrich Indus., 316 Pa.Super. 533, 463 A.2d 1026 [real estate lease]; but see Mollohan v. Black Rock Contr., 160 W.Va. 446, 235 S.E.2d 813 [declining to adopt section 251, except to the extent that failure to give adequate assurance on demand may be some evidence of repudiation]).

IV.

New York, up to now, has refrained from expanding the right to demand adequate assurance of performance beyond the Uniform Commercial Code.... The only other recognized exception is the insolvency setting.... Hence, the need for this certified question emerged so this Court could provide guidance towards a correct resolution of the Federal lawsuit by settling New York law with a modern pronouncement governing this kind of contract and dispute.

Niagara Mohawk, before our Court through the certified question from the Federal court, urges a comprehensive adaptation of the exceptional demand tool. This wholesale approach has also been advocated by the commentators.... Indeed, it is even reflected in the breadth of the wording of the certified question.

This Court's jurisprudence, however, usually evolves by deciding cases and settling the law more modestly.... The twin purposes and functions of this Court's work require significant professional discipline and judicious circumspection.

We conclude, therefore, that it is unnecessary, while fulfilling the important and useful certification role, to promulgate so sweeping a change and proposition in contract law, as has been sought, in one dramatic promulgation. That approach might clash with our customary incremental common-law developmental process, rooted in particular fact patterns and keener wisdom acquired through observations of empirical application of a proportioned, less than absolute, rule in future cases.

It is well to note the axiom that deciding a specific case, even with the precedential comet's tail its rationale illuminates, is very different from enacting a statute of general and universal application....

Experience and patience thus offer a more secure and realistic path to a better and fairer rule, in theory and in practical application. Therefore, this Court chooses to take the traditionally subtler approach, consistent with the proven benefits of the maturation process of the common law, including in the very area of anticipatory repudiation which spawns this relatively newer demand for assurance corollary. . . .

This Court is now persuaded that the policies underlying the UCC 2–609 counterpart should apply with similar cogency for the resolution of this kind of controversy. A useful analogy can be drawn between the contract at issue and a contract for the sale of goods. If the contract here was in all respects the same, except that it was for the sale of oil or some other tangible commodity instead of the sale of electricity, the parties would unquestionably be governed by the demand for adequate assurance of performance factors in UCC 2–609. We are convinced to take this prudent step because it puts commercial parties in these kinds of disputes at relatively arm's length equilibrium in terms of reliability and uniformity of governing legal rubrics. The availability of the doctrine may even provide an incentive and tool for parties to resolve their own differences, perhaps without the necessity of judicial intervention. Open, serious renegotiation of dramatic developments and changes in unusual contractual expectations and qualifying circumstances would occur because of and with an eye to the doctrine's application.

The various authorities, factors and concerns, in sum, prompt the prudence and awareness of the usefulness of recognizing the extension of the doctrine of demand for adequate assurance, as a common-law analogue. It should apply to the type of long-term commercial contract between corporate entities entered into by Norcon and Niagara Mohawk here, which is complex and not reasonably susceptible of all security features being anticipated, bargained for and incorporated in the original contract. Norcon's performance, in terms of reimbursing Niagara Mohawk for credits, is still years away. In the meantime, potential quantifiable damages are accumulating and Niagara Mohawk must weigh the hard choices and serious consequences that the doctrine of demand for adequate assurance is designed to mitigate. This Court needs to go no further in its promulgation of the legal standard as this suffices to declare a dispositive and proportioned answer to the certified question.

Accordingly, the certified question should be answered in the affirmative.

NOTES

(1) *Questions.* Did Niagara Mohawk have "reasonable grounds for insecurity"? What assurances from Norcon would have been "adequate"? Would PDM have had the right in appropriate circumstances to demand assurances from Brookhaven even if the court had determined that the contract was not one for the sale of goods?

The Code answers this question for Harrison in Walker & Co. v. Harrison, p. 748 above. If the contract was one of sale, UCC § 2–609 would apply. If the contract was one of lease, Article 2A, Leases, has a similar provision in UCC § 2A–401. In McCloskey v. Minweld, p. 776 above, would McCloskey have had a right under *Norcon Power* to demand assurances from Minweld on July 20?

(2) *Further Extension by Analogy.* In Conference Center Ltd. v. TRC—The Research Corp., 455 A.2d 857, 864–65 (Conn.1983), cited by the court in *Norcon*, a landlord sued a tenant for wrongful abandonment of the premises. The tenant, claiming constructive eviction, had summary judgment, but the Supreme Court of Connecticut reversed and remanded. Justice Ellen Peters noted "that courts in other jurisdictions have required a tenant who contemplates abandonment of the premises because of constructive eviction first to give his landlord notice and a reasonable opportunity to provide adequate assurance.... That case law provides a further link to Uniform Commercial Code § 2–609, for the cases and the statute both recognize the desirability of providing an opportunity for dialogue to establish whether the parties intend to repudiate or to fulfill their contractual obligations.... [W]e find support for recourse to § 2–609 as a source of general law in the provisions of § 251 of the Restatement (Second) of Contracts.... Only a full trial can establish whether the defendant was in fact constructively evicted or was entitled, for lack of adequate assurance, to infer that its lease had been terminated."

(3) Maddox *Redux.* In an omitted part of Judge Posner's opinion in C.L. Maddox v. Coalfield Services, p. 780 above, he observed that Coalfield would have had a right to demand assurance of Maddox's performance if the case had been governed by the Uniform Commercial Code, and that the principle behind UCC § 2–609 was a "sound one." "Coalfield's repeated requests to Maddox to sign a proposal that, so far as the record shows, contained no unusual, coercive, or one-sided terms ... were in effect reasonable requests for assurances, or close enough to be treated the same by the law. Maddox's failure to provide any assurances entitled Coalfield in the circumstances ... to anticipate that Maddox would commit a breach, to suspend its own performance for the sake of self-protection, and to demand payment for the work done to date.... Against this it can be argued that since the parties already had a contract, Coalfield need not have required Mr. Maddox to sign anything and therefore did not have to worry about his failure to respond to the repeated demands to sign Coalfield's written offer, and could treat Maddox's counteroffer as a request for modification and ignore it...."

"We are mindful of the standard formula ... that an anticipatory breach occurs only when a party makes a clear and unequivocal statement of his intention to break the contract when his performance comes due.... We have no quarrel with the formula. But obviously it is meant for cases in which the claim of anticipatory repudiation is based on a statement. Here, as in cases based on section 2–609 of the Uniform Commercial Code, the claim is based on silence in the face of a request for the equivalent of assurances.... By the time Coalfield brought its crew to the surface, Maddox had repeatedly failed to respond to Coalfield's demand for confirmation of their agreement. Had Coalfield not acted and instead had completed the job and sued, it might have been faced with a defense of failure to mitigate its damages."

Reconsider the questions in the Note, p. 782 above, following *Maddox.*

(4) *Self–Help Remedies Under the Code.* Under the doctrine of constructive conditions of exchange, an injured party may suspend performance and ultimately terminate. As long as the injured party does not claim damages, that party does not need to go to court. Suspension and termination are "self-help" remedies. In UCC §§ 2–609 and 2–717, the Code expands the array of such remedies available under contracts for the sale of goods. What might be the reason for this expansion? Do you see any drawback? See Celia Taylor, Self–Help in Contract Law: An Exploration and Proposal, 33 Wake Forest L.Rev. 839 (1998).

CHAPTER 9

Basic Assumptions: Mistake, Impracticability and Frustration

Sometimes a contracting party faces an obstacle to its performance that the parties did not take into account when the contract was made. Sometimes—and only sometimes—a contract obligation is excused, or is suspended, for that reason. And sometimes, when that is so, another obligation arises in its place. This chapter addresses occasions of these types.

When a party's performance is impeded, or when a party's expectations are seriously thwarted, by circumstances existing but unknown to the parties, a common ground for claiming an excuse is mistake. That is the focus of Section 1. In contrast, the next two sections largely feature obligations that are subverted by events occurring after the parties have contracted.

When a promisor seeks relief on the ground that a supervening turn of events has impeded its performance, the conventional legal basis is "impossibility" or—now more commonly—the word "impracticability." We have already seen a number of cases in which a performance was impeded by a "turn of events," such as floods (Gill v. Johnstown Lumber Co., p. 733), outbreak of war (McCloskey & Co. v. Minweld Steel Co., p. 776), freeze (Cosden Oil & Chemical Co. v. Karl O. Helm, p. 783) and subsequent price controls on oil (Eastern Air Lines v. Gulf Oil Corp., p. 76). The doctrine of impracticability, the topic of Section 2, describes the additional circumstances that must attend such events in order to excuse the performance of a party: although important, it is not sufficient that the party's performance is simply more difficult or costly than anticipated.

While our discussion of impracticability is significantly informed by considerations of the cost of performance, the topic of Section 3, "frustration of purpose," focuses on the value or purpose of performance. The typical situation presented in this section is somewhat singular in that the party claiming an excuse cannot say that its performance was impeded by a supervening event; rather, some turn of events has thwarted that party's object in making the contract.

Being relieved of an obligation through an excuse doctrine is often not the end of the story. There may well be a sequel to the story when one party's expectations are defeated because another party has succeeded, for one of the reasons mentioned above, in disclaiming an obligation. Some compensating adjustment may be possible, especially in the name of *restitution*. Section 4 gives instances.

SECTION 1. MUTUAL MISTAKE

We have already encountered one aspect of the doctrine of mistake in Chapter 2. In Elsinore School District v. Kastorff, p. 139 above, a bidder for building work got relief for mistake. That case concerned *unilateral* mistake. See, e.g., Restatement § 153. The cases considered in this section involve *mutual* mistake, where both parties to the contract are mistaken as to the same basic assumption. Mistaken beliefs and misunderstandings concerning material aspects of an agreement may undermine assent and the very basis of the contract. Restatement § 20, Comment *h*; Wichelhaus v. Raffles, p. 422 above. But even when a belief, contrary to fact, does not defeat formation of a contract, courts will sometimes allow a party to avoid performance of the contract through the doctrine of mistake.

The background principle against which the mistake doctrine operates is that agreements are to be observed—*pacta sunt servanda*—notwithstanding the regret that a party may experience when fresh information comes to light. This principle underlies a dictum in Watkins & Son v. Carrig, p. 331. The contract there called for the excavation of a cellar, and the parties seemed to be surprised when the excavator encountered rock. "In this situation," the court said, "a defense of mutual mistake is not available." Similarly, in the case that follows, a builder—Leonard—encountered an unfavorable soil condition. In writing about Leonard's responsibility, the court did not indicate that he made an explicit appeal to the law of mistake. But it is clear from the opinion that the court would have been deaf to that appeal.

Stees v. Leonard

Supreme Court of Minnesota, 1874.
20 Minn. 494, 20 Gil. 448.

[The statement of facts is taken in part from the 1882 edition by Gilfillan of 20 Minnesota Reports.] The action was brought to recover damages for a failure of defendants to erect and complete a building on a lot of plaintiffs, on Minnesota Street, between Third and Fourth streets, in the city of St. Paul, which, by an agreement under seal between them and plaintiffs, the defendants had agreed to build, erect, and complete, according to plans and specifications annexed to and made part of the agreement. The defendants commenced the construction of the building, and had carried it to the height of three stories when it fell to the ground. The next year, 1869, they began again and carried it to the height as before, when it again fell to the ground, whereupon defendants refused to perform the contract. They claimed that in their attempts to erect the building they did the work in all respects according to the plans and specifications and that the failure to complete the building and its fall on the two occasions was due to the fact that the soil upon which it was to be constructed was composed of quicksand, and when water flowed into it, was incapable of sustaining the building.... The specifications annexed to the contract are very full, and provide, (among other things,) that "All the walls shall be of the following thickness: foundation walls, two feet thick, and shall have footings six inches thick, which shall run clear across walls and project six inches on each side of wall above it." The specifications contain no other provisions relating to the character of the foundation for the building. [The plaintiffs alleged that the specifications, signed by both parties to the contract, had been prepared by a firm of architects named Sheire & Bro. Two persons named Sheire were named as defendants along with Leonard.]

The plaintiffs allege ... that the fall of the building was owing to the negligence and unskilful work of the defendants, and the poor quality of the material furnished by them. Judgment is demanded for the sum of $5,214.80, with interest, as the damages sustained by the plaintiffs; being $3,745.80 paid, pursuant to the contract, during the progress of the work, $1,000 as damages for loss of the use of the lot on which the building was to be erected, and $469, as damages, occasioned by the fall of the building, to an adjacent house of plaintiffs, and property stored therein....

The jury found for the plaintiffs. The defendants moved, upon a bill of exceptions, for a new trial, and appeal from the order denying their motion.

■ YOUNG, J. The general principle of law which underlies this case is well established. If a man bind himself, by a positive, express contract, to do an act in itself possible, he must perform his engagement, unless prevented by the act of God, the law, or the other party to the contract. No hardship, no unforeseen hindrance, no difficulty short of absolute impossibility, will excuse him from doing what he has expressly agreed to do. This doctrine may sometimes seem to bear heavily upon contractors; but, in such cases, the hardship is attributable, not to the law, but to the contractor himself, who has improvidently assumed an absolute, when he might have undertaken only a qualified, liability. The law does no more than enforce the contract as the parties themselves have made it....

School Trustees v. Bennett, 3 Dutcher, N.J., 513, is almost identical, in its material facts, with the present case. The contractors agreed to build and complete a schoolhouse, and find all materials therefor, according to specifications annexed to the contract; the building to be located on a lot owned by plaintiff, and designated in the contract. When the building was nearly completed it was blown down by a sudden and violent gale of wind. The contractors again began to erect the building, when it fell, solely on account of the soil on which it stood having become soft and miry, and unable to sustain the weight of the building; although, when the foundations were laid, the soil was so hard as to be penetrated with difficulty by a pickax, and its defects were latent. The plaintiff had a verdict for the amount of the installments paid under the contract as the work progressed. The verdict was sustained by the supreme court, which held that the loss, although arising solely from a latent defect in the soil, and not from a faulty construction of the building, must fall on the contractor....

[The court referred to Dermott v. Jones, 2 Wall. [69 U.S.] 1 (1864), a case in which "the foundation of the building sank, owing to a latent defect in the soil." From the opinion there the court quoted a statement that the applicable principle "regards the sanctity of contracts. It requires a party to do what he has agreed to do. If unexpected impediments lie in the way, and a loss ensue, it leaves the loss where the contract places it."]

Nothing can be added to the clear and cogent arguments we have quoted in vindication of the wisdom and justice of the rule which must govern this case, unless it is in some way distinguishable from the cases cited....

It is no defense to the action that the specifications directed that "footings" should be used as the foundation of the building, and that the defendants, in the construction of those footings, as well as in all other particulars, conformed to the specifications. The defendants contracted to "erect and complete the building." Whatever was necessary to be done in order to complete the building, they were bound by the contract to do. If the building could not be completed without other or stronger foundations than the footings specified, they were bound to furnish such other foundations. If the building could not be erected without draining the land, then they must drain the land, "because they have agreed to do everything necessary to erect and complete the building." (3 Dutcher, N.J., 520; and see Dermott v. Jones, supra, where the same point was made by the contractor, but ruled against him by the court.)

As the draining of the land was, in fact, necessary to the erection and completion of the building, it was a thing to be done, under the contract, by the defendants. The prior parol agreement that plaintiffs should drain the land, related therefore, to a matter embraced within the terms of the written contract, and was not, as claimed by defendants' counsel, collateral thereto. It was, accordingly under the familiar rule, inadmissible in evidence to vary the terms of the written contract, and was properly excluded.

[In the remainder of the opinion the court considered evidence offered by the defendants that *after* the work was begun the plaintiffs made promises to drain the site of the building, and that the failure to do so caused the collapse. The court held that the evidence was properly excluded because the defendants had failed to allege consideration for the promises, or justifiable reliance upon them.]

There was, therefore, no error in the exclusion of the evidence offered, and the order appealed from is affirmed.

NOTES

(1) *Questions.* Note that Stees did not get, nor did he ask for, his expectation interest—the value to him of the building less any savings. Do you see any significance in that? As a test of your answer, suppose this case: Leonard detected the problem before beginning work and refused to begin, whereupon Stees paid a higher price to another builder for doing the work. What of a claim for the additional cost?

Charles Fried, in his influential book *Contract as Promise* (1981, p. 64), has called the result in *Stees* a harsh and silly one. Do you agree? If so, do you object also to what was said in *Watkins & Son*, as quoted before the *Stees* opinion, about an excavator's liability?

(2) *Owner's Responsibility?* In Dermott v. Jones, relied on in *Stees*, counsel for the owner cautioned the Court against the theory that a building contract makes the owner "an insurer to the builder of the stability and solidity of the soil on which such builder contracts to build work." In *Stees*, the defendants urged a modified version of that theory on the court. The court rejected the argument, concluding that it was foreclosed by the pleadings. The argument has impressive support, however, at least when the contract requires building according to plans prepared by the owner. That being the case, it has been said that "the contractor will not be responsible for the consequences of defects in the plans and specifications." United States v. Spearin, 248 U.S. 132, 136 (1918). There the Court ruled that specifications in the contract about a projected sewer, including its location in the Brooklyn Navy Yard, "imported a warranty that, if the specifications were complied with, the sewer would be adequate." See also the "soft soil" case, Ridley Investment Co. v. Croll, 192 A.2d 925 (Del.1963) (plans and specifications "defective for the location in question").

Courts have distinguished between a "performance specification," which requires a contractor to produce a specific result without specifying the means for achieving that result, and a "design specification," which specifies the design, materials, and methods, and impliedly warrants their adequacy. Which kind of specification was involved in *Stees*? In *Spearin*?

(3) *Act of God.* Changing the facts in *Stees*, let it be supposed that Leonard had no foundation trouble in putting up the building, but that when he had nearly finished the job the building was struck by lightning and destroyed by an ensuing fire. He would have been accountable for breach, it seems, if he did not begin to build again. "It is well established law that where one contracts to furnish labor and materials, and construct a chattel, or build a house, on land of another, he will not ordinarily be excused from performance of his contract by the destruction of the chattel or building without his fault before the time fixed for the delivery of it." Butterfield v. Byron, 27 N.E. 667 (Mass.1891)—a case of lightning. (But the court found in the facts a reason to avoid applying the rule quoted.)

(4) *Parol Evidence.* Consider Leonard's offer to prove a "prior parol agreement" by Stees to drain the site, in relation to this statement: "The parol evidence rule does not preclude the use of prior or contemporaneous agreements or negotiations to establish that the parties were mistaken." Restatement § 152, Comment *a*. Evidence of the supposed agreement could not have helped Leonard to establish a mutual mistake, it seems. What, then, of using that evidence to establish that the parties were *not* mistaken? One can imagine that Stees—not Leonard—offered evidence of his own promise. Expecting that the parol evidence rule would prevent enforcement of the promise, Stees might want to use the evidence to show that no mistake was made. (Anyone believing the evidence would infer that the parties knew the site was waterlogged.)

Renner v. Kehl

Supreme Court of Arizona, 1986.
150 Ariz. 94, 722 P.2d 262.

[Two couples, the Kehls and the Moyles, doing business together, decided to sell their interest in unimproved land near Yuma, Arizona. They held leases on more than two thousand acres. Roy Renner and some associates contracted to pay about $100 an acre for the leases. Before that, the purchasers made it clear to the sellers that they were interested in the property only for the cultivation of jojoba and required adequate water supplies. The property appeared to be ideal for that purpose; the soil and climate were good and both parties were of the opinion that sufficient water was available beneath the land to sustain jojoba production. (Jojoba ["ha-ho'ba"] is a shrub, the seeds of which yield a valuable oil.)

The purchasers abandoned the project after making a down payment, taking a conveyance, and drilling five test wells. None of the wells produced water of sufficient quantity or quality for commercial jojoba cultivation. Then the purchasers brought an action against the sellers for rescission. The trial court directed the sellers to reimburse the purchasers, upon receiving a reassignment of the leases. The Court of Appeals affirmed, on a first appeal, and the sellers appealed again.]

■ GORDON, VICE CHIEF JUSTICE. . . . Mutual mistake of fact is an accepted basis for rescission. Amos Flight Operations, Inc. v. Thunderbird Bank, 112 Ariz. 263, 540 P.2d 1244 (1975); Mortensen v. Berzell Investment Company, 102 Ariz. 348, 429 P.2d 945 (1967). See Restatement (Second) of Contracts § 152. In Arizona a contract may be rescinded when there is a mutual mistake of material fact which constitutes "an essential part and condition of the contract." [*Mortensen* at 350, 947.] The trial court found that the sole purpose of the contract was to enable respondents to grow jojoba, which depends upon an adequate water supply. The trial court specifically found that "There would have been no sale if both sellers and buyers had not believed it was possible to grow jojoba commercially on the leased acres. . . ." and that "[b]ased upon the factual data available, all parties were of the opinion that there would be sufficient good quality water for commercial jojoba production, and that it would be close enough to the surface that it would be economically feasible to pump it for irrigation of large acreages." Consequently, the trial court concluded that "[p]laintiffs are entitled to rescind the purchase agreement because of the mutual mistake of fact and because there was a total failure of consideration."[1]

The belief of the parties that adequate water supplies existed beneath the property was "a basic assumption on which both parties made the contract," Restatement (Second) of Contracts § 152 Comment *b*, and their mutual mistake "ha[d] such a material effect on the agreed exchange of performances as to upset the very bases of the contract." Id. Comment *a*. The contract was therefore voidable and the respondents were entitled to rescission.[2]

---

1. The petitioner challenges the sufficiency of the evidence in support of the trial court's conclusions of fact and law, but failed to provide a record of the trial. . . . Without a record we must presume that the trial court properly exercised its discretion and that there was substantial evidence in the complete record to support the findings of the trial court. . . .

2. The failure of the parties to make a thorough investigation of the water supply prior to signing the contract does not preclude rescission where the risk of mistake was not allocated among the parties and the mistake is material and relates to a basic assumption on which the contract was made. Restatement (Second) of Contracts § 152 Comment *a*. See id., illustration 1:

[The trial court had ordered the sellers to reimburse the purchasers in the amount of $309,849.84. This amount included $80,200, which the sellers had received as a down payment for the leases. (The purchasers had agreed to pay $142,000 more in annual installments.) The remainder of the reimbursement consisted of expenses that the purchasers had incurred in developing the property, including the cost of drilling test wells.]

... The court of appeals upheld the full award.... The petitioners challenge the $229,649.84 awarded as an improper grant of "consequential damages".[3] [The parties and the court seem to have used this expression as an alias for a recovery of reliance expenses.]

... We are dealing with a rescission based upon mutual mistake, which implies freedom from fault on the part of both parties. [W]e hold that absent proof of breach for fraud or misrepresentation a party who rescinds a contract may not recover consequential damages....

This does not mean, however, that the respondents are entitled only to recover their down payment. When a party rescinds a contract on the ground of mutual mistake he is entitled to restitution for any benefit that he has conferred on the other party by way of part performance or reliance. Restatement (Second) of Contracts § 376. Restitutionary recoveries are not designed to be compensatory; their justification lies in the avoidance of unjust enrichment on the part of the defendant. D. Dobbs, Remedies § 4.1 p. 224 (1973). Thus the defendant is generally liable for restitution of a benefit that would be unjust for him to keep, even though he gained it honestly. Id; Restatement (Second) of Contracts § 376 Comment *a*. The issue we must now address is the proper measure of the restitutionary interest.

The first step determining the proper measure of restitution requires that the rescinding party return or offer to return, conditional on restitution, any interest in property that he has received in the bargain. Restatement (Second) of Contracts § 384(1)(a). In Arizona this includes reimbursement for the fair market value of the use of the property.... Thus the respondents were obliged to return the land to the petitioners in exchange for their down payment, and in addition to pay the petitioners the fair rental value of the land for the duration of their occupancy.

However, to avoid unjust enrichment the petitioners must pay the respondents a sum equal to the amount by which their property has been enhanced in value by the respondents' efforts. The Restatement (Second) of Contracts § 376 provides that "[i]f [a party] has received and must return land ... he may have made improvements on the land in reliance on the contract and he is entitled to recover the reasonable value of those

"A contracts to sell and B to buy a tract of land, the value of which has depended mainly on the timber on it. Both A and B believe that the timber is still there, but in fact it has been destroyed by fire. The contract is voidable by B."

3. Consequential or "incidental" damages represent a plaintiff's expenses incurred in reliance upon the contract. See Fousel v. Ted Walker Mobile Homes, Inc., 124 Ariz. 126, 602 P.2d 507 (App.1979). In *Fousel* these expenses included the cost of custom-made awnings, skirting and steps purchased for their mobile home, see discussion, infra; in this case they would represent the cost of developing the land for jojoba production.

improvements.... The rule stated in this section applies to avoidance on any ground, including ... mistake...." Comment *a*. The reasonable value of any improvements is measured by "the extent to which the other party's property has been increased in value or his other interests advanced." Restatement (Second) of Contracts § 371(b). Thus the petitioners must pay to the respondents that amount of money which represents the enhanced value of the land due to the respondents' development efforts. In short, the respondents are entitled to their down payment, plus the amount by which their efforts increased the value of the petitioners' property, minus an amount which represents the fair rental value of the land during their occupancy. They are not entitled to the $229,649.84 expended upon development, because that would shift the entire risk of mistake onto the petitioners, which is incompatible with equitable rescission.

CONCLUSION

The respondents were entitled to rescind the contract, but may not recover the costs of developing the land in the form of consequential damages. The respondents are entitled to restitution of their down payment and any amount by which the value of the land was enhanced, but in turn the respondents must pay petitioners the fair rental value of the tenancy. Accordingly, the trial court is affirmed in part and reversed in part and the court of appeals' decision is approved in part and vacated in part. The case is remanded to the trial court for further proceedings not inconsistent with this opinion.

NOTES

(1) *Enforcement Possibilities.* It is well to defer consideration of the court's rulings about restitution for the purchasers and the rental-value charge, and for the present to consider only the ruling that the purchasers were entitled to rescission. (As to monetary adjustments, see pp. 819–820 below.)

Suppose that the buyers had learned of the water problem earlier, and had refused to take a conveyance. Suppose also that the court had ruled otherwise on the issue of mistake. It would follow that the sellers could have recovered damages based on the contract price. Does it also follow that the sellers could have won an order for specific performance, as is usual for contracts for real-property transfers? Recall the element of judicial discretion in actions for specific performance, and see McKinnon v. Benedict, p. 455 above.

(2) *The Converse Case.* Changing the facts in *Renner*, let it be supposed that the buyers' test drilling had disclosed not only an ample and accessible supply of water but also valuable minerals. In that case one might anticipate an action for rescission brought by the sellers, not the buyers. Except that, by all indications, that action would fail. "[I]t is commonly understood that the seller of farm land generally cannot avoid the contract of sale upon later discovery by both parties that the land contains valuable mineral deposits, even though the price was negotiated on the basic assumption that the land was suitable only for farming and the effect on the agreed exchange of performances is material." Restatement § 154, Comment *a*. Can this be explained on any ground other than *caveat vendor*?

SALE OF GOODS: TWO FAMOUS CASES

We have so far considered land and building contracts. We now turn to two well-known sale of goods cases.

The first case is Wood v. Boynton, 25 N.W. 42 (Wis.1885), the so-called "Diamond in the Rough Case." S.B. Boynton, of the firm Boynton & Boynton, jewelers, was accepting a pin for repair when the customer (Clarissa Wood) showed him a stone she had found. "I thought I would ask him what the stone was," Wood said later. After Boynton looked over the stone, "I told him I had been told it was a topaz, and he said it might be." The conversation progressed something like this: B—"I would buy this; would you sell it?" W—"What would it be worth?" Boynton said he did not know; he would give me a dollar and keep it as a specimen. Wood said she would not sell, and that the stone was "certainly pretty to look at." Two or three months later Wood visited Boynton again. "I needed money pretty badly," she later said, "and thought every dollar would help, and I [told] Mr. Boynton ... I had brought back the topaz, and he says, 'Well, yes; what did I offer you for it?' and I says, 'One dollar;' and he stepped to the change drawer and gave me the dollar, and I went out." The stone was straw-colored, and about the size and shape of a canary egg. It was later found to be a rough diamond, worth about $700. Wood demanded that it be returned, tendering $1.10 (ten cents as interest) to the Boyntons. Wood brought an action for the return of the diamond. The foregoing report of the parties' dealings is drawn from her testimony at the trial. Boynton's testimony did not differ materially. He added that he had never seen an uncut diamond, and that "it never entered his brain at the time" that the stone was a diamond. The trial court dismissed the action and Wood appealed. *Held*: Affirmed. Aside from fraud, the court said, it knew of only one possible ground for recovery: "that there was a mistake made by the vendor in delivering an article which was not the article sold,—a mistake in fact as to the identity of the thing sold with the thing delivered."

The second case is Sherwood v. Walker, 33 N.W. 919 (Mich.1887): the "Pregnant–Cow Case." Hiram Walker, a cattle breeder, agreed with Theodore Sherwood, a banker, to sell him a cow of distinguished ancestry known as Rose 2d of Aberlone. The price was $80, both parties believing Rose to be sterile. When Walker discovered that she was pregnant and therefore worth between $750 and $1,000, he refused to deliver her. Sherwood sued in replevin and prevailed in the trial court, but lost on appeal. "A barren cow is substantially a different creature than a breeding one," the court explained. Rose "was not in fact the animal, or the kind of animal, the defendants had intended to sell or the plaintiff to buy."

NOTES

(1) *Distinctions*. Which of the following suggestions serves better as the operative distinction between the rough-diamond case and the pregnant-cow case? Is some other one still better? Or is there no adequate distinction?

a. In the former case the party adversely affected by the mistake (the seller, Wood) had delivered the diamond before the mistake was discovered, and sought to retrieve it, whereas in the latter that party (Walker) had not performed, and sought only to retain the cow. Though this distinction has been advocated, it is generally discounted. It would not explain Renner v. Kehl, above.

b. Possibly the price/value ratios differentiate the two cases. That is, $80 for a titled cow would indicate a basic assumption that she was not fertile, whereas one dollar is a fair compromise between the prospect of great value in a small rock—a dim prospect—and the going price of the vast majority of rocks, even those "pretty to look at" (zero).

(2) *Background Principles*. These cases preceded the UCC, but were they to arise today they would fall within the scope of Article 2. Yet Article 2 does not directly address mistake, but see UCC § 1–103.

(3) *Essence and Quality*. Courts use varying terminology when discussing the avoidance of a contract for mistake. One is represented in the expression, "basic assumption on which the contract was made," as used in the Restatement and in Renner v. Kehl, above. In an earlier period, discourse about "essences" and "attributes," or "substances" and "qualities," was common. For an English example, see Leaf v. International Galleries, [1950] 2 K.B. 86 (Court of Appeal), about the sale of a painting that was supposed to be, but was not, the work of a master. One justice observed that the mistake was one about "quality and value rather than [about] the substance of the thing itself." Such a mistake, Lord Denning said, "does not avoid the contract: there was no mistake at all about the subject-matter of the sale. It was a specific picture: 'Salisbury Cathedral' "—whether or not painted by Constable. Because the seller had told the buyer that the painting was a "Constable," might the buyer have recovered damages for breach of warranty?

Does it matter how the critical distinction is expressed? Reasoning about essences has been denounced as metaphysical and "conclusory." The Restatement speaks with disapproval of "such artificial and specious distinctions as are sometimes drawn between 'intrinsic' and 'extrinsic' mistakes or between mistakes that go to the 'identity' or 'existence' of the subject matter and those that go merely to its 'attributes,' 'quality' or 'value.' " Restatement § 154, Comment *a*. Is the Restatement criterion any less conclusory? Not all scholars think so. See Andrew Kull, Mistake, Frustration, and the Windfall Principle of Contract Remedies, 43 Hartings L.J. 1, 13 ("less quaint, but no less conclusory"). That criterion may be more conducive to relief. But reasoning about essences can be somewhat flexible. Witness the pregnant-cow case, in which the court said: "A barren cow is substantially a different creature than a breeding one."

Long after the Supreme Court of Michigan court decided the pregnant-cow case, it abandoned the test used there. Lenawee County Bd. of Health v. Messerly, 331 N.W.2d 203, 211 (1982). In the more recent case, the buyer and the seller of an apartment building mistakenly believed that the building was suitable for human habitation and would generate rental income. The court concluded that "the distinctions which may be drawn from [the opinion in the cow case] do not provide a satisfactory analysis of the nature of a mistake sufficient to invalidate a contract." The "better reasoned approach," it said, is that of the Restatement. The court held, however, that the buyer bore the risk of the parties' mistake because the contract contained an "as is" clause, stating that the buyer "has examined this property and agrees to accept the same in its present condition."

(4) *Defining Mistake*. The conception of "mistake" is open to differing views. The Restatement defines mistake as "a belief that is not in accord with the facts." Section 151. It speaks also of a situation in which it is "sometimes said . . . that, in a sense, there was not mistake but 'conscious ignorance.' " Comment *c* to § 154. That situation has also been characterized as one of "recognized uncertainty." For

that situation, however, the overarching solution is that one of the parties "bears the risk of a mistake." The divide between mistake and ignorance is more pronounced in some sources. And sometimes when a court denies relief, it may offer a curious combination of reasons: the risk of mistake was assumed, and there was "no mistake." See Note 1 below.

THE RISKS OF LIMITED KNOWLEDGE

What obligations do parties have to investigate facts concerning their dealings? The administrators of the Estate of Martha Nelson advertised a public sale of some Estate assets. At the sale, they asked $60 for two oil paintings bearing the signature "Martin Johnson Heade" (an American painter of scenery, 1819–1904). Carl Rice paid that price. He assumed the paintings were not originals, but he liked the frame on one and the subject matter of the other. Later, after consulting a notable dealer in art (Christie's), Rice sold the paintings at auction for more than $1 million. Rice's wife enjoyed some of the after-tax proceeds. "[T]he Rices paid income taxes of $337,000 on the profit from the sale of the paintings, purchased a home, created a family trust, and spent some of the funds on living expenses." Having learned of the Rices' good fortune, the administrators proceeded against the Rices, asking that the sale contract be either rescinded or reformed on ground of mutual mistake.[a] The trial court granted summary judgment for the Rices. It found that the Estate bore the risk of mistake. It relied on Restatement § 154(b), which states that a party bears the risk of mistake when "he is aware, at the time the contract is made, that he has only limited knowledge with respect to the facts to which the mistake relates but treats his limited knowledge as sufficient." On appeal, *held*: Affirmed. Estate of Nelson v. Rice, 12 P.3d 238 (Ariz.App.2000).

The court quoted, as "clearly" applicable, Comment *c* to § 154 ("Conscious ignorance"). The administrators cited Renner v. Kehl, above, saying that the facts of the two cases were similar. To that the court answered: "The Estate's reliance on *Renner* is unavailing because, as stated above, the Estate bore the risk of mistake based on its own conscious ignorance."[b]

In support of its ruling, the court recited findings that the administrators had consulted an appraiser before the sale—one who told them that she was not qualified to appraise fine art. That reservation did not concern one of the administrators, he testified, because he had supposed that the

---

a. Unconscionability was another ground asserted by the administrators. As to that the appellate court said: "In refusing to rescind the sale on [that basis], the trial court stated that, 'while the results of the transaction may seem unconscionable to the [Estate] in hindsight, the terms of the contract certainly were not.' We agree...."

b. In its reply brief, the Estate argues that a party's negligence does not bar avoid-

ance or reformation of a contract for mutual mistake, claiming that § 157 of the Restatement requires bad faith or gross negligence. This argument is waived by the Estate's failure to raise it in its opening brief. General Motors Corp. v. Arizona Dep't of Revenue, 189 Ariz. 86, 938 P.2d 481 (App.1996); Wasserman v. Low, 143 Ariz. 4, 691 P.2d 716 (App.1984).

Estate contained little of significant value. Is it possible that there was no mistake at all on the part of the administrators?

The court found yet another reason for denying relief based on § 154(c) of the Restatement. The court said—including quotations from Comment *d*—that it could "allocate the risk of mistake to one party 'on the ground that it is reasonable in the circumstances to do so.' In making this determination, 'the court will consider the purposes of the parties and will have recourse to its own general knowledge of human behavior in bargain transactions.' Here, the Estate had had ample opportunity to discover what it was selling and failed to do so; instead, it ignored the possibility that the paintings were valuable and attempted to take action only after learning of their worth as a result of the efforts of the Rices. Under these circumstances, the Estate was a victim of its own folly and it was reasonable for the court to allocate to it the burden of its mistake."

NOTES

(1) *Risk Controls.* A distinction like that in the pregnant-cow case appears in Watkins & Son v. Carrig, p. 331 above. There the court said that a contract for excavating a cellar was not voidable by reason of the parties' supposition that rock would not be encountered. Suppose it had been shown that excavators habitually make test borings before committing themselves. Would that have reinforced the court's view of the mistake issue? Changing the facts in the case, let it be supposed that, before making the contract, the *owner* had made a boring at the site to test for rock and, by mischance, had detected none. Would that have reinforced the court's view, or have changed it? Recall that, in Renner v. Kehl, the purchasers drilled test wells *after* committing themselves. Should the court have given weight to that fact? (See the court's footnote 2.)

(2) *Expert Knowledge.* Consider again the Diamond in the Rough (*Wood*) and the Pregnant–Cow (*Sherwood*) cases. One difference between *Wood* and *Sherwood* concerns the vocations of the parties. By vocation, the buyer of the diamond and the seller of the cow were presumably more discriminating with respect to pretty stones and breedable cattle, respectively, than the parties they dealt with. The buyer prevailed in the one case, and the seller in the other. Is this a difference without a distinction? Should expertness have counted against the winner in either case? Where a retail dealer in coins deals for a rare coin under a mutual mistake with a *part-time* dealer, would you expect the former to bear the risk of mistake? See Beachcomber Coins, Inc. v. Boskett, 400 A.2d 78 (N.J. Super. Ct. 1979).

PROBLEMS

(1) *A Case of Rare Gas.* The buyer of a tract of land is led to pay a premium for it by seismic studies indicating to both parties that a supply of natural gas may underlie the property. Upon drilling, the buyer finds instead a deposit of helium, making the property worth three times what the buyer paid. Is the seller entitled to rescission?

(2) *The Putative Poussin.* By family tradition, the owners of a painting understood that it was the work of the great 17th century painter Nicholas Poussin. They consulted an auctioneer about selling it. In turn, the auctioneer consulted an art expert, and the owners were persuaded that the painting was the work of an unknown minor painter. The painting was exhibited for sale under the modest

designation "school of the Carraci." The buyer was the "Reunion des musées nationaux," which, exercising a right of preemption under French law, paid about $500. The painting was later authenticated as a Poussin by an expert connected with the Louvre and exhibited there as a Poussin. Other experts continued to doubt this attribution, however, and the question remained in doubt. On these facts, can the owners recover the painting?

See (Réunion des Musées Nationaux c/Saint–Arromans), Versailles, Jan. 7, 1987, Gaz.Pal.1987 Jur. 34—the last of six opinions which, nearly twenty years after the sale, concluded a dispute that, as one commentator wrote, "had caused more ink than paint to flow." Compare Firestone & Parson, Inc. v. Union League of Philadelphia, 672 F.Supp. 819 (E.D.Pa.1987).

————

MISTAKE AND RESTITUTION

Review the opinion in Renner v. Kehl, p. 811 above, attending to the concluding paragraphs, in which the court instructed the trial court how to determine what amount of reimbursement the sellers should pay to the purchasers (no "consequential damages" as such). The court did not mention the payment of interest. In the case of the pretty stone (diamond), p. 815 above, Wood, the seller, met one condition on rescission by making a tender of money to Boynton, the buyer. She tendered $1.10—the price she had received plus interest of ten cents. Should one dollar be enough? In *Renner*, should the sellers have been charged with interest on the deposit they had received?

As a general question, to what extent should a court readjust the parties' legal relations to account for performances, expenditures, and lost opportunities prior to their discovery of the mistake? Should it matter whether the discovery was a pleasant or unpleasant one? (In a case of pleasant surprise, as in Wood v. Boynton, the result is a gain in the joint wealth of the parties as they perceive it. In a case of unpleasant surprise, as in *Renner*, there is a loss.) Professor Kull found in contemporary cases a strong inclination to make adjustments—stronger in "loss" cases than in "gain" cases, "though why this should be so is not entirely clear." Mistake, Frustration, and the Windfall Principle of Contract Remedies, 43 Hastings L.J. 1, 41 (1991).

Professor Kull argued for leaving matters as they stand.[a] The effect of his solution in *Renner* would have been, apparently, to confer the leases on the buyers, leaving the sellers with the down payment and no further rights. If the courts were to go that way, might there be a reaction against avoiding contracts for mistakes?

Support for monetary "reparations" in cases of rescission is found in the Restatement § 158 and in other scholarly work.[b] But attitudes differ

---

a. He was anticipated in this by Professor Victor Goldberg, who wrote: "Anglo–American law appears to be moving in the wrong direction." Impossibility and Related Excuses, 144 J. of Inst'l & Theoretical Economics 100, 112–14 (1988).

b. See Eric Kades, Windfalls, 108 Yale L.J. 1489, 1526 (1999); for a defense of loss about the appropriate computation. Opposing judgments depend on part on diverse views about why parties contract for "down payments," advance payments, and deferred payments. Why, in *Renner*, might the parties have agreed on a down payment of 36%?

Settlements of disputed claims, though intended to be conclusive, are sometimes not, owing to mistake. The overpayment of a claim often generates a right of restitution if it was based on a mistake, but usually not if the payment was one implementing the settlement of a disputed claim. Likewise, a claimant who settles for an underpayment usually has no further entitlement. As to consideration and compromise in a claim-release case, see Fiege v. Boehm, p. 40 above.

An exceptional case is one in which the settlement contract itself can be avoided for mutual mistake. Suppose, for example, a claim by a woman against an insurance company, based on a contract insuring the life of her husband (known as the *cestui que vie* (CQV), the person whose life determines the duration of a trust, an estate or, in this case, an insurance agreement), and on a report that he was a wartime casualty. Suppose also that the claim was compromised at 50%, owing to a dispute about premium payments. Upon the surprise reappearance of the husband, the CQV, it is likely that the insurer could recapture its payment—but would be embroiled again in a dispute about the premiums. The release of a personal-injury claim may become questionable when an injury comes to light that the parties were not aware of at the time of settlement.

Comment *f* to Restatement § 152 speaks to the problem. It indicates some circumstances bearing on the basic assumptions of the parties, including "the amount received by the claimant in settlement of his claim."

A settlement may be vitiated for a misperception of law as well as for one of fact, by the better view. Or, as the Restatement puts it, "Facts include law." Comment *b* to § 151. If, however, the parties have made an inference about the state of the law, relying on inconclusive precedents, and are taught by a later decision that their inference was wrong, the case is not one of relievable mistake. Krantz v. University of Kansas, 21 P.3d 561 (Kan.2001). In order to support a finding of *mistake*, as the word is defined in the Restatement, "the erroneous belief must relate to the facts as they exist at the time of the making of the contract." Comment *a* to § 151.

If the courts were to find a vitiating mistake in a large proportion of settlement agreements, what consequence would you expect in the practices of litigants?

NOTE

Arithmetic in the Rubble. Refer again to the amounts recovered in Stees v. Leonard, above. If in that case Leonard had sought to avoid the contract on the ground of mistake, and had succeeded, what reparations would have been appropriate?

sharing, see Charles Fried, *Contract as Promise* 69–73 (1981).

PROBLEMS

(1) *The Sham Stradivarius.* A violin supposed to be the work of a master craftsman of the Renaissance was sold for $9,000 by a collector of rare instruments (not a dealer). The buyer, a renowned concert violinist, paid $3,000 down. Before he paid more, the violin was found to be a recent knockoff, worth $500 at most. Each party has made a claim against the other: the seller for the unpaid part of the price, and the buyer (who has tendered the return of the item) for the down payment. How should the claims be decided? See Smith v. Zimbalist, 38 P.2d 170 (Cal.App. 1934).

(2) *Make or Change?* To settle a dispute under a contract, Creditor and Debtor make a settlement agreement under which Debtor is to pay Creditor $1,000,000 in return for a release from all of Creditor's claims based on the underlying contract. The parties assume that that contract does not offend public policy and is clearly enforceable. Their assumption rests on the advice of their lawyers and on a ten-year-old decision of the state's highest court. Soon after the settlement agreement is made, that court overrules its earlier decision, holding that contracts like the one that generated the dispute are unenforceable, being contrary to public policy. You represent Debtor. Mistake or erroneous prediction? (Do judges make the law or only declare it?) What difference does it make whether or not the settlement rests on a mistake? See Kleinwort Benson v. Lincoln City Council, [1998] 4 All.E.R. 513 (House of Lords).

SECTION 2. IMPRACTICABILITY OF PERFORMANCE

Recall Stees v. Leonard: "If a man bind himself, by a positive, express contract, to do an act in itself possible, he must perform his engagement, unless prevented by the act of God, the law, or the other party to the contract. No hardship, no unforeseen hindrance, no difficulty short of absolute impossibility, will excuse him from doing what he has expressly agreed to do."

Of course many contractual undertakings are not "absolute" in this sense. Take, for example, the obligations of Otis Wood (p. 83 above) and Falstaff Brewing (p. 532 above) to use reasonable efforts. In the rest of this chapter, however, we explore the limits of more specific undertakings. To what extent is even an "absolute" contractual undertaking affected by a change of circumstances after the contract is made? This principle underlies a dictum in *Watkins & Son.* "In this situation," the court said, "a defense of mutual mistake is not available." In the following case that follows, a contractor encounters unfavorable soil condition, raising the costs of its performance—similar to *Watkins & Son*, where a contractor unexpectedly encountered a boulder in the excavation of a cellar, and *Stees v. Leonard*, where a builder unknowingly erected a building on quicksand, twice.

Mineral Park Land Co. v. Howard

Supreme Court of California, 1916.
172 Cal. 289, 156 P. 458.

■ SLOSS, J. The defendants appeal from a judgment in favor of plaintiff for $3,650. The appeal is on the judgment roll alone.

The plaintiff was the owner of certain land in the ravine or wash known as the Arroyo Seco, in South Pasadena, Los Angeles county. The defendants had made a contract with the public authorities for the construction of a concrete bridge across the Arroyo Seco. In August, 1911, the parties to this action entered into a written agreement whereby the plaintiff granted to the defendants the right to haul gravel and earth from plaintiff's land, the defendants agreeing to take therefrom all of the gravel and earth necessary in the construction of the fill and cement work on the proposed bridge, the required amount being estimated at approximately 114,000 cubic yards. Defendants agreed to pay 5 cents per cubic yard for the first 80,000 yards, the next 10,000 yards were to be given free of charge, and the balance was to be paid for at the rate of 5 cents per cubic yard.

The complaint was in two counts. The first alleged that the defendants had taken 50,131 cubic yards of earth and gravel, thereby becoming indebted to plaintiff in the sum of $2,506.55, of which only $900 had been paid, leaving a balance of $1,606.55 due. The findings support plaintiff's claim in this regard, and there is no question of the propriety of so much of the judgment as responds to the first count. The second count sought to recover damages for the defendants' failure to take from plaintiff's land any more than the 50,131 yards.

It alleged that the total amount of earth and gravel used by defendants was 101,000 cubic yards, of which they procured 50,869 cubic yards from some place other than plaintiff's premises. The amount due the plaintiff for this amount of earth and gravel would, under the terms of the contract, have been $2,043.45. The count charged that plaintiff's land contained enough earth and gravel to enable the defendants to take therefrom the entire amount required, and that the 50,869 yards not taken had no value to the plaintiff. Accordingly the plaintiff sought, under this head, to recover damages in the sum of $2,043.45.

The answer denied that the plaintiff's land contained any amount of earth and gravel in excess of the 50,131 cubic yards actually taken, and alleged that the defendants took from the said land all of the earth and gravel available for the work mentioned in the contract.

The court found that the plaintiff's land contained earth and gravel far in excess of 101,000 cubic yards of earth and gravel, but that only 50,131 cubic yards, the amount actually taken by the defendants, was above the water level. No greater quantity could have been taken "by ordinary means," or except by the use, at great expense, of a stream dredger, and the earth and gravel so taken could not have been used without first having been dried at great expense and delay. On the issue raised by the plea of defendants that they took all the earth and gravel that was available the court qualified its findings in this way: It found that the defendants did take all of the available earth and gravel from plaintiff's premises, in this, that they took and removed 'all that could have been taken advantageously to defendants, or all that was practical to take and remove from a financial standpoint'; that any greater amount could have been taken only at a prohibitive cost, that is, at an expense of 10 or 12 times as much as the usual cost per yard. It is also declared that the word "available" is used in the findings to mean capable of being taken and used advantageously. It was not "advantageous or practical" to have taken more material from plaintiff's land, but it was not impossible. There is a finding that the parties were not under any mutual misunderstanding regarding the amount of available gravel, but that the contract was entered into without any calculation on the part of either of the parties with reference to the amount of available earth and gravel on the premises.

The single question is whether the facts thus found justified the defendants in their failure to take from the plaintiff's land all of the earth and gravel required. This question was answered in the negative by the court below. The case was apparently thought to be governed by the principle—established by a multitude of authorities—that where a party has agreed, without qualification, to perform an act which is not in its nature impossible of performance, he is not excused by difficulty of performance, or by the fact that he becomes unable to perform.

It is, however, equally well settled that, where performance depends upon the existence of a given thing, and such existence was assumed as the basis of the agreement, performance is excused to the extent that the thing ceases to exist or turns out to be nonexistent. . . .

We think the findings of fact make a case falling within the rule of these decisions. The parties were contracting for the right to take earth and gravel to be used in the construction of the bridge. When they stipulated that all of the earth and gravel needed for this purpose should be taken from plaintiff's land, they contemplated and assumed that the land contained the requisite quantity, available for use. The defendants were not binding themselves to take what was not there. And, in determining whether the earth and gravel were "available," we must view the conditions in a practical and reasonable way. Although there was gravel on the land, it was so situated that the defendants could not take it by ordinary means, nor except at a prohibitive cost. To all fair intents then, it was impossible for defendants to take it.

"A thing is impossible in legal contemplation when it is not practicable; and a thing is impracticable when it can only be done at an excessive and unreasonable cost." 1 Beach on Contr. § 216. We do not mean to intimate that the defendants could excuse themselves by showing the existence of conditions which would make the performance of their obligation more expensive than they had anticipated, or which would entail a loss upon them. But, where the difference in cost is so great as here, and has the effect, as found, of making performance impracticable, the situation is not different from that of a total absence of earth and gravel.

On the facts found, there should have been no recovery on the second count.

The judgment is modified by deducting therefrom the sum of $2,043.45, and, as so modified, it stands affirmed.

■ We concur: SHAW, J.; LAWLOR, J.

NOTES

(1) *Mistake or Impracticability?* A distinction is sometimes drawn between a performance that becomes impracticable because of some event occurring after the contract is formed and a performance that is impracticable for reasons that existed at the time of contract formation but were unknown to the parties. The former is called supervening impracticability, while the latter is often referred to as existing impracticability. A party who claims existing impracticability may also have a claim of mistake under the common law. What difficulties would Mineral Park have encountered if he had based his defense on mistake? What difficulties would the excavating contractor in Watkins & Son have encountered if he had claimed that he was relieved on the ground of impracticability?

(2) *Not Earth Moving.* Cases involving impracticability typically entail realized performance costs that are substantially greater than anticipated costs. In these cases, the value of performance, while exceeding anticipated cost, may be less than the actual cost of performance. Compelling performance in such circumstances, where the value of performance is less than the cost of performance, would be an inefficient allocation of resources. Should the doctrine of impracticability be motivated by efficiency, or basic fairness—or something else?

Does the opinion in *Mineral Park* suggest that Howard placed any value on the removal of the gravel beyond the price offered by Mineral Park? Do you think Howard would have objected if Mineral Park simply offered to pay 5 cents per cubic yard for the remaining 50,869 cubic yards (less the "10,000 yards [that] were to be given free of charge" after the first 80,000 cubic yard) without removing any more earth and gravel? Was there any risk that earth and gravel would have been inefficiently moved from the ground if Mineral Park's obligation was not excused?

(3) *Risky Business.* Though the excavating contractor, in *Watkins & Son*, struck solid rock, "a defense of mutual mistake [was] not available." The court said, "[i]f the plaintiff was unwise in taking chances, it is not relieved, on the ground of mistake, from the burden incurred in being faced with them." Courts often look to see if the risks of impracticability are assigned to one party or the other by the agreement or context of the parties. And what if the risks are not allocated by the agreement or the background rules against which the parties contract? Does the court make its own independent risk allocation decision by granting or refusing the sought-after excuse?

———

SUPERVENING EVENTS

Centuries ago, in Paradine v. Jane, Aleyn 26, 82 Eng.Rep. 897 (Kings Bench 1647), the court gave reasons for the proposition that a contract duty—in this instance, a duty to pay rent—is "absolute," in the sense that no excuse based on changed conditions has been recognized. First, the court said that even if a change makes a party's performance impossible, "he might have provided against it in his contract." (If that was ever the rule, it has long since been subjected to some important qualifications.) Second, the court said that because a party "is to have the advantage of casual profits, so he must run the hazard of casual losses." In other words, a contract should impose matching burdens on the parties, so that a party that could take advantage of a favorable change in circumstances ought to bear the risk of an unfavorable one. Both of these reasons are echoed in later cases and continue to be effective as argument, on occasion. The next case depicts an early departure from the absolute rule.

Taylor v. Caldwell

King's Bench, 1863.
3 B. & S. 826, 122 Eng.Rep. 309.

[Action for breach of a written agreement by which defendants contracted to "let" the Surrey Gardens and Music Hall, at Newington, Surrey, to plaintiffs, for four days, for the purpose of giving four "grand concerts" and "day and night fêtes" in the hall; plaintiffs agreeing to pay £100 at the close of each day. The defendants agreed to furnish a band and certain other amusements in connection with plaintiffs' entertainments, but the plaintiffs were to have all moneys paid for entrance to the music hall and gardens. The plaintiffs alleged the defendants' breach, "Whereby the plaintiffs lost divers moneys paid by them for printing advertisements of and in advertising the concerts, and also lost divers sums expended and expenses incurred by them in preparing for the concerts and otherwise in relation thereto, and on the faith of the performance by the defendants of the agreement on their part". The defendants pleaded that the Gardens and Music Hall were accidentally destroyed by fire on June 11, 1861, without the default of the defendants or either of them. A verdict was returned for the plaintiffs, with leave reserved to enter a verdict for defendants.]

■ BLACKBURN, J. In this case the plaintiffs and defendants had, on the 27th May, 1861, entered into a contract by which the defendants agreed to let the plaintiffs have the use of The Surrey Gardens and Music Hall on four days then to come, viz., the 17th June, 15th July, 5th August and 19th August, for the purpose of giving a series of four grand concerts, and day and night fêtes at the Gardens and Hall on those days respectively; and the plaintiffs agreed to take the Gardens and Hall on those days, and pay £100 for each day.

[The court interpreted the agreement not to be a lease, and concluded that the entertainments provided for in the agreement could not be given without the existence of the Music Hall.]

After the making of the agreement, and before the first day on which a concert was to be given, the Hall was destroyed by fire. This destruction, we must take it on the evidence, was without the fault of either party, and was so complete that in consequence the concerts could not be given as intended. And the question we have to decide is whether, under these circumstances, the loss which the plaintiffs have sustained is to fall upon the defendants. The parties when framing their agreement evidently had not present to their minds the possibility of such a disaster, and have made no express stipulation with reference to it, so that the answer to the question must depend upon the general rules of law applicable to such a contract.

There seems no doubt that where there is a positive contract to do a thing, not in itself unlawful, the contractor must perform it or pay damages for not doing it, although in consequence of unforeseen accidents, the performance of his contract has become unexpectedly burdensome or even impossible. The law is so laid down in 1 Roll.Abr. 450, Condition (G), and in the note (2) to Walton v. Waterhouse, 2 Wms.Saund. 421a. 6th Ed., and is recognised as the general rule by all the Judges in the much discussed case of Hall v. Wright (E.B. & E. 746). But this rule is only applicable when the contract is positive and absolute, and not subject to any condition either express or implied: and there are authorities which, as we think, establish the principle that where, from the nature of the contract, it appears that the parties must from the beginning have known that it could not be fulfilled unless when the time for the fulfillment of the contract arrived some particular specified thing continued to exist, so that, when entering into the contract, they must have contemplated such continuing existence as the foundation of what was to be done; there, in the absence of any express or implied warranty that the thing shall exist, the contract is not to be construed as a positive contract, but as subject to an implied condition that the parties shall be excused in case, before breach, performance becomes impossible from the perishing of the thing without default of the contractor.

There seems little doubt that this implication tends to further the great object of making the legal construction such as to fulfil the intention of those who entered into the contract. For in the course of affairs men in making such contracts in general would if it were brought to their minds, say that there should be such a condition.

Accordingly, in the Civil law, such an exception is implied in every obligation of the class which they call obligatio de certo corpore. The rule is laid down in the Digest, lib. XLV, tit. 1, de verborum obligationibus, 1.33. "Si Stichus certo die dari promissus, ante diem moriatur: non tenetur promissor." The principle is more fully developed in 1.23. "Si ex legati causa, aut ex stipulatu hominem certum mihi debeas: non aliter post mortem ejus tenearis mihi, quam si per te steterit, quominus vivo eo eum mihi dares: quod ita fit, si aut interpellatus non dedisti, aut occidisti eum." The examples are of contracts respecting a slave, which was the common illustration of a certain subject used by the Roman lawyers, just as we are apt to take a horse; and no doubt the propriety, one might almost say necessity, of the implied condition is more obvious when the contract relates to a living animal, whether man or brute, than when it relates to some inanimate thing (such as in the present case a theatre) the existence of which is not so obviously precarious as that of the live animal, but the principle is adopted in the Civil law as applicable to every obligation of which the subject is a certain thing. The general subject is treated of by Pothier, who in his Traite des Obligations, partie 3, chap. 6, art. 3, sec. 668, states the result to be that the debtor corporis certi is freed from his obligation when the thing has perished, neither by his act, nor his neglect, and before he is in default, unless by some stipulation he has taken on himself the risk of the particular misfortune which has occurred.[a]

Although the Civil law is not of itself authority in an English Court, it affords great assistance in investigating the principles on which the law is grounded. And it seems to us that the common law authorities establish that in such a contract the same condition of the continued existence of the thing is implied by English law.

[The court referred to instances of a performance unfulfilled at the death of the promisor, saying, "[I]t was very early determined that, if the performance is personal, the executors are not liable." (See Note 2 above.)]

These are instances where the implied condition is of the life of a human being, but there are others in which the same implication is made as to the continued existence of a thing. . . .

[In Williams v. Lloyd W. Jones, 179] the count, which was in assumpsit, alleged that the plaintiff had delivered a horse to the defendant, who promised to redeliver it on request. Breach, that though requested to redeliver the horse he refused. Plea, that the horse was sick and died, and the plaintiff made the request after its death; and on demurrer it was held a good plea, as the bailee was discharged from his promise by the death of the horse without default or negligence on the part of the defendant. "Let it be admitted," say the Court "that he promised to deliver it on request, if the horse die before, that is become impossible by the act of God, so the party shall be discharged as much as if an obligation were made conditioned to deliver the horse on request, and he died before it."[b]

It may, we think, be safely asserted to be now English law, that in all contracts of loan of chattels or bailments if the performance of the promise of the borrower or bailee to return the things lent or bailed, becomes impossible because it [sic] has perished, this impossibility (if not arising from the fault of the borrower or bailee from some risk which he has taken upon himself) excuses the borrower or bailee from the performance of his promise to redeliver the chattel.

The great case of Coggs v. Bernard (1 Smith's L.C. 171, 5th ed.; 2 L.Raym. 909) is now the leading case on the law of bailments, and Lord Holt, in that case, referred so much to the Civil law that it might perhaps be thought that this principle was there delivered direct from the civilians, and was not generally applicable in English law except in the case of bailments; but the case of Williams v. Lloyd (W. Jones, 179), above cited, shows that the same law had been already adopted by the English law as early as The Book of Assizes. The principle seems to us to be that, in contracts in which the performance depends on the continued existence of a given person or thing, a condition is implied that the impossibility of performance arising from the perishing of the person or thing shall excuse the performance.

a. For a criticism of the Roman law authorities relied upon by Blackburn, J., see Buckland, *Casus* and Frustration in Roman and Common Law, 46 Harv.L.Rev. 1281, 1287–89 (1933).

b. But at an earlier period the bailee was not excused. O.W. Holmes, The Common Law 176 et seq. (1881).

In none of these cases is the promise in words other than positive, nor is there any express stipulation that the destruction of the person or thing shall excuse the performance; but that excuse is by law implied, because from the nature of the contract it is apparent that the parties contracted on the basis of the continued existence of the particular person or chattel. In the present case, looking at the whole contract, we find that the parties contracted on the basis of the continued existence of the Music Hall at the time when the concerts were to be given; that being essential to their performance.

We think, therefore, that the Music Hall having ceased to exist, without fault of either party, both parties are excused, the plaintiffs from taking the gardens and paying the money, the defendants from performing their promise to give the use of the Hall and Gardens and other things. Consequently the rule must be absolute to enter the verdict for the defendants.

NOTES

(1) *"Tiger Days Excepted."* By 1922 it was possible, in a British court, to ridicule the notion that when a post-contract event impedes the performance of a party, and so excuses that performance, the result depends on a condition, explicit or implicit, in the parties' agreement. In that year a Scottish judge felt bound to that notion, owing to its acceptance in the House of Lords. But he expressed doubt, saying:

> It does seem to me somewhat far-fetched to hold that the non-occurrence of some event, which was not within the contemplation or even the imagination of the parties, was an implied term of the contract.... A tiger has escaped from a travelling menagerie. The milkgirl fails to deliver the milk. Possibly the milkman may be exonerated from any breach of contract; but, even so, it would seem hardly reasonable to base that exoneration on the ground that "tiger days excepted" must be held as if written into the milk contract.

Scott & Sons v. Del Sel, 1922 Sess.Cas. 592, 596–97, aff'd, 1923 Sess.Cas. (House of Lords) 37.

Compare this passage in the Restatement, introducing Chapter 11: "An extraordinary circumstance may make performance so vitally different from what was reasonably to be expected as to alter the essential nature of that performance. In such a case the court must determine whether justice requires a departure from the general rule that the obligor bear the risk that the contract may become more burdensome or less desirable. This Chapter is concerned with the principles that guide that determination.... In recent years courts have shown increasing liberality in discharging obligors on the basis of such extraordinary circumstances."

(2) *Death and Illness.* A duty to perform a "personal" service (one that cannot be delegated to another to perform) is usually excused when the person required to perform suffers death or illness. Cardozo stated the point in connection with the death of a person while engaged in decorative work on a structure: "The contract being personal, the effect of his death was to terminate the duty of going forward with performance...." Buccini v. Paterno Construction Co., 170 N.E. 910, 911 (N.Y.1930).

Not only a death, but also a malady, may discharge a contract obligation. In Oneal v. Colton Consolidated School District No. 306, 557 P.2d 11 (Wash.App.1976), a school teacher's duty was discharged by deterioration of his vision. Moreover, not only illness but the "apprehension" of illness may excuse. See Wasserman Theatrical Enterprise v. Harris, 77 A.2d 329 (Conn.1950), in which Walter Huston, the actor, was excused from appearing on stage because of a minor throat ailment.

(3) *Specific Result or Reasonable Efforts?* Whether a commitment is one to achieve a specific result, or only to use reasonable effort to do so, is sometimes unclear. The difference may be critical if changed circumstances have made the result harder to achieve. In City of Mounds View v. Walijarvi, 263 N.W.2d 420 (Minn.1978), the court that decided Stees v. Leonard rejected the argument that an architect's undertaking was to achieve a specific result—an implied warranty that the structure was fit for its intended purpose—and had this to say:

"Architects, doctors, engineers, attorneys, and others deal in somewhat inexact sciences and are continually called upon to exercise their skilled judgment in order to anticipate and provide for random factors which are incapable of precise measurement. The indeterminate nature of these factors makes it impossible for professional service people to gauge them with complete accuracy in every instance. Thus, doctors cannot promise that every operation will be successful; a lawyer can never be certain that a contract he drafts is without latent ambiguity; and an architect cannot be certain that a structural design will interact with natural forces as anticipated. Because of the inescapable possibility of error which inheres in these services, the law has traditionally required, not perfect results, but rather the exercise of that skill and judgment which can be reasonably expected from similarly situated professionals."

For a different view, see Tamarac Development Co., Inc. v. Delamater, Freund & Associates, P.A., 675 P.2d 361 (Kan.1984), reasoning that the "work performed by architects and engineers is an exact science; that performed by doctors and lawyers is not." Do professionals *never* undertake to achieve a specific result? See Sullivan v. O'Connor, p. 14 above.

Do nonprofessionals *ever* undertake to achieve a specific result? See Bloor v. Falstaff Brewing Corp., p. 532 above. Absent explicit provision, what factors other than professionalism might affect the classification? See Milau Associates, Inc. v. North Avenue Development Corp., 368 N.E.2d 1247 (N.Y.1977). For a distinction between a duty of best efforts and a duty to achieve a specific result, see articles 5.1.4 and 5.1.5 of the UNIDROIT Principles.

————

IMPOSSIBILITY AND IMPRACTICABILITY OF PERFORMANCE UNDER ARTICLE 2

Article 2 of the Uniform Commercial Code contains a series of provisions that may afford relief in the event of changed circumstances. The narrowest of these is UCC § 2–613, which provides that a contract is "avoided" if goods that are required for performance of the contract suffer a "casualty" without the fault of either party before the risk of loss passes to the buyer. ("Risk of loss" is an Article 2 term of art that indicates which party will bear the loss if something happens to the goods at any particular time.) UCC § 2–613 is limited to situations in which the goods that suffer the casualty are the only goods that would satisfy the contract. It does not apply when the seller could satisfy its obligation by tendering goods other than those destroyed. Section 2–613 is analogous to the common law doctrine of impossibility. Section 2–615 provides relief when the seller's performance "has been made impracticable by the occurrence of a contingency the non-occurrence of which was a basic assumption on which the contract was made." As noted in the comments to that section, the standard for impracticability is high—a mere increase in cost is not sufficient. Finally, UCC § 2–614 provides relief when the agreed method of delivery becomes commercially impracticable. Both UCC § 2–614 and UCC § 2–615 are considered in the *Transatlantic* case, which follows, even though the case is not governed by Article 2.

Transatlantic Financing Corporation v. United States

United States Court of Appeals, D.C.Circuit, 1966.
363 F.2d 312.

■ J. Skelly Wright, Circuit Judge. This appeal involves a voyage charter between Transatlantic Financing Corporation, operator of the SS CHRISTOS, and the United States covering carriage of a full cargo of wheat from a United States Gulf port to a safe port in Iran. The District Court dismissed a libel filed by Transatlantic against the United States for costs attributable to the ship's diversion from the normal sea route caused by the closing of the Suez Canal. We affirm.

On July 26, 1956, the Government of Egypt nationalized the Suez Canal Company and took over operation of the Canal. On October 2, 1956, during the international crisis which resulted from the seizure, the voyage charter in suit was executed between representatives of Transatlantic and the United States. The charter indicated the termini of the voyage but not the route. On October 27, 1956, the SS CHRISTOS sailed from Galveston for Bandar Shapur, Iran, on a course which would have taken her through Gibraltar and the Suez Canal. On October 29, 1956, Israel invaded Egypt. On October 31, 1956, Great Britain and France invaded the Suez Canal Zone. On November 2, 1956, the Egyptian Government obstructed the Suez Canal with sunken vessels and closed it to traffic.[a]

On or about November 7, 1956, Beckmann, representing Transatlantic, contacted Potosky, an employee of the United States Department of Agriculture, who appellant concedes was unauthorized to bind the Government, requesting instructions concerning disposition of the cargo and seeking an agreement for payment of additional compensation for a voyage around the Cape of Good Hope. Potosky advised Beckmann that Transatlantic was expected to perform the charter according to its terms, that he did not believe Transatlantic was entitled to additional compensation for a voyage

---

a. For another chronology of events see Fry, The Suez Crisis, 1956, 15, 19, and 24 (Georgetown Institute for the Study of Diplomacy 1992). Among the events listed are these:

Britain and France began military planning for an invasion of Egypt on August 2. On September 12, they informed the U.N. Security Council that Egypt's rejection of cer-tain proposals constituted a threat to international peace and security. The European canal pilots left Egypt on September 15. Israeli forces attacked Egypt in Sinai on October 29. Egypt sank ships in the canal, thereby blocking it, on November 4. On the following day British and French paratroops were dropped at the north end of the canal. On November 7 (Middle East time) a cease-fire went into effect.

around the Cape, but that Transatlantic was free to file such a claim. Following this discussion, the CHRISTOS changed course for the Cape of Good Hope and eventually arrived in Bandar Shapur on December 30, 1956.

Transatlantic's claim is based on the following train of argument. The charter was a contract for a voyage from a Gulf port to Iran. Admiralty principles and practices, especially stemming from the doctrine of deviation, require us to imply into the contract the term that the voyage was to be performed by the "usual and customary" route. The usual and customary route from Texas to Iran was, at the time of contract, via Suez, so the contract was for a voyage from Texas to Iran via Suez. When Suez was closed this contract became impossible to perform. Consequently, appellant's argument continues, when Transatlantic delivered the cargo by going around the Cape of Good Hope, in compliance with the Government's demand under claim of right, it conferred a benefit upon the United States for which it should be paid in *quantum meruit*.

The doctrine of impossibility of performance has gradually been freed from the earlier fictional and unrealistic strictures of such tests as the "implied term" and the parties' "contemplation." Page, The Development of the Doctrine of Impossibility of Performance, 18 Mich.L.Rev. 589, 596 (1920). See generally 6 Corbin, Contracts §§ 1320–1372 (rev. ed. 1962); 6 Williston, Contracts §§ 1931–1979 (rev. ed. 1938). It is now recognized that " 'A thing is impossible in legal contemplation when it is not practicable; and a thing is impracticable when it can only be done at an excessive and unreasonable cost.' " Mineral Park Land Co. v. Howard, 172 Cal. 289, 293, 156 P. 458, 460, L.R.A.1916F, 1 (1916). Accord, Whelan v. Griffith Consumers Company, D.C.Mun.App., 170 A.2d 229 (1961); Restatement, Contracts § 454 (1932); Uniform Commercial Code (U.L.A.) § 2–615, comment 3. The doctrine ultimately represents the ever-shifting line, drawn by courts hopefully responsive to commercial practices and mores, at which the community's interest in having contracts enforced according to their terms is outweighed by the commercial senselessness of requiring performance.[1] When the issue is raised, the court is asked to construct a condition of performance[2] based on the changed circumstances, a process which involves at least three reasonably definable steps. First, a contingency—something unexpected—must have occurred. Second, the risk of the unexpected occurrence must not have been allocated either by agreement or by custom. Finally, occurrence of the contingency must have rendered performance commercially impracticable.[3] Unless the court finds these three requirements satisfied, the plea of impossibility must fail.

---

1. While the impossibility issue rarely arises, as it has here, in a suit to recover the cost of an alternative method of performance, compare Annot., 84 A.L.R.2d 12, 19 (1962), there is nothing necessarily inconsistent in claiming commercial impracticability for the method of performance actually adopted; the concept of impracticability assumes performance was physically possible. Moreover, a rule making nonperformance a condition precedent to recovery would unjustifiably encourage disappointment of expectations.

2. Patterson, Constructive Conditions in Contracts, 42 Colum.L.Rev. 903, 943–954 (1942).

3. Compare Uniform Commercial Code § 2–615(a), which provides that, in the absence of an assumption of greater liability, delay or non-delivery by a seller is not a

The first requirement was met here. It seems reasonable, where no route is mentioned in a contract, to assume the parties expected performance by the usual and customary route at the time of contract.[4] Since the usual and customary route from Texas to Iran at the time of contract[5] was through Suez, closure of the Canal made impossible the expected method of performance. But this unexpected development raises rather than resolves the impossibility issue, which turns additionally on whether the risk of the contingency's occurrence had been allocated and, if not, whether performance by alternative routes was rendered impracticable.[6]

Proof that the risk of a contingency's occurrence has been allocated may be expressed in or implied from the agreement. Such proof may also be

breach if performance as agreed is made "impracticable" by the occurrence of a "contingency" the non-occurrence of which was a "basic assumption on which the contract was made." To the extent this limits relief to "unforeseen" circumstances, comment 1, see the discussion below, and compare Uniform Commercial Code § 2–614(1). There may be a point beyond which agreement cannot go, Uniform Commercial Code § 2–615, Comment 8, presumably the point at which the obligation would be "manifestly unreasonable," § 1–102(3), in bad faith, § 1–203, or unconscionable, § 2–302. For an application of these provisions see Judge Friendly's opinion in United States v. Wegematic Corporation, 2 Cir., 360 F.2d 674 (1966).

4. Uniform Commercial Code § 2–614, Comment 1, states: "Under this Article, in the absence of specific agreement, the normal or usual facilities enter into the agreement either through the circumstances, usage of trade or prior course of dealing." So long as this sort of assumption does not necessarily result in construction of a condition of performance, it is idle to argue over whether the usual and customary route is an "implied term." The issue of impracticability must eventually be met. One court refused to imply the Suez route as a contract term, and went on to rule the contract had been "frustrated." Carapanayoti & Co. Ltd. v. E.T. Green Ltd., [1959] 1 Q.B. 131. The holding was later rejected by the House of Lords. Tsakiroglou & Co. Ltd. v. Noblee Thorl G.m.b.H., [1960] 2 Q.B. 348.

5. The parties have spent considerable energy in disputing whether the "usual and customary" route by which performance was anticipated is defined as of the time of contract or of performance. If we were automatically to treat the expected route as a condition of performance, this matter would be crucial, and we would be compelled to choose between unacceptable alternatives. If we assume as a constructive condition the usual and customary course always to mean the one in use at the time of contract, any sub-

stantial diversion (we assume the diversion would have to be substantial) would nullify the contract even though its effect upon the rights and obligations of the parties is insignificant. Nor would it be desirable, on the other hand, to assume performance is conditioned on the availability of *any* usual and customary route at the time of performance. It may be that very often the availability of a customary route at the time of performance other than the route expected to be used at the time of contract should result in denial of relief under the impossibility theory; certainly if *no* customary route is available at the time of performance the contract is rendered impossible. But the same customarily used alternative route may be practicable in one set of circumstances and impracticable in another, as where the goods are unable to survive the extra journey. Moreover, the "time of performance" is no special point in time; it is every moment in a performance. Thus the alternative route, in our case around the Cape, may be practicable at some time during performance, for example while the vessel is still in the Atlantic Ocean, and impracticable at another time during performance, for example after the vessel has traversed most of the Mediterranean Sea. Both alternatives, therefore, have their shortcomings, and we avoid choosing between them by refusing automatically to treat the usual and customary route as of any time as a condition of performance.

6. In criticizing the "contemplation" test for impossibility Professor Patterson pointed out: " 'Contemplation' is appropriate to describe the mental state of philosophers but is scarcely descriptive of the mental state of business men making a bargain. It seems preferable to say that the promisee *expects* performance by [the] means ... the promisor expects to (or which on the facts known to the promisee it is probable that he will) use. It does not follow as an inference of fact that the promisee expects performance by *only* that means...." Patterson, supra Note 2, at 947.

found in the surrounding circumstances, including custom and usages of the trade. See 6 Corbin, supra, § 1339, at 394–397; 6 Williston, supra, § 1948, at 5457–5458. The contract in this case does not expressly condition performance upon availability of the Suez route. Nor does it specify "via Suez" or, on the other hand, "via Suez or Cape of Good Hope."[7] Nor are there provisions in the contract from which we may properly imply that the continued availability of Suez was a condition of performance.[8] Nor is there anything in custom or trade usage, or in the surrounding circumstances generally, which would support our constructing a condition of performance. The numerous cases requiring performance around the Cape when Suez was closed, see e.g., Ocean Tramp Tankers Corp. v. V/O Sovfracht (The Eugenia), [1964] 2 Q.B. 226, and cases cited therein, indicate that the Cape route is generally regarded as an alternative means of performance. So the implied expectation that the route would be via Suez is hardly adequate proof of an allocation to the promisee of the risk of closure. In some cases, even an express expectation may not amount to a condition of performance.[9] The doctrine of deviation supports our assump-

---

7. In Glidden Company v. Hellenic Lines, Limited, 2 Cir., 275 F.2d 253 (1960), the charter was for transportation of materials from India to America "via Suez Canal or Cape of Good Hope, or Panama Canal," and the court held performance was not "frustrated." In his discussion of this case, Professor Corbin states: "Except for the provision for an alternative route, the defendant would have been discharged, for the reason that the parties contemplated an open Suez Canal as a specific condition or means of performance." 6 Corbin, supra, § 1339, at 399 n. 57. Appellant claims this supports its argument, since the Suez route was contemplated as usual and customary. But there is obviously a difference, in deciding whether a contract allocates the risk of a contingency's occurrence, between a contract specifying no route and a contract specifying Suez. We think that when Professor Corbin said, "Except for the provision for an alternative route," he was referring, not to the entire *provision*—"via Suez Canal or Cape of Good Hope" etc.—but to the fact that *an alternative route* had been provided for. Moreover, in determining what Corbin meant when he said "the parties contemplated an open Suez Canal as a specific condition or means of performance," consideration must be given to the fact, recited by Corbin, that in *Glidden* the parties were specifically aware when the contract was made the Canal might be closed, and the promisee had refused to include a clause excusing performance in the event of closure. Corbin's statement, therefore, is most accurately read as referring to cases in which a route is specified after negotiations reflecting the parties' awareness that the usual and customary route might become unavailable. Compare Held v. Goldsmith, 153 La. 598, 96 So. 272 (1919).

8. The charter provides that the vessel is "in every way fitted for *the voyage*" (emphasis added), and the "P. & I. Bunker Deviation Clause" refers to "the contract voyage" and the "direct and/or customary route." Appellant argues that these provisions require implication of a voyage by the direct and customary route. Actually they prove only what we are willing to accept—that the parties expected the usual and customary route would be used. The provisions in no way condition performance upon nonoccurrence of this contingency.

There are two clauses which allegedly demonstrate that time is of importance in this contract. One clause computes the remuneration "in steaming time" for diversions to other countries ordered by the charterer in emergencies. This proves only that the United States wished to reserve power to send the goods to another country. It does not imply in any way that either was in a rush about the matter. The other clause concerns demurrage and despatch. The charterer agreed to pay Transatlantic demurrage of $1,200 per day for all time in excess of the period agreed upon for loading and unloading, and Transatlantic was to pay despatch of $600 per day for any saving in time. Of course this provision shows the parties were concerned about time, see Gilmore & Black, The Law of Admiralty § 4–8 (1957), but the fact that they arranged so minutely the consequences of any delay or speedup of loading and unloading operates against the argument that they were similarly allocating the risk of delay or speed-up of the voyage.

9. Uniform Commercial Code § 2–614(1) provides: "Where without fault of either party . . . the *agreed* manner of delivery tion that parties normally expect performance by the usual and customary route, but it adds nothing beyond this that is probative of an allocation of the risk.[10]

If anything, the circumstances surrounding this contract indicate that the risk of the Canal's closure may be deemed to have been allocated to Transatlantic. We know or may safely assume that the parties were aware, as were most commercial men with interests affected by the Suez situation, see The Eugenia, supra, that the Canal might become a dangerous area. No doubt the tension affected freight rates, and it is arguable that the risk of closure became part of the dickered terms. Uniform Commercial Code § 2–615, Comment 8. We do not deem the risk of closure so allocated, however. Foreseeability or even recognition of a risk does not necessarily prove its allocation.[11] Compare Uniform Commercial Code § 2–615, Comment 1; Restatement, Contracts § 457 (1932). Parties to a contract are not always able to provide for all the possibilities of which they are aware, sometimes because they cannot agree, often simply because they are too busy. Moreover, that some abnormal risk was contemplated is probative but does not necessarily establish an allocation of the risk of the contingency which actually occurs. In this case, for example, nationalization by Egypt of the Canal Corporation and formation of the Suez Users Group did not necessarily indicate that the Canal would be blocked even if a confrontation resulted.[12] The surrounding circumstances do indicate, however, a willing-

... becomes commercially impracticable but a commercially reasonable substitute is available, such substitute performance must be tendered and accepted." (Emphasis added.) Compare Mr. Justice Holmes' observation: "You can give any conclusion a logical form. You always can imply a condition in a contract. But why do you imply it? It is because of some belief as to the practice of the community or of a class, or because of some opinion as to policy...." Holmes, The Path of the Law, 10 Harv.L.Rev. 457, 466 (1897).

10. The deviation doctrine, drawn principally from admiralty insurance practice, implies into all relevant commercial instruments naming the termini of voyages the usual and customary route between those points. 1 Arnould, Marine Insurance and Average § 376, at 522 (10th ed. 1921). Insurance is cancelled when a ship unreasonably "deviates" from this course, for example by extending a voyage or by putting in at an irregular port, and the shipowner forfeits the protection of clauses of exception which might otherwise have protected him from his common law insurer's liability to cargo. See Gilmore & Black, supra Note 8, § 2–6, at 59–60. This practice, properly qualified, see id. § 3–41, makes good sense, since insurance rates are computed on the basis of the implied course, and deviations in the course increasing the anticipated risk make the insurer's calculations meaningless. Arnould, supra, § 14, at 26. Thus the route, so far as

insurance contracts are concerned, is crucial, whether express or implied. But even here, the implied term is not inflexible. Reasonable deviations do not result in loss of insurance, at least so long as established practice is followed.... The doctrine's only relevance, therefore, is that it provides additional support for the assumption we willingly make that merchants agreeing to a voyage between two points expect that the usual and customary route between those points will be used. The doctrine provides no evidence of an allocation of the risk of the route's unavailability.

11. See Note, The Fetish of Impossibility in the Law of Contracts, 53 Colum.L.Rev. 94, 98 n. 23 (1953), suggesting that foreseeability is properly used "as a *factor* probative of assumption of the risk of impossibility." (Emphasis added.)

12. Sources cited in the briefs indicate formation of the Suez Canal Users Association on October 1, 1956, was viewed in some quarters as an implied threat of force. See N.Y. Times, Oct. 2, 1956, p. 1, col. 1, noting, on the day the charter in this case was executed, that "Britain has declared her freedom to use force as a last resort if peaceful methods fail to achieve a satisfactory settlement." Secretary of State Dulles was able, however, to view the statement as evidence of the canal users' "dedication to a just and peaceful solution." The Suez Problem 369–370 (Department of State Pub. 1956).

ness by Transatlantic to assume abnormal risks, and this fact should legitimately cause us to judge the impracticability of performance by an alternative route in stricter terms than we would were the contingency unforeseen.

We turn then to the question whether occurrence of the contingency rendered performance commercially impracticable under the circumstances of this case. The goods shipped were not subject to harm from the longer, less temperate Southern route. The vessel and crew were fit to proceed around the Cape.[13] Transatlantic was no less able than the United States to purchase insurance to cover the contingency's occurrence. If anything, it is more reasonable to expect owner-operators of vessels to insure against the hazards of war. They are in the best position to calculate the cost of performance by alternative routes (and therefore to estimate the amount of insurance required), and are undoubtedly sensitive to international troubles which uniquely affect the demand for and cost of their services. The only factor operating here in appellant's favor is the added expense, allegedly $43,972.00 above and beyond the contract price of $305,842.92, of extending a 10,000 mile voyage by approximately 3,000 miles. While it may be an overstatement to say that increased cost and difficulty of performance never constitute impracticability, to justify relief there must be more of a variation between expected cost and the cost of performing by an available alternative than is present in this case, where the promisor can legitimately be presumed to have accepted some degree of abnormal risk, and where impracticability is urged on the basis of added expense alone.[14]

We conclude, therefore, as have most other courts considering related issues arising out of the Suez closure, that performance of this contract was not rendered legally impossible. Even if we agreed with appellant, its theory of relief seems untenable. When performance of a contract is deemed impossible it is a nullity. In the case of a charter party involving carriage of goods, the carrier may return to an appropriate port and unload its cargo, The Malcolm Baxter, Jr., 277 U.S. 323 (1928), subject of course to required steps to minimize damages. If the performance rendered has value, recovery in *quantum meruit* for the entire performance is proper. But here Transatlantic has collected its contract price, and now seeks *quantum meruit* relief for the additional expense of the trip around the Cape. If the contract is a nullity, Transatlantic's theory of relief should have been *quantum meruit* for the entire trip, rather than only for the extra expense. Transatlantic attempts to take its profit on the contract, and

---

13. The issue of impracticability should no doubt be "an objective determination of whether the promise can reasonably be performed rather than a subjective inquiry into the promisor's capability of performing as agreed." Symposium, The Uniform Commercial Code and Contract Law: Some Selected Problems, 105 U.Pa.L.Rev. 836, 880, 887 (1957). Dealers should not be excused because of less than normal capabilities. But if both parties are aware of a dealer's limited capabilities, no objective determination would be complete without taking into account this fact.

14. See Uniform Commercial Code § 2–615, Comment 4: "Increased cost alone does not excuse performance unless the rise in cost is due to some unforeseen contingency which alters the essential nature of the performance." See also 6 Corbin, supra, § 1333; 6 Williston, supra, § 1952, at 5468.

then force the Government to absorb the cost of the additional voyage.[15] When impracticability without fault occurs, the law seeks an equitable solution, see 6 Corbin, supra, § 1321, and *quantum meruit* is one of its potent devices to achieve this end. There is no interest in casting the entire burden of commercial disaster on one party in order to preserve the other's profit. Apparently the contract price in this case was advantageous enough to deter appellant from taking a stance on damages consistent with its theory of liability. In any event, there is no basis for relief.

NOTES

(1) *Unexpected Events.* "First, a contingency . . . must have occurred." So said the court in stating three requirements for an excuse by reason of impossibility. A seller that wants to be excused from delivering goods is unlikely to meet even this first requirement simply by showing that its cost of producing the goods has spiked upward. On inquiry, however, it may be possible to identify an unexpected event underlying the increase of cost that is more likely to count as a contingency— "something unexpected"—than higher cost. If, for example, the seller is a miller and supplier of lumber, and has encountered unusual cost in buying timber, it may be possible to attribute the added cost to new environmental regulations, to a sharp upswing in construction, or to the coincidence of vast forest fires. With respect to a lumber-sale contract, which of these events is the most likely to count as a contingency? As to which is the risk most likely have been allocated—"either by agreement or by custom"—to the seller?

(2) *Impracticability and Risk.* In response to an invitation from the Federal Reserve Board, the Wegematic Corporation submitted the winning proposal for a new computing system, which Wegematic described as "a truly revolutionary system utilizing all of the latest technical advances." Delivery was to be a year later. After delays of nearly four months, Wegematic finally announced that it was "impracticable to deliver the . . . Computing System at this time." After another year, the Board succeeded in procuring comparable equipment elsewhere. When sued by the United States, Wegematic argued that it was excused because it was unable to achieve the revolutionary breakthrough that it had anticipated because of "basic engineering difficulties" that would have taken up to two years and a million and a half dollars to correct, with success likely but not certain. The United States prevailed. (In *Transatlantic Financing* the court cited the decision in its footnote 3.)

Was there a "contingency" in the *Wegematic* case? The court referred to UCC § 2–615, and said that the "basic assumption" part of the Code's test "seems a somewhat complicated way of putting Professor Corbin's question of how much risk the promisor assumed." It went on: "We see no basis for thinking that when an electronics system is promoted by its manufacturer as a revolutionary breakthrough, the risk of the revolution's occurrence falls on the purchaser; the reasonable supposition is that it has already occurred or, at least, that the manufacturer is assuring the purchaser that it will be found to have when the machine is assembled. . . . If a manufacturer wishes to be relieved of the risk that what looks good on paper may not prove so good in hardware, the appropriate exculpatory language is well known and often used."

---

15. The argument that the Uniform Commercial Code requires the buyer to pay the additional cost of performance by a commercially reasonable substitute was advanced and rejected in Symposium, supra Note 13, 105 U.Pa.L.Rev. at 884 n. 205. In Dillon v. United States, 156 F.Supp. 719, 140 Ct.Cl. 508 (1957), relief was afforded for some of the cost of delivering hay from a commercially unreasonable distance, but the suit was one in which the plaintiff had suffered losses far in excess of the relief given.

Note that UCC § 2–615 begins with an exception where a seller has "assumed a greater obligation," recognizing that a party may assume the risk of being unable to do the impracticable—even the impossible. As compared with impracticability, would mistake have been a better ground for Wegematic's defense?

(3) *Other "Suez Cases."* The court relied for support on the *Glidden* case, partially described in footnote 7. A further fact in that case was a provision of the charter that gave the shipper power to designate a destination (on the Atlantic seaboard) "not later than on Vessel's passing Gibraltar." In which case—*Glidden* or the main case—did the carrier come closer to establishing a defense under the doctrine of impracticability?

In footnotes not reproduced here, the court referred also to two English "Suez cases" for support. One was *The Eugenia.* There the court said that performance is not excused by a cost increase that is merely onerous: "It must be positively unjust to hold the parties bound." Ocean Tramp Tankers Corp. v. V/O Sovfracht (The Eugenia), [1964] 2 Q.B. 226, 239. The other case concerned a sale-of-goods contract requiring the seller to pay, among other charges, the freight for transporting the goods from Sudan to Hamburg. (The case was *Tsakiroglou & Co.*, cited in the court's footnote 4.) Assume that, before the Canal closure, the seller had contracted for a carrier to move the goods. If the carrier were to be excused by the closure, does it follow that the seller should be? In *Transatlantic Financing*, Judge Wright seemed to be disconcerted by the thought that the seller might be committed to the buyer although the carrier was not committed to the seller. Are you?

———

FORESEEABILITY

"Foreseeability or even recognition of a risk does not necessarily prove its allocation." So said Judge Wright in *Transatlantic Financing*. A passage in the Restatement squares with this: Though anticipating a possible turn of events, "the parties may not have thought it sufficiently important a risk to have made it a subject of their bargaining." Introductory Note to Restatement Chapter 11. In some quarters—not all—the test of foreseeability has been treated with scorn, or, at best, with lukewarm regard.[a] Yet it is difficult, on hearing a party's plea of changed circumstances, to refrain from asking "Weren't you worried that . . .?" Notice that Judge Wright adverted to worrisome events before Transatlantic made the contract before him, and inferred its "willingness . . . to assume abnormal risks." A Comment to UCC § 2–615 contains a lengthy, Delphic sentence about an event "foreshadowed" at the time of contracting: that being so, possibly "the exemptions of this section do not apply." Do you find that thought in the text of the section?

If the foreseeability of an impeding event counts for little, what of a showing that the event was *not* foreseeable? This is significant, according to

a. See Hans Smit, Frustration of Contract: A Comparative Attempt at Consolidation, 58 Colum.L.Rev. 287 (1958); Paul Joskow, Commercial Impossibility, the Uranium Market and the Westinghouse Case, 6 J.Legal Stud. 119, 173 (1977)(test tolerated as imposing a penalty on the "suboptimal use of available information"). But it has been said that foreseeability "has been central to impossibility cases for as long as they have been around." Richard Duesenberg, Contract Impracticability: Courts Begin to Shape § 2–615, 32 Bus.Law. 1089, 1095 (1977).

the Restatement Introductory Note quoted above, as suggesting that the nonoccurrence of the impeding event was a basic assumption on which the contract was made. Is it easy to believe that foreseeability is less significant than unforeseeability?

NOTE

The Case of the Foreseeable Finale. By an agreement with the Wolf Trap Foundation for the Performing Arts, the Opera Company of Boston was to stage four summertime performances at the Foundation's concert center. The final performance was cancelled when a thunderstorm caused an electrical outage and left the stage dark. Wolf Trap declined to pay the price of that performance. In an action against it by the Opera Company, evidence was given of some remarks following the mishap that were unfortunate for Wolf Trap. "We have experienced power outages on several occasions," according to its agent who had negotiated the contract. He had also expressed his feeling that a theater without an adequate generator is incomplete. The trial court said, in granting judgment against Wolf Trap, that, if it could have foreseen the mishap, it was "absolutely barred" from relying on the doctrine of impossibility. Wolf Trap appealed. *Held*: Reversed and remanded.

The reviewing court was divided. According to the majority, "Foreseeability . . . is at best but one fact to be considered. . . ." Opera Company v. Wolf Trap Foundation, 817 F.2d 1094, 1102 (4th Cir.1987).

RISK–BEARING ANALYSES

Look again at three sentences in the opinion in *Transatlantic Financing*, those following the court's footnote 13. These sentences compare the capacities of the parties to anticipate "troubles" and to calculate additional costs of performance. As between Transatlantic and the United States, the court thought it reasonable to expect that Transatlantic be the one to insure itself against war risks. In a well-known economic analysis, this passage is quoted with approval and is amplified as follows:

> The shipowner is the superior risk bearer because he is better able to estimate the magnitude of the loss ... and the probability of the unexpected event. Furthermore, shipowners who own several ships and are engaged in shipping along several routes can spread the risks of delay on any particular route without purchasing market insurance. . . .

Richard Posner and Andrew Rosenfield, Impossibility and Related Doctrines in Contract Law, 6 J.Legal Stud. 83, 104 (1977). Having ready access to an appropriate insurance market is one mark of a well-qualified risk bearer, according to this analysis. A mode of risk distribution, alternative to buying insurance and more cost-effective, is open to some firms: diversification, as suggested in *Transatlantic Financing*. Other marks of a well-qualified risk bearer are some ability to avert the event that impeded performance, and to mitigate its loss when the event occurs.

The thesis of the authors is that, once a court has identified the "superior risk bearer" in a case like *Transatlantic Financing*, it should rule in favor of the other party as to the dispensing effect of a mischance. Some underlying assumptions are these: (i) If the parties had had the mischance in mind during their negotiations, as a possibility, they would have assigned the risk to the superior risk bearer—possibly adjusting the price or another term to balance that assignment. (ii) For the court to make the same assignment would spare the parties the cost, time, and effort ("transaction costs") of negotiating to the position they would prefer.

Posner and Rosenfield acknowledged that uncertainties creating the risk of error in identifying superior risk bearers tend to undercut the potential savings in transaction costs. As to *Transatlantic Financing*, they acknowledged also that the United States was a candidate for the position of superior risk bearer, as the holder of a well-diversified portfolio of contracts. But, they concluded, "decision should (and here did) turn on the characteristics of shippers *as a class*, if an unduly particularistic analysis is to be avoided." (emphasis supplied).

For a detailed rebuttal of the authors' analysis see John Elofson, The Dilemma of Changed Circumstances . . . , 30 Colum.J. of Law & Social Prob. 1 (1996), seizing on the acknowledgments just mentioned and on other supposed defects. Although the analysis has drawn widespread attention in academic circles, it has not been cited often in judicial opinions. The Supreme Court has referred to it, however, for these propositions: "parties generally rely on contract law 'to reduce the costs of contract negotiation by supplying contract terms that the parties would probably have adopted explicitly had they negotiated over them' "; and "subject to certain constraints, 'the contracting parties' chosen allocation of risk' should always be honored as the most efficient one possible." United States v. Winstar Corporation, 518 U.S. 839, 884 n. 27, 909 n. 56 (1996).

At a time when price inflation was unusually brisk in the United States, Professor Alan Schwartz developed an argument for imposing at least the inflation risk on sellers. To do so, he reasoned, would help to popularize price-indexing terms in sale contracts. And that, in turn, would complement government efforts to control inflation. See Schwartz, Sales Law and Inflation, 50 So.Cal.L.Rev. 1, 21–22 (1976).

Selland Pontiac–GMC, Inc. v. King

Minnesota Court of Appeals, 1986.
384 N.W.2d 490.

■ RANDALL, JUDGE. Buyer, Selland Pontiac–GMC, Inc., sued seller, George King, for breach of contract. After a one-day bench trial the court granted judgment for King. The trial court denied Selland's motion for a new trial and/or amended findings of fact and conclusions of law and entered judgment. Selland appeals. We affirm.

FACTS

Selland contracted with King (doing business as King's Superior Bus Sales) to buy four school bus bodies. The oral agreement made in April,

1983, was reduced to a writing dated May 12, 1983. King was to supply the bodies, which would be built on top of chassis provided by Selland. The written agreement indicates that the bodies would be manufactured by Superior Manufacturing, which was located in Morris, Manitoba. The written agreement contains no completion date. King was aware that Selland's customer needed the buses by late August for the start of the school year. The contract price was $47,660. The writing contained no escape clause excusing King's performance should his source of supply fail.

In reliance on the contract, Selland ordered four bus chassis from General Motors. They arrived at Superior's entry point in Pembina, North Dakota, in June and early July, 1983.

Superior went into receivership on July 7, 1983, and King learned of this on July 8. King informed Selland of the receivership on August 12. The parties do not agree on what happened afterwards. Selland claims that King assured Selland that the buses would be completed on time. King claims that Selland, fully advised of Superior's status, decided to wait and see if Superior would come out of receivership able to supply and install the bus bodies. The trial court found that "after receiving notice of the receivership, Selland acquiesced to the delay in production."

The bodies were never manufactured. The Superior plant was operated by a new company from approximately late July to September or October. For some time after that, different individuals expressed interest in buying and operating the plant. Finally it was purchased, moved to Oklahoma, and it began production in 1985. Superior went out of business. In December, 1983, Selland's customer (Chief Auto Sales) cancelled their order. Selland sold the chassis at a loss. . . .

ANALYSIS

On appeal this court will not set aside the trial court's findings unless they are clearly erroneous. Peterson v. Johnston, 254 N.W.2d 360, 362 (Minn.1977). Selland questions the trial court's finding that the contract identified Superior as King's supplier, and that the contract contemplated that the bodies would be manufactured by Superior. This finding is supported by the contract which states that Superior bus bodies were being sold.

[Selland contested the finding by the trial court that it had acquiesced in King's delay in making delivery. The court sustained that finding.]

[The court quoted from clauses (a) and (c) of UCC § 2–615, enacted as Minn.Stat. § 336.2–615.] Supply of Superior bus bodies was a basic assumption on which the contract was made. These became impracticable to supply when Superior ceased manufacturing.

Appellant argues that the trial court improperly applied § 336.2–615. In Barbarossa & Sons v. Iten Chevrolet, Inc., 265 N.W.2d 655 (Minn.1978) the supreme court applied § 336.2–615 and affirmed judgment for the buyer where the manufacturer's supply of seller's order was not a basic assumption of the contract and the contract contained no escape clause. The manufacturer, General Motors, was not mentioned in the contract as the source of supply. General Motors had cancelled several orders at this time due to a shortage. The court stated:

> A partial failure of a seller's source of supply generally has been treated as a foreseeable contingency, the risk of which is allocated to the seller absent a specific provision to the contrary in the contract.

Id. at 659–60 (citations omitted).

The trial court's finding of no breach of contract here is consistent with Barbarossa's holding that the contract was breached under § 336.2–615. Here the seller's supplier was specified in the contract. Superior was also specified in King's price quotation to Selland. In *Barbarossa* the supplier did not cease to manufacture, but simply cancelled the orders of some of its dealers. Here both parties testified that they had no knowledge of Superior's questionable financial circumstances when they contracted and King did not expressly assume the risk of Superior's ceasing production.

[Finally, the court dealt with Selland's contention that King had failed to give it seasonable notice of nondelivery. Although the court agreed with Selland that "notice of delay does not necessarily constitute notice of nondelivery," it sustained the trial court's conclusion on the point. Selland had cancelled the contract, the court said, before such notice could be given.]

DECISION

The trial court did not clearly err in finding that the contract contemplated that the bus bodies would be manufactured by Superior and that Selland acquiesced to the delay in delivery. The trial court did not err in its application of Minn. Stat. § 336.2–615.

Affirmed.

NOTES

(1) *Authorities.* The court suggested two ways of distinguishing the decision in Barbarossa & Sons v. Iten Chevrolet: (a) In that case, unlike this one, "[t]he manufacturer ... was not mentioned in the contract as the source of supply"; and (b) In that case the manufacturer (General Motors), unlike Superior Manufacturing, had not ceased producing, but had "simply cancelled the orders of some of its dealers." Which of these distinctions is the more satisfying one?

Restatement § 261, Comment *e* includes this statement: "Even if a party contracts to render a performance that depends on some act by a third party, he is not ordinarily discharged because of a failure by that party because this is also a risk that is commonly understood to be on the obligor." What made *Selland* an exceptional case, outside this observation?

(2) *Parol Evidence.* Because the King–Selland contract indicated that the bus bodies were to be manufactured by Superior Manufacturing, King had no need to rely on parol evidence that the parties had agreed on Superior as a particular source of supply. Would the decision have been different if the contract—an integrated one—had omitted any reference to Superior, but Selland could otherwise be shown to have known where King expected to get the bodies? Suppose that knowledge to be proved by convincing evidence of a conversation King had with Selland when the

contract was executed. Would the decision be the same on those facts? For the answer No, see Luria Bros. & Co. v. Pielet Bros. Scrap Iron, 600 F.2d 103, 112 fn. 7 (7th Cir.1979). Do you agree that the effect of the supposed evidence is to contradict the writing, or instead to introduce an additional term?

PROBLEM

The School–Bus Resale. "In December, 1983," we are told, "Selland's customer (Chief Auto Sales) cancelled their order." Let it be assumed that the "order" was in truth a contract of sale, Selland to Chief. Possibly Chief's cancellation was warranted by Selland's delay in delivery: Chief needed the buses for the start of the school year. But this question suggests itself: Was Selland's duty of timely delivery excused by commercial impracticability? A further question arises if it is assumed that Chief effected cover in September and claimed damages against Selland: Was Selland discharged of its duty to deliver by impracticability?

How would you answer these questions? What undisclosed facts would be especially helpful in answering them?

———

FORCE MAJEURE CLAUSES

When, during the negotiation of a contract, a party anticipates one or more events that it cannot readily prevent and that might impede its performance, it may well introduce a term intended to excuse it from performing if the impediment arises. "*Force majeure* clause" is the generic name for a provision so intended. Would you expect such a clause to be broader in scope in a seller's or a buyer's contract? In a short-term or long-term contract? In *Selland Pontiac* the court remarked that the written agreement between the parties "contained no escape clause excusing King's performance should his source of supply fail." If King had been quizzed about that at the trial, what answer might he have made?

The drafting of a *force majeure* clause calls for a certain level of craft. A threat to a careless drafter is the maxim *ejusdem generis*. (See the discussion of maxims, p. 399 above.)

An example of a *force majeure* clause appears in Kama Rippa Music, Inc. v. Schekeryk, 510 F.2d 837 (2d Cir.1975). The clause pertained to an undertaking by the company, a music publisher, to make prompt payment of royalties to a songwriter and performer known professionally as Melanie. In stated eventualities, it was provided, "Publisher may, upon notice to writers, suspend its obligations including its obligations to make payments hereunder for the duration of such delay, impossibility, impracticability, as the case may be." The clause contained a "specific enumeration" of some dozen excusing events, typified by these: Act of God, earthquake, strike, civil commotion, acts of government, and delays in the delivery of material and supplies. The list concluded with this phrase: "for any similar or dissimilar reason." The trial court disregarded this general term. On appeal, that was said to be "a tack supported by New York contract law." The appellate court said also:

Alternatively, the [trial] court might have assimilated the clause to the remainder of the provision by invoking *ejusdem generis* and, hence, construing this final and most generic term in a series in light of the more specific terms preceding it.

Id. at 841 fn. 5.

A similar fate has befallen other generic terms adjoining specific ones. See, for example, Rothenberg v. Lincoln Farm Camp, Inc., 755 F.2d 1017 (2d Cir.1985), accepting "any other *similar* reason" as a reading of "any other reason." But see Eastern Air Lines, Inc. v. McDonnell Douglas Corp., 532 F.2d 957 (5th Cir.1976). In that case, growing out of the Vietnam War, McDonnell Douglas had been persuaded by government officials to defer the production of civilian aircraft. As a seller, resisting Eastern's claim, it relied on a provision in the contract between them that referred to delays

due to causes beyond Seller's control and not occasioned by its fault or negligence, *including but not being limited to* ... governmental priorities [and other specific eventualities].

"Unambiguous," the court said, referring to the words italicized in this quotation. Are they any less ambiguous than those in *Kama Rippa Music* ("any similar or dissimilar reason")? How did the drafting on behalf of the music producer go wrong?

NOTES

(1) Force Majeure *Clauses and the UCC.* Agreed-upon restrictions on a party's undertakings, presumably including *force majeure* clauses, are broadly recognized in the Code. In a Comment to the section about discordant offers and acceptances (UCC § 2–207, Comment 5), mention is made of a clause "setting forth and perhaps enlarging slightly upon the seller's exemption due to supervening causes, similar to those covered by [UCC § 2–615]"; that is given as an example of a term in an acceptance that does not materially alter the offer. On the other hand, Comment 8 to UCC § 2–615 contains this obscure sentence:

Generally, express agreements as to exemptions designed to enlarge upon or supplant the provisions of this section are to be read in the light of mercantile sense and reason, for this section itself sets up the commercial standard for normal and reasonable interpretation *and provides a minimum beyond which agreement may not go.*

Does the phrase emphasized here mean a minimum of obligation or a minimum of exemption from obligation?

In Eastern Air Lines v. McDonnell Douglas Corp., cited in the foregoing text, the court referred to the sentence quoted above, and drew this conclusion: "where there is doubt concerning the parties' intention, exemption clauses should not be construed as broadening the excuses available under the Code's impracticability rule." Plainly the sentence is a bad omen for a drafter intent on writing an extensive *force majeure* provision. Why should that purpose require especially explicit drafting?

(2) *Opting In and Opting Out.* It has been suggested that express terms "offer two distinct options for using particularized instructions to enhance a framework of implied terms. The first of these enables one to augment or *supplement* the implied

terms ('opting in').... By contrast, parties sometimes desire to countermand or *trump* one or more of the pre-formulated provisions ('opting out')." Charles Goetz & Robert Scott, The Limits of Expanded Choice: An Analysis of the Interactions Between Express and Implied Contract Terms, 73 Calif.L.Rev. 261, 281 (1985). Did the *force majeure* clause used by McDonnell Douglas involve supplementing or trumping?

PROBLEMS

(1) *Practice.* As a test of your drafting skill, consider the word "strike" in the music publisher's contract quoted above. What would you add to the list of specifics in order to protect the publisher in the event of labor difficulties not amounting to a strike? An answer is suggested by the full provision, as set out in the opinion cited.

(2) *A Hospital Case.* The Brighten Company made a contract with T–Square Inc. to restore and replace a neon sign marquee on a theater that T–Square was renovating. Brighten's contract contained the following clause:

> The Company shall not be liable for any failure in the performance of its obligations under this agreement which may result from strikes or acts of labor unions, fires, floods, earthquakes, or acts of God, war or other conditions or contingencies beyond its control.

Shortly after making the contract, Brighten learned that its expert on sheetmetal work required hospitalization for an indeterminate period. Because this was the only employee who could do the sheet metal work on the marquee, Brighten explained to T–Square that it would be unable to do that part of the work, and it returned an uncashed deposit check. T–Square had work done by another firm, for a higher price, and brought an action against Brighten for the difference between the two prices. What result? Seitz v. Mark–O–Lite Sign Contractors, Inc., 510 A.2d 319 (N.J.Super.1986).

———

CANADIAN INDUSTRIAL ALCOHOL CO. v. DUNBAR MOLASSES CO., 179 N.E. 383 (N.Y.1932). [At the end of 1927 the plaintiff Alcohol Company contracted with Dunbar to purchase a quantity of molasses, shipments to begin after the following April 1, and to be spread out during the warm weather. The goods were described as "approximately 1,500,000 wine gallons Refined Blackstrap (Molasses) of the usual run from the National Sugar Refinery, Yonkers, N.Y., to test around 60 per cent sugars." While the contract was in force, that refinery produced much less molasses than its capacity—less than half a million gallons. Dunbar shipped to the Alcohol Company its entire allotment of the refinery's output (344,083 gallons), but failed to deliver any more molasses. Upon being sued for damages, Dunbar contended that its duty was conditioned, by an implied term, on the refinery's producing enough molasses to fill the plaintiff's order. From a judgment for the buyer, Dunbar appealed.]

■ CARDOZO, C.J. ... The contract, read in the light of the circumstances existing at its making, or more accurately in the light of any such circumstances apparent from this record, does not keep the defendant's duty within boundaries so narrow.... The defendant does not even show that it tried to get a contract from the refinery during the months that intervened between the acceptance of the plaintiff's order and the time when shipments were begun. It has wholly failed to relieve itself of the imputation of contributory fault (3 Williston on Contracts, sec. 1959). So far as the record shows, it put its faith in the mere chance that the output of the refinery would be the same from year to year, and finding its faith vain, it tells us that its customer must have expected to take a chance as great. We see no reason for importing into the bargain this aleatory element. The defendant is in no better position than a factor who undertakes in his own name to sell for future delivery a special grade of merchandise to be manufactured by a special mill. The duty will be discharged if the mill is destroyed before delivery is due. The duty will subsist if the output is reduced because times turn out to be hard and labor charges high. . . .

[Affirmed.]

NOTES

(1) *Back-to-Back Contracts.* If Dunbar had made a contract with the refinery, as Cardozo suggested, would the result in the case have been different? Could Dunbar, in its contract with Alcohol Company, have relieved itself of the risk that its source of supply would fail as it did? If so, would Dunbar be expected to turn over to Alcohol Company any rights of Dunbar against the refinery? Compare Comment 5 to UCC § 2–615 with InterPetrol Bermuda Ltd. v. Kaiser Aluminum International Corp., 719 F.2d 992 (9th Cir.1983).

(2) *Stranded Sellers.* Each seller in the two previous cases—George King in *Selland Pontiac*, and Dunbar Molasses in *Canadian Industrial Alcohol*—had a designated supplier, and the supply for each seller failed. "Stranded seller" is an apt name for a seller in that position. As to the seller's liability it matters why the supply fails, according to the latter case: "The [seller's] duty will be discharged if the mill is destroyed. . . ." Why is that? The result would be different, we are told, if the supply fails because "times turn out to be hard. . . ." Does this mean that what has been called "economic *force majeure*" does not count? If it does not, how can we explain the decision in *Selland Pontiac*?

(3) *Labor Difficulties.* In the foregoing opinion the court spoke dismissively of high labor costs. But what of strikes, sick-outs, and other job actions against a supplier of goods or services? In *force majeure* clauses, strikes are commonly associated with acts of God; see *Kama Rippa Music*, p. 842 above. Apart from a *force majeure* clause, might a work stoppage at the Yonkers refinery justify it in withholding molasses from Dunbar if there had been a sale contract between them? Might a work stoppage excuse a subcontractor from completing its work on time, under a contract with a general contractor?

It has been suggested that experience in the line of business concerned, as known to the parties, might be dispositive. Mishara Construction Co. v. Transit–Mixed Concrete Corp., 310 N.E.2d 363 (Mass.1974). Although the court had some difficulty envisaging an industry in which labor relations were consistently amicable, it indicated that the picketing of a firm in such an industry would be more likely to limit its contract obligations than the picketing of a firm engaged in a business "with a long record of labor difficulties."

(4) *International Solutions.* Article 79 of the CISG, in paragraph (1), relieves a party from liability "for a failure to perform any of his obligations if he proves that the failure was due to an impediment beyond his control and that he could not reasonably be expected to have taken the impediment into account at the time of

the conclusion of the contract or to have avoided or overcome it or its consequences." Does this test seem more or less strict than that of UCC § 2–615? The
article has been criticized as having a "chameleon-like character that permits it to
take on that meaning that best conforms to the reader's own legal background."
Farnsworth, Perspective of Common Law Countries, in La Vendita Internazionale
3, 19 (Congress at S. Margherita Ligure 1981). The comparable provision of the
UNIDROIT Principles is article 7.1.7. Note that it does not contain language like
that in article 79(2).

(5) *"Subjective" and "Objective" Impracticability.* A distinction is sometimes
drawn between "objective" impracticability ("the thing cannot be done") and
"subjective" impracticability ("I cannot do it"). Financial inability ("I cannot pay")
is a classic example of the latter. A promisor's want of financial resources is not an
"event," it has been said, that makes its performance unexpectedly and unreasonably difficult or costly. La Motte v. Hilgedick, 956 F.2d 274 (9th Cir.1992). The
Restatement retains a requirement of objective impracticability in other terms,
explaining that "a party generally assumes the risk of his own inability to perform
his duty. Even if a party contracts to render a performance that depends on some
act by a third party, he is not ordinarily discharged because of a failure by that
party because this is also a risk that is commonly understood to be on the obligor."
Comment *e* to § 261. See also Comment 5 to UCC § 2–615: "There is no excuse
under this section, however, unless the seller has employed all due measures to
assure himself that his source will not fail"—citing the main case.

<hr />

CASUALTY TO GOODS

When a "stranded seller" of goods seeks an excuse because an exclusive source of supply has failed—see Note 2 above—the applicable provision
is UCC § 2–615. We are told to look elsewhere for the solution to a problem
of damage or destruction occurring to the very goods that a buyer has
contracted for. Comment 5 to UCC § 2–615 draws a contrast between
applications of that section and other situations governed by "the provision
on destruction or deterioration of specific goods."

UCC § 2–613 states possible results of a loss ("casualty") to identified
goods. One is that the contract is avoided. But a different result is required,
generally, if the loss occurs after "the risk of loss passes to the buyer."
Under the section avoidance may occur by reason of a casualty *before* the
risk of loss passes "in a proper case under a 'no arrival, no sale' term
(Section § 2–324)." In that situation the contract is not avoided by the loss:
the buyer must pay the price even though the seller is excused from
delivering the goods. The usual case for avoidance is one in which the risk
has *not* passed, and "the contract requires for its performance goods
identified when the contract is made." (*E.g.*, "You to have, for $5 million,
the earliest van Gogh self-portrait when it has been restored.") According
to the general rule for situations like that, "if the loss is total the contract
is avoided." UCC § 2–613. (That provision speaks also to cases of partial
loss: the buyer may either treat the contract as avoided or require a price
adjustment.)

The Code states an array of rules for determining when the risk of loss has passed to the buyer. They are best considered in an advanced course. In brief and in general, it can be said that the seller remains at risk at least until the goods have been identified to the contract, and frequently beyond that time. (The contract might be for "one of the van Gogh self-portraits, to be selected by the buyer.")

NOTE

A Visit to the Farm. An opinion reported in the following section contains this passage about farming (omitted there):

> Suppose a grower agrees before the growing season to sell his crop to a grain elevator, and the crop is destroyed by blight and the grain elevator sues. Discharge is ordinarily allowed in such cases.... The grower has every incentive to avoid the blight; so if it occurs, it probably could not have been prevented; and the grain elevator, which buys from a variety of growers not all of whom will be hit by blight in the same growing season, is in a better position to buffer the risk of blight than the grower is.

Northern Indiana Public Service Co. v. Carbon County Coal Co., p. 866 below. This is an application, evidently, of Judge Posner's "superior risk bearer" method of dealing with problems of impossibility and the like.

Comment 9 to UCC § 2–615 speaks of the "case of the farmer who has contracted to sell crops to be grown on designated land." The farmer may be excused, we are told, "when there is a failure of a specific crop," either because of the failure of a basic assumption or "on the basis of the destruction of identified goods."

Growers are sometimes charged with liability, however, in crop-failure cases. See ConAgra, Inc. v. Bartlett Partnership, 540 N.W.2d 333 (Neb.1995); Unke v. Thorpe, 59 N.W.2d 419 (S.D.1953); and Colley v. Bi–State, Inc., 586 P.2d 908 (Wash.App.1978). In *Colley*, farmers and grain dealers testified that, by usage in the vicinity, sale agreements such as the one in question "were never contingent upon the success of the seller's crop." These cases point to a critical question, which may be put this way: Did the grower contract, on the one hand, to sell identified goods ("my crop"), or a crop "to be grown on designated land," or, on the other hand, a specified quantity of grain? In *Unke*, the contract called for the delivery of 600–800 bushels of alfalfa seed. The buyer testified to a conversation between him and the seller in which the buyer insisted on a quantity term and explained that he intended to resell against the contract. Is there a compelling reason to disregard this evidence?

PROBLEM

Risk of Loss and Impracticability. Seller and Buyer contracted for the sale of a specific carload of alfalfa seed on Seller's premises, "possession to be taken by Buyer no later than July 30 and risk of loss to pass to Buyer on Buyer's taking possession and in any event by the end of July."

(a) Suppose that the carload is destroyed by lightning while it is still on Seller's premises on July 20. Can Seller recover the price from Buyer? Can Buyer recover damages from Seller?

(b) Suppose that the carload is destroyed by lightning while it is still on Seller's premises on August 1, Buyer not yet having taken possession. Can Seller recover the price from Buyer? Can Buyer recover damages from Seller?

See UCC §§ 2–709(1)(a) and 2–613.

Eastern Air Lines, Inc. v. Gulf Oil Corporation

United States District Court, Southern District of Florida, 1975.
415 F.Supp. 429.

[The facts and part of the opinion in this case are at p. 76 above, and another part is at p. 526 above.]

■ James Lawrence King, District Court Judge.... Gulf's commercial impracticability defenses are premised on two sections of the Uniform Commercial Code specifically §§ 2–614 (F.S. 672.614) and 2–615 (F.S. 672.615).... The modern U.C.C. § 2–615 doctrine of commercial impracticability has its roots in the common law doctrine of frustration or impossibility and finds its most recognized illustrations in the so-called "Suez Cases", arising out of the various closings of the Suez Canal and the consequent increases in shipping costs around the Cape of Good Hope. Those cases offered little encouragement to those who would wield the sword of commercial impracticability. As a leading British case arising out of the 1957 Suez closure declared, the unforeseen cost increase that would excuse performance "must be more than merely onerous or expensive. It must be positively unjust to hold the parties bound." Ocean Tramp Tankers v. V/O Sovfracht (The Eugenia), 2 Q.B. 226, 239 (1964).... These British precedents were followed by the District of Columbia Circuit, which gave specific consideration to U.C.C. 2–615, Comment 4, in Transatlantic Financing Corp. v. United States, 124 U.S.App.D.C. 183, 363 F.2d 312, 319 (1966).

Other recent American cases similarly strictly construe the doctrine of commercial impracticability. For example, one case found no U.C.C. defense, even though costs had doubled over the contract price, the court stating, "It may have been unprofitable for defendant to have supplied the pickers, but the evidence does not establish that it was impossible. A mere showing of unprofitability, without more, will not excuse the performance of a contract." Schafer v. Sunset Packing Co., 256 Or. 539, 474 P.2d 529, 530 (1970)....

Gulf's argument on commercial impracticability has two strings to its bow. First, Gulf contends that the escalator indicator does not work as intended by the parties by reason of the advent of so-called "two-tier" pricing under Phase IV government price controls.[1] Second, Gulf alleges that crude oil prices have risen substantially without a concomitant rise in the escalation indicator, and, as a result, that performance of the contract has become commercially impracticable.[2]

The short and dispositive answer to Gulf's first argument under U.C.C. § 2–615, that the price escalation indicator (posting in Platt's Oilgram Crude Oil Supplement) no longer reflects the intent of the parties by

---

1. One tier being "old" price-controlled oil, and the second tier being the unregulated oil.

2. The average price paid by Eastern to Gulf has risen more than 40% over the life of the contract.

reason of the so-called "two-tier" pricing structure, is that the language of the contract is clear and unambiguous. The contract does not require interpretation and requires no excursion into the subjective intention of the parties. The intent of the parties is clear from the four corners of the contract; they intended to be bound by the specified entries in *Platt's,* which has been published at all times material here, which is published today, and which prints the contract reference prices. Prices under the contract can be and still are calculated[3] by reference to Platt's publication.[4]

It should be noted that Platt's Oilgram Crude Oil Supplement states on its face that its postings since the advent of "two-tier" are basically comparable to the postings historically quoted in Platt's, and that postings listed in Platt's were price controlled at the time of negotiation and execution of the contract, just as they are today and have been at all times in between. In addition, Gulf's expert witness Mr. Coates testified that oil companies, including Gulf, continue to use "old oil" prices (the prices reported in Platt's) for contracts between themselves. Finally, as to the indicator crude (West Texas Sour) there is no showing that the Platt's postings do not reflect the market price for that oil today. The testimony is in substantial dispute but the court finds, with respect to domestic oil, some 60 percent of Gulf's 1974 domestic production was old oil. With respect to foreign crude oil, domestic prices were considerably lower than imported price at the beginning of the period in question so that the West Texas Sour Crude postings unquestionably did not reflect foreign crude oil postings. In the absence of any evidence to the contrary it may be reasonably inferred that virtually all transactions in West Texas Sour Crude Oil take place at the postings reflected in *Platt's,* since most of the production in that field is "old" oil.

With regard to Gulf's contention that the contract has become "commercially impracticable" within the meaning of U.C.C. § 2–615, because of the increase in market price of foreign crude oil and certain domestic crude oils, the court finds that the tendered defense has not been proved. On this record the court cannot determine how much it costs Gulf to produce a gallon of jet fuel for sale to Eastern, whether Gulf loses money or makes a profit on its sale of jet fuel to Eastern, either now or at the inception of the contract, or at any time in between. Gulf's witnesses testified that they could not make such a computation. The party undertaking the burden of establishing "commercial impracticability" by reason of allegedly increased raw material costs undertakes the obligation of showing the extent to which he has suffered, or will suffer, losses in performing his contract. The

---

3. The parties have stipulated that Eastern has been paying prices mandated by the contract terms.

4. Gulf's contention that the publication of the postings has been "suspended" and therefore that a proviso of Article II of the contract, declaring the consequences of "suspension", has been triggered, is without merit. The Proviso deals, in the clearest of terms, with *Platt's* ceasing to publish either *in toto* or in regard to the specified postings, neither of which is the case here. Furthermore, the proviso contains its own prescription for remedial action in the case of suspension, including notice and substitution of other indicators. Gulf has never attempted to follow the prescribed remedy; thus its argument fails for procedural as well as substantive reasons.

record here does not substantiate Gulf's contention on this fundamental issue.

Gulf presented evidence tending to show that its "costs" of crude oil have increased dramatically over the past two years.

However, the "costs" to which Gulf adverts are unlike any "costs" that might arguably afford ground for any of the relief sought here. Gulf's claimed "costs" of an average barrel of crude oil at Gulf's refineries (estimated by Gulf's witness Davis at about $10.00 currently, and about $9.50 during 1974) include intra-company profits, as the oil moved from Gulf's overseas and domestic production departments to its refining department. The magnitude of that profit was not revealed.

With respect to Gulf's foreign crude oil "costs", the record shows that at the very time Gulf was in the process of repudiating its contract with Eastern (January 1974), Gulf's profit margin on foreign crude oil brought into the United States (Cabindan and Nigerian) was approximately $4.43 to $3.88 per barrel compared with profits of $0.92 and $0.88 respectively, one year earlier.[5] That margin may now have declined, but the record discloses that Gulf's overseas subsidiaries have enjoyed substantial profits from crude oil transactions and that those profits are included in the "average" crude oil "costs" of which Gulf now complains. The "transfer" prices at which Gulf "sells" its foreign oil to its domestic subsidiaries are set by a pricing committee in Gulf's Pittsburgh home office.[a]

Intra-company profit can be and is allocated among those 400—plus corporate subsidiaries of Gulf, largely through the transfer price device, to optimize overall benefit to the corporation, as documents from the committee reveal. Internal memoranda from the pricing committee introduced into evidence showed for instance that the committee had before it the view of one of its tax experts that every $1 increase in Nigerian oil prices resulted in a 50 to 90 cent benefit to the company; other memoranda describe how profits might be assigned, through intercompany sales, to various other offshore subsidiaries to obtain favorable tax treatment for the purpose of maximizing the advantages to the corporation for the benefit of the parent corporation. Similarly, there are memoranda reflecting a policy of charging the highest prices possible to the United States.

In like manner, the "per barrel" cost calculations which Gulf introduced at trial reflect "in house" profits from Gulf's domestic production. During the discovery process, Gulf developed for Eastern certain "cost" figures. Those data show that a Gulf-produced barrel of domestic crude oil is reflected on Gulf's books at a cost of approximately $2.44 for the nine-month period ending September 30, 1974. Yet, for purposes of computing an overall average "cost" to Gulf of a barrel of crude oil for trial purposes (estimated by Gulf's economist witness Davis on the stand at about $9.50 for that period), Gulf used, not the $2.44 actual booked cost, but a

5. Gulf's international oils expert, Mr. Blackledge testified that foreign oil costs were up four-fold during 1973–74 but Gulf's profits also went up four-fold in that period.

a. Transfer pricing is the practice, not unusual within segmented firms, of assigning a cost to goods as they are acquired by one segment from another (*e.g.*, by the assembly division from the parts division).

"transfer" price, equal to "postings" and including intra-company profit. To the extent "old oil" postings are reflected in the domestic oil "transfer price", the intra-company profit would be on the order of $2.76 per barrel, measured against the $5.20 posting listed in *Platt's* for West Texas Sour Crude; "new" oil "transfer prices" would include an even larger profit margin. Gulf estimated that some 70 percent of domestic oil going into Gulf's refineries was its own proprietary production.

Again, these are not the kinds of "costs" against which to measure hardship, real or imagined, under the Uniform Commercial Code. Under no theory of law can it be held that Gulf is guaranteed preservation of its intra-company profits, moving from the left-hand to the right-hand, as one Gulf witness so aptly put it. The burden is upon Gulf to show what its real costs are, not its "costs" inflated by its internal profits at various levels of the manufacturing process and located in various foreign countries.

No criticism is implied of Gulf's rational desire to maximize its profits and take every advantage available to it under the laws. However, these factors cannot be ignored in approaching Gulf's contention that it has been unduly burdened by crude oil price increases.

No such hardship has been established. On the contrary, the record clearly establishes that 1973, the year in which the energy crises began, was Gulf's best year ever, in which it recorded some $800 million in net profits after taxes. Gulf's 1974 year was more than 25% better than 1973's record-$1,065,000,000 profits were booked by Gulf in 1974 after paying all taxes.[6]

For the foregoing reasons, Gulf's claim of hardship giving rise to "commercial impracticability" fails.

But even if Gulf had established great hardship under U.C.C. § 2–615, which it has not, Gulf would not prevail because the events associated with the so-called energy crises were reasonably foreseeable at the time the contract was executed. If a contingency is foreseeable, it and its consequences are taken outside the scope of U.C.C. § 2–615, because the party disadvantaged by fruition of the contingency might have protected himself in his contract, Ellwood v. Nutex Oil Co., 148 S.W.2d 862 (Tex.Civ.App. 1941). . . .

The record is replete with evidence as to the volatility of the Middle East situation, the arbitrary power of host governments to control the foreign oil market, and repeated interruptions and interference with the normal commercial trade in crude oil. Even without the extensive evidence present in the record, the court would be justified in taking judicial notice of the fact that oil has been used as a political weapon with increasing success by the oil-producing nations for many years, and Gulf was well aware of and assumed the risk that the OPEC nations would do exactly what they have done.

---

6. Gulf stipulated in the parties' pre-trial stipulation that it had the capability to perform the contract.

With respect to Gulf's argument that "two-tier" was not "foreseeable", the record shows that domestic crude oil prices were controlled at all material times, that Gulf foresaw that they might be de-controlled, and that Gulf was constantly urging to the Federal Government that they should be de-controlled. Government price regulations were confused, constantly changing, and uncertain during the period of the negotiation and execution of the contract. During that time frame, high ranking Gulf executives, including some of its trial witnesses, were in constant repeated contact with officials and agencies of the Federal Government regarding petroleum policies and were well able to protect themselves from any contingencies.

Even those outside the oil industry were aware of the possibilities. Eastern's principal contract negotiator advised his superior in recommending this contract to him:

"While Gulf is apparently counting on crude price increases, such increases are a fact of life for the future, except as the government may inhibit by price controls, therefore all suppliers have such anticipation."

"1975 is the year during which the full effect of energy shortages will be felt in the United States according to most estimates."

Knowing all the factors, Gulf drafted the contract and tied the escalation to certain specified domestic postings in *Platt's*. The court is of the view that it is bound thereby.

The court is further of the opinion that U.C.C. § 2–614(2) is not applicable to this case.... It is clear that this section dealing with "means or manner of payment" speaks, by way of illustration, to the blocking by governmental interference with the contemplated mode of monetary exchange (e.g., when a contract provides for payment in gold specie and the government subsequently forbids payment in gold). No such issue appears in the case at bar and U.C.C. § 2–614 is inapposite here.

NOTES

(1) *Questions.* If Eastern's supplier had been a firm other than Gulf, one whose dealings in hydrocarbons was restricted to refining crude oil and marketing the products, might that firm have found it easier to establish the "great hardship" that Gulf failed to establish? Might it be possible to establish the requisite injury without showing that operations under the contract in question have begun to show a loss? How, exactly, was it germane that, overall, Gulf had record and rising profits in 1973 and 1974?

Consider the court's discussion of the cost to Gulf of crude oil, as affected by its transfer pricing. Is the court's reasoning linked to the concept of self-imposed impracticability?

(2) *Promisor's Good Faith?* An obstacle to a promisor's performance is not an excuse for the promisor if it might have been overcome easily. Neither are obstacles that the promisor has put in its own way. "A man may habitually leave his house by the front door to keep his appointments; but, if the front door is stuck, he would hardly be excused for not leaving by the back." So said Lord Radcliffe in Tsakiroglou & Co. v. Noblee Thorl G.m.b.H., [1960] 2 Q.B. 318. "To recognize impossibility where ... the party pleading the defense has intentionally incapacitated itself from

performing would defy ... all good sense." Kama Rippa Music, Inc. v. Schekeryk, 510 F.2d 837, 843–43 (2d Cir.1975).

These observations may be self-evident, but they do not solve all the problems about a promisor's responsibility. What of an obstacle that the promisor might have overcome by strenuous effort? And what of one resulting from the promisor's carelessness? Consider the following observations: (i) In *Kama Rippa Music*: "The party pleading impossibility as a defense must demonstrate that it took virtually every action within its power to perform its duties under the contract." (ii) According to Comment 5 to UCC § 2–615, concerning the defense of commercial impracticability for a "stranded seller," the section provides no excuse for a seller unless he has "employed all due measures to assure himself that his source will not fail." (iii) "Some day it may have to be finally determined whether a *prima donna* is excused by complete loss of voice from an executory contract to sing if it is proved that her condition was caused by her carelessness in not changing her wet clothes after being out in the rain." Viscount Simon, in Joseph Constantine Steamship Line v. Imperial Smelting Corp., [1942] A.C. 154, [1941] 2 All E.R. 165 (Court of Appeal). The limitations on a promisor's excuse indicated above might be ascribed, loosely, to its duty to perform in good faith.

(3) *Promisee's Good Faith?* A want of good faith on the part of the promisee may serve as an excuse for the promisor. More precisely, an obstacle to the promisor's performance that is chargeable to the promisee may well be an excuse for the promisor under the rubric "prevention." See the discussion of Hindrance and Prevention, p. 758 above.

(4) *Governmental Acts.* In United States v. Winstar Corporation, 518 U.S. 839 (1996), the Supreme Court considered an impracticability defense presented by the United States. It considered also the "sovereign act" doctrine, restricting contractual liability of the United States for engaging in "public and general acts." The claimants in the case were three banks. The Government pinned a defense on a change in federal banking law: the enactment of a statute known as FIRREA.[a] Earlier, the claimants had been promised favorable accounting treatment by federal authorities supervising them. This promise led them to absorb weaker institutions the failure of which would have been a drain on the Federal Savings & Loan Insurance Corporation. FIRREA sought to foreclose the accounting practice desired by and promised to the claimants. If considered as an ordinary litigant, the Government was in a poor position to rely on its inability to perform the promise, for the disabling statute was its own doing. But the United States is not an ordinary litigant. As a contractor, the Court said, it is relieved from "the traditional blanket rule that a contracting party may not obtain discharge if its own act rendered performance impossible." Hence, while rejecting the Government's defense, the Court proceeded to take it seriously.

Governmental interference with a seller's means of performance may and may not excuse the seller, according to Comment 10 to UCC § 2–615. "[T]his section," we are told, "disregards any technical distinction between 'law,' 'regulation,' 'order' and the like." But there are more-than-technical distinctions to be made. Judicial opinions commonly purport to refine existing law, rather than to promulgate fresh rules. It would not be surprising, therefore, to be told that a seller had assumed the risk of a new, pro-buyer precedent about, say, a reasonable time for tendering goods. When a court announces a novel ruling, should its effect on outstanding contracts depend on whether or not the court portrays the ruling as a novelty?

On occasion, a buyer has complained that its supplier acquiesced too readily in governmental opposition to performance of the supplier's undertaking. Officials, fearful that performance may give comfort to an enemy, have been known to

a. The Financial Institutions Reform, Recovery, and Enforcement Act of 1989.

forestall performance by "jawboning" a supplier rather than by promulgating a regulation. In Harriscom Svenska, AB v. Harris Corp., 3 F.3d 576 (2d Cir.1993), a seller found shelter under a *force majeure* clause ("governmental interference") without having resisted governmental influence to a degree that would have been, in the court's view, "unusually foolhardy." Compare MG Refining & Mktg. v. Knight Enters., 25 F.Supp.2d 175 (S.D.N.Y.1998).

(5) *Temporary Impracticability.* An obstacle to performance that makes it impracticable may prove to be temporary; it may abate before the period required for full performance has elapsed. Promisors have sometimes sought excuses from any further performance based on obstacles that endured only for a time. Gene Autry, for example, a star of cowboy movies, refused to resume the performance of an acting contract with his studio, following his Army service during World War II. That was not a breach, it was held. Autry v. Republic Productions, Inc., 180 P.2d 888 (Cal.1947). A different but related question is this: When may a party justifiably terminate a contract because the other party suffers from a short-term disability? A party who announces termination too hastily is chargeable with having repudiated the contract.

(6) *The Westinghouse Litigation.* The most widely observed litigation over UCC § 2–615 arose out of long term contracts made by Westinghouse Electric to supply uranium oxide ("yellowcake") to electric utility companies in connection with sales of nuclear power plants. The price of uranium oxide rose from about $6 a pound in 1972 to about $40 a pound in 1976. Late in 1975 Westinghouse wrote seventeen utilities, saying that it was excused because of commercial impracticability from delivering the total of some 80 million pounds that it had agreed to supply, and that it would prorate among the utilities some 15 million pounds that it could command. From that event a fountain of litigation flowed, resulting in many settlements. Most interesting is the interim decision in the Richmond case, in which the suits of several utilities were consolidated for trial.

Westinghouse arranged, with court approval, to deliver the uranium oxide at its disposal, subject to a later determination. After nine months of hearings, the judge ruled that Westinghouse was not wholly excused, but he expressed willingness to hear argument that a judicial limitation of the remedy was appropriate. Submissions on issues of damages and an "equitable adjustment" were then made. Eventually all claims were settled on terms relatively favorable to Westinghouse. For background, see Paul Joskow, Commercial Impossibility, the Uranium Market and the Westinghouse Case, 6 J.Legal Stud. 119 (1977).[b]

SECTION 3. FRUSTRATION OF PURPOSE

Krell v. Henry

Court of Appeal, 1903.
2 K.B. 740.

[By a contract in writing of June 20, 1902, the defendant agreed to hire from the plaintiff a flat in Pall Mall, London, for June 26 and 27, on which

---

b. For a later episode in Westinghouse's travails arising out of nuclear power contracts, see Florida Power & Light Co. v. Westinghouse Electric Corp., 826 F.2d 239 (4th Cir.1987). The court there noted a trial court's finding that "while Westinghouse was supposedly more expert in the field of nuclear energy, Florida was more expert in the drafting of agreements and that it had demonstrated this superior expertise by 'out-negotiating' Westinghouse."

days it had been officially announced that the coronation processions (i.e., to be held in connection with the coronation of Edward VII) would take place and pass along Pall Mall. The contract contained no express reference to the coronation processions, or to any other purpose for which the flat was taken. A deposit was paid when the contract was entered into. As, owing to the serious illness of the King, the processions did not take place on the days originally fixed, the defendant declined to pay the balance of the rent.]

■ VAUGHN WILLIAMS, L.J. The real question in this case is the extent of the application in English law of the principle of the Roman law which has been adopted and acted on in many English decisions, and notably in the case of Taylor v. Caldwell, (3 B. & S. 826).... I do not think that the principle of the civil law as introduced into the English law is limited to cases in which the event causing the impossibility of performance is the destruction or non-existence of some thing which is the subject matter of the contract or of some condition or state of things expressly specified as a condition of it. I think that you first have to ascertain, not necessarily from the terms of the contract, but, if required, from necessary inferences, drawn from surrounding circumstances recognized by both contracting parties, what is the substance of the contract, and then to ask the question whether that substantial contract needs for its foundation the assumption of the existence of a particular state of things. If it does, this will limit the operation of the general words, and in such case, if the contract becomes impossible of performance by reason of the non-existence of the state of things assumed by both contracting parties as the foundation of the contract, there will be no breach of the contract thus limited. Now what are the facts of the present case? The contract is contained in two letters of June 20 which passed between the defendant and the plaintiff's agent, Mr. Cecil Bisgood. These letters do not mention the coronation, but speak merely of the taking of Mr. Krell's chambers, or, rather, of the use of them, in the daytime of June 26 and 27, for the sum of 75*l.*, 25*l.* then paid, balance 50*l.* to be paid on the 24th. But the affidavits, which by agreement between the parties are to be taken as stating the facts of the case, show that the plaintiff exhibited on his premises, third floor, 56A, Pall Mall, an announcement to the effect that windows to view the Royal coronation procession were to be let, and that the defendant was induced by that announcement to apply to the housekeeper on the premises, who said that the owner was willing to let the suite of rooms for the purpose of seeing the Royal procession for both days, but not nights, of June 26 and 27.[a] In my

---

a. Two processions were planned in connection with the coronation: that on Coronation Day, and a "Pageant" on the following day. Experience of the Diamond Jubilee (1897) provided some guidance for the pricing of space to see the processions. At that time a club-house had been "let to a speculator for £200, who realized £500 by his bargain." C. Pascoe, The Pageant & Ceremony of The Coronation 213 (1902). But there were complications in the early summer of 1902, in that the routes of the processions had not been determined. Pall Mall—"club-land of the empire"—was thought to be a certainty for the Pageant procession; but for Coronation Day two shorter routes, not including Pall Mall, were thought to be under consideration. One writer of the time estimated that prices for the Pageant ought not to exceed those paid for Victoria's Jubilee—"that is to say, if the Route be not [curtailed]. Of course, the lesser the opportunity of seeing the Pagjudgment the use of the rooms was let and taken for the purpose of seeing the Royal procession. It was not a demise of the rooms, or even an agreement to let and take the rooms. It is a license to use rooms for a particular purpose and none other. And in my judgment the taking place of those processions on the days proclaimed along the proclaimed route, which passed 56A, Pall Mall, was regarded by both contracting parties as the foundation of the contract; and I think that it cannot reasonably be supposed to have been in the contemplation of the contracting parties, when the contract was made, that the coronation would not be held on the proclaimed days, or the processions not take place on those days along the proclaimed route; and I think that the words imposing on the defendant the obligation to accept and pay for the use of the rooms for the named days, although general and unconditional, were not used with reference to the possibility of the particular contingency which afterwards occurred. It was suggested in the course of the argument that if the occurrence, on the proclaimed days, of the coronation and the procession in this case were the foundation of the contract, and if the general words are thereby limited or qualified, so that in the event of the non-occurrence of the coronation and procession along the proclaimed route they would discharge both parties from further performance of the contract, it would follow that if a cabman was engaged to take someone to Epsom on Derby Day at a suitable enhanced price for such a journey, say 10*l.*, both parties to the contract would be discharged in the contingency of the race at Epsom for some reason becoming impossible; but I do not think this follows, for I do not think that in the cab case the happening of the race would be the foundation of the contract. No doubt the purpose of the engager would be to go to see the Derby, and the price would be proportionately high; but the cab had no special qualification for this particular occasion. Any other cab would have done as well.

Appeal dismissed.

NOTES

(1) *Twin Doctrines.* The foregoing decision is the best-known example of the doctrine known as "frustration of purpose." In this country frustration affords an excuse distinct from that of impracticability of performance. In Krell v. Henry the court pitched its decision on the "impossibility" principle of the music-hall case, Taylor v. Caldwell, above. But the postponement of the coronation did not impede performance of the contract either by Krell or by Henry. After the King's illness, as before, it was perfectly possible for Henry to occupy the rooms and to pay the agreed price; it was only that the occupancy would have been relatively valueless to him.

A comparable California case is Lloyd v. Murphy, 153 P.2d 47 (1944). Murphy's business as a car dealer, in leased quarters, was severely curtailed when wartime

eant, the higher will be the prices asked for accommodation." Id. at 212.

On June 22 Commons was informed that the King had just undergone an operation for appendicitis, and that the Coronation was indefinitely postponed. V. Cowles, Edward VII and His Circle 240 (1956). It was per-

formed on August 9. Though some of the captains and the princes (kings were not invited) had departed London, the splendor of the ceremony was "scarcely dimmed." Pall Mall was on the coronation route. London Illustrated News, Aug. 14, 1902.

orders of the federal government placed sharp restrictions on sales of new cars. When he withheld rent payments, his landlords brought an action to enforce the lease terms. The court identified Murphy's defense as one of frustration. "Although [that] doctrine is akin to the doctrine of impossibility of performance ... frustration is not a form of impossibility.... Performance remains possible but the expected value of performance to the party seeking to be excused has been destroyed by a fortuitous event...." For a tenant in a different kind of difficulty, see Kel Kim Corp. v. Central Markets, Inc., 519 N.E.2d 295 (N.Y.1987). Kel Kim sought to maintain its lease without complying with its undertaking to maintain a sizable amount of liability insurance; a crisis in the insurance market had prevented it from complying, Kel Kim said. The landlord prevailed in each case.

(2) *Efficient Non-performance?* When parties enter into a contract, the value of performance to each party often exceeds the cost of performance. In the introductory note on the Economics of Remedies, p. 20, we presented a hypothetical where a buyer purchased a piece of machinery from a seller. The machinery, which would cost the seller $300 to produce, was worth $1,000 to the buyer. The parties entered into a contract for the sale of the machinery for a price of $600.

However, the relationship between value and costs may change before performance is rendered. For example, a more valuable opportunity may present itself to the seller, as it did in the introductory note. Another occurrence that may change the relationship between value and costs is when a party's cost of performance increases significantly, as we saw in the cases on impracticability, such as *Transatlantic*.

Like impracticability, frustration of purpose may also lead to a change in the relative magnitude of value and cost of performance. With frustration of purpose, however, it is the value of performance to the party receiving it (rather than the cost) that turns out to be significantly different than expected.

Suppose, in our hypothetical, that before the seller produces and delivers the machinery to the buyer, the buyer's factory burns to the ground—frustrating the buyer's purpose of entering into the contract with the seller. The machinery now has little value to the buyer. In such a circumstance, does excusing the buyer promote efficiency? Does it promote fairness? What would inform your response? Different conceptions of efficiency? Different conceptions of fairness? Something else?

(3) *Occurrence and Assumption.* Was it so inconceivable that illness or bad weather or some other unfortunate event would lead to cancellation or postponement of the coronation of Edward VII, thereby frustrating Krell's purpose in letting the room on the announced day of the event? Perhaps it was difficult for a lay person to foresee this eventuality. But, "[i]n fact, Krell did not let his rooms directly; rather, he left that to his solicitor." Victor Goldberg, Framing Contract Law, (2006) at 340. Is this a significant fact? Should excuse doctrines apply equally to those represented by counsel and those not?

PROBLEMS

(1) *The Lost Weekend.* A major university, Gridiron U., is situated in the town of Touchdown, which is otherwise a small community, somewhat isolated. There is one hotel in the town, and a few motels, but rooms for transient visitors are not abundant. You represent several alumni of Gridiron who have suffered a disappointment. They had planned to attend the school's homecoming, a major annual event in Touchdown. This year the event was canceled, owing to a tragic tornado strike. Your clients, however, already arranged for weekend lodgings in Touchdown, paying

substantial advance deposits to the hotelkeeper. As your clients well knew, the usual room charges in Touchdown are more than doubled for homecoming weekends. If you can establish that your clients' lodging contracts were terminated by Gridiron's cancellation of its homecoming, you can expect to succeed in a class action on behalf of your clients and other alumni who have made similar arrangements, seeking recovery of the deposits.

Do you find support for that action in *Krell*? Can you distinguish the case of the cab on Derby Day, suggested by counsel for Krell? Are you prepared to dispute the court's dictum on that case?

(2) *A Bride Bereaved*. For a promise of $500 P promises to provide a wedding dress for D by June 1. D's marriage to X is scheduled for a week after that. When the dress is all but ready, X suffers a fatal accident. Is D bound to pay anything?

Swift Canadian Co. v. Banet

United States Court of Appeals, Third Circuit, 1955.
224 F.2d 36.

Action to recover from buyer of goods, for breach of contract. In the United States District Court for the Eastern District of Pennsylvania, George A. Welsh, District Judge, each party moved for summary judgment upon stipulated facts, and the buyer's motion was granted. The seller appealed to the Court of Appeals....

Judgment reversed with instructions to enter judgment for plaintiff.

■ GOODRICH, CIRCUIT JUDGE. This is an action on the part of a seller of goods to recover against the buyer for breach of contract. In the trial court each party, following the filing of a stipulation of facts, moved for summary judgment. The court granted the motion of the defendant. Plaintiff here says that it should have had the summary judgment or, at the worst, that the case should be remanded for trial on the facts.

The one point presented is both interesting and elusive. The seller is a Canadian corporation. It entered into an agreement with defendant buyers who do business as Keystone Wool Pullers in Philadelphia. By this contract Keystone agreed to purchase a quantity of lamb pelts at a stipulated price. Part of the quantity was delivered on board railroad cars at Toronto and shipped to Keystone in Philadelphia. On or about March 12, 1952, Swift advised Keystone of its readiness to deliver the remaining pelts to the buyer on board railroad cars in Toronto for shipment to Philadelphia. The parties have stipulated that on or about that day the government of the United States by its agency, the Bureau of Animal Industry, had issued stricter regulations for the importation of lamb pelts into the United States. The parties have stipulated that "pursuant to these regulations, the importation into the United States of these lamb pelts by Keystone was prevented." They have also stipulated that for the reasons just stated Keystone then and thereafter refused to accept delivery of the pelts and the loading and shipment of the car did not occur.

From an inspection of the contract made between the parties it appears that the seller agreed to sell the pelts:

"all at $3.80 each U.S. Funds"

"F.O.B. Toronto."[a]

Below this an approximate time was stipulated for shipment and then there were shipping directions in the following form:

Note --- Frankford

Via: Buffalo—Penna. R.R. to
~~Broad & Washington Ave.~~

Freight Sta. Penna. R.R. Delivery.

Following this appears the terms and method of payment.

Two additional conditions of sale should be stated. There was a provision that neither party is to be liable for "orders or acts of any government or governmental agency...." And there was a provision that "when pelts are sold F.O.B. seller's plant title and risk of loss shall pass to buyer when product is loaded on cars at seller's plant."

The one question in this case is the legal effect of this agreement between the parties. If the seller's obligation was performed when it delivered, or offered to deliver, the pelts to the railroad company in Toronto, we think it is entitled to recovery. If the seller did fulfill its obligation, when it did so deliver, of course it is clear that when it failed to load the pelts because the buyer had signified his refusal to accept them, the seller may assert the same rights as though he had loaded them. A party is not obligated to do the vain thing of performing, assuming that he is ready to perform, when the other party has given notice of refusal to accept performance. 3 Williston on Sales, § 586 (Rev. ed., 1948); Restatement, Contracts, §§ 280, 306; Leonard Seed Co. v. Lustig Burgerhoff Co., 1923, 81 Pa.Super. 499. See also Uniform Commercial Code, § 2–610(c); Pa.Stat.Ann. tit. 12A, § 2–610(c) (1954).

The argument for the buyer must rest on the fact that the shipping directions in the contract showed that what the parties had in mind was such kind of performance by the seller as would start the goods to the buyer in Philadelphia. This coupled with the stipulation that, in consequence of the stiffening of federal regulations, "the importation into the United States of these lamb pelts by Keystone was prevented," forms the basis for the argument that the carrying out of the agreement was prevented by governmental agency and the buyer is therefore excused.

The validity of this argument depends upon what effect we give to a provision for shipment of the goods to the buyer via Pennsylvania R.R., destination Philadelphia. We do not think that this is any more than a shipping direction which the buyer could have changed to any other destination in the world had it so desired. Suppose the buyer had found that it wanted the goods in New York, could it not have directed such a

---

a. F.O.B. is a common trade term that means, in this context, that for the stated price the seller will place the pelts "free on board" a train at the named place, here Toronto. See the similar term "F.A.S." described in footnote b, p. 402 above.

change in destination without any violation of the contract? Could the seller have insisted that it would ship to Philadelphia and nowhere else? We think that authority in general regards these shipping directions as simply inserted for the convenience of the buyer and subject to change by him. Dwight v. Eckert, 1888, 117 Pa. 490, 12 A. 32; Hocking v. Hamilton, 1893, 158 Pa. 107, 27 A. 836; Richter v. Zoccoli, 1930, 150 A. 1, 8 N.J.Misc. 289; 1 & 2 Williston on Sales, §§ 190, 457 (Rev. ed., 1948). See also Uniform Commercial Code, § 2–319(3); Pa.Stat.Ann. tit. 12A, § 2–319(3) (1954).

If the contract in this case had called for performance "F.O.B. seller's plant" a provision of the contract itself would clearly have indicated when the seller's responsibility was finished and the buyer's had begun.[1] Here the provision in the earlier part of the contract was simply "F.O.B. Toronto" and it was not specifically provided that the sale was delivery at the seller's plant. We think the provision shows what the parties meant by "F.O.B." and can see no difference, so far as this expressed meaning goes, between F.O.B. at seller's plant and F.O.B. Toronto.

The general rule on this subject is pretty clear. Williston points out that when goods are delivered "free on board" pursuant to contract the presumption is that the property passes thereupon. Williston on Sales, § 280(b) (Rev. ed., 1948). It is agreed that this is a presumption and that the phrase F.O.B. is not one of iron-clad meaning. Seabrook Farms Co. v. Commodity Credit Corp., 206 F.2d 93 (C.A.3, 1953). There is nothing in this case, however, to counteract the effect of such a presumption. When the shipper had made his delivery he was to send bill of lading and draft through a Philadelphia bank. His part of the agreement would have been fully performed when the goods were delivered F.O.B. at Toronto. We think both the risk of loss and the possibility of profit if the market advanced, were in the buyer from then on. Even if the goods could not be imported into the United States under the then existing regulations, the rest of the world was free to the buyer, so far as we know, as destination for the shipment. If he did not care to accept them under the circumstances and his expectation of a profitable transaction was disappointed, nevertheless, the seller having performed or being ready, able and willing to perform, was entitled to the value of his bargain.

[The court found that the law of Pennsylvania and that of Ontario were identical on the issue involved here, and that the seller's damages were sufficiently proved.]

The judgment of the district court will be reversed with instructions to enter judgment for the plaintiff for the difference between the contract price and the price at which the goods were sold.

NOTE

Variations. Would the decision have been different if the sale contract had provided for delivery F.O.B. Philadelphia rather than Toronto? UCC § 2–319(1) distinguishes between "F.O.B. the place of shipment" and "F.O.B. the place of

---

1. See the second additional condition of sale quoted in the text above.

destination." Given the latter expression, "the seller must at his own expense and risk transport the goods to that place and there tender delivery...." But the entire subsection is qualified by the opening phrase, "Unless otherwise agreed...."

If the seller had undertaken to deliver the pelts in Philadelphia, and had failed to do so because of United States import regulations, would that necessarily be a breach of its duty?

If Canada had regulated the *export* of lamb pelts, so as to require a license, would the Canadian seller have borne the risk that one could not be obtained? Look in the opinion for a remark that might be used to distinguish import from export restrictions. And see Amtorg Trading Corp. v. Miehle Printing Press & Mfg. Co., 206 F.2d 103 (2d Cir.1953).

Chase Precast Corp. v. John J. Paonessa Co.

Supreme Judicial Court of Massachusetts, 1991.
409 Mass. 371, 566 N.E.2d 603.

■ LYNCH, JUSTICE. This appeal raises the question whether the doctrine of frustration of purpose may be a defense in a breach of contract action in Massachusetts, and, if so, whether it excuses the defendant John J. Paonessa Company, Inc. (Paonessa), from performance.

The claim of the plaintiff, Chase Precast Corporation (Chase), arises from the cancellation of its contracts with Paonessa to supply median barriers in a highway reconstruction project of the Commonwealth. Chase brought an action to recover its anticipated profit on the amount of median barriers called for by its supply contracts with Paonessa but not produced. Paonessa brought a cross action against the Commonwealth for indemnification in the event it should be held liable to Chase. After a jury-waived trial, a Superior Court judge ruled for Paonessa on the basis of impossibility of performance.[1] Chase and Paonessa cross appealed. The Appeals Court affirmed, noting that the doctrine of frustration of purpose more accurately described the basis of the trial judge's decision than the doctrine of impossibility. Chase Precast Corp. v. John J. Paonessa Co., 28 Mass.App.Ct. 639, 554 N.E.2d 868 (1990). We agree. We allowed Chase's application for further appellate review, and we now affirm.

The pertinent facts are as follows. In 1982, the Commonwealth, through the Department of Public Works (department), entered into two contracts with Paonessa for resurfacing and improvements to two stretches of Route 128. Part of each contract called for replacing a grass median strip between the north and southbound lanes with concrete surfacing and precast concrete median barriers. Paonessa entered into two contracts with Chase under which Chase was to supply, in the aggregate, 25,800 linear feet of concrete median barriers according to the specifications of the department for highway construction. The quantity and type of barriers to be supplied were specified in two purchase orders prepared by Chase.

---

1. The judge also ruled that the Department of Public Works had the right to cancel the order for median barriers under its general contracts with Paonessa, particularly under subsection 4.06 of those contracts. See note [5], *infra*.

The highway reconstruction began in the spring of 1983. By late May, the department was receiving protests from angry residents who objected to use of the concrete median barriers and removal of the grass median strip. Paonessa and Chase became aware of the protest around June 1. On June 6, a group of about 100 citizens filed an action in the Superior Court to stop installation of the concrete median barriers and other aspects of the work. On June 7, anticipating modification by the department, Paonessa notified Chase by letter to stop producing concrete barriers for the projects. Chase did so upon receipt of the letter the following day. On June 17, the department and the citizens' group entered into a settlement which provided, in part, that no additional concrete median barriers would be installed. On June 23, the department deleted the permanent concrete median barriers item from its contracts with Paonessa.

Before stopping production on June 8, Chase had produced approximately one-half of the concrete median barriers called for by its contracts with Paonessa, and had delivered most of them to the construction sites. Paonessa paid Chase for all that it had produced, at the contract price. Chase suffered no out-of-pocket expense as a result of cancellation of the remaining portion of barriers.

This court has long recognized and applied the doctrine of impossibility as a defense to an action for breach of contract. See, e.g., Boston Plate & Window Glass Co. v. John Bowen Co., 335 Mass. 697, 141 N.E.2d 715 (1957); . . . Butterfield v. Byron, 153 Mass. 517, 27 N.E. 667 (1891). Under that doctrine, "where from the nature of the contract it appears that the parties must from the beginning have contemplated the continued existence of some particular specified thing as the foundation of what was to be done, then, in the absence of any warranty that the thing shall exist . . . the parties shall be excused . . . [when] performance becomes impossible from the accidental perishing of the thing without the fault of either party." Boston Plate & Window Glass Co., supra, 335 Mass. at 700, 141 N.E.2d 715, quoting Hawkes v. Kehoe, 193 Mass. 419, 423, 79 N.E. 766 (1907).

On the other hand, although we have referred to the doctrine of frustration of purpose in a few decisions, we have never clearly defined it. See Mishara Constr. Co. v. Transit–Mixed Concrete Corp., 365 Mass. 122, 128–129, 310 N.E.2d 363 (1974). . . . Other jurisdictions have explained the doctrine as follows: when an event neither anticipated nor caused by either party, the risk of which was not allocated by the contract, destroys the object or purpose of the contract, thus destroying the value of performance, the parties are excused from further performance. See Lloyd v. Murphy, 25 Cal.2d 48, 153 P.2d 47 (1944).

In Mishara Constr. Co., supra, 365 Mass. at 129, 310 N.E.2d 363, we called frustration of purpose a "companion rule" to the doctrine of impossibility. Both doctrines concern the effect of supervening circumstances upon the rights and duties of the parties. The difference lies in the effect of the supervening event. Under frustration, "[p]erformance remains possible but the expected value of performance to the party seeking to be excused has been destroyed by [the] fortuitous event...."[2] Lloyd v. Murphy, supra, 25 Cal.2d at 53, 153 P.2d 47. The principal question in both kinds of cases remains "whether an unanticipated circumstance, the risk of which should not fairly be thrown on the promisor, has made performance vitally different from what was reasonably to be expected." See Lloyd, supra at 54, 153 P.2d 47 (frustration); Mishara Constr. Co., supra, 365 Mass. at 129, 310 N.E.2d 363 (impossibility).

Since the two doctrines differ only in the effect of the fortuitous supervening event, it is appropriate to look to our cases dealing with impossibility for guidance in treating the issues that are the same in a frustration of purpose case.[3] The trial judge's findings with regard to those issues are no less pertinent to application of the frustration defense because they were considered relevant to the defense of impossibility.

Another definition of frustration of purpose is found in the Restatement (Second) of Contracts § 265 (1981):

"Where, after a contract is made, a party's principal purpose is substantially frustrated without his fault by the occurrence of an event the non-occurrence of which was a basic assumption on which the contract was made, his remaining duties to render performance are discharged, unless the language or the circumstances indicate the contrary."

This definition is nearly identical to the defense of "commercial impracticability," found in the Uniform Commercial Code, G.L. c. 106, § 2–615 (1988 ed.),[4] which this court, in Mishara Constr. Co., supra at 127–128, 310 N.E.2d 363, held to be consistent with the common law of contracts regarding impossibility of performance. It follows, therefore, that the Restatement's formulation of the doctrine is consistent with this court's previous treatment of impossibility of performance and frustration of purpose.

Paonessa bore no responsibility for the department's elimination of the median barriers from the projects. Therefore, whether it can rely on the defense of frustration turns on whether elimination of the barriers was a risk allocated by the contracts to Paonessa. Mishara Constr. Co., supra, 365 Mass. at 129, 310 N.E.2d 363, articulates the relevant test:

"The question is, given the commercial circumstances in which the parties dealt: Was the contingency which developed one which the parties could reasonably be thought to have foreseen as a real possibility which could affect performance? Was it one of that variety of risks

---

2. Clearly frustration of purpose is a more accurate label for the defense argued in this case than impossibility of performance, since, as the Appeals Court pointed out, "[p]erformance was not literally impossible. Nothing prevented Paonessa from honoring its contract to purchase the remaining sections of median barrier, whether or not the [department] would approve their use in the road construction." 28 Mass.App.Ct. 639, 644 n. 5, 554 N.E.2d 868 (1990).

3. Those issues include the foreseeability of the supervening event, allocation of the risk of occurrence of the event, and the degree of hardship to the promisor....

4. That section states that performance is excused when it has been made "impracticable by the occurrence of a contingency the non-occurrence of which was a basic assumption on which the contract was made." G.L. c. 106, § 2–615.

which the parties were tacitly assigning to the promisor by their failure to provide for it explicitly? If it was, performance will be required. If it could not be so considered, performance is excused."

This is a question for the trier of fact. Id. at 127, 130, 310 N.E.2d 363.

Paonessa's contracts with the department contained a standard provision allowing the department to eliminate items or portions of work found unnecessary.[5] The purchase order agreements between Chase and Paonessa do not contain a similar provision. This difference in the contracts does not mandate the conclusion that Paonessa assumed the risk of reduction in the quantity of the barriers. It is implicit in the judge's findings that Chase knew the barriers were for department projects. The record supports the conclusion that Chase was aware of the department's power to decrease quantities of contract items. The judge found that Chase had been a supplier of median barriers to the department in the past. The provision giving the department the power to eliminate items or portions thereof was standard in its contracts. See Standard Specifications for Highways and Bridges, Commonwealth of Massachusetts Department of Public Works § 4.06 (1973). The judge found that Chase had furnished materials under and was familiar with the so-called "Unit Price Philosophy" in the construction industry, whereby contract items are paid for at the contract unit price for the quantity of work actually accepted. Finally, the judge's finding that "[a]ll parties were well aware that lost profits were not an element of damage in either of the public works projects in issue" further supports the conclusion that Chase was aware of the department's power to decrease quantities, since the term prohibiting claims for anticipated profit is part of the same sentence in the standard provision as that allowing the engineer to eliminate items or portions of work.

In Mishara Constr. Co., supra at 130, 310 N.E.2d 363, we held that, although labor disputes in general cannot be considered extraordinary, whether the parties in a particular case intended performance to be carried out, even in the face of a labor difficulty, depends on the facts known to the parties at the time of contracting with respect to the history of and prospects for labor difficulties. In this case, even if the parties were aware generally of the department's power to eliminate contract items, the judge could reasonably have concluded that they did not contemplate the cancellation for a major portion of the project of such a widely used item as

---

5. The contracts contained the following provision:

"4.06 Increased or Decreased Contract Quantities."

"When the accepted quantities of work vary from the quantities in the bid schedule, the Contractor shall accept as payment in full, so far as contract items are concerned, payment at the original contract unit prices for the accepted quantities of work done."

"The Engineer may order omitted from the work any items or portions of work found unnecessary to the improvement and such omission shall not operate as a waiver of any condition of the Contract nor invalidate any of the provisions thereof, nor shall the Contractor have any claim for anticipated profit."

"No allowance will be made for any increased expenses, loss of expected reimbursement therefor or from any other cause."

concrete median barriers, and did not allocate the risk of such cancellation.[6]

Our opinion in Chicopee Concrete Serv., Inc. v. Hart Eng'g Co., 398 Mass. 476, 498 N.E.2d 121 (1986), does not lead to a different conclusion. Although we held there that a provision of a prime contract requiring city approval of subcontractors was not incorporated by reference into the subcontract, id. at 478, 498 N.E.2d 121, we nevertheless stated that, if the record had supported the conclusion that the subcontractor knew, or at least had notice of, the approval clause, the result might have been different. Id. at 478–479, 498 N.E.2d 121.[7] . . .

Judgment affirmed.

NOTE

Stranded Buyers. In Note 2, p. 845 above, the term "stranded seller" is used for sellers who plead impracticability because their supplies were choked off. The situation of Paonessa was the converse: its contract with Chase Precast designated a customer, and it lost the patronage of that customer. Paonessa was a "stranded buyer," one might say.

It is a striking fact about UCC § 2–615 that, on its face, the section has no bearing on the problem in *Chase Precast*: it makes no provision for a stranded buyer. In the case next presented, a buyer ("NIPSCO") sought to be excused under the doctrine of frustration. The court alluded to the question whether or not a buyer can ever claim excuse under UCC § 2–615. That part of the opinion is omitted; it provides no answer. If applicable, the court concluded, UCC § 2–615 would be of no more avail to the buyer than the common law of frustration. The enactment of the Code did not displace that law, the court said, citing UCC § 1–103.

As to the question whether or not UCC § 2–615 can be applied in favor of a buyer, in an appropriate case, the court considered Indiana law. It quoted from Comment 9 to the section: "the reason of the present section may well apply and entitle the buyer to the exemption." The court cited several precedents, although in none of the cases was a buyer exempted. The court noted, on the other hand, that the Indiana legislature had not enacted the Code comments. No legislature has.

---

6. The judge did not explicitly find that cancellation of the barriers was not contemplated and that the risk of their elimination was not allocated by the contracts. However, the judge's decision imports every finding essential to sustain it if there is evidence to support it. Mailer v. Mailer, 390 Mass. 371, 373, 455 N.E.2d 1211 (1983).

7. This court held in John Soley & Sons v. Jones, 208 Mass. 561, 566–567, 95 N.E. 94 (1911), that, where by its terms the prime contract could be cancelled if the defendant was not making sufficient progress on the work, and the plaintiff knew of the article of cancellation, nevertheless, even if it was mutually understood that the defendant did not intend to perform unless the prime contract remained in force, the defendant was not relieved from performance on the ground of impossibility where it failed to provide for the risk of cancellation in its contract with the plaintiff. To the extent that holding is contrary to our decision in this case, we decline to follow it, and refer to our adoption in Mishara Constr. Co., supra, 365 Mass. at 130, 310 N.E.2d 363, of the following statement: "Rather than mechanically apply any fixed rule of law, where the parties themselves have not allocated responsibility, justice is better served by appraising all of the circumstances, the part the various parties played, and thereon determining liability," quoting Badhwar v. Colorado Fuel & Iron Corp., 138 F.Supp. 595, 607 (S.D.N.Y.1955), aff'd, 245 F.2d 903 (2d Cir.1957). See West Los Angeles Inst. for Cancer Research v. Mayer, 366 F.2d 220, 225 (9th Cir.1966), cert. denied, 385 U.S. 1010 (1967) ("foreseeability of the frustrating event is not alone enough to bar rescission if it appears that the parties did not intend the promisor to assume the risk of its occurrence").

Most states, like Indiana, have their own state comments—none of them having been enacted either.

Laying aside the case of severe currency deflation, and the case of a buyer's cash shortage (usually an allocated risk), it is not easy to suppose situations in which it is impracticable for a buyer to pay. Considering the "reason" of UCC § 2–615, does it support the decision in the main case?

PROBLEMS

(1) Heavyside Company was a franchised dealer in farm equipment for the International Harvester Company (IH). After a dramatic downturn in the market for farm equipment, which caused IH to lose $4 billion in four years, it concluded that it had no alternative but to go into bankruptcy or to sell off its farm implement division. It decided to do the latter, receiving for its assets hundreds of millions, in cash and stock, from J.I. Case Company and an affiliate. Although Case did not acquire the IH franchise network, it offered franchises to many IH dealers. Heavyside was not one of these, for Case already had a dealer in the area. Heavyside sued IH for breach of contract. Does IH have the defense of impracticability? Of frustration? See Karl Wendt Farm Equip. Co. v. International Harvester Co., 931 F.2d 1112 (6th Cir.1991).

(2) The Precision Parts Company contracted with Micro Manufacturing, Inc. to produce and deliver a specialized machine part, a custom gear box. Micro cancelled the contract when Precision's work was almost complete. It did so as a consequence of the Gulf War. Micro's reason for buying the gear box was to incorporate it into a piece of equipment called a human centrifuge. Iraqi Airways had ordered that equipment from Micro. But Micro lost interest in the gear box when, in connection with the war, the United Nations placed an embargo on shipments to Iraq like the one Micro had counted on. In an action by Precision against Micro for breach of the gear-box contract, Micro defended on the ground of frustration of purpose. It appeared that (a) Precision had not been told, before the cancellation, what the gear box was wanted for. Also that (b) after the cancellation, Precision had completed work on the item and sold it to the Macro Corporation for very nearly the price Micro had agreed to pay. Do both of these circumstances—(a) and (b)—run counter to Micro's frustration defense? If so, which is the more compelling? See Power Engineering & Mfg. v. Krug International, 501 N.W.2d 490 (Iowa 1993).

Northern Indiana Public Service Co. v. Carbon County Coal Co.

United States Court of Appeals, Seventh Circuit, 1986.
799 F.2d 265.

■ Posner, Circuit Judge. These appeals bring before us various facets of a dispute between Northern Indiana Public Service Company (NIPSCO), an electric utility in Indiana, and Carbon County Coal Company, a partnership that until recently owned and operated a coal mine in Wyoming. In 1978 NIPSCO and Carbon County signed a contract whereby Carbon County agreed to sell and NIPSCO to buy approximately 1.5 million tons of coal every year for 20 years, at a price of $24 a ton subject to various provisions for escalation which by 1985 had driven the price up to $44 a ton.

NIPSCO's rates are regulated by the Indiana Public Service Commission. In 1983 NIPSCO requested permission to raise its rates to reflect increased fuel charges. Some customers of NIPSCO opposed the increase on the ground that NIPSCO could reduce its overall costs by buying more electrical power from neighboring utilities for resale to its customers and producing less of its own power. Although the Commission granted the requested increase, it directed NIPSCO, in orders issued in December 1983 and February 1984 (the "economy purchase orders"), to make a good faith effort to find, and wherever possible buy from, utilities that would sell electricity to it at prices lower than its costs of internal generation. The Commission added ominously that "the adverse effects of entering into long-term coal supply contracts which do not allow for renegotiation and are not requirement contracts, is a burden which must rest squarely on the shoulders of NIPSCO management." Actually the contract with Carbon County did provide for renegotiation of the contract price—but one-way renegotiation in favor of Carbon County; the price fixed in the contract (as adjusted from time to time in accordance with the escalator provisions) was a floor. And the contract was indeed not a requirements contract: it specified the exact amount of coal that NIPSCO must take over the 20 years during which the contract was to remain in effect. NIPSCO was eager to have an assured supply of low-sulphur coal and was therefore willing to guarantee both price and quantity.

Unfortunately for NIPSCO, as things turned out it was indeed able to buy electricity at prices below the costs of generating electricity from coal bought under the contract with Carbon County; and because of the "economy purchase orders," of which it had not sought judicial review, NIPSCO could not expect to be allowed by the Public Service Commission to recover in its electrical rates the costs of buying coal from Carbon County. NIPSCO therefore decided to stop accepting coal deliveries from Carbon County, at least for the time being; and on April 24, 1985, it brought this diversity suit against Carbon County in a federal district court in Indiana, seeking a declaration that it was excused from its obligations under the contract either permanently or at least until the economy purchase orders ceased preventing it from passing on the costs of the contract to its ratepayers. In support of this position it argued that the contract violated section 2(c) of the Mineral Lands Leasing Act of 1920, 30 U.S.C. § 202, because of Carbon County's affiliation with a railroad (Union Pacific), and that in any event NIPSCO's performance was excused or suspended—either under the contract's *force majeure* clause or under the doctrines of frustration or impossibility—by reason of the economy purchase orders.

On May 17, 1985, Carbon County counterclaimed for breach of contract and moved for a preliminary injunction requiring NIPSCO to continue taking delivery under the contract. On June 19, 1985, the district judge granted the preliminary injunction, from which NIPSCO has appealed. Also on June 19, rejecting NIPSCO's argument that it needed more time for pretrial discovery and other trial preparations, the judge scheduled the trial to begin on August 26, 1985. Trial did begin then, lasted for six weeks, and resulted in a jury verdict for Carbon County of $181 million. The judge entered judgment in accordance with the verdict, rejecting Carbon County's argument that in lieu of damages it should get an order of specific performance requiring NIPSCO to comply with the contract. Upon entering the final judgment the district judge dissolved the preliminary injunction, and shortly afterward the mine—whose only customer was NIPSCO—shut down. NIPSCO has appealed from the damage judgment, and Carbon County from the denial of specific performance. . . .

[Here the court considered a provision of the contract, saying, "This is what is known as a *force majeure* clause." The provision permitted NIPSCO to stop taking delivery of coal.]

[for any cause beyond (its) reasonable control . . . including but not limited to . . . orders or acts of civil . . . authority . . . which wholly or partly prevent . . . the utilizing . . . of the coal.]

[According to NIPSCO, the "economy purchase orders" of the Indiana Public Service Commission had prevented it, at least in part, from using the coal that it had agreed to buy. To that the court answered: "It is evident that the clause was not triggered by the orders."]

All that those orders do is tell NIPSCO it will not be allowed to pass on fuel costs to its ratepayers in the form of higher rates if it can buy electricity cheaper than it can generate electricity internally using Carbon County's coal. Such an order does not "prevent," whether wholly or in part, NIPSCO from using the coal; it just prevents NIPSCO from shifting the burden of its improvidence or bad luck in having incorrectly forecasted its fuel needs to the backs of the hapless ratepayers. . . . By signing the kind of contract it did, NIPSCO gambled that fuel costs would rise rather than fall over the life of the contract; for if they rose, the contract price would give it an advantage over its (hypothetical) competitors who would have to buy fuel at the current market price. If such a gamble fails, the result is not *force majeure*.

This is all the clearer when we consider that the contract price was actually fixed just on the downside; it put a floor under the price NIPSCO had to pay, but the escalator provisions allowed the actual contract prices to rise above the floor, and they did. This underscores the gamble NIPSCO took in signing the contract. It committed itself to paying a price at or above a fixed minimum and to taking a fixed quantity at that price. It was willing to make this commitment to secure an assured supply of low-sulphur coal, but the risk it took was that the market price of coal or substitute fuels would fall. A *force majeure* clause is not intended to buffer a party against the normal risks of a contract. The normal risk of a fixed-price contract is that the market price will change. If it rises, the buyer gains at the expense of the seller (except insofar as escalator provisions give the seller some protection); if it falls, as here, the seller gains at the expense of the buyer. The whole purpose of a fixed-price contract is to allocate risk in this way. A *force majeure* clause interpreted to excuse the buyer from the consequences of the risk he expressly assumed would nullify a central term of the contract.

[Here the court compared the market in which NIPSCO operated—a regulated one—with unregulated ones. Assuming an unregulated and fully competitive market, Judge Posner observed, if fuel costs were to drop after NIPSCO made a long-term, fixed price contract for coal, it could expect to suffer a loss. Conversely, if fuel costs were to increase, it could expect a gain at the expense of competitors. "The chance of this 'windfall' gain offsets, on an ex ante (before the fact) basis, the chance of a windfall loss if fuel costs drop."]

The Indiana Public Service Commission is a surrogate for the forces of competition, and the economy fuel orders are a device for simulating the effects in a competitive market of a drop in input prices. The orders say to NIPSCO, in effect: "With fuel costs dropping, and thus reducing the costs of electricity to utilities not burdened by long-term fixed-price contracts, you had better substitute those utilities' electricity for your own when their prices are lower than your cost of internal generation. In a freely competitive market consumers would make that substitution; if you do not do so, don't expect to be allowed to pass on your inflated fuel costs to those consumers." ... If as is likely the Public Service Commission would require NIPSCO to pass on any capital gain from an advantageous contract to the ratepayers ..., then it ought to allow NIPSCO to pass on to them some of the capital loss from a disadvantageous contract—provided that the contract, when made, was prudent. Maybe it was not; maybe the risk that NIPSCO took was excessive. But all this was a matter between NIPSCO and the Public Service Commission, and NIPSCO did not seek judicial review of the economy purchase orders.

If the Commission had ordered NIPSCO to close a plant because of a safety or pollution hazard, we would have a true case of *force majeure*. As a regulated firm NIPSCO is subject to more extensive controls than unregulated firms and it therefore wanted and got a broadly worded *force majeure* clause that would protect it fully (hence the reference to partial effects) against government actions that impeded its using the coal. But as the only thing the Commission did was prevent NIPSCO from using its monopoly position to make consumers bear the risk that NIPSCO assumed when it signed a long-term fixed-price fuel contract, NIPSCO cannot complain of *force majeure;* the risk that has come to pass was one that NIPSCO voluntarily assumed when it signed the contract.

The district judge refused to submit NIPSCO's defenses of impracticability and frustration to the jury, ruling that Indiana law does not allow a buyer to claim impracticability and does not recognize the defense of frustration....

Section 2–615 of the Uniform Commercial Code takes this approach. It provides that "delay in delivery ... by a seller ... is not a breach of his duty under a contract for sale if performance as agreed has been made impracticable by the occurrence of a contingency the non-occurrence of which was a basic assumption on which the contract was made...." Performance on schedule need not be impossible, only infeasible—provided that the event which made it infeasible was not a risk that the promisor had assumed. Notice, however, that the only type of promisor referred to is a seller; there is no suggestion that a buyer's performance might be excused by reason of impracticability. The reason is largely semantic. Ordinarily all the buyer has to do in order to perform his side of the bargain is pay, and while one can think of all sorts of reasons why, when the time came to pay, the buyer might not have the money, rarely would the seller have intended to assume the risk that the buyer might, whether through improvidence or bad luck, be unable to pay for the seller's goods or services. To deal with the rare case where the buyer or (more broadly) the paying party might have a good excuse based on some unforeseen change in circumstances, a new rubric was thought necessary, different from "impossibility" (the common law term) or "impracticability" (the Code term, picked up in Restatement (Second) of Contracts § 261 (1979)), and it received the name "frustration." Rarely is it impracticable or impossible for the payor to pay; but if something has happened to make the performance for which he would be paying worthless to him, an excuse for not paying, analogous to impracticability or impossibility, may be proper. See Restatement, supra, § 265, Comment *a* . . . .

NIPSCO is the buyer in the present case, and its defense is more properly frustration than impracticability; but the judge held that frustration is not a contract defense under the law of Indiana. . . . At all events, the facts of the present case do not bring it within the scope of the frustration doctrine, so we need not decide whether the Indiana Supreme Court would embrace the doctrine in a suitable case.

For the same reason we need not decide whether a *force majeure* clause should be deemed a relinquishment of a party's right to argue impracticability or frustration, on the theory that such a clause represents the integrated expression of the parties' desires with respect to excuses based on supervening events; or whether such a clause either in general or as specifically worded in this case covers any different ground from these defenses; or whether a buyer can urge impracticability under section 2–615 of the Uniform Commercial Code, which applies to this suit. [Much of what the court had to say about the latter question is indicated in the Note, p. 847 above.]

Whether or not Indiana recognizes the doctrine of frustration, and whether or not a buyer can ever assert the defense of impracticability under section 2–615 of the Uniform Commercial Code, these doctrines, so closely related to each other and to *force majeure* as well, . . . cannot help NIPSCO. All are doctrines for shifting risk to the party better able to bear it, either because he is in a better position to prevent the risk from materializing or because he can better reduce the disutility of the risk (as by insuring) if the risk does occur. . . .

Since impossibility and related doctrines are devices for shifting risk in accordance with the parties' presumed intentions, which are to minimize the costs of contract performance, one of which is the disutility created by risk, they have no place when the contract explicitly assigns a particular risk to one party or the other. As we have already noted, a fixed-price contract is an explicit assignment of the risk of market price increases to the seller and the risk of market price decreases to the buyer, and the assignment of the latter risk to the buyer is even clearer where, as in this case, the contract places a floor under price but allows for escalation. If, as is also the case here, the buyer forecasts the market incorrectly and therefore finds himself locked into a disadvantageous contract, he has only himself to blame and so cannot shift the risk back to the seller by invoking impossibility or related doctrines.... It does not matter that it is an act of government that may have made the contract less advantageous to one party.... Government these days is a pervasive factor in the economy and among the risks that a fixed-price contract allocates between the parties is that of a price change induced by one of government's manifold interventions in the economy. Since "the very purpose of a fixed price agreement is to place the risk of increased costs on the promisor (and the risk of decreased costs on the promisee)," the fact that costs decrease steeply (which is in effect what happened here—the cost of generating electricity turned out to be lower than NIPSCO thought when it signed the fixed-price contract with Carbon County) cannot allow the buyer to walk away from the contract....

[Affirmed.]

NOTES

(1) *We're All Frustrated.* In the case above, the court went on to hold that Carbon County was not entitled to specific performance which "would force the continuation of production that has become uneconomical." The workers and merchants where Carbon County's mine was located suffered hardship when the mine shutdown, although they were not parties to the contract or third party beneficiaries. But, assume that some of these workers and merchants entered into contracts with other parties, contracts of little value following the mine closing. Might some have plausible claims of frustration of purpose? How foreseeable is the closing of a coal mine in a highly fluctuating market for coal and electricity? More or less foreseeable than a King's coronation being cancelled?

(2) *Market Discipline and Government Discipline.* Judge Posner, in the opinion above, made these further observations about the market for electricity, assuming it to be unregulated and fully competitive:

> If NIPSCO signed a long-term fixed-price fixed-quantity contract to buy coal, and during the life of the contract competing electrical companies were able to produce and sell electricity at prices below the cost to NIPSCO of producing electricity from that coal, NIPSCO would have to swallow the excess cost of the coal. It could not raise its electricity prices in order to pass on the excess cost to its consumers, because if it did they would buy electricity at lower prices from NIPSCO's competitors.... Admittedly, the comparison between competition and regulation is not exact. [But the] purpose of public utility regulation is to provide a substitute for competition in markets (such as the market for electricity) that are naturally monopolistic. *Id.* at 275.

In discussing NIPSCO's prospect of a "windfall gain," the court did not suppose that this was NIPSCO's object in making the contract. Rather: "NIPSCO it appears was seeking a secure source of low-sulphur coal...." As one reason for thinking that, the court surmised that the Public Service Commission would not have permitted NIPSCO to translate such a gain into profit. Do you see a suggestion in the opinion that the Commission should—within limits—permit that?

(3) *Take-or-Pay: Reprise.* The character of a take-or-pay clause is described, and contrasted with that of a take-and-pay clause, p. 689 above. Consider a change of circumstances that would excuse a buyer from taking and paying, owing to frustration of purpose. Does it follow that the same buyer would be excused, in the

same circumstances, if its contract required it to take *or* pay? For an indication that *force majeure* clauses, identical in terms, might—other things being equal—excuse an "and pay" obligation, but not an "or pay" obligation, see International Minerals & Chemical Corp. v. Llano, Inc., 770 F.2d 879 (10th Cir. 1985). (There, however, the buyer got relief under a provision about adjusting its minimum purchase requirements.)

Section 4.   Half Measures

What further consequences follow when a party is excused from performance on the ground of impracticability or frustration? One consequence is that, because of the operation of the concept of constructive conditions of exchange, the other party is excused from having to render any further performance. But this will not serve to compensate either party for losses incurred in reliance on the contract before the parties were excused. To what extent have courts in such situations been receptive to "half measures"[a]—to relief that stands somewhere between strict enforcement and complete excuse?

If the contract can be treated as divisible, a court may hold that the parties are excused only as to part of their performances. See Gill v. Johnstown Lumber Co., p. 733 above. If the losses incurred in reliance have resulted in a benefit to the other party, usually restitution will be allowed. Beyond that, however, courts have not ventured far. The Restatement states, in one of its more audacious pronouncements, that if the traditional rules "will not avoid injustice, the court may grant relief on such terms as justice requires including protection of the parties' reliance interests." Restatement § 272. Materials below examine some of the support for that assertion.

NOTE

A Test Case. The problems addressed in this section are illustrated by the facts of a well-known British case. The outbreak of World War II made it impossible for a British firm to perform an export contract it had made to manufacture and deliver industrial (flax-hackling) machines. It had received an advance payment of £1,000 from the buyer, a Polish firm. The buyer brought the action to recover that payment. The seller objected that it had incurred expenses in preparing the machines that it could not recapture. For this discussion let it be assumed that these expenses amounted to £800.

Several ways of assigning rights to these parties can be imagined. One is to award £200 to the buyer, recognizing the buyer's restitution interest, but offsetting it by the seller's reliance interest. The House of Lords chose to award full recovery—£1000—to the buyer. Fibrosa Spolka Akcyjna v. Fairbairn Lawson Combe Barbour, Ltd., [1943] A.C. 32, 144 A.L.R. 1298. Being dissatisfied with that, Parliament redirected the law by a statute described below (p. 877).

Another possibility is to deny any recovery to the buyer, leaving matters as they stand. A "do nothing" rule has scholarly support in the United States, see p. 819

---

a. See William Young, Half Measures, 81 Colum.L.Rev. 19, 20 (1981), noting "that   half measure relief is equivalent to a court-imposed compromise."

above. That was once the so-called English rule: "that the loss must remain where it first falls, and that neither of the parties can recover of the other for anything done under the contract." Butterfield v. Byron, 27 N.E. 667, 668 (Mass.1891). In Krell v. Henry, above, it is reported that Henry made an advance payment of £25 for the use of Krell's rooms to view the coronation. The *Fibrosa* decision indicates that Krell would owe Henry restitution of that amount. Earlier, however, restitution had been denied in other cases concerning the coronation of Edward VII.

On reading the materials that follow, consider how a United States court might deal with the facts of *Fibrosa*.

IMPRACTICABILITY AND RELIANCE

To the extent that, before a party's performance became impracticable, it has conferred a benefit on the other party through part performance, the courts are receptive to a claim for restitution. Similarly, restitutionary relief is often available when a contract has been terminated by the doctrine of frustration. (*Fibrosa* is an example.) Restatement § 272 recognizes restitution as one form of relief available in these situations. A restitution award may be made also when a contract is rescinded for mistake. (Renner v. Kehl, p. 811 above, is an illustration.)

The amount of compensable benefit is sometimes debatable. A judicial pronouncement by Cardozo has been influential. The case was Buccini v. Paterno Construction Company, 170 N.E. 910 (1930). The company had engaged Alberto Buccini to give personal attention to some decorative design work, and he had died before completing it. As indicated in Note 2, p. 828 above, further performance by Buccini was excused. Recognizing that, Cardozo proceeded, in dictum,[a] as follows:

> The parties may say by their contract what compensation shall be made in the event of that excuse. The award will then conform to the expression of their will. They may leave the subject open, to be governed by the law itself. The award will then conform to the principles of liability in quasi-contract and to the considerations of equity and justice by which that liability is governed.... The interrupted work may have been better than any called for by the plans.... The value proportionately distributed may be greater than the contract price. Even so, the price, and not the value, will be the maximum beyond which the judgment may not go (Clark v. Gilbert, 26 N.Y. 279, 283). "The recovery in such a case cannot exceed the contract price, or the rate of it for the part of the service performed" (Clark v. Gilbert, *supra*). The question to be determined is not the value of the work considered by itself and unrelated to the contract. The question to be determined is the benefit to the owner in advancement of the ends to be promoted by the contract.

The final sentence suggests a generous measure of restitution claims.

a. The action was one brought by Flora Buccini, as executrix of her husband's estate, to compel arbitration of the estate's claim. The court approved an award of relief, relying on an arbitration term in the contract.

NOTES

(1) *The Case of Cutter's Contingency.* Cutter, a seaman of the 18th century, signed on in Jamaica as second mate aboard the ship *Governor Parry*. His pay was to be thirty guineas [one guinea being worth £1.05], "provided he proceeds, continues and does his duty as second mate in the said ship from hence to the port of Liverpool." The ship sailed from Jamaica on August 2 with Cutter on board and arrived at Liverpool on October 9, but Cutter had died on September 20. The usual wage for a second mate on such a voyage, if fixed by the month for a round-trip voyage, was £4 per month, roughly a quarter of what Cutter had been promised. Cutter's administratrix sued for the thirty guineas. *Held:* Judgment for defendant.

"[I]f there been no contract between these parties, all that the intestate could have recovered ... for the voyage would have been eight pounds; whereas here the defendant contracted to pay thirty guineas provided the mate continued to do his duty as mate during the whole voyage, in which case the latter would have received nearly four times as much as if he were paid for the number of months he served. He stipulated to receive the larger sum if the whole duty were performed, and nothing unless the whole of that duty were performed; it was a kind of insurance." Cutter v. Powell, 101 Eng.Rep. 573 (King's Bench 1795).

Do you agree? In what sense was there "a kind of insurance"? Does Cutter v. Powell illustrate what Cardozo said with reference to death as an excuse: "The parties may say by their contract what compensation shall be made in the event of that excuse"?

(2) *The Case of the House Halfway.* Owner contracted with Mover to have a building on Third Street relocated to First Street, at a fixed price. When Mover had gotten it about halfway, and quit work for the night, it was consumed by fire, through no fault of Mover. Owner disclaimed any liability, and Mover sued for the fair value of the services rendered in the work down to the time of the fire. Mover obtained a judgment on a jury verdict (amount unspecified), and Owner appealed. *Held:* Affirmed. Angus v. Scully, 57 N.E. 674 (Mass.1900). Do you find support for this decision in Cardozo's statement, "The question to be determined is the benefit to the owner in advancement of the ends to be promoted by the contract"?

Young v. City of Chicopee

Supreme Judicial Court of Massachusetts, 1904.
186 Mass. 518, 72 N.E. 63.

■ HAMMOND, J. This is an action to recover for work and materials furnished under a written contract providing for the repair of a wooden bridge forming a part of the highway across the Connecticut river. While the work was in progress the bridge was totally destroyed by fire without the fault of either party, so that the contract could not be performed. The specifications required that the timber and other woodwork of the carriageway, wherever decayed, should be replaced by sound material, securely fastened, so that the way should be in "a complete and substantial condition." As full compensation both for work and materials, the plaintiff was to receive a certain sum per thousand feet for the lumber used "on measurements made after laying and certified by the engineers"; or, in other words, the amount of the plaintiff's compensation was measured by the number of feet of new material wrought into the bridge. That the public travel might not be interfered with more than was reasonably necessary, the contract provided that no work should be begun until material for at least one-half of the repairs contemplated should be "upon the job." With this condition the plaintiff complied, the lumber, which, at the time of the fire had not been used, being distributed "all along the bridge" and upon the river banks. Some of this lumber was destroyed by the fire. At the trial the defendant did not dispute its liability to pay for the work done upon and materials wrought into the structure at the time of the fire (Angus v. Scully, 176 Mass. 357, 57 N.E. 674, 49 L.R.A. 562, 79 Am.St.Rep. 318, and cases there cited), and the only question before us is whether it was liable for the damage to the lumber which was distributed as above stated and had not been used. It is to be noted that there had been no delivery of this lumber to the defendant. It was brought "upon the job," and kept there as the lumber of the plaintiff. The title to it was in him, and not in the defendant. Nor did the defendant have any care or control over it. No part of it belonged to the defendant until wrought into the bridge. The plaintiff could have exchanged it for other lumber. If at any time during the progress of the work before the fire the plaintiff had refused to proceed, the defendant, against his consent, could not lawfully have used it. Indeed, had it not been destroyed, it would have remained the property of the plaintiff after the fire. Nor is the situation changed, so far as respects the question before us, by the fact that the lumber was brought there in compliance with the condition relating to the commencement of the work. This condition manifestly was inserted to insure the rapid progress of the work, and it has no material bearing upon the rights of the parties in relation to the lumber. It is also to be borne in mind in this connection that the compensation for the whole job was to be determined by the amount of lumber wrought into the bridge. The contract was entire. By the destruction of the bridge each party was excused from further performance, and the plaintiff could recover for partial performance. The principle upon which the plaintiff can do this is sometimes said to rest upon the doctrine that there is an implied contract upon the owner of the structure upon which the work is to be done that it shall continue to exist, and therefore, if it is destroyed, even without his fault, still he must be regarded as in default, and so liable to pay for what has been done. Niblo v. Binsse, 40 N.Y. 476; Whelen v. Ansonia Clock Co., 97 N.Y. 293. In Butterfield v. Byron, 153 Mass. 523, 27 N.E. 669, 12 L.R.A. 571, 25 Am.St.Rep. 654, it was said by Knowlton, J., that there was "an implied assumpsit for what has properly been done by either [of the parties], the law dealing with it as done at the request of the other, and creating a liability to pay for it its value." In whatever way the principle may be stated, it would seem that the liability of the owner in a case like this should be measured by the amount of the contract work done which at the time of the destruction of the structure had become so far identified with it as that, but for the destruction, it would have inured to him as contemplated by the contract. In the present case the defendant, in accordance with this doctrine, should be held liable for the labor and materials actually wrought into the bridge. To that extent it insured the plaintiff. But it did not insure the plaintiff against the loss of lumber owned by him at the time of the fire, which had not then come into such relations with the bridge as, but for the fire, to inure to the benefit of the defendant, as contemplated by the contract. The cases of Haynes v. Second Baptist Church, 88 Mo. 285, 57 Am.Rep. 413, and Rawson v. Clark, 70 Ill. 656, cited by the plaintiff, seem to us to be distinguishable from this case.

The exceptions therefore must be sustained, and the verdict set aside. In accordance with the terms of the statement contained in the bill of exceptions, judgment should be entered for the plaintiff in the sum of $584 damages, and it is so ordered.

NOTES

(1) *You're Both Excused*. In *Chicopee*, the court observes that "[b]y the destruction of the bridge each party was excused from further performance." On what basis do you imagine an excuse was granted for each party?

(2) *Multiple and Divisible Contracts*. As a variation on the facts of Young's case, suppose that he had made separate contracts with the City—one for the sale of materials, requiring payment by the City when they arrived at the work site, and another for doing the repair work. Would the fire have had different consequences? If so, how different?

Given a single contract, for work and materials, assume that the fire was confined to the bridge, not consuming lumber stacked aside the river. How would you assess a claim by the City that it could appropriate that lumber for other projects, on the ground that the contract was divisible?

(3) *Repair v. Building*. Young's case would have been quite different if he had contracted to erect a bridge from scratch, rather than to repair one. In that case the risk of chance destruction of the bridge would have rested entirely on him, it seems, absent an agreement to the contrary. See Note 3, p. 811 above. Aside from the analogy of Taylor v. Caldwell, above, what might account for the difference between construction contracts and repair contracts?

RELIANCE INTERESTS

Restatement Chapter 11, which states rules about impracticability of performance and frustration of purpose, concludes with the statement that, in some circumstances, a court may grant relief "on such terms as justice requires including protection of the parties' reliance interests." Section 272(2). Reliance expenditures were the basis of a recovery by a subcontractor against a general contractor in Albre Marble and Tile Co. v. John Bowen Co., 155 N.E.2d 437 (Mass.1959). The court took pains to distinguish Young v. Chicopee, above. One distinction was that the court was able to ascribe the dislocating event in *Albre Marble* to some degree of fault on the part of the general contractor, whereas the event that prevented performance in Young v. Chicopee was "a fire not shown to have been caused by the fault of either party." The court found some support in its decision in Angus v. Scully, represented as "The Case of the House Halfway" in Note 2, p. 874 above.

NOTES

(1) *Coordination of Interests*. What does justice require, when competing interests are deserving of protection: a restitution interest on one side and a reliance

interest on the other? Let it be supposed that a buyer has prepaid $1,000 and the seller has incurred preparatory expenses of $800, which cannot otherwise be recouped. (Compare Note, p. 872 above.) Two eminent Britishers have advocated differing solutions: $200 to the buyer, according to one, and $600 according to the other. Professor Glanville Williams would have each party shoulder half of the unavoidable loss ($800). Lord Chancellor Simon argued for giving more protection to the seller's reliance interest, saying, "I think that will commend itself to everybody as good sense." Glanville Williams, Law Reform (Frustrated Contracts) Act 35–36 (1944). For other proposals about apportioning losses, see Leon Trakman, Winner Take Some: Loss Sharing and Commercial Impracticability, 69 Minn.L.Rev. 471 (1985); Note, 69 Yale L.J. 1054 (1960).

(2) *Why the Hurry?* In setting an appropriate amount of recovery for a prepaying buyer, such as the Polish firm Fibrosa Spolka Akcyjna (see the note at p. 872 above), it may help to know what the seller's object was in requiring an advance payment. Possibly it was to maintain the seller's cash flow. Possibly it was to avert or limit loss to the seller if the buyer should lack the resources to pay. Possibly it was to avert or limit loss to the seller if it should happen that a supervening event (*e.g.*, a war) terminated the contract after the seller had made an investment in the contract. One of these objects might, of course, operate in conjunction with another. Buyers and sellers are not usually actuated to provide for prepayments by the latter object, it is said. If they contemplate a disabling event, "their usual reaction is to take out a policy of insurance, not to provide for payment in advance." Williams, Law Reform at 36. But see the discussion of "reparations," p. 819 above.

On facing a claim for restitution of an advance payment, might a seller undercut the claim by establishing that, as the buyer understood, the seller had negotiated for the payment for one of the reasons suggested above?

(3) *Statutes.* The note at p. 872 above mentions a English statute concerning reliance interests: the Law Reform (Frustrated Contracts) Act of 1943. The statute addresses the case of a seller of goods who has received a prepayment and has incurred expenses in preparing the goods. According to the Act, "the court may, if it considers it just to do so having regard to all the circumstances of the case, allow him to retain [part of the prepayment], not being an amount in excess of the expenses so incurred." Section 1(2). This text was the subject of the views reported in Note 1 above.

Section 1514 of the California Civil Code, part of the Field Code, provides for apportionment, upon excuse from performance of an obligation, "of the consideration to which [the obligor] would have been entitled upon full performance, according to the benefits" received by the other party.

Compare Restatement § 272(2). How does it differ from these enactments?

PROBLEM

Ex Post. Reconsider Chase Precast Corp. v. Paonessa Co., p. 861 above. What would have been the result if Chase had, in accordance with its contract, produced all of the median barriers before receiving Paonessa's letter notifying it to stop?

THE *ALCOA* CASE

One of the most controversial decisions dealing with changed circumstances is Aluminum Company of America v. Essex Group, Inc., 499 F.Supp. 53 (W.D.Pa.1980). Late in 1967, after more than six months of negotiations, ALCOA contracted with Essex to convert Essex's alumina into molten aluminum by a smelting process. Performance was to take place over 16 years, with an option in Essex to extend for another five years, for a flexible price. (Alan Greenspan, the economist, assisted ALCOA in devising the pricing formula.) One of the variables in the formula represented changing production costs other than labor; for this the Wholesale Price Index—Industrial Commodities (WPI) was used as a proxy. At all events the charge to Essex was limited to 65% of an aluminum market price periodically published (the "65% cap"). In each of the first six years of operations ALCOA's profit exceeded 4¢ a pound, but by the tenth year ALCOA was incurring losses that threatened to mount to more than 75 million dollars. Other than the labor cost, that of electricity is the chief outlay in converting alumina. Since energy costs are a relatively small component of the WPI, electricity rates had begun swiftly to outpace that index, owing to OPEC's influence on oil prices and to anti-pollution regulations.

In litigation between ALCOA and Essex, the trial court found, in an opinion of some forty pages, that though ALCOA had sought a profit of 4¢ a pound, the parties had foreseen that the profit might vary either way, between 1¢ and 7¢ a pound, and reformed the price term so as to yield ALCOA not less than a 1¢ per pound profit (unless the 65% cap should be less). The case was settled while on appeal.

NOTES

(1) *The Ground in ALCOA.* It is not certain that the *ALCOA* decision was one dependent on a change of circumstances. The court first concluded that the parties had contracted under the influence of a mutual mistake, warranting some kind of relief for ALCOA. Then it gave reasons for continuing with a discussion of changed circumstances.

The parties' mistake, according to the court, concerned the capacity of the WPI "to work as [they] expected it to work." The court found that they chose the WPI after a careful investigation, showing that it had, for a number of years, tracked fairly well ALCOA's non-labor costs. According to Comment *a* to Restatement § 151, a party's "prediction or judgment as to events to occur in the future, even if erroneous, is not a 'mistake' as that word is defined here." See also the discussion of claim settlements, p. 820 above. Is *ALCOA* consistent with the Comment? The court said that the parties had made an error "of fact rather than one of simple prediction of future events"—had made a mistaken assumption that "was essentially a present actuarial error." Are you convinced?

(2) *The Remedy in ALCOA.* The ALCOA case occasioned extensive scholarly comment. The court's remedy—reformation of the price—played to mixed reviews. Professor Richard Speidel expressed reservations, but was generally sympathetic. He referred to the case as "a trail blazer" and has written of its "new 'spirit' of contract law." See Speidel, Court–Imposed Price Adjustments Under Long–Term Supply Contracts, 76 Nw.U.L.Rev. 369 (1981). Professor John Dawson took issue with Speidel. He described the case as "grotesque." It was, he said "the only instance in which an American judge has tried to dictate entirely different substantive terms ... in a contract that was still being actively performed." Also: "Does anyone seriously contend that a judge ... becomes better equipped than the parties concerned to reconcile their divergent, often conflicting interests, to devise the terms that can govern a complex enterprise and ensure its future survival?" Dawson, Judicial Revision of Frustrated Contracts: The United States, 64 B.U.L.Rev. 1, 26, 35–36 (1984). For the results of a survey of general counsel,

indicating approval of judicial price adjustment, see Russell J. Weintraub, A Survey of Contract Practice and Policy, 1992 Wis.L.Rev. 1, 41–45. In Unihealth v. U.S. Healthcare, Inc., 14 F.Supp.2d 623 (D.N.J.1998), the court, relying on *ALCOA*, asserted its "right to fashion an equitable remedy by modifying the price term of a contract the principal purpose of which had been frustrated."

(3) *Significance of Concessions.* Scholars have occasionally suggested that changed circumstances may place a party under an obligation to negotiate in good faith with respect to a modification. See Speidel, as cited above. But courts have not been receptive to this suggestion. See, for example, L.C. Williams Oil Co., Inc. v. Exxon Corp., 625 F.Supp. 477 (M.D.N.C.1985), rejecting the argument "that Exxon was under a good faith obligation to modify the existing contract terms when Williams's circumstances changed."

This is not to say, however, that a court will ignore a party's reasonable proposal for a concession in the face of changed circumstances. See Lloyd v. Murphy, 153 P.2d 47 (Cal.1944), in which a dealer in new cars suffered from wartime restrictions and ultimately vacated his leased quarters. Before that, the landlords had offered to reduce the rent and to waive prohibitions in the lease against uses they had not consented to, and against subletting. In a major statement on the law of frustration of purpose, Justice Traynor denied relief to the tenant, emphasizing the value of the landlord's concession. The inference might be that the tenant's obligation turned on how the landlords chose to refashion the terms of the lease.

(4) *Renegotiation Clauses.* On entering into a long-term contract, the parties may perceive a high risk of changing conditions and so may choose to provide for renegotiation in specified circumstances. The drafter faces several challenging questions. How, first, to specify those circumstances? Second, what standards should govern the process of renegotiation? And third, what consequence should follow from a failure to agree? For a case involving a provision under which the parties to a long-term coal supply contract agreed to address revising the price on the occurrence "of material unforeseen events or changed conditions" which caused the price to be inequitable to one of the parties, see Kentucky Utilities Co. v. South East Coal Co., 836 S.W.2d 392 (Ky.1992).

The International Chamber of Commerce—the ICC—has addressed these questions in "drafting suggestions" for so-called hardship provisions. The suggested occasion for renegotiation is an occurrence "not contemplated by the parties [that] fundamentally alter[s] the equilibrium" of the contract and places "an excessive burden on one of the parties" in its performance, followed by a party's request for revision. Thereupon, according to the suggested term, the parties are to consult one another "with a view to revising the contract on an equitable basis, in order to ensure that neither party suffers excessive prejudice." For cases in which no agreed revision results, drafters are offered several choices. One is a provision that "the contract remains in force in accordance with its original terms." Another is to draw on third parties, either as advisers or as arbiters, leading possibly to a judicial revision. ICC, Force Majeure and Hardship 18 ff. (1985). Compare the orders entered in Oglebay Norton Co. v. Armco, p. 252 above.

PROBLEM

Seller contracted to sell a pile of lumber located on its premises to Buyer, who was to assume the risk of loss immediately and was to remove the lumber as soon as practicable. Unknown to either party, when the contract was made an underground fire was burning nearby and was likely to consume the lumber before it could be removed. In fact, it did. You represent Buyer. Mistake or erroneous prediction? What difference does it make? See Richardson Lumber Co. v. Hoey, 189 N.W. 923 (Mich.1922).

CHAPTER 10

THIRD PARTIES: RIGHTS AND RESPONSIBILITIES

When relief is sought for the breach of a contract, an objection often made is that the claimant is not in *privity* with the promisor. The claimant is a "stranger" to the contract, it is sometimes said. A claim for relief may fail on that ground, but the requirement of privity has limitations. This chapter deals with two of its major limitations. First, a claimant may be eligible to enforce a contract, although not a party to it, because the claimant is a *third-party beneficiary*. And second, a claimant may be eligible to enforce a contract right by virtue of a *transfer* (an assignment) to the claimant of that right, made by one who was a party to the contract. Also, one who has obtained a contract right by assignment may well be able to make a further assignment of the right, and so make another person eligible to enforce it. (That happened in Hamer v. Sidway, p. 34 above, in which the plaintiff acquired her claim through "several mesne assignments" from the promisee, William E. Story, 2d.) The chapter deals also with agreements in which a contracting party delegates to a third party, and that party assumes, a duty that the contract imposes on the one making the delegation. It will be seen that when an effective delegation is made, the other contracting party—the one entitled to the performance in question—is usually a third-party beneficiary of the delegation.

SECTION 1. THIRD–PARTY–BENEFICIARY CONTRACTS

The modern development of third-party-beneficiary law, at least in this country, is usually dated from the 1859 case Lawrence v. Fox, the first in this chapter. Long before then, however, claims on contracts had been made by persons who were not parties to them. The results were mixed. In 17th century England it was successfully argued that a promise to pay a woman £1,000 was enforceable by her, although it was made to her father, and although she gave nothing in exchange for the promise. Later this case was disapproved. According to a 19th century English judge, "It would be a monstrous proposition to say that a person was a party to the contract for the purpose of suing upon it for his own advantage, and not for the purpose of being sued." Tweddle v. Atkinson, 121 Eng.Rep. 762 (Q.B. 1861).

As the case law has developed in this country, it is generally accepted that an action may be maintained on a contract, in an appropriate case, by one who had no part in creating it. Probably the class of third-party-beneficiary contracts most familiar to the public at large is contracts of life insurance. It is perfectly well understood that the beneficiary of a life insurance policy may enforce a right to the death benefits even though the beneficiary did not apply for it, pay for it, or have any other connection with it.

Of course, many contracts are not in this category, and often a claimant's attempt to seize an advantage under a contract between other parties meets with failure. Together, the initial Restatement and the Restatement Second have popularized the term "incidental beneficiary" for a third party who may enjoy an advantage through the performance of a contract, but has no enforceable interest in its performance. A clear though admittedly unusual example may be helpful. A basketball referee called a foul in a game between Iowa and Purdue. Iowa lost. In Iowa City there was a novelty store stocked with Iowa University sports memorabilia. The store owners made a claim against the referee for losses due to his alleged incompetence; the game had cost Iowa its chance of a championship. One basis for the claim was an alleged contract between the referee and the Big Ten Conference, requiring him to exhibit competence in his calls. The trial court granted summary judgment for the referee. On appeal, *held:* Affirmed. Bain v. Gillispie, 357 N.W.2d 47 (Iowa App.1984).

Through the power of contracting parties to create rights in others many needs have been met, some commercial in nature, others not; and there are "procedural" conveniences also in recognizing third-party claims in contracts. Nevertheless, there are complications and inconveniences in the law of third-party beneficiaries. It will be well, in going through the chapter, to consider both aspects of the subject. When disadvantages are encountered in granting a third-party claim, it may be possible to think of an alternate arrangement that would serve the purpose better. And in many of the cases there is a challenge to skill in drafting, so as to remove doubts and promote the objects of the agreement.

———

RESTATEMENT FORMULATIONS

In the initial Restatement of Contracts, and in the Restatement Second, each of the chapters on contract beneficiaries opens with a section classifying beneficiaries. The two sections have much in common, but differ in significant ways. Each section identifies a class of "beneficiaries" called *incidental*; these are ineligible to enforce a contract between other parties, even though they would benefit from its performance. Beneficiaries eligible to enforce a contract between other parties are designated in the Restatement Second, § 302, as *intended* beneficiaries. A claimant is in this class only if "recognition of a right to performance in [the claimant] is appropriate to effectuate the intention of the [contracting] parties." (Although the parties' intention is a focus of the section, Comment *d* expands on that: "In some cases an overriding policy, which may be embodied in a statute, requires recognition of [a third party's right] without regard to the intention of the parties.")

According to Section 302, a claimant must also meet one of two qualifications. One of these is that "the performance of the promise will satisfy an obligation of the promisee to pay money to [the claimant]." The other is that "the circumstances indicate that the promisee intends to give [the claimant] the benefit of the promised performance." As to the first qualification, see the case that follows. As to the second, see Seaver v. Ransom, p. 888 below.

Section 302 is set out in full at p. 897 below, in Rathke v. Corrections Corporation. The corresponding section of the initial Restatement is set out, in part, at p. 900 below. A short selection of relevant statutes appears at p. 901 below.

NOTE

Circumventing Privity. A person or firm may qualify to enforce a contract because it was made on behalf of that entity by a person acting as an agent for the claimant—the claimant being known, in that case, as the "principal." This book, and the law reports generally, are permeated with successful actions brought by corporations on contracts negotiated for them by their agents. Also, a person having authority to act as an agent for another can make a contractual commitment on behalf of the other. Governments, as well as corporations, utilize the law of agency for taking part in commerce. When they do, the requirement of privity is affected by that body of law. The particulars of agency law are scarcely examined here.

In some situations various doctrinal ideas work together to moderate the requirement of privity. The following example is given in the Restatement: "[T]he rights of employees under a collective bargaining agreement are sometimes treated as rights of contract beneficiaries, sometimes as rights based on agency principles, sometimes as rights analogous to the rights of trust beneficiaries. Or the collective bargaining agreement may be treated as establishing a usage incorporated in individual employment contracts, or as analogous to legislation." Restatement Chapter 14, Introductory Note.

INTRODUCTION TO *LAWRENCE v. FOX*

Lawrence won a judgment in this case as what would now be called an *intended* beneficiary of a contract between the promisor (Fox) and the promisee (Holly). The judgment was affirmed by a vote of 6–2 in the Court of Appeals. But two of the six judges would have said that Holly made the contract as a self-professed agent of Lawrence. That left only four judges committed to the general proposition that when "a promise [is] made to one for the benefit of another, he for whose benefit it is made may bring an action for its breach."

The arguments about that proposition centered on the law of trusts, which provides a way around the requirement of privity. "If A delivers money or property to B, which the latter accepts upon a trust for the benefit of C, the latter can enforce the trust by an appropriate action for that purpose." All the judges were agreed about that, it seems. But what if no property has been placed in trust with B? Might C nevertheless enforce a promise made by B to A? On that question the judges were divided.

A person might become a trustee by having goods delivered to him and accepting responsibility for them. Say that the owner of a batch of lead, A, delivers it to B with instructions to mold the lead into a pig and to deliver the pig to C. If B accepts that charge, the lead is the subject of an express trust, B is the trustee, and C is the beneficiary (*"cestui que trust"*). It would not be so if B had simply contracted to buy lead, mold it, and deliver it to C. Having bargained for those promises, A could enforce them. As indicated above, some judges thought that C could not, distinguishing the case in which C is the beneficiary of a trust. What differentiates the two situations supposed is the existence in one of an asset—a batch or a pig of lead—as the subject of an agreement between A and B. The existence of a trust asset, or *res*, is a requisite of a trust. For a comparison of agency and trust relationships with those growing out of third-party-beneficiary contracts, see Restatement § 302, Comment *f*.

Lawrence v. Fox

Court of Appeals of New York, 1859.
20 N.Y. 268.

Appeal from the Superior Court of the City of Buffalo. On the trial before Mr. Justice Masten, it appeared by the evidence of a bystander that one Holly, in November, 1857, at the request of the defendant [Fox], loaned and advanced to him $300, stating at the time that he owed that sum to the plaintiff [Lawrence] for money borrowed of him, and had agreed to pay it to him the then next day; that the defendant, in consideration thereof, at the time of receiving the money, promised to pay it to the plaintiff the then next day. Upon this state of facts the defendant moved for a nonsuit, upon three several grounds, viz.: That there was no proof tending to show that Holly was indebted to the plaintiff, that the agreement by the defendant with Holly to pay the plaintiff was void for want of consideration, and that there was no privity between the plaintiff and defendant. The court overruled the motion, and the counsel for the defendant excepted. The cause was then submitted to the jury, and they found a verdict for the plaintiff for the amount of the loan and interest, $344.66, upon which judgment was entered, from which the defendant appealed to the Superior Court, at General Term, where the judgment was affirmed, and the defendant appealed to this court. The cause was submitted on printed argument.

■ H. GRAY, J. The first objection raised on the trial amounts to this: That the evidence of the person present, who heard the declarations of Holly giving directions as to the payment of the money he was then advancing to the defendant, was mere hearsay and, therefore, not competent. Had the plaintiff sued Holly for this sum of money no objection to the competency of this evidence would have been thought of; and if the defendant had performed his promise by paying the sum loaned to him to the plaintiff, and Holly had afterwards sued him for its recovery, and the evidence had been offered by the defendant, it would doubtless have been received without an objection from any source. All the defendant had the right to demand in this case was evidence which, as between Holly and the plaintiff, was competent to establish the relation between them of debtor and creditor. For that purpose the evidence was clearly competent; it covered the whole ground and warranted the verdict of the jury.

But it is claimed that notwithstanding this promise was established by competent evidence, it was void for the want of consideration. It is now more than a quarter of a century since it was settled by the supreme court of this state—in an able and painstaking opinion by the late Chief Justice Savage, in which the authorities were fully examined and carefully analyzed—that a promise in all material respects like the one under consideration was valid; and the judgment of that court was unanimously affirmed by the court for the correction of errors. Farley v. Cleveland, 4 Cow. 432, 15 Am.Dec. 387; s. c. in error, 9 Cow. 639. In that case one Moon owed Farley and sold to Cleveland a quantity of hay, in consideration of which Cleveland promised to pay Moon's debt to Farley; and the decision in favor of Farley's right to recover was placed upon the ground that the hay received by Cleveland from Moon was a valid consideration for Cleveland's promise to pay Farley, and that the subsisting liability of Moon to pay Farley was no objection to the recovery. The fact that the money advanced by Holly to the defendant was a loan to him for a day, and that it thereby became the property of the defendant, seemed to impress the defendant's counsel with the idea that because the defendant's promise was not a trust fund placed by the plaintiff in the defendant's hands, out of which he was to realize money as from the sale of a chattel or the collection of a debt, the promise although made for the benefit of the plaintiff could not inure to his benefit. The hay which Cleveland bought of Moon was not to be paid to Farley, but the debt incurred by Cleveland for the purchase of the hay, like the debt incurred by the defendant for money borrowed, was what was to be paid.

That case has been often referred to by the courts of this state, and has never been doubted as sound authority for the principle upheld by it. Barker v. Bucklin, 2 Denio 45, 43 Am.Dec. 726; Canal Co. v. Westchester County Bank, 4 Denio 97. It puts to rest the objection that the defendant's promise was void for want of consideration. The report of that case shows that the promise was not only made to Moon but to the plaintiff Farley. In this case the promise was made to Holly and not expressly to the plaintiff; and this difference between the two cases presents the question, raised by the defendant's objection, as to the want of privity between the plaintiff and defendant. . . .

But it is urged that because the defendant was not in any sense a trustee of the property of Holly for the benefit of the plaintiff, the law will not imply a promise. I agree that many of the cases where a promise was implied were cases of trusts, created for the benefit of the promisor. The case of Felton v. Dickinson, 10 Mass. 287, and others that might be cited are of that class; but concede them all to have been cases of trusts, and it proves nothing against the application of the rule to this case. The duty of the trustee to pay the cestui que trust, according to the terms of the trust, implies his promise to the latter to do so. In this case the defendant, upon ample consideration received from Holly, promised Holly to pay his debt to the plaintiff; the consideration received and the promise to Holly made it as plainly his duty to pay the plaintiff as if the money had been remitted to him for that purpose, and as well implied a promise to do so as if he had been made a trustee of property to be converted into cash with which to pay. The fact that a breach of the duty imposed in the one case may be visited, and justly, with more serious consequences than in the other, by no means disproves the payment to be a duty in both. The principle illustrated by the example so frequently quoted (which concisely states the case in hand) "that a promise made to one for the benefit of another, he for whose benefit it is made may bring an action for its breach," has been applied to trust cases, not because it was exclusively applicable to those cases, but because it was a principle of law, and as such applicable to those cases.

It was also insisted that Holly could have discharged the defendant from his promise, though it was intended by both parties for the benefit of the plaintiff, and, therefore, the plaintiff was not entitled to maintain this suit for the recovery of a demand over which he had no control. It is enough that the plaintiff did not release the defendant from his promise, and whether he could or not is a question not now necessarily involved. . . .

The cases cited and especially that of Farley v. Cleveland, established the validity of a parol promise; it stands then upon the footing of a written one. Suppose the defendant had given his note in which for value received of Holly, he had promised to pay the plaintiff and the plaintiff had accepted the promise, retaining Holly's liability. Very clearly Holly could not have discharged that promise, be the right to release the defendant as it may. No one can doubt that he owes the sum of money demanded of him or that in accordance with his promise it was his duty to have paid it to the plaintiff; nor can it be doubted that whatever may be the diversity of opinion elsewhere, the adjudications in this state, from a very early period, approved by experience, have established the defendant's liability; if, therefore, it could be shown that a more strict and technically accurate application of the rules applied, would lead to a different result (which I by no means concede), the effort should not be made in the face of manifest justice.

The judgment should be affirmed.

■ JOHNSON, CH. J., DENIO, SELDEN, ALLEN and STRONG, JJ., concurred. JOHNSON, CH. J., and DENIO, J., were of opinion that the promise was to be regarded as made to the plaintiff through the medium of his agent, whose action he could ratify when it came to his knowledge, though taken without his being privy thereto.

■ COMSTOCK, J. (dissenting). The plaintiff had nothing to do with the promise on which he brought this action. It was not made to him, nor did the consideration proceed from him. If he can maintain the suit, it is because an anomaly has found its way into the law on this subject. In general, there must be privity of contract. The party who sues upon a promise must be the promisee, or he must have some legal interest in the undertaking. In this case, it is plain that Holly who loaned the money to the defendant, and to whom the promise in question was made, could at any time have claimed that it should be performed to himself personally. He had lent the money to the defendant, and at the same time directed the latter to pay the sum to the plaintiff. This direction he could countermand, and if he had done so, manifestly the defendant's promise to pay according to the direction would have ceased to exist. The plaintiff would receive a benefit by a complete execution of the arrangement, but the arrangement itself was between other parties, and was under their exclusive control. If the defendant had paid the money to Holly, his debt would have been discharged thereby. So Holly might have released the demand or assigned it to another person, or the parties might have annulled the promise now in question, and designated some other creditor of Holly as the party to whom the money should be paid. It has never been claimed that in a case thus situated the right of a third person to sue upon the promise rested on any sound principle of law. We are to inquire whether the rule has been so established by positive authority....

If A. delivers money or property to B., which the latter accepts upon a trust for the benefit of C., the latter can enforce the trust by an appropriate action for that purpose.... There is some authority even for saying that an express promise founded on the possession of a trust fund may be enforced by an action at law in the name of the beneficiary, although it was made to the creator of the trust. Thus, in Comyn, Dig. "Action on the Case upon Assumpsit," B. 15, it is laid down that if a man promise a pig of lead to A. and his executor give lead to make a pig to B., who assumes to deliver it to A., an assumpsit lies by A. against him.... [P]erhaps there is no gross violation of principle in permitting the equitable owner of [a fund held in trust] it to sue upon an express promise to pay it over. Having a specific interest in the thing, the undertaking to account for it may be regarded as in some sense made with him through the author of the trust. But further than this we cannot go without violating plain rules of law. In the case before us there was nothing in the nature of a trust or agency. The defendant borrowed the money of Holly and received it as his own. The plaintiff had no right in the fund, legal or equitable. The promise to repay the money created an obligation in favor of the lender to whom it was made and not in favor of any one else....

The judgment of the court below should, therefore, be reversed, and a new trial granted.

■ GROVER, J., also dissented.

Judgment affirmed.

NOTES

(1) *History*. "Progressive, not retrograde" is the way a New York judge spoke of third-party entitlements. Kellogg, Presiding Justice, as quoted on p. 890 below. But there have been periods of retrogression. English common law recognized third-party rights long ago, but turned about. In 1918 the New York Court of Appeals stated the "present English rule" this way: "a contract cannot be enforced by or against a person who is not a party." (See Seaver v. Ransom, below at p. 888.) See also Beswick v. Beswick, [1967] 2 All E.R. 1197 (House of Lords). But English law veered again with the enactment of the Contracts (Rights of Third Parties) Act of 1999.

A further excerpt from the *Seaver* opinion is as follows: "The general rule, both in law and equity ... was that privity between a plaintiff and a defendant is necessary to the maintenance of an action on the contract. The consideration must be furnished by the party to whom the promise was made. The contract cannot be enforced against the third party, and therefore it cannot be enforced by him. On the other hand, the right of the beneficiary to sue on a contract made expressly for his benefit has been fully recognized in many American jurisdictions, either by judicial decision or by legislation, and is said to be 'the prevailing rule in this country.'

Hendrick v. Lindsay, 93 U.S. 143; Lehow v. Simonton, 3 Colo. 346. It has been said that 'the establishment of this doctrine has been gradual, and is a victory of practical utility over theory, of equity over technical subtlety.' Brantly on Contracts, 2d Ed., p. 253. The reasons for this view are that it is just and practical to permit the person for whose benefit the contract is made to enforce it against one whose duty it is to pay.''

(2) *Restitution.* Could the decision in Lawrence v. Fox have been based on quasi-contract? Does it seem that the court would have affirmed if there had been no evidence of a promise made by Fox to Holly? Compare Callano v. Oakwood Park Homes Corp., p. 110 above.

"The underlying premise on which the third-party beneficiary doctrine is based,'' it has been said, ''is the same as that of unjust enrichment. It must appear that one party is holding sums of money which *rightfully belong* to another party.'' Litton Systems, Inc. v. Frigitemp Corp., 613 F.Supp. 1377 (S.D.Miss. 1985). Does this statement ignore the discussion in Lawrence v. Fox of "cases of trusts"?

(3) *Durability of Rights.* In Lawrence v. Fox the dissenting judges saw no merit in recognizing an entitlement that was readily defeasible. They assumed that the contracting parties could have divested Lawrence of his right at will. "[T]he arrangement ... was under their exclusive control.... So Holly might have released the demand or assigned it to another person, or the parties might have annulled the promise now in question, and designated some other creditor of Holly as the party to whom the money should be paid.'' The other judges brushed this objection aside: "It is enough that the plaintiff [Lawrence] did not release the defendant from his promise, and whether he could or not is a question not now necessarily involved.'' (Both of these passages are omitted above.)

That question has generated controversy. It is addressed in the Note at p. 913 below, Vesting of Third-party Rights.

(4) *Commentary.* For a history of the litigation in Lawrence v. Fox see Anthony Waters, The Property in the Promise: A Study of the Third Party Beneficiary Rule, 98 Harv.L.Rev. 1109 (1985). Professor Waters's investigations led him to believe that the promisee (not "Holly'' but actually one Samuel Hawley) made the loan to Fox for the purpose of gambling, as Hawley knew. For an appraisal of the case see Melvin Eisenberg, Third Party Beneficiary Contracts, 92 Colum.L.Rev. 1358, 1392–93 (1992) [cited hereafter as "Eisenberg"].

(5) *Business Buyouts.* News items often appear in a form much like this: "S Corporation will be acquired by B Corporation for $x million in cash and the assumption of $y million of debt.'' The aggregate purchase price is, at least by inference, x + y million. The bulk of the debt referred to is commonly represented by outstanding issues of S Corp bonds; but it may also reflect heavy bank borrowing by S. The subject of the purchase may be all the stock of S Corporation. Or it may be all the assets of S, leaving that firm in place, and its stock outstanding.

The effect of the buyout on creditors of S, whether banks, bondholders, or others, is generally favorable. It cannot be the case that, without their consent, they lose their entitlements against S Corporation. The standard effect is that they now have entitlements against two firms, rather than one. Lawrence v. Fox is authority for their entitlements against B Corporation. No other facts being supposed, the addition of B as their debtor is an unqualified benefit. (What subsequent turn of events would be likely to produce special rejoicing over this benefit?)

Consider how the sale transaction might be shaped so as to prevent the creditors of S from realizing an unearned surplus.

Seaver v. Ransom

Court of Appeals of New York, 1918.
224 N.Y. 233, 120 N.E. 639.

Action by Marion E. Seaver against Matt. C. Ransom and another, as executors, etc., of Samuel A. Beman, deceased. From a judgment of the Appellate Division (180 App.Div. 734, 168 N.Y.S. 454), affirming judgment for plaintiff, defendants appeal. Affirmed.

■ POUND, J. Judge Beman and his wife were advanced in years. Mrs. Beman was about to die. She had a small estate consisting of a house and lot in Malone and little else. Judge Beman drew his wife's will according to her instruction. It gave $1,000 to plaintiff, $500 to one sister, plaintiff's mother, and $100 each to another sister and her son, the use of the house to her husband for life, and remainder to the American Society for the Prevention of Cruelty to Animals. She named her husband as residuary legatee and executor. Plaintiff was her niece, 34 years old, in ill health, sometimes a member of the Beman household. When the will was read to Mrs. Beman, she said that it was not as she wanted it. She wanted to leave the house to the plaintiff. She had no other objection to the will, but her strength was waning, and, although the judge offered to write another will for her, she said she was afraid she would not hold out long enough to enable her to sign it. So the judge said, if she would sign the will, he would leave plaintiff enough in his will to make up the difference. He avouched the promise by his uplifted hand with all solemnity and his wife then executed the will. When he came to die, it was found that his will made no provision for the plaintiff.

This action was brought, and plaintiff recovered judgment in the trial court, on the theory that Beman had obtained property from his wife and induced her to execute the will in the form prepared by him by his promise to give plaintiff $6,000, the value of the house, and that thereby equity impressed his property with a trust in favor of the plaintiff. Where a legatee promises the testator that he will use property given him by the will for a particular purpose, a trust arises. O'Hara v. Dudley, 95 N.Y. 103, 47 Am.Rep. 53; Trustees of Amherst College v. Ritch, 151 N.Y. 282, 45 N.E. 876, 37 L.R.A. 305; Aherns v. Jones, 169 N.Y. 555, 62 N.E. 666, 88 Am.St.Rep. 620. Beman received nothing under his wife's will but the use of the house in Malone for life. Equity compels the application of property thus obtained to the purpose of the testator, but equity cannot so impress a trust, except on property obtained by the promise. Beman was bound by his promise, but no property was bound by it; no trust in plaintiff's favor can be spelled out.

An action on the contract for damages, or to make the executors trustees for performance, stands on different ground. Farmers' Loan & Trust Co. v. Mortimer, 219 N.Y. 290, 294, 295, 114 N.E. 389. The Appellate Division properly passed to the consideration of the question whether the judgment could stand upon the promise made to the wife, upon a valid consideration, for the sole benefit of plaintiff. The judgment of the trial court was affirmed by a return to the general doctrine laid down in the great case of Lawrence v. Fox, 20 N.Y. 268, which has since been limited as herein indicated.

Contracts for the benefit of third persons have been the prolific source of judicial and academic discussion. Williston, Contracts for the Benefit of a Third Person, 15 Harvard Law Review, 767; Corbin, Contracts for the Benefit of Third Persons, 27 Yale Law Review, 1008. The general rule, both in law and equity (Phalen v. United States Trust Co., 186 N.Y. 178, 186, 78 N.E. 943, 7 L.R.A., N.S., 734, 9 Ann.Cas. 595), was that privity between a plaintiff and a defendant is necessary to the maintenance of an action on the contract. The consideration must be furnished by the party to whom the promise was made. The contract cannot be enforced against the third party, and therefore it cannot be enforced by him. On the other hand, the right of the beneficiary to sue on a contract made expressly for his benefit has been fully recognized in many American jurisdictions, either by judicial decision or by legislation, and is said to be "the prevailing rule in this country." Hendrick v. Lindsay, 93 U.S. 143; Lehow v. Simonton, 3 Colo. 346. It has been said that "the establishment of this doctrine has been gradual, and is a victory of practical utility over theory, of equity over technical subtlety." Brantly on Contracts, 2d Ed., p. 253. The reasons for this view are that it is just and practical to permit the person for whose benefit the contract is made to enforce it against one whose duty it is to pay. Other jurisdictions still adhere to the present English Rule (7 Halsbury's Laws of England, 342, 343; Jenks' Digest of English Civil Law, sec. 229) that a contract cannot be enforced by or against a person who is not a party. Exchange Bank v. Rice, 107 Mass. 37. But see, also, Forbes v. Thorpe, 209 Mass. 570, 95 N.E. 955; Gardner v. Denison, 217 Mass. 492, 105 N.E. 359.

In New York the right of the beneficiary to sue on contracts made for his benefit is not clearly or simply defined. It is at present confined: First. To cases where there is a pecuniary obligation running from the promisee to the beneficiary, "a legal right founded upon some obligation of the promisee in the third party to adopt and claim the promise as made for his benefit." [Cases cited.] Secondly. To cases where the contract is made for the benefit of the wife (Buchanan v. Tilden, 52 N.E. 724; Bouton v. Welch, 63 N.E. 539), affianced wife (De Cicco v. Schweizer, 117 N.E. 807), or child (Todd v. Weber, 95 N.Y. 181, 193; Matter of Kidd, 80 N.E. 924) of a party to the contract. The close relationship cases go back to the early King's Bench case (1677), long since repudiated in England, of Dutton v. Poole, 2 Lev. 211 (s.c., 1 Ventris, 318, 332). See Schemerhorn v. Vanderheyden, 1 Johns, 139, 3 Am.Dec. 304. The natural and moral duty of the husband or parent to provide for the future of wife or child sustains the action on the contract made for their benefit. "This is the furthest the cases in this state have gone," says Cullen, J., in the marriage settlement case of Borland v. Welch, 162 N.Y. 104, 110, 56 N.E. 556.

The right of the third party is also upheld in, thirdly, the public contract cases [cases cited] where the municipality seeks to protect its inhabitants by covenants for their benefit; and, fourthly, the cases where, at the request of a party to the contract, the promise runs directly to the beneficiary although he does not furnish the consideration [cases cited]. It may be safely said that a general rule sustaining recovery at the suit of the third party would include but few classes of cases not included in these groups, either categorically or in principle.

The desire of the childless aunt to make provisions for a beloved and favorite niece differs imperceptibly in law or in equity from the moral duty of the parent to make testamentary provision for a child. The contract was made for the plaintiff's benefit. She alone is substantially damaged by its breach. The representatives of the wife's estate have no interest in enforcing it specifically. It is said in Buchanan v. Tilden that the common law imposes moral and legal obligations upon the husband and the parent not measured by the necessaries of life. It was, however, the love and affection or the moral sense of the husband and the parent that imposed such obligations in the cases cited, rather than any common-law duty of husband and parent to wife and child. If plaintiff had been a child of Mrs. Beman, legal obligation would have required no testamentary provision for her, yet the child could have enforced a covenant in her favor identical with the covenant of Judge Beman in this case. De Cicco v. Schweizer, supra. The constraining power of conscience is not regulated by the degree of relationship alone. The dependent or faithful niece may have a stronger claim than the affluent or unworthy son. No sensible theory of moral obligation denies arbitrarily to the former what would be conceded to the latter. We might consistently either refuse or allow the claim of both, but I cannot reconcile a decision in favor of the wife in Buchanan v. Tilden, based on the moral obligations arising out of near relationship, with a decision against the niece here on the ground that the relationship is too remote for equity's ken. No controlling authority depends upon so absolute a rule. In Sullivan v. Sullivan, 161 N.Y. 554, 56 N.E. 116, the grandniece lost in a litigation with the aunt's estate, founded on a certificate of deposit payable to the aunt "or in case of her death to her niece;" but what was said in that case of the relations of plaintiff's intestate and defendant does not control here, any more than what was said in Durnherr v. Rau [135 N.Y. 219, 32 N.E. 49], on the relation of husband and wife, and the inadequacy of mere moral duty, as distinguished from legal or equitable obligation, controlled the decision in Buchanan v. Tilden. Borland v. Welch, supra, deals only with the rights of volunteers under a marriage settlement not made for the benefit of collaterals. Kellogg, P.J., writing for the court below, well said:

> "The doctrine of Lawrence v. Fox is progressive, not retrograde. The course of the late decisions is to enlarge, not limit, the effect of that case."

The court in that leading case attempted to adopt the general doctrine that any third person, for whose direct benefit a contract was intended, could sue on it. [Next the court referred to a number of later New York precedents, some stating the doctrine in general terms, and others narrowing its application.]

But, on principle, a sound conclusion may be reached. If Mrs. Beman had left her husband the house on condition that he pay the plaintiff $6,000, and he had accepted the devise, he would have become personally liable to pay the legacy, and plaintiff could have recovered in an action at law against him, whatever the value of the house.... That would be because the testatrix had in substance bequeathed the promise to plaintiff, and not because close relationship or moral obligation sustained the contract. The distinction between an implied promise to a testator for the benefit of a third party to pay a legacy and an unqualified promise on a valuable consideration to make provision for the third party by will is discernible, but not obvious. The tendency of American authority is to sustain the gift in all such cases and to permit the donee beneficiary to recover on the contract. Matter of Edmundson's Estate (1918) 259 Pa. 429, 103 A. 277. The equities are with the plaintiff, and they may be enforced in this action, whether it be regarded as an action for damages or an action for specific performance to convert the defendants into trustees for plaintiff's benefit under the agreement.

Judgment affirmed.

NOTE

Qualified Enforcers. The New York Court of Appeals has intimated that Marion Seaver prevailed because no one else was qualified to enforce Judge Beman's promise to his wife. See Fourth Ocean Putnam Corp. v. Interstate Wrecking Co., 485 N.E.2d 208 (1985). There, on re-reading the *Seaver* opinion, the court was struck by the statement that only Ms. Seaver was substantially damaged by Judge Beman's breach. The court wrote: "we have emphasized when upholding the third party's right to enforce the contract that no one other than the third party can recover if the promisor breaches the contract." Following this, the court cited *Seaver*. Was that citation apt?

According to § 307 of the Restatement, a duty owed to an intended beneficiary may be enforced by the promisee in an action for specific performance if that remedy is otherwise appropriate. A supporting authority is Croker v. New York Trust Co., 156 N.E. 81 (N.Y.1927). That was a case like *Seaver*, except that the promisee was the suitor. The court said: "That plaintiff's remedy in law would be inadequate is obvious." *Id.* at 82.

PROBLEMS

(1) Flo, the long-time owner of "Flo's Flower," recently sold her business to Leopold. When she began it she had help from her sister Sue, in the form of a startup loan. As part of the sale transaction, Leopold agreed to pay business debts as listed by Flo. One entry on Flo's list was Sue's name and the amount of Sue's loan. Actually, by that time Sue was barred from collecting from Flo by a statute of limitations. May she now collect from Leopold? See Spiklevitz v. Markmil Corp., 357 N.W.2d 721 (Mich.App.1984).

It can be imagined that Flo included Sue in the list of her creditors because she thought it would be unbecoming to use what some people regard as a "technical" defense so as to withhold payment from anyone who had given her credit. Is there another possible reason that would make Sue's claim stronger? One that would make it weaker?

(2) The United Kingdom Ministry of Defence (the Ministry) expected that its cruise missile program would benefit from goods supplied by Trimble Navigation

Ltd.; they would permit the Ministry to latch onto the global positioning system of the U.S. Air Force. The Air Force, having received payment from the Ministry for the goods in advance, contracted with Trimble for it to supply the goods to the Ministry. (The Congress has authorized sales of military goods to foreign authorities in this manner.) The Ministry has complained that defects in the goods have imposed a cost on it. The Air Force has decided not to take action against Trimble. May the Ministry do so, as a third-party beneficiary? See United Kingdom Ministry of Defence v. Trimble Navigation Ltd., 422 F.3d 165 (4th Cir. 2005).

DETROIT INSTITUTE OF ARTS FOUNDERS SOCIETY v. ROSE, 127 F.Supp.2d 117 (D.Conn.2001). [This case concerned the disposition of a puppet that was revered as the central figure in a popular children's TV show. The original "Howdy Doody" was owned by the National Broadcasting Company (NBC). After the show closed, the puppet was held in storage and for servicing by Rufus C. Rose. After some sparring, Rose and NBC entered into an agreement represented by letters between him and a member of the NBC legal department. According to one letter from NBC, Rose and another would "arrange for the disposition of the various Howdy Doody puppets (except for *the* HOWDY DOODY, of course)," and Rose would inform NBC which puppets would be "going into the PUPPET MUSEUM," along with Howdy Doody. (Several similar puppets had been created, including a "Double Doody" which appeared as a stand-in while repairs were made on "Howdy.") Read with others, the court said, this letter indicated that the puppet in question was to go to the Detroit Institute, which, according to Rose, housed "the recognized museum of Puppetry in America."

After the death of Rose and his widow, not having received the puppet, the Institute brought an action against several defendants named Rose (one being the executor of the widow's estate).]

■ CHRISTOPHER F. DRONEY, DISTRICT JUDGE. . . . Two parties may enter into a contract to benefit a third party beneficiary who is then entitled to enforce contractual obligations without being a party to the contract and thus may sue the obligor for breach. To be valid, there need not be express language in the contract creating a direct obligation to the third party beneficiary. See Grigerik v. Sharpe [p. 908 below]. However, a contract can only result in an obligation to a third party if both parties to the contract intended to created a direct obligation from the promisor to the third party. In other words, the fact a third party may gain an incidental benefit is not enough to support third-party beneficiary status. The intent of the parties is to be "determined from the terms of the contract read in light of the circumstances attending the making of the contract, including the motives and the purposes of the parties." Delacroix [v. Lublin Graphics, Inc., 993 F.Supp. 74 (D.Conn. 1997)] at 83.

[The court entered a partial summary judgment in favor of the Institute.]

NOTE

Tangled Strings? This case was the converse of Seaver v. Ransom, it appears. Although it featured a donative intent, the would-be donor was not the promisee (NBC), but was the promisor (R.C. Rose). Possibly NBC was indifferent about the disposition of the puppet.

Consult Restatement Second § 302(1), as set out at pp. 897–898 below. Can the Institute be fitted into either clause (a) or clause (b)? If not, it was only an incidental beneficiary, was it not? Possible conclusions are that the court was in error, and that the Restatement section is unduly restrictive.

————

DISTRIBUTION NETWORKS

Now and then, a distributor of goods holding an exclusive marketing license has portrayed itself as a third-party beneficiary of an agreement between its supplier and another licensee. A representative distribution network was described this way:

> Exercycle Corporation of New York sells its machines through a national system of territorial distributorships. During the period in question here, each contract between Exercycle Corporation and the various distributors, including those of plaintiff and defendants, granted the distributor an exclusive right to sell exercycles within a specified area and each contract contained a provision similar to that of clause 11 of defendants' contract. In that clause the distributor agreed "Not to sell Exercycles in any territory other than that assigned to him by the Company under clause 1."

Exercycle of Michigan, Inc. v. Wayson, 341 F.2d 335, 336 (7th Cir.1965). The complaint made by Exercycle of Michigan was that its territory had been invaded by the defendants, in violation of clause 11. That clause was intended, the court said, "for the protection of other distributors, including plaintiff." *Id.* at 337. The promisee was, of course, Exercycle of New York.

For a contrasting case see Piccoli A/S v. Calvin Klein Jeanswear Co., 19 F.Supp.2d 157 (S.D.N.Y. 1998), a case about sales of jeans in Scandinavia. Each of the contestants held a license to distribute gear trademarked by Calvin Klein Inc. (CKI). The agreement between CKI and the defendant Jeansware prohibited Jeansware from selling Calvin Klein products outside North America and also from selling to third parties whom it knew or should have known would sell the products outside North America. Piccoli charged that Calvin Klein jeans had showed up in Scandinavian discount stores owing to a breach of that part of the Jeansware license agreement.

Piccoli purported to be a third-party beneficiary of that agreement. The court rejected that characterization. It said:

> A third party is an intended beneficiary where either (1) "no one other than the third party can recover if the promisor breaches the contract" or (2) "the language of the contract otherwise clearly evidences an intent to permit enforcement by the third party."

Id. at 162. The court based that statement on Fourth Ocean Putnam Corp. v. Interstate Wrecking Co., 485 N.E.2d 208 (N.Y.1985), a case that has had considerable influence in distributorship cases.

NOTES

(1) *Eligible Enforcers—Reprise.* An effort to enforce a promise by someone other than the recipient may gain some traction from the assumption that the promisee could not enforce it: "*Someone* ought to be in a position to enforce." That effect was suggested in *Fourth Ocean Putnam*, as quoted in *Piccoli.*

Conversely, a third party's effort to enforce may lose traction because the court assumes that the recipient of the promise might have enforced it. So it happened when a bottler of Pepsi–Cola, Bottling Company of Pittsburg, sought to enforce a promise made by another bottler to PepsiCo, Inc. The other bottler's promise was to refrain from marketing PepsiCo products outside a specified territory. A reason given for repelling the bottler's claim was that PepsiCo might have enforced the promise. The court was influenced by Piccoli v. Jeanswear. Pepsi–Cola Bottling Company of Pittsburg v. PepsiCo, Inc., 2006 WL 925606 (C.A.10) (2006).

The enforcement power of a promisee is the subject of the Note at p. 891 above. That Note points out some apparent slippage in the reasoning in *Fourth Ocean Putnam*. Possibly some slippage occurred also in *Pepsi–Cola Bottling*, for the promisee had some solid business reasons to indulge the defendant in trespassing on the claimant's territory. One was a call by nationwide customers of PepsiCo (*e.g.*, Sam's Club) for the opportunity to purchase at a single point. Another was the creation by Coca–Cola of a single "anchor" distributor. Should considerations like these weigh in a decision whether or not to entertain a third-party-beneficiary claim?

(2) *A Question of Intent.* Suppose that a producer, enlisting distributors, exacts from each of them an undertaking not to trespass on another's territory, and does so because it supposes that any qualified distributor will expect others to be so bound, and for no other reason. Can it be said in any strong sense that the producer, as promisee, has acted with the intent to confer a benefit on others?

(3) *Anti-assignment Clauses.* An illustrative clause of this sort is this:

> Neither this Agreement nor any right, remedy, obligation or liability arising hereunder or by reason thereof shall be assignable by any party to this Agreement without the prior written consent of the other parties.

Anti-assignment clauses have been invoked against distributors asserting third-party-beneficiary status. One of them suggested, it was said, "an intent to limit the obligation of the contract to the original parties." Subaru Distributors Corp. v. Subaru of America, Inc., 425 F.3d 119, 125 (2d Cir.2005). See also Sazerac Co. v. Falk, 861 F.Supp. 253 (S.D.N.Y.1994). But see Piccoli v. Jeanswear, above, at 164: "Insofar as *Sazerac* stands for the proposition that the existence of a non-assignment clause alone suffices to preclude assertion of intended third-party beneficiary status, the Court cannot agree."

Something might be said for any of three positions about an anti-assignment clause in relation to a third-party-beneficiary claim: (a) It defeats the claim, (b) It indicates that the claim has no merit, and (c) It has no bearing on the issue. Which is the best position?

———

CONTRACTS FOR PUBLIC SERVICES

The opinion in Seaver v. Ransom cites "public contract" cases in which municipalities bargained for benefits to be conferred on their inhabitants. The first of these concerned a contract made on behalf of the State of New York with A. Bleecker Banks, a publisher. Banks had agreed to supply copies of the New York Reports "to all alike," and to allot a specified quantity to any other law-book dealer. In the event of his breach, Banks was to pay liquidated damages of $100 to any aggrieved person. Banks had declined to sell to another dealer, named Little. In Little v. Banks, 85 N.Y. 258 (N.Y. 1881), the court affirmed a judgment against Banks, citing Lawrence v. Fox. Apparently the court perceived a way to distinguish that case, for it said that it need not rely on the rule laid down there. It cited other New York cases in support of "a broad principle of public policy essential to the public welfare," and applicable where officers of the State had entered into a contract "for the advantage and welfare of the public." (It can hardly be imagined that judges of the Court of Appeals would not see an advantage to the public in having their opinions distributed widely.)

Subsequent decisions by the New York Court of Appeals have placed some bounds on the broad principle of Little v. Banks. One concerned a contract by a Water Company to supply the City of Rensselaer with water for homes and commercial users, and for various city purposes. In an action against the company, the claimant alleged that a fire had spread to its warehouse owing to the company's failure to supply enough water at the pressure needed for firefighting, and that the warehouse and its contents had been destroyed. The trial court dismissed the claim. The Court of Appeals approved. Distinguishing Lawrence v. Fox, the court said: "No legal duty rests upon a city to supply its inhabitants with protection against fire." City uses of water were the subject of separate "branches" of the contract. No intention was discernible to "assume an obligation of indefinite extension to every member of the public.... [Such an intention] is seen to be the more improbable when we recall the crushing burden that the obligation would impose." As to liability in the event that a fire should lay low an entire city, "A promisor will not be deemed to have had in mind the assumption of a risk so overwhelming for any trivial reward." The court applied the method of analogy: "A promisor undertakes to supply fuel for heating a public building. He is not liable for breach of contract to a visitor who finds the building without fuel, and thus contracts a cold." H.R. Moch Co. v. Rensselaer Water Co., 159 N.E. 896, 897 (1928). See also Ultramares Corp. v. Touche, 174 N.E. 441 (1931), in which the court spoke of liability "in an indeterminate amount for an indeterminate time to an indeterminate class."

In subsequent decisions the New York high court has moderated liabilities that might have been "crushing" by means other than rejecting third-party claims. It reversed a judgment, for some half a million dollars, based on the death of the claimant's husband which she ascribed to an undue delay in responding to a call for help after a mishap on the State Thruway. The defendant was an oil company which had contracted with the Thruway Authority to sell gas and make service calls. The court found in the contract an intention by the Authority to serve the interests of motorists in some ways, as well as its own interest. But the court said that a personal-injury claim was "another matter." It relied on the doctrine of Hadley v. Baxendale, p. 657 above. Kornblut v. Chevron Oil Co., 407 N.Y.S.2d 498, *aff'd on opinion below*, 400 N.E.2d 368 (1979). Similarly, in Koch v. Consolidated Edison Co., 468 N.E.2d 1 (1984), the court was concerned about the defendant's contemplation of losses from looting and vandalism that were said to attend a massive power failure in New York City. Some of the claimants relied on agreements made by the power supplier ("Con Ed") with the State's Power Authority to provide customers with service of a stated quality. Subject to a determination whether or not Con Ed should have foreseen various losses, the court said that power users were "precisely the consumers for whose benefit . . . the agreements [were] made."

The facts of the next principal case bring it within the realm of contracts for public services, although the claimant was not a member of the public at large. (The claimant, Rathke, was a prisoner.)

NOTES

(1) *Reasoning about H.R. Moch.* Most owners of improved real property maintain insurance against serious fire losses. If the Moch Company was insured against the damage to its warehouse, and the insurer had paid it for the loss, the insurer might well have made a claim against the Water Company. As between those parties, how should the loss be allocated? Thinking about that question might lead to a choice between raising the cost of fire insurance and raising the cost of water in fire hydrants. Is that an easy choice? All the City's taxpayers had to contribute to the cost of water, whereas some of them could have done without insurance. Does that matter? (It may be noted, for what it is worth, that the City had agreed to pay the Water Company $42.50 a year for supplying each of its hydrants.)

(2) *Salmon vs. Farmers.* Farmers, favorites of the Congress, have sought to qualify as third-party beneficiaries of contracts about waters subject to management by the U.S. Bureau of Reclamation. Decisions on the point are mixed. The Court of Appeals for the Ninth Circuit has resisted, saying:

> Parties that benefit from a government contract are generally assumed to be incidental beneficiaries, and may not enforce the contract absent a clear intent to the contrary. Government contracts often benefit the public, but individual members of the public are treated as incidental beneficiaries unless a different intention is manifested.

Orff v. United States, 358 F.3d 1137 (2004) (quoting).

Orff was one of a long line of cases involving the nation's largest federal water-management project, the Central Valley [California] Project. The farmers sought relief under a contract between their water district and the United States. The Bureau had reduced the diversion of water from the Sacramento River for the protection of Chinook salmon.

According to Professor Eisenberg, "a third party should be allowed to enforce a contract where enforcement is supported by an independent reason of policy or morality and would not conflict with the contracting parties' performance objectives"; and this proposition tends to favor the enforcement of government contracts by third-party beneficiaries. Eisenberg at 1409. Can the Ninth Circuit decision in *Orff* be made to comport with that? The case that follows is another test of the proposition.

INTRODUCTION TO *RATHKE* v. *CCA*

Gus Rathke was an inmate of a prison operated by the Corrections Corporation of America (CCA). He charged CCA with having imposed discipline on him in violation of CCA's contract with the Alaska Department of Corrections. Also, he charged a firm named PharChem, Inc. with error in having prompted the discipline. According to Rathke, PharChem had violated its contract with CCA.

The discipline was based on a test for Rathke's use of marijuana. The test result would have been within the limit allowed by Alaska law. It was over the limit allowed by Arizona law, however. Apparently the two firms applied the more stringent test because the prison was in Arizona. They should have applied the more lenient one because Rathke had been convicted under the law of Alaska, not the law of Arizona.

Rathke depicted himself as a beneficiary of both CCA's contract to operate the prison and PharmChem's contract with CCA. The trial court ruled against the contract claims. On Rathke's appeal, the Alaska Supreme Court made repeated references to something it called the *"Cleary* FSA," so designating the final settlement agreement in a prior class action by Alaska prisoners. That agreement, the court said, constituted a contract between the State and its prisoners. It was incorporated by reference in the Department–CCA contract. Moreover, there were parallels between terms of the FSA and those of CCA's contract.

Rathke v. Corrections Corporation of America, Inc.

Alaska Supreme Court, 2007.
153 P.3d 303.

■ CARPENETI, JUSTICE. . . . The superior court ruled that Alaska inmates in Florence [Arizona] may not sue CCA for breach of its contract with the state since the inmates are not intended third-party beneficiaries of the contract. On appeal, Rathke argues that he is an intended third-party beneficiary by virtue of the *Cleary* FSA and its incorporation into the state's contract with CCA. In determining whether a third party is an intended beneficiary of a contract, we refer to the Restatement (Second) of Contracts. According to § 302:

> (1) Unless otherwise agreed between promisor and promisee, a beneficiary of a promise is an intended beneficiary if recognition of a right to performance in the beneficiary is appropriate to effectuate the intention of the parties and either

(a) the performance of the promise will satisfy an obligation of the promisee to pay money to the beneficiary; or

(b) the circumstances indicate that the promisee intends to give the beneficiary the benefit of the promised performance.

(2) An incidental beneficiary is a beneficiary who is not an intended beneficiary.

When applying these provisions, we have declared that the motives of the parties in executing a contract—especially the promisee[1]—are determinative. A court looks to the parties' objective motive or intent, rather than their subjective motives.[2] As a general rule, if the promised performance is rendered directly to the beneficiary, "the intent to benefit the third party will be clearly manifested."[3] For instance, with regard to a promise to pay money, where a contract exists between a debtor and a lender to pay the debtor's debt to a creditor, if the loan contract calls for the lender to pay a sum directly to the creditor, then the creditor is presumed to be the intended beneficiary of the contract, and thus the creditor may enforce that contract against the lender. This general rule also applies in other contexts where the promisor has promised to perform a duty which the promisee owes to the beneficiary. The Restatement provides the following illustration for § 302: "B promises A to furnish support for A's minor child C, whom A is bound by law to support. C is an intended beneficiary under Subsection (1)(a)." The state owes legal duties to all Alaska inmates, including those housed like Rathke at the CCA's Florence, Arizona, facility. These duties are detailed in the *Cleary* FSA, which is an enforceable contract between Alaska inmates and the state.[4] In dismissing Rathke's claim, the superior court conceded that the *Cleary* FSA gives certain rights to prisoners, but it denied third-party beneficiary status to the prisoners with regard to the state/CCA contract. The court noted that the *Cleary* FSA duties run only from the state to the inmates, while the duties in the contract between the state and CCA run only between the state and CCA. On this basis, the court concluded that state prisoners are not third-party beneficiaries of the state/CCA contract. We disagree with the superior court's analysis. First, the *Cleary* settlement is incorporated by reference into the state/CCA contract. Even more, many of its provisions are repeated virtually word for word in the CCA contract. For example, portions of the discipline section of the state/CCA contract, allegedly breached in Rathke's case, are virtually identical to the *Cleary* FSA. [The court quoted terms from each document that it considered illustrative.]

1. State v. Osborne, 607 P.2d 369, 371 (Alaska 1980) ("Ordinarily, only the promisee's ... motives are relevant.") (citing 4 A. Corbin, Corbin on Contracts § 776 (1951)). *See also* 13 Williston § 37:8 at 71 ("According to the majority rule, there is no requirement of mutual intent, as to the right of enforcement, on the part of the contracting parties; instead, it is the intent or purpose of the promisee who pays for the promise that has been generally considered as governing....").

2. See Restatement (Second) of Contracts § 2 cmt. b....

3. 13 Richard A. Lord, Williston on Contracts § 37:8 at 70 (4th ed. 2000). *See also id. at 68–69* ("[U]nder the Restatement (Second) view, a party may be deemed an 'intended beneficiary' regardless of the actual intentions of the parties, a view consistent with the objective theory of contracts generally, in that it places primary emphasis on the objective, rather than the subjective intention of the parties.").

4. Smith v. Cleary, 24 P.3d at 1247 n.3, 1251.

Additionally, the *Cleary* FSA states: "An inmate is presumed innocent of an infraction until proven guilty, and the Department has the burden of establishing guilt by a preponderance of evidence.... The determination of the inmate's guilt must be based only on evidence presented at the hearing."[5] The state/CCA contract states: "A prisoner is presumed innocent until proven guilty by a preponderance of the evidence presented at the hearing." Given this identity of provisions between the FSA and the state/CCA contract, we conclude that the prisoners are intended third-party beneficiaries of the portions of the contract which are taken directly from the FSA. The result of the superior court's order is that, although Rathke may sue the state under the *Cleary* FSA, he may not sue the state or CCA under identical provisions contained in the state/CCA contract. Such an interpretation denies Florence inmates direct redress against the very institution charged with their day-to-day care and discipline. Accordingly, we hold that Florence inmates also have the right to sue CCA for violations of the *Cleary* FSA provisions contained in the CCA's contract with the state.[6]

[Finally, the court addressed Rathke's contract claim against Pharm-Chem.] Unlike CCA's contract with the state, its contract with PharmChem does not refer to inmates or prisoners except in its attachments. Indeed, it mentions only their "specimens" to be submitted for testing. Prisoners might be said to benefit from competent drug urinalysis results reported by PharmChem (when those results are negative), but given the fact that the prisoners are not even mentioned in the contract, it is impossible to say that "the circumstances indicate that [CCA or PharmChem] intends to give [the inmates] the benefit of the promised performance."[7] Accordingly, the superior court did not err in granting summary judgment to PharmChem on Rathke's contract claim.[8]

NOTE

Individual Defendants. In a part of the opinion omitted above the court addressed a claim that Rathke made against individual employees of CCA, based on his supposed status as a third-party beneficiary of the employment contracts. According to the court, that claim had been dismissed correctly. "Generally," the court said, "an employee cannot be held liable for the breach of a contract between the employer and another party." Jones v. Central Peninsula General Hospital, 779 P.2d 783, 791 (Alaska 1989).

---

5. [*Cleary FSA*] at 63.

6. CCA has also promised to indemnify the state for any claims arising from the CCA's performance of the contract....

7. Restatement (Second) of Contracts § 302(1)(b).

8. We make no determination as to whether Rathke's complaint can be read to support a claim for negligence against PharmChem (for failure to carry out testing duties as prescribed in the contract). On remand, if Rathke's unresponsiveness to PharmChem's motion for judgment on the pleadings is found by the superior court to be excused, the court may consider this question.

FIRST RESTATEMENT

§ 133. Definition of Donee Beneficiary, Creditor Beneficiary, Incidental Beneficiary

(1) Where performance of a promise in a contract will benefit a person other than the promisee, that person is [exception omitted]:

(a) a donee beneficiary if it appears from the terms of the promise in view of the accompanying circumstances that the purpose of the promisee in obtaining the promise of all or part of the performance thereof is to make a gift to the beneficiary or to confer upon him a right against the promisor to some performance neither due nor supposed or asserted to be due from the promisee to the beneficiary;

(b) a creditor beneficiary if no purpose to make a gift appears from the terms of the promise in view of the accompanying circumstances and performance of the promise will satisfy an actual or supposed or asserted duty of the promisee to the beneficiary, or a right of the beneficiary against the promisee which has been barred by the Statute of Limitations or by a discharge in bankruptcy, or which is unenforceable because of the Statute of Frauds;

(c) an incidental beneficiary if neither the facts stated in Clause (a) nor those stated in Clause (b) exist.

NOTE

New Diction; New Law. The comparable section in the Restatement Second (see p. 897 above) is different, at least in diction. It retains the expression "incidental beneficiary," but not some others. It introduced the expression "intended beneficiary." Probably the discard of other expressions is less momentous than it seems. In Seaver v. Ransom, Marion Seaver fit the definition of "donee beneficiary"; and she fits comfortably within the category of what may now be called "intended subsection (1)(b) beneficiary." In Lawrence v. Fox, Lawrence fit the definition of "creditor beneficiary"; and he fit comfortably within the category "intended subsection (1)(a) beneficiary." For these cases, at least, the revision was only a rewording. Some courts have continued to use the discarded expressions well into this century.

For other situations the revision made a substantive difference. Identify one or more of those.

PROBLEM

The Tenant Mix. In Gianni v. R. Russell & Co., p. 368 above, a provision of Gianni's lease was that he would not sell tobacco in any form. It may be supposed that the owner of the office building had leased other space for tobacco sales. If so, should the lessee of that space be treated as a third-party beneficiary of Gianni's lease? Is this case provided for in Restatement Second § 302(1)(a)? Is it in First Restatement § 133(2)(b)? Does the law of restitution warrant a claim against Gianni by the other tenant, on the facts supposed?

In a similar case, the claimant was defeated; but the ruling was based on a statute curtailing the rights of third-party beneficiaries. Tusa v. Roffe, 791 So.2d 512 (Fla.App.2001).

STATUTES

Statutes in every state deal with some aspect of third-party claims, either to support or to suppress them. With respect to claims on insurance contracts, the text at pp. 902–903 below refers to statutes supporting third-party claims. In a number of states more comprehensive statutes provide footing for third-party claims, giving more or less detail. Three of those statutes are presented here, with elisions as indicated.

Oklahoma: 15 Okla.Stat. § 29—Beneficiary may enforce

> A contract, made expressly for the benefit of a third person, may be enforced by him at any time before the parties thereto rescind it.

West Virginia: Code § 55–8–12

> If a covenant or promise be made for the sole benefit of a person with whom it is not made, or with whom it is made jointly with others, such person may maintain, in his own name, any action thereon which he might maintain in case it had been made with him only, and the consideration had moved from him to the party making such covenant or promise.

Michigan: Compiled Laws § 600.1405

Any person for whose benefit a promise is made by way of contract, as hereinafter defined, has the same right to enforce said promise that he would have had if the said promise had been made directly to him as the promisee.

> (1) A promise shall be construed to have been made for the benefit of a person whenever the promisor of said promise had undertaken to give or to do or refrain from doing something directly to or for said person. . . .

NOTES

(1) *Prisoners' Rights: Another Look.* Consider Rathke's claim against the Corrections Corporation in light of the foregoing statutes. Was the contract between the Corporation and the Alaska Department of Corrections one made expressly for Rathke's benefit? Was it made for his sole benefit?

(2) *Direct Performance.* "A's son C is indebted to D. With the purpose of assisting C, A secures from B a promise to pay the debt to D." On these facts, according to the Restatement, D is an intended beneficiary of the promise. And so is C. Illustration 6 to § 302. According to the Michigan statute, should the promise be construed to have been made for the benefit of D? For the benefit of C?

The test of direct performance is criticized in Eisenberg at 1380–81. See also Stowe v. Smith, 441 A.2d 81 (Conn.1981): "Contracts for the benefit of a third party are enforceable without any requirement that the promisor's performance be rendered directly to the intended beneficiary." *Id.* at 83.

(3) *Builders' Duties; Builders' Rights.* Sometimes builders represent themselves as third-party beneficiaries. An example was the claimant in Eastern Steel Constructors, Inc. v. City of Salem, 549 S.E.2d 266 (W.Va.2001). The city, meaning to replace a sewer line, engaged a design professional ("the pro") to prepare plans, on the basis of which—as the pro knew—bids were to be solicited. After hearing from bidders, the city contracted for the work to be done by one of them, Eastern Steel Constructors (ESC). That work was impeded by a deficiency in the plans. ESC

brought an action against the pro for delays and added expense. The pro resisted on the ground, among others, that it was not in privity with ESC.

One lesson from this case is that third-party-beneficiary law is not the only way to circumvent the requirement of privity. ESC based its action partly on that law, but it made claims also for professional negligence and for the breach of an implied warranty accompanying the pro's plans and specifications. The trial court granted summary judgment for the pro, and ESC appealed. *Held*: Affirmed with respect to the third-party-beneficiary claim, but reversed and remanded with respect to the other claims.

Of the three statutes set out above, which is the most favorable to the former claim?

PROBLEMS

(1) A college lets a contract for the renovation of its football stadium. The general contractor subcontracts the job of reinforcing the bleachers. Given a breach by the subcontractor, would it be plausible for the college to make a claim as a third-party beneficiary of the subcontract?

(2) Suppose that a breach by the subcontractor causes a delay in reopening the stadium, and cancellation of the first game of the season. Would it be plausible for a disappointed fan, holding a ticket for that game, to make a claim as a third-party beneficiary of the subcontract? Suppose, rather, that a breach by the general contractor caused the cancellation. Would it be plausible for the fan to make a claim as a third-party beneficiary of the general contract?

————

INSURANCE CONTRACTS

Large sets of insurance contracts confer rights on third parties in ways in which, although the intentions of the parties may be represented, those intentions are ones directed by the will of others. Illustrations are given here. They stand in contrast with most insurance bought by a person on his or her life, and made payable to a family member; the buyer does not act under compulsion. But in policies of that kind the rights of the beneficiaries are likely to become entrenched, over time, at the direction of a legislature. Statutes in a widespread form make life-insurance policies *incontestable* when they have been in force for two years—incontestable in the sense, for example, that an issuer cannot avoid its policy by reason of a misrepresentation. Some paragraphs that follow illustrate what might be called incontestability in policies of property insurance and of liability insurance.

1. A business or financial relation may impel one party to it to buy insurance for the benefit of the other. It is, for example, the practice for vocational lenders, when taking a security interest in the improved real property of a borrower, to require that the borrower hold insurance on the improvements, and to insist that the policy contain a *standard mortgagee clause*. This is that clause, in a form much litigated:

> Loss or damage, if any, under this policy, shall be payable to [name and address of mortgagee] ... as interest may appear, and this insurance, as to the interest of the mortgagee only therein, shall not be

invalidated by *any act or neglect* of the mortgagor or owner of the within described property.

The words put in italics here are comprehensive. They include fraud on the insurer, committed by the mortgagor, and the failure of that party to fulfill a condition on its right to payment. This is "incontestability" in the strongest sense. Often the effect of the clause is ascribed, rather fancifully, to the existence of a separate contract between the insurer and the mortgagee. (For a more recent standard version of the clause, and its application, see Iron Horse Auto, Inc. v. Lititz Mutual Ins. Co., 156 P.3d 1221 (Kan.2007). That version states some conditions on the mortgagee's entitlement.)

2. Statutes about compensation for road injuries by way of liability insurance are numerous, prevalent, and diverse. Many of them install one or another class of persons as third-party beneficiaries of insurance contracts. The broadest class is that of persons who suffer injuries, whether to person or to property, from the negligence of others while using vehicles. Many careless users are unwilling or unable to make compensation. As a corrective, owners of vehicles are required to provide themselves with insurance against this or that measure of liability, as a condition of registration.

Standing alone, that mandate falls short of the legislative purpose in several ways. It is supplemented by a requirement that coverage extend to a user of vehicle other than its owner, assuming that the owner has given permission for the use. A term so providing—known as an "omnibus clause"—routinely establishes third-party entitlements in friends of the person named as the one insured, and members of that person's family. Often, no doubt, it reflects benevolence toward those persons on the part of an insurance buyer, but it also enhances the compensation available to victims of road injuries.

Even so, that compensation is contingent, commonly, in several ways. It is contingent on a motorist's compliance with the mandate to buy insurance. (Noncompliance may bring into play another mandated coverage, one protecting motorists against harms at the hands of uninsured, or underinsured motorists.) Compensation is contingent, by the terms of policies, in that insurers will pay only after a motorist's liability has been established. (Those terms are overridden by a few statutes authorizing "direct actions.") Compensation is contingent also on the enforceability of a motorist's policy, in the face of a defense that, say, the policy was procured by a misrepresentation. In some states, however, statutes override that defense, and so entrench the entitlements of road-injury victims.

———

THIRD–PARTY CLAIMS FOR BAD–FAITH BREACH

Having in mind that the victim of a breach of contract can sometimes enhance recovery by showing that the breach was a *bad-faith* breach, one may wonder whether or not a third-party beneficiary may do so as well. If so, it can be imagined that courts would be inclined to withhold relief altogether from third-party claimants as a way to curtail the doctrine of bad-faith breach. That would be a poor match of the means to that end, however; a better means is to discriminate among classes of beneficiaries, or types of contracts, so that only some of them sustain recoveries for bad-faith breach.

Third-party claims on insurance contracts are of special importance in this connection, for the doctrine of bad-faith breach is focused largely on insurers. The precedents show discrimination among those claims.

Insurers' duty to deal fairly and act in good faith "does not extend," it has been said, "to every party entitled to payment of insurance benefits." Anderson v. American Internat'l Specialty Lines Ins. Co., 38 P.3d 240, 241 (Okla.App. 2001), echoing Roach v. Atlas Life Ins. Co., 769 P.2d 158, 161 (Okla. 1989). In deciding about third parties to whom that duty *does* extend, a court might nominate any or all of the following persons and firms:

—One that qualifies as a person insured by the policy in question;

—One on whom the insurer is bound by the policy to confer a direct payment or other benefit;

—One of whom, as the insurer should understand, a buyer of the coverage was solicitous.

Rather than endowing entities—persons and firms—with bad-faith claims according to the favor intended by a particular buyer, a court might select one or more *coverages* commonly bought as benevolences, and assign duties of good faith to those.

The opinion in *Roach* proceeds along that line. The court said: "There must be either a contractual or statutory relationship between the insurer and the party asserting the bad faith claim before the duty arises. The beneficiary of a life insurance contract meets both criteria for assertion of the right. . . . [T]he failure to afford a cause of action for bad faith to the beneficiary of a life insurance policy would negate a substantial reason for the insured's purchase of the policy—the peace of mind and security which it provides in the event of loss." *Id.* at 161–62.

Doubtless medical-expense coverages are bought, often, for the same purpose. But it was not so, Oklahoma courts have thought, in cases about that coverage bought in conjunction with premises-liability coverage. *Anderson*, above, and Rednour v. JC & P Partnership, 996 P.2d 487 (Okla.App. 1999). (In each case, a divided court, and certiorari denied). In *Rednour* the court said: "the primary purpose behind a business owner's purchase of liability insurance is the protection of assets. Medical expense provisions in such policies principally serve that goal by reducing the likelihood of further litigation through the prompt payment of medical expenses of parties injured on the premises without the necessity of them suing the business owner and proving negligence." *Id.* at 490. Hence punitive damages were unavailable to a third-party claimant who charged that the insurer was slow to pay expenses resulting from a fall he had suffered.

PROBLEM

Al bought auto liability insurance on his car. He allowed his son Jeff to drive it. That made Jeff an insured driver, according to an omnibus clause included in the policy. Jeff gave a lift to a friend named Gina. She was injured in a collision. Gina made a claim against Jeff, charging him with negligent driving, and a claim against Al under an owners' liability statute. Jeff and Al demanded that the insurer provide defenses against Gina's claims, as required by its policy. The insurer treated the demands with unwarranted contempt. Gina won judgments against Al and Jeff. She then demanded payment from the insurer, who treated that demand with the same contempt.

Now Al, Jeff, and Gina make claims against the insurer for punitive damages by reason of bad-faith breach. Going by Oklahoma law, which of those claims is viable, if any?

Does it matter that an Oklahoma statute required Al's policy to contain the omnibus clause? See Gianfillippo v. Northland Casualty Co., 861 P.2d 308 (Okla. 1993); 47 Okl.St. § 7–324.

Verni v. Cleveland Chiropractic College

Missouri Supreme Court, 2007.
212 S.W.3d 150.

[Leonard Verni was enrolled in a dermatology class conducted by Dr. Aleksandr Makarov at the College. The faculty handbook required that members of the faculty observe some standards of decency in dealing with students. Verni brought an action against Makarov, charging that Makarov had dealt with him in violation of the handbook, and so had violated Makarov's employment contract with the College. (Verni had been dismissed by the school for having sold advance copies of Makarov's exam. He made claims against the College also, but not on the same theory.) Verni won a verdict and judgment against Makarov for $10,000. Makarov appealed.]

■ MICHAEL A. WOLFF, CHIEF JUSTICE. . . .

Verni is not a third-party beneficiary of the contract.

Verni's breach of contract claim asserts that he is a third-party beneficiary of the employment contract between Dr. Makarov and Cleveland. Dr. Makarov argues that Verni was not a party to the contract or a third-party beneficiary of the contract and, thus, did not have standing to raise the claim.

Whether Verni had standing to raise the breach of contract claim is a matter of law that this Court reviews de novo. . . . Where a question of standing has been raised, this Court has a duty to resolve that question before reaching substantive issues. . . .

Only parties to a contract and any third-party beneficiaries of a contract have standing to enforce that contract. Andes v. Albano, 853

S.W.2d 936, 942 (Mo. banc 1993).... "To be bound as a third-party beneficiary, the terms of the contract must clearly express intent to benefit that party or an identifiable class of which the party is a member." Nitro Distributing, Inc. v. Dunn, 194 S.W.3d 339, 345 (Mo. banc 2006). "In cases where the contract lacks an express declaration of that intent, there is a strong presumption that the third party is not a beneficiary and that the parties contracted to benefit only themselves." *Id.* "Furthermore, a mere incidental benefit to the third party is insufficient to bind that party." *Id.*

This matter is resolved by examining the contract's language. OFW Corp. v. City of Columbia, 893 S.W.2d 876, 879 (Mo.App. 1995). The contract is a one-page document providing that Dr. Makarov would be a full-time faculty member of Cleveland for one year. The contract required him to be on campus a certain amount of time each week and outlined his teaching duties. In return, the contract provided Dr. Makarov's salary and employment benefits. Although the contract might incidentally provide a benefit to Cleveland students, it does not clearly express any intent that Dr. Makarov was undertaking a duty to benefit Verni or a class of students.

The contract also required Dr. Makarov to comply with the policies and procedures stated in Cleveland's faculty handbook and with any institutional modification thereof. Verni alleges that Dr. Makarov violated the handbook's requirement that faculty members treat students with courtesy, respect, fairness, and professionalism. The handbook also provides that students are entitled to expect such treatment. Assuming, for the sake of argument, that the faculty handbook is a binding part of the employment contract, this language does not overcome the strong presumption that the contract was executed solely for the parties' own benefit.

Undoubtedly, Verni and all of Cleveland's students are incidental beneficiaries of employment contracts between the college and faculty members, but not every person who is benefited by a contract may bring suit to enforce that contract. Rather, only those third-parties who are clearly intended beneficiaries may do so. Verni is not entitled to third-party beneficiary status under the contract between Cleveland and Dr. Makarov because the terms of the contract do not directly and clearly express the intent to benefit Verni or any class of which Verni claims to be a member.

The judgment of the circuit court against Dr. Makarov on Verni's breach of contract claim is reversed.

ATTORNEY–CLIENT CONTRACTS AND THIRD PARTIES

The courts have looked with some favor on charges against attorneys of substandard performance of contracts with their clients, brought by persons and firms other than clients. The Restatement, Third, of the Law Governing Lawyers states some circumstances in which a lawyer owes a duty of care to a non-client, and says that the enforcement of that duty "may promote the lawyer's loyal and effective pursuit of the client's objectives." Section 51. An illustration states a case in which an attorney botched the execution of a will, so that a person named in it—"Non-client"—was deprived of an intended benefit. According to the illustration, the attorney would be accountable to Non-client for negligence. A well-known supporting authority is Lucas v. Hamm, 364 P.2d 685 (Cal.1961). It happens also that an attorney pursuing a claim has an obligation to someone other than the client—someone whose hopes ride on the claim. See Oxendine v. Overturf, 973 P.2d 417 (Utah 1999).

On the other hand, courts and scholars have often taken note of countervailing considerations. The Maryland high court has expressed serious reservations about claims of the kind made in *Lucas*. Noble v. Bruce, 709 A.2d 1264 (1998), and Ferguson v. Cramer, 709 A.2d 1279 (1998). Indeed, in *Lucas* itself the court declined to castigate the defendant attorney, saying that he had stumbled over a rule of property law that had "long perplexed the courts and the bar." Also, the case is distinguishable when a non-client tries to show that a will is less favorable to him than the testator wished it to be. See Stowe v. Smith, 441 A.2d 81 (Conn.1981), where the court observed that a claim of that kind may be especially difficult to win. Difficult, perhaps, but winnable on extreme facts; see Young v. Williams, 645 S.E.2d 624 (Ga.App. 2007).

A non-client suing on a promise made by an attorney to a client cannot expect an easy victory when it appears that the interests of the claimant and the client were at odds. For illustrations, see California Public Employees' Retirement System [CalPERS] v. Shearman & Sterling, 741 N.E.2d 101 (N.Y.2000), and Baker v. Coombs, 219 S.W.3d 204 (Ky.App.2007). In *CalPERS*, the law firm was charged with fault in documenting an investment. The court observed that CalPERS and the client were on opposite sides of an agreement between the two, and "did not share at all times the same interests." Janice Baker's claim against Coombs grew out of his representation of James Collins when she brought a divorce proceeding against Collins. Disapproving her claim, the court said that Coombs "had a contractual obligation to represent Collins *against* Baker" (emphasis by the court).

NOTES

(1) *Putting the Client First.* The Restatement, Third, of the Law Governing Lawyers alludes to situations in which enforcement would "significantly impair the lawyer's performance of obligations to the client." One case supposed is that in which an attorney is hesitant to prepare a will for a client. If the attorney has a doubt about the client's mental capacity, and imagines a successful will contest, she might worry about being held liable to the winner of that contest—a rightful heir—for the legal expense of winning. A worry like that might deter an attorney, it is thought, from providing a service meritorious in itself. See § 51 and Comment *f* and Illustration 4 thereto. See also Caba v. Barker, 145 P.3d 174 (Or.2006), indicating that a client cannot fairly expect a lawyer, drafting a will, to make it invulnerable to a will contest—cannot, that is, absent an express undertaking to that effect.

(2) *Wanted: Enforcers.* A court resisting a third-party claim against a lawyer may take comfort in the fact that the client may press a claim for disservice by the lawyer. See Ferguson v. Cramer, above. But that is cold comfort if the client has died. Given a defective will, it has been said, the normal case is that the testator's

estate "is not injured ... except to the extent of fees paid.... Unless the beneficiaries can recover against the attorney, no one could do so and the social policy of preventing future harm would be frustrated." Bucquet v. Livingston, 129 Cal.Rptr. 514, 521 (Cal.App.1976). See also the Note at p. 891 above.

Grigerik v. Sharpe

Supreme Court of Connecticut, 1998.
247 Conn. 293, 721 A.2d 526.

[Joseph Grigerik contracted to buy a tract of undeveloped land from Edward Lang for $16,000. He had offered $9,000 for the property "as is," but agreed to the higher price because of Lang's undertaking to get the town's approval of the tract as a building lot. Because the tract was adjacent to a reservoir, the town sanitarian had told the parties that they needed an engineer to prepare a site plan for drainage. Lang contracted for that work—including the design of a septic sewage-disposal system—with Gary Sharpe and a firm with which Sharpe was associated. According to evidence in the case (although Sharpe denied it), Lang told Sharpe that he needed the site plan in order to obtain approval of the land as a building lot and that he had a buyer for the land if the town granted approval. The site plan having been prepared, and approved by the sanitarian, the sale went through. Later, however, when Grigerick applied for a building permit, it was denied. The town sanitarian (a new one) and state authorities concluded that the tract was not suited to a septic system.

Grigerik brought this action against Sharpe and his firm, alleging (i) professional negligence, and (ii) an entitlement as third-party beneficiary of the services contracts. A judgment was entered for Grigerik, on the jury's verdict. (The facts as stated above were those that might reasonably have been found by the jury.) On an appeal by Sharpe, the judgment was reversed by the Appellate Court. That court ruled that (i) the negligence claim was barred by a statute of limitations, and (ii) there was error in charging the jury about third party beneficiary law. For the latter point the Appellate Court relied on the decision in Stowe v. Smith, 441 A.2d 81 (Conn.1981), saying, "we have concluded that the implications of that decision have changed the law and that such a mutual intent of the promisor and promisee is no longer necessary for a beneficiary to have a right to enforce the contract." Grigerik v. Sharpe, 699 A.2d 189, 196 (Conn.App.1997).

Against those rulings Grigerik brought the present appeal. The court disagreed with the first, and wrote as follows about the second.]

■ BORDEN, J. The dispositive issues in this certified appeal are: ... (2) whether it is the intent of the promisee of a contractual obligation, rather than the intent of both of the parties to the contract, which determines whether a third party is a beneficiary of the contract in question.... We conclude that: (1) [a] seven year limitations period ... applies to this action; and (2) it is the intent of both parties to a contract that determines whether a third party is a beneficiary of a contract. Accordingly, we reverse the judgment of the Appellate Court.

... With respect to the breach of contract count, the trial court instructed the jury that, in order for the plaintiff to recover as a third party beneficiary to the contract, he was required to establish that he was either an intended, a contemplated, or a foreseeable beneficiary of the contract between Lang and the defendants.[1]

... With respect to the breach of contract count, the Appellate Court concluded that the trial court's instructions were flawed in two respects: first, in favor of the plaintiff, by permitting him to recover as a foreseeable, rather than an intended beneficiary of the contract; second, in favor of the defendants, by requiring that both parties, rather than just the promisee of the contractual obligation in question, intended to benefit the plaintiff. Accordingly, the Appellate Court reversed the judgment of the trial court, ordered that judgment be rendered for the defendants on the negligence count, and ordered a new trial on the breach of contract count....

... As noted earlier, the jury found that the plaintiff was a foreseeable third party beneficiary of the contract between the defendants and Lang, and returned a verdict in favor of the plaintiff on the plaintiff's breach of contract count.

[Here the court considered its decision in Stowe v. Smith, 441 A.2d 81 (1981), as support for the Grigerik's claim. The court concluded that its traditional rule about third-party-beneficiary claims had not been changed, "by *Stowe* or any other decision of this court," and that "the intent of both parties to a contract determines whether a third party has contract rights as a third party beneficiary." The court conceded that, in *Snowe*, it had made reference to some remarks by Professor Arthur Corbin in opposition to taking guidance from the intent of the parties.[a] But the passage, taken as a whole, did not support Grigerik's argument, the court said.]

1. The trial court instructed the jury as follows: "In light of all the evidence, you must determine whether [the plaintiff] was an intended, contemplated or foreseeable third party which was to derive a benefit from the contract for professional services entered into between the defendants and [Lang]. You must determine that it was intended, contemplated and foreseeable that any buyer of the property would derive a benefit from the contract or you may determine that it was intended, contemplated or foreseeable that [the plaintiff] specifically would derive a benefit from the contract. If you find that it was intended that [the plaintiff] was an intended, contemplated or foreseeable beneficiary to the contract, then you must find that [the plaintiff] was a third party beneficiary to the contract. In summary, if you determine that [the plaintiff] was a third party beneficiary to the contract and that the defendants breached the contract, then [the plaintiff] is entitled to the damages caused him as a result of the breach."

a. The passage in *Stowe* is this, as adapted from 441 A.2d 83 n. 1: "Commenta-

tors generally look upon the intent of the promisee, if the promisee had any relevant intent, as governing whether a third party may enforce a contract as a donee beneficiary. Restatement (Second), Contracts, c. 6, Introductory Note and § 133 (Tent. Draft 1973); 2 Williston, Contracts (3d Ed.) § 356A, pp. 836, 839 n.19; 4 Corbin, Contracts § 776, p. 16.

"Williston has criticized Colonial Discount Co. v. Avon Motors, Inc., 75 A.2d 507 (1950), and Byram Lumber & Supply Co. v. Page, 146 A. 293 (1929), for proposing as a universal test of third party rights the intent of the contracting parties to impose on the promisor a direct obligation to the third party. 2 Williston, op.cit. § 356A, pp. 838–39.

"Corbin views the ideas that lie behind such terms as 'purpose,' 'motive,' and 'intention' as obscure and elusive. 4 Corbin, op.cit. § 776, pp. 14–15. The problem before the courts, he says, 'is to draw the line between those third persons whose benefit is so indirect and incidental that it is not sound policy to let them enforce the contract, and those other persons whose benefit is so direct and

Moreover, we disagree with Professor Corbin's view that the concept of "intent" is too "obscure and elusive" to be helpful in determining the contract rights of third parties. 4 A. Corbin, Contracts (1951) § 776, pp. 14–15. We traditionally have relied on the intent of the parties to determine whether a contract has been formed, as well as to determine the meaning of the terms of the contract. See [three cases cited]. We are unpersuaded, therefore, that the concept of intent is any more elusive in the context of determining whether third parties have enforceable rights under the contract.

In support of the view that the presence of a third party beneficiary issue is determined solely by the intention of the promisee, the Appellate Court also relied on 2 Restatement (Second), Contracts § 302 (1981), and concluded that "the notion that the promisor and promisee must share the same intent is at variance with most authorities." Grigerik v. Sharpe, *supra*, 45 Conn.App. 784. Our reading of § 302 of the Restatement (Second) does not support that reliance. That provision provides in relevant part: "Unless otherwise agreed between promisor and promisee, a beneficiary of a promise is an intended beneficiary if recognition of a right to performance in the beneficiary is *appropriate to effectuate the intention of the parties and* ... the circumstances indicate that the promisee intends to give the beneficiary the benefit of the promised performance." 2 Restatement (Second), *supra*, § 302(1)(b). Thus, the language of the Restatement (Second) suggests that the right to performance in a third party beneficiary is determined both by the intention of the contracting parties and by the intention of one of the parties to benefit the third party.

We decline, therefore, to alter our traditional test for determining whether a third party has enforceable contract rights. We reaffirm that the intent of both parties, rather than just one of the parties to a contract, determines whether a third party is to be afforded third party beneficiary status under a contract.

Applying this standard to the facts of the present case, we conclude that the plaintiff cannot prevail on his breach of contract claim. The jurors specifically found that the plaintiff had not proven that he was an intended beneficiary of the contract between Lang and the defendants. See [editors' footnote a, above]. The plaintiff, therefore, did not establish that it was the intent of the parties that he be a third party beneficiary of the contract.

Although the jury found that the plaintiff was a foreseeable beneficiary of the contract, we agree with the Appellate Court that foreseeability is a tort concept, and the fact that a person is a foreseeable beneficiary of a contract is not sufficient for him to claim rights as a third party beneficiary. To import the concept of foreseeability into the law governing contracts, which is premised "on the concept that mutual obligations entered into voluntarily should be enforced," would significantly reduce contracting

substantial and so closely connected with that of the promisee that it is economically desirable to let them enforce it. The law would profit greatly if the courts would concentrate upon this aspect of the problem and cease to state the questions merely in terms of the supposed 'intent' of the parties. 4 Corbin, op.cit. § 786, p. 95."

parties' ability to control, through the negotiated exchange of promises and consideration, the scope of their contractual duties and obligations.

With respect to the negligence count, the judgment of the Appellate Court is reversed and the case is remanded to that court [with directions]. With respect to the breach of contract count, the judgment of the Appellate Court is reversed and the case is remanded to that court with direction to remand it to the trial court with direction to render judgment for the defendants on that count.

NOTES

(1) *Mutual Intent.* The court stood by an inquiry into the intent of the promisor, as well as an inquiry into the intent of the promisee. It found support in Section 302 of the Restatement. The section speaks both of "the intention of the parties" and the intention of the promisee. A reader might well wonder why.

Conceivably the "intention of the parties" is not an intention "to give the beneficiary the benefit of the promised performance," but is an intention about something else. What that something else might be is not clear. The *Grigerick* opinion simplifies matters, no doubt, with its test of mutual intent. But some readers of the Restatement may consider that test an over-simplification.

(2) *Beneficiaries of Construction Contracts.* A substantial number of third-party claims concern construction work. The contract in question is sometimes a subcontract, on which the owner makes a claim, sometimes the general contract, on which a subcontractor makes a claim, and sometimes a sub-subcontract, on which either the owner or the general contractor makes a claim. Compare Eastern Steel Constructors v. City of Salem, described above in Note 3, p. 901.

These claims are usually rebuffed. Can that be explained without reference to the intent of *both parties* to the contract in question?

(3) *A Professorial Principle.* Professor Melvin Eisenberg has harsh words for the test "intent to benefit the claimant," as generalized in the Restatement and elsewhere: *inadequate, largely meaningless.* "[T]he entire enterprise of finding [that] intent . . . is misguided. . . . [T]he intent of the contracting parties is typically to further their own interests. . . ." Eisenberg at 1381. He qualified this, however, in two ways. One concerns a promisee who acts in favor of a third party as a means to serve the promisee's own interests. The other concerns what he called "true donee beneficiaries" (*e.g.*, Marion Seaver, in Seaver v. Ransom). He was critical also of the reference in the Restatement to what the claimant might have relied upon with reason, believing that the reasonableness of reliance depends on the decision whether or not that party has an entitlement under the contract—the very issue in question. *Id.* at 1384.

What Professor Eisenberg proposed, instead, was a principle allowing for third-party entitlements "supported by reasons of policy or morality independent of contract law," and otherwise only as important means of effectuating the "objectives of the enterprise embodied in the contract"—objectives not necessarily manifested in the parties' language, but only those that the promisor knew or should have known. *Id.* at 1385.

———

THE *SEPTEMBERTIDE* CASE

Applying New York law, the Second Circuit Court of Appeals gave broad recognition to third-party rights in Septembertide Publishing, B.V. v. Stein & Day, Inc., 884 F.2d 675 (1989). Stein & Day had published, in hard cover, a book by the author Harry Patterson, who used the pseudonym "Jack Higgins." New American Library (NAL) published a paperback edition. Stein & Day was licensed to publish by an agreement with Patterson's firm, Septembertide. NAL was licensed by an agreement with Stein & Day, the "Paperback Agreement." The litigation concerned the disposition of a fund that NAL had paid into court, as required by that agreement, being uncertain about the proper payee. Septembertide—hereafter "the author"—made a claim to the fund, and was awarded the bulk of it by the district court.

That award depended, it was thought, on a finding that the author was an intended beneficiary of NAL's promise, in the Paperback Agreement, to pay Stein & Day. The other agreement, between the author and Stein & Day, required that Stein & Day pay to the author a major share of any licensing proceeds it received. The appellate court affirmed the ruling that the author was an intended beneficiary.

As to the intention of Stein & Day, the court relied on several other circumstances. One was that the two agreements had been entered into on successive days. Also, the Paperback Agreement identified the author and the book ("Confessional") by name. "The timing of the two agreements and the mention by name of the author and his Work suggest that Stein & Day intended [NAL's] payments to it under the Paperback Agreement to be used to satisfy its obligation to Septembertide under the [other agreement]." Stein & Day had already devoted one payment by NAL to satisfy its debt to the author.

The court seems to have thought it necessary to find also that NAL had intended a benefit to the author. As to that, the court relied largely on what NAL knew, or should have known, about the author's interest. NAL was chargeable, the court said, with knowledge of an industry practice for an author to share in a publisher's royalties resulting from sublicenses, "particularly under the present circumstances where the two agreements were executed simultaneously." Moreover, a term of the Paperback Agreement about using the publisher's influence with the author's agent "sufficiently alerted [NAL] to the fact that Septembertide had retained an interest in its Work and that Stein & Day maintained a working relationship with that author."

NOTE

Critique. The *Septembertide* court said: "The Restatement formulation captures the essence of New York law." Consider again Section 302 of the Restatement Second (p. 897 above). Does the section require a finding that a promisor—in this case NAL—intended to confer a benefit on the third party? If so, can that intention be established by proof that the promisor knew of the third party's interest? If not, how does the promisor's knowledge figure in the application of § 302, if at all?

Can *Septembertide* be squared with the following pronouncement? "In the case of a creditor-beneficiary, the established rule is that 'a contract to provide a borrower with funds to pay his debts does not give creditors a right to enforce the contract as third party beneficiaries.' Exchange Bank & Trust Co. v. Lone Star Life Ins. Co., 546 S.W.2d 948, 950 (Tex.Civ.App. 1977). Rights vest in the creditor only when the lender promises to make payment directly to the creditor. This distinction is illustrated in Restatement § 302, cmt. b, illus. 3: B lends money to A, who owes C, D, and E. 'If the promise is interpreted as a promise that B will pay C, D, and E, they are intended beneficiaries.' On the other hand, 'if the money is to be paid to A in order that he may be provided with money to pay C, D, and E, they are at most incidental beneficiaries.' " Alaska Cont'l., Inc. v. Trickey, 933 P.2d 528, 533 (Alaska 1997). See also this statement at p. 910 above: "the fact that a person is a foreseeable beneficiary of a contract is not sufficient for him to claim rights as a third party beneficiary."

VESTING OF THIRD-PARTY RIGHTS

Section 311 of the Restatement describes several circumstances in which the parties to a contract, having used it to set up an entitlement in a third party, are not at liberty to limit or eliminate that entitlement as they please. In other circumstances they are; that is a corollary of the general rule that a third-party beneficiary's entitlement is no better than that of the promisee. See p. 887 above.

The Restatement declares that the contracting parties can no longer discharge or modify a duty owed to an intended beneficiary once he has manifested assent to the promise at the request of one of the parties, or has brought suit on the promise, or has changed his position materially in justifiable reliance on it, and has so acted before receiving notification of the discharge or modification.

A stronger rule of vesting was invoked on behalf of Mrs. Roxanne Scott in Detroit Bank and Trust Co. v. Chicago Flame Hardening Co., 541 F.Supp. 1278 (N.D.Ind.1982). As her guardian, the Detroit Bank referred to a rule stated in the Restatement of 1932. By that rule, applicable to the rights of donee beneficiaries only, those rights vest when they arise. The court described the competing rules as follows:

> The old Restatement rule provided that the promisor and promisee could make no change in the promise made to a donee beneficiary unless such a power is reserved. Restatement of Contracts § 142.... Nor could a change be made by the promisor and promisee in their promise to a creditor beneficiary if he has changed his position in reliance on that promise. *Id.*; see Page, The Power of Contracting Parties to Alter a Contract for Rendering Performance to a Third Person, 12 Wis.L.Rev. 141, 149–50 (1937). Evolutionary changes in the law, however, have transformed the aforementioned position of the original Restatement. The Second Restatement of Contracts ... eliminates this distinction between a donee and creditor beneficiary and recognizes that modification on the part of the promisor and promisee is ineffective only if the agreement so provides, unless the third party

beneficiary has changed his position in reliance on the promise or has accepted, adopted or acted upon it....

Id. at 1282–83. The court rejected the "old Restatement rule," and said that it was "not followed by the vast majority of states even at the time of its adoption." The result was that the rescission of a contract for the benefit of Mrs. Scott deprived her of that benefit.

The Illinois Supreme Court espoused the Restatement Second rule in 1997, reversing its earlier position. Olson v. Etheridge, 686 N.E.2d 563.

NOTES

(1) *A Statutory Position.* The Michigan statute partly quoted on p. 901 above contains, in subsection (2), rules about the vesting of the rights of a third party as stated in subsection (1). A two-step sketch of those rules, omitting some significant features, is as follows:

(a) *Cases of the type Lawrence v. Fox.* The parties to a third-party-beneficiary contract may, subject to two qualifications, divest a right to payment that it confers on a creditor of the promisee, if performance of the promise in question was intended to discharge the promisee's debt. They may not do so with intent to hinder, delay or defraud the creditor, and may do so only *"before he has taken any legal steps to enforce said promise."*

(b) *General rule.* Otherwise, a third party's entitlement under the section becomes vested "without any act or knowledge on his part, the moment the promise becomes legally binding on the promisor." That rule can be overridden by a provision in the contract to the contrary. Also, it is subject to "conditions, limitations, or infirmities of the contract" to which the promise is subject.

What merits and demerits can be found in the Michigan statute, as described here?

(2) *Full and Partial Vesting.* The directors of a corporation adopt a resolution conferring a pension on Mrs. Anna Sachs Feinberg, a long-time employee, payment to begin when she chooses to retire. On being told of the resolution, Mrs. Feinberg transfers her holding of stock in the firm to her daughter as a gift. "I shan't need that for my retirement," she says. The stock is worth $10,000 at all material times.

Suppose that the cost to the corporation of the pension is anticipated, reasonably, to be at least $25,000. Compare two possibilities: (a) The corporation can withdraw the pension promise only upon paying Mrs. Feinberg $10,000, and (b) It cannot withdraw the promise at all. Which is the preferable rule? The Restatement appears to adopt the latter. But cf. Section 90: "The remedy ... may be limited as justice requires." And see Eisenberg at 1418–19.

SECTION 2. DELEGATION OF DUTIES

Some contractual duties are delegable, others not. A main object of this section is to examine the distinction. To say that a duty is delegable signifies that the holder of the reciprocal right cannot object to having the duty performed by someone other than the initial obligor. Many of the cases presented above illustrate delegable duties. One appears as far back as p. 299: Langman v. Alumni Association. Dr. Langman was an initial obligor, having incurred a debt upon acquiring a property that she later donated to the UVA Alumni Association. In connection with the "gift," the Alumni Association undertook to satisfy Langman's debt. That is, she *delegated* her duty to the Association. A money debt is a paradigm of delegable duty. If the Association had tendered payment to Langman's creditor, the creditor would not have been heard to object that the money should have come from her. It is not that the creditor would have been likely to make that objection; almost all creditors are content to take payment from any source. That fact goes a long way toward explaining why an obligation to pay a fixed sum of money is within the category "delegable duty." A similar delegation was made in Lawrence v. Fox, p. 883 above, Holly having delegated to Fox the duty to pay Lawrence.

At the extreme, nondelegable duties are easy to distinguish. A standard example is that of a singer, engaged to perform in public. In this connection, one court has mentioned the exceptional talent of the late Luciano Pavarotti ("the great tenor"). The court supposed this case: Pavarotti contracts with the agency operating a city airport to sing in its terminal "in order to soothe the souls of weary travelers." Pavarotti enters bankruptcy and a trustee is appointed to manage his bankruptcy estate. Relying on a provision of the Bankruptcy Code about executory contracts, the trustee attempts to delegate the responsibility for singing to the pop star Michael Jackson. After stating that case, the court said that the agency could not be compelled to accept performance by Jackson. The performance is of a type, the court suggested, "that depends upon the identity of the party that is to perform" (*e.g.*, Pavarotti). Metropolitan Airports Commm'n v. Northwest Airlines, Inc., 6 F.3d 492 (7th Cir. 1993). Presumably the converse would hold: If Jackson had made the contract and had entered bankruptcy, the agency could not be compelled to accept a vocal recital by Pavarotti instead. If a more extreme example of non-delegable duties is wanted, consider those undertaken by the parties entering into a contract of marriage. The Restatement criterion is whether or not the obligee has "a substantial interest in having [a particular] person perform or control the acts promised." Section 318(2).

Metropolitan Airports Comm'n was actually a case about a lease of airport space. The tenant being in bankruptcy, the question was whether or not the Airports Commission could be compelled to deal with a substitute tenant. As to that, the court said that the payment of rent pursuant to a lease is "hardly the type of performance that depends upon the identity of . . . the lessee." Of course a lease may require action by the lessee of some other type, as to which the lessor can decline to accept performance by a surrogate.

NOTE

Delegation as a Threat. It may be that the "substantial interest" test does not capture fully the interest of a promisee in shunning strangers as potential delegates of the promised undertaking. A commentator has suggested that a stranger "may have a greater willingness to breach [greater than that of the initial promisor] in the hope of getting some collateral gain." Richard Epstein, Why Restrain Alienation?, 85 Colum.L.Rev. 970, 983 (1985). (Oddly, this observation appears in connection with assignments, although many assignments are not accompanied by a delegation.)

Professor Epstein's observation can be countered, at least in part, by two others. First, a promisor is likely to be averse to making a delegation to anyone prone to breach; see the text that follows. And second, if a person or firm bargaining for a promise is fearful that the other party will delegate performance to someone prone to breach, the concern can be allayed by an appropriate "no delegation" term. See the text below at p. 917: UCC Article 2 and the Restatement.

———

DELEGATION ≠ ABSOLUTION

The delegation of a contract obligation does not of itself absolve the obligor of its duty. For absolution, the assent of the obligee is required. Given that assent, the result is a novation; see pp. 298–299 above. The rule of ongoing obligation is so firmly established that any deviation from it can be regarded as an aberration. (The case described in the Note that follows appears to be an aberration.) The rule is exemplified by the liability fixed on an insurer, CIGNA, as to which the court said:

. . . CIGNA is still liable.

Many a debtor wishes that by such an expression of an intention to delegate he could get rid of his debts. . . . [Nonetheless, t]he debtor's duty remains absolutely unchanged. The performance required by a duty can often be delegated; but by such a delegation the duty itself is not escaped.

In re Integrated Res. Life Ins. Co., 562 N.W.2d 179, 182–83 (Iowa 1997) (quoting 4 Arthur L. Corbin, Corbin on Contracts § 866 (1951) (citations and alterations omitted)).

NOTES

(1) *Running with the Land*. Aldon Companies, Inc., a housing developer, sold a lot in a "subdivision" unit (Lot 9, Unit 1) to John and Kathy Paniaguas ["the couple"], and improved it according to their specifications. According to Aldon's contract with the couple, it was required that a uniform quality of improvements be maintained on other lots within the subdivision. That covenant was not observed, the couple charged, saying that its breach diminished the value of their home. The trial court dismissed their claim against Aldon, and they appealed.

Another transaction critical to the decision had occurred some years after the Aldon–Paniaguas sale: Aldon had sold to another developer, Endor, Inc., the lots in Unit 1 that it had not disposed of. That sale transferred to Endor the rights and obligations of Aldon arising from its dealings with the couple, including the one stated above about quality. It was Endor's work on the lots it acquired that offended the couple.

The ruling below was affirmed in Paniaguas v. Endor, Inc., 847 N.E.2d 967 (Ind.App.2006). The court's reasoning followed this line:

(a) Aldon's obligation to the claimants was delegable. "[T]his court cannot conclude that Aldon's personal development of the . . . subdivision is so essential to the purchase agreements between [the claimants] and Aldon as to preclude the assignment of the obligation to Endor."

(b) Aldon "assigned" its obligation to Endor. Alson's obligation to "maintain a specified level of quality development was effectively transferred to Endor."

(c) Thereafter the obligation was Endor's, not Aldon's.

The court concluded that the claimants' remedy, if any, "lies . . . against Endor."

It is possible that the court was misled by its own observation, in an earlier case, about covenants affecting real property:

> Covenants are either personal, enforceable only by the original parties to an agreement, *or* they "run with the land." When covenants run with the land, they may be enforced against remote grantees. The ruling in *Paniaguas* appears to rest on reading the foregoing sentence as if it ended ". . . remote grantees *only*."

(2) *Duty Bonded to Status*. The expression "non-delegable duty" has a different meaning when used at one remove or more from contract law. It refers, often, to a duty attendant on a *status*.

According to the Restatement, Second, of Torts, the expression is used to describe, for example, a duty of one (an "employer") who engages an independent contractor—a duty that the employer "is not free to delegate to the contractor. [The duty] requires the person upon whom it is imposed to answer for it that care is exercised by anyone, even though he be an independent contractor, to whom the performance of the duty is entrusted." Liability may rest on an employer who has not himself been at fault. "The liability imposed is closely analogous to that of a master for the negligence of his servant." But it is not that. The quotations above are taken from the Introductory Note to a Restatement topic titled "Harm Caused by Negligence of a Carefully Selected Independent Contractor"—Chapter 15, Topic 2.

Another non-delegable duty is that of an attorney appointed as the guardian of an incompetent person. A sanction can be imposed on the attorney for having delegated responsibility for managing that person's assets to an assistant and having failed to supervise the assistant. Disciplinary Counsel v. Young, 862 N.E.2d 504 (Ohio 2007).

————

UCC ARTICLE 2 AND THE RESTATEMENT

The primary Article 2 provisions about delegation of duties appear in UCC § 2–210. They resemble those of the Restatement in important ways, but are more detailed. As to the Restatement, see § 318, quoted in part on p. 915 above. The Code section is similar in that it deprives a party—seller or buyer—of the power to perform its duties through a delegate if "the other party has a substantial interest in having the original promisor perform or control the acts required by the contract." Subsection (1). *Question*: As between a manufacturer of goods and its customer, which is the more likely to have that interest?

Both the Restatement and the Code use the phrase "unless otherwise agreed," but they do so in opposite directions. In the former the phrase serves to liberate a promisor to make a delegation that would otherwise be foreclosed by the "substantial interest" standard, whereas in the Code the phrase appears to foreclose delegation even when that standard would not. Compare Restatement § 318(2) with UCC § 2–210(1), and compare § 318(1): "... contrary to ... the terms of his promise."

Both sections concur with the statement above that the delegation of a contract obligation does not of itself absolve the obligor of its duty. Section 318(3) and UCC § 2–210(1).

The opinions in the case presented next (*Sally Beauty*, p. 919) concern the first sentence of UCC § 2–210(1): "A party may perform its duties through a delegate unless...."

TERMS OF DELEGATION

A hospital terminated a contract it had made with a firm it had engaged to do construction work; the firm ("Walsh") was in default. Walsh had engaged a subcontractor to do structural steel and other work on the project. Some of that work had been done before the termination, and not paid for; so the subcontractor alleged in a complaint against the hospital. Following the termination of the main contract, the hospital had received from Walsh a document reading, in part, "Walsh hereby assigns to Presbyterian Hospital ... the contract between Walsh and Metropolitan Steel [the subcontractor]." The subcontractor contended that, by accepting that assignment, the hospital became chargeable with making good on Walsh's duty to pay. *Held*: Complaint dismissed. A.C. Associates v. American Bridge Division of the U.S. Steel Industries, Inc., 1989 WL 1111034 (S.D.N.Y. 1989). Apparently the claimant was actually a sub-subcontractor; but the court dealt with the matter as if the facts were as stated here.)

UCC § 2–210 did not govern the case. But it speaks to analogous cases in which a seller or buyer of goods makes an assignment in terms that are similarly indeterminate: "of 'the contract' or of 'all my rights under the contract' or an assignment in similar general terms." For those cases Subsection (5) states that, unless the language or the circumstances indicate the contrary, the assignment "is also a delegation of performance of the duties of the assignor."

The Restatement tracks that statement in Subsection (1) of § 328. And in Subsection (2) it adds, as the Code does, a provision about the claim of Metropolitan Steel against Presbyterian Hospital ("intended beneficiary" vs. recipient of the assignment, given an acceptance).

NOTES

(1) *Land-sale Contracts*. With respect to land-sale contracts and the responsibilities of assignees, the authorities are in disarray. New York courts have never accepted that a person taking an assignment of the purchaser's "contract" thereby becomes accountable to the vendor. The leading case is Langel v. Betz, 164 N.E. 890 (1928). (The opinion there cites Seaver v. Ransom, p. 888 above.) When, in 1967, the matter came before the American Law Institute, in connection with the Restatement Second, there was a face-off between advocates of the *Langel* rule and advocates of a *Caveat*:

> The Institute expresses no opinion as to whether the rule stated in Subsection (2) applies to an assignment by a purchaser of his rights under a contract for the sale of land.

The *Caveat* won, 47–44.

(2) *Common Sense?* S, a manufacturer of goods, contracts to sell a quantity of them to a customer, B. The contract prohibits B from delegating its duty to pay for the goods. B makes an assignment to D of "all my rights under the contract," describing the contract, and D accepts. S now finds it desirable to deliver the goods to D and to collect the price from D. (The price is over-market, and B is insolvent.) An applicable statute provides that the prohibition on delegation is enforceable, and that an attempt at delegation in violation of the prohibition is "not effective." Does the statute bar S from enforcing the contract against D?

The statutory rule—"not effective"—appears in a proposed amendment to UCC Article 2: UCC § 2–210(2)(d). As in Article 2 as it stands, the proposed amendment makes B's assignment into a delegation of duties as well.

Question (a): What does common sense say about appending a delegation of duty to B's assignment of "all my rights"? Question (b): What does common sense say about nullifying the delegation, when enforcing it would be to the benefit of S?

INTRODUCTION TO *SALLY BEAUTY CO.* v. *NEXXUS PRODUCTS CO.*

There is an idea in the law that "in dealing with a corporation a party cannot rely on what may be termed the human equation in the company." New York Bank Note Co. v. Hamilton Bank Note Engraving & Printing Co., 73 N.E. 48, 52 (N.Y.1905). A reading of cases from New York courts has raised a doubt that they "would impose the same implied duty of personal service upon a contracting corporation as [they] would on an individual under the same circumstances." Arnold Productions, Inc. v. Favorite Films Corp., 298 F.2d 540 (2d Cir.1962). In contrast, when there is a change in the membership of a professional partnership having ongoing services contracts with clients, there is often good reason to doubt that the "new firm" may maintain the entitlements of the former partnership as of right.

Yet the decisions relating to delegation of contract obligations do not insist on a sharp dichotomy. Something of a "personal character" has been ascribed to a corporation, owing to its distinctive charter powers and the applicable laws governing the liabilities of its officers and stockholders. See the first case cited above. For partnership cases an illustration is City of North Kansas City v. Sharp, 414 F.2d 359 (8th Cir.1969). "The essence of the professional service cases," the court said, "is that the critical partner, for one reason or another, is no longer available to render those services. Here the critical partners were available and the record indicates ... that they were able to, and did, function collectively."

In the opinions that follow serious questions are raised about the degree of "personal trust and confidence" that existed in an inter-corporate relation, as compared with that between, say, a lawyer and a client.

Sally Beauty Co. v. Nexxus Products Co.

United States Court of Appeals, Seventh Circuit, 1986.
801 F.2d 1001.

[In July of 1981 the Best Barber Beauty & Supply Company was acquired by, and merged into, the Sally Beauty Company, a Dallas-based firm. Both firms were distributors of hair care and beauty products to retail stores and hair styling salons. Sally Beauty succeeded to Best's rights and interests in all of Best's contracts. One of these was a letter agreement of August 2, 1979, with Nexxus Products, a California firm founded in that year, which formulated and marketed hair care products through independent distributors. The agreement provided for introducing and promoting Nexxus products in the Texas market; it made Best the exclusive distributor of these in Texas (except for El Paso). Prices to Best were specified; and Nexxus agreed to provide support, such as maintaining a technician in the territory and helping to pay for an annual seminar, with a "guest artist." Nexxus agreed not to terminate the agreement except on an anniversary date, and then upon 120 days' notice and upon buying back Best's inventory of Nexxus products at cost. "[We] look forward to a long and successful business relationship," Best wrote.

Nexxus renounced its obligations when Best was merged into Sally Beauty. Sally Beauty was a wholly-owned subsidiary of a company (Alberto–Culver) which was a major manufacturer of hair-care products and, thus, a direct competitor of Nexxus in the hair-care market: "we have great reservations about allowing our NEXXUS products to be distributed by a company which is, in essence, a direct competitor."

Sally Beauty sued Nexxus, charging it with breach of contract and violation of antitrust laws. Nexxus made a motion for summary judgment on the former claim.]

■ CUDAHY, CIRCUIT JUDGE. ... Nexxus ... argued that the distribution agreement it entered into with Best was a contract for personal services, based upon a relationship of personal trust and confidence between Reichek and the Redding family. As such, the contract could not be assigned to Sally without Nexxus's consent.

In opposing this motion Sally Beauty argued that the contract was freely assignable because (1) it was between two corporations, not two individuals and (2) the character of the performance would not be altered by the substitution of Sally Beauty for Best....

In ruling on this motion, the district court [said]:

> ... [I]n this case the circumstances surrounding the contract's formation support the conclusion that the agreement was not simply an ordinary commercial contract but was one which was based upon a relationship of personal trust and confidence between the parties. Specifically, Stephen Redding, Nexxus's vice-president, travelled to Texas and met with Best's president personally for several days before making the decision to award the Texas distributorship to Best. Best itself had been in the hair care business for 40 years and its president Mark Reichek had extensive experience in the industry. It is reasonable to conclude that Stephen Redding and Nexxus would want its distributor to be experienced and knowledgeable in the hair care field and that the selection of Best was based upon personal factors such as these.

We cannot affirm this summary judgment on the grounds relied on by the district court.... Although it might be "reasonable to conclude" that Best and Nexxus had based their agreement on "a relationship of personal trust and confidence," and that Reicheck's participation was considered essential to Best's performance, this is a finding of fact....

We may affirm this summary judgment, however, on a different ground if it finds support in the record.... Sally Beauty contends that the distribution agreement is freely assignable because it is governed by the provisions of the Uniform Commercial Code (the "UCC" or the "Code"), as adopted in Texas.[1] ...

III.

... Texas applies the "dominant factor" test to determine whether the UCC applies to a given contract or transaction: was the essence of or dominant factor in the formation of the contract the provision of goods or services? ... We are confident that a Texas court would find the sales aspect of this contract dominant and apply the majority rule that such a distributorship is a contract for "goods" under the UCC.

IV.

We are concerned here with the delegation of Best's duty of performance under the distribution agreement, as Nexxus terminated the agreement because it did not wish to accept Sally Beauty's substituted performance.[2] ...

In the exclusive distribution agreement before us, Nexxus had contracted for Best's "best efforts" in promoting the sale of Nexxus products in Texas. UCC § 2–306(2).... It was this contractual undertaking which Nexxus refused to see performed by Sally.

... [We] hold that Sally Beauty's position as a wholly-owned subsidiary of Alberto–Culver is sufficient to bar the delegation of Best's duties under the agreement.

We do not believe that our holding will work the mischief with our national economy that the appellants predict. We hold merely that the duty of performance under an exclusive distributorship may not be delegated to a competitor in the market place—or the wholly-owned subsidiary of a competitor—without the obligee's consent. We believe that such a rule is consonant with the policies behind section 2–210, which is concerned with preserving the bargain the obligee has struck. Nexxus should not be required to accept the "best efforts" of Sally Beauty when those efforts are

1. The parties agree that the contract is governed by the law of Texas....

2. If this contract is assignable, Sally Beauty would also, of course, succeed to Best's rights under the distribution agreement. But the fact situation before us must be distinguished from the assignment of contract rights that are no longer executory (*e.g.*, the right to damages for breach or the right to payment of an account), which is consid-

ered in UCC section 2–210(2), Tex.Bus. & Com.Code Ann. § 2–210(b) (Vernon 1968), and in several of the authorities relied on by appellants. The policies underlying these two situations are different and, generally, the UCC favors assignment more strongly in the latter. See UCC § 2–210(2) (non-executory rights assignable even if agreement states otherwise).

subject to the control of Alberto–Culver. It is entirely reasonable that Nexxus should conclude that this performance would be a different thing than what it had bargained for. At oral argument, Sally Beauty argued that the case should go to trial to allow it to demonstrate that it could and would perform the contract as impartially as Best. It stressed that Sally Beauty is a "multi-line" distributor, which means that it distributes many brands and is not just a conduit for Alberto–Culver products. But we do not think that this creates a material question of fact in this case.[3] When performance of personal services is delegated, the trier merely determines that it is a personal services contract. If so, the duty is *per se* nondelegable. There is no inquiry into whether the delegate is as skilled or worthy of trust and confidence as the original obligor: the delegate was not bargained for and the obligee need not consent to the substitution.[4] And so here: it is undisputed that Sally Beauty is wholly owned by Alberto–Culver, which means that Sally Beauty's "impartial" sales policy is at least acquiesced in by Alberto–Culver—but could change whenever Alberto–Culver's needs changed. Sally Beauty may be totally sincere in its belief that it can operate "impartially" as a distributor, but who can guarantee the outcome when there is a clear choice between the demands of the parent-manufacturer, Alberto–Culver, and the competing needs of Nexxus? The risk of an unfavorable outcome is not one which the law can force Nexxus to take. Nexxus has a substantial interest in not seeing this contract performed by Sally Beauty, which is sufficient to bar the delegation under section 2–210,.... Because Nexxus should not be forced to accept performance of the distributorship agreement by Sally, we hold that the contract was not assignable without Nexxus' consent.[5]

The judgment of the district court is AFFIRMED.

■ POSNER, CIRCUIT JUDGE, dissenting....[a] My brethren find this a simple case—as simple (it seems) as if a lawyer had undertaken to represent the party opposing his client. But notions of conflict of interest are not the same in law and in business, and judges can go astray by assuming that the legal-services industry is the pattern for the entire economy. The lawyerization of America has not reached that point. Sally Beauty, though a wholly

---

3. We do not address here the situation in which the assignee is not completely under the control of a competitor. If the assignee were only a partially-owned subsidiary, there presumably would have to be fact-finding about the degree of control the competitor-parent had over the subsidiary's business decisions.

4. Of course, the obligee makes such an assessment of the prospective delegate. If it thinks the delegated performance will be as satisfactory, it is of course free to consent to the delegation. Thus, the dissent is mistaken in its suggestion that we find it improper—a "conflict of interest"—for one competitor to distribute another competitor's products. Rather, we believe only that it is commercially reasonable that the supplier in those circumstances have consented to such a state of

affairs. To borrow the dissent's example, Isuzu allows General Motors to distribute its cars because it considers this arrangement attractive.

Nor is distrust of one's competitors a trait unique to lawyers (as opposed to ordinary businessmen), as the dissent may be understood to suggest.

5. This disposition makes it unnecessary to address Nexxus' argument that Sally Beauty breached the distribution agreement by not giving Nexxus 120 days' notice of the Best–Sally Beauty merger.

a. Judge Posner observed that Alberto–Culver's products "mostly are cheaper than Nexxus's, and are sold to the public primarily through grocery stores and drugstores."

owned subsidiary of Alberto–Culver, distributes "hair care" supplies made by many different companies, which so far as appears compete with Alberto–Culver as vigorously as Nexxus does. Steel companies both make fabricated steel and sell raw steel to competing fabricators. General Motors sells cars manufactured by a competitor, Isuzu. What in law would be considered a fatal conflict of interest is in business a commonplace and legitimate practice. The lawyer is a fiduciary of his client; Best was not a fiduciary of Nexxus.

How likely is it that the acquisition of Best could hurt Nexxus? Not very. Suppose Alberto–Culver had ordered Sally Beauty to go slow in pushing Nexxus products, in the hope that sales of Alberto–Culver "hair care" products would rise. Even if they did, since the market is competitive Alberto–Culver would not reap monopoly profits. Moreover, what guarantee has Alberto–Culver that consumers would be diverted from Nexxus to it, rather than to products closer in price and quality to Nexxus products? In any event, any trivial gain in profits to Alberto–Culver would be offset by the loss of goodwill to Sally Beauty; and a cost to Sally Beauty is a cost to Alberto–Culver, its parent. Remember that Sally Beauty carries beauty supplies made by other competitors of Alberto–Culver; Best alone carries "hair care" products manufactured by Revlon, Clairol, Bristol–Myers, and L'Oreal, as well as Alberto–Culver. Will these powerful competitors continue to distribute their products through Sally Beauty if Sally Beauty displays favoritism for Alberto–Culver products? Would not such a display be a commercial disaster for Sally Beauty, and hence for its parent, Alberto–Culver? Is it really credible that Alberto–Culver would sacrifice Sally Beauty in a vain effort to monopolize the "hair care" market, in violation of section 2 of the Sherman Act? Is not the ratio of the profits that Alberto–Culver obtains from Sally Beauty to the profits it obtains from the manufacture of "hair care" products at least a relevant consideration?

Another relevant consideration is that the contract between Nexxus and Best was for a short term. Could Alberto–Culver destroy Nexxus by failing to push its products with maximum vigor in Texas for a year? In the unlikely event that it could and did, it would be liable in damages to Nexxus for breach of the implied best-efforts term of the distribution contract. Finally, it is obvious that Sally Beauty does not have a bottleneck position in the distribution of "hair care" products, such that by refusing to promote Nexxus products vigorously it could stifle the distribution of those products in Texas; for Nexxus has found alternative distribution that it prefers—otherwise it wouldn't have repudiated the contract with Best when Best was acquired by Sally Beauty.

Not all businessmen are consistent and successful profit maximizers, so the probability that Alberto–Culver would instruct Sally Beauty to cease to push Nexxus products vigorously in Texas cannot be reckoned at zero. On this record, however, it is slight. And there is no principle of law that if something happens that trivially reduces the probability that a dealer will use his best efforts, the supplier can cancel the contract.... At most, so far as the record shows, Nexxus may have had grounds for "insecurity" regarding the performance by Sally Beauty of its obligation to use its best efforts to promote Nexxus products, but if so its remedy was not to cancel the contract but to demand assurances of due performance. See UCC § 2–609; Official Comment 5 to § 2–306. No such demand was made. An anticipatory repudiation by conduct requires conduct that makes the repudiating party unable to perform. See Note, p. 741 below. The merger did not do this. At least there is no evidence it did. The judgment should be reversed and the case remanded for a trial on whether the merger so altered the conditions of performance that Nexxus is entitled to declare the contract broken.

NOTES

(1) *A Case for Contrast.* O.R. Concepts, Inc. (ORC) was a producer of health-care products, one of which was "Thermadrape," used to prevent hypothermia. Shareholders of the firm sold 95% of the stock in the firm to Vital Signs, Inc. (VSI). Thereafter the sales staff of VSI began distributing Themadrape. These developments led to an action against ORC, brought by the Baxter Healthcare Corporation (Baxter). Earlier, Baxter had contracted with ORC to buy quantities of Thermodrape at a price of at least $3 million, for distribution to Baxter's customers. Baxter charged ORC with having violated UCC § 2–210, and with breach of the implied covenant of good faith and fair dealing. Baxter relied on *Sally Beauty*. The court that decided that case approved the trial court's dismissal of Baxter's action. Baxter Healthcare Corp. v. O.R. Concepts, Inc., 69 F.3d 785 (1995).

What distinctions can be drawn between *Sally Beauty* and *Baxter Healthcare*? See In re Nedwick Steel Company, 289 B.R. 95 (Bankr.Ct.N.D.Ill. 2003). (The court offered distinctions between *Sally Beauty* and the trial court's decision in *Baxter Healthcare*, not noticing, apparently, the affirmance of the latter, as cited above.)

(2) *A Case for Comparison.* The decision in *Sally Beauty* was cited by the Bronco Wine Company when Bronco was sued by Scher Enterprises, Inc. Scher, formerly a wholesaler of wine, had sold its business to the J. Lewis Cooper Company. It had sold at a "greatly reduced price," Scher alleged, because Bronco had refused assent to the sale. That refusal, Scher contended, was a violation of the Michigan Liquor Control Code, in particular § 436.1305, the purpose of which is "to provide a structure for the business relations" between suppliers and wholesalers of wine. One provision of the section is this:

> A supplier shall not withhold consent to any transfer of a wholesaler's business if the proposed transferee meets the material and reasonable qualifications and standards required by the supplier.

At one point in discussion between Scher and Bronco, Bronco wrote: "you have sold your business to a distributorship which already represents our single largest competitor [Gallo]. It is simply not in the best interests of our brands to play 'second fiddle' to any product line where other alternatives are available."

Upon Bronco's motion for summary judgment, the court invited submissions by the parties which yielded much evidence. One telling bit of evidence was that Bronco supplied wine to 31 distributors who also distributed Gallo wine. A witness for Bronco sought to discount that fact in various ways. Among other things, he noted that Bronco used hundreds of distributors, and that the number 31 reflected "a 92.5% consistency in adhering to Bronco's requirements" about competing wines.

The court denied Bronco's motion. Of *Sally Beauty* it said simply that the case was "not factually analogous or legally relevant." Scher Enterprises, Inc. v. Bronco Wine Co., 178 F.Supp.2d 780, 788 (E.D.Mich. 2001). Is that right?

SECTION 3.   ASSIGNMENTS OF RIGHTS

(A)   ASSIGNABILITY OF RIGHTS; MEANS OF ASSIGNMENT

An illustration in the Restatement supposes that "B contracts with A to furnish A's family with all the oil it shall need for the ensuing year at a fixed price." Illustration 3 to § 334. The supposed contract suggests the question whether or not either party might transfer—"assign"—to someone else its rights: A to X, A's right to a supply of oil, or B to Y, B's right to payment.

Take first an attempt by B to assign to Y its right to payment for oil supplied. In all probability that will succeed, in the sense that A must pay Y for the oil that B delivers. It may succeed also in the sense that A cannot satisfy her debt by paying B. But that depends on the circumstances of the payment, as will be seen. B's attempt may fail in the sense that B retains the power to revoke the assignment. But that too depends on circumstances to be indicated.

On turning to an attempt by A to assign to X her right to a supply of oil, one must make a fundamental distinction. It is one thing to call it "success" if, should B fall short of supplying A's family with oil, it must pay damages to X. It is quite another to say that success in assigning means that B must thereafter supply the needs of *X's family*, rather than those of A's family. The Restatement Illustration mentioned above goes on to say that an assignment by A cannot confer on some other person a right that that person's family be supplied with oil. The Restatement rule on the subject appears in § 317(2), cited in the opinion that follows. The section begins: "A contractual right can be assigned unless...." One of the restrictions stated there applies when "the substitution of a right of the assignee [X] for the right of the assignor [A] would materially change the duty of the obligor [B]." That restriction appears to apply, unless the requirements of X's family are known to be nearly identical to those of A's family.

A comparable case, now dated, is Crane Ice Cream Co. v. Terminal Freezing & Heating Co., 128 A. 280 (Md. 1925), concerning a sale of ice. Terminal Freezing had agreed to supply, within limits, the requirements of one Frederick, the operator of a "simple" ice-cream plant in Baltimore. Frederick attempted to assign his rights and to delegate his duties under the contract to a much larger, multi-state operator, Crane Ice Cream. According to the court, that attempt constituted a repudiation by Frederick of his contract with Terminal.

Now that the Code is in place, it would govern on the facts of *Crane Ice Cream* and on the others supposed above, all of which concern sales of goods. UCC § 2–210(2) was the pattern for the Restatement rule quoted above. Subject to some stated exceptions, it provides that "all rights of either seller or buyer can be assigned." It is not so, however, "when the assignment would materially change the duty of the other party."

PROBLEM

Ice Lifting. Disregard the problem of delegation in *Crane Ice Cream*, and consider only the problem of assignment there, in relation to UCC § 2–210(2). Does the Code validate Frederick's assignment of his right to ice? Does it matter that Crane, having access to Terminal's ice, might adjust its production of ice cream as between its newly acquired Baltimore plant and one it already owned in Philadelphia, to take account of differences between its ice costs at the two points? How likely would that adjustment be?

NOTES

(1) *Delegation and Repudiation.* The Code does not track the statement about repudiation in *Crane Ice Cream.* What it says is that *any* assignment which delegates performance entitles the other party—B, in the illustrative case above—to demand adequate assurance of due performance from the assignee—X, in that case. It says also that the "other party" may treat the assignment as "creating reasonable grounds for insecurity." Presumably that would entitle B to demand assurance from the assigning party, A. See UCC § 2–609. One's failure to make an adequate response to a justified demand amounts, by that section, to a repudiation. (Both entitlements are stated in Subsection 6 of UCC § 2–210.)

It would seem sensible to say that B cannot require adequate assurances from *both* A and X, but must be content with an assurance from one or the other. But that is not what Subsection 6 says.

(2) *Lost Leverage.* Professor Richard Epstein has described a burden that an assignment may place on a promisor even though the assignment does not alter the prior legal position of the promisor. "The promisee is a known quantity chosen and selected by the promisor. Even if the legal system gives the promisor the same rights against the promisee's assignee, the value of those rights still may be reduced by the assignment. The promisor may not have any informal leverage against the assignee.... Preventing the assignment reduces the cost to the promisor by fixing the content of the obligation that would otherwise run to an unidentified party." Why Restrain Alienation?, 85 Colum.L.Rev. 970, 983 (1985).

Is any "informal leverage" against a chosen promisee lost if the promisee assigns only its rights and delegates none of its duties?

Herzog v. Irace

Supreme Judicial Court of Maine, 1991.
594 A.2d 1106.

■ BRODY, JUSTICE. Anthony Irace and Donald Lowry appeal from an order entered by the Superior Court (Cumberland County, *Cole, J.*) affirming a District Court (Portland, Goranites, J.) judgment in favor of Dr. John P. Herzog in an action for breach of an assignment to Dr. Herzog of personal injury settlement proceeds[1] collected by Irace and Lowry, both attorneys, on behalf of their client, Gary G. Jones. On appeal, Irace and Lowry contend that the District Court erred in finding that the assignment was valid and enforceable against them. They also argue that enforcement of the assignment interferes with their ethical obligations toward their client. Finding no error, we affirm.

The facts of this case are not disputed. Gary Jones was injured in a motorcycle accident and retained Irace and Lowry to represent him in a personal injury action. Soon thereafter, Jones dislocated his shoulder, twice, in incidents unrelated to the motorcycle accident. Dr. Herzog examined Jones's shoulder and concluded that he needed surgery. At the time, however, Jones was unable to pay for the surgery and in consideration for the performance of the surgery by the doctor, he signed a letter dated June 14, 1988, written on Dr. Herzog's letterhead stating:

> I, Gary Jones, request that payment be made directly from settlement of a claim currently pending for an unrelated incident, to John Herzog, D.O., for treatment of a shoulder injury which occurred at a different time.

Dr. Herzog notified Irace and Lowry that Jones had signed an "assignment of benefits" from the motorcycle personal injury action to cover the cost of surgery on his shoulder and was informed by an employee of Irace and Lowry that the assignment was sufficient to allow the firm to pay Dr. Herzog's bills at the conclusion of the case. Dr. Herzog performed the surgery and continued to treat Jones for approximately one year.

In May, 1989, Jones received a $20,000 settlement in the motorcycle personal injury action. He instructed Irace and Lowry not to disburse any funds to Dr. Herzog indicating that he would make the payments himself. Irace and Lowry informed Dr. Herzog that Jones had revoked his permission to have the bill paid by them directly and indicated that they would follow Jones's directions. Irace and Lowry issued a check to Jones for $10,027 and disbursed the remaining funds to Jones's other creditors. Jones did send a check to Dr. Herzog but the check was returned by the bank for insufficient funds and Dr. Herzog was never paid.

Dr. Herzog filed a complaint in District Court against Irace and Lowry seeking to enforce the June 14, 1988 "assignment of benefits." The matter was tried before the court on the basis of a joint stipulation of facts. The court entered a judgment in favor of Dr. Herzog finding that the June 14, 1988 letter constituted a valid assignment of the settlement proceeds enforceable against Irace and Lowry. Following an unsuccessful appeal to the Superior Court, Irace and Lowry appealed to this court. Because the Superior Court acted as an intermediate appellate court, we review the District Court's decision directly. See Brown v. Corriveau, 576 A.2d 200, 201 (Me.1990).

---

1. This case involves the assignment of proceeds from a personal injury action, not an assignment of the cause of action itself.

. . . [W]e will set aside trial court findings based solely upon documentary evidence and stipulated facts only if clearly erroneous . . .

Validity of Assignment

An assignment is an act or manifestation by the owner of a right (the assignor) indicating his intent to transfer that right to another person (the assignee). See Shiro v. Drew, 174 F.Supp. 495, 497 (D.Me.1959). For an assignment to be valid and enforceable against the assignor's creditor [debtor?] (the obligor), the assignor must make clear his intent to relinquish the right to the assignee and must not retain any control over the right assigned or any power of revocation. *Id.* The assignment takes effect through the actions of the assignor and assignee and the obligor need not accept the assignment to render it valid. Palmer v. Palmer, 112 Me. 149, 153, 91 A. 281, 282 (1914). Once the obligor has notice of the assignment, the fund is "from that time forward impressed with a trust; it is . . . impounded in the [obligor's] hands, and must be held by him not for the original creditor, the assignor, but for the substituted creditor, the assignee." *Id.* at 152, 91 A. 281. After receiving notice of the assignment, the obligor cannot lawfully pay the amount assigned either to the assignor or to his other creditors and if the obligor does make such a payment, he does so at his peril because the assignee may enforce his rights against the obligor directly. *Id.* at 153, 91 A. 281.

Ordinary rights, including future rights, are freely assignable unless the assignment would materially change the duty of the obligor, materially increase the burden or risk imposed upon the obligor by his contract, impair the obligor's chance of obtaining return performance, or materially reduce the value of the return performance to the obligor, and unless the law restricts the assignability of the specific right involved. See Restatement (Second) Contracts § 317(2)(a) (1982). In Maine, the transfer of a future right to *proceeds* from pending litigation has been recognized as a valid and enforceable equitable assignment. McLellan v. Walker, 26 Me. 114, 117–18 (1846). An equitable assignment need not transfer the entire future right but rather may be a partial assignment of that right. Palmer, 112 Me. at 152, 91 A. 281. We reaffirm these well established principles.

. . . Irace and Lowry contend that Jones's June 14, 1988 letter is invalid and unenforceable as an assignment because it fails to manifest Jones's intent to permanently relinquish all control over the assigned funds and does nothing more than request payment from a specific fund. We disagree. The June 14, 1988 letter gives no indication that Jones attempted to retain any control over the funds he assigned to Dr. Herzog. Taken in context, the use of the word "request" did not give the court reason to question Jones's intent to complete the assignment and, although no specific amount was stated, the parties do not dispute that the services provided by Dr. Herzog and the amounts that he charged for those services were reasonable and necessary to the treatment of the shoulder injury referred to in the June 14 letter. . . . Given that Irace and Lowry do not dispute that they had ample notice of the assignment, the court's finding on the validity of the assignment is fully supported by the evidence and will not be disturbed on appeal.

Ethical Obligations

Next, Irace and Lowry contend that the assignment, if enforceable against them, would interfere with their ethical obligation to honor their client's instruction in disbursing funds. Again, we disagree.

... The Bar Rules [of Maine] require that an attorney "promptly pay or deliver to the client, as requested by the client, the funds, securities, or other properties in the possession of the lawyer which the client is entitled to receive." M.Bar R. 3.6(f)(2)(iv). The rules say nothing, however, about a client's power to assign his right to proceeds from a pending lawsuit to third parties. Because the client has the power to assign his right to funds held by his attorney, McLellan v. Walker, 26 Me. at 117–18, it follows that a valid assignment must be honored by the attorney in disbursing the funds on the client's behalf.... Irace and Lowry were under no ethical obligation, and the record gives no indication that they were under a contractual obligation, to honor their client's instruction to disregard a valid assignment. The District Court correctly concluded that the assignment is valid and enforceable against Irace and Lowry.

MEANS OF ASSIGNMENT

Both the Uniform Commercial Code and the Restatement recognize that an intention to assign payment rights of some kinds can be implemented by making a delivery. These are rights represented by what the Restatement calls "a writing of a type customarily accepted as a symbol or as evidence of the right assigned." Restatement § 332. An instance is a passbook symbolizing a bank savings account. The Code provides for comparable transfers of certain interests that are not payment rights. It provides also for implementing transfers of some payment rights, and some other interests, by establishing "control" in the transferee. These include transfers of deposit accounts generally. See UCC § 9–203(b) as to both delivery and control. These modes of assignment are not addressed further in this book. What follows next is about language as a means of assignment.

According to § 324 of the Restatement, an intention to transfer a contract right may be manifested, except as provided by statute or by contract, either orally or by a writing. But what language to use requires some discrimination. The language used by Gary Jones, in *Herzog*, is less dispositive than that customarily used by competent attorneys wishing to effect an assignment. Several other forms of expression are now to be illustrated. Some of them constitute assignments; others do not. Each of them should be compared with the language used by Jones.

(a) Words of assignment were used by the firm JVS Powersports USA (JVS) with respect to payment rights it held against its customers, buyers of motorbikes and other vehicles. JVS used these payment rights—"accounts," or "accounts receivable"—to obtain several millions of dollars from a financier named Rexford Funding. The financing agreement contained this term:

> [JVS] hereby assigns and sells to [Rexford], as absolute owner, and [Rexford] hereby purchases from [JVS], certain Accounts which arise from [JVS's] sale of merchandise or rendition of services.

That was an assignment.

(b) One can imagine that Rexford transferred funds to JVS by way of a check much like this:

Rexford Funding, Inc.

                Date: <u>April 1, 2005</u>

PAY TO THE
ORDER OF   <u>   JVS Powersports USA   </u> $

<u>   </u> DOLLARS

YOUR BANK   <u>Rexford Funding by C.F.O.</u>

That would not be an assignment. A check is not an assignment. "A person with an account at a bank enjoys a claim against the bank for funds in an amount equal to the account balance. Under the U.C.C., a check is simply an order to the drawee bank to pay the sum stated, signed by the maker and payable on demand.... Receipt of a check does not, however, give the recipient a right against the bank. The recipient may present the check, but, if the drawee bank refuses to honor it, the recipient has no recourse against the drawee." Barnhill v. Johnson, 503 U.S. 393, 398 (1992). Also: "A check or other draft does not of itself operate as an assignment of any funds in the hands of the drawee available for its payment, and the drawee is not liable on the instrument until he accepts it." (The court quoted this from the 1989 Official Text of UCC Article 3. The current Official Text contains a virtually identical provision, § 3–408.)

(c) A writes to B, "Please pay to C the balance you owe me." That looks even less like an assignment than a check does.

(d) A firm named Fiberlast needs financing to fulfill a contract to build a "radome"; the work is to be done for the Counter Company. Fiberlast gets a substantial loan from a friendly investor named Gordon Drew, and gives him a memo, signed, saying:

> Any money advanced by Mr. Drew for the purpose of manufacturing the Radome will be paid immediately to him upon receipt of Counter's remittance, irrespective of any other demands from other creditors.

See Shiro v. Drew, 174 F.Supp. 495, 498 (D.Me. 1959): "Language of present transfer is wholly lacking."

A passage in the *Shiro* opinion is virtually quoted in *Herzog*; see the paragraph above that follows "Validity of Assignment". According to the *Shiro* opinion, at 497–98, "the courts have uniformly recognized that an agreement to pay out of a particular fund, without more, is not an assignment. . . ." For that the court cited Christmas v. Russell (1871) 14 Wall. 69, 84, 81 U.S. 69, 84.

NOTES

(1) *Ebb and Flow*. This sentence in Christmas v. Russell has been quoted often: "An agreement to pay out of a particular fund, however clear in its terms, is not an equitable assignment." In some quarters words of present transfer are regarded as essential to an effective assignment. But the courts have not been altogether faithful to the proposition quoted. Early in the 20th century the Supreme Court detoured around it. In Barnes v. Alexander, 232 U.S. 117 (1914), the Court ruled that a fee earned by William Barnes, an attorney, had become subject to an equitable lien because, in soliciting the assistance of another attorney, he had earlier said "I will give you one third of the [contingent] fee which I have coming to me. . . ."

After *Barnes*, it was still possible to think that the decision represented a limited exception to the general rule. See B. Kuppenheimer & Co. v. Mornin, 78 F.2d 261 (8th Cir.1935). There it was said that the Supreme Court had "mellowed" the strict requirements set down in the *Christmas* case, but only for certain situations—*e.g.*, "in cases involving contingent fees of attorneys." *Id*. at 264. Also:

> Many cases are to be found sustaining the rule that a promise to pay out of a particular fund, when it shall come into existence, does not create an equitable assignment of that fund. As counsel for defendants on argument aptly said, in effect, that business and commerce will be greatly harmed, hamstrung, and impeded if every agreement of an Iowa farmer to pay a debt out of a crop of corn, when he shall have sold the corn, is to be held to be an equitable assignment of the proceeds of such corn.

Id. at 265. The opinion in Spiro v. Drew cited *B. Kuppenheimer*, and distinguished *Barnes*.

In this century, however, *Barnes* was revivified. See Sereboff v. Mid Atlantic Medical Services, Inc., 547 U.S. 356 (2006), where a unanimous Court rebuffed an argument for applying the "typical rules regarding equitable liens by assignment," and denied that *Barnes* "announced a special rule for attorneys claiming an equitable lien over funds promised under a contingency fee arrangement." In *Barnes* the Court rested its ruling on an ancient principle of general law. Now that the Court defers largely to state courts in elaborating general law, it may well be that the ruling is authoritative only for questions strongly influenced by a federal interest. *Sereboff* was, in the main, a construction of the Employee Retirement Income Security Act (ERISA).

(2) *Legal Effect without Assignment*. To say that a check and the documents in (c) and (d) above do not amount to assignments is not to say that they are without legal significance. It is clear, for instance, that a bank may charge the checking account of a customer upon payment of a check properly drawn and issued, and indorsed and presented by the payee. Indeed, assuming that the account balance is ample, the bank usually owes it to its customer—the drawer of the check—to honor it. Are the elements of a contract apparent in the transactions described in (c) or (d) above?

(3) *Gift Assignments*. A striking distinction exists between "for value" assignments and gift assignments. As to many payment rights an oral assignment is ineffective as part of a commercial transaction. So it is provided in UCC § 9–203(b)(3), setting out some conditions on the enforceability of a "security agreement" with respect to the "collateral." As indicated above, if the collateral is

embodied in a document, handing over possession of the document may make the agreement enforceable. Otherwise the agreement may well be unenforceable unless the assignor has "authenticated" the agreement. In contrast, an oral assignment by way of gift is effective, given appropriate wording.

On the other hand, the recipient of an oral gift assignment is likely to have only a tenuous hold on the right transferred. According to Section 332 of the Restatement, "Except as stated in this Section, a gratuitous assignment is revocable," and is terminated by any one of a number of incidents, including the making of a conflicting assignment and the assignor's death.

The section states various ways in which a gift assignment may be made, or may become, more durable than that. One of these is the delivery of a written and signed assignment. (In this connection, a New York statute dispenses with delivery: Gen.Oblig.L. § 5–1107.) Another is the delivery of a symbolic or evidentiary writing. Another, sometimes operative, is expectable action or inaction on the part of the assignee, induced by the assignment. A California statute is largely parallel to the Restatement section (taking *verbal* to mean *oral*): "A verbal gift is not valid, unless...." Civil Code § 1147. It omits the thought of reliance, however.

SALE vs. LOAN

Two firms mentioned above, JVS Powersports and Rexford Funding, entered into a "factoring" agreement by which Rexford received an advance of some $3 million. Rexford does a like business across the United States. In litigation between the two firms, the court quoted as follows from Black's Law Dictionary (8th ed. 2004), saying: "Factoring is '[t]he buying of accounts receivable at a discount. The price is discounted because the factor (who buys them) assumes the risk of delay in collection and loss on the accounts receivable'." The accounts concerned were, of course, payment rights arising from sales by JVS to its customers, the "account debtors."

Some tension is apparent in the foregoing paragraph. A merchant making an outright *sale* of its accounts thereby sheds the risk of nonpayment by its customers, or by a disproportionate number of them. In contrast, in using its accounts as collateral for a loan ("advance"), a merchant retains that risk. The parties disagreed about the extent to which the factoring agreement shifted the nonpayment risk to Rexford.

A term of the agreement, quoted above at p. 930, used the word *sells*. On the other hand, the agreement assigned to JVS some responsibilities with respect to its nonpaying customers. To that end it defined the word *disputes*, making it mean "any cause for nonpayment of an Account ... except for financial inability of [JVS's] Customers to pay an Account at maturity." JVS undertook to give Rexford prompt notice of any disputes, and to "settle all Disputes at no cost or expense to [Rexford]...." Upon a failure by JVS to settle a customer dispute, it was to become liable for all of the unpaid factored accounts.

The court considered evidence about a representative nonpaying customer, and was unsure whether or not that customer's account was in dispute. Hence it denied a motion by Rexford for a partial summary judgment. Rexford Funding, LLC v. JVS Powersports USA, Inc., 2007 WL 2822771 (W.D.Mich.).

Whether or not Rexford's "advance" to JVS represented a loan is open to doubt; it might fairly be called a prepayment. JVS assigned to Rexford invoices having face values of nearly $6 million in the aggregate. The case illustrates the hybrid character of many assignments.

For many purposes the sale/loan distinction was reduced in importance by the Uniform Commercial Code. Section 9–109(a) provides that, subject to a number of qualifications, Article 9 (Secured Transactions) applies not only to a transaction that creates a personal-property security interest, but also to a sale of accounts. The Comment to a predecessor section (9–102) gave this explanation: "Commercial financing on the basis of accounts ... is often so conducted that the distinction between a security transfer and a sale is blurred, and a sale of such property is therefore covered...." Article 9 applies to transfers of payment rights by way of sales, as well as to those that support loans, a broadly applicable rule that an assignee's interest is enforceable only if the assignor has "authenticated a security agreement." UCC § 9–203(b)(3)(A). (Subparagraph (A) speaks of authentication by a *debtor*, but by definition that word comprises a selling assignor.) The rule is in effect a statute of frauds. Other parts of paragraph (3) describe some transactions not subject to it.

Although the Code has reduced the sale/loan distinction, it has not obliterated it: witness *Rexford Funding*.

ANTI–ASSIGNMENT PROVISIONS

A contract between a general contractor, Caristo Construction, and a subcontractor, Kroo Painting, contained this provision:

> The assignment by [Kroo] of this contract or any interest therein, or of any money due or to become due by reason of the terms hereof without the written consent of [Caristo] shall be void.

Without having obtained the written consent of Caristo, Kroo purported to assign to a bank its right to "moneys due and to become due" under the subcontract. In turn, the bank assigned the right to Herman Allhusen, who sought to enforce it. That action was dismissed by reason of the anti-assignment provision. Allhusen appealed twice, without success. The power to contract trumped the power to transfer. The ultimate ruling, made in 1952, is cited in the opinion that follows.

The enactment of the Uniform Commercial Code superseded the ruling in *Allhusen* and others like it. UCC § 9–406(d) provides, with some qualifications, that a term in an agreement between an *account debtor* [*e.g.*, Caristo] and an assignor ... is ineffective to the extent that it:

> (1) prohibits, restricts, or requires the consent of the account debtor ... to the assignment or transfer of ... the *account*....

The terms italicized here are given definitions in UCC § 9–102(a).

In the opinion that follows the court considered the possibility that an assignment of contract rights was barred by a provision in the contract that generated those rights. The court did not refer to the Code. That omission would be surprising but for the fact that the rights in question were not "accounts," as defined in Section 9–102(a). As defined there, the word is limited, among other ways, to a right to payment of a monetary obligation for goods, for services, or for various other benefits. Hence the Code would not have suppressed an anti-assignment provision, properly drafted. It would not have suppressed, either, a provision directed at the right of a buyer of goods to receive delivery. That sort of provision appears in Trubowitch v. Riverbank Canning Co., 182 P.2d 182 (Cal.1947), a case concerning a large quantity of canned tomato paste. The provision was: "This contract is not assignable and goods sold hereunder are not to be shipped or diverted to any destination other than that herein specified, without consent of seller."

An anti-assignment provision, as follows, appears in a standard form widely used for deals in California real estate: "Buyer may not assign any rights hereunder without the prior written consent of Seller." The Code definition of *account* does not comprise the principal entitlement conferred on a buyer by the form—the right to a conveyance of property. Nor does it comprise the seller's principal entitlement—the right to be paid.

The three anti-assignment provisions quoted above are perceptibly different in tenor, each from the others. Whether or not they differ in effect should be considered in light of the opinion that follows.

Bel–Ray Company v. Chemrite (Pty) Ltd.

United States Court of Appeals, Third Circuit, 1999.
181 F.3d 435.

[The Bel–Ray Company, a New Jersey corporation, makes specialty lubricants, using formulas and technology that it maintains in the highest confidentiality. Over a period of years, Bel–Ray entered into a series of agreements—the Trade Agreements, or "Agreements"—with a South African corporation, Chemrite Ltd., for the blending and distribution of Bel–Ray products in South Africa. In 1996, a newly formed firm named Lubritene Ltd. acquired Chemrite's lubricant business, including rights under the Agreements. Bel–Ray was informed of the transfer. Business went on as before, under the Agreements. Four persons who had been shareholders and officeholders in Chemrite took similar positions in Lubritene.

Bel–Ray brought an action in New Jersey against Lubritene, charging it with fraud and other torts, and with violations of the Agreements. In the trial court, Bel–Ray got an order compelling Lubritene to arbitrate the Bel–Ray claims. The basis for this order was a provision in the most recent Agreement requiring arbitration, in New Jersey, of "any and all disputes relating to the agreement or its breach."

Appealing, Lubritene relied on provisions in the Chemrite/Bel–Ray Agreements that required Bel–Ray's written consent to any assignment of Chemrite's interests under the Agreements.]

■ STAPLETON, CIRCUIT JUDGE: ... Under the Federal Arbitration Act ("FAA"), a court may only compel a party to arbitrate where that party has entered into a written agreement to arbitrate that covers the dispute. See 9 U.S.C. §§ 2 & 206. The arbitration clauses in the Trade Agreements are the only written agreements to arbitrate offered in this case. It is undisputed that these agreements were entered into by Chemrite and Bel–Ray, and that Chemrite subsequently assigned the agreements to Lubritene. If these assignments are effective, then the District Court's order should be affirmed. Lubritene, however, contends that the assignments are ineffective because Bel–Ray did not consent to the assignments in writing as the Trade Agreements require. They therefore argue that there is no written agreement to arbitrate and we must reverse the District Court's order.

Thus, according to Lubritene, this case turns on the effect to be given to the Trade Agreements' requirement that Bel–Ray consent in writing to any assignment of Chemrite's interest. . . .

[After observing that the law of South Africa might be controlling, the court concluded that it should apply New Jersey law—"forum law"—owing to Lubritene's failure both to raise the issue and to provide information about foreign law.]

. . . The New Jersey Supreme Court has not yet addressed the effect of contractual provisions limiting or prohibiting assignments. Nevertheless, we are not without guidance because the Superior Court's Appellate Division recently addressed this issue in Garden State Buildings L.P. v. First Fidelity Bank, N.A., 305 N.J. Super. 510, 702 A.2d 1315 (N.J.Super.Ct.App.Div.1997). There, a partnership had entered a loan agreement with Midatlantic Bank for the construction of a new hotel. The parties subsequently entered into a modification agreement to extend the loan's maturity date, which provided that: "No party hereto shall assign this Letter Agreement (or assign any right or delegate any obligation contained herein) without the prior written consent of the other party hereto and any such assignment shall be void." 702 A.2d at 1318. Midatlantic subsequently assigned the loan to Starwood without obtaining the partnership's prior written consent. The partnership acknowledged Starwood's rights under the loan agreement by making payments to, and eventually entering a settlement agreement with, Starwood. Nonetheless, the partnership filed suit against Midatlantic for damages arising from its breach of the modification agreement's assignment clause. It argued that it was not required to void the assignment, but could recognize its validity while still preserving its right to sue Midatlantic for breach of its covenant not to assign without the partnership's written consent.

To resolve this claim the Appellate Division looked to § 322 of the Restatement (Second) of Contracts, which provides in relevant part:

(2) A contract term prohibiting assignment of rights under the contract, unless a different intention is manifested. . . .

(b) gives the obligor a right to damages for breach of the terms forbidding assignment *but does not render the assignment ineffective....*

Restatement (Second) of Contracts § 322 (1981) (emphasis added). The Court, distinguished between an assignment provision's effect upon a party's "power" to assign, as opposed to its "right" to assign. A party's "power" to assign is only limited where the parties clearly manifest a different intention. According to the Court:

> "to reveal the intent necessary to preclude the power to assign, or cause an assignment violative of contractual provisions to be wholly void, such clause must contain express provisions that any assignment shall be void or invalid if not made in a certain specified way." Otherwise, the assignment is effective, and the obligor has the right to damages.

Garden State, 702 A.2d at 1321 (quoting University Mews Assoc's v. Jeanmarie, 471 N.Y.S.2d 457, 461 (N.Y.Sup.Ct.1984)). The Court concluded that the parties had sufficiently manifested their intent to limit Midatlantic's power to assign the loan because the anti-assignment clause clearly provided that assignments without the other party's written consent "shall be void." 702 A.2d at 1322.

In adopting § 322, New Jersey joins numerous other jurisdictions that follow the general rule that contractual provisions limiting or prohibiting assignments operate only to limit a parties' right to assign the contract, but not their power to do so, unless the parties' manifest an intent to the contrary with specificity. See Allhusen v. Caristo Const. Corp., 303 N.Y. 446, 103 N.E.2d 891, 893 (N.Y. 1952) [and six other cases cited]. To meet this standard the assignment provision must generally state that non-conforming assignments (i) shall be "void" or "invalid," or (ii) that the assignee shall acquire no rights or the non-assigning party shall not recognize any such assignment. See *Garden State*, 702 A.2d at 1321 ("clause must contain express provisions that any assignment shall be void or invalid if not made in a certain specified way").... In the absence of such language, the provision limiting or prohibiting assignments will be interpreted merely as a covenant not to assign, or to follow specific procedures—typically obtaining the non-assigning party's prior written consent—before assigning. Breach of such a covenant may render the assigning party liable in damages to the non-assigning party. The assignment, however, remains valid and enforceable against both the assignor and the assignee....

[After quoting from the Agreements,[a] the court continued:] None contain terms specifically stating that an assignment without Bel–Ray's

---

a. "(i) the Distributor Sales Agreement § 7.06 provides that the 'Agreement and the obligations and rights under this Agreement will not be assignable by [Chemrite] without express prior written consent of Bel–Ray, which may be withheld at the sole discretion of Bel–Ray'; (ii) the Blending and Manufac-

turing License Agreement § 7.05 provides that the 'Agreement and the obligations and rights hereunder will not be assignable by [Chemrite] without the express prior written consent of BEL–RAY'; and (iii) the License Agreement to Trade Name § 6.06 provides that the 'Agreement, and the obligations and written consent would be void or invalid. Several courts have considered virtually identical clauses and concluded that they did not contain the necessary express language to limit the assigning party's power to assign. . . .

The Trade Agreements' assignment clauses do not contain the requisite clear language to limit Chemrite's "power" to assign the Trade Agreements. Chemrite's assignment to Lubritene is therefore enforceable, and Lubritene is bound to arbitrate claims "relating to" the Trade Agreements pursuant to their arbitration clauses. We therefore agree with the District Court that Bel–Ray was entitled to an order compelling Lubritene to arbitrate. . . .

NOTES

(1) *Question*. Consider the three anti-assignment clauses quoted in the text preceding the main case. What differences among them, in legal effect, if any, are indicated in *Bel–Ray*?

(2) *Meddling with a Mortgage.* Roy Haggett was much disturbed by a letter he received from a person, K.E. Norton, with whom he had had some arguments. The letter said that Norton had bought, from a savings bank, a note that Haggett had given the bank, and the accompanying mortgage on Haggett's home. These facts emerged in litigation between the two men. Norton v. Haggett, 85 A.2d 571 (Vt.1952). The opinion does not say why Haggett was disturbed. One can speculate that he counted on the bank for mercy in the event of his delay in paying the note, and did not expect mercy from Norton. If so, Haggett may have wished he had gotten the bank's agreement not to make an assignment of the note and mortgage without his consent. In another case about a contested assignment, the court said that to withhold approval of it would have served no interest of the contestant. The court emphasized the somewhat singular facts. Trubowitch v. Riverbank Canning Co., 182 P.2d 182 (Cal.1947). These cases suggest the question why a debtor should care whether the creditor is this or that entity.

The suggestion has been made that a promisee's assignment may impose a burden on a promisor by depriving it of informal leverage that it had over the promisee; see Note 2, p. 926 above. Could that have been a concern for Haggett upon receiving Norton's letter? Eventually, federal and state officials began to put serious pressure on banks to defer home foreclosures. But that followed the decision in *Norton* by more than fifty years.

(Norton v. Haggett was an action bought by Norton. It emerged that he had made a mistake in dealing with the bank: instead of buying Haggett's note he had *paid* it. On learning of his mistake, he brought the action to reinstate the note and mortgage in his favor. Otherwise, Norton thought, Haggett would be unjustly enriched. The court thought otherwise, concluding that Norton had acted as a meddler in Haggett's affairs, and was simply out his money.)

----

rights under this agreement will not be assignable without the express written consent of all Parties to this Agreement.' "

(B) OBLIGOR'S DUTY TO ASSIGNEE: SOME VARIATIONS

If an assignment of an account has been made effective by Article 9 of the UCC, and the account debtor has received an appropriate notification of the assignment, a payment made on the account will not be credited to the account debtor. (As to the terms *account* and *account debtor* in this statement, see pp. 932–934 above.) The Restatement makes a comparable statement, generalized to *obligors* rather than account debtors. The Restatement section reads, in part,

> The right of an assignee is . . . not [subject to] defenses or claims [of the obligor] which accrue [after the obligor receives notification of the assignment] except as stated in this Section or as provided by statute.

Section 336(2). Observe that an obligor's defense "I have paid that," when faced with a claim by an assignee, constitutes a defense which "accrued" after notification unless the payment was made before the notification. The same section speaks also to the case of prior payment:

> The right of an assignee is subject to any defense or claim of the obligor which accrues before the obligor receives notification. . . .

The Code rule about post-notification payments appears, with particulars added, in UCC § 9–406.

The rule about pre-notification payments appears in paragraph (2) of UCC § 9–404(a), which, like the Restatement, speaks in terms of the time when a defense "accrues." The defense "I have paid that" is not one "arising from the transaction that gave rise to the contract." A defense so arising is, for example, "Your claim is based on a contract that I may avoid, owing to fraud by your assignor." The distinction is important because both the Code and the Restatement give more leeway to that kind of defense. As for the Code, a comparison between paragraphs (1) and (2) of Section 9–404(a) demonstrates this. As for the Restatement, see Section 336(1).

In the opinion that follows the court set out both paragraphs and applied paragraph (1). The defense concerned was based on a *failure* to pay—a failure on the part of the assignor to satisfy a debt that it owed to the account debtor.

INTRODUCTION TO *DELACY INVESTMENTS* v. *THURMAN*

The contestants in this appeal were Delacy Investments, as assignee, and Re/Max, as account debtor. Re/Max had won a default judgment below against Steven Thurman, assignor, owing to his failure to plead; he was not a party to the appeal. A Note after the opinion speaks to his legal position.

By reason of the assignment from Thurman to Delacy, Delacy held a *security interest* in the account in question. That interest was the nub of a *security agreement* between those parties. Hence Delacy was a *secured party*. The three terms in italics are the subject of interrelated definitions in the Uniform Commercial Code. See UCC § 1–201(b)(35), and paragraphs (72) and (73) of UCC § 9–102(a). The opinion reports that Delacy had "perfected its security interest by filing a UCC financing statement with the Minnesota Secretary of State." Something of the mechanics and effect of that precaution is described in text below at p. 943. It had little effect, if any, on the contest between Delacy and Re/Max.

The court quoted and referred to Minnesota statutes that track the Uniform Commercial Code; *e.g.*, "Minn. Stat. § 336.9–404," which tracks UCC § 9–404. As presented here, the opinion invariably substitutes "UCC" for the prefix "Minn. Stat. § 336."

The court stated the issue before it this way: "Did the district court err by granting summary judgment to respondent based on its interpretation of article 9 of the Uniform Commercial Code as to assignment of an account receivable?"

Delacy Investments, Inc. v. Thurman & Re/Max Real Estate Guide, Inc.

Minnesota Court of Appeals, 2005.
693 N.W.2d 479.

■ HALBROOKS, JUDGE. . . .

FACTS

Appellant Delacy Investments, Inc., d/b/a Commission Express (CE), is in the business of factoring receivables from real-estate agents. In this business, a real-estate agent can assign or sell his future receivable or commission to CE in exchange for immediate funds. Respondent Re/Max Real Estate Guide, Inc. (Re/Max) is a real-estate brokerage company.

On November 11, 2001, defendant Steven Thurman, a licensed real-estate agent, entered into a master repurchase and security agreement (MRSA) with CE. The substance of the MRSA "granted to CE a security interest under the [UCC] in all of [Thurman's] right, title and interest in and to [Thurman's] current and future accounts receivable...." CE perfected its security interest by filing a UCC financing statement with the Minnesota Secretary of State.

On February 25, 2003, Thurman entered into a standard independent-contractor agreement with Re/Max. The agreement details the employment relationship between the two, whereby Thurman agreed to pay Re/Max certain overhead expenses. The agreement explains how Thurman will receive his "commission" from Re/Max and certain "nonpayment remedies." In pertinent part, the agreement states:

> [Thurman] shall be deemed entitled only to 100 percent of the amount by which commissions generated by [Thurman's] efforts *exceed* past-due financial obligations imposed by the terms of Paragraphs 4 and 5 of the Agreement. That portion of commissions which *does not exceed* past-due financial obligations shall be deemed to belong to RE/MAX and shall be used by RE/MAX first to offset arrearages owed by [Thurman].

(Emphasis added.) Thus, in terms of the legal relationships that exist here, CE is an "assignee," having accepted Thurman's assignment of his commission by the MRSA. Thurman, in turn, is an "assignor," having assigned his right of commission to CE. Re/Max is an "account debtor" by virtue of its independent-contractor agreement with Thurman, whereby Re/Max possesses the potential right to receipt of that which Thurman assigned to CE.

In April 2003, Re/Max executed an acknowledgement of CE's security interest in Thurman's account receivable from the sale of a home on Javelin Avenue and directed that Thurman's commission from that sale be paid directly to CE. On April 22, 2003, CE and Thurman entered into an Account Receivable Sale and Assignment Agreement (assignment agreement), whereby CE agreed to purchase a $10,000 receivable related to Thurman's sale of a property on Keller Lake Drive in Burnsville (Keller Lake property).[1]

On June 7, Re/Max terminated Thurman as a real-estate agent for poor performance, failure to deposit earnest-money payments in a timely manner, and customer complaints. Re/Max asserts that at the time of his termination, Thurman had accumulated $11,126.38 in overhead debts owed to Re/Max. As a result, Re/Max refused to pay the assigned receivable and "applied the commission to Thurman's balance in accordance with [the independent-contractor agreement]," claiming a right of setoff based on the overhead expenses that Thurman owed. In Re/Max's words, "because the commissions earned by Re/Max as a result of Thurman's services did not exceed his past-due financial obligation to Re/Max, Thurman was entitled to no compensation at the Keller Lake closing, and so nothing was paid to CE pursuant to the assignment."

In June 2003, CE sent Re/Max a demand for immediate payment of the Keller Lake account receivable and sent a notice of default to Thurman. Re/Max did not pay. CE then filed a complaint in district court. Re/Max answered and counterclaimed against Thurman.[2] Both parties moved for summary judgment. The district court denied CE's motion and granted Re/Max's, finding that "[CE's] ability to receive a commission from Re/Max is based upon Thurman's assignment of a contractual right to receive a commission from Re/Max." Therefore, the district court determined that "Thurman was not entitled to a commission at the time of the Keller Lake property closing." As a result, it was "impossible for [CE] to obtain a greater right in the commission than Thurman had in the commission." This appeal follows....

ANALYSIS

On an appeal from summary judgment, we ask two questions: (1) whether there are any genuine issues of material fact, and (2) whether the district court erred in its application of the law....

A.   The District Court's Application of UCC 9–404

In granting Re/Max's motion for summary judgment, the district court determined that Thurman was not entitled to a commission at the time of the Keller Lake property closing. The court stated:

1. Pursuant to the assignment agreement, CE immediately paid $8,000 to Thurman and promised to pay him an additional $1,000 upon the receipt of the assigned receivable, in exchange for Thurman's assignment of a $10,000 receivable to be paid at the closing on the Keller Lake property.

2. Thurman is not a party to this appeal. A default judgment was entered against him following his failure to plead.

... Under UCC 9–404, an assignee's rights are subject to "(1) all terms of the agreement between the account debtor and the assignor ... [.]" ... "A valid assignment generally operates to vest in the assignee the same right, title, or interest that the assignor had in the thing assigned." Ill. Farmers Ins. Co. v. Glass Service Co. [], 669 N.W.2d 420, 424 (Minn.App. 2003) (citation omitted), [*rev'd on other grounds,* 683 N.W.2d 792 (Minn. 2004)].

In the present action, Thurman was not entitled to collect a commission while his fees were in arrears. There is no question that at the time of the closing on the Keller Lake property, Thurman was in arrears in his fees to Re/Max in the amount of approximately $11,126.38. The court, therefore, finds that Thurman was not entitled to a commission at the time of the Keller Lake property closing and that it is impossible for [CE] to obtain a greater right in the commission than Thurman had in the commission.

[The Court of Appeals quoted from UCC § 9–404 as follows, adding emphasis.]

(a) Assignee's rights subject to terms, claims, and defenses; exceptions. Unless an account debtor has made an enforceable agreement not to assert defenses or claims, and subject to subsections (b) through (e), *the rights of an assignee are subject to:*

(1) *all terms of the agreement between the account debtor and assignor* and any defense or claim in recoupment arising from the transaction that gave rise to the contract; and

(2) any other defense or claim of the account debtor against the assignor which accrues before the account debtor receives a notification of the assignment authenticated by the assignor or assignee.

The official comment to the provision further explains its meaning:

Subsection (a) ... provides that an assignee generally takes an assignment subject to defenses and claims of an account debtor. Under subsection (a)(1), if the account debtor's defenses on an assigned claim arise from the transaction that gave rise to the contract with the assignor, *it makes no difference* whether the defense or claim accrues before or after the account debtor is notified of the assignment.

UCC 9–404 cmt. 2 (emphasis added); *see also* Restatement (Second) of Contracts § 336, cmt. b (1981) (explaining that an assignor can assign "only what he has" and "is subject to limitations imposed by the terms of that contract [creating the right] and to defenses which would have been available against the [account debtor] had there been no assignment"). The particular issue presented here is one of first impression in Minnesota.[3]

Under UCC 9–404(a)(1), because the rights of CE are subject to *all* terms of the agreement between Re/Max and Thurman—namely, the

---

3. Both parties cite to Nat'l Trade Trust, Inc. v. Merrimac Constr., 524 N.W.2d 14 (Minn.App.1994). In that case, we held that "an account debtor that erroneously pays the assignor after receiving notice of assignment waives any claim to a setoff against the assignor raised for the first time *after* the assigned debt was paid." *Id.* at 17 (emphasis in original). Because that case was decided on narrow grounds factually distinguishable from the issue presented here, its application is of little value.

independent-contractor agreement giving CE a right to all of Thurman's commissions which *exceed* past-due financial obligations to Re/Max–we conclude that CE cannot collect from Re/Max because the commissions earned by Re/Max as a result of Thurman's sales do not exceed his past-due financial obligations to Re/Max. As we recently explained, "it is black-letter law that an assignee of a claim take no other or greater rights than the original assignor and cannot be in a better position than the assignor." *Ill. Farmers Ins. Co.*, 669 N.W.2d at 424. This most basic principle of commercial law is reflected in the Latin phrase *nemo dat qui non habet*—or, "no one may transfer more than he owns." Commerce Bank, N.A. v. Chrysler Realty Corp., 244 F.3d 777, 780 (10th Cir. 2001).

Our decision is further supported by a number of courts across the country interpreting former § 9–318(1) and revised § 9–404 of the UCC. . . . The Sixth Circuit has . . . interpreted the same UCC provision to "clearly limit[] the rights of . . . the assignee, to those of the assignor . . . and make[] its right to accounts receivable *subject to the provisions of* [the account debtor's] contract with [the assignor]." Nat'l. City Bank, Northwest v. Columbian Mut. Life Ins. Co., 282 F.3d 407, 410 (6th Cir. 2002) (emphasis added). In that case, the court concluded that "there is no authority for the proposition that a perfected assignment to a third person takes precedence over a right of recoupment created between the original contracting parties in their contract."[4] *Id.*

[The court found support in a decision that an assignee was bound by an arbitration term in the agreement between the account debtor and the assignor: Systran Fin. Servs. Corp. v. Giant Cement Holding, Inc., 252 F.Supp.2d 500 (N.D.Ohio 2003). From the opinion there the court quoted as follows:

> [If the assignee] did not want to arbitrate disputes over collections from account debtors, it could have contracted with [the assignor] to prevent it from entering into any agreement that contained arbitration clauses. Because it did not do so, it is bound by the arbitration clause.]

Similarly, here, if CE did not want to be bound by the independent-contractor agreement between Re/Max and Thurman, it could have contracted otherwise. But it did not, and CE is thereby bound by the independent-contractor agreement between Re/Max and Thurman. As the assignee, CE cannot assume greater rights than Thurman, the assignor.

B.   Subsection (a)(2)

But CE also argues that UCC 9–404(a)(2) does not permit an account debtor to contract away the rights of an assignee *after* having received notice of a previously-executed assignment. According to CE, subsection (a)(2) limits which setoffs an account debtor may assert against a payment to an assignee after notice of the assignment. CE contends that Re/Max had

---

4. The case distinguishes between a right of "recoupment" and "setoff." "[A] right of 'recoupment' arises from the same transaction or contract that creates an asset whereas 'setoff' is a broader term referring to any claim or demand, however created, that the holder of the asset has against the debtor." [*Id.*] at 409 (citing *Black's Law Dictionary* 1439–40 (4th ed. 1968)).

notice of the assignment on three separate occasions: (1) statutory notice by CE's filing of the financing statement with the Secretary of State on November 14, 2001, after Thurman's execution of the MRSA; (2) actual notice that CE was entitled to all of the Thurman receivables when a notice of default regarding the Javelin Avenue property was delivered by certified mail on March 12, 2003; and (3) actual notice from the assignment of the Keller Lake receivable on April 22, 2003. CE argues that Thurman signed the MRSA with CE, giving CE a right to his commission, before Thurman signed the independent-contractor agreement with Re/Max.

[The court quoted from UCC § 1–201(25) and (26), as enacted in Minnesota.] It therefore appears that Re/Max had notice of the assignment between Thurman and CE before its independent-contractor agreement with Thurman.

A perfected security interest is generally effective against creditors *"except as otherwise provided* in the Uniform Commercial Code." UCC 9–201(a) (emphasis added). UCC 9–404(a)(1) provides otherwise.... UCC 9–404(a)(2) does not govern the dispute here.

The plain language of UCC 9–404(a)(1) makes clear that the rights of CE (as an assignee) "are subject to ... all terms of the agreement between the account debtor and assignor." *Id.* Here, the independent-contractor agreement between Re/Max and Thurman limited payment to Thurman to those commissions that exceeded his past-due financial obligations to Re/Max. Because CE can take no greater rights nor be in a better position than Thurman by recovering a commission when Thurman, himself, was not entitled to the commission, the district court did not err by granting summary judgment to Re/Max.

DECISION

[W]e affirm the district court's grant of summary judgment in favor of respondent.

NOTES

(1) *The Thurman Factor.* The court indicated, inferentially, that Delacy made a claim against Thurman, without indicating the character of that claim. Perhaps it was a claim of fraud, or other tort. Or perhaps Delacy contended that the account in question was collateral for an unpaid loan, or that Thurman had warranted that the account was collectible. Whatever the terms of the assignment were, they did not impair Re/Max's defense. Recall that a sale of the account, by which Delacy took all the risk of collectibility, would have generated an Article–9 security interest just as much as a transfer securing a loan. See the text, Sale vs. Loan, at p. 932 above.

(2) *Financing Statements, and "Perfection."* "UCC–1" is the style of an official form used to put the public on notice of a security interest like that of CE, and of a host of other security interests governed by Article 9. It is designed for filing in one or more public offices, as designated by the adopting state. It is a simple, one-page document. It requires few entries, chiefly these three: names and addresses for the debtor and the secured party, and something in a space after "This FINANCING STATEMENT covers the following collateral...." A suitable entry for that space would be "accounts that have arisen and may arise against Re/Max." CE could have

achieved the same effect by filing its agreement with Thurman, or another document they might have devised.

The object of a filing is to achieve *perfection* of a security interest. The object of that is to prevent competing claimants from appropriating the collateral at the expense of the secured party. The court alluded to an important class of competitors, saying that a perfected security interest "is generally effective against creditors." As applied to the facts of *Delacy Investments*, that would be a reference to creditors of Thurman. If he had entered bankruptcy, it would include that gargantuan hypothetical creditor, the bankruptcy trustee. Some further particulars about perfection, and about competitors of assignees, are presented in Section 3 of this chapter.

The *attachment* of a security interest is another matter, having to do with its efficacy against not only against competitors but even against the debtor.

(3) *Timing*. The Thurman–CE security agreement was made in 2001. The Thurman–Re/Max agreement was made in 2003. Because the account in question was generated by the latter, CE could not have had a security interest in it before 2003. UCC § 9–203(a) and (b)(2).

The court was not required to say when CE received a notification of the assignment. It did say that Re/Max had notice of the assignment before it agreed to pay commissions to Thurman. That was a rash statement, perhaps. It can be argued that notification could not occur until the Re/Max–Thurman agreement was in place. That would have been important if Re/Max's only defense was that it had paid the account to Thurman. CE offered three possible "notification dates," one in 2001 and two in 2003. Assignees have a natural disposition to favor early notification dates.

MODIFICATION

Following an assignment of rights under a contract, it is sometimes possible for the parties to the contract to impair the assignee's interest by agreeing on a modification of the contract. The Code addresses the matter in Section 9–405, "Modification of Assigned Contract." Subsection (a) states rules about the effect on the assignee. The first rule stated is:

> A modification of or substitution for an assigned contract is effective against an assignee if made in good faith.

But the rules of subsection (a) are qualified in further subsections. They do not, for example, permit the contracting parties to reduce an assigned payment right once it has been fully earned by the assignor's performance *and* "the account debtor has ... received notification of the assignment under Section 9–406(1)." That qualification leaves much room for modifications effective against assignees, many of whom must rely for protection on the requirement of good faith. "Good faith" means, in this context, "honesty in fact and the observance of reasonable commercial standards of fair dealing." UCC § 1–201(b)(20).

Further rules in subsection (a) are that, upon a modification or substitution, the assignee acquires "corresponding rights" under the modified or substituted contract, and that the assignment may provide that the modification or substitution is a breach of contract by the assignor.

NOTE

Rescission. When a bank made a claim as assignee of rent due under a computer-equipment lease, it was faced with the defense that the parties to the lease had rescinded it. (Under the Code, a lease gives rise to accounts.) On a review of Article 9, it was found that no such defense works against an assignee. Modification, yes, in the right circumstances, but not rescission. The defendant contended that the distinction creates an anomaly. The court conceded that "the functional difference between a modification of the lease amount to a dollar and the rescission of the contract is nugatory in financial terms." As to the former, the legislature may have supposed that a trier of fact would withhold a finding of good faith. "But regardless of the reason the Legislature chose to differentiate between modification and rescission, it did." Wells Fargo Bank Minnesota, N.A. v. B.C.B.U, 49 Cal.Rptr.3d 324, 332 (Cal.App.2006). (Also, an agreement to rescind does not amount to *paying* the assignor, as described in UCC § 9–406.)

PROBLEMS

(1) Mayflower Motel, Inc. received this letter from the Plymouth Bank:

> The Plank Company tells us that it expects you to call on it to supply you with lumber, on credit, as needed to repair your property damaged in the recent fire. We notify you hereby that Plank is a customer of ours, that we have extended a line of credit to it, and that we hold an assignment from Plank of all its accounts now on its books and of those hereafter to arise. That assignment secures all advances we have made and will make to Plank. You are to make payment for any lumber you buy from Plank directly to us.

After that, Mayflower did indeed contract to purchase lumber from Plank, on credit. Plank has yet to deliver most of the goods. Now the parties to the lumber-sale contract wish to reduce the price by 10%, owing to a general drop in lumber prices. They want to know whether or not, if they do, the change will affect the bank's entitlement against Mayflower.

In part, the answer is determined by UCC § 2–209(1), and in part by UCC § 9–405. How would you advise Mayflower and Plank?

(2) The facts are the same as in Problem 1, except that Plank delivered all the lumber ordered by Mayflower before the drop in prices. Might it be argued that a good-faith reduction in the lumber price would be effective against the bank, in that there has not yet been notification to the account debtor of the assignment?

A dictum in *Delacy Investments*, above, indicates the answer No. (The court said that Re/Max had notice of Thurman's assignment before it entered into the contract that generated the account in question.) Does that make sense? As to UCC § 9–406(a), the juncture specified there is when "the account debtor receives a notification ... that the amount due or to become due has been assigned and that payment is to be made to the assignee." When Mayflower received the bank's letter, was it an account debtor? Should that matter?

(3) Let it be supposed that UCC § 9–405 would make effective, against the bank, a 10% change in the contract price, as suggested in the foregoing problems. Suppose also, however, these further facts: On learning of the lumber-sale contract, the bank increased Plank's line of credit by the amount of the contract price, and Plank drew down the full amount of the credit. Mayflower has been informed of these transactions. How might it be argued that Mayflower cannot now, as against the bank, enjoy the benefit of a price reduction? Would it matter that Mayflower does not know of the two transactions described?

AGREEMENT NOT TO ASSERT DEFENSES AGAINST ASSIGNEE

(Waiver-of-Defenses Clause)

UCC § 9–403 empowers the parties to some agreements—account debtor and assignor—to contract, to some extent, around this other provision, also mentioned above: "[T]he rights of an assignee are subject to ... any defense or claim in recoupment arising from the transaction that gave rise to the contract." UCC § 9–404(a)(1). Clauses having that object are known commonly as *waiver-of-defenses* clauses. The Restatement touches only lightly on the subject, referring to statutes affecting certain defenses.

For several reasons waiver-of-defenses clauses are the subject of widespread obloquy. Almost always they appear in standard-form contracts, at the instance of firms that take assignments as a vocation. They may lead to serious misfortune for subscribing obligors, who may not appreciate the threat when subscribing. Hence both federal and state authorities have moved to counteract them. Moves of that kind are exemplified in Title 16, § 433.2, of the Code of Federal Regulations ("Preservation of consumers' claims and defenses ..."), and in § 2986.10 of the California Civil Code, both quoted in Notes below.

An example of misfortune occasioned by a waiver-of-defenses clause is that of a firm desiring the use of computer equipment. During negotiations for a lease, the prospective lessor induced an agent of the firm to sign lease documents, saying that it was common industry practice to execute undated documents "in advance," and promised to hold the documents in escrow until a deal was reached. No deal was reached, and the would-be lessee never received the equipment. Nevertheless, it had to pay according to the "lease" because of an assignment and because of a waiver-of-defenses clause in the documents. (The waiver-of-defenses clause was, "Lessee shall not assert against the assignee any defense, counterclaim or set-off that Lessee may have against Lessor.") Wells Fargo Bank Minnesota, N.A. v. B.C.B.U., 49 Cal.Rptr.3d 324 (Cal.App.2006). For another example of misfortune for a lessee, this one a law firm, see Chemical Bank v. Rinden Professional Ass'n, p. 949 below. The leased property was an office telephone system.

One might think that a waiver-of-defenses clause cannot override defenses more appealing than the ones in those cases—fraud, for example. But a waiver-of-defenses clause can override a defense based on fraud of the worst type.

The Code places significant limits on the class of assignees who can enjoy the benefit of waiver-of-defenses clauses under Section 9–403. An assignee qualifies only if it has taken the assignment for value, and in good faith. The definition of "good faith" is that appearing at p. 451 above. A further requirement is that the assignee take without notice of some truly fundamental defenses, including an especially egregious kind of fraud and most defenses of duress and incapacity. This qualification manifests some mistrust of the good-faith requirement. (The qualification speaks of defenses "of a type that may be asserted against a holder in due course of a negotiable instrument under Section 3–305(b)." The particulars of negotiable-instrument law are not pursued here.)

Section 9–403 makes two references to "other" laws protective of obligors. One of the laws referred to is the federal regulation cited above, 16 C.F.R. § 433.2. It requires that certain contracts include a prominent "anti-waiver-of-defenses" clause; see Note 1 below. In the absence of the required clause, subsection (d) of UCC § 9–403 undercuts a waiver-of-defenses clause to the extent that the required clause would have done if included.

Subsection (e) of Section 9–403 provides that the section is "subject to law other than this article which establishes a different rule for an account debtor who is an individual and who incurred the obligation primarily for personal, family, or household purposes." A "different rule" would be one preserving an account debtor's defenses against an assignee. The subsection has no bearing on the cases last cited, *Wells Fargo Bank* and *Chemical Bank*, for the goods concerned in those cases were wanted for business purposes. But the subsection was applicable in LaChapelle v. Toyota Motor Credit Corp., 126 Cal.Rptr.2d 32 (Cal.App.2002), assuming that the Toyota 4–Runner concerned was leased to Ms. LaChapelle for her personal use. See Note 2 below.

NOTES

(1) *A Federal Riposte.* "ANY HOLDER OF THIS ... CONTRACT IS SUBJECT TO ALL CLAIMS AND DEFENSES WHICH THE DEBTOR COULD ASSERT AGAINST THE SELLER OF GOODS OR SERVICES OBTAINED PURSUANT HERETO OR WITH THE PROCEEDS HEREOF.... "

A failure to include this text, in ten-point bold-face type, in a consumer credit contract, may be a federal offense, in connection with a sale or lease of goods or services to a consumer. The offense is that of the "seller." It can be committed only in a transaction "in or affecting commerce as 'commerce' is defined in the Federal Trade Commission Act." 16 C.F.R. § 433.2.

(2) *A California Riposte.* "An assignee of the lessor's rights is subject to all equities and defenses of the lessee against the lessor, notwithstanding an agreement to the contrary...."

This provision applies to leases by which a natural person acquires the use of a registered motor vehicle, primarily for personal, family or household purposes, for a term exceeding four months. Cal.Civil Code §§ 2985.7(d) and 2986.10. In UCC § 9–403, according to subsection (e), the section is subject to these provisions of the California Vehicle Leasing Act.

Note the word "all" in the California statute ("all equities and defenses") and in the notice quoted in Note 1 ("ALL CLAIMS AND DEFENSES"). Presumably the word comprises some defenses that would preclude recovery by a holder in due course.

––––––––

FINANCIERS vs. CONSUMERS

The Uniform Commercial Code is relatively dispassionate about consumers who express assent to waiver-of-defenses clauses. See Robert Skilton and Orrin Helstad, Protection of the Installment Buyer of Goods under the UCC, 65 Mich.L.Rev.1465 (1967). That may be so partly because the topic has engendered much passion.

To some extent rules that protect consumers against waiver-of-defenses clauses reflect only concern about the more general problems of standard form contracts. But attempts have been made to show that the waiver-of-defenses problem is a singular one, deserving of specialized treatment. The following considerations figure in the argument. (1) Financing institutions are in a superior position, by comparison with ordinary consumers, to evaluate the reliability of a retail merchant or firm. A bank or finance company supplying a merchant with funds is equipped to form judgments about the matter more accurately than the merchant's ordinary customers. (2) Customers of a retail firm are poorly situated to exercise discipline against it for substandard business practices, whereas corrective measures may readily be forced on it by a financier if its retail operations give rise to an undue number of complaints. (3) Pooling of information is an effective means of reducing substandard performance by merchants. Financing institutions are capable of organizing exchanges of information, such that a merchant who proves unworthy of trust will be promptly foreclosed from the credit market. By contrast, information exchanges among consumers are feebly organized, so that a retail firm may maintain a certain reputation with the public even though many of its customers suffer from its delinquencies.

None of these arguments need be taken at face value, of course. What countervailing considerations are there? It has been argued forcefully that, if merchants cannot give the assurances to financing institutions through waiver-of-defenses clauses, they will find credit more expensive, or inaccessible, and that the cost to merchants must be reflected in retail prices. Persuasive? If so, would the effect show in cash transactions, or only in credit transactions?

It is instructive to compare the remedies of a disappointed buyer who uses credit with those of one who does not. Withholding payment, while not a remedy available to a cash buyer, may be a remedy available to a buyer on credit. Possibly, then, a disappointed cash buyer never has a better prospect of relief than one who uses credit, and often has a worse one. Does that state of affairs make sense?

―――――

LINKAGE, ASSIGNOR AND ASSIGNEE

A firm that takes assignments repeatedly or continuously from a merchant whose dealings with customers are substandard may become entangled with defenses of customers, notwithstanding waiver-of-defenses clauses. At some point a question may arise about that firm's good faith.

Aside from that, customers' defenses have succeeded simply because of the ongoing link between assignor and assignee. Notable authorities on the subject are Unico v. Owen, 232 A.2d 405 (N.J.1967), and Leasing Service Corp. v. River City Const., Inc., 743 F.2d 871 (11th Cir.1984). In each case the claimant sought to override a buyer's defense by presenting itself as a holder in due course of a negotiable instrument.

In *Unico* the court wrote an elaborate opinion, referring to Williams v. Walker–Thomas Furniture Co., p. 497 above, among other cases. "Many courts have solved the problem," the court said, "by denying to the holder of the paper the status of holder in due course where the financer maintains a close relationship with the dealer whose paper he buys...." The court described signs of close cooperation between dealers and assignees. "The transaction is looked upon, as a species of tripartite proceeding, and the tenor of the cases is that the financer should not be permitted 'to isolate itself behind the fictional fence' of the Negotiable Instruments Law, and thereby achieve an unfair advantage over the buyer." *Unico* at 412.

In *Leasing Service Corp.* the court said: "There are, of course, commercial cases in which a court has held that the seller and the alleged holder in due course were so closely linked that the entities were indistinguishable for purposes of the holder in due course doctrine.... In those cases the manufacturer's representative either assisted or participated in the sale by the dealer, and the manufacturer's course of dealing was, to furnish blank sales contracts to its dealer and to have the dealer assign the contract routinely as soon as the sale was made."

Is a decision like that justifiable on the ground that a closely-connected financier is in a position to monitor the merchant's selling practices and the quality of its products? The opinion that follows speaks to the point.

INTRODUCTION TO *CHEMICAL BANK* v. *RINDEN PROFESSIONAL ASSOCIATION*

The ruling here depended on the following sentence in a Massachusetts statute now superseded:

> Subject to any statute or decision which establishes a different rule for buyers of consumer goods, an agreement by a buyer that he will not assert against an assignee any claim or defense which he may have against the seller is enforceable by an assignee who takes his assignment for value, in good faith and without notice of a claim or defense, except as to defenses of a type which may be asserted against a holder in due course of a negotiable instrument under the Article on Negotiable Instruments (Article 3).

The sentence was very like the first of three in a section of the Uniform Commercial Code—Section 9–206—that was the predecessor of current UCC § 9–403. The current section was later enacted in Massachusetts as Gen.Laws ch. 106, § 9–402.

The sentence quoted above differs notably from the corresponding one in UCC § 9–403. The closing "except" phrase entrenched certain defenses which can be foreclosed under the section as revised. But that difference is not germane to the case.

As presented here, the opinion does not include chapter or section references to the General Laws, and refers to former Code Section 9–206 as "the Code section."

Chemical Bank v. Rinden Professional Association

Supreme Court of New Hampshire, 1985.
126 N.H. 688, 498 A.2d 706.

[A firm named Intertel installed an office telephone system for a law firm (Rinden) under a lease-purchase agreement made in April, 1974. The contract required monthly payments into 1982, at which time Rinden might purchase the equipment for a dollar. Thereafter Rinden received written notice that the Chemical Bank expected to purchase from Intertel the payment rights. This document required Rinden's assent to its terms; and on June 11 Rinden's office manager, John Satterfield, read and signed it. One of its terms included this provision:

> As Lessee, you ... agree as follows: (a) that your obligation to pay directly to the Assignee [bank] the amounts which come due as rentals as set forth in said Lease shall be absolutely unconditional and shall be payable whether or not the Lease is terminated [in any way] and you promise to pay the same notwithstanding any defense, set-off or counterclaim whatsoever, [by] breach or otherwise, which you may or might now or hereafter have as against the Lessor [Intertel].

After the bank received the signed document, it received also an assignment by Intertel of Intertel's payment rights, for which it paid. About a week after Satterfield signed, Rinden received a letter from the bank saying that the assignment had been completed and that Rinden was obligated to make its monthly payments to the bank.

After nearly three years of payments to the bank, the phone system began to malfunction seriously. Rinden replaced it and refused to make further payments to the bank. A three-party lawsuit ensued, which resulted in a master's report in 1984. In the meanwhile, Intertel had gone into bankruptcy.

The report favored the bank. Rinden appealed, contesting a finding that the waiver clause was enforceable.]

■ DOUGLAS, JUSTICE. ... This case is governed by the Uniform Commercial Code (UCC) as enacted in Massachusetts. The version of the provision of article 9 of the UCC applicable to this case is entitled "Agreement Not to Assert Defenses Against Assignee; Modification of Sales Warranties Where Security Agreement Exists".... [Here the court set out the statute. With one qualification, it was identical to UCC § 9–206(1), as it stood prior to the revision of Article 9 effective 2001. The difference was that the statute omitted references, found in the Code section, to lessors and lessees of goods, as well as to sellers and buyers. The court concluded, however, that the statute applied because the Intertel–Rinden "lease" fit the UCC definition of a security agreement.]

... The requirements of a valid waiver are that there was an agreement by a buyer, who is not a consumer, to waive defenses against an assignee and that the assignment was made for value, in good faith, and without notice of a claim or defense.... We find that these requirements were met so that the defendant validly waived his defenses against Chemical Bank.

The master found that Rinden agreed to the waiver of defenses clause, and the evidence supports this view....

The defendant does not claim that it is a consumer so as to make [the statute] inapplicable on that account. The defendant is a professional association, a law firm, not in need of special protections often provided for unwary consumers....

Next we must determine whether there is sufficient evidence to support the master's findings that Chemical Bank took the assignment for value, in good faith, and without notice of a claim or defense. As to the first issue, Chemical Bank paid Intertel over $8,800 for the assignment of Intertel's rights in the defendant's contract.

As to the next requirement, the defendant asserts that Chemical Bank is not a good faith purchaser, mainly because the plaintiff and Intertel were too closely connected. Nothing in the record indicates, however, that the relationship between Intertel and Chemical Bank was anything other than an arms-length commercial relationship.

William Tupka, the Chemical Bank employee in charge of the Intertel account, testified that Chemical Bank's course of dealing in purchasing the rights to the Rinden contract from Intertel was typical of its transactions with hundreds of other clients with which it had entered into similar agreements. Chemical Bank and Intertel were not related corporations, having common directors or owning shares of stock in each other. Nor was Chemical the only bank to lend to Intertel.

Finally, the facts that Chemical Bank checked Rinden's credit rating and insisted upon an insertion of a waiver of defenses clause, before it would purchase the assignment, certainly do not prove lack of good faith as Rinden claims. Both Mr. Tupka and Kenneth Barron, former president of Intertel, testified that these actions were standard procedure for a bank extending credit. Moreover, even if there was any evidence of interrelatedness, Massachusetts law appears to look with disfavor on the admission of past dealings between parties to show bad faith, absent some other indications of bad faith by the holder. See Bowling Green, Inc. v. State Street Bank and Trust Co., 425 F.2d 81, 85 (1st Cir. 1970) (citing Universal C.I.T. Credit Corp. v. Ingel, 196 N.E.2d 847, 852 (Mass. 1964)).

There is also no basis to conclude that the master erred in finding that Chemical Bank took the assignment without notice of a claim or defense. Mr. Tupka testified that he came across nothing in his investigation of the Intertel account which would indicate that Rinden might have some kind of claim or defense relating to the lease agreement between it and Intertel. No evidence was introduced to contradict this testimony. . . .

The defendant next argues that even if the terms of [the statute] were complied with, the waiver of defenses is ineffective because it was given without consideration. The short answer to this is that none was required. Mass.Gen.Laws Ann. ch. 106 § 2–209(1) states that "[a]n agreement modifying a contract within this Article needs no consideration to be binding." . . .

[The argument next focused on the defendant's contention that a provision of Article 2, such as that last cited, is inapplicable to a transaction within Article 9 of the Code. The court concluded that "Article 2 does apply to transactions in goods which involve both a sales contract and a security agreement." The court rejected an argument grounded in public policy.]

We note that our decision today is in accord with the policy of the UCC in general, and of [the Code section] in particular, "to encourage the supplying of credit for the buying of goods by insulating the [institutional] lender from lawsuits over the quality of the goods." Massey–Ferguson Credit Corp. v. Brown, 547 P.2d 846, 850 (Mont. 1976) (quoting Massey–Ferguson, Inc. v. Utley, 439 S.W.2d 57, 60 (Ky.1969)). "A contrary holding would not only have a chilling effect on loans made by financial institutions but would mean that the law allows the plain meaning of covenants to be declared nugatory whenever a bad bargain results." B.V.D. Co. v. Marine Midland Bank—New York, 360 N.Y.S.2d 901, 904 (App.Div. 1974). . . .

Affirmed.

NOTES

(1) *Unconscionability.* Rinden argued that the waiver-of-defense clause it had assented to was unenforceable because it was unconscionable. The court rejected that argument in a part of the opinion omitted here. What were the weaknesses in the argument?

(2) *Alternate Rationale.* The facts of *Chemical Bank* might have supported a finding that Rinden made a promise directly to the bank that the bank would be paid notwithstanding any defense that Rinden might have against Intertel. If that promise was made, would it have served as a basis for the decision without reference to Article 9 of the Code?

There might be a question of consideration for the promise: What was given in exchange for Rinden's undertaking? The question would be especially acute if the supposed promise was made after the bank had invested in the contract. (Rinden could of course bargain with the bank for it to make an advance, or a payment, to Intertel, if the bank had not already acted.) Possibly a promise by Rinden to the bank, if one was made, could be enforced on the basis of promissory estoppel. A showing of something in the way of reliance by the bank would be required. What kind of reliance might be shown?

(3) *Variant State Rules.* The stance of Article 9 toward waivers by consumers of their defenses was sharply debated in the councils of the Code sponsors. As to the Code's neutrality on consumer-credit issues see Robert Skilton and Orrin Helstad, Protection of the Installment Buyer of Goods under the UCC, 65 Mich.L.Rev. 1465 (1967). The decision was, of course, not to strive for uniformity on the issue of consumer protection. Does that fact suggest any attitude that should be taken toward the business buyer?

The issue of consumer protection has also been hard-fought in the legislatures and the courts. A number of states virtually deprive waiver-of-defense clauses—and holder-in-due-course status, with respect to notes—of their efficacy in ordinary consumer transactions. See Uniform Consumer Credit Code § 3.307 and other sections cited in the Comment. Other statutes provide the consumer with a limited period for raising objections against paying the assignee. In states of this persuasion, the inception and the duration of this period are variables. A description and compilation of retail installment sales statutes as they affect assignment law appear in the Introductory Note to Chapter 15 of the Restatement.

———

ASSIGNEES' LIABILITIES

Efforts, now to be described, have been made to impose no-fault liabilities on assignees, sometimes by consumers, sometimes by others. The end point of these efforts, which is not even in sight, might be put this way: When a dispenser of goods or services has obtained financing by assigning a customer's account, and the dispenser is found to have imposed on the customer, the customer may require the assignee to account for its gain or may charge the assignee with the customer's loss.

Statutory and regulatory texts have given some impetus to claims against assignees, but also have put them in check. An example is the FTC "holder rule," which requires that consumer credit contracts contain this notice: ANY HOLDER OF THIS ... CONTRACT IS SUBJECT TO ALL CLAIMS ... WHICH THE DEBTOR COULD ASSERT AGAINST THE SELLER OF GOODS OR SERVICES OBTAINED PURSUANT HERE-TO. ... (For a fuller quotation see p. 954 above.)

Restitution Claims

Long before that rule was thought of, restitution was thought of as a basis for a claim against an assignee. In Merchants' Insurance Company v. Abbott, 131 Mass. 397 (1881), the facts were such that, if the company had paid anything to Abbott, "it could be recovered back as money paid under the influence of a mistake." The mistake was that the company was indebted to Abbott under a policy of insurance on a mill which had been destroyed by fire. In fact, the company owed him nothing because he had instigated the fire. And it had paid him nothing. Instead, the company had paid the amount of the loss to a firm—Denny, Rice & Company ("Denny Rice")—to which Abbott had assigned his "claim" on the policy. On learning of the arson, the company sought to recover from Denny Rice the payment it had made. Denny Rice was exonerated. Abbott had made the assignment to satisfy a debt that he owed to Denny Rice. Hence it took the assignment "for value." Denny Rice was not unjustly enriched by having received money that Abbott owed to it. Merchants' Ins. Co. v. Abbott, 131 Mass. 397 (1881).

A comparable claim was made in Michelin Tires (Canada) Ltd. v. First Nat. Bank of Boston, 666 F.2d 673 (1st Cir. 1981). This one had some support in UCC Article 9: "the rights of an assignee are subject to ... all the terms of the contract between the account debtor and assignor and *any* ... *claim arising therefrom* ...." (emphasis supplied). Nevertheless, the assignee was exonerated. The section quoted was the predecessor of what is now subsection (a) of UCC § 9–404. The current provision contains language disfavoring the claim. For one thing, the former reference to "any ... claim" has been changed to "any ... claim in recoupment." Also, the revision inserted subsection (b), the rule of which, applicable to the facts of *Michelin Tire*, is: "[T]he claim of an account debtor against an assignor may be asserted against an assignee under subsection (a) only to reduce the amount the account debtor owes."

NOTE

Monitoring Costs. In *Michelin Tires* the court made a policy argument against affirmative actions, based on transaction costs. Michelin complained of its contractor, one Corrigan, in an action against his assignee, the bank. The court compared the Corrigan–Michelin connection with the Corrigan-bank connection. To charge financiers with liability would compel them, the court thought, to supervise performance by their customers of the job being financed. A party in Michelin's position would not, however, relax its supervision. "The party most interested in adequate performance would be the other contracting party. . . . Given this natural interest, it seems likely to us that while [on charging them with affirmative actions] the banks will be given additional burdens of supervision, there would be no corresponding reduction in vigilance by the contracting parties, thus creating two inspections where there was formerly one. Costs for everyone thus increase, without any discernible benefit." Also: "We simply do not believe that the banks are best suited to monitor contract compliance."

Does this reasoning cut too deep? That is, does it tend to show that Corrigan's default should be no defense for Michelin when the bank is the claimant?

Holder Rules

By an act of the Michigan legislature concerning the financing of motor-vehicle sales, an installment sale contract governed by the act is to contain this notice:

> Any holder of this consumer credit contract is subject to all claims and defenses which the debtor could assert against the seller of goods or services obtained pursuant hereto or with the proceeds hereof. Recovery hereunder by the debtor shall not exceed amounts paid by the debtor hereunder.

Mich. Comp. Laws § 1114a(c). Before the second sentence was added, this provision was held (as that sentence intimates) to impose vicarious liability on a holder.

It may be noticed that the first sentence parallels the language required by the Federal Trade Commission in its "holder rule." One might suppose, then, that federal law also opens financiers to vicarious liability. But the Congress has acted to limit that liability. It added the following provision to the Truth-in-Lending Act (15 U.S.C. § 1601 *et seq.*), which governs applications of the F.T.C. holder rule:

> [Subject to a qualification] any civil action for a violation of this subchapter . . . which may be brought against a creditor may be maintained against any assignee of such creditor only if the violation for which such action or proceeding is brought is apparent on the face of the disclosure statement, except where the assignment was involuntary.

The statute goes on to restrict the kinds of "apparent" violation.

Among the debtors who have been balked by this provision was Susanne Ramadan, when she made a claim against the Hyundai Motor Finance Corporation. See Ramadan v. Chase Manhattan Corp., 229 F.3d 194 (3d Cir. 2000) (Chase Manhattan was another of her targets). That case is of special interest, in part because it evoked an interesting response from Judge Louis H. Pollak, formerly eminent as a law school dean. Dissenting, he wrote:

> [I]t seems to me that a finance company, feeling that the Holder Notice is in place via force majeure and intending to defend against its applicability in any litigation that may arise, should, before accepting

assignment of a finance agreement, insist that the Holder Notice be garlanded with caveat emptors that warn the purchaser-borrower of the finance company's view that the 1980 TILA amendment robs the Holder Notice of substantive effect. A finance company has no ground for supposing that more than one in tens of thousands of purchaser-borrowers (the Ramadans of the world) will be conversant with the interplay between the FTC regulation and TILA. Given the disparity in the possession of crucial information, I would conclude that an assignee finance company that failed to insist on inclusion of an appropriate warning adjacent to the Holder Notice should be estopped from invoking the Holder Notice in litigation.

Id. at 203, 204.

(C) ASSIGNEES IN CONTESTS WITH THIRD PARTIES

This part concerns contests between a transferee and a competing claimant to the asset transferred. The claimants considered are creditors of the transferor, and other transferees. The transfers considered are those subject to Article 9 of the Uniform Commercial Code, and not others except for some mentioned in a reference to Restatement priority rules below.

Part 1 below depicts a contest between two assignees of the same payment rights, and indicates how Article 9 assigns priority to them.

Something is said above about a contest between the assignee of an account and creditors of the assignor. Part 2 pursues that subject.

1. CONFLICTING SECURITY INTERESTS

In the main, this part concerns what the Restatement refers to as priority as among "Successive Assignees [of the same right] From the Same Assignor." The paragraphs that follow paraphrase the Restatement section on that subject, Section 342. Aside from that, this part deals only with priorities declared in the Uniform Commercial Code. Hence the heading, "conflicting security interests."

Restatement priority rules. The primary Restatement rule about priority is a "first in time" rule: If an assignment is effective, is not revocable, and is not voidable by the assignor, the assignee's right is superior to that of a subsequent assignee of the same right. In various circumstances the Restatement reverses its first-in-time rule. One is that the first assignment is voidable by the subsequent assignee. Another has to do with assignments of a right represented in a writing—a writing "of a type customarily accepted as a symbol or as evidence" of the right. An assignee of that right will outrank the recipient of a prior assignment if, "without knowledge or reason to know of the prior assignment," it gives value and obtains possession of the writing. That provision makes way for the seniority accorded to transferees who qualify as holders in due course of negotiable instruments.

Other reversals of the first-in-time rule are likewise confined to subsequent assignees who give value and act, in this way or that, "without knowledge...." The action specified may be getting payment, or getting a judgment against the obligor, or entering into a novation with the obligor.

Comment *c* to § 342 states that the subject is "now largely governed by the Uniform Commercial Code." It gives instances of claims not so governed, naming wage claims, deposit accounts, and some rights under insurance policies.

———

U.S. CLAIMS, INC. v. FLOMENHAFT & CANNATA, LLC, 519 F.Supp.2d 515 (E.D.Pa.2006). [U.S. Claims ("USC") and the Stillwater Asset–Backed Fund LP ("Stillwater") had conflicting interests in assets of a New York attorney and the law firm in which he was a partner ("the other defendants"). So it was alleged in an action that USC brought against Stillwater, seeking a declaratory judgment that its interest was senior to that of Stillwater. The assets in question were fees that the other defendants expected to earn in pursuing clients' personal-injury claims.

The other defendants had made a series of sales to USC of interests in those fees. Thereafter they had procured a loan from Stillwater, giving as collateral all their assets. USC alleged that Stillwater knew of its interests at that time, in that the later transaction was arranged by a former representative of USC—in fact the one who had arranged the earlier transactions.

The USC claim was a difficult one because it had never filed a financing statement respecting its interests in the fees, whereas Stillwater had done so. The primary Code rule about priority in these circumstances is "first to file or perfect." USC sought to overcome this difficulty by pointing to Stillwater's knowledge of USC's interests, and by reference to parts of UCC § 9–309, including clause (2). That clause is as follows:

> The following security interests are perfected when they attach:
>
> ... an assignment of accounts or payment intangibles which does not by itself or in conjunction with other assignments to the same assignee transfer a significant part of the assignor's outstanding accounts or payment intangibles.

As to Stillwater's supposed knowledge, the court referred to the "clear dictates of Article 9 that a creditor's subjective knowledge is wholly irrelevant to the question of lien priority." (Contrast § 342 of the Restatement, as described above.)

As to the automatic perfection of sales of payment intangibles, the court ruled that the fees to be earned were accounts—as to which USC should have filed—and not payment intangibles. Being accounts, they were not even general intangibles.

As to clause (2), the court ruled that USC had not pleaded it properly. What follows is footnote 3 of the court's opinion.]

■ DAVIS, J. In any event, the Court notes that the [clause] is unlikely to aid Plaintiff in its position . . . While nothing in the plain text of the provision appears to bar its application to this case, the official comments make patently clear that the exception is not intended to apply to assignors like U.S. Claims: "[t]he purpose of [the clause] is to save from *ex post facto* invalidation casual or isolated assignments—assignments which no one would think of filing. Any person who regularly takes assignments of any debtor's accounts or payment intangibles should file." UCC § 9–309, cmt. 4. . . . Plaintiff is a financial enterprise engaged in the business of purchasing attorneys' fee interests. . . . Furthermore, as U.S. Claims' interests at issue are alleged to have totaled in excess of three million dollars, it is hard to believe that a sophisticated corporation like Plaintiff would have regarded the transactions as "casual" such that it failed to consider that it may be necessary to file in order to protect its interests.

NOTES

(1) *Questions.* The action appears to have been brought a good while after the controversy arose. What can account for USC's failure to file a financing statement in the interim?

(2) *Significant Part.* The court conceded that "nothing in the plain text [of UCC § 9–309(2)] appears to bar its application to this case," but quoted a Code Comment in opposition to that. How is it that a comment overrides the statutory text? Possibly the Comment (". . . should file") means that prudence calls for a filing, sometimes, when it may prove ultimately to be needless.

(3) *Sale* vs. *Loan.* It is possible to doubt that the assignments to USC were sales, as they purported to be. The aggregate interest of USC in the fees assigned was determined by the amount it had "advanced," plus monthly increases, but was to diminish as fees were paid. If the expectation of a particular fee should fail (not every contingent fee materializes), the attorneys were to replace it with a fee or fees—"makeups"—equal in amount to the failing one. If that might signify *loan*, there was all the more reason for USC to file.

2.   ASSIGNEE vs. CREDITORS OF ASSIGNOR

As noted above, Article 9 of the UCC applies not only to transactions in which property is collateral for an obligation but also to sales of accounts (and most other contractual payment rights). Article 9 refers to the right of the buyer of an account as a "security interest" even though the right does not "secure" anything. It provides that a creditor who acquires a lien on an asset of her debtor (typically as a result of the judicial enforcement of a claim against the debtor) is senior in right to a security interest earlier granted by the debtor in that asset, if that security interest has not been perfected. This provision applies to assets of many types, including accounts. It appears, along with various extensions and qualifications, in UCC § 9–317. The rule poses a serious threat to an assignee who fails, by inadvertence or otherwise, to be prompt in taking action to perfect its interest. (That action is usually the filing of a financing statement, often taking a form referred to above as a "UCC–1.") As Section 9–317 describes the danger, it is that a security interest—including the right of a buyer of an account—becomes "subordinate" to the rights of one who becomes a lien creditor before the security interest is perfected.

The loss suffered as a result of subordination to a competitor's lien is limited to the amount of the claim that the lien secures. But a delay in perfecting a security interest created by an assignment, or a failure to perfect it at all, poses a threat more serious than subordination: *avoidance* of the security interest entirely.

The most notable occasion of avoidance is the bankruptcy of the entity that sold the account—one who may be called the assignor for present purposes. The voidability of assignments in bankruptcies is among the most intricate aspects of a formidable body of law, one not suited to study in connection with contract law in general. A few words are in order, however, as reinforcement for some practical lessons for financiers.

In a liquidation bankruptcy, a trustee is chosen to administer the assets of the "estate," distributing them according to a scheme in the Bankruptcy Code. A bankruptcy estate comprises, with some exceptions, all the assets of the debtor. But that is not all it comprises. Trustees are equipped by the bankruptcy statute with various powers to avoid transfers of assets that the debtor has made. The effect of avoidance is to bring the asset into the estate. A trustee can augment the estate by exerting one or more of these powers, and should do so as the Bankruptcy Code permits. A transfer that was made by a debtor in bankruptcy before the inception of the bankruptcy, and that is unperfected at that time, is almost invariably voidable.

What is more striking, a trustee can sometimes avoid even a perfected transfer, if the transfer, or its perfection, occurred while the debtor was insolvent, given some other circumstances. (One who knows the Bankruptcy Code will recognize this statement as a glancing reference to a section titled "Preferences.") A more specific statement about the law of preferences in bankruptcy, especially germane to this chapter, is this: If a debtor has assigned an account, the trustee may be able to avoid the assignment, even if it was perfected before the bankruptcy, if the assignee delayed in perfecting it for more than thirty days. The trustee may do so, however, only on establishing other facts. A notable requisite is that perfection was achieved within a specified period before the bankruptcy. The period is usually ninety days.

For financiers and others taking assignments of accounts and other contractual payment rights, the foregoing observations lead to the conclusion that they should hasten to take any steps necessary to perfect their interests. Article 9 eases that task: It allows assignees, and other secured parties, to file a financing statement effective with respect to a particular asset before its transfer occurs; and it gives effect to a financing statement covering assets a debtor has yet to acquire, as well as those already booked.

INDEX

References are to pages.

†